NEW

WITHDRAWN

W9-BYQ-393

NEW

# ENCYCLOPEDIA OF
# WORLD BIOGRAPHY

**4**

# ENCYCLOPEDIA OF WORLD BIOGRAPHY

## SECOND EDITION

Chippendale
Dickinson

**4**

GALE

DETROIT • NEW YORK • TORONTO • LONDON

## Staff

*Senior Editor:* Paula K. Byers
*Project Editor:* Suzanne M. Bourgoin
*Managing Editor:* Neil E. Walker

*Editorial Staff:* Luann Brennan, Frank V. Castronova, Laura S. Hightower, Karen E. Lemerand, Stacy A. McConnell, Jennifer Mossman, Maria L. Munoz, Katherine H. Nemeh, Terrie M. Rooney, Geri Speace

*Permissions Manager:* Susan M. Tosky
*Permissions Specialist:* Maria L. Franklin
*Permissions Associate:* Michele M. Lonoconus
*Image Cataloger:* Mary K. Grimes

*Production Director:* Mary Beth Trimper
*Production Manager:* Evi Seoud
*Production Associate:* Shanna Heilveil
*Product Design Manager:* Cynthia Baldwin
*Senior Art Director:* Mary Claire Krzewinski

*Research Manager:* Victoria B. Cariappa
*Research Specialists:* Michele P. LaMeau, Andrew Guy Malonis, Barbara McNeil, Gary J. Oudersluys
*Research Associates:* Julia C. Daniel, Tamara C. Nott, Norma Sawaya, Cheryl L. Warnock
*Research Assistant:* Talitha A. Jean

*Graphic Services Supervisor:* Barbara Yarrow
*Image Database Supervisor:* Randy Bassett
*Imaging Specialist:* Mike Lugosz

*Manager of Data Entry Services:* Eleanor M. Allison
*Data Entry Coordinator:* Kenneth D. Benson

*Manager of Technology Support Services:* Theresa A. Rocklin
*Programmers/Analysts:* Mira Bossowska, Jeffrey Muhr, Christopher Ward

Copyright © 1998
Gale Research
835 Penobscot Bldg.
Detroit, MI 48226-4094

ISBN 0-7876-2221-4 (Set)
ISBN 0-7876-2544-2 (Volume 4)

**Library of Congress Cataloging-in-Publication data is available.**

Printed in the United States of America
10 9 8 7 6 5 4 3 2

# ENCYCLOPEDIA OF
# WORLD BIOGRAPHY

# 4

# C

## Thomas Chippendale

**Thomas Chippendale (1718-1779), an English cabinetmaker, was one of the most distinguished of all furniture designers. His "Director" was the first comprehensive design book for furniture ever to appear, and it remains probably the most important.**

The son of a joiner and the grandson of a carpenter, Thomas Chippendale was born at Otley, Yorkshire, on June 5, 1718. There is a tradition that as a young apprentice he made the dollhouse at Nostell Priory, Yorkshire, and also worked at Farnley Hall near Otley. He moved to London and married in 1748; his eldest son, also named Thomas, was born in 1749. In 1753 Chippendale went into partnership with James Rannie and took residence on St. Martin's Lane, where he remained until his death.

Chippendale's *The Gentleman and Cabinet-Maker's Director* appeared in 1754. This work, containing 160 plates and some descriptive notes, was intended to serve as a trade catalog and guide to clients. Its special significance is that it forms an important expression of the gay and lively rococo taste which became fashionable in the mid-18th century in the reaction against the somewhat ponderous character of early Georgian furniture. All three aspects of the rococo style were represented: the French, the Gothic, and the Chinese. At one time it was believed that many of the designs in the *Director* were not the work of Chippendale, but Anthony Coleridge (1968) suggests Chippendale himself was responsible for the original drawings. The *Director* was so successful that a second edition appeared in 1755 and a third edition, revised and enlarged, in 1762.

One of Chippendale's important early commissions was the furnishing of Dumfries House in Scotland in 1759. This house was the first independent work of the architect Robert Adam, and it was probably here that the long association between the two men began. Both were members of the Society of Arts, to which Chippendale was elected in 1760.

The *Director* was the principal inspiration behind the characteristic mahogany furniture of the mid-18th century, and Chippendale's designs were used, often in greatly simplified form, by innumerable provincial and rural craftsmen. The most distinguished furniture produced from the Chippendale workshops, however, was the handsome marquetry pieces inspired by the neoclassic designs of Robert Adam. It was for many years hotly debated whether Chippendale ever actually made furniture to the architect's designs, but that he did so is conclusively proved by Chippendale's bill of July 9, 1765, for the supply to Sir Lawrence Dundas of armchairs and sofas which correspond exactly to an Adam design dated 1765. It appears that henceforth Chippendale absorbed the Adam manner so successfully that the architect had the fullest confidence in leaving the design of movable articles to Chippendale, who supplied furniture in the neoclassic style to Harewood House, Newbey Hall, and Nostell Priory, all in Yorkshire, and to other houses with which Adam was concerned. The pair of important satinwood and mahogany marquetry china cabinets at Firle Place, Sussex, is in Chippendale's neoclassic style (ca. 1770).

Chippendale died in London in November 1779. His eldest son continued the family business.

## Further Reading

The first monograph on Chippendale was Oliver Brackett, *Thomas Chippendale: A Study of His Life, Work, and Influence* (1924). This was superseded by the monumental study of Anthony Coleridge, *Chippendale Furniture: The Work of Thomas Chippendale and His Contemporaries in the Rococo Taste* (1968). Two volumes of selections of Chippendale designs were published by Alec Tiranti, with notes and preface by R. W. Symonds: *Chippendale Furniture Designs* (1948) and *The Ornamental Designs of Chippendale* (1949).

The first systematic account of Chippendale and his contemporaries was Ralph Edwards and Margaret Jourdain, *Georgian Cabinet-Makers* (1944; rev. ed. 1955); this work was partially superseded by later studies. Chippendale's designs are discussed in Peter Ward-Jackson, *English Furniture Designs of the Eighteenth Century* (1958). For the most comprehensive general account of Chippendale's furniture in the Adam style see Clifford Musgrave, *Adam and Hepplewhite and Other NeoClassical Furniture* (1966). Other useful works are Ralph Fastnedge, *English Furniture Styles from 1500 to 1830* (1955), and Helena Hayward, ed., *World Furniture: An Illustrated History* (1965).

## Additional Sources

Gilbert, Christopher, *The life and work of Thomas Chippendale,* London: Studio Vista, 1978. □

# Jacques Chirac

**Jacques Chirac (born 1932) was an influential French technocrat under Presidents Charles de Gaulle and Georges Pompidou. He served as prime minister under President Valéry Giscard d'Estaing (1974-1976), was an unsuccessful presidential candidate in 1981, became prime minister again in 1986 under President François Mitterrand, and was elected President of France in 1995.**

Jacques Chirac was born in Paris on November 29, 1932. Young Jacques had a meteoric career. Like many upper middle class Parisians he first headed for the bureaucracy. He graduated from the prestigious Institute for Political Studies and the National School for Administration, one of the training grounds for the French elite.

In 1959 Chirac began his bureaucratic career in accounting at the Cour des Comptes. Like many bureaucrats of his day, he found his own commitment to growth and modernization coincided with the policies of the new Gaullist government. He was tapped to join a politician's personal staff, in this case Prime Minister Pompidou's, in 1962. For the remainder of Pompidou's tenure, Chirac was a valuable economic adviser who played a critical role in the dramatic economic growth France was experiencing. Chirac entered the electoral arena in 1965, when he was elected to the municipal council of the tiny Corrèzian town of Sainte-Féréol, his family's home town. In 1967 he was elected to the National Assembly from that area and was repeatedly re-elected after that.

Chirac was also appointed to a series of cabinet posts, beginning as secretary of state for social affairs in charge of

employment in 1967. After that he served as secretary of state for the economy and finance (1968-1971), minister delegate to the premier for relations with Parliament (1971-1972), minister of agriculture and rural development (1972-1974), and minister of the interior (February-May 1974).

## Appointed Prime Minister

Chirac's political influence within the Gaullist party grew during those years. His personal political career really took off with the 1974 presidential election. President Georges Pompidou died while in office that April. Chirac supported the successful Valéry Giscard d'Estaing in the ensuing elections rather than the Gaullist Jacques Chaban-Delmas.

The new president named Chirac prime minister. And, despite some grumbling from the old Gaullist "barons," he took control of the Gaullist party, which had been left in a shambles following Chaban's disastrous showing in the elections.

His years as prime minister were difficult. He and President Giscard had different styles and images of the proper role for the state. Chirac, in particular, had difficulty with the president's frequently expressed desire to limit the role of the state in guiding the economy. In addition, Prime Minister Chirac's strong ambitions often conflicted with the president's. Finally, in 1976, the president requested and received Prime Minister Chirac's resignation.

## Member of the Opposition

That December Chirac restructured the Gaullist party, calling it the Rally for the Republic (RPR), and became the "new" party's first leader as a first step in his own presidential campaign. In 1977 he was elected the first mayor of Paris since the commune of 1870-1871. He used that office, which he held until 1995, as a vehicle to criticize the national government and to demonstrate his own ability to head a team that had remarkable success in redeveloping much of the city and improving its social services. He also headed the RPR slate in the 1978 legislative elections and continued his critical support of the Giscard-Barre government from then until the end of Giscard's seven year term in 1981.

That year, Jacques Chirac chose to run in the presidential elections and did rather well, winning 18 percent of the first ballot vote. At the second ballot, he only gave Giscard lukewarm support, which undoubtedly helped contribute to the president's defeat by President François Mitterrand. Chirac remained one of the leading opposition politicians. When the Socialist Party of President Mitterrand lost its majority in the National Assembly in the 1986 election, Chirac became prime minister again in a power-sharing agreement called cohabitation. It was the first time in the 28 years of the Fifth Republic that the French government was divided between a conservative parliament, led by Chirac, and a socialist president, Mitterrand. In 1988 Chirac ran for president a second time and was again defeated by Mitterrand. Mitterrand's election ended cohabitation and Chirac's term as prime minister. In 1995, Mitterrand, in declining health, decided not to seek another term in office.

In the May election to replace him, Chirac won nearly 53 percent of the vote to capture the presidency on his third attempt.

## President of France

As the President of France, Chirac faced the daunting challenge of restoring public confidence and generating higher levels of economic growth to decrease the country's alarming unemployment rate. In addition to creating more jobs, Chirac also promised to lower taxes, overhaul the education system, and create a volunteer army. The President also signalled his intention of continuing Mitterrand's move toward European integration and a single European currency.

Chirac's popularity dropped, however, when, later in 1995, France restarted its nuclear weapons test program in the South Pacific. Over 20 countries officially protested, demonstrators across the globe took to the streets, and international boycotts of wine and other French products were erected. Riots erupted in Tahiti, near the test site, injuring 40 people and causing millions of dollars in property damage. Chirac defended his decision by claiming that Mitterrand had prematurely ceased testing during his term in office. Chirac promised, however, to sign the Comprehensive Test Ban Treaty provided the current round of testing offered sufficient data to make future computer simulations feasible.

Chirac's closest political advisor was his daughter Claude who handled the President's communications, organized his trips, and played an important role in his election.

Despite the serious burdens that Chirac shouldered as French President, he embraced the lighter side of life and had a penchant for Americana that probably began in 1953 when he traveled to the United States and attended summer courses at Harvard. To help support himself, the 20-year-old Chirac worked as a soda jerk and dishwasher in a Howard Johnson's restaurant. The *New York Times,* speaking of Chirac's common touch, reported, "He prefers a cold Mexican beer to a glass of wine, and a genuine American meal like a hot turkey sandwich with gravy to a pseudo-Escoffier meal. While he strongly supports the law that requires French television stations to show mainly French films, . . . friends say he would rather watch a Gary Cooper western than a mannered French romance." Chirac's habit of frequenting McDonald's and Burger King restaurants led Prime Minister Alain Juppé to joke in *Time,* "As soon as he sees a fast-food place, he has to stop the car, rush up to the counter, and order a hamburger."

## Further Reading

For an article on Chirac's presidency, see Paris bureau chief, Craig R. Whitney's article in the *New York Times,* February 11, 1996.
None of Jacques Chirac's books have been translated into English. The best material on him and his political circumstances can be found in Jean Charlot, *The Gaullist Phenomenon* (London, 1971) and in Frank L. Wilson, *French Political Parties Under the Fifth Republic* (1982). □

# Giorgio de Chirico

**The Italian painter Giorgio de Chirico (1888-1978), acclaimed by the surreallists as a forerunner of their movement, founded the school of metaphysical painting.**

Giorgio de Chirico was born on July 10, 1888, in Volos, Greece, the son of an engineer from Palermo. The family settled in Athens, where De Chirico studied art at the Polytechnic Institute. His earliest works were landscapes and seascapes.

After the death of his father in 1905 De Chirico, attracted by the German neoromantic school of painting, moved to Munich. There he saw the paintings of Arnold Böcklin and discovered the writings of Friedrich Nietzsche, which exercised a great influence on him.

The attraction of Böcklin for De Chirico is best understood from the artist's own words: "Böcklin knew how to create an entire world of his own of a surprising lyricism, combining the preternaturalism of the Italian landscape with architectural elements." De Chirico also spoke of the metaphysical power with which "Böcklin always springs from the precision and clarity of a definite apparition." These statements describe the characteristics of De Chirico's own art.

In 1909 De Chirico went to Italy. The following year he began to execute the paintings that became characteristic of his style, such as the *Enigma of the Oracle* and the *Enigma of an Autumn Afternoon*. This style he developed further in Paris between 1911 and 1915, where he worked in isolation and in poor health. When he exhibited at the Salon des Indépendants in 1913, Guillaume Apollinaire called him "the most astonishing painter of his time."

De Chirico had to return to Italy for his military service and was stationed in Ferrara (1915-1918). The architecture of that city, with its far perspectives, deepened his sense of the mysterious. In 1917 he met the painter Carlo Carrà at the military hospital in Ferrara, and they launched the metaphysical school (Scuola Metafisica) of painting, which attempted to create a new order of reality based on metaphysics. Giorgio Morandi, Ardengo Soffici, Filippo de Pisis, Alberto Savinio (De Chirico's brother), and Mario Sironi soon became members of the circle.

## Characteristics of His Art

The art of De Chirico centers upon the antithesis between classical culture and modern mechanistic civilization. These two elements are locked in a desperate struggle, and the tragic quality of this situation exudes an aura of melancholy of which De Chirico is a prime exponent. The iconographic elements of his early art—modern railways and clock towers combined with ancient architecture—are to be sought in the artist's childhood memories of Greece. For the strange visual images in which De Chirico cast his mature works (1911-1918), he used an airless dreamlike space in his townscapes with an exaggerated perspective artificially illuminated, with long sinister shadows, and strewn about with antique statues. There is an elegiac loneliness too (the *Delights of the Poet*, 1913) and the disturbing juxtaposition of such banal everyday objects as biscuits and rubber gloves with those of mythical significance. And De Chirico's new man has no face; he is a dummy (*Hector and Andromache*, 1917).

A favorite amusement of ancient Greece was the composition of enigmas. In De Chirico's art they symbolize an endangered transitional period of European culture. From the enigma to the riddle presented by one's dream life is but a short step.

## Late Works

De Chirico moved to Rome in 1918, and on the occasion of an exhibition that year he was hailed as a great avant-garde master. A year later he became one of the leaders of Valori Plastici, a group of painters espousing traditional plastic values which dominated the artistic scene in Italy at that time. In 1919 an exhibition of De Chirico's works in Berlin made a deep impression on the central European Dadaists. Between 1920 and 1924 his art underwent numerous fluctuations.

In 1925 De Chirico returned to Paris, where the French proclaimed him one of the masters of surrealism. He, however, had quarreled with the Dadaists and surrealists (he corresponded intensely between 1920 and 1925 with Paul Éluard and André Breton) and had left this stage of his development far behind.

In Paris, De Chirico designed scenery and costumes for the Ballets Suédois and the Ballets Monte Carlo and began to paint a series of ruins, wild horses, and gladiators. After 1929, the year in which he published a strange dream novel, *Hebdomeros*, he changed his style entirely, renounced his adherence to the modern movement, and from then on, living in Rome, became not only a fierce critic of modernism but an academic painter of neoclassic character. He died in 1978.

## Further Reading

James Thrall Soby, *Giorgio de Chirico* (1955), is a searching and comprehensive study of De Chirico's life, work, and philosophy. Isabella Far, *Giorgio de Chirico* (1953), has a text in Italian and English. See also James T. Soby and Alfred H. Barr, Jr., *Twentieth-Century Italian Art* (1949), and Massimo Carrà, ed., *Metaphysical Art* (1970). De Chirico's novel, *Hebdomeros*, is discussed in J. H. Matthews, *Surrealism and the Novel* (1966). □

# Caroline Chisholm

**Caroline Chisholm (1808–1877) was a British-born author and philanthropist, whose work with immigrant families, women and children ensured the successful colonization of Australia.**

Caroline Jones Chisholm was born in a time of turmoil. On the continent, Napoleon was wreaking havoc, and the wars undertaken to defeat him were sapping Great Britain of her resources. The Industrial Revolution was in full swing, and by the late 18th century there had emerged a massive underclass of "deserving" poor, many without means of subsistence. To deal with the poverty, a support system loosely based on the Christian principle of charity was espoused. Foremost among the early protagonists of this social philosophy were John Howard, Robert Owen, and Elizabeth Fry—philanthropists who perceived the need for outright abolition of state poor laws in favor of a more personal reliance on voluntary charitable support of the poor by the upper class.

Not without its opponents, this system of poor relief and quasi-state aid persisted not only in Great Britain, but in most cases throughout the empire until the end of World War I (1914-18). Born in 1808 into the reasonably well-to-do family of William Jones, a yeoman farmer in Northampton, Caroline Chisholm received an education that reflected the times. As a young girl, she visited the sick of the neighboring village, providing them with help and care, and was, in the words of one biographer, educated to "look on philanthropic labor as a part of her everyday life."

At seven, she displayed a passionate interest in immigration. Having heard wondrous tales of far-off lands in what has been characterized as an enlightened household, she invented an immigration game. Using a wash basin as the sea, she "made boats of broad-beans; expended all [her] money in touchwood dolls, removed families, located them in the bed-quilt and sent the boats, filled with wheat, back to the friends." This early interest in immigration would later provide a focus for her rising philanthropic passion.

When Captain Archibald Chisholm asked her to marry him, the 22-year-old accepted on the condition that she maintain the freedom to pursue any philanthropic concern she desired; his acceptance of her terms forged a loving compromise that would endure throughout their marriage. Indeed, he assisted Chisholm, becoming somewhat of a partner in her great works. But another problem confronted the young couple. Archibald was a Roman Catholic. Raised Protestant—in an age and nation where Catholicism was viewed with suspicion and mistrust—Chisholm faced a difficult decision. Deeply in love with her husband, she converted to Catholicism and lest one think that her conversion was one of mere convenience, "the record of her life," as one biographer put it, "shows that she was a most devout Catholic." Her Catholicism would, later in life, furnish opponents with dangerously powerful ammunition in their fight against her work.

For the first two years of their marriage, the couple lived in Brighton until, in the early months of 1832, Archibald received a posting to Madras, India. When Chisholm followed him there a few months later, she immediately discovered a viable outlet for her philanthropic passions. Living in a military encampment, she observed the soldiers' families and found the condition of their children, especially the daughters, appalling. As they ran about without discipline or structured education, she decided to establish a school for these unattended young ladies. As the wife of a junior officer with limited resources, Chisholm would have to raise the necessary funds through private donations. She enlisted the help of a few friends and set out to appeal to the generosity of "a few gentlemen." At the end of five days, they had raised 2,000 rupees, and The Female School of Industry for the Daughters of European Soldiers was founded. The school, which taught cooking, housekeeping, and the "three R's," was a significant first step in Chisholm's philanthropic career.

During their sojourn in Madras, she gave birth to two sons whose care coupled with the maintenance of the school kept her busy. In 1838, Archibald was granted sick leave, and the Chisholms headed for Australia. The difficult journey took over seven months, acquainting Chisholm with the inherent difficulties of travel to Australia, a lesson that would partly fuel her philanthropic concern for the plight of immigrants in the years to come.

By the end of the Napoleonic Wars in Europe, free immigration slowly began to transform Australia from a reputedly desolate penal colony to a thriving, prospering, proud member of the British Empire. Sydney, the pearl of New South Wales (NSW) and the visible symbol of an ascendant Australia, stretched at its seams, bustling with activity and opportunity. Initially, all immigration had been unassisted, but in 1831 the Home government instituted a system of assisted immigration. This new step was taken because the majority of the free immigrants had been single men, and since the transported convicts were predominantly male as well, a poor male-female ratio existed in the colony. The disparity between the sexes was, according to some, "causing grave moral evils," and assisted immigration, it was hoped, would provide a balance between the sexes and encourage civilized conduct in this less than civilized outpost of the empire. The British government, however, emptied the slums, tenements, orphanages, and asylums of England, and by 1835 this system was suffering severe criticism. A program of bounties was instituted, by which agents of Australian settlers in England would offer bounties to qualified immigrants. Gradually, bounties were handed out by shipping companies and ship-owners. These shipowners were granted bounty permits in their name, with no mention of specific immigrants, by the governor of Australia. Spotting an opportunity for immense profit, shipowners packed as many immigrants as possible on their ships, without regard for their suitability or comfort. Regardless of the obvious corruption of this system, the settlers were contented with these new immigrants.

One of the main flaws associated with assisted immigration and the bounties was the lack of provision for immigrants after disembarkation. Whereas in 1838, when Chisholm arrived in Australia, less than 7,000 immigrants entered the country, by 1841, a surge in immigration swelled the number of newcomers to over 20,000. Even in the best of times, such a number would have overwhelmed the system. In the depressionary times of the early 1840s, the effects were disastrous. Immigrants—largely taken from large urban centers in England, Scotland, and Ireland—

preferred starvation in Sydney to an uncertain future in the bush. Although a demand existed in the interior for labor, these immigrants were unwilling, without assistance, to venture far from Sydney's familiar trappings.

The foremost concern of Caroline Chisholm was the plight of the young immigrant girls. When Captain Chisholm sailed for China in 1841, his wife decided to come to the aide of the abandoned and penniless women of Sydney. Assisted by a committee, Chisholm set out to establish an immigrants' home where these women could reside until suitable employment could be found. Immediately, she met opposition from the colony's governor, Sir George Gipps, who believed as did most people of the day, that women had no place in public life. Her Catholicism, as well, raised the suspicions of some opponents to the plan, though the opposition remained muted in the beginning. While praying in Church on Easter Sunday, 1841, Chisholm made a solemn vow:

> . . . to know neither country nor creed, but to serve all justly and impartially. I asked only to be enabled to keep these poor girls from being tempted by their need to mortal sin, and resolved that to accomplish this, I would in every way, sacrifice my feelings— surrender all comfort—nor, in fact, consider my own wishes or feelings, but wholly devote myself to the work I had in hand.

Invigorated by her new pledge, she proved a formidable adversary to Gipps. Eventually, after striking a bargain that no state funds would be used, Gipps acquiesced, giving Chisholm part of the old immigration barracks. Thus, in 1841, the Female Immigrants' Home was established. In the first year alone, it served approximately 1,400 women, helping to settle most of them in the interior of the continent. Situating these young women in suitable homes, Chisholm traveled extensively and by the end of 1842 had established 16 branch homes throughout northeastern New South Wales. That year, she authored *Female Immigration Considered in a Brief Account of the Sydney Immigrants Home,* the first book published in Australia by a woman.

With the advent of a crippling economic depression, Chisholm began to concentrate on settling whole families of immigrants on land of their own. Demand for labor in the bush remained high, but British land-settlement policies had kept the price of land high enough to make land purchase impossible for all but the wealthiest immigrant families. Chisholm regarded permanent settlement of the lands in the interior as both a way to combat the depression and a way to alleviate the problem of overpopulation in Great Britain. She devised a system of land settlement by which families would be distributed in the bush in small settlements, with 10- to 15-year clearing leases (as opposed to rent), allowing these families to prosper.

This idea interested several important landowners, most notably Captain Robert Towns, who offered her 4,000 acres at Shell Harbor, NSW, for the settlement of 50 families. But, fearing that the plan would create a new class of landowners and thus upset the prevailing political structure of the colony, the Select Committee on Distressed Labourers

stated that the Committee was "afraid we should find that these people becoming employers of labour would do us a mischief." Undaunted by her lack of support, Chisholm pressed on, publishing a survey entitled "Voluntary Information from the People of New South Wales," in order to further stimulate acceptance of the organized settlement of Australia by Britons.

Determined to take her fight directly to the British people, the family visited England upon Archibald's 1845 retirement from the army. With her organization firmly established in Australia, Chisholm felt the need to furnish it with a steady flow of immigrants. Explaining her philosophy, she wrote:

> for all the clergy you can dispatch, all the schoolmasters you can appoint, all the churches you can build and all the books you can export will never do much good without "God's Police"—wives and little children.

In England, she could appeal more directly to philanthropic and social reformers, and she hoped to do this by circulating the "Voluntary Information" among all classes of people in Great Britain. Thus, upon arrival in England, Chisholm developed the three-point agenda that she thought necessary to promote the successful settlement of Australia: (1) to organize a viable colonization system; (2) to arrange for unwanted and mistreated orphans a chance at a new life; and (3) to convey to Australia the wives and children of men transported by the British government earlier, either as ticket-of-leave men or emancipated convicts.

First, she wanted to organize a national scheme for sustained colonization. A few months after her arrival, Chisholm set up an office in London where she could interview prospective immigrants. She published "Emigration and Transportation Relatively Considered," extolling the virtues of systematic emigration over forced transportation, and soon gained popularity in some powerful circles of Victorian society. Charles Dickens wrote several articles in his periodical *Household Words* championing her cause, and with such support the Family Colonization Loan Society was founded in 1847. By the end of 1849, 200 families had been enrolled and plans for chartering a ship were begun. In providing for passage to Australia, the Society effectively eradicated overcrowding and other injurious conditions on ships which had plagued earlier immigration schemes. The first vessel to be chartered, the *Slains Castle,* sailed in September of 1850 with 250 families on board. Soon, other ships followed, and Chisholm succeeded in convincing whole families to undertake emigration. In 1852, the Legislative Council of NSW granted the Family Colonization Loan Society the sum of £10,000 in support of continued immigration. Chisholm's work had gained the support of the Australian government, and the success of the Family Colonization Loan Society had been assured.

Concerning the second and third goals of her stay in England, Chisholm had little problem securing transport, and later homes, for two shiploads of children taken from several orphanages around England. She managed as well to secure assistance from the British government for the transport of the families of convicts sent to Australia in the previous decades. But while her work in England ensured a sustained, successful colonization of Australia, Chisholm was not without her detractors.

In Australia, in fact, the Presbyterian minister Dr. John Dunmore Lang stirred up old religious bigotries, crying, "No Popery!" (no pope) to all who would listen. Fearful that Chisholm's efforts might lead to the creation of a Catholic majority in Australia, Lang devised his own reactionary and divisive immigration scheme and vowed to "deliver this Colony and Hemisphere for all time coming, from the justly apprehended and intolerably degrading despotism of Rome." Lang later vowed to "live and die amongst his own people," and not among Catholics. In response, Chisholm wrote:

I have lived happily amongst pagans and heathens, Mahometans and Hindoos—they never molested me at my devotions, nor did I insult them at theirs; and am I not to enjoy the same privilege in New South Wales?

Ironically, the feud between Lang and Chisholm only served to promote the colonization of Australia. Since she had secured the only viable means of accomplishing this task, British support, the subsequent success of her venture was guaranteed.

But by 1854, with the advent of the Crimean War, ships became scarce, and Chisholm decided to return to New South Wales. Upon her arrival, she discovered a new problem which required her attention. With the discovery of gold in the wilderness, vast tracts of land beyond the original boundaries of the 19 counties of NSW originally surveyed in the 1830s were deemed off-limits by the local government. Chisholm toured the goldfields, becoming a champion of the cause of the small farmers and demanding that the government "Unlock the Lands!"

Our aim must be to make it as easy for a working man to reach Australia as America, and we must hold out a certainty of being able to obtain land. Nothing else will tempt the honest working man of the right sort to emigrate.

Still, her call for this opening of the land and the sale of tracts of land at an affordable price, initially fell on deaf ears. When her health failed in 1857, she was forced to leave this fight half-fought as her tenure in public life drew to an end. Archibald Chisholm's pension from the Honourable East India Company had all but dried up, and in an effort to address her family's economic hardship, she opened a ladies' school at Rathbone House, Newtown, in 1862, which subsequently closed in 1864. By 1866, Archibald and Caroline Chisholm had returned to England. A few months later, she was granted a government pension of £100 a year. The last five years of her life were spent bedridden and ill.

At the age of 69, Caroline Chisholm died on Sunday, March 25th, 1877, in London. The Times' obituary outlined her achievements in about ten lines, and Australian papers barely marked her passing. The inscription on her headstone reads: "The Emigrant's Friend." Renowned

French historian Michelet praised her thus: "The fifth part of the world, Australia, has up to now but one saint, one legend. This saint is an Englishwoman." Florence Nightingale, slightly more militant in her method, nevertheless characterized herself as Chisholm's "friend and pupil," and Robert Lorne, member of the Legislative Council of New South Wales wrote of her life and work: "It was the most original ever devised or undertaken by man or woman, and the object, the labor and the method were beyond all praise."

## Further Reading

"Chisholm, Caroline" in The Australian Encyclopedia. Vol. 2, Michigan State University Press, 1958.

Hoban, Mary C. Fifty-one Pieces of Wedding Cake: A Biography of Caroline Chisholm. Lowden, 1973.

Kiddel, Margaret. Caroline Chisholm. Melbourne University Press, 1950.

Younger, R. M. Australia and the Australians: A New Concise History. Humanities Press, 1970.

Clark, C. M. H. A History of Australia. Vol. 3, Melbourne University Press, 1973.

Kennedy, Richard, ed. Australian Welfare History: Critical Essays. Macmillan of Australia, 1982.

Malony, John. The Penguin Bicentennial History of Australia: The Story of 200 Years. Viking, 1987. □

# Shirley Anita St. Hill Chisholm

**Shirley Anita St. Hill Chisholm (born 1924) was the first Black woman to serve in the United States Congress. She served as the representative for the 12th district of New York from 1969 until 1982. In 1972, when she became the first black woman to actively run for the presidency of the United States, she won ten percent of the votes at the Democratic National Convention.**

Born in Brooklyn, New York, to Barbadian parents, Chisholm was raised in an atmosphere that was both political and religious. Her father was a staunch follower of the West Indian political activist Marcus Garvey, who advocated black pride and unity among blacks to achieve economic and political power. Chisholm received much of her primary education in her parents homeland, Barbados, under the strict eye of her maternal grandmother. Chisholm, who returned to New York when she was ten years old, credits her educational successes to the well-rounded early training she received in Barbados.

Attending New York public schools, Chisholm was able to compete well in the predominantly white classrooms. She attended Girls' High School in Bedford-Stuyvesant, a section of the city with a growing poor black and immigrant population. She won tuition scholarships to both Oberlin and Vassar, but at the urging of her parents decided to live at home and attend Brooklyn College. While training to be a teacher she became active in several campus and community groups. Developing a keen interest in politics, she began to learn the arts of organizing and fund raising. She deeply resented the role of women in local politics, which consisted mostly of staying in the background, sponsoring fund raising events, and turning the money over to male party leaders who would then decide how to use it. During her school years, she became interested in the Delta Sigma Theta Sorority and the National Association for the Advancement of Colored People and eventually joined both groups.

### From Classroom to Congress

After graduating *cum laude* from Brooklyn College in 1946 Chisholm began to work as a nursery school teacher and later as a director of schools for early childhood education. In 1949 she married Conrad Chisholm. She continued to teach but her political interest never waned. After a successful career as a teacher, Chisholm decided to run for the New York State Assembly in 1964. She won the election.

During the time that she served in the assembly, Chisholm sponsored 50 bills, but only eight of them passed. The bills she sponsored reflected her interest in the cause of blacks and the poor, women's rights, and educational opportunities. One of the successful bills provided assistance for poor students to go on for higher education. Another provided employment insurance coverage for personal and domestic employees. Still another reversed a law that caused female teachers in New York to lose their tenure while they were out on maternity leave.

Chisholm served in the State Assembly until 1968 and then decided to run for the U.S. Congress. Her opponent was the noted civil rights leader James Farmer. Possibly because Chisholm was a well-known resident of Bedford-Stuyvesant and Farmer was not, she won easily. Thus began her tenure in the U.S. House of Representatives from the 91st through the 97th Congress (1969-1982). Always considering herself a political maverick, Chisholm attempted to focus as much of her attention as possible on the needs of her constituents. She served on several House committees: Agriculture, Veterans' Affairs, Rules and Education, and Labor. During the 91st Congress when she was assigned to the Forestry Committee, she protested saying that she wanted to work on committees that could deal with the "critical problems of racism, deprivation and urban decay." (There are no forests in Bedford-Stuyvesant.)

Chisholm began to protest the amount of money being expended for the defense budget while social programs suffered. She argued that she would not agree that money should be spent for war while Americans were hungry, ill-housed, and poorly educated. Early in her career as a congresswoman she began to support legislation allowing abortions for women who chose to have them. Chisholm protested the traditional roles for women professionals—secretaries, teachers, and librarians. She argued that women were capable of entering many other professions and that they should be encouraged to do so. Black women, too, she felt, had been shunted into stereotypical maid and nanny roles from which they needed to escape both by legislation and by self-effort. Her antiwar and women's liberation views made her a popular figure among college students, and she was beseiged with invitations to speak at college campuses.

### Presidential Contender

In 1972 Chisholm made the decision that she would run for the highest office in the land—the presidency. In addition to her interest in civil rights for blacks, women, and the poor, she spoke out about the judicial system in the United States, police brutality, prison reform, gun control, politician dissent, drug abuse, and numerous other topics. She appeared on the television show "Face the Nation" with three other democratic presidential candidates: George McGovern, Henry Jackson, and Edmund Muskie. George McGovern won the presidential nomination at the Democratic National Convention, but Chisholm captured ten percent of the delegates' votes. As a result of her candidacy, Chisholm was voted one of the ten most admired women in the world.

After her unsuccessful presidential campaign, Chisholm continued to serve in the U.S. House of Representatives for another decade. As a member of the Black Caucus she was able to watch black representation in the Congress grow and to welcome other black female congresswomen. Finally, in 1982, she announced her retirement from the Congress.

## Final Years

From 1983 to 1987 Chisholm served as Purington Professor at Massachusetts' Mt. Holyoke College where she taught politics and women's studies. In 1985 she was the visiting scholar at Spelman College, and in 1987 retired from teaching altogether. Chisholm continued to be involved in politics by cofounding the National Political Congress of Black Women in 1984. She also worked vigorously for the presidential campaign of Jesse Jackson in 1984 and 1988. "Jackson is the voice of the poor, the disenchanted, the disillusioned," Chisholm was quoted as saying in *Newsweek*, "and that is exactly what I was."

In 1993 President Bill Clinton nominated Chisolm as Ambassador to Jamaica, but due to declining health, she withdrew her name from further consideration.

## Further Reading

Chisholm has written two autobiographical accounts, *Unbought and Unbossed* (1970) and *The Good Fight* (1973). There are several other books about her political career which are especially geared to young readers. A few of them are: Lenore K. Itzkowitz, *Shirley Chisholm for President* (1974); James Haskins, *Fighting Shirley Chisholm* (1975); and Nancy Hicks, *The Honorable Shirley Chisholm, Congresswoman from Brooklyn* (1971). The *Congressional Record* for the 91st through 97th Congress can be used to find the texts of Chisholm's speeches. □

# Joaquim Alberto Chissano

**Joaquim Alberto Chissano (born 1939), one of the leaders of the war of liberation against Portugal, became his nation's first foreign minister when Mozambique won its independence in 1975. Upon the accidental death of President Samora Machel in 1986 Chissano became president.**

Joaquim Alberto Chissano was born on October 22, 1939, at Chibuto in the province of Gaza in the south of Mozambique. He went through an impoverished childhood, as did the great majority of Mozambicans of his generation. Nevertheless, he was able to go through primary and secondary high school at Tai-Xai and Liceu Salazar in Lourenco Marques (now Maputo), respectively. After lonely school years he emerged as one of the first Black children to graduate from the Liceu Salazar. He then left for Portugal in pursuit of further studies.

After failing anatomy at the end of his first year at a Portuguese university he moved to France, where he soon emerged as one of the founders of the exile organization Front for the Liberation of Mozambique (Frente de Libertacao de Moçambique), on June 25, 1962. This FRELIMO movement was the merger of three nationalist parties: The Uniáo Democrática Nacional de Moçambique (UDENAMO), the Mozambique African Nationalist Union (MANU), and the Uniáo Africana de Moçambique Independence (UNAMI). In August 1963 he was one of the FRELIMO guerrilla leaders sent to Algeria for training.

## Student and Political Activist

Chissano's political career had been shaped during his early school days in Lourenco Marques. He was a member of the Nucleus of African Secondary Students of Mozambique and was the founder of the National Union of Mozambique Students. His involvement in student politics later proved valuable when he entered nationalist politics. The leadership qualities developed during the early period allowed Chissano to emerge as one of the three leading figures in FRELIMO.

In 1963 he became a member of the central and executive committee of the party. Between 1964 and 1974 he was FRELIMO's secretary and minister of defense, and until the death of the first FRELIMO leader, Eduardo Mondlane, who was killed by a parcel bomb on February 3, 1969, Chissano shared the responsibility for security and defense with Samora Moises Machel. Chissano was, however, absent at the time of Mondlane's death.

In the ensuing struggle for leadership following the death of Mondlane, Chissano played a crucial conciliatory role. He brought together Samora Machel, Marcelino dos Santos, and Uria Simango in a temporary uneasy alliance, the Presidential Council. Chissano himself continued to hold the position of secretary and minister of defense.

Chissano was also FRELIMO's representative to the Tanzanian government during the 1964-1974 period.

While in Dar es Salaam he was also the director of the Mozambique Institute (now the Mozambique-Tanzania Centre for Foreign Relations) up to 1973. That position made him the person in charge of conduct and coordination of the liberation war against the Portuguese Army.

As the liberation war intensified, and aided by the April 25, 1974, military coup in Portugal, it became clear that Portuguese colonialism was coming to an end. By September 1974 Portugal agreed to grant Mozambique independence under FRELIMO. Chissano, the moderate of the three leading figures in FRELIMO, was appointed prime minister of the transitional government, which lasted from September 1974 until independence on June 25, 1975. Machel and dos Santos preferred to remain outside the transitional government in order to cushion themselves against the possible short-comings, and even failures, of the new government.

As prime minister of the transitional government, Chissano came directly under Portuguese colonial officials. Directly above him was the governor general, who continued to represent Portugal under the new arrangement. Chissano found himself in a difficult situation, especially in dealing with the Portuguese residents. Other FRELIMO leaders, such as Amando Guebuza, wanted the Portuguese expelled from Mozambique, but Chissano was against unnecessary expulsions of Portuguese people.

## Independence Comes to Mozambique

At independence on June 25, 1975, Chissano became Mozambique's minister of foreign affairs, a position he held until the death of Machel in October 1986. During this period he also had a less-publicized role as chief of security, which won him the support of the country's military commanders. In that post he kept a close watch over possible infighting in the party. Although Chissano was a committed Marxist, he was urbane and articulate. A pragmatist, he won wide respect internationally.

Chissano always remained committed to party discipline, even though at times he disagreed with his leader. For instance, because Chissano never trusted the South African government, he neither took active participation in the drawing up of the Nkomati Accord in 1984 nor was involved in the signing ceremony. But as minister of foreign affairs he tried to have good relations with the West, where he found both Great Britain and the United States more sympathetic to the Mozambique situation than to the Angolan government on the other side of the continent.

## Chissano, the President

Following the death of President Samora Moises Machel in a plane crash on October 19, 1986, Chissano was elected by the 130-member Central Committee of FRELIMO on November 3 to succeed Machel as president of the party, head of state, and commander-in-chief of the armed forces. He was sworn into office on November 6. Chissano was a close associate of Machel. They both trained in Algeria, and Chissano had risen during the liberation war to the rank of major general.

In his inaugural speech on November 6 Chissano pledged Mozambique's continued adherence to the Nkomati Accord, even though he had always doubted South Africa's commitment to the agreement. On the home front, Chissano announced that rehabilitation of the economy was the central objective in the economic sphere. Chissano also announced on December 17, 1987, that an amnesty for rebels and a reduction in jail sentences was to be introduced in order to rehabilitate the rebels of the Mozambique National Resistance (MNR) and make political progress.

## Fifth Congress of FRELIMO

During the fifth congress of FRELIMO held in Maputo on July 24 to 30, 1989, Chissano was unanimously re-elected as party president by the 700 delegates. At the congress Chissano indicated that he was ready to consider negotiating with the rebels in order to end the 14-year-long war. The congress adopted Chissano's proposals for a negotiated peaceful settlement with the rebels. The congress also adopted his other proposal that people previously excluded from FRELIMO on ideological grounds be admitted into the party. Property owners and local entrepreneurs were also to be admitted.

The fifth congress, the first since 1983, was marked by the conspicuous absence of Marxist-Leninist rhetoric in the FRELIMO works. The congress was more concerned with dealing with the real issues and finding solutions. Thus little time was wasted on Marxist-Leninist rhetoric. This change of direction in Mozambican international alignments was reflected in the March 29, 1989, meeting between British Prime Minister Margaret Thatcher and President Chissano in neighboring Zimbabwe at Nyanga where British instructors helped train Mozambican troops. At the meeting the two leaders discussed the possibility of increasing the training program to assist Mozambique in combating the MNR rebels and the increasing pressure coming from South Africa.

President Chissano continued to make amends with the West. He made his first official visit to the United States and met with President George Bush for two hours on March 13, 1990. Since Mozambique abandoned rigid Marxist-Leninist ideology in the course of 1989, the United States, on January 24, 1990, removed Mozambique from the list of Marxist-Leninist nations denied preferential loan and trade agreements. Later that year, on December 2, Mozambique adopted a constitution establishing a multi-party democracy. These moves were encouragements to Mozambique's goal of free-market economics.

## The End of Civil War

His early years in office steered Mozambique onto a different political and economic course, and the eventual conclusion of a 16-year-old civil war. Presidential elections were held in 1994, which Chissano won.

In reviewing 1996, Chissano noted his country's improvements in national reconciliation, the justice system and increased efforts at crime control, while improving the economy and lowering the inflation rate. He lobbied Western governments for debt forgiveness to promote political and economic stability throughout Africa. Despite progresses, Mozambique remains one of the absolute poorest in the world. He vowed to develop a strong private sector composed of various races through its ongoing privatization process. Towards national reconciliation, he visited Maringue, a county where the headquarters of the former rebel movement was situated.

While president, Chissano welcomed Chinese Premier Li Peng to discuss bilateral relations. He accepted an award for opening the Mozambique economy to the global marketplace during the ''Attracting Capital to Africa'' summit in April 1997, sponsored by the Corporate council on Africa. He officially visited Uganda, and granted final approval for a private game reserve planned to be the largest in the world. He called for an international devotion to the issue of children's human rights, acknowledging that Mozambique children have an especially rough time after 16 years of civil war. He also held talks with Tanzanian President Benjamin Mkapa. He visited France for official meetings. He met with Archbishop Desmond Tutu about regional issues in southern Africa. He signed a controversial deal with Nelson Mandela in which South African farmers would move into Mozambique and farm underdeveloped areas of Mozambique.

In May 1997, the ruling FRELIMO Party re-elected head of state Chissano as president of the party and many speculate that he will represent the party in 1999 presidential elections. Chissano was an experienced linguist who spoke fluent Portuguese, French, English, and Swahili. He was married to Marcelina Rafael Chissano, and they had four children.

## Further Reading

Biographical material in English on Chissano is scarce. A detailed biographical essay appeared in *New African* in December 1986, and he is listed in *Africa Year Book and Who's Who in Africa 1977*, published by Africa Journal Limited, and in *African Biographies*. Nevertheless, students will find the following material, which generally explores Mozambique's experience since Chissano became president, useful: *Keesing's Contemporary Archives*, volumes 32-36; *The Europa Year Book, 1989*, vol. II (earlier volumes are also useful); *African Contemporary Record: Annual Survey and Documents*, edited by Colin Legum. *Mozambique: A Country Study* (1984), edited by Harold D. Nelson, is also useful. □

# John Simpson Chisum

**American rancher John Simpson Chisum (1824-1884) was one of the first cattlemen in New Mexico, and he was identified with the Lincoln County War of 1878-1879.**

John Chisum was born on his grandfather's plantation in western Tennessee on Aug. 16, 1824. When he was 13, his parents settled in the growing community of Paris, Tex. Apparently he had no formal education but worked at odd jobs. At 28 he became county clerk and began speculating in real estate in the surrounding counties. For reasons

of health he wanted work outdoors as a rancher, so 2 years later he formed a partnership with Stephen K. Fowler of New York, who invested $6,000 in cattle, with Chisum agreeing to manage the enterprise for a share in the profits. They placed stock on a range north of present Fort Worth and applied for a land patent. By 1860 Chisum evaluated his half interest at $50,000.

When Texas joined the Confederacy in 1861, Chisum, exempt from military service, became a beef supplier for the troops in the Trans-Mississippi Department. At the close of the war he was among the first to drive Texas cattle into eastern New Mexico to sell to the military and Native American reservations. He had a thousand head near Roswell, N. Mex., in 1867. He made an agreement with Charles Goodnight to deliver additional herds to that point to be driven northward by Goodnight's trail hands. Chisum became a New Mexico resident and established a series of ranches along the Pecos River for 150 miles. In 1875 he won the contract to furnish beef to all agencies for Native Americans in Arizona Territory. Employing a hundred cowboys to handle 80,000 head, he became known as the ''Pecos Valley Cattle King.''

Many aspects of Chisum's career have been subject to debate. Considered a man of integrity, he was involved in business deals that led to prolonged litigation, and he spent at least one short period in jail. He employed gunmen to protect his herds from cattle rustlers and Indians. With two other men he established the Lincoln County Bank in Sante Fe, but the murder of one led to an outbreak of violence. In this Lincoln County War the outlaw Billy the Kid was rumored to be in Chisum's employ. Chisum was largely responsible for the election of a new sheriff of Lincoln County, and when the sheriff shot Billy the Kid, Chisum breathed more easily. Chisum also claimed friendship with Lew Wallace, who had been sent to New Mexico as territorial governor to restore peace.

Chisum died in 1884 in Eureka Springs, Ark., where he was recuperating from an operation. He left an estate estimated at $500,000.

## Further Reading

General histories of New Mexico and accounts of the Lincoln County War in particular have brief biographical sketches of Chisum. Among the more recent are William A. Keleher, *The Fabulous Frontier: Twelve New Mexico Items* (1945; rev. ed. 1962); Frederick W. Nolan, ed., *The Life and Death of John Henry Tunstall: The Letters, Diaries and Adventures of an Itinerant Englishman* (1965); and Maurice Garland Fulton, *History of the Lincoln County War*, edited by Robert N. Mullin (1968). The most authoritative study on Chisum for the 1877-1884 period is by Harwood P. Hinton in the *New Mexico Quarterly Review* (vols. 31 and 32, 1956-1957). Lewis Atherton made some penetrating observations on Chisum's career in *The Cattle Kings* (1961).

## Additional Sources

Clarke, Mary Whatley, *John Simpson Chisum: jinglebob king of the Pecos*, Austin, Tex.: Eakin Press, 1984. □

# Ch'i-ying

**The Manchu official and diplomat Ch'i-ying (ca. 1786-1858) was chief negotiator for the first series of treaties concluded between China and the Western nations between 1842 and 1844.**

B orn an imperial clansman of the Ch'ing dynasty, Ch'i-ying began his official career in 1806. He first achieved international prominence in August 1842 at Nanking, which the British, who had been engaged in the Opium War in China since 1839, were threatening to bombard if China did not capitulate. Ch'i-ying had been granted full authority to negotiate peace.

The ensuing Treaty of Nanking (Aug. 29, 1842), which Ch'i-ying signed for China, granted to the British the island of Hong Kong, which was turned back over to China in July of 1997; an indemnity of $21 million; the opening of five ports—Canton, Amoy, Foochow, Ningpo, and Shanghai—to foreign trade; and diplomatic equality between Chinese and British officials. On Oct. 8, 1843, Ch'i-ying also signed the supplementary Treaty of the Bogue, which established tariffs and granted consular jurisdiction and other extra-territorial rights to the British. It also contained the "most-favored-nation clause," by which any privileges granted by China to one country might be demanded by other treaty powers. Ch'i-ying also negotiated similar treaties with the United States, France, Sweden, and Norway.

During the negotiations Ch'i-ying was severely criticized for his unorthodox conduct. His camaraderie and conciliation were regarded as a betrayal of Chinese traditional procedures vis-à-vis foreigners. In his defense, Ch'i-ying stated, in a memorial in 1844, that these foreigners were so ignorant of normal Chinese procedures, so suspicious of Chinese motives, and so arrogant that the normal methods of dealing with barbarians could not be applied. Ch'i-ying, in effect, was questioning Chinese values and inadvertently took the first step toward the destruction of traditional China.

Under the treaties, the British claimed the right to enter Canton, but the xenophobic Cantonese refused. Ch'i-ying, as the governor general of Canton between 1844 and 1848, was thus placed in an untenable position. His appeasement policy had failed, and he was recalled to Peking in 1848.

When British and French forces threatened Peking in 1858 as a consequence of the Arrow War (1856-1860), Ch'i-ying was ordered to participate in the peace negotiations. However, when the British presented him with a copy of his memorial of 1844, Ch'i-ying fled. For having left his post he was arrested, tried, and permitted to commit suicide.

## Further Reading

The only complete biography of Ch'i-ying in English is by Arthur W. Hummel, ed., *Eminent Chinese of the Ch'ing Period,* vol. 1 (1943). John K. Fairbank, *Trade and Diplomacy on the China Coast, 1842-1854* (2 vols., 1953), and Immanuel C. Y. Hsü,

*The Rise of Modern China* (1970), describe Ch'i-ying's appeasement policy. Ch'i-ying's policies in Canton are discussed by Frederic Wakeman, Jr., *Strangers at the Gate: Social Disorder in South China, 1839-1861* (1966). □

# Bogdan Chmielnicki

**The Cossack leader Bogdan Chmielnicki (1595-1657) led the Dnieper Cossacks in the Ukrainian war of liberation against Polish rule in 1648.**

B ogdan Chmielnicki, or Khmelnitskii, was born in Pereyaslav in the Polish-controlled Ukraine. His father was a registered Cossack and proprietor of a small farm and flour mill at Czehrin near the Dnieper River. Bogdan was educated in the school of one of the Orthodox brotherhoods and also studied at the Jesuit school in Yaroslav.

When his father died, Chmielnicki assumed management of the small family estate. He ran into difficulty, however, when a Polish lord claimed ownership of the land. Chmielnicki was summoned before a tribunal and dispossessed of his small estate. He eventually fled to the south, where he joined the Zaporozhan Cossacks. Anxious for revenge, Chmielnicki raised an army from among the Cossacks, and he also gained wide support from the Crimean Tatars and the oppressed Russian peasantry of the Ukraine. In the spring of 1648, with a force of about 300,000 men, he defeated two Polish armies sent against him.

The rather limited character of Chmielnicki's ambitions enabled a peace treaty to be concluded with the Polish king in August 1649. Chmielnicki was recognized as hetman, or Cossack leader, and allowed to retain an armed force of 40,000 Cossacks, but no provision was made for the peasantry, thousands of whom had immigrated to the Donets Basin under Russian protection. War broke out again in 1650, and Chmielnicki, now deserted by the Crimean Tatars, was compelled to accept a peace which reduced the number of registered Cossacks to 20,000.

At this point Chmielnicki sent an urgent appeal to Alexis, the Russian czar, for support. Although he had ignored earlier appeals, Alexis agreed to take Hetman Chmielnicki and his entire army, "with their towns and lands," under his protection. The final agreement was made at Pereyaslav in January 1654. Although there is some debate over its meaning, the agreement seems to have represented unconditional Ukrainian acceptance of Moscow's authority. It should be noted, however, that in later years the Ukrainians acquired good reason to complain of the Russian government, which eventually abrogated entirely the considerable autonomy granted to the Ukrainians after they had sworn allegiance to the Muscovite czar.

Chmielnicki died on Aug. 6, 1657. His death opened the way for a succession of hetmans, who thought of Poland as a lesser danger than their Russian protectors. Their policy split the Ukraine; the left bank of the Dnieper tended to support Muscovy and carried on a civil war with the Polish sympathizers on the right bank. The Treaty of Andrusovo in 1667 confirmed this division.

## Further Reading

The only biography of Chmielnicki in English is George Vernadsky, *Bogdan, Hetman of the Ukraine* (1941). Brief sketches of Chmielnicki are presented in William Cresson, *The Cossacks: Their History and Country* (1919), and Maurice Hindus, *The Cossacks: The Story of a Warrior People* (1945). The best general history of the period is V. O. Kliuchevskii, *A History of Russia,* vol. 3 (1931). □

# Ch'oe Ch'ung-hn

**Ch'oe Ch'ung-hn (1149-1219) was a Korean general who in 1196 established a hereditary military dictatorship which lasted until 1258.**

A descendant of a military family, Ch'oe Ch'ung-hn rendered conspicuous service to the Korean king in quelling a rebellion in the Western Capital (1174-1176). In 1196 Ch'oe assassinated a rival general and cleared the way for his own dictatorship. A year later he deposed King Myngjong and enthroned his own candidate to preserve the technical legitimacy of his position. During his lifetime Ch'oe enthroned four kings and deposed two. Ch'oe ruthlessly eliminated any opposition, including his own family members. In 1197, when his younger brother attempted to marry off his daughter to the heir apparent, Ch'oe opposed him and had him killed. Ch'oe also succeeded in severing the traditional alliance between monks and the nobility, thus forestalling a possible powerful opposition.

Ch'oe's "administration" was harsh, corrupt, and unfair. He sold offices, arbitrarily distributed merits and honors, and tyrannized the people. Outraged peasantry and slaves rose in revolt year after year, the most noteworthy, though unsuccessful, uprising occurring in 1198 in the capital. By 1203 Ch'oe was finally able to suppress the uprisings that had disrupted the social fabric of the country for 30 years.

In order to bolster the power of his clan, Ch'oe organized a private guard corps in 1200, first divided into 6 and later into 36 units, the upper stratum of which comprised elite retainers, and the lower, slaves. Other sources of power were great estates which the clan owned but never directly managed and a large holding of slaves. In 1209 Ch'oe established a supreme council, the chief governing organ of military rule, akin to the Japanese *bakufu,* and he himself occupied the position of chief councilor, the highest office. In this position he supervised personnel administration, levying of taxes, and surveillance of officials.

## Legacy and End of the Clan

In 1225 Ch'oe Ch'ung-hn's son U (died 1249) extended the Ch'oe clan's power to the civil service. He also founded the "Three Special Service Corps," a private army designed to suppress internal dissension and to fight foreign invaders.

The undoing of the Ch'oe rule was the Mongol invasions, which started in 1231. U transferred the capital to Kanghwa Island (1232), determined to fight to the end. The civilian officials, however, allied with dissatisfied military groups, advocated peace, and in 1258 the last Ch'oe dictator was murdered.

## Further Reading

There is no book in English on Ch'oe Ch'ung-hn. Takashi Hatada, *A History of Korea* (1951; trans. 1969), and the chapter on Korea in Edwin O. Reischauer and John K. Fairbank, eds., *East Asia: The Great Tradition* (1958), contain information on Ch'oe Ch'ung-hn and his times. W. E. Henthorn, *Korea: The Mongol Invasions* (1963), is a detailed but inaccurate study. Frederick M. Nelson, *Korea and the Old Order in Eastern Asia* (1945), discusses the international relations of the Koreans. □

# Noam Avram Chomsky

**Noam Chomsky (born 1928), American linguist and philosopher, was responsible for the theory of transformational grammar. As a political commentator he was critical of American foreign and domestic policy.**

N oam Avram Chomsky was born in Philadelphia on December 7, 1928. He studied at the University of Pennsylvania, receiving his Ph.D. in linguistics in 1955. After that year, he taught at the Massachusetts Institute of Technology, where he was Institute Professor of Linguistics.

Chomsky received international acclaim for his work in linguistics, philosophy, and social/political theory. A prolific writer, he revolutionized linguistics with his theory of transformational-generative grammar. His work in epistemology and philosophy of mind was controversial; his social and political writings were consistently critical of American foreign and domestic policy.

## Transformational Grammar

In two seminal books on linguistic theory—*Syntactic Structures* (1957) and *Aspects of the Theory of Syntax* (1965)—Chomsky argued that the grammar of human language is a formal system consisting of abstract logical structures which are systematically rearranged by operations to generate all possible sentences of a language. Chomsky's theory is applicable to all components of linguistic description (phonology, morphology, syntax, semantics, and so forth). In phonology, for example, Chomsky argues that the sound system of a language consists of a set of abstract binary features (phonemic level) which are combined and

recombined by means of phonological processes to produce the sounds which people actually say (phonetic level) (see Chomsky and Halle's *The Sound Pattern of English,* 1968). In syntax, which has received the most attention by linguists, the theory specifies a set of abstract phrase-structure rules (deep structures) which undergo transformations to produce all possible sentences (surface structures).

Chomsky's assumption was that a grammar is finite, but that the sentences which people produce are theoretically infinite in length and number. Thus, a grammar must generate, from finite means, all and only the infinite set of grammatical sentences in a language. Chomsky has further argued that all languages have the same underlying, abstract structure—universal grammar.

Evidence for these claims is strong. The most commonly cited evidence is that children learn language rapidly, totally, and similarly by the age of five or six, irrespective of the culture into which they are born or the language which they learn. Chomsky thus claimed that children have innate linguistic competence, a reflection of universal grammar.

Chomsky broke from previous structuralist dominance of linguistics and revolutionized the field in several ways. First, he converted linguistics into a theoretical discipline. Second, he pluralized the word "grammar": he showed that there are many possible theories of language—grammars—and he argued that the purpose of scientific linguistics is to demonstrate which of all possible grammars is the most explanatory feasible. Third, he linked linguistics to mathe-

matics, psychology, philosophy, and neuropsychology, thereby broadening the discipline immensely.

Chomsky's later work in linguistics focused on spelling out the details of universal grammar. He was particularly concerned with the sorts of constraints that limit the power of transformations (see, for example, *Lectures on Government and Binding,* 1981).

Critics of Chomsky generally argued that grammar is not a formal system, but a social tool. They raised as counter-evidence such things as language variation, social and cultural differences in language use, and what they claim to be the unprovability of the innateness hypothesis: that innateness is a theorist's intuition, not an empirical fact. In all fairness to Chomsky, he never ruled out variation or the functional aspect of language, but preferred instead to focus on the similarities across languages. His work, furthermore, generated considerable interest in both the neuropsychology and biology of language, which provided considerable evidence for innateness.

## Rationalist Philosopher, Political Theorist

Chomsky demolished any connection between linguistics and behaviorist psychology with the scathing "Review of B. F. Skinner's *Verbal Behavior*" (1959), in which he argued that stimulus-response theory could in no way account for the creativity and speed of language learning. He then produced a series of books in favor of rationalism, the theory that a human is born with innate organizing principles and is not a tabula rasa (blank slate): *Cartesian Linguistics* (1966), *Language and Mind* (1972), *Reflections on Language* (1975), and *Rules and Representations* (1980).

Chomsky's rationalism engendered a resurgence of work in faculty psychology, the theory that the human mind consists of discrete modules which are specialized for particular cognitive processes: vision and language, for example. One of his statements in rationalist philosophy was *Modular Approaches to the Study of Mind* (1984).

## Critic of American Policy Motives

Chomsky was also an ardent critic of American domestic and foreign policy. His libertarian socialist ideas can be found in such works as *American Power and the New Mandarins* (1969), *For Reasons of State* (1973), *The Political Economy of Human Rights* (1979), and *Towards a New Cold War* (1982). Chomsky's position was always that American international aggression is rooted in the American industrial system, where capitalism, by its aggressive, dehumanizing, and dominating nature, spawns a corresponding militaristic policy. Historian Michael Beschloss, writing for the *Washington Post Book World* found in Chomsky's *American Power and the New Mandarins* a strong denunciation of the "system of values and decision-making that drove the United States to the jungles of Southeast Asia." Chomsky's strongest vitriol, however, was directed toward the so-called "New Mandarins"—the technocrats, bureaucrats, and university-trained scholars who defended America's right to dominate the globe. *Times Literary Supplement* contributor, Charles Townshend noted that

Chomsky "[sees] a totalitarian mentality" arising out of the mainstream American belief in the fundamental righteousness and benevolence of the United States, the sanctity and nobility of its aims. Yet "the publicly tolerated spectrum of discussion" of these aims is narrow. Chomsky transcended that narrow spectrum by offering examples to illuminate how American policies proved otherwise. Chomsky's political views, though, caused his historical/political scholarship to be taken less seriously than his work in linguistics. Steve Wasserman wrote in the *Los Angeles Times Book Review* that Chomsky had been "banished to the margins of political debate. His opinions have been deemed so kooky—and his personality so cranky—that his writings no longer appear in the forums . . . in which he was once so welcome."

In later years Chomsky continued his criticism of American foreign policy in works such as *The ABC's of U.S. Policy Toward Haiti* (1994), *Free Trade and Democracy* (1993), *Rent-A-Cops of the World: Noam Chomsky on the Gulf Crisis* (1991), and *The New World Order Debate* (1991). Appreciation, if not acceptance, attended Chomsky's later works. According to Christopher Lehmann-Haupt in the *New York Times,* Chomsky "continues to challenge our assumptions long after other critics have gone to bed. He has become the foremost gadfly of our national conscience." *New Statesman* correspondent Francis Hope concluded of Chomsky's lingering suspicions of government motives: "Such men are dangerous; the lack of them is disasterous."

## Further Reading

Noam Chomsky's positions, written in readable form, are presented in his own two books, *Language and Responsibility* (1979) and *The Generative Enterprise* (1982). Good accounts of, and commentaries on, his ideas and theories can be found in Lyons' *Noam Chomsky* (1970), Newmeyer's *Linguistic Theory in America* (1980), Smith and Wilson's *Modern Linguistics: The Results of Chomsky's Revolution* (1979), and Piattelli-Palmarini's *Language and Learning: The Debate between Jean Piaget and Noam Chomsky* (1980).
For more insight on Chomsky's political views see Robert F. Barsky, *Noam Chomsky: A Life of Dissent,* 1997. □

# Chong Chung-bu

**Chong Chung-bu (1106-1179) was a general in the Korean kingdom of Kory; after a massacre of civil officials in 1170 he instituted military rule in Kory.**

From the beginning of the 12th century, factious nobles struggled for political supremacy, creating a period of unrest and instability. The fall of the Yi clan of Inju in 1126 was followed by rivalry among the nobility and a revolt at the Western Capital in 1135, led by the monk Myoch'ong. It was suppressed by a capital-based power group headed by the famous historian Kim Pu-sik.

Kim's appointment as a commander of government forces had precedents in early Kory, where a civilian was made a leader of expeditionary forces, symbolizing the supremacy of the civilian branch over the military. However, the military chafed under civilian suppression and abuse. In one instance, simply to abuse a general at a court gathering, a young scholar, Kim Pu-sik's son, lifted a candle and managed to burn the mustache of Chong Chung-bu. Chong beat him down and swore to avenge the civilian affront.

With the enthronement of the 18th ruler Ŭijong in 1127, a less than ideal monarch given to wine, women, and song, the situation worsened. Surrounded by sycophants, the frivolous and dissolute monarch enraged the military. On Oct. 11, 1170, when the royal pleasure party was on its way to Pohynwn in Changdan, Chong, then a member of the palace guard, and his associates initiated a coup and massacred all civil officials accompanying the King. Chong then sent troops to the capital to massacre the remaining officials. Following this, he banished Ŭijong and the heir apparent, killed the royal grandson, and set up the King's younger brother as Myngjong. Three years later, on Nov. 7, 1173, Ŭijong was murdered in Kyngju.

Thus the military achieved administrative control and filled all the chief positions at court and in the provinces. Soon, however, Chong and his principal associates began to fight among themselves, expanding their estates and increasing their private armies. Several unsuccessful revolts ensued—in 1173 by a commander of the northeast province and in 1174 by a commissioner of the Western Capital—but they could not topple Chong. On the night of Oct. 18, 1179, Chong was killed by a young rival general, Kyng Tae-sŭng.

The local peasant and slave uprisings which had broken out under Chong continued through the turn of the century. They were finally quelled by the general Ch'oe Ch'ung-hn, who seized control of the government in 1196.

## Further Reading

Three works useful for a study of Chong are Homer B. Hulbert, *The History of Korea* (4 vols., 1901-1903; rev. ed., 2 vols., 1962); Takashi Hatada, *A History of Korea* (1951; trans. 1969); and the South Korean government's publication, *Korea: Its Land, People and Culture of All Ages* (1960; 2d ed. 1963). □

# Chongjo

**Chongjo (1752-1800) was king of Korea and one of the outstanding monarchs of the Yi dynasty. His reign culminated the great 18th-century revival of traditional Korean civilization.**

Chongjo, born Yi Sng on Oct. 28, 1752, was the son of Crown Prince Changhn and the grandson of King Yngjo, whose 52-year reign preceded his own. Studious as a youth, Chongjo exhibited an early maturity which helped him to cope with the tragedy of 1762, when his father was tortured and murdered by a crazed and provoked King Yngjo. Chongjo came to the throne on April 27, 1776, upon his grandfather's death.

Chongjo's reign was a watershed between the 18th-century heyday of Korean civilization and its troubled decline in the 19th century. For most of Yngjo's reign Koreans had felt secure in their traditional social system and values, and the country had been at peace with its neighbors. But they were less secure by the time of Chongjo's death. There were economic problems, the aristocracy was under attack by satirists, and Catholicism and Western learning had begun to flood the country, threatening native values. Chongjo responded to these problems by proclaiming Confucian verities: respect for authority, diligence in agriculture, and frugality in expenditure. He confidently issued regulations for everything and was certain that these, together with sincerity and good Confucian principles, would produce solutions.

But Chongjo also encouraged practical measures and supported progressive scholars seeking better ways of administration. In this innovative spirit he was ahead of most officials, who with their outmoded practices blunted or nullified many of his measures. He was also open in his policies on Catholicism despite constant pressure from advisers to persecute the converts. Fundamentally he was opposed to persecutions, believing that the new religion could best be fought by emphasizing Confucianism. He followed this policy steadily to the end of his reign, though it was reversed by his successors.

Chongjo was an enthusiastic bibliophile, probably the greatest Korea ever had. He was concerned with almost every aspect of books, supporting as royal patron authors, librarians, lexicographers, typographers, and printers. The splendid Kyujanggak Library, which he founded in 1776, has been largely preserved and is now part of the library of Seoul National University. Chongjo died on Aug. 18, 1800. He may be said to be the last king of Korea to achieve greatness.

### Further Reading

There is no biography of Chongjo in any Western language. His bibliophilic activities are interestingly and accurately told in Chao-ying Fang, *The Asami Library: A Descriptive Catalogue,* edited by Elizabeth Huff (1969), which also contains much information on Chongjo's reign in general. A more comprehensive account of his reign is found in a standard history, such as Takashi Hatada, *A History of Korea* (1951; trans. 1969). □

# Frédéric François Chopin

**Frédéric François Chopin (1810-1849), a Polish-French composer and pianist, was one of the creators of the typically romantic character piece. All of his works include the piano.**

The imaginative schemes of Frédéric Chopin for his piano pieces include the following features: concentration on one motive in preludes and études; elaboration of dance forms in mazurkas, waltzes, polonaises, the Bolero, and the Tarantella; improvisational effects from piano figurations in the nocturnes; and episodic, vigorous writing in the larger works such as the scherzos, ballades, impromptus, and the Fantasy. Thus, in an era when the piano was becoming the preeminent solo instrument in both the home and the concert hall, Chopin devised new figurations, delicate traceries, and elaborate quasivocal fioriture and fashioned them for use at the keyboard. He wrote no symphonies, no operas, no string quartets, and only one trio (piano, violin, and cello). Besides his two significant sonatas and two piano concertos, he is best known for his musical miniatures, many of which are within the technical grasp of amateurs.

Chopin was not a conductor, or a writer on music, or a great teacher—although he earned substantial amounts from his teaching—nor did he concertize extensively. Indeed, he represents the curious phenomenon of a legendary pianist who gave approximately 30 public performances in his entire lifetime. From all reports, his playing was extraordinary: quiet, controlled, exquisitely shaded, varying from pianissimo to mezzo forte with only a very occasional forte.

Chopin was born on Feb. 22, 1810, near Warsaw, the second of four children of a French father, Nicholas Chopin, and a Polish mother, who had been a well-educated but impoverished relative in the Skarbek household, where

Nicholas had been a tutor. Young Chopin had a good education and studied music privately with Joseph Elsner, founder and director of the Warsaw Conservatory. In 1817 Chopin's first composition was performed publicly; a year later he himself performed in public, playing a concerto by Adalbert Gyrowetz.

## Musical Training

In 1826 Chopin became a full-time student at Elsner's conservatory, where he received an excellent foundation in theory, harmony, and counterpoint. The earliest work to display Chopinesque figurations as we know them today is the set of variations on Wolfgang Amadeus Mozart's theme *Là ci darem' la mano,* from the opera *Don Giovanni.* Elsner, after recognizing that Chopin's style was too original to force into traditional patterns, granted him the freedom to develop along distinctly personal lines. Indeed, Chopin is one of the few composers whose style crystallized in his formative years and remained the same throughout his lifetime.

Chopin's first acquaintance with the musical world beyond Warsaw occurred in 1828, when Johann Nepomuk Hummel, a Viennese pianist-composer, visited that city. Italian opera had been the exclusive local musical fare, and Hummel's visit made Chopin aware of happenings in the west. After visiting Berlin, where he was exposed to the music of George Frederick Handel and Felix Mendelssohn, Chopin heard Nicolò Paganini in Warsaw on his return and recognized that he must leave the city for exposure to other musicians. The government rejected his father's request for financial aid to send the boy abroad, so on his own Chopin went to Vienna to try to arrange the publication of several of his works. After a successful debut at the Kärntnerthor Theater on Aug. 11, 1829, he returned home only to prepare for a concert tour, this time through Germany and Italy. His two concertos (the F Minor is the earlier), which he performed in a public concert in Warsaw in 1830, several fantasies incorporating national themes, and the first set of études stem from this period.

After a trip through Breslau, Dresden, and Prague, Chopin arrived in Vienna, but owing to the unsettled political conditions he never reached Italy. He composed the B Minor Scherzo and the G Minor Ballade, as well as some songs, while he waited in Vienna. These works show Chopin's fully developed personal style long before he had met Franz Liszt, Vincenzo Bellini, or Hector Berlioz, all of whom were said to have influenced his writing. Besides Hummel, the only musician whose piano style inspired Chopin was the Irish composer John Field, who first used the term nocturne on several of his short, lyrical pieces.

## Middle Period

When the 20-year-old Chopin arrived in Paris, he first considered—then rejected—the idea of studying with F. W. M. Kalkbrenner, the renowned virtuoso. Poor physical health as well as an unsuitable temperament prevented Chopin from giving public performances. Nevertheless, he became a significant figure in Parisian artistic circles, numbering among his friends musicians, writers, and painters as well as many wealthy and talented women. His pupils were all aristocratic ladies who paid well for their lessons. Some were gifted, but not one was sufficiently accomplished to establish or to preserve a method derived from her teacher.

Chopin recognized that he did not have the stamina to compete in public against such virtuosos as Liszt and Sigismund Thalberg. So long as he was able to earn enough by teaching, Chopin preferred to forgo concertizing for composition. His musical tastes are public knowledge. Friendly with Berlioz and Mendelssohn, he was not impressed with their music. Nor, for that matter, did he appreciate Robert Schumann's work, despite the latter's warm welcome written for the *Neue Zeitschrift für Musik* when Chopin first arrived in Paris. Schumann introduced Clara Wieck to Chopin's work, and eventually her performances of Chopin's pieces made favorable impressions on innumerable audiences.

## Final Years

Several young ladies appear to have been the object of Chopin's affections over the years, but the most celebrated female with whom he had a relationship was Aurore Dudevant, known as George Sand, whom he met in 1836. For 9 years, beginning in 1838, after he had composed the *Funeral March* (which later became part of the B-flat Minor Sonata), she was his closest associate. They spent the winter of 1838-1839 in Majorca, where she took Chopin in the belief that his health would improve. Unfortunately the weather was bad, Chopin's health deteriorated, and his Pleyel piano did not arrive until a week before they left. Nevertheless, the composer completed his 24 Preludes there at Valldemosa, which today is a Chopin museum. Chopin and Sand spent the following summer at Nohant, Sand's country place near Châteauroux, where Chopin composed the B-flat Minor Sonata and the F-sharp Minor Impromptu. From 1839 to 1846, with the exception of 1840, they passed every summer at Nohant.

Chopin kept to himself in Paris and played only occasionally at social gatherings in the homes of the aristocracy. Because he did not enjoy copying his music, his friend Julian Fontana, who as a student had boarded with the Chopin family in Warsaw, was his copyist. When Fontana left for America at the end of 1841, Chopin's output slowed considerably.

In 1846 Sand's children became a problem. Chopin sided with Solange, her daughter, in arguments against Sand and her son Maurice. Separation became inevitable, and the beginning of the end for Chopin. His health failed, and he lost all interest in composition. The Revolution of 1848 brought Chopin to England, where he accepted a long-standing invitation from Jane Stirling, a Scottish pupil. He gave several private performances in London and on May 15 played for Queen Victoria. After a rest in Scotland he returned to London in the fall of 1848, where on November 16 he played a benefit for Polish refugees at the Guildhall. He returned to Paris shortly afterward, living virtually on the generosity of the Stirlings. He died of tuberculosis on Oct. 17, 1849, in Paris.

### His Achievements

Chopin's achievements are closely related to the improvements in the piano, particularly the extension of the keyboard. He was adroit in his use of the pedal to obtain gradations of color and sonority. He experimented with new fingerings, using the thumb or the fifth finger on black notes, sliding the same finger from a black note to a white one, and passing the fourth finger over the fifth. Even his most complicated pieces lie easily under a pianist's fingers because the works are idiomatically suited to the instrument. His creative imagination raised the étude from a practice piece to the concert stage. Chopin's harmonic innovations, often concealed beneath a soaring lyricism, place him on an equal footing with Liszt and Richard Wagner, both of whom extended conventional concepts of tonality. The popularity of Chopin's works has led to a multiplicity of editions, but the best publication today is the Polish national edition issued under the name of his compatriot Ignace Jan Paderewski.

### Further Reading

*Selected Correspondence of Fryderyk Chopin,* edited and translated by Arthur Hedley (1963), includes much biographical information as well as peripheral material on Paris in the 1840s. Hedley's *Chopin* (1947; rev. ed. 1963) is the most useful book in English on the composer. Frederick Niecks, *Frederick Chopin as a Man and Musician* (2 vols., 1888; rev. ed. 1902), is particularly important for its insights into Chopin's character. James Huneker, *Chopin the Man and His Music* (1900), provides extensive discussion of the music. Alan Walker, ed., *Frédéric Chopin: Profiles of the Man and the Musician* (1966), offers accounts by several specialists.

Maurice J. E. Brown, *Chopin: An Index of His Works in Chronological Order* (1960), is the only work of its kind but does not supply sufficient information on the significantly different editions of Chopin's music; fortunately, the Chopin Institute in Poland is continuing publication of a series of facsimiles that provide insight into the reasons for variant editions. For those who read even a little French, Robert Bory's picture history, *La Vie de Frédéric Chopin par l'image* (1951), is a delight. An excellent scholarly work on the period is Alfred Einstein, *Music in the Romantic Era* (1947). See also Rey M. Longyear, *Nineteenth-Century Romanticism in Music* (1969). □

# Katherine Chopin

**A popular local colorist during her lifetime, Katherine Chopin (1851-1904) is best known today for her psychological novel *The Awakening* (1899) and for such often-anthologized short stories as "Desiree's Baby" and "The Story of an Hour."**

C hopin was born to a prominent St. Louis family. Her father died in a train accident when Chopin was four years old, and her childhood was most profoundly influenced by her mother and great-grandmother, who descended from French-Creole pioneers. Chopin also spent much time with her family's Creole and

mulatto slaves, becoming familiar with their unique dialects. She read widely as a child, but was an undistinguished student at the convent school she attended. She graduated at age seventeen and spent two years as a belle of fashionable St. Louis society. In 1870 she married Oscar Chopin, a wealthy Creole cotton factor, and moved with him to New Orleans. For the next decade, Chopin pursued the demanding social and domestic schedule of a Southern aristocrat, her recollections of which would later serve as material for her short stories. In 1880, financial difficulties forced Chopin's growing family to move to her father-in-law's home in Cloutierville, a small town in Natchitoches Parish located in Louisiana's Red River bayou region. There, Chopin's husband oversaw and subsequently inherited his father's plantations. Upon his death in 1883, Chopin insisted upon assuming his managerial responsibilities, which brought her into contact with almost every segment of the community, including the French-Acadian, Creole, and mulatto sharecroppers who worked the plantations. The impressions she gathered of these people and Natchitoches Parish life later influenced her fiction.

In the mid-1880s Chopin sold most of her property and left Louisiana to live with her mother in St. Louis. Family friends who found her letters entertaining encouraged Chopin to write professionally, and she began composing short stories. These early works evidence the influence of her favorite authors: the French writers Guy de Maupassant, Alphonse Daudet, and Moliere. At this time Chopin also read the works of Charles Darwin, Thomas Huxley, and Herbert Spenser in order to keep abreast of trends in scien-

tific thinking, and she began questioning her Roman Catholic faith as well as socially imposed mores and ethical restraints. After an apprenticeship marked by routine rejections, Chopin began having her stories published in the most popular American periodicals, including *America, Vogue,* and the *Atlantic.* The success of the collections *Bayou Folk* (1894) and *A Night in Acadie* (1897) solidified her growing reputation as an important local colorist. Financially independent and encouraged by success, Chopin turned to longer works. Although she had published the novel *At Fault* in 1890, that work displays many of the shortcomings of an apprentice novel and failed to interest readers or critics. Publishers later rejected a novel and a short story collection on moral grounds, citing their promotion of female self-assertion and sexual liberation. Undaunted, Chopin completed *The Awakening,* the story of a conventional wife and mother who, after gaining spiritual freedom through an extramarital affair, commits suicide when she realizes that she cannot reconcile her new self to society's moral restrictions. The hostile critical and public reaction to the novel largely halted Chopin's career; she had difficulty finding publishers for later works and was ousted from local literary groups. Demoralized, she wrote little during her last years.

The stories in *Bayou Folk,* Chopin's first collection, largely reflect her skills as a local colorist and often center on the passionate loves of the Creoles and Acadians in her native Natchitoches Parish. For example, "A Lady of Bayou St. John" portrays a young widow who escapes the sexual demands of a suitor by immersing herself in memories of her dead husband, while "La Belle Zoraide" chronicles a mulatto slave's descent into madness after her mistress sells her lover and deprives her of their child. Recent critics occasionally detect in *Bayou Folk* the melodramatic conventions of popular magazine fiction. Nevertheless, they laud Chopin's meticulous description of setting, precise rendering of dialects, and objective point of view. In addition, commentators perceived in several stories universal themes that transcend the restrictions of regional fiction. One such story, the often-anthologized "Desiree's Baby," examines prejudice and miscegenation in its portrayal of Armand Aubigny, a proud aristocratic planter, and his wife Desiree. When she gives birth to a son possessing African characteristics, Aubigny assumes that Desiree is of mixed racial heritage and turns his wife and child out of his house. However, while burning his wife's possessions, Armand discovers a letter written by his mother, which reveals that she and therefore Armand belong to the race "cursed by the brand of slavery."

In *A Night in Acadie* Chopin continued to utilize the Louisiana settings that figured in *Bayou Folk.* However, the romanticism of the earlier collection is replaced by a greater moral ambivalence concerning such issues as female sexuality, personal freedom, and social propriety. Bert Bender observed that Chopin's "characters transcend their socially limited selves by awakening to and affirming impulses that are unacceptable by convention. Unburdened of restricting social conventions, her characters come to experience the suffering and loneliness, as well as the joy, of their freedom; for the impulses that they heed are a mere part of a world in which change and natural selection are first principles." For example, in "A Respectable Woman" a happily married woman becomes sexually attracted to Gouvernail, a family friend invited by her husband to visit their home for a week. Disturbed by her feelings, she is relieved when Gouvernail leaves, but as the following summer approaches, she encourages her husband to contact him again, ambiguously promising that "this time I shall be very nice to him." Chopin later expanded upon this essentially amoral perception of adultery in "The Storm," a story written near the end of her career, which portrays a woman's extra-marital affair as a natural impulse devoid of moral significance.

Chopin also explored the connection between selfhood and marriage in *A Night in Acadie.* Several stories reflect her contention that security and love cannot compensate for a lack of control over one's destiny. In "Athenaise," for instance, the title character, a naive young bride, leaves Cazeau, her devoted yet insensitive husband, twice; first returning home to her parents, then traveling to New Orleans. Although Cazeau retrieves her from her parents, he refuses to follow her to the city after drawing an unsettling parallel between his actions toward her and his father's treatment of a runaway slave. A month after arriving in New Orleans, however, Athenaise learns that she is pregnant, and, thinking of her husband, experiences "the first purely sensuous tremor of her life." Now accepting her role as wife and mother, she reconciles with Cazeau. While some critics contend that Chopin likely formulated this conclusion, like other happy endings to her stories, to appease the moral sensibilities of her editors and publishers, most regard it as an appropriate ending to an incisive portrait of the limitations and rewards of marriage.

Early reviewers of *A Night in Acadie* objected to the volume's sensuous themes. Similar concerns were later raised by publishers who rejected Chopin's next volume, *A Vocation and a Voice.* Although Chopin continuously pursued its publication until her death, the volume did not appear as a single work until 1991. In these stories Chopin largely abandons local setting to focus upon the psychological complexity of her characters. Tales such as "Two Portraits," "Lilacs," and "A Vocation and a Voice," examine contrary states of innocence and experience and ways that society divides rather than unites the two. In "The Story of an Hour," the best known work in the collection, Chopin returns to the issue of marriage and selfhood in her portrayal of Mrs. Mallard, a woman who learns that her husband has died in a train accident. Initially overcome by grief, she gradually realizes that his "powerful will" no longer restricts her and that she may live as she wishes. While she joyfully anticipates her newfound freedom, however, her husband returns, the report of his death a mistake, and Mrs. Mallard collapses upon seeing him. Doctors then ironically conclude that she died of "heart failure—of the joy that kills." In evaluating *A Vocation and a Voice,* Barbara C. Ewell observed: "[The] collection, which includes some of Chopin's most experimental stories, reveals how intently she had come to focus her fiction on human interiority, on the interplay of consciousness and circumstance, of unconscious motive and reflexive action. Such psychological elements, combined with technical control, indicate a writer not only in command of her craft but fully in tune with the intellectual currents of her time. In many ways, *A Vocation and a Voice* represents the culmination of Chopin's talents as a writer of the short story.''

*The Awakening* is considered Chopin's best work as well as a remarkable novel to have been written during the morally uncompromising America of the 1890s. Psychologically realistic, *The Awakening* is the story of Edna Pontellier, a conventional wife and mother who experiences a spiritual epiphany and an awakened sense of independence that change her life. The theme of sexual freedom and the consequences one must face to attain it is supported by sensual imagery that acquires symbolic meanings as the story progresses. This symbolism emphasizes the conflict within Pontellier, who realizes that she can neither exercise her new-found sense of independence nor return to life as it was before her spiritual awakening: the candor of the Creole community on Grand Isle, for example, is contrasted with the conventional mores of New Orleans; birds in gilded cages and strong, free-flying birds are juxtaposed; and the protagonist selects for her confidants both the domesticated, devoted Adele Ratignolle and the passionate Madame Reisz, a lonely, unattractive pianist. The central symbol of the novel, the sea, also provides the frame for the main action. As a symbol, the sea embodies multiple pairs of polarities, the most prominent being that it is the site of both Edna Pontellier's awakening and suicide.

After the initial furor over morality and sexuality in *The Awakening* had passed, the novel was largely ignored until the 1930s, when Daniel S. Rankin published a study of Chopin's works that included a sober assessment of *The Awakening*'s high literary quality and artistic aims. During the succeeding decades, critical debate surrounding *The Awakening* has focused on Chopin's view of women's roles in society, the significance of Pontellier's awakening, her subsequent suicide, and the possibility of parallels between the lives of Chopin and her protagonist. George Arms, for example, has contended that Chopin was a happily married woman and devoted mother whose emotional life bore no resemblance to Pontellier's, while Per Seyersted has noted her compelling secretive, individualistic nature and her evident enjoyment of living alone as an independent writer. Priscilla Allen has posited that male critics allow their preconceptions about ''good'' and ''bad'' women to influence their interpretations of Chopin's novel, arguing that they too often assume that Edna's first priority should have been to her family and not to herself. Like Allen, Seyersted brings a feminist interpretation to *The Awakening,* and points out that the increasing depiction of passionate, independent women in Chopin's other fiction supports the theory that she was in fact concerned about the incompatibility of motherhood and a career for women living during the late nineteenth century. These questions about Chopin's depictions of women's roles in society have led to a debate about the significance of Pontellier's suicide. The ambivalence of the character as she wrestles with the new choices that confront her has left the suicide open to many interpretations. Carol P. Christ, like Seyersted, interprets the death as a moral victory and a social defeat—the act of a brave woman who cannot sacrifice her life to her family, but will

not cause her children disgrace by pursuing a scandalous course. In a contrasting assessment of Pontellier's choice to die, James H. Justus likens the protagonist's gradual withdrawal from society and responsibility to a regression into childhood selfishness because she refuses to compromise and cannot control her urge for self-assertion. Often compared to the protagonist of Gustave Flaubert's *Madame Bovary,* Pontellier differs primarily in her desire for selfhood, even at the risk of loneliness, while Madame Bovary seeks romantic fulfillment.

Once considered merely an author of local-color fiction, Chopin is today recognized for her pioneering examination of sexuality, individual freedom, and the consequences of action—themes and concerns important to many later twentieth-century writers. While their psychological examinations of female protagonists have made Chopin's short stories formative works in the historical development of feminist literature, they also provide a broad discussion of a society that denied the value of sensuality and female independence. Per Seyersted asserted that Chopin ''was the first woman writer in America to accept sex with its profound repercussions as a legitimate subject of serious fiction. In her attitude towards passion, she represented a healthy, matter-of-fact acceptance of the whole of man. She was familiar with the newest developments in science and in world literature, and her aim was to describe—unhampered by tradition and authority—man's immutable impulses. Because she was vigorous, intelligent, and eminently sane, and because her background had made her morally tolerant, and socially secure, she could write with a balance and maturity, a warmth and humor not often found in her contemporaries.''

## Further Reading

Cather, Willa, *The World and the Parish,* Volume II: *Willa Cather's Articles and Reviews, 1893-1902,* edited by William M.Curtin, University of Nebraska Press, 1970.

Chopin, Kate, *The Complete Works of Kate Chopin* (two volumes), edited by Per Seyersted, Louisiana State University Press, 1969.

Chopin, Kate, *The Storm and Other Stories, with The Awakening* edited by Seyersted, Feminist Press, 1974.

*Concise Dictionary of American Literary Biography: Realism, Naturalism, and Local Color, 1865-1917,* Gale, 1988.

Diamond, Arlyn and Lee R. Edwards, *The Authority of Experience: Essays in Feminist Criticism,* University of Massachusetts Press, 1977.

*Dictionary of Literary Biography,* Gale, Volume 12: *American Realists and Naturalists,* 1982, Volume 78: *American Short-Story Writers, 1880-1910,* 1988. □

# Chou En-lai

**Chou En-lai (1898-1976) was a Chinese Communist leader and premier of the People's Republic of China. From the 1920s on Chou was among the top leaders of the Chinese Communist party.**

Chou En-lai was born in Huaian, Kiangsu Province, into a landed family. Both of his parents died while he was a child, and Chou was sent to live with an uncle in Mukden, where he was given a traditional primary education.

## Early Foreign Travels

In 1917 Chou went to Japan to continue his education. He joined in the activities of a nationalistic Chinese student organization and was introduced to Marxist thought through Japanese sources. When the May Fourth student movement broke out in 1919, he returned to Tientsin to join in the active political ferment among Chinese students. He enrolled at Nank'ai University, where he became editor of a radical student newspaper. Early in 1920 he was arrested with other students after a demonstration and imprisoned for 4 months.

After his release from prison, Chou went to France on a work-study program and soon came under the influence of French and Chinese socialists active in France. He became a member of the Chinese Socialist Youth Corps, a young Communist organization, and founded its Berlin branch in 1922. In the same year he was elected to the executive committee of the European branch of the Chinese Communist party (CCP). As the Communist party was at that time allied with Sun Yat-sen's Kuomintang (KMT), Chou also joined the KMT and served on the executive committee of its European headquarters. During these years he formed close attachments with many future leaders of the CCP, including Chu Teh and Ch'en Yi.

## Work with the Kuomintang

Late in 1924 Chou returned to China and began working in Canton at the joint Communist-KMT revolutionary headquarters established there by Sun. Chou soon became deputy director (and in effect acting director) of the political department of the Whampoa Military Academy, just established with Chiang Kai-shek as its commander. In this capacity Chou formed connections with many cadets who were later to form the core officer group of the Red Army, among them Lin Piao.

In August 1925 Chou was made political commissar to the 1st Division of the 1st Army of the KMT, which was the chief military force under Chiang Kai-shek's control at the time. In the winter of 1925 he became special commissioner of the recently captured East River District of Kwangtung Province. Chou lost both these posts, however, after the Chung-shan gunboat incident of March 1926, when Chiang Kai-shek seized control of the KMT by a military coup.

When the Kuomintang armies began the Northern Expedition against the warlords in the summer of 1926, Chou went to Shanghai and worked to organize a labor revolt in the city. Chou then directed the general strike that captured Shanghai just before Chiang's troops entered the city. Chou, however, escaped the terror instituted by Chiang and fled to Wuhan, where the official leadership of the KMT still supported the Communist alliance. At the Fifth National Congress of the Communist party there in April, he was elected for the first time to the Central Committee and the Politburo and became head of the Military Committee. When the KMT at Wuhan also broke with the Communists in the summer of 1927, Chou fled again. He took charge of a small military force created by the defection of Communist officers and led the Nanchang uprising on August 1. After the failure of this insurrection Chou remained with the Communist forces through a series of abortive campaigns aimed at setting up a base in Kwangtung Province.

With the Communist party in disarray as a result of these events, Chou went to Moscow for the Sixth National Congress of the Communist party and was reelected to his positions. He returned to China in 1929 and created the Red Guards, a secret police that tried to protect the party leadership in Shanghai. In the spring of 1931 Chou was sent to Ch'ingkan Mountain Soviet, controlled by Mao Tse-tung and Chu Teh, to establish a closer connection with the party headquarters. There he became political commissar of Chu Teh's army. When this base had to be abandoned in 1934, Chou served as a military officer on the Long March to Yenan in the northwest.

In Yenan, Chou began to emerge as a major negotiator for the Communist party. He worked out cease-fire arrangements with Gen. Chang Hsüeh-liang that eventuated in Chang's kidnaping of Chiang Kai-shek at Sian in December 1936. As leader of the Communist delegation summoned to Sian, Chou is widely believed to have saved Chiang Kai-shek's life. From this point to the end of the Sino-Japanese war, Chou was largely involved in negotiations with Chiang Kai-shek and his government over common anti-Japanese issues. Chou spent much of the war period in Chungking, the Nationalist capital, where his personal charm, intelligence, and tact made him an effective spokesman for the Communist position to the press, foreign diplomats, and uncommitted Chinese.

From November 1944 Chou was regularly involved in negotiations between U.S. ambassador Patrick J. Hurley, the Nationalist government, and the Communists. Early in 1946 he headed the Communist team in negotiations with Gen. George Marshall over the future of China. When these discussions broke down, Chou returned to Yenan.

## People's Republic of China

After the Communist victory in 1949, Chou became premier of the People's Republic. He was largely responsible for the creation and guidance of the new governmental bureaucracy and until 1958 was also foreign minister. After 1949 he was also largely responsible for maintaining relations with the non-Communist political groups that supported the People's Republic.

Early in 1950 Chou negotiated in Moscow a treaty of alliance with the Soviet Union, and in 1952 he again went to Moscow, where he negotiated further agreements. In 1957 he played a significant role in negotiating settlements of issues arising from Polish and Hungarian conflicts with the Soviet Union. After Sino-Soviet relations deteriorated, he led the Chinese delegation that walked out of the Twenty-second Congress of the Soviet party in October 1961.

Chou also had to deal with acute crises in Sino-American relations that arose largely as a result of the Korean War. On Oct. 2, 1950, he delivered through the Indian ambassador a warning that China would intervene in the war if American troops crossed the 38th parallel. The American rejection of this warning brought a direct confrontation of American and Chinese troops in Korea. However, on Chou's initiative in 1955, Sino-American ambassadorial talks began in Warsaw.

Chou also was prominent in forming and implementing Chinese policy toward the Afro-Asian nations. He made extensive tours of Asia and Africa. In 1954 he led the Chinese delegation at the Geneva Conference and was instrumental in drawing up terms for the French evacuation of Indo-China. In 1960 he played a leading role in negotiating treaties delimiting Chinese frontiers with Burma, Nepal, Mongolia, Pakistan, and Afghanistan but failed to resolve the Indian frontier question despite a visit to New Delhi for talks with Prime Minister Jawaharlal Nehru.

Domestically, Chou played an essential role both as head of the administrative system and as peacemaker in the party. He actively supported Mao Tse-tung during the Great Proletarian Cultural Revolution that developed in 1965, the major objective being to reinfuse revolutionary enthusiasm into Chinese society. At the end of this movement in 1969, Chou was the third-ranking member of the Chinese leadership, and later, after Lin Piao disappeared, the second-ranking member.

In 1975, Chou was dying of cancer, but he continued to serve China. In January, his report to the Fourth National People's Congress justified the Cultural Revolution as a battle against bourgeois tendencies and at the same time proposed the Four Modernizations (of agriculture, industry, national defense and technology). Chou died on January 8, 1976.

## His Family

In 1925 Chou married Teng Ying-ch'ao, whom he had met in 1919 when they were both active in student demonstrations in Tientsin. She remained an active revolutionary leader and was one of the few women who made the Long March. When she was trapped in Peking by the Japanese occupation of the city, she was smuggled through Japanese lines by Edgar Snow. She was deputy chairman of the All-China Federation of Women. They had no children.

## Further Reading

The best account of Chou's life is Hsu Kai-yu, *Chou En-lai: China's Gray Eminence* (1968). Hsu tends to exaggerate Chou's importance but presents a convincing picture of his character-his human warmth versus his devotion to revolution. See also Edgar Snow, *The Other Side of the River: Red China Today* (1962), which contains interviews with Chou En-lai, as well as other Chinese leaders; Donald S. Zagoria, *The Sino-Soviet Conflict, 1956-1961* (1962); and Franz Schurmann and Orville Schell, eds., *The China Reader* (3 vols., 1967), especially volume 3. □

# Chou Kung

**Chou kung (active ca. 1116 B.C.) was one of the most revered figures in Chinese history. Confucius considered him the model minister whom all potential officials should emulate.**

Chou kung, or the Duke of Chou, was born during the Shang dynasty (1766-1122 B.C.). His original name was Chi Tan and his family came from the Wei River valley of Shensi Province. His father, known as Wen wang, or the Cultured King, had revolted against the Shang, and Chou kung's older brother, Wu wang, or the Martial King, overthrew the Shang and established the Chou dynasty (1122 B.C.). Chou kung was his brother's chief adviser in planning military and political strategy. After the conquest Chou kung was given the fief of Lu, located on the eastern seaboard in what is now Shantung Province.

Chou kung did not immediately go to his fief but remained with his brother to help him run the government. Many of the policies Wu wang adopted were originally suggested by Chou kung. Wu wang died in 1116 B.C. and was succeeded by his infant son, known as King Ch'eng. Since Ch'eng was too young to assume full power, Chou Kung set himself up as regent. Chou kung's action was interpreted by some as an attempt to assume the throne for himself, and his two brothers, Kuan Shu and Ts'ai Shu, were particularly suspicious of his motives. Just after the conquest they had been put in charge of supervising the son of the conquered Shang king, who had been given a small fief in eastern China. When Chou kung declared himself regent, the two brothers revolted and rallied around the Shang heir in an ostensible attempt to reestablish the Shang rule. Chou kung immediately sent out an army to the east and defeated the rebellious forces. He put to death the Shang heir and Kuan Shu and exiled Ts'ai Shu.

Chou kung served as regent for 7 years; he resigned when King Ch'eng reached maturity but continued to advise him. Chou kung was responsible for supervising the building of the new capital, which was moved from the Wei valley to Loyang in north-central China. He also is credited with composing instructions to the young king in administering his government. The exact date of Chou kung's death is unknown, but it must have been shortly after King Ch'eng took power.

## Further Reading

There are no studies of Chou kung in Western languages. The definitive work is in Japanese. For background information see Marcel Granet, *Chinese Civilization* (1929; trans. 1930); Fung Yu-Lan, *A History of Chinese Philosophy: The Period of the Philosophers* (1931; trans. 1937); and Herrlee Glessner Creel, *The Birth of China: A Study of the Formative Period of Chinese Civilization* (1937). □

# Chrestien de Troyes

**The French author Chrestien de Troyes (active 12th century) was one of the greatest medieval poets. His works include the earliest extant Arthurian romances.**

Very little is known of the life of Chrestien de Troyes. His productive literary career extends from a little after the middle of the 12th century to about 1190. He was associated with the court of Marie de Champagne in or after 1164 and with that of Philippe d'Alsace, Comte de Flandres, sometime between 1168 and 1190. In 1190 Philippe left on the Third Crusade, and it is generally assumed that Chrestien died about the time of Philippe's departure. Chrestien's name and some traces of the dialect of Champagne in his works show that he was from northeastern France. Various hypotheses about Chrestien's life have been advanced, for example, he was a herald at arms, but they are not well founded.

Two lyric poems can be attributed to Chrestien, and four others have been dubiously ascribed to him. He translated Ovid's *Art of Love* and *Cures of Love* and wrote an adaptation of an episode from Ovid's *Metamorphoses* and a version of *Tristan and Isolt;* these four works have, however, been lost. *Philomena*, a short, tragic romance, survives. Another surviving romance, *William of England,* is partly didactic and partly adventurous, but the authorship of this poem has been disputed.

## Arthurian Romances

*Erec and Enide,* written about 1160, is the first of Chrestien's Arthurian romances which has survived. The hero marries the heroine fairly early in the romance, after which most of the story consists of demonstrations of prowess by which Erec proves himself free of uxoriousness. A tone of aristocratic refinement and of celebration of youthful joys and vigor runs throughout this work.

*Cligès,* composed about 1175, is at once Arthurian and Byzantine. It tells of Alexander, Prince of Constantinople, who goes to Britain to serve King Arthur. Alexander marries and returns to Constantinople with his wife and their son, Cligès. The second and longer part of this work consists of the dramatic love adventures of Cligès and Fenice.

*Lancelot, or The Knight of the Cart,* Chrestien's third major romance, was written for Marie de Champagne about 1179. The hero, Lancelot, goes in search of Queen Guenievre, who is being held captive. He meets a dwarf with a cart and is told to get into the cart if he wants to find the Queen. Although Lancelot hesitates to climb into this disgraceful conveyance, he finally does so. He then must overcome numerous obstacles, including the painful crossing of a sword bridge, before he finds the Queen. At last Lancelot kills the captor in combat and frees Guenievre. The theme of *Lancelot* is courtly love, which commits a knight to unlimited service to his lady. Therefore Lancelot's hesitation in climbing into the cart is a crime against courtly love and his long suffering is deserved. The last 988 lines of this romance were written by Godefroy de Leigny.

*Yvain,* or *The Knight of the Lion,* written about 1184, is a superb work. The hero, Yvain, marries Laudine, who grants him leave to engage in knightly activity. But he overstays his time and is banished by Laudine. During his wanderings he saves a lion from a dragon. The lion then becomes Yvain's companion and saves his life on two occasions. Yvain performs many feats at arms, all of which are directed to the needs of others. Due to the efforts of his benefactress, Lunette, he is reunited with Laudine. In this work the hero becomes aware of his weaknesses and renounces self-interest completely. His acts become deeds of expiatory charity, and his new spirit of compassion redeems him before his wife and his peers.

*Perceval,* or *The Story of the Grail,* Chrestien's unfinished masterpiece, was begun for Philippe de Flandres before 1190. The hero, Perceval, is raised by his mother in a remote region, since she fears that, like his father and brothers, he will meet death as a knight. However, he sees knights by chance and, much to his mother's sorrow, determines to become a knight. Although received by King Arthur, he is actually knighted by Gournement de Goort. Later Perceval visits the Grail Castle but fails to ask the significant questions; he soon learns the importance of the questions he did not dare to ask. A number of episodes follow, intermixed with parallel adventures of Gauvain, and then at line 9234 Chrestien's poem abruptly ends.

In the course of over 55,000 additional lines, four continuators put their hands to bringing the story to a conclusion, but their efforts fall far short of the genius, and probably the intention, of Chrestien. Like the composer Richard Wagner, Chrestien undertook this highly spiritual theme for his last work: the character who plays the great fool is to evolve into the Grail hero.

Chrestien's works show courtly tastes, detailed psychological insight, an unusual ease in versification, which at times reaches lyric quality, and a narrative technique that was closely imitated for two generations.

### Further Reading

The vast bibliography on Chrestien de Troyes is made up largely of French and German titles, of which the most concise short study is Jean Frappier, *Chréstien de Troyes* (1957), in French. The two most valuable studies in English are James Douglas Bruce, *The Evolution of Arthurian Romance* (2 vols., 1923), and Roger Sherman Loomis, *Arthurian Tradition and Chréstien de Troyes* (1949). Foster E. Guyer, *Chréstien de Troyes: Inventor of the Modern Novel* (1957), is useful. William W. Comfort's 1914 translation of Chrestien's romances is still the best in English; it does not, however, include *Perceval,* which was translated into modern French by Lucien Foulet in 1957. ☐

# Joseph-Jacques-Jean Chrétien

**Joseph-Jacques-Jean Chrétien (born 1934) had one of the remarkable careers in modern Canadian politics. He was elected ten times as a Liberal to the House of Commons, held almost every major cabinet office, served as the country's first French Canadian finance minister, and in October 1993 was elected as his nation's 20th prime minister.**

Jean Chrétien was born on January 11, 1934, in Shawinigan, Quebec, the 18th of 19 children of paper mill machinist Wellie Chrétien and his wife, Marie Boisvert-Chrétien. His father was a grassroots Liberal Party organizer, and Chrétien described his family as "Liberal in the free-thinking, anti-clerical, anti-establishment tradition of the nineteenth century." As a teenager he found himself defending Liberal policy in a local poolroom during the national election of 1949. A good student, he won a scholarship to Laval University law school in Quebec City, supplementing his income with summer work at the Shawinigan paper mill. He was called to the Quebec bar in 1958, a year after marrying Aline Chaîne.

In 1963 Chrétien became the federal member of Parliament for his home area of St. Maurice-Laflèche. He went to Ottawa speaking scarcely a word of English, but his energy and likability brought him quickly to the attention of Prime Minister L.B. Pearson and his powerful colleague Mitchell Sharp. Named Pearson's parliamentary assistant in July 1965, he was given the same position under Sharp, then the finance minister, in January 1966. Sharp liked his quick mind, solid political instincts, and straightforward manner,

as well as his ability to convey to audiences his genuine Canadian patriotism and commitment to a strong national government, this at a time when some of his fellow Quebecers were calling for policies that would make their province master of its own destiny within or perhaps outside Canada. Chrétien was given cabinet rank under Sharp as minister of state for finance in April 1967, and he became minister of national revenue in January 1968.

Pearson was replaced as Liberal leader and prime minister by Pierre Elliott Trudeau in the spring of 1968, and Chrétien was appointed his minister of Indian affairs and northern development in the summer. Early on in his six-year tenure, his department suggested a package of reforms to Canada's native peoples, including an end to their separate legal status, that was received with outrage. Chrétien retreated but rebounded quickly, making it clear in actions and words that he hated paternalism and had no desire to act as "the great white father."

Chrétien was then given a series of senior economic portfolios. "Let the philosophers philosophize elsewhere," he said. He enjoyed being where the cash was. He was president of the Treasury Board, 1974 to 1976; minister of industry, trade, and commerce, 1976 to 1977; and then the first francophone minister of finance, 1977 to 1979. The symbolism was important. A government had been elected in Quebec bent on independence for the province. The federal government wanted to make the point that Quebecers had real power in Ottawa and that their grievances could be solved in a national context. A difficult moment came in August 1978, when Trudeau announced major spending cuts without clearing them with his finance minister. Rather than resign, Chrétien swallowed his pride, knowing that the departure of a senior francophone minister would give comfort to the separatists in Quebec.

The Trudeau Liberals were briefly out of office in 1979, but they swept back into power in February 1980. Chrétien was minister of justice with special responsibility to lead the federal forces in a referendum campaign that had been called by the Quebec government to determine whether the province ought to secede from Canada. The referendum (which rejected the plan) was won by the Chrétien side in dramatic and convincing fashion, and he next tackled the national constitution. After a bruising 18-month battle, all of the provinces were satisfied with the federal proposals, including a charter of rights and freedoms, except Quebec. Chrétien and his colleagues decided to proceed without his home province, reinforcing the impression in some quarters of Quebec that he had other priorities than its welfare.

Chrétien served as minister of energy, mines, and resources from 1982 to 1984. When Trudeau announced his retirement, Chrétien ran to become chief of the Liberal Party, finishing second in June 1984 to John Turner, who took over as prime minister. The relationship with Turner was strained, but Chrétien was appointed deputy prime minister and secretary of state for external affairs. He won his seat in the September 1984 election, but the party lost badly to Brian Mulroney's Conservatives. Chrétien returned to the private practice of law in 1986.

After Turner's resignation in 1990, Chrétien again contested the leadership of the Liberal Party, this time winning easily. Preferring to be constructive, he hated his new role as leader of the opposition. Media critics were everywhere—he was labeled "yesterday's man"—and a long illness in 1991 sapped his strength over many months. In the national election of October 1993, however, experience showed, and all the former decisiveness and roughhewn confidence returned. Chrétien ran a brilliant campaign, taking 178 of 295 seats. The only blot was Quebec, where many of the old suspicions lingered and the separatist Bloc Quebeçois won 54 seats.

Chrétien assumed control as prime minister on November 4, 1993. The first months were marked by an emphasis on integrity in government, policy review, and budget-cutting. Polls taken at the time showed his party to be immensely more popular than it had been even at election time.

Chrétien successfully championed his federalist cause in 1995 with the Quebec Referendum. The Referendum was yet another attempt to make Quebec a separate entity from Canada. He has often been described as a major political player against Quebec separatists.

## Further Reading

The only in-depth study of Chrétien is his own autobiography, *Straight from the Heart* (Toronto, 1985; revised edition, 1994).
☐

# Agatha Christie

**Agatha Christie (1890-1976) was the best selling mystery author of all time and the only writer to have created two major detectives, Poirot and Marple. She also wrote the longest-running play in the modern theater, *The Mousetrap*.**

The daughter of an American father and a British mother, Agatha Mary Clarissa Miller was born at Torquay in the United Kingdom on September 15, 1890. Her family was comfortable, although not wealthy, and she was educated at home, with later study in Paris. In 1914 she was married to Col. Archibald Christie; the marriage produced one daughter.

In 1920 Christie launched a career which made her the most popular mystery writer of all time. Her total output reached 93 books and 17 plays; she was translated into 103 languages (even more than Shakespeare); and her sales have passed the 400 million mark and are still going strong.

It was in her first book, *The Mysterious Affair at Styles* (1920), that Christie introduced one of her two best-known detectives, Hercule Poirot, and his amanuensis, Captain Hastings. Her debt to the Sherlock Holmes stories of Sir Arthur Conan Doyle is manifest in the books in which this pair appears. Like Holmes, Poirot is a convinced and convincing spokesman for the human rational faculty (he places his faith in "the little grey cells"), uses his long-suffering companion as a sort of echo-chamber, and even has a mysterious and exotically-named brother who works for the government. Captain Hastings, like Dr. John Watson a retired military man, has much in common with his prototype: he is trusting, bumbling, and superingenuous, and by no means an intellectual. Yet occasionally he wins applause from the master by making an observation which by its egregious stupidity illuminates some corner previously dark in the inner recesses of the great mind. There is even a copy of Conan Doyle's ineffectual Inspector Lestrade in the person of Inspector Japp.

While writing in imitation of Conan Doyle, Christie experimented with a whole gallery of other sleuths.

Tuppence and Tommy Beresford, whose specialty was ferreting out espionage, made their debut in *The Secret Adversary* (1922); their insouciant, almost frivolous approach to detection provided a sharp contrast to that of Poirot.

The enigmatic, laconic Colonel Race appeared first in *The Man in the Brown Suit* (1924), but, since his principal sphere of activity was the colonies, he was used only sporadically thereafter.

Superintendent Battle, stolid, dependable, and hardworking, came onto the scene in *The Secret of Chimneys* (1925) and later solved *The Seven Dials Mystery* (1929), but probably because of a lack of charisma was relegated to a subordinate role after that.

Also in 1930, writing under the penname of Mary Westmacott, she published *Giant's Bread,* the first of six romances, none of which showed distinction. In that same year in *Murder at the Vicarage,* undoubtedly the best-written Christie novel, she first presented Jane Marple, who became one of her favorite sleuths and showed up frequently thereafter. Miss Marple was one of those paradoxes in whom readers delight: behind the Victorian, tea-and-crumpets, crocheted-antimacassar facade was a mind coldly aware of the frailty of all human beings and the depravity of some.

In the mid-1930s Christie began to produce novels that bore her unique stamp. In them she arranged a situation which was implausible, if not actually impossible, and into this unrealistic framework placed characters who acted realistically for the most realistic of motives. In *Murder in the Calais Coach* (1934) the murder is done with the connivance of a dozen people; in *And Then There Were None* (1939) nine murderers are invited to an island to be dispatched by an ex-judge with an implacable sense of justice; in *Easy to Kill* (1939) four murders are committed in a miniscule town without any suspicions being aroused; in *A Murder Is Announced* (1950) the killer advertises in advance. Also interesting in these books is Christie's philosophy that it is quite acceptable to kill a killer, particularly one whose crime is a heinous one.

In addition to her fiction, her archaeological reminiscences, the children's book *Star over Bethlehem* (1965), a collection of her poetry (1973), and her autobiography (1977), Christie authored 17 plays. Her own favorite was *Witness for the Prosecution* (1953), based on one of her novellas, but the public disagreed. *The Mousetrap* opened in London in 1952 and played there for over three decades, a run unparalleled in theater history. Many of her mysteries were made into movies—*And Then There Were None* three times—with the most successful those in which Margaret Rutherford portrayed Miss Marple.

Named a Dame of the British Empire in 1971, Christie died on January 12, 1976.

## Further Reading

Besides *An Autobiography* (1977), there is a good biography by Gwen Robyns, *The Mystery of Agatha Christie* (1978). It contains a bibliography, although not as complete a one as that in *Contemporary Authors.* Janet Morgan's *Agatha Christie: A Biography* (1985) traces the writer's career through her first marriage and 1928 divorce. Christie is also a central figure in Sir Max Mallowan's *Mallowan's Memoirs* (1977). A semi-factual, semi-fictional look at the 1926 disappearance can be found in Kathleen Tynan's *Agatha* (1978). □

Others who debuted during this experimental period were the weird pair of the other-worldly Harley Quin and his fussbudgety, oldmaidish "contact," Mr. Satterthwaite, and the ingenious Parker Pyne, who specialized not in solving murders, but in manipulating the lives of others so as to bring them happiness and/or adventure. Pyne was often fortunate enough to have the assistance of Mrs. Ariadne Oliver, the mystery novelist who bore an uncanny resemblance to her creator.

The year 1926 was a watershed year for Christie. It saw the publication of her first hugely successful novel, *The Murder of Roger Ackroyd,* in which the narrator is the murderer, a plot twist that provoked great controversy about the ethics of the mystery writer. It was also a year of personal tragedy: her mother died, and then she discovered that her husband was in love with another woman. She suffered a nervous breakdown and on December 6 disappeared from her home; subsequently her car was found abandoned in a chalk-pit. Ten days later, acting on a tip, police found her in a Harrogate hotel, where she had been staying the entire time, although registered under the name of the woman with whom her husband was having his affair. She claimed to have had amnesia, and the case was not pursued further. The divorce came two years later.

In 1930 she married Sir Max Mallowan, a fellow of All Souls College, Oxford, and one of Britain's foremost archaeologists. She often accompanied him on his digs in Iraq and Syria and placed some of her novels in those countries. In *Come, Tell Me How You Live* (1946) she wrote a humorous account of some of her expeditions with her husband.

# Christina of Sweden

**Christina (1626–1689), Queen of Lutheran Sweden, who abdicated at the height of Sweden's power during the Thirty Years' War, converted to Catholicism, and spent the second half of her life in Rome.**

Queen Christina is one of the most unusual monarchs in European history. Inheriting her throne at the age of six, she was raised by brilliant tutors to face a complex and dangerous political world. Intellectually gifted, with a highly complex personality, she confounded her advisors first by refusing to marry, then by voluntarily surrendering her throne, and finally by converting to Catholicism in an age of bitter religious warfare, although her Swedish kingdom was then leader of the Protestant powers. The 1933 movie *Queen Christina,* starring Greta Garbo, which made the queen's name familiar to 20th-century audiences is entirely misleading about the historical Queen Christina, but it is not alone; she has been the subject of extravagant praise from some observers and detestation from others—so much so, that reliable information in English has remained the exception rather than the rule.

Christina was the daughter of King Gustavus II Adolphus, one of the great military heroes of Swedish history. Entering the Thirty Years' War in 1630 when the "Protestant Cause" was at its lowest ebb, Gustavus Adolphus won a succession of sweeping victories over the armies of the Catholic Holy Roman Empire, culminating in the triumphs of Breitenfeld (1631) and Lützen (1632). At this second battle, however, Gustavus was killed, and although his generals fought on through the following two decades, none could quite match him for strategic daring or tactical elan. At his death Christina, his only child, inherited his throne. For the immediate future, power went to her regent, Axel Oxenstierna, a brilliant politician who continued Gustavus's active policy in northern Europe. He negotiated favorable terms for Sweden in its war against Denmark, settled at Bromsebro in 1644. By winning title to extensive south Baltic lands and ports for Sweden in the general pacification of Westphalia (1648), Oxenstierna showed unmistakably that Christina's Sweden had become the major power of northern Europe.

Not until December 1644, her 18th birthday, did Christina become queen in her own right, though by then she had been attending meetings of the Regency Council for two years. In the meantime, Oxenstierna had taken her away from her mentally unbalanced mother and put her education in the hands of Johannes Matthiae, a broadminded and widely learned man, who gave her a thorough grounding in history, philosophy, theology, and the sciences, in accordance with her father's early orders that she should be raised like a boy. Matthiae nourished in her a passion for philosophy and whetted her intellectual appetite, preparing for the days when she would be one of the chief patrons of European intellectual life. She became a confident speaker of French, German, Latin, Spanish, and Italian, but her written works—letters, aphorisms, and an autobiography—suggest that, although she was surely bright, she was not the genius whom flattering courtiers described in their dedications.

As she matured, Sweden faced domestic and international crises. In the late 1640s, Swedish statesmen watched anxiously as a revolution overthrew the English monarchy and beheaded King Charles I. In Paris, the *Fronde* rebellion came close to unseating the French monarchy, and the boy-

king Louis XIV had to flee for his life. Revolutions in these and other parts of Europe alarmed Oxenstierna, and he feared that the high taxes he had levied for war and for Christina's court expenses might spark a peasant revolt at home. In 1650, Sweden's representative assembly, the Diet, met at a time of widespread hunger following a poor harvest and protested against the power and privileges of the aristocracy, the price of food, and the costs of a foreign policy from which ordinary Swedes gained nothing. The Diet also argued that Oxenstierna's policy of giving away crown lands, in the hope that they would yield more revenue when taxed than when farmed, benefited none but the aristocracy.

Noting the Diet's formal *Protestation,* Oxenstierna tried to curb Christina's lavish tastes in art, architecture, and music when she began to rule in her own right—one of several sources of tension between the old servant and his new mistress. She, however, scorned Oxenstierna's efforts at frugality and defied him by giving large gifts of lands to returning veterans when the long series of wars came to an end. As the leading historian of Sweden, Michael Roberts, notes: "She had neither interest in, nor grasp of, finance; and after 1652 seems to have been cynically indifferent to the distresses of a crown she had already decided to renounce." She also rewarded her favorites, such as Magnus de la Gardie, lavishly and tactlessly, and angered Oxenstierna further by introducing men into the royal council whom he thought unsuitable but could no longer oppose.

Every 17th-century European monarchy had to think about and plan for the succession. The presence of a queen made matrimonial diplomacy even more hazardous and more necessary than usual because the wrong husband could be politically disastrous. As an adolescent Christina was in love with, and planned to marry, her cousin Charles (the future Charles X), with whom she was educated at Stegeborg Castle. The attraction was mutual and led him to hope for a throne. But as she matured Christina's ardor cooled. Though she kept alive the possibility of a marriage to Charles, it was more as a tactic to secure the succession than from affection. Her Council of Regents and her Parliament were also eager to assure a politically suitable royal marriage of this kind, which could eventuate in the birth of heirs.

But once she was queen in fact as well as in name, Christina was in no hurry to tie the knot. Like Queen Elizabeth I of England a generation earlier, she realized that the promise of her hand in marriage was a more potent instrument than marriage itself. Once wed, her power would probably decline, whereas the hope of it beforehand would keep Charles, and other possible suitors, guessing as to her intentions and assure her dominance. Meanwhile, she endured rumors which alleged that she was involved in a lesbian affair with her friend Countess Ebba Sparre.

After lengthy disputes with her councillors, she agreed in 1649 to the principle that *if* she married it would be to Charles, but added that she could not be compelled to marry at all. She was more eager to have Charles formally recognized as her heir. Since the two of them were nearly contemporaries, it was unlikely that Charles would enjoy a long reign after her. In the meantime, he had to skulk on his estates where, according to the court gossip of the day, he spent much of his time in a drunken stupor.

Christina was therefore still unmarried when, in 1651, she told Parliament of her intention to abdicate. A collective cry of dismay from the Swedish statesmen delayed her, but in 1654 she renewed the project and this time carried it out, leaving Sweden permanently in June of that year, and traveling to the Spanish Netherlands. From there, traveling in fine style and assured (as it then seemed) of a lifelong income from her Swedish estates, she went to Innsbruck in Austria, and during her stay openly declared her conversion to Roman Catholicism. To nearly all Swedes her conversion, even more than her abdication, appeared as a horrific form of betrayal. In that age of bitter, protracted religious wars, in which Lutheran Sweden had been pitted for 30 years against the Catholic Empire, a conversion of this sort seemed not so much an act of personal conscience as a symbolic declaration of allegiance to the enemy. Why she took these steps has always been a mystery, and has continued to be the subject of a keen dispute among Swedish historians. Her often-voiced conviction that women were unsuited to rule may have played a part in the decision, but religious conviction was probably more decisive.

Generations of historians have also debated the exact sequence of events and causes surrounding this amazing set of actions. While still in Sweden, Christina had been secretive about her interest in Catholicism, because of its politically volatile implications. She had certainly been strongly impressed by the Catholic French ambassador to her court, Chanut, and by the French philosopher Rene Descartes, also a dedicated Catholic, who spent the last year of his life at her court in Stockholm (he died there of pneumonia in 1650). Next she had encountered Antonio Macedo, who was a Jesuit priest posing as the Portuguese ambassador's interpreter. Christina had several conversations with Macedo and told him that she would welcome the chance to discuss Catholicism with more members of his order. When he hurried to Rome with this news, the Father General of the order responded by sending two learned Jesuit professors, Fathers Malines and Casati, also incognito, to her court. After winning her notice by their pose as Italian noblemen, they quickly recognized that she was a thoughtful and gifted person, "a twenty-five year old sovereign so entirely removed from human conceit and with such a deep appreciation of true values that she might have been brought up in the very spirit of moral philosophy." They recalled later that "our main efforts were to prove that our sacred beliefs were beyond reason, yet that they did not conflict with reason. The queen, meanwhile, shrewdly absorbed the substance of our arguments; otherwise we should have needed a great deal of time to make our point."

Christina may have converted as early as 1652, more than a year before her abdication, but if so she did it secretly. When she went to the Netherlands in 1654, she was still accompanied by a retinue which included a Lutheran chaplain. But while there, he died and was not replaced. Christina, meanwhile, gained a reputation in those

years, 1654 and 1655, for having a caustic and dismissive attitude towards all forms of Christianity, which may have been a smokescreen to allay suspicions of her conversion. At any rate, after her open confession of her new faith, scandalous tales of her atheism died away. On the other hand scurrilous rumors of her real motives, printed in an avalanche of hostile and lurid pamphlets, were to follow her to the grave and to mislead historians in the ensuing three centuries.

Arriving at Rome in high style after her stately progress through Europe, she took up residence in the Farnese Palace, alarmed Pope Alexander VII by meeting him in a red dress (the color usually reserved for Roman prostitutes) and entertained lavishly, but with little outward sign of religious fervor. Her home quickly became a salon, where intellectuals, cardinals, and noblemen met, and it inevitably became the focus of political intrigues. Despite Christina's lack of outward piety, she was the most prominent convert of the century, and Rome countered Protestant taunts with an avalanche of its own propaganda, singing her praises. She declared that other European princes should follow her lead and end the Reformation rift which had divided Europe for the last 150 years, but none did so.

Charles X, her successor in Sweden, gained a crown sooner than he had dared hope. He proved an effective—and sternly Protestant—monarch, carrying on the policy which Gustavus Adolphus had initiated, of gaining conquests in what is now Poland and North Germany, on the south shore of the Baltic. One pamphleteer noted that while the Pope had gained one lamb in Queen Christina he had lost an entire flock in Poland at the hands of Charles. Lands and tax revenues from this area strengthened the monarchy in its continuing conflict with the aristocracy, and facilitated the paradox of Sweden, a nation of very small population and indigenous resources, remaining a major European power for the best part of a century.

As for Christina, the second half of her life saw her embroiled in the complex politics of baroque Rome, in which she gained the greatest possible leverage from her royal position and felt constrained only by lack of money. When she arrived, the city was one of the focal points of a conflict between pro-French and pro-Spanish factions: France and Spain themselves were at war. At first the common view was that she was pro-Spanish, but her old friend Chanut reassured his master, Cardinal Mazarin, Louis XIV's chief minister, that this was not true. Sure enough, the early months of 1656 bore witness to a gradual deterioration of Christina's courtesy towards the Spanish ambassadors and her cultivation of French envoys and diplomats. She recognized that France was becoming the dominant power in Europe and that it could better serve her interests than any other nation. Among other things her income had fallen precipitously despite her precautions at the time of abdication. Since less than a quarter of the anticipated revenue was coming to her from her Swedish estates, she hoped Mazarin might offer her a substitute. In late 1656, therefore, she traveled to Paris and was again accorded a sumptuous royal welcome; she then settled down to debating with Mazarin the possibility that she might be made queen of Naples. The

Kingdom of Naples, constituting what is now southern Italy, was then in Spanish hands, and making it an independent, pro-French monarchy was one of the central aims of Mazarin's diplomacy. Christina seemed a likely candidate for monarch, and the two of them signed an accord at Compiegne which drew up a timetable for the achievement of this plan.

The expedition of conquest, prepared in secrecy, was due to sail from Marseilles to Naples in February 1657, but French military commitments elsewhere led to a delay. Christina returned from Italy to France and urged Mazarin to hurry, lest he lose the element of surprise. Sure enough, an Italian member of her own entourage whom she had treated lavishly in the past but who now felt slighted, the Marquis of Monaldesco, warned the Spanish Viceroy in Naples of the impending attack. The Viceroy prepared his fortifications to repel it, and Mazarin canceled the expedition. In a fury of disappointment and rage, Christina retaliated against Monaldesco, whose mail she had intercepted, by having his throat cut in her presence at Fontainbleau Palace, despite his agonized pleas for mercy. News of this bloody act, undertaken while she was a foreign king's guest and in his house, undermined her reputation and nullified the Neapolitan scheme altogether. She had fatally underestimated its consequences for her future. Some pamphlets appeared on the streets of Paris which said Monaldesco had been her lover and that she had killed him to keep the fact a secret; others added that he was just one in a long line of murdered lovers. These allegations were groundless, but the killing was politically inept, especially for a woman who prided herself on her Machiavellian skills and diplomatic tact. In 1659, France and Spain signed the Treaty of the Pyrénées and any lingering hopes of a Neapolitan kingdom for Christina fizzled.

From then on Mazarin would make no more schemes with her and Pope Alexander VII now referred to her as "a woman born a barbarian, barbarously brought up, and living with barbarous thoughts." She returned to Rome without further hope of political power but was still resourceful enough to create one of the most refined and brilliant salons in Europe at the Palazzo Riario. For 30 more years, she remained the great anomaly in Europe, a skilled and talented queen without a realm. A circle of friends and retainers still surrounded her, led by Cardinal Azzolino, who did everything he could to repair her tarnished reputation but was careful always to answer her passionately loving letters in a tone of cold severity, lest further scandal attach itself to her name.

Unable to break the habits of a lifetime, she remained an inveterate intriguer (including an effort to become queen of Poland, and a plan to have Azzolino elected pope) but died in 1689 without making any further impact on the course of events. Without the backing of another monarchy, she lacked the resources for further expeditions, and her Swedish successor, Charles X, himself an ally of France, was careful to do nothing to encourage her. Vatican dismay at the Monaldesco affair had cooled sufficiently after 30 years that Christina the eminent convert could be given the final honor, by Pope Innocent XI, of burial in St. Peter's.

## Further Reading

Elstob, Eric. *Sweden: A Political and Cultural History.* Rowman & Littlefield, 1979.
Masson, Georgina. *Queen Christina.* London: Secker & Warburg, 1968.
Roberts, Michael. *Essays in Swedish History.* University of Minnesota Press, 1967.
Scott, Franklin D. *Sweden: The Nation's History.* University of Minnesota Press, 1977.
Stolpe, Sven. *Christina of Sweden.* Macmillan, 1966.
Weibull, Curt. *Christina of Sweden.* Bonniers: Svenska Bokforlaget, 1966. □

# Christine de Pisan

**The French author Christine de Pisan C. (c. 1364-ca. 1430) wrote lyric poetry and also prose and verse works on a great variety of philosophical, social, and historical subjects.**

Thomas de Pisan, father of Christine de Pisan, was an astrologer and medical doctor in the service of the republic of Venice when he accepted a similar appointment at the court of Charles V of France. Born in Venice, Christine was taken to Paris in 1368, where she was brought up in courtly surroundings and enjoyed a comfortable and studious childhood and adolescence. At 15 she married Étienne de Castel. In 1380 Charles V died, thereby dissolving the royal appointment of her father, who died 5 years later. Christine's husband, secretary of Charles VI, died in 1390, leaving her a widow at 25, with three children, considerable debts, and impatient creditors. Two years later Charles VI became insane, leaving the nation open prey.

Impoverished by multiple blows of adversity, Christine determined to earn her living by writing, composing her first ballades in 1393. Her works were successful, and richly illuminated copies of some of them were presented to noted patrons of letters. Thirty major titles followed until she retired to the convent at Poissy, where her only daughter had been a religious for 22 years. She wrote no more except one religious work and a eulogy on Joan of Arc after the victory at Orléans.

In verse, Christine's first work appears to be her *Hundred Ballades,* followed by 26 virelays, 2 lays, 69 rondeaux, 70 framed poems, 66 more ballades, and 2 complaints. In her *Epistle to the God of Love* (1399) she begins her battle for feminism, reproaching Ovid and Jean de Meun for their misogyny; a second attack appears in her *Tale of the Rose* (1402). Of her 15 other long poems the best is the *Changes of Fortune* (1403), in the 23,636 lines of which she traces changing "fortune" from the time of the Jews down to her own time.

In prose, after her allegorical *Epistle from Othea* (1400), Christine vigorously continues her feminism in the *City of Ladies* and the *Book of the Three Virtues* (both 1405). Other works in prose include the *Deeds and Good Morals of Wise*

*King Charles V* (1404), a book on arms and knighthood (1410), and the *Book of Peace* (1414), which holds up Charles V as a model for the Dauphin. Her *Hours of Contemplation on the Passion,* containing lessons on patience and humility, was written during her last retreat.

## Further Reading

There is little material on Christine de Pisan. A study of her is in Alice Kemp Welch, *Of Six Medieval Women* (1913). See also Lula McDowell Richardson, *The Forerunners of Feminism in French Literature of the Renaissance from Christine of Pisa to Marie de Gournay* (1929).

## Additional Sources

McLeod, Enid, *The Order of the Rose: the life and ideas of Christine de Pizan,* Totowa, N.J.: Rowman and Littlefield, 1976 and London: Chatto & Windus, 1976.
Pernoud, Regine, *Christine de Pisan,* Paris: Calmann-Levy, 1982.
Willard, Charity Cannon, *Christine de Pizan: her life and works,* New York, N.Y.: Persea Books, 1984. □

# Christo Vladimiroff Javacheff

**Christo Vladimiroff Javacheff (born 1935) is a Bulgarian-born sculptor who gained world-wide fame for his unique large-scale environmental artworks such as *Running Fence* and *Valley Curtain.***

Christo Vladimiroff Javacheff, who is known professionally only by his first name, was born on June 13, 1935, in Gabrovo, a small town in the Balkan Mountains of Bulgaria. Bulgaria was invaded by the Nazis during his early childhood, and later occupied by the Soviets at the end of World War II when Christo was about ten-years-old. He was the second of three sons born to Ivan Javacheff, a chemist and prominent businessman and industrialist, and Tzveta (Dimitrova) Javacheff, a political activist. His family was prominent in Bulgarian artistic circles in the 1950s and young Christo studied at the Fine Arts Academy in Bulgaria's capital city, Sofia. There the curriculum followed the tenets of Soviet Social Realism and Christo learned to paint in the strict realistic styles advanced by the Soviet government. As a member of the Communist Youths he participated in art propaganda projects while in school. In 1956, he went to Prague, Czechoslovakia to study theater design, and there he saw for the first time modern paintings by Matisse, Miro, Klee, and Kandinsky which were relegated to basements and storerooms.

## Early Work

When the Hungarian uprising of 1956 broke out, Christo managed to defect to Austria. He studied art briefly in Vienna, Austria, and then, after a short stay in Switzerland, moved to Paris in 1958.

Once in Paris, Christo supported himself by painting and met a group of artists who used everyday objects and events as the subjects of their work. The group included Arman, Daniel Spoerri, Jean Tinguely, and Yves Klein. Roughly corresponding to American and British Pop Art, they gathered around the critic Pierre Restany and were identified as "Nouvelle Realism" (New Realism). In this milieu Christo made the first wrapped sculptures that became his hallmark. Christo also met his future wife and business and artistic partner, Jeanne-Claude Guillebon, in Paris. Guillebon was the daughter of a noted French World War II general and was born on the same day as Christo. She would play the role of organizer and administrator of their corporation, which controls the finances of these ventures. On many of the projects, Guillebon is also enrolled as a photographer.

## Began Wrapping

Christo began wrapping objects for display purposes soon after his arrival in Paris. He started with small items, like beer cans and wine bottles, then moved on to bicycles, road signs, and cars. He also wrapped huge piles of crates along a harbor in Cologne, Germany, and covered shop windows and corridors of shops. His first major foray was his *Iron Curtain—Wall of Oil Barrels,* which he displayed in Paris in 1962. The origin of this approach is unclear; he told one writer that it may have developed when he and other art students in Sofia were "drafted" to decorate a railway embankment at the local train station. Decorating an actual location with common materials appealed to him.

## "Christos"

In 1964 Christo moved to New York where he continued to make what he called "temporary monuments," and at one point he wrapped live female models. His sculpture often passed as ordinary objects walking a line between art and life. His projects began to grow in size, and after several unsuccessful attempts he erected a 280-foot sausage-like column filled with air at the international exhibition *Documenta* in 1968, the first of his monumental environmental sculptures. He followed that success by wrapping a medieval tower in Spoleto, Italy and the city hall of Bern, Switzerland. In 1969, he wrapped the Museum of Contemporary Art in Chicago and revealed his *Wrapped Coast,* which entailed wrapping one mile of Australian coastline near Sydney. The *Valley Curtain,* built in the Grand Hogback Mountain Range near Aspen, Colorado in 1972, spanned a distance of 1,250 feet from one side of Rifle Gap, a narrow valley, to the other with 200,000 square feet of bright orange nylon fabric. *Running Fence,* built in 1976 of two million square feet of a white fabric "fence," ran across 24 miles of California landscape from Sonoma and Marin Counties into the Pacific Ocean. These large projects were known as "Christos" and brought an ever increasing amount of both scorn and praise to Christo.

In the spring of 1980, he completed *Surrounded Islands* in Biscayne Bay near Miami, Florida, by encircling eleven man-made islands with 200-foot-wide sheets of flamingo pink polypropylene fabric. Christo called this project his version of Monet's water lilies, in reference to Claude Monet's large cycle of paintings of water lilies, often considered the quintessential Impressionist painting. Christo's project was made with the help of 430 assistants, cost $3.4 million, and lasted two weeks. To realize *Surrounded Islands* the artist had to file numerous permits and go through seven public hearings. Much of the initial local opposition to it turned to support by its conclusion. In 1985, Christo unveiled his *Pont Neuf Wrapped*. He wrapped the Pont Neuf bridge, the oldest bridge in Paris, and one of the most famous crossings of the Seine River.

He followed this achievement with his 1991 "Christo," *The Umbrellas, Joint Project for Japan and USA*. This project would not be as successful as his previous ones had been. The project consisted of a line of thousands of yellow and blue umbrellas arrayed in a wandering line along the coasts of Japan and California. After years of preparation and planning, environmental studies, wind tests, and negotiations, a line of umbrellas stretching for about 12 miles in Japan and 16 in California was unfurled on the same day in October. Unfortunately, a gust of wind lifted one of the large umbrellas out of its metal mooring, killing one person and injuring three more. Christo immediately ordered the closing of the umbrellas. Then, in the course of dismantling one of the umbrellas, a Japanese worker was electrocuted as he lifted the metal poles onto a truck near a high-power electric line.

These deaths made it increasingly difficult for Christo to gain permission for his projects and made it more difficult for Christo to gain the support of insurance companies and other organizations. Nonetheless, some progress was made on what Christo called "the project that is more important to me than all of the others put together." This "Christo" was called *Wrapped Reichstag, Project for Berlin* and had been in Christo's mind for nearly 20 years. He wrapped the Reichstag, the center of Germany's government and an important and symbolic monument in that nation's history. The project had faced rigid opposition for many years, but in 1993 the president of the German parliament announced that she would support the wrapping. It took another year, but in February of 1994, a parliamentary vote of 292 to 223 okayed Christo's wrapping of the Reichstag.

The *New York Times* Holland Cotter wrote that, for Christo, the Reichstag "is both a monument to democracy and a symbol of the possibility of renewed relationships between Eastern and Western Europe. In that light, his project can be viewed as the bandaging of old wounds." In June of 1995, Christo, his wife, and over 100 mountain climbers and assistants wrapped the Reichstag in thousands of yards of silver fabric. When the wrapping came off after nearly two weeks, the German government went ahead with plans to remodel the building so as to house the newly-unified German parliament.

In 1996, Christo traveled back to Colorado for his *Over the River, Project for Western USA*. This involved wrapping roughly five miles of the Arkansas River near Canon City, Colorado with a translucent fabric.

Christo's latest idea involves lining all the paths in New York City's Central Park with rectangular steel gates that would hold saffron-colored banners. The project has drawn fire from many in New York and is still under consideration.

The environmental projects of Christo are temporary events that require hundreds of assistants, cost large sums of money, and are the result of years of complicated negotiations between government officials, financial backers, environmentalists, and the public-at-large. The artist considered these efforts as part of artwork. No public or corporate funds are used for any "Christo," and all funds were raised through the sales of his drawings and prints. His work always generated controversy which he welcomed claiming that "the worst thing that can happen to any artist is that no one cares about his work."

Like many contemporary artists Christo wanted to defy convention and demanded that old definitions and expectations of art be expanded. He challenged the idea that sculpture is a permanent object and circumvented the world of art galleries and museums by placing his art in the world-at-large. While the projects cost millions of dollars they cannot be bought, sold, or owned. William Rubin, curator at the Museum of Modern Art, described Christo as "an artist functioning more in the realm of events than in that of painting and sculpture," where the emphasis has been on the end product and not on the process. As sculpture, his work is environmental, built to relate to a specific site and to be part of it. None of his projects can be moved. In the process of making the work Christo, along with hundreds of collaborators, must be a diplomat, publicist, fund-raiser, and politician as well as form-giver. This complex role goes against the modern myth of the artist as a lone individual.

In general Christo's projects get more and more ambitious and the planning stages become very complicated, especially in relationship to the amount of time that the artwork lasts. Like the artist Judy Chicago, he had a wide following outside of art circles, and he is often criticized by art critics for being a "megalomaniac" and for relying too much on the single theme of envelopment. Christo says of this, "For me, the real world involves everything: risk, danger, beauty, energy."

### Further Reading

*Christo* (1972), with a text by critic David Bourdon, is a good summary of Christo's work up to the 1970s and contains many photographs of sculptures and projects that no longer exist. *Christo, Complete Editions, 1964-1982* (1982), by Per Hovdenakk, is a more up-to-date listing of the graphic work which accompanied his large projects. Information about Christo's work is constantly being updated and often appears first in the general press. A thorough examination of the process of making *Surrounded Islands* can be found in an article in *Art News* (January 1984) entitled "Christo's Blossoms in the Bay," written by Lisbeth Nelson.

Information on Christo's project in Colorado can be found in the *Denver Post*, July 10, 1995; July 16, 1995; and November 16, 1996. Biographical information on Christo can be found in the May 23, 1997 issue of the *Denver Post*. Information on Christo's latest project in New York City can be found in the March 31, 1996 issue of the *New York Times*. □

# Henri Christophe

**Henri Christophe (1767-1820) was a Haitian patriot and king. Though he is mostly remembered for the Citadelle, the fortress he built, equally impressive was his organizational genius, which created a prosperous and solvent Haiti.**

Born a slave, Henri Christophe originally came from the British island of St. Christopher (St. Kitts), from which he took his name. He bought his freedom in Saint Domingue and later added the English name of Henry (French, Henri) as a token of his admiration of England.

Christophe gained an early reputation as an independence fighter under Toussaint L'Ouverture in the 1791 antislavery rebellion. When French troops invaded Haiti in 1802 to reassert France's right to the former colony, Christophe was commanding Haitian troops in Cap-Français (modern Cap-Haitien). After Toussaint's capture by the French, Christophe served as a general under Haiti's military ruler, Jean Jacques Dessalines.

Following Dessalines's assassination in 1806, Christophe took over as president. However, the southern and western parts of Haiti had chafed under the authoritarian regime of Dessalines. To prevent a repetition of such a regime, a new constitution was promulgated which would have curtailed the power of the executive. Christophe refused to accept the office with such restrictions and gained control of the northern part of the country.

## A Prosperous Kingdom

Recognizing the need for outside help in developing the country, Christophe did not have the customary xenophobic hatred of whites and thus welcomed them, especially the English, to his part of the country. During the 13 years of his rule, agriculture and commerce prospered in the north, and the treasury was full. Though he inherited the feudal economic and social structure from Toussaint and Dessalines, Christophe contributed a superb administration. He also promulgated a body of laws which he called the Code Henri.

In 1811 Christophe changed Northern Haiti from a republic to a kingdom and had himself crowned King Henri I. He then catered to the vanity of his associates by granting them nobility, thereby assuring their personal loyalty and identifying their interests with his own. Enforcement of costly court etiquette made the "nobility" exert every effort to make their plantations pay. In the words of James G. Leyburn, "Vanity was to serve an economic and a political purpose."

Generally, the masses accepted this feudalistic arrangement. In spite of the discipline, lack of mobility, and hard work, the farmers stayed reasonably content because they were permitted to keep one-fourth of their crops and to grow staples for personal consumption on private plots. Standards were set for personal appearance and for honesty. To achieve the latter, valuables were "planted," and those failing to turn them in were punished. Christophe's corps of enforcers was the Dahomets, an elite group of soldiers also trained in administration. They enforced the King's law, impartially and efficiently, toward worker and nobleman alike.

Ultimately, Christophe became an egocentric tyrant, discipline became repressive, and in spite of border patrols the lure of the easy life in Southern Haiti drew many northerners. Although uneducated himself, Christophe supported the arts, created a school system (though it served mostly the nobility), and built magnificent edifices. Among them were Sans Souci, his residential palace, and the Citadelle la Ferrière, a massive and impregnable fortress dominating the northern plains from a 3,000-foot peak. Never finished despite an enormous number of workmen (20,000 of them are supposed to have died in its construction), the citadel nevertheless symbolized the defiance by a newly independent black republic still fearful of French reconquest.

Christophe's death was indicative of the man. After suffering a massive stroke while attending Mass, he was carried to Sans Souci. His army revolted, his friends and retainers deserted him, and on Oct. 8, 1820, he committed suicide, according to legend shooting himself with a silver bullet.

## Further Reading

The definitive work on Christophe is John W. Vandercook, *Black Majesty: The Life of Christophe, King of Haiti* (1928). An excellent source of information on Haiti is James G. Leyburn, *The Haitian People* (1941; rev. ed. 1966). Other useful works include C. L. R. James, *The Black Jacobins* (1938; 2d ed. 1963); Selden Rodman, *Haiti: The Black Republic* (1954; rev. ed. 1961); and Charles Moran, *Black Triumvirate* (1957). □

# Warren Minor Christopher

**Lawyer and government official Warren Minor Christopher (born 1925) became U.S. secretary of state in 1993 by appointment of President Bill Clinton.**

Warren Minor Christopher was born on October 27, 1925, in Scranton, North Dakota. His parents were Ernest W. and Catherine Anne (Lemen) Christopher. His father, a banker, died when Christopher was young. His mother moved the family to California.

Christopher attended Hollywood High School. In 1942 he entered the University of Redlands, but transferred to the University of Southern California to complete his studies. He graduated in 1945 with a B.S. degree with honors and finished serving his three years, from 1943 to 1946, in the U.S. Naval Reserve.

Christopher's plan to become a lawyer began by enrolling in Stanford University's law school in 1946. He earned his LL.B. degree in 1949. After graduation he was selected for a very prestigious position: law clerk to Justice William O. Douglas of the U.S. Supreme Court.

After one year in Washington, D.C., Christopher returned to his hometown and joined a law firm. From 1950 on he split his career between practicing law and public service. He was a special counsel to California Governor Edmund Brown and vice-chairman of a commission the governor established in 1965 to investigate the causes of the urban riots in Watts, Los Angeles. Christopher also served as a consultant to the U.S. State Department and helped negotiate several international trade agreements.

President Lyndon Johnson appointed Christopher as deputy attorney general in June 1967. Johnson selected him to assist federal efforts to combat the urban riots in Detroit during July 1967 and in Chicago during April 1968. He served in that office until Johnson's term expired in January 1969. Christopher returned to his law firm in California.

President Jimmy Carter called Christopher back to work in the nation's capital in 1977. Christopher was appointed as deputy secretary of state. A highlight of his term in office occurred after militants in Iran seized the United States embassy and held its occupants as hostages from November 1979 to January 1981. Carter put Christopher in charge of negotiating the release of the 52 captured Americans. For his skillful and successful negotiations, he was awarded the Medal of Freedom, the nation's highest civilian award. When Carter left office in 1981, Christopher returned to California and resumed his law practice. He

headed a commission to investigate charges of brutality and racism in the Los Angeles Police Department in 1991.

In 1992 Christopher was again called back into national public service. His record of having worked in every Democratic presidential administration since he was an adult continued with the election of President Bill Clinton. When Clinton won enough votes in the 1992 campaign to be assured of the Democratic Party's nomination, he asked Christopher to head the team to select a vice presidential running mate (Albert Gore). After the November 1992 election, Clinton asked Christopher to help select members to the new cabinet and to head the transition staff for the newly elected president. Clinton appointed Christopher as secretary of state in his first round of cabinet choices.

In 1993, Christopher was sworn in as the 63rd U.S. secretary of state. A series of international problems gave the new secretary of state little time to relax. After establishing some degree of order in Somalia, American troops were withdrawn by the end of March 1994. Meanwhile, in April the civil war among the states of the former Yugoslavia entered its second year and peace negotiations in the Middle East continued to be a sensitive issue. After Clinton was re-elected in 1996 to a second presidential term, Christopher resigned. During his four years with the cabinet, he played an important role in several foreign policy successes, including a historic peace accord between Israel and the Palestinian Liberation Organization (PLO).

Christopher married Marie Josephine Wyllis on December 21, 1956. An earlier marriage had ended in divorce. He had four children: Lynn, Scott, Thomas, and Kristen.

### Further Reading

Warren Christopher co-edited a book on the negotiations to free the Americans held in the embassy takeover, *American Hostages in Iran: The Conduct of a Crisis* (1985). Christopher is listed in *Who's Who in America*.

### Additional Sources

*New Republic*, February 1, 1993.
*Time*, June 7, 1993, pp. 32-33; June 26, 1995, pp. 31-33.
*U.S. News & World Report*, July 5, 1993, p. 24. □

# Petrus Christus

**The Flemish painter Petrus Christus (ca. 1410-c. 1472) synthesized inherited styles in a creative manner. His work is distinguished by extreme clarity, precision of form, and advanced rendering of linear and aerial perspective.**

P etrus Christus was born in the Flemish town of Baerle. His early training probably took place in the workshop of Jan van Eyck in Bruges, and Christus is his only known follower. He is first mentioned in 1444, when he became a free master in Bruges and was granted citizenship in the town. With the possible exception of a visit to Milan in 1457, he remained active in Bruges until his death in 1472 or 1473.

The earliest work by Christus dates from about 1441, when he appears to have completed the *Rothschild Madonna,* a painting begun by Jan van Eyck. The diminutive *St. Jerome* is also thought to be a collaboration between master and pupil.

About 1445 Christus was also exposed to the influence of the great painter from Brussels, Rogier van der Weyden. The *Nativity* in Washington from this period shows an awareness of Rogier's fluid compositions and the sharpened emotional content of his works, while retaining Van Eyck's strong sense of form. At the same time the advanced landscape background transcends the work of either master in clarity and organization. Further pictorial innovations can be seen in the *St. Eligius,* which Christus signed and dated in 1449. Despite its muted religious overtones, this panel is rightly considered the first genre painting in northern art. In the *Lamentation* in Brussels, Christus set for himself the additional problem of integrating a figural composition derived from Rogier with his own subtle interests in lighting and the ordering of space.

The portraits by Christus reveal a major development of the schemes inherited from both Van Eyck and Rogier. In *A Donor and His Wife* (ca. 1460) Christus localizes the figures in an amplified architectural setting and reduces the sitters to simple, blocklike volumes. This ability to attain "progress through renunciation" is also present in the beguiling *Portrait of a Young Woman* (ca. 1470), which reveals an unprecedented directness in the approach to the sitter in combination with a subtlety of modeling and lighting that found no rival in northern painting until the time of Jan Vermeer.

### Further Reading

The best treatment of Christus is in Max J. Friedländer, *Early Netherlandish Painting,* vol. 1 (1924; trans. 1967). This magistral study contains a sensitive stylistic analysis of his works as well as an up-to-date *catalogue raisonné* of the major paintings. Also important is Erwin Panofsky, *Early Netherlandish Painting: Its Origins and Character* (2 vols., 1953). □

# Edwin P. Christy

**The American minstrel Edwin P. Christy (1815-1862) was not the originator of the minstrel show, but the Christy Minstrels set the pattern which almost all other companies followed.**

L ittle is known about Edwin P. Christy's early life. He was born in Philadelphia in 1815 and worked for a time as an office boy in New York. He was subsequently a hotel clerk and a traveling salesman. It is known that about 1840 "Ned" Christy gave performances on the banjo and tambourine in the hotels and barrooms in Buffalo and a short time later blackened his face, dressed himself in

old "plantation" clothes, and performed as a minstrel in Harry Meech's Museum in Buffalo. He was expert on the banjo, the instrument which was to provide the minstrel show its special musical character.

Christy's original company was formed in 1842. At first they called themselves the Virginia Minstrels, probably in imitation of an earlier group led by another famous minstrel, Dan Emmett, composer of *Dixie.* But when the original group of four was expanded to seven, the name was changed to the Christy Minstrels. It was the "Christy's" that became world famous.

### History of the Minstrel Show

Christy never claimed to have created this theatrical form, as indeed no one could, for it was a kind of entertainment that gradually grew out of folk roots over the years. Christy merely credited his group with being "the first to harmonize and originate the present style of Negro minstrelsy."

The minstrel show's true source was the songs and dances of African American slaves in the antebellum South. From the touching melodies of joy and lament of these subject people grew an elaborate theatrical imitation which in time developed stereotypes far removed from their human origins. (The stage African American, characterized as a lazy, careless, fun-loving, rhythmic fellow, dressed in gaudy clothes, persisted as stereotype well into the 20th century.) Though the minstrel's portrait doubtless contributed to the white man's condescension toward African

Americans, the minstrel show itself was not malicious in intent, for its endeavor was always to provide simplehearted entertainment, and the performers early learned that their material was more appealing in blackface than in white. The show's presentation of human foibles and sentiments was directed toward its white audience, not its African American progenitors.

The most famous of those actors who early darkened their faces for the stage to render plantation songs was T. D. "Daddy" Rice, to whom most properly belongs the title "Father of American Minstrelsy." It was his presentation of the song and dance *Jim Crow* (at first merely between acts of a play) that initiated the vogue of the minstrels. In 1832 at the Bowery Theater in New York, he gave 20 encores and probably brought more into the box office than any other performer of his time.

Christy's contribution came in formalizing the structure of the minstrel show. He settled upon the semicircular seating arrangement of the large company with the interlocutor at the center and with two end men, one with a set of bones (or castanets) and the other with a tambourine. The role of the interlocutor—the only performer not blackfaced and the role which Christy usually assumed—was to introduce the various acts, to harmonize and pace the activity, and to be the pompous butt of the jokes of the witty "Tambo" and "Bones" at the ends.

Christy's minstrel show was set up in three parts. It began with the elaborate entrance of the entire group in brilliant costume, a regalia of brightly colored dress suits, striped trousers, high hats. With the interlocutor's famous command, "Gentlemen, be seated!" the second portion, known as the "First Part," began. It consisted of a variety of individual and choral songs, dances, and the chatter between the end men and the interlocutor. The "Olio," or last part, was an assortment of individual specialty acts, much as was found later in vaudeville, concluded by the entire company participating in the "breakdown," or "hoedown."

Christy also made elaborate use of the minstrel's parade, a bright musical march down the main street of American towns to announce the arrival of the company—a scene which was to become part of the nostalgic myth of 19th-century America.

## Success of the Christy Minstrels

After their original performances in Buffalo in 1842, Christy's troop, growing in size and popularity, toured the West and South, arriving in New York in 1846 to give a brief series of concerts. But they were so successful that in 1847 they moved into Mechanics Hall, where they played for almost 10 years, giving over 2500 performances. The popularity of the "burnt-cork players" spawned many other companies, but until his retirement Christy was the king of his profession.

Christy's group toured England with such success that thereafter all such organizations came to be called "Christy's." There were the Royal Christy Minstrels, the Queen's Christy Minstrels, and even a group which performed in the costumes of the English court.

Christy himself introduced the melodies of Stephen Foster to the public long before their rich simplicity was to make them American favorites.

By 1854 Christy had decided to retire. His company, however, continued to prosper under the leadership of George Christy (whose real name was Harrington), who had been a member of the original troop in Buffalo. Though Edwin retired a wealthy man, he fell increasingly into moods of melancholy in which he imagined himself penniless. In 1862, during one of these periods of temporary insanity, this man, who had brought laughter and music to so many, jumped from a window in his New York home and killed himself.

## Further Reading

No full-length biography of Christy exists, though sketches of his career are given in various histories of the American stage that deal with minstrel shows. The most scholarly treatment of minstrelsy is in Carl F. Wittke, *Tambo and Bones: A History of the American Minstrel Stage* (1930), which provides a valuable record of the major minstrels and their companies. Dailey Paskman and Sigmund Spaeth, *Gentlemen, Be Seated!* (1928), gives details about individual companies and provides examples of songs and jokes of the minstrels, along with numerous drawings and photographs. Isaac Goldberg, *Tin Pan Alley* (1930), relates minstrel music to the popular music of a later period. □

# Chrysippus

**The Greek philosopher Chrysippus (ca. 280-ca. 206 B.C.) was the first systematizer of Stoic doctrine and should probably be credited with much of that Stoic logic and language theory which has impressed a number of 20th-century philosophers.**

Chrysippus was born in Soli in Cilicia. As a young man, he made his way to Athens, where Cleanthes was head of the Stoic school. For a while Chrysippus seems to have been drawn to the teachings of Arcesilaus, head of the Platonic Academy and initiator of the skeptical phase in the history of Platonism, but eventually threw in his lot with Stoicism.

Any influence exercised by Cleanthes, however, must have been at a doctrinal level only; their personal relations do not appear to have been of the happiest. Chrysippus clearly had more respect for Cleanthes' beliefs than for his ability to defend them; on one occasion he asked Cleanthes to supply him with the doctrines, and he himself would supply the proofs. According to his ancient biographer, he eventually broke with Cleanthes and set up as a Stoic teacher in his own right. In 232 B.C. he succeeded Cleanthes as head of the Stoa and retained the chair till his death.

Chrysippus's numerous writings—he wrote 705 pieces, all of which are lost—mark a move away from the "poetic" stoicism of Cleanthes to a more rigid and logical systematization of the doctrine. There was a saying in antiquity that "but for Chrysippus there would have been no Stoa." A cardinal point of his system, indeed the one which underpinned the whole structure, was his conviction that absolute certitude is attainable by man. In this he was attacking the fundamental tenet of the Skeptical Academy, which laid stress on the Socratic method and the epistemological open-endedness of so many of Plato's dialogues. The continuing influence of the same skepticism on Chrysippus, however, can be seen in his willingness to examine counter-arguments; in this respect he seems to have worried fellow Stoics, who felt that he often stated the anti-Stoic case more forcibly than his own.

While in general Chrysippus systematized doctrines propounded less systematically by his predecessors Zeno and Cleanthes, he seems to have made contributions of his own in the matter of basic epistemology; in his assertion that feelings are in fact judgments of the mind; in his conviction that the mind is purely rational, rather than a composite of rationality and irrationality; and, perhaps, in his anthropocentric view of the plant and animal kingdom.

## Further Reading

For the fragmentary remains of Chrysippus's doctrines the most convenient source is the third volume of C. J. de Vogel, ed., *Greek Philosophy* (3 vols., 1950-1959; 3d ed. 1963). For discussion of particular doctrines see Josiah B. Gould, *The Philosophy of Chrysippus* (1970). □

# Walter Percy Chrysler

**The American manufacturer Walter Percy Chrysler (1875-1940) was a self-trained engineer who formed one of the three major automobile companies in the United States.**

The son of a Union Pacific Railroad engineer, Walter Chrysler was fascinated by machinery at an early age. He turned down a chance to go to college to become an apprentice in the Union Pacific shops at Ellis, Kans. Hard-working, intelligent, and determined to master every aspect of his craft, Chrysler then worked as a machinist in a series of railroad shops throughout the Midwest. Moving into positions of greater responsibility, he emerged in 1910 as superintendent of motive power for the Chicago Great Western Railroad. As an official in the mechanical branch of railroading, Chrysler knew he had little chance of moving into the top echelons of the corporate structure, and so in 1910 he took a position as works manager of the American Locomotive Company in Pittsburgh, beginning at a salary of $8,000 per year.

At this time General Motors Corporation, formed by William C. Durant in 1908, was in financial difficulties. In order to avoid bankruptcy for the $60-million group of plants manufacturing both automobiles and components, a syndicate of bankers holding GM securities forced Durant

out in 1910 and made Charles W. Nash, a self-trained engineer, president. Aware of Chrysler's efficient management of American Locomotive, Nash in 1912 persuaded Chrysler to become works manager of Buick at a cut in salary from $12,000 to $6,000.

## Increased Production at Buick

Production methods at Buick were inefficient and expensive because cars were still being made by slow, hand-work methods traditional in the manufacture of expensive carriages. Chrysler immediately reorganized the Buick shops into efficient units centered on construction by machinery and introduced the production-line method of automobile building inaugurated by Henry Ford. The results were impressive. The output of cars rose from 45 to 200 per day. At the same time Buick was chiefly responsible for a rise in GM's profits from $7 million to $28 million between 1913 and 1916.

Through skillful financial manipulations, Durant returned to the presidency of GM in 1916 and appointed Chrysler president of Buick at a salary of $500,000 per year, payable largely in stock. During the next 4 years production surged ahead, and Buick continued to provide most of the profits for GM. But Chrysler found Durant's interference in Buick's affairs increasingly irritating. He disapproved strongly of Durant's wholesale purchase of new plants for GM, some of them of marginal value to the combination, financially unstable, and difficult to integrate into GM's operations. Finally, in 1920 Chrysler resigned, intending to retire on his considerable savings. But in 1922, at the behest

of a banking syndicate, he took on the job of salvaging the Willys-Overland Company from bankruptcy at a salary of $1 million per year.

An important part of the recovery program was the designing of a high-performance car in the $1,500 range which would compete with luxury cars selling for $5,000 and up. Shortly after the start of the Willys-Overland undertaking, Chrysler accepted responsibility for a similar reorganization of the Maxwell Motor Company. Through the efforts of three capable engineers the new Chrysler car was completed at the Maxwell plant in 1924 and exhibited in New York.

## Birth of Chrysler Corporation

Public enthusiasm for his new car enabled Chrysler to raise the funds to get it into mass production, and in 1925 the Maxwell Company was rechartered as the Chrysler Corporation. Because of increasing demand for the car, Chrysler purchased the Dodge Brothers Manufacturing Company in 1928. Capitalized at approximately $432 million, Chrysler Corporation was the second-largest automobile producer in the nation.

During the Depression, Chrysler followed a policy of rigorous reduction of debt and improvements on the line of cars—Chrysler, DeSoto, and Plymouth. Thus by 1937, when demand surged back, the company was in a secure position.

A bluff, abrupt man, Chrysler nevertheless had a warm, outgoing personality which enabled him to make and keep friends even in times of disagreement. His success was due primarily to his ability to rationalize production, cut costs to the bone, and constantly improve his product. Moreover, he showed a remarkable ability to grow with his job. During his automotive years he became as adept at managing the financial and marketing ends of his business as in the actual production of automobiles. He retired in 1935 and died 5 years later.

## Further Reading

The most detailed information on Chrysler is in his autobiography, written with Boyden Sparkes, *Life of an American Workman* (1938). Chrysler describes his managerial methods in B. C. Forbes and O. D. Foster, *Automotive Giants of America: Men Who Are Making Our Motor Industry* (1926). Thomas C. Cochran gives an excellent account of Chrysler's business career in John A. Garraty, ed., *The Unforgettable Americans* (1960). Chrysler's years at Buick and the history of the Chrysler Corporation receive good coverage in two volumes by John B. Rae, *American Automobile Manufacturers: The First Forty Years* (1959) and *The American Automobile: A Brief History* (1965). □

# Paul Ching-Wu Chu

**A Chinese-American experimentalist in solid-state physics, Paul Ching-Wu Chu's (born 1941) leadership in superconductivity research in 1986-1987 led**

**to revolutionary advances world-wide in materials which carry electric current without resistance at high temperatures.**

Paul Ching-Wu Chu was born in China's Hunan Province on December 2, 1941. In 1949 he was taken to Taiwan where he grew up and received his formative education. Both his family and his country were supportive of his youthful interests in radios, electronics, and transistors. By the time he finished high school in Taichung, central Taiwan, he knew enough of the physical sciences to want to become an experimental physicist.

Chu attended Cheng-Kung University from 1958 to 1962, where he obtained his B.S. degree. After a year's service as an officer in the Nationalist Chinese Air Force, he migrated to the United States, where he earned his Master's degree in physics at Fordham University in the Bronx (1965). Then he moved to the University of California at San Diego in order to study solid-state physics in the laboratory of Bern T. Matthias (1918-1980), where he earned his Ph.D. in 1968. Matthias, an expert in superconductivity, exerted a strong influence on Chu, counseling him to think daringly within his discipline. Known to his American friends by his baptismal name, Paul, Chu published his first scientific papers in 1967 and 1968 on the relationships of high pressure and low-temperature superconductivity in various metallic compounds.

## What is Superconductivity

The Dutch physicist Kamerlingh Onnes first made liquid helium in 1908 and, by means of a series of experiments utilizing that discovery, discovered the phenomenon of superconductivity in 1911. Superconductivity is the ability of electric currents to float through certain materials completely untouched, without an ounce of energy loss. Until 1986, superconductivity had only been seen at extremely cold temperatures, a few dozen degrees above the absolute zero mark. As a technology, that rendered it practically useless because of the enormous expense required to cool something to those frigid depths. Supercold and superconducting go hand in hand because superconductivity is a state of matter that's frozen beyond solid. Take a familiar substance, like water. Hot water molecules careen around in steamy disarray; cooler water gets organized enough to flow, or stay put in a glass; really cold water can freeze rock solid. The atoms in superconductors line up in an even more ordered array—so well ordered, in fact, that they all behave like a single atom. When electricity flows through this super-crystalline arrangement, it doesn't collide with atoms in the metal, scattering its energy this way and that, as normal currents do. It doesn't waste its energy as heat. So the current loses none of its punch.

But just as ice won't freeze above 32 degrees Fahrenheit, materials won't superconduct above their transition temperature, which is different for each material. Like a freezing point, it is the temperature at which the transformation from solid to superconducting takes place.

Traditional (pre-1986) superconductors all had transition temperatures below about 40 degrees above absolute zero. The only way to get something that cold is to surround it with liquid helium, the coldest liquid that can be created on Earth. But liquid helium is so expensive that any efficiency savings from superconductivity are quickly eaten up in cooling costs.

The miracle of 1986 was twofold: First, the new materials were ceramics, and no one could figure out how a ceramic could carry electricity at all—much less without resistance. Second the materials became superconducting at temperatures "warm" enough to be cooled with liquid hydrogen, which physicists point out is cheaper than beer.

## What Can Superconductivity Do?

Since 1986, dozens of new high-temperature superconducting materials have been discovered. The one currently holding the record for the highest transition temperature was created by Chu, who hosted the anniversary workshop; it becomes superconducting at 164 degrees above absolute zero. Still, high temperature alone does not make a practical superconductor. The applications with the most potential to benefit from superconductor technology require strong electric currents and powerful magnets; nuclear magnetic imaging, for example, or power supply cables and motors.

But many of the new materials can't carry a strong current without destroying their own superconductivity—melting, in effect. Others fall apart in the presence of a strong magnetic field. Others can carry currents so high that they would evaporate a traditional copper wire. But unfortunately, Chu says, they are very unstable. "Instability and [high temperature superconducting] go hand in hand," Chu said.

Some applications of superconductors—like magnetically levitating trains—rely on still another property of these magic materials. A true superconductor strongly repels magnetic fields. A magnet brought near a superconductor floats on an invisible cloud of magnetic force like a boat on water. Trains riding on such clouds should be able to fly from city to city at 500 mph or more, but for now, only the Japanese are seriously pursuing such a project.

High-temperature superconducting is especially useful in applications that require exquisite sensitivity. Because superconducting atoms move in lockstep, it's very easy to pick up even the most minute variations in magnetic fields. Thus, IBM is already developing mine detectors for the Navy that can pick up magnetic fields smaller than those created by a moving paper clip.

Indeed, the most developed applications to date are supersensitive magnetic field detectors (call SQUIDS, for Superconducting Quantum Interference Devices) that are used in everything from geology to oil prospecting. Developers see huge markets in medicine, for example, in high-temperature devices for listening to the magnetic fluctuations of the heart and brain. Of course, none of these promises will become reality until a host of technological problems is overcome. Cooling systems have to get better, and cheaper, and high-temperature superconducting components have to get rugged enough to stand up to the hard knock of everyday use and mass production. Researchers who make these materials are still hoping that the theorists—whose job it is to explain how they work—will offer some guidance in the future. Without a workable theory, they've had to rely on guesswork and intuition. "I really have no idea what the mechanism is behind high-temperature superconducting," Chu said.

## A History of Chu's Work

In 1926 W. H. Keesom first produced solid helium by using high pressures at low temperatures. It was Matthias who carried on this tradition, looking for more and better superconductive materials and ever higher critical temperatures ($T_c$) at which these materials might show superconductivity. Matthias found more than a thousand such compounds and achieved a record $T_c$ of 18.3 K (Kelvin) in a nickel/tin alloy in 1953. Using his basic approach, a new record of 23.2 K was obtained by John Gavaler and Lou Testardi in metallic niobium/germanium films in 1973, seven years before his death. Chu's inspiration, like Keesom's, came largely from his mentor. But whereas Matthias had been constrained by having to work with the very expensive cryogenics of liquid helium, Chu, in his early research, was able to use the much cheaper but dangerous cryogenics of liquid hydrogen. The holy grail, a cryogenic of benign liquid nitrogen, which is cheaper than milk or beer, remained the animating motive for superconductivity research throughout the 1970s and 1980s.

After two years with the technical staff of Bell Laboratories in New Jersey, Paul Chu was appointed to his first academic post at Cleveland State University in Ohio. There, in 1973, he became a U.S. citizen and rose to the rank of full professor by 1975, creating an energetic research team in superconductivity, magnetism, and dielectrics. In 1978, with J. A. Woolam, he co-edited the book *High Pressure and Low Temperature Physics*. This work, plus more than 50 refereed scientific papers, led him to be wooed by and won to the Department of Physics at the University of Houston in 1979.

For the better part of the next decade Chu and his colleagues worked steadily toward realizing his dream of fabricating a superconducting material that could perform above the unbelievably high temperature of 77 K. Methods of all sorts were tested and their results appraised, but the 1973 record remained unbroken for 13 years. A 50 K leap to a "practical" high temperature above 77 K, the boiling point of liquid nitrogen, seemed insurmountable to many scientists. But then, in 1986-1987, everything changed and high temperature superconductivity (HTS) was born.

Johannes Georg Bednorz and Karl Alex Müller at the Zürich research center of the IBM Corporation published a report in the September 1986 issue of *Zeitschrift für Physik* that they had observed "possible high $T_c$" superconductivity at 35 K in a $La_2Ba_1Cu_4O$ (or lanthanum 214) mixture. A worldwide race to understand the chemistry and physics of this phenomenon started. Research teams around the world such as Bell Labs in New Jersey and laboratories in Tokyo, Zürich, Berkeley, Houston (of course), and many other cities were trying to understand the occurrence of superconductivity in the La214 compound. Chu's group chemically purified the compound, isolated the superconducting phase, and then exerted great physical pressure on it, thereby successfully raising the $T_c$ into the mid-50s K by the end of 1986.

By January 12, 1987, they had unambiguously established superconductivity above 77 K for the first time. Since physical pressure had such a phenomenal effect on $T_c$, they decided to recreate the same effect by substituting smaller atoms for the lanthanum and barium in the compound. It seemed reasonable to substitute calcium for barium, but that didn't work. Another attempt at substitution, this time using strontium, was successful. Lanthanum was easily replaced by yttrium. Thus, by the end of January 1987, together with M. K. Wu (his former student, then at the University of Alabama at Huntsville), Chu's group was convinced that they had stabilized and observed unambiguously superconductivity above 90 K in their $Y_1Ba_2Cu_3O$ (or Yttrium 123) compound. Within a few weeks, replacement of yttrium with nearly all the rare earth elements demonstrated that a whole new class of superconductors had been discovered.

For the first time, superconductivity research could proceed using cheap liquid nitrogen. The copper-oxygen layers in these ceramics seems to be where the superconductivity is occurring. Unusual electrical and magnetic behavior, suggesting the existence of superconductivity at much higher temperatures, has subsequently been reported.

However, these anomalies fail to meet the four criteria to prove unambiguously that they were superconducting. Those criteria are zero electrical resistivity, the Meissner effect, high stability, and reliable reproducibility. By the end of 1987, despite anomalies and a prevailing pessimism that any further discoveries would be made, Chu was confidently predicting HTS well above 100 K:

High $T_c$ is a real possibility, and known applications pose great promises and challenges as well to all of us. But I think the area of novel applications tailored to the unusual properties of this class of materials will hold even greater promise. Indeed, the year 1987 is a "super" year in physics. We have witnessed superconductivity, [a] supernova, [the] superstring (theory), and superconducting supercollider (authorization). Let us enjoy these super-events in physics.

Almost immediately, in the spring of 1988, superconductivity up to 125 K was observed in a thallium compound (TlCaSrCuO) by S. Sheng and A. Hermann.

Bednorz and Müller won the 1987 Nobel Prize for Physics, but Chu won respect and support as he continued to work toward "super high," and "super tech"—that is, room-temperature superconductivity and superconducting technology, respectively.

Room-temperature superconductivity was reported by the French research team of Jean-Pierre Bastide and Serge Contreras of the National Institute of Applied Science in Lyon in December of 1996. Room-temperature conductivity represents a jump of 200 degrees Fahrenheit, and researchers are conducting experiments to verify the French results.

## Further Reading

Paul C. W. CHU achieved great fame in 1987 and 1988 with numerous awards and much coverage in newspapers and magazines. In addition to his own popular articles on "Lasers" and "Superconductivity" in *Funk and Wagnall's New Encyclopedia* (1982) and on "Superconductivity" in *McGraw-Hill Yearbook of Science and Technology 1989*, one might consult his favorite paper, "The Discovery and Physics of Superconductivity above 100 K," in *AIP Conference Proceedings 169: Modern Physics in America, A Michelson-Morley Centennial Symposium*, W. Fickinger and K. Kowalski, editors (1988). The most popular article on the subject is "Superconductors! The Startling Breakthrough that Could Change Our World," in *TIME* (May 11, 1987). Other popular articles include James Gleick, "In the Trenches of Science," in *The New York Times Magazine* (August 16, 1987); and Al Reinert, "The Inventive Mr. Chu," in *Texas Monthly* (August 1988). An absorbing and fast-paced history of Chu's work leading to the discovery of high temperature superconductivity, intended for the non-scientist, can be found in *The Breakthrough, The Race for The Superconductor*, by R. M. Hazen (1988). Basic scientific background on superconductivity may be found in V. Daniel Hunt's *Superconductivity Source Book* (1989). For the history of low-temperature sciences and technologies, see K. Mendelssohn's *The Quest for Absolute Zero, the Meaning of Low Temperature Physics* (1966). □

# Chuang Tzu

**The Chinese philosopher Chuang Tzu (ca. 369-ca. 286 B.C.), also known as Chuang Chou, was the most brilliant of the early Taoists and the greatest prose writer of his time.**

Not much is known of the life of Chuang Tzu. The *Shih Chi* (Historical Records, written about 100 B.C.) tells us that he was a contemporary of King Hui of Liang (370-319) and King Hsüan of Ch'i (319-301). Thus Chuang Tzu seems to have been a contemporary of Mencius (372-289), but neither was mentioned by the other in his extant writings. The *Shih Chi* also says that Chuang Tzu was born in Meng on the border of Shantung and Honan and that he held a petty official post for a time in Ch'iyüan. However, he seems to have lived most of his life as a recluse, "to be intoxicated in the wonder and the power of Nature."

Legend has it that Chuang Tzu declined the honor of being prime minister to King Wei of Ch'u (339-329), saying that he much preferred to be a live tortoise wagging its tail in the mud than a dead one venerated in a golden casket in a king's ancestral shrine. (The story is apocryphal, but it is highly illustrative of the mentality of the Taoist mystic, who cared more for personal freedom than for high office.)

Chuang Tzu's greatness lay in his bringing early Taoism to its full completion. While he was true to the Taoist doctrine of *wu-wei* (refraining from action contrary to Nature), he extended the Taoist system and carried out metaphysical speculations never heard of by the early Taoists. The philosophy of Chuang Tzu, as characterized by its emphasis on the unity and spontaneity of the Tao, its assertion of personal freedom, and its doctrine of relativity of things, is essentially a plea for the "return to Nature" and free development of man's inherent nature. It is in fact a kind of romantic philosophy that favors anarchistic individualism and condemns Confucian virtues and institutions—a philosophy, in short, that idealizes the state of natural simplicity marked by no will, no consciousness, no knowledge.

All these ideas are well illustrated in the book bearing Chuang Tzu's name. The *Chuang Tzu* as it stands today contains 33 chapters, in 3 sections: 7 "inner chapters," 15 "outer chapters," and 11 "miscellaneous chapters." It was probably compiled by Kuo Hsiang (died A.D. 312), the great commentator of the *Chuang Tzu*. As in the case of the *Lao Tzu* (also known as the *Tao Te Ching*), there has been much controversy over the authorship of the *Chuang Tzu*. The first section is generally regarded as the work of the man called Chuang Tzu. Some of the best chapters of the *Chuang Tzu* representing the naturalistic aspects of Taoism are not included in the first section, and no definite answer has so far been given as to who else would have written them. In view of the frequent repetitions, many interpolations, and differences of styles in the various parts of the work, most scholars agree that the *Chuang Tzu* is a compilation of Taoist writings from various hands. However this may be, the *Chuang Tzu*, which consists of beautiful allegories and lively anecdotes, has rarely been surpassed for beauty of style and felicity of expression.

## Further Reading

English versions of the *Chuang Tzu* were edited by Herbert A. Giles (1889; repr. 1961) and Fung Yu-lan (1963). Extracts may be found in Arthur Waley, *Three Ways of Thought in Ancient China* (1939; repr. 1956), and in the Modern Library's *Wisdom of China and India* and *Wisdom of Laotse*. For discussions of Chuang Tzu see Fung Yu-lan, *History of Chinese Philosophy*, vol. 1 (1952), and Herrlee G. Creel, *Chinese Thought from Confucius to Mao Tse-tung* (1953). □

# Chu Hsi

**Chu Hsi (1130-1200) was one of the greatest Chinese scholars and philosophers. The system of Neo-Confucianism of which Chu Hsi is regarded as the spokesman represents a summary of doctrines of his predecessors as well as original ideas of his own.**

Sung-dynasty (960-1279) China, in which Chu Hsi lived, combined a high point in cultural development with a singular weakness in political administration and military power. The popularization of printing stimulated the establishment of numerous libraries and academies and the compilation of several encyclopedic works. There was also a phenomenal economic growth, as evidenced by largescale overseas commerce and the introduction of paper money. Politically and militarily, however, the Sung period had a bad start and grew steadily worse during its 3-century tenure. Sung never achieved a unified rule over the Chinese Empire, and it had to coexist, successively, with the Liao (the Khitans), the Chin (the Jürched), and the Yüan (the Mongols), who were in control of an ever-expanding territory in North China.

In 1123 the Chin replaced the Liao, and in 1127 they ransacked the Sung capital at Kaifeng, carrying away Emperor Ch'in Tsung; his father and predecessor, the artist-emperor Hui Tsung; and about 3,000 courtiers. The remnants of the Sung court rallied around Emperor Kao Tsung and established the national capital in Hangchow—hence the designation Southern Sung (1127-1279). National policy polarized the court officials into two camps: those who upheld national pride and advocated military recovery of the North, and those who counseled prudence and espoused a peace settlement with the Chin. Eventually Ch'in Kuei, leader of the "peace" group, won out, and a peace treaty was concluded with the Chin in 1142.

While serving as a court official, Chu Sung, father of Chu Hsi, had voiced his opposition to the peace policies of Ch'in Kuei. Chu Sung was promptly relieved of his post at the capital and, as a punishment, appointed magistrate of Yu-hsi Prefecture in mountainous central Fukien. There Chu Hsi was born in October 1130, although the family came from Anhui in the Yangtze River valley. Chu Sung retired from his government post in 1134 and devoted himself to the instruction of his precocious heir. When his father died, the 13-year-old boy continued his studies with three noted scholars whom his father had recommended. At the early age of 17 Chu Hsi passed the rigorous final civil service examination and was awarded the highest degree, a remarkable feat of scholarly achievement.

## Early Career

Three years later Chu Hsi was appointed to his first official post, as recorder in the T'ung An Prefecture. During his tenure, from 1151 to 1157, he introduced reforms in taxation and police, expanded the community library, raised the standard of the schools, and promulgated a code of proper and decorous conduct. This initial appointment turned out to be also the longest continuous period of public life on the part of Chu Hsi, as he spent only a total of about 3 more years in public service much later in life and amid intermittent dismissals and recalls. He was offered imperial appointments more than 20 times, but divergence in public policy, as well as recurrent attacks of beriberi, compelled Chu Hsi to decline most of them in favor of a succession of sinecures, such as the superintendency of one temple or another.

Chu Hsi spent the long stretches of semi-self-imposed leisure in vigorous pursuit of scholarship and development of his system of philosophy. First, he sought out Li T'ung, one of the ablest followers of the 11th-century Neo-Confucians. Under Li T'ung's influence Chu Hsi renounced his affiliation with Buddhism and Taoism and turned his allegiance completely to Confucianism. Chu Hsi was a diligent scholar and prolific writer. During the period of 15 years from 1163 to 1178 he completed a formidable list of 18 scholarly works.

## As Government Official

Chu Hsi did not accept another appointment to office until 1179. By this time his literary accomplishments had firmly established him as a leading scholar and interpreter of the Northern Sung philosophers. The court desired Chu Hsi's participation for its prestige value but had no use for his criticisms and moralistic preachments. Chu Hsi, on the other hand, had to go through the struggle between the Confucian teaching that a good man should undertake leadership in government and the possible compromise of his principles by serving superiors of whose policies, and even of whose character, he disapproved. Eventually, Chu Hsi was appointed to serve, not in the central government at the national capital, but as prefect of Nan-k'ang, in modern Kiangsi Province. After much hesitation, Chu Hsi accepted the appointment and assumed his duties.

In Nan-k'ang, Chu Hsi reduced taxes and restored the White Grotto Academy, which flourished under his direction and attracted many students. Among the scholars invited to lecture at the academy was Lu Chiu-yuan, with whom Chu Hsi had held a vehement philosophical debate a few years earlier. When famine struck, Chu Hsi instituted several important relief measures, including repairs of the dikes along the Yangtze River, while working energetically for the welfare of the people. He thus gained a considerable reputation as a capable and compassionate administrator.

After a 2-year term at Nan-k'ang, Chu Hsi was appointed as tea and salt commissioner of Chekiang Province, an area suffering from famine. He indicted a number of remiss and corrupt officials. One of the officials indicted happened to be related by marriage to a powerful minister at court, and mounting obstructions to his office and attacks on Chu Hsi himself began to occur. The weak Emperor vacillated between Chu Hsi and his enemies, and several imperial appointments to Chu Hsi were not implemented. When Emperor Kuang Tsung ascended the throne in 1189, Chu Hsi was conferred high honors and persuaded to accept the post of prefect of Chang-chou (modern Amoy) which he held for less than a year. He next served, in 1194, as prefect of T'an-chou (modern Changsha), where he restored the famous Yü-li Academy. But within a month he resigned in protest of a gross misconduct at court. Chu Hsi was highly recommended to the attention of the new emperor Ning Tsung, who had replaced Kuang Tsung, and summoned to the capital to serve as court academician and lecturer. Within a matter of weeks, however, he was "granted leave" and permanently relieved of government posts.

## As His Majesty's Loyal Opposition

Chu Hsi's avoidance of public office was by no means an indication of a lack of interest in public affairs. As a matter of fact, he expressed himself only too freely and forcefully in a number of memorials presented to and at audiences with the succession of emperors during his lifetime. Chu Hsi assumed the role of guardian of Confucian principles and His Majesty's mentor and loyal opposition. The sealed memorial which he presented to Emperor Hsiao Tsung in 1188 in response to a summons to the court was especially lengthy and noteworthy. It began with an explanation of Chu Hsi's reasons for declining repeated appointments; namely, it would be inconsistent both for him and for the government if he occupied a government post while his advice and policies were rejected. Then it proceeded to the key point of the memorial—a basic teaching of Confucius— that good government could be achieved only through the "rectification" of the person of the Emperor. Chu Hsi stressed this theme repeatedly, because he held the conviction that the rectification of the Emperor would set off a chain reaction of moral regeneration leading from the Emperor to his family, the court officials, the civil servants, and ultimately the whole population. The welfare of the state therefore depended on the moral state of the mind of the Emperor. Conversely, the moral turpitude in the palace and corruption in the bureaucracy, which were prevalent, were symptoms of the Emperor's failure to achieve rectitude. To correct this serious defect, the Emperor must surround himself with wise and righteous ministers. Emperor Hsiao Tsung got up from bed to read the memorial by candlelight but decided that he could not make use of Chu Hsi's advice. Instead, the Emperor abdicated a few months later in favor of his son.

Chu Hsi's frank and forceful criticisms were not confined to the Emperor. During the few months he served as court lecturer in 1194, he warned the young emperor Ning Tsung of the scheming ambitions of Han T'o-chou, a high minister. This action triggered a broad purge from government of Chu Hsi and his friends and followers and also brought on vehement denunciations and fantastic rumors against him and his doctrines. In 1196 the Emperor proscribed Tao-hsueh (a term referring mainly to the Neo-Confucian system), and in 1198 a list was drawn up of 59 men guilty of belonging to the "rebel clique of false learning," which significantly included four of Han T'o-chou's major political enemies.

Chu Hsi devoted the last 5 years of his life exclusively to study and teaching; he died in 1200. In spite of himself he had become the center of a politicointellectual struggle, and the attendance at his funeral by thousands of friends, pupils, and admirers was considered by his enemies as a gathering to mourn the "teacher of rebellious falsehoods." After the public execution of Han T'o-chou in 1206 and the disgrace of his followers, opinion became more favorable to Chu Hsi. In 1208 Chu Hsi was accorded the posthumous title of master of literature, and in 1241 his tablet was admitted to the Confucian Temple.

### Exemplification of the Sage Ideal

Chu Hsi objected to Buddhism on the grounds of its teachings and its practice of monasticism and tried to conduct his life according to Confucian teachings, to stand as a living example of Confucian sagehood. Chu Hsi's daily life is vividly described in a eulogistic account written by Huang Kan, his disciple and son-in-law: "As regards his conduct and character, his appearance was dignified and his language to the point. He moved with an easy gait and he sat in an erect posture. Ordinarily he rose before dawn, wearing his long robe, a hat, and square shoes, and began the day by paying respects to his departed ancestors and the early sages at the ancestral temple. Then he repaired to his study, where the desks and tables, books and stationery were all arranged in good order. For his meals, the soups and dishes and spoons and chopsticks were placed each in its appointed place. When it was time to retire, he would first rest a while by closing his eyes while sitting erect. Then he would rise and walk to his bed in measured steps. By midnight he was asleep, and if he awoke in the night he would sit up in bed until dawn. This ordered life pattern remained constant for him from youth to old age, from one season to another, and under all circumstances.

"Within the family, he practiced utmost filial piety toward his parents and compassion toward his inferiors. There was a sweet harmony resulting from mutual kindness and propriety among the members of the clan. . . . Toward the relatives and townspeople, proper expressions were given on all occasions of joy or sorrow and assistance offered to all in need. At the same time, his own wants were few: enough clothes to cover his body, enough food to satisfy his hunger, lodging to keep out wind and rain. Living conditions which other people might have found unbearable, he accepted in contentment."

It is evident that in his private life the philosopher strove to live according to what he conceived of as the rigorous standards of a Confucian sage. Chu Hsi has been respected and admired as a superior man after the Confucian model not only by posterity but also by his contemporaries, even including Lu Chiu-yuan (1139-1192) and Ch'en Liang (1143-1194), who vigorously disagreed with his philosophic views. It is with good reason that the Chinese refer to Chu Hsi as Chu Fu-tzu, the "Great Master" Chu.

### System of Neo-Confucianism

With the passage of time the political controversies and factional struggles involving Chu Hsi have receded in importance, and he has come to be remembered—and revered—as a great scholar and philosopher. Chu Hsi's complete works, in 62 volumes, cover all fields of Chinese learning. In the field of classics Chu Hsi's commentaries were accorded the recognition of orthodoxy in the government examinations from 1313 until 1905, when the examinations were abolished. These commentaries often served as occasions for the author to express his own ideas and tenets, expositions of which are also preserved in the voluminous letters he wrote and in the lecture notes and dialogues kept by his disciples.

Chu Hsi's system of philosophy, known as Li-hsueh, or Li learning, represents a synthesis of the ideas of a number of his predecessors with the imprint of his own genius. The term *li,* which means principle, came into prominence first in the ancient classic *I Ching* and became central in the thought of Ch'eng I, whom Chu Hsi acknowledged as his master. Identifying *li* with the Supreme Ultimate in the system of the philosopher Chou Tun-i, Chu Hsi regarded it as the underlying order or rationale of all existence. He said: "There is nothing in the universe but motion and quiescence alternating with each other without cease: this is called *i,* change. There must be a *li,* principle, governing this motion and quiescence: this is called the T'ai-chi, the Supreme Ultimate."

*Li,* according to Chu Hsi, is "without birth and indestructible" and it is "the intrinsic nature of all things." In its actualization in existent things, *li* is combined with *ch'i,* the material force, a concept advanced by Chang Tsai. With regard to the relation between *li* and *ch'i,* Chu Hsi said: "Before creation, there is *li.* When there is *li* there is the world. If there were no *li* there would be no world." But also, "When there is no condensation of *ch'i, li* will have no place to inhere." Hence the principle element and the material element are mutually dependent in the phenomenal world, but in the realm "above shape," *li* is prior and can subsist without *ch'i.*

The material force, *ch'i,* provides also a basis for individuation. In each thing there is its *li,* and the totality of the individuated *li* might be called the total *Li,* or the Supreme Ultimate. The relation between the individual *li* and the total *Li* is not one of whole and part but is like that of the moon and its reflections. It is interesting to note that Leibniz had a fair knowledge of Chu Hsi's system of *Li,* and the close similarity between this system and Leibniz's system of monadology is perhaps no mere coincidence.

Man's nature, according to Chu Hsi, is his *li,* and therefore Chu Hsi could repeat after Confucius that "by nature all men are alike" and after Mencius that "the nature of man is good." Evil in man is accounted for by the *ch'i* element, which is clear in some people and turbid in some others. Personal cultivation consists in cleansing the *ch'i* of the turbidity and recovering the purity of one's original nature, which is also said to be establishing the supremacy of the "laws of heaven" over the "desires of men." For this undertaking Chu Hsi recommended the procedures found in the *Great Learning,* namely, "the extension of knowledge through the investigation of things," which should also be accompanied by "the attentiveness of the mind."

## Further Reading

The only volume on Chu Hsi is J. Percy Bruce, *Chu Hsi and His Masters* (1923). Substantial chapters are also found in Fung Yu-lan, *A History of Chinese Philosophy,* vol. 2 (trans. 1953); Carson Chang, *The Development of Neo-Confucian Thought,* vol. 1 (1957); Conrad M. Schirokauer, "Chu Hsi's Political Career," in Arthur F. Wright and Denis Twitchett, eds., *Confucian Personalities* (1962); and Wing-tsit Chan, *A Source Book in Chinese Philosophy* (1963).

## Additional Sources

Chan, Wing-tsit, *Chu Hsi, life and thought,* Hong Kong: Chinese University Press; New York: St. Martin's Press, 1987. □

# Chulalongkorn

**Chulalongkorn (1853-1910) was king of Thailand from 1868 to 1910. When Thailand was seriously threatened by Western colonialism, his diplomatic policies averted colonial domination and his domestic reforms brought about the modernization of his kingdom.**

Born in the Grand Palace in Bangkok, Thailand (Siam), on Sept. 20, 1853, Chulalongkorn was the ninth child of King Mongkut but the first son to be born to a royal queen. He was thus regarded from an early age as the logical heir to the throne, especially by the consuls of European powers, and was educated accordingly. It was for him and his younger brothers that Anna Leonowens was engaged as governess at the court (1862-1867). She later recalled the slight and frail youth as studious, gentle, and awed by the responsibilities which lay before him. These came upon him much earlier than he expected when, after a trip with his father to the Malay Peninsula to view a solar eclipse, both he and his father fell ill of malaria and Mongkut died on Oct. 1, 1868.

## Regency Period

Supposing the 15-year-old Chulalongkorn also to be dying, the most powerful government official of the day, the "prime minister" Suriyawong (Chuang Bunnag), stage-managed the succession of Chulalongkorn to the throne. He also arranged his own appointment as regent and the appointment of Prince Wichaichan, Chulalongkorn's cousin, as heir apparent, confident that Wichaichan could be manipulated after Chulalongkorn's death. But Chulalongkorn's health improved, and he was tutored in public affairs, traveled to Java and India to observe modern administration, and was crowned king in his own right as Rama V on Nov. 16, 1873.

## Politics of Reform

With the support of his brothers and young friends, the King began, in 1873, to attack the injustices of the old order and the power of his political rivals by attempting to impose centralized budgeting and accounting, streamlining a judicial system beset by delays and corruption, and inaugurating consultative legislative councils dominated by his young friends. These actions, accompanied by a decline in Wichaichan's prospects, brought on the "Front Palace Crisis" of early 1875, when Wichaichan fled to the British consulate and demanded protection; had it been granted, Thailand would have become an Anglo-French protectorate in all but name. Britain and France, by refusing to support their consuls, treated the matter as an internal quarrel, and Chulalongkorn was able to bring about a resolution of the crisis. Peace, however, was bought at a high price, for the King's supporters were disbanded, the councils ceased to meet, and no further reforms were undertaken for a decade.

The decade which followed was in some ways the most critical of the reign. Chulalongkorn felt thwarted by the former regent and older conservatives who dominated public office; and they, for their part, were more than ever distrustful of him and the modern reforms with which he was identified. When the king managed, from 1879, to begin establishing modern schools for the education of civil servants, the sons of the old noble families were conspicuously absent. Several lesser noble families from whom the King expected support disgraced themselves in public scandals. Chulalongkorn found that he could rely only on his younger half brothers—of whom 26 survived into the 1880s—for educated and loyal leadership. He supervised their formal education and worked with them in his personal secretariat to assess their abilities before placing them in offices under his control. Together he and his brothers labored as clerks in the new audit office, discussed means of improving the royal bodyguard corps and ultimately the army, and carefully kept abreast of foreign affairs and all the details of domestic administration. As the ministers of the older generation began to die or retire, the King at last had his opportunity to initiate change.

Chulalongkorn was convinced of both the rightness and the necessity of reform. His father had imbued him with the Buddhist ideals of the "just king" (*dhammaraja*), and Mrs. Leonowens with parallel Western ideas of social justice and democracy, and to these ideals he was genuinely committed. At the same time, he was constantly reminded by Western representatives that his only hope of avoiding colonial control lay in undertaking far-reaching reforms to facilitate Western commercial penetration. The crisis of 1875 had made the King painfully aware of the limits of his powers and of the strength of his conservative rivals, so that he moved only gradually and slowly to reform as his position improved. The Western consuls, however, were impatient and only dimly aware of this tense political situation, which the Thai tried to conceal from them; and by the time Chulalongkorn moved, it was almost too late.

## Governmental Reform

As in 1873-1874, when the king began to take over the old ministries by appointing his brothers, the more radical among them wished to move faster than he did. A group including three of his brothers and five officials with foreign experience petitioned him on Jan. 8, 1885, for the creation of a constitutional monarchy and elective legislature. In a gentle and thoughtful reply he argued that parliamentary democracy was not yet possible in a country without education and in which the small educated elite was completely absorbed in administration. What was needed immediately, he stated, was a "reform government." He rapidly constructed one in the following 7 years by placing young men gradually in all the old ministries, by transferring departments from one ministry to another to group responsibilities functionally, and by personally supervising the training of the men who were to run the new system.

The six ministries of traditional Thai government had been omnicompetent, each with its own tax collections, law courts, provinces to administer, and rights to unsupervised expenditure; and they tended to be dominated by the minister of the North (*mahatthai*) and the minister of the South (*kalahom*), whom the King had been almost powerless to control. The new system, introduced on April 1, 1892, had 12 functionally defined ministries responsible to the King. Nine of the 12 ministers were half brothers of the King, and they met regularly as a cabinet to formulate state policy.

Central to the reform program was the work of the ministry of interior, directed from 1892 by Prince Damrong Rajanubhab. By grouping almost 100 provinces into just 14 "circles," Damrong was able to make effective use of a very small body of educated young men in rapidly strengthening Bangkok's control over hitherto semiautonomous provinces. As a result, state revenues doubled within 7 years, and the new administrative structure brought the rule of law, public works, and elementary public education to the most distant provinces by the turn of the century. Chulalongkorn's son Prince Rabi was appointed as minister of justice in 1896, and all Thai law was recodified along European lines by the end of the reign, and a centralized modern judicial system was introduced. Railway construction, financed until 1904 entirely out of current revenues, rapidly linked the country together as never before. The King took great care in choosing the men for these tasks and followed daily the progress of the work. He encouraged and supported the most able of them and gave them a free hand, while ever goading and criticizing the less decisive and mediocre.

## Foreign Relations

Until the 1880s Chulalongkorn generally could assume that he had the goodwill of the Western powers and counted on British support for Thai independence and upon the skillful diplomacy of Prince Devawongse, whose appointment as foreign minister in 1886 marked the resumption of reform. From the mid-1880s, however, French ambitions in Indochina began to clash with Thai rights of suzerainty over Laos. The Thai were powerless to halt the demands which escalated into the Franco-Thai War of 1893 and ended with French gunboats forcing their way up the Chaophraya River to Bangkok to demand the cession to France of the east bank of the Mekong River and the payment of a large indemnity. Britain, counted on to support the Thai, refused to intervene, and Laos was ceded to France.

Chulalongkorn was disheartened and went into an almost year-long period of illness and depression. Once recovered, he began to take initiatives and responsibility he had earlier been more willing to share with his brothers. The Anglo-French Declaration of 1896 guaranteed the integrity of central Siam but left the northeast threatened by France and the south by Britain. Chulalongkorn's European tour of 1897 was, among other things, an attempt to secure new European interest in Thailand's continued independence, especially on the part of Russia and Germany. Whether the tour achieved this object or not, it did give Chulalongkorn a new self-confidence and a realization that modernization did not necessarily mean Westernization: "We must try to imitate what is good elsewhere, and at the same time not only to keep but to develop what is good and worthy of respect in our own national character and institutions," he declared upon his return.

During the remainder of Chulalongkorn's reign rapid progress was made toward the resolution of Thailand's most serious problems in the field of foreign affairs. Small areas of Laos on the western bank of the Mekong and the western provinces of Cambodia were ceded to France in 1904 and 1907, and in return the Thai regained legal jurisdiction over French Asian subjects in Thailand. The cession to Britain of the four Malayan states of Kelantan, Trengganu, Kedah, and Perlis in 1909 brought Thailand similar legal concessions (although the abolition of extraterritoriality was still several decades away) and capital for the extension of the railways toward Singapore. Most of all, by the end of his reign the King could feel that his country's independence at last was secure.

## Personal Life

Chulalongkorn's personal life was filled with tragedies no less severe than the public crises he successfully surmounted. His beloved Queen Sunantha died in a boating accident in 1880; Crown Prince Vajirunhis died in 1894. Of his 77 children (by four queens and many concubines, as was customary), only two-thirds lived to maturity. Though he took great satisfaction in his accomplishments, he did not enjoy being king. Especially in the 1880s, he was fond of traveling incognito and would wander the slums and streets of Bangkok at night clad as a peasant. He once stopped a royal procession to join, unannounced, a peasant wedding; and his numerous travel diaries are filled with recorded conversations with peasant farmers who told him local folklore or complained about local conditions. He was a man of broad interests, and his zeal for change did not diminish his appreciation of his country's traditions.

Chulalongkorn was a prolific writer in many fields. Numerous volumes of his correspondence, as well as 25 volumes of his diary, have been published. His *Far from Home,* the collection of letters written to his daughter when he toured Europe in 1908, is still widely read. His historical study *The Royal Ceremonies of the Twelve Months* (written 1888) has never been superseded. His best historical works are his commentary on the memoirs of Princess Narinthewi and his lengthy "Speech Introducing Governmental Reform" in 1888. He wrote much verse and drama, his best-known drama probably being *Ngo Pa* (1905). After the longest reign in Thai history, he died on Oct. 23, 1910.

## Further Reading

There is no biography of Chulalongkorn. Prince Chula Chakrabongse, *Lords of Life* (1960), has a long hagiographic chapter on Chulalongkorn, and a good account by a contemporary of Chulalongkorn is in J. G. D. Campbell, *Siam in the Twentieth Century* (1902). The first scholarly treatment of Chulalongkorn's reign is David K. Wyatt, *The Politics of Reform in Thailand: Education in the Reign of King Chulalongkorn* (1969). Recommended for general historical background are D. G. E. Hall, *A History of South-East Asia* (1955; 3d ed. 1968), and David J. Steinberg, *In Search of Southeast Asia: A Modern History* (1971). □

# Chun Doo Hwan

**Chun Doo Hwan (born 1931), an army general turned politician, was elected to a seven-year term in 1981 as president of the Republic of Korea (South Korea).**

Chun Doo Hwan was born on January 18, 1931, in a remote mountainous farm village in Hapch'ongun, South Kyongsang Province. He was the second son of a family of ten children. He studied the Chinese classics at an early age but started his formal primary school rather late. In 1940, at the age of nine, his family migrated to Manchuria where he entered Horan primary school in Jilin Province. After a little more than a year, his family moved back to Korea and settled down in Taegu, the third largest city in Korea. Following a period of irregular education, Chun was finally admitted to Hido Primary School in Taegu as a fourth grader in April 1944. It is said that Chun earned part of his school expenses as a newspaper delivery boy to help his father who was engaged in the Chinese medicine business. In 1947 Chun was admitted to a six-year Taegu technical middle school, only to have this education interrupted by the onset of the Korean War in June 1950.

## Military Career

Chun passed the competitive entrance examination to the newly-inaugurated four-year course in the Korean Military Academy in December 1951. For the next four years from 1952 to 1955, which included the Korean War years, Chun spent his days as a cadet at the academy. As a cadet Chun was oriented more athletically than intellectually, serving at one time as captain of the academy's soccer team. He had ample opportunity to display his leadership role while a cadet. His close classmates, such as Roh Tae Woo and Kim Bok-dong, who would later play important roles in assisting the military coups led by Chun in 1979 and 1980, were more intellectually-oriented than was Chun. In 1955 Chun was commissioned as a second lieutenant, graduating with the first class to receive four years of training at the Korean Military Academy.

In December 1958 Captain Chun married Lee Soon Ja, the daughter of a retired general, Lee Kyudong, who once had served in the Korean Army Headquarters and was also a military academy classmate of former President Park Chung Hee. Lee's two uncles were also army officers. At the time of their wedding Chun was recruited as a founding member of the paratrooper special forces stationed at a base in Kimpo, outside of Seoul. In 1959 Chun went to the United States for a five-month training program on psychological warfare at the United States special combat school at Fort Black in North Carolina.

In April 1960 Chun became operations officer in the special forces and was on United States-Republic of Korea joint maneuvers in Okinawa when the April 19, 1960, student revolution took place in Korea. This resulted in the overthrow of President Syngman Rhee's government. On May 16, 1961, then-Major General Park Chung Hee and his followers led a military coup ousting the Posun Yun govern-

ment. Chun gave Park his allegiance and service and was credited, for instance, with having persuaded the cadets of the Korean Military Academy to march through the Seoul streets in support of Park. During the junta rule in the following months Chun was appointed one of Park's senior secretaries in charge of civilian petitioning affairs.

The subsequent career pattern of Chun in the military was smooth and rapid. He served in the Korean Central Intelligence Agency and at the Army headquarters and trained as a paratrooper. It is said that he took part in paratrooper sky jumping exercises more than 500 times. As a lieutenant colonel Chun became deputy commander of the First Paratrooper Special Forces in 1966 and battalion commander of the Metropolitan Defense Division in 1967.

### Becoming More Political

In November 1969 Chun, now promoted to full colonel, served in the Army headquarters as senior aide to the Army chief of staff. He was the first in his class to be promoted to full colonel, and later general, although ranking only in the middle range of his class of 156 graduates. In November 1970 Chun volunteered to serve in Vietnam and was made commander of the 29th Regiment of the Republic of Korea 9th Division. After one year's field experience in combat Chun returned home to assume the position of commander of the First Paratrooper Special Forces. Incidentally, while in Vietnam Chun allegedly suggested to President Park in a letter the idea of establishing "Democracy Korean style," which Park took favorably. Park later wrote back that he had made an address on this theme before to the graduating class of the Korean Military Academy in 1971.

As of January 1, 1973, Chun was made brigadier general and was appointed to serve in the Blue House (presidential mansion) Protective Forces as assistant deputy chief. On February 1, 1977, he was promoted to major general, and in 1978 he was appointed as commander of the Republic of Korea First Division. It was during his tenure as commander of the First Division that on January 10, 1978, his unit was credited with having uncovered North Korea's third invasion tunnel along the Demilitarized Zone (DMZ) near Panmunjom. On March 5, 1979, Major General Chun was appointed to a key position, commander of the Army Security Command, which subsequently enabled him to plot coups in 1979 and 1980.

On October 26, 1979, President Park was assassinated, ending 18 years of military rule. A civilian government under Choi Kyu-ha took office. As commander of the powerful Army Security Command, Chun investigated the Park assassination. On December 12, 1979, Chun acted against his military superiors by arresting Martial Law Commander General Chung Sung-hwa, who was also the Army chief-of-staff, in a violent confrontation charging him with possible implication in the assassination plot. This was the first of the two military coups which subsequently led to the founding of South Korea's Fifth Republic, officially proclaimed with the adoption of a new constitution by national referendum on October 22, 1980.

Meanwhile, on May 17, 1980, then-Lieutenant General Chun led the second coup establishing a military gov-

ernment to replace that of Choi. After proclaiming martial law and prohibiting assemblies and free speeches, Chun and his fellow coup leaders, including General Roh Tae Woo, went on to arrest the opposition leaders. Dissident Kim Dae-jung and New Democratic Party President Kim Young Sam, as well as the political leaders of the old regime, such as former prime minister and Democratic Republican Party President Kim Jong-pil were among those arrested. The arrest of Kim Dae-jung, however, led to a nationwide protest by Kim's followers and to the bloody riots of Kwangju, the provincial capital of South Cholla, Kim's home province. The Kwangju riot initially started as a campus demonstration, but turned into a major insurrection lasting for nine days between May 18 and May 27. Chun dispatched a paratrooper unit to recapture the city. In the process many civilians and rebel students were killed. Casualties were estimated at around 183 dead and several hundred wounded, according to an official account, although eyewitness accounts placed the figure much higher—at over 2,000 dead and wounded. "Kwangju" became an emotional and evocative issue for many South Koreans, who blamed Chun for what they considered a massacre and national disgrace.

### The Presidency of Chun

During his tenure as president, Chun maintained a strong, sometimes brutal police state, but at the same time encouraged and oversaw the country's vast economic growth. Overall, South Koreans enjoyed prosperity and an improved standard living. He was invited to Washington, D.C. by U.S. President Ronald Reagan twice, in January 1981 and April 1985. He also paid an official state visit to Japan in October 1984, the first such visit by a Korean head of state. He actively toured other foreign countries, including the five ASEAN countries in 1981, four African countries and Canada in 1982, and several Asian countries in 1983. It was during his 1983 diplomatic tour that he was the target of an assassination attempt by a bomb explosion in Rangoon, Burma, on October 9, reportedly the work of North Korean commandos, which killed some of his closest aides. He also pursued an active policy of North-South Korean dialogue and negotiation on unification, including a proposal for a summit meeting between the leaders of the two Koreas.

The challenge of his administration was to maintain internal political stability, continue the momentum of economic growth, and successfully complete the 1988 Seoul Summer Olympics, in which North Korea refused to participate. Despite the public's skepticism, Chun left office, as promised, when his seven-year presidential term expired in 1988—though not as he originally planned. In 1987 he named his long-time friend and military colleague, Roh Tae Woo, as his successor. Violent demonstrations erupted until Roh made a dramatic speech endorsing direct presidential elections, restoration of civil rights for Kim Dae Jung and other dissidents, and lifting press restrictions. The turbulence was quelled, and Roh went on to win the presidential elections despite charges of fraud.

## From Power to Disgrace

Chun left power amid widespread accusations of corruption, and was embarrassed by an investigation that officially spared him but sent several family members (also in government) to prison for having raised illegal funds from corporations. The former president sought to mollify public anger by leaving his luxurious home in Seoul to live an ascetic life in a Buddhist monastery for over a year. During Roh's presidency, which lasted until 1993, South Korea moved steadily toward a more democratic government and gained respect around the world. Domestically, however, accusations of fraud still persisted, particularly against Roh who faced charges of amassing a large slush fund while president.

A former dissident turned party leader, Kim Young Sam, was elected president in 1993—the first civilian to hold office after three decades of military leadership. Almost immediately, Kim came under pressure to right the wrongs of the military government's past transgressions. After a long investigation, former Presidents Chun and Roh were found to have initiated the 1979 coup, now referred to as a "premeditated military rebellion," that led them to power. At first, it appeared the two men would not be prosecuted; however, public outrage demanded that they be tried for staging the 1979 coup and the Kwangju massacre. They each faced separate bribery charges.

## Trial of the Century

On December 3, 1995 the government reversed its decision, and announced the two men would be indicted for their actions in the 1979 coup, as well as the military action in Kwangju that crushed the uprising against martial law. Chun immediately denied the charges and protested by going on a hunger strike that lasted for 26 days, but recovered to stand trial in early 1996. The most serious charge, which can be punished by execution, was for sending troops to Kwangju with orders to kill demonstrators. In September he was convicted of mutiny and treason and sentenced to death for the 1979 coup that brought him to power and for instigating the massacre in Kwangju. A panel of three judges tried and sentenced the case (South Korea does not have juries). The court also convicted Rho, and sentenced him to 22 years in prison. In separate but related cases involving political bribes, nine leading businessmen, including the chairmen of Samsung and Daewoo and 21 former presidential aides and military officers, were convicted on charges of corruption or assisting the coup. All received jail terms of at least three years, except the chairman of the Samsung group whose two-year sentence was suspended.

Both men appealed their sentences. The Appeals Court overturned Chun's sentence of death (usually by hanging), and reduced it to life imprisonment. Rho's sentence was reduced to 17 years in prison. In a final appeal to Korea's Supreme Court, both sentences were upheld. The only remaining possibility for leniency was a presidential pardon, which was unlikely given the public's strong desire to rectify past military actions and corruption of power. Even President Kim was not above scrutiny as he faced increasing

questions about his own relationship with the previous leaders and the possibility that he took substantial sums of money from them.

## Further Reading

For Korea's political history since 1945 see: Young Whan Kihl, *Politics and Policies in Divided Korea: Regimes in Contest* (1984) and "Korea's Fifth Republic: Domestic Political Trends," in *Journal of Northeast Asian Studies* (June 1982). Additional articles can be found in *World Press Review* (November 1996). □

# Connie Chung

**In 1993 when Connie Chung (born 1941) became the co-anchor of the "CBS Evening News," she was the first Asian American and the second woman ever to be named to the coveted post of nightly news anchor at a major network.**

Constance Yu-hwa Chung was born on August 20, 1946, in suburban Washington, D.C., to Margaret Ma and William Ling Ching Chung. Her father had been an intelligence officer in China's Nationalist Army who fled his war-torn homeland for the United States in 1944.

Chung earned a degree in journalism from the University of Maryland in 1969. Her first job was with WTTG-TV, an independent television station in the nation's capital. Later she secured a job at CBS' Washington bureau, aided in part by the Federal Communications Commission's timely mandate for stations to hire more minorities. In her early years with CBS, Chung covered stories such as the 1972 presidential campaign of George McGovern, anti-Vietnam War protests, and the presidency of Richard M. Nixon.

In 1976, Chung moved to Los Angeles to becom an anchor at the local CBS affiliate, KNXT (now KCBS). She began hosting three news broadcasts a day, and the station went from third to second place in ratings. In 1983, she took a drastic pay cut and moved to NBC where she worked as a correspondent and anchored several shows and prime-time news specials. She also served as political analysis correspondent for the network. In 1989, Chung announced that she would leave NBC for CBS when her current contract expired. Her contract with CBS was reported to be worth $1.5 million annually. Her initial duties at CBS included hosting "West 57th," "The CBS Sunday Night News," and serving as the principal replacement for Dan Rather on "The CBS Evening News."

On June 1, 1993, Connie Chung became the co-anchor of the "CBS Evening News." She became the first Asian American and only the second woman ever to named to the coveted post of nightly news anchor at a major network, traditionally thought of as the pinnacle of broadcast journalism. In addition to her role as co-anchor, Chung began hosting "Eye to Eye with Connie Chung," a popular prime-

time television news magazine that highlighted interviews with controversial newsmakers, a specialty of Chung's. Her time in the limelight was limited. Her desire for higher level interviews caused a stir with the network and Chung's credibility suffered as she continued to cover the tabloid stories assigned to her. Her 1995 firing from the co-anchor position and subsequent loss of "Eye to Eye with Connie Chung" disturbed many who were pleased to see a woman reaching new heights in journalism. Dan Rather's seeming indifference to Chung's firing fueled the rumor that he pulled strings to have her let go.

Chung received numerous accolades for her work, including three National Emmy Awards, a Peabody, a 1991 Ohio State Award, a 1991 National Headliner Award, two American Women in Radio and Television National Commendations, a 1991 Clarion Award, and in 1990 she was chosen as favorite interviewer by *U.S. News and World Report* in their annual "Best of America" survey.

On December 2, 1984, Chung married television journalist Maury Povich, host of "The Maury Povich Show," a syndicated day-time television talk show. Their adoption of a son, Matthew Jay Povich, came shortly after Chung's firing from CBS. She has been a full-time mother since her departure from the network, but talks have surfaced suggesting she and Povich will collaborate on a news show, to be produced by Dreamworks Televsion, once his contract with "The Maury Povich Show" runs out in 1997. □

# Tung Chung-shu

**Tung Chung-shu (ca. 179-104 B.C.) was a Chinese man of letters best known for his work in formulating a mode of thought which was to become known, somewhat loosely, as Confucianism.**

Well versed in Chinese literature, Tung Chung-shu made his name at court during discussions with the Emperor (Han Wu-ti) and held official posts in the provinces. Tung's writings are preserved in the Standard History of the Western Han dynasty (*Han-shu*) and in a collection of essays entitled *Ch'un-Ch'iu fan-lu,* or *Luxurious Gems of the Spring and Autumn Annals.*

Very little of Tung Chung-shu's work was due to original thinking; his importance lies in his synthesis of a number of elements under a single system which could be adopted as the ideological basis for the exercise of imperial authority. He venerated Confucius as one of the earliest of China's teachers, who had clearly linked the exercise of temporal powers with moral standards. Tung's study of the past was directed to clarifying the moral precepts that could be learned and applied for the guidance of mankind; and he commented at length on the lessons to be found in the *Spring and Autumn Annals,* a text which Confucius was believed to have edited.

Tung Chung-shu accepted the principle that the creation of the universe and its maintenance in correct balance derived from the harmonious relationship of the two forces *yin* (female, dark) and *yang* (male, light) and the actions of the five elements (wood, fire, earth, metal, and water), which possessed both a control of material substances and a moral and symbolic effect. He also accepted the existence of *t'ien* (heaven) as the final arbiter under whose protection these powers operated. As part of the same regulated system, the son of heaven, the emperor, holds authority that was deputed to him from heaven in order to regulate the affairs of man and to impart to them a balanced and ordered development.

According to Tung Chung-shu, heaven, earth, and man have complementary parts to play within the single system of the universe, and in a well-ordered state of affairs they work together harmoniously. Heaven holds a perpetual interest in the welfare of man; man is endowed with a natural willingness to obey heaven; and the earth lies ready for man's cultivation and nourishment.

## Role of the Emperor

So that human beings will cooperate effectively, heaven deputes temporal authority to a select individual, the emperor, who is thereby entitled to command the loyal obedience of the inhabitants of the world. This mandate is never bestowed indiscriminately and can be held properly only by an individual who possesses the characteristics, power, and personality that fit him for the just exercise of his authority; and this must always be designed to benefit humanity, not simply to enrich or strengthen his own position.

Tung Chung-shu lived at a time when the imperial dynasty of Han was being actively consolidated and its grasp of authority purposefully extended. In his knowledge of the past he could look back to earlier periods of Chinese history before the first empire had been formed (221 B.C.) and discern the circumstances in which heaven had bestowed a mandate to rule over small territories and how this had been forfeited by unworthy incumbents.

## Warning Omens

With the establishment of the hereditary empire of Han (from 202 B.C.) the principle of heaven's mandate and its requirements had to be reconciled with a practical problem that could easily arise should an emperor conduct himself unsuitably, show himself unfit for the responsibilities that had been thrust upon him, and arouse opposition, disobedience, or rebellion. Tung Chung-shu's answer to this problem could satisfy the needs of imperial authorities who were anxious to find support for their measures. He believed that when it is clear that an emperor is abusing his position or failing to conduct the world in a sufficiently harmonious manner, heaven responds by giving an obvious warning so that the emperor can mend his ways and restore a balanced and just dominion on earth. Such warnings take the form of abnormalities or rarities, either in the heavens or on earth, for instance, eclipses, comets, earthquakes, or the birth of freak creatures.

In addition, the phenomena whereby heaven's warnings are manifested are of a symbolic type whose characteristics correspond with those of the improper or offensive activities perpetrated on earth under the dispensation of the emperor. For this reason the purpose of the warning may be determined easily, and appropriate steps may be taken to avert further phenomena. The system is based on a belief in a correspondence between the natural actions of heaven, man, and earth whereby the actions of one order may stimulate a similar reaction from the other two.

Tung Chung-shu linked the successful operation of dynastic rule with the teachings of Confucius, the benevolent dispensation of heaven, and an ordered explanation of the workings of the universe. This system comprised many of Confucius's own teachings regarding social relationships, the importance of education, and the operation of government. Later it was adopted as a state cult throughout China's imperial period, and in the course of those 2,000 years the cult became subject to very considerable changes of emphasis, doctrine, and practice.

## Further Reading

For the place of Tung Chung-shu in the development of Chinese thought see Feng Yu-lan, *History of Chinese* Philosophy, translated by Derk Bodde (2 vols., 1952-1953); Joseph Needham and others, *Science and Civilisation in China*, vol. 2 (1956); W. T. de Bary, *Sources of Chinese Tradition* (1960); and Wing-tsit Chan, *A Source Book in Chinese Philosophy* (1963). ☐

# Frederick Edwin Church

**The works of American painter Frederick Edwin Church (1826-1900) marked the culmination of romantic landscape painting in America and the final great expression of the group of artists identified as the Hudson River school.**

Frederick Edwin Church was born in Hartford, Conn., into a prominent family. At an early age he decided to become an artist. He studied for a short time with Benjamin Coe, then went to Catskill, N.Y., in 1844 to study with Thomas Cole, one of the foremost painters of the Hudson River school. Though Cole died 4 years later, Church had already formed his style in the tradition of his master. He wished to travel and he read with interest *Kosmos,* a book by the young German scientist Alexander von Humboldt. This description of a 4-year trip to unexplored areas of Latin America inspired Church, who went to Ecuador and Colombia in 1853 and again in 1857. On these trips Church made many beautifully executed pencil drawings, which he later worked up into paintings showing detailed tropical foliage with Mt. Cotopaxi or Mt. Chimborazo in the distance.

In the summer of 1859 Church went to Labrador with Cole's biographer. Church was impressed by the dramatic aspect of icebergs and made many sketches. In 1865 he went to Jamaica and once again enjoyed sketching in a tropical environment. On his first trip to Europe, in 1868, he visited the Bavarian Alps, Italy, and Greece, as well as Palestine and Syria. A remarkable series of small oil sketches gives a pictorial account of these travels and indicates a very important side of his work, for they have a brilliance and spontaneity often lacking in his large canvases. Church made full use of his sense of the dramatic when depicting grandiose scenery. He had a remarkable feeling for light and atmosphere. His vividly painted sunsets seem almost explosive and anticipate 20th-century expressionism.

When he returned to America, Church built "Olana," a large country house on a mountaintop commanding an unsurpassed view of the Hudson River and the Catskill Mountains beyond. This semi-Moorish structure designed by the artist with the help of the architect Calvert Vaux has been preserved as a museum. Here Church assembled paintings collected in Italy, Turkish carpets, Moorish tiles, and Near Eastern brass. After subsequent trips to Mexico, he added religious paintings and pre-Columbian sculpture and terra-cottas. Some paintings by Cole and some of Church's own hang in the house.

Church was enormously successful as a painter in his own time, and he amassed a considerable fortune. However, he was crippled by arthritis and unable to paint during the last 20 years of his life.

ally loomed large in his works—the politician and the business tycoon.

*Richard Carvel* (1899) is a romantic historical novel of the American Revolutionary period. Though carefully written, the book has the episodic structure characteristic of Churchill. It became a best seller because of the conscientious research that gave remarkable authenticity to events and characters.

Churchill determined to cover "the most emphasized epochs in the history of this country" in a series of novels. *The Crisis* (1901), set mainly in St. Louis, where northern and southern emigrants and German immigrants had commingled in a border region, pictures the Civil War in a new way. *The Crossing* (1904), a panorama of America's westward movement and the newly settled frontier during the Revolution, is generally considered Churchill's best historical novel. Like its predecessors, this narrative vividly characterizes a number of outstanding historical figures.

By 1904, however, public interest in historical fiction had waned, and a group of "muckraking" journalists were exposing graft and corruption in the United States. Churchill was affected by the trend and began to write about contemporary issues. *Coniston* (1906) shows the long-lasting ethical conflicts in New England's politics; *Mr. Crewe's Career* (1908) examines a railroad's attempt to dominate a state. *A Modern Chronicle* (1910) deals with divorce, *The Inside of the Cup* (1913) with religion, *A Far Country* (1915) with the need for the control of corporations, and The *Dwelling-*

### Further Reading

David C. Huntington, *The Landscapes of Frederick Edwin Church* (1966), is a sympathetic study of the man and his art and is the only critical work. Frederick A. Sweet, *The Hudson River School and the Early American Landscape Tradition* (1945), includes a short discussion of Church. Further background material is in Oliver W. Larkin, *Art and Life in America* (1949; rev. ed. 1960). □

# Winston Churchill

**The American author Winston Churchill (1871-1947) was known during his lifetime for his historical and political novels.**

B orn in St. Louis, Winston Churchill went to Smith Academy, then attended Annapolis. He served briefly in the U.S. Navy, working as an editor for the *Army and Navy Journal,* and then joined the staff of *Cosmopolitan Magazine.* He had been encouraged to write during his years in the Naval Academy and soon began a career as an author.

Churchill's first novel, *The Celebrity: An Episode* (1898), satirized the era's literary and fashionable world. This book introduced him to the public and gave him practice in portraying two kinds of characters that eventu-

*Place of Light* (1917) with the rise of radicalism. His work established the value of research to the historical novelist.

### Further Reading

Charles Child Walcutt, *The Romantic Compromise in the Novels of Winston Churchill* (1951), and Warren Irving Titus, *Winston Churchill* (1963), treat Churchill's life and work. General studies which discuss Churchill's novels include Ernest Erwin Leisy, *The American Historical Novel* (1950); Grant C. Knight, *The Strenuous Age in American Literature* (1954); and Joseph L. Blotner, *The Political Novel* (1955). □

# Sir Winston Leonard Spencer Churchill

**The English statesman and author Sir Winston Leonard Spencer Churchill (1874-1965) led Britain during World War II and is often described as the "savior of his country."**

S ir Winston Churchill's exact place in the political history of the 20th century is, and will continue to be, a subject of debate and polemical writing. Where he succeeded, and how much he personally had to do with that success, and where he failed, and why, remain to be established. That he was a political figure of enormous influence and importance, belonging in many ways to an age earlier than the 20th century, and that he fitted uneasily into the constraints of British party politics until his moment came in 1940 are not in doubt. Until recently his reputation during the years from 1940 onward was scarcely questioned. But now historians are beginning to reassess his career in just the same way as Churchill himself tried to revise T. B. Macaulay's account of the Duke of Marlborough by writing a multivolumed *Life* of his distinguished ancestor (completed in 1938).

Churchill's record both before 1939 and after 1945 was for the most part undistinguished. But as Anthony Storr writes: "In 1940 Churchill became the hero that he had always dreamed of being. . . . In that dark time, what England needed was not a shrewd, equable, balanced leader. She needed a prophet, a heroic visionary, a man who could dream dreams of victory when all seemed lost. Winston Churchill was such a man; and his inspirational quality owed its dynamic force to the romantic world of phantasy in which he had his true being."

### Early Life

Winston Churchill was born on Nov. 30, 1874, at Blenheim Palace—the home given by Queen Anne to his ancestor the Duke of Marlborough. He was the eldest son of Lord Randolph Churchill, a Tory Democrat who achieved early success as a rebel in his party but who later failed and was cruelly described as "a man with a brilliant future behind him." His mother was Jenny Jerome, the beautiful and talented daughter of Leonard Jerome, a New York businessman.

Winston was conventionally educated following the norms of his class. He went to preparatory school, then to Harrow (1888), then to the Royal Military College at Sandhurst. He was neither happy nor successful at school. Winston idolized his mother, but his relations with his father, who died in 1895, were cold and distant. It is generally agreed that as a child Winston was deprived of openly expressed warmth and affection.

Churchill very early exhibited the physical courage and love of adventure and action that he was to keep throughout his political career. His first role was that of a soldier-journalist. Having joined the 4th Hussars in 1895, he immediately went to Cuba to write about the Spanish army for the *Daily Graphic.* He took part in the repulse of the insurgents who tried to cross the Spanish line at Trochem. In 1896 he was in India, and while on the North-West Frontier with the Malakand Field Force he began work on a novel, *Savrola, a Tale of the Revolution in Laurania,* which was published in 1900. More important, however, were his accounts of the military campaigns in which he participated. A book about the North-West Frontier and the Malakand Field Force was followed by a book about the reconquest of the Sudan (1899), in which he had also taken part. He went to Africa during the Boer War as a journalist for the *Morning Post,* and the most romantic of his escapades as a youth was his escape from a South African prison during this conflict.

## Young Politician

In 1899 Churchill lost in his first attempt at election to the House of Commons. This was to be the first of many defeats in elections and by-elections during his career—he lost more elections than any other political figure in recent British history. But in 1900 he entered the House of Commons, in which he served intermittently until 1964. Throughout this long span his presence and oratory exercised a magnetic attraction in an institution he always refused to leave for the House of Lords.

Churchill's early years in politics were characterized by an interest in the radical reform of social problems. In 1905 he completed a biography of his father, which is perhaps his best book. Lord Randolph had tried to give coherence and organization to a popular socially oriented Toryism; Churchill carried that effort into the Liberal party, which he had joined in 1904 because of his disagreement with the revived demands for protectionism by the Chamberlain section of the Tory party. The major intellectual achievement of this period of Churchill's life was his *Liberalism and the Social Problem* (1909). In this work he stated his creed: "Liberalism seeks to raise up poverty. . . . Liberalism would preserve private interests in the only way in which they can be safely and justly preserved, namely by reconciling them with public right." Churchill was very active in the great reforming government of Lord Asquith between 1908 and 1912, and his work in palliating unemployment was especially significant.

In 1912 Churchill became first lord of the Admiralty—the range of offices which he held was as remarkable as the number of elections which he lost. He switched his enthusiasm away from butter toward guns, and his goal was the preparation of Britain's fleet for impending war. While at the Admiralty, Churchill suffered a major setback. He became committed to the view that the navy could best make an impact on the 1914-1918 war in Europe by way of a swift strike through the Dardanelles. This strategy proved unsuccessful, however, and Churchill lost his Admiralty post. In 1916 he was back in the army and served for a time on the front lines in France.

## Interwar Years

Churchill soon reentered political life. Kept out of the Lloyd George War Cabinet by conservative hostility to his style and philosophy, by 1921 Churchill held a post in the Colonial Office. A clash with Mustapha Kemal in Turkey, however, did not help his reputation, and in 1922 he lost his seat in the House of Commons. The Conservative party gained power for the first time since 1905, and Churchill now began long-term isolation, with few friends in any part of the political spectrum.

In 1924 Churchill severed his ties with liberalism and became chancellor of the Exchequer in Stanley Baldwin's government. His decision to put Britain back on the gold standard was a controversial one, attacked by the economist John Maynard Keynes, among others. Although he held office under Baldwin, Churchill did not agree with the Conservative position either on defense or on imperialism. In 1931 he resigned from the Conservative "shadow cabinet"

as a protest against its Indian policy. Ever the romantic imperialist, he did not want to cast away "that most truly bright and precious jewel in the crown of the King." Baldwin and he also disagreed on how to react to the crisis caused by the abdication of King Edward VIII.

Churchill's interwar years were characterized by political isolation, and during this period he made many errors and misjudgments, among them his bellicosity over the general strike of 1926. Thus he cannot be viewed simply as a popular leader who was kept waiting in the wings through no fault of his own. In fact, it is not completely evident that he was aware of the nature of the fascist threat during the 1930s.

## World War II

The major period of Churchill's political career began when he became prime minister and head of the Ministry of Defense early in World War II. "I felt as if I was walking with destiny, and that all my past life had been but a preparation for this hour," he wrote in the first volume of his account of the war. (This account was later published in six volumes from 1948 to 1953). His finest hour and that of the British people coincided. His leadership, which was expressed in noble speeches and ceaseless personal activity, stated precisely what Britain needed to survive through the years before United States entry into the war.

The evacuation of Dunkirk and the air defense of the Battle of Britain have become legend, but there were and are controversies over Churchill's policies. It has been argued that Churchill's oversensitivity to the Mediterranean as a theater of war led to mistakes in Crete and North Africa. The value of his resistance to the idea of a second front as the Germans advanced into Russia has also been questioned. And there has been considerable debate over the wisdom of the course he pursued at international conferences (such as those at Yalta in February 1945) which reached agreements responsible in large part for the "cold war" of the 1950s and 1960s. But although criticisms may be made of Churchill's policies, his importance as a symbol of resistance and as an inspiration to victory cannot be challenged.

## Last Years

The final period of Churchill's career began with his rejection by the British people at the general election of 1945. At that election 393 Labour candidates were elected members of Parliament as against 213 Conservatives and their allies. It was one of the most striking reversals of fortune in democratic history. It may perhaps be explained by Churchill's aggressive vituperation during the campaign combined with the electorate's desire for patient social reconstruction rather than for a return to prewar economic mismanagement.

In 1951, however, Churchill again became prime minister. He resigned in April 1955 after an uneventful term in office. For many of the later years of his life, even his iron constitution was not strong enough to resist the persistent cerebral arteriosclerosis from which he suffered. He died on

Jan. 24, 1965, and was given a state funeral, the details of which had been largely dictated by himself before his death.

## Further Reading

Churchill's own works, combining a very personal perspective with grand historical themes, are written with great style and lucidity. They include *The World Crisis* (6 vols., 1923-1931), an account of World War I; *The Second World War* (6 vols., 1948-1953); and the less satisfactory but sometimes elegant *History of the English Speaking Peoples* (4 vols., 1956-1958).

An official multivolume biography of vast scope, with separate companion volumes of documents, was started by Churchill's son, Randolph S. Churchill: *Winston S. Churchill,* vol. 1: *Youth, 1874-1900* (1966); *Winston S. Churchill: Companion Volume I,* pts. 1 and 2 (1967); *Winston S. Churchill,* vol. 2: *Young Statesman, 1901-1914* (1967). The best introductory assessment of Churchill is A. J. P. Taylor and others, eds., *Churchill Revised: A Critical Assessment* (1969), a volume of essays. For the best example of what will be a growing industry of revisionism on Churchill's reputation see Robert Rhodes James, *Churchill: A Study in Failure, 1900-1939* (1970).

There are many other studies of Churchill: Alan Moorehead, *Winston Churchill in Trial and Triumph* (1955); Alfred L. Rowse, *The Churchills* (2 vols., 1956-1958; 1 vol., 1966); Herbert Feis, *Churchill, Roosevelt, Stalin: The War They Waged and the Peace They Sought* (1957; rev. ed. 1966); American Heritage, *Churchill: The Life Triumphant; the Historical Record of Ninety Years* (1965); Malcolm Thomson, *Churchill: His Life and Times* (rev. ed. 1965; published 1949 as *Life and Times of Winston Churchill*); Charles McMoran Wilson Moran, *Churchill: The Struggle for Survival, 1940-1965, Taken from the Diaries of Lord Moran* (1966); Kenneth Young, *Churchill and Beaverbrook: A Study in Friendship and Politics* (1966); Brian Gardner, *Churchill in His Time: A Study in Reputation, 1939-1945* (1968); Dennis Bardens, *Churchill in Parliament* (1969); and John Wheeler-Bennett, *Action This Day: Working with Churchill* (1969). Harold MacMillan's memoirs have much material on Churchill: *Winds of Change, 1914-1939* (1966); *The Blast of War, 1939-1945* (1967); and *Tides of Fortune, 1945-1955* (1969).

## Additional Sources

Charmley, John, *Churchill, the end of glory: a political biography,* New York: Harcourt Brace, 1993.

Churchill, Winston S. (Winston Spencer), *Memories and adventures,* New York: Weidenfeld and Nicolson, 1989.

*Churchill,* Oxford; New York: Oxford University Press, 1992.

Gilbert, Martin, *Churchill: a life,* London: Heinemann, 1991.

Pelling, Henry, *Winston Churchill,* Houndmills, Basingstoke, Hampshire: Macmillan, 1989.

Robbins, Keith, *Churchill,* London; New York: Longman, 1992.

Rose, Norman, *Churchill: the unruly giant,* New York: Free Press, 1995.

Sandys, Celia, *The young Churchill: the early years of Winston Churchill,* New York: Dutton, 1995.

Soames, Mary, *Winston Churchill: his life as a painter: a memoir by his daughter,* London: Collins, 1990.

*Winston Churchill: resolution, defiance, magnanimity, good will,* Columbia: University of Missouri Press, 1996. □

# José Benito de Churriguera

**José Benito de Churriguera (1665-1725) was a Spanish architect and sculptor in the late baroque style. His artistic expression fused, with elaborate theatricality, the influences of Spain's late Renaissance style and that of the Roman baroque.**

Until recently both Salamanca and Barcelona were cited as the probable birthplace of José Benito de Churriguera, but it is now known that he was born and died in Madrid. His obituary hailed him as "the Spanish Michelangelo," and his death occurred just in time for him to escape knowing the hysterically adverse criticism hurled at his works by the neoclassicists, who coined the term "Churrigueresque" to signify an accursed style of excess and extravagance. Ironically, these academicians sometimes praised works by him, believing them to have had other authors.

José Benito was one of a family of artists, of which he became the head after the death of his father, José Simón de Churriguera, in 1679. José Benito's brothers were Joaquin, Alberto, Manuel, and Miguel. Of the works of the three sons of José Benito—Matías, Jerónimo, and Nicolás, all architects—very little is known, no doubt because they were trained in a style rejected by their generation.

King Charles II named José Benito an architect for the royal works in 1690, although he did not begin to receive a salary for this office until 1696. In 1702 Teodoro Ardemans was named chief architect by King Philip V, and shortly thereafter Churriguera was accused of insubordination and presumption. The loss of royal patronage was balanced by the acquisition of a private patron, the banker Juan de Goyeneche. In addition, Churriguera had become the architect of Salamanca Cathedral in 1690. Although he worked almost exclusively in Madrid during the last 26 years of his life, his Salamanca appointment proved an "open sesame" to important commissions for his brothers and at least one of his sons.

Churriguera first attracted fame when he won the competition for the catafalque for Charles II's first queen, Maria Luisa d'Orleáns. This temporary monument was erected in the Church of the Encarnacíon, Madrid, and a sketch of it was published. His most famous altarpiece is that in the church of S. Esteban, Salamanca (1693). It is an architectural frame for sculptures, carved and gilded, with projections and recessions in monumental proportions and featuring Solomonic (twisted) columns. Despite the lavish ornament, the altarpiece has an impressive dignity achieved by rhythmic unity and harmonious proportions.

The most original architectural work by Churriguera is his urban layout for a new town, Nuevo Baztán, near Madrid. It was commissioned by Goyeneche to include a glass factory, workers' dwellings, a church, and a palace in a complex with three plazas. Its architectural austerity is reminiscent of the work of Juan de Herrera, and its asymmetry is unique as well as visually effective.

## Further Reading

George Kubler and Martin Soria, *Art and Architecture in Spain and Portugal and Their American Dominions, 1500-1800* (1959), lacks recently discovered facts on Churriguera and is often biased. Bernard Bevan, *History of Spanish Architecture* (1938), also contains information on him. □

# Chu Teh

**Chu Teh (1886-1976), or Zhu De, was a Chinese Communist military leader. He became closely associated with Mao Tse-tung (Mao Zedong) in 1928 and was for many years afterward commander in chief of the Communist military forces.**

One of 14 children in a poor, frugal peasant family, Chu Teh was born in the village of Ma'an Chung, Szechwan Province, on Dec. 18, 1886. The Chu family had moved to Szechwan from Kwangtung in the early 1800s and although his grandparents were buried in Szechwan, the family's customs and dialect remained that of Kwangtung. It was only in Chu Teh's generation that family members began to speak the Szechwan dialect in addition to Cantonese. Through careful scrimping by the entire family, Chu alone was given an education, studying in the nearby town of Tawan, where he came under the influence of a reform-minded Confucian scholar. In 1905 Chu entered a modern school at Nanch'ung but continued to study for the traditional examinations. He passed the first civil service examination in 1906, just after the examinations had become meaningless because of government reforms. He continued for another year at Nanch'ung and then studied physical education at the Chengtu Higher Normal School. He left school in 1908 to help support his family by teaching physical education in a school near home. His family, which had expected to gain prestige and an easier living through making him a government official, was horrified.

## Military Career

In 1909 Chu entered Yunnan Military Academy at Kunming, where he became involved in the T'ung Meng Hui, an association dedicated to the overthrow of the Manchus, and the Ko-lao-hui, a Chinese secret society with strong roots in the country's southwestern region. He also joined the Revolutionary Party of Sun Yat-sen. Toward the end of his course of studies at Yunnan, Chu established a relationship with one of his teachers, Ts'ai O, a patriot from the province of Hunan and military leader who had come to Yunnan in the spring of 1911 to command a local brigade and to teach at the military academy. When Chu graduated from the academy in June 1911, he became a second lieutenant in the brigade of Ts'ai O, who was a secret revolutionist. Under Ts'ai's command, Chu participated in the revolution against local Manchu authority. The coup brought Ts'ai to power as the first republican governor of

Yunnan. Chu and his Szechwanese regiment next returned to their native province to attack the headquarters of Chao Erh-feng, Manchu governor general, at Suifu. Chu and his troops patrolled the Suifu region of Szechwan until the spring of 1912, when he went back to Kunming as an instructor at Yunnan Military Academy. He also joined the Kuomintang and was promoted to the command of a detachment. After his promotion to major in 1913, Chu was stationed on Yunnan's border with Indochina until 1915.

In 1915 Chu became a colonel in Ts'ai O's command, participating in a revolt organized by Ts'ai and Liang Ch'i-cha'o against would-be monarch Yuan Shih-k'ai. In early 1916 Ts'ai led his forces from Yunnan into southern Szechwan, where Chu commanded troops which fought pro-Yuan forces to a bloody stalemate. Only the death of Yuan in June 1916 brought the conflict to an end. The following month Ts'ai was named governor of Szechwan. Ts'ai in turn appointed Chu commander of the 13th Mixed Brigade of the 7th Division of the Yunnan Army in Szechwan and when Ts'ai became governor of Szechwan in 1916, Chu was made a brigadier general and commander of provincial forces in the southwest. For several years he fought the warlords in Szechwan but slipped into the habits of a warlord himself. By 1921 he and his allies were badly defeated, and Chu was forced to flee to Shanghai for his life.

## Convert to Communism

In October 1922 Chu went from Shanghai to Berlin, where he met Chou En-lai and joined the Chinese Socialist Youth League. Chu's subsequent membership in the Communist party was kept secret. He attended the University of Göttingen for a year and then returned to Berlin for political work. He assisted Chou in organizing the German headquarters of the Kuomintang (KMT), with which the Communists were allied. Twice arrested in connection with demonstrations, Chu was expelled from Germany in June 1926.

Chu arrived in China at the height of the Northern Expedition and became director of the Nationalist training school for new officers in Nanchang, Kiangsi, and in effect became garrison commander and head of the Nanchang police. When the Nationalists broke with the Communists in the summer of 1927, the Communist leadership unsuccessfully attempted to capture Nanchang. Chu and a part of the Communist force retreated toward Canton and eventually to the Kiangsi Soviet base of Mao Tse-tung. Chu became commander in chief, and Mao political commissar, of the forces there. Their alliance became the major basis of later Communist success.

In the next four years Chu successfully defended and extended the base area, and early in 1934 he was made a member of the Political Bureau of the party. By late 1934, however, Nationalist attacks on the Kiangsi region forced the abandonment of the base. Chu planned the evacuation and subsequent Long March to northwestern China of about 100,000 men, breaking through three encircling lines of KMT troops and then following an 8,000-mile route through hostile and difficult terrain. Chu commanded the force through the most difficult portion of the march but was apparently ''kidnapped'' by Chang Kuo-t'ao, leader of a Soviet base in Szechwan, in an obscure inner-party quarrel. Mao proceeded with the main force to Paoan, Shensi, where Chu finally arrived in October 1936.

Chu spent the years of the Sino-Japanese War largely in the Communist capital of Yenan, serving as commander-in-chief of the Eighth Route Army, the chief force in the Communist movement. In August 1937 Chu Teh's armies, now a part of the regular Nationalist forces, began attacking the Japanese. For eight years Chu Teh, who had been appointed to his command by Chiang Kai-shek, was in direct command of all Communist military operations against the Japanese. On Aug. 14, 1945, however, he refused to obey Chiang's order that he halt independent action, and thereafter Chu's troops began resisting new attempts launched by the Kuomintang to annihilate them. Warfare spread, and by the end of 1948 all Manchuria had fallen to the People's Armies commanded by Chu Teh. Forces under Chu's command swept inexorably southward, taking Peking (Beijing), Nanking (Nanjing), Shanghai, and, finally in November 1949, Canton. Chu's military successes were attributed to a number of his policies, including the maintenance of very close ties between soldiers under his command and the peasants, organizing operations behind enemy lines, effective use of propaganda, and his mobile tactics of ''concentration and dispersal.'' In September 1949, Chu was named to the Consultative Council of the new (Communist) Chinese People's Republic, and in October he was named commander in chief of the People's Liberation Army. In 1954 he became vice chairman of the republic. In

1958, when Mao announced his plan to relinquish his administrative responsibilities as chief of staff, it was thought that Chu might succeed him. However, the following year, in April, the National People's Congress tapped Liu Shao-chi'I for chairman. At that time, Chu gave up his post as vice chairman of the National Defense Council and became chairman of the standing committee of the People's Congress.

## His Family

Chu's first wife, whom he married in 1912, died in 1916 shortly after giving birth to Chu's only child, a son, who was apparently killed during a Nationalist police raid on his home in 1935. Chu married again in 1917; the marriage ended in separation in the 1920s, and she was killed by police in 1935. He remarried in 1928; his third wife was executed by the government in 1929. About 1930 he married K'ang K'o-ch'ing, who survived the Long March and became a leader of the women's movement in the People's Republic. After 1949, she served her country on a number of overseas cultural missions. She was named vice chairman of the Women's Federation of China in 1957. On July 6, 1976, at the age of 89, Chu died in Peking.

## Further Reading

Chu's most important publication, a 1945 report on military affairs during the Sino-Japanese War, was translated into English as *On the Battlefronts of the Liberated Areas* (1952). The only full-length study of Chu is Agnes Smedley, *The Great Road: The Life and Times of Chu Teh* (1956), a sensitive presentation based on extended interviews with Chu in 1937, written by an American woman who traveled with the Red Army in its fight against the Japanese. Her earlier work, *China Fights Back* (1938), also contains personal accounts of Chu. Chu is discussed in Edgar Snow, *Red Star over China* (1938; rev. ed. 1968) and *The Other Side of the River: Red China Today* (1961); Samuel B. Griffith, *The Chinese People's Liberation Army* (1967); and John Gittings, *The Role of the Chinese Army* (1967). Further information on Chu may be found in S.T. Ludwig's entry on him in *Colliers Encyclopedia* (1996), *Britannica Online* at http//www.eb.com, and *Biograpical Dictionary of Republican China* (1967), edited by Howard L. Boorman. □

# Marcus Tullius Cicero

**Marcus Tullius Cicero (106-43 B.C.) was Rome's greatest orator and a prolific writer of verse, letters, and works on philosophy, politics, and rhetoric that greatly influenced European thought.**

C icero was born on Jan. 3, 106 B.C., at Arpinum near Rome, the elder son of a wealthy landowner. At an early age Cicero saw military service during the Social War (90-89), but he managed to avoid involvement in the civil wars that followed. He wanted to follow a career in politics and decided first to gain a reputation as an advocate.

Cicero's first appearances in court were made during the dictatorship of Sulla (81-80). In one case, while defending Sextus Roscius of Ameria on a trumped-up charge of murder, he boldly made some outspoken comments on certain aspects of Sulla's regime, and in 79 he left Rome to study in Rhodes. By 76 Cicero was back in Rome, where he married Terentia, whose family was wealthy and perhaps aristocratic. In 75 he held the office of quaestor, which brought him membership in the Senate, and in 70 he scored his first great success, when he prosecuted Caius Verres for gross misgovernment in Sicily. As Verres was defended by the leading advocate of the day, Quintus Hortensius, Cicero's success in this case won him great acclaim and considerably helped his political career.

In 69 Cicero held the office of aedile and that of praetor in 66, in which year he made his first major political speech in support of the extension of Pompey's command in the Mediterranean. During the following years he acted as a self-appointed defender of that general's interests. When Cicero stood for the consulship of 63, he reached the highest political office at the earliest legal age, a remarkable achievement for a complete outsider. His consulship involved him in a number of political problems which culminated in the conspiracy of Catiline.

### Disillusion and Exile

In the years after his consulship Cicero, politically helpless, watched Caesar, Pompey, and Crassus form the dictatorial First Triumvirate. Cicero refused offers to become a fourth member of this alliance, and his publicly expressed dislike of the violent methods Caesar employed in his consulship (59) led to Cicero's exile to Macedonia. There he lived for 16 months in abject misery, until the efforts of his friends secured his recall in August 57 B.C.

During the next 8 months Cicero tried to separate Pompey from his partners, but early in the summer of 56 Pompey brusquely ordered Cicero to stop his efforts. For the next 4 years he was largely out of politics, devoting himself to writing and occasionally emerging to defend (inconsistent behavior on his part) various supporters of the Triumvirate.

In 51 Cicero was sent off to govern Cilicia for a year. He was a conscientious and unusually honest administrator, but he was bored by the whole business and hated every moment of his absence from Rome. He finally returned in December 50 B.C., too late to be able to do anything to stop the outbreak of war between Pompey and Caesar. He accepted a commission from Pompey but did little for him, and when Pompey left Italy, Cicero stayed behind.

After Pompey's death Cicero took no part in politics and devoted himself to writing works on philosophy and rhetoric. Apart from his increasing dislike of Caesar's autocratic rule, Cicero's life was made unhappy during these years by domestic sorrows. In the winter of 47/46 he divorced Terentia after 30 years' marriage, and in the following summer he was deeply grieved by the death of his much-loved daughter Tullia.

### Second Triumvirate

Cicero was not involved in the conspiracy against Caesar, though he strongly approved of it, and after the assassination he took a prominent part in establishing a compromise between Antony and the conspirators. But before long he concluded that Antony was as great a menace to liberty as Caesar had been. During the winter of 44/43 with a series of vigorous speeches, the "Philippics," he rallied the Senate to oppose Antony in concert with Octavian. But Octavian, having seized power at Rome by force, reached an agreement with Antony and Lepidus to set themselves up as a three-man dictatorship. They started by proscribing many of their enemies, and among the first names on the list was that of Cicero. He could perhaps have escaped, but his efforts were halfhearted, and in December 43 B.C. he met his death at the hands of Antony's agents with courage and dignity.

As a politician, Cicero was ultimately unsuccessful, since he was not able to prevent the overthrow of the republican system of government. Devoted to peace and reason, he lived in an age when political power depended more and more on sheer force. Moreover, he was blind to many of the defects of the republican system and did not realize how much it failed to meet the real needs of the provincials and even of the poorer citizens of Italy and Rome itself.

### The Speeches

The texts of 57 speeches have survived, though 2 or 3 are not complete, and Cicero delivered at least 50 more, nearly all of which were published but have since been lost.

As Cicero normally edited and polished his speeches before publication, we do not have the text of what he actually said, but in most cases a more or less close approximation.

However, five speeches against Verres were never delivered but were written by Cicero to present material not used in court; the "Second Philippic" is a political pamphlet cast in the form of an imaginary speech; and *Pro Milone* represents what Cicero would have said in Milo's defense in 52 if he had not been flustered by a hostile mob into making a poor and ineffective speech.

The corpus of the extant speeches is impressive both for its bulk and its quality. It is hard not to be impressed by their vigor, by their variety of tone, and above all by the lucidity with which Cicero could present a complicated series of facts. Of the forensic speeches, *Pro Cluentio* (66) is the longest and most complicated, but it gives a vivid picture of life in a small Italian town. The much shorter *Pro Archia* (62) is notable for its sincere and eloquent defense of a life devoted to literary pursuits, and *Pro Murena* (63) is an excellent example of Cicero's ability to win a case by disregarding the basic facts and concentrating with charm and wit on such irrelevancies as the Stoic beliefs of one of the prosecutors. Of the political speeches, although the "Catilinarians" are the most famous, the 14 "Philippics" are probably the finest, because in them Cicero was concentrating all his energy and skill with a directness that he did not always achieve.

## The Dialogues

Nearly all of Cicero's works on philosophy, politics, or rhetoric are in dialogue form, though Cicero had little of Plato's dramatic instinct for the genre. They are written in that elegant and sonorous Latin prose of which Cicero was such a master. Several are devoted to ethics, religion, or other philosophical subjects, but they cannot be regarded as original contributions to philosophy, for Cicero himself acknowledged, "I provide only the words, of which I have a very large stock." Nevertheless, they are extremely valuable because in them he reproduced the theories of many of the leading Greek philosophers of the post-Aristotelian schools, such as the Stoics and the Epicureans, whose own works have not survived.

Among the more attractive are the short essays on friendship and old age, *De amicitia* and *De senectute* (both 44). Of the longer works, the most important are probably *De finibus* (45), a systematic discussion of ethics; *De natura deorum* (45), a hastily written and disjointed but valuable survey of contemporary religious beliefs; and *De officiis* (winter 44/43), a treatise on moral duties.

Another group is concerned with political theory, especially *De republica* (54-51), of which barely one-third is extant, and *De legibus*, started in 52 but perhaps never completed. These works also are to some extent based on Greek ideas, but the theoretical basis is reinforced by the Roman practical genius for the art of government and Cicero's own considerable experience of politics.

In the works on Cicero's own art of rhetoric there is a similar blend of Greek theory and Roman practical experience. The most important are *De oratore* (55), which is basically a discussion of the training of the ideal orator but takes in many aspects of the art of speaking, such as humor; *Brutus* (45), which contains an account of Roman oratory of great historical importance, with sketches of nearly 200 speakers; and *Orator* (45), in which Cicero discusses the different styles of oratory and various technical aspects of rhetoric, including a detailed examination of prose rhythms.

## The Poetry

In his youth Cicero wrote a quantity of verse, none of which has survived, and he won a considerable reputation as a poet. In later years he composed a short epic on the great soldier Marius and a longer poem on his own consulship. Of such poetry, only a few scattered lines have been preserved, in one or two cases because they are so very bad. We do have, however, several hundred lines of the *Aratea,* a translation of a poem on astronomy by the Alexandrian poet Aratus, and a number of shorter passages also translated from Greek originals. It is clear that Cicero had little real poetic inspiration but was a highly competent craftsman who did much for the development of the dactylic hexameter in Latin, and metrical analysis suggests that in this respect Virgil owed as much to him as to any other poet.

## The Letters

The collection of Cicero's letters is undoubtedly the most interesting and valuable part of all his enormous literary output. It includes nearly 800 letters written by him, and nearly another 100 written to him by a wide variety of correspondents. The two major collections are the letters *Ad Atticum* in 16 books, and *Ad familiares,* also in 16 books, published by his freedman secretary Tiro. This latter set includes practically all the letters written to Cicero. There are also two smaller sets, three books of *Ad Quintum fratrem* and two books of *Ad M. Brutum,* both the remains of what were at one time larger collections. Other sets of letters to his son Marcus, to Julius Caesar, to Octavian, and to others have all been lost. The surviving letters belong mainly to his last years; there are only 12 dating before his consulship, while over a quarter of the collection were written in the last 18 months of his life.

Some of the letters are as carefully composed as the speeches or dialogues, but most of them, especially those to his brother or to close friends like Atticus, have a spontaneity which is often lacking in the more calculated prose. In these intimate letters Cicero uses a very colloquial style, with frequent use of slang, ellipse, diminutive forms, and words or phrases in Greek.

But however rapidly they may have been written, Cicero never loses his instinctive sense of style, and their combination of immediacy with stylishness makes them some of the most attractive reading in the whole of Latin literature, quite apart from the fascination of their subject matter, for they cover an immense range of topics. But above all, they give an incredibly vivid picture of Cicero himself: his vanity, his facile optimism and equally exaggerated despair, his timidity and his indecisiveness, but also his energy and industry, his courage, his loyalty, and his basic honesty, kindliness and humanity. Thanks to his letters, we can know Cicero as we know no other Roman, and with all his faults he was a man worth knowing.

## Further Reading

Cicero's major works and his correspondence are available in English translation. The best brief account of his career and personality comprises the essays by H. H. Scullard, T. A. Dorey, and J. P. V. D. Balsdon in T. A. Dorey, ed., *Cicero* (1965), a rather uneven collection of studies by various authors. Of the numerous longer accounts, Torsten Petersson, *Cicero: A Biography* (1920), is balanced and reliable, and H. J. Haskell, *This Was Cicero* (1942), is very readable and generally sensible. R. E. Smith, *Cicero the Statesman* (1966), concentrates on the political side of his career and, though generally reliable on facts, is not very profound and is perhaps too favorable to Cicero. David Stockton, *Cicero: A Political Biography* (1971), is a straightforward account of Cicero's public career. Hartvig Frisch, *Cicero's Fight for the Republic* (1946), is an extremely detailed discussion of the last stage of Cicero's career. There is a good brief discussion of Cicero as a philosopher in H. A. K. Hunt, *The Humanism of Cicero* (1954).

For Cicero as an orator and for Roman rhetoric generally, S. F. Bonner, *Roman Declamation in the Late Republic and Early Empire* (1949), and M. L. Clarke, *Rhetoric at Rome* (1953; rev. ed. 1963), should be consulted. The best account of the history of Rome in Cicero's lifetime is in H. H. Scullard, *From the Gracchi to Nero* (1959; 2d ed. 1964), and a more detailed account is in T. Rice Holmes, *The Roman Republic and the Founder of the Empire* (1923). ☐

# The Cid

**The Cid (1043-1099), or Cid Campeador, was the greatest Spanish medieval warrior and remains one of Spain's national heroes. At a time when Berber invaders threatened Castile, the Cid alone was able to rally his countrymen and emerge victorious.**

Rodrigo Diaz, later called the Cid was born in Vivar, a village north of Burgos. Vivar was the fief of his father, Diego Lainez, a minor nobleman. About 1058 his father died, and Rodrigo went to live in the household of Prince Sancho. When the prince became King Sancho II in 1065, he gave Rodrigo the highest position at court, that of standard bearer or head of the royal armies. Soon after, in order to settle a jurisdictional dispute between Navarre and Castile, Rodrigo defeated a Navarrese knight in single combat, gaining thereby the epithet of Campeador (from the Latin *campidoctoris,* "one who captures fields").

In 1067 Sancho and Rodrigo besieged the Islamic kingdom of Saragossa. Rodrigo was the outstanding figure in this siege, and it may have been at this time that Christians and Arabs alike began to call him Cidi or Cid (from the Arabic *sayyidi,* "my lord"). In January 1072 Sancho and his brother Alfonso, the king of León, battled at Golpejera. Sancho won the day and forced Alfonso into exile. Their sister Urraca then began to conspire against Sancho at Zamora. Sancho besieged this city and was murdered there in October 1072.

After the Cid forced Alfonso to swear that he had no complicity in Sancho's assassination, Alfonso became also king of Castile.

The Cid continued in the royal service and married Alfonso's niece Jimena in 1074. But he was too powerful and popular for Alfonso's taste. The Cid's enemies at court declared that he was not a faithful vassal but a traitor, and the King believed them. Thus after a victorious campaign against Toledo, the Cid was exiled from Castile in the summer of 1081. He spent his first decade of exile fighting for various Christian and Moslem rulers. Throughout he remained loyal to Alfonso, despite the King's steadfast refusal to forgive him.

In 1090 the Cid, in coalition with the kings of Saragossa and Aragon, concentrated on repelling the advance of the Berber Almoravids in eastern Spain. In November 1092 he began a siege of Valencia, and the city finally fell in June 1094. As ruler of Valencia, which he captured in the name of Alfonso VI but governed as an autonomous territory, the Cid strove to build up the Christian presence in the largely Moslem town. He ruled there until his death on July 10, 1099. His widow Jimena continued to rule, but in 1102 she was forced to abandon Valencia to the Almoravids.

## Further Reading

The most thorough study of the Cid is by Ramón Menéndez Pidal, Spain's foremost Cid scholar, *The Cid and His Spain* (2 vols., 1929; trans. 1934). A popular account is Stephen Clissold, *In Search of the Cid* (1965).

## Additional Sources

Matthews, John, *El Cid, champion of Spain,* Poole, Dorset:
Firebird Books; New York, NY: Distributed in the U.S. by
Sterling Pub. Co., 1988.
Matthews, John, *Warriors of medieval times,* Poole, Dorset En-
gland: Firebird Books; New York, N.Y.: Distributed in the U.S.
by Sterling Pub., 1993. □

# Tansu Çiller

**The controversial politician and leader of the True Path Party, Tansu Çiller (born 1946), served as the prime minister of Turkey from 1993 until 1996, during a period of extreme political upheaval and economic volatility. She began her career as a professor of economics before entering politics in 1990.**

Tansu Çiller was born in 1946 in Istanbul into a comfortable middle-class home, the daughter of a retired government official. She went to the American Girls' School and then on to Bosphorus University (formerly Robert College), from which she graduated with a degree in economics in 1967. In 1963, at the age of 17, she married Özer Üçuran, who adopted her second name; he soon became an influential figure in her life. Çiller came to the United States for higher education and received her Master's degree and Ph.D. in economics from the Universities of New Hampshire and Connecticut, respectively. Before returning to Turkey in 1973 she taught economics at Franklin and Marshall College in Pennsylvania.

Çiller joined the faculty as assistant professor of economics at Bosphorus University in Istanbul in 1974 and was promoted to associate professor in 1978 and professor in 1983. During these years she established good relations with Turkey's business community and wrote a number of reports on the country's economic problems for TÜSIAD, the acronym for the Turkish Association of Businessmen and Industrialists. These reports account for most of her academic publications. Meanwhile her husband had gone into business, acquiring the franchise for "7-Eleven" stores in Turkey and the directorship of a bank that went bankrupt in the economic crisis of the 1980s. However, this did not undermine the financial fortunes of the Çillers, who had acquired great wealth through speculation in land and real estate.

The 1980s were a turbulent decade politically for Turkey. After the military takeover of September 12, 1980, all political activity was frozen, parties were dissolved, and politicians banned from politics. When politics was restored in 1983 only new and untainted people were allowed to form parties. The door was thrown open to a new generation of politicians, of whom Turgut Ozal became the most famous. Tansu Çiller did not enter politics at that point; she came into the public eye in the late 1980s as one of the critics of Turgut Ozal's economic policies. The support she enjoyed in the business community enabled her to enter

Süleyman Demirel's circle as a consultant on economic matters. With the fortunes of his True Path Party (TPP) on the rise, Demirel had her join the party in 1990. When general elections were held in October 1991, she was one of the architects of her party's economic policy. The TPP emerged as the largest party in Parliament with 178 seats but without the majority necessary to form its own government. Çiller won the seat for Istanbul and entered Parliament.

Demirel formed a coalition government with the Social Democratic Populist Party (SHP) and appointed Çiller to be minister of state responsible for the economy. Her economic stabilization program was presented on January 17, 1992. Its goal was to stabilize the economy by sustaining a reasonable growth rate of 5.5 percent in 1992 (as compared to 2 percent in 1991); by tackling inflation, which stood at around 70 percent, and reducing it to 42 percent; and by narrowing the budget deficit. Çiller proposed reforming the taxation system to broaden the base and restructuring the state-owned economic enterprises so that they would become profitable and therefore attractive to private buyers. The success of the program also depended on foreign investments and loans, and therefore Çiller traveled around the world selling her ideas, especially in Germany, the United States, and Japan.

One can only speculate as to how Tansu Çiller's political career would have progressed had not certain events intervened to open new doors. The death of President Turgut Ozal in April 1993 left the presidency vacant, leading to Süleyman Demirel's election on May 16. That left the posts of leader of the True Path Party and prime minister vacant. Çiller was not the obvious choice; she was a new-comer to the party and relatively inexperienced, and there were more seasoned candidates (such men as Cindoruk and Ismet Sezgin) who had stronger claims to leadership. But Çiller had the advantage of being younger, female, attractive, and well educated as compared to her rivals. Not only was she an economist, she was fluent in English and German, had a cosmopolitan outlook, and was well acquainted with the West. Around the world voters seemed to prefer young, dynamic leaders, and Turkey was no exception. The young Mesut Yilmaz had taken over the Motherland Party from Ozal; İnönü's SHP went in the same direction when he retired and a younger leader was elected in September 1993. It made good political sense to elect an attractive woman, happily married with two sons, as TPP's leader and thereby strengthen the party's position in the coming election. She would counter the qualities of her rivals, especially among female voters, who made up over half the electorate. The open support that the business community gave Çiller could not be ignored either. Moreover, in the West her success was expected to enhance Turkey's image as a forward-looking Muslim country in an Islamic world which too often seemed to be looking to the past for inspiration.

Tansu Çiller was elected leader of the TPP on June 13, 1993, and was appointed Turkey's first woman prime minister. Her coalition with the SHP won the vote of confidence on June 25 and Tansu Çiller took charge of Turkey's destiny. Her success would depend on her ability to find answers to Turkey's many problems, especially the economy and the Kurdish question, and these would test the abilities of any leader.

As time passed Tansu Çiller proved ineffective at controlling the parliament, much less the dire problems facing the Turkish people. Kurdish uprisings, runaway inflation, and a desperately shrinking economy plagued her tenure as prime minister. The intrinsic instability of the Turkish government further aggravated the situation. By 1995 Çiller was beset by personal accusations. She resigned under pressure in September of that year. One month later, on October 15, a vote of confidence was taken and Çiller was permitted to continue as acting prime minister until the matter could be resolved. Early in 1996 Çiller agreed to a coalition government whereby Mesut Yilmaz of the Motherland Party would serve as prime minister until 1997, at which time Çiller would reclaim the job. Çiller, however, never returned to her post as the serious allegations against her continued to mount. On June 6, 1996 Yilmaz was himself censured by the Parliament, and the government collapsed. By July 8 a new coalition had been formed. This time Çiller agreed to serve as deputy prime minister under Necmettin Erbakan of the Welfare Party. According to the arrangement Çiller would be reinstated as prime minister the following year. On June 18, 1997 Erbakan resigned in an effort to force an early election, which in turn would prevent Çiller from reclaiming the position of prime minister.

## Further Reading

For more information on Çiller, see *The Economist,* March 25, 1995; October 21, 1995; March 9, 1996; June 8, 1996; June 15, 1996; June 21, 1997. On the Internet, visit the site http://www.mfa.gov.tr:80/grupb/ciller.htm. □

# Cimabue

**The Italian painter Cimabue (active last quarter of 13th century) worked in an Italo-Byzantine style characterized by a vigor and vivacity that set it apart from the more conventional art of his times and anticipated the more natural style of the 14th century.**

Cimabue whose given name was Cenno de' Pepi, was probably born before 1250. The earliest document associated with him dates from June 8, 1272. The only other documented phase of Cimabue's life relates to his apse mosaic, *St. John the Evangelist,* in the Pisa Cathedral, dated 1301-1302. He died sometime after mid-1302.

Some hint of Cimabue's personality comes from literary sources. Dante mentioned Cimabue in the *Divine Comedy* but was more concerned with the moral lesson to be taught about the transitory nature of fame than with Cimabue's character: "Once, Cimabue thought to hold the field/ In painting; Giotto's all the rage today;/ The other's fame lies in the dust concealed" (*Purgatory,* Canto XI, 94-96, trans. Dorothy L. Sayers).

In an early-14th-century commentary on the *Divine Comedy,* Cimabue was described as arrogant and haughty; however, Lorenzo Ghiberti's account of the legend, later repeated by Giorgio Vasari, of how Cimabue discovered Giotto as a shepherd drawing on a flat stone and offered to train the boy in the artist's craft would suggest that Cimabue's disposition had a charitable side as well.

The majority of extant examples of Cimabue's art consists of frescoes and panel paintings. The most extensive of these are the frescoes in the transept and apse of the Upper Church of S. Francesco in Assisi (ca. 1290). Vasari declared that Cimabue was responsible for all the decorations in the Upper Church except for the series of frescoes given over to the legend of St. Francis. Modern critics have tended to see Cimabue as the guiding spirit behind the decoration of the transept and apse but not necessarily the author of every scene.

The large *Crucifixion* scene in the left transept is the masterpiece among Cimabue's works in Assisi. The fresco, which now has the appearance of a photographic negative, the result of the blackening of lead pigments, is powerful and evocative. Cimabue took a Byzantine iconographic form, the dead Christ on the cross, and filled it with human drama. From the gentle rhythms among the faithful on the left to the pulsating hysteria of the angels fluttering about the cross, Cimabue related the story of the Crucifixion in direct, humanly comprehensible terms. The firmly rendered figures possess a plasticity and fullness not commonly found in late-13th-century painting and certainly explain why he was cited as the first painter to break away from the "Greek" manner and develop a more natural style of painting.

The Evangelists' portraits in the vaults of the crossing also reveal Cimabue's skill in creating full and plastic forms. Placed in half of the rather awkward triangular format, balanced in the other half with a cityscape, the Evangelists sit on wooden thrones drawn in distorted perspective. Their heads and hands have a volume quite consistent with the three-dimensional rendering of the drapery.

In the Lower Church of S. Francesco is the fresco *Madonna Enthroned with Angels and St. Francis.* It is one of Cimabue's most touching works, although it is in poor condition now.

Two painted wood crucifixes demonstrate the evolution of Cimabue's style. In the earlier work, in S. Domenico, Arezzo, which probably dates from before the frescoes in Assisi (that is, before ca. 1290), the artist retained traditional Italo-Byzantine conventions, especially in the linear definition of muscles, treatment of the hair, gold striations in the opaque loincloth, and two bust-length portraits in the terminals. The later work, formerly in Sta Croce, Florence (destroyed 1966), which probably dates from about the same time as the murals in Assisi, showed a new softness of modeling and abandonment of some Byzantine conventions, like gold striations. The torso of Christ was modeled with broad, widely varied tones which tended to suppress the tortoiseshell appearance seen in the Arezzo crucifix. In the Florence crucifix Cimabue was moving further along the path toward greater naturalism.

The large *Madonna Enthroned* from the Church of Sta Trinita in Florence (1280-1285) is one of the best paintings to study in order to understand Cimabue's art. The artist retained a number of Byzantine motifs but forsook the austere, hieratic remoteness of the typical Byzantine Virgin for a softer, more human warmth. She is more accessible, more loving, more the earthly mother. Cimabue, furthermore, showed a concern for the realistic depiction of space in his arrangement of the angels around the throne and in the perspective of the throne itself. The four busts which appear in openings below the throne are without precedent. They give the panel an architectural stability and importance not found in any other work of the period.

## Further Reading

The literature on Cimabue is substantial, with most of the work in Italian and German. Among English language works Eugenio Battisti's monograph *Cimabue* (1963; trans. 1967) is the most useful. It includes complete transcriptions of all documents, most of the earliest sources, a *catalogue raisonné,* a good bibliography, and especially fine color and black-and-white reproductions. Alfred Nicholson, *Cimabue: A Critical Study* (1932), is basic for an understanding and appreciation of Cimabue's role in the evolution of Italian painting. It includes very useful appendices, with summaries of documents and sources and lists of authentic and attributed works. ☐

# Domenico Cimarosa

**The works of the Italian opera composer Domenico Cimarosa (1749-1801) typify the style of Italian opera buffa, or comic opera, in the late 18th century.**

Domenico Cimarosa was born in Averso near Naples, the son of a very poor family. At the age of 12 he entered the Conservatory of S. Maria di Loreto; he studied composition, voice, and keyboard and sang major parts in conservatory performances.

Cimarosa's first opera, *Le stravaganze del cante,* was produced in Naples in 1772, the year he left the conservatory. From then until 1780 he moved between Rome and Naples, composing 15 operas for the two cities. By the 1780s he was the rival of Giovanni Paisiello, until then the acknowledged leader among opera composers in Italy. Italian companies performed Cimarosa's works in London, Paris, Dresden, and Vienna.

In 1787 Cimarosa went to St. Petersburg, Russia, as chamber composer to Catherine II, joining a long line of Italians who had held posts there beginning in the early 18th century. He composed two operas, *Cleopatra* and *La vergine del sole,* as well as cantatas and vocal and instrumental works during his stay. His constitution was not strong enough to stand St. Petersburg's weather, so he left in 1791 to become conductor to Leopold II in Vienna. It was here that he composed his masterpiece, *Il matrimonio segreto,* in 1792. This, his most popular work, is the only one to remain in the repertory. When Leopold II died that year, Cimarosa lost his position and returned to Naples, where he became conductor to the king and music teacher to the royal children in 1793. In 1799 he was imprisoned for publicly expressing his sympathy for Napoleon. After his release he left Naples for St. Petersburg; on the journey he died in Venice in 1801.

In addition to 61 operas, many with two versions, Cimarosa composed oratorios, cantatas, miscellaneous vocal works, and instrumental works, including 32 one-movement piano sonatas. His melodic gifts so impressed Goethe that he wrote two texts, *Die Spröde* and *Die Bekehrte,* to be sung to Cimarosa's melodies.

Cimarosa's operatic style is similar to that of many of his Italian contemporaries. The speed at which he composed is reflected in his tendency to use conventional procedures. However, he wrote dramatic ensembles very well, both within acts and as finales, to carry forward the dramatic action. Although these ensembles do not show the breadth and depth of a Mozart, they are well above the standard of contemporary practice.

## Further Reading

Both Paul Henry Lang, *Music in Western Civilization* (1941), and Donald J. Grout, *A Short History of Opera* (1947; 2d ed. 1965), survey the 18th-century Italian tradition and discuss Cimarosa. See also George T. Ferris, *The Great Italian and French Composers* (1883).

## Additional Sources

Iovino, Roberto, *Domenico Cimarosa: operista napoletano,* Milano: Camunia, 1992. □

# Joseph Cinque

**Joseph Cinque (ca. 1813-ca. 1879) was a West African who led a slave mutiny on the Cuban *Amistad* ship in 1839. It led to a celebrated trial in United States courts, which held that slaves escaping from illegal bondage should be treated as free men.**

Joseph Cinque was born the son of a Mende headman in the village of Mani, in modern Sierra Leone. A rice farmer and trader, he was enslaved for debt and sold to the notorious Spanish slaver Pedro Blanco, on Lomboko Island at the mouth of the Gallinas River, in April 1839. Cinque was then carried to Havana, where he was resold with 51 others, many of them Mendians, and shipped aboard the coasting schooner *Amistad* bound for the Cuban sugar plantations near the port of Guanaja, Puerto Principe.

On June 30 Cinque incited the slaves to revolt at sea, killing the captain and cook and taking prisoner their owners, two merchants named Ruiz and Montez. Cinque tried to force Montez to pilot the vessel to Africa, but Montez reversed the course repeatedly, zigzagging up the North American coast. They were captured off Montauk Point, Long Island, by the U.S. Coast Guard vessel *Washington* and were brought to New London, where the ship, cargo, and rebellious slaves were claimed for salvage money, while Ruiz and Montez sought to regain possession of them.

President Van Buren and Secretary of State John Forsyth, sympathetic to the slaveholders' claims and pressured by the Spanish government, tried to remove the case from the courts and transport the Africans to Cuba. But the Connecticut courts would not release them, and the plight of Cinque and his companions, jailed in New Haven, aroused abolitionist forces led by the New York merchant Lewis Tappan.

Cinque's heroic figure and commanding personality lent itself to the drama, and he was widely lionized as a symbol of the abolitionist cause. The abolitionists argued that the Africans, illegally enslaved, were justified in revolting to regain freedom and were innocent of any true crime in killing their captors to achieve freedom. In a dramatic appeal before the Supreme Court in 1841, the 73-year-old former president John Quincy Adams charged the Federal government with wrongful interference in the courts and obstruction of justice through partiality for slaveholders and antipathy toward blacks. The Court's decision, given on March 9, 1841, went for the abolitionists and set the Africans free.

Tappan and his associates then intended to found an African mission, using Cinque's party as a nucleus. Once in Sierra Leone, however, the not ungrateful but independent-minded Africans clashed with their mentors and soon deserted the enterprise. Cinque established himself as an independent power and became, according to rumors, a successful slave trader himself. Years later, in 1879, he was reported to have reappeared, to die and be buried at the old mission on Sherbro Island.

## Further Reading

The fullest account of Cinque is William A. Owens, *Slave Mutiny: The Revolt on the Schooner Amistad* (1953), a dramatized account based on research into the documents of the *Amistad* collection of the New Haven Historical Society, Supreme Court case records, personal papers, and records of the American Missionary Association. Cinque and the *Amistad* mutiny are discussed in the context of the slave trade and the international efforts to suppress it in John R. Spears, "The Story of the Amistad," in *The American Slave Trade: An Account of Its Origin, Growth and Suppression* (1900; reissued 1967 with a new introduction), and in Daniel P. Mannix and Malcolm Cowley, *Black Cargoes* (1962). Contemporary accounts and documentation are found in John W. Barber, *A History of the Amistad Captives . . . with Biographical Sketches . . . also, an Account of the Trials* (1840). The key judicial decisions in the *Amistad* case are contained in Helen Tunnicliff Catterall, ed., *Judicial Cases Concerning American Slavery and the Negro,* vol. 4 (1936). □

# Henry G. Cisneros

**Politician, college professor, cabinet member, and network executive, Henry G. Cisneros (born 1947) was elected mayor of San Antonio in 1981, the first Hispanic mayor in Texas, and became by the mid-1980s the nation's most prominent and publicly visible Hispanic leader.**

Born in 1947, Henry Cisneros was the eldest of five children of Mexican-American George and Mexican-born Elvira Cisneros. Henry was raised in what was later described as a model home environment for an upwardly mobile ethnic family. His father, a civil servant at a nearby military base, and his mother were keenly ambitious for their children, prescribing piano lessons, Scout memberships, visits to the opera and symphony, and limited television viewing only after their homework and family responsibilities had been fulfilled.

The Cisneros family switched from Spanish to English use in the home when the children were born because the language of the schools was English and home use of the language of instruction would certainly help them to do better. It paid off. All five children became college graduates, including two Ph.Ds. Future mayor Henry Cisneros, who received a B.A. degree from Texas A&M University, an M.A. from Harvard University, and a Ph.D. in public administration from George Washington University in 1975, was selected as a White House Fellow and later worked for the Department of Health, Education, and Welfare when it was under Elliott Richardson.

## Entry Into Politics

In 1974 doctoral candidate Cisneros returned to San Antonio, where he was employed as an assistant professor at the University of Texas branch campus. Always interested in public policy and politics, Cisneros won a seat on the city council in 1975 and was reelected in 1977 and 1979. Although sensitive to the special needs of the Hispanic community, Cisneros studiously avoided an association with one of the city's most controversial advocacy groups, Communities Organized for Public Service (COPS), which specialized in Saul Alinsky style 1960s confrontation politics with the city fathers, planners, and future employers. It was not only a matter of style but a deep conviction on Cisneros's part that confrontation tactics could be counterproductive to the city's economic health. He also had a strong belief in the socially redeeming power of economic growth.

Elected mayor in 1981 at the age of 33 by a landslide 63 percent of the vote, which included solid Hispanic support and a sizable Anglo vote, Cisneros went on to enlarge his election majority in 1983 to an astonishing 94 percent of the vote and to 73 percent in 1985. Clearly his style and programs had won over the hearts and minds of residents of all colors and creeds. Downtown development, job expansion, and new factories and businesses were the hallmarks of the Cisneros administrations. The mayor boasted that he spent 85 percent of his time recruiting and luring high technology industry to his city. An unabashed booster, he was a firm believer in the benefits of economic

expansion and business growth. No growth, he warned, translates into fewer opportunities and stunted mobility for the citizens.

He described himself as a "technocrat" and seemed to be in tune with the temper of the times in helping to re-start the economic engines and rekindle economic growth. He stressed the need for economic expansion and not the expansion of welfare as a solution to social problems. As one observer noted: "A Martin Luther King he is not." The mayor backed up his boosterism with substance. When once told by a potential industrial re-locator that the city's University of Texas branch lacked programs in key engineering fields, Cisneros got together a committee that persuaded the state educational authorities to remedy that need.

## Scandal Tarnishes Reputation

Cisneros married his high school sweetheart, Mary Alice Perez, in 1969 and was the father of two daughters and a son. In 1988 his public announcement of an extra-marital affair with Linda Medlar led to his resignation as mayor and the near destruction of his marriage. He reunited with his wife primarily because his infant son had been born the previous year with a defective heart. Although Cisneros supposedly ended the affair with Medlar, he continued making support payments to her after he left office and founded Cisneros Assets Management Company. In 1993 Cisneros was appointed Secretary of Housing and Urban Development (HUD) by President Bill Clinton. As HUD secretary Cisneros worked hard to reverse decades of Federal housing policy that promoted racism and to make the department's programs more efficient. Despite his efforts, though, the Medlar controversy would not go away. Upon accepting his position with HUD, Cisneros had ended his payments to Medlar. In 1994 the former mistress sued Cisneros, citing that she had been promised $4,000 a month until her daughter graduated from college. For his part, Cisneros claimed that his $148,000 annual salary as HUD secretary was much less than he received as a private sector consultant and speaker, and made continued payments a financial impossibility. The core of Cisneros's problems, however, centered around his claim to the FBI of having provided $60,000 to Medlar between 1990 and 1992 while Medlar's records showed payments of $213,000.

The scandal worsened in late 1994 as tapes of conversations between Cisneros and Medlar surfaced in the press. From 1992 to 1993, Medlar had secretly taped her conversations with Cisneros. She sold the tapes to the tabloid TV news show *Inside Edition*. The fall-out from this unwanted publicity led to a further FBI investigation of Cisneros's financial reports used during his cabinet background check. In 1995 Attorney General Janet Reno appointed a special counsel to ascertain whether or not Cisneros had lied to the FBI. National Public Radio (NPR) reported Cisneros response as "I regret any mistakes that I may have made but affirm once again that I have at no point violated the public's trust." That same year Cisneros settled the Medlar suit for $49,000

## Resignation From HUD

Throughout his ordeal, Cisneros continued to receive the support of the Clinton administration, but decided in 1996 not to remain in his post during the president's second term in office. The *Associated Press* reported Cisneros's reasoning as financial. "Really, I came to do this for four years. I prayed I could stretch the finances that far," he said. "This is about as far as I can stretch it." At the time of Cisneros's departure from HUD in 1997, the investigation into his financial records was still ongoing.

In January of 1997 Cisneros was named president and chief operating officer of Univision Communications, the parent company of the dominant Hispanic network in the United States.

## Further Reading

For his early life, see Richard Erickson, "Cisneros: Media Creation or Right Man," *Advertising Age* (June 1981), and biographical file from the mayor's office. For his later life and public career, see Nicholas Leman, "First Hispanic," *Esquire* (December 1984); Irwin Ross, "Mayor Cisneros of San Antonio," *Readers Digest* (December 1984); and *U.S. News and World Report* (December 10, 1984; May 20, 1985). A full-length biography *Cisneros: Portrait of a New American* by Kemper Diehl and Jan Jarboe, was published in 1985.

For more information on Cisneros's resignation from HUD, see *Lubbock Online* (http://lubbockonline.com/news/112296/cisneros.htm). In-depth coverage of Cisneros's move to Univision Communications can be found in an article by Tony Cantu at http://www.hisp.com/apr97/cisneros.html. (July 1997). □

# Sandra Cisneros

**Drawing heavily upon her childhood experiences and ethnic heritage Sandra Cisneros (born 1954) creates characters who are distinctly Hispanic and often isolated from mainstream American culture by emphasizing dialogue and sensory imagery over traditional narrative structures.**

B orn in Chicago, Cisneros was the only daughter among seven children. Concerning her childhood, Cisneros recalled that because her brothers attempted to control her and expected her to assume a traditional female role, she often felt like she had "seven fathers." The family frequently moved between the United States and Mexico because of her father's homesickness for his native country and his devotion to his mother who lived there. Consequently, Cisneros often felt homeless and displaced: "Because we moved so much, and always in neighborhoods that appeared like France after World War II— empty lots and burned-out buildings—I retreated inside myself." She began to read extensively, finding comfort in such works as Virginia Lee Burton's *The Little House* and Lewis Carroll's *Alice's Adventures in Wonderland.* Cisneros periodically wrote poems and stories throughout her child-

hood and adolescence, but she did not find her literary voice until attending the University of Iowa's Writers Workshop in the late 1970s. A breakthrough occurred for Cisneros during a discussion of French philosopher Gaston Bachelard's *The Poetics of Space* and his metaphor of a house; she realized that her experiences as a Hispanic woman were unique and outside the realm of dominant American culture. She observed: "Everyone seemed to have some communal knowledge which I did not have—and then I realized that the metaphor of *house* was totally wrong for me. . . . I had no such house in my memories. . . . This caused me to question myself, to become defensive. What did I, Sandra Cisneros, know? What *could* I know? My classmates were from the best schools in the country. They had been bred as fine hothouse flowers. I was a yellow weed among the city's cracks."

Shortly after participating in the Iowa Workshop, Cisneros decided to write about conflicts directly related to her upbringing, including divided cultural loyalties, feelings of alienation, and degradation associated with poverty. Incorporating these concerns into *The House on Mango Street,* a work that took nearly five years to complete, Cisneros created the character Esperanza, a poor, Hispanic adolescent who longs for a room of her own and a house of which she can be proud. Esperanza ponders the disadvantages of choosing marriage over education, the importance of writing as an emotional release, and the sense of confusion associated with growing up. In the story "Hips," for example, Esperanza agonizes over the repercussions of her body's physical changes: "One day you wake up and there

they are. Ready and waiting like a new Buick with the key in the ignition. Ready to take you where?'' Written in what Penelope Mesic called ''a loose and deliberately simple style, halfway between a prose poem and the awkwardness of semiliteracy,'' the pieces in *The House on Mango Street* won praise for their lyrical narratives, vivid dialogue, and powerful descriptions.

*Woman Hollering Creek and Other Stories* is a collection of twenty-two narratives revolving around numerous Mexican-American characters living near San Antonio, Texas. Ranging from a few paragraphs to several pages, the stories in this volume contain the interior monologues of individuals who have been assimilated into American culture despite their sense of loyalty to Mexico. In ''Never Marry a Mexican,'' for example, a young Hispanic woman begins to feel contempt for her white lover because of her emerging feelings of inadequacy and cultural guilt resulting from her inability to speak Spanish. Although Cisneros addresses important contemporary issues associated with minority status throughout *Woman Hollering Creek and Other Stories,* critics have described her characters as idiosyncratic, accessible individuals capable of generating compassion on a universal level. One reviewer observed: ''In this sensitively structured suite of sketches, [Cisneros's] irony defers to her powers of observation so that feminism and cultural imperialism, while important issues here, do not overwhelm the narrative.''

Although Cisneros is noted primarily for her fiction, her poetry has also garnered attention. In *My Wicked Wicked Ways,* her third volume of verse, Cisneros writes about her native Chicago, her travels in Europe, and, as reflected in the title, sexual guilt resulting from her strict Catholic upbringing. A collection of sixty poems, each of which resemble a short story, this work further evidences Cisneros's penchant for merging various genres. Gary Soto explained: ''Cisneros's poems are intrinsically narrative, but not large, meandering paragraphs. She writes deftly with skill and idea, in the 'show-me-don't-tell-me' vein, and her points leave valuable impressions.'' In her poetry, as in all her works, Cisneros incorporates Hispanic dialect, impressionistic metaphors, and social commentary in ways that reveal the fears and doubts unique to Hispanic women. She stated: ''If I were asked what it is I write about, I would have to say I write about those ghosts inside that haunt me, that will not let me sleep, of that which even memory does not like to mention. . . . Perhaps later there will be a time to write by inspiration. In the meantime, in my writing as well as in that of other Chicanas and other women, there is the necessary phase of dealing with those ghosts and voices most urgently haunting us, day by day.''

## Further Reading

*Americas Review,* Spring, 1987, pp. 69-76.
*Bloomsbury Review,* July-August, 1988, p. 21.
*Chicano-Riquena,* Fall-Winter, 1985, pp. 109-19.
*Glamour,* November, 1990, pp. 256-57.
*Los Angeles Times,* May 7, 1991, p. F1.
*Los Angeles Times Book Review,* April 28, 1991, p. 3.
*Mirabella,* April, 1991, p. 46. □

# Souleymane Cissé

**The Malian filmmaker Souleymane Cissé (born 1940), known in Africa for his documentary and feature films, was considered one of the major African filmmakers of the late 20th century. He was the first African to win a major award at the Cannes Film Festival in France.**

Souleymane Cissé was born in Bamako, Mali, in 1940. He attended his first film at age seven, and thereafter his enthusiasm for film sometimes interfered with his school work, since by age ten he was attending theaters daily. He was educated in Bamako and in Dakar, Senegal, where his family lived for several years. After completing his schooling, Cissé was trained as a film projectionist in Moscow on a three-month scholarship in 1961. He returned to Moscow in 1963, again on scholarship, and studied filmmaking at the State Institute of Cinema until 1969. When Cissé returned to Mali he became the first director of SCINFOMA (Service Cinémato-graphique du Ministère de l'Information du Mali).

Cissé made three films with other students in Moscow, one of which, *L'Aspirant* (*The Aspirant;* 1968), was awarded special mention by the State Institute of Cinema. However, he has said that he learned how to make films in his early years at SCINFOMA, where he made more than thirty newsreels and documentary films, carefully examining the results of his work. Cissé made films so that people could understand African societies. He aimed to depict faithfully the cultural heritage, problems, and aspirations of Malian and other African people. The inspiration for his films came from his observations of life around him.

Cissé's feature films photographed in Mali are in the Bambara language and have received awards at African and other international film festivals. In contrast, *Waati,* about apartheid and the need for Africans to get to know each other, was filmed in Abidjan, Ivory Coast, Namibia, and South Africa.

*Den Muso* (*The Young Girl;* 1974), Cissé's first feature film, is about a deaf-mute urban Muslim girl who becomes pregnant by one of her father's employees and is rejected by her family. In addition to telling Tenin's story, Cissé examined problems of young women who live in urban areas and the moral conflicts that arise from adhering to ''traditional'' values in contemporary urban society. *Den Muso* won the bronze prize at the Carthage Film Festival.

*Baara* (*Work;* 1978) won major awards at FESPACO (Festival Panafricain du Cinéma d'Ouagadougou) and the Carthage, Nantes, and Namur film festivals. It is about a young porter who has come from the countryside to the city where he eventually finds work at a textile factory with an engineer whose ideas about labor organization are too democratic for his employer. The film exposes the greed and corruption of the business elite and highlights the emerging social awareness of workers and women. The musical score by Lamine Katé is based on contemporary folk tradition and its lyrics are used as additional commentary on the condition of workers.

*Finyé* (*The Wind;* 1982), which also takes place in an urban setting, won major awards at FESPACO and Carthage and was shown in the A Certain Regard section at Cannes in 1983. It is about love between two students whose parents, respectively a military governor and a traditional chief, disapprove of the relationship. The two students participate in a protest over the falsification of exam results and are jailed. Cissé's theme is the recognition of the power of mass protests against the government. Like Cissé's two earlier feature films, it is grounded in realities of Malian life that are meaningful elsewhere in Africa.

*Yeelen* (*Brightness;* 1987) is about the cultural heritage of the Bambara and other Mande-speaking peoples of West Africa. It is based on oral tradition and includes a complete initiation ritual of the Komo secret society, which Malians know about but few have ever seen. The plot concerns the conflict between generations, a father and son, and the search for and acquisition of knowledge. In *Yeelen* Cissé deliberately changed his style from that of a didactic sociopolitical filmmaker to a more expressive style grounded in Bambara cosmology and concepts of time and space. Yet Cissé considered *Yeelen* his most political film. Critics praised *Yeelen* for its dazzling photography, excellent musical score, superb acting, embodiment of mythology, and universal accessibility and significance. In 1987 Mali awarded Cissé the Chevalier du Mérit National for *Yeelen,* which was awarded the Jury Prize at Cannes.

Cissé, like some other African filmmakers, formed his own production company, Les Films Cissé, and produced low-budget films in natural settings. He used local actors and actresses who had not been trained in a drama school and many of whom had not previously acted in a film. Les Films Cissé produced videos of his later feature films, which enabled many Malians who could not attend a theater to enjoy his films. Cissé's feature films have been subtitled in many languages and have been shown worldwide. In 1991 Cissé established the N'Fa Cissé, an award which is given annually in Mali for artistic creation.

Cissé's productions retain their perennial appeal at film festivals, and reviewers never tire of expressing approval and providing further insight into the meaning and implications of his works. He was featured in assorted commemorative documentary collections including the souvenir manual of the Cannes film festival in 1992. In 1994 Rithy Panh produced a videocassette about Souleymane Cissé as part of a series of tapes on contemporary cinema, and Hegel Goutier interviewed Cissé for *Courier* in 1996.

## Further Reading

There is a large literature on Cissé written in French. Biographical background and an analysis of his early films is included in Françoise Pfaff, *Twenty-five Black African Filmmakers* (1988). An interview by Manthia Diawara, "Souleymane Cissé's Light on Africa" in *Black Film Review* (1988) focuses on *Yeelen.* James Leahy comments briefly on all of Cissé's feature and student films in "Stories of the Past—Souleymane Cissé," *Monthly Film Bulletin* (November 1988).

## Additional Sources

Shiri, Keith, *Directory of African Film-Makers and Films,* Greenwood Press, 1992.
Nowell-Smith, Geoffrey (Ed.), *The Oxford History of World Cinema,* Oxford University Press, 1996.
*Courier, Africa-Caribbean-Pacific-European,* November-December 1996. □

# André-Gustave Citroën

**French automobile manufacturer André-Gustave Citroën (1878-1935) brought the cost-and time-saving methods of mass-production to the European automotive industry. His Type A car, introduced in 1919, became the European version of Henry Ford's Model T, bringing the automobile within the grasp of the average consumer. His TA 7 was another long-running success, becoming the first popular car to feature front-wheel drive.**

André-Gustave Citroën revolutionized the French automobile industry in the early 1900s with his creation of mass-produced vehicles that were affordable to the average consumer. His cars were known for their innovation designs and features that focused on the comfort and practical needs of the driver, rather than placing a priority on style. The durability of Citroën's vehicles was highlighted in the 1920s with a series of strenuous long-distance scientific expeditions over the continents of Africa and Asia that used specially adapted caterpillar tractors supplied by the manufacturer. Although he eventually lost control of his business in 1935, Citroën is remembered for his daring engineering and business ideas that brought Europe into the technological and consumer age. David Owen, in an *Automobile Quarterly* article, summed up the ongoing influence of Citroën in the company he founded and throughout the automotive industry: "His ideas, attitudes and influences have lived on through successive takeovers and mergers [in his Citroën automobile company] in such an extraordinary way that even now Citroën cars owe far more to him than those of most other firms have inherited from their original creators."

Citroën was born on February 5, 1878, in Paris, France. He was the fifth child of a Jewish family originating in Amsterdam that had accumulated a substantial fortune in the diamond trade. As a young child, however, his home was filled with financial and personal tragedy. His parents were the victims of an investment scam which claimed most of their money. When the boy was six, he lost both parents with his mother's death and father's suicide. He was subsequently placed in the Lycé Concordat at age seven and then distinguished himself as a top student at the Lycée Louis le Grand, graduating in 1894. His excellent grades won him entrance to the highly-regarded École Polytechnique. But there his interest in academics lagged. When he left the school in 1900 he did not follow his more successful class-

particularly drawn to the automobile industry personally. But after a fact-finding trip to the American auto plants of Henry Ford in 1912, he began to see the improvements that could be made to the French auto industry using assembly-line techniques.

Citroën's musings on automobile production were interrupted by the beginning of World War I in 1914. He was drafted to serve in the French artillery, where he saw that the French were at a severe disadvantage due to their limited supply of ammunition. He drafted a proposal to build a factory that could efficiently mass-produce artillery shells. The idea was immediately accepted by the French government, which provided him with the resources to establish a munitions factory on the Quai de Javel in Paris. Not only did Citroën successfully create a system for producing tens of thousands of shells a day, he was also instrumental in improving processes at all factories participating in the war effort. His other wartime activities included securing a steady supply of coal for factories and power plants as well as organizing civilian food distribution through the use of ration cards.

## Produced Affordable Cars for Europeans

When the war ended, the factory at Quai de Javel was left in Citroën's hands. The engineer decided to use the site to launch his plan for producing a practical, affordable car. His goal was to obtain the kind of success that Henry Ford had had in the United States by changing the image of the automobile from an exotic toy of the rich to a pragmatic item within the financial reach of the working class. His Type A automobile began production in 1919. This initial model featured an efficient four-cylinder engine, an electric starter and lights, and a top speed of 40 miles per hour. Citroën's cars were completely assembled when they left the factory, an innovative development in Europe, where autos had previously required individual assembly in a specialty workshop. Word of the low-cost Type A generated consumer excitement even before the first public demonstration of the vehicle, and thousands of orders began to pour in. 2,000 cars were produced in the first year of business; that number increased to 8,000 in 1920, making Citroën the leading manufacturer of automobiles in Europe.

The Type A was soon being offered in a number of styles and sizes to meet consumer needs, including the Coupé, Limousine, City Coupé, Torpedo, and a delivery van. In 1922 a new model, the 5CV Type C, was introduced as sporty option for younger buyers. Sales continued to grow thanks to this wide variety of products as well as Citroën's uncanny marketing instinct. He gained the confidence of buyers by becoming the first company to offer test drives. By opening his own insurance company that offered low rates to Citroën owners, he was able to overcome the financial concerns of many people. He also was a talented promoter who staged exciting stunts and tests of his products to demonstrate their quality. He sent one car over a cliff and photographed the wreck to show how a collision affected it. Another automobile was burdened with a ten-ton weight in a show of strength. His most elaborate schemes were a series of long-distance scientific journeys over diffi-

mates into the professional sphere but joined the French Army as an engineer officer.

## Founded Thriving Gear Company

During a leave from the military, Citroën went to visit some relatives in the textile center of Ludz, Poland. It was there that he seized upon the idea for his first engineering success. He observed the wooden gear drives used in the cotton mills and developed an improved design. After returning to duty in Paris, he obtained a patent for a steel gear using a herringbone, or V-shaped, pattern that provided increased strength. In 1904, he started up a small workshop to produce the gears with two friends. The business grew quickly, and by 1910 it had annual sales of one million francs. By 1913, the company had tripled its sales and taken on the name of Société Anonyme des Engrenages Citroën. His first venture had at that point produced more than 500 gears, including the steering gear for the famed ocean-liner the Titanic. To accommodate the expanding company, a new factory was procured in Paris on the Quai Grenelle.

Citroën's business had attracted the attention of other engineers and manufacturers impressed with his mass-production techniques. Around 1909, he was hired as a consultant by Emile and Louis Mors, brothers who owned a prominent automobile company known for its racing vehicles. The Mors wanted to find a way to bring their quality designs to a wider clientele and increase sales by reducing costs and improving marketing techniques. Under Citroën's guidance, sales at Mors improved from 10 cars a month in 1909 to 100 a month by 1914. The engineer was not cult terrain featuring specially adapted Citroën vehicles. In December of 1922, a group of Citroën-built caterpillar tractors began the first crossing of the 2,000 mile wide Sahara Desert by motorized vehicles, completing the trip in 20 days. Eight similar tractors undertook a journey across the African continent in 1924, beginning in Algeria and passing through Central Africa before finally reaching Cape Town, Mozambique, and Madagascar. During the nine-month trip, which covered 15,000 miles, scientists and technical crews took enormous amounts of film footage and photographs of the little-known Central African regions. Another massive trek left Beirut in 1931 for a trans-Asian drive that was to end in Beijing and included the crossing of the Himalayan mountain range.

## Forced to Hand Over Business

Throughout his years of success, Citroën continued to push for innovations in his cars and production methods. His passion for new ideas led him to invest huge sums in buying out patents and developing new concepts. He also drained the company of funds with his excessive gambling habits. By the 1930s, his creditors had becoming increasingly uneasy about his financial status. Citroën hoped to quell their fears and boost the lagging sales of the Depression-era years with the introduction of his revolutionary passenger car, the Traction Avant, or TA 7. The Citroën TA 7 was the first successful car to feature front-wheel drive; it also incorporated such concepts as hydraulic brakes and an overhead valve engine. In March of 1934, Citroën arranged a demonstration of his new model to encourage financiers to support the company. During the event, the prototype's transmission fell apart, dashing all confidence in Citroën's ability to keep his company afloat.

His creditors called upon the French government to declare Citroën bankrupt and take control of the company. In 1935, the Michelin Tire Company—one of Citroën's creditors—assumed the task of running the auto company. Forced into retirement, Citroën grew despondent at the loss of his business. He became ill within a few months, and apparently having lost the will to live, he died in Paris on July 3, 1935. He never witnessed the astounding success of the TA 7, which became an incredibly popular vehicle that remained in production for more than 20 years. Through the years, the Citroën company has undergone a number of transformations, including a merger with the Peugot car company in 1974. But the spirit of its founder has accompanied the evolution of the company, which maintains a desire to produce innovative styles designed to serve the practical needs of the consumer.

## Further Reading

See also Baldwin, Nick, *The World Guide to Auto Manufacturers,* Facts on File, 1987; Dumont, Pierre, *Citroën, the Great Marque of France,* translated by Tom Ellaway, Interante, 1976; LeFevre, Georges, *An Eastern Odyssey,* translated by E. D. Swinton, Little, Brown, 1935; and Owen, David, "The Legacy of André Citroën," *Automobile Quarterly,* second quarter, 1975. □

# Liz Claiborne

**Founder of one of the world's most successful women's apparel manufacturing companies, Liz Claiborne (born 1929) was a pioneer in designing reasonably priced, good quality clothing for modern working women.**

L iz Claiborne (Elisabeth Claiborne Ortenberg) was born March 31, 1929, in Brussels, Belgium, where her father, Omer V. Claiborne, was a banker for the Morgan Guaranty Trust Company. In the 1930s Omer, his wife Louise Fenner Claiborne, and their young daughter returned to their home in New Orleans, where Liz received a strict Roman Catholic upbringing. Her father did not consider formal education important, and before Claiborne graduated from high school he sent her to Europe to study art in Belgium and France. Although her parents expected her to become an artist, Claiborne, whose mother had taught her to sew, wanted to study fashion and pursued a career as a clothing designer.

When she was 21 years old her sketch for a woman's coat won a Jacques Heim design competition sponsored by *Harper's Bazaar* magazine. With this award and her sketching ability, Claiborne began working on Seventh Avenue in New York City's garment district as a design assistant and a model. From 1950 to 1955 she held several positions designing sportswear, tailored clothing, and high fashion. From 1955 to 1960 she was a dress designer for the Dan Keller company. From 1960 to December 1975 she was the principal designer for Youth Guild, the junior dress division of Jonathan Logan, a major women's apparel manufacturer. During this time Claiborne also raised her son from her first marriage to Ben Schultz and two step-children from her second marriage to Arthur Ortenberg, a textile manufacturer and consultant.

Claiborne saw a need in the marketplace for more comfortable but professional apparel for working women. Claiborne's fashion sense told her women could use clothing that was easier to wear and softer than the tailored business suits, blouses, and bow ties then sold in department stores. Unable to convince her employer to enter the mix-and-match coordinated sportswear market for working women, Claiborne started her own company.

Liz Claiborne, Inc. was founded on January 19, 1976, with approximately $250,000, including $50,000 of Claiborne's and her husband's savings. Ortenberg was the company's secretary and treasurer; industry executive and friend Leonard Boxer was in charge of production; and the fourth key executive, Jerome Chazen, joined the company in 1977 to direct marketing operations. Sales for the first year were over $2 million, as Claiborne's collection of pants, skirts, shirts, sweaters, and jackets was instantly popular.

Priced in a moderate range, from about $40 to $100, and sold in department stores, the Liz Claiborne label became known for its good quality materials, comfortable fit, good construction, color selection, and clean silhouettes.

Not a couture designer but more of a stylist, Claiborne produced a collection of fashionably appropriate clothing that perfectly matched late-20th-century working women's clothing needs.

As sales increased from $2.6 million in 1976 to $117 million in 1981, production, delivery, and marketing demands increased in proportion. Credit for a well managed company belonged to the original management team of Ortenberg, Boxer, and Chazen. The company was regarded as one of the best managed in the highly competitive and volatile women's fashion apparel business.

Liz Claiborne, Inc. became a public company in 1981. Within a few years their stock holdings made Claiborne and Ortenberg millionaires. The company's market share continued to expand and the profits were high. To continue increasing its market share as well as to diversify its product, Claiborne expanded her fashion lines to include petites, dresses, shoes, accessories, menswear, and perfume between 1981 and 1986. Six years later there were 19 divisions. Computer analysis of sales and traveling consultants provided the company with constant feedback, making it possible to quickly fill or reduce merchandise orders. The majority of merchandise was manufactured in the Far East with an overseas staff to monitor quality control.

The company's success was partly due to what Ortenberg described as an "exploding market" of millions of baby-boomer women who during the 1980s were graduating from college and graduate schools to enter the professions. Encouraged by Claiborne's merchandise selection,

women were becoming more confident about dressing for work and selected clothing that was appropriate for work and reflected their personalities.

In 1986, when company sales reached $1.2 billion, it joined the list of *Fortune* magazine's 500 largest industrial companies in the United States; it was one of only two companies started by a woman included on the list. Also in 1986 Claiborne, who was company president, became chairman of the board and chief executive officer. Until she retired in 1989, Claiborne remained the creative force behind the company's success and advised its design teams. She always emphasized fit, color, comfort, and good value as the company's goals.

In spring 1988 the company opened its first retail stores, and by spring 1992 it had approximately 45 stores. Sales were $2.1 billion for 1992. However, by early 1993 the company began to feel the effects of a growing popularity of discount stores compared to department stores in their decreasing sales.

Claiborne and her husband retired from active management of the company in 1989 to pursue their environmental and philanthropic interests. The Liz Claiborne and Art Ortenberg Foundation was established in 1989 with assets of $10 million; it provides substantial support for wilderness preservation. They spent six months of each year at a ranch house in Swan Valley, Montana; they also had a home on Fire Island, New York, and one on the Caribbean Island of St. Barts.

In 1990 Claiborne and her husband were elected to the National Business Hall of Fame, sponsored by Junior Achievement. A few of the many honors awarded Claiborne were induction into the National Sales Hall of Fame in 1991 and an honorary Doctorate degree from the Rhode Island School of Design the same year.

Liz Claiborne Inc. remains a fashion mainstay in mid-1997. Sales for 1996 reached $2.2 billion and the company now employs over 7000. Liz Claiborne herself remains active through a variety of charities. She and her husband still travel between their homes and avoid the public eye as much as possible.

## Further Reading

There are several sources for additional information on Liz Claiborne's business and fashion sense. Elsa Klensch's interview article in *Vogue* (August 1986) gives Claiborne's views on how fashion had changed since 1976. "Can Ms. Fashion Bounce Back?" *Business Week* (January 16, 1989) discusses the company's growth, market share, and history. Valerie Steele, *Women of Fashion, Twentieth Century Designers* (1991) provides a brief perspective on the Liz Claiborne label, emphasizing its practicality and clothing for ordinary working women. *Liz Claiborne, Inc. 1992 Annual Report* describes each division and indicates its relative success. □

# Tom Clancy

**Tom Clancy (born 1947) writes novels of adventure and espionage in the international military-industrial complex that have earned him enormous popularity in the 1980s as a creator of the "techno-thriller" genre.**

Tom Clancy was born in Baltimore, Maryland, in 1947, the son of a mail carrier and a credit employee. After graduating Loyola College in Baltimore in 1969, Clancy married Wanda Thomas, an insurance agency manager, and became an insurance agent in Baltimore, and later in Hartford, Connecticut. In 1973, he joined the O.F. Bowen Agency in Owings, Maryland, becoming an owner there in 1980. His poor eyesight made him ineligible for a military career, but Clancy maintained an interest in the military and researched various aspects of the armed forces and military technology. The ideas for several novels and main characters he wrote in the 1980s were formed in the late 1970s while he was conducting research. During this time, Clancy wrote in his spare time while working and raising a family, and in 1984, his first novel, *The Hunt for Red October,* was published by The Naval Institute Press, a noncommercial publisher in Annapolis. The story of the defection of a Soviet submarine commander to the United States, the novel captured the spirit of the Reagan-era Cold War politics that called attention to Soviet military capabil-

ity and the United States' capacity to meet and surpass the Soviet challenge. *The Hunt for Red October* was noticed by President and Mrs. Reagan, who praised the book publicly and helped boost the novel to bestseller lists. Casper Weinberger, Reagan's Secretary of Defense, reviewed the book for *The Times Literary Supplement,* calling it "a splendid and riveting story" and praising the technical descriptions as "vast and accurate." Clancy's subsequent novels continued to feature plots based upon critical world political issues from the perspective of military or CIA personnel, including the international drug trade and terrorism. All of Clancy's popular novels have resided on bestseller lists, and *Clear and Present Danger* (1989) sold more copies than any other novel published in the 1980s, according to Louis Menand of *The New Yorker.* Today Clancy continues to write successful novels. Several of his books have been adapted as popular films, including *The Hunt for Red October, Patriot Games* (1987), and *Clear and Present Danger.*

Although, according to an interview with *Contemporary Authors* in 1988, Clancy claimed he did not create the "techno-thriller," his use of highly involved technical detail incorporated into complex, suspenseful plots made him the most successful practitioner of the genre and added a new level of military realism and sophistication to the traditional adventure novel. His books take their plots from the most pressing international concerns of his times. When the arms race was escalating in the 1980s, Clancy's novels *The Hunt for Red October, Red Storm Rising* (1986), and *The Cardinal of the Kremlin* (1988) used different aspects of the Soviet-American conflict for story lines. In the post-Cold War era, Clancy turned to the South American drug trade in *Clear and Present Danger,* IRA terrorism in *Patriot Games,* and Middle East peace and nuclear proliferation in *The Sum of All Fears* (1991). Clancy takes his characters from various levels of military establishment insiders, from elite soldiers and crewman to commanders, generals, espionage operatives, and government officials. Their goals and motives are often clearly good or evil, and while later novels feature some ambivalence or introspection in lead characters, most of the moral choices characters face are straightforward questions of right and wrong. In addition to using declassified documents and tours of vessels and bases, Clancy conducted interviews with personnel in order to draw his characters accurately. The hero in many Clancy novels is Jack Ryan, a sometime CIA agent who epitomizes integrity, bravery, and ingenuity in a changing, high stakes world. Whether he is assigned to resolve a crisis, as in *Clear and Present Danger,* or stumbles accidently into an international incident and becomes a target for revenge, as in *Patriot Games,* Ryan is adept at using available technology to achieve his mission; as Clancy stated in the CA interview, "the superior individual is the guy who makes use of [new technology]." The accuracy of Clancy's descriptions of military-industrial technology and personnel has been characterized as remarkable for one outside the establishment, and his favorable portrayal of the American armed forces has earned him respect in military circles.

Ronald Reagan called *The Hunt for Red October* "the perfect yarn." This comment could be a summation of critical reception to Clancy's novels. Although some critics found the plots of *The Sum of All Fears* and *Clear and Present Danger* too lengthy and bogged down by the detailed technical descriptions, most agree that Clancy is successful in creating suspenseful, thrilling action stories. Appreciation of Clancy's technological details varies among critics; some find the insider's glimpse of weaponry and tactics presented with clarity, accuracy, and interest, while others, perhaps more knowledgeable about the technology described, find Clancy's renderings inaccurate and implausible. Critics are almost unanimous in their negative reaction to Clancy's skill at characterization, finding them underdeveloped, and the hero Jack Ryan too flawless and unbelievably virtuous. Clancy responded to criticism about Ryan by giving him some vices in later novels, a change some critics found unbelievable. Clancy's novels usually are received by critics in the spirit they are written, to entertain and educate while highlighting the important international issues of the times and showing how the United States can meet difficult challenges with moral integrity, courage, and the wise use of modern technology.

## Further Reading

*Bestsellers 89,* Issue 1, Gale, 1989.
*Bestsellers 90,* Issue 1, Gale, 1990.
*Contemporary Literary Criticism,* Volume 45, Gale, 1987.
*American Legion,* December, 1991, p. 16.
*Chicago Tribune Book World,* September 7, 1986.
*Detroit News,* January 20, 1985.
*Fortune,* July 18, 1988; August 26, 1991. □

# Sir John Harold Clapham

**The English economic historian Sir John Harold Clapham (1873-1946) established economic history as a significant and independent field of study in Great Britain.**

John Harold Clapham was the son of a Wesleyan Jeweler in Salford, Lancashire. He attended King's College, Cambridge, on a scholarship, graduating with first-class honors in history in 1895. He received the Lightfoot scholarship in ecclesiastical history the following year and the Prince Consort Prize in 1897 and then was made a fellow of King's. He was influenced most in these early years by the economist Alfred Marshall.

In 1902 Clapham went to the University of Leeds as a professor of economics and a pioneer in economic history. He returned to Cambridge in 1908 as dean of King's and was deeply involved in university affairs until his death. In 1928 the Cambridge chair in economic history was established for him, and he held it for a decade.

Clapham was a member of the Board of Trade on the Cabinet Committee on Priorities (1916-1918), president of the British Academy (1940-1945), editor of *Studies in Economic History,* and joint editor of the first volume of the epochal *Cambridge Economic History of Europe* (1941). He was knighted in 1944.

In 1945 Clement Atlee appointed Clapham chairman of a committee to study economic and social research in England. The committee's recommendations, published after Clapham's death, were accepted and implemented by the government.

## Major Efforts and Achievements

Clapham was essentially uninterested in the role of ideas, and in 1922 his famous essay "Of Empty Boxes" attacked theory and analysis which "outran verification." During the 1930s and 1940s, when disagreements on methodology and meaning stirred historians and social scientists, he continued to support narrative histories of institutions based on accumulations of economic data. In his monumental three-volume *Economic History of Modern Britain* (1926-1938), Clapham traced with admiration the achievements of 19th-century free enterprise. Personally sympathetic to the economically displaced, Clapham wrote little about them and even less about the causes for their displacement. His views of economic history as the "story of how men have kept alive and as comfortable as might be" dominated the practice of economic history at Cambridge until recent times.

Although Clapham wrote two studies in political history, his major efforts and achievements were in economic history. Beginning with *The Woolen and Worsted Industries* (1907), his other works of importance are *The Economic Development of France and Germany, 1815-1914* (1921); *The Bank of England: A History* (3 vols., 1944-1958); and *A Concise Economic History of Britain from the Earliest Times to 1750* (published post-humously in 1949 and revised in 1959).

## Further Reading

The most complete biographical sketch of Clapham's life and work is G. N. Clark's "Sir John Harold Clapham, 1873-1946" in the *Proceedings of the British Academy,* vol. 32 (1944). A biographical sketch of Clapham by W. H. B. Court is in *Architects and Craftsmen in History,* edited by Joseph T. Lambie (1956). The inaugural address of M. M. Postan as professor of economic history at Cambridge, succeeding Clapham, *The Historical Method in Social Science* (1939), illustrates the continuity of Clapham's influence. □

# Margaret Antoinette Clapp

**The winner of the 1948 Pulitzer Prize for biography, Margaret Antoinette Clapp (1910-1974) was a distinguished American educator who served as president of Wellesley College from 1949 to 1966.**

Margaret Clapp was born April 10, 1910, in East Orange, New Jersey, the daughter of Anna Roth and Alfred Chapin Clapp, an insurance agent. She graduated from East Orange High School in 1926 and from Wellesley College in 1930. She received an A.B. from the latter with a focus on history and economics. While in college she was named a Wellesley College Scholar, an award given for academic excellence.

Following graduation she taught English literature at the Todhunter School for Girls in New York City. She stayed in this position for 12 years, during which time she also worked at Columbia University for her master's degree in history, which she received in 1937. During World War II and shortly thereafter she taught in the history departments of various universities in the New York City area, including the City College of New York (1942-1944), Douglass (1945-1946), and Columbia (1946-1947). At the same time Clapp continued her graduate studies at Columbia in American history.

Her doctoral dissertation was on John Bigelow (1817-1911), an intriguing 19th-century political figure who was an active supporter of the Free Soil movement in the pre-Civil War period (the attempt to ensure that all subsequent territories admitted to the union be free and not slave states). Known also for other progressive ideas such as prison reform, Bigelow served as editor of the New York *Evening Post,* as New York secretary of state, and as American ambassador to France. Philosophically, he was attracted to Swedenborgianism, a 19th-century mystical doctrine derived from the writings of Emmanuel Swedenborg (1688-1772).

In the biography which grew from her thesis Clapp stressed the influence of Swedenborg's theories upon Bigelow. She wrote the dissertation under the direction of Allan

Nevins. *Forgotten First Citizen: John Bigelow* was published in 1947 and won the Pulitzer Prize for biography in 1948.

Following a brief term at Brooklyn College, Clapp assumed the presidency of Wellesley College in 1949. At the time there were only four other women in the country serving as presidents of major colleges. An effective administrator, Clapp expanded Wellesley's facilities and resources considerably. The endowment multiplied threefold during her tenure, and three new dormitories, a faculty club, and a new library wing were added to the campus. In addition, Clapp instituted a generous leave policy for junior faculty and increased faculty salaries by 150 percent. In 1950 Clapp edited a collection of articles, *The Modern University,* to which she contributed a chapter on the national postsecondary education scene following World War II.

A feminist during the 1950s when conventional notions of feminine identity were at a peak, Clapp maintained that women's sole purpose in life was neither motherhood nor wifedom. Against the then popular Freudian "mystique" (that women violated their natural destiny by becoming educated professionals), Clapp urged that women pursue careers and that social programs such as day care centers and domestic services be provided to allow women to combine work with domestic commitments.

In 1966 Clapp retired from Wellesley and the following year served briefly as chief administrator of a women's college (Lady Doak) in Mandurai, India. In 1968 she accepted a position as United States cultural attaché to India. Later she served as minister-councilor of public affairs in the United States Information Agency (USIA), an office she held from 1970 to 1971.

Clapp retired from public life in the early 1970s and returned to Tyringham, Massachusetts, where she died of cancer in 1974. The library at Wellesley is named in her honor, a fitting tribute to a woman who furthered the cause of women's education during a period when national interest in it was at a low ebb.

### Further Reading

No biography of Clapp yet exists. Short summaries may be found in *Notable American Women* and *American Women Writers.* She was the subject of a cover story in *Time* on October 10, 1949. Clapp's papers are at Wellesley College. Several issues of the *Wellesley Alumnae Magazine* (notably those of March 1958, November 1961, and July 6, 1966) include articles by or about her. □

# Hugh Clapperton

**A Scottish explorer of Africa, Hugh Clapperton (1788-1827) extended knowledge of the Fulani empire in what is now northern Nigeria and reached the Niger River in an effort to solve the mystery of that river's course and terminal point.**

ugh Clapperton was born in Annan, the son of a surgeon. He received little formal education and at age 13 went to sea. He joined the Royal Navy and saw service in the Mediterranean, the East Indies, and Canada.

Clapperton returned to Scotland on half pay in 1817 and 3 years later met Dr. Walter Oudney, who was preparing an expedition to west-central Africa. Clapperton accepted Oudney's invitation to accompany him, and in 1822, with Maj. Dixon Denham, they set out from Tripoli to cross the Sahara. On Feb. 4, 1823, they reached Lake Chad, being the first Europeans to see it. Thinking it the key to western African river systems, they explored the kingdoms around the lake and discovered the Shari River, which emptied into Lake Chad.

Quarreling over leadership of the party, the three parted, Denham going southeastward and Clapperton and Oudney going west, through the Hausa states, toward the Niger River. Oudney died at Murmur in January 1824, but Clapperton continued, visiting Kano and then Sokoto, where the Fulani Sultan Muhammed Bello refused to allow him to continue on to the Niger, only 150 miles away. Bello, however, was friendly to Clapperton and expressed interest in developing trade with Britain. Clapperton and Denham met near Lake Chad and returned to England on June 1, 1825.

Only 3 months later Clapperton left again on a second expedition, this time starting from the Bight of Benin and traveling through Yoruba lands in what is now western Nigeria. He crossed the Niger River near Boussa and reached Kano by July 1826. At Sokoto, Clapperton found that Sultan Bello had become suspicious of British imperialism and refused to enter into agreement with him. Clapperton became ill, and the failure of his expedition helped destroy him. He died on April 13, 1827, near Sokoto. Clapperton's belief that the Niger emptied into the Atlantic at the Bight of Benin was proved by his servant, Richard Lander, in a later expedition.

## Further Reading

Clapperton and Oudney's role in the first expedition to Lake Chad was minimized by Dixon Denham, who claimed most of the credit for himself in his *Narrative of Travels and Discoveries in Northern and Central Africa, in the Years 1822, 1823, and 1824* (1826). For Clapperton's second journey see his *Journal of a Second Expedition into the Interior of Africa* (1829), edited and commented on by his servant, Richard Lander. See also Lander's *Records of Captain Clapperton's Last Expedition to Africa* (2 vols., 1830). An excellent secondary source that gives an evaluation of Clapperton's accomplishments is E. W. Bovill, *The Niger Explored* (1968). □

# 1st Earl of Clarendon

**The English statesman and historian Edward Hyde, 1st Earl of Clarendon (1609-1674), was the first minister of Charles II in exile and then in England until 1666.**

he son of Henry Hyde of Dinton, Wiltshire, Edward Hyde was born on Feb. 18, 1609. He attended Oxford University and earned a bachelor of arts degree in 1626, the year after he had begun legal studies at the Middle Temple. Noted for his intellectual abilities, he associated with prominent scholars and writers, and among his friends were the playwright Ben Jonson and the statesman, poet, and literary patron Lord Falkland.

Hyde's first wife died 6 months after their marriage in 1629, and in 1634 he married Frances Aylesbury. Having been called to the bar in 1633, he soon built up a profitable legal practice and was also awarded government posts, owing in part to the influence of his father-in-law, Sir Thomas Aylesbury.

Hyde's political ideals were formed in the period before the English civil war as a member of the Falkland circle. He believed in a balanced sovereignty between Parliament and the monarchy, such as he felt had existed in the time of Queen Elizabeth. It was his tragedy that such a balance was never obtained during his career; he was driven from position to position, never truly leading policy but largely fighting rearguard actions.

In the late 1630s Hyde felt the main violation of this balanced concept of government proceeded from the king. Elected to Parliament in 1640, he was extremely active in the original movements to check royal power and was a leading formulator of the impeachment proceedings against

Lord Strafford. But by late 1641 he began to oppose the revolutionary tendencies, particularly in religious matters, among the controlling parliamentary leaders. He successfully obstructed the Root and Branch Bill to destroy the Church and became an adherent of the royal minority in the Lower House.

By 1643 Hyde had become a leading councilor of King Charles I and was among those who proposed the calling of the Parliament at Oxford that opened the civil war. Appointed chief adviser to the heir apparent, Prince Charles, he followed the prince into exile in 1646. During the years of exile, although his advice was not always heeded, he was the principal figure at the prince's court.

## Later Career

With the restoration of the monarchy in 1660, Hyde continued as the first minister of the returned prince, who was then styled King Charles II. In 1660 Hyde was created Baron Hyde and in 1661 Earl of Clarendon. For the first year of his ministry he, like the King, favored programs of moderation, amelioration, and toleration, but with the election of the Cavalier Parliament in 1661, Clarendon's position had to change. Since his principal responsibility was to lead Parliament into cooperation with the King, his policy had to be based on accommodation. The new Parliament being rigidly Cavalier royalist and stridently Anglican, Clarendon was forced into a similar posture. Thus the religious laws of the early 1660s, which established persecutive measures against Dissenters, are known as the Clarendon code but

were framed largely by those whom Clarendon needed for support in other matters.

Clarendon's position was further complicated by the fact that a number of very ambitious courtiers constantly attacked him on nearly every issue. There were impeachment attempts made upon him as early as 1663. Clarendon was the subject of considerable envy over the marriage in 1660 of his daughter Anne to the heir apparent, James, Duke of York. When the marriage of Charles II and Catherine of Braganza of Portugal proved to be barren, it was rumored that Clarendon had purposely married the King to a barren princess to secure the throne for his own grandchildren. Clarendon was also wrongly blamed for the sale of Dunkirk to the French and for the failure of the English project at Tangier. Finally his obvious disapproval of the manners at court and his increasing high-handedness in council irritated the King.

Clarendon's fall, however, proceeded mainly from the loss of the Dutch War in 1666. Although he had been less than enthusiastic in the pursuit of this war, the defeat did not stem principally from his mishandling of the situation. But the blow to his prestige because of the English loss destroyed his already-weakened influence at court and shattered his party in Parliament. Thus, despite support of Clarendon by the Duke of York's faction and the Anglican bishops, in 1667 Parliament began impeachment proceedings against him. The court party and the King, along with almost every dissident interest in England, including many of the Cavaliers, advocated impeachment. Clarendon was persuaded to flee into exile, and the impeachment was turned into a bill for perpetual banishment.

Clarendon spent the rest of his life in France. He had the satisfaction of seeing many of his enemies shatter themselves in the scramble for office which followed his own fall. During his years in exile he wrote his memoirs and completed his *History of the Rebellion and Civil Wars.* His writings supply historians with some of the best available source material for the period. Clarendon died at Rouen on Dec. 9, 1674.

## Further Reading

The best biographies of Clarendon are T. H. Lister, *Life and Administration of Edward, First Earl of Clarendon* (3 vols., 1837-1838), and B. H. G. Wormald, *Clarendon* (1951), which covers only the civil war period. The serious student of Clarendon or his times should also turn to Clarendon's own writings. The general works on the period, David Ogg, *England in the Reign of Charles II* (2 vols., 1934; 2d ed. 1962), and G. N. Clark, *The Later Stuarts, 1660-1714* (1934; 2d ed. 1955), may be supplemented by such special works as Keith Feiling, *A History of the Tory Party, 1640-1714* (1924), which deals extensively with Clarendon's political career.

## Additional Sources

Brownley, Martine Watson, *Clarendon and the rhetoric of historical form,* Philadelphia: University of Pennsylvania Press, 1985.

Clarendon, Edward Hyde, Earl of, *Selections from the History of the rebellion and the Life by himself,* Oxford; New York: Oxford University Press, 1978.

Harris, R. W. (Ronald Walter), *Clarendon and the English Revolution,* Stanford, Calif.: Stanford University Press, 1983.

Harris, R. W. (Ronald Walter), *Clarendon and the English Revolution,* London: Hogarth Press, 1983.

Ollard, Richard Lawrence, *Clarendon and his friends,* New York: Atheneum, 1988, 1987.

Wormald, B. H. G., *Clarendon—politics, history, and religion, 1640-1660,* Cambridge England; New York: Cambridge University Press, 1989, 1951. □

# George Rogers Clark

**George Rogers Clark (1752-1818) was an American Revolutionary War soldier. His capture of British posts on the far frontier was of considerable importance, though the idea that Clark "won the Northwest" is an oft-repeated exaggeration.**

S tanding 6 feet tall, topped by flaming red hair, George Rogers Clark was a true frontiersman. He talked the language of his men and shared in all their hardships. With a flair for the dramatic, he was known to the Native Americans as "Long Knife" and was skilled in the high-flown, metaphorical oratory that they appreciated.

Born on a small plantation near Charlottesville, Va., Clark had only a rudimentary education before becoming a surveyor. By the age of 20, he had staked out his own land claims on the Ohio River and obtained "a good deal of cash by surveying." Commissioned a captain in the Virginia militia, Clark saw extensive campaigning in Lord Dunmore's War against the Shawnee Indians in 1774. The next year the Ohio Land Company engaged him to lay out its tracts on the Kentucky River. Clark made his home in Harrodsburg, the first settlement in Kentucky. Quickly emerging as a dominant figure, he led the Kentuckians in their successful efforts to be formally annexed as a county of Virginia.

## Revolutionary Career

Kentucky's survival against the Native Americans—who looked upon "the dark and bloody ground" as their own and who were mainly pro-British during the Revolution—was Clark's great concern. Consequently, he went to Williamsburg, the capital of Virginia, to sell the state leaders on a plan for the capture of the British-held villages north of the Ohio and eventually Detroit as well. In January 1778 the Virginia Legislature commissioned Clark a lieutenant colonel, granted him £1,200, and authorized him to take as much of the interior as possible. It was no easy task to get men to leave their thinly populated settlements exposed, but at length, with 175 recruits, he floated down the Ohio and, before its juncture with the Mississippi, set off on foot across southern Illinois. Early in July 1778, Clark took the hamlets of Kaskaskia and Cahokia without bloodshed, and Vincennes a little later. Soon the entire region became known as the county of Illinois in the state of Virginia.

But Clark had to defend his conquests, for Lieutenant Governor Henry Hamilton and a mixed force—Indians, French Canadians, and regulars—swept down from Detroit to restore royal control. Initially, the advantage belonged to Hamilton, who easily wrested Vincennes from the Americans and with superior numbers threatened Clark at Kaskaskia. But Hamilton decided to sit out the winter at Vincennes before attacking and soon saw many of his Frenchmen and Native Americans return to their northern homes.

Clark, in contrast, would not let adversity bar the door. Believing that "great things have been affected by a few men well conducted," he and his "boys" marched 180 miles through torrential rains and other discomforts to recapture Vincennes on Feb. 5, 1779. He also bagged Hamilton himself, who was hated by the Americans for his allegedly indiscriminate use of Indians—"the Famous Hair-Buyer General," boasted Clark of his prize prisoner.

## Clark's Significance

Clark's conquest of the Illinois country stood as a dramatic feat accomplished under tremendous physical and material handicaps by a bold and resourceful leader. Unfortunately, he failed to receive the reinforcements that would have enabled him to move against Detroit. Therefore it seems dubious to accept such extreme statements as that Clark "added three—perhaps five—states to the Union;" or that his "rearguard operations" on the frontier "saved the American Revolution from collapse." Moreover, the diplomats who negotiated the Treaty of Paris in 1783 were only very dimly aware of the military events in the back country. In fact, Clark was on the defensive along the Ohio during the last 2 years of the war as the Indians continued to devastate the frontier. In his last important action Clark launched a counteroffensive against the Shawnee tribe, driving it back into central Ohio.

When Clark retired from the Virginia service as a brigadier general, he became chief surveyor of the military lands granted to his soldiers north of the Ohio. In 1784 Congress appointed Clark one of several commissioners to settle outstanding differences, such as land claims, with the Indians of the Old Northwest. His efforts failed, and 2 years later Clark was again in the field with the Kentucky militia. At Vincennes he impressed much-needed supplies owned by Spanish merchants. James Wilkinson, a former Continental general and a paid secret agent of the Madrid government, used the episode to try to destroy Clark's character. Clark also had trouble with Virginia authorities attempting to settle the accounts of his campaign against Henry Hamilton. In the absence of records that had disappeared (they were discovered in the attic of the Virginia Capitol in 1913), Clark was never compensated for heavy personal losses in the public service. Financially ruined and filled with bitterness, he turned increasingly to liquor as an escape.

Visions of glory prompted Clark to join a French-sponsored expedition aimed at taking Spanish Louisiana in 1793, but President Washington prevented its departure and the scheme collapsed. When still another military venture in behalf of France failed in 1798, Clark returned to Louisville. Later, following the loss of one leg and a stroke, he made his home with a nearby sister. Impoverished, partially paralyzed, and plagued by alcoholism and creditors, he was once heard to say on learning of a friend's passing, "Everybody can die but me." For Clark the end came on Feb. 13, 1818.

## Further Reading

The two standard biographies of Clark are James A. James, *The Life of George Rogers Clark* (1928), and John Bakeless, *Background to Glory: The Life of George Rogers Clark* (1957; 1992). Both are factually reliable, and Bakeless is especially interesting. Both, however, tend to exaggerate the importance of Clark's conquests in the Northwest. Recommended for general historical background are Milo M. Quaife, ed., *The Capture of Old Vincennes: The Original Narratives of George Rogers Clark and of His Opponent Gov. Henry Hamilton* (1927); Randolph C. Downes, *Council Fires on the Upper Ohio* (1940); and Francis S. Philbrick, *The Rise of the West, 1754-1830* (1965).

## Additional Sources

Bakeless, John Edwin, *Background to glory: the life of George Rogers Clark,* Lincoln: University of Nebraska Press, 1992.

Harrison, Lowell Hayes, *George Rogers Clark and the war in the West,* Lexington: University Press of Kentucky, 1976.

Rankin, Hugh F., *George Rogers Clark and the winning of the West,* Richmond: Virginia Independence Bicentennial Commission, 1976.

Schrodt, Philip A., *George Rogers Clark, frontier revolutionary,* Bloomington, Ind.: Buffalo Wallow Press, 1976. □

# John Bates Clark

**The American economist John Bates Clark (1847-1938) was the first economic theorist from the United States to achieve an international reputation.**

John Bates Clark was born and raised in Providence, R. I. In 1872, after an absence due to his father's illness and death, Clark graduated from Amherst College. Abandoning earlier plans to enter divinity school, he turned to economics. From 1872 to 1875 he studied at the University of Heidelberg under Karl Knies, leader of the German historical school, and at the University of Zurich.

On his return Clark participated actively in the creation of a "new" economics, becoming the third president of the young reformers' American Economic Association. He was professor of history and political economy at Carleton College until 1882. He then taught at Smith College, Amherst, and Johns Hopkins University. From 1895 until his retirement as professor emeritus in 1923, Clark was part of the influential faculty of political science at Columbia University, where he edited the *Political Science Quarterly* (1895-1911). After 1911 he devoted himself to pacifist causes and served as the first director of the Carnegie Endowment for International Peace.

Near the turn of the century, rapid industrial development and serious discontent, especially with the anomalous distribution of wealth, prompted Clark to examine problems of production and distribution. The indisputable influence which he exercised upon at least a generation of economists lay more in his development of analytical tools than in the conclusions he drew from them. Through his marginal utility principle, developed independently of Léon Walras, Carl Menger, and W. S. Jevons, Clark became the leading theorist of a marginal productivity theory of distribution which idealized the relationship between income and an individual's contribution to goods or services.

Clark's first important work, *The Philosophy of Wealth* (1885), attacking the hedonistic and atomistic assumptions of classical economics, attempted to tie economics to social ethics. Clark's major contribution, *The Distribution of Wealth* (1899), discarded his early reformist tendencies to present a deductive system of economic harmony based upon the competition of rational, self-interested men inevitably progressing. Clark began by assuming that society was a biological organism subject to collective moral judgment. Then he divided economics into "static" and "dynamic" analysis, a distinction which continues to characterize American economics. Clark's own analysis was a static description of economic laws in an unchanging society where perfect competition led to economic equilibrium. Static phenomena were not analytical abstractions but real economic forces isolated from dynamic laws of social change so that the mechanics of distribution were revealed. Dynamic laws, to be discovered by future generations using refined empirical techniques, were formulated tentatively by Clark in the last chapters of *Distribution* and in his later *Essentials of Economic Theory* (1907) on the basis of static

economics and an optimistic justification of the status quo. To Clark, population growth, improvement in tastes, capital accumulation, technological innovation, and industrial organization were dynamic, necessarily progressive forces.

Clark's other important works included *The Modern Distributive Process* (with Franklin H. Giddings, 1888); *The Control of Trusts* (1901); *The Problem of Monopoly* (1904), influential in the antitrust legislation of 1914; *Social Justice without Socialism* (1914); and *A Tender of Peace.*

## Further Reading

There is no biography of Clark. The essay on Clark in Paul T. Homan, *Contemporary Economic Thought* (1928), remains the clearest exposition of his economic theory. The discussion by Clark's distinguished economist son, "J. M. Clark on J. B. Clark," in Henry W. Spiegel, ed., *The Development of Economic Thought: Great Economists in Perspective* (1952; abr. ed. 1964), is warm, filial, and defensive but not very useful. John Rutherford Everett, *Religion in Economics: A Study of John Bates Clark, Richard T. Ely, Simon N. Patten* (1946), lifts whole sections from other commentators without adding anything new. Jacob H. Hollander, ed., *Economic Essays Contributed in Honor of J. B. Clark* (1967), which includes a brief memoir by Hollander, shows the development of Clark's thought.

## Additional Sources

Henry, John F., *John Bates Clark: the making of a neoclassical economist,* New York, N.Y.: St. Martin's Press, 1995. □

# John Maurice Clark

**The American economist John Maurice Clark (1884-1963) is perhaps the best-known forerunner of the American economists who are sometimes referred to as the pragmatic school.**

J ohn Maurice Clark was born in Northampton, Mass. He graduated from nearby Amherst College in 1905 and did his graduate study in economics at Columbia University, where he received his doctorate in 1910. He instructed at Colorado College (1908-1910) and at Amherst College (1910-1915) until he joined the faculty of political economy at the University of Chicago, where his colleagues included Jacob Viner and Frank Knight. In 1926 he left Chicago to accept a professorship at Columbia, where he remained until he retired in 1957, completing a half century of uninterrupted teaching and productive scholarship.

Clark's works, while primarily theoretical in content, were almost always directed toward clarifying and solving practical economic issues. He skillfully built his own analytical treatises upon the logic underlying the rigorously formulated models of others, first the marginalists and later Edward H. Chamberlin and Joan Robinson. In contrast with the methodology of these scholars, and of the younger mathematical economists who rose to prominence during the latter part of his professional life, Clark's methodology relied on the written word rather than geometric and algebraic formulations.

## Dynamics of a Market Economy

Clark has been singled out as one of the few economists (John Maynard Keynes was another) born into the profession. He was the son of the distinguished John Bates Clark, a founder and the third president of the American Economic Association. John Maurice Clark, following in his father's footsteps, was the association's thirty-seventh president. The senior Clark had a pronounced influence on Clark's professional and personal life. The father directed the son's doctoral dissertation at Columbia (*Standards of Reasonableness in Local Freight Discriminations*), and in turn the younger Clark was the coauthor of the revised edition of his father's *The Control of Trusts* (1914). Clark dedicated his highly praised *Studies in the Economics of Overhead Costs* to his father, and in his last major work published before his death, *Competition as a Dynamic Process* (1961), he attributed his concern with the dynamics of economics to his father's basic conception that static equilibrium analysis was properly an introduction to the study of dynamics rather than an end in itself.

Virtually all of Clark's works were concerned with the dynamics of a market economy. His article "Towards a Concept of Workable Competition" (1940) greatly influenced the later writings of others concerned with the policy standards applicable to the functioning of a dynamic market economy.

Clark received honorary degrees from Amherst College, Columbia University, the University of Paris, the New School of Social Research, and Yale University. In 1951 Columbia appointed him to the John Bates Clark chair, established in his father's honor. A year later the American Economic Association bestowed on him its highest honor by awarding him the Francis A. Walker Medal for distinguished service in the field of economics.

## Further Reading

Detailed biographies of Clark are in Joseph Dorfman, *The Economic Mind in American Civilization* (5 vols., 1946-1959), and Ben B. Seligman, *Main Currents in Modern Economics: Economic Thought since 1870* (1962). See also T.W. Hutchison, *A Review of Economic Doctrines, 1870-1929* (1953).

## Additional Sources

Hickman, Charles Addison, *J. M. Clark,* New York: Columbia University Press, 1975. □

# Kenneth B. Clark

**An American social psychologist, Kenneth B. Clark (born 1914) was the best known and most highly regarded black social scientist in the United States. Clark achieved international recognition for his re-**search on the social and psychological effects of racism and segregation.

Kenneth Clark was born on July 14, 1914, in the Panama Canal Zone. At the age of five Clark's mother moved him and his younger sister to Harlem, New York, where he was educated in the public schools. Clark received his bachelor's and master's degrees at Howard University where he met Mamie Phipps, who became his wife and life-long collaborator and colleague. While at Howard the Clarks began studying the effects of racism on the identity and self-esteem of Washington, D.C., school children.

In 1940 they moved to New York City to pursue doctoral studies at Columbia University and to continue their work on the psychological effects of racism. Clark's early career includes work on the Carnegie-Mydral Project, a brief teaching stint at Hampton Institute while holding a Rosenwald Fellowship, a staff research position at the Office of War Information, and, finally, an appointment to the faculty of the City College of New York. Based on their studies of the pathology of racism and volunteer work with emotionally disturbed children, the Clarks in 1946 established the Northside Center for Child Development.

As a part of their research on the psychological damage caused by racism the Clarks developed the famous "doll tests." Black children in the early school ages were shown four identical dolls, two black and two white, and were asked to identify them racially and to indicate which doll was best, which was nice, which was bad, and which they would prefer to play with. The tests, administered to children in varying communities around the country, showed that a majority of the children rejected the black doll and expressed a preference for the white doll. For the Clarks these tests were indisputable evidence of the negative effects of racism on the personality and psychological development of black children. As a result of this research, Clark was asked to prepare a report on the problems of minority youth for the White House Mid-Century Conference on Youth held in 1950. This report, published in revised form as *Prejudice and Your Child* (1955), summarized the results of the doll tests and related research and brought the young Clark to the attention of the National Association for the Advancement of Colored People (NAACP), which was preparing to challenge the laws requiring segregation in the nation's schools.

Clark's work for the NAACP played a major role in the Supreme Court's 1954 decision *Brown v. Board of Education,* which declared school segregation unconstitutional. In his testimony in several of the trials and in the social science brief submitted to the Court, Clark and his colleagues argued that segregation tended to create in black children feelings of inferiority, self-rejection, and loss of self-esteem which affected negatively their ability to learn. The influence of Clark on the Court's decision is apparent in the unanimous opinion written by Chief Justice Earl Warren. The Chief Justice wrote " . . . the policy of separating the races is usually interpreted as denoting the inferiority of the

Negro group. A sense of inferiority affects the motivation of the child to learn. Segregation with the sanction of law, therefore, has a tendency to retard the educational and mental development of Negro children. . . ." To support this central finding of the *Brown* decision the Chief Justice cited (in footnote 11) several social science studies, the first being Clark's *Effects of Prejudice and Discrimination on Personality Development.*

As a result of his work on the *Brown* case, Clark in subsequent years became a leading advocate of school integration and an intellectual leader of the civil rights movement, while continuing his research on the effects of racism and urging the application of social science research to the resolution of the nation's race problems. In 1966 he authored *Dark Ghetto,* a prize winning study of the dynamics of racial oppression and the resulting pathologies of the American ghetto. Clark was also instrumental in the establishment of the Metropolitan Applied Research Center and the Joint Center for Political Studies, institutions devoted to making social science research relevant to the civil rights movement and to the process of social change.

Appointed visiting professor at Harvard, Columbia, and the University of California, Berkeley, Clark was also a member of the boards of trustees at the University of Chicago and at Howard University and was the winner of numerous awards, including in 1961 the NAACP's Spingarn Medal. In 1966 he was appointed to the New York State Board of Regents, the first black to serve on that state's highest education decision-making body. Clark was also Distinguished Professor of Psychology at the City University of New York and was generally recognized as one of the nation's leading social scientists.

## Further Reading

Richard Kluger's *Simple Justice: The History of* Brown *v.* Board of Education, *and Black America's Struggle for Equality* (1975) contains an analysis of Clark's work on the *Brown* case. Clark's life and career are profiled by Nat Hentoff in "The Integrationists" in the *New Yorker* (August 23, 1982). □

# Kenneth M. Clark

**During his long and varied career, English art historian Kenneth M. Clark (1903-1983) served as director of the British National Gallery and of Britain's first commercial television network. He also helped establish government patronage of the arts.**

Kenneth Mackenzie Clark was born in London on July 13, 1903, the only child of parents he described as members of the Edwardian "idle rich." While his parents spent the family fortune (amassed by Clark's Scottish great-great grandfather, the inventor of the cotton spool), Clark developed into a lonely, serious young man with a passion for art and complete confidence in his judgment. Lacking a mentor at home or school, he groped his way toward knowledge, winning a scholarship to Oxford. There, he gave up early hopes of becoming a painter to become an aesthete. " . . . Nothing could destroy me," he said, "as long as I could enjoy works of art and for 'enjoy' read 'enjoy': not codify or classify, or purge my spirit or arouse my social consciousness." Clark was able to fulfill another childhood ambition: to assist art critic Bernard Berenson in the revision of his *Florentine Drawings.* Clark spent two years in Italy working for Berenson, during which time he married Jane Martin, an Oxford classmate.

Then, in 1928, he delved into a project on Leonardo da Vinci, whose work at that time was still largely undocumented. The resulting catalogue established Clark's reputation. He was invited to help organize a major exhibit of Italian art in London. Though dissatisfied with his contributions to its catalogue, thinking himself still too young and inexperienced, Clark was soon being invited to lecture widely.

In 1931 he became Keeper of the Department of Fine Arts at Oxford's Ashmolean Museum. The next year marked the beginning of what he called the "great Clark boom." From 1933 to 1945 he was the British National Gallery's youngest director and a major force in the expansion of its collection. Also in 1934, King George V convinced him to be surveyor of the King's pictures. In 1938 he was knighted.

When war broke out in 1939 Clark served as director of the Film Division of the Ministry of Information after he saw to it that the National Gallery's collection was safely hidden in caves in Wales. He had already begun collecting and

championing the work of contemporary artists, particularly that of his friends Henry Moore and Graham Sutherland, and he took advantage of his ministry position to convince the government to begin supporting the arts on a large scale, at that time a novel concept in Britain. He helped launch what became the Arts Council. A lover of classical music, he also introduced a series of lunchtime concerts at the National Gallery, one of which he conducted himself. Later he would establish the National Opera at Covent Garden.

After the war he resigned his post at the gallery and from 1945 to 1950 held the prestigious Slade professorship of fine arts at Oxford. He spent much of that time lecturing and writing on John Ruskin and was chiefly responsible for reestablishing Ruskin's reputation. During this period he wrote *Piero della Francesca* (1951), *Moments of Vision* (1954), and, culled from a series of Mellon lectures delivered in Washington, D.C., *The Nude* (1956), which he considered his best work and which was heavily influenced by the art theories of Aby Warburg.

Though Clark's catalogue on Leonardo da Vinci had established him as a scholar, he eschewed the title. "I have not got a first class mind," he wrote, "only a love of art, a good visual memory and a certain amount of commonsense." With his enthusiasm for sharing this love and his articulate but conversational style, Clark was a popular lecturer. Later he was able to transfer these skills successfully to television. In the intervening years he served as director of Britain's first commercial television network, ITA, setting to rest, with his trustworthy name, the grumblings of a public who feared the crassness of commercial "tellie." When he left ITA in 1957 the BBC immediately hired him, launching him in the final, and best known, stage of his career, as a television personality, albeit not a flashy one.

In 1969 he wrote and narrated the 13-part "Civilisation" series, a survey of European art which included a segment on his favorite period, the early quattrocento (14th century) in Florence. "Civilisation" was a huge success in both England and the United States (and also became a best-selling book). Clark felt both awed and ill at ease with his new status as a star. He went on to do other television programs, but resigned all his duties when his wife took ill in 1974. At Saltwood Castle in England, their home since 1955, Clark wrote on Botticelli, Rembrandt, and his friend Edith Wharton, as well as completing a second volume of his autobiography. His wife died in 1977. Soon thereafter Clark was remarried, to Nolwen de Janze-Rice, a family friend. As his health declined, he suffered bouts of depression alternated with periods of productivity. He died shortly before his 80th birthday, leaving behind two sons and a daughter.

## Further Reading

For two different accounts of the life and work of Kenneth Clark, see Clark's two volumes of autobiography, *Another Part of the Wood* (1974) and *The Other Half* (1977). Both are charming, witty, and readable, if less than complete, portraits. Meryle Secrest's *Kenneth Clark: A Biography* (1984) fills in many of the gaps. Many of Clark's books are widely available, including *The Gothic Revival* (1929), *Leonardo da Vinci* (1939 and

1952), *Florentine Painting: the Fifteenth Century* (1945), *Landscape Into Art* (1950), *Piero della Francesca* (1951), *Moments of Vision* (1954), *The Nude* (1956), and *Looking at Pictures* (1960).

## Additional Sources

Clark, Kenneth, *Another part of the wood: a self portrait,* New York: Harper & Row, 1974.

Clark, Kenneth, *The other half: a self portrait,* New York: Harper & Row, 1977.

Secrest, Meryle, *Kenneth Clark: a biography,* New York: Fromm International Pub. Corp.: Distributed to the trade by Kampmann & Co., 1984. □

# Mark Wayne Clark

**The American army officer Mark Wayne Clark (1896-1984) held important commands in Europe and Asia and became one of America's leading anti-Communist propagandists.**

M ark Clark was born in Madison Barracks, N.Y., on May 1, 1896. After graduating from the U.S. Military Academy in 1917, he fought during World War I as an infantry officer in France, where he was wounded and decorated. He attended the Army's postgraduate schools between the wars and was widely known as a competent, ambitious officer.

In June 1942 Clark became Gen. Dwight Eisenhower's deputy for the invasion of French North Africa that began on Nov. 8, 1942. The next day Clark—whose code name, "Eagle," fitted both his personality and his appearance, since he had a thin but prominent nose—flew into Algiers, where he worked out an armistice with the French. The basis of the deal was American recognition of the French fascist Adm. Jean Darlan as governor of French North Africa. The "Darlan deal" brought a storm of abuse on Clark's and Eisenhower's heads; placing a fascist in charge of the first territory occupied by the Americans in World War II appeared to make a mockery of the principles for which the Allies claimed to be fighting. After Darlan's assassination on Dec. 24, 1942, the indignation faded.

Much to his annoyance, Clark did not hold a combat command in either the Tunisian or Sicilian campaigns. Instead, Eisenhower had him train the U.S. 5th Army for the invasion of Italy that would begin on Sept. 8, 1943.

At the outset Clark's forces just managed to cling to their first beachhead at Salerno south of Naples, and the Italian campaign that followed was one of endless frustration. Clark and the British forces on his right flank were always short of supplies and manpower, and progress up the Italian peninsula was painfully slow. Not until June 5, 1944, did Clark drive the Germans from Rome, a feat almost ignored by the world since the Normandy invasion began the next day. During the remainder of 1944 and the first 4 months of 1945, Clark's troops crept up the peninsula, forgotten by most of the world. For a man of Clark's ambition and keen desire for publicity, it was a trying time.

After the German surrender Clark became commander in chief of the American occupation forces in Austria. He quickly adopted an attitude of extreme hostility toward his Soviet counterparts on the Allied Control Commission for Austria. He was impatient with what he called the "cream puff and feather duster approach to communism" and advocated a get-tough policy with the Russians. He loudly protested against what he considered to be the "appeasement" of the Soviet Union by the United States.

In 1947 Clark served as deputy secretary of state, meeting with the Council of Foreign Ministers to negotiate a peace treaty for Austria. No progress was made at the talks, and late in the year Clark returned to the United States to take command of the 6th Army. Two years later he became chief of Army Field Forces, which made him responsible for the training of the Army. In the spring of 1952 he became commander in chief of the United Nations command in Korea, as well as commanding general of the U.S. Army Forces in the Far East. By the time Clark took over in Korea there was a virtual stalemate on the battlefront, and his major concerns were a prisoner-of-war mutiny and the armistice negotiations. On the military front his tactic was to inflict maximum casualties on the Chinese enemy. Fourteen months after he arrived, he signed the armistice agreement and fighting ended. Clark was unhappy with the outcome of the Korean War. He had hoped the United Nations would be able to defeat the North Koreans and Chinese and reunify Korea under Syngman Rhee.

Clark left the Army in 1954 to become president of the Citadel Military College of South Carolina, a position he held until his retirement in 1966. He remained a prominent anti-Communist, especially sensitive to what he considered a serious threat of communism from within the United States. He died on April 17, 1984.

## Further Reading

Clark wrote two volumes of memoirs: *Calculated Risk* (1950), a full and sprightly account of his World War II career, and *From the Danube to the Yalu* (1954), in which he describes his dealings with the Communists from 1946 to 1953. Kenneth G. Crawford, *Report on North Africa* (1943), and Alan Moorehead, *The End in Africa* (1943), provide information on the North African campaign. For general background on the war in Italy see Pietro Badoglio, *Italy in the Second World War: Memories and Documents* (trans. 1948), and Chester G. Starr, ed., *From Salerno to the Alps: A History of the Fifth Army* (1948). □

# Tom Campbell Clark

**Tom Campbell Clark (1899-1977) served the United States for more than 20 years as President Harry S. Truman's attorney general and as a Truman appointee to the Supreme Court.**

Dallas-born Tom Campbell Clark's soft-spoken drawl never disguised what for 22 years was one of the most influential legal minds in post World War II America. During four years as President Harry S. Truman's first attorney general (1945-1949) and for 18 years as one of Truman's four Supreme Court appointments (1949-1906), Tom Clark shaped American legal history.

Born September 23, 1899, to a prominent public family in Dallas Democratic party circles, Clark was raised a Presbyterian, as his Scotch-Irish ancestry predicted. He served for a short time in World War I and afterwards attended the University of Texas, graduating with a Bachelor's degree and an L.L.B. He joined his family's law firm in 1922. Two years later he married Mary Jane Ramsey, daughter of a Texas judge.

Clark's interest in politics and his family connections brought him to the attention of Congressman Sam Rayburn, later Speaker of the House, and of Senator Tom Connolly. During the 1920s and early 1930s, Clark engaged in private practice with occasional sallies into government service. An appearance on behalf of oil interests before the Texas legislature brought him censure from that body. In 1937 he joined the Justice Department and worked his way through that expanding agency in its New Deal heyday. A hard worker, politically reliable and well-connected, Clark rose rapidly under the benign protection of Rayburn, Connolly, and other patrons.

Clark was to spend the principal part of his public career as a Truman appointee and thus the relationship

between the two is crucial. The public record is historically ambivalent, however. Clark and Truman first became associated during the work of the World War II "Truman Committee" (Special Committee to Investigate the National Defense Program) which uncovered waste and fraud in the war effort. Established in 1941, the committee functioned as a watchdog working closely with the Justice Department's War Fraud Unit, then headed by Tom Clark.

In 1944, when Senator Truman sought the vice presidential nomination in Chicago, Clark was one of his supporters while then-Attorney General Francis Biddle was not. Inaugurated in January 1945, Truman served a mere three months as vice president, succeeding President Franklin D. Roosevelt in April 1945. One month later Truman took steps to remove Biddle, informing him to his apparent dismay that Clark was his replacement at Justice.

Clark served Truman as attorney general for somewhat over four years, from July 1, 1945, to August 14, 1949. A dutiful Cabinet officer, he took an active role in antitrust cases and prosecuted subversives as part of Truman's anti-Communist activities. Unwilling to go beyond the bounds of moderation in loyalty cases, he was sometimes at odds with the House Un-American Activities Committee. Unique among his duties as attorney general were the thorny legal problems arising out of the war: black marketeering, alien internment and deportation, and disposition of government financed war factories.

Clark vigorously supported Truman's hard line against the Soviet Union which manifested itself in the Doctrine of Containment and the Truman Doctrine. In 1948 he was one of the president's most avid supporters, defending the administration's record on internal security matters.

Clark's tenure was marked by congressional criticism and by some scandal, including the famous case of T. Lamar Caudle, a tax expert he brought into the department who later went to jail for conspiracy involving tax fraud. By the time the Caudle scandal came to light, Clark had been appointed Associate Justice of the Supreme Court, his judicial skirts raised clear of any mud by an overwhelming confirmation vote of 73 to eight (all eight dissenters being Republicans) taken on August 19, 1949.

Clark's 18 years on the Court spanned the most active period in its history, when it was the center of such vital and controversial issues as presidential power to seize private property, legislative reapportionment, school prayer, censorship, and civil rights.

Truman's appointment of Clark was generally attributed to the intervention of Chief Justice Fred Vinson, whom the president had chosen in 1946. In Clark, Vinson found a moderate Southerner he could work with.

As attorney general Clark had been thoroughly loyal to his chief, but his appointment to the Court freed him from that fealty and left him free to follow his own Constitutional dictates.

In the Steel Seizure case of 1952, both Truman and Vinson discovered Clark's independent mind when he joined five other Justices to overrule the seizure of the steel industry based on emergency inherent executive power.

*The Youngstown Sheet and Tube Co.* v. *Sawyer* decision declared Truman's act unconstitutional, thereby providing a significant check on presidential power.

A widely read biography of Truman later quoted the former president as describing his appointment of Clark as his "biggest mistake." According to oral biographer Merle Miller, Truman said: "He was no damn good as Attorney General, and on the Supreme Court . . . it doesn't seem possible, but he's been even worse." It is possible that Truman's disenchantment—if the quotation is accurate—was founded on the Youngstown decision.

In other instances of Court decisions Clark showed himself a moderate libertarian, somewhat to the right of William O. Douglas but certainly within Franklin D. Roosevelt's oft-quoted description of his own ideological position: slightly to the left of center. Clark wrote the unanimous decision in *Burstyn* v. *Wilson* (1952) which removed a state's right to censor a film on grounds of sacrilege. He joined the majority in striking down the use of the New York State Regents prayer in public schools (*Engle* v. *Vitale,* 1962). He supported the landmark *Baker* v. *Carr* reapportionment decision, although with reservations. And, in what was one of the most far-reaching judicial decisions of modern times, Clark was part of a unanimous Court's ruling on school desegregation when in 1954 *Brown* v. *Board of Education* reversed *Plessy* v. *Ferguson* of 1896.

Rising up the ladder of national prominence in the 1960s was Justice Clark's lawyer son, (William) Ramsey Clark. Paternal pride gave way to embarrassment, however, when President Lyndon Johnson selected the younger Clark to be his attorney general in 1967. To avoid potential conflicts of interest, Justice Clark resigned his seat, at the time calling his decision a "happy" one. Still a young man (67) by judiciary standards, he continued an active life on the Federal Court of Appeals until shortly before his death on June 13, 1977.

## Further Reading

Tom Clark's role as attorney general can be studied from memoirs such as those of Forrestal and Ickes, as well as by standard works such as Robert J. Donovan's *Conflict and Crisis* (1977) and *Tumultous Years* (1982), dealing with the Truman era. He coauthored (with Philip B. Perlman) *Prejudice and Proper, an Historic Brief Against Racial Covenants* (1969). Standard works such as Alfred H. Kelly's and Winfred A. Harbison's *The American Constitution* (1977) put Clark's judicial career in context.

## Additional Sources

Larrimer, Don, *Biobibliography of Justice Tom C. Clark,* Austin: Tarlton Law Library, School of Law, University of Texas at Austin, 1985. □

# William Clark

**The American explorer and soldier William Clark (1770-1838) was second in command of what has been called the American national epic of explora-**

tion, the Lewis and Clark expedition of 1804-1806, which traveled from the Missouri River to the Pacific Ocean.

William Clark was born on Aug. 1, 1770, in Caroline County, Va. He joined militia companies fighting local tribes in the Ohio country in 1789 and 3 years later won a lieutenant's commission in the U.S. infantry. He was on the Native American and Spanish frontier of the United States and served in Mad Anthony Wayne's successful campaign, terminated by the victory of Fallen Timbers (1794) over the Native Americans.

Clark resigned his commission in 1796, became a civilian, and tried to straighten out the chaotic financial condition of his famous brother, a hero of the Revolution, George Rogers Clark. However, when Meriwether Lewis offered him a role in what would be known as the Lewis and Clark expedition, he leaped at the opportunity.

In 1801 President Thomas Jefferson had chosen his White House secretary, Capt. Meriwether Lewis, to lead a corps of discovery up the Big Muddy (or Missouri) River and across the Rockies to the Pacific via the Columbia River. He gave Lewis complete freedom to choose his second in command. Without hesitation the Virginian picked his old Army buddy William Clark. When the Army failed to give Clark the promotion he deserved, Lewis ignored the ''brass'' and addressed Clark as captain, treating him as a virtual co-commander of the expedition.

It was Clark who led the fleet of boats upriver on May 14, 1804, while Lewis was detained in St. Louis by diplomatic and administrative matters. The two officers led their men up the Missouri to the Mandan Indian country of North Dakota, where they wintered before continuing in the spring of 1805. With great difficulty they shifted from canoes to horses and back to canoes as they crossed the unknown Rockies and followed the Columbia River to the sea. Clark was sharing leadership with Lewis in one of the most successful partnerships in the history of the nation.

After wintering at Ft. Clatsop on the Oregon coast, Lewis decided to split the party on its return to Missouri. He sent Clark to explore the Yellowstone River while he reconnoitered the Marias River. Although Lewis never yielded his command to Clark (except when accidentally wounded and incapacitated during a hunting expedition), Clark's wilderness and leadership skills contributed to the success of the corps of discovery. While Lewis was more brilliant and intellectual, Clark got along better with the men and was a fine map maker. Both men kept diaries, although spelling was not one of Clark's strong points.

Safe in St. Louis in September 1806, Clark resigned his commission to become brigadier general of militia and superintendent of Indian affairs for Louisiana Territory (later Missouri Territory) under the new governor, Meriwether Lewis. Clark was governor himself from 1813 to 1821, then became an unwilling—and unsuccessful—candidate for governor of the new state of Missouri. He devoted much of his time during the War of 1812 to Native American affairs and kept Missouri Territory almost unharmed by British-

inspired Native American raids. He continued in Indian diplomacy after the conflict and by his good sense was able to avert trouble with the Indians, who came to trust him more than any other white man.

Clark died in St. Louis on Sept. 1, 1838. Highly respected as an administrator, soldier, and explorer, for a half century he had served his country well, particularly in keeping the peace on the Native American frontier.

### Further Reading

There is no biography of Clark, although one has long been in preparation. The best sources are those on Meriwether Lewis, including John Bakeless, *Lewis and Clark: Partners in Discovery* (1947), and Richard Dillon, *Meriwether Lewis* (1965). An interesting retracing of Lewis and Clark's exploration is Calvin Tomkins, *The Lewis and Clark Trail* (1965). A one-volume abridgment of *The Journals of Lewis and Clark* was edited by Bernard DeVoto (1953).

### Additional Sources

Ambrose, Stephen E., *Undaunted courage: Meriwether Lewis, Thomas Jefferson, and the opening of the American West,* New York: Simon & Schuster, 1996.

Bakeless, John Edwin, *Lewis and Clark: partners in discovery,* Mineola, N.Y.: Dover Publications, 1996. □

# William Andrews Clark

**The American copper entrepreneur and politician William Andrews Clark (1839-1925) was a key figure in forging statehood for Montana.**

William Andrews Clark was born on Jan. 8, 1839, near Connellsville, Pa. He was educated in private academies in Pennsylvania and in Iowa, and after a short stint as a schoolmaster in Missouri, he studied law at Iowa Wesleyan College. At the outbreak of the Civil War, Clark enlisted in an Iowa regiment. Discharged in 1862, he moved to Colorado Territory.

Although Clark's career in Colorado was brief, it was productive, for it was his experience in the mines of the Central City district that brought into focus his lifelong obsession with the accumulation of wealth and political power. In 1863, attracted by the opportunities a new frontier offered an ambitious young man, Clark left Colorado for Montana. From a lucky strike in a claim near Bannack, he extracted $1500 worth of gold, which became the nucleus of an immense fortune.

Over the next few years Clark alternated between mining during the spring and summer and merchandising during the fall and winter. A typical frontier entrepreneur, he operated stores at several mining camps, lent money to men needing a grubstake, sold timbers to the miners, and operated a mail route between Missoula, Mont., and Walla Walla, Wash. In 1867 he formed a partnership to engage in wholesaling. He then established a bank at Deer Lodge in 1870 and at Butte in 1877.

## Mining King

In 1872 Clark had set up headquarters in the booming mining town of Butte. He purchased several mines. Realizing that the day of the untrained independent prospector was ending and that the time for scientific mining was dawning, he spent a year at Columbia University School of Mines. Back in Butte he built the Old Dexter mill and organized the Colorado and Montana Smelting Company. But he always sought to diversify his holdings, and soon he founded a newspaper, the *Butte Miner,* and went into lumbering, farming, and ranching. In Butte he established the city waterworks and a streetcar line. He also built, and for a time operated, the San Pedro, Los Angeles, and Salt Lake Railroad, later sold to the Union Pacific.

Branching out from Montana, Clark established the Los Alamitos Sugar Corporation in Los Angeles and bought the United Verde copper prospect in Arizona. A significant aspect of Clark's business techniques was his refusal to become deeply involved in any commercial enterprise unless he could own it in its entirety.

## Political Aspirant

In 1884, when Montanans sought unsuccessfully to win statehood, Clark served as president of an abortive constitutional convention. Four years later he ran as a Democrat for the post of territorial delegate to Congress. To Clark's astonishment he lost by 5,000 votes to Thomas H. Carter, a virtually unknown Republican. Clark had failed to carry either the mining towns or the lumbering districts,

both nominally Democratic and areas he had considered safe. With justification Clark attributed his loss to the machinations of Marcus Daly, the founder of the Anaconda Company, a potent rival of Clark's in the copper business. Thus began a political struggle that eventually placed virtually every Montana voter in the camp of either one man or the other.

In 1889, Clark was again chosen as president of a Montana constitutional convention. He was instrumental in incorporating a clause in the constitution fixing the maximum tax rate for mining property at the price paid to the Federal government for a claim. This meant that a claim worth millions could not be assessed at more than $5. Clark ran unsuccessfully for the U.S. Senate in 1889 and 1893.

## Elusive Senatorial Seat

Clark made yet another attempt to capture his long-cherished senatorial post in 1899. The moment seemed auspicious because the Democrats had captured control of the state legislature. After an 18-day contest the legislators chose Clark. Immediately, political foes in and out of his party charged that the election had been won by bribery. Although Clark freely admitted spending several hundred thousand dollars to elect legislators favorable to his political ambitions, he stubbornly denied any involvement in corrupt electoral practices. A grand jury refused to indict him, and he proceeded to Washington, D.C. There Thomas H. Carter, now a senator, introduced petitions from Montana citizens demanding that Clark be denied his seat. After a lengthy hearing, the Senate Committee on Privileges and Elections recommended unanimously that Clark be unseated.

Not yet willing to give up the fight, Clark waited until Governor Robert B. Smith was out of Montana on business and then sent a letter of resignation to Lieutenant Governor A. E. Spriggs, one of Clark's political henchmen. Spriggs immediately appointed Clark to fill the vacancy caused by his own resignation. A travesty of the political process was prevented only by the timely arrival of Governor Smith, who nullified the appointment and sent a replacement for Clark to Washington.

In 1901 Clark was finally elected to the Senate. He served one term (1901-1907) and distinguished himself only in a negative way, by opposing all measures designed to further the conservation of forest and mineral lands.

After leaving the Senate, Clark moved permanently to New York City. He devoted his last years to assembling a fine collection of art, now part of the collection of the Corcoran Gallery in Washington, D.C. Clark died in New York City on March 2, 1925, the last of the West's great copper kings.

## Further Reading

There is no full-length biography of Clark, but a family history appears in William D. Mangam, *The Clarks: An American Phenomenon* (1941). Other books containing important material on Clark include C. B. Glasscock, *The War of the Copper Kings* (1935); Joseph Kinsey Howard, *Montana: High, Wide, and Handsome* (1943); and K. Ross Toole, *Montana: An Uncommon Land* (1959).

## Additional Sources

*William Andrews Clark, Jr., his cultural legacy: papers read at a Clark Library seminar, 7 November 1981,* Los Angeles (2520 Cimarron St., Los Angeles 90018): William Andrews Clark Memorial Library, University of California, Los Angeles, 1985. □

# Kenneth Harry Clarke

**An experienced and popular Conservative politician, Kenneth Harry Clarke (born 1940) became Great Britain's chancellor of the exchequer in May 1993. Many observers predicted that he was destined to take over leadership of his party.**

Kenneth Harry Clarke was born in Nottingham on July 2, 1940. The descendant of coal miners, whose grandfather was an avid Communist, Clarke was raised in modestly upwardly-mobile circumstances. His father was initially a colliery electrician and, after World War II, the owner of a watch repair and jewelry business. An intelligent boy, Clarke was sent to Nottingham High School, where he excelled in academics and won a college scholarship to Caius College, Cambridge.

Clarke's Cambridge career was a great and unlikely success. Despite an undistinguished lineage and an unprepossessing appearance, he was popular and admired for his incisive mind, frankness, sense of humor, and amusing conversation. At Cambridge he focused his interests and found his true vocation—politics. Although he studied law and received a respectable degree, much of his time was spent in non-academic pursuits: he was active in campus Conservative (Tory) politics, serving as chairman of the Cambridge University Conservative Association in 1961 and, at the national level, as chairman of the Federation of Conservative Students from 1963 to 1965. He also was involved in the famous university debating society, the Cambridge Union, and in 1963 was named its president.

While at Cambridge Clarke met Gillian Edwards, a brilliant graduate student in medieval history, and the two were married in 1964. Like Clarke, unconventional in appearance, Gillian gave up her studies and devoted herself to making a home for Clarke and, later, their two children, a son and a daughter; to needlecraft (she was a national champion quilter); to gardening; and to philanthropy.

## Clarke Enters Politics

In 1963 Clarke was admitted to the bar, and he was a practicing barrister from 1963 to 1979. Specializing in criminal cases, he was able to utilize his skills in debate and soon established a flourishing career. His goal, however, was a political career, and he remained active in the Conservative Party. In the general election of 1970 he was elected member of Parliament for Rushcliffe, in Nottinghamshire, a seat he held well into the 1990s.

In Parliament Clarke's potential was quickly noticed. He became parliamentary private secretary to the solicitor general in 1971 and was an assistant whip in the Heath government from 1972 to 1974. In 1974 he was named secretary of the Conservative parliamentary health and social security committee, lord commissioner of the treasury, and member of the parliamentary delegation to the Council of Europe and was appointed opposition spokesman on social services. Two years later he became opposition spokesman on industry. For the next several years, however, his career stalled, not because of any lack of talent but because he was not a staunch advocate of Thatcherism and party leader Margaret Thatcher did not care for him personally. As a Tory politician Clarke represented everything Thatcher was not. He was a left-wing or "wet" Tory and a social and religious liberal, proudly provincial in orientation, and pro-European. He criticized his party's obsession with social class while himself exemplifying, like John Major, a new breed of "classless" Tory politician.

Despite her personal views on Clarke, in 1985 Thatcher named Clarke to his first cabinet position, minister for employment. Henceforth his progress was steady. In 1988 he was appointed secretary of state for health. In this capacity he took on the daunting task of reforming the glaringly inefficient management practices of the National Health Service in the face of intense opposition from the medical establishment and a significant portion of the electorate. Rising to the challenge, Clarke became known as the government's "bruiser" and was able to implement much of his reform policy.

During the Tory leadership crisis of November 1990 Clarke played a critical role. Though personally opposed to Thatcher's continued leadership, he believed that the threat posed by her opponent, Michael Heseltine, was a more immediate danger to the solidarity of the party. Accordingly, he at first defended Thatcher. Like most of his colleagues, he thought that she would withdraw from the contest when she realized the gravity of the situation. When she did not do so, he was the first cabinet minister to tell her she should resign and, in the interest of the party, let others—i.e., centrist John Major, the chancellor of the exchequer, and Clarke's old friend and fellow "wet" Tory, foreign secretary Douglas Hurd—have a chance. At length Thatcher did resign, apparently blaming Clarke for "leading the rout from the Cabinet Room." Clarke was then asked by his cabinet colleagues to urge Hurd, whom he supported, to run for the party leadership. Clarke's career was not disrupted, however, when Major, with whom Clarke always had maintained friendly relations, was elected leader and became the new prime minister.

## Appointment to Major's Cabinet

Major appointed Clarke secretary for education in his cabinet, and in his two years in the job Clarke initiated important reforms, empowering individual local schools at the expense of the local education authorities, often bastions of the "looney left," and strengthening educational standards. Named home secretary in December 1992, Clarke continued as a reformer, this time taking on the police. He sought to rationalize the byzantine police regulations, finances, and structure, and conducted an inquiry into policy pay and internal management. Here too, despite much criticism, the "bruiser" triumphed.

By mid-1993 Clarke's political position was assured. He had a significant following in the country and in the party. In Parliament he had a reputation for skill and was named "most impressive parliamentarian" in an informal, non-partisan poll of MPs (members of Parliament). He had shown he was able to stand up to the vested interests. Unlike representatives of the faltering right-wing of the Tory Party, the "wet" Tory Clarke exuded confidence and common sense. In the post-Thatcher era of "grey" politicians, Clarke was manifestly not boring. He was, in short, not merely viewed as a "coming man," but the "coming man," and the most likely and logical heir to John Major.

## Appointment to Chancellor of the Exchequer

In May 1993, in a bid to bolster his government by sacking the unpopular chancellor of the exchequer Norman Lamont, Major reshuffled his cabinet and named Clarke as chancellor. Although the appointment came as something of a surprise—Clarke had no substantial experience in economics—the appointment was hailed by most of the party because of Clarke's public credibility and political following. The appointment also was seen as a great opportunity for Clarke: the chancellor is the second most powerful position in the British cabinet, and Clarke, if able to improve Britain's fragile economy, would be in a very strong political position. Much of the press speculated that as chancellor Clarke was poised to replace Major, who was depicted as dull, indecisive, and melancholy. Nonetheless, Clarke consistently supported Major and his leadership. At the Conservative Party conference in October 1993 he defended Major against his critics ("an enemy of John Major is an enemy of the Conservative Party"), and in November 1993 he endorsed Major's much maligned "Back to Basics" policy.

From the time of his appointment as chancellor there was much speculation about the budget Clarke would produce on November 30, 1993. Clarke's 75-minute budget speech, in which he self-assuredly declared he was presenting the "no-nonsense budget . . . of a responsible government," was generally recognized as a political *tour de force*. Contrary to expectation, he did not propose massive new taxes. He did, however, propose higher taxes on gasoline, cigarettes, and wine; new taxes on air travel and insurance; and reduced tax breaks for home mortgages. In addition, he called for a 3.5 billion pound reduction in government spending through a freeze on public sector pay and government costs, and changes in unemployment (redubbed "job-seeking") and disability benefits. He predicted that the increased taxes and reduced spending would significantly decrease the public debt. The budget clearly strengthened Clarke's political position. Although it was termed "a vicious attack on the welfare state" by Labour leader John Smith, it was received enthusiastically by the Tories, by the financial markets, and by major economists and analysts at home and abroad.

Chancellor Clarke was able to deal adroitly with the problems confronting him. For example, the agreement in February 1994 with the public sector employees' unions for a 3 percent pay raise, which Clarke initially opposed, was reached after he stipulated that the money for the raise would come either from lay-offs or greater efficiency and would not nullify the provisions of his budget. His position as Major's heir apparent was not an easy one, and he was admittedly an ambitious man, but he carried it out with dignity and loyalty. And, as political analyst John Grigg observed, in the early 1990s Clarke was "young enough to be patient."

At the end of 1994 Clarke proposed to deregulate the government bond "repo" market as part of his 1995 budget proposal, and this was received with great approval. Repos are similar to stock futures in the corporate sector, and the move to open this market was seen as an incentive to foreign investment which in turn would strengthen the pound. By February of that year however the pound was still in a decline, and the Chancellor stubbornly persisted in his refusal to raise interest rates, despite intense pressure from the governor of the Bank of England. Clarke's subsequent endorsement of privatization for public projects did little to enhance his appeal. He held to his course regardless, and the economy continued to wane over the course of that year. Then in the spring of 1996 a serious confrontation with Prime Minister John Major antagonized Clarke to the point of resignation. This time the issue concerned the proposed EuroDollar, a common currency system for all of Europe. Clarke vehemently opposed the entire concept, and reportedly resigned over the issue of whether or not there should be a public referendum if the other European countries would pass the resolution. John Major assuaged Clarke's ire and convinced him to continue as Chancellor, and the critics had a field day until later that year when none could deny that the British economy had taken a turn for the better despite the Chancellor's idiosyncratic policies. At the end of 1996 Chancellor Clarke finally conceded to an increase in interest rates, most likely to stave off a relapse of the sluggish economy.

With the dawn of the new year, 1997, Kenneth Clarke's political future was hanging in the balance. His controversial budget proposal for 1997 was ballyhooed by critics as politically expedient but otherwise useless. The ongoing flap over acceptance of the EuroDollar served to antagonize the situation. In a seething editorial in *The Economist* he was labeled a "closet New Labourite . . . doing his tactical best to keep the Tories in power." However, in 1997 elections, John Major's Tories failed to hold a majority of seats in the House of Commons and lost the prime minister's office to Labour's Tony Blair.

## Further Reading

Two biographies of Clarke are reportedly in progress in Britain. The single best source of general information on Kenneth Clarke is John Grigg's admiring article "Primed Minister" in the *London Times Magazine* (October 2, 1993). The more left-wing *Guardian*'s profile of Clarke, by Alex Brunner (September 29, 1993), is less effusive. A portrait of an amiably eccentric Gillian Clarke is provided by Alice Thomson in

"Patchwork Provincial Shares Limelight with Cocktail Set," *London Times* (May 29, 1993). Penny Junor's *The Major Enigma* (1993) is a sympathetic biography of John Major. Clarke's role in the Tory leadership crisis of November 1990 is discussed in Robert Shepherd's factual and balanced *The Power Brokers: The Tory Party and Its Leaders* (1991). For an anti-Clarke perspective on the same topic see Alan Clark's *Diaries* (1993). Journalists have enjoyed speculating on Clarke's possible future as prime minister. Of particular interest is William Rees-Mogg's "Clarke for PM," *London Times* (May 31, 1993). Clarke's first budget attracted attention even in the United States—see Nicholas Bray's "Britain's Budget Mixes Tax Increases with Promise of Public Spending Cuts," *Wall Street Journal* (December 1, 1993). Simon Heffer's "The Day of the Job Seeker" in the *Spectator* (December 4, 1993) is highly critical of Clarke and his budget.

Clarke wrote or coauthored three pamphlets. In 1966 he, with John Lenton and Nicholas Budger, produced "Immigration, Race, and Politics: A Birmingham View." With fellow Conservative MP Elaine Lellett-Bowman he wrote "Britain in Europe—New Hope for the Regions" in 1979, and in 1987 the Conservative Political Centre published his "The Free Market and the Inner Cities." All the pamphlets are indicative of Clarke's political views: a positive attitude and an enthusiastic embracing of the need for an activist government to reform unacceptable conditions.

## Additional Sources

*The Economist,* December 3, 1994; February 18, 1995; May 13, 1995; October 28, 1995; March 16, 1996; April 6, 1996; November 16, 1996; November 30, 1996; November 30, 1996. □

# Marcus Andrew Hislop Clarke

**Marcus Andrew Hislop Clarke (1846-1881) was an English-born journalist and author who achieved eminence in colonial Australia. He is noted for his novel of early-19th-century convict transportation.**

Marcus Clarke was born on April 24, 1846, in Kensington, London. His mother died while he was an infant, and he was brought up by his father, a lawyer with literary interests. When he was 16 his father died and, seeing no future for him in London, relations persuaded the boy to try his fortunes in Australia, where he could be under the eye of an uncle who owned a sheep run and held a judgeship.

After trying and disliking work in a Melbourne bank, Clarke at 19 went into the backcountry to taste the rustic life and gain "colonial experience." He began writing sketches for the *Australian Magazine* and in 1867 returned to Melbourne as a newspaper reporter. Energetic, restless, and unable to settle at any task for long, he found routine tasks intolerable but succeeded as a columnist commenting on people and events. He thus established himself as a leader among the writers and poets who were making Melbourne the literary center of Australia.

At the age of 23 Clarke acquired a magazine which he named the *Colonial Monthly*. In it he serialized his first novel, *Long Odds* (later to be renamed *Heavy Odds*), a lively but unsubstantial story about a young Australian sheep grazier on a visit to England. When the story was complete, Clarke's interest flagged, and the magazine subsequently closed.

## "The Great Australian Novel"

Visiting Tasmania, Clarke studied the records of transportation to the island's penal settlements and set about writing a novel recapturing the atmosphere of the old convict days. Under the title *His Natural Life* the story was serialized in the *Australian Journal* (1870-1872). Written mostly a chapter at a time—some portions while the typesetter stood by—it was to rank as Clarke's great achievement. In 1874 a substantially edited version was published in book form; later it appeared as *For the Term of His Natural Life,* the title by which it became established. Meanwhile Clarke was appointed secretary to the trustees of Melbourne's Public Library; later he became the assistant librarian.

Contrasting strongly with his witty and exuberant writings as a columnist, *For the Term of His Natural Life* deals in gloomy and powerful terms with the brutishness of the convict system. As in all his writing, Clarke intensified every phase, making it more striking, if less real. In the story injustice is heaped upon misfortune as Clarke unfolds an agitated drama of bitter human relationships. From melodramatic opening to sentimental conclusion, the story has compelling narrative power and strong human interest. In spite of exaggeration, both action and characterization are extraordinarily vivid. The language is sometimes theatrical; occasionally pathos turns to banality—yet overall the novel manages to outstrip its faults. In its day it was highly regarded and even considered to be "the great Australian novel." It can more correctly be regarded as representing a landmark of the colonial period—the Anglo-Australian phase—of Australia's literary development. In fact, it is Australian only in subject (and only insofar as Australia can be identified with convictism), and its author was Australian in nothing but residence.

Clarke's third novel, *'Twixt Shadow and Shine* (1875), was a light and pleasantly written story; it gained only minor attention. Meanwhile his extravagance had run him into insolvency in 1874. Pressures built up, and he left his public library post. He continued to contribute to newspapers and was active in the theater as an original author and translator, but he remained in hopeless debt. Dispirited, he overworked himself to the point of exhaustion. Early in 1881 he was declared bankrupt for the second time. He died on Aug. 2, 1881. Clarke's fourth novel, *Chidiock Tichbourne, or the Catholic Conspiracy,* a swashbuckling romance of Elizabethan England, was published in 1893.

## Further Reading

A favorable biography of Clarke is A. W. Brazier, *Marcus Clarke: His Work and Genius* (1902). A concise sketch of Clarke, together with a full listing of his essays, drama, and fiction, is contained in E. Morris Miller and others, *Australian Literature* (1940). See also Brian Robinson Elliott, *Marcus Clarke* (1958). For an appreciation of Clarke's *For the Term of His Natural Life* and comments on his place in the literary development of Australia see H. M. Green, *A History of Australian Literature*, vol. 1 (1966).

### Additional Sources

McLaren, Ian Francis, *Marcus Clarke, an annotated bibliography*, Melbourne: Library Council of Victoria, 1982.
Simmons, Samuel Rowe, *Marcus Clarke: an annotated checklist, 1863-1972*, Sydney: Wentworth Press, 1975. □

# Samuel Clarke

**The English theologian and moral philosopher Samuel Clarke (1675-1729) was in his time the foremost exponent of rationalist ethics and a prominent defender of Newtonian physics.**

S amuel Clarke was born on Oct. 11, 1675, in Norwich, where his father was alderman and at one time representative in Parliament. He entered Cambridge University at 16. There he discovered Sir Isaac Newton's *Principia mathematica* and resolved to advance Newton's theories against those of René Descartes, which were then dominant. His translation of Jacques Rohault's popular physics textbook, with notes and comments reflecting Newton's ideas, was used at Cambridge for several decades.

Clarke's ecclesiastical career began as vicar to the bishop of Norwich. In 1704 and 1705 he gave the Boyle Lectures; these were published as *A Demonstration of the Being and the Attributes of God* (1705-1706) and *The Verity and Certitude of Natural and Revealed Religion* (1705). They are his chief contributions to philosophy and theology, along with *Discourse Concerning the Unchangeable Obligation of Natural Religion* (1708). He moved to London in 1706 as rector of St. Benet's Church and later served as chaplain at court. In 1709 he became rector of St. James, Westminster, and he held this position, despite charges of heresy provoked by his *Scripture Doctrine of the Trinity* (1712), until his death.

Clarke became a friend of Newton in London, and his translation of Newton's *Opticks* into Latin, warmly praised by the author, was published in 1706. Later he was asked by the Princess of Wales to defend Newton against the German philosopher Gottfried Wilhelm von Leibniz. In the controversy with Leibniz, Clarke supported Newton's theory of absolute space and time. The Clarke-Leibniz correspondence, conducted during 1715-1716, appeared in print in 1717. Clarke also wrote numerous treatises on theology, philosophy, and mathematics; an edition of Caesar's *Commentaries;* and a translation of the first 12 books of the *Iliad*. He died on May 17, 1729.

Clarke is best known for his ethical theory, which compares moral and mathematical truths. Right and wrong are known self-evidently, like the axioms of mathematics, and depend on "the necessary eternal different relations that different things bear to one another." They express "fitness or suitableness of certain circumstances to certain persons, and unsuitableness of others." He also argued against materialism and atheism and for free will and the immortality and spirituality of the soul.

### Further Reading

*The Works of Samuel Clarke* (4 vols., 1738-1742) was edited, with a biographical preface, by Benjamin Hoadly, Bishop of Salisbury. A modern edition of the Leibniz-Clarke correspondence was prepared by H. G. Alexander, *The Leibniz-Clark Correspondence, together with Extracts from Newton's Principia and Opticks* (1956). William Whiston, *Historical Memoirs of the Life of Dr. S. Clarke* (3d ed. 1748), includes A. A. Sykes's "Elogium" and Thomas Emlyn's "Memoirs of the Life and Sentiments of Dr. Clarke." For Clarke's ethical theory see James Edward LeRossignol, *Ethical Philosophy of Samuel Clarke* (1892). Background studies which discuss Clarke include W. R. Sorley, *A History of English Philosophy* (1920); Gerald R. Cragg, *Reason and Authority in the Eighteenth Century* (1964); and Charles Vereker, *Eighteenth-Century Optimism* (1967).

### Additional Sources

Ferguson, James P., *Dr. Samuel Clarke: an eighteenth century heretic*, Kineton: Roundwood Press, 1976. □

# Claude Lorrain

**The French landscape painter, draftsman, and etcher Claude Lorrain (1600-1682) was regarded as the prince of landscape painters until the days of impressionism in the mid-19th century.**

Claude Lorrain and Nicolas Poussin were the most distinguished exponents of the French classical baroque style, though fulfilling antithetically expressive ends within the theoretical precepts established by the French for painters from the middle of the 17th century. Whereas Poussin was interested in rendering the archeologically precise and imposing monumentality of imperial Rome objectively, Lorrain preferred to depict the romantic deserted ruins in a rolling countryside. To Lorrain's admirers, his paintings remain the visual counterpart of the profound sentiment of the beauty of the natural world found in the *Eclogues* and *Georgics* of the ancient Roman poet Virgil. Lorrain, however, largely deemphasized the role of man in nature in order to enhance the presence and play of cosmic forces, though classical tradition precluded his unbalancing the two to any pronounced degree. If Poussin's art is the last phase of rational formalism in the history of landscape painting, Lorrain's can be considered the first in the long development of autonomous pictorialism leading to the 19th-century romantics and impressionists. A synthesis of the divergent artistic messages of Poussin the scholar

and Lorrain the poet might be said to have been reached in the landscape art of Paul Cézanne, where the poetic content of nature is unified within the formal elements of classical composition.

Claude Lorrain was born Claude Gellée in the village of Chamagne near Nancy. Orphaned at about the age of 12, he moved to Freiburg im Breisgau to live with his brother, who apparently was equipped to teach him engraving. In 1613 he set off with another relative, a dealer in lace, for Rome, where, because of the talent common to many Lorrainers, he found employment as a pastry cook in the house of the landscape painter Agostino Tassi. The position of apprentice soon replaced that of cook, the master teaching the young boy the rudiments of painting.

About 1623 Lorrain went to Naples, where he studied for a short time with the Flemish artist Goffredo Wals. The impression of the Gulf of Naples from Sorrento to Pozzuoli and the islands of Capri and Ischia was overwhelming and indelibly imprinted upon his memory, for reminiscences of these awesome views of water, earth, sky, and light recurred in his art until the end of his life. In 1625 he returned to Nancy, where he briefly assisted Claude Deruet by executing the architectural backgrounds to the latter's ceiling paintings for the Carmelite church (now destroyed). He then made his way back to Rome—sketching all the way. No record reveals Lorrain's ever leaving Rome again, and he lived out his life quietly and industriously as a respected member of the colony of foreign artists, though some scholars believe the vividness of the Neapolitan recollections in his paintings implies the necessity of his having returned to Naples and its environs.

After the 1630s his reputation as a landscape painter was firmly established. By the 1640s he counted among his clients the French ambassador Philippe de Béthune, cardinals Bentivoglio and Crescenzio, and Pope Urban VIII. As a clue to the degree of his early success, the French artist Sébastien Bourdon in 1634 imitated Lorrain's style and passed the work off as an original. Because copyists and imitators of his style abounded, he created, to offset this plagiarizing tendency by contemporaries, a catalog of 200 drawings of his original compositions and entitled it *Liber veritatis*.

## Artistic Style

This visual record, as well as all other authenticated works by the artist, reveals relatively little change in Lorrain's style from his early to his late period. The structural formula of composition, transmitted through Tassi, his first teacher, from such late mannerist artists as Paul Brill and Adam Elsheimer, who utilized stage-set structural devices, remains constant in him. He sets his scenes consistently as spatial areas receding from picture plane to infinity. The picture plane is established by placing a mass of dark greenish-brown foliage on both sides of the composition, with usually a tall, feathery tree element on one side, as in *The Mill* (1631). When human activity does occur, as in *The Mill*, the action takes place quite animatedly in the front area of the middle distance, set upon or against a barge landing, bridge, or farmhouse. This central focus then is systematically reduced by subtly placed flanking motifs, like stage flats, creating wings, or coulisses, which carry the eye to the far distance of mountains, rivers, or the rolling Roman campagna, as in *Apollo Guarding the Herds of Admetus* (1654).

The real subject of Lorrain's work is not, however, the forms of nature or the activities of men, but rather the animating power of light, emanating in varied intensities, depending upon the time of day chosen for the theme, playing upon the material realm and transforming it into a peculiar mood impression.

Chiaroscuro, or the play of patterns of dark and light contrasts, is the method Lorrain generally uses in drawing and painting. Modulation plays down the violence of blindingly dramatic sun and moon effects of such a mannerist precursor as Elsheimer. His drawings, though great in variety, uniformly reveal a preoccupation with values of light and dark rather than with color. As with his paintings, the magic of mood, the veiling of earth and man in an infinite variety of gently controlled radiation and reflection of light which issues from a known but unobtrusive source, is the subject.

Lorrain's influence was both catalytic and mediating of divergent national talents. In his art he melded the northern emotive response to nature, such as that found in the works of the German Albrecht Altdorfer and the Fleming Joachim Patinir, with the more palpable control of the southern temperament. In this sense his contribution to art is more universal than that of his habitually more formalistic contemporary and countryman Poussin.

## Further Reading

A scholarly and interesting summary in English of all previous studies of Claude is Marcel Röthlisberger, *Claude Lorrain: The Drawings* (2 vols., 1968). Röthlisberger's *Claude Lorrain: The Paintings* (2 vols., 1961) is also valuable. Roger Fry's essay on Claude in his *Vision and Design* (1920) is rich in esthetic and philosophical wisdom and refutes the literary attacks on the artist in John Ruskin's *Modern Painters* (5 vols., 1846-1860). See also Martin Davies's detailed discussion of the *Liber veritatis in French School* (1946-1950; 2d ed. 1957), published by the National Gallery in London. There is a discussion of Claude and the general historical period in Anthony Blunt, *Art and Architecture in France, 1500-1700* (1953).

## Additional Sources

Russell, H. Diane (Helen Diane), *Claude Lorrain, 1600-1682,* Washington, D.C.: National Gallery of Art, 1982. □

# Paul Louis Charles Claudel

**The French author and diplomat Paul Louis Charles Claudel (1868-1955) is best known for his plays, in which he explored the relationship between man, the universe, and the divine in a highly poetic and original style.**

Paul Claudel was one of a group of celebrated writers, all born about 1870, who gave French literature a new orientation. Though quite different from one another, Paul Valéry, Marcel Proust, André Gide, Charles Péguy, Colette, and Claudel all revolted against 19th-century positivism, as well as against the extremes of symbolism which denied reality to the external world. Each, in his own way, experimented with new ways of using the French language and offered new visions of the world and new views of the function of art.

Claudel was born on Aug. 6, 1868, at Villeneuve-sur-Fère-en-Tardenois on the border between the provinces of Champagne and the Ile-de-France. His family, of peasant and petit bourgeois stock, was Roman Catholic but not particularly devout. He received his early education in the various provincial towns where his father worked as a civil servant. In 1882 the family moved to Paris and enrolled young Paul in the famous lycée Louis-le-Grand. As a schoolboy, he was solitary and pessimistic and rebelled against the pervading philosophies of determinism and positivism, which denied man his free will and made him merely a product of his heredity and environment. He rejected his whole traditional literary education to take refuge in the poetry of Charles Baudelaire, Paul Verlaine, and especially Arthur Rimbaud, who was to be a lifelong source of inspiration. Rimbaud, he wrote later, revealed the supernatural to him and was in part responsible for his return to the Catholic faith, which he had abandoned.

## Claudel's Conversion

While studying for a diplomatic career, Claudel underwent on Christmas Day 1886, in the Cathedral of Notre Dame, a profound mystical experience which was to shape his destiny. During the singing of the Magnificat, he suddenly knew that he believed in a living and personal God. His complete conversion and return to the Church were accomplished only after 4 years of study and spiritual struggle to reconcile the opposition between his intuition and his intellect.

This spiritual crisis is evident in Claudel's first works. *Tête d'Or* (1889), his only non-Christian play, is the tragedy of an adventurer who tries to find salvation solely through his own strength and intelligence and ignores an inner voice counseling humility. This play, like all that were to follow it, rejects all the conventions of the French theater, be they classical, romantic, or realistic. It offers a new conception of poetic drama in which psychology and logical dramatic action give way to symbolism and imaginative truth. The play also uses the completely original line of verse, known as the *verset claudélien,* in which Claudel wrote all his poems and plays. The rhythmic pattern of the lines of different lengths is intended to reproduce the natural breathing and heartbeat of the poet or actor in order to indicate the emotional intensity of the passage. In Claudel's second play, *La Ville* (1890), he sees the city, and eventually the entire world, as a single body, a *maison fermée* (closed house) in which each member is responsible for the salvation of the other members.

## Diplomatic Career

In February 1893 Claudel received his first diplomatic post, as vice-consul in New York. From then until his retirement in 1935, he lived almost continuously outside France. He served as French ambassador to Japan (1921-1927), the United States (1927-1933), and Belgium (1933-1935).

Claudel's experiences outside France, and especially outside Europe, influenced his work and thought in many ways. His discovery of non-Western conceptions of the theater encouraged him to experiment with revolutionary and, at the time, largely misunderstood dramatic techniques. Most importantly, however, Claudel's travels throughout the world contributed a cosmic dimension to his Catholicism, rendering it often unacceptable to his more orthodox coreligionists.

## Major Works

The moving religious drama *Partage de Midi* (1906) is partly based on an episode in Claudel's life that occurred in 1905, the year before his marriage. Like the hero of this play, after considerable spiritual anguish Claudel had rejected a religious vocation. He also fell in love with a young married woman and learned for the first time the meaning of great love, suffering, and sacrifice.

Claudel's long lyric poems *Cinq Grandes Odes* (1910) and *La Cantate à trois voix* (1931) are meditations on the relationship between the Creator and the created world, on the role of the poet, and on the function of love. These themes reappear in *L'Annonce faite à Marie* (1912; *Tidings Brought to Mary*), Claudel's best-known play. In a medieval setting, the apparent paradox of human relationships is resolved when Violaine, the heroine, reveals how love, separation, suffering, and even evil lead men to understand both their role in the salvation of others and also the divine order of the universe.

*Le Soulier de satin* (1929; *The Satin Slipper*), considered by many to be his greatest play, is a complicated and gigantic drama of the Renaissance, a period Claudel believed to be the beginning of a new era of Catholicism. Against a background of violence, conquest, and passion, the characters work out their destinies in a plot that reveals Claudel's characteristic themes: man's desire for the infinite, the limitations of human love, and the necessity of human love as an instrument of salvation.

## Last Years

Claudel divided the last 20 years of his life between an apartment in Paris and his Château de Brangues. Although he wrote no more poems or plays, he composed lengthy reflections on various scriptural texts. During these years, when his plays were staged, he often attended rehearsals and made changes in his texts for the stage. In 1946 he was elected to the French Academy. He died in Paris on Feb. 23, 1955, and was accorded a state funeral at the Cathedral of Notre Dame before his burial at Brangues. He was survived by his widow, five children, and many grandchildren.

## Further Reading

Jacques Madaule has made the most comprehensive study of Claudel to date. Especially recommended are three of his volumes, in French: *Le Génie de Paul Claudel* (1933; rev. ed. 1947), *Le Drame de Paul Claudel* (1936; rev. ed. 1964), and *Claudel et le langage* (1968). In English, Wallace Fowlie, *Paul Claudel* (1957), is an excellent short study. Joseph Chiari, *The Poetic Drama of Paul Claudel* (1954), is a sympathetic treatment of his theater. Recommended for general background material on modern French poetry and theater are Marcel Raymond, *From Baudelaire to Surrealism* (1950); Wallace Fowlie, *A Guide to Contemporary French Literature: From Valéry to Sartre* (1957); Roger Shattuck, *The Banquet Years* (1958; rev. ed. 1960); and Jacques Guicharnaud, *Modern French Theatre from Giraudoux to Genet* (1967).

## Additional Sources

Chaigne, Louis, *Paul Claudel: the man and the mystic,* Westport, Conn.: Greenwood Press, 1978, 1961. □

# Tiberius Claudius Germanicus

**Tiberius Claudius Germanicus (10 B.C.-A.D. 54) was the fourth emperor of Rome. Deemed a weak emperor, he nevertheless extended the borders of the empire and reformed its administration.**

orn in Lugdunum (modern Lyons) on Aug. 1, 10 B.C., Claudius was the son of Drusus and Antonia and the grandnephew of Augustus. Although Claudius was the sole surviving heir of Augustus after the assassination of Caligula, he was given the throne primarily because of the support shown him by the imperial troops. He assumed the throne unwillingly in 41; indeed, he is said to have been found cowering in a closet after Caligula's death was announced.

Kept in the background and often ignored during the reigns of Augustus, Tiberius, and Caligula, Claudius gained a reputation for stupidity, gluttony, and licentiousness. Although he is pictured by contemporary historians as a man incapable of anything, Claudius seems to have been, in fact, an excellent scholar, linguist, and writer.

Claudius began his rule with a great deal of enthusiasm and effort. He respected and frequently consulted both the Senate and the magistrates, groups whose prerogatives had been absorbed previously by the emperors. He built many monuments and public works in Rome. He began the campaign that led to the eventual conquest of Britain, and the imperial armies were successful in repelling the threatened German invasions. The Emperor initiated a number of reforms of the Roman legal and administrative systems, and he reestablished sound fiscal policies.

However, Claudius was a man of extremely weak character, easily swayed and led. That same elasticity of nature which had enabled him to survive his predecessor's reign of terror now made him an emperor completely governed by those around him. The aristocracy, which had hoped for a restitution of their former powers and privileges after the death of Caligula, was disappointed and angered when the new emperor surrounded himself with his friends, mainly slaves and freedmen. The middle class was shocked, feeling that Claudius's associates were degrading the dignity of the imperial power. This dissatisfaction led to the first conspiracy against the Emperor, in A.D. 42.

The plot was crushed, but further trouble arose in 48. Claudius's third wife, Messalina, who had previously influenced the Emperor to retaliate against the aristocracy, became involved in a scandal with a Roman senator, Silius. The affair rocked Roman society, and Claudius ordered Messalina to commit suicide.

The Emperor's next wife was Agrippina, his niece and the mother of his successor, Nero. A woman of immense capability and driving ambition, she persuaded Claudius to set aside his own son, Britannicus, and adopt Nero as his heir.

The details surrounding Claudius's death are unclear, although many ancient historians, including Tacitus, say that he may have been poisoned by Agrippina. Claudius died in Rome on Oct. 13, 54.

## Further Reading

The two ancient sources for the life of Claudius are Tacitus's *Annals* and Suetonius's *The Lives of the Twelve Caesars.* Modern references include Arnaldo Momigliano, *Claudius: The Emperor and His Achievement* (1932; trans. 1934; new ed. 1962), and Vincent M. Scramuzza, *The Emperor Claudius* (1940).

## Additional Sources

Levick, Barbara, *Claudius,* New Haven: Yale University Press, 1990.
Momigliano, Arnaldo, *Claudius: the Emperor and his achievement: with a new bibliography (1942-59) by Arnaldo Momigliano; translated by W. D. Hogart,* Westport, Conn.: Greenwood Press, 1981. □

# Rudolf Julius Emanuel Clausius

**The German physicist Rudolf Julius Emanuel Clausius (1822-1888) was one of the chief architects of thermodynamics and the kinetic theory of gases.**

orn on Jan. 2, 1822, in Köslin, Pomerania, R. J. E. Clausius was the sixth son of the 18 children of the Reverend C. E. G. Clausius, a Lutheran pastor and councilor of the Royal Government School Board in Köslin. Young Clausius received much of his primary and secondary education in the private school which his father established in Uckermünde. After graduating from the gymnasium in Stettin, Clausius enrolled at the University of Berlin, and in 1844 he obtained his teacher's certificate.

During the next 6 years Clausius taught physics at the Friedrich Werder Gymnasium in Berlin. He received his doctoral degree in 1848 from the University of Halle with a dissertation which gave for the first time the explanation of the blue sky and red sunset in terms of the selective reflection of various wavelengths of light by particles present in the atmosphere. In 1850 Clausius became professor of physics at the Royal Artillery and Engineering School in Berlin and also obtained the rank of privat-dozent at the University of Berlin.

## Theories of Heat

Clausius presented his paper "On the Motive Power of Heat and on the Laws Which Can Be Deduced from It for the Theory of Heat" in 1850. Its significance can best be gauged by the comments of James Clerk Maxwell, who years later wrote that Clausius "first stated the principle of Carnot in a manner consistent with the true theory of heat." The "true theory" was the consideration of heat as a mechanical process.

Sadi Carnot's explanation of his very successful theory of the efficiency of steam engines seemed, however, to contradict the mechanical theory. In Carnot's words, "no heat was lost" when a steam engine produced work by going through its cycles. Clausius insisted that the "new theory" could only be a mechanical one. More importantly, he showed that it was quite consistent with the mechanical theory to assume that when work was done by heat one part of the heat was "lost," or rather was transformed into work.

task in two papers: "On the Kind of Motion Which We Call Warmth" (1857) and "On the Average Length of Paths Which Are Traversed by Single Molecules in the Molecular Motion of Gaseous Bodies" (1858). From the assumption that molecules move in a straight path Clausius calculated the average velocity of hydrogen molecules at normal temperature and pressure. Because the value, about 2,000 meters per second, seemed to contradict the low rate of gaseous diffusion, Clausius offered as explanation the important notion of the free mean path of molecules.

A few years later, in 1862, Clausius published his paper "On the Thermal Conductivity of Gaseous Bodies," in which he successfully derived from theoretical considerations the experimentally known data in question. He deserved indeed the praises heaped on him by Maxwell, who referred to Clausius as the first who "gave us precise ideas about the motion of agitation of molecules." Maxwell also described the adoption of mechanical principles to molecular studies as being "to a great extent the work of Prof. Clausius."

The year 1862 also saw the return of Clausius's full attention to thermodynamics. The results spoke for themselves. In the paper known as his sixth memoir, "On the Application of the Theorem of the Equivalence of Transformations to Interior Work," he concluded that it was "impossible practically to arrive at the absolute zero of temperature by any alteration of the condition of a body."

## Concept of Entropy

On April 24, 1865, Clausius read before the Philosophical Society of Zurich his best-remembered paper, or ninth memoir, "On Several Convenient Forms of the Fundamental Equations of the Mechanical Theory of Heat." In it the word "entropy" was used for the first time. The word, as Clausius noted, was coined by him from the Greek $\tau\rho o\pi\epsilon$, or transformation: "I have intentionally formed the word *entropy* so as to be as similar as possible to the word *energy;* for the two magnitudes to be denoted by these words are so nearly allied in their physical meanings, that a certain similarity in designation appears to be desirable."

In nontechnical parlance, entropy stands for the inevitable transformation of some part of the energy in any real physical process into a form which is no longer utilizable. Clausius disclosed the far-reaching, cosmic consequences of his analysis of the foundations of thermodynamics: "If for the entire universe we conceive the same magnitude to be determined, consistently and with due regard to all circumstances, which for a single body I have called entropy, and if at the same time we introduce the other and simpler conception of energy, we may express in the following manner the fundamental laws of the universe which correspond to the two fundamental theorems of the mechanical theory of heat. (1) The energy of the universe is constant. (2) The entropy of the universe tends to a maximum."

In 1869 Clausius accepted an invitation to become professor of physics at the University of Bonn after having spent 2 years in the same capacity at the University of Würzburg. The University of Bonn represented the last phase of Clausius's academic career. There he wrote in

This part of the heat and the other part which was rejected into the cold reservoir of the engine stood, in Clausius's words, in a "certain definite relation to the quantity of work produced."

Two subsequent papers published in 1851 by Clausius clarified merely some details of his first memoir, but in 1854 he confronted once more the fundamentals. What became known as his fourth memoir carried the title "On a Modified Form of the Second Fundamental Theorem in the Mechanical Theory of Heat." In it Clausius proposed to make Carnot's theorem a particular form of the general proposition, "Heat can never pass from a colder to a warmer body without some other change, connected therewith, occurring at the same time." With a penetrating analysis, Clausius showed that the Carnot cycle corresponded to the integral $\int (dQ/T)$, the value of which was zero for a reversible, or ideal, process. For an irreversible, or real, process the corresponding value could only be positive.

Herein lay a proposition of utmost importance, but its full meaning was not spelled out by Clausius until about 10 years later. Meanwhile, he moved to Zurich to serve as professor of physics at the Swiss Federal Technical Institute. Two years later he also assumed professorship at the University of Zurich. In Zurich he married Adelheid Rimpau; they had six children.

## Kinetic Theory of Gases

The scientific fruits of Clausius's first years in Zurich related to the kinetic theory of gases. Clausius achieved his

1870 his last important paper on thermodynamics, which contained the notion of virial. In 1876 he published a second, considerably enlarged and revised version of what was mainly a collection of his memoirs which had been printed in 1864 under the title *Abhandlungen über die mechanische Wärmetheorie*. The new edition, entitled *Die mechanische Wärmetheorie* (The Mechanical Theory of Heat), was for several decades the standard for textbooks on thermodynamics. The second part of the book deals with the analysis of electrical phenomena on the basis of mechanical principles, a topic which dominated Clausius's attention in Bonn.

Clausius's wife died in 1875. Eleven years later he married Sophie Sack, by whom he had one son. In the summer of 1886 he began to show symptoms of acute anemia. Nevertheless he carried on with the work of seeing to print the third edition of his *Wärmetheorie,* and he even held examinations from his sickbed. He was the embodiment of sincerity and conscientiousness to the end, which came on Aug. 24, 1888.

## Further Reading

In French, *R. Clausius, sa vie, ses travaux et leur portée métaphysique* (1890), is a booklet by F. Folie, a close friend of the Clausius family and director of the Brussels Observatory. The major documents representing the emergence of thermodynamics as a full-fledged branch of physics are collected in W. F. Magie, ed., *The Second Law of Thermodynamics: Memoirs by Carnot, Clausius and Thomson* (1899). A good critical account of the steps leading to the full formulation of the second law of thermodynamics is given in Frederick O. Koenig's essay, "On the History of Science and of the Second Law of Thermodynamics," in Herbert McLean Evans, ed., *Men and Moments in the History of Science* (1959). □

# St. Peter Claver

**St. Peter Claver (1580-1654) was a Spanish Jesuit missionary to Latin America. He is known as the "Apostle of the West Indies" and the "Slave to the Slaves."**

Peter Claver was born in Verdu, Catalonia, on July 26, 1580, of prosperous parents. Little is known of his early years. In 1602 he entered the Society of Jesus. Three years later he began to study with Alphonsus Rodriquez in Majorca, with whom he shared a spiritual model of life focused on "suffering with Christ," which he would try to emulate for the rest of his life.

Haunted by a vision of going where he was really needed, Claver left his theological studies before completion and in 1610 went to Cartagena, New Granada (now Colombia). "Why stay in Europe," he asked, "when there are so many men of God needed in America?" He finished his Jesuit requirements and was ordained a priest in 1616 in Bogotá. In his profession he stipulated that he would "never admit any inferiority in the Negro slaves," and so that there

would be no doubt of this, he proclaimed himself their slave, adding to his signature *ethiopium semper servus* (slave of the Negroes forever). One of his biographers states that "there have been few saints so specialized."

For the remaining 38 years of his life, Claver lived in Cartagena, one of the major Caribbean ports in Latin America to which slaves were imported. He had no social program but simply geared his life to the primary needs of the often sick and broken slaves who arrived on American shores. He was not a "revolutionary" priest, intent on changing the fabric of society; he simply cared for the slaves and exhorted the slave masters to be humane.

Claver made himself available to the black slaves. He met them at the port of the city, inquired about their Christian state, catechized those who had had no instruction before crossing the Atlantic, and allegedly baptized more than 300,000. After baptism he tried to nurture his "children," visiting the plantations and mines where the slaves were employed. In accordance with Pauline maxims, he urged slaves to be obedient but exhorted slave masters to be generous. In order to humanize these people hardly regarded as humans, he visited prisoners, nursed lepers and the sick, and worked for the release of some. He often protected fugitive slaves while seeking out good masters for them.

In 1650 Peter Claver became a victim of the plague and lived the rest of his life in almost complete solitude, dying on Sept. 8, 1654. He was canonized in 1887 and 3 years later was declared the patron saint of the missions to the Negroes.

## Further Reading

Angel Valtierra, *Peter Claver, Saint of the Slaves* (trans. 1960), is a critical biography by a Colombian admirer. Also useful is Arnold Lunn, *A Saint in the Slave Trade: Peter Claver, 1581-1654* (1935). □

# Henry Clay

**The American political leader and secretary of state Henry Clay (1777-1852) came to national prominence as leader of the "War Hawks," who drove the country into the War of 1812. For the next 40 years he worked for international peace and sought to reconcile warring factions in the nation.**

Henry Clay was born on April 12, 1777, in Hanover County, Va., the seventh of nine children of the Reverend John Clay and Elizabeth Hudson Clay. Henry's father died in 1781, the year British and loyalist soldiers raided the area and looted the Clay home. Ten years later his mother remarried and his stepfather moved the family to Richmond, where Henry worked as a clerk in a store and then, from 1793 to 1797, as secretary to George Wythe, chancellor of the High Court of Chancery. Henry had little regular education, but he read in Wythe's library and learned to make the most of scanty information. He moved to Lexington, Ky., in November 1797 and made a reputation as a lawyer. In 1799 he married Lucretia Hart, of a leading family in the community. They had 11 children.

Clay's life-style was that of the frontier South and West; he drank and gambled through the night for high stakes. John Quincy Adams commented, "In politics, as in private life, Clay is essentially a gamester." He fought two duels, one in 1809 and the other in 1826. This did not hinder a public career in young America, and Clay had attributes which served him well in politics. He was tall and slim with an air of nonchalance, and he had a sensitive, expressive face, a warm spirit, much personal charm, and an excellent speaker's voice. Adams, who had observed him closely, said Clay was "half-educated" but added that the world had been his school and that he had "all the virtues indispensable to a popular man."

## Early Political Career

In 1803 Clay was elected to the Kentucky Legislature. In 1806 and again in 1810 he was sent to the U.S. Senate to fill out short terms. In 1811 he was elected to the House of Representatives. He was immediately chosen Speaker and was elected six times to that office, making it a position of party leadership.

By 1811 Clay was fanning the war spirit and the aggressive expansionism of the young republic. He said that the "militia of Kentucky are alone competent" to conquer Montreal and Upper Canada, and he organized the war faction in the House of Representatives. Clay was one of five men selected to meet British representatives at Ghent in 1814; there the failure of American arms forced them to a treaty in which no single objective of the war was obtained.

In the House again from 1815 to 1825 (except for the term of 1821-1823, when he declined to be a candidate), Clay developed his "American System," a program designed to unite the propertied, commercial, and manufacturing interests of the East with the agricultural and entrepreneurial interests in the West. It would establish protection for American industries against foreign competition, Federal financing of such internal improvements as highways and canals, and the rechartering of the United States Bank to provide centralized financial control. Clay succeeded for a time in part of his program: the Bank was rechartered and protective tariffs were enacted, reaching a climax in 1828 with the "Tariff of Abominations." But the internal improvements were not carried out in his lifetime (it required the Civil War to nationalize the country sufficiently for such measures), and long before Clay's death the Bank and the protective tariff had fallen at the hands of the Democrats.

## Slavery and Politics

Missouri's application for statehood in 1819 raised the issue of slavery and shocked the nation "like a firebell in the night," as the aged Thomas Jefferson said. Clay had advocated gradual emancipation in Kentucky in 1798, asserting that slavery was known to be an enormous evil. Though he came to terms with the institution in practice—owning, buying, and selling slaves—he was never reconciled to it in principle. When he died he owned some 50 slaves. His will distributed them among his family but provided that all children born of these slaves after Jan. 1, 1850, should (at age 25 for females and 28 for males) be liberated and transported to Liberia. In 1816, Clay was one of the founders of the American Colonization Society, which promoted sending freed slaves to Africa. The racism which he shared with most Americans was an important motivation in the society. (His racism was not restricted to African Americans; he said Native Americans were "not an improvable breed," and that they were not "as a race worth preserving.")

In the Missouri debate he did not devise the basic compromise—that is, that Missouri be a slave state but that slavery henceforth be prohibited in territory north of 36°30'. But he resolved the second crisis caused by the Missouri constitutional provision that free Negroes could not enter the state; Clay got assurance from the Missouri Legislature that it would pass no law abridging the privileges and immunities of United States citizens. The role which Clay played in the debate was, in fact, as spokesman for the interests of the slave South. In the controversy over the activities of the abolitionists in the 1830s he defended the right of petition but secured the passage of resolutions in the Senate censuring the abolitionists and asserting that Congress had no power to interfere with the interstate slave trade.

## Secretary of State

Clay was a candidate for the presidency in 1824, but three others received more votes, so that his name did not go to the House for election. He defied Kentucky's instruction to cast the state's votes for Jackson, saying he could not support a "military chieftain"; instead, his support elected John Quincy Adams. When Clay subsequently became secretary of state, the traditional steppingstone to the presidency, the cry of "corrupt bargain" was raised. The charge was unwarranted—he had merely supported the man whose views were closest to his own—but the charge lingered for the rest of his life.

Foreign affairs were not particularly important from 1825 to 1829, and most of Clay's diplomatic efforts did not succeed. The United States failed in efforts to purchase Texas from Mexico, nor was progress made toward acquiring Cuba. The State Department was unsuccessful in settling the Maine-Canadian boundary dispute, in securing trade with the British West Indies, and in getting payment from France for losses suffered by Americans during the Napoleonic Wars. Clay had taken a strong position in support of recent Latin American independence movements against Spain, and he tried unsuccessfully to promote active American participation in the Congress of Panama in 1826.

The Adams administration was defeated overwhelmingly in 1828; Clay's own state voted for Andrew Jackson. Adams offered to appoint Clay to the Supreme Court, but he declined and returned to Kentucky. In 1831 he was elected to the Senate and remained in that office until 1842. During these years of Jacksonian democracy Clay fought a losing battle for his American System. In 1833 he devised the compromise on the tariff which brought the nullification threat from John C. Calhoun's South Carolina; his measure provided that duties be lowered gradually until none were higher than 20 percent by 1842. He favored higher duties but said he made the concession to get past the crisis and on to saner times.

Clay correctly estimated that Martin Van Buren was unbeatable in 1837, but he expected the Whig nomination in 1840 and was bitterly disappointed when the aging military hero William Henry Harrison won nomination and election. Clay then anticipated that he would be the actual leader of the administration, but Harrison resisted him for the short time that he lived and Harrison's successor, John Tyler, proved to be opposed in principle to Clay's Whig program. Clay resigned from the Senate in disgust.

Clay was the Whig presidential candidate in 1844, but his equivocation on the expansionist issue of the annexation of Texas cost him the election. He made an abortive effort for the 1848 nomination, which went to the Mexican War general Zachary Taylor. Clay had condemned the initiation of the war but supported it once it got under way.

## Compromise of 1850

The fruits of that war brought on another sectional crisis, with threats to dissolve the Union. Clay returned to the Senate in poor health and led in working out the Compromise of 1850. This series of measures admitted California as a free state, organized the new territories without reference to slavery, assumed the public debt of Texas while restricting its area, abolished the slave trade in the District of Columbia, and enacted a fugitive slave law which denied due process and equal protection of the laws to African Americans living in the North. Thus was the rupture of the Union delayed for a decade. Clay died in Washington on June 29, 1852.

## Further Reading

The definitive edition of Clay's writings is James B. Hopkins, ed., *The Papers of Henry Clay* (3 vols., 1959-1963). The best biography of Clay, comprehensive and temperate in interpretation, is Glyndon G. Van Deusen, *The Life of Henry Clay* (1937). An excellent brief study is Clement Eaton, *Henry Clay and the Art of American Politics* (1957), which has a useful bibliographical essay. A fine study of Clay's early life is Bernard Mayo, *Henry Clay: Spokesman of the New West* (1937). The best 19th-century biography, and still very valuable, is Carl Schurz, *Life of Henry Clay* (2 vols., 1887-1889).

## Additional Sources

Clay, Henry, *The life and speeches of Henry Clay,* Littleton, Colo.: F.B. Rothman, 1987.
Colton, Calvin, *The life and times of Henry Clay,* New York, Garland Pub., 1974.
Remini, Robert Vincent, *Henry Clay: statesman for the Union,* New York: W.W. Norton, 1991.
Schurz, Carl, *Henry Clay,* New York: Chelsea House, 1980.
Van Deusen, Glyndon G. (Glyndon Garlock), *The life of Henry Clay,* Westport, Conn.: Greenwood Press, 1937, 1979. □

# John Middleton Clayton

**The American lawyer and statesman John Middleton Clayton (1796-1856) served as U.S. secretary of state during 1849-1850.**

John M. Clayton was born in Dagsboro, Del., on July 24, 1796. As a young man, he showed exceptional abilities, and in 1815 he graduated from Yale College with highest honors. After studying law in the office of his cousin and at the famous Litchfield Law School in Connecticut, Clayton was admitted to the Delaware bar in 1819. Soon he became one of the state's leading lawyers and orators.

Clayton served Delaware in a number of offices and became active in national politics in 1824 as a partisan of John Quincy Adams in his battle against Andrew Jackson. Conservative in background and outlook, Clayton became a leader of the Delaware Whig party. In 1828 he was elected to the U.S. Senate and became a noted anti-Jacksonian and a confidant of Henry Clay. In 1833 Clayton was effective in securing passage of Clay's compromise tariff. Reelected to the Senate in 1834, he resigned in 1836. From 1836 to 1839 he was chief justice of Delaware.

In 1839 Clayton supported the presidential candidacy of William Henry Harrison. In 1845, after acquiring a national reputation as a scientific farmer, Clayton returned to the U.S. Senate. He opposed President James Polk's expansionist policies on Oregon and Mexico, although he supported the Mexican War after it began. In 1848 Clayton broke with Clay, supporting the successful presidential candidacy of Zachary Taylor. Taylor appointed Clayton secretary of state in 1849.

As secretary of state, Clayton was intensely nationalistic and an ardent advocate of commercial expansion. But his strict interpretation of international law created unnecessary crises with Spain, Portugal, and France. His interest in commercial expansion was clear in his advocacy of increased trade with the Orient—later implemented by the mission of Matthew Perry to Japan—and his negotiation of the Clayton-Bulwer Treaty in 1850. This treaty won British recognition of an equal American interest in the Central American canal area, and it remained in effect until 1901, when the United States acquired full dominance there.

After Taylor's death in 1850, Clayton resigned his office and returned to his Delaware farm. In 1853 he returned to the Senate, chiefly to defend his treaty with England against attackers who suggested he had yielded unnecessarily to the British. By 1856 declining health rendered him inactive. He died of a kidney disease that year at his home.

## Further Reading

There is no modern biography of Clayton. Mary W. Williams's chapter, "John Middleton Clayton," in volume 6 of Samuel Flagg Bemis, ed., *The American Secretaries of State and Their Diplomacy* (10 vols., 1927-1929; rev. ed., 17 vols., 1963-1967, with vols. 11-17 edited by Robert H. Ferrell), emphasizes Clayton's career as secretary of state but also has other biographical material. □

# Leroy Eldridge Cleaver

**Leroy Eldridge Cleaver (born 1935), an American writer and a leader of the Black Panther party, was noted for advocating violent revolution within the United States.**

Leroy Eldridge Cleaver was born August 31, 1935 in Wabbaseka, Arkansas, the son of Leroy Cleaver, a waiter and piano player, and Thelma Cleaver, an elementary school teacher. When his father became a dining car waiter on the Super Chief, a train running from Chicago to Los Angeles, the family moved to Phoenix, Arizona, one of the train's stops. Young Cleaver earned money by shining shoes after school. Two years later, the family moved to the Watts section of Los Angeles. Cleaver dropped out of Abraham Lincoln Junior High School after his parents separated. His petty crime record began at the age of 12 with the theft of a bicycle. He was sent to the Fred C. Nelles School for Boys in Whittier, California, where he was inspired to commit more sophisticated crimes. In 1953, he was released from Nelles and was soon sent to the Preston School of Industry for selling marijuana. Soon after his release from Preston, he was again arrested for possession of marijuana and, now an adult, was sentenced to a two-and-one-half-year sentence at the California State Prison at Soledad in June of 1954.

At Soledad, Cleaver completed his high school education and read the works of Karl Marx, W.E.B. Du Bois, and Thomas Paine. After his release from Soledad, he went back to selling marijuana and became a rapist on the weekend. This led him to be arrested for "assault with intent to murder" at the end of 1957 and was sentenced to two to fourteen years at San Quentin Prison. He later was transferred to Folsom Prison in Represa, California.

In the early 1960s, while in jail, Cleaver decided to give up crime. He was influenced by the teachings of the Black Muslims and became a follower of Malcolm X. When Malcolm broke with the Black Muslims, so did Cleaver. Then he became an advocate of "black power," as this position was enunciated by Stokely Carmichael.

Also while in jail, Cleaver wrote essays, some published in 1962 in the *Negro History Bulletin;* these dealing mainly with racial pride and black nationalism. Out of these autobiographical essays came his first book, *Soul on Ice* (1968).

*Ramparts* magazine, which had brought Cleaver to public attention by publishing some of his prison articles, and Cleaver's lawyer were instrumental in securing his parole in 1966. He immediately began a new life as a writer and political activist. He helped found Black House, a social center for San Francisco youth. In 1967, he met the men who had founded the Black Panther party the year before. He became the party's minister of information, responsible for editing its newspaper. Later that year, he married Kathleen Neal. She became the communications secretary of the Black Panther party. The couple had two children.

With *Soul on Ice* Cleaver gained national prominence. On April 15, 1968, along with the widow of Martin Luther King Jr., and others, he addressed a mass rally against the Vietnam War in San Francisco.

As he became increasingly outspoken against racial, economic, and political injustices in America, Cleaver's parole officer advised him to discontinue his political activities. But Cleaver was becoming convinced that conditions for African-American people could not be alleviated without a violent revolution. To effect this, he felt, massive education was required to politicize the people. One method was to utilize a political campaign. In 1968, he urged the Black Panther party to unite with the predominantly white Peace and Freedom party in California to nominate candidates for local and state offices. Cleaver's wife became a candidate on the Peace and Freedom party ticket for the California State Assembly, along with the Black Panther's Huey P. Newton and Bobby Seale.

In April 1968, following the assassination of Martin Luther King Jr., and after harassment by the police of the Black Panther party, Cleaver was involved in a shoot-out with the Oakland police. One man was killed, and Cleaver was wounded in the foot and arrested. He was accused of violating his parole by possessing a gun, associating with people of bad reputation, and failing to cooperate with his parole agent. He was released on $50,000 bail.

In the next few months, Cleaver became a prominent spokesman of the radical, revolutionary left. He had moved from cultural, African-American nationalism to a more Marxist interpretation of revolutionary change. Cleaver believed that African-Americans should ally themselves with radical whites, and he criticized those African-American nationalists who refused such coalitions. During this period, he toured America as the presidential candidate of the Peace and Freedom party. He lectured on racism at the University of California in the fall of 1968.

Cleaver was scheduled to surrender to prison authorities in November 1968 for hearings on the charge of parole violation. Instead, he disappeared. He went to Cuba, North Korea, and Algeria and in September 1970 announced the establishment of an international office for the Black Panther party in Algiers.

While in exile, Cleaver championed "the angels of destruction" and the "great educational value" of murder. Cleaver accused Newton of putting the Black Panthers in the past by advocating community service programs over armed revolution. Cleaver was accused by others of abusing his wife while in Algeria and of having other Black Panthers killed. In March of 1971, Cleaver and Newton expelled each others' faction from the party, thus ending its heyday as the major voice for African-American activism in America.

In 1976, Cleaver returned to America to vote for Jimmy Carter and to face his accusers in California. Cleaver had changed his beliefs again while in Africa and now "stopped being a communist or socialist and developed an understanding and respect for free enterprise and the democratic political system." He joined the Mormon church and began to lecture on conservative issues and sell ceramic pots. He eventually set up a recycling business and tried, unsuccessfully, to get the backing of the Republican party for the a 1984 run for the US Senate.

Cleaver later divorced his wife and went to Harvard Law School. Cleaver then moved back to Berkeley, California and became a preacher. A recovering drug addict, Cleaver now speaks in school, prisons, and churches about the importance of resolving conflicts without violence and is working on a new autobiography.

## Further Reading

*Eldridge Cleaver: Post Prison Writings and Speeches* was edited by Robert Scheer in 1968. Lee Lockwood's talks with Cleaver were published as *Conversations with Eldridge Cleaver: Algiers* (1970). Books about the Black Panthers that include Cleaver are Gene Marine *The Black Panthers* (1969), Ruth Marion Baruch and Pirkle Jones *The Vanguard: A Photographic Essay on the Black Panthers* (1970), Philip S. Foner, ed. *The Black Panthers Speak* (1970), and Bobby Seale *Seize the Time* (1970). Two books critical of the Black Panthers are Earl Anthony *Picking Up the Gun* (1970), and *I Was a Black Panther,* as told to C. J. Moore (1970). Cleaver's own autobiography is *Soul On Fire* (1978). Much biographical information on Cleaver can be found in David Leon *Leaders From the 1960s: A Biographical Sourcebook of American Activism* (1994), and a biography of Cleaver to that point can be found in the 1970 issue of *Current Biography*. Cleaver also appears in August 1996 issue of *Ebony* magazine. □

# Cleisthenes

**Cleisthenes (active 6th century B.C.) was an Athenian political leader and constitutional reformer. The first avowed democratic leader, he introduced important changes into the Athenian constitution.**

Son of Megacles, leader of the powerful Alcmeonid clan in Athens, and of Agariste, daughter of Cleisthenes, the tyrant of Sicyon, Cleisthenes was destined for a public career. Accommodating himself to the regime of the tyrants, he was chief magistrate of Athens in 525 B.C., but he and other Alcmeonids were in exile when the tyranny fell in 510.

Cleisthenes ran for leadership of Athens at the head of a noble faction favoring oligarchy; he was defeated by Isagoras, a friend of the Spartan king Cleomenes. Cleisthenes then turned democrat, threatening the position of Isagoras, who asked Cleomenes for help. The Spartan king arrived with troops and tried to disband the Council of 300 and install Isagoras as head of a new council, but the people rose and forced Cleomenes and Isagoras to withdraw. Cleisthenes returned, a committed democrat, to reform the constitution in favor of a moderate democracy.

## Constitutional Reforms

Athens had suffered from faction, or tyranny born of faction, for a century, and Cleisthenes aimed at the root of the trouble—clan affiliations in politics. In the past, clans had grouped themselves around a particular clan leader, such as Isagoras, Megacles, or Peisistratus, and had exerted pressure upon elections and policies by their organized votes. Cleisthenes provided an alternative to clan loyalty by registering the citizens by residence as members of a deme, a small area analogous to an English parish. Moreover, he extended the franchise to vote not only to clansmen but also to members of guilds, who hitherto had inferior rights.

To facilitate central government administration, Cleisthenes brigaded the demes, 170 or so in number, into 10 artificial tribes, allocating to each tribe a number of demes drawn from the three divisions of Attica. In many elections the citizens voted by tribe, returning a tribal official who might also serve the central government.

Since in this democracy the ultimate power was vested in the Assembly of all adult males, Cleisthenes set up a Council of 500 to make government less unwieldy and to steer the Assembly. Each of the 10 tribes selected by lot 50 persons who were councilors for a year (reelection was allowed only once). The council was in permanent session, and each tribal group of 50 served as governing committee in office for a tenth of the year, conducting day-to-day business and presiding over the council and the Assembly.

These reforms lasted as long as democracy in Athens. Cleisthenes is also credited with the invention of ostracism, but this is uncertain.

## Further Reading

Ancient sources on Cleisthenes are Aristotle's *Politics* and the *Athenian Constitution,* translated by John Warrington (1959). Two modern works are Charles Hignett, *A History of the Athenian Constitution to the End of the Fifth Century B.C.* (1952), and N. G. L. Hammond, *A History of Greece to 322 B.C.* (1959; 2d ed. 1967). □

# Georges Clemenceau

**The French statesman Georges Clemenceau (1841-1929) was twice premier of France, in 1906-1909 and 1917-1919. He led France through the critical days of World War I and headed the French delegation to the Paris Peace Conference.**

Georges Clemenceau was born on Sept. 28, 1841, at Mouilleron-en-Pareds in the Vendée. Following the family tradition, he studied medicine at Nantes and Paris. In 1865 he traveled to the United States, where he served as correspondent for a Paris newspaper and taught riding and French in a girls' academy at Stamford, Conn. He married one of his pupils, Mary Plummer. They had two daughters and one son but separated after 7 years.

## Early Political Career

In 1869 Clemenceau returned to France; after the Revolution of 1870 he was appointed mayor of the 18th *arrondissement* of Paris, comprising Montmartre. After being elected as a representative to the National Assembly from Paris in February 1871, he voted against the Treaty of Frankfurt. When the Communard uprising began on Montmartre on March 18, he tried unsuccessfully to prevent bloodshed. Later Clemenceau tried to mediate between the Commune and the Versailles government. Failing again, he resigned his position at Paris and his seat in the Assembly. He was elected in July 1871 to the municipal council of Paris, where he remained until 1876, becoming president in 1875.

In 1876 Clemenceau returned to national politics and was elected to the Chamber of Deputies as representative of the 18th *arrondissement* of Paris. At that time his graying hair was close-cropped, his bushy eyebrows overhung large, black eyes, and his thick, drooping moustache was still black. His highly individual debating style, marked by a caustic wit, soon won him undisputed leadership of the radicals. While he was uncompromisingly atheistic and anticlerical, advocating separation of church and state, Clemenceau believed in human perfectibility through scientific knowledge and moral effort. He firmly upheld liberty and natural rights and was influenced by the ideas of Auguste Comte, J. S. Mill, and Charles Darwin.

Clemenceau possessed a genius for destructive criticism and won the appellation of the "Tiger" for his role in destroying Cabinets. Strongly opposed to imperialism, he

brought down the Ferry Cabinet on the Tunisian question in 1881, attacked the Freycinet Cabinet for its desire to intervene in Egypt the following year, and destroyed the Ferry Cabinet of 1885 during the Indochinese crisis.

In 1886 Clemenceau first supported Gen. Boulanger as minister of war in the Freycinet Cabinet but later actively opposed him. Clemenceau also played a prominent role in the Wilson scandal, forcing President Grévy to resign. He subsequently backed Sadi Carnot for the presidency against Jules Ferry and is credited with having said, "I shall vote for the stupidest." This incident contributed to the tradition of a weak presidency that plagued the Third Republic. Clemenceau was denounced as a friend and associate of Cornelius Hertz, a key figure in the Panama scandal, and was also accused of being in the pay of the English. He was greeted with campaign posters showing him juggling English coins, and he failed to win reelection in 1893.

## Journalistic Career

Between 1893 and 1903 Clemenceau built a new career in journalism. At first he wrote daily articles for *La Justice,* but in 1897 he began writing for *L'Aurore,* which had a larger circulation. Selections of his articles were published as *Le Mêlée sociale* (1895) and *Le Grand Pan* (1896). In 1898 he published a novel, *Les Plus forts,* and a volume of sketches on Jewish subjects, *Au pied de Sinai.* Another book of articles, *Au fil des jours,* appeared in 1900.

On Jan. 13, 1898, Clemenceau ceded his usual space in *L'Aurore to Emile Zola's* inflammatory article on the Dreyfus Affair, which Clemenceau headlined "J'accuse." Henceforth Clemenceau became a dedicated partisan of the Dreyfus cause. In 1900 he began publishing a weekly, *Le Bloc,* most of which he wrote himself, but he soon returned to *L'Aurore* as editor. Meanwhile, he published his Dreyfusard articles in five volumes.

## Senator and Premier

In 1902 Clemenceau was elected senator for the Var, and he accepted the post of minister of interior in the Sarrien ministry in 1906. He used troops to control a strike of miners in the Pas-de-Calais following a mine disaster in that district and employed military engineers to break a strike of electrical workers in Paris.

When the Sarrien ministry resigned in October 1906, Clemenceau became premier. He was confronted with new strikes and used the army to control the most formidable, which involved agricultural workers of the Midi. When Paris postmen struck, Clemenceau denounced strikes by civil servants. Later he created a ministry of labor and negotiated nationalization of the Western Railway. In foreign affairs Clemenceau continued to cultivate close relations with Great Britain and to build up the French alliance system. He refused to apologize to Germany for an incident in Morocco. He was forced out of office in July 1909 in a dispute on naval policy.

After a lecture tour through Brazil and Argentina in 1910, Clemenceau became a member of the senate commissions for foreign affairs and for the army. In 1913 he founded a daily paper, *L'Homme Libre* (The Free Man), to express his views on armaments and the German menace.

## World War I

In September 1914 Clemenceau's paper was suppressed because of its criticism of government weaknesses, but it reappeared immediately with the title *L'Homme Enchaîné* (The Enchained Man). In this journal Clemenceau strove to foster the French will to victory, and to expose all forms of inefficiency in the war effort.

On Nov. 17, 1917, when French morale was near its nadir, President Poincaré asked Clemenceau to form a ministry. He served as minister of war, as well as premier, and summed up his policy: "Je fais la guerre" (I wage war). Clemenceau restored France's self-confidence. He welcomed Marshal Ferdinand Foch's appointment as commander in chief of the Allied armies in April 1918 and gave him unqualified support. When the Germans had advanced to Château Thierry, 18 miles from Paris, Clemenceau proclaimed: "The Germans may take Paris, but that will not prevent me from going on with the war. We will fight on the Loire, we will fight on the Garonne, we will fight even on the Pyrenees. And if at last we are driven off the Pyrenees, we will continue the war at sea. But as for asking for peace, never!" Clemenceau's confidence in his military commanders proved justified, and by June, Foch and Pétain were able to take the offensive. On Nov. 11, 1918, Germany signed the armistice.

## Peace Conference

As leader of the French delegation at the Paris Peace Conference, Clemenceau played a major role in drafting the Treaty of Versailles and determining conference policies. He tried to obtain a strong League of Nations backed by military force, and when this failed he proposed other measures to ensure French security: German reparations to pay the whole cost of the war; French annexation of the Saar basin; and creation of a separate Rhineland state under protection of the League of Nations. U.S. president Woodrow Wilson and British prime minister David Lloyd George offered an Anglo-American guarantee of France's frontiers as compensation and forced Clemenceau to compromise all these points. Consequently, the French legislators, who found Clemenceau's rule autocratic and resented being excluded from the peace negotiations, condemned the peace treaty as too lenient and debated 3 months before ratifying it. After the elections of 1919 Clemenceau resigned as premier. An attempt to elect him president in 1920 failed.

Clemenceau retired from parliamentary politics. In 1922 he made a tour of the United States in an attempt to recall that country to its obligations after American rejection of the Versailles Treaty and the Anglo-American guarantee of French security. During the remaining years of his life he divided his time between Paris and the Vendée and devoted himself to writing. In 1927 he had completed a two-volume philosophical testament, *Au soir de la pensée (In the Evening of My Thought).* His memoirs of the war and the peace settlement were published after his death as *Grandeurs et misères d'une victoire* (*Grandeur and Misery of Victory*) in 1930. He died in Paris on Nov. 24, 1929.

## Further Reading

The most detailed and judicious biography of Clemenceau written in English is Geoffrey Bruun, *Clemenceau* (1943). Probably the best of the many biographies written at the height of his career is H. M. Hyndman, *Clemenceau: The Man and His Time* (1919). Interesting sidelights are in Clemenceau's *Clemenceau: The Events of His Life as Told by Himself to His Former Secretary, Jean Martet* (trans. 1930). A specialized study of one aspect of Clemenceau's policy is Jere Clemens King, *Foch versus Clemenceau: France and German Dismemberment, 1918-1919* (1960). One of the best works for general historical background is Sir D. W. Brogan, *The Development of Modern France, 1870-1934* (1940; rev. ed. 1966). David Thomson, *Democracy in France* (1946; 4th ed. 1964), provides information on the political and social dynamics of the Third Republic.

## Additional Sources

Dallas, Gregor, *At the heart of a tiger: Clemenceau and his world, 1841-1929,* New York: Carroll & Graf, 1993.

Duroselle, Jean Baptiste, *Clemenceau,* Paris: Fayard, 1988.

Ellis, Jack D., *The early life of Georges Clemenceau, 1841-1893,* Lawrence: Regents Press of Kansas, 1980.

Erlanger, Philippe, *Clemenceau,* Paris: Perrin, 1979.

Holt, Edgar, *The Tiger: the life of Georges Clemenceau, 1841-1929,* London: Hamilton, 1976.

Jackson, J. Hampden (John Hampden), *Clemenceau and the Third Republic,* Westport, Conn.: Hyperion Press, 1979.

Newhall, David S., *Clemenceau: a life at war,* Lewiston, N.Y., USA: E. Mellen Press, 1991.

Watson, David Robin, *Georges Clemenceau; a political biograph,* London Eyre Methuen 1974. ☐

himself from a priest-poet active in Ypres at the time who bore the same name and called himself Jacobus Papa.

The extant works of Clemens—all works for unaccompanied voices—include 15 Masses, 231 motets, a number of songs in French and in Flemish, and 4 books of *Souterliedekens,* or "little psalter songs." These last are simple three-part settings of the Psalms in Flemish that Clemens based on popular melodies of the day. These Psalm settings were intended as devotional pieces for the home, which accounts for their simplicity and easy tunefulness. By contrast, in his Masses and motets, Clemens wrote a rich and varied polyphony, with a seriousness and thoroughness typical of the Renaissance Netherlandish composers. His motets, in which Clemens shows himself ever responsive to the moods and images of his texts, are especially remarkable for both their clarity and expressive power. Many of his motets are remarkable, as well, for their unusual use of chromaticism, much of it notated in the scores, but more of it, many scholars believe, implied and meant to be added to the music only in its performance by the initiate.

Clemens was an outstanding composer in an epoch that produced many composers of genius. His contributions to the genres of the Mass and the motet, in particular, stand as great monuments of the art of polyphony in the Renaissance.

## Further Reading

Sources in English that contain material on Clemens are Edward E. Lowinsky, *Secret Chromatic Art in the Netherlands Motet* (1946), and Gustave Reese, *Music in the Renaissance* (1954; rev. ed. 1959). ☐

# Jacobus Clemens non Papa

**Jacobus Clemens non Papa (ca. 1510-ca. 1556) was a Flemish composer whose a cappella Masses, motets, and chansons represent high points in the history of Renaissance polyphonic vocal music.**

Jacobus Clemens non Papa was born in Ypres, Flanders. Nothing is known of his education except that he was trained as a priest, and little is known about his career. He seems to have spent his early creative years in Paris, where his first works were published, but he returned to the Low Countries in 1540. It is known that he was in Bruges until 1545, where he served as priest and choirmaster of the children at St. Donatien. In subsequent years Clemens was active as a singer and composer at the cathedrals in Antwerp and's Hertogenbosch, at Ypres, and finally at Dixmuide, where he died and was buried.

Clemens published under the name Jacques Clément or Jacobus Clemens until 1546, after which he added the appellation "non Papa" to the Latin form of his name. Why he did this is not known, though scholars have suggested it may have been done so that Clemens might distinguish

# Clement V

**Clement V (1264-1314) reigned as pope from 1305 to 1314. He was the first pope of the "Babylonian Captivity," when the papacy was located in Avignon, France.**

Bertrand de Got, who became Pope Clement V, was a nobleman and a native of Gascony, France. He became archbishop of Bordeaux in 1299. His election to the papacy in 1305 followed the pontificate of Boniface VIII (and the brief rule of Benedict XI), during which a long quarrel between France and the papacy culminated in Boniface's capture and mistreatment by henchmen of the French king, Philip IV, at Anagni, Italy, in 1303. France had humiliated the papacy, and the cardinals chose de Got as a compromise candidate who had neither opposed Boniface nor displeased Philip. Although Clement V was not a mere tool of France, throughout his reign he was pressured by Philip IV. At Philip's request Clement was crowned at Lyons; there he suffered a fall from his horse which may have affected his health permanently, for chronic illness contributed to his submission to French demands. Philip IV urged a posthumous heresy trial of Boniface VIII, and it was probably to avoid this that Clement agreed to settle in Avignon in 1309. Further submission is shown by Clement's approval of Philip's bloody suppression of the Knights Templar; his withdrawal of Boniface VIII's bull *Clericis laicos;* and his withdrawal of support for Emperor Henry VII's activities in Italy.

Clement V took important financial and political actions as pope. He introduced the annates, a lucrative papal tax, and thus refilled the papal treasury; but he spent the money unwisely, much of it on his relatives and on loans to France and England. He created 24 cardinals, of whom 23 were French and Gascon, thus producing a French majority. He was condemned for his nepotism, accused of simony, and disliked for his luxurious style of living. But he was also a scholarly man, and he ordered the study of the Hebrew, Syriac, and Arabic languages at the universities of Paris, Bologna, Oxford, and Salamanca. He added to canon law the sixth book of the Decretals, named "Clementines" after him.

Clement's reputation today is predominately unfavorable because of his submission to French domination and his role in creating the Avignon papacy. But much evidence suggests that his intentions were good. It was always his wish to return the papacy to Rome, but poor health and fear of "another Anagni" made him unable to resist Philip IV. Clement died on April 14, 1314.

## Further Reading

The best source of information about Clement V is Guillaume Mollat, *The Popes at Avignon, 1305-1378* (9th ed. 1949; trans. 1963), translated from the French, this is the classic book on the Avignon papacy and sets Clement's career in the context of his time. The ideology and consequences of the Avignon period are presented in Walter Ullmann, *The Origins of the Great Schism* (1948). □

# Clement of Alexandria

**The Christian theologian Clement of Alexandria (ca. 150-ca. 215) sought to integrate Greek classical culture with Christian faith.**

The date and place of birth of Clement of Alexandria, born Titus Flavius Clemens, are not known, though it is likely that he was born in the decade 150-160, possibly in Athens. Having studied with religious and philosophical teachers in Greece, southern Italy, and Syria, he settled in the Egyptian city of Alexandria. There he was deeply impressed by the teachings of Pantaenus, who had been converted to Christianity from stoicism and who was at the time head of the Christian catechetical school in Alexandria. Clement, remaining a layman, eventually succeeded Pantaenus in this office and held the post for a number of years, probably not more than a decade. In

relation to his activities as a Christian teacher Clement produced his three most important writings: *The Exhortation to Conversion, The Tutor,* and *Miscellanies.*

In Alexandria, Clement was at one of the leading intellectual centers of the Hellenistic world. Highly speculative and heretical Gnostic forms of Christian thought had been prominent there for decades among those who professed any form of Christianity. Gnosticism itself represented one way of synthesizing Christian faith with Hellenistic culture. Clement was of the firm conviction that Greek philosophy, particularly Platonic metaphysics and Stoic ethics, represented one of the ways in which God had prepared the world for the coming of Christ. His task, then, was to work toward an orthodox Christian appropriation of Greek thought.

The reader senses in Clement's writings the presence of three groups of critics against whom he constantly defends himself. To the pagan representatives of classical culture he argues the defensibility of any kind of "faith" and of Christian faith in particular. To the heretical Christian Gnostics he shows that the experience of redemption in Christ does not entail a depreciation of the material world created by God. To the simple and orthodox Christians he gives assurance that faith and intellectual sophistication are not incompatible and that philosophy does not inevitably lead to Gnostic heresy.

Clement left Alexandria on the outbreak of persecution against the Christians in 202. There is a fleeting glimpse of him in Syria shortly afterward. Later still he appears in the

company of an old pupil, now a bishop in Asia Minor; the bishop sends his old teacher with a letter of congratulation to a newly elected bishop of Antioch. It is generally thought that Clement died about 215.

## Further Reading

The classic study in English, R.B. Tollinton, *Clement of Alexandria: A Study in Christian Liberalism* (2 vols., 1914), is particularly useful for the way in which it synthesizes widely scattered materials, though it is sometimes dull. A splendid treatment of much smaller scope is Henry Chadwick, *Early Christian Thought and the Classical Tradition: Studies in Justin, Clement, and Origen* (1966).

## Additional Sources

Ferguson, John, *Clement of Alexandria,* New York, Twayne Publishers 1974. □

# Cleomenes I

**Cleomenes I (active ca. 520-490 B.C.) was a brilliant but unstable Spartan king who attempted to extend his country's influence outside the Peloponnesus.**

A son of Anaxandridas, Cleomenes first displayed his genius in diplomacy in 519 B.C., when the city of Plataea asked Sparta for help against Thebes. He suggested Plataea ask the assistance of Athens, which accepted and promptly became embroiled with Thebes. Aiming thus to divide and conquer, Cleomenes chose as his next step in central Greece to expel the tyrant Hippias from Athens in 510 and try to bring the city into the Peloponnesian League, of which Sparta held the military command. But Cleomenes, failing to install the pro-Spartan oligarch Isagoras as ruler, was forced to withdraw.

In 508 Cleomenes realized that Athens was an implacable opponent of Spartan power in central Greece. He therefore organized a concerted attack against Athens. In 506 a Boeotian army, led by Thebes, invaded western Attica; the Chalcidians of Euboea invaded northern Attica; and the two Spartan kings, Cleomenes and Demaratus, led the army of the Peloponnesian League into southwestern Attica. When it became known that Cleomenes planned to make Isagoras tyrant of Athens, some Peloponnesians withdrew in protest, and King Demaratus took his force out of the line. The Spartan army disbanded, and Athens defeated Boeotia and Chalcis. Cleomenes proposed in 505 to make Hippias tyrant of Athens but failed. The only rival to Sparta in the Peloponnesus was Argos. Cleomenes led a surprise seaborne attack against it about 495 and won a great victory which disabled Argos for a generation.

Overseas, Cleomenes pursued a cautious policy since Sparta was not a naval power. About 515 he had rejected Samos's plea for help against the Persians. When the Ionians under Aristagoras revolted against the Persians in 499, Cleomenes again refused to lend Sparta's help. But when the Persians threatened to invade Greece in 491, Sparta

allied itself with Athens, and Cleomenes went to Sparta's ally Aegina to arrest the leaders of a government which had submitted to Persia. He was rebuffed on the grounds that both Spartan kings were required to make a diplomatic intervention valid. Cleomenes knew that he could not obtain the cooperation of Demaratus, and he therefore plotted to oust him. A potential rival, Leotychidas, disputed the legitimacy of Demaratus, and the case was referred to Delphi, where Cleomenes bribed the priests and obtained the god's verdict against Demaratus. Leotychidas replaced Demaratus and, with Cleomenes, arrested the Aeginatans.

But the bribery became known. Cleomenes fled to Thessaly and then to Arcadia, where he fomented opposition to Sparta. Though Sparta reinstated him late in 491, Cleomenes apparently went insane and committed suicide.

## Further Reading

Information on Cleomenes is in W. W. How and J. Wells, *A Commentary on Herodotus,* vol. 2 (1912), and in G. L. Huxley, *Early Sparta* (1962). □

# Cleomenes III

**Cleomenes III (ca. 260-219 B.C.), the king of Sparta from 235 to 219, passed important reforms, revived Sparta's power, and was utterly defeated by Macedon. A vivid personality and dashing leader, he unfortunately lacked vision in politics.**

C leomenes III was the son of King Leonidas of Sparta. He married Agiatis, the widow of Leonidas's murdered coruler Agis IV, and she influenced Cleomenes deeply in the direction of social change. Since Leonidas was an archconservative, Cleomenes's feelings must have been torn between conservatism and socialism, between father and wife. When Cleomenes succeeded Leonidas in 235 B.C., he inherited policies of conservatism and of the king's subordination to the ephors, or magistrates.

## Expansion Policies

When the expansion of the Achaeans under Aratus made war inevitable in 229, the ephors authorized Cleomenes to defend the frontiers of Sparta. Not content with defense, he took the offensive with 5,000 men and in 228 forced an Achaean army of 20,000 to withdraw. Cleomenes's reputation soared. Ptolemy III, King of Egypt, now supported Cleomenes instead of Aratus. When Cleomenes hired mercenaries, the ephors scented danger, and after Cleomenes defeated the Achaeans in 227, King Archidamus was recalled to restore Sparta's dual kingship and check Cleomenes. But Archidamus was assassinated, and on winning a decisive victory over the Achaeans, Cleomenes left his citizen troops to occupy Arcadia, slipped back to Sparta with his mercenaries, and seized power. Killing four ephors and banishing 80 opponents, he named his brother successor to Archidamus's throne but from then on was sole military dictator.

## Reforms in Sparta

Cleomenes at once introduced the reforms sponsored by Agis and frustrated by Leonidas. Though he may have believed in the socialist doctrines advocated by Agiatis and the Stoic philosopher Sphaerus, Cleomenes's immediate aim was to increase and improve the army. All debts and mortgages were canceled; all land was nationalized; and enough *perioeci,* or noncitizens who served in the forces, and aliens resident in Laconia were enfranchised to raise the number of male citizens to 4,000. Public land was divided into 4,000 equal lots, and each citizen received one. The 4,000 citizens were equipped in Macedonian style with long pikes, the messes (*syssitia*) were reestablished, and the young were educated in the traditional manner.

With his enlarged army Cleomenes won a decisive victory in Achaea in 226. He offered generous terms if Achaea would enter his revived Peloponnesian League under Spartan leadership. But Achaea opened negotiations with Macedon.

## War against Macedon

In 225 city after city—even Argos—joined Cleomenes in the expectation that he would revolutionize their societies as well. The Peloponnesian League was almost complete as a military alliance when, in 224, Achaea accepted Macedon's terms, the cession of Corinth. By now Cleomenes held Corinth but not its fortress, Acrocorinth. The Macedonian king, Antigonus Doson, failed to pierce Cleomenes's defenses at the Isthmus, but his political position was precarious. He had neither spread the socialist revolution nor supported the wealthy; thus the revolutionaries acted on their own, while the wealthy decided to rely on Macedon to reinstate them to their former status of power.

A popular rising at Argos, in concert with Macedonian and Achaean troops, overwhelmed the Spartan garrison in Argos. Abandoning the Isthmus and Corinth, Cleomenes fought his way into Argos and had the upper hand when the Macedonian cavalry appeared. Routed, Cleomenes fled to Tegea, where he heard of Agiatis's death. Antigonus reinstated the wealthy, formed the Hellenic League, condemned Cleomenes as a revolutionary, and declared he had no quarrel with Sparta.

Cleomenes turned to Ptolemy III. In exchange for subsidies he sent his mother and children as hostages to Egypt. In 223 Antigonus captured Tegea, Orchomenus, and Mantinea, entrusting the last to the Achaeans, who sold the population into slavery. Cleomenes captured Megalopolis, but the people escaped. When he offered to return the city if the people would support him, they refused. He sacked Magalopolis, an act of temper which only confirmed his isolation. For the final campaign Cleomenes freed many helots, raising his army to 20,000 men.

In 222 the decisive battle was fought at Sellasia. With 30,000 men Antigonus attacked Cleomenes's prepared position. When his troops overbore the left flank, Cleomenes

committed his center to the attack. Charging downhill, the Spartans drove back the Macedonian phalanx but failed to break its formation. Antigonus's forces completed a pincer movement, and the encircled Spartan army was almost annihilated.

Cleomenes escaped, advising Sparta to submit, and sailed to Egypt. Antigonus spared Sparta, but Cleomenes's hopes of return faded. When Ptolemy III died, Ptolemy IV was unsympathetic to the Spartans, and the refugees found themselves virtually interned at Alexandria. In 219 Cleomenes conceived a plan which was as courageous as it was impracticable. Tricking their guards, he and 12 others escaped armed into the streets of Alexandria, called on the people to rise against Ptolemy, and tried to capture the prison of the citadel. Failing, they killed one another, the last committing suicide over the King's body. Ptolemy executed the women and children and had the corpse of Cleomenes flayed and hung on a gibbet.

## Further Reading

Ancient accounts of Cleomenes are in the writings of Plutarch and Polybius. A modern discussion is in J.B. Bury and others, eds., *The Cambridge Ancient History,* vol. 7 (1928). □

# Cleon

**Cleon (ca. 475-422 B.C.) was an aggressive Athenian political leader. He was the first member of the nonaristocratic classes to reach a prominent position in Athens's political structure.**

From humble origins, Cleon rose to prominence by attacking the Athenian strong man Pericles and endeavored to succeed him after 429. Exploiting the reaction against Pericles and the angry mood of the people during the Peloponnesian War with Sparta, Cleon advocated in 427 the execution of every adult male and enslavement of the rest of the population of Mytilene. A nominally free ally of Athens, the city had joined Sparta and had then been forced to capitulate to Athens. Cleon's policy was adopted at first but defeated by a small majority upon reconsideration. The news reached Mytilene just in time to stop the executions. Cleon's proposal to execute the ringleaders—more than 1,000 according to the text of Thucydides—was carried out.

Thus Cleon identified himself with methods which more civilized Athenians, such as Thucydides and Aristophanes, regarded as savage and cruel. When Aristophanes denounced such methods in the comedy *The Babylonians* in 426, it was significant that Cleon prosecuted the producers of the play. Aristophanes retaliated in *The Knights* in 424, pinning on Cleon (whether justly or unjustly, it is not known) all the faults of the bullying demagogue and warmongering agitator.

Between the productions of these two plays, Cleon was very successful in the military field, though he had no experience of command. The opportunity had come in 425, when Athens had a temporary advantage in the war, having isolated a Spartan force on the island of Sphacteria near Pylos. Sparta offered peace and alliance on terms which Thucydides thought favorable. But Cleon persuaded the people to reject the offer. When this temporary advantage seemed to be slipping away, Cleon was criticized, but he turned the criticism against the generals at Pylos. One of them, Nicias, present in the Assembly, offered to resign when Cleon accused the generals at Pylos of incompetence for failing to capture the Spartans at nearby Sphacteria. The Assembly voted the command to Cleon, and with characteristic bluster Cleon said he would return within 20 days with the Spartans. With the help of Demosthenes, the general on the spot, Cleon succeeded.

Cleon now led the state in an aggressive policy, exacting more tribute from allies and attempting to regain lost territory. Sparta replied by opening a new front in Chalcidice, where allies of Athens defected. Cleon tried to deter them by making an example of the Thracian town of Scione. All adult males were executed and the women and children sold into slavery. But defections continued, and the Spartan commander, Brasidas, captured Amphipolis. In an attempt to redeem his prestige, Cleon obtained the command in this theater, was trapped by Brasidas, and perished with 600 Athenians in 422. Cleon's death cleared the way for an inconclusive peace.

## Further Reading

Ancient sources for Cleon are Aristophanes, in *The Knights,* and Thucydides, both of them hostile. A useful modern study, which includes a discussion of Cleon, is H. D. Westlake, *Individuals in Thucydides* (1968). For background material, including a discussion of Cleon, see N. G. L. Hammond, *A History of Greece to 322 B.C.* (1959; 2d ed. 1967), and Charles A. Robinson, *Athens in the Age of Pericles* (1959). □

# Cleopatra

**Cleopatra (69-30 B.C.) was the last of the Ptolemaic rulers of Egypt. She was notorious in antiquity and has been romanticized in modern times as the lover of Julius Caesar and Mark Antony.**

Third daughter of Ptolemy XII Auletes, Cleopatra VII Philopator (her full name) learned her political lessons by watching the humiliating efforts of her father to maintain himself on the throne of Egypt by buying the support of powerful Romans. When he died in 51 B.C., the ministers of Cleopatra's brother Ptolemy XIII feared her ambition to rule alone and drove her from Egypt in 48.

## Cleopatra and Julius Caesar

Cleopatra made preparations to return by force, but when Caesar arrived in Alexandria after the Battle of Pharsalus, she saw the opportunity to use him. She had herself smuggled to him in a rug. Ptolemy XIII died fighting Caesar, who restored Cleopatra to the throne with another brother, Ptolemy XIV, as coregent.

Contrary to legend, Caesar did not dally in Egypt with Cleopatra. Although in 46 she gave birth to a son whom she named Ptolemy Caesarion, Caesar never formally recognized him. That same year Caesar invited her to Rome. Although he spent little time with her, her presence in Rome may have contributed to the resentment against him which led to his assassination.

In April 44 B.C. Cleopatra returned to Alexandria, where Ptolemy XIV had died under mysterious circumstances. She made Caesarion her partner on the throne and awaited the outcome of the political struggle in Rome. When, after the Battle of Philippi, Antony summoned her and other puppet rulers to Tarsus in Cilicia, she responded eagerly. Matching her preparations to the man whose weaknesses she knew, she dazzled Antony and bent him to her will. She easily cleared herself of a charge of helping Brutus and Cassius, and at her request Antony put to death three persons she considered a threat to her throne.

## Cleopatra and Mark Antony

In the winter of 41/40 Antony followed Cleopatra to Alexandria, where he reveled in the pleasures of the Ptolemaic court and the company of the Queen. Cleopatra hoped to tie him emotionally to her, but Antony left Egypt in the spring of 40.

In the autumn of 37 Antony sent his wife, Octavia, back to Italy on the excuse that she was pregnant and went to

Antioch to make final preparations for his invasion of Parthia. In Antioch he again sent for Cleopatra and went through a ritualistic marriage not recognized under Roman law. He also recognized the twins Cleopatra had with him and made extensive grants of territory to her, including Cyprus, Cyrene, and the coast of Lebanon, all of which had once been part of the Ptolemaic empire.

In 36 Cleopatra returned to Alexandria to await the birth of her third child by him. The failure of the Parthian campaign and Octavian's exploitation of Antony's misadventure drove Antony further into the arms of Cleopatra, who gave him immense financial help in rebuilding his shattered army. When Antony defeated Artavasdes of Armenia in 34, he celebrated his triumph not in ·Rome but in Alexandria. On the following day he declared Cleopatra and Ptolemy Caesarion joint rulers of Egypt and Cyprus and overlords of all lands west and east of the Euphrates. For Cleopatra this meant the potential union of the Ptolemaic and Seleucid empires under her control, and Antony staked out his claims on the wealth of Egypt for the coming struggle with Octavian.

In Italy, Octavian used the donations at Alexandria and Antony's relations with Cleopatra to turn public opinion against him. The Battle of Actium (Sept. 2, 31), fought for the control of the Roman Empire, led to the final disaster. Because Cleopatra's money built the fleet and supported it, she insisted on fighting at sea. When she fled from the battle with the war chest, Antony had little choice but to follow.

After Actium, Cleopatra tried to negotiate with Octavian for the recognition of her children as her successors in Egypt. But as his price Octavian demanded the death of Antony, and Cleopatra refused. After the final battle outside Alexandria on Aug. 1, 30 B.C., in which his troops deserted him, Antony stabbed himself when he received a false report that Cleopatra was already dead. Antony died in Cleopatra's arms inside her mausoleum, where she had barricaded herself with the treasures of the Ptolemies to keep them from Octavian.

Tricked into surrendering herself, Cleopatra tried again to negotiate with Octavian. Rebuffed, she carefully planned her own death. On August 10, after paying last honors to Antony, she retired to her quarters for a final meal. How Cleopatra died is not known, but on her left arm were found two tiny pricks, presumably from the bite of an asp.

## Further Reading

The principal ancient sources on Cleopatra are Plutarch and Dion Cassius. H. Volkmann, *Cleopatra: A Study in Politics and Propaganda* (1953; trans. 1958), offers a well-balanced and penetrating analysis of the political implications of Cleopatra's relations with Julius Caesar and Antony. Arthur Weigall, *The Life and Times of Cleopatra* (1914; new ed. 1923), and Oscar von Wertheimer, *Cleopatra: A Royal Voluptuary* (trans. 1931), overemphasize Cleopatra's domination of Antony. In S. A. Cook and others, eds., *The Cambridge Ancient History*, vol. 10 (1934), W. W. Tarn views Cleopatra as dominated more by ambition for empire than by love. To Ronald Syme in *The Roman Revolution* (1939), both Antony and Cleopatra were playing a cynical game of politics with each other. □

# James Cleveland

**The Reverend James Cleveland (c. 1931-1991) combined his talents as minister, singer, composer, and philanthropist to become known as the Crown Prince of Gospel Music.**

Variously hailed as the King of Gospel Music and the Crown Prince of Gospel, the Reverend James Cleveland combined his talents as preacher, composer, singer, producer, and philanthropist to become one of the most outstanding exponents of the modern gospel sound. Indeed, with a voice that has earned acclaim as one of gospel's greatest, and a religious fervor that has refused the lure of secular music, Cleveland, more than any artist of his generation, served as a champion of gospel in its purest form. As he explained to Ed Ochs in an interview for *Billboard,* gospel is not only "a music, but . . . a representation of a religious thinking. Gospel singing is the counterpart of gospel teaching. . . . It's an art form, true enough, but it represents an idea, a thought, a trend."

## Grew up Where Gospel Flourished

Born in Depression-era Chicago, the son of hard-working, God-fearing parents, Cleveland grew up in an environment where gospel flourished. His grandmother introduced him to Chicago's Pilgrim Baptist Church, where the budding musician was influenced by choir director Thomas A. Dorsey—also known as the father of gospel music. Under Dorsey's tutelage, the youth made his solo debut with the choir at the age of eight. The vocalist subsequently taught himself to play piano, often recounting how he practiced on imaginary keys until his parents could afford to purchase an upright for him. As Tony Heilbut quoted the star in *The Gospel Sound:* "My folks being just plain, everyday people, we couldn't afford a piano. So I used to practice each night right there on the windowsill. I took those wedges and crevices and made me black and white keys. And, baby, I played just like Roberta [Martin]. By the time I was in high school, I was some jazz pianist."

Roberta Martin, a Dorsey disciple and one of the Chicago gospel pioneers to gain international recognition, was among Cleveland's idols. It was her group, the Roberta Martin Singers, who first helped shape the youth's singing and piano style, with Roberta Martin herself inspiring the youngster to begin composing. By the time he was a teenager, Cleveland was singing with a neighborhood group, the Thorn Gospel Crusaders. And once the group began featuring Cleveland's compositions, the artist found himself piquing the interest of prominent gospel talents. In 1948 Cleveland's "Grace Is Sufficient," performed at a Baptist convention, prompted Martin to begin publishing the new composer's work.

## Founded the Gospel Chimes

The next decade proved a productive one for Cleveland. He made his recording debut on the Apollo label in 1950, singing "Oh What a Time" with the Gospelaires. He

## Worked to Preserve Gospel Tradition

Indeed, in the early sixties Cleveland became a minister and served Los Angeles's New Greater Harvest Baptist Church as pastor until he was able to build his own Cornerstone Institutional Baptist Church in 1970. For him, gospel music and gospel teaching were inseparable—different mediums conveying the same message. As the minister-musician explained to Ochs: "If we can't preach to people in a dry, talking sermon and get their attention, we'll sing it to them, as long as we get the message across. We have been instrumental in drawing more people to the church in recent years through singing and getting them to find favor with something in the church they like to identify with. Then when we get them into church, putting the same message into words without music is not as hard, for we have set some type of precedent with the music to get them into the church and get them focused on where we're coming from."

For Cleveland, gospel music was so vital that in 1968 he organized the first Gospel Music Workshop of America. Designed both to help preserve the gospel tradition and to feature new talent, the workshop has grown to include more than five hundred thousand members representing almost every state. "My biggest ambition is to build a school somewhere in America, where we can teach and house our convention," Cleveland told *Village Voice* interviewer David Jackson. This was the best way, in the artist's opinion, to assure that gospel's legacy continues.

## One Last Message

Cleveland perpetuated an understanding of gospel music and gospel teaching as part of the same religious experience, believing that the music devoid of the mission is not genuine gospel. As Jackson articulated: "Through classics like 'Peace Be Still,' 'Lord Remember Me,' 'Father, I Stretch My Hands to Thee,' and 'The Love of God,' Reverend Cleveland retells a biblical love story for the plain purpose of reconciling people to God and to one another." And as his scores of devoted followers attest, concluded Jackson, "his message is widely appreciated and applauded."

Cleveland died of heart failure on February 9, 1991, in Los Angeles, California. He had not been able to sing for a year before his death due to respiratory ailments. But the last Sunday of his life, he faced his congregation at the Cornerstone Institutional Baptist Church and told them, "If I don't see you again and if I don't sing again, I'm a witness to the fact that the Lord answers prayer. He let my voice come back to me this morning," the *Los Angeles Times* reported. The same source reverently opined that Cleveland had been "not just . . . a record maker, but a mentor, producer, primary source of new material and fountainhead of artistic recognition for the form."

composed songs for Roberta Martin, including "Stand By Me," "Saved," and "He's Using Me." He worked frequently with the Caravans, first establishing himself as a superlative gospel arranger, then emerging as a singer—the Caravans scored their earliest hits, in fact, with Cleveland as lead vocalist on such tunes as "Old Time Religion" and "Solid Rock." And he founded the first of his own groups, the Gospel Chimes, which helped showcase his talents as composer, arranger, and singer.

By 1960 Cleveland, who had incorporated blues riffs and what Heilbut described as "sheer funkiness" in his work, had become associated with a new tenor in gospel music. That year "The Love of God," a song he recorded with Detroit's Voices of Tabernacle choir, was a sensation, and its success helped Cleveland secure a recording contract with Savoy Records, for whom he recorded more than sixty albums. The artist passed another milestone with Savoy's 1963 release *Peace Be Still*. A recording pairing Cleveland with the Angelic Choir of Nutley, New Jersey, the album, which held a spot on the gospel charts for more than fifteen years, has sold more than one million copies, an almost unheard of achievement for a gospel recording.

During the 1960s Cleveland also formed the James Cleveland Singers, gradually built an international reputation, and became one of the best paid of the gospel music entertainers. And although two of Cleveland's former pupils—Aretha Franklin and Billy Preston—went on to achieve celebrity status, the master himself declined to expand his audience by moving into secular music, and instead chose to devote himself strictly to gospel.

## Further Reading

Broughton, Viv, *Black Gospel: An Illustrated History of the Gospel Sound,* Blandford Press, 1985.
Heilbut, Tony, *The Gospel Sound: Good News and Bad Times,* Simon & Schuster, 1971.
*Billboard,* September 27, 1980.

*Chicago Tribune,* February 17, 1991.
*Detroit Free Press,* February 18, 1991.
*Ebony,* December, 1984.
*Los Angeles Times,* February 10, 1991; February 15, 1991.
*Village Voice,* April 16, 1979.
*Washington Post,* February 11, 1991.
Baker, Barbara, "Black Gospel Music Styles: 1942-1979," Ph.D.
    dissertation, University of Maryland, 1978.
Casey, M. E., "The Contributions of James Cleveland," thesis,
    Howard University, 1980. □

# Stephen Grover Cleveland

**Twice elected president of the United States, Stephen Grover Cleveland (1837-1908) owed his early political successes to reformism. His efforts to stem economic depression were unsuccessful, and the conservative means he used to settle internal industrial conflicts were unpopular.**

Grover Cleveland's political career developed while the wounds of the Civil War and Reconstruction were healing and just as the serious social and economic problems attendant upon industrialization and urbanization were unclearly emerging. Although a lifelong Democrat, Cleveland was not skilled in party politics; he had emerged from a reform wing of his party and had only a few years of public experience before becoming president. Interested in public issues, he used the presidency to try to shape legislation and public opinion in domestic areas. Yet, by his second term of office, the old, familiar debates over tariffs and currency had been called into question and traditional political alignments began to tear apart. Cleveland, however, was not sensitive to the problems of party harmony; instead, he stood on principle at the price of party unity and personal repudiation. In the depression of the 1890s, his concern for the flow of gold from the Treasury led him to force Congress to repeal the Sherman Silver Purchase Act, and this action caused division of the Democratic party. The depression worsened, and by his intervention in the Pullman strike of 1894 he alienated the laboring class, thus losing all effectiveness as president. In 1896 Cleveland was rejected by his party.

Cleveland was born in New Jersey but spent most of his life in New York. Despite the early death of his father, a Presbyterian minister, and his consequent family responsibilities, he studied law in a respected Buffalo firm and gained admission to the New York bar in 1859. He joined the Democratic party, acting as ward delegate and ward supervisor before being appointed assistant district attorney for Erie County in 1863. Diligent and devoted, Cleveland set a good, though not brilliant, record. Enactment of the Conscription Act of 1863 caught him in the dilemma of whether to serve in the Army or find a substitute. To continue supporting his mother and sisters, he took the latter option, remaining in Buffalo to practice law. This was a costly decision, for a military record was expected of almost

any aspirant to public trust. Though without public office from 1865 to 1870, he steadily enlarged his law practice and gained stature in the community.

Cleveland became sheriff in 1870, a post which promised large fees as well as frustrating experiences with graft and corruption. Although he was respected for his handling of official responsibilities, he made many enemies and won few admirers, for most citizens looked with disfavor on the office of sheriff. After 3 years he returned to legal practice, concentrating now on corporate law. His legal aspirations (and fees) were modest. His qualities as a lawyer were a good index to the whole of his public service: he was thorough, careful, slow, diligent, serious, severe, and unyielding. His sober approach to his career contrasted sharply with the boisterous humor of his private life, for he was a popular, if corpulent, bachelor.

## Quickly Up the Political Ladder

In 1881 Buffalo Democrats, certain that a reform candidate could sweep the mayoralty election, turned to Cleveland. In his one-year term as mayor he stood for honesty and efficiency—exactly the qualities the New York Democrats sought in a candidate for governor in 1882. New York State was alive with calls for reform in politics; a trustworthy candidate was much in demand. Elected governor by a handsome margin, Cleveland favored reform legislation and countered the interests of the New York-based political machine called Tammany Hall and its "boss," John Kelly, to such an extent that it caused a rift between them. After one term as governor, Cleveland was seen as a leading contender for the presidential nomination of 1884. His advantages lay in his having become identified with honesty and uprightness; also, he came from a state with many votes to cast, wealthy contributors, and a strong political organization. Pitted against Republican nominee James G. Blaine, Cleveland even won the support of reform-minded Republican dissidents known as Mugwumps. Several forces favored him: Tammany's eventual decision to support him in New York State, blame for the depression of the 1880s falling on the Republicans, and temperance workers' ire with the Republican party.

Thus, in 4 years, riding a crest of reform movements on municipal, state, and national levels, Cleveland moved from a modest law practice in upstate New York to president-elect. The rapidity of this political success had several implications for the balance of his career—he had not had to make compromises in order to survive, he had not become identified with new programs or different systems, he owed fewer debts to special-interest groups than most new presidents, and he had come to the presidency on the strength of his belief in simple solutions of honesty and reform.

## First Term as President

Cleveland's victory margin in 1884 was slim. His Cabinet appointees were men of substance, though not of prominence: Thomas Bayard as secretary of state, Daniel Manning as secretary of the Treasury, and William Endicott as head of the War Department. All shared the conviction that government should be neither paternalistic nor favorable to any special group and that contesting economic groups should settle their differences without government intervention. With little administrative experience and few reasons to think highly of party organization, Cleveland in his first term advocated improved civil service procedures, reform of executive departments, curtailment of largesse in pensions to Civil War veterans, tariff reform, and ending coinage based on silver. He failed to stop silver coinage but achieved at least modest success in the other areas. In one regard Cleveland was an innovative president: he used his office to focus attention on substantive issues, to pressure for legislation, and to define and determine the lines of congressional debate. Previously (and again after Cleveland), U.S. presidents left issues of legislation to Congress, spending most of their efforts on party leadership. Thus, in 1887 Cleveland took a strong position on tariff reform and later supported passage of the Mills Bill of 1888. Although the Mills Bill provided for only moderate tariff reductions, it was viewed as a step in the right direction, a way of reducing the embarrassingly large annual government surpluses.

## Private Citizen

The Republicans mobilized to meet tariff reduction head on, stopping the Mills Bill and substituting a protective tariff measure, going into the election of 1888 with the tariff as the key issue. Renominated for the presidency in 1888 without challenge, Democrat Cleveland was opposed by Republican Benjamin Harrison of Indiana, who had the support of businessmen and industrialists favoring protec-

tive tariffs. Superior Republican organization, Democratic party feuding, and election fraud lost the 1888 election for Cleveland, although he won a plurality of the popular vote. He moved back to New York to practice law and enjoy his family.

Out of office, Cleveland withdrew from politics for a year but then began again to behave like an interested candidate. Stirred into attacking the McKinley tariff of 1890 and taking a strong position against currency expansion through silver-based coinage, he gained the Democratic presidential nomination in 1892.

Cleveland's campaign against incumbent President Harrison was a quiet one, with the Democrats aided by the 1892 Homestead strike, in which prominent Republicans were involved in the effort to break labor power and to maintain special benefits for the powerful steel magnates. The Democrats scored smashing victories in 1892, not only electing Cleveland but winning control of both House and Senate.

## Second Term As President

To his second Cabinet, Cleveland named Walter Gresham as secretary of state, John G. Carlisle as secretary of the Treasury, Daniel S. Lamont as head of the War Department, and Richard Olney as attorney general. Like Cleveland's earlier Cabinet, these men agreed on extreme conservatism in handling economic issues. It was to Carlisle, Lamont, and Olney that Cleveland listened most closely, although in the final analysis he made his own decisions.

## Policies in Time of Depression

Cleveland had scarcely taken his oath of office when the worst financial panic in years broke across the country. A complex phenomenon, the Panic of 1892-1893 had its roots in overexpansion of United States industry, particularly railroad interests; in the long-term agricultural depression that reached back to the 1880s; and in the withdrawal of European capital from America as a result of hard times overseas. As the panic broadened into depression, the American public tended to focus debate about its cause and cure on one item: the money question. On one side the argument was that businessmen (alarmed by the Sherman Silver Purchase Act requiring a purchase of silver each month) had lost confidence in the monetary system and feared depletion of the gold reserves; to regain their confidence and a return to prosperity, the buying of silver by the Federal government had to be halted. On the opposite side of the argument, silver exponents maintained that what was needed was more money in circulation, which could be achieved only if more, not less, silver was purchased by the government and used as a basis for coinage.

Cleveland, long afraid of silver as a threat to economic stability, determined that repeal of the Sherman Silver Purchase Act would stem the drain of gold reserves and end the depression by restoring confidence to businessmen; he called a special session of Congress for its repeal. Protracted and bitter debate ensued. The Democratic party divided along sectional lines, with western and southern Democrats standing against repeal. The repeal, however, was voted, but it was ineffective, and gold reserves continued to dwindle. Meanwhile the depression became worse during 1893 and 1894.

Wounds that had opened during the silver-repeal debate were not healed when Cleveland's administration turned to the long-promised issue of tariff reform. Cleveland had been identified for many years with downward revision of tariffs and more equitable distributions. Pressured by sectional interests, the Democrats in Congress were more divided than united over tariff legislation. In addition, the silver battle had virtually torn the party in half, leaving many Democrats with nothing but hatred for the President. The Wilson bill, from the viewpoint of the President, a fairly satisfactory measure for tariff reduction, was amended almost beyond recognition as it passed through the Senate, emerging with tariff rates only slightly lower than previous ones and carrying a host of provisions for special-interest groups. Highly dissatisfied but unsuccessful in his attempts to improve it, Cleveland allowed the Wilson-Gorman Act to become law without his signature.

To avert what he viewed as financial disaster, Cleveland became involved with four bond issues to draw gold into the Treasury. Not only was this effort to maintain gold reserves unsuccessful, but Cleveland was charged with having catered to Wall Street millionaires when other governmental policies had failed.

Beset by currency and tariff failures and hated by a large segment of the general population and by many in his own party, Cleveland further suffered loss of prestige by his actions in the Pullman strike of 1894. Convinced that the strike of the American Railway Union under Eugene V. Debs against the Pullman Company constituted an intolerable threat to law and order and that local authorities were unwilling to take action, Cleveland and Olney sent Federal troops to Chicago and sought to have Debs and his associates imprisoned. Although Cleveland prevailed and order was enforced, laborers throughout the country were angered by this use of Federal force.

### Foreign Policies

The congressional elections of 1894 marked a sharp decline in Democratic power. Bitter at Cleveland and disheartened by worsening depression, American voters turned against the Democrats. Although Cleveland felt betrayed by his party and misunderstood by his constituents, he remained confident that his money policy had been correctly conceived and reasonably executed. Perhaps his party had split, but for him the defense of principle was more important than political harmony. Confronted with possibilities for compromise, Cleveland spurned such options and withdrew into isolation.

More successful in foreign policy, Cleveland exhibited the same determination and toughness. He would not be drawn into the Cuban rebellion against Spain; he would not sanction the Hawaiian revolution engineered by American commercial interests. Yet he took an equally stern posture vis-á-vis the boundary dispute between Venezuela and Great Britain in 1895-1896. Concerned about European influence in the Western Hemisphere, Cleveland and Olney carried the United States to the brink of war by insisting that the dispute be arbitrated. Business interests, clamoring for guarantees of open markets for their products, had considerable influence in shaping Cleveland's policy, which succeeded when Great Britain accepted arbitration.

### Again a Private Citizen

Distrusted now and detested, Cleveland was convincingly repudiated by the Democratic Convention of 1896, which nominated William Jennings Bryan on a platform demanding free and unlimited coinage of both silver and gold at the rate of 16 to 1. Cleveland took no role in the campaign. He retired to Princeton, N.J., as soon as his term ended. He occupied himself with writing, occasional legal consultation, the affairs of Princeton University, and very occasional public speaking, but after 1900 he became less reluctant to appear in public. Sympathetic crowds greeted his appearances as the conservative Democratic forces with which he had been identified took party leadership from William Jennings Bryan. Briefly stirred into activity in 1904 to support Alton B. Parker's candidacy for the presidency, Cleveland spent most of his retirement years outside political battles, increasingly honored as a statesman. After offering to assist President Theodore Roosevelt in an investigation of the anthracite coal strike of 1902, he was active in the reorganization of the affairs of the Equitable Life Assurance Society in 1905. His death in 1908 was the occasion for general national mourning.

### Further Reading

There is an abundant literature on Cleveland. Allan Nevins, *Grover Cleveland: A Study in Courage* (1944), is the best overall treatment. A less sympathetic portrayal of Cleveland is Horace S. Merrill, *Bourbon Leader: Grover Cleveland and the Democratic Party* (1957). Robert Wiebe, *The Search for Order, 1877-1930* (1967), credits Cleveland's efforts to shape legislation, whereas J. Rogers Hollingsworth, *The Whirligig of Politics: The Democracy of Cleveland and Bryan* (1963), criticizes him as a party leader. Cleveland's diplomacy is discussed in Walter LaFeber, *The New Empire: An Interpretation of American Expansion, 1860-1898* (1963). A detailed account of the 1892 campaign is George H. Knoles, *The Presidential Campaign and Election of 1892* (1942), and of the 1896 campaign, Stanley L. Jones, *The Presidential Election of 1896* (1964). Arthur M. Schlesinger, Jr., ed., *History of Presidential Elections* (4 vols., 1971), is valuable as a source on the four campaigns of 1884-1896. □

# Patsy Cline

**Vocalist Patsy Cline (1932-1963) was one of the first women to break into the country and western music scene, which was, until then, dominated by men.**

Up until Patsy Cline's recordings in the late 1950s and early 1960s there were only a handful of country and western female singers; and the title of queen belonged solely to Kitty Wells. It was Cline who dethroned Wells with classic performances on cuts like "Walkin' After Midnight" and the Willie Nelson composition "Crazy," which combined the pop characteristics of Patti Page and Kay Starr with the hillbilly traits of Hank Williams. All three singers were major influences on Cline's style.

## Career Began at Age Four

Cline's entertainment career began at the tender age of four, when she won a local amateur contest for tap dancing in her hometown of Winchester, Virginia. By age eight she was playing the piano and singing in her church's choir. In 1948 the drugstore counter girl began singing in nightclubs with Bill Peer and his Melody Boys. Wally Fowler of the Grand Ole Opry convinced the 16-year-old to go to Nashville for an appearance on Roy Acuff's "WSM Dinner Bell" radio program. Cline hung around Nashville trying to break into the industry but ended up working as a club dancer.

Cline headed back home shortly thereafter and continued singing with Peer's band until 1954, when she returned to Nashville and signed a contract with William McCall's 4 Star Sales Co. out of Pasadena, California. Cline's first recording session was on June 1, 1955, and her first three songs were leased to Coral Records, a subsidiary of Decca. Part of her deal with 4 Star, which included one-time session fees with no royalties, stipulated that she could only

record material that belonged to McCall's company. This may have been part of the reason that the majority of her early work did not sell very well. She was also tackling a wide variety of styles that made it hard to categorize her.

## Radical Image

Producer Owen Bradley was trying to create a new genre with Cline by bathing her voice in full, jazzy orchestrations at his Quonset Studios in an effort to counter the rising popularity of rock and roll. According to *The Listener's Guide to Country Music,* "Patsy Cline was his ultimate country success. For him, she played down her country characteristics. For her, he played down his popular music background. The results were records full of tension and dynamics."

It would, however, take some time before the formula caught on, as the country scene was changing from hillbilly to country and western and was still mainly dominated by male artists. Cline's radical image as a two-fisted, hard-drinking woman definitely made her stand out from the rest of the Nashville crowd, but any chance of success would rely on her voice and songs. Her talents shined on both slow torchers and up-tempo cuts but her 4 Star sessions never did fully realize her potential, with the exception of "Walkin' After Midnight."

## "Walkin' After Midnight" a Hit

Cline recorded the tune on November 8, 1956, but it was the rendition of the song she performed on *Arthur Godfrey's Talent Scouts* television program on January 28, 1957, that got the industry's attention. She had debated performing the song but was finally convinced by one of the regulars on Godfrey's show, Janette Davis. The television audience went wild and gave Cline a standing ovation.

4 Star rushed to release the single on February 11 and it shot all the way to number three on *Billboard'* s country chart. More importantly, however, "Walkin'" also rose to number 17 on the pop charts. Donn Hecht had originally written the tune for Kay Starr, who turned it down, but Cline and Bradley managed to use it as a vehicle to bridge the gap between hillbilly and pop. McCall, whose company was eventually shut down as a result of questionable business dealings, was unfortunately too slow in following up on the hit. He did convince Cline to renew her contract, but it took another six months before she recorded another session, "Fingerprints"/"A Stranger in My Arms." Her remaining work with 4 Star was unspectacular and in 1959 she jumped to Decca Records, insisting upon a $1,000 advance.

## Vocals Soared to New Heights

It wasn't until 1961, one year after she became a regular cast member of the Grand Ole Opry, that Cline had her second hit, "I Fall to Pieces." The song went to number one on the country charts and was joined by "Crazy," another Top 10 hit of 1961. Cline's vocals began to soar to new heights on material that was less restrictive than 4 Star's catalog. For the next two years she recorded major hits with "She's Got You" (a number-one hit), "When I Get Through

With You, You'll Love Me," "Faded Love," and "Leavin' On Your Mind" (all Top 10's).

Cline was just coming into her own when tragedy struck on March 5, 1963. On the way home from a Kansas City benefit for disc jockey Cactus Jack Callat, Cline, Randy Hughes, Cowboy Copas, and Hawkshaw Hawkins were killed when the airplane they were flying in crashed near Camden, Tennessee. At the age of 31 she had been performing for over twenty years, yet recording for less than eight.

## A Legend

Ironically, perhaps her most identifiable tune, "Sweet Dreams," was released posthumously and also broke the Top 10. Even with her relatively small collection of songs, Cline managed to break new ground and influence hundreds of female, and some male, country singers since. Loretta Lynn, undoubtedly Cline's most successful pupil, recorded a tribute LP, *I Remember Patsy,* featuring nine of Cline's songs.

"Patsy Cline knew how to cry on both sides of the microphone," wrote Donn Hecht in *The Country Music Encyclopedia.* "And the why of it all, explained by many, understood by few, is slowly becoming a legend unparalleled by any other country entertainer since Hank Williams."

## Further Reading

Lazarus, Lois, *Country Is My Music!,* Messner, 1980.
Malone, Bill, *Country Music U.S.A.—A Fifty-Year History,* American Folk Society, 1968.
Oermann, Robert K., with Douglas B. Green, *The Listener's Guide to Country Music,* Facts on File, 1983.
Stambler, Irwin, and Grellun Landon, *The Encyclopedia of Folk, Country & Western Music,* St. Martin's Press, 1983.
*Stars of Country Music—Uncle Dave Macon to Johnny Rodriguez,* edited by Bill C. Malone and Judith McCulloh, University of Illinois Press, 1975.
Shestack, Melvin, *The Country Music Encyclopedia,* KBO, 1974.

□

# DeWitt Clinton

**The American politician DeWitt Clinton (1769-1828) was mayor of New York City, governor of New York State, and a tenacious sponsor of the state's Erie Canal.**

DeWitt Clinton was born in Orange County, N.Y., the son of Gen. James Clinton and Mary DeWitt Clinton. Educated at Kingston Academy and Columbia College, from which he graduated in 1786, he studied law for 3 years. At the age of 18 the precocious youth became an Antifederalist propagandist for his uncle, New York governor George Clinton, writing newspaper articles in 1787 and 1788 opposing the ratification of the Federal Constitution. Entering politics in 1789, at the age of 20, he was appointed private secretary to Governor Clinton. He

served as a transitional leader between the factional politics of the postrevolutionary period and the party politics of the new professionals which coalesced around New York's U.S. senator Martin Van Buren, who controlled the state political machine.

When John Jay was elected governor in 1795, Clinton aligned himself with the Democratic-Republican party, entering the New York Assembly in 1797, moving to the state Senate in 1798, and joining the Council of Appointment in 1801. In 1802 Clinton was chosen to fill a vacant seat in the U.S. Senate. His chief contribution as senator was the initiation of the 12th Amendment to the Constitution.

In 1803 Clinton resigned his Senate seat to become mayor of New York City, serving until 1815 with the exception of two annual terms. He also served as state senator from 1806 to 1811, lieutenant governor from 1811 to 1813, and political boss of the Democratic-Republicans in New York. But his break with the faction of Robert R. Livingston in 1807 and his opposition to the Embargo Act in 1808 led to strained relations with presidents Thomas Jefferson and James Madison. In 1812 New York Republicans nominated him for the presidency instead of Madison. After Madison's reelection, Clinton failed to be renominated as lieutenant governor and in 1815 was ousted from his position as mayor.

Clinton promptly turned to his favorite project, the promotion of a state canal between the Hudson River and Lake Erie. Since 1810 he had served as one of the canal commissioners; he now organized a campaign advocating

state support of the project. In April 1816 the legislature adopted Clinton's plan, which carefully outlined the engineering problems and procedures, the financial necessities, and the commercial potential. In 1817 a Republican caucus nominated Clinton, and he was elected governor by an overwhelming majority. Reelected in 1820, he lost support because of internal dissension in his party. He refused to run again in 1822.

When the group headed by U.S. senator Martin Van Buren overplayed its hand in 1824 and removed Clinton as canal commissioner, the Anti-Regency party nominated Clinton as their gubernatorial candidate. He won easily. Thus Governor Clinton in 1825 presided over the celebration of the opening of both the Champlain Canal and the Erie Canal, the greatest engineering project of its day. Reelected in 1826, he died in office on Feb. 11, 1828.

Clinton had been an active participant in literary, educational, and cultural affairs in New York. He organized the Public School Society in 1805, became the chief patron of the New York City Hospital and the New York Orphan Society, and secured the charter of the New York Historical Society, serving as its president in 1817. Clinton was a founder of the New York Literary and Philosophical Society, also serving as president of the American Academy of Art and vice president of the American Bible Society.

By his first wife, Maria Franklin, Clinton had 10 children. In 1819 he married Catherine Jones, who survived him.

### Further Reading

The standard account of Clinton is by Dorthie De Bear Bobbé, *DeWitt Clinton* (1933; rev. ed. 1962). For Clinton's role in the organization of the New York State canal system see Ronald E. Shaw, *Erie Water West: A History of the Erie Canal, 1792-1854* (1966). Specialized studies include Howard L. McBain, *DeWitt Clinton and the Origin of the Spoils System in New York* (1907), and Edward A. Fitzpatrick, *The Educational Views and Influence of DeWitt Clinton* (1911).

### Additional Sources

Hanyan, Craig, *De Witt Clinton: years of molding, 1769-1807*, New York: Garland, 1988. □

# George Clinton

**The American patriot and statesman George Clinton (1739-1812) was the governor of New York for 21 years and vice president of the United States for two terms.**

George Clinton's father, Charles, was an Ulster County, N.Y., farmer who had emigrated from Ireland in 1729. Charles Clinton achieved modest prominence through military and political office, but it was the marriage of his sons, James to Mary DeWitt in 1765 and George to Cornelia Tappen in 1769, that gave the Clintons

status in New York society and future political allies among influential Dutch families.

### Revolutionary Radical

Born in Ulster County, on July 26, 1739, George Clinton was educated at home and under a tutor, with the advantage of his father's better-than-average library. After studying law in New York City under William Smith, Jr., one of the famous Whig "triumvirate," he began practice in 1764. His political career was launched in 1768 with his election to the Assembly from Ulster County. There he allied himself with the minority "popular party" of the Livingstons against the DeLancey "court party" which controlled the legislature. For the next 7 years Clinton consistently opposed grants for supporting the king's troops, and he was one of a mere five assemblymen who in 1770 voted against jailing Alexander McDougall, a Whig "firebrand" who had publicly criticized the House for betraying its trust by its military appropriations. In the broader quarrel with Britain, Clinton sided with the radicals, denouncing parliamentary taxation and the Coercive Acts and urging support for the resolves of the First Continental Congress. A delegate to the Second Continental Congress, he was absent when independence was approved, having military obligations in New York, where he had been appointed brigadier general of the Ulster and Orange County militia in December 1775. Despite military shortcomings, the Continental Congress placed him in command of the forts in the Hudson Highlands. However, his energetic efforts did not prevent capture of the forts by the British in late 1777.

## War Governor

The new state constitution of 1777 provided for a popularly elected governor. New York's aristocrats, led by Philip Schuyler, John Jay, John Morin Scott, and the Livingstons, expected Schuyler to be chosen. To their consternation the elections brought victory to Clinton—a tribute to his appeal to middle-class and small farmers and his popularity with the soldiers. Schuyler's postelection judgment that neither Clinton's family nor connections entitled him "to so distinguished a predominance" but that he was "virtuous and loves his country, has abilities and is brave" is an apt commentary on Clinton's entire political career. He attracted the majority of New Yorkers by his loyalty to the Revolutionary cause, his honesty, and his devotion to his state. His reputation was enhanced by his able service as war governor, a post which was more often military than political. He organized the defenses of the frontier, procured supplies, suppressed loyalists, quieted the Native Americans, and organized campaigns against Tory and British raiders. His universal popularity was attested to by his successive elections to the governorship, often without opposition, until his voluntary retirement in 1795.

## Antifederalist and Republican

Conservative in his administration during the Confederation period, committed to the protection of property and a stable financial system, Clinton was equally sensitive to popular liberties and republican government. It was the latter that made him suspicious of the movement for the U.S. Constitution in 1787. Willing to strengthen congressional powers under the Articles of Confederation, he feared the substitution of a "consolidated" for a "federal" government. The acknowledged leader of New York's Antifederalists, he was not so virulent an opponent of the Constitution as Alexander Hamilton made him out to be. He presided over the state's ratifying convention at Poughkeepsie with impartiality and spoke seldom, and then with moderation. There is some doubt that he wrote the Antifederalist essays attributed to him which appeared in the *New York Journal* (September 1787 to January 1788) as "Cato's Letters." Preferring ratification conditional upon amendments, he nevertheless promised to support the new Constitution when New York ratified it 30 to 27, on July 26, 1788, without such conditions.

## Vice President

While Clinton continued to be popular personally, his political followers hereafter faced stiff opposition from the Federalists, who in 1789 secured control of the legislature and in 1792 just missed placing John Jay in the governor's chair. Pleading ill health and perhaps sensing defeat, Clinton declined to stand in 1795, and his party was beaten. For the next 6 years his nephew DeWitt Clinton led the newly formed Democratic-Republican party in New York, an alliance of Clintonites, Livingstons, and the followers of Aaron Burr. George Clinton returned as governor for a term in 1801, but his political mantle remained with his nephew. Clinton played out the remainder of his political career on the national scene. In 1792 he was the unsuccessful candi-

date of Republicans in New York, Virginia, North Carolina, and Georgia for the vice presidency in place of John Adams. In 1804 he replaced Burr for the second place on the Republican ticket and served as vice president during Jefferson's second term. Four years later his followers promoted his candidacy for president on a ticket with James Monroe. When this failed, he settled for another term as vice president under James Madison. His 7 years in Washington (1805-1812) did not enhance his reputation. He had little influence with either administration, presided over the Senate without much skill, and disliked Washington society. Perhaps his most important action was his tiebreaking vote in 1811 to prevent the recharter of the Bank of the United States. He died in office on April 20, 1812.

A moderate reformer who during his governorship promoted road and canal building, lent support for manufactures and reform of the criminal code, and gave aid to libraries and public funds for common schools, Clinton appealed to the middle-class democracy of New York State. He lacked the felicity of language and the talented pen of a Jefferson to extend his influence much beyond his state.

## Further Reading

The standard biography of Clinton is E. Wilder Spaulding, *His Excellency George Clinton: Critic of the Constitution* (1938; 2d ed. 1964). It has been revised in many details by more recent works on early New York political history, most notably Linda Grant De Pauw, *The Eleventh Pillar: New York State and the Federal Constitution* (1966), and Alfred F. Young, *The Democratic Republicans of New York: The Origins, 1763-1797* (1967). *Public Papers of George Clinton* (10 vols., 1899-1914) is an essential source, although the introductory sketch of Clinton's life by the editor, Hugh Hastings, is inaccurate. The Clinton era in New York politics may be traced in Jabez D. Hammond, *History of Political Parties in the State of New York* (2 vols., 1842; 4th ed., 3 vols., 1852), and in De Alva Stanwood Alexander, *A Political History of the State of New York* (4 vols., 1906-1923). Clinton's war governorship is ably analyzed and evaluated in Margaret Burnham Macmillan, *The War Governors in the American Revolution* (1943).

## Additional Sources

Kaminski, John P., *George Clinton: yeoman politician of the new republic,* Madison: Madison House, 1993. □

# Sir Henry Clinton

**Sir Henry Clinton (c. 1738-1795) was commander in chief of the British armies during the crucial years of the American Revolution.**

Henry Clinton was the only son of George Clinton, governor of colonial New York. He entered the military, serving first in the New York militia and then in 1751 as a regular army lieutenant in the Coldstream Guards. He rose steadily in rank and displayed gallantry and capability during the French and Indian War in America. In the peace that followed 1763 he became colonel of the 12th

Regiment and, after May 1772, major general. At this same time he was given a seat in the British Parliament, which he retained for 12 years.

Clinton's most sustained military service occurred during the American Revolution. He fought bravely at Bunker Hill but botched his command in the 1776 expedition to capture Charleston, S.C. He participated successfully, however, in the Battle of Long Island. Irritation with William Howe led Clinton to consider resigning, a threat he made periodically during his American command. (In 1777, he returned to England, now a lieutenant general, and was made a Knight of the Bath.) In the British battle design of 1777 Clinton was put in command at New York, while Howe moved against Philadelphia and John Burgoyne marched down from Canada. After Burgoyne's defeat and Howe's meaningless capture of Philadelphia, Clinton was the obvious choice to succeed Howe as commander in chief. In mid-1778 Clinton violated orders to evacuate Philadelphia by sea and instead led the British in a land retreat—under difficult conditions and with considerable skill—that included the Battle of Monmouth. For the next 2 years Clinton concentrated his forces around New York, undertaking successful though minor raids against coastal towns.

Clinton's greatest triumph—ironically also the beginning of the end of England's efforts to subdue its former colonies—was his second expedition against Charleston. He captured the city and 6000 American soldiers. This victory encouraged British hopes of conquering the Southern states. However, Charles Cornwallis was left in com-

mand when Clinton returned to New York. The relations between Clinton and Cornwallis revealed the same problems earlier apparent in Clinton's disagreements with William Howe. A flurry of orders and counterorders from Clinton in New York and George Germaine in London in effect left Cornwallis free to follow his own inclinations to Yorktown, and the result was his crushing defeat in October 1781. Clinton left his command the following May. While Cornwallis had a friendly reception in England, Clinton—his nominal commander—was blamed, and an acrimonious public debate between the two military leaders ensued.

In and out of Parliament, quarreling with relatives and critics, Clinton was nevertheless promoted to general in 1793 and became governor of Gibraltar the following year. He died at Gibraltar on Dec. 23, 1795. His two sons both rose to the rank of general in the British army.

Clinton was undoubtedly a difficult man. His short, happy marriage—ended by the death of his wife in 1772—was followed by a period of extreme depression. He was unsuccessful as a subordinate to Howe, frequently offering him what was regarded as impertinent advice. He was equally unsuccessful as a commander over Cornwallis, in part because he feared the latter as his chosen successor.

### Further Reading

Clinton's own account of his role in America may be found in William B. Willcox, ed., *The American Rebellion: Sir Henry Clinton's Narrative of His Campaigns, 1775-1782* (1954). An interesting biography is William B. Willcox, *Portrait of a General: Sir Henry Clinton in the War of Independence* (1964). For a careful study of the overall British problems of command see Piers Mackesy, *The War for America, 1775-1783* (1964). □

# Hillary Rodham Clinton

**Described as the first major U.S. female political figure since Eleanor Roosevelt, Hillary Rodham Clinton (born 1947) was considered a force to be reckoned with in American politics. Married to Bill Clinton, the 42nd president of the United States, she figured prominently in the Clinton administration with substantial influence on domestic policy-making.**

A First Lady with an independent professional identity, Hillary Rodham Clinton had experience as a corporate lawyer, a tenacious fighter for educational reform, a nationally recognized expert on children's legal rights, and a director of both corporate and nonprofit boards. Hillary Diane Rodham was born on October 26, 1947, in Chicago, Illinois. She grew up with two younger male siblings in Park Ridge, a conservative, upper-class suburb north of the city. Her parents, Hugh and Dorothy Howell Rodham, reared their three children with traditional mid-American values that stressed family, church, school, and social obligations that evolved from the adage that "to whom much is given, much is expected."

As a youth Rodham was influenced by her religious training in Methodism, with its emphasis on personal salvation and active applied Christianity. A seminal influence in her teen years was a youth minister, the Reverend Don Jones, who introduced Rodham and her peers to some of the issues, causes, and movements of the time and who encouraged involvement in direct social action. It was under Jones's guidance that she read religious philosophers such as Soren Kierkegaard and Dietrich Bonhoeffer; babysat the children of migrant farm workers; and met the Reverend Dr. Martin Luther King, Jr., when he came to Chicago on a speaking tour.

Rodham attended the public schools of Park Ridge and in 1965 enrolled in Wellesley College, where she majored in political science and took a minor in psychology. Her undergraduate years were important to her developing world view and growing sense of personal empowerment. An exceptional communicator, she was a catalyst for many of the movements for change occurring on the Wellesley campus and was involved also in a number of off-campus activities. She spent her final undergraduate summer in Washington, D.C., working for the House Republican Conference and returned to campus to spend her senior year as president of the student government. Graduating with highest distinction in 1969, Rodham gave the first student address delivered during commencement in the history of the college. In the fall she enrolled in Yale University Law

School, where she was among 30 women in the class of 1972.

## Experience in Washington, D.C.

Rodham's experiences at Yale helped to focus her areas of interest and commitment toward issues related to children, particularly poor and disadvantaged ones. She became acquainted with Marian Wright Edelman, a civil rights attorney who headed up the Washington Research Project, a non-profit group based in Washington, D.C., later to be known as the Children's Defense Fund. Spending a summer internship in Washington, D.C., Rodham was assigned by Edelman to Walter Mondale's Senate subcommittee, which was studying the plight of migrant families. In subsequent years at Yale she volunteered to work in the Yale Child Studies Center and the Yale-New Haven Hospital, assisted the New Haven Legal Assistance Association, and engaged in several other projects aimed at improving understanding of, and effecting improvements in, the legal system where children were concerned. An extra year of study at Yale prior to her graduation in 1973 further refined her expertise in child law issues.

After graduation Rodham moved to Washington and took a full-time position with the Children's Defense Fund. As staff attorney, she worked on juvenile justice problems, traveling the country comparing census data with school populations and becoming involved in litigations related to juvenile issues. In January 1974 she was chosen as one of 43 lawyers handpicked to work on the legal staff of the House Judiciary Committee, which was charged with preparing impeachment proceedings against President Richard Nixon resulting from the Watergate scandal. When Nixon resigned on August 9, 1974, and the legal staff disbanded, she accepted a teaching position at the University of Arkansas Law School. It was in Arkansas in 1975 that she married Bill Clinton, whom she had met while attending Yale.

## A Life in Little Rock

Two years after their marriage Bill Clinton became attorney general of Arkansas, and the couple moved to Little Rock. In 1977 Hillary Clinton joined the prestigious Rose Law Firm, said to be one of the oldest law firms west of the Mississippi River, and became involved in an area of law known as "intellectual property." Her primary focus, however, remained in the area of children's rights, and she helped found Arkansas Advocates for Children and Families. She continued to write on the rights of children, revising an earlier article published in the *Harvard Educational Review.* The revised essay, "Children's Rights: A Legal Perspective," appearing in *Children Rights: Contemporary Perspectives,* developed and refined her arguments for the implementation of children's legal rights. She also was appointed by President Jimmy Carter to the board of the Legal Services Corporation in Washington (1978 to 1981), a federally-funded program that provided legal assistance to the poor. In January 1978, following her husband's successful bid for the governorship, Clinton became Arkansas' first lady. Later that year she also became the first woman ever to become a partner in the Rose Law Firm. In

February 1980 she gave birth to a daughter, Chelsea Victoria.

In her 11 years as first lady of Arkansas, Clinton continued to pursue activities aimed at public service and policy reforms in the state. In her husband's second term she served as chair of the Arkansas Education Standards Committee, established to study the state's educational system and to recommend changes in the standards for public schools. Released to the public in September 1983, the standards report was controversial in several aspects, although it would eventually become state law. In 1985 Hillary Clinton also gave leadership to the establishment in Arkansas of the Home Instruction Program for Pre-School Youngsters (HIPPY). The program, which brought instruction and tutorials into impoverished homes to teach four- and five-year-olds, became one of the largest programs in the country, with over 2,400 mothers participating.

In 1987 she was elected chairperson of the board of the Children's Defense Fund and of the New World Foundation, a philanthropic organization headquartered in New York that had helped launch the Children's Defense Fund. In that year, too, Hillary and Bill Clinton were awarded the National Humanitarian Award by the National Conference of Christians and Jews. Enjoying a national prominence, Hillary Clinton held directorships on the boards of directors of several corporations, including Wal-Mart, TCBY Enterprises (yogurt), and Lafarge (cement). She would also be cited by the *National Law Journal* in 1988, and again in 1991, as one of the "One Hundred Most Influential Lawyers in America."

Analyses of Clinton were varied; however, they generally pointed to her "spiritual center" and her "continuous textured development." *People* magazine, as one example, noted that "her social concern and her political thought rest on a spiritual foundation" (January 25, 1993). The "politics of virtue" according to the *The New York Times Magazine,* informed the actions of the newest First Lady (May 23, 1993).

### In the White House

As the wife of the president of the United States Clinton remained an advocate for many of the programs and issues to which she earlier devoted her time and professional expertise. Her stated goal of "making a difference" in the world led her to press for reforms in many aspects of the American system, including health care and child welfare. Hers is said to be "the most purely voiced expression of the collective spirit of the Clinton administration, a spirit that is notable . . . for the long reach of its reformist ambitions . . . ." (*The New York Times,* May 23, 1993). She provided leadership in a number of areas, with the most notable appointment in the first year of the Clinton administration being head of the Task Force on National Health Care, with responsibility for preparing legislation, lobbying proposals before Congress, and marshaling strategy for passage of a comprehensive reform package.

Her White House agenda beyond health care reform included promoting diversity in personnel appointments— an effort she began with her role in the transition group—

and pushing for children's issues. With an office in the White House's west wing, close to the center of power, Clinton was expected to remold the role of First Lady for the 21st century.

Clinton has remained an active and vital figure in the White House throughout her husband's presidency. In August of 1995, Hillary Clinton was invited to deliver the keynote address at the United Nations International Conference on Women near Beijing, China. Early in 1996 Clinton and her daughter Chelsea made a goodwill trip to South Asia, addressing women's issues in Pakistan and India.

In November 1996 Bill Clinton was re-elected president of the United States. In that same year Hillary Clinton published her first book entitled *It Takes a Village: And Other Lessons Children Teach Us.*

### Further Reading

Several biographies provide coverage of Hillary Rodham Clinton's personal and professional life as well as her philosophical development and early tenure in the White House. These include the following: Norman King, *Hillary: Her True Story* (1993); Donnie Radcliffe, *Hillary Rodham Clinton: A First Lady for Our Time* (1993); Judith Warner, *Hillary Clinton: The Inside Story* (1993); and Joyce Milton, *The First Partner: Hillary Rodham Clinton* (1999). Short biographical articles and political analyses are found in a variety of magazines and newspapers. Recommended among these are Patricia O'Brien, "The First Lady with a Career?" *Working Woman* (August 1992); Margaret Carlson, "All Eyes on Hillary," *TIME* (September 14, 1992); Michael Kelly, "Saint Hillary," *The New York Times Magazine* (May 23, 1993); and "The Clintons: Taking Their Measure," *U.S. News and World Report* (January 31, 1994). Additional information may be obtained from the White House web site at http://www.whitehouse.gov □

# William Jefferson Clinton

**William Jefferson (Bill) Clinton (born 1946) won the Democratic nomination for the presidency in 1992 and then defeated incumbent George Bush to become the 42nd president of the United States. He was re-elected to a second term in 1996**

William Jefferson (Bill) Clinton was born in Hope, Arkansas, on August 19, 1946. He was a fifth-generation Arkansan. His mother, Virginia Kelly, named him William Jefferson Blyth, IV, after his father, who had been killed in a freak accident several months before Bill's birth. When Bill was four years old his mother left him with her parents, Hardey and Mattie Hawkins, while she trained as a nurse-anesthesiologist. His grandparents ran a small store in a predominantly African American neighborhood and, despite the racist practices of the South in the early 1950s, Bill's grandparents taught him that segregation was wrong.

After his mother's marriage to Roger Clinton when Bill was eight, the family moved to Hot Springs, Arkansas. They lived outside of the town in a house that had no indoor plumbing, which was not unusual for rural Arkansas in the late 1950s and early 1960s. Though Bill changed his last name to Clinton when he was 15 in an expression of family solidarity, the Clinton household was a troubled one. Roger Clinton was an alcoholic, and the family was frequently disrupted by incidents of domestic violence. At the age of 15 Bill made it clear to his stepfather that he would protect his mother and half brother, Roger, Jr., from any further assaults.

Clinton considered several careers as a child. At one point he wanted to be a musician (a saxophonist), and at another he wanted to be a doctor, but in 1963, as part of a delegation of the American Legion Boys' Nation, he met then-President John F. Kennedy. As a result of that meeting Clinton decided that he wanted a career in politics.

### Education of a Future President

He entered college at Georgetown University in 1964. As a college student Clinton was committed to the movement against the Vietnam War, as well as to the civil rights struggle. In 1966 he worked as a summer intern for Arkansas Senator J. William Fulbright, who was at that time the leader of antiwar sentiment in the U.S. Senate. He was still a college student in Washington, D.C., when Martin Luther King, Jr., was killed, and he and a friend used Clinton's car to deliver food and medical supplies to besieged neighborhoods during the unrest that followed King's assassination.

Bill Clinton graduated from Georgetown University in 1968 with a B.S. in International Affairs. It was already clear

to those who knew him that he was a natural politician. Clinton was awarded a Rhodes scholarship and spent the next two years as a postgraduate student at Oxford University. It was in 1969, while at Oxford, that Clinton wrote a letter to an army colonel in the University of Arkansas ROTC program concerning his draft eligibility and his opposition to the war in Vietnam. In his letter he expressed concern about his position both in terms of the draft and in terms of his later "political viability." At the age of 23 Clinton was already concerned with his electability.

In 1970 Clinton entered law school at Yale University. In his first year at Yale Clinton served as a campaign coordinator for Joe Duffy, an antiwar candidate for the U.S. Senate from Connecticut. While still a law student, Clinton worked with the writer Taylor Branch as campaign coordinator in Texas for presidential candidate George McGovern.

At Yale Clinton met Hillary Rodham, a fellow law student. After graduation Clinton and Rodham were offered jobs on the staff of the House of Representatives committee that was considering the impeachment of Richard Nixon. Clinton chose to return to Arkansas while Hillary Rodham went to work as a member of the House staff. Clinton went into private practice in Fayetteville, the center of Arkansas politics, and also began teaching at the University of Arkansas Law School.

### A Political Career in Arkansas

In 1974 he ran for Congress against John Paul Hammerschmidt, who was a strong Nixon supporter. He lost the election, but it was a very close vote. In a heavily Republican district, running as the incumbent, Hammerschmidt got only 51.5 percent of the vote.

Hillary Rodham moved to Fayetteville in 1974 and also began teaching at the University of Arkansas Law School. On October 11, 1975, Bill Clinton and Hillary Rodham were married. In 1976 the Clintons moved to Little Rock when Bill was elected attorney general of the State of Arkansas, an office he held from 1977 to 1979.

In 1978 Bill Clinton ran for the office of governor of Arkansas. He was elected, and was the youngest-ever governor of Arkansas; in fact, he was the youngest person to be elected governor of any state since Harold E. Stassen was elected in 1938 at the age of 31. In his first term in office Clinton attempted to make numerous changes, many of which were extremely unpopular, including an attempt to raise automobile licensing fees.

On February 27, 1980, Bill and Hillary Clinton had a daughter they named Chelsea Victoria. In November of that same year Ronald Reagan won a landslide victory against Jimmy Carter, and Bill Clinton lost his bid for reelection as governor of Arkansas to Republican candidate Frank White. Clinton was a strong Carter supporter, which accounted for some of his difficulties, but Clinton recognized that many of his own policies had cost him reelection. When Clinton campaigned for election in 1982 against White, he explained he had learned the price for hubris and the importance of adaptability and compromise. He was elected with 55 percent of the vote.

Clinton served as governor of Arkansas until 1992. He was considered to be an activist, pushing for school reform and for health care and welfare reform with mixed results. He continued in these years to be active in Democratic national politics. Increasingly, Clinton attracted interest as a new voice in post-segregation southern politics. In 1988 Clinton came to national prominence at the Democratic convention when he gave a lengthy speech nominating Massachusetts Governor Michael Dukakis as the party's presidential candidate. Clinton's speech was considered to be excessively long and was not well received. The audience, in fact, began to shout, "Get off, get off."

In spite of this unsuccessful debut, Clinton continued to be active in national politics. In 1991 he was voted most effective governor by his peers. That same year he was chosen as chair of the Democratic Leadership Conference. Along with such other southerners as Albert Gore of Tennessee, he worked to shift control of the party away from the northeastern liberal wing and to reshape a new party constituency. In October of 1991 Clinton announced that he was entering the 1992 race for president.

## 1992 Campaign and Election

Clinton had a lot of competition for the Democratic nomination, and many of those candidates claimed to be the alternative who offered a change from the party's past and a chance to beat the incumbent president, George Bush. Even before the New Hampshire primary in early 1992 Clinton had suffered many embarrassments and difficulties. He came from a state that was small and was regarded by many as unsophisticated and economically underdeveloped. Critics felt he had no experience on the federal level and no understanding of foreign policy. Clinton in turn insisted that his strengths lay in the fact that he was not connected to a Washington power base and therefore had a fresh perspective to bring to government.

Clinton's campaign was also plagued by charges of personal scandal that included allegations of sexual liaisons with women other than his wife and questions about his draft status during the Vietnam War. Clinton remained in the race, however, slowly gaining momentum until the 1992 Democratic convention, where he became his party's nominee. He selected Senator Albert Gore as his running mate. Clinton focused his campaign on economic issues, especially stressing his understanding of the plight of the unemployed and the underemployed as well as general concern over access to health care. In November 1992 Clinton was elected president, defeating Republican incumbent George Bush and third-party candidate Ross Perot.

Once in office Clinton addressed economic issues as interest rates and unemployment began to drop. He also appointed Hillary Rodham Clinton as the head of a task force mandated to explore possibilities for large-scale health care reform.

Helped by a Democratic majority in both the Senate and the House of Representatives, Clinton was able to have enacted most of his proposals for the "change" issue that keyed his campaign. Probably the most enduring of the passed legislation was the 1993 North American Free Trade Agreement (NAFTA) making a single trading bloc of the United States, Canada, and Mexico. As the end of Clinton's term approached a new scandal threatened the President's credibility. The scandal was termed Whitewater for the suspicious Arkansas land deal in which Bill and Hillary Clinton were involved.

In 1996 Clinton was re-elected to a second term as the United States President. He won the election by a landslide, defeating Bob Dole with 49 percent of the popular vote and 379 electoral votes. Bill Clinton continues campaigning for the issues in which he believes. He remains the nation's youngest President since John F. Kennedy in 1960. Clinton has left a mark on not only the nation, but on the world as well.

### Further Reading

There are a number of biographies of Bill Clinton, including *The Comeback Kid: The Life and Career of Bill Clinton* (1992) by Charles F. Allen and Jonathan Portis, *Clinton, Young Man in a Hurry* (1992) by Jim Moore with Rich Ihde, *America: A Place Called Hope?* (1993) by Conor O'Clery, *The Clinton Revolution: An Inside Look at the New Administration* (1993) by Koichi Suzuki, and *Partners in Power: The Clintons and Their America* (1996) by Roger Morris. Additional information may be obtained from the White House web site at http://www.whitehouse.gov □

# Robert Clive

**The English soldier and statesman Robert Clive, Baron Clive of Plassey (1725-1774), extended British power in India. He checked French aspirations in that area and made possible 200 years of British rule in the Indian subcontinent.**

Robert Clive was born of an old and prominent family on Sept. 29, 1725, at Styche in Moreton Say, Shropshire. An unruly youngster, he attended several schools and at 18 was sent to Madras as a clerk and bookkeeper in the East India Company. A moody young man, he once fought a duel and twice attempted suicide.

The rivalry between French and British interests in southern India gave Clive his opportunity for fame and fortune. He volunteered for military service, received an ensign's commission, and participated in several battles against the French; he distinguished himself at Pondicherry in 1748, before the Treaty of Aix-la-Chapelle temporarily ended hostilities. In 1749 he was appointed captain of commissary to supply provisions to the troops, and he began to amass a fortune. But recurring clashes between the French and English East India companies brought him back to active military service.

In 1751 Clive offered to lead an expedition to relieve Trichinopoly (Tiruchirappalli), where Mohammed Ali, the British candidate for nawab, or ruler, was besieged by Chanda Sahib, the French candidate. With only 200 European and 300 Indian troops, plus three fieldpieces, Clive

now enabled him to buttress the authority of the new nawab, Mir Jafar, to launch successful military expeditions against the French and to thwart Dutch expansion.

In declining health Clive went to England in 1760. He was given an Irish peerage, knighted, and made a member of Parliament. In 1765, when administrative chaos and fiscal disorder brought the company near disaster in Bengal, he returned to Calcutta as governor and commander in chief.

Clive limited the company to Bengal, Bihar, and Orissa, bringing these states under direct company control. He reformed the company's administrative practices, restored financial discipline while abolishing abuses, and reorganized the army. His efforts made the company sovereign ruler of 30 million people who produced an annual revenue of £4 million sterling.

Clive left India in February 1767. Five years later, in the absence of his strong hand in Bengal, the company appealed to the British government to save it from bankruptcy caused by widespread corruption. Clive's enemies in Parliament claimed that he was responsible for the situation. After a long trial he was exonerated; but continuing attacks on his integrity, together with illness and physical exhaustion, led him to commit suicide in London on Nov. 22, 1774. Somewhat above average height, with a commanding presence though melancholic mien, Clive brought a measure of peace, security, prosperity, and liberty to Indian natives who had been oppressed for many years.

## Further Reading

There are three standard biographies of Clive: Sir George Forest, *The Life of Lord Clive* (2 vols., 1918); R. J. Minney, *Clive of India* (1931; rev. ed. 1957); and A. Mervyn Davies, *Clive of Plassey* (1939). H. H. Dodwell, *Dupleix and Clive: The Beginning of Empire* (1920), is a classic account of French-British rivalry in India. Lucy Sutherland, *The East India Company in Eighteenth-Century Politics* (1952), clarifies the relationship of government and business.

## Additional Sources

Bence-Jones, Mark, *Clive of India,* New York: St. Martin's Press, 1975, 1974.

Chaudhuri, Nirad C., *Clive of India: a political and psychological essay,* London: Barrie & Jenkins, 1975.

Edwardes, Michael, *Clive: the heaven-born general Michael Edwarde,* London: Hart-Davis, MacGibbon, 1977.

Garrett, Richard, *Robert Clive,* London: A. Barker, 1976.

Lawford, James Philip, *Clive, Proconsul of India: a biography,* London: Allen & Unwin, 1976.

Malleson, G. B. (George Bruce), *The founders of the Indian empire,* Delhi: Mayur Publications; New Delhi: Distributed by D.K. Publishers Distributors, 1985.

Spear, Thomas George Percival, *Master of Bengal: Clive and his India,* London: Thames and Hudson, 1975.

Turnbull, Patrick, *Clive of India,* Folkestone: Bailey and Swinfen, 1975.

Watney, John Basil, *Clive of India,* Farnborough, Hants.: Saxon House, 1974. □

seized Arcot, Chanda Sahib's capital, thereby diverting 10,000 of Chanda Sahib's men from Trichinopoly.

Clive withstood a 50-day siege and, when he received reinforcements, began guerrilla warfare against the French and French-supported troops. The siege of Trichinopoly was finally lifted, and a truce in 1754 recognized Mohammed Ali as nawab. The Treaty of Paris in 1763 confirmed this, and in 1765 the emperor at Delhi admitted British hegemony in southern India.

Clive's brilliant leadership at Arcot gave him an immense reputation in Europe. When he went home in 1753, William Pitt the Elder called him a "heaven-born general." After running unsuccessfully for Parliament, Clive returned to India in 1755 as governor of Fort St. David and as lieutenant colonel in the royal army.

In 1756 Suraja Dowla (Siraj-ud-Daula), the new nawab, seized and plundered Calcutta, the principal city of Bengal and the most valuable trading center in India. Many English fled to ships and escaped, but 146 were imprisoned in a small underground dungeon called the Black Hole. Only 23 would emerge alive. Clive led a relief expedition from Madras in October; he rescued the English prisoners in December, took Calcutta in January, and defeated the nawab's army in February. Peace was made, and the East India Company's privileges were restored.

Displeased with the nawab's friendly attitude toward the French, Clive decided to replace him. In June 1758, at the Battle of Plassey, he defeated Suraja and became company governor and virtual master of Bengal. His position

# Clodion

**The French sculptor Clodion (1738-1814) is best known for small terra-cotta groups in the rococo style, depicting nymphs and fauns in an erotic and playful manner.**

Clodion, whose real name was Claude Michel, was born in Nancy on Dec. 20, 1738, into a family of sculptors. He studied with his uncle, Lambert Sigisbert Adam, a prominent sculptor whose work was significant in transforming the vigorous and dynamic baroque style into the more delicate rococo. Clodion also worked with the famous rococo sculptor Jean Baptiste Pigalle. In 1759 the Royal Academy awarded Clodion the Grand Prize for Sculpture, and he was in Rome between 1762 and 1771. In 1773 he became a member of the academy. He created his most important works during the 1770s and 1780s.

Clodion possessed great technical virtuosity and executed many types of sculpture in a variety of media. During the 1770s he completed two important commissions for the Cathedral of Rouen: the marble *St. Cecilia* and the bronze *Crucified Christ.* In 1779 the royal government commissioned him to produce a monumental statue of the Baron de Montesquieu, one of the leading philosophers of the Enlightenment. This marble statue shows the subject seated in a chair and wearing an impressive judge's robe. It is in no way formal or solemn, however, but is a sprightly and vibrant image of one of the most clever intellectuals of the time.

Clodion is most noted for small, intimate terra-cotta sculptures or statuettes of nymphs, fauns, satyrs, and bacchantes, mythological creatures symbolic of erotic pleasure. Such works as the *Intoxication of Wine* (*Nymph and Satyr*) and *Seated Bacchante Playing with a Child* are typical examples and are wholly within the decorative rococo traditions of 18th-century art. These graceful productions convey a mood of exuberant gaiety and depend for their effect upon a delicate play of highly refined textures; the soft medium of terra-cotta allowed Clodion to exploit fully and sensually the contrasting textural values of flesh, hair, fabric, fur, and foliage.

As early as the 1760s, the rococo style was under attack as frivolous and trivial, and during the last half of the century it was gradually replaced by a return to the relative severity of the art of antiquity. Clodion, however, was unaffected by the encroaching neoclassicism, and his statuettes remained popular until the French Revolution. During the Revolutionary and Napoleonic periods neoclassicism triumphed in the arts, and in his later works, such as the reliefs (1806) for the Arc du Carrousel in Paris, Clodion finally accepted the new style. He died in Paris on March 28, 1814.

## Further Reading

The most important works on Clodion are in French. General background studies in English include Lady Emilia Francis Dilke, *French Architects and Sculptors of the 18th Century* (1900); Chandler R. Post, *A History of European and American Sculpture,* vol. 2 (1921); Germain Bazin, *History of Western Sculpture* (trans. 1968); and Herbert Keutner, *Sculpture: Renaissance to Rococo* (trans. 1969). ☐

# Publius Clodius Pulcher

**The Roman politician Publius Clodius Pulcher (died 52 B.C.) was one of the leading demagogues in the 1st century B.C. As tribune, he wielded nearly as much power as Julius Caesar or Pompey.**

Clodius came from one of the most distinguished of Roman families, the Claudii, which later included Roman emperors. His early career showed signs of the turmoil that was a major feature of his later life. In 68 B.C. he preached mutiny to the troops of the aristocratic general Lucullus in Asia Minor. Clodius was also accused of collusion with the revolutionary noble Catiline in 64, although this was disputed. By these acts he established a reputation as an opponent of the entrenched aristocracy and also built a future power base for himself. In 64-63 he served on the staff of Lucius Murena in Transalpine Gaul but was accused of lining his own pockets at the expense of the provincials.

In 62 Clodius became a source of public scandal when, disguised as a woman, he invaded the exclusively female sacred rites dedicated to Bona Dea (the Good Goddess). Clodius was charged with sacrilege, and although Cicero demolished the alibis of Clodius, the latter managed to win acquittal by the extensive use of bribery. This produced a lifelong enmity between Clodius and Cicero.

In this period when Caesar, Pompey, and Crassus were struggling against the conservatives in the Senate, Clodius's talent as a political organizer and goon became increasingly useful. He was advancing through the usual progression of Roman offices, being quaestor in 61, but he soon saw that his talents and connections could best be used as tribune, a representative of the people. Unfortunately, as an aristocrat he was ineligible for this office. However, Caesar also favored Clodius for tribune and in 59 arranged for Clodius's adoption into a plebeian family, at which time his name was changed from the patrician Claudius to the plebeian Clodius. Thus Clodius was elected tribune for the year 58.

## Tribune and Power Broker

As tribune, Clodius rapidly set to work to aid his and his patrons' interests. To curry favor with the people he instituted distribution of free corn. To strengthen his operating base he arranged for the legalization of guilds, which had been prohibited 6 years earlier. From these guilds Clodius could draw gangs of toughs to terrorize Rome. Finally, to hamstring the oligarchic senatorial officials Clodius introduced a law which limited the power of the censors to expel members of the Senate and another which restrained magistrates from using religious omens to block public business, a device much used against Caesar the previous year.

Clodius also settled private grudges. He struck at Cicero by means of a law which outlawed any official who had condemned to death a Roman official without trial. Cicero had done this in the case of supporters of Catiline and was forced to go into exile. Clodius tore down the house of Cicero on the Palatine hill, purchased the property himself, and dedicated a part of it as a shrine to liberty. Clodius also removed Cato, another senator dangerous to him, by securing him a special commission to organize Cyprus as a Roman province.

Clodius now emerged as one of the most powerful men in Rome. Caesar had departed for Gaul, and Clodius's gangs spread terror through the city, so that as prominent a person as Pompey was forced to spend the last period of Clodius's tribunate at home for fear of his life. But Clodius by his attacks united his enemies against him. T. Annius Milo, another demagogic politician of the type of Clodius, began to organize gangs with the support of Pompey and the Senate, and the return of Cicero was engineered.

In 56 Clodius was elected curile aedile, and he used this office to continue his attacks on Cicero, accusing him of sacrilege when Cicero repossessed his property on the Palatine. When Caesar, Pompey, and Crassus renewed their alliance at the conference of Luca, they agreed that Clodius must be controlled.

Clodius was aiming to be praetor when, in 52, his gang met that of Milo on the Appian Way, and in the ensuing brawl Clodius was killed. At his funeral in the forum his supporters started a fire which burned down the senate house.

### Further Reading

Much information on Clodius comes from the writings of his enemy Cicero. Information also appears in Dio Cassius's history of Rome and in the accounts of the lives of Pompey, Cicero, and Lucullus in Plutarch's *Lives*. The best modern account of Clodius and his times is H. Scullard, *From the Gracchi to Nero* (1959). For the political activity of the period see L. R. Taylor, *Party Politics in the Age of Caesar* (1949).

### Additional Sources

Beesly, Edward Spencer, *Catiline, Clodius, and Tiberius,* Tustin, Calif.: American Reprint Service, 1985. ☐

# Jean and François Clouet

**The French painters Jean (ca. 1485-ca. 1541) and François (ca. 1516-ca. 1572) Clouet were masters of an elegantly mannered, aristocratic style of portrait painting and of colored chalk portrait drawing.**

J ean Clouet was court painter to King Francis I. His son, François, succeeded him as court painter and maintained that position under Henry II, Francis II, and Charles IX.

## Jean Clouet

Jean, or Janet, Clouet was the son either of Michel Clouet, known to have painted in Valenciennes, or of the Brussels painter Jan Clouet. In any case, Jean's early training must have exposed him to the formal, cool, and detached Flemish mannerist portrait type as seen in the works of Jan Gossart and Joos van Cleve.

Jean was appointed painter to the court of Francis I in 1516, the year of the monarch's accession to the throne. Though Jean was never naturalized, he became the chief court painter in 1523, a position he held until his death. In France he developed his own courtly style to comply with the French preference for decorative elegance and sophistication. The problem of attribution of his works is difficult, but it seems likely that eight oil portraits and nine miniatures known today are by him. He is recorded as having painted altarpieces at Tours, but these have disappeared, probably destroyed during the religious struggles of the mid-16th century.

Jean's chief claim to fame lies in his establishment as a medium in its own right of chalk (or hard crayon) drawing in hues of red, white, and black. About 130 examples are attributed to him. Typical is the drawing of Admiral Bonnivet (1516), with its fine feeling for the placement of the head in the usual quarter-turn to the right and the delicate system of shading in diagonal lines that he learned from

**Jean Clouet**

Leonardo da Vinci, whom Jean would have met at Francis I's château of Amboise, where the great Italian died in 1519.

One of Jean's oils is a half-length portrait of the French humanist Guillaume Budé (ca. 1535). Restrained and nearly monochrome in color, the portrait reflects the drawings in its stress on a patterned silhouette.

Of greatest inherent interest are two portraits of Francis I (both ca. 1525). The one in Florence, which has been questioned as a work by Jean himself, depicts the monarch in monumental fashion, regally erect upon a static, caparisoned horse which fills the space of the tiny panel. The setting is in the Italian mode, with a hint of architecture at the right and a generalized landscape with low horizon to enhance the grandeur of the sitter. The portrait in Paris is a half-length, nearly life-sized presentation of Francis I in dazzling robes, before a tapestried background. There is the trace of a supercilious smile on the face of this unscrupulous and dissolute Renaissance ruler. It is Jean's best-known painting, not because of its quality, which is not great, but because of the historical importance of the subject.

## François Clouet

François Clouet, also called Janet, was born at Tours and was active as a painter by 1536. He succeeded his father as chief court painter and maintained that position until his death in 1572.

More gifted than his father, the son continued the conventions of the international portrait style prevalent throughout the courts of Europe. Under the influence of such supreme Italian mannerist portraitists as Bronzino and of the Netherlander Anthonis Mor van Dahorst (Antonio Moro), François introduced into French court painting a greater naturalism with more emphasis on modeling. This may be seen in the portrait of the apothecary Pierre Quthe (signed and dated 1562). Now posed in the newly fashionable three-quarter-length view, which permits full extension of the arms and a more natural placement of the hands, the sitter's courtly station in life and his calling are indicated by an opened herbal and by a portion of a velvet drape, a space-creating device invented by Titian. François may be fairly said to have surpassed his father in imbuing his subjects with a more natural air; yet they remain restrained and very dignified.

The most interesting painting by François that has survived is ostensibly a genre scene, *Lady in Her Bath* (perhaps painted ca. 1550). It features in outspoken fashion a half-length, bejeweled nude lady seated in her "bath" before a still life of assorted fruits. Immediately behind her are a lad who reaches for the fruit and a nursemaid who suckles a baby swaddled in the Italian fashion. Drapes are drawn to reveal, in a manneristic plunge into deep space, a kitchen maid at a fireplace in an elegant room and, beside her, a pictorial representation of a unicorn, the fabled beast that symbolized virginity. Quite possibly the lady represented is Diane de Poitiers, famous mistress of Henry II. The beautifully rendered nude torso was surely derived from the undraped version of Leonardo's *Mona Lisa* (now lost), but the principal inspiration of the composition was taken from contemporary Flemish interior genre scenes, such as those

by Pieter Aertsen, which often have symbolic overtones that are obscure in meaning.

François continued the portrait drawing technique established by his father, with whose works François's are sometimes confused.

## Further Reading

The only monograph on the Clouets is in French, but there is a detailed discussion of them in Louis Dimier, *French Painting in the Sixteenth Century* (trans. 1904). See also H. W. Janson, *History of Art* (1962). □

# Arthur Hugh Clough

**The English poet Arthur Hugh Clough (1819-1861) epitomized in his life and poetry the religious crisis experienced by many Englishmen of the mid-Victorian period.**

Arthur Hugh Clough was born in Liverpool in Jan. 1, 1819. In 1829 he entered Rugby, where he quickly distinguished himself as a scholar and an athlete and became a favorite of Rugby's famous headmaster, Thomas Arnold. In 1837 he entered Balliol College, Oxford, and became friends with Benjamin Jowett and Matthew Arnold, the son of Thomas.

The controversy between members of the conservative Oxford movement and more liberal theologians undermined Clough's faith in orthodox Christianity. He maintained his general belief in God; but he became deeply disturbed, and his attempt to keep an open mind on all points of view tended to paralyze his will to act. Thus Clough came to typify his whole generation, which seemed, as Matthew Arnold noted in "Stanzas from the Grande Chartreuse," to be "wandering between two worlds, one dead, the other powerless to be born." Clough himself made this indecision the subject of many poems, such as "Say Not the Struggle Naught Availeth," "Thesis and Antithesis," "Qua Cursum Ventus," and "Easter Day."

In 1842 Clough was granted a fellowship at Oriel College and became a tutor in 1843, but in 1848 he resigned both positions. He then entered into an "after-boyhood" which enabled him to write and publish *The Bothie of Tober-na-Vuolich, a Long Vacation Pastoral*. This long narrative poem reveals the lighter, charming side of his personality.

In 1848, turning his attention from religious to political crises, Clough journeyed to Paris to observe the revolution and was in Rome in June 1849, when the French attacked the city. While in Rome, he wrote *Amours de Voyage*, his second long poem and perhaps his best. This poem explores the indecisive personality of the central character, whose inability to act destroys his love affair. Also in 1849, Clough and Thomas Burbidge published a volume of their shorter poems, entitled *Ambarvalia*. In 1850 Clough began but never finished *Dipsychus,* a long poem modeled after Goethe's Faust.

In October 1852 Clough sailed for Boston, where he was befriended by Ralph Waldo Emerson, James Russell Lowell, and Charles Eliot Norton. He returned to England in 1853 and in 1854 married Blanche Smith. Giving up his poetry, he turned to the philanthropic work being done by his wife's cousin Florence Nightingale. But his health began to fail, and in 1861 he left England to tour the Mediterranean. He began another long poem, *Mari Magno,* but never finished it, for he died in Florence on Nov. 13, 1861.

Clough's fame grew after his death. Many of his verses first appeared in a posthumous edition of *Poems* (1862), and a two-volume edition of *Poems and Prose Remains* (1869) was reprinted 14 times before 1900.

## Further Reading

The best biography of Clough is Katherine Chorley, *Arthur Hugh Clough: The Uncommitted Mind* (1962). Additional insight into Clough's personality can be gained from Frederick L. Mulhauser's edition of Clough's *Correspondence* (2 vols., 1957). An excellent modern critical study is Walter E. Houghton, *The Poetry of Clough* (1963).

## Additional Sources

Osborne, James Insley, *Arthur Hugh Clough,* Norwood, Pa.: Norwood Editions, 1976; Philadelphia: R. West, 1978.
Waddington, Samuel, *Arthur Hugh Clough: a monograph,* New York: AMS Press, 1975. □

# Clovis I

**The Frankish king Clovis I (465-511) founded the Merovingian kingdom of Gaul, the most successful of the barbarian states of the 5th century. He is widely regarded as the originator of the French nation.**

The son of Childeric I and Basina, Clovis inherited the kingship of the Salian Franks in 481, at the age of 15. In 486 he led his army against Soissons, the last of the Gallo-Roman strongholds, and defeated the Roman governor. He then engaged in a series of campaigns against other barbarian kingdoms, and it was during one of these military ventures that Clovis was converted to non-Arian Christianity. According to Gregory of Tours, Clovis was at a disadvantage in his fight against the Alamans and sought the aid of the God of his Christian wife Clotilde, promising that if he were given victory he would become a Christian. In 506 Clovis inflicted a crushing defeat on the Alamans at Tolbiac (Zülpich).

After the battle Clovis adopted Christianity and by so doing won the support of the Gallo-Roman bishops who controlled a significant portion of the wealth of Gaul and were exceedingly influential with the population. Moreover, his conversion automatically made Clovis's wars into holy wars against heretics and nonbelievers. Many historians have seen Clovis's conversion as a shrewd political move; but it is also likely that the victory of Tolbiac was instrumental in his religious shift and that without a sign of some variety he might never have abandoned his ancestral gods.

Within the Frankish portion of his kingdom Clovis, who was ruthless in his desire for power, gradually eliminated the other kings who had previously been his allies, and by a combination of military expertise and treachery he emerged as the supreme ruler in Gaul.

The period of Frankish expansion, which had begun in 486, ended with the battle against the Visigoths at Vouillé (near Poitiers) in 507. Clovis then turned his attention to the government of his newly conquered territories. His reign, which combined elements of Germanic kingship with traditional Roman fiscal and administrative systems, owed much of its success to the cooperation between Clovis and his Germanic followers and the Gallo-Roman episcopate. His policy toward the Church was essentially one of overlordship tempered with consideration for ecclesiastical needs and privileges. In the latter years of his reign, Clovis devoted much energy to the promulgation and codification of the *Lex Salica* (Salic Law), the customary unwritten laws of the Franks, and thus he provided jurisdictional unity for his kingdom.

Clovis died at Paris on Nov. 27, 511, at the age of 45. In keeping with Frankish tradition, his four sons (Chlodomer, Childebert I, Clothar I, and Theuderic) divided his kingdom.

## Further Reading

The most important source for the life of Clovis and the character of Merovingian Gaul is the *History of the Franks* by Gregory of Tours, written between 575 and 585 and available in several English translations. The best modern descriptions of the life and times of Clovis are *The Cambridge Medieval History,* vol. 3 (1913), and J.M. Wallace-Hadrill, *The Long-Haired Kings* (1962). □

# Tyrus Raymond Cobb

**Tyrus Raymond Cobb, better known as Ty Cobb (1886-1961), was most probably the greatest all-around baseball player who ever lived and also universally acknowledged as the "most hated man in baseball."**

Ty was born on December 18, 1886, in Narrows, Banks County, Georgia, to William Herschel Cobb, a school administrator and state senator, and Amanda Chitwood. Cobb grew up in Royston, Georgia, and began playing sandlot ball as soon as he could swing a bat. Over his family's objections he signed with the Augusta baseball team of the South Atlantic League in 1904 and soon attracted notice. Grantland Rice, the famous sportswriter, saw him play for Augusta and named him the "Georgia Peach," a title that Cobb wore proudly.

At a time when pitchers dominated the game and batting averages were low, Cobb was a brilliant exception, hitting .326 in his last season in the minors before joining the Detroit Tigers of the American League on August 27, 1905. In 1906 Cobb hit .320, the fifth best average in the league and 35 points ahead of the nearest Tiger. The next year he won the American League batting championship, hitting .350 and leading Detroit to the World Series. He quickly became the biggest gate attraction in baseball and would hit .300 or better for 23 straight years. During that time he hit over .400 in three different seasons, his all-time high being .420 in 1911. Cobb led the league in hitting 12 times, nine of them in a row. During his peak years, 1909-1919, he so dominated baseball that historians refer to it as the era of the "Cobbian game."

In 1909, for example, he had the best year of any baseball player to that date, leading both leagues in hitting with an average of .377 and leading the American League in hits, runs, stolen bases, runs batted in, total bases, and home runs. Once again he led the Tigers to a pennant, though as usual they lost the World Series. As most of his teammates were markedly less talented than Cobb, he would never be on a world championship team, about the only honor available to a ball player that he did not win. This remained so even during his years as a player-manager for Detroit from 1921 to 1926, when the team never finished better than second place.

In addition to his peerless batting skills, amazing fielding, and audacity as a base runner, Cobb was the fiercest competitor in baseball. Not satisfied with simply winning, he had to run up the highest possible score and therefore put unrelenting pressure on the opposition until the last man was out. The terror of pitchers as a hitter and base runner, he was also the terror of infielders and catchers as he stormed down the base paths. A perfectionist in an era of what was called "inside baseball," which emphasized hit-and-run plays, base stealing, and bunting, he mastered every aspect of his craft. Cobb was also a supremely intelligent player, a kind of baseball genius. "Know thy enemy" was his guiding rule, and his thorough knowledge of every competitor enabled him to "read" the opposition as no one else could.

Why his brains were so much admired in his playing days can be seen in his autobiography. The chapter on hitting is a brilliant essay on how to keep the opposition off balance by never doing the same thing twice. "I tried to be all things to all pitchers," Cobb wrote, summing up his teachings nicely. If this chapter is all about technique, the next one, "Waging War on the Base Paths," is all about psychology. To Cobb base stealing was largely a matter of deceiving and demoralizing the enemy. Once Cobb, annoyed by a catcher who was always telling journalists that Cobb's reputation was overblown, performed an astonishing feat. On stepping up to the plate he told the catcher that he was going to steal every base. After singling to first, Cobb then stole second, third, and home on four straight pitches. Cobb's explanation of how he accomplished this is itself a masterpiece.

Cobb remained a star after 1920 when the rise of Babe Ruth and the introduction of a livelier ball changed the game to one in which sheer batting power mattered more than finesse and guile. But the new "Ruthian game" was not to Cobb's taste, and, although he remained a skillful batter, his legs began to give out. In 1927 Cobb signed with the Philadelphia Athletics, but, though he averaged .357 at the plate, it was clear that his days as a player were numbered. He spent most of 1928 on the bench and retired at season's end. When he left baseball Cobb held 43 records. Although all but one have since been broken, his fantastic lifetime batting average of .367 appears safe. That he was the best all-around player who ever lived was recognized in 1936 when he led everyone in votes for the first group of Baseball Hall of Fame inductees, coming in ahead of Babe Ruth, Honus Wagner, Christy Mathewson, and Walter Johnson—the other four original selectees.

As a player Cobb was godlike, but as a man he had little to offer. Angry, abrasive, touchy, a loner, he was hated by his teammates at first for what one called his "rotten disposition" and was tolerated only after his phenomenal value became evident. A brawler and bully on the field, Cobb was the same off it. In a racist age he was notably abusive to African Americans. Cobb was a poor husband and father too. Both his marriages ended in divorce and, though he had five children by his first wife, his relations with them were not close. As sometimes happens, he did better as a grandfather.

Like many ex-athletes Cobb was restless in retirement, living simply despite his wealth—much of which he gave away. In 1953 he founded the Cobb Educational Foundation, which awarded college fellowships to needy Georgia students. Among his other charitable endeavors was the hospital Cobb built in Royston as a memorial to his parents. This was a defiant act in part, as his mother had shot his father to death in 1905 under suspicious circumstances—although a jury found her not guilty of manslaughter. Cobb died in Atlanta, Georgia, on July 17, 1961, widely admired but not loved, unlike his great counterpart Babe Ruth.

### Further Reading

The best biography is *Ty Cobb* (1984) by Charles C. Alexander. Must reading is *My Life in Baseball* (1961, paperback 1993) by Ty Cobb with Al Stump, a unique mixture of score-settling, revisionist self-history, and outstanding baseball analysis. The movie*Cobb* (1994) starring Tommy Lee Jones was based on Stamp's biography. □

# William Cobbett

**The English radical journalist and politician William Cobbett (1763-1835) was an advocate of parliamentary reform and a critic of the new industrial urban age.**

William Cobbett was born at Farnham, Surrey, on March 9, 1763. His father, a small farmer, could afford him little schooling. Cobbett worked briefly with a copying clerk in London in 1783; he enlisted in the army in 1784 and served until 1791, mostly in Canada. In 1792 he wrote a pamphlet exposing military corruption but was unable to supply adequate evidence to press his case and fled to France and then to America.

Writing under the name of "Peter Porcupine" in Philadelphia, he attacked the French Revolution and defended England, then at war with France. During his American sojourn Cobbett wrote numerous pamphlets and founded and edited several small periodicals, including the *Political Censor* and *Porcupine's Gazette*. At this stage in his career he was clearly anti-Radical and anti-Jacobin (pro-Federalist and anti-Democrat in American terms). Cobbett savagely criticized the English scientist Joseph Priestley, who had also settled in Philadelphia, for his support of the French Revolution. But criticism of Dr. Benjamin Rush ended Cobbett's American journalistic career; he accused the famous physician and Democrat of killing patients (George Washington, among others) through his bleeding and purging technique. This brought a charge of libel against Cobbett, and he returned to England in 1800.

Britain's Tory government welcomed him as a literary asset in the struggle against republican France. He opened a bookshop in London and in 1802 began his famous *Weekly Political Register*. Gradually moving toward radicalism, he criticized the government's conduct of the long Napoleonic War. He was especially concerned about the war's eco-

nomic repercussions on the home front. Because of his criticism of the government's handling of an army mutiny, in 1810 Cobbett was convicted of sedition and imprisoned for 2 years. Upon his release in 1812, he emerged as the great popular spokesman for the working classes. In his new, cheaper *Register,* he championed parliamentary reform and attacked the government for the high taxation and widespread unemployment of the postwar period.

Cobbett's newfound radicalism alarmed the government, and he went to America in 1817. On his return to England in 1819 Cobbett discovered a new enemy of the people—industrialism—and he repeatedly attacked this development in his famous *Rural Rides*. These essays, which praise old agricultural England, were first published in the *Register* and in book form in 1830.

Although his grand projects, the *Parliamentary Debates* and the *Parliamentary History of England,* were taken over by others while he was in prison, Cobbett never lost his interest in politics. He ran for Parliament unsuccessfully twice but was elected in 1832 from Oldham, following the acceptance of the Great Reform Bill. The parliamentary reform implemented by the bill fell far short of the demands of Cobbett and the Radicals, since the working class was still denied the vote. He opposed much of the legislation of the new Whig government in the reformed Parliament, especially the New Poor Law of 1834. He died on his farm near Guilford on June 18, 1835.

Cobbett has been praised as the prophet of democracy, but most of his writings look back to the old agrarian England of responsible landlords and contented tenants. He was not a profound thinker; his comments on economic matters were nearly always erroneous. Emotion rather than reason dictated many of his conclusions. But his passion for the interests of the common man and his ability to write in a jargon that was understood by the working class made him the leading English Radical of the early 19th century.

## Further Reading

The range in the evaluation of Cobbett is suggested by the two standard biographies: G.D.H. Cole, *William Cobbett* (1925), views him as a Radical leader of the working classes, while G.K. Chesterton, *William Cobbett* (1925), considers him a Conservative. More recent biographies of Cobbett are William Baring Pemberton, *William Cobbett* (1949), and John W. Osborne, *William Cobbett: His Thought and His Times* (1966). Osborne more than the earlier biographers minimizes Cobbett's significance, calling him "a failure in politics . . . and of very limited influence in his lifetime." Mary Elizabeth Clark wrote a specialized study, *Peter Porcupine in America* (1939). There is a provocative chapter on Cobbett in Crane Brinton, *English Political Thought in the Nineteenth Century* (1933).

## Additional Sources

Booth, Simon, *William Cobbett: an introduction to his life and writings,* Farnham Eng.: Farnham Museum Society, 1976.

Clark, Mary Elizabeth, *Peter Porcupine in America: the career of William Cobbett, 1792-1800,* Philadelphia: R. West, 1977 1939.

Cole, G. D. H. (George Douglas Howard), 1889-1959., *William Cobbett,* Norwood, Pa.: Norwood Editions, 1976; Philadelphia: R. West, 1977.

Green, Daniel, *Great Cobbett: the noblest agitator,* Oxford Oxfordshire; New York: Oxford University Press, 1985, 1983.

Osborne, John Walter, *William Cobbett, his thought and his times,* Westport, Conn.: Greenwood Press, 1981, 1966.

Schweizer, Karl W., *Cobbett in his times,* Savage, Md.: Barnes & Noble Books, 1990.

Spater, George, *William Cobbett, the poor man's friend,* Cambridge; New York: Cambridge University Press, 1982.

Williams, Raymond, *Cobbett,* Oxford Oxfordshire; New York: Oxford University Press, 1983. □

# Richard Cobden

**The English politician Richard Cobden (1804-1865) was leader of the free-trade movement. He strenuously opposed war and worked unceasingly for the cause of international peace.**

The son of a farmer, Richard Cobden was born on June 3, 1804, near Midhurst, Sussex. There were 11 children in the Cobden family, and poverty was an obstacle in Cobden's youth. His formal education was an unhappy experience. He worked for a time for his uncle in London; then in 1828 he became a calico merchant near Manchester. Prosperity followed, and he soon added Manchester municipal politics to his interests. Repeal of the Corn Laws was the issue that attracted him, and Manchester was the center of the Anti-Corn Law League, which was founded in 1838. This led him to national politics, as he emerged the leader of the free-trade movement.

During these years Cobden visited Europe, America, and Africa, and his travels gave him a perspective in international affairs. Cobden believed that free trade would promote international cooperation. His first attempt at a parliamentary career failed, but he was successful in 1841, when he was elected to Parliament from Stockport. In the same year he persuaded the orator and statesman John Bright to work toward repeal of the Corn Laws. Bright's oratory coupled with Cobden's organizational skills made the Anti-Corn Law League a great success. Prime Minister Peel's conversion to free trade was the final step, and the repeal of the Corn Laws came in 1846.

## Opposition to British Policies

Cobden was victorious, but he was also bankrupt; politics and the league had swallowed up his fortune. But a public subscription in 1847 returned him to financial solvency, and his interests turned more to foreign affairs. He became increasingly alarmed by the bellicose policies of Lord Palmerston. Cobden supported a reduction in armaments and suggested a possible trade alliance with Russia in direct opposition to Palmerston's position. Cobden wrote a number of pamphlets condemning the traditional "balance of power" approach in international politics.

At the Great Exhibition of 1851 Cobden's position of "free trade and peace" seemed triumphant; Palmerston was dismissed from office at the end of the year. But the Crimean War (1853-1856) changed all that as the anti-Russian crusade became the order of the day. In 1855 Palmerston returned as prime minister and war leader, and Cobden, who opposed the war, was severely criticized in the press and was defeated in the parliamentary election of 1857. He was, however, returned to Parliament in 1859. He was offered a position in Palmerston's Cabinet but declined. Cobden, partly through William Gladstone's influence, was sent to Paris to prepare an Anglo-French commercial treaty; his efforts led to the signing in 1860 of a 10-year reciprocal "most favored nation" treaty (Cobden-Chevalier Treaty). This was one of his greatest accomplishments.

Britain's colonial policy was also a target of Cobden's criticism. His attacks in this area were closely related to his opposition to British foreign policy. Britain had acquired huge areas of land all over the world without any regard for basic economic laws; extent of territory, not commercial value, had dictated acquisition. Cobden held that the colonies, if given up, would remain good customers of England but would cease to involve the nation in international difficulties.

America always attracted Cobden's interest. He visited the United States twice and was impressed by the absence of an entrenched landed aristocracy. In contrast to England, the United States was essentially a middle-class nation. The American Civil War deeply disturbed Cobden. He wavered (hating Southern slavery but also disliking Northern protectionism) but finally supported the North. He died in London on April 2, 1865.

## Assessment of Political Role

Cobden's outlook was based on an intense internationalism. He firmly believed that free trade would create prosperity at home and introduce a new era of international peace. The main obstacle to both free trade and peace, in Cobden's view, was the aristocracy. He felt that as a class aristocrats were naturally bellicose and believed that the sooner power was transferred from the aristocracy to the middle class, the better for the destiny of all nations.

To the historian Cobden appears as a strange combination of realist and visionary. His work for the Anti-Corn Law League was that of a hard-headed businessman, a man of action. The practical implications for manufacturers (new markets for products) were stressed. But in foreign affairs he was not so well informed; and although his conclusions, dogmatic as they were, may have been correct, he was not able to convince the majority of his countrymen. The bulk of his career in domestic politics, however, must be considered a success. Cobdenite reforms in education as well as in economics were adopted. He was, according to one biographer, "the greatest non-party statesman ever to figure in British politics."

## Further Reading

The standard biography of Cobden is John Morley, *The Life of Richard Cobden* (1881; 12th ed. 1905). There are newer biographies· by Ian Ivor Bowen, *Cobden* (1935), and by Donald Read, *Cobden and Bright: A Victorian Political Partnership* (1967). A specialized study of value is Norman McCord, *The Anti-Corn Law League* (1958; 2d ed. 1968). Recommended for general historical background are E.L. Woodward, *The Age of Reform* (1938; 2d ed. 1962); Norman Gash, *Politics in the Age of Peel* (1953); and George Sidney Roberts Kitson Clark, *The Making of Victorian England* (1962).

## Additional Sources

Edsall, Nicholas C., *Richard Cobden, independent radical,* Cambridge, Mass.: Harvard University Press, 1986.

Hinde, Wendy, *Richard Cobden: a Victorian outsider,* New Haven: Yale University Press, 1987. □

# Cochise

**Cochise (ca. 1825-1874) was both hereditary and war chief of the Chiricahua Apache band of American Indians. His ability earned him the designation "the Apache Napoleon."**

B orn probably in southern Arizona, Cochise grew to imposing manhood. A newspaper correspondent in 1870 described him as 5 feet 9 1/2 inches tall, weighing 164 pounds, with broad shoulders, a stout frame, black eyes, high forehead, hair straight back, large nose, "scarred all over his body with buckshot," and "for an Indian, straight."·

As leader of the Chiricahua Apache, Cochise fought the Mexicans relentlessly, as had been his tribe's custom for

centuries. Often these raids were conducted in concert with the Warm Springs Apache, who were led by Mangas Coloradas.

Cochise maintained a strong friendship for Americans when they began arriving in numbers in Arizona during the 1850s until the "Bascom affair" of 1861, when Cochise was wrongly accused of kidnapping the stepson of an Arizona rancher, John Ward, and of stealing Ward's cattle. Troops commanded by Lt. G.N. Bascom were sent from nearby Ft. Buchanan to secure the boy's release. Bascom arrested Cochise, who escaped, but hanged his other six prisoners, mainly relatives of Cochise. This sent Cochise on the warpath, determined to kill all white men in Arizona.

In June 1861 Cochise attacked Ft. Buchanan but was driven off. Then, as American troops were withdrawn from Arizona during the Civil War, he led his braves in bloody assaults against the Americans. In 1862 he attacked 700 troops of the California Column at Apache Pass in southeastern Arizona, but howitzer fire drove him off.

Yet Cochise could make exceptions to his hatred of the white man. Thomas J. Jeffords, government superintendent of the mails from Ft. Bowie to Tucson, walked into Cochise's camp to plead for the safety of his mail carriers, which Cochise granted, and thereafter the two men became close friends. In 1869 Henry Clay Hooker, a contract supplier of beef to reservations, was surrounded by Apache warriors and boldly rode into Cochise's camp; there Cochise entertained him and returned his guns, and Hooker was allowed to depart in peace. When he evinced surprise at this treatment, Cochise said he had not been killed because he was supplying beef eaten by Indians.

Jeffords led Gen. Oliver Otis Howard, special Indian commissioner sent by President U.S. Grant to secure peace in the Southwest, to Cochise's camp in October 1872. Cochise signed a peace treaty giving the Chiricahua a reservation some 55 miles square in southeastern Arizona with Jeffords as agent.

Cochise spent his last 2 years in peace, honoring the treaty. He died on June 8, 1874, while visiting Jeffords at the reservation and was buried there.

## Further Reading

Two contemporary views of Cochise are offered in Samuel Woodworth Cozzens, *The Marvellous Country, or Three Years in Arizona and New Mexico* (1873; repr. 1967), and James Henry Tevis, *Arizona in the '50's* (1954). A general history of the period that gives an excellent overview is Dan L. Thrapp, *The Conquest of Apacheria* (1967). But the best book for understanding the life of Cochise is a novel: Elliot Arnold, *Blood Brother* (1947). □

# Johnnie Cochran

**Although he has been well known in west coast law circles for many years, Johnnie Cochran (born 1937) entered the national spotlight as a member of O. J. Simpson's defense team.**

Johnnie L. Cochran, Jr. led the winning team of lawyers in the "trial of the century," and in the process became arguably the most famous lawyer in the world. Cochran's successful defense of former football great O. J. Simpson against charges of murder in the televised trial was followed by millions of Americans. Although his trial tactics are still sparking debate, his legal acumen and ability to sway a jury have characterized his legal career. In fact, the *People v. O. J. Simpson* is only the most recent and most visible of a string of Cochran's courtroom victories, some involving superstars such as Michael Jackson and others involving ordinary people thrust into extraordinary circumstances. *Ebony* magazine once described Cochran as "a litigator who'd taken the cases people said he *might* win when hell freezes over, then laughed all the way to the bank when the multimillion-dollar verdicts came rolling in."

Handsome and well-spoken, Cochran was established in the West-Coast power elite well prior to his defense of O. J. Simpson. Today he is more sought-after than ever as both an attorney and a celebrity. If he is detested in some circles as an opportunist, he is just as widely admired as a black American success story. Cochran told *Essence* that he has never been bothered by his detractors. "I have learned not to be thin-skinned, especially when I think I'm doing the right thing," he said. "It's not about money, it's about using the law as a device for change."

Johnnie Cochran, Jr. was born in 1937 in Shreveport, Louisiana, and is the great-grandson of a slave. He grew up in a stable and prosperous family, with a father and mother who stressed education, independence, and a color-blind

attitude. While Cochran was still young the family moved to Los Angeles, and he attended public schools there, earning excellent grades. Although his father had a good job with the Golden State Mutual Life Insurance Company, Cochran always managed to find friends who had more money and more luxuries than he did. "If you were a person who integrated well, as I was, you got to go to people's houses and envision another life," he recalled in *The American Lawyer*. "I knew kids who had things I could only dream of. I remember going to someone's house and seeing a swimming pool. I was like, 'That's great!' Another guy had an archery range in his loft. An archery range! I could not believe it. I had never thought about archery! But it made me get off my butt and say, 'Hey, I can do this!'"

## Law Career Beckoned

Cochran earned a bachelor's degree from the University of California, Los Angeles, in 1959, supporting himself by selling insurance policies for his father's company. He was accepted by the Loyola Marymount University School of Law and began his studies there in the autumn of 1959. "I was the kind of student that didn't want to look like a jerk, always raising my hand," Cochran recalled in *The American Lawyer*. "But I would sit there and pray that I would be called on. That was my competitive spirit lying in wait."

Having finished his law studies and passed the California bar by 1963, Cochran took a job with the city of Los Angeles, serving as a deputy city attorney in the criminal division. There he worked as a prosecutor. In 1965 he entered private practice with the late Gerald Lenoir, a well-known local criminal lawyer. After a short period with Lenoir, he formed his own firm, Cochran, Atkins & Evans. "That was the closest to a storefront I ever had," Cochran remembered in *The American Lawyer*. Johnnie Cochran's career was launched from this office with a highly-publicized and inflammatory case.

In May of 1966, a young black man named Leonard Deadwyler was shot dead by police as he tried to rush his pregnant wife to the hospital. Cochran represented Deadwyler's family, who accused the police of needless brutality in their son's murder. The Los Angeles Police Department insisted that the officers had acted in self-defense. "To me, this was clearly a bad shooting," Cochran maintained in *The American Lawyer*. "But the [district attorney] did not file charges, and when our firm filed a civil suit we lost. Those were extremely difficult cases to win in those days. But what Deadwyler confirmed for me was that this issue of police abuse really galvanized the minority community. It taught me that these cases could really get attention."

Another memorable case further steered Cochran toward working on behalf of his race. In the early 1970s he went to court in defense of Geronimo Pratt, a former Black Panther who stood accused of murder. Cochran lost that case too, but he insists to this day that Pratt was railroaded by the F.B.I. and local police. "White America just can't come to grips with this," Cochran explained in *Essence*. "To them the police are as they should be: saving children, acting like heroes in the community. They aren't setting up people, they're not lying, they aren't using their racist beliefs as an excuse to go after certain people." Cochran has continued to press for a re-trial in the Pratt case.

## "Best in the West"

Such headline-grabbing cases quickly made Cochran's name among the black community in Los Angeles, and by the late 1970s he was handling a number of police brutality and other criminal cases. In an abrupt about-face in 1978, however, he joined the Los Angeles County district attorney's office where one of his subordinates was a young lawyer named Gil Garcetti. Cochran has said that he took the job because he wanted to broaden his political contacts and refashion his image. "In those days, if you were a criminal defense lawyer, even though you might be very good, you were not considered one of the good guys, one of the very top rung," he explained in *The American Lawyer.*

Cochran's position at the district attorney's office did not spare him a brush with racist police. One afternoon as he drove his two young daughters across town in his Rolls Royce, he was pulled over. The police yelled at him to get out of the car with his hands up, and when he did he could see that they had drawn their guns. "Well, talk about an illegal search and seizure!" Cochran exclaimed in *The American Lawyer,* recalling the event. "These guys just go through ripping through my bag. Suddenly this cop goes gray. He sees my number three badge from the D.A.'s office! He's like, 'Ahh! Ahh!' They all go apoplectic. I never got stopped again, but I'm careful not to make any weird moves. I might get shot!"

Cochran never publicized the incident, but he was deeply disturbed about its effect on his two daughters. "I didn't want to tell them it was because of racism," he added. "I didn't want to tell them it happened because their daddy was a black guy in a Rolls, so they thought he was a pimp. So I tried to smooth things over. . . . As an African American, you hope and pray that things will be better for your children. And you don't want them to feel hatred."

Returning to private practice in 1983, Cochran established himself as "the best in the West," to quote *Ebony* magazine. One of his first major victories occurred in the case of Ron Settles, a college football player who police said had hanged himself in a jail cell after having been picked up for speeding. On the behalf of Settles's family, Cochran demanded that the athlete's body be exhumed and examined. A coroner determined that Settles had been strangled by a police choke hold. A pre-trial settlement brought the grieving family $760,000.

The Settles case settlement was the first in a series of damage awards that Cochran has won for clients—some observers estimate he has won between $40 and $43 million from various California municipalities and police districts in judgments for his clients. *Essence* reporter Diane Weathers wrote: "Cochran is not just another rich celebrity lawyer. His specialty is suing City Hall on behalf of many fameless people who don't sing, dance or score touchdowns and who have been framed, beaten up, shot at, humiliated and sometimes killed at the hands of the notorious LAPD."

Success begot success for Cochran. The Settles case was followed by another emotional case in which an off-duty police officer molested a teenager and threatened her with bodily harm if she told anyone. In that case Cochran spurned an out-of-court settlement in six figures and took the issue to the courtroom—where a jury awarded his client $9.4 million. A post-verdict settlement paid the young woman $4.6 million.

As Cochran's fame grew, his client list began to include more celebrities, of which pop singer Michael Jackson is the best known. On Jackson's behalf, Cochran arranged an out-of-court settlement with a boy who had accused the singer of molestation. Cochran had the case retired in such a way that the charges against Jackson were withdrawn, and Jackson could publicly proclaim his complete innocence. Cochran also engineered an acquittal for *Diff'rent Strokes* star Todd Bridges, who stood accused of attempted murder.

## The "Trial of the Century"

No celebrity trial was more followed than O. J. Simpson's trial, however. In the summer of 1994, Simpson was arrested and charged with the murders of his ex-wife, Nicole Brown Simpson, and her friend Ron Goldman. Simpson declared that he was innocent, and he engaged Cochran as part of an expensive "dream team" of lawyers dedicated to his defense. Before long, Cochran had replaced Robert Shapiro as leader of the "dream team" as the matter was brought to trial. Calling the O. J. Simpson trial a "classic rush-to-judgment case," Cochran vowed to win an acquittal for the football star-turned-television celebrity. Responding to questions about the nickname for his legal team, Cochran told *Time:* "We certainly don't refer to *ourselves* as the Dream Team. We're just a collection of lawyers just trying to do the best we can."

One week into the Simpson trial in February of 1995, *Time* reported that Cochran had "unveiled an unexpectedly strong defense." With his engaging manner and sincerity, Cochran sought to poke holes in the case against Simpson as presented by district attorneys Marcia Clark and Christopher Darden. Piece by piece he challenged the evidence, paying special attention to the racist attitudes of one of the investigating officers, Mark Fuhrman.

Cochran was effective—and controversial—in his closing arguments on Simpson's behalf. He claimed his client had been framed by a racist police officer, and that if such injustice were allowed to persist, it could lead to genocide as practiced by Nazi dictator Adolf Hitler. Speaking to the jury, Cochran concluded: "If you don't speak out, if you don't stand up, if you don't do what's right, this kind of conduct will continue on forever." After deliberating only four hours, the mostly black jury found Simpson not guilty on all counts.

Observers called Cochran's remarks the "race card," and some castigated the attorney for proceeding in this manner. Cochran offered no apologies for his strategy, claiming that his scenario represented the truth as he saw it. "I think race plays a part of everything in America, let alone this trial," he maintained in a *Newsweek* interview. "That's one of the problems in America. People don't want to face up to the fact that we do have some racial divisions."

After handling the post-trial publicity, Cochran returned to other cases, including pending civil litigation against Simpson. The trial has had its impact on Cochran's life. Once a celebrity lawyer only in Los Angeles, he is now a celebrity lawyer across America, receiving a million-dollar advance to write his memoirs and a hefty fee for any personal appearances he makes. Cochran has had his share of negative publicity, however. His first wife, Barbara Cochran Berry, wrote a memoir during the Simpson trial in which she accused Cochran of abuse and infidelity. Cochran's longtime mistress, Patricia Cochran, also claims to be writing her own memoir. "I did a lot of stupid things," Cochran admitted in *Essence* when asked about his private life. "I paid a price with my eldest daughter and with my [first] marriage. I would like young lawyers not to make the mistakes I made."

Married for a second time, Cochran lives in a luxurious home with a commanding view of the Los Angeles basin. His father, whom he calls "the Chief," lives with him. He has written a book, *Journey to Justice,* and is planning to take part in a once-a-week commentary for "Court TV" with Atlanta prosecutor Nancy Grace. Having won an acquittal for O. J. Simpson—and having made himself famous in the process—Cochran concluded in *Newsweek* that he wants to initiate a "healing" between the races in America. If that is to happen, he believes, white America will have to become more sympathetic to the hardships facing African Americans. "It doesn't make sense for us to go back into our individual camps after this is over," he noted. "African Americans . . . respond to what I have to say. I spoke what they feel is happening, and I spoke it as an African American lawyer. This case cried out for that. . . . I don't want to exacerbate racial problems. But you have to be true to who you are. . . . This is not for the timid."

### Further Reading

*American Lawyer,* May 1994, p. 56.
*Ebony,* April 1994, pp. 112-16.
*Essence,* November 1995, p. 86.
*Newsweek,* January 16, 1995, p. 60; October 9, 1995, pp. 31, 34; October 16, 1995, pp. 37-39, 42.
*People,* April 10, 1995, pp. 55-56.
*The Source,* January 1996, p. 34.
*Time,* January 30, 1995, pp. 43-44; February 6, 1995, pp. 58-63; January 1, 1996, pp. 102-03.
*U.S. News and World Report,* January 23, 1995, pp. 32-35.
*Los Angeles Times* January 13, 1997, sec: 1, pp. 5. □

# John Douglas Cockcroft

**John Douglas Cockcroft (1897-1967) was an English physicist. His main contribution to physics consisted in designing a linear accelerator capable of giving such a speed to charged particles as to produce the transmutation of atomic nuclei.**

John Cockcroft was born in Todmorden, Lancashire, on May 27, 1897. He attended the University of Manchester, where he studied mathematics under Horace Lamb in 1914-1915. Following service with the Royal Field Artillery in World War I, Cockcroft joined Metropolitan-Vickers, an engineering company, which sent him back to the University of Manchester to study electrical engineering. He transferred to St. John's College, Cambridge, where he took honors in mathematics in 1924.

Cockcroft was one of the gifted young physicists whom Ernest Rutherford gathered at the Cavendish Laboratory. By 1928 Cockcroft was at work on the problem of accelerating protons by high voltages, a task in which he was greatly helped by E.T.S. Walton. At the meeting of the Royal Society on April 28, 1932, it was announced that Cockcroft and Walton "had successfully disintegrated the nuclei of lithium and other light elements by protons entirely artificially generated by high energy potentials." Cockcroft and Walton shared the Nobel Prize in physics for 1951.

Cockcroft's rise in the British scientific establishment was spectacular. In 1934 he became the head of the Royal Society's Mond Laboratory in Cambridge. In 1939 he obtained the coveted Jacksonian chair in experimental physics and that year took charge of the practical implementation of the principle of radar for Britain's coastal and air defense. Following his return in 1940 from the United States as a member of the Tizard Mission, he became head of the Air Defense Research and Development Establishment. By 1944 he was in Canada directing the Canadian Atomic Energy Project, and upon returning to England in 1946 he

was appointed director of the Atomic Energy Research Establishment at Harwell. His 12 years there saw the production of the British atomic bomb and also an impressive advance in the peaceful use of atomic energy, exemplified by the construction of the famous nuclear energy power station at Calder Hall.

From 1959 until his death on Sept. 18, 1967, he was master of Churchill College while retaining a part-time membership in the British Atomic Energy Authority. At the last meeting which Cockcroft attended in July 1967, he made interesting predictions about the future of technology and offered the following advice to youth: "Never finish your education. I did not know much about physics when I started to do research. Go on with your reading and going to meetings and continue to work in your spare time on your own subject. It is the only way." Perhaps the finest personal characteristic of Cockcroft was his disarming kindness. It earned him countless friends both within and outside his professional field. The same quality made him also a much admired family man. He married Eunice Elizabeth Crabtree in 1925, and they had four daughters and a son.

## Further Reading

Biographical material on Cockcroft is in the Nobel Foundation's publication *Nobel Lectures, Physics, 1942-1962: Including Presentation Speeches and Laureates' Biographies* (1964). The voltage multiplier of Cockcroft and Walton is explained in Irving Kaplan, *Nuclear Physics* (1955; 2d ed. 1963). Volume 2 of Henry A. Boorse and Lloyd Motz, eds., *The World of the Atom* (2 vols., 1966), contains a chapter on Cockcroft and describes the Cockcroft-Walton experiments. □

# Jean Cocteau

**The French writer Jean Cocteau (1889-1963) explored nostalgia for childhood and adolescence, frustration in love, and fear of solitude and death.**

Jean Cocteau was born in a suburb of Paris and brought up in a well-to-do home frequented by the artistic notables of the day. As a schoolboy at the Lycée Condorcet, he was anything but a model pupil, but he charmed his teachers by his verve and brilliance. His official debut was at the age of 18, when the renowned actor Édouard de Max gave a lecture on Cocteau's poetry. Cocteau soon visited Edmond de Rostand, Anna de Noailles, and Marcel Proust; everybody and everything fashionable attracted him.

When the Russian ballet performed in Paris, Jean Cocteau was there. Soon he proposed to its director, Sergei Diaghilev, a ballet of his own. The resulting *Blue God*, which was not presented until 1912, was not a success. Not daunted, Cocteau started the ballet *David*, for which he hoped Igor Stravinsky would do the music. Although the ballet did not materialize, *Potomak*, a curious prose work of fantasy dedicated to Stravinsky, did get written, and texts composed for both works were finally incorporated in a ballet called *Parade*. Erik Satie and Pablo Picasso collabo-

rated with Cocteau on this production, for which Guillaume Apollinaire, in a program note, coined the word surrealistic.

After World War I, when Dada and surrealism replaced cubism and the "new spirit," Cocteau played about with the new ideas and techniques without adhering strictly to any group. The mime dramas of *The Newlyweds of the Eiffel Tower* and *The Ox on the Roof* as well as the poems of *The Cape of Good Hope* all demonstrate the manner of the day without, however, following any prescribed formula. Subsequently, in verse Cocteau reverted to more conventional prosody, and in fiction, to an uncomplicated narrative style. *The Big Split* and *Thomas the Impostor* present in forthright prose the themes of the author's life and times.

*Antigone* opened Cocteau's series of neoclassic plays, which enjoyed great success from the late 1920s on with their sophisticated props such as oracular horses, symbolic masks and mirrors, angels, and mannequins. The same trappings would be maintained for his plays of romantic or medieval inspiration and would constitute, as well, recognizable features of Cocteau's films.

In the universe that Cocteau's work evokes, the boundaries between what is real and what is unreal disappear, and none of the conventional oppositions such as life and death or good and bad remains fixed. Enveloping the work is a hallucinatory atmosphere that is characteristic. Cocteau was elected to the French Academy in 1955.

## Further Reading

Francis Steegmuller's sympathetic *Cocteau* (1970) is the most comprehensive biography. Margaret Crosland deliberately avoids gossip in her *Jean Cocteau* (1955). Neal Oxenhandler in *Scandal and Parade: The Theater of Jean Cocteau* (1957) expressed indignation at what he considers unfair treatment of Cocteau. Wallace Fowlie is frankly admiring in *Jean Cocteau: The History of a Poet's Age* (1966). Elizabeth Spigge, collaborating with a French biographer (Jean Jacques Kihm) on *Jean Cocteau: The Man and the Mirror* (1968), handles her subject with bland discretion. Not so, however, Frederick Brown, whose hostile treatment of Cocteau has given *An Impersonation of Angels: A Biography of Jean Cocteau* (1968) particular notoriety. Brutal though it is, this is a witty and well-written book.

## Additional Sources

*Album Masques, Jean Coctea,* Paris: Masques, 1983.
Cocteau, Jean, *The difficulty of being,* New York: Da Capo Press, 1995.
Cocteau, Jean, *Souvenir portraits: Paris in the Belle Epoque,* New York: Paragon House, 1990.
Peters, Arthur King, *Jean Cocteau and the French scen,* New York: Abbeville Press, 1984.
Steegmuller, Francis, *Cocteau, a biography,* Boston: D.R. Godine, 1986, 1970.
Touzot, Jean, *Jean Cocteau,* Lyon: Manufacture, 1989. □

# Jan Pieterszoon Coen

**The Dutch merchant Jan Pieterszoon Coen (ca. 1586-1629) founded Batavia as governor general of the Dutch East India Company. Possessed of great administrative and military ability, he contributed greatly to the expansion of Dutch influence in the East Indies.**

Born at Hoorn probably at the end of 1586 (he was baptized on Jan. 8, 1587), Jan Coen at the age of 13 obtained employment with a firm of former Dutch merchants in Rome, where he remained for almost 7 years and where he learned bookkeeping, other commercial skills, and several languages.

Returning to Holland in 1607, Coen sailed on December 22 of that year for the Dutch East Indies as an employee of the Dutch East India Company. He returned home in 1610, and 2 years later the company dispatched him to the Indies as commander of two ships. At the end of 1614 Coen was named director general, the second highest post, and on April 30, 1618, he was appointed governor general at the age of 31.

Coen had difficulties with the Bantamese and English over the spice trade and transferred the seat of the company in Java from Bantam to Jacatra, where the company storehouse was located. He reinforced this building, making it a reliable fortress. The English, however, concentrated a large fleet off Bantam and seized a heavily laden Dutch ship, *De Swarte Leeuw.* Coen demanded its return, and when this

was refused, a fight ensued. Coen's fleet held its own against a superior force until its ammunition was exhausted. He then sailed for the Moluccas, where he obtained reinforcements of 16 ships. Upon his return to Jacatra at the end of May 1619 he found that his garrison had held out, so Coen built a Dutch center which he named Batavia.

In 1621 Coen led a punitive expedition against the Bandanese in East Indonesia, who had been trading with the English. He decimated the population and resettled the survivors. In 1623 he resigned as governor general, but the following year the company persuaded him to take up this post again. British opposition delayed his return, however, until 1627, when he sailed secretly for the Indies and assumed without proper credentials the governor generalship. Shortly after his arrival at Batavia, he was confronted with sieges by the Bantamese and by the kingdom of Mataram. The latter made two unsuccessful attempts to dislodge the Dutch, and during the second attack Coen was suddenly stricken with a tropical disease and died on Sept. 21, 1629.

## Further Reading

There is an extensive bibliography on Coen in Dutch. In English see E. S. De Klerck, *History of the Netherlands East Indies* (2 vols., 1938), and Bernard H. M. Vlekke, Nusantara: *A History of the East Indian Archipelago* (1943; 2d ed. 1959). A valuable background study is J.H. Parry, *The Age of Reconnaissance* (1963). □

# J. M. Coetzee

**J. M. Coetzee (born 1940) was a white South African novelist whose writings reflected strong anti-imperialist sentiments.**

John M. Coetzee, the son of a sheep farmer, was born in Cape Town in 1940 and was educated in both South Africa and the United States. He earned his B.A. at the University of Cape Town, and his Ph.D. from The University of Texas. After the Sharpeville crisis in South Africa in 1960 he spent ten years outside the country as a student, a lecturer, and an employee in a multi-national corporation. Returning to teach English at the University of Cape Town in 1971, he had a highly cosmopolitan outlook which tended to set him apart from most white South African writers. Indeed, he felt that his writing fit into no recognizably South African literary tradition and was more influenced by the vogue of postmodernist writing in Europe and America of the 1960s, which was also fired by a strongly anti-imperialist commitment, prompted by opposition to the Vietnam War. Thus, though he listed his interests as crowd sports, "apes and humanoid machines," and images such as photographs "and their power over the human heart," he remained a rather isolated figure in Cape Town, separated from his wife and tending to shun human company. In 1984 he did not travel to London to receive in person the Booker Prize for his novel *The Life and Times of Michael K.*

Coetzee's cosmopolitan outlook helped shape his first novel, *Dusklands* (1974), which consists of two separate stories which skillfully interweave fact and fiction. Exploring the theme of the western imperial imagination, the novel contrasts the experiences of Eugene Dawn, an American government official put in charge of the New Life project to transform Vietnamese society, who eventually goes insane, and the account of the travels of Jacobus Coetzee into the interior of the Cape in the 18th century. The novel embraces, however, a binding thread in the mental dualism between mind and body prompted by imperial expansion and conquest and, through the ancestor figure of Jacobus Coetzee, the author's search for his own roots in South African society and history.

The publication of *Dusklands* caused a considerable stir in South African literary circles, as the novel broke with many of the traditions of the colonial novel. Some radical critics, however, charged Coetzee with only partially undermining the colonial conventions of literary realism and taking the western vogue of exploration of the individual self to its extremes.

The publication of Coetzee's second novel, *In the Heart of the Country,* in 1976, however, confirmed his proficiency as a writer and developed especially the theme of the violence and alienation at the roots of western white colonialism. The novel is the first person account of a lonely white spinster, Magda, and of her solitude and incestuous relationship with her father on an isolated Cape farm, sometime in the 19th century. There are many allegorical features to this story, which strips away the thin western veneer

behind colonial society to reveal its culturally rootless quality. After being raped by the colored servant, who also kills her father, Magda is left alone on the farm and invents her own metaphysical skygods to worship in the absence of any other meaningful cultural symbols. The author's rejection of the traditional mode of linear and teleological mode of writing was reflected in the numbering of individual paragraphs, and there was no obvious progress through time, but rather a state of mental and emotional timelessness. The novel was received with considerable enthusiasm in both South Africa and Western Europe and North America. It established Coetzee as a writer of international repute.

In 1980 Coetzee published his third novel, *Waiting for the Barbarians,* which continued his allegorical examination of the imperial theme through the eyes of a benevolent liberal imperial official on the frontier of an empire on the verge of collapse. An amateur collector of historical records, the official is concerned to retain a memory of the empire's history before it disappears at the hands of nameless and faceless barbarians who progressively intrude over the empire's borders. Though he tries unsuccessfully to form a relationship with a blind woman barbarian taken prisoner, the official fails in this endeavor and, after returning her to her society, is tortured by new militaristic imperial rulers who are trying to shore up the empire before its final collapse. The novel clearly embraces many themes at the heart of the South African condition, as well as universalizing the dilemma at the heart of imperial conquest generally.

Coetzee was received as a writer who had, in some measure, stepped outside the tight limits of his own society, and his fourth novel, *The Life and Times of Michael K* (1983), was eagerly awaited.

*Life and Times* marked in some respects a new departure for Coetzee, for the story had far more naturalistic qualities than his previous novels. The setting in Cape Town, in a near future of riots and breakdown of law and order, had a strongly realistic quality and was undoubtedly shaped by the unrest in South Africa. Michael K, the central character, is a typically Coetzee character: lonely, isolated, and stigmatized with a harelip. Interspersing Michael K's own thoughts within the narrative, the novel follows the progress of its character away from Cape Town, back into the rural terrain, as Michael K flees with his ill mother (who dies on the way) and tries to survive in a situation of social breakdown. The novel was significant for refusing to recognize any racial identities and was concerned with the suffering and redemption of humanity as a whole. Michael K, though, cannot escape the clutches of the disintegrating society and is captured on an abandoned farm and accused of aiding guerrillas. Returning to Cape Town, Michael is left alone, though finds solace in some human company and in the idea that he is a gardener and has in some manner returned to the roots of his society. Concerned to the end with revealing the essential truth about existence, the novel manifested a more puritanical commitment to humanity in the abstract than any particular contemporary political creed or ideology.

In 1987 Coetzee released his next novel, *Foe,* a clever reinterpretation of Daniel Defoe's classic, *Robinson Crusoe.*

Critics were divided in their assessment of this somewhat unusual work from Coetzee. Some contended that the material seemed a stylistic departure from his previous works, while others held that the new novel was on a continuum with material such as Michael K. In *Southern Humanities Review,* Ashton Nichols wrote, "Like all of Coetzee's earlier works, *Foe* retains a strong sense of its specifically South African origins, a sociopolitical subtext that runs along just below the surface of the narrative."

Whereas *Foe* dealt with South African political issues symbolically, *Age of Iron* was Coetzee's first novel to address the South African political situation directly. It is the story of Mrs. Curren, a retired teacher, dying of cancer, who for the first time faces the reality of apartheid in her home country. At the end of her life, she's forced for the first time to confront a system that she has never before questioned. Sean French wrote in *New Statesman and Society,* "Dying is traditionally a process of withdrawal from the world. . . . Coetzee tellingly reverses this."

Coetzee also delivered an impressive body of nonfiction, with works such as *White Writing: On the Culture of Letters in South Africa* (1988) and *Doubling the Point: Essays and Interviews* (1992). In 1996 he published *Giving Offense: Essays on Censorship* to favorable reviews.

Coetzee lectured at numerous universities, including the University of Cape Town and Johns Hopkins University. He was distinguished by being a truly multilingual writer, translating work into Dutch, German, French, and Afrikaans. He was the recipient of numerous awards, including the Booker-McConnell Prize, CNA Literary Award, and the Jerusalem Prize for the Freedom of the Individual in Society.

## Further Reading

Further information can be found in Stephen Watson, "Speaking: J. M. Coetzee" in *Speak* (May-June 1978); Peter Knox-Shaw, "Dusklands: A Metaphysics of Violence" in *Contrast* (September 1982); Paul Rich, "Tradition and Revolt in South African Fiction" in *Journal of Southern African Studies* (October 1982), and "Apartheid and the Decline of the Civilization Idea: An Essay on *July's People* and *Waiting for the Barbarians*" in *Research in African Literature* (Fall 1984); and Landeg White and Tim Couzens, *Literature and Society in South Africa* (London, 1984). □

# Levi Coffin

**A leading American antislavery reformer and a conductor of the Underground Railroad, Levi Coffin (1789-1877) contributed to the good repute in the North of illegal and contested fugitive slave activities.**

Levi Coffin came of an old Nantucket, Mass., family, part of which had settled with a Quaker community in New Garden, N.C. There he was born of farmer parents on Oct. 28, 1789, and raised with little schooling.

What he learned came by his own efforts. Coffin aspired at the time to be a teacher and taught a number of seasons in the area. North Carolina still permitted moderate antislavery measures. Coffin, already a friend of runaway slaves, sought means for helping them. In 1821 he opened a Sunday school for slaves. It was successful but stirred the antagonism of white neighbors, who discouraged friendly slaveholders from permitting their slaves to attend its sessions.

Increasing repression in the state dissatisfied many of Coffin's Quaker associates, and in 1826 they moved to Newport (later Fountain City), Ind., where African Americans resided freely. There Coffin opened a country store, which became a successful enterprise, soon including pork curing and the manufacture of linseed oil. By this time Coffin was wholly dedicated to peaceful measures for opposing the institution of slavery. His home became a center of secret activity for conducting runaways north to freedom on the Underground Railroad, and he gained fame as informal "president" of what was largely a loose federation of people and routes for encouraging fugitive slave enterprises. He also continued his educational efforts in behalf of African Americans.

Coffin was outstanding in his search for alternatives to slave labor and was a major advocate of "free produce," that is, goods produced by free labor. He hoped to persuade Southerners as well as Northerners of its virtues, and he visited the South in his efforts to win partisans for his program. While there he expressed himself freely in criticism of the morals and economics of slavery.

In 1847, with the cooperation of Quaker associates, Coffin moved to Cincinnati, Ohio, to build a business dealing in free produce. Thanks to his commercial abilities, it operated at a profit, though its success did not advance the free-labor movement significantly. He also continued his Underground Railroad and educational work. During the Civil War he gave much thought to the future of slaves who were being freed by military actions or proclamations. He contributed to the work of the Freedmen's Aid Associations set up to ease their plight. In 1864 he visited England to appeal for funds from auxiliary associations there and received more than $100,000 to help feed, clothe, and educate freedmen. The adoption of the 15th Amendment to the Constitution in 1869, giving the vote to African American men, marked his retirement from active service. He died on Sept. 16, 1877.

## Further Reading

Coffin's autobiography, *Reminiscences of Levi Coffin* (1876; 3d ed. 1898), is the major source. See also Wilbur H. Siebert, *The Underground Railroad from Slavery to Freedom* (1898), and Carter G. Woodson, *The Education of the Negro Prior to 1861* (1915). □

# William Sloane Coffin Jr.

**William Sloane Coffin, Jr. (born 1924) was a Yale University chaplain who spoke out against the Viet-**

**nam War and was indicted as a criminal by the United States government for conspiring to aid young men to avoid the military draft.**

William Sloane Coffin, Jr. was born to considerable wealth and social position on June 1, 1924, in New York City. When he was 11 his father died, and he grew up in the company of tutors and teachers in New England and Paris, France. He graduated from Andover Academy in 1942, spent a year of piano study at the Yale School of Music, and then, in the middle of World War II, he enlisted in the U.S. army. He emerged from Officer's Candidate School as a second lieutenant and was sent to Europe in 1945. Already fluent in French and German, he now mastered the Russian language and served for two years as a liaison officer with the American and Soviet forces. He returned to Yale University from 1947 to 1949 for the completion of his college degree and for religious training at Union Theological Seminary. However, because of his ability to speak Russian, he allowed himself to be recruited for a three year tour of duty in Europe with the Central Intelligence Agency.

In 1953 Coffin came back to Yale University, this time to Yale Divinity School for training which would lead him to become an ordained Presbyterian minister. In spite of his army-CIA background, the pulpit was a natural progression. After all, he had been named for his uncle, Henry Sloane Coffin, who had been president of Union Theological Seminary for 19 years (1926-1945). Somewhat aggressively ath-

letic in behavior, young Coffin did not fit the image of a prelate. He rode a motorcycle wherever he went. He played classical piano and married the daughter of famed violinist Arthur Rubinstein. Finally, he was fearlessly outspoken in calling attention to discrimination and injustice.

After becoming a minister, Coffin took a one year job as acting chaplain at Andover Academy. The next year (1957-1958) he was the chaplain at Williams College in Massachusetts. The year after that he was appointed chaplain at Yale University in New Haven, Connecticut, the position which he held for the following 17 years.

The coming of Coffin to Yale coincided with the beginnings of social protest throughout America. Black Americans under the leadership of the Martin Luther King, Jr. had already transformed a segregated bus system in Alabama. Courageous young white students were traveling southward to help end racism. Still others were on the streets of the nation protesting against the death penalty, against nuclear war, and against injustice everywhere. This had been Coffin's approach to society's problems from the start, and he now embarked on his own campaigns.

His first protest was against anti-Semitism at Yale. His second was to gain the admittance of more African students at Yale. He was successful in both endeavors.

Coffin's third protest in the spring of 1961 was to join several other black and white ministers and students for a "freedom ride" on a Trailways bus through Alabama and Georgia. Such rides provoked the racist fears of some southern whites, spurring them to attack and burn the busses and to beat the riders. Coffin and his friends were jailed before any mob reached them, but the reaction of the Yale faculty and administration was anything but approving that their chaplain had put himself in the position of doing time in a southern jail.

Within the next five years, American participation in the fateful Vietnam War increased. At first, the majority of young Americans heeded the nation's call to arms. But as casualty lists lengthened, debate over U.S. policy sharpened and the numbers of people disapproving of America's Vietnam intervention grew. Coffin and a huge number of other ministers never harbored any doubt that the anti-Communist foreign policies of the government were wrong. The slaughter of the Vietnamese was for them a positive evil. Once more, to the consternation of many of his Yale colleagues, Chaplain Coffin began to protest. He helped to establish committees for re-appraising U.S. foreign policy. He was one of the founders of Clergy and Laity Concerned About Vietnam, a powerful peace group.

By 1967 the United States had hundreds of thousands of fighting men in Vietnam. Antagonism to the war within America had moved from verbal protest to outright resistance and to draft-card burning. These were called acts of civil disobedience. They had been justified in America since the Pilgrims first fled the persecution of the British Crown. The writings of Henry David Thoreau had also sustained their use. According to the theory of civil disobedience, whenever governments or majorities behave immorally, those who are harmed may appeal beyond the civil law to "conscience" or to "higher law." Chaplain Coffin appealed

to higher law in October 1967 when he and four other people (Benjamin Spock, Marcus Raskin, Michael Ferber, and Mitchell Goodman) received draft cards from men who refused to serve in Vietnam and returned them to the attorney general of the United States. The federal government did not recognize civil disobedience as anything other than the breaking of the law. It promptly indicted them for conspiracy to aid draft resistance—a felony for which those convicted could receive prison sentences and heavy fines. The court refused to permit Coffin and his friends to place the Vietnam War itself on trial, and Coffin was found guilty. He appealed his case, and finally, in 1970, the whole matter was simply dropped.

Coffin was a favorite speaker at anti-war demonstrations in the early 1970s. He flew to Hanoi, North Vietnam, in September 1972 to bring home two prisoners of war who had been released. In 1976 he resigned his post at Yale, and a year later he became the senior minister at Riverside Church in New York City.

At Riverside, a church built by John D. Rockefeller, Coffin found a platform for his political ideology. The interdenominational church was known for its focus on social programs and issues, and while Coffin served as minister he focused on unemployment, juvenile delinquency, and drugs. During this time Coffin continued his work with Clergy and Laity Concerned, only instead of focusing on Vietnam, the group worked internationally for arms control.

One of Coffin's more controversial actions occurred in 1979 when he was one of four Christian laypeople to travel to Teheran to visit the American hostages who were being held at the American embassy. Ostensibly, the role of the four ministers was to inspect the hostages and vouch to the world that they were not being mistreated. It seemed that he was acting more the role of political activist, when upon his return he urged the United States government to assume a more "humble (and) religious stance toward the captors and acknowledge the justice of some of Iran's grievances against the United States."

In 1989 Coffin left his position at Riverside Church to assume executive directorship of SANE/FREEZE, an anti-nuclear organization later known as Peace Action. In his capacity as executive director, Coffin sought the dissolution of NATO and the elimination of short-range nuclear weapons. In 1990 Coffin was made national president of SANE/FREEZE.

Later in the 1990s Coffin opposed the United States involvement in the Gulf War, and urged the deployment of troops in Bosnia. In *Christian Century* Coffin was quoted as saying, "I first realized when the Cambodian genocide of the Pol Pot regime came to light that violence within borders could be even worse than violence across borders." Many applauded Coffin for his radical political stances, for instance when the President of Yale, A. Bartlett Giamatti said, "You gave us energy." Others weren't so laudatory, such as Carl McIntyre of the International Council of Christian Churches who said, "During the Vietnam years, he contributed to the spirit of surrender that finally gripped our country."

## Further Reading

William Coffin has written his own immensely readable autobiography, *Once to Every Man* (1977). The American Enterprise Institute for Public Policy Research has published two of Coffin's debates on civil disobedience, one with Charles E. Whittaker (1967), the other with Morris I. Leibman (1972). In 1985 Coffin published some of his reflections on religion in *Living the Truth in a World of Illusions.* Good biographical information on Coffin's later years can be found in *Leaders from the 1960s: A Biographical Sourcebook of American Activism* (1994), edited by David DeLeon, and also in *American Social Leaders* (1993), by William McGuire and Leslie Wheeler. □

# George Michael Cohan

**The American actor and playwright George Michael Cohan (1878-1942) was one of the most versatile personalities in the American theater. His shows glorified Broadway and patriotism.**

George M. Cohan was born July 3, 1878 (legend has it as July 4), in Providence, R.I., the son of vaudevillians. He first appeared on stage as a violinist in the family act and then as a "buck and wing" dancer. He was the star of *Peck's Bad Boy* in 1890, and at age 15 he made his Broadway debut. At the concluding curtain call, his words to the audience, "My mother thanks you, my father thanks you, my sister thanks you, and I thank you," became a sentimental trademark of his act. His first wife, Ethel Levey, whom he married in 1899, was his dancing partner after his sister left the act. He married a second time in 1908.

The first Broadway production which he wrote, composed, and directed was *The Governor's Son* (1901). Among the more than 50 plays, comedies, and revues he wrote, produced, or acted in were *Little Johnny Jones* (1904), *Forty-five Minutes from Broadway* (1906), *George Washington, Jr.* (1906), *The Man Who Owns Broadway* (1908), *The Yankee Prince* (1908), *Seven Keys to Baldpate* (1913) (which earned him a reputation as a serious playwright), and *The Cohan Revues* (1916 and 1918). He also wrote over 100 vaudeville sketches. The stage style for which he was famous included dapper costumes, a derby or straw hat cocked jauntily over one eye, wisecracks, and lively capers across the stage with a fast swinging cane.

The many popular songs he composed include "Mary's a Grand Old Name," "Give My Regards to Broadway," "So Long Mary," "I'm a Yankee Doodle Dandy," and "You're a Grand Old Flag." His famous World War I song, "Over There" (1917), sold 2 million copies of sheet music and 1 million records. President Woodrow Wilson described it as an inspiration to American manhood, and President Franklin Roosevelt cited the song when presenting Cohan with a congressional medal.

Cohan's role in Eugene O'Neill's *Ah Wilderness* (1933) proved his competence as a serious actor. His imper-

sonation of President Roosevelt in the satire *I'd Rather Be Right* (1937-1938) was also praised.

Cohan made a movie in 1932, *The Phantom President*, but was generally unhappy with Hollywood. In 1942 James Cagney portrayed him in the film biography *Yankee Doodle Dandy* and won the Academy Award. A musical play, *George M!*, featuring his music, was produced on Broadway in 1968.

Cohan died on Nov. 5, 1942. A protean talent, he often wrote his own books and lyrics and sang and danced in, produced, and directed his own shows. Essentially a "song and dance" man, he energized the American musical theater. However uncomplicated and sentimental his works are, they have an important place in theatrical history.

## Further Reading

Cohan's autobiography, *Twenty Years on Broadway and the Years It Took to Get There* (1925), is cheerful and brash but without real insight. A witty, fond, and anecdotal treatment is Ward Morehouse, *George M. Cohan, Prince of the American Theater* (1943).

## Additional Sources

McCabe, John, *George M. Cohan, the man who owned Broadway,* New York: Da Capo Press, 1980. □

# Hermann Cohen

**The German philosopher Hermann Cohen (1842-1918) founded the Marburg Neo-Kantian school of philosophy. His ethical socialism, based on the biblical Jewish moral law, greatly influenced German social democracy.**

Hermann Cohen was born in Coswig, Anhalt, on July 4, 1842. After attending the Jewish Theological Seminary of Breslau, he studied at the universities of Breslau, Berlin, and Halle. In 1873 he became instructor at the Philipps University of Marburg, where he was appointed professor in 1876 and taught until his resignation in 1912. He died in Berlin on April 4, 1918.

## Cohen's Thought

Cohen started his philosophical career as an interpreter of the philosophy of Immanuel Kant, and he slowly developed his own system of Neo-Kantianism in three major works: *Logik der Reinen Erkenntnis* (The Logic of Pure Perception), *Ethik des Reinen Willens* (The Ethics of the Pure Will), and *Ästhetik des Reinen Gefühls* (The Esthetics of Pure Feeling). Reacting against materialism and Marxism, Cohen denied the existence of a real external world and interpreted experience as man's subjective creation of objects. Thus, thinking is the source of reality; being is nothing but pure knowledge produced by thought.

Just as the subject of logic is "being" or "whatness," the subject of ethics is "oughtness" or "pure will." Thus, Cohen separated human will from psychologism and ethics from logic, rejecting not only materialism but all monism. The supreme value and measure became the idea of man, who finds his realization in the community of men or the ethical socialistic state.

According to Judaism, God is both the creator of nature and the proponent of moral law, so that the truth of God means a harmonious combination of physical nature with morality. God in Judaism is not a mythological figure but an idea whose essence is revealed in His law. Therefore Cohen was not interested in the study of the nature of God but, rather, in the doctrine of the Messiah, which is the Jewish religious expression of the eternity of morality.

In 1880 Cohen announced his renewed belief in Judaism and began to defend the Jewish faith against the anti-Semitic German historian Heinrich von Treitschke. He started lecturing at the Berlin Institute for Jewish Studies and immensely influenced several generations of Jewish thinkers. Although he repudiated Zionism, he took a direct interest in the life of the Jewish people and felt a responsibility for its destiny.

Among Cohen's other major works are *Kants Theorie der Erfahrung* (Kant's Theory of Experience), *Kants Begründung der Ethik* (Kant's Proof of Ethics), and *Kants Begründung der Ästhetik* (Kant's Proof of Esthetics). Among his specifically Jewish works are *Religion und Göttlichkeit* (Religion and Divinity), *Das Gottesreich* (The Kingdom of

God), *Der Nächste* (The Fellow Man), and the posthumously published *Die Religion der Vernunft aus den Quellen des Judentums* (The Religion of Reason from the Sources of Judaism).

## Further Reading

The important literature on Cohen is in German. For background material in English see Emile Bréhier, *Contemporary Philosophy since 1850,* vol. 7 (1932; trans. 1969), and Ernst Cassirer, *The Problem of Knowledge* (trans. 1960).

## Additional Sources

*Hermann Cohen,* Frankfurt am Main; New York: P. Lang, 1994.
Kluback, William, *The legacy of Hermann Cohen,* Atlanta, Ga.: Scholars Press, 1989. □

# Morris Raphael Cohen

**The American philosopher Morris Raphael Cohen (1880-1947) distinguished himself as an expositor of the nature of a liberal society, as a teacher, and as a defender of academic freedom.**

Morris R. Cohen was born probably on July 25, 1880, and spent his first years in a Jewish ghetto in Minsk, Russia. He early displayed a preference for the contemplative life. His education was that of an Orthodox Jew. In 1892 the family emigrated to New York, where, during the next 7 years, Cohen drifted away from organized religion and eventually gave up all belief in a personal God.

Cohen entered the College of the City of New York in 1895. His family's penurious, hand-to-mouth existence stimulated Cohen's interest in socialism. From his study of Marx and Hegel developed his earliest preoccupation with the technical aspects of philosophy. In 1898 he met Thomas Davidson, the Scottish scholar whose example would inspire Cohen throughout his life; under his tutelage Cohen read Aristotle, Plato, Hume, and Kant.

After graduating in 1900, Cohen continued his pursuit of philosophy, discovering in Bertrand Russell's *Principles of Mathematics* a "renewed faith" in logic. In 1904 the Ethical Culture Society awarded Cohen a fellowship to do graduate work at Harvard. Two years later, shortly after he completed his doctorate, he married Mary Ryshpan; they had three children.

Ensconced in the philosophy department of the College of the City of New York, Cohen came into his own as a teacher. Demanding of his students and responding sarcastically to careless thinking, he nonetheless drew overflow crowds of students and won great affection and respect. Outside the classroom he led the struggle to uphold academic freedom against authoritarian interference. He was one of the founding members of the American Association of University Professors. As a tide of anti-Semitism rose in the 1930s, he helped organize the Conference on Jewish

Relations to study modern Jewry scientifically; he was also editor of its journal, *Jewish Social Studies.*

Meanwhile Cohen was writing scholarly articles and books. In 1923 his edition of C. S. Peirce's essays, *Chance, Love and Logic,* appeared. In 1931 in his most important work, *Reason and Nature: An Essay on the Meaning of Scientific Method,* he developed the concept that characterized all his thought and came closest to representing a metaphysical position. That concept, polarity, held that ideas such as "unity and plurality, similarity and difference, dependence and independence, form and matter, change and permanence" were "equally real," and "the way to get at the nature of things" was to "reason" from such "opposing considerations." Hence the necessity of society's tolerating conflicting points of view.

Ever since he had shared a room with Felix Frankfurter at Harvard, Cohen had indulged a lively interest in jurisprudence, which resulted in *Law and the Social Order: Essays in Legal Philosophy* (1933). He believed that logical reasoning was critically important to all fields of thought. *An Introduction to Logic and Scientific Method* (1934), written with a former student, Ernest Nagel, became a popular college textbook.

In 1938 Cohen left teaching to devote himself to writing. His *Preface to Logic* (1944) elucidated logic's place in the universe. *Faith of a Liberal* (1946) sought to rescue the term "liberal" from connotations of sentimentality. Cohen had already manifested his lifelong fascination with history by helping found the *Journal of the History of Ideas.* He selected the philosophy of history as his topic when the American Philosophical Association chose him to deliver its Carus Lectures, later published as *The Meaning of Human History* (1947).

Cohen died on Jan. 28, 1947. He left many works half finished, which his son Felix, a scholar in his own right, published: *A Source Book in Greek Science* (1948), *A Dreamer's Journey* (1949), *Studies in Philosophy and Science* (1949), *Reflections of a Wondering Jew* (1950), *Reason and Law: Studies in Juristic Philosophy* (1950), *Readings in Jurisprudence and Legal Philosophy* (1951), *King Saul's Daughter: A Biblical Dialogue* (1952), and *American Thought: A Critical Sketch* (1954). Cohen's publications stand as a positive statement of his faith in a liberal civilization and answer those critics who found in him only the sharp tongue of a nihilist.

## Further Reading

Cohen's autobiography, *A Dreamer's Journey* (1949), is a candid depiction of the life of a Jewish immigrant. In *Portrait of a Philosopher: Morris R. Cohen in Life and Letters* (1962), Cohen's daughter, Leonora Cohen Rosenfield, supplements lively anecdotes with extensive quotations from his diary and other unpublished manuscripts. For further appreciation and commentary see Salo W. Baron, Ernest Nagel, and Koppel S. Pinson, *Freedom and Reason: Studies in Philosophy and Jewish Culture in Memory of Morris Raphael Cohen* (1951).

**Additional Sources**

Cohen, Morris Raphael, *A dreamer's journey: the autobiography of Morris Raphael Cohen,* New York: Arno Press, 1975. ☐

# Daniel Cohn-Bendit

**Daniel Cohn-Bendit (born 1946) only occupied center stage in French politics for a few weeks in 1968. Still, more than anyone else, Cohn-Bendit came to personify the new left that swept Western Europe and North America in the late 1960s and early 1970s.**

I n early 1968, Daniel Cohn-Bendit was a little known leader of a tiny student movement at the brand new Nanterre campus of the University of Paris. He was only 22, having been born in France of German Jewish parents in 1946. Because he held dual citizenship he had chosen to pursue his studies in sociology at the newly opened campus in one of the grimier industrial suburbs of Paris.

That campus represented everything that was troubling the overcrowded French university system. It had been built without planning for the social lives of the students. The educational system suffered from the same problems as the rest of the huge university centered at the Sorbonne.

Gradually the students' discontent with the university merged with more general opposition to the Gaullist regime, which seemed to run everything in a heavy-handed manner. In March 1968 those resentments began to surface. On March 22 a ceremony was held to open officially the Nanterre campus's swimming pool, which Cohn-Bendit and a small group of his fellow students disrupted. They were summoned to a disciplinary hearing which, given the centralization of the university, was to be held at the Sorbonne on May 3.

That hearing marked the beginning of the "events" of May and June 1968, the largest protest movement in the history of the new left. While the accused students were inside, a small group of supporters held a sympathy demonstration in the courtyard. To everyone's surprise, for the first time in centuries the police entered the courtyard to break up a demonstration. That fact, plus the brutality of the police action, rippled throughout Paris.

Students, whose anger had been building and repressed for months, reacted quickly. Throughout the next week demonstrations occurred in the streets of the Latin Quarter. As the police grew more violent, sympathy for the students and their seemingly modest demands grew. Finally, on the night of May 10-11, things truly got out of hand. The police became more violent, and the students and other demonstrators responded by erecting barricades. The police moved in with armored personnel carriers, tear gas, and billy clubs. Echoes of past revolutions could be heard throughout Paris.

In the meantime, Daniel Cohn-Bendit had emerged as the informal leader of the protests. No organization had called or could control what was happening. And, even though Danny the Red—as Cohn-Bendit was called—was by no means in charge, his role at Nanterre thrust him onto the front line.

After the "night of the barricades" support for the students spread, especially into the trade unions who had their own grievances with the government, the same enemy the students were attacking. They called for a sympathy protest the following Monday. The students marched behind the workers, and afterward Cohn-Bendit led them down a few blocks to begin occupying the Sorbonne.

Within hours the occupations spread as workers began taking over factories, newspapers, even the radio and television system. Within days the country was at a virtual standstill.

At first, Danny the Red seemed even more important, especially after a senior government official referred to him as "that German Jew," prompting thousands of people to march through Paris chanting "we are all German Jews." Then Cohn-Bendit was forced into the background. On May 24 he was expelled from France. De Gaulle seized that opportunity to deny him permission to reenter France, even though he did have joint French-German citizenship. He was not able to legally reenter the country for more than a decade.

Within another week President de Gaulle had reassumed control and dissolved the National Assembly. The

Gaullists, not the left, won an overwhelming victory in the parliamentary elections held in June.

For many years, Danny the Red receded from the public eye. After his exile, he settled in Frankfurt, Germany, where he held a variety of jobs while remaining active in politics. In the 1970s he founded RK, a German group which encouraged common action between students and workers, and took part in various housing-related protests and reforms. For employment, he taught at an "anti-authoritarian kindergarten," and worked as a salesperson in the Karl-Marx Bookstore near the city's main university. In the 1980s, Cohn-Bendit founded a radical city magazine, *Pflasterstand,* whose name referred to a slogan of the 1968 revolts: "Underneath the surface structures of cement [*das Pflaster*] and steel lies the beach [*der Strand*]." He also worked as publicist for a number of books and publications, and wrote extensively on radical issues.

In 1984, Cohn-Bendit became a member of the Green Party, which changed its name to the Alliance Green Party in 1989. The Greens made common cause with the German Socialist Party (SPD) in the so-called "Red-Green Coalition," which elected Cohn-Bendit to the honorary position of Commissioner for Multicultural Affairs in July 1989.

In 1994, Cohn-Bendit reemerged onto the world, or at least the Continental, stage with his election to the European Parliament as a member of the Alliance Green Party. Sitting on the Committees for External Affairs, Security, and Defense, he opposed nationalism and promoted a globalist agenda. (Because of his Franco-German background, Cohn-Bendit has often humorously referred to himself as a "bastard," someone who is not tied to a specific national identity.) He also served on the Committee for Basic Freedoms and Internal Affairs, and on the "Delegation Maghreb," which is concerned with issues relating to the nations of the Maghreb region of north Africa: Algeria, Morocco, and Tunisia. He has also been an active figure behind the European Forum for Active Conflict Avoidance (FEPAC.)

When he was only 22, Daniel Cohn-Bendit left an indelible mark on the history of the 1960s. The movement he helped spawn led to many improvements in the lives of students and workers in the short run; even more importantly, the events set the agenda for French politics for many years, culminating in the 1981 election of President Francois Mitterrand's socialist government. But Cohn-Bendit himself remained modest about his achievements. In his brief autobiography on the World Wide Web in the 1990s, he made scant reference to his role in the 1968 events, and concentrated more on his current activities in the European Parliament. Summing up his interests, he said, "In any event I remain: a wanderer through the worlds, cultures, languages, occupations, generations, and classes, and last but not least: still an active soccer-nut, as player and fan."

## Further Reading

On Daniel Cohn-Bendit and the "events of May," see his *Obsolete Communism: The Left Wing Alternative* (1968) or Patrick Seale and Maureen McConville, *Red Flag/Black Flag* (1968). Other books with which Cohn-Bendit has been involved,

either as writer, cowriter, or contributor, include *The Grand Bazaar* (1976), *We Loved Her So Much, the Revolution* (1987), *1968: The Last Revolution That Was Unaware of the Hole in the Ozone Layer* (with Reinhard Mohr, 1988), and *At Home In Babylon: The Risk of a Multicultural Democracy* (1992, with Thomas Schmid.) His English-language Web site is at http://www.oeko- net.de/eurospeed/dcbeng.htm. ☐

# Sir Edward Coke

**The English jurist and parliamentarian Sir Edward Coke (1552-1634) fought to prevent royal interference with the independent common-law courts.**

Edward Coke was born at Mileham, Norfolk, and was educated at Trinity College, Cambridge, from 1567 to 1571. Thereafter he rapidly rose in the legal profession from a student at Lincoln's Inn to barrister, reader at Lyon's Inn, and senior member of the Inner Temple. In 1592 Queen Elizabeth I appointed Coke solicitor general, and in the following year he became attorney general. As attorney general, Coke was a forceful prosecutor on behalf of the Crown, and among his most famous prosecutions were those of the Earl of Essex, Sir Walter Raleigh, and the "Gunpowder" plotters. Coke's ascendancy was at the expense of Sir Francis Bacon, whom Essex had supported for the attorney generalship, and the two were rivals throughout their careers.

In 1582 Coke married Bridget Paston, who brought him a fortune. She died in 1598, and Coke then married the beautiful and rich Elizabeth Hatton, who had also been courted by Bacon.

In 1606 James I made Coke chief justice of the Court of Common Pleas. Coke opposed James on the question of the king's right to interpret the common law and to encroach on judicial independence. In accord with his belief in the divine right of kings, James felt that God had endowed him with the wisdom to interpret the traditional English common law. Coke insisted that the interpretation of common law must be left to lawyers. He also opposed James's policy of discussing cases with the judges before they gave judgment. In 1610 he argued that the king could not lawfully create new offenses through his own proclamation. Coke's chief rival during this period, the chancellor, Baron Ellesmere, supported James's view of the royal prerogative.

Coke was appointed chief justice of the King's Bench in 1613. Both Bacon and Ellesmere favored this shift; though it accorded Coke a higher status and greater wages, it made conflict with the Crown less likely. In the same year Coke was brought into the Privy Council. The battle between Coke and James was not easily avoided, however, and in 1616 the King dismissed his obstreperous judge from both the bench and the government.

Coke returned to favor the following year, when his daughter married the elder brother of George Villiers, the King's favorite courtier and later the powerful Duke of Buckingham. The vain and stubborn Coke again sat in the Privy

Council and enjoyed great respect at court for his unrivaled knowledge of the common law. But in 1621 he sat in Commons and was active in the debates against the King's lax enforcement of the anti-Catholic laws and against royal grants of monopoly; as a result he was sent to the Tower for 9 months. Thus 1621 marked the end of his hopes for attaining a high government position and the start of the last phase of his career, as a leader of the parliamentary opposition.

In 1625 Coke was a leader of the attack on the Duke of Buckingham and later supported his impeachment. He held that Commons should withhold further grants of revenue until it was provided with an accounting of government expenditures. In 1628, when Commons sought to place restraints upon royal power, Coke initiated the idea of a Petition of Right. Its principal terms required parliamentary consent for taxation and a statement of charges against those placed under arrest. In 1629 Coke retired to Stoke Poges, where he died in 1634, at the age of 82.

Coke's main writings are the *Reports* and the *Institutes*. Compiled between 1578 and 1615, the former contains cases argued before the royal courts. The four parts of the *Institutes* deal with tenures, statutes, the criminal law, and the jurisdiction of courts. Coke was not above twisting earlier law to the advantage of the 17th-century causes he favored. His holding in Dr. Bonham's case (1610) has attracted the interest of students of American constitutional law, some of whom view it as the first enunciation of the principle of judicial review.

## Further Reading

The sole modern biography of Coke is Catherine Drinker Bowen, *The Lion and the Throne: The Life and Times of Sir Edward Coke, 1552-1634* (1957). This work makes very pleasant reading, while maintaining a high standard of scholarship, and contains a lengthy list of older works and journal articles on Coke.

## Additional Sources

Bowen, Catherine Drinker, *The lion and the throne: the life and times of Sir Edward Coke (1552-1634),* Boston: Little, Brown, 1990.

Lyon, Hastings, *Edward Coke: oracle of the law: containing the story of his long rivalry with Francis Bacon . . . ,* Littleton, Colo.: F.B. Rothman, 1992. □

# Jean Baptiste Colbert

**The French statesman Jean Baptiste Colbert (1619-1683) was one of the greatest ministers of Louis XIV and is generally regarded as the creator of the economic system of prerevolutionary France.**

Jean Baptiste Colbert was born at Reims on Aug. 29, 1619, of a family of prosperous businessmen and officials. He entered the service of the French monarchy under Michel le Tellier, the father of the Marquis de Louvois. In 1651 he became the agent of Cardinal Mazarin, whom he served so well that the cardinal bequeathed him to King Louis XIV in 1661. Almost immediately Colbert became the most important minister in France. He was made intendant of finances in 1661 and in the next few years assumed responsibility for public buildings, commerce, and the administration of the royal household, the navy, and the merchant marine. His only serious rival was the war minister, Louvois. The two men intrigued against each other for royal favor, with Louvois, especially after 1679, gradually winning the upper hand. Colbert, however, remained immensely powerful until his death.

Colbert's most successful years were from 1661 to 1672. The neglect and corruption of the Mazarin period were replaced by a time of prosperity with expanding industry and mounting employment. The tax system was made slightly fairer and much more efficient, thereby greatly increasing Louis XIV's revenues.

In a mercantilist age Colbert was the supreme mercantilist. His program was to build up the economic strength of France by creating and protecting French industries, encouraging exports, and restricting imports (especially of luxury goods). By endless regulation and supervision, he tried to make French industry, particularly in luxury items, first in Europe; he was partially successful, for the French tradition of high quality in certain fields (for example, tapestry and porcelain) dates from his time.

Colbert organized royal trading companies to compete with the English and the Dutch for the trade of the Far East

and the Americas. Although these companies were almost all failures, he was successful in building up one of the strongest European navies and a more than respectable merchant marine. At the same time he laid the foundations of the French overseas empire in Canada, the West Indies, and the Far East. The great expansion of French commerce and industry in the next century was largely due to his groundwork.

Colbert carried through a series of legal codifications of enormous importance, and the Code Napoleon was partly inspired by, and based on, his monumental work. He also made himself responsible for the artistic and cultural life of France. He encouraged, patronized, and regimented artists and writers, and the magnificent building program of Louis XIV was primarily his work.

Colbert was not an innovator. His ideas came from other men, particularly Cardinal Richelieu, and his interpretation of them was often mistaken. But for 22 years he controlled the economic fortunes of France, and he did so with an all-embracing scope and an incredible capacity for work. Some of his projects, however, were unsuccessful. He was unable to unify the diverse systems of weights and measures in France or to secure free trade within the country. His regulation of industry by constant inspection was largely ineffective, as his orders were often disregarded.

The major failure of Colbert stemmed from his determination to end Dutch domination of Far Eastern and European trade. Unable to damage the Dutch by a vindictive tariff war, he supported Louis XIV's unprovoked invasion of

Holland in 1672 in the hope that the Dutch would be overrun in a few weeks. But the resultant war lasted until 1679, and the strain on the French economy undid many of the good results of Colbert's work.

Colbert died on Sept. 6, 1683, to the great relief of the general public, with whom he was (for the most part undeservedly) very unpopular. The immense concentration of responsibilities in one minister was never repeated under the monarchy.

## Further Reading

Most of the work on Colbert is in French. The definitive work in English is Charles Woolsey Cole, *Colbert and a Century of French Mercantilism* (2 vols., 1939). A useful general treatment is in Pierre Goubert, *Louis XIV and Twenty Million Frenchmen* (1966; trans. 1970). Goubert considers that Colbert has been overpraised by French historians and stresses his lack of originality and the elementary nature of his views on economics. However, he does justice to the wide range and great importance of Colbert's work.

## Additional Sources

Murat, Ines, *Colbert,* Charlottesville: University Press of Virginia, 1984.
Trout, Andrew P., *Jean-Baptiste Colbert,* Boston: Twayne Publishers, 1978. □

# William E. Colby

**William E. Colby (1920–1996) former CIA director, Colby was thought to have damaged the CIA's reputation by cooperating with congressional investigations and disclosing information many felt should have remained covered, in order to pacify critics of the agency.**

William E. Colby was the most controversial director of the Central Intelligence Agency (CIA). He became director in 1973, when, for the first time in the agency's history, it had to explain its actions to hostile critics. Hoping to put the agency's problems behind it quickly, Colby decided to cooperate with congressional investigations. For a time he so demoralized the CIA that his harshest critics inside the agency argued that even if he were a Soviet agent he could not have done more harm.

William Egan Colby was born on 4 January 1920 in Saint Paul, Minnesota, the son of an army officer. The family moved around a lot and spent three years in China. After graduating from Princeton University in 1940, Colby entered law school at Columbia University. He dropped out to enter the army, becoming a lieutenant in the paratroops. He later joined the Office of Strategic Services, the forerunner of the CIA, and participated in commando missions behind German lines in France and Norway in 1944 and 1945. Colby returned to Columbia after the war and entered the law profession in 1947. In 1950, bored by his law practice, he joined the newly created CIA.

### Strategic Hamlet Program

Colby's first years in the CIA were spent abroad under the cover of the State Department. He served in Stockholm, Sweden, for two years and in Rome, Italy, for five. In 1959 Colby went to Saigon as head of the CIA's operations in South Vietnam. There results were mixed. He moved South Vietnamese peasants into what were called strategic hamlets in an unsuccessful effort to deprive the Vietcong guerrillas of bases from which to operate. He had better luck recruiting Vietnamese Montagnard tribesmen to fight alongside the United States. In 1962 Colby returned to the United States to become chief of the Far East division of the CIA's plans directorate. He oversaw much of what the CIA was doing in Vietnam.

### Operation Phoenix

In 1968 Colby returned to Saigon, technically on leave from the CIA, to direct Operation Phoenix, a State Department-administered "pacification" program developed by the intelligence agency. Supplied with a force of some five thousand American troops, Colby was charged, in what became a famous phrase, with winning the hearts and minds of the people, ostensibly through the establishment of health and social service programs. But it was the counter-terror aspect of the program that made Colby and his some-time boss Robert W. Komer notorious. Designed to destroy the infrastructure of the Vietcong's operations in South Vietnam, the Phoenix counter-terror operation quickly degenerated into a series of massive episodes of destruction, torture, and assassination in which American and South Vietnamese troops killed to fulfill quotas and to settle old scores. Before it was discontinued in 1969, almost 29,000 suspected Vietcong were captured, 18,000 were persuaded to defect, and 21,000 were killed. While the CIA was not directly responsible for the killings, it clearly condoned them.

In 1970 the Phoenix program came to the attention of the Senate Foreign Relations Committee, the center of congressional opposition to the war. Senator Frank Church, who headed a 1975 investigation into the agency, regarded Phoenix as evidence that the CIA was a rogue elephant on a rampage, "uncontrolled and uncontrollable." Cooler analyses consider Phoenix a well-conceived program clumsily executed. It earned Colby a reputation as a tough, ruthless operator with religious intensity, extremely dedicated, but with too little imagination. After he became CIA director Colby conceded that there had been excesses and many innocent people had been murdered, but most of the deaths — more than 85 percent — came in clashes between American and Vietnamese troops.

### CIA Director, 1973

Returning to the United States in 1971, Colby was reassigned to covert operations, where he had spent his entire career except for the Phoenix years. In 1972 he became the CIA's executive director-controller and in March 1973 director for operations, responsible for covert activities. Two months later President Richard M. Nixon chose Colby to succeed James R. Schlesinger as CIA director. At his Senate confirmation hearings that summer, Colby found himself caught in a fire-storm. In the past the CIA had enjoyed a certain immunity on Capitol Hill and rarely underwent close examination. But Congress had heard of various agency misdeeds, and Colby had to answer for them. He agreed that the CIA had no business gathering intelligence in the United States, and that the agency had erred in helping one of the men charged in the Watergate break-in. Moreover he declared he would resign if ordered to engage in anything illegal. He was confirmed as director on 4 September 1973.

### CIA Re-organization and Congressional Investigation

As CIA director Colby seemed to experience a major change of heart, what his enemies even called a personality change, caused in part by the attacks he received for Phoenix and in part by the anguish he experienced over the terminal illness of his oldest daughter. He came to believe that if he cooperated with congressional critics and made a clean breast of matters, the easier the CIA could go about its legitimate business. His decision to go public aroused a bitter controversy within the agency; its staff was already demoralized over budget cuts, a reorganization, and firings instituted by Schlesinger. To many Colby's going public was incomprehensible, even if the agency was culpable. Colby's strategy was more clever than it first appeared. Since Congress would learn its secrets anyway, it was better that the agency control how the story got out.

Colby had already ordered an in-house investigation to assemble a list of every CIA operation that had been in violation of its charter. Later known to the press as the "Family Jewels" and within the agency as the "Skeletons," the list filled 693 typed pages. On 22 December 1974 the *New York Times* broke a major story that the CIA had spied on the antiwar movement, igniting an intense two-year public scrutiny of the CIA. Colby released the Skeletons list in sanitized form. The House and Senate initiated several investigations, and President Gerald R. Ford named Vice-president Nelson A. Rockefeller to head another inquiry.

The dirt was out. The most damaging revelations concerned assassination attempts against various foreign leaders — some were successful. But it was soon clear that while Colby's cooperation was tarnishing the agency, he was doing a better job of tarnishing the reputations of previous presidents, John F. Kennedy especially. Colby admitted that the CIA had erred, but he never confessed that the agency was to blame. It had never been a rogue elephant, and it had always followed presidential orders. Colby's cooperation probably headed off legislation limiting the agency's activities. Though it was demoralized and the scope of its covert activities was strictly curtailed by the political climate, the agency suffered no lasting damage.

Colby's tenure as CIA chief was marked by another development. Disclosure that the CIA had illegally opened mail gave Colby the excuse to fire James J. Angleton, the 20-year head of the agency's counterintelligence efforts who was charged with ferreting out infiltrators. Angleton was brilliant, paranoid according to some, and his suspicions that the CIA had been penetrated by a high-level Soviet agent eventually paralyzed the agency. He suspected everyone. Colby decided the agency would be better off without him and the mail incident was Colby's excuse to let him go.

## Failures of CIA Analysis

While the airing of the dirty laundry focused on covert operations, the agency's analytical capabilities were also under attack. The CIA had failed to anticipate developments such as the Soviet invasion of Czechoslovakia in 1968 and the 1973 Arab-Israeli War. In 1975 critics of the Strategic Arms Limitation Treaty (SALT) with the Soviet Union charged that the CIA did not possess accurate information of Soviet capabilities, limiting its ability to detect Soviet violations. The dispute had a political dimension. Ronald Reagan, getting ready to challenge President Gerald R. Ford for the 1976 Republican presidential nomination, charged that the United States was tolerating Soviet violations as a way to undermine the entire Nixon-Ford foreign policy toward the Soviets. There was also a bureaucratic consideration, for the CIA traditionally issued fewer doomsday scenarios than the Pentagon's analysts. Their estimates usually kept expenses in mind.

Colby responded with the A Team/B Team evaluation of the Soviet Union's capabilities and intentions. The A Team was composed of the CIA's own experts. They were matched against outside experts, all conservative, anti-Soviet hardliners, many of whom would receive positions in the Reagan administration in 1981. The B Team concluded that the Soviets were pursuing a policy of global domination and had a credible first-strike war-winning military capability. Its report helped shape Reagan's defense policies.

Ford fired Colby on 2 November 1975 as part of a general housecleaning of his administration. The firing was regarded as inevitable. It signaled an end to disclosures and investigations. The energy behind the need to reveal and come clean had spent itself. Had Colby chosen not to be so forthcoming or attempted to justify what in retrospect should not have been undertaken, two courses many in the CIA urged upon him, Congress may have responded by curtailing certain operations. Instead, Congress created more oversight committees. Also Ford ordered the agency not to engage in political assassination.

After he left the CIA he worked in the Washington, District of Columbia, office of the New York law firm for which he worked before he joined the CIA. Retired from government duty, Colby diversified his activities. In addition to practicing law, he became active in a campaign against the nuclear arms race of the 1980s, speaking out with former Defense Secretary Robert S. McNamara. He also founded the American Committee for a Free Vietnam, an organization that focused on the development of a democratic Vietnam and the strengthening of human-rights within the country.

Shortly before his death in April of 1996, Colby was marketing a CD-ROM game about espionage and counterterrorism, a project he developed with former Soviet intelligence officer Oleg Kalogin. Colby died suddenly, apparently of drowning, while on a solo canoe trip on the Wicomoco River. ☐

# Cadwallader Colden

**The American botanist and politician Cadwallader Colden (1688-1776), a diverse thinker whose scholarship encompassed natural history, the nature of the universe, and medicine, was also lieutenant governor of New York.**

Cadwallader Colden was born on Feb. 7, 1688, in Ireland of Scottish parents; his father was a minister. He received a degree from the University of Edinburgh and then studied medicine in London. He emigrated to Philadelphia in 1710 and went to New York in 1718 at the request of Governor Robert Hunter, who made Colden surveyor general of the colony in 1720. This sinecure allowed him the leisure for a scientific career, although he remained interested in politics, serving as a member of the Governor's Council.

In 1739 Colden left New York City to live at his farm, Coldengham, where he spent much of his time in scientific study. He began corresponding with Peter Collinson, the London botanist, who brought Colden into the international natural history circle. Colden became one of the first men in Europe or America to completely master the new Linnaean system of plant classification, which he rigorously applied to the flora surrounding his farm. These descriptions, which he circulated in Europe, drew praise even from Linnaeus himself. Colden criticized the Linnaean reliance on sexual characteristics and suggested a more natural system.

Being located in America had been an advantage for his botanical work, but when Colden turned from natural history to speculations on the nature of the universe, even his finely honed, highly rational mind could not make up for his geographical isolation. *An Explication of the First Causes of Action in Matter* (1745) was his attempt to discover the cause of gravity, postulating a division of the material world into matter, light, and ether. Although it is possible to read an equation of energy with matter in the work, it was in general a rationally deduced system in no way based on the observations of scientists in Europe. He sent copies to European scientists, most of whom refused to comment, but the German scientist Leonhard Euler called it absurd. Colden never accepted the verdict and hoped, by tinkering, to perfect his theory. He consistently produced respectable medical treatises, although his abstract rational tendencies led him to write a dissertation on yellow fever without ever actually having seen a case of the disease.

In 1760 he realized an old ambition to be lieutenant governor of New York. He was a confidant of Governor George Clinton and wrote many speeches and papers for him. In 1764 he declared his intention to enforce the Stamp Act and the following year was burned in effigy by a mob. He tried to balance himself between the radicals and conservatives in the 1770s. After the Battle of Lexington, Colden retired to his Long Island estate, where he died on Sept. 28, 1776.

The son of a builder in West London, G. D. H. Cole went from St. Paul's School to Balliol College, Oxford. He coedited the *Oxford Reformer,* acted in social causes, and joined the Fabian Society. He attempted to reconcile syndicalism and socialism in *World of Labour* (1913), a plea for public ownership of major industries under the democratic control of unions modeled upon medieval guilds. With a first class in classical moderns and greats, he was awarded a fellowship at Magdalen College. Elected to the Fabian executive in 1915, he rebelled against the old guard to head the quasi-independent Fabian Research Bureau.

During the next decade Cole was away from Oxford writing, often with his wife and fellow Fabian rebel, Margaret Postgate Cole; directing tutorial classes at the University of London; and organizing professional trade unions. He returned to Oxford in 1925 as fellow of University College and university reader in economics and was to have compelling influence upon students such as Hugh Gaitskell. From 1944 until his retirement in 1957 Cole was at All Souls College as first Chichele professor of social and political theory.

Cole was for many years chairman of the Fabian weekly, the *New Statesman,* contributing to almost every issue during his lifetime. In 1931 he formed the Society for Socialist Information and Propaganda but broke with the society when it moved toward communism. That year he formed the New Fabian Research Bureau as a politically neutral agency for accumulating objective information. This group formed the basis for union in 1938 with the older,

Colden had married Alice Cristie in 1715 and among their children, a daughter, Jane, became the first woman botanist. Their son David was also a scholar of some standing.

### Further Reading

There is no up-to-date biography of Colden. Different aspects of his career are treated in Alice M. Keys, *Cadwallader Colden, a Representative Eighteenth Century Official* (1906), and in Isaac Woodbridge Riley, *American Philosophy: The Early Schools* (1907). General background may be found in Brooke Hindle, *The Pursuit of Science in Revolutionary America, 1735-1789* (1956).

### Additional Sources

Fingerhut, Eugene R., *Survivor, Cadwallader Colden II in Revolutionary America,* Washington, D.C.: University Press of America, 1983. □

# George Douglas Howard Cole

**George Douglas Howard Cole (1889-1959) was an English historian, economist, and guild socialist. His teaching, writing, and commitment to political activism affected three generations of Englishmen.**

badly splintered Fabian Society. Collectivization was omitted from the new rules as a concession to Cole.

Cole's prodigious writings (over 130 works) may be divided into five broad and overlapping categories: guild socialism; history; biography; economic, political, and social analysis; and fiction. His strongest treatment of guild socialism, *Self-government in Industry* (1917), was an appeal for the pluralistic and romantic socialism which moved Cole all his life. In *Case for Industrial Partnership* (1957) he tried to adjust the earlier plea to new times.

Cole's historical and biographical work provided the evidence against which he tested his socialist faith and reliance upon the individual. This was especially true in his classic five-volume *History of Socialist Thought* (1953-1960).

Of Cole's perceptive biographies, the two best are *The Life of William Cobbett* (1924) and *The Life of Robert Owen* (1925). The analytical writings, intended to influence or explain, include *Principles of Economic Planning* (1935) and *An Intelligent Man's Guide to the Post-war World* (1947). For recreation he wrote, largely with his wife, more than 15 detective novels.

## Further Reading

Although there is no biography of Cole, various aspects of his life and thought are discussed in the book by his wife, Margaret Cole, *The Story of Fabian Socialism* (1961). See also Anne Fremantle, *This Little Band of Prophets: The British Fabians* (1959), and Asa Briggs and John Saville, eds., *Essays in Labour History: In Memory of G. D. H. Cole* (1960; rev. ed. 1967), which contains personal recollections of Cole by Ivor Brown, Hugh Gaitskell, Stephen K. Bailey and G. D. N. Worswick. The discussion of Cole's thought in Henry M. Magid, *English Political Pluralism: The Problem of Freedom and Organization* (1941), suffers from an inadequate historical context. □

# Johnnetta Cole

**A distinguished scholar, Johnnetta Cole (born 1936) has served on the faculties of Washington State University, University of Massachusetts, Hunter College, and Spelman College, the historically black women's institution in Atlanta where she was president.**

Spelman College is the oldest, most respected institution of higher learning for black women in the United States. It is somewhat ironic, therefore, that 107 years of the school's history passed before a black woman filled its presidential office. Johnnetta Cole is that woman, and since taking responsibility for Spelman in 1987, she has proven to be a dynamic administrator, an energetic fundraiser, and a source of inspiration to both faculty and student body. At a time when historically black colleges have been deemed obsolete by some commentators, Cole has emerged as one of their most passionate advocates. Discussing Spelman with an interviewer from *Dollars and Sense*, Cole stated: "I

think that our students are being pulled here by the ambiance, by the affirming environment, by our insistence that African American women can do anything that they set out to do."

Higher education and high standards of achievement are traditions in Cole's family. In 1901 her great-grandfather, Abraham Lincoln Lewis, cofounded the Afro-American Life Insurance Company of Jacksonville, Florida. That business grew and thrived, eventually employing both of Cole's parents, each of whom had graduated from a black college. Her mother had worked as an English teacher and registrar at Edward Waters College prior to becoming a vice-president of Afro-American Life Insurance, and it was assumed that Johnnetta would also join the family business after completing her education.

Johnnetta was precocious, finishing high school by the age of fifteen. She earned outstanding scores on an entrance examination for Fisk University's early admissions program and began studying there in the summer of 1952. Her stay at Fisk was brief, yet pivotal. While there, a world of intellectual endeavor far beyond anything she'd experienced in Jacksonville's segregated schools was revealed to her. She had frequent contact with Arna Bontemps, the noted writer who also held a job as Fisk's librarian. Seeing this respected author in a work setting was important to her because, as she later wrote in a *McCall's* column, "When our . . . heroes are portrayed as bigger than life, living, working, accomplishing beyond the realm of the normal, when they are depicted as perfect human beings, . . . they are placed so far

from us that it seems impossible that we could ever touch them or mirror who they are in our own lives."

After just one year at Fisk, Cole was eager to move on to new horizons. In 1953 she transferred to Oberlin College, where her sister was majoring in music. Seventeen-year-old Johnnetta was by then tightly focused on a career in medicine, but an anthropology course (taken to fulfill a liberal arts requirement) and its enthusiastic instructor changed her direction permanently. "On my own little track, I would have simply taken my science courses, and never would have taken a class with George E. Simpson. This white American professor played Jamaican cult music in the classroom, jumping up and down, beginning to hyperventilate, talking about African retentions in the New World! 'This is what anthropologists try to understand,' said he. 'Good-bye, premed and hello, anthropology!' said I," she was quoted as saying in a *Ms.* magazine article by Susan McHenry.

After earning her bachelor's degree in anthropology at Oberlin in 1957, Cole went on to graduate study at Northwestern University. There she worked under noted anthropologists Paul J. Bohannan and Melville J. Herskovits. To her surprise, she also fell in love with a white graduate student in the economics program. "It was not my plan to fall in love with Robert Cole," she remarked in *Ms.* "And I doubt seriously that this man coming from an Iowa dairy farming family . . . intended to fall in love with a black woman from Jacksonville, Florida." Nevertheless, the two were married. Robert Cole shared his wife's fascination with Africa, and after their wedding day, they traveled to Liberia to work cooperatively on research that would form the basis of both their dissertations.

## Conducted Anthropological Studies Abroad

She did anthropological field studies in villages while he conducted economic surveys of the area. Cole has stated that the experience of living in Africa imparted a unique perspective to her and her husband that helped their interracial marriage endure for more than twenty years, despite the fact that they returned to the United States at the beginning of the black power movement. It was "a time when for many *black* folk interracial marriage was a problem," she was quoted as saying in *Ms.* "But perhaps because I was working largely in an academic setting, with students, it was not just manageable, it was all right."

By 1967 Cole had completed her dissertation, "Traditional and Wage Earning Labor in Liberia," received her Ph.D. from Northwestern, and joined her husband as a faculty member at Washington State University. Beginning as an assistant professor of anthropology, she went on to become a key player in the creation of the school's Black Studies program, also serving as director of the program. In 1970, Cole and her husband moved to New England, where she had been offered a tenured position at the University of Massachusetts at Amherst. She spent thirteen productive years there, developing the existing Afro-American Studies program, increasing the interaction between her school and the others in the Connecticut River valley, teaching courses

in anthropology and Afro-American studies, and serving as provost of undergraduate education.

Cole's marriage ended in 1982, and the following year she moved on to Hunter College of the City University of New York. She remained on the staff of the anthropology department until 1987 and was director of the Latin American and Caribbean Studies program. She continued her field work, which since her days in Liberia had encompassed studies of households headed by women, the lives of Caribbean women, Cape Verdean culture in the United States, and racial and gender inequality in Cuba.

## Wrote on Issues of Culture, Race, and Gender

Cole's focus on cultural anthropology, Afro-American studies, and women's issues all came together in a groundbreaking book published in 1986. *All-American Women: Lines That Divide, Ties That Bind* was cited by numerous reviewers for its perceptive synthesis of issues concerning race, class, gender, and ethnicity. Cole remarked in *Ms.* that her field work has definitely influenced the administrative side of her career: "I tend to look at problems in ways that I think are very, very much in the anthropological tradition. Which means, first of all, one appreciates the tradition, but second, one also at least raises the possibility that there are different ways of doing the same thing. And it's in that discourse where interesting things can happen."

When Spelman College began looking for a new president in 1986, finding a black woman for the job was a top priority. When the school was founded in 1880 by white abolitionists from New England, it was conceived as a missionary school where emancipated slave women could learn literacy, practical skills, and Christian virtues. Its first four presidents were white women; the first black to fill the office, Albert Manley, was not hired until the 1950s. When he left in the mid-1970s, a small but very vocal group of students demanded a black woman president for this black woman's school. The search committee had three excellent candidates that fit the criteria, but two of them withdrew from the selection process before it was completed. The third was offered the job, but had already accepted another. Donald Stewart, former associate dean at University of Pennsylvania, was hired. A group of Spelman students reacted angrily to the announcement, locking the trustees in their boardroom for twenty-six hours.

## Became President of Spelman College

When Stewart left office ten years later, Cole was clearly the standout choice of all the applicants for the vacancy, not just because of her race and sex but because of her strong background as a scholar, a feminist, and a student of black heritage. "Her credentials were not only impeccable, but her incredible energy and enthusiasm came through during the personal interview. She showed certain brilliance in every sense of the word," Veronica Biggins, co-vice-chair of Spelman's board of trustees, was quoted as saying in *Working Woman.* "Cole's charismatic personality, cooperative leadership style, and firm 'black womanist' attitude . . . raise[d] expectations for an exciting new era at

Spelman," according to a *Ms.* article published shortly after Cole took office. "While [she] is a highly qualified, purposeful, serious-minded individual, she is also a thoroughly warm and unpretentious *sister*—in both the black and feminist senses of the term."

Cole's presidency had an exciting kickoff—during her inauguration, Bill and Camille Cosby announced a gift of $20 million to Spelman. Delighted with the donation, Cole was nevertheless quick to point out that there is never enough money. She estimates that fund-raising took up 50 percent of her time. The other half was divided between teaching (one class per term), building up academics, and starting new traditions such as her Mentorship Program, in which CEOs of six major Atlanta corporations are paired with promising students from Spelman. She is committed to building and maintaining a powerful liberal arts program at the school, for it is her belief that a good liberal arts education is the proper foundation for any career. "I tell my students to write, to learn to think, and the rest will fall in place," she told *Working Woman* contributor Audrey Edwards.

## Looking to the Future

Cole firmly believes that African American colleges are vital to African American success. She has frequently quoted statistics showing that although only 17 percent of African American students enter African American colleges, 37 percent of those who make it to graduation were attending African American colleges, and a full 75 percent of African American professional women are graduates of African American colleges. She is convinced that these schools give African American students more opportunities to excel, to discover their heritage, and to see role models in their own image. "I am obviously not an objective soul. I happen to think that this school is the greatest women's college in America," she told an interviewer for *Dollars and Sense.* When asked what lies ahead, she responded: "I would like to think that Spelman has in her future a good deal of continuity and some intriguing changes. . . . Tradition is important at this institution, not just for its own sake, but because it works."

In September 1996, Cole announced that she would by relinquishing her Spelman College presidency in the spring of 1997. She said that she planned to take a year off before moving on to Emory University to teach anthropology.

In her 1993 book *Conversations: Straight Talk with America's Sister President,* Cole broadens her call for a new order, targeting "a multiplicity of audiences" with her message of equality. Mixing enthusiastic discourse on race, gender, and learning with ruminations on her own experiences as an African American woman, she argues for the eradication of racist and sexist views through education, tolerance, and expanded social awareness. While reaching readers of both sexes and all races, Cole marshals the forces of young African American women in the United States to act for change, stating, "We African American women must cure whatever ails us."

## Further Reading

Bateson, Catherine, *Composing a Life,* Atlantic Monthly Press, 1989.
Cole, Johnnetta, *Conversations: Straight Talk with America's Sister President,* Doubleday, 1993.
*Art in America,* September 1990.
*Change,* September/October 1987. *Dollars and Sense,* March 1992.
*Ebony,* February 1988.
*Essence,* November 1987; July 1990.
*McCall's,* October 1990; February 1991.
*Ms.,* October 1987.
*New York Times,* July 20, 1987.
*Publishers Weekly,* July 13, 1992; November 30, 1992.
*SAGE: A Scholarly Journal on Black Women,* Fall 1988.
*USA Today,* October 11, 1990
*Working Woman,* June 1989; November 1991.
*Atlanta Journal and Atlanta Constitution* September 8, 1996. □

# Nat Cole

**The American musician Nat Cole (Nathaniel Adams Coles; 1919-1965) was beloved by millions as a singer of popular songs, but his forte was piano, in the "cool" jazz idiom.**

Nathaniel Adams Coles, the youngest son of the Reverend Edwards Coles and Perlina (Adams) Coles, was born on March 17, 1917 (St. Patrick's Day), in Montgomery, Alabama. Cole and his family were moved to Chicago, Illinois, in 1921 by his father, who served as pastor of the Truelight Spiritual Temple on the South Side of Chicago. By the time he reached the age of 12, Cole was playing the organ and singing in the choir of his father's church under his mother's choir direction.

He took piano lessons "mostly to learn to read, you know. I could play more piano than the teacher." Infatuated with show business, Cole formed his own big band, the Rogues of Rhythm, joined by his older brother Eddie, previously bassist with Noble Sissle's orchestra. First recordings of the Rogues, for Decca Records, are now collector's items.

Working with the band in Chicago nightclubs and dance halls enabled Cole to develop both as a pianist and a singer. He was early influenced by the piano styling of Earl Hines and Jimmy Noone's band. Of Noone's theme song, "Sweet Lorraine," he said, "Man, that was the first song I ever sang." The tune, written by the New Orleans clarinetist Mitchell Parish, became a Cole classic.

Leaving the Chicago circuit, Cole and the band joined the Shuffle Along show scheduled to play the West Coast. Brother Eddie declined the engagement and Cole went along to California where, in 1937, he met and married Nadine Robinson, a chorus girl with the show. When the show folded, he and the band played a short-lived booking at the Ubangi Club in Maywood. "Old musicians never die; they just run out of gigs," said Louie Armstrong once, and when Cole's Ubangi gig was over the band broke up and he

went on to do a solo act at the Century Club. From the Century, Cole was hired by Bob Lewis, owner of the Swanee Inn in Hollywood. Lewis insisted on a trio. The booking was for two weeks, but lasted six months.

### The Genius of Cole, Moore, and Miller

Cole's first bass player, later to be replaced by the legendary Johnny "Thrifty" Miller, was Wesley Prince, who introduced him to Oscar Moore, a movie studio-guitarist. Although the phenomenal Moore was replaced years later by the excellent guitarist Irving Ashby, the trio reached its apex with the combination of the genius of Cole, Moore, and Miller.

The trio wove a fabric of blues licks, riffs, runs, arpeggios, and scalewise invented melodies, classically composed in an original and precise musical logic, as if nothing were left to chance, when, in fact, every note was a calculated risk controlled by the artists' innate rhythmic, harmonic, and melodic sensibilities—absolute freedoms contained by absolute rules of the musical art. Head arrangements were worked up from sheet music in rehearsals, but were not written down. Rehearsal time nods of the head by Cole signaled Moore and Miller and resulted in smooth transitions from piano to guitar solos and piano-guitar riffs, in the Benny Goodman mode. The three musicians each possessed exceptional improvisational melodic gifts which melded original inventions with jazz conventions.

Their harmonic genius added to a constantly swinging rhythm rooted in Miller's unswerving bass line and Moore's driving four to the measure chordal accompaniment—a beat which inspired the envy of contemporary big bands. Cole's accompaniment style, which backed up Moore's improvisational guitar lines and his own singing, was characterized by piano bass-note rockers and comped (chopped) chords executed by the left hand against exquisitely tasteful fill-ins executed by the right hand.

The trio was an original of the jazz combo which prepared future audiences for the small ensembles later to emerge as a consequence of economic retrenchment in the music industry, causing the demise of the big bands on the road circuit at a time when live radio and television broadcasting costs, too, became, for a while, prohibitive of orchestration on the grand scale.

Legend has it that upon an occasion of Cole's after-hours venture into vocalization with the previously predominantly instrumental trio, a young woman present in the club figuratively crowned him the "King," an affectionate nickname which stuck ever after. Among the "Counts" of Basie and the "Dukes" of Ellington, the title of "King" was reverential and emphasized Cole's high place in the enduring art and history of jazz.

After the Swanee Inn, the trio worked night spots in Hollywood and its environs; later, in Chicago, they played on the same bill with the Bob Crosby band and cut eight sides with Decca, including an early rendition of "Sweet Lorraine," one almost identical to their eventual hit on the Capital label. Moving on through Washington, D.C., they arrived in Manhattan in 1941 to play Nick's in Greenwich Village, Kelly's Stable (uptown), and one week at the Paramount, but the pay was "slim pickens," impelling the trio to return to the West Coast, where they played the 331 Club followed by a 10-week tour of Omaha and a return engagement at the 331 for almost a year, which got them through the winter of 1943-1944.

Lean times were followed by big hits. With the arrival of the spring of 1944 came a second Capital recording of "Straighten Up and Fly Right" and, on the flip side, "I Just Can't See for Lookin'," a novelty lyric derived from an old preacher's joke that Cole had composed and set to music about a buzzard who took a monkey for a ride. With personification came gratification and a series of hits: "Gee, Baby, Ain't I Good to You?" "Bring Another Drink," "If You Can't Smile and Say Yes," "Shy Guy," and then, two real winners, "Frim Fram Sauce" and "Route 66."

Constantly together on the road, Cole, Moore, and Miller lived and breathed their music at work and at play, until they played as one. Most often Cole sang solo, but some tunes were rendered in a unison band chant. His piano talent, synthesized from cross-fertilization of Earl "Fatha" Hines, Fats Waller, Frankie Carl, Count Basie, Fletcher Henderson, Mel Powell, and Teddy Wilson, was the bridge between the preceding style of Art Tatum and the styles to follow of George Shearing and Oscar Peterson. This lineage is, perhaps, best exemplified in Cole's solo rendition of "Body and Soul." Such is the family way in which jazz musicianship develops: first imitation and then innovation; first convention and then invention. Moore had picked up a few tricks along the way from Django Rinehardt, Eddie Lang

(Salvatore Mussaro), Charley Christian, and Danny Perri; Miller had profited from listening to "Slam" Stewart and "Bobby" Haggert—but the trio's synthesis was original.

## Huge Success as a Single

Cole and some of his Californian friends, including songwriter-singer Frankie Laine, prepared original compositions for what proved to be a successful concert tour, but as success mounted, so the jazz lessened and the popular vocalization increased, and so, too, the trio faded into the background, sometimes appearing with full orchestra in concerti sections; sometimes not appearing at all. With his recording of Mel Torme's "Christmas Song," a new career was launched for Cole which left little room for Moore and Miller; the trio broke up, to be restaffed later on by Cole for occasional gigs. Unfortunately, new success marked the end of old friendship.

There are three major lineages in modern American popular singing. The earliest is the Neapolitan School, which resulted from a fusion of Al Jolson's and Carlo Buti's styles by Russ Columbo, who was the leader in a family of crooners including Harry Lillis "Bing" Crosby, Buddy Clark, Perry Como, Dean Martin, and Elvis Presley. The second, the Big Band School, traded Rudy Valley's megaphone for the more sensitive microphone and includes Bob and Ray Eberly, Frank Sinatra, Vic Damone, Steve Lawrence, and Jack Jones. The youngest of the three pre-rock schools is the Cool School, deriving from the harsher toned ancestry of Louis Armstrong, Jimmy Rushing, and Louis Prima to culminate in the smooth, relaxed delivery of Cole, who established a style out of which others grew, including the styles of Mel Torme, Johnny Ray, Johnny Mathis, Oscar Peterson (whose similarity of style with Cole's caused a lifetime contract between them requiring Peterson to refrain from singing), Frankie Laine, Tony Bennett, early Ray Charles, and later, John Pizzarelli, Jr. (son of Bucky).

After seven film contracts with the trio, a long-term contract with the NBC Kraft Music Hall, recording contracts with Decca and Capital, top-ten hits, Metronome Poll awards, Gold Piano and Silver Singing Esquire awards, and a Gold Esquire Guitar award for Moore; after the constant friendship, the countless one-night stands, the concert engagements, and the fame and the fortune, the trio gig was up and Cole was on his own.

Cole never belted a song in his life, but depended on interesting subtleties of vocal timbre and texture and the art of nuance. Even Sinatra admired his intonation. Cole never sang a sour note in his life. He well knew how to hold the vowels and let go of the consonants. He was master of the art of understatement and knew how to capitalize on brief spaces of pregnant silence, as dramatically important to music as sound itself. He mastered the art of rubato, which resulted in an intricate ability to phrase a melodic line and tell a lyric story. The consummate jazz artist became the consummate balladeer, the singer of art and folk songs of the future, an American troubadour.

Cole bought a home in Los Angeles—"my own home," he said, but two lives spent in show business had led to divorce from Nadine. He married for a second and last time to singer Marie Ellington, who, although not related, sang with Duke Ellington's band. He and Marie had three daughters: Carol, Timlin, and Natalie. Natalie followed in her father's swinging footsteps.

After the successes of "Dance, Ballerina, Dance," "Nature Boy," and "Lush Life," there came the sudden and most sad end to the artist's life and the beginning of a landmark of native American music. The sound quality of Cole's voice derived not only from his broad Southern dialect (the vowel sounds almost Italian in pronunciation), his impeccable ear, the microphonic amplification of his tone color, his idiosyncratic pronunciation of "I", or from his velvet falsetto, but also from his cigarette smoking. On a WNEW New York interview shortly before his untimely death in 1965 by throat cancer, he was asked by host William B. Williams how he could smoke so much and still be a singer. Cole responded by saying he had learned two things, the first thing being that the choice of the right key for a song meant everything, and the second being that smoking helps a singer get a husky sound in his voice that the audience loves—"so, if you want to sing, keep on smoking."

When Cole died, a consummate jazz artist and a voice millions knew as the voice of a friend was irreplaceably lost to the world.

## Further Reading

Additional information on Nat "King" Cole can be found in *Look* (April 19, 1955); *Newsweek* (August 12, 1946); *TIME* (July 30, 1951); *Saturday Evening Post* (July 17, 1954); *ASCAP Biographical Dictionary of Composers, Authors, and Publishers* (1952); and *Who Is Who in Music* (1951). □

# Thomas Cole

**Thomas Cole (1801-1848) was the founder of the Hudson River school of romantic American landscape painting. He treated the idyllic as well as the formidable aspects of nature in great detail and was also noted for his allegorical subjects.**

Thomas Cole was born in Bolton-le-Moors, Lancaster, England, and emigrated with his family to Philadelphia in 1818. They soon moved to Steubenville, Ohio, where Thomas, who had studied engraving briefly in England, taught art in his sister's school. He then tried to be an itinerant portrait painter. Seeking better patronage, he returned to Philadelphia in 1823 to paint landscapes and decorate Japan ware. He took drawing lessons at the Pennsylvania Academy and exhibited there for the first time in 1824.

Moving to New York the following year Cole began to receive recognition and may at this time be said to have set in motion the taste for romantic landscape—a genre which would later become known as the Hudson River school. Taking a trip up the Hudson River, he painted three landscapes. Placed in the window of Coleman's Art Store, they were purchased at $25 apiece by three well-known artists of the day: John Trumbull, Asher Durand, and William Dunlap. Cole was now established and able to support himself by his landscapes.

Cole moved up the Hudson in 1826 to Catskill. After seeing the great scenic wonders of the White Mountains and Niagara, he sailed for England in 1829 under the patronage of Robert Gilmore of Baltimore. Although Cole admired the paintings of Claude Lorrain and Gaspard Poussin, he spent little time in European museums, preferring to sketch out of doors. After a brief visit to Paris he went down the Rhone River and then to Italy. After nine weeks in Florence he went to Rome, accomplishing most of the journey on foot.

Returning to New York in 1832, Cole was given a commission by an art patron to execute five panels. Known as the *Course of Empire,* these were considerably influenced by J.M.W. Turner's *Building of Carthage,* which Cole had seen in London.

In November 1836 Cole married Maria Barton, whose family home in Catskill became their permanent residence. Commissions came in from William P. Van Rensselaer for *The Departure* and *The Return,* from P. G. Stuyvesant for *Past and Present,* and from Samuel Ward for four panels, the *Voyage of Life.*

In 1841 Cole went to Europe again. On returning home he visited Mount Desert on the coast of Maine and Niagara. At the time of his death on Feb. 11, 1848, he was at work on a religious allegory, the *Cross of the World.*

With the overland expansion of America, people took great interest in their land and the various aspects of nature. Cole established landscape painting as an accepted form of art. He was a Swedenborgian mystic, and his paintings reflect his intensely religious feelings; never dealing with the trivial, his work has a high moral tone. He had a profound reverence for nature, which he depicted sometimes in a tranquil mood and at other times in a state of violence. He makes the viewer feel man as a helpless creature overwhelmed by the all-powerful forces of nature. He frequently placed a highly detailed tree at the right or left foreground (an inheritance from baroque stage settings), and the landscape beyond unfolds as on a stage. His was a highly romanticized version of nature often overlaid with elements of fantasy and sometimes even including medieval or classical ruins.

## Further Reading

In the absence of a modern study of Cole, the best source is Louis Legrand Noble, *The Life and Works of Thomas Cole* (1853; edited, with an introduction, by Elliot Vesell, 1964); it includes correspondence and other documents. Howard S. Merritt, *Thomas Cole* (1969), an exhibition catalog, includes a critical introduction. For shorter notices see Frederick A. Sweet, *The Hudson River School and the Early American Landscape Tradition* (1945), and Esther Seaver, ed., *Thomas Cole: One Hundred Years Later* (1949).

## Additional Sources

Baigell, Matthew, *Thomas Cole,* New York: Watson-Guptill Publications, 1981.

Parry, Ellwood, *The art of Thomas Cole: ambition and imagination,* Newark: University of Delaware Press, 1988. □

# Bessie Coleman

**Bessie Coleman (1892-1926) was the first African American to earn the coveted international pilot's license, issued in Paris (June 15, 1921) by the Fédération Aéronautique Internationale.**

B essie Coleman was born on January 26, 1892, in a one-room, dirt-floored cabin in Atlanta, Texas, to George and Susan Coleman, the illiterate children of slaves. When Bessie was two years old, her father, a day laborer, moved his family to Waxahachie, Texas, where he bought a quarter-acre of land and built a three-room house in which two more daughters were born.

When George Coleman's hopes for a better living in Waxahachie remained unfulfilled, and with five of his nine living children still at home, he proposed moving again, this time to Indian territory in Oklahoma. There, on a reservation, his heritage of three Native American grandparents would give him the civil rights denied to both African Americans and Native Americans in Texas. In 1901, after Susan refused to go with him, he went to Oklahoma on his own, leaving his family behind in Waxahachie. Susan found work as a domestic, her two sons became day laborers, and Bessie was left to be the caretaker of her two younger sisters.

Education for Coleman was limited to eight grades in a one-room schoolhouse that closed whenever the students were needed in the fields to help their families harvest cotton. Already responsible for her sisters and the household chores while her mother worked, Coleman was a reluctant cotton picker but an intelligent and expert accountant. The only member of the family who could accurately add the total weight of the cotton they picked, she increased the total whenever she could by putting her foot on the scale when the foreman wasn't looking.

Coleman easily established her position as family leader, reading aloud to her siblings and mother at night, winning the prize for selling the most tickets for a church benefit, and assuring her ambitious church-going mother that she intended to "amount to something." After completing school she worked as a laundress and saved her wages until 1910 when she left for Oklahoma to attend Langston University. She left after one year when her funds were exhausted.

Back in Waxahachie Coleman again worked as a laundress until 1915 when she moved to Chicago to live with her older brother, Walter, a Pullman porter. Within months she became a manicurist and moved to a place of her own while she continued to seek—and finally, in 1920, to find—a goal for her life: aviation.

Cultivating the friendship of leaders in South Side Chicago's African American community, Coleman found a sponsor in Robert Abbott, publisher of the nation's largest

achieved occasional brief notice from the press of the time, which ordinarily confined its coverage of African Americans to actors, athletes and entertainers or those involved in sex, crime, or violence. But the African American press of the country, primarily weekly newspapers, quickly proclaimed her "Queen Bell."

In December 1922, after a number of successful air shows on the East Coast and in Chicago, Coleman walked out on the starring role of a New York movie in production, publicly denouncing the script as "Uncle Tom stuff" demeaning to her race. The abrupt move alienated a number of influential African American critics and producers and threatened to end her career. But Coleman bounced back by going to California and air-dropping advertising leaflets for a tire company in exchange for money to buy a JN4, or "Jenny"—a surplus U.S. Army training plane from World War I.

On February 4, 1923, however, within only days of getting her plane, Coleman crashed shortly after takeoff from Santa Monica en route to her first scheduled West Coast air show. The Jenny was destroyed and Coleman suffered injuries that hospitalized her for three months. Returning to Chicago to recuperate, it took her another 18 months to find backers for a series of shows in Texas. Her flights and theater appearances there during the summer of 1925 were highly successful, earning her enough to make a down payment on another surplus Jenny she found at Love Field, Dallas.

To raise the rest of the money, in January 1926 she returned to the East Coast, where she had signed up for a number of speaking engagements and exhibition flights in borrowed planes in Georgia and Florida. In Florida she met the Rev. Hezekiah Keith Hill and his wife, Viola Tillinghast, community activists from Orlando who invited her to stay with them. She also met Edwin M. Beeman, heir to the Beeman Chewing Gum fortune, whose interest in flying led him to give her the payment due on her airplane in Dallas. At last, she wrote to one of her sisters, she was going to be able to earn enough money to open her school for fliers.

Coleman left Orlando by train to give a benefit exhibition for the Jacksonville Negro Welfare League, scheduled for May 1, 1926. William D. Wills, the young white mechanic-pilot who flew her plane to her from Love Field, made three forced landings en route. Two local pilots who witnessed his touchdown at Jacksonville's Paxon Field said later that the Jenny was so worn and so poorly maintained they couldn't understand how it made it all the way from Dallas. On April 30 Wills piloted the plane on a trial flight while Coleman sat in the other cockpit to survey the area over which she was to fly and parachute jump the next day. Her seat belt was unattached because she had to be able to lean out over the edge of the plane while picking the best sites for her program. At an altitude of 1,000 feet, the plane dived, then flipped over, throwing Coleman out. Moments later Wills crashed. Both were killed.

Coleman had three memorial services—in Jacksonville, Orlando, and Chicago, the last attended by thousands. She was buried at Chicago's Lincoln Cemetery and gradu-

African American weekly, the *Chicago Defender.* There were no African American aviators in the area and, when no white pilot was willing to teach her to fly, Coleman appealed to Abbott, who suggested that she go to France. The French, he said, were not racists and were the world's leaders in aviation.

Coleman took French language lessons while managing a chili parlor and, with backing from Abbott and a wealthy real estate dealer, Jessie Binga, she left for France late in 1920. There she completed flight training at the best school in France and was awarded her F.A.I. (Fédération Aéronautique Internationale) license on June 15, 1921. She returned to the United States in September 1921 but soon realized that she needed to expand her repertoire and learn aerobatics if she were to make a living giving exhibition flights. She went back to Europe the following February and for the next six months gained further flying experience in Holland, France, and Germany.

Back in New York in August 1922, Coleman outlined to reporters the objectives she intended to pursue for the remainder of her life. She would be a leader, she said, in introducing aviation to her race. She would found a school for aviators of any race, and she would appear before audiences in churches, schools, and theaters to arouse the interest of African Americans in the new, expanding technology of flight.

Intelligent, beautiful, and eloquent, Coleman often exaggerated her remarkable-enough accomplishments in the interest of better publicity and bigger audiences. She even

ally, over the years following her death, achieved recognition at last as a hero of early aviation and of her race.

## Further Reading

The best source of information on Bessie Coleman is *Queen Bess—The Life of Bessie Coleman* (1993), written by Doris Rich in large part to correct the many misstatements in contemporary sources. Two reliable places where information can be found are the DuSable Museum of African American History in Chicago and the National Air and Space Museum, Smithsonian Institution, Washington, D.C.

## Additional Sources

Fisher, Lillian M., *Brave Bessie: flying free,* Dallas, Tex.: Hendrick-Long Publishing Co., 1995.
Freydberg, Elizabeth Hadley, *Bessie Coleman, the brownskin lady bird,* New York: Garland Pub., 1994.
Rich, Doris L., *Queen Bess: daredevil aviator,* Washington: Smithsonian Institution Press, 1993. □

# Samuel Taylor Coleridge

**The English author Samuel Taylor Coleridge (1772-1834) was a major poet of the romantic movement. He is also noted for his prose works on literature, religion, and the organization of society.**

B orn on Oct. 21, 1772, Samuel Taylor Coleridge was the tenth and last child of the vicar of Ottery St. Mary near Exeter. In 1782, after his father's death, he was sent as a charity student to Christ's Hospital. His amazing memory and his eagerness to imbibe knowledge of any sort had turned him into a classical scholar of uncommon ability by the time he entered Jesus College, Cambridge, in 1791. Like most young intellectuals of the day, he felt great enthusiasm for the French Revolution and took his modest share in student protest against the war with France (1793). Plagued by debts, Coleridge enlisted in the Light Dragoons in December 1793. Discharged in April 1794, he returned to Cambridge, which he left in December, however, without taking a degree.

The reason for this move, characteristic of Coleridge's erratic and impulsive character, was his budding friendship with Robert Southey. Both young men were eagerly interested in poetry, sharing the same dislike for the neoclassic tradition. They were both radicals in politics, and out of their feverish conversations grew the Pantisocratic scheme—the vision of an ideal communistic community to be founded in America. This juvenile utopia came to nothing, but on Oct. 4, 1795, Coleridge married Sara Fricker, the sister of Southey's wife-to-be. By that time, however, his friendship with Southey had already dissolved.

## Poetic Career

In spite of his usually wretched health, the years from 1795 to 1802 were for Coleridge a period of fast poetic growth and intellectual maturation. In August 1795 he be-

gan his first major poem, "The Eolian Harp," which was published in his *Poems on Various Subjects* (1796). It announced his unique contribution to the growth of English romanticism: the blending of lyrical and descriptive effusion with philosophical rumination in truly symbolic poetry.

From March to May 1796 Coleridge edited the *Watchman,* a liberal periodical which failed after 10 issues. While this failure made him realize that he was "not *fit* for *public* life," his somewhat turgid "Ode to the Departing Year" shows that he had not abandoned his revolutionary fervor. Yet philosophy and religion were his overriding interests. His voracious reading was mainly directed to one end, which was already apparent in his *Religious Musings* (begun 1794, published 1796)—he aimed to redefine orthodox Christianity so as to rid it of the Newtonian dichotomy between spirit and matter, to account for the unity and wholeness of the universe, and to reassess the relation between God and the created world.

Perhaps the most influential event in Coleridge's career was his intimacy with William and Dorothy Wordsworth, in whose neighborhood he spent most of his life from 1796 to 1810. This friendship was partly responsible for his *annus mirabilis* (July 1797 to July 1798), which culminated in his joint publication with Wordsworth of the *Lyrical Ballads* in September 1798. As against 19 poems by Wordsworth, the volume contained only 4 by Coleridge, but one of these was "The Ancient Mariner." Coleridge later described the division of labor between the two poets—while Wordsworth was "to give the charm of novelty to things of every day by awakening the mind's attention from the lethargy of custom, and directing it to the loveliness and the wonders of the world before us," it had been agreed that Coleridge's "endeavours should be directed to persons and characters supernatural, or at least romantic." But the underlying world view of the two poets was fundamentally similar. Like Wordsworth's "The Thorn," for example, Coleridge's "The Ancient Mariner" deals with the themes of sin and punishment and of redemption through suffering and a loving apprehension of nature.

A second, enlarged edition of Coleridge's *Poems* also appeared in 1798. It contained further lyrical and symbolic works, such as "This Lime-Tree Bower, My Prison" and "Fears in Solitude." At this time Coleridge also wrote "Kubla Khan," perhaps the most famous of his poems, and began the ambitious narrative piece "Christabel."

In September 1798 Coleridge and the Wordsworths left for Germany, where he stayed until July 1799. In the writings of post-Kantian German philosophers such as J. G. Fichte, F. W. J. von Schelling, and A. W. von Schlegel, Coleridge discovered a world view so congenial that it is almost impossible to disentangle what, in his later thought, is properly his and what may have been derived from German influences. *Sibylline Leaves* (1817) contains lively, humorous accounts of his German experiences.

## Personal Difficulties

The dozen years following Coleridge's return to England were the most miserable in his life. In October 1799 he settled near the Wordsworths in the Lake District. The cold, wet climate worsened his many ailments, and turning to laudanum for relief, he soon became an addict. His marriage, which had never been a success, was now disintegrating, especially since Coleridge had fallen in love with Sara Hutchinson, sister of Wordsworth's wife-to-be. Ill health and emotional stress, combined with his intellectual absorption in abstract pursuits, hastened the decline of his poetic power. Awareness of this process inspired the last and most moving of his major poems, "Dejection: An Ode" (1802). After a stay in Malta (1804-1806) which did nothing to restore his health and spirits, he decided to separate from his wife. The only bright point in his life during this period was his friendship with the Wordsworths, but after his return to the Lake District this relationship was subject to increasing strain. Growing estrangement was followed by a breach in 1810, and Coleridge then settled in London.

Meanwhile, however, Coleridge's capacious mind did not stay unemployed; indeed, his major contributions to the development of English thought were still to come. From June 1809 to March 1810 he published the periodical the *Friend.* Coleridge's poetry and his brilliant conversation had earned him public recognition, and between 1808 and 1819 he gave several series of lectures, mainly on Shakespeare and other literary topics. His only dramatic work, *Osorio,* which was written in 1797, was performed in 1813 under the title *Remorse.* "Christabel" and "Kubla Khan" were published in 1816.

## Later Works

In April 1816 Coleridge settled as a patient with Dr. Gillman at Highgate. There he spent most of the last 18 years of his life in comparative peace and in steady literary activity, bringing out several works which were to exert tremendous influence on the future course of English thought in many fields: *Biographia literaria* (1817), *Lay Sermons* (1817), *Aids to Reflection* (1825), and *The Constitution of Church and State* (1829). His apparently rambling style was well suited to a philosophy based on an intuition of wholeness and organic unity.

Although Coleridge's conservative idea of the state may appear both reactionary and utopian, his religious thought led to a revival of Christian philosophy in England. And his psychology of the imagination, conception of the symbol, and definition of organic form in art brought to the English-speaking world the new, romantic psychology and esthetics of literature which had first arisen in Germany at the turn of the century.

When Coleridge died on July 25, 1834, he left bulky manuscript notes, which scholars of the mid-20th century were to exhume and edit. The complete publication of this material will make it possible to realize the extraordinary range and depth of his philosophical preoccupations and to assess his true impact on succeeding generations of poets and thinkers.

## Further Reading

The standard work on Coleridge is E. K. Chambers, *Samuel Taylor Coleridge* (1938; rev. ed. 1950). Norman Fruman, *Coleridge: The Damaged Archangel* (1971), is a comprehensive study of the man and the poet. Two fine works that combine biography with literary criticism are William Walsh, *Coleridge: The Work and the Relevance* (1967), and Walter Jackson Bate, *Coleridge* (1968).

General critical introductions are Humphry House, *Coleridge* (1953); John B. Beer, *Coleridge the Visionary* (1959); Marshall Suther, *The Dark Night of Samuel Taylor Coleridge* (1960); Max F. Schulz, *The Poetic Voices of Coleridge* (1963); Kathleen Coburn, ed., *Coleridge: A Collection of Critical Essays* (1967); and Patricia M. Adair, *The Waking Dream* (1968).

Increasing attention is given to the poet's thought in a great variety of fields. See John H. Muirhead, *Coleridge as Philosopher* (1930). On esthetics see I. A. Richards, *Coleridge on Imagination* (1935; 3d ed. 1962); James V. Baker, *The Sacred River: Coleridge's Theory of the Imagination* (1957); Richard Harter Fogle, *The Idea of Coleridge's Criticism* (1962); and J. A. Appleyard, *Coleridge's Philosophy of Literature: The Development of a Concept of Poetry, 1791-1819* (1965). On religion see Charles Richard Sanders, *Coleridge and the Broad Church Movement* (1942); James D. Boulger, *Coleridge as Religious Thinker* (1961); and J. Robert Barth, *Coleridge and Christian Doctrine* (1969). For general background information the reader is referred to the bibliography in W. L. Renwick, *English Literature, 1789-1815* (1963).

## Additional Sources

Ashton, Rosemary, *The life of Samuel Taylor Coleridge: a critical biography,* Cambridge, Mass.: Blackwell Publishers, 1996.

Bate, Walter Jackson, *Coleridge,* Cambridge, Mass.: Harvard University Press, 1987, 1968.

Campbell, James Dykes, *Samuel Taylor Coleridge: a narrative of the events of his life,* Norwood, Pa.: Norwood Editions, 1977.

Chambers, E. K. (Edmund Kerchever), *Samuel Taylor Coleridge: a biographical study,* Westport, Conn.: Greenwood Press, 1978, 1938.

Doughty, Oswald, *Perturbed spirit: the life and personality of Samuel Taylor Coleridge,* Rutherford N.J.: Fairleigh Dickinson University Press; East Brunswick, N.J.: Associated University Presses, 1981.

Garnett, Richard, *Coleridge,* Philadelphia: R. West, 1977.

Gillman, James, *The life of Samuel Taylor Coleridge,* Philadelphia: R. West, 1977.

Holmes, Richard, *Coleridge: early visions,* London: Hodder & Stoughton, 1989. □

# Robert Martin Coles

**Robert Martin Coles (born 1929) was a social psychiatrist, social critic, and humanist whose work was centered on the daily lives of those Americans—the poor, minorities, the elderly, and especially children—who confront an often oppressive society with dignity and resilience.**

Robert Martin Coles was born in Boston, Massachusetts, on October 12, 1929. His parents, especially his father, an engineer, impressed upon him the importance of keen observation and commitment to a better social world, whatever one's professional career. He took his undergraduate degree at Harvard and his medical degree at Columbia University in 1954, with a specialization in child psychiatry. But as a young doctor he was not happy with conventional medical practice in Boston; it did not satisfy his deep interest in the humanities, in literature, in the intersection of the human spirit and the social order. Nor could it resolve his restless conflict: the desire to achieve and succeed and, at the same time, make a real contribution to the understanding of the human condition.

## The Opportunity to Integrate Social Idealism

Drafted into the Air Force and sent to Mississippi to a psychiatric hospital, he began to see in the racially segregated society just beyond the military base the opportunity for integrating his social idealism, his psychiatric training, and his literary sensibility (with its debt owed to such writers as James Agree and George Orwell). This included his desire to be an active part of the African American struggle to overcome racial discrimination. With his wife and lifelong collaborator, Jane Halowell Coles, he worked out a method for listening to, and drawing out, those young African American children who were courageously running the gauntlet of jeering mobs in order to take their rightful place in school. This field work, and in particular the story of Ruby Bridges, who integrated the first grade of a school in New Orleans in 1960, laid the foundation for his life's work: the need to understand the most challenging and complex social and economic problems as refracted through the daily lives of ordinary people. (In the process we come to see that we must bring insight and compassion to the analysis of bigoted whites as well as courageous African American children, to the affluent as well as to the poor, to the successful as well as to the failed. It is this quality which David Riesman stressed in his evaluation of Coles: "There is one important theme he has contributed: antistereotype. Policemen are not pigs, white Southerners are not rednecks, and African Americans are not all suffering in exotic misery. What he is saying is 'People are more complicated, more varied, more interesting, have more resiliency and more survivability than you might think!'")

Coles' first book, *Children of Crisis,* which resulted from his work with African American children, lent its title to a series of volumes. In the decade 1967-1977 he settled in Concord, Massachusetts, earning his living as a writer, staff psychiatrist, and lecturer at Harvard. (Students described his course, Social Science 33, with affection as "Guilt 33.") He went on to study in the other four volumes of the series migrant and sharecropper families; Southern, poor families moving north; Indian, Chicano, and Eskimo children; "the privileged ones," rich children; and the spiritual and moral lives of children. Despite the material deprivation, he writes, of children who are poor, they are no more unhappy than rich kids. "The pathology of childhood depression—and indeed other pathologies we physicians try to treat—are by no means epidemic among the poor, and may be just as common and conspicuous among the well-to-do who have so much and who want so much." With Jane Coles he also wrote *Women of Crises,* two volumes (1978 and 1980) about women across the class-race spectrum: "What it is that certain American women have to struggle for or against as a consequence of their 'background,' and what it is they share (in the way of concrete realities, or hopes and fears)."

## A Proflific Writer

Coles was an enormously prolific writer; by the early 1980s there were more than thirty books and more than five hundred articles. By early 1997, that number climbed to over 53 books. Many of them carried on the same conception and approach. They are about miners in Appalachia, children in strife-torn Belfast and apartheid-ridden South Africa, middle Americans, the elderly Spanish-speaking of the Southwest, troubled adolescents. Throughout there is a steady vision of what is wanted, a "method," as Coles was careful to say in quotes. "Eventually we pull together the words of others and our own observations into what (we can only pray) is a reasonably coherent and suggestive series of portraits, comments, reflections." The technique is by no means new. The books of the anthropologist Oscar Lewis, in the same vein, predated Coles's work by a decade. But Coles's psychiatric background deepened the portraits. And the connection of personal lives to oppressive social conditions was made more explicit. We must not only record how the miners talk about the terrible devastation of "black lung"; we must get rid of black lung.

As the years went by, Coles came to emphasize more and more his role as a writer, a creative writer, with a particular interest in the life of the spirit as well as the mind. His was a broadly religious outlook, a sense of the Judaic-Christian ethic at work rather than a formal elaboration of a given theology. His many biographies—of the psychiatrist Erik Erikson (1970), of the poet William Carlos Williams (1975), of the writers Flannery O'Connor (1980), James Agee (1985), and Walker Percy (1978)—engaged Coles in this contest, as did the collections of essays, whose titles provide a clue to Coles's central concern: *Harvard Diary: Reflections on the Sacred and Secular* (1988); *A Spectacle unto the World: the Catholic Worker Movement* (1973); *The Moral Life of Children* (1986); *The Call of Stories: Teaching and the Moral Imagination* (1989), and so on.

*The Moral Intelligence of Children* hopes to further the idea that moral development is every bit as important as intellectual and emotional growth. "It's interesting how we make these generalizations about ghetto children and forget the parallels among the privileged. In some privileged precincts of America, you have well-educated parents with plenty of money who give their children toys and travel and credit cards. What they don't offer them is moral attention, a sense of connection to the community. The result can be staggering morally. And teachers are left to pick up the pieces."

In what Coles said was his last book about children he produced *The Spiritual Life of Children* (1990). From interviews of hundreds of children, ages 8 to 13—Christian, Jewish, Islamic, Hopi, secular—he reported what they had to say about how God speaks to them and how they listen and react.

### The Core of Social Psychiatry

The core of Coles's social psychiatry is that it shows not only the mental stresses and strains in individual lives but the way in which powerful social and economic forces impinge on those lives and how those persons respond: well and poorly, emotionally and stoically, in resistance and defeat. Since the portraits, the heart of Coles's matter, do not end in solutions or policies, a number of critics of his work argue that we are left only with the sum of these voices; it is all too diffuse, the analysis and the compassion not focused on what is to be done and how. But that was not Coles's task, as he saw it. Rather, he wanted readers to understand, through the depth and complexity of these profiles, how, in the words of C. Wright Mills, personal problems and public issues connect. From that connection we can move on to social change.

*1995, The Mind's Fate: A Psychiatrist Looks at His Profession—Thirty Years of Writings* is a 1995 collection of his popular articles—book review, memoirs, essays and musings from publications like the *New Yorker,* the *New England Journal of Medicine,* the *New Republic, Commonweal* and the *New York Review of Books,* among others. What we have here is a collection of snapshots of Coles's thinking on this and that, which is valuable to have as Coles has a lot to say.

Coles had little use for many of his colleagues, whom he saw as narrow-minded and condescending, too quick to apply textbook labels and psuedo-diagnoses. In one book review, he extols R.D. Laing, the contrarian and controversial British psychiatrist who is something of a pariah for challenging the distinction between sanity and madness: "Freud called himself a conquistador, and if the bookkeepers and bureaucrats have now descended upon the psychoanalytic movement' in droves to claim his mantle, all the more reason for a man like Laing to stand fast as the psychoanalyst he is," Coles writes. "I am overpowered by the challenges he issues to what has become a rather conventional profession, very much the property of (and source of solace to) the upper-middle-class American, this century's civis Romanus. To Laing, we psychiatrists are something else, too: willing custodians, who for good pay agree to do the bidding of society by keeping tabs on various deviants,' and in the clutch taking care' of them—the double meaning of the verb being exactly the point."

Indeed, with the death of Christopher Lasch, Coles stands out as one of a diminishing group of scholars who refute the destructive and anti-democratic specialization that has nearly eliminated the general intellectual—once found in the hard sciences as well as in the history and English departments of the great universities—from public and political life.

### Further Reading

In Robert Coles's prodigious output the most accessible work is *The Children of Crisis Series,* 5 volumes, (1967-1977). Among the biographies the studies of the writers Flannery O'Connor and Walker Percy are especially to be recommended: *Flannery O'Connor's South* (1980) and *Walker Percy; An American Search* (1978), and among the essays *The Call of Stories* (1988) and *The Mind's Fate: Ways of Seeing Psychiatry and Psychoanalysis* (1975). A brief but insightful profile of Coles and his work is Paul Wilkes, "Doctor of Crisis," in *New York Times Magazine* (March 26, 1978). □

# John Colet

**The English theologian and moral reformer John Colet (ca. 1446-1519) founded St. Paul's School and influenced the humanist Erasmus.**

The father of John Colet was Sir Henry Colet, twice mayor of London. He was a wealthy man and the father of 22 children, none of whom survived to maturity except John. After early schooling in London, John went to Oxford, where he spent some 20 years as a scholar and lecturer, eventually receiving a doctorate in divinity about 1504.

After earning a master of arts degree, in 1493 Colet went to Italy and France for 3 years, visiting both Rome and Paris. On Colet's return to Oxford, Erasmus reports: "He publicly and gratuitously expounded all St. Paul's epistles. It was at Oxford that my acquaintance with him began." Moreover, wrote Erasmus, Colet's "opinions differed widely from those commonly received. When I was once praising Aquinas to him as a writer not to be despised among the moderns, since he appeared to me to have studied both the Scriptures and the early Fathers, and had also a certain unction in his writings, he checked himself more than once from replying and did not betray his dislike."

In contrast to the elaborate scriptural exegesis then prevalent, Colet preferred to pay careful attention to the context of St. Paul's letters. Although Colet stressed the importance of the literal meaning of the books of the Bible, he was not a fundamentalist.

Colet received priestly orders in 1498 and left Oxford 6 years later to become dean of St. Paul's Cathedral in London. In 1510 he founded St. Paul's School for boys. The essential moral earnestness that suffused all of Colet's teaching and writing was plainly evident in the great trouble he took over the founding of this establishment, which is still one of the great schools of England. As he said in the statutes he devised for it, "My intent is by this school specially to increase knowledge and worshiping of God and our Lord Jesus Christ and good Christian life and manners in the children."

At his death Colet left one published work, his convocation sermon of 1512. A fierce attack on the lives of the clergy, this sermon declared that there "is no need that new laws and constitutions be made, but that those that are made already be kept."

## Further Reading

The standard biography of Colet is J. H. Lupton, *A Life of John Colet* (1887; 2d ed. 1961). Among numerous modern studies the most important are Ernest W. Hunt, *Dean Colet and His Theology* (1956), and Sears R. Jayne, *John Colet and Marsilio Ficino* (1963); both works have excellent bibliographies.

## Additional Sources

Gleason, John B., *John Colet,* Berkeley: University of California Press, 1989.

Lupton, Joseph Hirst, *A life of John Colet, D.D., dean of St. Paul's, and founder of St. Paul's School,* New York, B. Franklin 1974.

□

# Sidonie Gabrielle Colette

**The French author Sidonie Gabrielle Colette (1873-1954) was concerned with feminine independence in experiencing the joys and sorrows of love. She succeeded in translating a delicate sensibility into a vivid, sensual, and highly imagistic prose.**

On Jan. 28, 1873, Sidonie Gabrielle Colette was born in a small Burgundian town, Saint-Sauveuren-Puisaye. In 1893 she married Henri Gauthier-Villars, a Parisian littérateur of doubtful talents and morals. Gauthier-Villars, or Monsieur Willy, as he was known, forced his young wife to produce novels that would satisfy his prurient and financial interests. Her first attempt, *Claudine à l'école* (1900), signed Colette Willy, was quickly a best seller. Three more Claudine novels (*Claudine à Paris, Claudine en ménage, Claudine s'en va*), *Minne,* and *Les Égarements de Minne* were produced in the following five years.

The marriage did not fare as well. After divorcing Willy in 1906, Colette became a music hall mime and traveled the circuits with moderate success for six years. But the discipline of writing imposed by Willy continued to hold her. Before her divorce she had published *Dialogues des bêtes* (1904) under her maiden name, and she continued to sign in this way her subsequent works, *La Retraite sentimentale* (1907), *Les Vrilles de la vigne* (1908), *L'Ingénue libertine* (1909), and *La Vagabonde* (1911). In 1909 she produced and starred in her first play, *En Camarades.*

From 1910 to 1923 Colette was the literary correspondent for the newspaper *Le Matin.* In 1912 she married her editor in chief, Henri de Jouvenel, and the following year they had a daughter, Colette de Jouvenel, whom Colette called "Bel-Gazou" in her writings. Although the marriage ended after 12 years, these were especially full years for Colette. She published *La Paix chez les bêtes* (1916), a collection of animal stories, and *Les Heures longues* (1917), a collection of her articles and travel notes; with *Mitsou* (1919) and *Chéri* (1920), she entered into her maturity as a novelist and artist, producing a string of masterpieces of the love novel that was to end with *Gigi* (1944). The heroes and heroines of these novels, which include *Le Blé en herbe* (1923), *La Fin de Chéri* (1926), *La Seconde* (1929), *Duo* (1934), *Le Toutounier* (1939), and *Julie de Carneilhan* (1941), resemble in many respects those of Colette's early

Dormann, Genevieve, *Colette, a passion for life,* New York: Abbeville Press, 1985.

Lottman, Herbert R., *Colette: a life,* Boston: Little, Brown, 1991.

Massie, Allan, *Colette,* Harmondsworth, Middlesex, England; New York, N.Y., U.S.A.: Penguin Books, 1986.

Mitchell, Yvonne, *Colette: a taste for life,* New York: Harcourt Brace Jovanovich, 1977.

Richardson, Joanna, *Colette,* New York: F. Watts, 1984, 1983.

Sarde, Michele, *Colette: free and fettered,* New York: Morrow, 1980. □

# Gaspard de Coligny

**The French admiral and statesman Gaspard de Coligny (1519-1572) was the most prominent leader of the French Protestants, or Huguenots, during the first decade of the religious wars in France.**

Gaspard de Coligny was born on Feb. 16, 1519, at his family's château of Châtillon-sur-Loing, the third of four sons of Gaspard de Coligny, Seigneur de Châtillon, and Louise de Montmorency. His mother came from an old and powerful noble house which was headed during Coligny's youth by his uncle, Anne de Montmorency, constable of France and one of the most influential figures in the courts of Francis I and Henry II.

Because of their kinship with Montmorency, Coligny and his brothers Odet and François came into important and lucrative offices and commands. Gaspard was named admiral of France and governor of two major French provinces. As admiral, he became France's first active exponent of colonial expansion in the New World. Between 1555 and 1571 he authorized and supported several colonizing expeditions in an effort to reduce the power of Spain, to find wealth for France, and to provide a haven for French Protestants.

### Conversion to Protestantism

Because they belonged to the Montmorency clientage, the Coligny brothers became enmeshed in the bitter rivalry between the constable and the powerful Guise family. This rivalry, originally a political struggle for influence over Henry II, acquired ideological overtones when Gaspard and his brothers converted to Calvinism and the Guises emerged as the foremost defenders of Catholicism. Among the many French nobles to take up the Protestant faith, Coligny stood out because of the sincerity of his conversion and the depth of his attachment to the new faith.

Coligny assumed the role of spokesman for the French Protestants, and his initial hope was to ally with the queen mother, Catherine de Médicis, and work through her to secure toleration for his fellow Huguenots. But the massacre of a Protestant congregation at Vassy in 1562 by the Duke of Guise drove the Protestant nobility, Coligny with them, into armed opposition to the Crown. Three times (1562-1563, 1567, and 1568-1570) Coligny led the Protestants against the armies of the King. After 1562 Catherine de Médicis

---

novels. Her preoccupations are still childhood, adolescent love, jealousy, love rebuked, and the search for absolute happiness in physical love.

In 1925 Colette met Maurice Goudeket, a young businessman turned journalist, with whom she was to have her longest and happiest liaison. They were married on April 3, 1935, and were not separated until Colette's death. During her later years Colette was progressively immobilized by arthritis, but she continued to record her impressions, recollections, and fantasies. She published *De ma fenêtre* (1942), *L'Étoile vesper* (1946), and *Le Fanal bleu* (1949), all semiautobiographical works reflecting the years of World War II in Paris.

Official recognition came soon after the war. In 1945 Colette was elected to the Académie Goncourt, over which she presided beginning in 1949, and in 1952 to the Légion d'Honneur. She died in Paris on Aug. 3, 1954.

### Further Reading

Two important critical studies of Colette's life and work are Elaine Marks, *Colette* (1960), and Margaret Davies's succinct *Colette* (1961). Also useful are Margaret Crosland, *Madame Colette* (1953), and Maurice Goudeket, *Close to Colette* (1957).

### Additional Sources

*Album Colette: iconographie,* Paris: Gallimard, 1984.

Colette, *Recollections: includes Journey for myself and The evening star,* New York: Collier Books, 1986.

Crosland, Margaret, *Colette—the difficulty of loving: a biography,* Indianapolis: Bobbs-Merrill, 1973.

## St. Bartholomew's Night Massacre

When Charles IX initiated an investigation and announced that those involved would be punished severely, Catherine and the others fabricated a supposed Huguenot plot against his life. The overwrought Charles then authorized the assassination of Coligny and other Protestant leaders who had gathered in Paris to celebrate the marriage of the Protestant prince Henry of Navarre to Charles's sister. On the night of Aug. 24, 1572, Coligny was slain in his bed by the attendants of the Duke of Guise and thus became the first of countless victims of the St. Bartholomew's Night massacre.

## Further Reading

The best biography of Coligny, sympathetic in tone, is A. W. Whitehead, *Gaspard de Coligny, Admiral of France* (1904). Good for the early years is Eugène Bersier, *Coligny: The Earlier Life of the Great Huguenot* (1884). See also Sir Walter Besant, *Gaspard de Coligny* (2d ed. 1879). Background information is in James Westfall Thompson, *The Wars of Religion in France, 1559-1576* (1909); Paul Van Dyke, *Catherine de Médicis* (2 vols., 1922); and Philippe Erlanger, *St. Bartholomew's Night: The Massacre of Saint Bartholomew* (trans. 1962).

## Additional Sources

Crete, Liliane, *Coligny,* Paris: Fayard, 1985. □

alternated reprisals against the admiral with attempts to reconcile him to the King and the Catholic party.

## Advocate of War with Spain

In 1571 Coligny returned to the royal court armed with a policy that he was determined to have Charles IX adopt. He yearned for a war against Spain, France's traditional enemy, which would be precipitated by French intervention on behalf of the rebelling Spanish Netherlands. He believed that this war would unite Frenchmen in spite of their religious differences and would help the cause of international Protestantism (the leaders of the revolt in the Netherlands were Calvinists). War against Spain would also allow Coligny to abandon the unwanted role of leader of an opposition faction and would remove the accusation of his enemies that he had been a traitor. This last charge grew out of a treaty with Elizabeth I of England that he had signed in 1562 on behalf of the Protestants of France and which had led to English occupation of Le Havre on the Normandy coast.

Believing that a war with Spain would be disastrous, Catherine de Médicis fought desperately during the summer of 1572 to convince the royal council and her son Charles IX to reject the proposal of war, but Coligny persisted in discussing it with the young king. On August 22 Coligny was fired upon and wounded while walking in Paris. Catherine, the King's brother (later Henry III), and the Duke of Guise were involved in this assassination attempt, which they kept secret from the King.

# John Collier

**John Collier (1884–1968) was a proponent of American Indian culture. His appointment as Commisioner of Indian Affairs helped shape federal policy toward Native Americans, especially through the Indian Reorganization Act.**

A lifelong proponent of social reform, John Collier first became involved in the fight to preserve American Indian culture in the early 1920s, after spending time among the Pueblo of New Mexico. His work led to his appointment as commissioner of Indian Affairs in 1933. In this position he played a vital role in reshaping federal policy toward Indians, primarily through the Indian Reorganization Act of 1934. Rather than forcing Indians to assimilate, the new policy encouraged self-sufficiency among tribes and provided them with the land rights, religious and educational freedom, and organization to achieve it.

Collier was born in Atlanta, Georgia, on May 4, 1884. He was educated at Columbia University and at the College de France in Paris. During his years at Columbia, Collier began to form the social philosophy that would shape his later work on behalf of the American Indians. Under the guidance of teacher Lucy Crozier, Collier began to worry about the adverse effects of the industrial age on mankind. He felt that it made people too materialistic and individualistic, and he argued that American culture needed to reestablish a sense of community and responsibility. "He believed that dignity and power for the average person, the future of leisure and of realized life, could be ensured only by revitalizing and enriching the primary social group until it was adequate to human nature, and that, to this end, the preservation and nurture of ethnic values was essential," Kenneth R. Philp wrote in his essay "John Collier and the American Indian."

Collier's philosophy led him to enter the field of social work in 1905, and to concentrate his efforts on assisting immigrants. For ten years, beginning in 1909, he worked at the People's Institute, an organization which tried to build a sense of community in the immigrant neighborhoods of New York City. One of Collier's successes in this role was to convince the city's board of education to keep public schools open after class hours for community activities. From 1915 to 1919 Collier acted as director of the National Training School for Community Workers created by the People's Institute.

Collier moved to California in 1919 to run the state's adult education program. Since this was the era of the red scare, however, he was soon placed under surveillance by the Department of Justice for his "communistic" beliefs. As a result, Collier resigned his post within a year and accepted the invitation of bohemian artist Mabel Dodge to visit the Indian Pueblo at Taos, New Mexico. He spent much of the next two years at an art colony near Taos, where he studied the history and current life of American Indians. He soon came to view the communal and cooperative existence of the tribes as a possible solution to the problems he saw in

white culture. "He believed that Pueblo culture offered a model for the redemption of American society because it concerned itself very little with the material aspects of life," Philp explained. "Instead, its goals were beauty, adventure, joy, comradeship, and the relationship of man to God." From that point on Collier dedicated himself to preserving Indian culture and securing reforms in the federal administration of Indian affairs.

Collier led the opposition to the Bursum Bill of 1922, which would have taken 60,000 acres of treaty-guaranteed New Mexico lands away from the Pueblos. After successfully defeating the bill, Collier helped form the American Indian Defense Association and became its executive secretary. One of his duties was to serve as editor of the organization's magazine, *American Indian Life*. Through this publication, and through his work as a lobbyist in Washington, D.C., Collier fought for a liberalization of government policy toward the Indians. The trend until this time was toward confiscating Indian lands and suppressing tribal customs and self-government. Collier and his group instead promoted placing increased land and other resources into Indian hands and allowing greater religious and educational freedom.

In recognition of Collier's work, Harold Ickes, Secretary of the Interior under President Franklin D. Roosevelt, appointed Collier commissioner of Indian Affairs in 1933. According to Philp, Ickes chose Collier to lead the beleaguered federal agency because he believed the activist would be "the best equipped man who ever held this office." In the early years of his tenure, Collier initiated reforms at a rapid pace under the Indian New Deal. For example, he issued two executive orders limiting the influence of Christian missionaries on the tribes by prohibiting coercion and restricting religious education at reservation schools. Though his orders met with protests among clergymen of several denominations—and led some to call him an "infidel" and an "atheist"—Collier insisted that "liberty of conscience in America was never meant to be liberty only for those who professed Christianity," Philp noted.

Collier's "most spectacular attempt to preserve Indian heritage," in the view of Philp, occurred in June 1934, when he secured passage in Congress of the Indian Reorganization Act. In its overall effect, this act radically changed the government's official policy on American Indians from one of forced assimilation to one of cultural pluralism. Some of the specific provisions of the act replaced a complex system of individual land allotments with a simpler system of communal lands belonging to tribes; established a fund to buy more land for the reservations; encouraged the tribes to organize their own governments and services; and removed the bans on traditional languages and religions. The act was also used to create an Arts and Crafts board to expand the markets for handmade goods and to provide funds for the college education of qualified Indians.

Collier resigned from his post in 1945 after serving longer than any previous Indian commissioner. Throughout his tenure he was known for his vigorous defense of American Indian rights and culture. Though Collier's successors retreated somewhat from his positions, young American

Indians raised under his Indian New Deal often demonstrated a new militancy in dealing with the government and seemed better prepared to secure their own rights. Collier remained active in the following years, serving as director of the National Indian Institute, as a professor of sociology at the College of the City of New York, and as president of the Institute of Ethnic Affairs. He was also the author of several books, including *Indians of the Americas* (1947), *Patterns and Ceremonials of the Indians of the Southwest* (1949), and *From Every Zenith* (1963). He died in Taos, New Mexico, on May 8, 1968. □

# Robin George Collingwood

**The English historian and philosopher Robin George Collingwood (1889-1943) did important historical research on Roman Britain and made original contributions to esthetics, the philosophy of history, and the philosophy of mind.**

B orn at Coniston, Lancashire, R.G. Collingwood received his early education from his father, a painter and a friend and biographer of John Ruskin. Under Ruskin's precepts Collingwood was trained in the arts and crafts in addition to the classical languages. At the age of 14 he went to Rugby to prepare for college. He did brilliant work at Oxford and was elected to a fellowship at Pembroke College in 1912. During World War I he worked in the Admiralty Intelligence Division in London; after the armistice he returned to teaching at Oxford and was elected Waynflete professor of metaphysical philosophy in 1934.

Throughout his teaching career Collingwood spent his summers working on archeological digs in Britain. He regarded this work as a laboratory in which he could test his philosophical theories about the logic of inquiry and about the relationship between history and philosophy. His many publications in this field culminated in his contribution to the *Oxford History of England*.

Collingwood's philosophical work falls into three periods. There was first a youthful period in which he sought to free himself from the realist doctrines of his Oxford teachers. This culminated in his *Speculum mentis,* a comparative study of five forms of experience arranged in an ascending order of truth: art, religion, science, history, and philosophy.

In the middle period of his writing Collingwood produced *Essay on Philosophical Method.* He expanded the insights of this work in *The Idea of Nature* and *The Idea of History.* His overall conclusion was that it is the task of philosophy to explore the presuppositions by which earlier cultures produced their characteristic views on nature and life. The implication is that once the historical part of this task is done, one can raise philosophical questions about the adequacy or truth value of the varying presuppositions. In his last period Collingwood seemed to deny philosophy any independent role—it is absorbed into the history of thought.

Collingwood's work in the last 5 years of his life shows defects and inconsistencies that can be traced in some measure to his rapidly declining health. In 1938 he suffered the first of a series of strokes which finally incapacitated him. He died on Jan. 9, 1943, leaving a number of manuscripts and incompleted works, some of which were published by his literary executors.

## Further Reading

Collingwood's *An Autobiography* (1939) follows his maxim that "all history is the history of thought" and describes the development of his ideas with only scattered biographical details. Alan Donagan, *The Later Philosophy of R. G. Collingwood* (1962), is the best critical work on Collingwood and also contains a bibliography.

## Additional Sources

Collingwood, R. G. (Robin George), *An autobiography,* Oxford etc.: Oxford University Press, 1978. □

# Edward Knight Collins

**The American shipowner Edward Knight Collins (1802-1878) operated transatlantic and coastwise packet ships and was the leading figure in America's most ambitious challenge to Great Britain's merchant marine supremacy in the 19th century.**

E dward Collins was born on Aug. 5, 1802, in Truro, Mass. He was a member of an old New England family which had emigrated to Massachusetts from England in the 1630s. His father, Israel Gross Collins, was a sailing ship captain, and Edward followed his father's example in choosing a maritime career.

In 1817 Collins moved to New York City, where he was to live for the rest of his life. He worked in a mercantile house for a time and then made several voyages to the West Indies. He later went into business with his father, conducting a general shipping and commission firm. The association with his father brought some profits, which Collins used to begin his lifetime career as a shipowner.

The first venture of Collins was the purchase of a line of packet ships that sailed between New York and Veracruz, Mexico. In 1831 he acquired a similar packet line in the coastwise trade with New Orleans, his ships carrying general merchandise to the South and returning laden with raw cotton. In 1837 he established a sailing line in the transatlantic commerce between New York and Liverpool. The Liverpool line was known as the "Dramatic Line" because the vessels were all named after leading stage actors.

Collins soon became convinced that the future of commercial shipping lay with steam, not sail. Once England awarded Samuel Cunard a subsidy mail contract in 1838 to underwrite expected losses on Cunard's proposed steam line, the age of steamships had begun. Collins became an enthusiastic lobbyist for American subsidies similar to those

# Eileen Collins

**On February 4, 1995, at 12:22 a.m. in Cape Canaveral, Florida, thousands of people held their breath as Lieutenant Colonel Eileen Collins (born 1956) launched the U.S. Space Shuttle Discovery into the heavens on her first mission as pilot.**

Flames burst from the shuttle's engines as smoke enveloped the launch pad. During the shuttle's violent ascent, acceleration is so forceful that the astronauts are pinned against their seats and breathe with difficulty as G-forces pound against their chests. The shuttle approaches an escape velocity of 3,000 miles per hour and later accelerates to 17,500 miles per hour. From her position inside the craft, U.S. Air Force Lieutenant Colonel Eileen Collins handled the takeoff with extraordinary confidence.

Perhaps piloting the shuttle seemed to be all in a day's work for Collins because she had rehearsed the takeoff hundreds of times in a simulator. She spent the previous month practicing takeoffs and landings for up to 14 hours per day and, during the previous six months, spent an average of three hours per day in the simulator. But the morning of February 4 was the real thing, and there was no room for error. Fear and excitement undoubtedly swelled in Collins as the price of failure was contemplated.

## First Woman to Pilot Shuttle

Although Collins's trip was the Discovery's twentieth flight and the sixty-seventh for the shuttle program, the voyage was a special one for a few reasons. First, the Discovery made a history-making rendezvous with the Russian Mir space station. Second, Collins was the first female pilot ever to fly the shuttle. Nineteen other women have been astronauts, beginning with Sally Ride in 1983, and have performed research and made space walks and repairs, but Collins was the first to actually pilot the craft.

Collins's responsibility for the flight included steering the space ship by firing small rockets, monitoring flight instruments, and handling the function of radar and navigation systems. Although the space shuttle was like no other aircraft she had ever been in, she mentioned in an interview with *Ad Astra* magazine before the launch, "I would say that every aircraft I have ever flown will have some transfer to flying the space shuttle." And Colonel Collins has flown many planes, logging over 4,000 hours in 30 different types of aircraft.

With all the flying experience Collins has under her belt, it would seem that she has been flying all of her life, but in fact, she had never stepped into a plane until she was 19 years old. Since Collins's parents could not afford the flying lessons she longed to take, she took part-time jobs to save up the $1,000 she would need. Alan Davis, the retired air force pilot who trained her, told the *New York Times*, "She was very quick to pick it up. She was very quiet and very reserved, but also very determined and very methodical."

enjoyed by Cunard. In 1847 Congress agreed to such a plan, authorizing the secretary of the Navy to contract with Collins and his associates for the creation of an Amerian version of the Cunard line.

The venture was ill-starred from the first, poorly advised and poorly managed. Five steamships were to be built, all designed for possible conversion to warships. The Collins line (officially the New York and Liverpool Mail Steamship Company) was to run 20 round-trip passenger voyages annually for 10 years, for which the line was to receive $385,000 a year in Federal funds. But the ships cost almost twice the original estimates, and the company was in financial difficulties from the first. Although the ships drew many passengers and were very swift vessels (they were superior to their British competition), the firm lost money consistently even after the subsidy was paid. Poor management, higher than anticipated operating costs, and a series of maritime disasters spelled failure for the effort to outdo British merchant marine supremacy. In 1858 Collins dissolved his company. He died in New York City on Jan. 22, 1878.

## Further Reading

For an account of the Collins shipping line see William E. Bennett (pseudonym of Warren Armstrong), *The Collins Story* (1957). Additional information and good background material are available in William S. Lindsay, *History of Merchant Shipping and Ancient Commerce* (4 vols., 1874-1876); in Robert G. Albion, *The Rise of New York Port* (1939); and in John G. B. Hutchins, *The American Maritime Industries and Public Policy, 1789-1914* (1941). □

## Dreams of Flight

Collins's flying lessons were a long awaited gift to herself. Since her childhood, she loved going to the airport with her parents and sitting on the hood of their car to watch planes take off as she drank root beer. They would also go to Harris Hill and watch gliders sail off cliffs while she told herself that one day she would be in the cockpit when one of those planes took off. As a teen, she read military books on flying, but she recalled even earlier memories of a love for flight. In fifth grade, she read an article on the pros and cons of the space program. "Even then, I couldn't understand why we shouldn't spend money on the space program," she told *Ad Astra*.

Those were big dreams for a little girl born in the small town of Elmira, New York. Collins is the second of four children of James and Rose Marie Collins, who separated when she was nine years old. Part of Collins's childhood was subsequently spent in public housing, living on food stamps. Apparently, in school, she made a favorable impression on her teachers. Her high school chemistry instructor still remembers exactly where she sat in his class. He told the *New York Times,* "Second seat, second row," pointing to a picture of a shy, long-haired girl in a yearbook.

Collins graduated from Elmira Free Academy in 1974 and registered at Corning Community College. She received her associate's degree in math two years later and had intentions of being a math teacher. She also went on to receive a bachelor of arts in math and economics from Syracuse University. Some interesting things, however,

were happening elsewhere in the world. In the same year she graduated from high school, the U.S. Navy accepted its first female pilots. Two years later, the U.S. Air Force accepted their first female pilots. And in 1978, they chose four female applicants from the 120 who applied for Air Force Undergraduate Pilot Training. One of the accepted applicants was Collins.

Also in 1978, the National Aeronautics and Space Administration (NASA) began accepting women into the space program. Ironically, the first female astronauts did their parachute training at Vance Air Force Base in Oklahoma at the same time Collins was there for air force training. Although always intrigued with space, it was the first time Collins realized that being an astronaut was possible. She later credited the other female astronauts who have gone before her. She told *Ad Astra,* "The fact that women have been in the NASA program since 1978 has helped me assimilate to the program. The first female astronauts were so excellent that it really paved the way for the future of women." Nevertheless, Collins felt there was tremendous pressure on her and commented in the *New York Times,* "I realize I can't afford to fail because I would be hurting other women's chances of being a pilot."

After graduating from pilot training in 1979 at the age of 23, Collins became the first female flight instructor. From 1979 to 1990, she taught in Oklahoma, California, and Colorado. In addition to giving soldiers flying lessons, she was also a math instructor at the U.S. Air Force Academy in Colorado Springs. A student as well as a teacher, she took pilot training classes at the Air Force Institute of Technology and, at age 32, was the second woman ever to attend Air Force Test Pilot School. Collins also received a master of science degree in operations research from Stanford University in 1986 and a master of arts degree in space systems management from Webster University in 1989.

## Chosen by NASA

Then, in January of 1990, NASA selected Collins to become an astronaut. According to NASA biographical data, she was initially assigned to Orbiter systems support. She also served on the astronaut support team responsible for Orbiter prelaunch checkout, final launch configuration, crew ingress/egress, and landing/recovery, and as a spacecraft communicator (CAPCOM). She was later, of course, made space shuttle pilot for the Mir space station rendezvous flight in February of 1995.

The Mir space station is an artificial Russian satellite designed to revolve in a fixed orbit and serve as a base for scientific observation and experimentation. Eventually, the Mir will be permanently occupied, and space shuttles will transport astronauts to and from the station. This mission of February 4, 1995, was a dry run to lay the groundwork for an actual landing scheduled for the summer of that year. Collins explained the mission to a reporter in *Ad Astra:* "The best comparison to what we are going to do is the Apollo 10 mission that descended to within 15 kilometers of the lunar surface, and the Apollo 11 mission that landed on the Moon." The rendezvous continued a trend of international cooperation between Russia and the United States.

Space exploration has also strengthened relationships between other nations, including Canada, Japan, and European countries.

A change in the Spacehab module that the shuttle would be carrying into orbit caused a postponing of the launch, which was originally scheduled for May of 1994. Although the nine-month delay was frustrating, Collins took the extra time to learn the Russian language and familiarize herself with the Mir. Then, just before the next scheduled flight, there was a failure in one of the three navigation units required to control the shuttle's steering. Engineers worked around the clock, and NASA delayed the trip another 24 hours. When the launch finally took place, the astronauts discovered a minor propellant leak on one of the jet thrusters. Though the leak would be manageable, the Russian astronauts became worried about the Mir's exposure to damage by such a close encounter and rearranged the rendezvous for a safer 1,000 feet, instead of the scheduled 38 feet. NASA scientists negotiated with the Russians, reassuring them that their space station was in no danger. The Russians were eventually convinced and agreed to the original 38 foot close encounter. Throughout the obstacles and delays, Collins handled the pressure with amazing calmness.

Collins credits her rugged astronaut training for preparing her for adversity. Although her pilot experience helped, NASA stretched her far beyond anything she thought possible. She recounted in *Ad Astra*, "20% of our basic astronaut training takes us through land and water survival, parachute training, field trips to all the NASA centers, and geology field trips. . . . About 70% of our basic course concerns learning the space shuttle [and] another part is called enrichment training where we learn a little bit about everything—oceanography, the history of the space program, astronomy, orbital mechanics, weather, medicine—all taught at various intervals to give us a feel for the big picture."

Collins later noted that the simulator was one of the hardest parts of her training. During an eight-minute artificial launch, trainers input up to 20 different malfunctions. She remarked in *Ad Astra*, "You have to prioritize and organize quickly: What's wrong? How to fix it? Find the procedure, then do the procedure. Then you get interrupted with another malfunction. Then you have to decide which one will 'kill me' now, in ten seconds, or in minutes."

As hard as training is in the 1990s, it was much more barbaric 30 years before. Concerning the training of the 1960s, the *Irish Times* wrote, "[The astronauts later claimed] the physical and psychological tests were devised by a sadist. . . . [They] rode exercise bikes to exhaustion, swallowed a meter-long rubber hose, drank radioactive water and were prodded, tilted, and spun until they couldn't stand." Such tests were given to the women who were almost the first female astronauts and who share a special relationship with Collins. Known as FLATS (fellow lady astronaut trainees), the 26 women were tested in 1961 along with male astronauts. Thirteen of them passed, becoming known as the Mercury 13. NASA, however, canceled the project before the women ever soared into the galaxy. Sarah

Ratley, one of the Mercury 13, told the *Kansas City Star* after Collins's takeoff, "We all knew Eileen and just kind of felt like we were there going up with her saying, 'Go, go, go.' It was a feeling as if we had finally made it."

In April of 1994, the FLATS had an official gathering, to which they had invited Collins. She returned the favor by offering the 11 surviving women special seats for the Mir launch. Collins told a Cable News Network (CNN) correspondent, "I feel like so many of them have become friends of mine now, and I'm sort of carrying on their dream." She offered to carry with her on the shuttle such mementos as a scarf worn by aviator Amelia Earhart, known for various female "firsts," and a pilot's license signed by Orville Wright for the famed flier Evelyn (Bobbi) Trout in 1924. Everyone gave something except Jerri Truhill, who explained on National Public Radio (NPR), "I told [Collins] she was carrying my dreams, that was all that was necessary."

When the space shuttle thundered into the horizon early in the morning on February 4, 1995, some of the onlookers cried. Women have come a long way in the field of aviation and astronautics, and Collins took them one step further.

## Further Reading

*Ad Astra*, July/August 1994, p. 30; January/February 1995, pp. 32-36.
*Detroit Free Press*, January 30, 1995, p. 5A.
*Gannet News Service*, February 11, 1995.
*Houston Chronicle*, February 11, 1995, p. 16.
*Irish Times*, February 11, 1995, p. 8.
*Kansas City Star*, February 16, 1995, p. C1.
*New York Times*, February 1, 1995, p. A7; February 5, 1995, p. 15;
*Pittsburgh Post-Gazette*, February 4, 1995, p. A6; February 9, 1995, p. A1.
*U.S. News & World Report*, February 13, 1995, p. 22.
*Washington Post*, February 3, 1995, p. A8; February 4, 1995, p. A3.
*Washington Times*, March 12, 1995, p. A2.
*Working Woman*, February 1995, p. 14.
Additional information for this profile was obtained from *The Week in Review*, CNN, February 12, 1995; *Weekend Edition*, NPR, February 11, 1995; and NASA biographical data, January 1994. □

# Marva Collins

**Schoolteacher Marva Collins's (born 1936) dedication to Chicago's Westside Preparatory School, which she opened in 1975, moved the producers of television's *60 Minutes* to do a feature on her and inspired a made-for-TV film.**

Teachers need nothing more than "books, a blackboard, and a pair of legs that will last the day," Marva Collins told Dan Hurley in *50 Plus* magazine. These three things were essentially all that Collins had when she opened the Westside Preparatory School in Chicago, Illinois, in 1975 with the $5,000 she had contributed to her pension fund. Disillusioned after teaching in the public school system for 16 years, Collins decided to leave and open a school that would welcome students who had been rejected by other schools and labeled disruptive and "unteachable." She had seen too many children pass through an ineffective school system in which they were given impersonal teachers, some of whom came to school chemically impaired.

A firm believer in the value of a teacher's time spent with a student, Collins rejected the notion that the way to solve the problems faced by U.S. schools was to spend more money. Collins also shunned the audiovisual aids so common in other classrooms because she believed that they created an unnecessary distance between the teacher and the student. By offering a plethora of individual attention tempered with strict discipline and a focus on reading skills, Collins was able to raise the test scores of many students, who in turn went on to college and excelled. "It takes an investment of time to help your children mature and develop successfully," declared Collins in *Ebony*.

### Indelible Impression Left by Father

Collins was born Marva Delores Nettles on August 31, 1936, in Monroeville, Alabama. Collins has described her childhood as "wonderful" and filled with material comforts that included riding in luxury cars and having her own horse. Her father, Alex Nettles, was a successful merchant, cattle buyer, and undertaker. He lavished attention and

praise on his daughter and her younger sister, Cynthia. By challenging Collins to use her mind, he instilled in her a strong sense of pride and self-esteem.

"[My father] never presumed that any task was too challenging for me to try nor any concept too difficult for me to grasp," noted Collins in *Ebony*. "He gave me assignments that helped build my confidence and gave me a sense of responsibility." As a child, Collins managed the store's inventory, kept track of invoices, and deposited the store's money in the bank. From these early experiences, she developed the philosophy she would use later in life to teach children, one that entailed providing encouragement and positive reinforcement.

Collins attended Clark College in Atlanta, Georgia. After graduating in 1957 with a bachelor's degree in secretarial sciences, she returned to Alabama to teach typing, shorthand, bookkeeping, and business law at Monroe County Training School. Having never intended to be a teacher, she left the profession in 1959 to take a position as a medical secretary at Mount Sinai Hospital in Chicago. While in the city she met Clarence Collins, a draftsman, whom she married on September 2, 1960.

### Left Teaching to Start Her Own School

In 1961 Collins returned to teaching as a full-time substitute in Chicago's inner-city schools because she missed helping youngsters discover the joy of learning. Working against a tide of indifferent teachers who, in Collins' words, were creating "more welfare recipients" soon left her weary and angry. With her pension money and the support of her husband, Collins opened the Westside Preparatory School in the basement of Daniel Hale Williams University.

Collins made a point of not accepting federal funds because she did not want to abide by all the regulations that such backing required. Craving more independence than she had in the university setting, Collins soon moved the school into the second floor of her home, which she and her husband had renovated to accommodate approximately twenty children ranging from four to fourteen years old. Located in one of Chicago's poorest neighborhoods, the school was eventually moved to its own building near Collins's home. Shortly after this move, enrollment increased to over two hundred students.

### The Media Focus on Collins

Collins started attracting media attention in 1977 after an article on her and the Westside Preparatory School appeared in the *Chicago Sun-Times*. Several national publications printed her story, and she was featured on the popular television program *60 Minutes* in an interview with Morley Safer. In 1981 CBS presented a Hallmark Hall of Fame special entitled *The Marva Collins Story*, starring Cicely Tyson.

Late in 1980 Collins was considered for the post of secretary of education by U.S. President Ronald Reagan. Preferring to continue teaching and running her school, Collins announced that she would not accept the position if it were offered to her. She believed that she could make a bigger difference by working with the children in Chicago than she could by immersing herself in the paperwork the job in Washington, D.C., would surely bring. The Chicago school board and the Los Angeles County school system also offered her positions. Again, she declined.

Collins's method of teaching, spelled out in her 1982 book *Marva Collins' Way,* provides students with a nurturing atmosphere in which they learn the basics—reading, math, and language skills. Gym class and recess are considered superfluous. When writing about Collins and her school, many journalists comment on the familiar sight of young children reading such classics as *Aesop's Fables* and works by William Shakespeare and Geoffrey Chaucer. Each day students write papers and memorize a quotation of their choice. In addition, they are expected to read a new book every two weeks and to report on it.

Collins guides all of this activity with a strong dose of love and personal concern for each student. Any child who has to be disciplined understands that it is the behavior, not the child himself, that is objectionable. In an interview in the *Instructor,* Collins pointed out that "teacher attitude is very important" and that she believed that the "children should be given a lot of my time."

## Collins and School Criticized

In 1982, however, Collins was assailed by criticism from several fronts. Charges against her ranged from accepting federal funds—she had always adamantly claimed that she would not—to reports that she had exaggerated her students' test scores. An independent investigation revealed that Collins received $69,000 through the Comprehensive Employment and Training Act (CETA). Collins refuted these charges early in 1982 as a guest on the *Phil Donahue Show,* during which she claimed that the CETA money had come to her through a social services agency and that she had no idea the money had originated in Washington, D.C.

A majority of the parents of Westside's students rallied behind her, declaring that they were pleased with the work Collins was doing with their children. Support also came from Morley Safer who had stayed in contact with Collins after her appearance on *60 Minutes.* In the March 8, 1982, issue of *Newsweek,* Safer was quoted as saying: "I'm convinced that Marva Collins is one hell of a teacher."

Kevin Ross, a former Creighton University basketball star, would no doubt agree with Safer. Ross came to the Westside Preparatory School in the fall of 1982 because he had not acquired basic education skills after four years of college. Working with Collins, Ross was able to double his reading and math scores and triple his language score within one school year.

Collins chose Ross to deliver the commencement address at Westside's eighth grade graduation. He was quoted in *Newsweek* as telling the graduating class to "learn, learn, and learn some more" so that the debate on the potential of inner-city school children would become "as obsolete as covered wagons on the expressway." Others also support Collins's work. She received donations from many individuals, most notably rock star Prince, who became cofounder and honorary chairman of Collins's National Teacher Train-

ing Institute, created so Collins could retrain teachers using her methodology.

Shortly before her 50th birthday, Collins was interviewed by *50 Plus* magazine and was asked if she felt, after all the media hype, that she had passed her peak. She responded: "All of that means nothing, except what I get for the children. Those were fleeting moments. . . . Being a celebrity isn't important. It's what the children learn that's important." Material possessions are not what matters to Collins; what does matter is that she be remembered for her contribution to society. She expressed the fundamental purpose of her work when she told an *Instructor* correspondent, "I take the children no one else wants."

## Further Reading

*American Spectator,* April 1983.
*Black Enterprise,* June 1982.
*California Review,* April 1983.
*Chicago Tribune Book World,* October 31, 1982.
*Christian Science Monitor,* November 20, 1981; September 9, 1982.
*Ebony,* February 1985; August 1986; May 1990.
*Essence,* October 1981; November 1985.
*50 Plus,* June 1986.
*Good Housekeeping,* September 1978.
*Harper's Bazaar,* December 1981.
*Instructor,* January 1982.
*Jet,* November 6, 1980; October 4, 1982; February 7, 1983; July 29, 1985; August 10, 1987; August 1, 1988.
*Life,* spring 1990.
*Los Angeles Times Book Review,* December 12, 1982.
*Newsweek,* March 8, 1982; June 27, 1983.
*New York Times,* December 19, 1980; December 21, 1980; March 7, 1982; November 4, 1990.
*People,* December 11, 1978; February 21, 1983.
*Saturday Review,* April 14, 1979.
*Time,* December 26, 1977.
*TV Guide,* November 28, 1981.
*Variety,* June 18, 1986.
*Wall Street Journal,* March 15, 1981.
*Washington Monthly,* February 1980.
*Washington Post Book World,* November 14, 1982. □

# Michael Collins

**The Irish revolutionary leader Michael Collins (1890-1922) was a founder of the Irish Free State.**

Michael Collins was born near Clonakilty, County Cork, on Oct. 16, 1890. He was educated at local primary schools and went to London in 1906 to enter the civil service as a postal clerk. For 10 years Collins lived in London, where he became active in various Irish organizations, the most important of which was the Irish Republican Brotherhood (IRB), a secret society dedicated to the overthrow of British rule in Ireland.

Collins returned to Ireland in 1916 to take part in the Easter Rising and after its suppression was interned in North Wales with most of the other rebels. When the internees were released in December 1916, he went to Dublin, where his keen intelligence and dynamic energy soon secured him a position of leadership in the reviving revolutionary movement.

After their victory in the general election of December 1918, the revolutionaries established an Irish Parliament, Dail Eireann, in January 1919. The Dail proclaimed an Irish Republic and set up an executive to take over the government of the country. British attempts to suppress the republican movement were met with guerrilla warfare by the Irish Republican Army (IRA). Collins played the most important role in this struggle. As director of intelligence of the IRA, he crippled the British intelligence system in Ireland and replaced it with an effective Irish network. At the same time he performed other important military functions, headed the IRB, and, as minister of finance in the Republican government, successfully raised and disbursed large sums on behalf of the rebel cause. Despite constant efforts the British were unable to capture Collins or stop his work. The "Big Fellow" became an idolized and near-legendary figure in Ireland and won a formidable reputation in Britain and abroad for ruthlessness, resourcefulness, and daring.

After the truce of July 1921, Collins reluctantly agreed to President Eamon De Valera's request to serve on the peace-making delegation headed by Arthur Griffith. During the autumn negotiations in London, the British government firmly rejected any settlement that involved recognition of the republic. Instead its representatives offered Dominion status for Ireland, with the right of exclusion for loyalist Northern Ireland. Collins decided to accept these terms, in the belief that rejection meant renewal of the war and quick defeat for Ireland and that the proposed treaty would soon lead to unity and complete freedom for his country. Using these arguments, he and Griffith persuaded their fellow delegates to sign the treaty on Dec. 6, 1921, and Dail Eireann to approve it on Jan. 7, 1922.

De Valera and many Republicans refused to accept the agreement, however, contending that it constituted a betrayal of the republic and would mean continued subjection to Britain. As the British evacuated southern Ireland, Collins and Griffith did their best to maintain order and implement the treaty but found their efforts frustrated by the opposition of an armed Republican minority. Collins sought desperately to pacify the antitreaty forces without abandoning the treaty but found it impossible to make a workable compromise.

In late June 1922, after the population had endorsed the settlement in an election, Collins agreed to use force against the dissidents. This action precipitated civil war, a bitter conflict in which the forces of the infant Irish Free State eventually overcame the extreme Republicans in May 1923. Collins did not live to see the end of the war; he was killed in ambush in West Cork on Aug. 22, 1922, just 10 days after the death of Arthur Griffith.

Much of Collins's success as a revolutionary leader can be ascribed to his realism and extraordinary efficiency, but there was also a marked strain of idealism and humanity in his character which appealed to friend and foe alike. The treaty that cost him his life did not end partition, as he had hoped, but it did make possible the peaceful attainment of full political freedom for most of Ireland.

## Further Reading

Frank O'Connor (pseud. of Michael O'Donovan), *The Big Fellow: Michael Collins and the Irish Revolution* (1937; rev. ed. 1965), offers penetrating insight into Collins's complex personality. Piaras Béaslaí, *Michael Collins and the Making of a New Ireland* (2 vols., 1926), is the most detailed biography. Rex Taylor, *Michael Collins* (1958), fills in important details of the treaty negotiations.

## Additional Sources

Coogan, Tim Pat, *Michael Collins: a biography,* London: Hutchinson, 1990.

Dwyer, T. Ryle, *Michael Collins: "the man who won the war,"* Cork: Mercier Press, 1990.

Dwyer, T. Ryle, *Michael Collins and the treaty: his differences with de Valera,* Dublin: Mercier Press, 1981.

Feehan, John M., *The shooting of Michael Collins,* Dublin: Mercier Press, 1981.

*Michael Collins,* Dublin: Gill and Macmillan, 1980.

Ryan, Meda, *The day Michael Collins was shot,* Swords, Co. Dublin, Ireland: Poolbeg, 1989. □

# William Collins

**The English poet William Collins (1721-1759) excelled in the descriptive or allegorical ode. He also**

wrote classical odes and elegies and lyrics marked by delicate and pensive melody.

William Collins was born on Dec. 25, 1721, in Chichester. His father was a prosperous merchant who was twice elected mayor. In 1733 Collins entered Winchester, intending to study for the clergy. There he began his lifelong friendship with Joseph Warton and his own poetic career. In 1739 his short poem ''To a Lady Weeping'' was published in the *Gentleman's Magazine.* The following year he entered Queen's College, Oxford, but soon transferred to Magdalene. While at Oxford, he published his *Persian Eclogues* (1742), the only one of his works that was highly regarded during his lifetime.

Having abandoned his plan to enter the clergy, Collins left Oxford. With a small inheritance from his mother, in 1744 he settled in London to become a man of letters. Here he frequented the coffee houses and made friends with David Garrick and Samuel Johnson, who described him as a man ''with many projects in his head and little money in his pocket.'' Among Collins's many projects which came to nothing were a commentary on Aristotle's *Poetics* and a history of the Renaissance.

In 1746 Collins and Warton planned the joint publication of their odes, but Robert Dodsley, to whom they submitted their manuscript, judged that Collins's work would have little public appeal and published only Warton's. Although Collins's *Odes on Several Descriptive and Allegorical Subjects* was soon undertaken by another publisher, Dodsley's rejection and the subsequent failure of the *Odes* mortified Collins deeply.

Collins continued to write and to practice the pictorial technique announced in the *Odes.* He made literary friendships with James Thomson and with lesser writers such as John Home and Christopher Smart. His most personal poem, the *Ode Occasioned by the Death of Mr. Thomson* (1749), was the last of his works published during his lifetime. Shortly after Thomson's death he sent John Home a manuscript of *An Ode on the Popular Superstitions of the Highlands of Scotland,* a superb poem which anticipates many of the attitudes of the romantic revival.

About this time Collins received a legacy from his uncle and retired to Chichester to carry out some of his ambitious projects. But he became threatened with insanity and sought relief in a trip abroad. When this failed to restore his health, he was committed to an institution. He was later released to the care of his sister, but he never recovered. Collins died on June 12, 1759.

## Further Reading

There are two full-length biographies of Collins: H. W. Garrod, *Collins* (1928), and Edward Gay Ainsworth, Jr., *Poor Collins: His Life, His Art, and His Influence* (1937). Chester F. Chapin, *Personification in Eighteenth-Century Poetry* (1955), offers a fine analysis of Collins's poetic technique. □

# William Wilkie Collins

**The English author William Wilkie Collins (1824-1889) wrote intricately plotted novels of sensational intrigue which helped establish the conventions of modern detective fiction.**

Wilkie Collins was born in London on Jan. 8, 1824, the son of a successful painter. Leaving school in his sixteenth year, he was apprenticed to a tea importer but had little enthusiasm for business. As a young man, he both wrote and painted. He published a number of articles and stories, exhibited a picture at the Royal Academy, and was an early supporter of the Pre-Raphaelite Brotherhood. His first published novel, *Antonina, or the Fall of Rome* (1850), was modeled on the historical fiction of the popular Edward Bulwer-Lytton.

Collins met Charles Dickens in 1851 and became one of his closest friends. Most of his early stories and novels appeared in Dickens's magazines *Household Words* and *All the Year Round,* and through participation in Dickens's elaborate amateur theatricals he was encouraged to try his hand at drama. However, Collins's melodramas, although popular in their day, are now largely forgotten.

In the novels *Basil* (1852), *Hide and Seek* (1854), and *The Dead Secret* (1857), Collins placed sensational incident in a realistic contemporary middle-class setting and developed the technique of gradually unfolding a mystery introduced at the beginning of the story.

*The Woman in White* (1860), based on an incident that had occurred in France some 70 years earlier, marked the maturing of Collins's art and was an immediate popular success on both sides of the Atlantic. In it a scheme to rob a woman of her fortune turns on the existence of a mysterious double who dies and is substituted for the victim. The extraordinarily complex maneuvers of the villain are made even more mystifying by Collins's device of narrating the events through a series of limited observers. Although *Armadale* (1866) contained no mystery, its plot was even more complex and its atmosphere even richer. *The Moonstone* (1868) was Collins's greatest achievement and set a permanent standard for detective fiction. Told, like *The Woman in White,* from a number of limited points of view, it dealt with the recovery by three Brahmins of a diamond stolen from an Indian idol.

After *Man and Wife* (1870), a novel on the problem of the marriage laws, Collins's works concentrate on social issues. But his style was not suited to this type of novel, and he was also becoming deeply addicted to opium after taking laudanum for rheumatic gout.

Collins never married but maintained a rather enigmatic relationship with two women, one of whom lived with him for almost 30 years. He died on Sept. 23, 1889, after prolonged illness.

## Further Reading

The standard biography of Collins is Kenneth Robinson, *Wilkie Collins* (1952). Also of interest are Stewart Marsh Ellis, *Wilkie Collins, Le Fanu and Others* (1931), and the chapter on Collins in Malcom Elwin, *Victorian Wallflowers: A Panoramic Survey of the Popular Literary Periodicals* (1934).

## Additional Sources

Ashley, Robert Paul, *Wilkie Collin,* Folcroft, Pa. Folcroft Library Editions, 1974.

Ashley, Robert Paul, *Wilkie Collins,* Brooklyn, N.Y.: Haskell House Publishers, 1976.

Ashley, Robert Paul, *Wilkie Collins,* Norwood, Pa.: Norwood Editions, 1976.

Clarke, William M. (William Malpas), *The secret life of Wilkie Collins,* Chicago: I.R. Dee, 1991.

Peters, Catherine, *The king of inventors: a life of Wilkie Collins,* Princeton, N.J.: Princeton University Press, 1993.

Robinson, Kenneth, *Wilkie Collins: a biography,* London: Davis-Poynter, 1974.

Sayers, Dorothy L. (Dorothy Leigh), *Wilkie Collins: a critical and biographical study,* Toledo, Ohio: The Friends of the University of Toledo Libraries, 1977. □

# Fernando Collor de Mello

**Brazilian businessman and politician Fernando Collor de Mello (born 1949) became that nation's youngest president in 1990. He brought a dynamic, effervescent style to the leadership of a nation saddled with enormous debt and pressing social problems.**

Fernando Collor de Mello was elected president of Brazil on December 15, 1989, and inaugurated on March 15, 1990. A former journalist and media entrepreneur, Collor was the first popularly-elected president of Brazil since 1960, and, at age 40, that republic's youngest chief executive ever.

Born in Rio de Janeiro on August 12, 1949, Collor was raised largely in the poverty-ridden interior state of Alagoas, far from the centers of Brazilian power. His father, a wealthy businessman, served as governor of Alagoas, and other members of the Collor family served in government and business in positions of influence. He studied economics and journalism at the state's Federal University in Brasilia and began his career within the Collor family empire. Phenomenally successful as a media businessman, Collor gathered both wealth and renown, and gained some international notoriety as somewhat of a playboy. He first married Lilibeth Monteiro de Carvalho, a teenage aristocratic heiress in 1975, with whom he had two sons, but they divorced in 1981. He entered politics in 1979 when he became mayor of Maceió, capital city of Alagoas. He served ably in that capacity until 1982, and then decided to take advantage of the policy of *abertura,* or gradual political democratization, permitted by General João Batista

Figueiredo, last of the five generals who ruled Brazil from 1964 to 1985.

In 1982 he was elected to the Brazilian Chamber of Deputies, serving the nation in Brasilia for four years as its youngest congressman, representing Alagoas. While in Congress his interest in, and official concern with, economic matters became marked, and he achieved sufficient publicity as a no-nonsense financial reformer. His special cause was the long-neglected northeast, including Alagoas, and he was easily elected governor of his home state in 1986. Meanwhile, in 1984, he had been remarried to Rosane Malta, a college freshman from Alagoa.

As governor, Fernando Collor won a reputation for his statewide economic reforms, focusing on administrative efficiency, campaigns against corruption, and championship of major new social welfare measures. Regardless of his own personal wealth and good looks, the energetic governor gained a strong and devoted following among his state's less-advantaged. A national reputation was assured for his prosecution of highly paid state bureaucrats, and he became known as "the hunter of the Maharajahs."

The young governor and his wife were the center of a Brazilian state "Camelot," his outgoing, charming personality enhanced by an almost fanatical devotion to physical fitness and sports—he was national karate champion, among other distinctions. Able to communicate easily in English, French, Spanish, and Italian as well as his native Portuguese, Collor was often in the company of distin-guished foreign visitors. He was, in short, something of a media event himself.

In 1989 Collor began his campaign for the presidency as candidate of the small National Reconstruction party, which controlled but five percent of the seats in Congress. Pledging to restructure the national economy, to protect the environment and ecology, and to initiate a responsible fiscal policy (which includes privatization of inefficient publicly-owned industries), Collor unleashed a media blitz unparalleled in Brazilian history. A bitter reaction by his two opponents revived long-standing class and religious antagonisms.

Although polls showed some erosion in support as the November 15 election approached, Collor's vision of "O Brasil Novo" ("The New Brazil") inspired enough voters of all social classes to lead the field of six candidates in the election, albeit with less than the constitutionally-mandated majority of votes cast.

Thus, a run-off election was scheduled for December 15, pitting Collor, an admirer of free-market economics and (more than any other Brazilian leader) the United States, against Leftist Luis "Lula" da Silva, candidate of the Workers' party. The final campaign was fierce and vitriolic, but despite Collor's elite status, his vision of a strong and modern Brazil, tied to the world's advanced democracies and combating both horrific inflation (up to 80 percent monthly) and government corruption, was sufficient to give him a slender electoral majority of 53 percent.

To help boost his image at home and give himself credibility abroad, the president-elect launched himself into a whirlwind of visits to foreign leaders. Following trips to neighboring Argentina, Paraguay, and Uruguay, his next official venue was—pointedly—the United States, where he conferred with President George Bush and other government and international lending organization officials. He then continued on, maintaining an exhausting pace, to Tokyo, Moscow, Bonn, Rome, Paris, London, Lisbon, and Madrid. All made for colorful and heartening headlines in Brazil while generating goodwill and initial trade and debt talks abroad. Somehow, amidst this whirlwind, he also restructured Brazil's executive branch, reducing the 23 Cabinet departments to 12 "super ministries." The key Ministry of the Economy he surprisingly gave to 36-year-old economist Zelia Cardoso de Mello.

By the date of his March 15 inauguration it was clear that Collor was poised to act immediately on two crucial fronts, both of them sensitive in the extreme. Announcing that "Brazil's efforts with the Third World have not given us anything concrete," Collor signaled a major shift in Brazilian foreign policy designed to bond and integrate the nation with the United States (and other nations of the hemisphere) and the other important Western industrialized states. Domestically, in an attempt to curtail inflation, he announced a return to the *cruzeiro* unit of currency and a draconian package of economic austerity measures. Within this package was abandonment of wage and price indexing, temporary freezes of both, a crackdown on tax-dodgers, severe paring of the ranks of the federal bureaucracy, a freeze of 18 months on bank accounts, and a start on renegotiating Brazil's $110 billion foreign debt.

Collor confronted truly daunting problems, but he did so with a stronger rating in the polls than he enjoyed on election day, and many Brazilians were betting that his youth, optimism, "can do" attitude, and seemingly boundless energy would triumph. In 1991 Collor focused government attention on the need for creating home reservations for Brazil's native peoples. He also mounted a campaign urging the Group of Seven, the creditor nations, to help Brazil protect the Amazon Rainforests.

His reform efforts failing to produce progress in the eyes of the Brazilian public, Collor was impeached by the Chamber of Deputies on corruption charges in the fall of 1992. Before the trial began in December, and maintaining his innocence, he stepped aside to allow Vice-President Itamar Franco to become acting president. At the opening of his impeachment trial before the Brazilian Senate, Collor announced his resignation. He was convicted of corruption charges by a vote of 76 to 3. He was then barred from holding public office for eight years, and also faced possible criminal prosecution. In 1994, Collor was exonerated by the highest court in the land of all charges brought against him.

## Further Reading

Information about Fernando Collor de Mello is scarce, but some can be obtained from the Brazilian Embassy, the *New York Times,* and *Times of the Americas,* as well as Brazilian newspapers. For recent background, see E. Bradford Burns, *History of Brazil* (1987), and the citation of Collor in *Current Biography Yearbook* (1990). His acquittal is reported on in the Dec. 24, 1994 issue of *Time.* ☐

# Samuel Colt

**The American inventor and manufacturer Samuel Colt (1814-1862) first developed and popularized the multishot pistol, or revolver, which found wide use in the last half of the 19th century, especially in the American West.**

Samuel Colt was born in Hartford, Conn., the son of a prosperous cotton and woolen manufacturer. In 1824 his father sent him to work in one of his dyeing and bleaching establishments; Colt attended school at the same time. His behavior in school, however, was such that his father sought to discipline him by sending him on a sea voyage as an ordinary seaman. It was a one-year trip to India and the Orient, and it was apparently on this voyage that young Colt began to work on a revolving pistol. On his return he worked for a year in his father's bleachery and then left to travel on his own. Little is known of his activities for the next few years, but for at least a part of that time he billed himself as "Dr. Coult" and gave popular lectures on chemistry and demonstrated the effects of laughing gas.

Colt continued to work on his idea for a pistol and by 1831 had constructed at least two versions of it. By 1833 he had made both a pistol and a rifle on the principles which he later patented in the United States. Just about this time he

wandered off to Europe, where he acquired patents in both France and England. He returned to America in 1836 and received an American patent that year. The primary feature of his pistol was a revolving cartridge cylinder which automatically advanced one chamber when the gun was cocked.

During 1836 Colt built a factory in Paterson, N.J., to make his revolvers, but failing to receive a contract from the government he was unable to produce and sell the gun in quantity. Forced to sell the patent for his revolver, he turned to the problem of submarine warfare, receiving some financial help from the government to build an experimental submarine battery.

In 1846, with the declaration of war against Mexico, the demand for guns rose, and Colt was given a government contract for 1000 of his revolving pistols. Quickly he bought back his patents and opened an armory in New Haven, Conn. This new government patronage, coupled with the growing popularity of the gun in the West (where it was ideally suited to the new kind of horseback warfare being carried out against the Indians) brought Colt financial success at last. His exhibit at the 1851 Crystal Palace international exhibition in London caused widespread comment—for the excellence of his weapons, but most importantly for the example they gave of the mass production of interchangeable parts, which came to be known as the American system of manufactures. In 1855 Colt built his great armory at Hartford, Conn. (the largest private armory of its time), and he lived out his life as a prosperous and respected manufacturer.

## Further Reading

A good introduction to Colt's life and works is William B. Edwards, *The Story of Colt's Revolver: The Biography of Col. Samuel Colt* (1953). There is a vast literature on guns, written for buffs and collectors, much of which contains references to Colt and his pistol.

## Additional Sources

Barnard, Henry, *Armsmear: the home, the arm, and the armory of Samuel Colt: a memoria,* s.l.: s.n., 1976.

Grant, Ellsworth S., *The Colt legacy: the Colt Armory in Hartford, 1855-1980,* Providence, RI: Mowbray Co., 1982.

Keating, Bern, *The flamboyant Mr. Colt and his deadly six-shooter,* Garden City, N.Y.: Doubleday, 1978. □

# John Coltrane

**Saxophone player John Coltrane (1926-1967) created an innovative form of music that continues to influence modern jazz musicians, even more than two decades after his death.**

Legendary saxophone virtuoso John Coltrane continues to influence modern jazz even from the grave. Coltrane's death more than two decades ago only enhanced his reputation as an artist who brought whole new dimensions to a constantly innovative musical form. The "sheets of sound" and other bizarre stylistic elements that characterize Coltrane's jazz sparked heated debate at the time of their composition. Today his work is still either hailed as the very pinnacle of genius or dismissed as flights of monotonous self-indulgence. In an *Atlantic* retrospective, Edward Strickland calls Coltrane "the lone voice crying not in the wilderness but from some primordial chaos" whose music "evokes not only the jungle but all that existed before the jungle." The critic adds: "Coltrane was attempting to raise jazz from the saloons to the heavens. No jazzman had attempted so overtly to offer his work as a form of religious expression. . . . In his use of jazz as prayer and meditation Coltrane was beyond all doubt the principal spiritual force in music."

## "Last Great Leader"

Andrew White, himself a musician and transcriber of many of Coltrane's extended solos, told *Down Beat* magazine that the jazz industry "has been faltering artistically and financially ever since the death of John Coltrane. . . . Besides being one of our greatest saxophonists, improvisors, innovative and creative contributors, Coltrane *was* our last great leader. As a matter of fact, he was the *only* leader we've had in jazz who successfully maintained an evolutionary creative output as well as building a 'jazz star' image. *He merged the art and the money.*"

John William Coltrane, Jr., was born on the autumn equinox, September 23, 1926. He was raised in rural North Carolina, where he was exposed to the charismatic music of the Southern church—both of his grandfathers were minis-

ters. Coltrane's father also played several instruments as a hobby, so the young boy grew up in a musical environment. Quite on his own, he discovered jazz through the recordings of Count Basie and Lester Young. He persuaded his mother to buy him a saxophone, settling for an alto instead of a tenor because the alto was supposedly easier to handle.

## Showed Saxophone Talent Immediately

Coltrane showed a proficiency on the saxophone almost immediately. After briefly studying at the Granoff Studios and at the Ornstein School of Music in Philadelphia, he joined a typical cocktail lounge band. Then he played for a year with a Navy band in Hawaii before landing a spot in the Eddie Vinson ensemble in 1947. He was twenty-one at the time. For Vinson's band Coltrane performed on the tenor sax, but his ears were open to jazz greats on both alto and tenor, including Charlie Parker, Ben Webster, Coleman Hawkins, Lester Young, and Tab Smith. After a year with Vinson, Coltrane joined Dizzy Gillespie's group for one of his longest stints—four years. By that time he had "paid his dues" and was experimenting with composition and technical innovation.

The 1950s saw a great flowering of modern jazz with the advent of artists such as Miles Davis and Thelonious Monk. Coltrane played horn for both Davis and Monk; the latter showed him tricks of phrasing and harmony that deepened his control of his instrument. Coltrane can be heard playing tenor sax on Davis's famous Columbia album *Kind of Blue,* a work that hints of the direction Coltrane would ultimately follow. Strickland writes of the period:

"Coltrane's attempt 'to explore all the avenues' made him the perfect stylistic complement to Davis, with his cooler style, which featured sustained blue notes and brief cascades of sixteenths almost willfully retreating into silence, and also Monk, with his spare and unpredictable chords and clusters. Davis, characteristically, paid the tersest homage, when, on being told that his music was so complex that it required five saxophonists, he replied that he'd once had Coltrane."

### Exhausted Every Possibility for His Horn

What Coltrane called "exploring all the avenues" was essentially the quest to exhaust every possibility for his horn in the course of a song. He devoted himself to rapid runs in which individual notes were virtually indistinguishable, a style quickly labeled "sheets of sound." As Martin Williams puts it in *Saturday Review*, Coltrane "seemed prepared to gush out every conceivable note, run his way a step at a time through every complex chord, every extension, and every substitution, and go beyond that by reaching for sounds that no tenor saxophone had ever uttered before him." Needless to say, this music was not easily understood—critics were quick to find fault with its length and monotony—but it represented an evolution that was welcomed not only by jazz performers, but by composers and even rock musicians as well.

In 1960 Coltrane formed his own quartet in the saxophone-plus-rhythm mode. He was joined by McCoy Tyner on piano, Elvin Jones on drums, and Jimmy Garrison on bass, all of whom were as eager as Coltrane to explore an increasingly free idiom. Finally Coltrane was free to expand his music at will, and his solos took on unprecedented lengths as he experimented with modal foundations, pentatonic scales, and triple meter. His best-known work was recorded during this period, including "My Favorite Things," a surprising theme-and-variations piece based on the saccharine Richard Rogers tune from "The Sound of Music." In "My Favorite Things," writes Williams, Coltrane "encountered a popular song which had the same sort of structure he was interested in, a folk-like simplicity and incantiveness, and very little harmonic motion. . . . It became a best seller."

### Extent of Jazz Legacy Realized

By 1965 Coltrane was one of the most famous jazz artists alive, acclaimed alike in Europe, Japan, and the United States. Critics who had once dismissed his work "all but waved banners to show their devotion to him," to quote Strickland. Not surprisingly, the musician continued to experiment, even at the risk of alienating his growing audience. His work grew ever more complex, ametric, and improvisatorial. Coltrane explained his personal vision in *Newsweek*. "I have to feel that I'm after something," he said. "If I make money, fine. But I'd rather be striving. It's the striving, man, it's that I want."

Coltrane continued to perform and record even as advancing liver cancer left him racked with pain. He died at forty, only months after he cut his album *Expression*. The subsequent years have revealed the extent of his legacy to jazz, a legacy based on the spiritual quest for meaning and involvement between man, his soul, and the universe. Strickland concludes: "Those who criticize Coltrane's virtuosic profusion are of the same party as those who found Van Gogh's canvases 'too full of paint.' . . . In Coltrane, sound—often discordant, chaotic, almost unbearable— became the spiritual form of the man, an identification perhaps possible only with a wind instrument, with which the player is of necessity fused more intimately than with strings or percussion. . . . The whole spectrum of Coltrane's music—the world-weary melancholy and transcendental yearning that ultimately recall Bach more than Parker, the jungle calls and glossolalic shrieks, the whirlwind runs and spare elegies for murdered children and a murderous planet—is at root merely a suffering man's breath. The quality of that music reminds us that the root of the word *inspiration* is 'breathing upon.' This country has not produced a greater musician."

### Further Reading

Cole, Bill, *John Coltrane,* Schirmer, 1977.
Terkel, Studs, *Giants of Jazz,* Crowell, 1975.
*Atlantic,* December 1987.
*Down Beat,* July 12, 1979; September 1986.
*New Republic,* February 12, 1977.
*Newsweek,* July 31, 1967.
*New York Times,* July 18, 1967.
*Saturday Review,* September 16, 1987. □

# Padraic Colum

**The Irish-American author Padraic Colum (1881-1972), best known for his poetry and plays, was active in the Irish Literary Revival.**

Padraic Colum was born in County Longford and as a youth met many who had lived through the Great Famine, which ravaged Ireland in the mid-19th century. His father was master of the workhouse (home for the destitute), and thus Padraic saw much of the poverty and land hunger of the people. His uncle was a poultry dealer, and the young Colum traveled with him to fairs and markets. There he met the wandering people of the roads, ballad singers, and storytellers and found inspiration for some of the poems which have become part of Ireland's literary heritage. "She Moves through the Fair" and "The Old Woman of the Roads" are among his numerous simple lyrics which have often been anthologized.

Colum became deeply interested in poetry and theater, and he brought to the great Irish Literary Revival a young man's vision together with an inheritance from the ancient voice of the people. He was one of the founders of the *Irish Review*, and his early poems were published by Arthur Griffith, of whom he later wrote a biography (*Ourselves Alone,* 1959). Among his volumes of poetry were *The Road Round Ireland* (1926) and *Images of Departure* (1969). His collected poems were published in 1953.

Colum was a founder-member of the Irish National Theatre Society (forerunner of the Abbey Theatre) and a friend of William Butler Yeats, John Millington Synge, Lady Gregory, AE, and James Stephens. He later celebrated some of these friendships in a book of poems, *Irish Elegies* (1958). His realistic plays—*The Land* (1905), *The Fiddler's House* (1907), and *Thomas Muskerry* (1910)—were an important influence in the development of the modern Irish theater. Their early productions were by the Fay brothers, and it was Frank Fay who taught Colum how to recite verse, an art which he perfected over the years.

Colum was much occupied with contemporary events, especially Ireland's struggle for freedom, and numbered among his friends the Irish patriots Patrick Pearse, Thomas McDonagh, and Roger Casement. In 1912 Colum married the author Mary Maguire, and 2 years later they emigrated to the United States. He retained close ties, however, with literary and political events in Ireland, and his writings continued to derive much of their inspiration from his native country.

The Colums wrote about their long and close friendship with James Joyce and his family many years later in *Our Friend James Joyce* (1958). They cared for Joyce's invalid daughter at a critical period. Colum's fondness for young people is also reflected in his many books for children, best known of which is *The King of Ireland's Son* (1916).

Although a resident of New York, Colum remained something of the traditional wandering Irish poet, traveling widely to give lectures and readings. In 1924 he accepted

an invitation from the Hawaii Legislature to make a survey of native myth and folklore; his versions of the Hawaiian tales were published in *The Bright Islands* (1925). He also retold Irish legends in *A Treasury of Irish Folklore* (1954). Colum was always interested in other cultures, from those of classical Greece and Rome to that of the South Sea Islands, which he visited at the age of 86.

After his wife's death in 1957, Colum published the long, semiautobiographical novel *The Flying Swans,* a saga of life in Ireland before the turn of the century. Colum's unfailing kindness in encouraging new poets and writers of talent perhaps contributed to his vitality and the continuing freshness of his ideas throughout his life. He died at Enfield, Conn., on Jan. 11, 1972.

## Further Reading

A comprehensive biographical and critical study of Colum is Zack Bowen, *Padraic Colum* (1970). The autobiography of his wife, Mary Colum, *Life and the Dream: Memories of a Literary Life in Europe and America* (1947; rev. ed. 1966), contains information about their life together. Ernest A. Boyd, *The Contemporary Drama of Ireland* (1917), discusses Colum's early career as an Irish folk dramatist. □

# St. Columba

**The Irish monk St. Columba (ca. 521-597) was a powerful preacher and leader of men. He founded monasteries in Ireland and Scotland, which were influential missionary centers.**

The son of a tribal chieftain, Columba was given the name Crimthann when he was baptized shortly after his birth in Gartan, County Donegal. When he was a boy, he was so often found praying in the town church that his friends called him Colm Cille (Dove of the Church), and it was as Colm, or its Latin form Columba, that he was known for the rest of his life.

In his early 20s Columba was strongly influenced by one of his teachers, Finian of Clonard, and asked to be ordained a priest. When a prince cousin gave him some land at Derry, he decided to start a monastery. Because of his love of nature Columba refused to build the church facing east, as was the custom; he wanted to spare the lives of as many oak trees as he could. His foundation of another monastery at Durrow 7 years later was the beginning of an extraordinary decade during which he traveled through northern Ireland teaching about Christianity and inspiring many people by his personal holiness. He founded some 30 monasteries in those 10 years.

Columba's strong personality and forceful preaching aroused considerable antagonism. He was accused in 563 of starting a war between two Irish tribes and was sentenced by the high king never to see Ireland again, to spend the rest of his life in exile. With 12 companions he sailed from the shores he loved, and settled on a bleak island called Iona off the coast of Scotland. The monks made occasional visits to the Scottish mainland, where they preached their kind of Christianity. Soon their community had 150 members.

In 575 Columba was persuaded to visit Ireland to mediate a dispute between the high king and the league of poets. Insisting on remaining faithful to the terms of his exile, that he never see Ireland again, he traveled blindfolded. Although his sympathies were with the poets, his reputation was respected by everyone. He spoke to the assembled nobles and clergy with such force and authority that the king was persuaded to reverse his original decree, and the hostility between the two parties was calmed.

Columba spent the rest of his life on Iona, praying, fasting, and teaching his monks to read and copy the Scriptures. He provided inspiration for their missionary efforts and was influential for a time in the politics of Scotland. Long before his death in 597 he was regarded as a saint by his fellow monks and is today a beloved figure in Irish tradition.

## Further Reading

*The Life of Saint Columba,* written about a hundred years after his death by a monk of his community, Adamnan of Iona, describes him as a poet and miracle worker. It was edited and translated into English by Alan Orr Anderson and Marjorie Ogilvie Anderson (1961). Benedict Fitzpatrick, *Ireland and the Making of Britain* (1922), pays tribute to Columba's influence in shaping the character of the British Isles. There is a charming chapter on Columba (Colm Cille) in Seumas MacManus, *The Story of the Irish Race* (1921).

## Additional Sources

Adamnan, Saint, 625?-704, *Adomnan's life of Columba,* Oxford; New York: Clarendon Press, 1990.
Finlay, Ian, *Columba,* London: Gollancz, 1979.
Jenkin, Roger, *Two local patron saints,* Ilfracombe: Stockwell, 1975. □

# St. Columban

**The Irish missionary St. Columban (ca. 543-615) traveled throughout Europe, preaching a strict, penitential version of Christianity. He founded influential monasteries in France, Switzerland, and Italy.**

As a young student, Columban was so impressed by the dedicated Irish monks who introduced him to religion and literature that he decided to join their ranks. He entered a monastery at Bangor, County Down, not far from his home, and placed himself under the spiritual guidance of its founder, Comgall. For some 30 years he lived quietly in prayer, work, and study. Desiring greater self-sacrifice, Columban asked his abbot if he could go into voluntary exile, leaving his native Ireland to start a monastery on the Continent. Twelve other monks set out with him in 590 for the land of the Franks.

They settled for a while in Burgundy at the invitation of King Childebert, founding three monasteries. So many young men were inspired by their religious zeal that soon more than 200 monasteries were formed, looking to Columban as their spiritual father. The Irish monks with their new, forceful kind of Christianity, stressing self-discipline and purity of life, presented a striking contrast to the complacent churchmen already living among the Franks. Columban spoke out repeatedly against the cruelty and self-indulgence of the kings and royal families, stressing the necessity of penance and introducing a new custom of frequent personal confession.

Columban's Irish brand of Christianity proved so annoying that the local clergy looked for opportunities to discredit him. They seized upon his different method of calculating the date of Easter as an excuse for attacking his orthodoxy and were happy when King Theuderic in 610 expelled him from Burgundy after he had censured the King for living with a mistress.

Other kings welcomed Columban into their territories, and he eventually made his way into what is now Switzerland, founding a monastery near Zurich. Columban refused, however, to settle down into a quiet monastic life and again ran into trouble. He preached so vigorously against the pagan customs of the surrounding Alemani that he was asked to leave their territory. With considerable difficulty Columban and a few faithful followers crossed the Alps and started what was to be their most important monastery in Bobbio in northern Italy. From there the Irish influence spread still further, although in time the harsh personal life of the monks softened as they came in contact with the more moderate ideas of Benedict.

Columban died in his monastery in Bobbio in 615. Many of his letters and sermons were preserved. These, together with his poems and the rules he composed for his monks, influenced European life and culture well into the Middle Ages.

## Further Reading

Of the several biographies of St. Columban available in English, the one by Francis MacManus, *Saint Columban* (1962), is helpful for its use of contemporary historical scholarship. Most church history studies present the effect of Columban's missionary efforts on the history of Europe, for example, John Ryan, *Irish Monasticism: Origins and Early Development* (1931). □

# Christopher Columbus

**The Italian navigator Christopher Columbus (1451-1506) was the discoverer of America. Though he had set out to find a westward route to Asia, his explorations proved to be as important as any alternate way to the riches of Cathay and India.**

The archives of Genoa show that the famous discoverer was born Cristoforo Colombo (Spanish, Cristóbal Colón) there between August and October 1451. His father, Domenico Colombo, followed the weaver's craft, and his mother, Suzanna Fontanarossa, came of equally humble stock. Christopher was the eldest child, and two brothers make some appearance in history under their Hispanicized names, Bartolomé and Diego.

Columbus had a meager education and only later learned to read Latin and write Castilian. He evidently helped his father at work when he was a boy and went to sea early in a humble capacity. Since he aged early in appearance and contemporaries commonly took him for older than he really was, he was able to claim to have taken part in events before his time.

In 1475 Columbus made his first considerable voyage to the Aegean island of Chios, and in 1476 he sailed on a Genoese ship through the Strait of Gibraltar. Off Cape St. Vincent they were attacked by a French fleet, and the vessel in which Columbus sailed sank. He swam ashore and went to Lisbon, where his brother Bartolomé already lived. Columbus also visited Galway, in Ireland, and an English port, probably Bristol. If he ever sailed to Iceland, as he afterward claimed to have done, it must have been as a part of this voyage. He made his presumably last visit to Genoa in 1479 and there gave testimony in a lawsuit. Court procedure required him to tell his age, which he gave as "past 27," furnishing reasonable evidence of 1451 as his birth year.

Columbus returned to Portugal, where he married Felipa Perestrelo e Monis, daughter of Bartolomeu Perestrelo, deceased proprietor of the island of Porto Santo. The couple lived first in Lisbon, where Perestrelo's widow showed documents her husband had written or collected regarding possible western lands in the Atlantic, and these probably started Columbus thinking of a voyage of investigation. Later they moved to Porto Santo, where his wife died soon after the birth of Diego, the discoverer's only legitimate child.

## Formation of an Idea

After his wife's death, Columbus turned wholly to discovery plans and theories, among them the hope to discover a westward route to Asia. He learned of the legendary Irish St. Brandan and his marvelous adventures in the Atlantic and of the equally legendary island of Antilia. Seamen venturing west of Madeira and the Azores reported signs of land, and ancient authors, notably Seneca and Pliny, had theorized about the nearness of eastern Asia to western Europe, though it is not known just when Columbus read them. He acquired incunabular editions of Ptolemy, Marco Polo, and Pierre d'Ailly, but again it is uncertain how early he read them. He possibly first depended on what others said of their contents.

From Marco Polo, Columbus learned the names of Cathay (north China) and Cipango (Japan). The Venetian traveler had never visited Japan and erroneously placed it 1,500 miles east of China, thus bringing it closer to Europe. Furthermore, Columbus accepted two bad guesses by Ptolemy: his underestimate of the earth's circumference and his overestimate of Asia's eastward extension. With the earth's sphericity taken for granted, all Columbus's mistaken beliefs combined to make his idea seem feasible.

In 1474 the Florentine scientist Paolo dal Pozzo Toscanelli sent a letter and map to Fernao Martins of Lisbon, telling Martins that a western voyage in the Atlantic would be a shorter way of reaching the Orient than circumnavigation of Africa. Columbus obtained a copy of the letter and used it to clarify his own ideas.

In 1484 Columbus asked John II of Portugal for backing in the proposed voyage. Rejected, Columbus went to Spain with young Diego in 1485, and for nearly 7 years he sought the aid of Isabella of Castile and her husband, Ferdinand of Aragon. The sovereigns took no action but gave Columbus a small annuity that enabled him to live modestly. He found influential friends, including the powerful Duke of Medinaceli and Juan Pérez, prior of La Rábida monastery.

While waiting, the widowed Columbus had an affair with young Beatriz Enriquez de Harana of Cordova, who in 1488 bore his other son, Ferdinand, out of wedlock. He never married her, though he provided for her in his will and legitimatized the boy, as Castilian law permitted.

## Preparations for the First Voyage

In 1492 Columbus resumed negotiations with the rulers. The discussions soon broke down, apparently because of the heavy demands by Columbus, who now prepared to abandon Spain and try Charles VIII of France.

Father Pérez saved Columbus from this probably fruitless endeavor by an eloquent appeal to the Queen. Columbus was called back, and in April he and the rulers agreed to the Capitulations of Santa Fe, by which they guaranteed him more than half the future profits and promised his family the hereditary governorship of all lands annexed to Castile.

Financing proved difficult, but three ships were prepared in the harbor of Palos. The largest, the 100-ton *Santa Maria,* was a round-bottomed nao with both square and lateen sails; the caravel *Pinta* was square-rigged; and the small *Niña ,* also a caravel, had lateen sails. Recruitment proved hard, and sailing might have been delayed had not the Pinzón brothers, mariners and leading citizens of Palos, come to Columbus's aid and persuaded seamen to enlist. The eldest brother, Martin Alonso, took command of the *Pinta,* and a younger brother, Vicente Yañez, commanded the *Niña.*

### The Departure

The fleet left Palos on Aug. 3, 1492, and, visiting the Canaries, followed the parallel of Gomera westward. Weather remained good during the entire crossing, "like April in Andalusia," as Columbus wrote in his diary, and contrary to popular tales, there was no serious threat of mutiny.

By mid-Atlantic, Columbus evidently concluded he had missed Antilia, so Cipango became his next goal. Landfall came at dawn of October 12, at the Bahama island of Guanahani, straightway renamed San Salvador by Columbus (probably modern San Salvador, or Watlings Island). Arawak natives flocked to the shore and made friends with the Spaniards as they landed. Believing himself in the East Indies, Columbus called them "Indians," a name ultimately applied to all New World aborigines.

The ships next passed among other Bahamas to Colba (Cuba), where the gold available proved disappointing. Turning eastward, Columbus crossed to Quisqueya, renamed Española (Hispaniola), where on Christmas Eve the *Santa Maria* ran aground near Cap-Haitien. No lives were lost and most of the equipment was salvaged. As relations with the local Taino Arawaks seemed good and Columbus wished to return to Spain immediately, he built a settlement named Navidad for the *Santa Maria*'s crew and left, promising to return in a few months.

### The Return

Columbus recrossed the Atlantic by a more northerly route than on his outward passage and reached Europe safely. He had an interview with John II of Portugal, who, by a farfetched interpretation of an old treaty with Castile, claimed the new western islands for himself. Columbus then sailed to Palos and crossed Spain to the court at Barcelona, bearing the artifacts he had brought from Hispaniola and conducting several natives he had induced or forced to accompany him. Strong evidence also suggests that his crew brought syphilis, apparently never reported in Europe before and known to have been endemic in mild form among the Arawaks.

Regarding John II's territorial claims, Isabella and Ferdinand appealed to Pope Alexander VI, an Aragonese Spaniard, for confirmation of their rights, and in 1493 the Pope obliged, granting Castile complete rights west of a line from pole to pole in the Atlantic. But the Treaty of Tordesillas (1494) established a new line, from pole to pole, 370 leagues west of the Cape Verde Islands. Spain was entitled to claim and occupy all non-Christian lands west of the line, and Portugal all those to the east.

### Second Voyage

Following an enthusiastic reception by Ferdinand and Isabella, "Admiral" Columbus prepared for a second voyage. He sailed from Cadiz with 17 ships and about 1,200 men in September 1493. Columbus entered the West Indies near Dominica, which he discovered and named. Passing westward and touching Marie Galante, Guadeloupe, and other Lesser Antilles, the fleet came to large Borinquén (modern Puerto Rico).

On reaching the Navidad settlement on Hispaniola, Columbus found the place destroyed. The Spaniards had made themselves so hated in their quest of gold and women that Chief Caonabo, more warlike than the others, had exterminated them. Another settlement, Isabela, proved an equally unfortunate location, and in 1495 or 1496 Bartolomé Columbus founded Santo Domingo on the south side of Hispaniola.

From Isabela the Admiral sent home most of the ships, though retaining the bulk of the men. He dispatched expeditions into the center of the island in search of gold and accompanied one in person. Meanwhile, he installed himself as governor of Hispaniola, intending it to be a trading post for commerce with the rich Oriental empires he expected soon to discover.

### Exploration in the Caribbean

Columbus now decided to explore Cuba further by tracing the island's southern coast. With three ships, including his favorite *Niña,* he left Isabela in the spring of 1494 and followed the Cuban coast nearly to its western end. Indians told him of Jamaica not far to the south, and the Admiral turned that way, discovered the island, and had several fights with hostile natives. Returning to the Cuban shore, Columbus sailed to Bahía Cortés, where leaky ships and sailors' complaints forced him to put back.

Back in Hispaniola, Columbus found the Spanish settlers unruly and nearly impossible to govern. Complaints against Columbus reached the Castilian court in such numbers that he at last decided to go to Spain to clear his name. He left in the *Niña* in March 1496 and reached Cadiz in June. Bartolomé, with the rank of *adelantado ,* remained to govern the colony in his absence.

### Third Voyage

The Admiral's reception at court was visibly cooler, but Vasco da Gama's departure from Portugal for India in 1497 caused the Spanish rulers to dispatch Columbus again the following year. There were reports of a great continent south of the Admiral's previous discoveries, and Columbus left Sanlúcar de Barrameda with six ships late in May 1498.

The first land sighted had three hills in view, which suggested the Holy Trinity, and Columbus promptly named the island Trinidad. Since it lies by the Gulf of Paria and the Venezuelan mainland, the Admiral became the discoverer of South America on Aug. 1, 1498. The welcome discovery of pearls from oysters in the shallow waters of offshore islands caused the name "Pearl Coast" to be applied for a time to Venezuela, which Columbus even then recognized as a land of continental proportions because of the volume of water flowing from one of its rivers.

## Rebellion and Arrest

The Admiral had left Hispaniolan affairs in bad condition 2 years earlier and now hastened to return there and relieve his hard-pressed brother. On arrival he succeeded in partially quieting by compromise a revolt headed by Francisco Roldán, an officeholder, and resumed his governorship. But so many letters of complaint had gone back to Castile regarding the Columbus brothers that the rulers sent out a royal commissioner, Francisco de Bobadilla, with full powers to act as he saw best.

Bobadilla was honest and meant well, but he had already formed a bad opinion of the Columbus family. He put the Admiral and the *adelantado* in chains and sent them to Spain. Andrés Martin, commanding the ship in which they sailed, offered to remove the shackles, but the Admiral refused permission, as he meant to appear fettered before the sovereigns. On arrival in Cadiz in late November 1500, Columbus went to court to receive a kind welcome and assurance by the monarchs that the chains and imprisonment had not been by their orders.

In 1501 the Admiral began preparing for a fourth voyage. The fleet, consisting of four ships, left Cadiz on May 9, 1502, arriving in Santo Domingo on June 29. The Admiral next sailed to Guanaja Island off Honduras, then down the coast of Central America. When Columbus learned from the natives about another saltwater body, the Pacific, not far away, he felt certain that he was coasting the Malay Peninsula, of which he had learned through the writings of Ptolemy. A strait or open water should permit entry to the Indian Ocean. Although Columbus followed the coast nearly to the Gulf of Darien, he found no strait.

In April 1503 the ships left the mainland, but the hulls were thoroughly bored by teredos and had to be abandoned as unseaworthy in Jamaica. The Admiral and his crews were marooned in Jamaica for a year, during which time Diego Mendez and Bartolomeo Fieschi fetched a small caravel from Hispaniola. Columbus finally reached Sanlúcar de Barrameda, Spain, on Nov. 7, 1504.

Columbus had 18 months of life remaining, and they were unhappy. Though only 53 he was physically an aged man, a sufferer from arthritis and the effects of a bout of malaria. But financially his position was good, as he had brought considerable gold from America and had a claim to much more in Hispaniola. He died in Valladolid on May 20, 1506.

## Further Reading

The best works on Columbus are Samuel Eliot Morison, *Admiral of the Ocean Sea: A Life of Christopher Columbus* (2 vols. and 1 vol. condensation, 1942), which concentrates on the nautical aspects, and, in Spanish, Antonio Ballesteros y Beretta, *Cristóbal Colón y el descubrimiento de América* (2 vols., 1945), which discusses all phases of Columbus's career. Invaluable as a source is the 1959 translation by Benjamin Keen of Fernando Colón, *The Life of the Admiral Christopher Columbus by His Son Ferdinand* (1571). Marianne Mahn-Lot, *Columbus* (1960; trans. 1961), gives a brief and accurate account of the discoverer's life.

More specialized works are Samuel Eliot Morison, *The Second Voyage of Christopher Columbus* (1939), which traces this voyage until the arrival at Hispaniola, and George E. Nunn, *The Geographical Conceptions of Columbus: A Critical Consideration of Four Problems* (1924), which has not found general acceptance. A more convincing work by Nunn is *The Columbus and Magellan Concepts of South American Geography* (1932). Columbus's voyages are discussed in Samuel Eliot Morison, *The European Discovery of America: The Northern Voyages* (1971). Older works that still have considerable value are Washington Irving, *A History of the Life and Voyages of Christopher Columbus* (3- and 4-vol. eds., 1828), and John Boyd Thacher, *Christopher Columbus: His Life, His Work, His Remains* (3 vols., 1903-1904).

Writings devoted to unusual theses are Henry Vignaud, *Toscanelli and Columbus: The Letter and Chart of Toscanelli* (1901; trans. 1902), which maintains that the Toscanelli letters were forgeries; Salvador de Madariaga, *Christopher Columbus* (1939; 2d ed. 1949), which proves to the author's satisfaction that Columbus was a Jew; and Edmundo O'Gorman, *The Invention of America* (1958; trans. 1961), which asserts that Columbus was not a discoverer because he had no intention of making a discovery and never thought he had made one. □

# Rita R. Colwell

**As a scientist and professor, Rita R. Colwell (born 1934) has investigated the ecology, physiology, and evolutionary relationships of marine bacteria.**

Rita R. Colwell is a leader in marine biotechnology, the application of molecular techniques to marine biology for the harvesting of medical, industrial and aquaculture products from the sea. As a scientist and professor, Colwell has investigated the ecology, physiology, and evolutionary relationships of marine bacteria. As a founder and president of the University of Maryland Biotechnology Institute, she has nurtured a vision to improve the environment and human health by linking molecular biology and genetics to basic knowledge scientists had gleaned from life and chemistry in the oceans.

Rita Rossi was born in Beverly, Massachusetts, November 23, 1934, the seventh of eight children to parents Louis and Louise Di Palma Rossi. Her father was an Italian immigrant who established his own construction company, and her mother was an artistic woman who worked to help ensure her children would have a good education. She died when her daughter was just thirteen years old, but she had been proud of her success in school. In the sixth grade, after Rossi had scored higher on the IQ exam than anyone in her school's history, the principal asked sternly whether she understood that she had the responsibility to go to college. Rossi had answered, "Yes, ma'am," and eventually received a full scholarship from Purdue University. She earned her bachelor of science degree with distinction in bacteriology in 1956. Although she had been accepted to medical school, Rossi chose instead to earn a master's degree so that she could remain at the same institution as graduate student Jack Colwell, whom she married on May 31, 1956. Colwell would have continued her studies in bacteriology, but the department chairman at Purdue informed her that giving fellowship money to women would have been a waste. She instead earned her master's degree in the department of genetics. The University of Washington, Seattle, granted her a Ph.D. in 1961 for work on bacteria commensal to marine animals, which is the practivce of an organism obtaining food or other benefits from another without either harming or helping it. Colwell's contributions included establishing the basis for the systematics of marine bacteria.

In 1964, Georgetown University hired Colwell as an assistant professor, and gave her tenure in 1966. Colwell and her research team were the first to recognize that the bacterium that caused cholera occurred naturally in estuaries. They isolated the bacterium from Chesapeake Bay and in ensuing years sought to explain how outbreaks in human populations might be tied to the seasonal abundance of the host organisms in the sea, particularly plankton. In 1972, Colwell took a tenured professorship at the University of Maryland. Her studies expanded to include investigations on the impact of marine pollution at the microbial level. Among her findings was that the presence of oil in estuarine and open ocean water was associated with the numbers of bacteria able to break down oil. She studied whether some types of bacteria might be used to treat oil spills. Colwell and her colleagues also made a discovery that held promise for improving oyster yields in aquaculture—a bacterial film formed on surfaces under water attracted oyster larvae to settle and grow.

In the spirit of using knowledge gained from the sea to benefit humans and the environment, Colwell prepared a seminal paper on marine biotechnology published in the journal *Science* in 1983. It brought attention to the rich resources of the ocean that might be tapped for food, disease-curing drugs, and environmental clean-up by the applications of genetic engineering and cloning. In order to realize the potential of marine biotechnology as originally outlined in her 1983 paper, Colwell helped foster the concept and growth of the University of Maryland Biotechnology Institute, established in 1987. As president of the U.M.B.I., she has formed alliances between researchers and industry and has succeeded in raising funds to develop the center as a prestigious biotech research complex.

In addition, Colwell has held numerous professional and academic leadership positions throughout her career and is a widely published researcher. At the University of

Maryland, Colwell was director of the Sea Grant College from 1977 to 1983. She served as president of Sigma Xi, the American Society for Microbiology, and the International Congress of Systematic and Evolutionary Biology, and was president-elect of the American Association for the Advancement of Science. Colwell has written and edited more than sixteen books and over four hundred papers and articles; she also produced an award-winning film, *Invisible Seas.* Her honors included the 1985 Fisher Award of the American Society for Microbiology, the 1990 Gold Medal Award of the International Institute of Biotechnology, and the 1993 Phi Kappa Phi National Scholar Award.

Colwell is the mother of two daughters who pursued careers in science. She is an advocate for equal rights for women, and one of her long-standing aspirations is to write a novel about a woman scientist. Her hobbies include jogging and competitive sailing.

## Further Reading

Andrews, Joan Kostick, "Lady With A Mission," in *Natural Science,* May, 1991, pp. 304–310.
Henderson, Randi, "Scientist Plays Many Roles," in *The Baltimore Sun,* October 13, 1991.
Sherman, Scott L., "The Long Road From the Laboratory," in *Warfield's,* August, 1990. □

# John Amos Comenius

**The Moravian theologian and educational reformer John Amos Comenius (1592-1670) is often called the father of modern education.**

John Amos Comenius was born on Mar. 28, 1592, in southeastern Moravia. His early education was irregular. After deciding to become a priest of the Bohemian Unity of Brethren (a German Baptist sect), he received his higher education in Germany at Herborn, Nassau, and Heidelberg. In 1614 he returned to Bohemia, where he taught in the schools of the Brethren. He was ordained a priest 2 years later and appointed pastor of a parish in Fulneck in 1618.

The sack of Fulneck by the Catholic forces after the outbreak of the Thirty Years War forced Comenius into hiding in Bohemia. Shortly afterward he wrote the allegory *The Labyrinth of the World and the Paradise of the Heart.* In this classic of Czech literature, man finds true happiness in mystical union with Christ.

Because of persecution, the Brethren were forced to leave Bohemia in 1628. Comenius went to Leszno, Poland, where his position as corector of the Brethren's school led him to become interested in educational reform. Many of the educational ideas expressed in his *Didactica magna* (1657; *The Great Didactic*) were developed during this period. Among the reforms that he advocated were gentler discipline; use of the vernacular instead of Latin in the primary schools; and free, universal, compulsory education for both sexes and all social classes. His book *Janua linguarum reserata* (1631; *The Gate of Languages Unlocked*) revolutionized the teaching of Latin and helped establish his reputation throughout Europe as an educational reformer.

Elected a bishop of his church in 1632, Comenius expressed his great interest in Christian unity and was conspicuous in the 17th century for his ecumenical beliefs. His development of a universal system of human knowledge among all men and nations, called pansophy, led to his being invited to England. From there he went to Sweden in 1642 and was employed in reforming the nation's school system. In 1650 he established a pansophic school in Hungary as a model for others, but conflicts caused his return to Leszno in 1655. After the sack of the city in 1656, he fled to Amsterdam, where he resided until his death on Nov. 4, 1670.

## Further Reading

In English, the best biography of Comenius is Matthew Spinka, *John Amos Comenius: That Incomparable Moravian* (1943). The earliest biography is S. S. Laurie, *John Amos Comenius, Bishop of the Moravians: His Life and Educational Works* (1881; new ed. 1892). Otakar Odloziik wrote a brief biographical sketch, *Jan Amos Komensky* (1942). Two books focus on his educational reforms: Will S. Monroe, *Comenius, and the Beginnings of Educational Reform* (1900), and John E. Sadler, *Comenius and the Concept of Universal Education* (1966). ☐

# Philippe de Comines

**The French chronicler Philippe de Comines (ca. 1445-1511) wrote an extensive memoir of the reigns of Louis XI and Charles VIII.**

Born in the château of Renescure in Flanders before 1447, probably in 1445, Philippe de Comines, or Commynes, was orphaned early. His formal education was limited, but his godfather, Philip V of Burgundy, reared him in his court. In 1464 Comines entered the service of Philip's son Charles the Bold, who became Duke of Burgundy in 1467. As Charles's chamberlain and councilor, he took an important part in the negotiations between the duke and King Louis XI when the latter was held prisoner at Péronne in 1468, and in fact did much to save the King's life.

In 1472 Comines abandoned Charles the Bold to enter the service of Louis XI; he was soon made chamberlain and councilor and was given a generous pension and a confiscated property. In 1473 Louis arranged his marriage with Helen of Chambes, who brought him the lands of Argenton. Comines and the King were in harmony in effecting many a political ruse, but Comines did not approve of Louis's domestic abuses.

After the death of Louis in 1483, Comines engaged in subversive plots against Charles VIII and in 1488 was exiled to one of his own estates. Recalled in 1492, he cooperated with Charles's Italian expedition, even representing the King at the Treaty of Vercelli. After the death of Charles VIII in

1498, Comines received no appointments of importance; he died at Argenton in 1511.

The *Memoirs* of Comines, his only permanent contribution, covers the period from 1464 to 1498. This work is not filled with charming anecdotes but abounds in explanations of the deep-seated and secret causes of political events, and thus Comines is the first French writer to deserve the title of historian in the modern sense. The earlier French chroniclers were content to report events, but Comines was a penetrating observer and a specialist in the secrets of the human mind. He presented some theories that were influential in the 18th century. Both he and his contemporary Niccolò Machiavelli shared the hardheaded view that success alone matters; but, unlike Comines, Machiavelli did not pervert Providence to consecrate reprehensible acts.

## Further Reading

The best French edition of Comines's *Memoirs* is that of Joseph Calmette and Georges Durville (3 vols., 1924-1925). A new translation undertaken by Isabelle Cazeaux, *The Memoirs of Philippe de Commynes,* edited by Samuel Kinser (vol. 1, 1969), promises to replace Sir Andrew Richard Scoble's translation of 1855-1856. The most useful monograph on Comines is in French: Gustave Charlier, *Commynes* (1945). An excellent background study is Joseph Calmette, *Golden Age of Burgundy* (1949; trans. 1963). ☐

# Henry Steele Commager

**Henry Steele Commager (born 1902) was an American historian who achieved much fame as a textbook author and as an editor of books of documents. He also earned a reputation as an historian of ideas and as a participant in the debates on the public issues of his day.**

Henry Steele Commager was born in Pittsburgh, Pennsylvania on October 25, 1902, the son of James Williams and Anne Elizabeth (Dan) Commager. His parents moved to Toledo and then to Chicago when Commager was growing up, necessitating several changes in schools.

Commager matriculated at the University of Chicago, earning three degrees in history, a Ph.B. in 1923, an A.M. in 1924, and a Ph.D. in 1928. In 1924 Commager spent a year in Copenhagen doing research on his dissertation, "Struensee and the Reform Movement in Denmark."

Although his early interest was in Danish history and although that interest persisted throughout his life, Commager made his reputation and did most of his writing on American history. In 1926 he became an instructor of history at Columbia University. He married Evan Carroll on July 3, 1928, and the couple had three children, Henry Steele, Elizabeth Carroll, and Nellie Thomas McCall.

In 1929 he received the Herbert Baxter Adams Prize for a first book in the field of European history, but his reputa-

tion was made the next year when he became the co-author of *The Growth of the American Republic* with Samuel Eliot Morison. The book became one of the best-selling texts in the subject and went through many editions. He next wrote several texts in collaboration with others and published *Documents of American History* (1934), which was also widely used. In 1936 he wrote *Theodore Parker,* a biography of the New England radical. In 1939 he edited, with Allan Nevins, another book of documents, *The Heritage of America.* In the 1930s Commager was a Progressive historian, a self-styled Parrington, who was isolationistic and a believer in an economic interpretation of American history.

World War II changed his views. In 1942 he gave the James W. Richards' Lectures at the University of Virginia. These appeared under the title *Majority Rule and Minority Rights* (1943) and argued for the implementation of the will of the majority. In 1942 Commager and Allan Nevins also published *America: The Story of a Free People,* which presented a sympathetic view of American life. Commager lectured for the Office of War Information in England in 1943 and was active in writing and giving broadcasts all during the war. In the spring and summer of 1945 he assumed the temporary rank of colonel and acted as an information and education specialist for the United States Army in Paris.

His experience in the war led him to publish *The Story of the Second World War* in 1945. This popular account consisted of a series of stories and vignettes which was not a critical success. In 1947-1948 he became Pitt Professor of American History at Cambridge University.

In 1950 he published what was probably his best book, *The American Mind,* an intellectual history of America from 1890 through the 1940s. The book became a classic and moved Commager into the rank of one of the top intellectual historians in the nation. The same year he also edited a two-volume work, *The Blue and the Grey,* which included eyewitness accounts from participants on each side during the Civil War. In 1953 he was Gottesman Professor at the Royal University of Uppsala; the next year he was the Zuskin Professor at Brandeis.

By this time Commager's concern had shifted to preserving minority rights, particularly against the witch-hunting techniques of Senator Joseph McCarthy. His book *Freedom, Loyalty, Dissent* (1954) spoke to issue of constitutional protection of free speech and won a Special Award from the Hillman Foundation.

In 1956, in a surprising move, Commager left Columbia to become a professor of history at Amherst College. Amherst made him Emerson Professor of History and Simpson Lecturer in 1971. The move to Amherst did not diminish his tremendous productivity. The year he arrived was also the year of the publication of *Joseph Story,* a biography that Commager had been working on for years.

Commager continued to write in a number of areas: contemporary political events, constitutional rights and theory, historiography, and the enlightenment. He also wrote books for juveniles as well as editing books of documents and historical series. By 1967 Harold W. Hyman and Leonard W. Levy counted over 400 items in the Commager corpus, including the authorship of 19 books and the editorship of 22 others. In this list were such books as *Freedom and Order: A Commentary on the American Political Scene* (1966), which was retrospective of his own work, and *Was America a Mistake?* (1967), an edited collection of the European arguments over the consequences of America's discovery.

Reaching his 65th birthday did not still Commager. The 1970s were a particularly fertile period as Commager wrote *The Discipline of History* (1972), ideas about historiography; *Britain Through American Eyes* (1974), selections from traveler's accounts; *The Defeat of America: Presidential Power and the National Character* (1974), a book inspired by the Nixon debate; *Jefferson, Nationalism and Enlightenment* (1975), a consideration of that leader's ideas; and *The Empire of Reason: How Europe Imagined and America Realized the Enlightenment* (1977), a comparative study of the impact of ideas on two continents.

In 1979, Commager wrote the text for *Mort Kuenstler's 50 Epic Paintings of America,* and he continued to write prolifically into the 1980s and 1990s. He co-authored *The Study and Teaching of History* (1980) with Raymond Muessig, and wrote the introduction for *The Civil War Almanac* (1983). In 1992 he published two new works, *Commager on Tocqueville,* which met mixed reviews, and *The Story of the Second World War,* a critical success. In 1994 he wrote the text for a book of paintings by Mort Kuenstler, *The American Spirit.*

In 1984, Commager suffered a personal loss when his son, Henry Steele Commager, Jr., also an historian and author, died of cancer. His son's death created some confusion in biographies, as it was sometimes reported incorrectly to be the death of Commager, Sr.

Commager also continued as a visiting professor or lecturer at a number of universities, including the Massachusetts Institute of Technology (1975 and 1977), McGill University (1977), Indiana University (1978), University of Washington (1981), and University of Illinois (1982). He had collected over 45 honorary degrees to add to his Guggenheim Fellowship, his Fellowship in the American Scandinavian Society, and his membership in the American Academy of Arts and Letters, as well as the Gold Medal for History the academy had bestowed on him. His career was a tribute to hard work and a wide interest in the world of both past and present.

## Further Reading

There is an appreciation of Commager by two of his students, Harold W. Hyman and Leonard W. Levy, in *Freedom and Reform: Essays in Honor of Henry Steele Commager* (1967), which was published on the occasion of his 65th birthday. Robert Allen Skotheim analyses Commager's approach to the history of ideas in his *American Intellectual Histories and Historians* (1966). Commager is mentioned briefly in John Higham's *History* (1965). There is an interview with Commager in John A. Garratys' *Interpreting American History* (1970) which sheds light on Commager's ideas on nationalism. There is biographical information in *Twentieth-Century American Historians* (1983) and *Contemporary Authors* (1989), Volume 26. □

before joining the faculty of Washington University in St. Louis, first as associate professor of plant physiology, later as chairman of the Botany Department, and finally as university professor of environmental science (1976-1981). It was here that he began the Center for the Biology of Natural Systems (CBNS). Although he published numerous professional research papers, he rejected the conventional view that what non-scientists do with scientific knowledge is none of the scientists' business. He became a social activist and vocal public educator.

What brought him out of the laboratory in 1953, Commoner declared afterward, was strontium-90, one of the radioisotopes contained in the fallout from nuclear tests in the atmosphere. His Committee for Nuclear Information set parents all over St. Louis to collecting their offspring's baby teeth for testing, and found out that in addition to the normal element calcium, those teeth contained also ominous proportions of strontium-90, which behaves physically and chemically much like calcium and can combine in building bones and teeth in much the same way, except that strontium-90 is highly radioactive.

In the first sentence of a book published in 1966, *Science and Survival*, Barry Commoner announced that "the age of innocent faith in science and technology may be over." A massive electric power failure all over the Northeast, the admission of children to a St. Louis hospital 15 years after they had been exposed to radio-iodine from Nevada nuclear bomb tests, the disturbing news about DDT, and the potential menace of recombinant DNA—not to mention the threat of "nuclear winter" in the event of

# Barry Commoner

**Barry Commoner (born 1917) was a biologist who became an environmental activist, leading efforts to inform the general public about the many environmental dangers posed by various scientific advances and common practices. He was one of the founders of the modern environmental movement who was referred to as the "Paul Revere of Ecology."**

Barry Commoner was born in Brooklyn, New York, on May 28, 1917. As a boy he lived the rugged life of the city streets, but on weekends he prowled Brooklyn's Prospect Park looking for microscope specimens. Educated at James Madison High School, which fostered his interest in biology, he put himself through Columbia University by doing odd jobs and got his bachelor's degree with honors in 1937. Earning master's and doctoral degrees at Harvard (1938, 1941), he began his teaching career as a biology instructor at Queens College (1940-1942). Serving in the Navy in World War II, he took part in spraying Pacific islands against insect-borne diseases with the new wonder chemical DDT, unaware as yet that indiscriminate use of such toxins was an invitation to environmental disaster.

Married after the war to Gloria Gordon, a psychologist, Commoner served as associate editor of *Science Illustrated*

thermonuclear war, a prospect Commoner discussed years before most Americans even heard of it—led him to the conclusion that science, like the magic practiced by the legendary Sorcerer's Apprentice, was getting out of control. Therefore, scientists could no longer simply remain at their work; they had to go out and alert the nonscientists to the problems that their work was creating. "Science can reveal the depth of this crisis," the book concluded, "but only social action can resolve it."

By 1970 *Time* magazine was calling Barry Commoner "the Paul Revere of Ecology." It said that Commoner was "endowed with a rare combination of political savvy, scientific soundness and the ability or excite people with his ideas." Commoner was not trained professionally as an ecologist. He came to it in reaction against the dismemberment of modern science by over-specialization, such that its practitioners could not see the forest for their own narrow trees. Scientists as well as laypeople, he believed, had to be educated to the fact that in nature "everything is connected to everything else," which is the primary message of ecology. From the 1950s Commoner played a leading role in every aspect and important phase of the environmental movement. He stated his opposition to nuclear weapons testing in the 1950s, was part of the science information movement of the 1960s, joined the energy debates of the 1970s and the organic farming/pesticides, waste management/recycling, and toxic chemicals issues of the 1980s and 1990s.

Commoner's best-known book, *The Closing Circle* (1971), concluded that "human beings have broken out of the circle of life, driven not by biological need, but by the social organization which they have devised to 'conquer' nature. . . . We must learn how to restore to nature the wealth that we borrow from it." The political lesson to be learned from Los Angeles smog, from fertilizer-poisoned water supplies in Illinois, from algal bloom in Lake Erie, and from detergent foam everywhere was that the older forms of both capitalism and socialism, with their emphases respectively on profit and productivity, were quite inadequate to cope with a deteriorating planet. At the same time Commoner did not want to sit back and contemplate nature fatalistically, or, as he called it, "inactivism."

In the 1970s, as Congress passed laws for clean air, pure water, and the protection of the environment, Barry Commoner's warnings seemed to be generating serious political and legal action because, as *Time* warned in its cover story on Commoner (February 2, 1970), "the price of pollution could be the death of man." Gradually, however, Commoner came to believe that much of the politicians' concern with the environment and with energy conservation was sham. He was particularly disappointed in President Jimmy Carter's national energy policy, which Commoner said was "not designed to solve the energy crisis . . . but merely to delay it."

In *The Politics of Energy* (1979) Commoner called for "a national policy for the transition from the present, nonrenewable energy system to a renewable one"—a transition which he believed a traditional free market economy would be unable to accomplish. He wanted Americans to use solar rather than conventional power, trains rather than automobiles, and methane or gasohol rather than gasoline— proposals which ran not only up against powerful vested interests but also against come basic American habits and preferences. This theme of the evils of an increased dependence on technology remained a theme for the rest of Commoner's career appearing again in 1995 in his book *Making Peace with the Planet.*

Since none of the presidential candidates of 1980 seemed to be dealing with environmental issues in the most superficial way, Barry Commoner ran for president on a ticket of his own, the Citizens Party. It polled only a quarter of one percent of the vote.

Commoner returned to Queens College in 1981 as professor of earth and environmental sciences, serving also as visiting professor of community health at the Albert Einstein College of Medicine. He also moved his Center for the Biology of Natural Sciences to Queens as well. The research conducted at Queens continued to make major advances in environmental science. He discovered the origin of dioxin in trash-burning incinerators, developed alternatives to incinerators and the economic benefits to communities of recycling their trash and developed a computer model that tracks the long-range transport of dioxin and other pollutants from their sources through the food chain into the human diet. This model became invaluable to evaluating dioxin contamination of milk on Wisconsin and Vermont dairy farms.

The 1980s saw a slight diminution of Commoner's influence as capitalist sway was on the rise and environmental concerns fell by the wayside. With the advent of the 1990s, however, increased interests in the environment returned Commoner and his theories to the forefront. In 1995, he was one of the featured speakers at the Dartmouth College Earth Day Conference, commemorating the 25th anniversary of Earth Day. There he called for the government to include in its "industrial policy" a promotion of organic farming and the improvement of electric motors as a clean energy source. He encouraged the development of a preventive strategy that encourages production without polluting in the first place.

*The Earth Times* (October 21, 1995) cited Commoner as one of the "100 Who Made A Difference" world-wide and called him "the dean of the environmental movement, who has influenced two generations." In May 1997, on the occasion of his 80th birthday and to commemorate his 50 year career in environmental research and activism, a symposium was sponsored by CBNS, entitled "Science and Social Action: Barry Commoner's Contribution to the Environmental Movement." The purpose of this event was to both honor Commoner's career of outspoken activism, even before it was fashionable, and to create a momentum for a strong future environmental movement.

In a directory of scientists published in 1984 Barry Commoner listed among his special concerns "alterations in the environment in relation to modern technology" and "the origins and significance of the environmental and energy crises"—realities which would not go away just because people for the moment chose to ignore them.

## Further Reading

Barry Commoner, together with other outstanding figures in the modern environmental movement such as Lewis Mumford, Rene Dubos, F. Fraser Darling, and Paul Ehrlich, is discussed in an informative account by Anne Chisholm, *Philosophers of the Earth* (1972). He made the cover of *Time* (February 2, 1970) in conjunction with an in-depth essay on the ecological issues he helped to publicize. Several of Commoner's own books are written for lay people in non-technical language, including *Science and Survival* (1966), *The Closing Circle* (1971), and *The Politics of Energy* (1979) *Making Peace with the Planet* (1990). *Newsweek* took note of his presidential campaign in an article titled "Dr. Ecology for President" (April 21, 1980). More information can be found on the CBNS Web site at http://o2eqc@qcunix1.acc.qc.edu/CBNS as well as in articles such as "Earth Day with Bella, Barry and friends" *America,* May 13, 1995. ☐

# John Rogers Commons

**The American historian John Rogers Commons (1862-1945) pioneered the study of labor movements in the United States.**

John Commons was born on Oct. 13, 1862, in Richmond, Ind. He was educated at Oberlin College and at Johns Hopkins, where he studied under Richard T. Ely. He sat in the same seminars with another fledgling historian, Frederick Jackson Turner. In 1890 Commons married and became an instructor at Wesleyan University. He returned to Oberlin in 1891 and taught at the University of Indiana the next year. He did not complete his doctorate.

Commons's first book, *Distribution of Wealth* (1894), was based on a Turnerian framework. Commons claimed that a turning point had been reached in the economic affairs of the United States because of the disappearance of easily available land. In 1896 Commons went to Syracuse University to fill a chair in sociology, and the following year he published *Proportional Representation*. This work reflected his belief in a democratic, voluntary society and in a system where balance was attained as a result of conflicting pressures.

In 1899 Commons lost his chair in sociology at Syracuse and worked for several nonacademic groups before going to the University of Wisconsin in 1904. The atmosphere was congenial there, as Commons shared faith in adult education and in the "Wisconsin idea"; that is, the state government would utilize the expertise of university professors in reforming and running this same government. His interest at this time had moved toward the study of labor movements. This culminated in two important books: *Trade Unions and Labor Unions* (1905) and his best-known work, *History of Labor in the United States* (4 vols., 1918-1935). The latter was written in collaboration with his students. In his study of labor unions, Commons concluded that they had resulted as a reaction to industrial concentration and reflected an American attitude of job rather than class orientation.

Commons's ideas found expression in other books, the most important of which are *Legal Foundations of Capitalism* (1924) and *Institutional Economics* (1934). The former portrayed the law as a necessary link to hold society together; the latter held that unemployment was the greatest hazard of capitalism but that collective action could eliminate it. Historical development, Commons believed, came from the bottom up, and the function of scholars was to aid in the reconstruction of society in a classic, progressive way.

Commons died on May 11, 1945. He was acknowledged as the most significant labor historian of his day, and his ideas were perpetuated by his students, the best-known of whom was Selig Perlman at Columbia.

## Further Reading

Commons's autobiography, *Myself* (1934), while pessimistic, catches much of the flavor of the midwestern progressive's character. A discussion of economic ideas may be found in Allen G. Gruchy, *Modern Economic Thought: The American Contribution* (1947), and in volume 3 of Joseph Dorfman, *The Economic Mind in American Civilization* (1949). Commons's *Institutional Economics: Its Place in Political Economy* (1934) presents his mature economic views and contains a complete bibliography of his books and articles published after 1893. ☐

# Anna Comnena

**The Byzantine princess and historian Anna Comnena (1083-1148) was one of the major court figures of the Comneni period. She was the author of the "Alexiad," a history of her father's reign.**

Anna Comnena was the oldest daughter of the emperor Alexius I, a member of the military aristocracy who seized Constantinople and the throne in 1081, and Irene Ducas. Comnena was born in the room reserved for imperial infants and entered the world as heiress to the throne. At an early age she was betrothed to Constantine Ducas, son of Michael VII and a cousin in her mother's family, who also had a claim to the crown. In 1088 a son, John, was born to Irene and Alexius; and as the male heir, the rights of succession were soon transferred to him. Comnena never reconciled herself to this turn of fortune's wheel, and she nurtured a pathological hatred of her younger brother. A second blow to her ambitions was the premature death of her fiancé.

Anna entered into a conspiracy with her mother against John. In 1097 she married Nicephorus Bryennius, a competent commander who took part in the Byzantine defense in the First Crusade, and a pretender to the throne. This man then joined mother and daughter in an attempt to convince Alexius to disinherit his eldest son. It is well known that at various times in Byzantine history imperial court politics were dominated by strong-minded women, and the reign of Alexius was such a time. Comnena took her place beside Maria, the mother of Constantine Ducas, and Anna Dalassena, the Emperor's forceful mother, as a member of the

circle that exerted extraordinary influence. Alexius, however, withstood the assault, although even on his deathbed Comnena tried to make Alexius change his mind.

John moved quickly to have himself proclaimed emperor on his father's death in 1118. Such was Comnena's rancor and her obsession with her brother's success that she made an attempt on his life. It failed; John pardoned her and Comnena came to terms with the situation. She spent her final years in a convent. "I mostly keep in a corner," she wrote, "and occupy myself with books and God."

Comnena's reputation rests upon the history of her father's life and reign, the *Alexiad,* which she completed many years after his death. It is the chief source for this dynamic period in Byzantine history. Comnena was a capable historian. Her high position allowed her access to information that would ordinarily never have been known, and her intelligent handling of a vast amount of material makes an engaging narrative. Her classical instruction is apparent in her references to Homer, Plato, Aristotle, and Euripides, and in her use of heroic figures such as Achilles and Heracles to portray the virtues of valor and prowess among her contemporaries. She had the Greek fondness for physical beauty and a horror of the barbarian, views encouraged by her aristocratic upbringing. Thus she was both attracted and repelled by the crusader Bohemund, so perfect in body and speech, yet the leader of the bellicose Westerners and the main adversary of her father.

Comnena placed great emphasis on the violent nature of Byzantine political life and on the disruptive tendencies

of religious heresy. She wrote of the difficulties connected with raising troops and keeping them in the field. Her history is marred by some confusion in chronology, an anti-Western bias, and an overenthusiastic appreciation of the Emperor. Yet as a narrative of the reign, it rises above these defects to become one of the great contributions to Byzantine history and literature.

### Further Reading

Georgina Buckler, *Anna Comnena* (1929), is a detailed study of the princess as seen through the pages of the *Alexiad.* There is a sparkling profile in Charles Diehl, *Byzantine Portraits* (trans. 1927). Naomi Mitchison, *Anna Comnena* (1928), provides useful information on her career. Ferdinand Chalandon, *Essai sur le règne d'Alexis I^{er} Comnène* (1900; repr. 1960), in French, is fundamental. □

# Arthur Holly Compton

**The American physicist Arthur Holly Compton (1892-1962) discovered the "Compton effect" and the proof of the latitude intensity variation. He also played a critical role in the development of the atomic bomb.**

Arthur Compton was born in Wooster, Ohio, on Sept. 10, 1892, the youngest child of Elias and Otelia Compton. It was midway during Arthur's early formal education that he became interested in science and carried out his first amateur researches. Although he wrote an intelligent student essay on the mammoth, it was chiefly astronomy and aviation that stimulated him. He purchased a telescope and photographed constellations and (in 1910) Halley's comet. Later he constructed and flew a 27-foot-wingspan glider.

During his undergraduate years at the College of Wooster (1909-1913) Compton had to choose a profession. His father encouraged him to devote his life to science. On his graduation from Wooster, therefore, Arthur decided to pursue graduate study, obtaining his master's degree in physics from Princeton University in 1914; in 1916 he obtained his doctoral degree. Immediately after receiving his degree, Compton married Betty Charity McCloskey, a former Wooster classmate; the Comptons had two sons.

### Compton Effect

Compton's first position was as an instructor in physics at the University of Minnesota (1916-1917), where he continued his x-ray researches. Leaving Minnesota, he became a research engineer at the newly established Westinghouse laboratory in East Pittsburgh, where he remained from 1917 to 1919, doing original work on the sodium-vapor lamp and developing instrumentation for aircraft. He left Westinghouse because he came to recognize that fundamentally his interest was not in industrial research but in pure research. In particular, he had become intrigued by a recent observation of the English physicist C. G. Barkla, who had scattered

the Compton effect, a discovery for which he was awarded the Nobel Prize of 1927. The historical significance of Compton's discovery was that it forced physicists for the first time to seriously cope with Einstein's long-neglected and revolutionary 1905 light-quantum hypothesis: in the Compton effect an x-ray behaves exactly like any other colliding particle.

## Cosmic-ray Work

While the discovery of the Compton effect was undoubtedly Compton's single most important contribution to physics, he made many others, both earlier and later. He proved in 1922 that x-rays can be totally internally reflected from glass and silver mirrors, experiments which eventually led to precise values for the index of refraction and electronic populations of substances, as well as to a new and more precise value for the charge of the electron. After Compton left Washington University for the University of Chicago in 1923 (where he later became Charles H. Swift distinguished service professor in 1929 and chairman of the department of physics and dean of the physical sciences in 1940), he reactivated a very early interest and developed a diffraction method for determining electronic distributions in atoms. Still later he and J. C. Stearns proved that ferromagnetism cannot be due to the tilting of electronic orbital planes.

Perhaps the most important work Compton carried out after going to Chicago was his work on cosmic rays. Realizing the importance of these rays for cosmological theories, Compton developed a greatly improved detector and convinced the Carnegie Institution to fund a world survey between 1931 and 1934. The globe was divided into nine regions, and roughly 100 physicists divided into smaller groups sailed oceans, traversed continents, and scaled mountains, carrying identical detectors to measure cosmic-ray intensities.

The most significant conclusion drawn from Compton's world survey was that the intensity of cosmic rays at the surface of the earth steadily decreases as one goes from either pole to the Equator. This "latitude effect" had been noted earlier by the Dutch physicist J. Clay, but the evidence had not been conclusive. Compton's survey therefore proved that the earth's magnetic field deflects at least most of the incident cosmic rays, which is only possible if they are charged particles. Compton's world survey marked a turning point in knowledge of cosmic rays.

## Atomic Bomb and Postwar Endeavors

When World War II broke out, Compton was called upon to assess the chances of producing an atomic bomb. If it were possible to develop an atomic bomb, Compton believed it should be the United States that had possession of it. Detailed calculations on nuclear fission processes proved that the possibility of developing this awesome weapon existed. Compton recommended production, and for 4 years thereafter, as director of the U.S. government's Plutonium Research Project, he devoted all of his administrative, scientific, and inspirational energies to make the bomb a reality.

hard x-rays from aluminum and found that the total amount of scattered radiation was less than that predicted by a wellknown formula of J. J. Thomson. Compton found that he could account for Barkla's observation by assuming that the electrons in the scatterer were very large and therefore diffracting the incident radiation.

Anxious to pursue these studies further, Compton applied for and received a National Research Council fellowship to work with perhaps the foremost experimentalist of the day, Ernest Rutherford, at the Cavendish Laboratory in England. Compton's year in the extremely stimulating intellectual atmosphere at the Cavendish, during which time he carried out gamma-ray scattering experiments and pondered his results, marked a turning point in his career, as he became convinced that he was on the track of a very fundamental physical phenomenon.

Desiring to pursue it further on his own, Compton returned to the United States in 1920 to accept the Wayman Crow professorship of physics at Washington University in St. Louis. There he scattered x-rays from various substances and, eventually, analyzed the scattered radiation by use of a Bragg spectrometer. By the fall of 1922 he had definite experimental proof that x-rays undergo a distinct change in wavelength when scattered, the exact amount depending only on the angle through which they are scattered. Compton published this conclusion in October 1922 and within 2 months correctly accounted for it theoretically. He assumed that an x-ray—a particle of radiation—collides with an electron in the scatterer, conserving both energy and momentum. This process has since become famous as

Compton was under extraordinary pressure as he made arrangements for the purification of uranium and the production of plutonium and many other elements that went into the construction of the atomic bomb. Ultimately, Compton was asked for his personal opinion as to whether the bomb should be dropped on Hiroshima. He gave an affirmative response in the firm conviction that it was the only way to bring the war to a swift conclusion and thereby save many American and Japanese lives.

Between 1945 and 1953 Compton was chancellor of Washington University in St. Louis and strove unceasingly to make that institution a guiding light in higher education. Between 1954 and 1961, as distinguished service professor of natural philosophy, he taught, wrote, and delivered lectures to many groups and, as always, served on numerous boards and committees. In 1961 he became professor-at-large, intending to divide his time between Washington University, the University of California at Berkeley, and Wooster College. His plans were cut short by his sudden death on March 15, 1962, in Berkeley.

Compton was an extraordinarily gifted human being. At the age of 35 he won the Nobel Prize and was also elected to the National Academy of Sciences; later, he was elected to numerous other honorary societies, both foreign and domestic. He received a large number of honorary degrees, medals (including the U.S. government's Medal for Merit), and other honors. In spite of his many achievements and honors, however, he remained a modest and warm human being.

## Further Reading

*The Cosmos of Arthur Holly Compton,* edited by Marjorie Johnston (1968), contains Compton's "Personal Reminiscences," a selection of his writings on scientific and nonscientific subjects, and a bibliography of his scientific writings. Compton discusses his role in the development of the atomic bomb in *Atomic Quest* (1956). The early life of the Compton family is the subject of James R. Blackwood, *The House on College Avenue: The Comptons at Wooster, 1891-1913* (1968). General works on modern physics which discuss Compton include Gerald Holton and Duane H.D. Roller, *Foundations of Modern Physical Science* (1958); Henry A. Boorse and Lloyd Motz, eds., *The World of the Atom* (2 vols., 1966); and Ira M. Freeman, *Physics: Principles and Insights* (1968). □

# Anthony Comstock

**The American antivice crusader Anthony Comstock (1844-1915) fought what he personally defined as immoral and obscene acts and publications. Though his crusades were somewhat fanatic, he did help clarify issues in civil liberties relating to art and free speech.**

Anthony Comstock was born in New Canaan, Conn., the son of a well-to-do farmer. It has been conjectured that his deep love of his mother, who died when he was 10 years old, contributed to his intense morality. The powerful, stocky young man went to work in a general store. During the Civil War he enlisted and served without incident; he was concerned about moral fitness while in the service.

After the war Comstock became a clerk but found no fit outlet for his energies until 1868. Then, having settled in New York and inspired by activities of the Young Men's Christian Association (YMCA), he secured the arrest of two purveyors of pornographic publications. One of them later attacked him with a bowie knife and inflicted a wound on his face, which Comstock hid under the whiskers that became his trademark.

In 1871 Comstock, with the aid of the YMCA, organized a committee to further his work. Two years later he conducted a successful campaign in Washington, D.C., for a strong Federal law (known popularly as the "Comstock Law") making illegal the transmission of obscene matter through the mails. He was appointed a postal inspector, serving without pay. In 1873 he organized the New York Society for the Prevention of Vice and made it a national symbol of tireless defense of traditional values.

In 1871 Comstock married Margaret Hamilton, a woman 10 years his senior. He was a dedicated husband and citizen. As an agent of the government and secretary of his society, Comstock was fearless and resourceful. He did

patently useful work in tracking down, raiding, and prosecuting a wide variety of frauds who advertised false services, including abortions. In 1914 his annual report could note his arraignment over the years in state and Federal courts of some 3,697 persons, of whom 2,740 pleaded guilty or were convicted. Among these were a small number of persons of intelligence and moral fiber concerned for free speech or the right to disseminate knowledge respecting birth control.

But since Comstock's standards remained rigid, they became increasingly impractical. Thus in 1906 his attack, implemented by police, on the Art Students League of New York was not well regarded. Bernard Shaw's denunciation of "Comstockery" evoked considerable agreement. Comstock's 1913 crusade against an innocuous nude painting, Paul Chabas's *September Morn,* did nothing less than make it in reproduction a national sensation.

Comstock's last days were shadowed by reports that he was to lose his post as inspector and by his belief that he was the victim of a conspiracy. He died on Sept. 21, 1915.

## Further Reading

Anthony Comstock, *Traps for the Young* (1883), was edited, with an introduction, by Robert Bremmer in 1967. Charles Gallaudet Trumbull, *Anthony Comstock, Fighter* (1913), is a partisan account. Heywood Broun and Margaret Leech, *Anthony Comstock: Roundsman of the Lord* (1927), treats Comstock with sympathy and good humor.

## Additional Sources

Bates, Anna Louise, *Weeder in the garden of the Lord: Anthony Comstock's life and career,* Lanham, MD: University Press of America, 1995. □

# Henry Tompkins Paige Comstock

**Henry Tompkins Paige Comstock (1820-1870) was a flamboyant American gold prospector whose name is attached to one of the world's most productive mining districts, the Comstock Lode.**

Henry Comstock was born in Trenton, Ontario. From a difficult life on the American frontier he developed a rugged body, an independent spirit, an acquisitive nature, and a shrewd way of dealing. He also became a boaster, braggart, and bully.

Trapping for fur in Canada, Michigan, and Indiana, Comstock was later employed by the American Fur Company. After serving in the Black Hawk and the Mexican wars, he guided overland travelers and also engaged in business in Santa Fe and in Mexico.

Though Comstock was attracted back to the United States by the California gold rush, he returned to Mexico. In 1856 he appeared in Nevada tending a flock of sheep. He claimed 160 acres of unoccupied land for a ranch. Although

he maintained good relations with the Paiute Indians, they were starving and decimated his flock.

In the late 1850s California prospectors began investigating the Nevada slopes of the Sierra range, locating numerous small but promising claims. Comstock joined them and helped organize the first mining district in the Washoe Valley. In 1859 two prospectors struck a particularly rich body of ore. Comstock appeared on the scene, blustering that the two had "jumped his claim." Although they knew that Comstock had neglected to perfect his claim, to quiet his rage they accepted him as a partner. None of the partners realized that an extremely valuable discovery had been made, a discovery now recognized as the beginning of the fabulous Comstock Lode. Unfortunately, none of the partners kept his claim long enough to greatly profit from it. Comstock sold his share to a California syndicate for $11,000—a fraction of its true worth. He remained in the area just long enough to see his name attached to a mining district he had neither discovered nor developed.

Unsuccessful at merchandising in Carson City, Comstock moved to the Pacific Northwest. He constructed a road in Oregon and prospected in Idaho and Montana. In 1870, after an expedition to the Big Horn Mountains, he returned to the Washoe Valley to testify in one of the numerous court suits over his old mine. On Sept. 27, 1870, during a period of mental depression, he took his own life near Bozeman, Mont.

## Further Reading

There is no biography of Comstock. Sketches of his life may be found in Dan De Quille, *The Big Bonanza* (1876; enlarged ed. 1947); in Carl B. Glasscock, *The Big Bonanza: The Story of the Comstock Lode* (1931); and in George D. Lyman, *The Saga of the Comstock Lode: Boom Days in Virginia City, Nevada* (1957). □

# Auguste Comte

**The French philosopher Auguste Comte (1798-1857) developed a system of positive philosophy. He held that science and history culminate in a new science of humanity, to which he gave the name "sociology."**

Born in Montpellier, Auguste Comte abandoned the devout Catholicism and royalism of his family while in his teens. He entered the École Polytechnique in 1814 and proved himself a brilliant mathematician and scientist. Comte was expelled in 1816 for participating in a student rebellion. Remaining in Paris, he managed to do immense research in mathematics, science, economics, history, and philosophy.

At 19 Comte met Henri de Rouvroy, Comte de Saint-Simon, and as a "spiritually adopted son," he became secretary and collaborator to the older man until 1824. The relationship between Saint-Simon and Comte grew increasingly strained for both theoretical and personal reasons and finally degenerated into an acrimonious break over disputed authorship. Saint-Simon was an intuitive thinker interested in immediate, albeit utopian, social reform. Comte was a scientific thinker, in the sense of systematically reviewing all available data, with a conviction that only after science was reorganized in its totality could men hope to resolve their social problems.

In 1824 Comte began a common-law marriage with Caroline Massin when she was threatened with arrest because of prostitution, and he later referred to this disastrous 18-year union as "the only error of my life." During this period Comte supported himself as a tutor. In 1826 he proposed to offer a series of 72 lectures on his philosophy to a subscription list of distinguished intellectuals. After the third lecture Comte suffered a complete breakdown, replete with psychotic episodes. At his mother's insistence he was remarried in a religious ceremony and signed the contract "Brutus Napoleon Comte." Despite periodic hospitalization for mental illness during the following 15 years, Comte was able to discipline himself to produce his major work, the six-volume *Course of Positive Philosophy* (1830-1842).

## Positivist Thought

Positivism as a term is usually understood as a particular way of thinking. For Comte, additionally, the methodology is a product of a systematic reclassification of the sciences and a general conception of the development of man in history: the law of the three stages. Comte, like the Marquis de Condorcet whom he acknowledged as a prede-

cessor and G. W. F. Hegel whom he met in Paris, was convinced that no data can be adequately understood except in the historical context. Phenomena are intelligible only in terms of their origin, function, and significance in the relative course of human history.

But unlike Hegel, Comte held that there is no *Geist,* or spirit, above and beyond history which objectifies itself through the vagaries of time. Comte represents a radical relativism: "Everything is relative; there is the only absolute thing." Positivism absolutizes relativity as a principle which makes all previous ideas and systems a result of historical conditions. The only unity that the system of positivism affords in its pronounced antimetaphysical bias is the inherent order of human thought. Thus the law of the three stages, which he discovered as early as 1820, attempts to show that the history of the human mind and the development of the sciences follow a determinant pattern which parallels the growth of social and political institutions. According to Comte, the system of positivism is grounded on the natural and historical law that "by the very nature of the human mind, every branch of our knowledge is necessarily obliged to pass successively in its course through three different theoretical states: the theological or fictitious state; the metaphysical or abstract state; finally, the scientific or positive state."

These stages represent different and opposed types of human conception. The most primitive type is theological thinking, which rests on the "empathetic fallacy" of reading subjective experience into the operations of nature. The theological perspective develops dialectically through fetishism, polytheism, and monotheism as events are understood as animated by their own will, that of several deities, or the decree of one supreme being. Politically the theological state provides stability under kings imbued with divine rights and supported by military power. As civilization progresses, the metaphysical stage begins as a criticism of these conceptions in the name of a new order. Supernatural entities are gradually transformed into abstract forces just as political rights are codified into systems of law. In the final stage of positive science the search for absolute knowledge is abandoned in favor of a modest but precise inquiry into the relative laws of nature. The absolutist and feudal social orders are replaced gradually by increasing social progress achieved through the application of scientific knowledge.

From this survey of the development of humanity Comte was able to generalize a specific positive methodology. Like René Descartes, Comte acknowledged a unity of the sciences. It was, however, not that of a univocal method of thinking but the successive development of man's ability to deal with the complexities of experience. Each science possesses a specific mode of inquiry. Mathematics and astronomy were sciences that men developed early because of their simplicity, generality, and abstractness. But observation and the framing of hypotheses had to be expanded through the method of experimentation in order to deal with the physical sciences of physics, chemistry, and biology. A comparative method is required also to study the natural sciences, man, and social institutions. Thus even the history of science and methodology supports the law of the three stages by revealing a hierarchy of sciences and methodological direction from general to particular, and simple to complex. Sociology studies particular societies in a complex way since man is both the subject and the object of this discipline. One can consider social groups from the standpoint of "social statics," which comprises the elements of cohesion and order such as family and institutions, or from the perspective of "social dynamics," which analyzes the stage of continuous development that a given society has achieved.

## Later Years

By 1842 Comte's marriage had dissolved, and he was supported by contributions from various intellectuals, including the English philosopher J.S. Mill. In 1844 he met Clothilde de Vaux, and they fell deeply in love. Although the affair was never consummated because Madame de Vaux died in the next year, this intense love influenced Comte in his later work toward a new religion of humanity. He proposed replacing priests with a new class of scientists and industrialists and offered a catechism based on the cult of reason and humanity, and a new calendar replete with positivist saints. While this line of thought was implicit in the aim of sociology to synthesize order and progress in the service of humanity, the farcical elements of Comte's mysticism has damaged his philosophical reputation. He died in obscurity in 1857.

## Further Reading

Comte's various writings have never been gathered into a critical edition. But Comte personally approved of Harriet Martineau's English redaction of the six volumes of his main work into *The Positive Philosophy of Auguste Comte* (3 vols., 1896). Secondary studies of Comte include J. S. Mill, *Auguste Comte and Positivism* (2d ed. rev. 1866; 5th ed. 1907); L. Lévy-Bruhl, *The Philosophy of Auguste Comte* (trans. 1903); and a chapter in Frank E. Manuel, *The Prophets of Paris* (1962). For Comte's relationship with Saint-Simon see Manuel's *The New World of Henri Saint-Simon* (1956); and for his relation to the history of positivism see Leszek Kolakowski, *The Alienation of Reason* (trans. 1968). Also useful are the two works of Richmond Laurin Hawkins, *Auguste Comte and the United States, 1816-1853* (1936) and *Positivism in the United States, 1853-1861* (1938), and F. S. Marvin, *Comte: The Founder of Sociology* (1936).

## Additional Sources

Gould, F. J. (Floyd Jerome), *The life story of Auguste Comte: with a digest review of ancient, religious, and "modern" philosophy,* Austin, TX: American Atheist Press, 1984.

Pickering, Mary, *Auguste Comte: an intellectual biography,* Cambridge; New York: Cambridge University Press, 1993.

Standley, Arline Reilein, *Auguste Comte,* Boston: Twayne Publishers, 1981. □

# Barber B. Conable Jr.

**Barber B. Conable, Jr. (born 1922), headed the most important lending institution committed to financing economic projects in developing countries, the World Bank, from 1986 to 1991. His tenure was noted for a complete overhaul of the bank and its personnel and a vital capital increase campaign. He piloted the bank through times of turbulent Third World debt defaults and restructuring.**

arber B. Conable, Jr., was born in Warsaw, New York, on November 2, 1922. After receiving his Bachelor's degree from Cornell in 1942, Conable joined the United States Marine Corps, serving out the end of World War II (1942-1946) and serving again during the Korean conflict (1950-1951), reaching the rank of colonel. He graduated with honors from Cornell's law school in 1948 and became a member of the New York State Bar that same year. Conable practiced law first in Buffalo (until 1950), then Batavia (until 1964). His career in the public sector began in the New York State Legislature (1963-1964), and from there he went on to become the 30th District representative to the U.S. House of Representatives, a post he successfully held for 20 years (1965-1985).

As the ranking Republican on the House Ways and Means Committee, Conable was respected as one of the most influential and knowledgeable legislators on tax issues, with important contributions to laws on trade (1974), capital gains (1977), and social security (1977). Yet his appointment to head the World Bank in 1986 was seen as somewhat of a surprise, since Conable had no banking

experience, only slight management experience, and virtually all of his legislative experience related to domestic rather than international issues. Nevertheless, what the Reagan administration desired was an insider on Capitol Hill who could successfully lobby for a capital increase for the institution, but an outsider to the bank who could reign in its perceived bloated bureaucracy and change its culture away from central planning toward market-oriented solutions.

The World Bank was created after World War II to channel funds for economic and social development projects from modern industrial nations to poor agricultural and newly industrializing nations in Latin America, Africa, and Asia. Because the United States provided the largest share of equity capital, the bank's president had traditionally been an American and its headquarters located in Washington, D.C. Three affiliated institutions make up the bank—the International Bank for Reconstruction and Development (IBRD), the International Development Association (IDA), and the International Finance Corporation (IFC).

The IBRD makes interest-bearing loans for public development projects (roads, dams, energy, communications, schools) and provides technical assistance, using funds raised by issuing bonds on world capital markets. These bonds are backed by the 151 member countries of the bank, thus generating a pool of funds for poor countries that on their own would lack the necessary credit rating to issue bonds. The IDA provides additional capital to the poorest countries on a below-market interest rate (i.e., part grant), while the IFC makes additional capital available to private industrial enterprises in developing countries.

During the 1970s, developing countries also borrowed heavily from private commercial banks in the United States, Europe, and Japan. Following the second oil shock of 1979 and the world-wide recession in the early 1980s, however, developing countries could not find export markets for their products except at much lower prices. While export revenues declined, debt service payments rose owing to much higher interest rates, creating a financial squeeze. Unable to obtain dollars to repay the interest and principal on the $1 trillion debt, many countries in Latin America and Africa suspended payments, leading to the crisis. As a result, new loans dried-up, thereby reducing economic growth by preventing countries from importing capital equipment, spare parts, and other items needed to expand production.

The World Bank acted slowly in seeking a solution. To switch from project lending to broader adjustment lending for macroeconomic assistance meant a capital campaign was needed. While the other member nations of the World Bank were in support, the U.S. Congress had its own fiscal deficits and resisted helping the bank, which was perceived to be over-staffed and inefficient. To rectify this perception, Conable's first task was reorganizing the bank's structure and personnel in 1987. This created internal conflict and a lowering of morale as 10 percent of the work force of 6,500 professionals was retired or fired.

Critics charged that Conable's handling of the restructuring was inept since he was an outsider and relied too heavily on the advice of those who stood to gain by internal politics. Many top managers, particularly those skilled in financial market aspects, resigned the bank in favor of private sector jobs. Furthermore, since the multilateral bank is staffed by a pool of international civil servants, intense nationalism and favoritism were alleged in the selection process.

Despite these pitfalls, the reorganized bank was able to obtain the desired capital increase in 1988 and to expand lending to over $21 billion by 1989. Conable led the bank toward a greater emphasis on market-oriented solutions to development over central planning, in keeping with the debt solution put forth by U.S. Treasury Secretary Nicholas Brady in 1989. The Brady Plan called for private commercial banks to write off some of their outstanding loans, thereby reducing the crippling indebtedness of poor countries. In return, the remaining private claims would be guaranteed, and a new infusion of loans from wealthier nations would occur through the auspices of the World Bank and the International Monetary Fund.

After retiring from Congress, Conable served on the boards of directors of the New York Stock Exchange and various corporations, in addition to being senior fellow at the conservative "think-tank" the American Enterprise Institute and distinguished professor at the University of Rochester. He also served as chairman of the Museum of the American Indian in New York City and on the boards of the Urban Institute, the Dole Foundation, and the Smith Richardson Foundation.

Citing his age and poor health, Conable announced his resignation from the World Bank effective September 1, 1991. At the end of his successful five-year term, he retired to his home in Alexander, New York. The Bush White House announced that his successor would be Lewis T. Preston (born 1926), a long-time executive with J. P. Morgan & Company.

## Further Reading

A general overview of international mechanisms and institutions may be found in J. C. Pool and S. Stamos, *The ABCs of International Finance* (1987). For an evaluation of the handling of the debt crisis see Shafigul Islam, "Going Beyond the Brady Plan," *Challenge* (July/August 1989). Excellent statistics on developing nations are incorporated in the *World Bank Development Report,* which is updated annually. □

# James Bryant Conant

**James Bryant Conant (1893-1978) was an American chemist, president of Harvard University, U.S. Ambassador and educational critic. He was an effective spokesman for the support of national policies by private and public scientific and educational institutions.**

James Conant was born on March 26, 1893, in Dorchester, Massachusetts. Both his father's and his mother's families trace themselves back to 17th-century New England settlers. After graduating *magna cum laude* from Harvard College in 1914, Conant pursued graduate studies in organic chemistry and received his doctorate in 1916. During the next three years he served as instructor at Harvard, tried unsuccessfully to set up a private chemistry laboratory, and joined the Army's Chemical Warfare Service. Engaged in the secret production of poison gases, Conant advanced to the rank of major, belonging to the elite group of organic chemists who constituted the nucleus of a growing profession in universities, industry, foundations, and the armed forces.

Returning to Harvard, Conant was appointed assistant professor in 1919, associate professor in 1925, and professor in 1927. He served as chairman of the Division of Chemistry, as consultant to the Du Pont Company, and on the Board of Scientific Advisers of the Rockefeller Institute for Medical Research. In 1933 he became president of Harvard University (until 1953). Following the policies of Harvard's recent presidents, Conant placed heavy emphasis on bringing talented students and faculty to Harvard. He devised interdisciplinary studies in American civilization and the history of science to improve the liberal education of the undergraduates. He sought to strengthen the graduate school of education by introducing the master of arts in teaching program.

In 1934 Conant joined the Board of Trustees of the Carnegie Foundation for the Advancement of Teaching.

During World War II he directed the resources of Harvard in support of the war effort, and he himself became an adviser to the Manhattan Project, which produced the first atomic bomb. He was a member of the General Advisory Committee of the Atomic Energy Commission from 1947 to 1952 and, after his retirement from Harvard in 1953, ambassador to West Germany from 1955 to 1957. Following that, from 1957 to 1959 he undertook a study of American secondary education for the Carnegie Foundation and thereafter served in various roles as educational consultant. He died on February 11, 1978 in Hanover, New Hampshire.

## Further Reading

Conant's educational views are contained in the series of books he wrote on secondary education: *The American High School Today* (1959); *The Child, the Parent and the State* (1959); *Slums and Suburbs: A Commentary on Schools in Metropolitan Areas* (1961); and *The Comprehensive High School* (1967). In *On Understanding Science: An Historical Approach* (1947) Conant wrote on the place of science in the general education curriculum of the undergraduate, and in *The Education of American Teachers* (1963) he discussed teacher education.

A more personal account is Conant's autobiography, *My Several Lives: Memoirs of a Social Inventor* (1970). Paul Franklin Douglass, *Six upon the World: Toward an American Culture for an Industrial Age* (1954), examines Conant's achievements in the context of the postwar technological society. See also Lawrence A. Cremin, *The Transformation of the School: Progressivism in American Education, 1876-1957* (1961); Edgar Z. Friedenberg, *The Dignity of Youth and Other Atavisms* (1965), which has a chapter critical of Conant; Adolphe E. Meyer, *An Educational History of the American People* (1967); and Robert E. Potter, *The Stream of American Education* (1967). □

# Prince de Condé

**The French general Louis de Bourbon, Prince de Condé (1621-1686), became known as the "great Condé" because of his victories in the Low Countries. As the principal French nobleman, he was important in politics but egotistical, imprudent, and stubborn.**

Louis de Bourbon was born in Paris on Sept. 8, 1621, to Henri de Bourbon, Prince de Condé, second cousin of Louis XIII, and Charlotte de Montmorency. He was entitled Duc d'Enghien until his father's death in 1646. From 1630 to 1636 he attended the Jesuit school in Bourges, studying Latin classics, Aristotelian philosophy, mathematics, the *Institutes* of Justinian, and political history. He retained intellectual tastes all his life and was long a freethinker on religious matters. His education was completed at the royal military school in Paris.

In accordance with his father's wishes, in 1641 Enghien married Claire-Clémence de Maillé-Brézé, daughter of Cardinal Richelieu's younger sister. He lived with his wife infrequently for brief periods. They had a son in late 1643 and a daughter in 1656.

Enghien's military ability was discernible in his first three campaigns (1640-1642). In the spring of 1643 he was put in command of the army in Picardy, and on May 18 he won an overwhelming victory at Rocroy northwest of Sedan. His cavalry turned the flank of the Flemish cavalry and scattered the enemy's rear regiments; he rallied the French infantry and finally overcame the immobile firepower of the veteran Spanish infantry, then the most feared in Europe.

Other victories followed. With his cousin the Vicomte de Turenne, Enghien took the west bank of the Rhine in 1644 and defeated the Bavarian army in 1645. He captured Dunkerque and other northern towns in 1646. Commanding the French forces in Spain in 1647, Condé was unable to take Lerida in Catalonia. But in 1648 he returned north to Hainaut and routed the cavalry of Lorraine and the Spanish infantry at Lens on August 20, a victory that finally brought about the Treaty of Münster.

In the ensuing period of sporadic revolt in France, Louis, now Prince de Condé, aided the queen regent and Cardinal Mazarin by organizing a blockade around rebellious Paris in early 1649. But the queen regent eventually found Condé intolerable and had him arrested with his brother and brother-in-law on Jan. 18, 1650. Finally a realignment of factions in Paris persuaded Mazarin that the princes were more dangerous in prison than at large. He freed them on Feb. 13, 1651. Yet Condé was increasingly dissatisfied.

In September, Condé went to Bordeaux to organize an independent base in the southwest. In 1652, his position there crumbling, he returned to Paris but found his forces locked out of the city. Turenne, now in command of a royal army, tried to pin Condé against the eastern walls of Paris on July 2, 1652. Condé's forces were suddenly let into the city, and cannon were fired from the Bastille on Turenne's troops. Condé's popularity in Paris, however, rapidly declined. He soon departed northward, was named commanding general for Spain, and proceeded to Brussels in March 1653.

While Condé opposed Turenne in a series of inconclusive campaigns in the Low Countries, one of Condé's agents attempted to establish friendly relations with Oliver Cromwell in England. But Cromwell formed an alliance instead with the French king, and in 1658 the allies defeated Condé decisively in the Battle of the Dunes outside Dunkerque. The Spanish negotiators made amnesty for Condé a condition of the peace settlement of 1659 and he returned to France. In 1667 he was again given command of a French army. During February 1668 he captured all the principal towns of Franche-Comté. The province was restored to Spain 3 months later.

In the summer of 1673 the young stadtholder William III was eager to use the imperial, Spanish, and Dutch armies against Condé. On Aug. 11, 1674, they fought an all-day battle near Seneffe south of Brussels, with heavy losses on both sides but no victor.

After 1675 Condé lived at Chantilly. He was reconverted to Catholicism the year before his death in 1686.

## Further Reading

The most extensive work on Condé is by King Louis Philippe's second son, Henri d'Orléans, Duc d'Aumale, *Histoire des princes de Condé pendant les XVI et XVII siècles,* vols. 3-7 (1863-1896). It includes hundreds of letters from, to, and about Condé and is generally sympathetic. Material on Condé is also in John B. Wolf, *Louis XV* (1968). □

# Étienne Bonnot de Condillac

**The French philosopher and educator Étienne Bonnot de Condillac (1715-1780) was a Lockean psychologist and early positivist who greatly influenced economic and political thought in prerevolutionary France.**

On Sept. 30, 1715, Étienne Bonnot was born to Gabriel Bonnot, Vicomte de Mably. He later became the Abbé de Condillac, a territory purchased by his father in 1720. Educated in Paris at the Sorbonne and at St-Suplice, he was ordained a priest in 1740 but chose to become a writer and a tutor. From 1740 to 1758 he frequented the literary salons of Paris and worked at his own education. John Locke's psychology and empiricism and Sir Isaac Newton's search for fundamental principles were strong influences in his reading.

Condillac's *Essai sur l'origine des connaissances humaines* (1746) followed Locke's principles but reduced the operations of human understanding to one principle—sensation—and treated reflection as a sequence and comparison of sensations. The work stated language to be the source of man's superiority to animals and recognized interest as an intimate part of any perception. *Traité des systèmes* (1749) was a study on proper method and the proper use of hypothesis and system.

In the *Traité des sensations* (1754) Condillac showed how ideas originate through sensation. The work stressed the integration of man's senses and stated that the higher forms of understanding develop from mere animal sensation because of man's needs. Condillac's *Traité des animaux* (1755) opposed Buffon's and Descartes's view of animals by declaring that man is like the animals, although more complex because of his more numerous needs, and that neither man nor animal is mere machine.

In 1758 Condillac went to Parma for 9 years to tutor Louis XV's grandson, Ferdinand de Parma. During this time he composed a 16-volume *Cours d'études pour l'instruction du Prince de Parme.* Opposition from the bishop of Parma delayed publication until 1775, when the volumes appeared in France, under the relaxed censorship of the Turgot ministry.

On returning to France in 1767, Condillac declined an offer to tutor the Dauphin's sons and retired instead to a

quiet life of writing at Flux. His 1776 work, *Le Commerce et le gouvernement consideres relativement l'un à l'autre,* considered the consequences of his basic psychological ideas in relation to political economy. Asked to compose an elementary logic for Palatinate schools, Condillac finished *La Logique* in 1779. He died from a fever on Aug. 2, 1780. His unfinished *Langage des calculs* was published posthumously.

In his opposition to obscurantist metaphysics Condillac was an early positivist. He insisted that, although man is ignorant of the thing-in-itself, he need not be in error if he will use a language of analysis, observation with thoroughness, and systems with circumspection.

## Further Reading

The best introduction to Condillac in English is *Condillac's Treatise on the Sensations,* translated by Geraldine Carr (1930). Zora Schaupp, *The Naturalism of Condillac* (1926), is a fine introduction to Condillac's thought in relation to early-20th-century psychology. A less readable but still useful work is Isabel F. Knight, *The Geometric Spirit: The Abbé de Condillac and the French Enlightenment* (1968). □

# Marquis de Condorcet

**The French thinker Marie Jean Antoine Nicolas Caritat, Marquis de Condorcet (1743-1794), expressed the spirit of the Enlightenment in reform** proposals and writings on progress. He was the only philosophe to participate in the French Revolution.

Born in Ribemont in Picardy on Sept. 17, 1743, the Marquis de Condorcet was educated at the Jesuit college in Reims and later at the College of Navarre in Paris. He excelled in mathematics and in 1765 wrote the *Essay on Integral Calculus.* In 1769 he became a member of the Academy of Science, later becoming its perpetual secretary, and in 1782 was elected to the French Academy. He married Sophie de Grouchy in 1786, and their home became one of the famous salons of the period.

Prior to the French Revolution, Condorcet wrote biographies of A.R.J. Turgot and Voltaire and essays on the application of the theory of probabilities to popular voting, on the American Revolution and the Constitutional Convention, and on the abolition of the slave trade and slavery. In 1791 he was elected to the Legislative Assembly and later to the National Convention, where he continued to manifest his liberal and egalitarian sentiments.

In the report of the Committee on Public Education, Condorcet advocated universal primary school education and the establishment of a self-regulating educational system under the control of a National Society of Sciences and Arts to protect education from political pressures. However, the Legislative Assembly was hostile to all autonomous corporate structures and ignored Condorcet's plan. His proposal for a new constitution, establishing universal male suffrage, proportional representation, and local self-government, was similarly set aside by the Jacobin-dominated National Convention, which considered it too moderate.

Condorcet's moderate democratic leanings and his vote against the death penalty for Louis XVI led to his being outlawed by the Jacobin government on July 8, 1793. He went into hiding in the home of a close friend, Madame Varnet, where he wrote the *Sketch of an Historical Picture of the Progress of the Human Mind,* his most famous and most optimistic work. This capsulized history of progress presented a set of intellectual and moral goals toward which men ought to work, and it was based on the utilitarian conviction that invention and progressive thought arise out of social need. According to Condorcet, the future progress of reason had become inevitable with the invention of the printing press and the advances in science and criticism. Rather than emphasizing the role of the solitary genius as the agent of progress, the *Sketch* stressed the dissemination of useful knowledge among the masses.

After 8 months of hiding, Condorcet fled Paris but was arrested on March 27, 1794, and imprisoned in Bourgla-Reine. On March 29 he was found dead in his cell. His identity was unknown, and it is ironic that this critic of classical education was eventually identified by a copy of Horace's *Epistles* that he had been carrying at the time of his arrest.

## Further Reading

The best biography of Condorcet is Jacob Salwyn Schapiro, *Condorcet and the Rise of Liberalism* (1934; new ed. 1962).

There is an excellent analysis of Condorcet's philosophy in Frank Edward Manuel, *The Prophets of Paris* (1962). Ann Elizabeth Burlingame, *Condorcet: The Torch Bearer of the French Revolution* (1930), is still useful. ☐

# James Hall Cone

**The American theologian James Hall Cone (born 1938) was the author of the first major attempt to integrate Black Power philosophy with theology. He became the leading exponent of *Black theology* in the decades following the 1960s.**

James Hall Cone was born in Fordyce, Arkansas, on August 5, 1938. After attending the local schools, he received a B.A. degree from Philander Smith College (Arkansas) in 1958, a B.D. degree from Garrett Theological Seminary (Wisconsin) in 1961, and M.A. and Ph.D. degrees from Northwestern University in 1963 and 1965, respectively. He taught religion at Philander Smith College, Adrian College (Michigan), and beginning in 1970 at Union Theological Seminary in New York City, where he was awarded the distinguished Charles A. Briggs Chair in systematic theology in 1977. He was visiting professor at several colleges and universities throughout the United States, including Drew University, Princeton Theological Seminary, University of Notre Dame, and Howard University. He lectured throughout the world and in virtually every state in the Union. Cone received the American Black Achievement Award, in the category of Religion in 1992.

James Cone became the preeminent Black theologian in the United States and the leading exponent for what is termed *Black theology*. The decade of the 1960s was a period of great social and racial turmoil in the United States. The civil rights movement of the early and mid 1960s with its model of passive resistance, led by the Reverend Martin Luther King, Jr., had become more militant and separatist toward the end of that decade, with Malcolm X the most charismatic leader of this more revolutionary approach on the part of some Blacks. "Black power" became the clarion call for this more radical segment. The time was ripe for Black theologians to articulate a new vision of theology that would be geared to the Black Power movement.

The first major attempt to integrate Black Power with theology was James Cone's book *Black Theology and Black Power* (1969). Here Cone developed the thesis that Black Power is "Christ's central message to twentieth century America," that Black Power means "complete emancipation of Black people from white oppression by whatever means Black people deem necessary," and that "Whether whites want to hear it or not, *Christ is Black, baby,* with all the features which are so detestable to white society." Such rhetoric was not likely to win friends among white people, so consequently Cone became the target of a barrage of white criticism. What his critics failed to do was to read Cone's book from cover to cover, for in the final paragraph of his book he explains: "Being black in America has very

little to do with skin color. To be black means that your heart, your soul, your mind, and your body are where the dispossessed are. . . . Being reconciled to God does not mean that one's skin is physically black. It essentially depends on the color of your heart, soul, and mind." For Cone, then, blackness is a symbol for the oppressed and whiteness is a symbol for the oppressor.

In his subsequent writings Cone consistently maintained the use of these symbols. In his second book, *A Black Theology of Liberation* (1970), Cone's rhetoric sounds strident if one fails to understand his use of the terms *black* and *white*. For example: "To be black is to be committed to destroying everything this country loves and adores." Or again, "Black theology will accept only a love of God which participates in the destruction of the white enemy." In looking back on these earlier books, Cone later admitted that he would no longer use such extreme language, but, nevertheless, his condemnation of racism and oppression was as strong as ever.

James Cone's influence continued to grow after the publication of his first book in 1969. He played a major role as catalyst in the emergence of liberation theologies throughout the Third World in their concern to free the oppressed from political, social, and economic misery. He was an effective spokesperson at the meetings of the Ecumenical Association of Third World Theologians, which beginning in 1976 brought together theologians from Africa, Asia, and Latin America. One of the most remarkable qualities about James Cone was his ability and willingness to grow and change with the times as he confronted new challenges. As early as 1977 he had come to see that Christian theology must develop a world-embracing vision that extends far beyond the immediate concerns of Black America and the particularities of the Christian faith. He wrote in *Cross Currents* in 1977: "I think that the time has come for black theologians and church people to move beyond a mere reaction to white racism in America and begin to extend our vision of a new socially constructed humanity in the whole inhabited world. . . . For humanity is whole, and cannot be isolated into racial and national groups." Cone readily admitted that in his earlier years as a theologian he failed to appreciate that he was guilty of male chauvinism and sexist language, especially with respect to Black women. In the introduction to the revised edition of *Black Theology and Black Power* he wondered aloud, "With black women playing such a dominant role in the African-American liberation struggle, past and present, how could I have been so blind?"

Twenty years after the first release of *A Black Theology of Liberation,* Cone's *Martin & Malcolm & America* compared the messages and missions of Martin Luther King and Malcolm X. "Paradoxically, in some ways Malcolm has more to say to us today than Martin does. Malcolm had seen the nightmare early on and had learned to carve out hope. Martin began with the dream and faced the nightmare toward the end of his life when he began to see the massive poverty in the ghettos of Los Angeles and Chicago. He began to recognize the sickness of American society and widened his vision to include the black urban poor and the poor of the Third World.''

Cone's willingness to learn as well as to teach was a mark of his true greatness. He ranks in the top echelon of theologians of all races and faiths today who are most admired and respected. In addition to his incisive writings he was a brilliant lecturer and a fiery preacher. And if the medium is the message, then the teachings of James Cone find their most eloquent testimony in the charisma and quality of his personal life and human relationships.

## Further Reading

There is little published information on James Cone. One biographical work is Rufus Burrow *James H. Cone and Black Liberation Theology* (1994). Cone is listed in the *Dictionary of American Scholars* and the *Encyclopedia of Black America*. His best known book is *Black Theology and Black Power* (1969; rev. ed., 1989). Other important books include *A Black Theology of Liberation* (1970) (1990, 20th anniversary edition), *The Spirituals and the Blues: An Interpretation* (1972), *God of the Oppressed* (1975), *Black Theology: A Documentary History* (1979), *My Soul Looks Back* (1982), *For My People: Black Theology and the Black Church* (1984, 1986), *Martin & Malcolm & America: A Dream or a Nightmare* (1991) and *Black Theology: A Documentary History* (1993). □

# Confucius

**The Chinese teacher and philosopher Confucius (551-479 B.C.) was the founder of the humanistic school of philosophy known as the Ju or Confucianism, which taught the concepts of benevolence, ritual, and propriety.**

In the 6th century B.C. China had begun to disintegrate into a loose confederation of city-states. The nominal ruler of China was the King of Chou, who occupied the imperial capital at Loyang in northcentral China. The Chou had been the supreme rulers of the entire Chinese Empire 500 years earlier, but now they were simply a pawn of the competing Chinese states. This period is generally depicted as a time of great moral decline, when principles and integrity meant little to the official classes.

Confucius, an obscure school teacher, found this situation horrifying, and he attempted to seek a remedy by reviving the great moral teachings of the sages of the past. That he failed is unimportant, for his teachings had a profound influence on later Chinese thought and formed the basis for the dominant Chinese ideology, known as Confucianism.

## Traditions and Sources on His Life

Confucius is the Latinized name of K'ung Fu-tzu (Great Master K'ung). His original name was K'ung Ch'iu; he is also known by the style name of K'ung Chung-ni. After he died, a large number of myths and legends grew up around his name, making difficult an accurate description of the historical Confucius. Traditionally, Confucius was venerated as a Chinese saint, and for a long time a critical, objective appraisal of his life was impossible. In more recent times both Chinese and Western scholars have ventured to discard some of the legends and myths and to reconstruct a biography from more reliable sources. As a result, a variety of new images of Confucius have emerged, many of them contradicting each other, and the demythologized picture of Confucius is as confusing as the traditional, mythical one.

The most detailed traditional account of Confucius' life is contained in the *Records of the Historian* (*Shih chi*) by Ssu-ma Ch'ien, who lived 145-86 B.C. Many modern scholars have dismissed this biography as a fictionalized, romanticized legend by a Confucian apologist. Nevertheless, in spite of obvious anachronisms, when used with the *Analects* (*Lun yü*), which purports to record actual conversations between Confucius and his disciples, one can reconstruct a satisfactory outline of the philosopher's family background, his career, and the role he played in 6th-century society.

According to the *Records of the Historian*, Confucius was a descendant of a branch of the royal house of Shang, the dynasty that ruled China prior to the Chou. His family, the K'ung, had moved to the small state of Lu, located in the modern province of Shantung in northeastern China. There is an early tradition that Confucius' father at an advanced age divorced his first wife because she had borne him only daughters and one disfigured son and married a 15-year-old girl from the Yen clan, who gave birth to K'ung Ch'iu. Ssu-ma Ch'ien refers to the relationship as a ''wild union,'' which very possibly indicates that Confucius was an illegitimate child.

Confucius' birth date is given in early sources as either 551 or 552, although the former is more commonly accepted. The exact status of his family at the time of his birth is obscured by later attempts to create for him an illustrious lineage. In the *Analects,* Confucius says that during his youth he was in humble circumstances and forced to acquire many different skills. It is clear that even though the fortunes of his family had declined, he was no commoner. Confucius unquestionably belonged to the aristocratic class known as the *shih.* By the time of Confucius most *shih* served as court officials, scholars, and teachers, and Confucius' first occupation appears to have been as keeper of the Lu granary and later as supervisor of the fields, both low positions but consistent with his *shih* status.

## Career as a Teacher

We do not know exactly when Confucius embarked on his teaching career, but it does not appear to have been much before the age of 30. In 518 he may have served as tutor to one of the prominent clans of Lu, the Meng, who wished their sons to be educated in the *li,* or ritual. He is alleged to have journeyed to Loyang that year to instruct himself in the traditional Chou ritual. Here he is said to have met the famous Taoist teacher Lao Tzu, who reportedly bluntly rebuked Confucius for his stuffiness and arrogance. This story is undoubtedly apocryphal and belongs to the corpus of anti-Confucian lore circulated by the Taoist school.

The nominal head of state in Lu at this time was a duke (*kung*), but the actual power lay in the hands of three clans: the Meng, Shu, and Chi. The most powerful of the three in Confucius' time was the Chi, which was frequently in conflict with the ducal house and the other clans. In 517 Duke Chao of Lu took prisoner the prime minister, Chi P'ing-tzu, and was immediately attacked by the other two clans. The duke fled to the neighboring state of Ch'i, Confucius apparently felt a certain loyalty to the duke and fled with him. There are a number of stories about Confucius' adventures in Ch'i, but most of them appear spurious.

Confucius eventually returned to Lu; one suggested date is 515. For several years after his return he does not appear to have accepted a governmental position and instead spent most of his time studying and teaching. He gathered around him a large number of students. Although we can only guess at the exact curriculum of the school, it undoubtedly included instruction in ritual, music, history, and poetry.

In 510 Duke Chao died without ever having returned to Lu, and the Chi clan set up another member of the ducal house as Duke Ting. Shortly thereafter, in 505, a swashbuckling adventurer named Yang Hu, who had been a supporter of the Chi family, rebelled and seized power in Lu.

The clans were able to gather enough strength to expel Yang Hu from Lu in 501, but at the same time another military commander, Kung-shan Fu-jao, gained control of the fortified city of Pi, which was the fief of the Chi clan.

Kung-shan Fu-jao issued an invitation to Confucius to join his government. The *Analects* records that Confucius was tempted to accept the offer, and only after being rebuked by his disciple Tzu-lu, who was in the employ of the Chi clan, did the master reluctantly decline. The decision to violate his own principles and serve a man in open revolt against the constituted authority of his state is a good indication of Confucius' intense desire to obtain a position, no matter how compromising, from which to implement his ideas.

## Political Career

Confucius finally did obtain the post he wanted in 501, this time with the legitimate government of Lu. He first served as magistrate of the city of Chang-tu and later was promoted to the important position of minister of justice (*ssu-k'ou*). There are a number of stories about Confucius' actions in this office, most of which cannot be verified. One of these stories concerns Confucius' role at the Chia-ku convention in the state of Ch'i, a meeting between the dukes of Ch'i and Lu in 500. At least five sources record that Confucius was responsible for thwarting a plot by Ch'i to kidnap the Duke of Lu and was able to force Ch'i to restore territory it had seized from Lu. Scholars have questioned the historicity of Confucius' participation in this event, but the wide currency of the account must indicate some grain of truth.

Confucius probably owed his position in Lu to the influence of the Chi family, which was still the dominant power. We know from the *Analects* that he was on especially good terms with Chi K'ang-tzu, the son of the head of the Chi clan. Several of Confucius' disciples were employed by the Chi family. Because of his close association with the Chi clan, which in effect was a usurper of the ducal power, it might be supposed that Confucius had compromised his integrity. However, Confucius and his disciples actually seem to have worked to reduce the power of the three clans. For example, in 498 they were able to extract promises from the Chi, Meng, and Shu families to demolish their fortified cities, which were their bases of power. The Chi and Shu actually had begun preparations to dismantle their cities when the Meng reneged and the plan was abandoned. Nevertheless, the episode is a clear example of Confucius' interest in restoring legitimacy in Lu.

## His Travels

It must have been shortly after the failure of his plan to dismantle the fortified cities that Confucius decided to leave his home in Lu and embark on a long journey throughout eastern China. The traditional explanation for Confucius' decision to leave is that Ch'i believed that if Confucius continued to advise the Duke of Lu, Lu would become more powerful and eventually dominate the other states around it. Therefore, in order to distract the duke from his political duties, Ch'i sent him 80 beautiful dancers and 30 teams of horses. The duke accepted them and became so engrossed that he did not hold court for 3 days, which so incensed Confucius that he resigned his post. This story clearly is a fabrication designed to disguise a less noble motive for Confucius' departure, namely, pressure from the clans, who must have been alarmed by Confucius' attempt to reduce their power.

Confucius left Lu accompanied by several of his disciples, including the former soldier Chung Yu (Tzu-lu) and Yen Hui, his favorite. They wandered throughout the eastern states of Wei, Sung, and Ch'en and at various times had their lives threatened. Confucius was almost assassinated in Sung by one Huan T'ui. On another occasion he was mistaken for the adventurer Yang Hu and was arrested and held in confinement until his true identity became known.

Confucius was received with great respect by the rulers of the states he visited, and he even seems to have received occasional emoluments. He spent much of his time developing and expounding his ideas on the art of government, as well as continuing his teaching. He acquired a large following, and the solidification of the Confucian school probably occurred during these years of exile. Not all of his disciples followed him on his travels, and several of them actually returned to Lu and assumed positions with the Chi clan. It may have been through their influence that in 484 Confucius was invited back to Lu.

## Final Years

Confucius was warmly received in Lu, but there is no indication that he was given a responsible position. Little is known about his last years, although this would have been a logical time for him to work on the many texts and documents he is reputed to have acquired on his journey. Much of his time was devoted to teaching, and he seems to have remained more or less aloof from political affairs.

This was an unhappy period for Confucius. His only son died about this time; his favorite disciple, Yen Hui, died the very year of his return to Lu; and in 480 Tzu-lu was killed in battle. All these losses Confucius felt deeply, and his despair and frustration must have been intensified by the realization that his political ideas had found no sympathetic ear among the rulers of his own state. Confucius died in 479. His disciples conducted his funeral and observed a mourning period for him.

## Confucius' Writings

Confucius has been considered responsible for editing and writing some of the most important works in the Chinese tradition. According to relatively early sources, he arranged the classical anthology of early Chinese poetry, the *Book of Odes* (*Shih ching*), into its present order and discarded spurious material from a historical work known as the *Book of Documents* (*Shu ching*). He is also credited with writing parts of the great divination classic, the *Book of Changes* (*I ching*), and the book of ritual, the *Records of Rites* (*Li chi*). His name is also associated with a work on music, the *Book of Music* (*Yüeh ching*), which is now lost. Few modern scholars accept any of these traditional attributions, and Confucius' connection with these books is simply another aspect of the traditional Confucian myth.

One work that cannot be dismissed so easily, however, is the *Spring and Autumn Annals* (*Ch'un ch'iu*), which is a chronological record of the reigns of the 12 dukes of Lu, beginning with the year 722 and ending in 479 B.C. As early

as the philosopher Mencius (ca. 317-289 B.C.), Confucius has been credited with compiling or editing this work, which was claimed to contain hidden criticisms of many of the Lu rulers. Later Confucian scholars tried to discover these hidden criticisms, but most scholars now agree that the *Spring and Autumn Annals* is simply a dry chronicle, containing no hidden meanings, and in spite of Mencius's testimony, Confucius had nothing to do with it.

## Confucius' Teachings

Although we cannot be certain that Confucius wrote any of the works attributed to him, it is still possible to know something about the general nature of his philosophy. Shortly after his death his disciples compiled a work known as the *Lun yü*, commonly translated as the *Analects* but more accurately rendered as the *Edited Conversations*. This work consists of conversations between Confucius, his students, and an occasional ruler.

The primary emphasis of the *Lun yü* is on political philosophy. Confucius was concerned about the rampant immorality and amorality of much of the government of his time, and he spent much of his life trying to find a ruler who would accept his teaching that ethical considerations should be the guiding principle of government. Confucius taught that the primary task of the ruler was to achieve the welfare and happiness of the people of his state. To accomplish this aim, the ruler had first to set a moral example by his own conduct, and this example would in turn influence the people's behavior. Confucius rejected the use of a rigid legal system and believed instead that moral custom and voluntary compliance were the best ways of maintaining order in society.

Confucius considered the early years of the Chou dynasty as the embodiment of the perfect form of government. It was not the rulers of this period that he admired so much as the chief minister, Chou Tan, or the Duke of Chou. The Duke of Chou was known in early Chinese tradition as the founder of the state of Lu, and he was probably the chief culture hero in this state. Because Confucius came from Lu, some scholars have claimed that much of Confucius' teachings were simply a revival of this cult. It is certainly true that Confucius himself never claimed to be teaching original ideas but rather termed himself a "transmitter."

Nevertheless, Confucius is the first Chinese thinker to introduce concepts that became fundamental not only to Confucian philosophy but to Chinese philosophy in general. The most important of these are *jen* (benevolence), *yi* (propriety), and *li* (ritual). Confucius believed that the *chün-tzu*, or "gentleman," must set the moral example for others in society to follow. The word *chün-tzu* originally meant "ruler's son," but in the *Lun yü* it refers to the educated "man of virtue," who was not necessarily an aristocrat. The *chün-tzu* was expected to follow a set of ethical principles, of which *jen*, *yi*, and *li* were the most important. *Jen* meant in the *Lun yü* what has been translated as humaneness or benevolence, a quality a *chün-tzu* should cultivate and, once acquired, attempt to transfer to others. *Li* was considered the rules of decorum and ritual that were observed in religious and non-religious ceremonies and, as applied to the *chün-tzu* , composed his rules of behavior. According to the *Lun yü,* it was through a knowledge of the *li* that *yi,* or propriety, could be attained. *Yi* represents what is right and proper in a given situation, and the *chün-tzu,* by observing the ritual and because of his inclination toward goodness, always knows what is right.

Confucius was basically a humanist and one of the greatest teachers in Chinese history. His influence on his immediate disciples was profound, and they continued to expound his theories until, in the first Han dynasty (206 B.C.-A.D. 8), they became the basis of the state ideology.

## Further Reading

The *Lun yü* has been translated many times. There are two acceptable translations: James Legge, *Confucian Analects* (1861), and Arthur Waley, *The Analects of Confucius* (1938). Because of the nature of the sources, there is no definitive account of Confucius' life. Herrlee Glessner Creel, *Confucius the Man and the Myth* (1949; republished as *Confucius and the Chinese Way,* 1960), is an attempt to discard the Confucian myth and write a biography based on historical material. Creel concludes that Confucius was basically a democrat and revolutionary. At the other extreme is Wu-chi Liu, *Confucius: His Life and Times* (1955), which accepts almost all of the legends rejected by Creel. It is a good example of the traditional Chinese approach to Confucius. A good balance between these two works is Shigeki Kaizuka, *Confucius,* translated from the Japanese by Geoffrey Bownas (1956). Kaizuka critically examines the apocryphal stories but does not dismiss them as readily as Creel.

The significance of Confucius for Chinese thought and society can be studied in any history of Chinese civilization. The best of these are C. P. Fitzgerald, *China: A Short Cultural History* (1938) and *The Horizon History of China* (1969); William Theodore de Bary and others, eds., *Sources of Chinese Tradition* (1960); and Wing-Tsit Chan, *A Source Book in Chinese Philosophy* (1963). □

# William Congreve

**The English dramatist William Congreve (1670-1729) was the most brilliant of the writers of the Restoration comedy of manners. He possessed the wit and charm of the heroes of his plays and was universally admired by his contemporaries.**

The Restoration comedy of manners was similar to the satiric comedy of Ben Jonson in that it ridiculed violations of moral and social standards, but it centered upon the intrigues of ladies and gentlemen who lived in a highly polished, artificial society, and much of its effectiveness depended upon repartee and brisk and witty dialogue. In 1698 Jeremy Collier attacked the immorality of situation and indecency of dialogue characteristic of Restoration comedy. A change of taste followed, and William Congreve was forced to abandon the stage.

Congreve was born at Bardsey near Leeds on Jan. 24, 1670. His father was a soldier and a descendant of an old English family which owned considerable property in Staffordshire. When Congreve was 4, his father was commissioned to command the garrison at Youghal in Ireland. Later he became agent for the estates of the Earl of Cork, and ultimately the family moved to Lismore. Congreve received all of his education in Ireland. In 1681 he was sent to Kilkenny School, where he met his lifelong friend the satirist Jonathan Swift. In April 1686 Congreve followed Swift to Trinity College, Dublin. While at Trinity, Congreve seems to have written the novel *Incognita; or, Love and Duty Reconciled,* which was published under the assumed name of Cleophil in 1692.

After the Glorious Revolution of 1688 Congreve and his family returned to the family home in Staffordshire, where he seems to have remained for 2 years. It is most probable that it was here that he wrote his first play, *The Old Bachelor,* "to amuse himself in a slow recovery from a fit of sickness." In the spring of 1691 he went to London and enrolled at the Middle Temple to study law, but most of his energy was diverted to literature. Within a year he had made the friendship of John Dryden, the former poet laureate. In 1692 the two collaborated on a translation of the satires of Juvenal and Persius. That year he also contributed some verses to Charles Gildon's *Miscellany.*

## The Dramatist

In 1693 *The Old Bachelor,* which had been revised by Dryden, was produced at the Theatre Royal in Drury Lane with the best actors and actresses of the time taking part in it—including Betterton, Mrs. Barry, and Mrs. Bracegirdle,

who was to have the leading role in all of Congreve's plays. The play was a great success and ran for the unprecedented length of a fortnight. Congreve was so encouraged by its reception that he hastened to put forth a second play, *The Double Dealer,* before the end of the year. This play was more complex and better structured than the first, but it was not nearly so well received.

While Congreve was writing his third comedy, *Love for Love,* Betterton and other leading actors rebelled against the management of the Theatre Royal, the only theater in London at the time. They were given permission to build a new theater at Lincoln's Inn Fields, which opened with the production of *Love for Love* in the spring of 1695. Probably Congreve's best acting play, it met with immediate success and placed him among the leading dramatists of the day. He became one of the managers of the new theater and agreed to give the new company a play a year.

At this time he also began to write public occasional verse. He was well established in his literary career, and through Charles Montague, later Earl of Halifax, to whom he had dedicated *The Double Dealer,* he was appointed one of the five commissioners to license hackney coaches at a salary of £ 100 a year.

Congreve was unable to produce a play a year as promised, but early in 1697 he gave the company the tragedy *The Mourning Bride.* It met with instantaneous success and was the most popular English tragedy for almost a century. The following year he launched an unsuccessful counterattack on Collier's charges against the stage. But by 1700 the taste in comedy had so changed that his next play, *The Way of the World,* failed miserably, and he determined to leave the stage.

## Later Career

Although Congreve associated briefly with Sir John Vanbrugh at the Queen's Theatre and wrote librettos for two operas (*The Judgment of Paris* and *Semele*), he spent the rest of his life at leisure. In 1705 he was appointed commissioner for wines and retained this post until 1714, when he received a more lucrative appointment as secretary of Jamaica. In 1710 he published the first collected edition of his works in three volumes. He continued to write poetry and made translations of Homer, Juvenal, Horace, and Ovid. He was highly regarded as a person and colleague by Swift, Pope, Addison, and Gay. Voltaire was annoyed at Congreve's affecting the role of gentleman in preference to that of author, but Congreve's considerateness of his fellow authors was held to be remarkable.

Congreve never married, but he was intimate for many years with Mrs. Bracegirdle, the leading lady of his plays. In later years he was in constant attendance upon the Duchess of Marlborough and is believed to have been the father of the duchess's daughter, Lady Mary Godolphin. His life of pleasure was pursued at the expense of his health, and he suffered greatly from blindness and gout. In the summer of 1728 he went to Bath with the Duchess of Marlborough and John Gay to recover from a long illness. While there his carriage was overturned, and he suffered internal injuries from which he never recovered. He died on Jan. 19, 1729,

and was buried in Westminster Abbey. He left the bulk of his fortune to the Duchess of Marlborough, who built a monument to his memory in the abbey.

## Further Reading

Edmund Gosse, *Life of William Congreve* (1888; rev. ed. 1924), was the first full biography. The fullest and most accurate is John C. Hodges, *William Congreve, the Man: A Biography from New Sources* (1941). Other useful biographical accounts are D. Crane Taylor, *William Congreve* (1931), and Kathleen M. Lynch, *A Congreve Gallery* (1951). Studies of the Restoration comedy of manners include John Palmer, *The Comedy of Manners* (1913); Kathleen M. Lynch, *The Social Mode of Restoration Comedy* (1926; rev. ed. 1965); and Norman N. Holland, *The First Modern Comedies: The Significance of Etherege, Wycherley, and Congreve* (1959).

## Additional Sources

Gosse, Edmund, *Life of William Congreve,* Norwood, Pa.: Norwood Editions, 1977, c1924.

Taylor, D. Crane (Daniel Crane), *William Congreve,* Norwood, Pa.: Norwood Editions, 1976.

Taylor, D. Crane (Daniel Crane), *William Congreve,* Philadelphia: R. West, 1977. ☐

# Roscoe Conkling

**Roscoe Conkling (1829-1888) represented the most unabashed sort of American political partisanship in the 1860s and 1870s. A leader of the "Stalwart" faction of the Republican party, he became a symbol of spoilsmanship in politics.**

Roscoe Conkling was born on Oct. 30, 1829, in Albany, N.Y. He attended Mount Washington Collegiate Institute, read law, and became district attorney of Albany. He moved to Utica, where in 1858 he was Whig party mayor. He sat in the House of Representatives from 1859 to 1863 and 1865 to 1867. A staunch supporter of Thaddeus Stevens and the Radical Republicans, Conkling once defended the dying Stevens from physical attack and sat on the "Committee of 15," which drafted the Radical program of reconstruction.

In 1867 Conkling seized effective control of the New York State Republican organization and got himself elected to the Senate. A devoted follower of Ulysses S. Grant, Conkling was at home only in the rough-and-tumble world of "gilded age" politics. Grant offered to make him chief justice of the Supreme Court in 1873, and Chester Arthur offered him a seat on the Court a decade later. But he rejected both.

"I do not know how to belong to a party a little," Conkling said, and he was indeed the sort of partisan that has since vanished from the political scene. He was frank; he insisted loudly where others equivocated; he believed that party workers should receive benefits from winning elections, that is, jobs and other financial rewards; in return

ceedingly petulant child." For all his arrogance and pomposity, however, Conkling clung to causes such as African American rights long after better-remembered contemporaries had abandoned them. And one ultimate conclusion about his spoilsmanship must be that he spoke frankly while others were hypocritical. He died in New York City on April 18, 1888.

## Further Reading

A relative, Alfred R. Conkling, published the customary 19th-century biography upon the death of Conkling, *The Life and Letters of Roscoe Conkling: Orator, Statesman, and Advocate* (1889). David M. Jordon, *Roscoe Conkling of New York: Voice in the Senate* (1971), is a penetrating and detailed biography. An incisive portrayal of Conkling is contained in H. Wayne Morgan, *From Hayes to McKinley* (1969). □

# John Bowden Connally Jr.

**Former Texas governor John Bowden Connally, Jr. (1917-1993), political adviser and confidant to both Democratic and Republican presidents and a candidate for the presidency in 1980, helped shape American economic policy as secretary of the treasury during the Richard M. Nixon administration.**

J ohn B. Connally, Jr., one of seven children, was born in Floresville, Texas, on February 27, 1917, to John Bowden Connally, a tenant farmer, and Lela (Wright) Connally. After attending public schools in San Antonio and Floresville he entered the University of Texas where he earned a law degree in 1941. Connally's introduction to politics occurred in 1937 when Lyndon B. Johnson, a former administrator of the Texas division of the National Youth Administration entered the race for the 10th District congressional seat vacated by the death of Walter Buchanan. Connally, then a University of Texas undergraduate and former student body president, volunteered for Johnson's successful campaign. When Congressman Johnson was elected to a full term in 1938 he hired Connally as his administrative assistant, thus beginning a 30-year political association. Connally remained in Washington one year and then returned to Austin to complete his law degree. In 1940 he married Idanell Brill, a University of Texas student.

Immediately upon graduating from law school Connally entered the U.S. Navy. While serving in the Office of Naval Operations he worked on General Dwight D. Eisenhower's staff and helped plan the allied invasion of Italy in 1943. Later Connally won a Bronze Star for bravery while serving as a fighter-plane director aboard the aircraft carrier *USS Essex.* Connally returned to civilian life in 1946 and founded radio station KVET in Austin. Two years later he managed Lyndon Johnson's successful Senate campaign and again served as Johnson's administrative assistant for one year before returning to Texas.

he demanded that they support the party as if it were a holy cause. He had a brilliant, quick mind in debate but saved his most scathing remarks for reformers who sought to eliminate political patronage through civil service reform which would distribute political appointments according to merit only.

Conkling battled President Hayes for control of the patronage in New York and hoped in 1880 to reelect Grant to the presidency. But the Republicans nominated James A. Garfield of Ohio. Conkling at once joined battle with President Garfield over patronage. In an attempt to rebuff him Conkling resigned his Senate seat: the idea was to be reelected in the face of Garfield's opposition, thus demonstrating his personal power in New York. But Garfield was killed in the meantime by a madman claiming to be a "Stalwart," and the shocked New York Legislature refused to follow Conkling's will. He effectively retired from politics, noting characteristically, "How can I speak into a grave? How can I battle with a shroud? Silence is a duty and a doom."

Conkling retired to a lucrative legal practice and to the fashionable New York City society that he adorned very well. A large, handsome man with a boxer's physique, he inspired nicknames such as the "Curled Darling of Utica" because of his affectation of gay, fashionably cut clothing. James G. Blaine matched Conkling's invective when he ridiculed Conkling's "haughty disdain, his grandiloquent swell, his majestic, supereminent, overpowering, turkey-gobbler strut." Garfield incisively characterized Conkling as "a singular compound of a very brilliant man and an ex-

In 1952 Connally became the attorney for oil multimillionaire Sid W. Richardson. Connally's frequent jumps between government and business continued throughout his career and established his image as a "wheeler-dealer" willing, according to his critics, to parlay his position for private profit. Connally, however, argued that financially successful public servants were less subject to compromise and thus could best act in the public interest.

Connally skillfully manipulated his political and business ties. While serving as a Washington lobbyist for the oil and national gas industry he remained active in Texas politics and helped Lyndon Johnson gain control over the state Democratic Party in 1956. In 1960 he managed Johnson's unsuccessful presidential campaign and later helped Johnson obtain the vice-presidential nomination at the Democratic convention. When the Kennedy-Johnson ticket was elected in 1960 Vice-President Johnson helped obtain Connally's 1961 appointment as secretary of the Navy. Connally held the Navy post 11 months before resigning to successfully run for governor of Texas, his only elective office.

Ten months after becoming governor John Connally was abruptly thrust into the national prominence. On November 22, 1963, President John F. Kennedy was assassinated while being driven through Dallas, Texas. Governor Connally, also in the presidential limousine, was wounded. While Connally and Kennedy differed on most issues the two men were linked in the public's mind and the notoriety aided the governor in his 1964 and 1966 reelection campaigns.

Connally was a politically conservative governor who promoted economic growth and aggressively expanded the Texas University system. He opposed the Voting Rights Act of 1965, the anti-poverty campaign, Medicare, federal aid to education, and most of the other "Great Society" programs created by President Lyndon Johnson, his former boss and mentor. Johnson frequently remarked that his former congressional aide had no compassion for the poor despite Connally's own childhood poverty. Connally fully supported American involvement in Vietnam and while heading the Texas delegation to the 1968 Democratic convention he pushed through a pro-war plank despite determined liberal opposition and anti-war demonstrations outside the convention hall. However, Connally gave lukewarm support to Democratic presidential candidate Hubert Humphrey.

At the end of his third term as governor Connally moved to Houston to become a senior partner in Vinson and Elkins, one of the largest law firms in the nation. However, in December 1970 President Richard Nixon in a surprise move appointed Connally secretary of the treasury. When skeptical reporters asked his qualifications for a post normally held by a banker, Connally quipped, "I can add." Connally's candor and wit won praise in Washington, and he quickly emerged as the principal administration spokesman for economic policy. But his abrasive style offended European and Japanese trade negotiators, while his unconditional endorsement of the government bailout of the nearly bankrupt Lockheed Corporation sparked opposition from Defense Secretary David Packard and Federal Reserve Board Chairman Arthur Burns. Connally's hard bargaining tactics eventually alienated Secretary of State William Rogers and national security adviser Henry Kissinger. As opposition in the Nixon administration grew, Connally was ultimately forced to resign in June 1972.

Despite his cabinet experience Connally remained a loyal Nixon supporter who in August 1972 organized the "Democrats for Nixon" committee. Connally soon became one of the president's closest political advisers, and on May 1, 1973, he joined the Republican Party. Connally's close association with the White House prompted allegations of his involvement in the Watergate scandals. In March 1973 a House subcommittee charged he had interfered with a Securities and Exchange Commission investigation of the International Telephone and Telegraph Corporation. Three months later White House counsel John Dean testified that Connally had participated in top level discussions on stopping the Watergate probe. On July 28, 1974, a federal grand jury indicted Connally for taking an illegal gratuity, conspiracy to obstruct justice, and perjury in connection with his alleged acceptance of $10,000 from the Associated Milk Producers, a dairy lobby, in 1971. Connally pleaded not guilty, and in April 1975 he was acquitted.

With the milk scandal trial four years past, Connally in 1979 began his quest for the 1980 Republican presidential nomination. Declaring "business is the lifeblood of our country, the source of our greatness," he called for corporate tax cuts, accelerated depreciation, less governmental regulation, and unlimited nuclear power development while promising to slash wasteful federal social programs and "parasitic, burgeoning government bureaucracy." Connally entered the early 1980 presidential primaries confident of victory. But after three grueling months of campaigning and spending $12 million, far more than his political opponents, he had only one delegate to show for his efforts. Connally then staked his political future on a decisive win over the GOP front-runner, former California governor Ronald Reagan, in the March 8 South Carolina primary. When Reagan won the primary, 63-year-old John Connally withdrew from the race and retired from politics.

No longer a political figure, Connally joined the oil industry. With the oil shortage of the early 1980s looming over the United States, Connally and a few business partners started Chapman Energy in 1981. For the next few years, Connally and his partners developed shopping centers, office buildings, other businesses, and real estate ventures. By 1983, Chapman Energy was worth an estimated $300 million. But disaster struck as the price of oil took a nose-dive, under $10 per barrel, in the mid-1980s. Chapman Energy was forced to liquidate all of its assets and ownings, and on July 31, 1987, Connally filed for personal bankruptcy.

Connally managed to recover from this setback, and appeared in several commercials for University Savings, promoting financial prudence. He was made a member on the board of pipeline operator at Coastal Corporation in 1988, and continued to live comfortably with his wife, Nellie, in their ranch house in Floresville. Connally succumbed to his long-term battle with pulmonary fibrosis, a condition caused by the gunshot wounds he received almost 30 years earlier, on June 15, 1993. He was 76.

## Further Reading

The best biographies of Connally are Charles Ashman, *Connally: The Adventures of Big Bad John* (1979) and A. F. Crawford and J. Keever, *John B. Connally: Portrait in Power* (1973). Other information on Connally can be found in Ronnie Dugger, *The Politician: The Life and Times of Lyndon Johnson* (1982) and Robert A. Caro, *The Years of Lyndon Johnson: The Path to Power* (1983). For a discussion of Connally's years as governor of Texas see Robert Sobel and John Raimo, editors, *Biographical Directory of the Governors of the United States, 1789-1978* (1978). □

# Cyril Connolly

**A British novelist and literary and social critic, Cyril Connolly (1903-1974) is best known for two works which combine criticism with autobiography, *Enemies of Promise* (1938) and *The Unquiet Grave* (1944).**

Cyril (Vernon) Connolly was born on September 10, 1903, in Coventry, England, to Matthew and Muriel (Vernon) Connolly and died in London on November 25, 1974. The father, an army major, was an eccentric, according to critic Peter Quennell, who had known

Connolly since their school days, and the mother, judging by Connolly's own account of her, was a rather restless person for whose love the son yearned in vain. Whether she might actually have loved him more is less important than the fact that he perceived that she might have and that he felt this yearning in later years. Eventually the parents separated.

Shortly after the author's death Quennell, in describing Connolly in their days together at Balliol College, Oxford, called him "gaily cynical," and noted in his young schoolmate a lack of ambition which was also apparent to Stephen Spender, the poet, who was also a friend of Connolly. Far from denying the charge of laziness, Connolly refused to make any excuses for not having accomplished more in his lifetime: "I would say only myself prevented me from doing the writing" was his candid confession. He confessed, too, that his parents had been ambitious for him and had wanted him to enter the Foreign Office or to clerk in the House of Commons or Lords. He doubted, he said, that he would ever write his masterpiece.

Like Quennell, another friend, John Lehmann, also remembered Connolly's gift for parody, a gift which prompted Spender to term him "the spectator of his own life," because parody, especially self-parody, presumably enabled him to achieve a kind of detachment.

Lehmann looked on *Enemies of Promise* (1938) as Connolly's attempt to write a masterpiece, but like a number of others he considers the last essay of the book, "A Georgian Boyhood," to be the most memorable one. Pritchett declared himself impressed with the earlier sections which try to put even present English literature in perspective by comparing past and present trends; yet certainly it is the last section in which the poignancy and immediacy of the description narrow the gap between writer and reader.

The account of the British public (actually private) school system—the sometimes sadistic headmasters, the severe or stupid teachers, the institution known as "fagging," which made it possible for the boys of the upper forms or classes to make virtual slaves of the boys of the lower classes—is unforgettable. According to colleague David Pryce-Jones, Connolly asked the adult Eric Blair (George Orwell) "to corroborate the horror of the past they had once shared at St. Cyprian's, then a relatively new school where both had been students before going on to Eton. Out of this request came Orwell's *Such, Such Were the Joys,* in which, Pryce-Jones says, St. Cyprian's "and all its work stand, in miniature, for everything that Orwell thought wrong with England."

To Spender *The Unquiet Grave,* which was first issued in 1938 but then revised in 1944, is "a masterpiece-non-masterpiece of a peculiarly modern kind" which deliberately aimed at fragmentariness. To Pritchett the book is "Connolly's mythical confession and elegy," and he points out the author's obsession with Palinurus whose name Connolly adopted as a pseudonym in writing the book. He took the name from Virgil's *Aeneid* in which Palinurus is the pilot who falls overboard with the ship's rudder and uses it as a kind of raft which enables him to reach shore. Here, however, he is killed by the natives. It is during Aeneas's visit to the underworld that he learns of Palinurus's fate. Now that unfortunate begs help in finding rest from his ceaseless tossing in the sea. His is the "unquiet grave."

The book is also filled with, as Pritchett puts it, "exotic flowers, fruits, animals, birds and insects" which were to Connolly "texts." One rather moving but brief section of the book is devoted to a pet lemur that had died. Pritchett thinks that the book had the effect on Connolly of "curing himself of guilt."

Connolly's novel *The Rock Pool* well repays reading today. In the 1930s British publishers were reluctant to publish it, Lehmann recalled, and Quennell suggested in his introduction to the 1981 re-issuing of the novel that its theme of lesbianism had been objectionable. Quennell disclosed that the novel, though no *roman a clef* is actually based on people whom Connolly had known, and that in the protagonist, Naylor, a good deal of the author is to be found. He sees the book as an attack on the English social system and on the competitiveness stemming from it, but he sees the true subject of the novel as the collision of two cultures, the elitist culture of the English world as it is represented by the unhappy Naylor and the remnants of pagan culture that Naylor himself sees as stubbornly persisting among the inhabitants of Trou-sur-Mer (Cagnes), who stubbornly follow their most primitive instincts. On the other hand, Pritchett regards the book as a kind of satire on what he calls "the typical sententious English youth" who deserted his public school and Oxford for "his first spree." The book also demonstrated Connolly's fascination with the Mediterranean and "the passing dissipation of foreign artists" of the town. Quennell thought the novel showed Connolly's "satirical wit and unfailing grasp of the cruelly descriptive image." This was no doubt an accurate judgment; yet the author lacked the more mordant wit and savage satire of, say, Evelyn Waugh, whom he knew. Still, as a picture of the France which was a mecca to many expatriates, including many Americans, in the 1920s and 1930s, the novel should be of interest today. Connolly tells a story well, shows an eye for detail, and makes the reader want to know more about the characters.

David Pryce-Jones, who met Connolly when the author was 50, speculated that he had allowed himself to grow fat and may have been unhappy with himself. Connolly struck him as "sloppy" and "bad-mannered." Pritchett used the metaphor of Connolly in a baby carriage to capture for the reader Connolly's character in middle age: willful, wanting what he could not have, and throwing it away if he got it and then wanting it again. He calls Connolly a good critic, inveterate traveller, and frank autobiographer who was kept back from greater things by his desire for pleasure, good food, women, "spendthrift habits," and his love of talk. As a literary critic Connolly had "a clinching gift for images," according to Pritchett. Apparently no critic would say that any one of Connolly's books was a masterpiece, and certainly no one book made him wealthy. As he confessed: "I don't think I could have lived on the profits of any single one of my books." Still, though he may have been a disappointment to himself as well as friends and family, many of his

works continue to interest readers and his reputation survived his death. Nor must one forget Connolly's career as a journalist: from 1927 until the time of his death he was a practicing journalist, working for such newspapers as the *New Statesman* and the *Sunday Times*. He even founded *Horizon,* a journal for which he was editor and writer from 1939 to 1950.

## Further Reading

For information about Connolly, see "Connolly, Cyril," in *Contemporary Authors-Permanent Series* (1978); Stephen Spender, "Cyril Connolly," *Times Literary Supplement* (December 6, 1974), a "memoir" by a poet and man of letters which reveals things of interest about Connolly's life and character and tells something about his *oeuvre;* Peter Quennell, "Cyril Connolly," *Encounter* (May 1975), in which, despite a friendship of long standing with the author, nevertheless estimates his friend, man and work, without glossing over the defects of either; John Lehmann, "Friend of Promise," *Encounter* (May 1975), in which another man of letters and old friend of Connolly reminisces about the man and his work; J. W. Lambert, "To Hell with Masterpieces," *Encounter* (May 1975); David Pryce-Jones, *Journal and Memoir* (1983); V. S. Pritchett, "Surviving in the Ruins," a review of various works of Connolly which were re-issued, some with interesting introductions or afterwords.

Sources by Connolly include "Richard Kershaw Speaks to Cyril Connolly," *The Listener,* April 11, 1968; David Pryce-Jones, editor, *Journal: 1928-1937,* which glitters with the names of the British cultural, scientific, and political worlds though his comments are brief to the point of being almost cryptic.

## Additional Sources

Fisher, Clive, *Cyril Connolly: the life and times of England's most controversial literary critic,* New York: St. Martin's Press, 1996.

Hobson, Anthony, *Cyril Connolly as a book collector,* Edinburgh: Tragara Press, 1983.

Pryce-Jones, David, *Cyril Connolly: journal and memoir,* New York: Ticknor & Fields, 1984.

Shelden, Michael, *Friends of promise: Cyril Connolly and the world of Horizon,* New York: Harper & Row, 1989.

Spender, Stephen, *Cyril Connolly: a memoir,* Edinburgh: Tragara Press, 1978. □

# Joseph Conrad

**The Polish-born English novelist Joseph Conrad (1857-1924) was concerned with men under stress, deprived of the ordinary supports of civilized life and forced to confront the mystery of human individuality. He explored the technical possibilities of fiction.**

Józef Teodor Konrad Nalecz Korzeniowski (to use the name which Joseph Conrad later drastically simplified for his English readers) was born on Dec. 3, 1857, in Berdyczew. Conrad's childhood was harsh. His parents were both members of families long identified with the movement for Polish independence from Russia. In 1862

Conrad's father, himself a writer and translator, was exiled to Russia for his revolutionary activities, and his wife and child shared the exile. In 1865 Conrad's mother died, and a year later he was entrusted to the care of his uncle Thaddeus Bobrowski.

In 1868 Conrad attended high school in Lemberg, Galicia; the following year he and his father moved to Cracow, where his father died. In early adolescence the future novelist began to dream of going to sea, and in 1873, while on vacation in western Europe, Conrad saw the sea for the first time. In the autumn of 1874 Conrad went to Marseilles, where he entered the French marine service.

For the next 20 years Conrad led a successful career as a ship's officer. In 1877 he probably took part in the illegal shipment of arms from France to Spain in support of the pretender to the Spanish throne, Don Carlos. At about this time Conrad seems to have fallen in love with a girl who was also implicated in the Carlist cause. The affair ended in a duel, which Conrad fought with an American named J. M. K. Blunt. There is evidence that early in 1878 Conrad made an attempt at suicide.

In June 1878 Conrad went for the first time to England. He worked as a seaman on English ships, and in 1880 he began his career as an officer in the British merchant service, rising from third mate to master. His voyages took him to Australia, India, Singapore, Java, Borneo, to those distant and exotic places which would provide the background for much of his fiction. In 1886 he was naturalized as a British citizen. He received his first command in 1888. In 1890 he

made the ghastly journey to the Belgian Congo which inspired his great short novel *The Heart of Darkness*.

In the early 1890s Conrad had begun to think about writing fiction based on his experiences in the East, and in 1893 he discussed his work in progress, the novel *Almayer's Folly,* with a passenger, the novelist John Galsworthy. Although Conrad by now had a master's certificate, he was not obtaining the commands that he wanted. *Almayer's Folly* was published in 1895, and its favorable critical reception encouraged Conrad to begin a new career as a writer. He married an Englishwoman, Jessie George, in 1896, and 2 years later, just after the birth of Borys, the first of their two sons, they settled in Kent in the south of England, where Conrad lived for the rest of his life. John Galsworthy was the first of a number of English and American writers who befriended this middle-aged Polish seaman who had come so late to the profession of letters; others were Henry James, Arnold Bennett, Rudyard Kipling, Stephen Crane, and Ford Madox Hueffer (later known as Ford Madox Ford), with whom Conrad collaborated on two novels.

## Early Novels

The scene of Conrad's first novel, *Almayer's Folly* (1895), is the Dutch East Indies, and its complicated plot is concerned with intrigues among Europeans, natives, and Arabs. At the center of the novel is Almayer, a trader of Dutch extraction, who is married to a Malay woman and has by her one daughter, Nina. He dreams endlessly of returning to Europe with his daughter, but he is powerless to act. Nina runs away with her young Malay lover, and her father takes refuge in opium and dies pathetically.

*An Outcast of the Islands* (1896) deals with the same milieu, and in fact Almayer appears again in this work. The main character is a shabby trickster, Willems, who betrays the man who gives him a chance to make something of himself and thus plays a part in Almayer's ruin. The novel ends melodramatically: Willems is shot by the beautiful native woman Aissa, for whom he has abandoned his wife.

In *The Nigger of the "Narcissus"* (1897) Conrad turns to the life of the merchant seaman and to one of his commonest themes, the ambiguities of human sympathy. Just before the *Narcissus* leaves on a long journey, it takes on as one of its crew a huge Black named James Watt. From the beginning Watt is marked for death, and Conrad studies the effects on the crew of his steady physical deterioration. At first, his fellow seamen are compassionate, but then Watt's recalcitrance and his ingratitude after they have heroically saved his life drive the crew to the brink of mutiny. Watt dies, as the older sailors predict he will, when the ship is finally in sight of land. The novel contains one of Conrad's great set pieces, a wonderfully sustained account of a storm at sea.

*The Heart of Darkness* (1899) is based on Conrad's voyage up the Congo 9 years before. Narrated by the sympathetic and experienced seaman Marlow, the novel is at once an account of 19th-century imperialist greed and a symbolic voyage into the dark potentialities of civilized man. Marlow is fascinated by the figure of Kurtz, a Belgian whose self-imposed mission is to bring civilization into the

Congo. Marlow tracks him down, and he finally finds the dying Kurtz, who has been corrupted by the very natives he has set out to save. Marlow, at the conclusion, visits Kurtz's fiancée, and he cannot find the courage to tell her the truth about her dead lover.

The first phase of Conrad's career culminates in *Lord Jim* (1900). Marlow is again the principal narrator, although Conrad entrusts his complex story to several other voices. Like all of Conrad's mature fiction, *Lord Jim* is a typical work of the 20th century in that a first reading does not begin to exhaust its subtleties of design and meaning. The hero begins as an inexperienced officer on the pilgrim ship *Patna*. In the night the ship, crowded with pilgrims to Mecca, strikes something in the water and seems about to sink. Urged by the other officers and not really aware of what he is doing, Jim deserts the ship. But the *Patna* does not sink, and the officers, Jim among them, are considered cowards. Disgraced, Jim wanders from job to job, moving ever to the East.

Marlow takes a sympathetic interest in the young man and finds him a job in the remote settlement of Patusan. Jim does well and he wins the respect of the natives, who call him Tuan Jim—Lord Jim. But the past catches up with him in the person of Gentleman Brown, a scoundrel who knows about Jim's past and insists that they are brothers in crime. Jim persuades the natives to let Brown go, whereupon Brown murders their chief, Dain Waris. Jim accepts responsibility for the murder, and he is executed by the natives. Once again, Conrad is concerned with the ways in which sympathy and imagination blur the clear judgment which is essential for the life of action.

## Political Novels

*Nostromo* (1904) is probably Conrad's greatest novel. It is set in Costaguana, an imaginary but vividly realized country on the north coast of South America. Symbolically and realistically the novel is dominated by the silver of the San Tomé mine and its effects on the lives of a large cast of characters. The treasure attracts greedy men, who impose on the country a succession of tyrannies, and it tests and eventually corrupts men who are devoted to high ideals of personal conduct. *Nostromo* is concerned with the relationship between psychology and ideology, between man's deepest needs and his public actions and decisions.

The London of *The Secret Agent* (1907) is a far cry from the exotic settings of Conrad's first fiction. It is a city of mean streets and shabby lives, and in his depiction of these scenes Conrad surely owes something to the works of Charles Dickens. Verloc is a fat, lazy *agent provocateur* who is paid by a foreign power (probably Russia) to stir up violent incidents which will encourage the British government to take repressive measures against political liberals. His wife, Winnie, married him in the hope that he will provide a safe home for herself and especially for her dim-witted, pathetic brother, Stevie. Verloc plots to blow up the Greenwich Observatory. Stevie is drawn into the plot; he stumbles, carrying an explosive, and is killed. Winnie kills her husband when she learns of Stevie's death—the dying Verloc

cannot understand the violence of her reaction—and then kills herself.

*Under Western Eyes* (1911) is Conrad's study of the Russian temperament. Razumov, who may be the illegitimate son of Prince K—-, is a solitary and devoted student. Haldin, another student, bursts into Razumov's apartment after he has assassinated an autocratic politician. Haldin turns to the Prince K—-but is immediately captured by the police. Razumov now goes to Switzerland, where he finds himself in the midst of a group of émigré revolutionaries, among them Haldin's sister, with whom Razumov falls in love. Tortured by his isolation, Razumov finally confesses his responsibility for Haldin's capture and death. He is punished by the revolutionaries and returns to Russia, where he lives out his alienated life.

## Later Novels

Thanks to the efforts of his American publisher, Conrad's next novel, *Chance* (1914), was a financial success, and for the rest of his life he was without worries about money. The novel is concerned with a young girl, Flora, and her relationship with her father, an egotistical fraud who spends some time in prison, and with an idealistic sea captain with whom she finds happiness after she has freed herself from her father.

*Victory* (1915), Conrad's last important novel, is another study in solitude and sympathy. Warned by his father to remain aloof from the world, the hero, Heyst, is twice tempted by sympathy into the active life—with tragic results. The second temptation is offered by the girl Lena, whom Heyst rescues and carries off to his island retreat. Their solitude is invaded by three criminals on the run, and in a melodramatic finale Lena dies saving Heyst's life.

Among Conrad's last novels are *The Shadow Line* (1917), a somber and ultimately triumphant story of another testing sea voyage, and *The Rover* (1923), a historical novel set in France in the years just after the Revolution.

Although there is a valedictory quality about Conrad's last novels—and some evidence of failing powers—he received many honors. In 1923 he visited the United States with great acclaim, and the year after, he declined a knighthood. He died suddenly of a heart attack on Aug. 3, 1924, and he is buried at Canterbury. His gravestone bears these lines from Spenser: Sleep after toyle, port after stormie seas,/ Ease after warre, death after life, does greatly please.

## Further Reading

Two older major biographical studies, G. Jean-Aubry, *Joseph Conrad: Life and Letters* (2 vols., 1927), and Jessie Conrad, *Joseph Conrad and His Circle* (1935; 2d ed. 1964), have been superseded by a definitive biography, Jocelyn Baines, *Joseph Conrad: A Critical Biography* (1960). Important critical studies of Conrad's work include M. C. Bradbrook, *Joseph Conrad: Poland's English Genius* (1941); F. R. Leavis, *The Great Tradition* (1954); Paul L. Wiley, *Conrad's Measure of Man* (1954); Thomas Moser, *Joseph Conrad: Achievement and Decline* (1957); Albert Joseph Guerard, *Conrad the Novelist* (1958); and Eloise Knapp Hay, *The Political Novels of Joseph Conrad* (1963). □

# John Constable

**John Constable (1776-1837), one of the greatest English landscape painters, represented the naturalistic aspect of romanticism. His calm, deeply poetic response to nature approximated in painting the insights of William Wordsworth in poetry.**

John Constable was born in East Bergholt, Suffolk, on June 11, 1776, the son of a well-to-do mill owner. The lush, well-watered Suffolk landscape with its rolling clouds and generally flat, but in parts undulating, terrain made a deep impression on his imagination, and no painter has referred more frequently to the scenes of his childhood as a recurrent source of inspiration. "Those scenes," he later wrote to a friend, "made me a painter," and again, "The sound of water escaping from mill-dams, etc., willows, old rotten planks, slimy posts and brickwork, I love such things."

Constable was encouraged first by a local amateur and later by his friend Sir George Beaumont, the painter and collector, who advised him to study the watercolors of Thomas Girtin. Constable said that a painting by Claude Lorrain that he saw at this time marked an important epoch in his life. Beaumont's collection later included the *Château de Steen* by Peter Paul Rubens, which Constable stable studied closely.

On a visit to London in 1796 Constable met the engraver and antiquary J. T. Smith, under whose influence he made sketches of picturesque cottages. In 1799 Constable became a student at the Royal Academy, where he worked diligently at anatomy under a system of instruction concentrating on the human figure as the basis of history painting.

## Nature Paintings

In 1802 Constable exhibited at the Royal Academy for the first time, declaring his intention to become a "natural painter." The following year he sailed from London to Deal, making drawings of ships in the tradition of the English Thames Estuary school. "I saw," Constable wrote to a friend, "all sorts of weather," and what he described as "the natural history of the skies" became a lifelong object of research, culminating in a series of cloud sketches inspired by the cloud classifications of the meteorologist Luke Howard, who published *The Climate of London* in 1818-1820.

In 1806 Constable spent 2 months touring the Lake District, and the following year he exhibited three paintings from the trip at the Royal Academy. After this, however, he broke with the tradition of picturesque travel, preferring to paint the scenes he knew and loved best, notably his native Suffolk; Salisbury, where he stayed with his friend Bishop Fisher and his family; Hampstead Heath; and the Thames Estuary.

A happy marriage to Maria Bicknell, with whom Constable fell in love in 1809, was delayed until 1816 by the opposition of her maternal grandfather, the wealthy rector of East Bergholt. From these 7 years of uncertainty date

those attacks of nervous depression which were occasionally to cloud a life of otherwise singular felicity.

In 1824 three of Constable's oil paintings, including *The Hay Wain,* were exhibited at the Paris Salon, where they were acclaimed by Eugène Delacroix and other painters and won a gold medal. The question of their influence on French contemporaries and ultimately on impressionism has been widely discussed. All that can safely be said is that his break with academic convention made a profound impact and was invoked as a sanction by Delacroix not for imitating the English painter but for greater boldness in his own work.

Constable's wife, with whom he had seven children, died in 1828, shortly after he inherited a fortune from her father. Constable had been elected an associate of the Royal Academy in 1819, and 10 years later he became a full member. He died on March 31, 1837, working on the day before his death on *Arundel Mill and Castle.*

## Original Contribution

Constable's finished landscapes were always greatly admired. He was revolutionary in painting large canvases consistently as sketches, and he later allowed himself considerable painterly freedom in finished pictures, like the magnificent *Hadleigh Castle,* subtitled *Mouth of the Thames, Morning after a Stormy Night.* Today it is his large sketchlike paintings that are most sought after, particularly those celebrating the themes that had haunted him from childhood: the mill, the lock, and water reflecting sunlight and clouds.

Constable's original contribution was to combine a scientific approach to nature with a romantic intensity of feeling. "Painting," he wrote, "is a science, and should be considered as an enquiry into the laws of nature." But he described his cloud studies as organs of his sentiment, and in a much-quoted passage declared, "painting is with me but another word for feeling."

## Further Reading

The best source for information on Constable is still his own writings. *The Letters of John Constable, R. A., to C. R. Leslie, R. A., 1826-1837,* edited by Peter Leslie (1931), contains both the letters, rich in observations on nature and art and illustrating Constable's genius for friendship, and the notes for Constable's critical lectures on the history of landscape painting delivered to the Royal Institution of Great Britain in 1836. Also extremely useful are R. B. Beckett, *John Constable and the Fishers: The Record of a Friendship* (1952), and a six-volume edition of Constable's *Correspondence,* edited by R. B. Beckett (1962-1968). Besides C. R. Leslie's classic, *Memoirs of the Life of John Constable, R. A., Composed Chiefly of His Letters* (1943; new ed. 1951), there is a scholarly literature of distinction on Constable. Preeminent is Graham Reynolds, *Constable: The Natural Painter* (1965). Sydney J. Key, *John Constable: His Life and Work* (1948), is a sound account. One of the best sources of illustrations, reproducing 597 works, is the Victoria and Albert Museum, *Catalogue of the Constable Collection,* written by Graham Reynolds (1960). A masterly specialized study, establishing Constable's relation to both poets and painters, is Kurt Badt, *John Constable's Clouds* (trans. 1950).

## Additional Sources

Constable, Freda, *John Constable: a biography, 1776-1837,* Lavenham: Dalton, 1975. □

# Constantine I

**Constantine I (ca. 274-337) was a Roman emperor. He is frequently called "the Great" because of his successes as a general, administrator, and legislator and because of his support of the Christian Church and efforts to maintain Christian unity.**

Born Flavius Valerius Constantinus at Naissus (in modern Yugoslavia), Constantine was the son of Constantius Chlorus and his concubine Helena. In 293 his father became the son-in-law and caesar (successor-designate) of Emperor Maximian, who was coruler of the Roman Empire with Emperor Diocletian. In 305 Diocletian and Maximian abdicated, and Chlorus became coruler, having superintendence of the West, while Galerius, Diocletian's son-in-law, superintended the East. The new emperors chose caesars (Maximinus Daia and Falvius Valerius Severus) who were not their relatives. Galerius kept Constantine, who had distinguished himself as a soldier, at

his own court, apparently fearing that he might develop imperial ambitions if left with his father. In 306, however, Constantine managed to escape to the West and joined Chlorus in campaigns in northern Britain. Chlorus died at York in July 306, and his troops immediately proclaimed Constantine his successor. Galerius acknowledged Constantine as a caesar, and he raised Severus to the role of emperor (augustus) in the West.

## Struggles for Empire

Constantine's dynastic elevation set a bad example. Thereupon Maxentius, old Maximian's son, proclaimed himself augustus in Italy, killed Severus, and obtained Africa as well. He quarreled with his father, however, and Maximian fled to Constantine, gave him his daughter Fausta in marriage, and supported Constantine's pretensions as an augustus. From 307 to 311 five men claimed the rank of augustus: Galerius, Maxentius, Maximinus Daia, Licinius (Severus's successor), and Constantine. But in 310 Maximian entered into a conspiracy against Constantine, and upon its discovery Constantine had his father-in-law strangled. This event was immediately followed by war with Maxentius, who was defeated and drowned at the Battle of the Milvian Bridge in 312. In the East, Galerius had died in 311; and in 313 Maximinus Daia died after being defeated by Licinius.

By 313 Constantine and Licinius were established as corulers of the Roman world. Their relationship was cemented in that year by the marriage of Licinius to Constantine's half sister Constantia; but jealousy and ambition

generated friction and suspicion between the emperors, and in 323 war broke out after Constantine had violated Licinius's territory. Licinius was defeated and deposed, but his life was spared at the intercession of Constantia. The following year, however, Constantine found it expedient to execute him.

## Constantine and Christianity

Constantine's conversion to Christianity has generated much discussion. In later years he told the historian Eusebius that before his encounter with Maxentius he had seen a cross of light superimposed on the sun with the inscription above it: *in hoc signo vinces* (in this sign you shall conquer). Since the cross was the Christian symbol, he had his troops inscribe the monogram of Christ on their shields before the Battle of the Milvian Bridge, and his subsequent success in battle convinced him that he had the protection of the Christian god. Theretofore Constantine had probably been a worshiper of the Unconquered Sun, and in the beginning he appears to have thought that Christ and the Sun were identical. Constantine's coinage for some time continued to celebrate the Sun, and as late as 321 his order for the observation of Sunday gave as a reason that the day was solemnized "by the veneration of the Sun."

But Constantine's early involvement in the theological disputes of the Christians soon disabused him of any syncretistic notions. Early in his reign a group of puritanical followers of Donatus in Africa charged that the orthodox Catholics were too lenient toward penitent apostates, and their quarrels reached the Emperor. He tried for years to reconcile or suppress the dissidents but ultimately gave up his efforts in despair. More serious were the quarrels concerning the nature of the godhead. A heresy called Arianism, which maintained that Christ was not coeternal with the Father, scandalized many churchmen. Roman emperors, as heads of the state religion, had always been responsible for keeping the gods at peace with men (*pax deorum*). Now it appeared that the Emperor must secure a *pax dej*, lest God be offended at His people's view of His nature. Therefore, in May 325 Constantine convened a council of bishops at Nicaea in Bithynia. This convocation created the Nicene Creed, which established the orthodox view that Christ was of the same substance (*homoousios*) as the Father but was a separate individual. The decisions of the council by no means pleased everyone, and Constantine was engaged in attempts to heal theological schisms right up to his death. Indeed, he was baptized on his deathbed by an Arian.

Constantine's personal religious views have been a puzzle to historians. He continued throughout his life to hold the post of pontifex maximus of the old religion. And he allowed the continued celebration of ancient cults and even the erection of temples in honor of his family, though he specified that worship in them must not include "contagious superstition." The Edict of Milan (313) by Constantine and Licinius conferred toleration on all religious sects but did not establish a state church.

But as time went on, Constantine showed increasing favor to the Christians. He built and endowed magnificent churches at Constantinople and Rome and in the Holy Land, Asia Minor, and Africa. He established allowances of grain for the support of the clergy and the poor. He legalized bequests to churches and gave bishops the right to free slaves as well as the right to judge quarrels between Christians without the right of appeal to civil courts. Many of his favorite officials were Christians, and the education of his sons was put in Christian hands. While the celebration of pagan rites continued, a few temples were ordered closed, and others were destroyed by Christian mobs without subsequent imperial punishment. Indeed, Constantine himself had some temples plundered, and only the wooden frames of chryselephantine cult statues were left for the worshipers. Here the decisive factor seems to have been the need for the gold and silver sheathing of the statues to help finance the Emperor's elaborate building program.

## Constantine's Administration

Constantine continued and elaborated the army reforms begun by Diocletian. He created a large central and mobile army which could be quickly dispatched to any troubled frontier. Civil and military authority in the provinces was carefully divided; and the new army appears to have been under the command of a master of infantry and a master of cavalry. The number of barbarians in the army increased, and Constantine is said to have favored Germans.

Constantine also followed Diocletian in the elaboration of court ritual. He instituted the order of imperial companions (*comites*) and classified them by grades, depending on the offices they held. Grandiloquent titles abounded, and recipients were favored by reduced tax burdens and fewer civic duties. He also gave the ancient title of patrician to close friends and high officials.

## Building of Constantinople

After his defeat of Licinius, Constantine was inspired to found a new imperial residence on the Bosporus at the site of ancient Byzantium. Constantinople had a magnificent harbor, the site was easily defensible, and strategically it was more or less equidistant from the dangerous Danubian and Persian frontiers. Constantine ransacked the pagan world for treasures with which to adorn his city, and he spirited a population to it by offering estates in Asia Minor to nobles who would build palaces there and, in an analogy to the Roman dole, by inaugurating rations of food for humbler immigrants.

The founding of Constantinople had far-reaching consequences. Rome was reduced in importance as the capital of the Roman Empire, and the western part of the empire continued to achieve increasing autonomy. The Roman Senate, hitherto a powerful instrument of government, became little more than Rome's city council. The establishment of Constantinople as a de facto second capital hastened the bipartition of the Roman Empire.

## Financial Policy

The cost of Constantinople, increased pay for the army and bureaucracy, and lavish grants to the Church and to favorites combined to create multiple financial problems. To meet these Constantine had the accumulated wealth of the parsimonious Licinius and the confiscated treasures of pagan temples. These were supplemented by new taxes on merchants and craftsmen, surtaxes on the land, and a gradual increase of customs dues and other local levies. Constantine's most constructive financial contribution was the creation of the gold solidus, struck at 72 to the pound, which maintained its purity until the 11th century.

But the economy remained weak and the burdens of government heavy. To ensure the performance of essential services, Constantine became more and more authoritarian. As early as 313 he had ordered local senators (*curiales*) bound to their positions because they were liable for the collection and guarantee of taxes. By the end of his reign their duties had become hereditary. Similarly, shipmasters were compelled to remain on their jobs, for the transport of food to cities was not financially attractive. And in 332 tenant farmers were threatened with a reduction to slavery if they left their districts, thus swiftly moving agricultural workers to serfdom. These measures of Constantine rapidly moved the Roman world from a regime of contract to a regime of status, wherein citizens were tied from birth to their places of origin and their professions.

Constantine's relations with his family were not marked by Christian love or charity. He was a calculating and suspicious man, perhaps as a result of his struggle to survive as a youth among the intrigues at the court of Galerius. In any case, during his career he contrived the death of his father-in-law (Maximian) and of two brothers-in-law (Maxentius and Licinius); in 326 he suddenly, and for obscure reasons, executed his eldest and much admired son, the Caesar Crispus, and apparently at the same time he killed his nephew Licinianus, who was only 11 years old. It is widely believed that Crispus's fall may have been due to the jealous ambition of his stepmother, Empress Fausta, in behalf of her own three sons. If so, there was an early revulsion of feeling, for she was drowned in her bath in less than a year. By her Constantine had three sons, Constantine II, Constantius, and Constans. They, along with Dalmatius and Hannibalian, sons of Constantine's brother Dalmatius, were made caesars and given the administration of various parts of the empire as though it were Constantine's personal estate. Except for these three sons and two infant nephews (Gallus and Julian) all of Constantine's close relatives, including his half brothers Dalmatius and Julius Constantius, were lynched by the army at Constantine's death, leaving Fausta's brood to fight over the inheritance. The one person that Constantine seems consistently to have trusted was his mother, Helena. Indeed, her grief at her grandson's execution may have been instrumental in Fausta's subsequent fall.

Constantine's effect on subsequent history through his rigorous systemization of society and his foundation of Constantinople was profound, and probably the success of the Christian Church can most reasonably be credited to him. In other lands where Christianity was tolerated but not embraced by the rulers, it remained a minority sect; but Constantine's partiality for Christians during a long reign, and the education of his sons as Christians, gave the Church a

half century of such advantages and strengths that the efforts of Julian the Apostate to return to the old ways some 30 years later probably were doomed to failure even had he lived to press his program. Constantine died near Nicomedia on May 22, 337.

## Further Reading

There is no continuous ancient account of Constantine and his reign, but material may be found in Eusebius's 4th-century *History of the Church and the Life of the Blessed Emperor Constantine,* a biased panegyric, and in the works of Zosimus, a Greek historian of the late 5th century. Biographies include Lloyd B. Holsapple, *Constantine the Great* (1942), and John Holland Smith, Constantine the Great (1971). Discussions of Constantine's Christianity may be found in A. Alföldi, *The Conversion of Constantine and Pagan Rome* (trans. 1948), and A. H. M. Jones, *Constantine and the Conversion of Europe* (1948; new rev. ed. 1962). A good account of the administrative, social, and economic aspects of the reign is in A. H. M. Jones, *The Later Roman Empire, 284-602* (2 vols., 1964). □

# Constantine XI

**Constantine XI (1405-1453) was the last Byzantine emperor. A gallant prince, he completed the conquest of the Peloponnesus from the Latins and heroically commanded the futile defense of Constantinople against the Turks.**

The fourth son of Emperor Manuel II Palaeologus (reigned 1391-1425), Constantine was born on Feb. 8, 1405. Following the Palaeologan custom of apportioning territorial responsibilities to each member of the reigning family, as a young man Constantine was assigned authority in the Black Sea coastal towns. His eldest brother, who had always favored him, became Emperor John VIII in 1425.

In 1427 Manuel's second son, Despot Theodore II of the Morea, announced his decision to resign his power in this important Peloponnesian territory. The Emperor designated Constantine to take Theodore's place. When Constantine arrived, however, Theodore had changed his mind. It was then agreed that Constantine should renew Byzantine efforts to conquer the areas of the Peloponnesus still in Latin hands, thus making an enclave for himself. He attacked Glarentza and finally won the city in 1428 by marrying the ruler's niece. By 1430 Constantine had conquered Patras and thus controlled the northern Peloponnesus. Two years later his younger brother Thomas annexed the last segments of Achaea, thereby placing all of the Peloponnesus in Byzantine hands for the first time since the Fourth Crusade (1204).

While John VIII attended the Council of Ferrara-Florence from 1437 to 1440, Constantine served as regent in Constantinople. During the following years he presided over what was to be the final flowering of Byzantine unity and prosperity in the Peloponnesus. At John VIII's death at

**Constantine XI (being fatally wounded)**

the end of 1448, Constantine succeeded to the imperial throne. He proceeded cautiously regarding the hated agreements for Church union with the Latins, which John had accepted at Florence in hopes of winning Latin aid but which he had never implemented. Finally, under pressure from Rome, Constantine allowed the union to be proclaimed in Hagia Sophia on Dec. 12, 1452. This act greatly antagonized the bulk of his subjects, while it actually won him little effective help from the Latin West.

With only token help from outside, Constantine had to face the empire's last agony, as the Turkish sultan Moham-med II launched his great siege against Constantinople in early April 1453. The Turks finally broke into the city on May 29, 1453. Constantine died bravely during the ensuing sack.

**Further Reading**

The only biography of Constantine is Chedomil Mijatovich, *Constantine: The Last Emperor of the Greeks* (1892), which is out of date. For material on Constantine in the Peloponnesus see William Miller, *The Latins in the Levant: A History of Frankish Greece, 1204-1566* (1908). His central role in the final siege is discussed in Edwin Pears's old but still admirable *The Destruction of the Greek Empire and the Story of the Capture of Constantinople by the Turks* (1903); Steven Runciman's newer but less satisfactory *The Fall of Constantinople, 1453* (1965); and David Dereksen, *The Crescent and the Cross: The Fall of Byzantium, May 1453* (1964).

**Additional Sources**

Nicol, Donald MacGillivray, *The immortal emperor: the life and legend of Constantine Palaiologos, last emperor of the Romans,* Cambridge England; New York: Cambridge University Press, 1992. □

# Niccolò de' Conti

**The Venetian merchant-adventurer Niccolò de' Conti (ca. 1396-1469) contributed greatly to Europe's knowledge of the Eastern world.**

Niccolò de'Conti was from a noble mercantile family; at an early age he decided to follow in the family tradition by establishing a lucrative trading operation in the East. Unlike most of his fellow Venetians, however, Conti did not concentrate solely on trade with Egypt. In 1419 he began a journey—reminiscent of that of Marco Polo—which lasted nearly a quarter of a century and took him to the Near and Far East. Like Marco Polo, Conti displayed a facility for language and for recording his observations for posterity.

The first phase of Conti's odyssey included a stay in Syria, where he spent enough time to learn to speak the Arabic language. He traveled overland through the desert to Baghdad; from there he moved on to Persia (modern Iran), where he founded a trading company with local merchants. In the course of his business activities, Conti added the Persian language to his repertory. With Persia as his base, Conti extended his operations into India. Sailing extensively in the Indian Ocean, Conti recorded many of his impressions as he landed at various cities. During these years he had an opportunity to experience Indian life personally, since he married an Indian woman and began to raise a family. It was probably at this time that Conti renounced Christianity. It is not clear whether this was done out of conviction or necessity.

Conti eventually extended his visit to the East Indies. His trip there included stops at Sumatra and the Malay Peninsula, a venture that proved extremely profitable. He returned with a shipload of Sumatran spices, gold, and precious stones. From the Malay Peninsula he sailed northward to Burma, which provided more cargo as well as numerous exotic stories. This part of his long travels included a stop at Java, after which he sailed for Venice.

The trip home was marked by frequent trading stops. He returned via the Red Sea and Suez and finally arrived in Venice in 1444. The reaction to his return was mixed. He was lionized because of the glamour of his long, lucrative trip, while his Indian wife and children were objects of a great deal of curiosity. But Conti's renunciation of Christianity, for whatever reasons, could not be officially condoned. Thus, as Conti's penance, Pope Eugene IV ordered him to provide a detailed, accurate account of what he had done and seen. The result was an account that remains one of the most informative narratives of southeastern Asia to emerge from the early Renaissance period. Like Marco Polo, Conti helped shape Europe's concept of the outside world.

### Further Reading

There is no biography of Conti. Useful background studies are Boies Penrose, *Travel and Discovery in the Renaissance: 1420-1620* (1952), and J. H. Parry, *The Age of Reconnaissance* (1963). ☐

# Jill Kathryn Ker Conway

**Jill Kathryn Ker Conway (born 1934) was a historian interested in the role of women in American history. She became the first woman president of Smith College in 1975.**

J ill Kathryn Ker was born in Hillston, New South Wales, Australia, a small town 75 miles from her parents' sheep station, on October 9, 1934. She earned her B.A. and a university medal at the University of Sydney in 1958 and received her Ph.D. from Harvard University in 1969. Her unpublished but widely-cited dissertation, "The First Generation of American Women Graduates," an intellectual history of Jane Addams and other progressive women reformers, almost single-handedly rekindled scholarly interest in women's contributions to Progressive Era America.

While attending Harvard University Jill Ker met and married John Conway, a history professor in whose course she was a teaching assistant. She followed him to Toronto, where he became one of the founders of York University and she joined the faculty of the University of Toronto. There she lectured on American history while completing her dissertation. Jill Conway rose to the rank of associate professor in 1972. From 1973 to 1975 she served as the first woman vice president for internal affairs at the University of Toronto.

In the mid-1970s, Toronto, like other major universities, was struck with student rebellions, giving Conway an opportunity to demonstrate her cool and unflappable administrative style. In 1975 she was appointed the first woman president of Smith College, the largest privately-endowed college for women in the United States. For this achievement, *Time* magazine named her one of its 12 "Women of the Year." Conway's appointment heralded a change in leadership of the so-called Seven Sisters Colleges, and as a result of this breakthrough all of them became headed by women by the early 1980s.

Initially, Conway found herself at the helm of a prestigious but flagging educational institution. In the early 1970s, Smith, like the other Seven Sisters, suffered a decline in status as bright women flocked to the newly coeducational Ivy League universities. Conway helped to restore Smith's luster as the premier women's college in the United States. A superb fund-raiser, she increased the endowment from $82 million to $220 million. To accomplish this, Conway became a peripatetic president, criss-crossing the

country to solicit alumnae, foundation, and corporate support. Her executive abilities were well recognized, as she served as director of IBM World Trade Americas/Far East Corporation, Merrill Lynch, and on the board of overseers of Harvard University. Despite a hectic administrative schedule Conway maintained her commitment to teaching and scholarship. She taught a course on the "Social and Intellectual Context of Feminist Ideologies in Nineteenth and Twentieth Century America." In 1982 she published *The Female Experience in 18th and 19th Century America.*

In the first portion of her presidency, Conway changed the college from a genteel institution which eschewed feminist ideals into a women's college that respected and reflected feminist values. Through a strong financial aid program, Smith for the first time admitted older, working women and welfare recipients as Ada Comstock scholars. Conway expanded the career development office and took pride in promoting the "old girl" network among alumnae. She endorsed the expansion of athletic facilities, enabling Smith to become the first women's college to join the National Collegiate Athletic Association. Conway articulated a concern that Smith tenure more women faculty, and she frequently publicized the plight of women scholars and the value of women's institutions in educational journals. While not in favor of a women's studies program at Smith per se, Conway did encourage the development of the Smith College Project on Women and Social Change funded by the Andrew W. Mellon Foundation. Out of her presidential budget she helped launch The Society of Scholars Studying Women's Higher Educational History, a group of researchers studying women's intellectual history.

Some highly publicized conflicts erupted in the closing years of Conway's presidency. In 1983, following student and faculty protests, Conway had to inform the U.S. ambassador to the United Nations, Jeane J. Kirkpatrick, that she could not guarantee that Kirkpatrick would receive her honorary degree and be heard as the commencement speaker without incident. The ambassador declined the offer to speak and was given her degree by the Smith trustees in a private ceremony. When newly unionized food-service workers tried to organize Smith's Davis Student Center acrimony developed between the workers and the administration. The unionized workers claimed they were being unfairly treated by a "paternalistic and male dominated" management. The dispute was quietly settled.

While funding for privately endowed, small, liberal arts colleges diminished throughout the early 1980s, Conway's capable leadership allowed Smith College to survive and grow. In an era that some term "post-feminist," Conway's contributions to women's higher education and her sponsorship of separate women's institutions made her an important spokeswoman for contemporary feminism. By the end of her presidency Conway was perturbed by a new generation of women students, less overtly feminist but strongly career-oriented. According to her, this change in the attitudes of the Smith student body was "the only disappointment in a decade." She called for women students to retain an interest in service to society and not to embrace unthinkingly high-earning professions. In this she remained faithful to the ideals of the social feminists of the Progressive generation whose careers she so well illuminated in her pioneering research. Conway also served as a visiting scholar at Massachusetts Institute of Technology. In March of 1996, she succeeded to vice-chairman of the John S. and James L. Knight Foundation, and in February of 1997, Conway was made a member on the Board of Trustees at Adelphi University in New York.

### Further Reading

Jill Conway is listed in *Canadian Who's Who* (1984) and in *Who's Who of American Women,* 14th edition (1985-1986). Conway is discussed in "Women of the Year: Great Changes, New Chances, Touch Choices," *Time* (January 5, 1976); Elizabeth Stone, "What Can an All Women's College Do for Women," *Ms* (1979); and Hal Langur, "Jill Conway," *Daily Hampshire Gazette* (June 27, 1985).

Two fascinating autobiographies recount Conway's life—from her childhood in Australia, and her decision to come to the United States (*The Road From Coorain,* 1990), to her life in the United States up until she was about to assume the presidency at Smith College (*True North,* 1994). □

# James Cook

**The English explorer, navigator, and cartographer James Cook (1728-1779) is famous for his voyages in the Pacific Ocean and his accurate mapping of it, as**

**well as for his application of scientific methods to exploration.**

James Cook was born in Yorkshire on Oct. 27, 1728, into a poor family. At the age of 18 he found employment with a shipowner in his native village of Whitby and made several voyages to the Baltic Sea. When the Anglo-French war broke out in 1755, he enlisted in the Royal Navy and saw service on the *Eagle* as an able-bodied seaman. In a month's time he was promoted to master's mate and 4 years later to master. In 1759 he also received command of a ship and took it to Canada, where he joined the operations in the St. Lawrence River. He performed well enough so that the senior officer of the British fleet put him in command of the flagship.

After the war ended in 1763, Cook was given a schooner, *Grenville,* and was charged with surveying the coasts of Newfoundland, Labrador, and Nova Scotia. For 4 years he sailed up and down these coasts, and when the task was done his findings were of such importance and usefulness that the government had them published.

### First Voyage

Upon his return to England in 1767, Cook found the British Admiralty planning to send a ship to the Pacific Ocean to observe the transit of Venus and also to explore new lands in that area. Cook was picked to command the vessel, and on Aug. 26, 1768, in the *Endeavour* he left

Plymouth, accompanied by an astronomer, two botanists, a landscape artist, and a painter of natural history. Sailing south and west, he touched the Madeira, Canary, and Cape Verde islands, then went to Rio de Janeiro, rounded Cape Horn into the Pacific, and reached Tahiti on April 13, 1769. On June 3 the transit of Venus was observed, and on July 13 he left the place.

Arriving at New Zealand on October 7, Cook set about at once to make an accurate chart of the waters of the two islands; it took him 6 months. He then sailed along the east coast of Australia, which he named New South Wales and for which he claimed possession in the name of the king. He sailed on through the strait separating Australia from New Guinea, to Java, around the Cape of Good Hope, and reached England on June 12, 1771. In recognition of his achievements—circumnavigating the globe, charting new waters, and discovering new land—he was promoted from lieutenant to commander.

## Second Voyage

One year later Cook stood ready for a second voyage, this time to verify the report of the existence of a great southern continent. On July 13, 1772, he left Plymouth in the *Resolution* and, accompanied by another vessel, *Adventure,* sailed southward along the African coast and around the Cape of Good Hope, crossing the Antarctic Circle in January 1773. Finding no great southern continent, he pointed his ship toward New Zealand. This was the starting point for a long cruise in the South Pacific, as he explored the New Hebrides, charted Easter Island and the Marquesas, visited Tahiti and Tonga, and discovered New Caledonia and the islands of Palmerston, Norfolk, and Niue. In January 1775 he was on his way back to England by way of Cape Horn, reaching home on July 29. Thus Cook completed his second Pacific voyage, once again having made a significant contribution by his mapping and charting and his explorations and discoveries.

To those accomplishments Cook added one in nautical medicine, for he had proved that a crew, if properly fed, could make a long voyage without ill effects. He lost only 1 man to disease out of a crew of 118. This feat won him the Copley Gold Medal of the Royal Society and election as a fellow of that distinguished scientific and philosophic association.

## Third Voyage

Then came the third and last voyage of Cook's life. Advanced to captain in August 1775, he was now given command of a new expedition to the northern Pacific to search for a passage around North America to the Atlantic Ocean. Once again the great seaman sailed in the *Resolution,* with another vessel, *Discovery,* leaving Plymouth on July 12, 1776. He went down the African coast, around the Cape of Good Hope, across the Indian Ocean to the Pacific, to New Zealand (which he reached in March 1777), northward to Tahiti and to an island sighted on Christmas Eve and named for the occasion, then to the discovery of the Hawaiian Islands, reaching in February 1778 the coast of North America at 44°55′ (present Oregon). He continued north-

ward along the coast to the Bering Sea and through the Bering Strait to the Arctic, but no northern passage could be found. He turned southward to Hawaii for much-needed repairs, fresh supplies, and sunshine in preparation for a return to northern Pacific waters.

But, as fate would have it, Cook did not live to continue the voyage. On Feb. 14, 1779, he was stabbed to death in a skirmish with some natives. Where he fell, an obelisk later would be erected but, as one of his biographers noted, his true monument was the map of the Pacific Ocean.

## Further Reading

*The Journals of Captain James Cook on His Voyages of Discovery,* edited by J.C. Beaglehole (3 vols., 1955-1967), is an invaluable source. The best biography of Cook is Allan Villiers, *Captain Cook, a Seaman's Seaman: A Study of the Great Discoverer* (1967). See also Hugh Carrington, *Life of Captain Cook* (1939); John Reid Muir, *The Life and Achievements of Captain James Cook* (1939); Christopher Lloyd, *Captain Cook* (1952); and R.W. Cameron, *The Golden Haze: With Captain Cook in the South Pacific* (1964). More general works are J.C. Beaglehole, *The Exploration of the Pacific* (1934; 3d ed. 1966); Ian Cameron, *Lodestone and Evening Star: The Epic Voyages of Discovery, 1493 B.C.-1896 A.D.* (1966); and Alan Moorehead, *The Fatal Impact: An Account of the Invasion of the South Pacific, 1767-1840* (1966). □

# Jay Cooke

**From 1862 to 1873 Jay Cooke (1821-1905) was the outstanding merchant banker in the United States. During the Civil War he made possible the sale at par of hundreds of millions of dollars' worth of Union government bonds to the American public.**

Born at Sandusky, Ohio, on Aug. 12, 1821, Jay Cooke was the son of a frontier lawyer and politician. He stopped his schooling at 14 and worked as a clerk in his own community and in St. Louis, Mo. He arrived in Philadelphia in 1839; from that time on his activities were virtually always associated with this city, which he made the leading financial center of the country for a brief time. He learned banking in the firm of E. W. Clarke and Company, where he worked until 1857. In 1861 Cooke set up his own banking house, a partnership, Jay Cooke and Company, engaging in the characteristic activities of private or merchant bankers: dealing in gold; buying and selling the notes of state banks; trading in foreign exchange; and acting as "note" broker, that is, the discounting of commercial paper.

## Great Financier

The outbreak of the Civil War gave Cooke his great opportunity, and his many fruitful ideas pushed him to the top of the business. Salmon Chase, the secretary of the Treasury and a fellow Ohioan, sought to sell the Treasury's first issues of war bonds and notes through banks and failed

(at this time it was customary to dispose of public securities by competitive bidding). Cooke persuaded Chase to appoint him a special "fiscal agent." Using the then unheard-of methods of advertising and personal solicitation by salesmen all over the country, Cooke sold at par (from October 1862 to January 1864) more than $500 million of the 6 percent bonds to as many as 1 million individual investors and country bankers. As fiscal agent, Cooke played another important role: he supported the price of government securities in the New York money market. "Pegging the market" from this time on became a necessary part of such financing. In January 1865 Cooke was called again to handle a large issue of 3-year Treasury notes bearing 7.3 percent interest; in 6 months he sold more than $600 million.

By the end of the war Cooke had three banking houses, each with a separate group of partners, in Philadelphia, New York, and Washington. In 1870 a similar bank was set up in London, and the next year all were brought together as a single partnership. Cooke expanded (and overexpanded) into many fields. He had been friendly to the National Banking Act of 1863 and obtained charters for national banks in Washington and New York; the national banks were the prime source of Cooke's strength.

To these banks and to small investors at home and abroad Cooke, now an investment banker, sold participation in state and railroad loans; the largest loans went to the great land-grant Northern Pacific Railroad, which was chartered to run from Duluth, Minn., to Tacoma, Wash. In this connection Cooke introduced two new ideas into banking: the establishment of banking syndicates as underwriters to handle particular issues, and the active participation by bankers in the affairs of the companies they were helping finance. Thus, Cooke became the banker and fiscal agent of the Northern Pacific in 1869, and he made short-term loans to the railroad out of his own house's resources—a fatal step.

In 1870, although Cooke was responsible for the proposal, he was only one (and a lesser participant) of the investment banking houses taking part in the great refunding operations of the Civil War loans. Congress authorized the sale of $1.5 billion worth of Treasury securities of various types bearing 4 to 5 percent interest in exchange for the higher-priced wartime issues. J. S. Morgan and Company, and Drexel, Morgan and Company, and their English connections now had their opportunity, and they pushed Cooke into the background.

## End of an Empire

Meanwhile, Cooke's troubles with the Northern Pacific Railroad were piling up. In addition to making loans to the railroad, he undertook the underwriting of its initial issue of first-mortgage bonds. But sale of these bonds moved slowly, and the firm of Jay Cooke and Company continued to make advances to the railroad out of the demand liabilities of its customers; this was a risky business. All the western rails required large funds for building and improvements, and when the national economy turned downward in early 1873, investment markets dried up. Cooke's banks and his associated houses were caught in illiquid form—they could not meet the demands of their depositors—with the result that on Sept. 18, 1873, the New York office of Jay Cooke and Company shut its doors, as did the banks with which it was associated.

This started the large-scale Panic of 1873; one of its results was the complete collapse of the Cooke financial empire and the end of Cooke's influence in the money markets; his personal fortune was wiped out. Later in the 1870s he invested a small sum in a silver mine which turned out to be a bonanza, and Cooke was able to sell his holdings for $1,000,000, thus assuring a comfortable old age. He died on Feb. 16, 1905, in Philadelphia.

## Further Reading

The best biography of Cooke is Henrietta M. Larson, *Jay Cooke: Private Banker* (1936). An earlier work, drawing extensively on private papers, is Ellis Paxson Oberholtzer, *Jay Cooke: Financier of the Civil War* (2 vols., 1907). Indispensable to an understanding of the role and early development of merchant and investment banking in the United States is Fritz Redlich, *The Molding of American Banking: Men and Ideas* (1951). □

# Charles Horton Cooley

**The American social psychologist, sociologist, and educator Charles Horton Cooley (1864-1929) showed that personality emerges from social influ-**

ences and that the individual and the group are complementary aspects of human association.

Charles Horton Cooley was born in Ann Arbor, Mich., on Aug. 17, 1864, the son of a well-known jurist, Thomas M. Cooley. After graduating from the University of Michigan (1887), Charles studied mechanical engineering and then economics. In 1889 he entered government work, first with the Civil Service Commission and then with the Census Bureau. He taught political science and economics (1892-1904) and then sociology (1904-1929) at the University of Michigan.

Cooley's first major work, *The Theory of Transportation* (1894), was in economic theory. This book was notable for its conclusion that towns and cities tend to be located at the confluence of transportation routes—the so-called break in transportation. Cooley soon shifted to broader analyses of the interplay of individual and social processes. In *Human Nature and the Social Order* (1902) he foreshadowed George Herbert Mead's discussion of the symbolic ground of the self by detailing the way in which social responses affect the emergence of normal social participation. Cooley greatly extended this conception of the "looking-glass self" in his next book, *Social Organization* (1909), in which he sketched a comprehensive approach to society and its major processes.

The first 60 pages of *Social Organization* were a sociological antidote to Sigmund Freud. In that much-quoted segment Cooley formulated the crucial role of primary groups (family, play groups, and so on) as the source of one's morals, sentiments, and ideals. But the impact of the primary group is so great that individuals cling to primary ideals in more complex associations and even create new primary groupings within formal organizations. Cooley viewed society as a constant experiment in enlarging social experience and in coordinating variety. He therefore analyzed the operation of such complex social forms as formal institutions and social class systems and the subtle controls of public opinion. He concluded that class differences reflect different contributions to society, as well as the phenomena of aggrandizement and exploitation.

Cooley's last major work, *Social Process* (1918), emphasized the nonrational, tentative nature of social organization and the significance of social competition. He interpreted modern difficulties as the clash of primary group values (love, ambition, loyalty) and institutional values (impersonal ideologies such as progress or Protestantism). As societies try to cope with their difficulties, they adjust these two kinds of values to one another as best they can.

## Further Reading

The most detailed biography of Cooley is Edward Jandy, *Charles Horton Cooley: His Life and Social Theory* (1942). A shorter review, by Richard Dewey, appears in Harry Elmer Barnes, ed., *An Introduction to the History of Sociology* (1948). Albert J. Reiss, Jr., ed., *Cooley and Sociological Analysis* (1968), contains a personal account by Robert Cooley Angell.

## Additional Sources

Cohen, Marshall J., *Charles Horton Cooley and the social self in American thought,* New York: Garland Pub., 1982. □

# John Calvin Coolidge

**John Calvin Coolidge (1872-1933) was the thirtieth president of the United States. He has become symbolic of the smug and self-satisfied conservatism that helped bring on the Great Depression.**

Calvin Coolidge (he dropped the John after college) was born July 14, 1872, at Plymouth Notch, a tiny, isolated village in southern Vermont; he was descended from colonial New England stock. His father was a thrifty, hard-working, self-reliant storekeeper and farmer, active in local politics. Calvin was a shy and frail boy, sober, frugal, industrious, and taciturn. But he acquired from his mother, whom he remembered as having "a touch of mysticism and poetry," a yearning for something better than Plymouth Notch.

Coolidge entered Amherst College in 1891 and graduated *cum laude*. While there he became an effective debater, and his professors imbued him with the ideal of public service. Unable to afford law school, he read law and clerked in a law office in Northampton, Mass. In 1897 he was admitted to the bar and the following year opened an office in Northampton. He built a modestly successful local practice. In 1905 he married Grace Goodhue, a charming and vivacious teacher. They had two sons: John, born 1906, and Calvin, born 1908.

## Apprentice Politician

Coolidge became active in local Republican politics, serving as a member of the city council, city solicitor, clerk of the Hampshire County courts, and chairman of the Republican city committee. He spent two terms in the Massachusetts House of Representatives and two terms as mayor of Northampton. In 1911 he was elected to the state senate and 2 years later—thanks to luck, hard work, and cautious but skillful political maneuvering—he became president of the state senate. This was a traditional stepping-stone to the lieutenant governorship; he was elected to this post in 1915 and reelected in 1916 and 1917. Meanwhile, he gained a reputation as a loyal party man and follower of the powerful U.S. senator W. Murray Crane, a safe and sound man as regards business and a champion of governmental economy and efficiency. And Coolidge won the friendship of Boston department store owner Frank W. Stearns, who became his enthusiastic political booster.

But Coolidge was no narrow-minded standpatter. His credo was the promotion of stability and harmony through the balancing of all legitimate interests. Thus, he supported woman's suffrage, popular election of U.S. senators, establishment of a public service commission, legislation to prohibit the practice of undercutting competition by charging

less than cost, protection of child and woman workers, maternity aid legislation, and the state's savings-bank insurance system.

## Governor of Massachusetts

Elected governor in 1918, Coolidge pushed through a far-reaching reorganization of the state government, supported adoption of legislation against profiteering, and won a reputation for fairness as a mediator in labor disputes. But what brought him national fame was the Boston police strike of 1919. He avoided involvement in the dispute on the ground that he had no legal authority to interfere. Even when the police went out on strike, Coolidge failed to act until after Boston's mayor had brought the situation under control. Yet again Coolidge's luck held; and he, not the mayor, received the credit for maintaining law and order. His reply to the plea of the American Federation of Labor president Samuel Gompers for reinstatement of the dismissed strikers—"There is no right to strike against the public safety by anybody, anywhere, any time"—made him a popular hero and won him reelection that fall with the largest vote ever received by a Massachusetts gubernatorial candidate. At the Republican National Convention the following year the rank-and-file delegates rebelled against the party leaders' choice for the vice-presidential nominee and named Coolidge on the first ballot.

## Sudden Thrust to the Presidency

Coolidge found the vice presidency frustrating and unrewarding. He presided over the Senate and unobtru-

sively sat in on Cabinet meetings at President Warren G. Harding's request but took no active role in administration decision making, gaining the nickname "Silent Cal."

Harding's death in 1923 catapulted Coolidge into the White House. The new president's major problem was the exposure of the corruption that had gone on under his predecessor. But his own reputation for honesty and integrity, his early appointment of special counsel to investigate the Teapot Dome oil-lease scandal and prosecute wrongdoers, and his removal of Attorney General Harry Daugherty when Daugherty refused to open Justice Department files to Senate investigators, effectively defused the corruption issue. Simultaneously, he smoothed the path for his nomination in 1924 through skillful manipulation of patronage. The Republican themes in the 1924 election were prosperity, governmental economy, and "Keep Cool with Coolidge." He won decisively.

Except for legislation regulating and stabilizing the chaotic radio industry, the subsidization and promotion of commercial aviation, and the Railroad Labor Act of 1926 establishing more effective machinery for resolving railway labor disputes, the new Coolidge administration's record in the domestic sphere was largely negative. Coolidge was handicapped by the split in Republican congressional ranks between the insurgents and regulars; furthermore, he was not a strong leader and remained temperamentally averse to making moves that might lead to trouble. He was also handcuffed by his conviction that the executive's duty was simply to administer the laws Congress passed. Most important, he was limited by his devotion to governmental economy, his belief in allowing the widest possible scope for private enterprise, his faith in business self-regulation, his narrow definition of the powers of the national government under the Constitution, and his acceptance of the "trickle-down" theory of prosperity through the encouragement of big business.

## Domestic Program

Coolidge's domestic program was in line with this philosophy. He strongly backed Secretary of the Treasury Andrew Mellon's proposals for tax cuts to stimulate investment, and the Revenue Act of 1926 cut the maximum surtax from 40 to 20 percent, abolished the gift tax, and halved the estate tax. He vetoed the World War I veterans' bonus bill (1924), but Congress overrode his veto. He packed the regulatory commissions with appointees sympathetic to business. He twice vetoed the McNary-Haugen bills for the subsidized dumping of agricultural surpluses abroad in hopes of bolstering domestic prices. Coolidge unsuccessfully urged the sale or lease of Muscle Shoals to private enterprise and in 1928 pocket-vetoed a bill providing for government operation. He succeeded in limiting expenditures for flood control and Federal development of water resources. He resisted any reductions in the protective tariff. And he not only failed to restrain, but encouraged, the stock market speculation that was to have such disastrous consequences in 1929.

## Foreign Affairs

Coolidge left foreign affairs largely in the hands of his secretaries of state, Charles Evans Hughes and then Frank B. Kellogg. The administration's major achievements in this area were its fostering of a professional civil service, its cautious sympathy toward Chinese demands for revision of the tariff and extraterritoriality treaties, and its efforts to restore friendship with Latin America.

Coolidge had a vague, idealistic desire to promote international stability and peace. But he rejected American membership in the League of Nations as then constituted and, whatever his personal feelings, regarded the League as a dead issue. He felt bound by Harding's prior commitment to support American membership on the World Court, but he never fought for its approval and dropped the issue when other members balked at accepting the reservations added by the Senate anti-internationalists. Although Coolidge did exert his influence to secure ratification of the Kellogg-Briand Pact (1928) outlawing war, his hand was forced by public opinion and he had no illusions about its significance. He supported Hughes's efforts to resolve the reparations tangle; but he was adamant against cancellation of the World War I Allied debts, reportedly saying, "They hired the money, didn't they?" His major effort in behalf of disarmament, the Geneva Conference of 1927, was a failure.

## Leaving the White House

Yet Coolidge was popular and could have been reelected in 1928. But on Aug. 2, 1927, he publicly announced, "I do not choose to run for president in 1928." The death of his son Calvin in 1924 had dimmed his interest in politics; both he and his wife felt the physical strain of the presidency, and he had doubts about the continued soundness of the economy. He left the White House to retire to Northampton, where he died on Jan. 5, 1933, of a coronary thrombosis.

Coolidge was not a leader of foresight and vision. But whatever his shortcomings as seen in retrospect, he fitted the popular yearning of his day for stability and normalcy.

## Further Reading

Two illuminating works are *The Autobiography of Calvin Coolidge* (1929) and a record of his press conferences, *The Talkative President: The Off-the-Record Press Conferences of Calvin Coolidge,* edited by Howard H. Quint and Robert H. Ferrell (1964). The most thorough and scholarly biography of Coolidge is Donald R. McCoy, *Calvin Coolidge: The Quiet President* (1967). Two earlier but still useful biographies are Claude M. Fuess's sympathetic *Calvin Coolidge: The Man from Vermont* (1940) and William Allen White's more hostile and less accurate *A Puritan in Babylon: The Story of Calvin Coolidge* (1938). □

# Herbert Cole Coombs

**The economist Herbert Cole Coombs (born 1906) was appointed to a series of public positions which allowed him more influence on the shape of post-war Australia than all except a few prime ministers. Widely respected by all sections of the Australian community, he was committed to government participation in economic reform and social betterment programs.**

Herbert Cole Coombs, the oldest surviving child of a family of six, was born on February 24, 1906. He was known as "Nugget" all his life, after the gold mined in his native Western Australia, because of his small size but great and universal worth.

After a small town education he won scholarships to teachers college and university and then to London as a research student. London, in the grip of the depression years, had a life-long effect on him. He observed the effects on people of the squalor and social injustice caused by economic conditions. His study of banking in British dominion countries examined how the central banks were dealing with the problems of the depression and brought into sharp relief the relationship between government inaction and society's ills. Coombs shared with John Maynard Keynes, who was then developing his "General Theory" at Cambridge, a passionate zeal which saw people's welfare as being the object of social and economic organization. If Coombs could ever have been labeled a socialist it was during this period.

## The Economist

After Coombs returned to Australia with his young family and doctorate in 1934 he was appointed as an economist first in the Commonwealth (government controlled) Bank, and then in the treasury in Canberra to work on financial and economic policy. Here, in the intimate political and bureaucratic circles of the national capital, Coombs's star shone brightly. He began to strike up personal relationships, nearly all of warmth and respect, with those who would be active in Australian government over the next two and more generations. He was especially close to both J. J. Curtin and J. B. Chifley, successive Labor prime ministers. He became director general of the Department of Postwar Reconstruction and had a chance, together with leading politicians, to develop a strategy for the whole of Australian society. Postwar reconstruction, he said looking back, "was a very innovative thing . . . the whole business of government, because it was a government department which was concerned not simply to administer the status quo, but to change the status quo."

Coombs's commitment to a program of reform and social betterment initiated through positive government action showed in the 1945 White Paper on full employment, an influential policy paper of originality and of international note, and in the beginnings of Commonwealth participation in education, out of which grew university scholarships and a national university. He was active also on the international economic scene. In 1943, for example, he participated in the first Australian bilateral discussions with the U.S. Treasury about the international financial organizations which later became the International Monetary Fund and the World Bank.

## The Educator

But he was not a "dismal" economist. In the midst of traditional Australian insularity, Coombs was remarkably internationalist in outlook, and his interests ranged widely beyond his official duties. Two significant strands of his thinking—social intervention of governments and development of the young—thus came together in the plan to establish a special kind of university which would make Canberra not only Australia's political but also its intellectual capital. Australians at that time were ignorant about the countries of Asia and those bordering the Pacific and had no organization whose aim was to study Australia's relations with these countries. The Research School of Pacific Studies was intended to fill this gap. And, as it was recognized that governments would require economic and social knowledge to enable policies planned for the postwar period to be made effective, the Research School of Social Science was created. In much the same way the idea for the Research School of Physical Sciences arose because of the importance attached to the field of physical science, especially with the development of atomic power.

When Coombs returned to the Commonwealth Bank as governor in 1949, at the age of 42, the work of implementing post-war reconstruction was well under way. Coombs knew how important it was that significant social institutions be under the leadership of those who understood the needs of the time. Yet the next 20 years or so brought him no smooth transitions. The Labor government which he had so outstandingly served fell at the elections in 1949 and was replaced by a government under Sir Robert Gordon Menzies which was suspicious of the "socialist planner" Coombs. The new government did eventually come to see his worth, however. He was re-appointed governor in 1956 and again in 1960 (to what then became the Reserve Bank).

## The Humane Man

"Neither withdrawal nor revolution are for me," he wrote. "There remains, therefore, only reform—the creation of new institutions, the recasting of those already existing, the revitalization of the moral and social imperatives which lend them vigour." His achievements in those years were considerable. His presence continued to be felt internationally as well as at home. Within Australia he became one of the best-known living Australians and probably the country's best-known public servant. His name was synonymous with the world of high finance and high politics, yet his public image as a humane and humorous man of great tolerance was accurate. The signature of "the doctor" on every Australian banknote was for years the sign to average Australians that all in the financial world was well. He worked officially with every Australian prime minister from Curtin to Whitlam and became personally close to them all, excepting Gorton but including the long-serving and initially hostile Menzies. He was the senior and almost the only adviser to span the long gap from one Labor government in 1949 to the next in 1972.

He used his position as bank governor to make efforts in artistic and Aboriginal policy which touched many Australians. He became the first chairman of the Australian Elizabethan Theatre Trust in 1954, for example, and held that position until 1968. In that year he retired from the Reserve Bank to become chairman of the Australian Council for Aboriginal Affairs and of the Australian Council for the Arts. In the same year he also became chancellor of the Australian National University.

On Aboriginal issues, the outstanding tolerance, sense of fair play, and cultural humility that he brought to his work was always rounded out by a shrewd understanding of economic realities and an advocacy of policies that made financial sense both for Aborigines and for other Australians. He traveled regularly to outback Australia to spend time among unknown Aborigines in their camps and stations. He espoused a Makarita, or treaty, between Aboriginal and white Australians. In 1986 he published *Towards a National Aboriginal Congress,* which truly brought the plights and concerns of the Aborigines to the entire world. In 1989 he co-wrote with three other authors, Helen McCann, Helen Ross, and Nancy M. Williams *Land of Promises: Aborigines and Development in the East Kimberley,* which reported on economic and social changes arising from resource development. As of May, 1989, Coombs was Visiting Fellow at the Australian National University. He was an Honorary Fellow of the London School of Economics and current Visiting Fellow at the Centre for Resource and Environmental Studies at ANU.

"We must rely on governments for reform," he wrote. "Since governments reflect fairly accurately the prejudices, hopes and intellectual preconceptions of the community generally, the broad requirements of policy suggested by theory must be thrashed around and mulled over in communication and controversy between academics, scientists, politicians and the community generally until they become, as did the objectives of full employment, part of the ethos of the community." Coombs's life was one of a brilliant intellectual, doyen of public servants, a powerful government banker, an avid supporter of Australia's arts, a mentor of prime ministers, and one of the rare white people who earned the respect and trust of Aborigines. A generous though modest tiller of the country's intellectual soil, he remained one of the most celebrated Australians whose impact on that society will be recognized still more fully in the decades to come.

## Further Reading

Little has been written to cover Coombs's time and place and his own books, though reporting only fragments of his life, are best, including: *Other People's Money* (ANU Press, 1971), *Kulinma: Listening to Aboriginal Australians* (ANU Press, 1978), and *Trial Balance* (1981, Sun 1983). □

# James Fenimore Cooper

**Novelist and social critic James Fenimore Cooper (1789-1851) was the first major American writer to**

**deal imaginatively with American life, notably in his five "Leather-Stocking Tales." He was also a critic of the political, social, and religious problems of the day.**

James Cooper (his mother's family name of Fenimore was legally added in 1826) was born in Burlington, N.J., on Sept. 15, 1789, the eleventh of 12 children of William Cooper, a pioneering landowner and developer in New Jersey and New York. When James was 14 months old, his father moved the family to a vast tract of wilderness at the headwaters of the Susquehanna River in New York State where, on a system of small land grants, he had established the village of Cooperstown at the foot of Otsego Lake.

Here, in the "Manor House," later known as Otsego Hall, Cooper grew up, the privileged son of the "squire" of a primitive community. He enjoyed the amenities of a transplanted civilization while reading, in the writings of the wilderness missionary John Gottlieb Heckewelder, about the Native Americans who had long since retreated westward, and about life in the Old World in the novels of Sir Walter Scott and Jane Austen. Meanwhile, he attended the local school and Episcopal church. The lore of the wilderness learned from excursions into the surrounding forests and from local trappers and hunters, the stories of life in the great estates of neighboring Dutch patroons and English patentees, and the gossip of revolution-torn Europe brought

by refugees of all classes furnished him with materials for his later novels, histories, and commentaries.

For the present, however, Cooper was a vigorous and obstreperous young man who was sent away to be educated, first by a clergyman in Albany, and then at Yale, from which he was dismissed for a student prank. His father next arranged for him to go to sea, first in a merchant vessel to England and Spain, and then in the Navy; these experiences stimulated at least a third of his later imaginative writing.

When Cooper returned to civilian life in 1811, he married Susan Augusta DeLancey of a formerly wealthy New York Tory family and established himself in Westchester County overlooking Long Island Sound, a gentleman farmer involved in the local militia, Agricultural Society, and Episcopal church. It was here, at the age of 30, that he published his first novel, written on a challenge from his wife.

## First Period of His Literary Career

*Precaution* was an attempt to outdo the English domestic novels Cooper had been reading, which he imitated in choice of theme, scene, and manner. But he soon realized his mistake, and the next year, in *The Spy,* he deliberately attempted to correct it by choosing the American Revolution for subject, the country around New York City he knew so well for scene, and the historical romance of Scott for model. Thereafter, although many of his novels combined the novel of manners with the historical romance, as well as with other currently popular fictional modes, he never again departed from his concern for American facts and opinions, even though for some of his tales he chose, in the spirit of comparative analysis, scenes in foreign lands and waters.

All of the novels of the first period of Cooper's literary career (1820-1828) were as experimental as the first two. Three dealt with the frontier and Native American life (*The Pioneers, The Last of the Mohicans,* and *The Prairie*), three with the sea (*The Pilot, The Red Rover,* and *The Water Witch*), and three with American history (*The Spy, Lionel Lincoln,* and *The Wept of Wish-ton-Wish*).

## Discovering the "American Problem"

The success of his first America-oriented novel convinced Cooper that he was on the right track, and he decided to turn to his childhood memories for a truthful, if not wholly literal, tale of life on the frontier: *The Pioneers* (1823). Judge Temple in the novel is Judge Cooper, and Templeton is Cooperstown; and originals for most of the characters can be identified, as can the scenes and much of the action, although all of it is given what Cooper called "a poetical view of the subject." Though the traditional novel of manners deals realistically with a group of people in a closed and stable community using an agreed-upon code of social ethics, Cooper tried to adapt this form to a fluid and open society, thereby illuminating the core of the "American problem": how could the original trio of "unalienable rights"—life, liberty, and property (not, as Jefferson had it, the pursuit of happiness)—be applied to a society in which the rights of the Native American possessors of the land were denied by the civilized conqueror who took it from them for his own profit, thus defying the basic Christian ethic of individual integrity and brotherly love?

Natty Bumppo (or Leather-Stocking as he is called in the series as a whole) is neither the "natural man" nor the "civilized man" of European theorists such as John Locke and Jean Jacques Rousseau; he is the American individualist who is creating a new society by a code of personal fulfillment under sound moral self-guidance, improvising as he goes along. In *The Pioneers* Natty is a somewhat crotchety old man whose chief "gift" is his ability to argue his rights with both Indian John and Judge Temple. The central theme which knits this complex web of people and adventures into the cycle of a single year is the emergence of Leather-Stocking as the "American hero."

At this point Cooper was feeling his way toward a definition of his social concern, but in the novel itself the problem is almost submerged in the excitement, action, and vivid description and narrative. In the next of the Leather-Stocking series, *The Last of the Mohicans,* Natty is younger and the romantic story line takes over, making it the most popular of all Cooper's novels. In *The Prairie* Natty in his last days becomes a tragic figure driven west, into the setting sun, in a futile search for his ideal way of life. To most of Cooper's readers these stories are pure romances of adventure, and their social significance is easily overlooked.

In *The Pilot* (1824) Cooper was drawn to the sea by what he felt was Scott's mishandling of the subject, and he thus discovered a whole second world in which to explore his moral problem. The American hero, John Paul Jones, like other patriots of the time, is in revolt against the authority of the English king, and yet, in his own empire of the ship, he is forced by the dangers of the elements to exert an even more arbitrary authority over his crew. There is a similar problem in *The Red Rover,* the story of a pirate with a Robin Hood complex, and in *The Water-Witch,* a tale of a gentleman-rogue, which is less successful because Cooper turned from the technique of straight romantic narrative to that of symbolism.

Cooper's two historical novels of the period (other than *The Spy*), *Lionel Lincoln* and *The Wept of Wishton-Wish,* are set in New England, where Cooper was never at home. The former, although thoroughly researched, is trivial, but in the latter, in spite of lack of sympathy, Cooper made a profound study of the conflict between Puritan morality and integrity and the savage ethic of the frontier.

## Second Period

His reputation as a popular novelist established, Cooper went abroad in 1826 to arrange for the translation and foreign publication of his works and to give his family the advantages of European residence and travel. He stayed 7 years, during which he completed two more romances, but thereafter, until 1840, he devoted most of his energy to political and social criticism—both in fiction and in nonfiction. Irritated by the criticisms of English travelers in America, in 1828 he wrote a defense of American life and institutions in a mock travel book, *Notions of the Americans Picked Up by a Travelling Bachelor.*

Settling his children in a convent school in Paris, he traveled from London to Sorrento, Italy, and also stayed in Switzerland, Germany, France, and England. Europe was astir with reform and revolutionary movements, and the outspoken Cooper was drawn into close friendships with the Marquis de Lafayette and other liberal leaders. One product of this interest was a trio of novels on European political themes (*The Bravo, The Heidenmauer,* and *The Headsman*), but the American press was so hostile to them that Cooper finally declared, in his 1834 *A Letter to His Countrymen,* that he would write no more fiction.

This resolution, however, lasted only long enough to produce five volumes of epistolary travel essay and commentary on Europe (*Gleanings in Europe* and *Sketches of Switzerland* ); *The Monikins,* a Swiftean political allegory; and various works on the American Navy, including a definitive two-volume history, a volume of biographies of naval officers, and miscellaneous tracts.

In 1833 Cooper returned to America, renovated Otsego Hall in Cooperstown, and settled his family there for the rest of his life. There is much autobiography in the pair of novels *Homeward Bound* and *Home as Found* (1838), in which he reversed himself to attack the people and institutions of his own land with the same keen critical insight that he had applied to Europe. One reason for this was that a series of libel suits against Whig editors helped personalize his quarrel with the equalitarian and leveling tendencies of the Jacksonian era. He won the suits but lost many friends and much of his reading public. His social and political position is succinctly summed up in *The American Democrat* (1838).

## Third Period

The third period of Cooper's literary career began in 1840-1841 with his return to the Leather-Stocking series and two more chapters in the life of Natty Bumppo, *The Pathfinder,* in which Cooper used his own experiences on Lake Ontario during the War of 1812, and *The Deerslayer,* which fills in the young manhood of his hero. These romances were followed by equally vigorous tales of the sea, *The Two Admirals* and *Wing-and-Wing.*

But the most significant development of this period was Cooper's final success in blending the romantic novel of action and the open spaces with the novel of manners and social concern. Returning for subject to the scenes of his first interest, the estates and villages of early upstate New York (with their mixed population of Dutch patroons, English patentees, small farmers and woodsmen, and variegated adventurers carving out civilization in a wilderness peopled by Native Americans and rife with unexploited wildlife of all kinds), he wrote five novels in two series: *Afloat and Ashore* (1844) and its sequel, *Miles Wallingford,* and the "Littlepage Manuscripts" (1845-1846), depicting in a trilogy (*Satanstoe, The Chainbearer,* and *The Redskins*) the four-generation history of a landed family from their first days of settlement to the days of the disintegration of their privileged way of life in the face of rampant, classless democracy. Largely unread and unappreciated in their day, these five novels, especially *Satanstoe,* have since become recognized as Cooper's most successful fulfillment of his intention. He had always wished to write a chronicle of his times in fictional form in order to interpret for his countrymen and the world at large the deeper meanings of the "American experiment" in its formative years.

Meanwhile, Cooper's concerns for individual and social integrity and for change had hardened into moral and religious absolutes, and the novels of his last 4 years were less story and more allegory. The best of these, *The Crater* (1847), succeeds where *The Water-Witch* and *The Monikins* failed, in using symbolism to convey a narrative message.

## Cooper's Achievement

The power and persistence of this first major American author in attempting a total imaginative redaction of American life, coupled with an equal skill in the description of place and the depiction of action, overcame the liabilities of both the heavy romantic style current in his day and his substitution of the character type for the individual character. Appreciated first in Europe, the most action-packed of his novels survived the eclipse of his reputation as a serious literary artist (brought about through attacks on his stormy personality and unpopular social ideas) and have led to a restudy of the whole of his work in recent years. In this process Cooper has been restored to his rightful place as the first major American man of letters.

## Further Reading

Probably the most satisfactory short biography of Cooper is James Grossman, *James Fenimore Cooper* (1949), although Donald A. Ringe, *James Fenimore Cooper* (1962), gives fuller critical treatment of Cooper's works, and Robert E. Spiller, *Fenimore Cooper: Critic of His Times* (1931), provides more background analysis of Cooper's social ideas. None of these biographers had the advantage of James F. Beard, who edited *The Letters and Journals of James Fenimore Cooper* (6 vols., 1960-1968), and a new biography is needed. □

# Peter Cooper

**American inventor and manufacturer Peter Cooper (1791-1883) was considered New York City's "first citizen" because of his philanthropy and civic activities. He was a self-made millionaire, and his ideas of government were, for his time, politically radical.**

Peter Cooper's father, John, was a craftsman whose restlessness and lack of success resulted in less than a year of formal education for his son, although the boy early became an accomplished mechanic. At 17 Cooper apprenticed himself to a New York City coach maker. Subsequently he was employed by a cloth-shearing factory, where he invented a new shearing device that became the basis for his first independent enterprise. He also bought a grocery store in New York. He married in 1813 and his wife, Sarah, baked the bread sold in the store. In 1827 he bought the glue factory which was the nucleus of his later fortune.

Through experimentation he produced a product as good as that imported from Europe and gained a monopoly of the American market. Returns from the glue factory enabled him to participate in the iron and telegraph industries.

Cooper's capital backed the development of a large-scale iron industry centered by 1845 in New Jersey, the Trenton Iron Company, managed by his son-in-law, Abram S. Hewitt, and his son, Edward. Cooper was a dedicated supporter of Cyrus Field in the effort to lay the Atlantic cable, and he was an early sponsor and organizer of the telegraph industry. He was president of the New York, Newfoundland and London Telegraph Company from 1854 to 1874 and, for shorter periods in the 1860s, of the American Telegraph Company and the North American Telegraph Association. His mechanical ingenuity, displayed in inventions as various as a lawn mower and a steam-propelled torpedo, enabled him in 1830 to construct the model locomotive "Tom Thumb," which demonstrated that the Baltimore and Ohio Railroad could be made practicable for sharply curved terrain.

Cooper's philanthropy, however, was more significant than his inventions. The Cooper Union, opened in 1859, reflected Cooper's special desire to provide education for working people. It was a significant contribution to adult education, offering professional and coeducational courses in science, technology, and art at night so that working people could take advantage of them. A well-stocked reading room and weekly public lectures were some of the services offered the public for more than 100 years. Coo-

per's work provided one model for Andrew Carnegie's later concept of the stewardship of wealth.

Beginning in 1828, when he was elected assistant alderman of the City of New York, Cooper was continuously occupied with civic projects, which included the building of the Croton Reservoir and participation in the Public School Society, which until 1842 oversaw the public schools of the city. His political convictions made him an unusual millionaire in the decades following the Civil War, perhaps America's first "socialist" millionaire. In his 80s he became the presidential candidate of the Greenback party (1876). He sought government management of the currency in the interest of the working classes and proposed government ownership of railroads and public works programs. "Ideas for a Science of Good Government," published in 1883, contained his reform proposals.

## Further Reading

For a biography of Cooper see Edward C. Mack, *Peter Cooper, Citizen of New York* (1949). Allan Nevins, *Abram S. Hewitt* (1935), gives an account of Cooper. □

# Thomas Cooper

**English-born American scientist and educator Thomas Cooper (1759-1839) was also a controversial political pamphleteer.**

Thomas Cooper was born in Westminster, England, on Oct. 22, 1759. He studied at Oxford but failed to take a degree. He then heard anatomical lectures in London, took a clinical course at Middlesex Hospital, and attended patients briefly in Manchester. Having also qualified for the law, he traveled as a barrister, engaged briefly in business, and dabbled in philosophy and chemistry.

Being a materialist in philosophy and a revolutionist by temperament, Cooper believed that the English reaction against the French Revolution proved that freedom of thought and speech was no longer possible in England; in 1794 he emigrated to the United States with the scientist Joseph Priestley. He settled near Priestley at North-umberland, Pa., where he practiced law and medicine and began writing political pamphlets on behalf of the Jeffersonian party. In 1800 Cooper was jailed and fined under the new Alien and Sedition Acts.

After Thomas Jefferson's election to the U.S. presidency, Cooper served as a commissioner and then as a state judge, until in 1811 he was removed on a charge of arbitrary conduct by the Pennsylvania Legislature. Driven from politics, Cooper was elected to the chair of chemistry in Carlisle (now Dickinson) College and then served as professor of applied chemistry and mineralogy at the University of Pennsylvania until 1819. The following year (when clerical opposition denied him the chair Jefferson had created for him at the University of Virginia) Cooper became professor of chemistry in South Carolina College (now University of

South Carolina). Elected president of the college, he maintained his connection with it until 1834.

Cooper served mainly as a disseminator of scientific information and as a defender of science against religious encroachments. He edited the *Emporium of Arts and Sciences;* published practical treatises on dyeing and calico printing, gas lights, and tests for arsenic; and edited several European chemistry textbooks for American use. In *Discourse on the Connexion between Chemistry and Medicine* (1818) he upheld the materialist position. In *On the Connection between Geology and the Pentateuch* (1836) Cooper attacked those who sought to correlate geological findings with the biblical account of creation.

A member of the American Philosophical Society, Cooper received an honorary medical degree from the University of New York in 1817. He was twice married: to Alice Greenwood, with whom he had three children; and in 1811 to Elizabeth Hemming, with whom he had three children. He died on May 11, 1839.

## Further Reading

The only biography of Cooper is Dumas Malone, *The Public Life of Thomas Cooper, 1783-1839* (1926). Benjamin Fletcher Wright, Jr., *American Interpretations of Natural Law: A Study in the History of Political Thought* (1931), analyzes Cooper's political ideas. Bernard Jaffe, *Men of Science in America: The Role of Science in the Growth of Our Country* (1944), includes material on Cooper. □

# Jacques Copeau

**The theorist, director, and actor Jacques Copeau (1879-1949) established the Vieux Colombier—one of the most important theaters of the 20th century—in Paris to put his theories of theater reform into practice.**

Jacques Copeau was born on February 4, 1879, in Paris. From his youth he was greatly interested in literature, poetry, and theater. As a young man he became acquainted with some of the leading writers and theater people of his day. As a young theorist who was impatient with the commercial theater, he became known as an advocate of theater reform. In 1909 he was one of the founders of the *Nouvelle Revue Francaise,* in which he published critiques and articles on the art of the modern theater.

Copeau was not only a theorist, however. In 1913 he founded what was to become one of the most important theaters of the century: The Vieux Colombier. Copeau formed a company of young actors that included Louis Jouvet, Charles Dullin, and Suzanne Bing. Jouvet not only became an important actor for Copeau, but he also served as stage manager and designer for the theater. As such he was instrumental in putting into actuality Copeau's vision of a theater space.

Copeau wanted a theater that was simple in conception, harmonious, and also functional. Taking his inspiration from the Elizabethans and from his long discussions with important artists such as Gordon Craig, Adolphe Appia, and Emile Jacques-Dalcroze, Copeau designed a space with a fixed, presentational stage that was free of complicated machinery, footlights, or other cumbersome paraphenalia. His theater seated approximately 400 people, had a forestage that allowed close contact with the audience, and depended upon simple curtains and lighting. Copeau's theater was functional, without being ornate, and versatile. It was here that he staged his adaptation of *Brothers Karamazov,* Shakespeare, Molière, and other classical as well as popular drama.

The significance of the Vieux Colombier was not only due to its size and physical layout. Just as important was the ensemble of actors Copeau organized and trained. They were young actors who could be molded by Copeau. Before opening the theater, Copeau and his troupe retired to the country outside Paris for a period of research and training. They studied, rehearsed out of doors, and performed demanding exercises in order to reach peak physical conditions. Copeau's goal, in part, was to eliminate affectation and to get the group to work together harmoniously. He wanted his company to be as physically skillful and as artistically versatile as the Elizabethan acting companys had been.

The repertory company he created could play many roles and perform just about any play. They took their leadership from the director, who, as Copeau believed, was the dominating intelligence of the group. A strong believer in the integrity of the text, Copeau strove to discover the inner rhythms and meanings in the play and to perform it as the author had intended. For Copeau, mounting a production of what an author had written was not a separate function, but, rather, another phase of the same intellectual conception. Thus the director's task was to discover the author's ideas and give them life on the stage.

To accomplish his goal, Copeau believed the writer, director, actor, and theatrical space must all work together as part of a unity and thus capture and enhance the central intellectual integrity of the drama itself. It was a formidable task that Copeau set for himself. In spite of the success of the Vieux Colombier (it became a focal point for some of Europe's leading writers and artists) and of his moderately successful tour of the United States (1917 and 1918), Copeau ultimately shifted his attention from directing to acting. With the help of Bing he opened a school of acting for young men and women aged 20. In 1924 he once again retired to the country to train his young actors. His training included improvisations, mime, experimenting with sounds, and, of course, strenuous physical exercises. Naturally, at the center of his teaching was his focus on the integrity of the text: students were trained to gain a thorough knowledge of the play in order to put on stage all that was inherent in the text itself. Copeau thus anticipated many of the developments in the modern theater, even the "researches" and experiments of Jerzy Grotowski.

Copeau's career as director and teacher made him an important figure in French drama in the early decades of the 20th century. He was a flexible, talented director who felt at home with the works of contemporary writers like André Gide or the works of Shakespeare and Molière. In most of his early presentations he strove for small, intimate, beautiful productions; later in his career, in the late 1920s and early 1930s, he strove to produce larger scale productions for larger audiences. After being passed over several times for head of the Comedie Française, he finally assumed that post for a short time in 1940. He left the post after a few months and retired to the country, where he died in 1949.

## Further Reading

Additional material on Copeau and his work can be found in Maurice Kurtz, *Jacques Copeau: Biographie D'Un Theatre* (1950); Oscar G. Brockett, *History of the Theatre* (1968); Terry Cole and Helen Krich Chinoy, editors, *Directors on Directing* (1963); Bettina Liebowitz Knapp, "The Vieux Colombier" in *Louis Jouvet: Man of the Theatre* (1957); and Norman H. Paul, "Jacques Copeau Looks at the American Stage, 1917-1919," in *Educational Theatre Journal* (March 1977).

## Additional Sources

Copeau, Jacques, *Appels,* Paris: Gallimard, 1974.
Copeau, Jacques, *Journal, 1901-1948,* Paris: Seghers, 1991.
Paul, Norman H., *Bibliographie, Jacques Copeau,* Paris: Societe Les Belles lettres, 1979.
Rudlin, John, *Jacques Copeau,* Cambridge Cambridgeshire; New York: Cambridge University Press, 1986. □

# Nicolaus Copernicus

**The Polish astronomer Nicolaus Copernicus (1473-1543) was the founder of the heliocentric ordering of the planets.**

Nicolaus Copernicus was born on Feb. 19, 1473, in Torun about 100 miles south of Danzig. He belonged to a family of merchants. His uncle, the bishop and ruler of Ermland, was the person to whom Copernicus owed his education, career, and security.

Copernicus studied at the University of Cracow from 1491 to 1494. While he did not attend any classes in astronomy, it was during his student years there that Copernicus began to collect books on astronomy and mathematics. Some of these contain marginal notes by him dating back to that period, but it remains conjectural whether Copernicus had already made at that time a systematic study of the heliocentric theory.

Copernicus returned to Torun in 1494, and in 1496, through the efforts of his uncle, he became a canon at Frauenburg, remaining in that office for the remainder of his life. Almost immediately Copernicus set out for Bologna to study canon law. In Bologna, Copernicus came under the influence of Domenico Maria de Novara, an astronomer known for his admiration of Pythagorean lore. There Copernicus also recorded some planetary positions, and he did the same in Rome, where he spent the Jubilee Year of 1500.

In 1501 there followed a brief visit at home. His first official act as canon there was to apply for permission to spend 3 more years in Italy, which was granted him on his promise that he would study medicine. Copernicus settled in Padua, but later he moved to the University of Ferrara, where he obtained in 1503 the degree of doctor in canon law. Only then did he take up the study of medicine in Padua, prolonging his leave of absence until 1506.

Upon returning to Ermland, Copernicus stayed in his uncle's castle at Heilsberg as his personal physician and secretary. During that time he translated from Greek into Latin the 85 poems of Theophylactus Simacotta, the 7th-century Byzantine poet. The work, printed in Cracow in 1509, evidenced Copernicus's humanistic leanings. At this time Copernicus was also mulling over the problems of astronomy, and the heliocentric system in particular. The system is outlined in a short manuscript known as the *Commentariolus,* or small commentary, which he completed about 1512. Copies of it circulated among his friends eager to know the "Sketch of Hypotheses Made by Nicolaus Copernicus on the Heavenly Motions," as Copernicus referred to his work. In it, right at the outset, there was a list of seven axioms, all of which stated a feature specific to the heliocentric system. The third stated in particular: "All the spheres revolve about the sun as their midpoint, and therefore the sun is the center of the universe." The rest of the work was devoted to the elaboration of the proposition that in the new system only 34 circles were needed to explain the motion of planets.

The *Commentariolus* produced no reaction, either in print or in letters, but Copernicus's fame began to spread. Two years later he received an invitation to be present as an astronomer at the Lateran Council, which had as one of its aims the reform of the calendar; he did not attend. His secretiveness only seemed to further his reputation. In 1522 the secretary to the King of Poland asked Copernicus to pass an opinion on *De motu octavae spherae* (On the Motion of the Eighth Sphere), just published by Johann Werner, a mathematician of some repute. This time he granted the request in the form of a letter in which he took a rather low opinion of Werner's work. More important was the concluding remark of the letter, in which Copernicus stated that he intended to set forth elsewhere his own opinion about the motion of the sphere of stars. He referred to the extensive study of which parts and drafts were already very likely extant at that time.

Copernicus could pursue his study only in his spare time. As a canon, he was involved in various affairs, including legal and medical, but especially administrative and financial matters. In fact, he composed a booklet in 1522 on the remedies of inflation, which then largely meant the preservation of the same amount of gold and silver in coins. For all his failure to publish anything in astronomy, to have his manuscript studies circulate, or to communicate with other astronomers, more and more was rumored about his theory, still on the basis of the *Commentariolus.*

Not all the comments were flattering. Luther denounced Copernicus as "the fool who will turn the whole science of astronomy upside down." In 1531 a satirical play was produced about him in Elbing, Prussia, by a local schoolmaster. In Rome things went better, for the time being at least. In 1533 John Widmanstad, a papal secretary, lectured on Copernicus's theory before Pope Clement VII and several cardinals. Widmanstad's hand was behind the letter which Cardinal Schönberg sent in 1536 from Rome to Copernicus, urging him to publish his thoughts, or at least to share them with him.

It was a futile request. Probably nobody knew exactly how far Copernicus had progressed with his work until Georg Joachim (Rheticus), a young scholar from Wittenberg, arrived in Frauenburg in the spring of 1539. When he returned to Wittenberg, he had already printed an account, known as the *Narratio prima,* of Copernicus's almost ready book. Rheticus was also instrumental in securing the printing of Copernicus's book in Nuremberg, although the final supervision remained in the care of Andrew Osiander, a Lutheran clergyman. He might have been the one who gave the work its title, *De revolutionibus orbium coelestium,* which is not found in the manuscript. But Osiander certainly had written the anonymous preface, in which Copernicus's ideas were claimed to be meant by their author as mere hypotheses, or convenient mathematical formalism, that had nothing to do with the physical reality.

The printed copy of his work, in six books, reached Copernicus only a few hours before his death on May 24, 1543. The physics of Copernicus was still Aristotelian and could not, of course, cope with the twofold motion attributed to the earth. But Copernicus could have done a better job as an observer. He added only 27 observations, an exceedingly meager amount, to the data he took over uncritically from Ptolemy and from more recent astronomical tables. The accuracy of predicting celestial phenomena on the basis of his system did not exceed the accuracy achieved by Ptolemy. Nor could Copernicus provide proof for the phases of Mercury and Venus that had to occur if his theory was true. The telescope was still more than half a century away. Again, Copernicus could only say that the stars were immensely far away to explain the absence of stellar parallax due to the orbital motion of the earth. Here, the observational evidence was not forthcoming for another 300 years. Also, while Ptolemy actually used only 40 epicycles, their total number in Copernicus's system was 84, hardly a convincing proof of its greater simplicity.

Still, the undeniable strength of Copernicus's work lay in its appeal to simplicity. The rotation of the earth made unnecessary the daily revolution of thousands of stars. The orbital motion of the earth fitted perfectly with its period of 365 days into the sequence set by the periods of other planets. Most importantly, the heliocentric ordering of planets eliminated the need to think of the retrograde motion of the planets as a physical reality. In the tenth chapter of the first book Copernicus made the straightforward statement: "In the center rests the sun. For who would place this lamp of a very beautiful temple in another or better place than this wherefrom it can illuminate everything at the same time."

The thousand copies of the first edition of the book did not sell out, and the work was reprinted only three times

prior to the 20th century. No "great book" of Western intellectual history circulated less widely and was read by fewer people than Copernicus's *Revolutions.* Still, it not only instructed man about the revolution of the planets but also brought about a revolution in human thought by serving as the cornerstone of modern astronomy.

## Further Reading

A popular modern account of Copernicus's life is A. Armitage, *The World of Copernicus* (1947). In Thomas Kuhn, *The Copernican Revolution* (1957), Copernicus's theory is discussed in the framework of the process leading from ancient to modern science through the medieval and Renaissance centuries. For a rigorous discussion of Copernicus's theory the standard modern work is A. Koyré, *The Astronomical Revolution: Copernicus, Kepler, Borelli* (1969). □

# Aaron Copland

**Aaron Copland (1900-1990) was one of the most important figures in American music during the second quarter of the 20th century, both as a composer and as a spokesman who was concerned about making Americans conscious of the importance of their indigenous music.**

Aaron Copland was born on November 14, 1900, in Brooklyn, New York, the youngest of five children born to Harris Morris Copland and Sarah (Mittenthal) Copland. He attended Boys' High School and studied music privately (theory and composition with Rubin Goldmark, beginning in 1917). In 1921 he went to France to study at the American Conservatory in Fontainebleau, where his principal teacher was Nadia Boulanger. During his early studies, he had been much attracted by the music of Scriabin, Debussy, and Ravel; the years in Paris provided an opportunity to hear and absorb all the most recent trends in European music, notably the works of Stravinsky, Bartók, and Schoenberg.

Upon completion of his studies in 1924, Copland returned to America and composed the *Symphony for Organ and Orchestra,* his first major work, which Boulanger played in New York in 1925. *Music for the Theater* (1925) and a Piano Concerto (1926) explored the possibilities of jazz idioms in symphonic music; from this period dates the interest of Serge Koussevitzky, conductor of the Boston Symphony Orchestra, in Copland's music—a sponsorship that proved important in gaining a wider audience for his own and much of America's music.

In the late 1920s Copland turned to an increasingly abstract style, characterized by angular melodic lines, spare textures, irregular rhythms, and often abrasive sonorities. The already distinctive idiom of the early works became entirely personal and free of identifiable outside influence in the *Piano Variations* (1930), *Short Symphony* (1933), and

Copland's concern for establishing a tradition of music in American life was manifested in his activities as teacher at The New School for Social Research and Harvard and as head of the composition department at the Berkshire Music Center in Tanglewood, Massachusetts, founded by Koussevitzky. His Norton Lectures at Harvard (1951-1952) were published as *Music and Imagination* (1952); earlier books, of similar gracefully didactic intent, are *What to Listen for in Music* (1939) and *Our New Music* (1941).

Beginning with the Quartet for Piano and Strings (1950), Copland made use of the serial methods developed by Arnold Schoenberg, amplifying concerns of linear texture long present in his music. The most important works of these years include the *Piano Fantasy* (1957), *Nonet for Strings* (1960), *Connotations* (1962), and *Inscape* (1967); the opera *The Tender Land* (1954) represents an extension of the style of the ballets to the lyric stage.

After his return from France, Copland resided in the New York City area. He engaged in many cultural missions, especially to South America. Although he had been out of the major spotlight for almost twenty years, he remained semi-active in the music world up until his death, conducting his last symphony in 1983.

Copland died on December 2,1990 in New York City and was remembered as a man who encouraged young composers to find their own voice, no matter the style, just as he had done for six decades.

## Further Reading

An autobiographical sketch is included in Copland's *The New Music, 1900-1960* (titled *Our New Music*) (1968). Arthur V. Berger *Aaron Copland* (1953), contains more penetrating observations about Copland's music, but Julia F. Smith *Aaron Copland: His Work and Contribution to American Music* (1955), is also useful. A detailed biography up to that point appears in the 1951 issue of *Current Biography*.
Copland's obituary appears in the December 17, 1990 issue of *Time* magazine. □

*Statements,* and the basic features of these works remained in one way or another central to his musical style thereafter.

The 1920s and 1930s were a period of intense concern about the limited audience for new (and especially American) music, and Copland was active in many organizations devoted to performance and sponsorship, notably the League of Composers, the Copland-Sessions concerts, and the American Composers' Alliance. His organizational abilities earned him the sobriquet of *American music's natural president* from his colleague Virgil Thomson.

Beginning in the mid-1930s, Copland made a conscious effort to broaden the audience for American music and took steps to adapt his style when writing works commissioned for various functional occasions. The years between 1935 and 1950 saw his extensive involvement in music for theater, school, ballet, and cinema, as well as for more conventional concert situations. In the ballets, *Billy the Kid* (1938), *Rodeo* (1942), and *Appalachian Spring* (1944; Pulitzer Prize, 1945), he made use of folk or folklike melodies and relaxed his previous highly concentrated style, to arrive at an idiom broadly recognized as "American" without the sacrifice of craftsmanship or inventiveness. Other well-known works of this period are *El Salón México* (1935) and *A Lincoln Portrait* (1942), while the Piano Sonata (1943) and the Third Symphony (1946) continue the line of development of his concert music. Among his widely acclaimed film scores are those for *Of Mice and Men* (1939), *Our Town* (1940), *The Red Pony* (1948), and *The Heiress* (1949).

# John Singleton Copley

**The portraits of the American painter John Singleton Copley (1738-1815), outstanding for their realism and psychological penetration, are the finest of the colonial period. In England from 1775, he executed historical paintings as well as portraits.**

John Singleton Copley was born on July 3, 1738, in Boston. His father died shortly afterward. When Copley was 10, his mother married the engraver, painter, and schoolmaster Peter Pelham. Copley's earliest art instruction came from Pelham and from the leading Boston painter, John Smibert, both of whom died in 1751. Copley then studied with Joseph Blackburn, an English painter working in Boston.

## Boston Period

From about 1760 until 1774 Copley painted the finest portraits the Colonies had ever known. In these works Copley's sitters are invariably shown as no more and no less than what they are. His approach is quite different from the flattering, contemporary English society portrait. Yet, for all his directness of observation, Copley never demeaned his sitters. Instead, an innate nobility, a steadfast, almost heroic quality seems to reside within them.

Copley's Boston portraits include those of Henry Pelham, his half brother (1765), Mrs. Thomas Boylston (1766), Paul Revere (1768-1770), Mrs. Ezekiel Goldthwaith (1770-1771), and Samuel Adams (1770-1772). The painting of Henry Pelham (also known as *The Boy with the Squirrel*), one of Copley's few uncommissioned portraits, shows Henry holding a pet squirrel that sits beside a half-filled glass of water on a polished table top. For its time and place the picture is strikingly novel.

Boylston's portrait shows a plain but rather handsome woman who looks out of the picture, it seems, with deeply felt, steadfast convictions. In the portrait of Paul Revere the famous silversmith sits calmly in shirt sleeves at a table displaying the tools of his trade. Goldthwaith is fittingly placed beside a bowl of ripe fruit, whose warm colors are made to cleverly complement the brown tones of her rich satin dress. Copley showed Samuel Adams, the most uncompromising of the American revolutionary patriots, standing rigidly, his face grim and almost masklike.

## Departure for England

In the spring of 1774, as America's revolutionary spirit began to mount, Copley's house was surrounded by a mob who believed he was sheltering a loyalist. Fearing for his safety, Copley sailed from America that June. In 1775 he toured Italy. In Naples he painted Mr. and Mrs. Ralph Izard; this double portrait was Copley's most elaborate to date. He surrounded the sitters with various classical artifacts, and in the background he painted the Colosseum. After a quick tour of Germany and the Low Countries, Copley settled with his family in London in October 1775.

Haunted by his sense of America's cultural mediocrity, Copley felt that in Europe he would have a chance to make his way where it "counted." When, in 1765, he had sent his portrait of Henry Pelham to London to be exhibited, Joshua Reynolds, the president of the British Royal Academy, had replied: "Considering the disadvantages you labored under, it is a very wonderful performance. . . . You would be a valuable acquisition to the art . . . provided you could receive these aids . . . before your manner and taste were corrupted or fixed by working in your little way in Boston."

Copley's first English painting was a family portrait that included his prosperous father-in-law, Richard Clarke (1776-1777). The figures are placed easily in comfortable poses, and the tone is one of happy nonchalance.

## Historical Paintings

Besides portraits, Copley began painting significant events of contemporary life as imposing history pieces. *Watson and the Shark* (1778) was the first of these. Copley dramatically painted Brooke Watson, helpless in the water, perhaps about to be devoured by an enormous shark, as his friends frantically try to pull him into the boat. The figures in the boat, grouped in a tight triangular format, make this one of Copley's greatest compositions. The brushstrokes, especially in the depiction of the water in the foreground (as would be true of most of his English work), are handled more loosely than before.

Because of the acclaim accorded *Watson and the Shark,* in 1779 Copley was elected to full membership in the Royal Academy and, appropriately, devoted much of his time thereafter to painting elaborate history pieces, as such were considered a higher form of painting than portraiture. The *Death of Major Pearson* (1782-1784) celebrates the 1781 defeat of the French at the Isle of Jersey. The *Death of the Earl of Chatham* (1781) depicts William Pitt's death of a stroke in the House of Lords in April 1778, as he rose to debate the war with the Colonies.

The enormous *Siege of Gibraltar* (1791), finished after at least 5 years' work, commemorates the bombardment of Gibraltar by the Spanish and French. Copley employed something of the meticulous realism of his Boston period but on a vast scale. He made models of the fortress and gunboats and even traveled to Germany to get accurate likenesses of the Hanoverian commanders of the siege. But the artistic control of his Boston period was lost in these increasingly grandiose works. Critical reception was lukewarm, and Copley's portrait commissions began to dwindle.

### Late Works

Copley never regained his former status. In his late work, parts of paintings are well done, but often the parts do not hang together. In *George IV as Prince of Wales* (1804-1810) the chief figure is brilliantly done in a bright red costume, but the troops in the background look like ants between the legs of his horse.

At the end of his life, criticism of Copley's painting became harsh, and he regretted having left America. Perhaps, had he remained in Boston, he would not have found it necessary to involve himself with elaborate allegories and intricate perspectival schemas. But he simply seems to have declined. Samuel F. B. Morse, who visited Copley in 1811, wrote: "His powers of mind have almost entirely left him; his late paintings are miserable; it is really a lamentable thing that a man should outlive his faculties." Copley died in London on Sept. 9, 1815.

### Further Reading

A collection of Copley's work is the Boston Museum of Fine Arts, *John Singleton Copley, 1738-1815: Loan Exhibition* (1938). Jules D. Prown, *John Singleton Copley* (1966), writes more warmly of Copley's English period than previous American writers. For reproductions and biographical sketches see Barbara Neville Parker and Anne Bolling Wheeler, *John Singleton Copley* (1938), and James Thomas Flexner, *America's Old Masters* (1939; 2d ed. 1967).

### Additional Sources

Flexner, James Thomas, *John Singleton Copley,* New York: Fordham University Press, 1993.
Klayman, Richard, *America abandoned, John Singleton Copley's American years, 1738-1774: an interpretative history,* Lanham, MD: University Press of America, 1983. □

# Arcangelo Corelli

**Arcangelo Corelli (1653-1713) was an Italian composer and violinist. His instrumental works established the chamber music style and form of the late baroque era, and he founded the modern school of violin playing.**

Arcangelo Corelli was born in Fusignano on Feb. 17, 1653. At the age of 13 he went to Bologna, where his main teacher was Leonardo Brugnol, a native of Venice. Corelli studied in Bologna until 1670 and then entered the famous Accademia Filarmonica. In 1671 he left for Rome, where he completed the study of composition under Matteo Simonelli. It has been said that Corelli visited Germany, but this cannot be proved.

In 1689, when Alexander VIII ascended the papal throne, his nephew, Cardinal Pietro Ottoboni, appointed Corelli to conduct weekly concerts at his palace, where

Corelli lived for the rest of his life. These concerts helped to establish Corelli as "master of masters."

Corelli's music was published in six opera, each opus containing 12 compositions: Opus 1 (1681), 2 (1685), 3 (1689), and 4 (1694) are trio sonatas; Opus 5 (1700), solo sonatas for violin and continuo; and Opus 6 (1714), concerti grossi for string orchestra.

The trio sonatas of Opus 1 and 3 were intended for church performance (*da chiesa*) with figured bass for organ, and those of Opus 2 and 4 were chamber music (*da camera*) with harpsichord and/or archlute accompaniment. The church sonatas are generally abstract: slow-fast-slow-fast, with the first fast movement being fugal. The chamber sonatas begin with a prelude, followed usually by an allemande, a sarabande, and a gigue. A gigue was also occasionally used in a church sonata.

The most influential of Corelli's works was his Opus 5 for violin, containing the *Folía* variations. Like the trio sonatas, the 12 solo sonatas are generally divided between church and chamber sonatas. As is true of much music of the time, the printed page only partially reflects the composer's intent; the performer of these sonatas was expected to improvise elaborate virtuoso ornaments, particularly in slow movements. There are contradictory reports about the ornaments to Corelli's Opus 5, which were published in Amsterdam in 1716 with the "graces" added to the slow movements as the composer "would play them." Later in the century Roger North challenged the authenticity of these graces, but an equally reliable authority, Johann Joachim

Quantz, did not. Supporting the latter view is the fact that they are excellent and the germ of them can be found in the first edition in the penultimate measure of the first movement.

Corelli's crowning achievement is his Opus 6, the concerti grossi for string orchestra. In this group is his famous *Christmas* Concerto (No. 8). Although these concerti grossi were not published until the year after his death, Georg Muffat reports that he heard concerti grossi by Corelli in 1682, which could give reason to believe that he, and not Giuseppe Torelli, was the originator of this form. Once again the opus comprises both church and chamber works. Concerti 1-8 are *concerti da chiesa*; 9-12 are *concerti da camera*.

Although famous for the calmness and nobility of his music, Corelli is also known for the "Corelli clash," a bold harmonic suspension. From the standpoint of performing technique his music is less advanced than that of his German contemporaries. That the German violin school was at that time farther advanced than the Italian school might be assumed from the fact that when Corelli heard Nicolas Adam Strungk play he exclaimed, "I am called Arcangelo, but you one might justly call Archidiavolo." But though tamer than the German works, his music when first brought to France was too difficult for the violinists there and was performed by the singers. This would seem to contradict the report by John Mainwaring (1760) that George Frederick Handel found Corelli's playing lacking in fire and demonstrated how he wished to have a passage played, whereupon Corelli said, "This music is the French style, of which I have no experience." Nevertheless, Francesco Geminiani, a pupil of Corelli, reported that Corelli was influenced by Jean Baptiste Lully.

Owing to the modern objective style of playing, Corelli's music sounds very calm today; however, he was noted for his passionate playing, and one observer said that Corelli was so moved that his "eyeballs rolled." Because of the modern smoothly connected bow strokes, his music sounds organlike; however, North reports that Corelli tried to make his violin "speak" and that he said, "Do you not hear it speak?" To obtain this effect today, it would be necessary to follow the instructions of North, Leopold Mozart, and others, who said that every bow stroke must begin with a small softness.

Manfred F. Bukofzer (1947) well states Corelli's historical position: "The decisive step in the development of the concerto proper was taken by Corelli and Torelli, both closely associated with the late Bologna school. Corelli can take the credit for the full realization of tonality in the field of instrumental music. His works auspiciously inaugurate the period of late baroque music." Corelli died in Rome on Jan. 8, 1713.

## Further Reading

Marc Pincherle, *Corelli: His Life, His Work* (1933; trans. 1956), analyzes Corelli's music and its unique position in the baroque era and discusses Corelli's influence on other composers. A contemporary appraisal of Corelli is in *Roger North on Music,* edited by John Wilson (1959). See also Manfred F.

Bukofzer, *Music in the Baroque Era: From Monteverdi to Bach* (1947); William S. Newman, *The Sonata in the Baroque Era* (1959); and David D. Boyden, *The History of Violin Playing: From Its Origins to 1761* (1965).

## Additional Sources

Pincherle, Marc, *Corelli: his life, his work,* New York: Da Capo Press, 1979, 1956. □

# Gerty T. Cori

**The scientist Gerti T. Cory (1896-1957) made important discoveries in biochemistry, especially carbohydrate metabolism, and in 1947, along with her husband, received the Nobel Prize in medicine or physiology. She later studied glycogen storage diseases and the role of enzymes in sugar metabolism.**

Collaborating with her husband, scientist Gerty T. Cori made important discoveries about the human body's metabolism of sugar. She won the Nobel Prize in physiology or medicine in 1947 and later went on to study diseases known as glycogen storage disorders, demonstrating the significant role enzymes play in metabolism.

Gerty T. Cori made significant contributions in two major areas of biochemistry, which increased understanding of how the body stores and uses sugars and other carbohydrates. For much of her early scientific career, Cori performed pioneering work on sugar metabolism (how sugars supply energy to the body), in collaboration with her husband, Carl Ferdinand Cori. For this work they shared the 1947 Nobel Prize in physiology or medicine with Bernardo A. Houssay, who had also carried out fundamental studies in the same field. Cori's later work focused on a class of diseases called glycogen storage disorders. She demonstrated that these illnesses are caused by disruptions in sugar metabolism. Both phases of Gerty Cori's work illustrated for other scientists the importance of studying enzymes (special proteins that permit specific biochemical reactions to take place) for understanding normal metabolism and disease processes.

Gerty Theresa Radnitz was the first of three girls born to Otto and Martha Neustadt Radnitz. She was born in Prague, then part of the Austro-Hungarian Empire, on August 15, 1896. Otto was a manager of sugar refineries. It is not known if his work helped shape his eldest daughter's early interest in chemistry and later choice of scientific focus. However, her maternal uncle, a professor of pediatrics, did encourage her to pursue her interests in science. Gerty was first taught by tutors at home, then enrolled in a private girls' school. At that time, girls were not expected to attend a university. In order to follow her dream of becoming a chemist, Gerty first studied at the Tetschen *Realgymnasium*. She then had to pass a special entrance exam (*matura* ) that

tested her knowledge of Latin, literature, history, mathematics, physics, and chemistry.

In 1914 Gerty Radnitz entered the medical school of the German University of Prague (Ferdinand University). There she met a fellow classmate, Carl Ferdinand Cori, who shared her interest in doing scientific research. Together they studied human complement, a substance in blood that plays a key role in immune responses by combining with antibodies. This was the first of a lifelong series of collaborations. In 1920 they both graduated and received their M.D. degrees.

Shortly after graduating, they moved to Vienna and married. Carl worked at the University of Vienna's clinic and the University of Graz's pharmacology department, while Gerty took a position as an assistant at the Karolinen Children's Hospital. Some of her young patients suffered from a disease called congenital myxedema, in which deposits form under the skin and cause swelling, thickening, and paleness in the face. The disease is associated with severe dysfunction of the thyroid gland, located at the base of the neck, which helps to control many body processes, including growth. Gerty's particular research interest was in how the thyroid influenced body temperature regulation.

## Immigrates to United States

In the early 1920s, Europe was in the midst of great social and economic unrest in the wake of World War I, and in some regions, food was scarce; Gerty suffered briefly from malnourishment while working in Vienna. Faced with

these conditions, the Coris saw little hope there for advancing their scientific careers. In 1922 Carl moved to the United States to take a position as biochemist at the New York State Institute for the Study of Malignant Diseases (later the Roswell Park Memorial Institute). Gerty joined him in Buffalo a few months later, becoming an assistant pathologist at the institute.

Life continued to be difficult for Gerty Cori. She was pressured to investigate malignant diseases, specifically cancers, which were the focus of the institute. Both she and Carl did publish studies related to malignancies, but studying cancer was not to be the focus of either Gerty's or Carl's work. During these early years in the United States, the Coris' publications covered topics from the biological effects of X rays to the effects of restricted diets on metabolism. Following up on her earlier work on the thyroid, Gerty published a report on the influence of thyroid extract on paramecium population growth, her first publication in English.

Colleagues cautioned Gerty and Carl against working together, arguing that collaboration would hurt Carl's career. However, Gerty's duties as an assistant pathologist allowed her some free time, which she used to begin studies of carbohydrate metabolism jointly with her husband. This work, studying how the body burns and stores sugars, was to become the mainstream of their collaborative research. During their years in Buffalo, the Coris jointly published a number of papers on sugar metabolism that reshaped the thinking of other scientists about this topic. In 1928 Gerty and Carl Cori became naturalized citizens of the United States.

In 1931 the Coris moved to St. Louis, Missouri, where Gerty took a position as research associate at Washington University School of Medicine; Carl was a professor there, first of pharmacology and later of biochemistry. The Coris' son, Carl Thomas, was born in 1936. Gerty become a research associate professor of biochemistry in 1943 and in 1947 a full professor of biochemistry. During the 1930s and 1940s the Coris continued their work on sugar metabolism. Their laboratory gained an international reputation as an important center of biochemical breakthroughs. No less than five Nobel laureates spent parts of their careers in the Coris' lab working with them on various problems.

For their pivotal studies in elucidating the nature of sugar metabolism, the Cori's were awarded the Nobel Prize for physiology or medicine in 1947. They shared this honor with Argentine physiologist Bernardo A. Houssay, who discovered how the pituitary gland functions in carbohydrate metabolism. Gerty Cori was only the third woman to receive a Nobel Prize in science. Previously, only Marie Curie and Iréne Joloit-Curie had been awarded such an honor. As with the previous two women winners, Cori was a co-recipient of the prize with her husband.

## Significance of the Coris' Research

In the 1920s, when the Coris began to study carbohydrate metabolism, it was generally believed that the sugar called glucose (a type of carbohydrate) was formed from another carbohydrate, glycogen, by the addition of water molecules (a process known as hydrolysis). Glucose circulates in the blood and is used by the body's cells in virtually all cellular processes that require energy. Glycogen is a natural polymer (a large molecule made up of many similar smaller molecules) formed by joining together large numbers of individual sugar molecules for storage in the body. Glycogen allows the body to function normally on a continual basis, by providing a store from which glucose can be broken down and released as needed.

Hydrolysis is a chemical process that does not require enzymes. If, as was believed to be the case in the 1920s, glycogen were broken down to glucose by simple hydrolysis, carbohydrate metabolism would be a very simple, straightforward process. However, in the course of their work, the Coris discovered a chemical compound, glucose–1-phosphate, made up of glucose and a phosphate group (one phosphorus atom combined with three oxygen atoms—sometimes known as the Cori ester) that is derived from glycogen by the action of an enzyme, phosphorylase. Their finding of this intermediate compound, and of the enzymatic conversion of glycogen to glucose, was the basis for the later understanding of sugar metabolism and storage in the body. The Coris' studies opened up research on how carbohydrates are used, stored, and converted in the body.

Cori had been interested in hormones (chemicals released by one tissue or organ and acting on another) since her early thyroid research in Vienna. The discovery of the hormone insulin in 1921 stimulated her to examine its role on sugar metabolism. Insulin's capacity to control diabetes lent great clinical importance to these investigations. In 1924 Gerty and Carl wrote about their comparison of sugar levels in the blood of both arteries and veins under the influence of insulin. At the same time, inspired by earlier work by other scientists (and in an attempt to appease their employer), the Coris examined why tumors used large amounts of glucose.

Their studies on glucose use in tumors convinced the Coris that much basic research on carbohydrate metabolism remained to be done. They began this task by examining the rate of absorption of various sugars from the intestine. They also measured levels of several products of sugar metabolism, particularly lactic acid and glycogen. The former compound results when sugar combines with oxygen in the body.

The Coris measured how insulin affects the conversion of sugar into lactic acid and glycogen in both the muscles and liver. From these studies, they proposed a cycle (called the Cori cycle in their honor) that linked glucose with glycogen and lactic acid. Their proposed cycle had four major steps: (1) blood glucose becomes muscle glycogen, (2) muscle glycogen becomes blood lactic acid, (3) blood lactic acid becomes liver glycogen, and (4) liver glycogen becomes blood glucose. Their original proposed cycle has had to be modified in the face of subsequent research, a good deal of which was carried out by the Coris themselves. For example, scientists learned that glucose and lactic acid can be directly inter-converted, without having to be made into glycogen. Nonetheless, the Coris' suggestion generated much excitement among carbohydrate metabolism re-

searchers. As the Coris' work continued, they unraveled more steps of the complex process of carbohydrate metabolism. They found a second intermediate compound, glucose–6-phosphate, that is formed from glucose–1-phosphate. (The two compounds differ in where the phosphate group is attached to the sugar.) They also found the enzyme that accomplishes this conversion, phosphoglucomutase.

By the early 1940s the Coris had a fairly complete picture of carbohydrate metabolism. They knew how glycogen became glucose. Rather than the simple non-enzymatic hydrolysis reaction that, twenty years earlier, had been believed to be responsible, the Coris' studies painted a more elegant, if more complicated picture. Glycogen becomes glucose–1-phosphate through the action of one enzyme (phosphorylase). Glucose–1-phosphate becomes glucose–6-phosphate through the action of another enzyme (phosphoglucomutase). Glucose–6-phosphate becomes glucose, and glucose becomes lactic acid, each step in turn mediated by one specific enzyme. The Coris' work changed the way scientists thought about reactions in the human body, and it suggested that there existed specific, enzyme-driven reactions for many of the biochemical conversions that constitute life.

## Resumes Early Interest in Pediatric Medicine

In her later years, Cori turned her attention to a group of inherited childhood diseases known collectively as glycogen storage disorders. She determined the structure of the highly branched glycogen molecule in 1952. Building on her earlier work on glycogen and its biological conversions via enzymes, she found that diseases of glycogen storage fell into two general groups, one involving too much glycogen, the other, abnormal glycogen. She showed that both types of diseases originated in the enzymes that control glycogen metabolism. This work alerted other workers in biomedicine that understanding the structure and roles of enzymes could be critical to understanding diseases. Here again, Cori's studies opened up new fields of study to other scientists. In the course of her later studies, Cori was instrumental in the discovery of a number of other chemical intermediate compounds and enzymes that play key roles in biological processes.

At the time of her death, on October 26, 1957, Cori's influence on the field of biochemistry was enormous. She had made important discoveries and prompted a wealth of new research, receiving for her contributions, in addition to the Nobel Prize, the prestigious Garvan Medal for women chemists of the American Chemical Society as well as membership in the National Academy of Sciences. As the approaches and methods that she helped pioneer continue to result in increased scientific understanding, the importance of her work only grows greater.

## Further Reading

Cori, Carl F., *American Chemists and Chemical Engineers: Gerty Theresa Cori*, American Chemical Society, 1976.
*Dictionary of Scientific Biography*, Scribner, 1971.

Magill, Frank N., *The Nobel Prize Winners, Physiology or Medicine: 1944–1969,* Salem Press, 1991 ☐

# Lovis Corinth

**Lovis Corinth (1838-1925) was a leading German artist of the late 19th-early 20th century with a prodigeous output of work.**

L ovis Corinth was born in 1838 in the town of Tapiau in East Prussia (now the Soviet Union), the son of a tanner. He was named Louis, but came to be called Lovis because he later signed his name with a Latin-style "u" which is written as a "v". Corinth grew up in a rural setting, with little or no exposure to works of art. From a very early age, however, he enjoyed sketching and painting. At the age of nine he was enrolled first in the public school in nearby Konigsberg and then at the Konigsberg Academy of Art.

Corinth continued his artistic training in Munich (1880-1882), and then in Antwerp and Paris (1884-1886), where he studied with the well-known academic painter Adolphe William Bouguereau. During this period Corinth remained uninfluenced by the "modern" painters of the day, such as Manet and Monet; he preferred instead the naturalistic style of Wilhelm Leibl, who had been a pupil of Gustave Courbet. He also admired works by Rubens in the Louvre in Paris and by Rembrandt.

Corinth returned to Germany in 1891 and continued his painting career. He became a part of the art world of Berlin at the turn of the century and in 1901 he opened a school for painters there. His first student, Charlotte Berend, became his wife two years later.

In the first decade of the 20th century, Corinth's palette became brighter and he began to employ the freer brushwork characteristic of the German Impressionists, represented by Max Liebermann. In addition to his landscapes and figure compositions, he achieved great success as a portrait painter, and his services were much in demand. Corinth was elected chairman of the Secession, the Berlin artists' association to which he had belonged since 1899, in 1911. In that same year he completed 61 oils, as well as many drawings, etchings, and lithographs, and all of his work was selling well.

At the end of the year, however, Corinth suffered a massive stroke which threatened to end his career. His left side was paralyzed, but through great perserverance and determination he was able to resume painting the following year. From 1912 until his death in 1925 Corinth continued to work and to struggle against his increasing debility. He produced some 500 oils and about 1,000 prints, in addition to drawings and watercolors. He was named president of the Berlin Secession in 1915.

In Corinth's late work expressive elements dominate, reflecting his own personal struggles against his illness and, perhaps, an increased perception of the world around him.

He created numerous portraits and self-portraits, notable for their profound psychological insights, and his work influenced later generations of German artists.

Corinth died in July 1925 while on a visit to Holland to see paintings by Rembrandt and Frans Hals. One of his most famous paintings, *Ecce Homo,* was done earlier in the year. His late work was condemned by the Nazis as degenerate. Today, however, Corinth is seen as a major artist whose paintings combined elements from the Old Masters he admired, such as Rembrandt, with late 19th-century Impressionism to create, in his late work, a fully modern idiom. His paintings, drawings, and prints are included in numerous public and private collections throughout the world.

## Further Reading

The majority of writings on Lovis Corinth and his art are in German. His widow, Charlotte Berend-Corinth, published a catalogue of all of his works in 1958. Corinth was included in a major exhibition titled *German Art in the 20th Century, Painting and Sculpture 1905-1985,* held at the Royal Academy of Arts, London, in 1985. The accompanying catalogue contains numerous reproductions of his works, as well as biographical information.

## Additional Sources

Uhr, Horst, *Lovis Corinth,* Berkeley: University of California Press, 1990. ☐

# Pierre Corneille

**The French dramatist Pierre Corneille (1606-1684) wrote more than 30 plays and is often called the father of French tragedy. His tragedies characteristically explore the conflict between heroic love and heroic devotion to duty.**

P ierre Corneille was born on June 6, 1606, in Rouen. Educated in the Jesuit school of the city, he completed law studies and became a lawyer there in 1624. In 1628 his father purchased for him, according to the custom of the times, the post of king's advocate in Rouen. Corneille continued for many years to discharge his legal duties as king's advocate, but his real interest was literature. At some time between 1625 and 1629 he wrote the comedy *Mélite,* which was taken up by a traveling theatrical troupe and subsequently presented in Paris, where it was an immense success.

## French Classical Drama

In 1629 the French theater was moving away from the exuberant baroque style of the early 17th century toward a dramaturgy based on the theatrical precepts of Aristotle and his commentators since the Renaissance. The general rules included the famous principle of "three unities" (time, place, and action), according to which a play must present a single coherent story, taking place within one day in a single palace or at most a single city. They also included the principles of theatrical verisimilitude (the events presented must be believable) and of *bienséance* (standards of "good taste" must be followed to avoid shocking the audience). These three major precepts structured the great classical theater of the following decades in France.

Corneille apparently first encountered the theatrical mainstream while attending performances of *Mélite* in Paris, and he recalled in later years that his first play was "certainly not written according to the rules, since I didn't know then that there were any." Although Corneille observed the rules more conscientiously in his subsequent plays, he was never completely bound by them. His ambivalent attitude toward the Aristotelian precepts is evident in his highly baroque plays—the extravagant tragicomedy *Clitandre* (1630/1631), the violent tragedy *Médée* (1635), and the fascinating comedy *L'Illusion comique* (1636)—and remains apparent in his first masterpiece, *Le Cid* (1637).

## Major Tragedies

Corneille's *Le Cid* is based on traditional stories about the Cid, a medieval warrior and Spanish national hero. In it the young Cid (Don Rodrigue) must avenge his father's honor by fighting a duel with the father of his own fiancée (Dona Chimène). Rodrigue thus finds himself torn between a duty to avenge family honor and a duty to act consistently with the precepts of love. To neglect either would tarnish his *gloire*. The concept of *gloire*, which combines elements of noblesse oblige, virtue, force of will, and self-esteem, seems to have formed the highest ideal of Corneille's world view.

In the course of the play Rodrigue fights Chimène's father and kills him, thus forcing Chimène to choose between family honor and her love for Rodrigue. Rodrigue distinguishes himself by defending the city against a Moorish attack, and Chimène distinguishes herself by implacably pursuing vengeance against Rodrigue. In the end the King judges that both have acted according to the most heroic conception of *gloire;* he declares that Chimène has fulfilled her obligation to her father and commands her to marry Rodrigue within a year.

*Le Cid* was one of the greatest theatrical successes of the 17th century. And although its success was marred by a literary quarrel in which lesser authors attacked its sins against the literary rules, it marked Corneille as a major dramatist and opened the most important epoch of his career. During this period Corneille showed great pride in his literary accomplishments but continued to practice law in Rouen and remained very much a bourgeois provincial who had made good. He was both resentful of, and deferential to, the literary "authorities" who attacked his play. When the newly founded French Academy decided against him, he was genuinely discouraged and apparently abandoned the theater for some time. An academician who remained friendly with Corneille wrote: "I encouraged him as much as I could and told him to avenge himself by writing some new *Cid*. But he talked of nothing but the rules and the things he could have replied to the academicians."

Overcoming his discouragement, Corneille wrote the successful tragedy *Horace* (1640), which was soon followed by *Cinna* (1640) and *Polyeucte* (1642). In these tragedies he continued to explore the concepts of *gloire*, heroism, and moral conflict.

*Horace,* based on an incident from early Roman history, depicts a young man who with his brothers, the Horatii, is obliged to defend Rome in combat against three brothers (the Curatii) from an enemy town. Horace's wife, however, is a sister of the Curatii, and his own sister is engaged to one of them. In *Cinna* a conspirator hesitates between his fidelity to the state and the desire for vengeance of the woman he loves; and the Roman emperor Auguste, who discovers the conspiracy, must choose between vengeance or clemency for the conspirators. In *Polyeucte* the hero is converted to Christianity during the Roman persecution of the Christians. He openly attacks the pagan religion, and thus he, his wife, his father-in-law (the Roman governor), and a noble Roman envoy must reconcile personal feelings and religious or political duty.

## Later Career

In 1644 Corneille returned successfully to comedy with *Le Menteur* and to tragedy with *Pompée,* but thereafter his success as a playwright was less consistent. Although such tragedies as *Nicomède* (1651), *Oedipe* (1659), and *Sertorius* (1662) were favorably received, Corneille wrote a larger number of unsuccessful plays. He tried one formula after another to make a comeback, and courtiers, great ladies, and men of letters took sides for or against him. But the success of each new play became more and more uncertain, and Corneille himself more and more embittered. His last play, *Suréna* (1674), skillfully imitated the style of the playwright who had eclipsed him, Jean Racine, but was less successful than Racine's play of the same year. Although Corneille remained active in the literary world, he wrote nothing more for the theater. He died on Oct. 1, 1684, in Paris.

## Critical Judgment

In his tragedies Corneille's treatment of his heroes' moral dilemmas is ambiguous and has inspired divergent views of his meaning. Although his heroes typically possess almost superhuman virtue and courage, each tragedy is resolved by the intervention of superior authority. Some critics have therefore asserted that Corneille's tragic works do not inspire terror or pity, the reactions that Aristotle stated were proper to tragedy. In the 17th century, however, the critics and poet Nicholas Boileau pointed out that in differing from the Aristotelian model Corneille had written "tragedies of admiration."

Such romantics as Victor Hugo, while unfavorable to classical theater in general, admired the heroic and optimistic virtue of Cornelian personages, a characteristic that has also been noted by more recent critics. Others, however, have spoken deprecatingly of the curious innocence or naiveté of even the most admirable of Corneille's heroes and have depicted Rodrigue, Horace, Polyeucte, and the rest as prisoners of a rigid virtue and exaggerated *gloire*. These criticisms possess some validity but also indicate the subtlety of Corneille's tragic vision.

## Further Reading

Some of Corneille's plays were translated into English verse by Lacy Lockert, ed., *Chief Plays* (2d ed., 1957). The best recent work on Corneille in English is Robert J. Nelson, *Corneille: His Heroes and Their Worlds* (1963). Nelson also reprinted selected Cornelian criticism in his excellent *Corneille and Racine: Parallels and Contrasts* (1966). Herbert Fogel surveyed critical opinion, *The Criticism of Cornelian Tragedy* (1967). The best work in English on the baroque esthetic in French literature is Imbrie Buffum, *Studies in the Baroque from Montaigne to Rotrou* (1957), which has chapters on some of Corneille's early plays. E. B. O. Borgerhoff, *The Freedom of French Classicism* (1950), and Will Grayburn Moore, *French Classical Literature* (1961), study the richness of 17th-century literary styles, including Corneille's.

## Additional Sources

Corneille, Pierre, *Polyeuctus; The liar; Nicomedes,* Harmondsworth, Middlesex, England; New York: Penguin Books, 1980.
Couprie, Alain, *Pierre Corneille, Le Cid,* Paris: Presses universitaires de France, 1989. □

# Ezra Cornell

**American capitalist and philanthropist Ezra Cornell (1807-1874) was the founder of Cornell University, which soon became one of the more advanced educational establishments of the United States.**

Ezra Cornell was the son of Elijah and Eunice Barnard Cornell. The family, of New England Quaker stock, settled in De-Ruyter, Madison County, N.Y., in 1819, where Ezra's father farmed and made pottery. Ezra learned something of both, as well as carpentry from his father, a former ship's carpenter. At 18 he set out on his own and in 1828 he settled in Ithaca, N.Y., where he worked as a carpenter and millwright. His employment in building and maintaining flour mills there came to a close when they were converted to textile mills in 1841.

Cornell's interest in promoting a patent plow brought him into contact with the promoters of the Morse magnetic telegraph; from that time on he was involved in the telegraph industry—organizing, building, and operating lines. He constructed lines which connected New York and Washington, Philadelphia and New York, New York and Albany, then turned to the Midwest to construct a network of lines connecting major points. Cutthroat competition in these early days of the industry led to the combination of many of the leading companies into Western Union Telegraph Company. The concern grew rapidly until it dominated the business in the United States and much of Canada. Cornell's considerable personal fortune was the result of his involvement in such activities during the first 30 years of the industry.

Once he had achieved great personal wealth, Cornell became concerned with public affairs. He financed the construction of a great public library in Ithaca and built and stocked a model farm. His interest in agricultural affairs led to his presidency of the State Agricultural Society. He was a

leading member of the New York State Legislature during the 1860s, first as an assemblyman and subsequently as a senator. Here he became concerned with higher education.

Cornell's pledge of his farm as a site plus a half-million-dollar endowment was the essential step that led to the enactment of legislation to found Cornell University. The school opened in 1868. Thereafter Cornell took a keen interest in the university, bestowing sizable gifts and encouraging its adherence to some of his egalitarian ideas of education. The university's freedom from religious ties, interest in the education of women, emphasis upon agricultural and engineering training, and interest in educational opportunities for poor students made it one of the more advanced educational institutions in America. Cornell, a frequent sight on campus, also carefully administered the disposition of the university's Morrill Act land-grant, husbanding that unique resource and eventually producing substantial returns for the university.

Cornell died in 1874. He was survived by his wife, Mary Anne Wood Cornell, and a son, Alonzo B. Cornell, later governor of New York.

## Further Reading

There are two full-length biographies of Cornell: Alonzo B. Cornell, *True and Firm: Biography of Ezra Cornell* (1884), and Albert W. Smith, *Ezra Cornell: A Character Study* (1934), which contains an extensive bibliography. There is considerable material relating to Cornell in Andrew Dickson White, *Autobiography*, vol. 1 (1905), and *My Reminiscences of Ezra Cornell* (1890). Histories of Cornell University also contain material of interest. □

# Joseph Cornell

**Joseph Cornell (1903-1972) was an American artist best known for his small collage boxes as well as for his experimental films.**

Joseph Cornell was born on December 24, 1903, in Nyack, New York, to parents descended from old Dutch families, his maternal grandfather being the wealthy and prominent Commodore William Voorhis. After his father's death in 1917 Cornell, along with his mother, two sisters, and an invalid brother, was faced with a financial set-back that forced them to leave Nyack and move to Flushing, Queens, where he lived until his death in 1972. Educated at Phillips Academy in Andover, Massachusetts, Cornell worked at a variety of jobs such as selling refrigerators door-to-door, designing textiles, and working in the garment industry to help support his family. He never married or travelled, living most of his life in a white frame house on Utopia Parkway in Queens. Cornell was an active Christian Scientist all of his adult life.

It is speculated that Cornell first made his toy-like artworks to amuse his brother who was confined to a wheelchair and cared for by Cornell. He filled them with all sorts of ephemera, of which he was an avid collector. Cornell

was known to haunt old book and print shops and junk stores during his daily trips to Manhattan, and he had extensive collections of old photographs, recordings, movies, opera librettos, souvenirs, and other memorabilia. He was enamoured of all forms of theater and was well read in literature and poetry.

A very private man, it is thought that he first began making boxes in which he collaged images and objects from his various collections in the early 1930s. The boxes, often containing words, were each based on themes developed by the relationships between collage elements. These connections were sometimes direct but more often allusive, giving the boxes a poetic quality. Cornell did many boxes that were homages to ballerinas, opera singers, and film stars he revered and sometimes corresponded with. The boxes were nostalgic worlds filled with people and places that Cornell admired from a distance. One such box entitled *A Pantry Ballet for Jacques Offenbach* contains a ballet corps of red plastic fish set against a background of shelf-paper which turns the box into a stage with paper doily curtains and menacing stagesets of toy silverware. The scale and nature of Cornell's boxes did not change much, but in the 1950s he began to make two-dimensional collages without the framework of the boxcontainer.

While considered something of a recluse, Cornell did make contacts with the small art circles in New York in the 1930s. He visited Alfred Stieglitz's pioneering gallery "291," and he became friendly with the dealer Julian Levy where he first showed his collages in 1932. Through Levy, Cornell met many of the European Surrealists who were in New York during the war, and he often showed with them. His work had superficial similarities to theirs, especially in his use of association between seemingly unrelated elements, but in general he criticized them as a group and was not one of their inner circle. His closest friends were the photographer Lee Miller, the artist Marcel Duchamp, and the painter Pavel Tchelitchew.

Cornell also made short, experimental films from the 1930s into the 1950s, an interest that sprung no doubt from his love for the cinema and from the film showings he frequently organized from his collection. In his films Cornell experimented with sequencing where he cut and juxtaposed images to depict a narrative in ways that had never been tried before. He used a collage effect similar to his boxes which film critics contend foreshadowed effects later adapted by commercial cinema. The most noted of these films was *Rose Hobart,* made in 1936. Cornell wrote scenarios and directed his films, allowing others to photograph them. Photographer Rudy Burckhardt and filmmaker Stan Brakhage worked with Cornell when they were young. Cornell also wrote and edited for the Surrealist magazine *View* and for *Dance Index.*

Cornell is often associated with the Surrealists and is footnoted in every history of the movement. But his work is essentially different. Less based on psychoanalytic theories, Cornell's boxes evoke conscious memories rather than unconscious ones. His admiration for the "ineffable beauty and pathos of the commonplace," gleaned from one of his diaries, is at odds with the Surrealist fascination with the bizarre, the shocking, and the inexplicable. Cornell's sensibility was of gentle nostalgia, a difference in temperament from the exaggerated drama of Salvador Dali, Max Ernst, or Andre Breton. At one point Cornell remarked that he thought Surrealizm as an idea had "healthier possibilities" than he saw expressed by the Surrealist artists.

As an artist, Cornell was a loner with only peripheral attachments to larger art currents of his time. Within the sophistication that overtook New York during World War II when many European artists were in exile, Cornell was something of a Yankee anomaly, connected yet separate, interested but skeptical. Like many American artists he chose isolation rather than the cafe society camaraderie to which most European artists were accustomed. Yet his spiritual ties were with their sense of history and memory. When a new American-based abstraction grew in part out of these war-time contacts, Cornell was not a part of it, continuing to refine the obsessions of his early work.

## Further Reading

Since his death a great deal has been written about Joseph Cornell, and there have been numerous exhibitions of his work. A retrospective exhibition at the Museum of Modern Art in 1980 was accompanied by an extensive catalogue, *Joseph Cornell* (1980) edited by Kynaston McShine with many illustrations and a good biographical section. Diane Waldman, curator at the Guggenheim Museum, also wrote a book *Joseph Cornell* (1977). A less historical study by critic Dore Ashton, a friend of Cornell's, entitled *A Joseph Cornell Album* (1974), is a homage to the artist in something of his own collage style. It includes anecdotes about him, photos of his family and house, an essay by Mexican poet Octavio Paz, and reprints of Cornell's writing and editing.

## Additional Sources

Cornell, Joseph, *Joseph Cornell,* Tokyo: Gatodo Gallery, 1987.

Cornell, Joseph, *Joseph Cornell portfolio,* New York: Leo Castelli Gallery, 1976.

Cornell, Joseph, *Joseph Cornell's theater of the mind: selected diaries, letters, and files,* New York: Thames and Hudson, 1993.

*Joseph Cornell,* New York: Museum of Modern Art, 1980. □

# Erastus Corning

**American merchant and financier Erastus Corning (1794-1872) was an early leader in the development of railroads in New York State and the first president of the New York Central Railroad. He became a notable political figure in the Democratic party.**

Erastus Corning was born on Dec. 14, 1794, in Norwich, Conn. He was an all-round entrepreneur; at one time or another and frequently simultaneously he was a merchant, iron manufacturer, railroad contractor, railroad president, banker, land speculator, and politician. Each phase of his multifaceted career connected with and strengthened the others.

Corning was among those who early recognized the economic growth possibilities inherent in the new railroad. He was already a prominent businessman when he helped organize the Utica and Schenectady Line in 1833. As president, he was paid no salary; instead he sold it iron and steel products. The multiplicity of railroads between Albany and Buffalo, N.Y., reduced efficiency so that it soon became apparent that a new, longer, and continuous railroad joining these two cities was desirable. A convention was held by the various railroads concerned, and the enabling consolidation act was passed by New York State in 1853. Corning was a primary actor in the negotiations which eventuated in the formation of the New York Central Railroad and was chosen the first president. He held that post until he resigned in 1864 for reasons of poor health but remained a director until 1867, when Commodore Cornelius Vanderbilt secured control of the railroad. Corning was also a member of the board of directors of several other major railroads, such as the Chicago, Burlington and Quincy.

Corning pioneered in the practice of making favorable contracts between his own companies, with himself as merchant and manufacturer selling supplies to his railroads; this form of business activity was highly profitable. The relation between Corning and the New York Central, similar to that he had enjoyed with the Utica and Schenectady, finally resulted in an investigation by a stockholders' committee. Even though the committee was composed of his friends, the report criticized Corning. Although the report noted that buying from stockholders was not recommended, the Cen-

tral continued to buy from Corning. In 1863 the New York newspapers criticized Corning's conflict of interest.

Corning had a reasonably distinguished political life. He supported Andrew Jackson and was elected mayor of Albany, state senator, and member of the House of Representatives as part of the Democratic Albany Regency. Despite his public offices, Corning's political influence came largely behind the scenes. He participated in the peace conference in 1861 in Washington, which was one of several last-ditch efforts to avert the Civil War. Though he had been an antiwar Democrat, he managed to make money in the iron business during the Civil War.

Corning's manifold business activities made him a millionaire. The town of Corning, N.Y., exemplifies his successful land speculation. He had provided the New York Central with superior executive leadership. He made early use of the Bessemer steel process, introducing it in 1865. Entrusting his associates with routine matters, he left himself free to expand in the entrepreneurial role. He died on April 9, 1872, in Albany.

## Further Reading

The prime source on Corning is Irene D. Neu, *Erastus Corning, Merchant and Financier, 1794-1872* (1960). A selection of Corning's letters is included in Thomas C. Cochran, *Railroad Leaders, 1845-1890: The Business Mind in Action* (1953). Several railroad studies also contain useful material: Frank Walker Stevens, *The Beginnings of the New York Central Railroad: A History* (1926); Edward Hungerford, *Men and Iron: The History of the New York Central* (1938); Alvin Fay Harlow, *The Road of the Century: The Story of the New York Central* (1947); and John F. Stover, *American Railroads* (1961). George Rogers Taylor, *The Transportation Revolution, 1815-1860* (1951), places Corning's role as a railroad magnate in perspective.

## Additional Sources

Neu, Irene D., *Erastus Corning, merchant and financier, 1794-1872,* Westport, Conn.: Greenwood Press, 1977, 1960. □

# Cornplanter

**Cornplanter (1732-1836) was a leading warrior and village leader among the Seneca, one of six nations of the Iroquois Confederacy. He earned his role as leader largely through military command and personal influence, which attracted friends and relatives to live on his reserved lands.**

Cornplanter was born sometime between 1732 and 1746, in the village of Conewaugus on the Genesee River in New York, the son of a Seneca woman and a Dutch trader named John Abeel (O'Bail). It should be noted that Lewis Henry Morgan erroneously states that it was Cornplanter's mother who was white rather than his father. This is important in that the Seneca, like other Iroquois people, are matrilineal, reckoning membership in the tribe through their mothers. Cornplanter had two half siblings who were born to his mother and a Seneca father: a brother, Handsome Lake, the Seneca prophet; and a sister who became the mother of Governor Blacksnake, the Seneca political leader. Little is known about Cornplanter during his early years, although many scholars contend that he was a warrior during the French and Indian War at the defeat of Edward Braddock in 1755 while he was in his early teens. It was also noted in a letter to the governor of Pennsylvania that Cornplanter, while playing with the other Indian boys, noticed that his skin color was lighter than that of the other boys, whereupon his mother told him of his white father who lived in Albany. As a prospective bridegroom, he visited his father who treated him kindly, but gave him nothing in the way of either material goods or expected information, particularly regarding the coming rebellion of the colonists against the British. This rebellion, however, was to play a major role in Cornplanter's life.

## Political Importance around the Time of the American Revolution

Cornplanter's importance in American Indian history derives from his major role in Iroquois Confederacy politics before and during the American Revolution and the subsequent political adaptation of the Seneca to the new government of the United States. Although the date of its beginnings is the subject of ongoing discussion, the Iroquois Confederacy was begun as an alliance of five northern Iroquoian-speaking tribes: the Mohawk, Onondaga, Oneida, Cayuga, and Seneca. This alliance was formed in order to harness the strength of these five groups in fighting common enemies as well as to foster economic cooperation among them. The confederacy was governed by the Grand Council of Fifty Chiefs, made up of the following: eight Seneca chiefs, ten Cayuga chiefs, fourteen Onondaga chiefs, eight Oneida chiefs, nine Mohawk chiefs, and the person who held the title of Tadadaho, an Onondaga chief who presided over confederacy meetings. The Tuscarora, a southern Iroquoian-speaking group in coastal North Carolina, came north after their defeat in the Tuscarora War in 1711, joined the confederacy at the invitation of the Oneida, and therefore had no direct voice in the Grand Council, speaking only through the Oneida.

Among the Grand Council, one of the cardinal governing rules was that any decision made required a unanimous vote of the chiefs. Among the major diplomatic and political decisions made in this manner were decisions of war. While it is not known if ideal rule of unanimity was always reached in such decisions, it is well known that a major disagreement arose within the confederacy over the impending colonial rebellion against the British.

The Grand Council of the Chiefs usually met before the central fire at Onondaga due to the fact that it was the home of the Tadadaho, or head chief, of the confederacy. In the months prior to the outbreak of the revolution, both the loyalists and the rebelling colonists had been busy soliciting the partisanship of the Indian nations, including the mighty Iroquois. Discussions ranged back and forth on the issue of which side to support if any. The Mohawk were firmly on the side of the British, but the Seneca, long willing to war against the British, in this case spoke for neutrality. Among those Senecas speaking strongly for neutrality were both Cornplanter and his half brother Handsome Lake, who held one of the major chiefly Seneca titles in the confederacy. In opposing this stand, Cornplanter was reminded of his clan brotherhood with Joseph Brant, a Mohawk captain for the British. This clan relationship obliged Cornplanter to support his fellow clansman, and thus he was reminded that duty lay in fighting with the British against the colonists.

In the end, the arguments of the pro-British Seneca prevailed, and the Seneca agreed to side with the British in the conflict. While the Seneca made this decision, however, several of the other members of the confederacy were not willing to accept this decision, notably the Oneidas and Tuscarora, with the latter remaining neutral for the most part and the Oneida taking the side of the colonists. Since there was no confederacy unanimity on this question, the Grand Council agreed to "cover the fire," meaning that they agreed to disagree and each member was left to decide for himself how he would affiliate in the coming war.

Despite his original misgivings about entering the war on the side of the British, Cornplanter, with Old Smoke, served as commanders for the Seneca throughout the war. It should be noted that Old Smoke was of advanced age by this time, being in his seventies or eighties. Nevertheless, these two were the primary field commanders of the tribe.

Perhaps most indicative of Cornplanter's character is a perhaps apocryphal encounter described by Governor Blacksnake during the Battle of Canajoharie, located in the Mohawk Valley, during August of 1780. Cornplanter supposedly recognized his father, John Abeel, among the captive survivors of the attack and burning of the village. Even after the earlier disappointment he felt at not receiving a wedding gift from his father at their first meeting, Cornplanter still accorded him the respect and kindness due a kinsman by offering his apology for the burning of his house and the option of his father returning to Seneca country to be supported by his son, or being released immediately. According to Thomas S. Abler in *Chainbreaker: The Revolutionary War Memoirs of Governor Blacksnake,* Abeel chose the latter and was allowed his freedom by the council of leaders out of respect for Cornplanter.

Around this time, the American revolutionaries began to discuss ideas for removing the Indians from their land. They not only wanted to punish them for their aid to the British by destroying the political importance of the confederacy, they also looked at the monetary gain to be had by first confiscating, then selling, Indian land to help pay for the expenses of the war. When General George Washington ordered an invasion of the Iroquois homeland to punish them for their role in the revolution, Cornplanter sent an urgent message in July of 1779, saying: "Father. You have said that we are in your hand and that by closing it you could crush us to nothing. Are you determined to crush us? If you are, tell us so that those of our nation who have become your children and have determined to die so, may know what to do. But before you determine on a measure so unjust, look up to God who made us as well as you. We

hope He will not permit you to destroy the whole of our nation."

While this plea was not successful, it was indicative of Cornplanter's attempts to reconcile the Seneca with the colonists. He attended the treaty council held at Fort Stanwix (1784) between the Iroquois and the newly successful republic, in which large amounts of Indian land was ceded to the new government. Because of his conciliatory stance and the great loss of land with this treaty, Cornplanter became very unpopular with his tribe and his rivals, including the influential Red Jacket, who began to work against him politically. Although he was not a signatory, Cornplanter's apparent agreement to the Fort Harmar Treaty (1789), in which another great tract of land was ceded to the United States, only worsened his position with the tribe.

## Involvement in "Right of Pre-emption" Controversy

Cornplanter was involved in another major dispute over land which has implications lasting to the present day. During this period of treaty-making, arguments arose over which of the newly formed states would encompass Indian territories. Recognition was made of the Indians' first right to ownership of their land, but the question was raised concerning who would have first rights to purchase the land should the Indians decide to sell it. Robert Morris, an early colonial and American financier, purchased this right, called a "right of pre-emption" from the state of Massachusetts. He eventually decided to sell this right of pre-emption to the Holland Land Company, agreeing in the bargain to extinguish Indian claim to the land by buying the land from the Indians. Finances ultimately kept him from accomplishing this, but he still attempted to extinguish Indian claim to the land through political channels. He met with Cornplanter in Philadelphia in August of 1797 to begin preliminary discussions of this issue, which led to full-scale negotiations between Morris and the Seneca at Genesee, New York. The Seneca rejected all of Morris's offers and Red Jacket eventually proclaimed negotiations to be at an end. However, other warriors and women eventually agreed to cede the land and signed a treaty in September of 1797. Since Cornplanter was one of the signers of this treaty, it signaled a major break between him and his political opponents led by Red Jacket, and for a while Cornplanter's life was in danger.

Fortunately for him, in 1795 the Pennsylvania Commonwealth awarded him in fee simple 1,500 acres of land in western Pennsylvania. Cornplanter directed the survey of this land into three strategic and valuable tracts and a patent was issued in 1796. He eventually lost two of the tracts, those at Oil City and Richland. The third tract he kept, encompassing about 750 acres along the Allegany River including the site of the old Seneca town Jenuchshadago and two islands in the river. He was also awarded a yearly pension by the U.S. government as a result of the 1797 treaty, which he collected for some time. An additional tract of land given to Cornplanter in what is now Marietta, Ohio, continues to be claimed by the contemporary heirs of Cornplanter who feel that he was defrauded out of the ownership of this land.

## Imbroglio with Handsome Lake over Religious Issues

Cornplanter retired to his land grant where he raised horses and cattle and maintained his own political community. It was not, however, the end of his political strife. According to O. Turner in *Pioneer History of the Holland Purchase of Western New York,* Cornplanter later quarreled with his messianic half brother Handsome Lake over some of the religious teachings which Handsome Lake had introduced to the Seneca.

In 1807, at the primary instigation of Handsome Lake, a woman at Allegany was executed for witchcraft. Cornplanter was not present at the time, but on his return, he expressed his regret over this action. Cornplanter eventually became a Christian, against the teachings of Handsome Lake, and allowed the invited Quakers to build a school on his land grant. It is reported, however, that he became very disillusioned with white men and the effects of their culture on the Seneca and publicly destroyed the formal regalia and various awards that he had received from the president of the United States. He died on February 18, 1836, in his village on the Cornplanter Grant at about the age of 100 years. Portraits of Cornplanter were painted by F. Bartoli in 1796 (now in the collection of the New York Historical Society).

The passage of time allowed Cornplanter to regain some of the recognition that he lost through his involvement in political and religious controversies. His efforts to bring peace between the Seneca and the U.S. government were not forgotten. His delicate and successful role as mediator between the new government and the Iroquois in creating a new political balance for his people in a drastically changed Indian world is generally recognized in the history of the Iroquois and the Seneca. A monument was erected on his grave by the grateful Commonwealth of Pennsylvania, reputedly the first monument in the United States erected in memory of an American Indian.

The majority of the Cornplanter Grant acreage was flooded during the Kinzua Dam Project which created the Allegany Reservoir, spelling the end to residence on the grant by Cornplanter's heirs. As a consequence of the construction of the Kinzua Dam in the 1960s, the remaining homes and outbuildings on the Cornplanter Grant, including the church and school, were bulldozed and burned. The trees were leveled and burned, and the Spring of Handsome Lake, reputedly the source of water used to initially revive the Prophet at the end of his first vision, was destroyed in the process of construction of the dam. Today, many of the nearly six-hundred descendants of Chief Cornplanter still meet at an annually family picnic on the Allegany Reservation in August and formally recognize their proud ties to both Cornplanter, a major figure in Iroquois history, and to the land granted to him.

## Further Reading

Abler, Thomas S., *Chainbreaker: The Revolutionary War Memoirs of Governor Blacksnake,* Lincoln, University of Nebraska Press, 1989.

Abler, Thomas S., and Elisabeth Tooker, "Seneca," *Handbook of North American Indians,* 15, edited by W. Sturtevant, Washington, DC, Smithsonian Institution, 1978; 505-517.

Hodge, Frederick Webb, *Handbook of American Indians North of Mexico,* New York, Rowman and Littlefield, 1965; 349-350.

Morgan, Lewis Henry, *League of the Ho-de-no-sau-nee or Iroquois,* Rochester, NY, Sage Books, 1851, reprinted as *League of the Iroquois,* Corinth Books, 1962.

Schaaf, Gregory, *Wampum Belts and Peace Trees: George Morgan, Native Americans, and Revolutionary Diplomacy,* Golden, CO, Fulcrum Publishing, 1990.

Turner, O., *Pioneer History of the Holland Purchase of Western New York,* Buffalo, NY, George H. Durby, 1850.

Wallace, Anthony F. C., "Origins of the Longhouse Religion," *Handbook of North American Indians,* 15, edited by W. C. Sturtevant, Washington, DC, Smithsonian Institution, 1978; 442-448.

Abrams, George H. J., "Cornplanter Cemetery," *Pennsylvania Archaeologist,* 1965, 25 (2); 59-73. □

# Charles Cornwallis

**Charles Cornwallis, 1st Marquess Cornwallis (1738-1805), was a British soldier and statesman. Although remembered best because of his defeat at Yorktown in the American Revolution, Cornwallis was more often successful in his military activities in India and Ireland.**

The Cornwallis family traced its roots to the 14th century in England and its titles back to Stuart times. Charles Cornwallis was educated at Eton, received his ensign's commission in the Grenadier Guards in 1756, then briefly attended a military academy at Turin. During the Seven Years War he participated in many engagements on the Continent. His rise to positions of military and political influence was rapid: he went to the House of Commons from the family borough in 1760, became a lieutenant colonel of the 12th Regiment the following year, and upon the death of his father the next year joined the Lords as the 2d Earl Cornwallis.

In the years of peace Cornwallis was a friend and supporter of Lord Shelburne. Critical of ministerial harshness toward the Colonies, he associated with the Whig peers. Nevertheless, he enjoyed favor at the court: the earl was made constable of the Tower of London in 1770 and promoted to major general 5 years later.

## American Revolution

Even though he had opposed Lord North's American policy, Cornwallis was trusted with the command of reinforcements sent to Gen. William Howe in 1776. He participated in the New York campaign and in the occupation of

**Charles Cornwallis (center, on horse)**

New Jersey. His failure to catch George Washington at this time and later before the Battle of Princeton led to some criticism by Sir Henry Clinton and a feeling that Cornwallis was too cocksure. In 1777 Cornwallis commanded one of Howe's divisions in the Battle of Brandywine. When Clinton took command in the American theater, Cornwallis rapidly became disgruntled over his limited policy. Relations between the two generals were complicated by the fact that Cornwallis held a dormant commission as Clinton's successor; Clinton regarded this as a threat to his position. Thus the two generals were hardly happy companions in arms, and Cornwallis in pique submitted his resignation just as Clinton tried to do. In 1778 Cornwallis commanded one of the forces in the Battle of Monmouth during Clinton's retreat from Philadelphia. For much of the succeeding year he was in England attending to his dying wife.

In mid-1780 after the siege of Charleston, S.C., Cornwallis received a semi-independent command in the southern states. Nominally still subordinate to Clinton, he was at such a distance from his commander and enjoyed such political favor with George Sackville Germaine (the English secretary of state for the Colonies) in London that he could conduct operations without worrying about restrictions from above. The consequence was Cornwallis's march through the Carolinas—with some real victories, as at Camden, and some Pyrrhic ones—that ultimately led him to Yorktown. His notion was that the best defense of British

reconquests in the south was an offensive against Virginia. Lacking sufficient troops, subject to conflicting whims, failing to rally the great loyalist support he had hoped for, and using every loophole in his orders from Clinton and Germaine, he was responsible for the loss of about one-quarter of the British forces in America when he surrendered his command to Washington in October 1781. Cornwallis surrendered in bad grace: he was "sick" and absent from the public ceremonies. While he has had later defenders of his American conduct, Cornwallis undertook far too ambitious a campaign for the means at his disposal and left the British cause in the south in disastrous condition.

## In India

Yet Cornwallis's political connections and personal standing were high enough so that he was quickly given new and greater responsibilities. After repeated refusals, he was persuaded to accept the post of governor general of Bengal in early 1786. And in India he was successful enough both as a reform administrator and military leader to acquire a reputation as one of the foremost builders of British rule in Asia. He tried to reduce the corruption endemic in the services of the India Company and to improve the quality of the company's European levies or to reduce English dependence upon them. He was reasonably successful in improving the civil administration, less successful in devising a permanent system for collecting land revenues, and not at all successful in improving the quality of the company's troops. Nonetheless, compelled by threats from Tippoo, Sultan of Mysore, to turn away from his avowed policy of nonintervention in the relations of the native states, Cornwallis led a triumphant army in the Third Mysore War (1790-1792). While he stopped short of total victory, Cornwallis compelled the cession of much of Tippoo's territory and payment of a large indemnity and effectively eliminated this threat to the company's power.

Returning to England, Cornwallis was rewarded with the title of marquess. He subsequently was widely used as a diplomatic and military troubleshooter. He served in Flanders trying to coordinate efforts against the French and next in the Cabinet, preparing England against an expected French invasion, and then was ready to set off for India against as governor general. Compromise in India and new threats from Ireland changed his direction. As the Irish troubles deepened, Cornwallis was called to act as viceroy and commander in chief of British forces there. In mid-1798 he disrupted the plans of Irish rebels, compelled the surrender of a small French invading force, and pacified the countryside with—for the time and place—a moderate policy of punishing only the rebel ringleaders. He then sought reforms for Ireland which would prevent future outbreaks. He proposed Catholic emancipation and the abolition of the unrepresentative Irish Parliament in favor of an Act of Union with Great Britain itself. While Cornwallis—with the free use of bribery—was able to push the Act of Union through the Irish Parliament, he was unable to gain royal acquiescence to Catholic emancipation in Ireland and resigned in protest.

Still Cornwallis continued his services to the government. He was British plenipotentiary during the negotiations at Amiens that led to the brief peace of 1802-1803 with France. Then, in 1805, he was sent off again to Bengal; he died shortly after his arrival. A gentleman born to wealth and influence, he had possessed a sense of duty that led him to serve his country well for many years.

## Further Reading

The standard source on Cornwallis's life is Charles Ross, ed., *Correspondence of Charles, First Marquis Cornwallis* (3 vols., 1859). Evaluations of Cornwallis's American activities are found in books dealing with military aspects of the American Revolution. Especially recommended are Piers Mackesy, *The War for America, 1775-1783* (1964), and William B. Willcox, *Portrait of a General: Sir Henry Clinton in the War of Independence* (1964). For another aspect of Cornwallis's career see W.S. Seton-Karr, *The Marquess Cornwallis and the Consolidation of British Rule* (1890), vol. 9 of *Rulers of India*.

## Additional Sources

Wickwire, Franklin B., *Cornwallis, the imperial years,* Chapel Hill: University of North Carolina Press, 1980. □

# Bert Corona

**Bert Corona (born 1918), a union organizer who worked to provide Mexican Americans with better wages and living conditions.**

Bert Corona was born into a revolutionary family. At the age of thirteen, his father, Noe, began to fight in the Mexican Revolution to overthrow the long and corrupt rule of Porfirio Díaz. He joined the forces of Pancho Villa, one of the most powerful rebels.

About 1911 Noe Corona was assigned to seal off Chihuahua City, which threatened to send out federal troops against Villa's forces. There he met Margarita Escápite Salayandía. Margarita and her mother, Ynez Salayandía y Escápite, were rebels in their own right. Both had decided to ignore the general feeling in Mexico that women should stay home, bear children, and restrict themselves to tending the household. Ynez became one of the few female doctors in Mexico, and Margarita became director of a teacher's college. Also, they were Protestants in a mostly Catholic country.

After fighting in the Battle of Juárez, which resulted in Díaz's fleeing the country, Noe returned to woo Margarita. The two married twice, in the Mexican city of Juárez and in El Paso, Texas. They settled in El Paso, and their first two children were born there. Bert was the second child and first son, born May 29, 1918.

## Early life

Corona attended primary schools in El Paso. It was in these schools that he first experienced racism. Although he was spared because he already spoke English, other stu-

dents were spanked and forced to wash their mouths with soap for speaking their own language, Spanish. Margarita objected to these actions so strongly that she took Bert out of the El Paso schools and sent him to a boarding school in Albuquerque, New Mexico. He attended Harvard Boys School for the fourth and fifth grades. One of Corona's early protest experiences occurred in the fifth grade.

The Mexican students at Harvard often objected to the ideas of history presented by their Anglo teachers. For talking back to the teachers, some students were sent to the physical education teacher to be spanked. When the students protested, school administrators threatened to throw some of them out of school. The students organized a strike, refusing to attend class until their demands were met. It was successful in keeping the students from being expelled, forcing the physical education teacher to apologize, and putting a stop to spankings for just questioning a teacher. In his oral biography, Corona proudly remembers that "This was my first strike!" It would not be his last.

## Athletic scholarship

Corona returned to El Paso and attended El Paso High School. There he played basketball on the varsity team, despite his young age—he had advanced through school so rapidly that he graduated high school at age sixteen. Corona was very young, so he played two years on El Paso community teams before accepting an athletic scholarship to the University of Southern California.

In 1936 a full athletic scholarship was very different from the scholarships of later years. Corona found that his scholarship was really a recommendation to a company that was willing to hire him. An athletic scholarship meant that a student could work full- or part-time while playing university sports and studying. Corona began taking a full course of studies in commercial law while working nearly full-time at his "scholarship" job. Because he had worked for a medical drug company in El Paso, he found a job at the Brunswick Pharmaceutical Company. It was there that he got his first taste of labor organizing.

### The Longshoremen's Union

Brunswick hired nearly 2,000 employees who were not yet organized by the labor unions. When the Longshoremen's Union decided to organize farm workers in Orange County, south of Los Angeles, Brunswick seemed to the union officers to be a good place to find help. The union asked Brunswick employees to help organize the farm workers. Corona accepted the invitation. He was always ready to support any cause he thought would help Mexican Americans, and many of the farm workers were Mexican immigrants.

Corona helped recruit union members and led them in strikes for better wages and better treatment by the farmers. In 1936, for example, he led 2,500 Mexican workers in a strike that stopped work on the region's $20-million orange crop.

### Abandons college

Soon after he agreed to help the Longshoremen's Union with farm workers, the union also decided to organize warehouse workers, starting with the Brunswick company. At that time, medical warehouse workers were receiving half the pay of warehouse workers in the food industries. Corona agreed to help organize a union for Brunswick workers and was fired for his efforts. By this time, he had decided that helping unions was more important than his studies at the university. When Harry Bridges of the Congress of Industrial Organizations (CIO) offered him another job as a union organizer, Corona decided to temporarily abandon his college education. For nearly a decade, he served the CIO as an organizer for the canning and packing industries and for Allied Workers of America. Working with more seasoned organizers such as César Chávez, he learned to be an excellent organizer and his fame grew.

### Politics

By 1948 Corona had grown concerned about the mistreatment of people who came from Mexico without the permission of the United States government. Two years later, he became regional organizer for the National Association of Mexican Americans. He gained a reputation for being able to influence Mexican American citizens. Becoming a member of the Northern California Democratic Campaign Committee, Corona actively supported Democratic candidates for the next two decades.

### Undocumented workers

Corona also served as a consultant to the U.S. Department of Labor and stepped up his efforts for those he called undocumented workers (and which the Immigration and Naturalization Service [INS] called illegal aliens). Corona spent more and more energy on behalf of the workers who had entered the United States without proper authorization.

After World War II, the INS stepped up its efforts to cancel work visas of Mexicans living in the San Diego area. As early as 1951, union leaders Phil and Albert Usquiano organized La Hermandad Mexicana Nacional (The Mexican National Brotherhood). Its purpose was to struggle against the INS in the San Diego area. In 1968 Corona brought this organization to Los Angeles and began to spread it across the nation. The Hermandad offered advice to undocumented workers about their rights under the United States Constitution. Corona and the other organizers of Hermandad believed that, once in the United States, the workers were entitled to the same protection under the Constitution as United States citizens.

The Hermandad also showed Mexicans in the United States how to organize to achieve better working conditions and better housing. Corona's Hermandad proved that undocumented workers could unite and win victories in the courts and in the fields. It offered support to those who had previously accepted terrible living and work conditions out of fear that the INS would deport them if they caused trouble. Soon the Hermandad was so busy with political action and recruiting that Corona found a need for a new social service organization.

### CASA

The idea was that social services (rent control or assistance, medical aid, legal advice, and even some labor organization) would be better obtained by forming local groups. People within a given area would be served from an office in their own community. Each office could sometimes operate independently to serve special needs of the local community. Corona and his friends established CASA (Centros de Acción Social Autónomo, or Centers for Autonomous [Independent] Social Actions). But the word *casa,* which in Spanish means "home," was significant for another reason, too. It pointed up the community-based plan behind the organization. CASA began to serve Mexican communities in the United States much like earlier mutual assistance groups had served towns in Mexico. From time to time, CASA organized other groups for special purposes. The Coalition for Fair Immigration Laws and Practices began in 1978. The Casa Carnalismo was organized to fight drug dealing in Mexican communities. Sin Fronteras became an organization that stood for open borders, taking a stand in the controversy over illegal immigration. Women as well as men were active in organizing CASA and its offshoot organizations. Outstanding among them were Soledad "Chole" Alatorre and Blanche Taff.

### "Chole" Alatorre

Alatorre was born in San Luis Potosí, Mexico, where her father served as an officer in the Railroad Workers'

Union. From him, she learned the value of organizing large groups of people to fight for a single cause. Alatorre married in Mexico, and she and her husband moved to Los Angeles, where many Mexican nationals were working for low pay in the garment industries.

Alatorre easily found work making swimsuits in the Rosemary Reid Company. Soon the company made her a section supervisor, but because she was beautiful, its managers found they could save money by also using her as an advertising model. The freedom of the two jobs allowed Alatorre to inspect the whole plant, which led to her deciding that the garment workers needed to organize. But before she could organize enough workers, the plant moved.

Alatorre changed jobs and became a union steward and contract negotiator. In one company, she organized a strike that won better wages and work conditions. The unhappy owner then called the INS. Immigration agents found thirty-three undocumented workers in the company and threatened to take them back to Mexico. Alatorre sought help and found it in the Hermandad, which was led by Corona. She joined Hermandad and eventually became its national coordinator. Meanwhile, she joined Bert Corona in organizing CASA.

## Blanche Taff

The daughter of Polish Jewish immigrants, Blanche Taff was active in the Democratic Youth Federation. It was at one of the federation's fund-raising parties that she met Bert Corona. Taff dated Corona and began to support him on the picket lines of various strikes. Eventually the two eloped to Yuma, Arizona.

Blanche Corona faced a difficult situation. She supported Corona's efforts and wanted to join him in some of his activities. At first, however, Corona held to the old-fashioned notion about marriage that "the woman works at home." He had to yield to Blanche, though, when his own activities failed to bring in enough money to support a growing family. Thereafter, Blanche Corona became an active supporter of Corona's efforts and influenced the change of his view of women's roles. The couple formed a lasting bond and raised a family of three children: Margo, David, and Frank.

## The fall of CASA

The Hermandad continued its efforts to recruit and support Mexicans everywhere in the United States. Corona believed that every organization required good and steady workers and recruited Hermandad members from the working-class Mexicans. By contrast, the home-based CASA was an organization in which college students, young business-people, and emerging politicians were the strongest workers. Eventually, these younger people took over CASA. They also took over Sin Fronteras in San Antonio and moved it to Los Angeles in 1975. The young people proved less patient than the older organizers and seemed unwilling to learn how to enlist others to work with them. In 1977 the director of Sin Fronteras objected to their tactics and resigned. CASA began to fade. Eventually, Corona withdrew from the orga-

nization. He still worked in Hermandad, however, and turned his attention to immigration laws.

## The immigration laws

Throughout most of its history, the United States has had laws aimed at controlling the influx of immigrants to the country. The 1798 Alien and Sedition Act authorized the president to throw out any citizens believed to be a threat to the nation. Economic conditions in the 1800s encouraged importing low-wage workers to help with such activities as railroad building. Once here, however, the immigrants were viewed as threats. New laws banned immigration from some countries and limited them from others. In 1882 Chinese immigrants, at first welcomed as needed laborers, were refused admittance to the United States. In 1907 President Theodore Roosevelt threatened even stronger laws and persuaded the Japanese government to refuse to allow Japanese laborers to sail for America.

World War I upset Europe and resulted in large emigrations from that continent. The result was a wave of laws that set quotas, or limits, on immigrants to the United States. By 1929 the flow of new citizens to the United States had been reduced to 142,000 each year. Movement to the United States was further slowed by laws that demanded that immigrants be able to read and write English and show proof of the ability to support themselves. Not until 1965 were the quotas removed. Even then, newcomers to America were allowed to stay only if they had close relatives in the country, they had a profession, they had job skills needed in the United States, or they were refugees from their native countries.

## Mexican immigrants

Mexico had once owned a large part of the southwestern United States, and many Mexicans thought they had claims to the land. Furthermore, Mexican workers had been encouraged to cross the border over the years to provide labor in industries such as agriculture and clothing manufacture. Also, many Mexican leaders in the United States believed that the border was an artificial one—that geography really made the Southwest and Mexico a single country. The thousand-mile-long border between the two countries had never been very well controlled, and for years Mexicans and U.S. citizens moved freely both ways across the line. Thus, Mexican workers had difficulty seeing why immigration authorities began to view Mexican workers who remained in the United States as "illegals." Over the years, the authorities placed stricter and stricter limits on immigration from Mexico. By the 1970s, as few as 20,000 Mexicans were allowed to enter the United States legally.

Corona and Hermandad began to oppose the INS in the late 1960s and early 1970s. He prepared information packages that told Mexican workers how they were protected under the U.S. Constitution. They did not have to incriminate themselves by giving information to the INS. Nor did they have to allow INS investigators into their homes without warrants. Agents of the INS often raided homes, farms, and businesses looking for illegal aliens. As the government stepped up such activity, some U.S. citizens were caught in raids and deported just because they looked Mexican. Corona's organization, Hermandad, began to take the INS to court. He helped find birth certificates and other legal documents that saved many people from being sent out of the country.

### Stricter laws

New immigration laws were proposed to help the INS. These new laws tried to stop Mexicans from entering the United States for work by discouraging the employer from hiring them. Under the proposed laws, an employer would be guilty of a crime if the employer hired an "illegal."

Corona and his aides objected to such proposals. For example, Corona opposed the proposed Dixon Arnett Bill, which would have made employers liable for penalties if they hired "illegal aliens." This state bill was soon made a national issue by a proposal in Congress called the Rodino Bill. Corona also opposed this bill and succeeded in preventing its passage for several years. He argued that such a bill illegally turned employers into agents of the government. The idea would also be a burden on Mexicans who were working in the United States legally and even U.S. citizens who were of Mexican descent, who would become subject to suspicion because of their looks. To prevent this mistreatment of Mexican Americans, Father Theodore Hesburgh and his commission had proposed that Mexican immigrants be required to carry a national identification card. Corona argued that this would be an insult to Mexicans everywhere and would not solve the problem. Despite Corona's efforts, public pressure and prejudice against job competition from Mexicans finally led to the passage of a 1982 law that imposed penalties for hiring Mexican "illegals."

The public pressure stemmed from controversy over the illegal population, and debate continued after the 1982 law was passed. Like Corona, some Americans rose up to defend the rights of illegal immigrants. Others pointed to their effects on the larger population, arguing that they used up badly needed social services, which belonged to U.S. citizens.

### The Immigration Act of 1986

In 1986 Congress passed a new immigration law. Although it stopped short of requiring Mexican immigrants to carry identification cards, it did hold employers responsible if they hired undocumented workers (workers without visas or work permits, called green cards). By this time, several million Mexican workers had settled in the United States. Many of them had not tried to become U.S. citizens for fear that the INS would deport them. The 1986 act attempted to remedy this situation by providing amnesty—Mexicans in the United States without documents could apply for citizenship without interference by the INS or other government agencies. The act appeared to be a step forward for Mexican Americans, and some accepted the invitation to become citizens.

Corona and Hermandad began to advise these potential citizens so they could benefit from the 1986 law. At the same time, Corona spoke out against it. In his view there

were many flaws in the new law. The most serious problem was that it ignored millions of Mexican immigrants. The new law provided amnesty only for those who had come to the United States without documents before 1982. Strictly applied, even students and workers who had entered on visas before 1982 and stayed when the visas expired could not apply for citizenship under the new law.

The law also required proof that those applying for citizenship would not be a financial burden to the United States. While at times many American workers of all ethnic backgrounds request short-term welfare help, Mexicans could not apply for citizenship if they were on welfare during the amnesty period.

### Mexican culture and heritage

Corona also opposed the act because it required applicants for citizenship to prove that they were learning the English language. This seemed to him to be an attempt to take away from the immigrants their Mexican culture and heritage, leaving Mexican Americans without roots to their past. He continued to speak out about these "flaws" in the 1986 Immigration Act even as he helped workers with their applications and need for instruction.

In spite of these "flaws," Corona's Hermandad encouraged Mexicans in the United States to take advantage of the opportunity to gain citizenship. Hermandad organized offices to help with the paperwork involved and classes to help with the English-language requirement. Altogether, Corona and Hermandad helped more than 160,000 Mexican Americans gain citizenship under the new act.

### The struggle continues

In his lifetime, Bert Corona served as a union organizer, a champion of Mexican Americans, and a university teacher (Stanford University and California State University at Los Angeles). He has participated in many of the organizations that are considered to be politically left, even far left. (Left describes groups that sometimes advocate extreme measures to achieve equality and freedom for citizens.) While never joining the Communist party, Corona earnestly studied communism and socialism to find the good in these political movements. He has not been afraid to join any movement to defend the rights of workers and organize them for action, particularly workers of Mexican descent. Moreover, Corona himself has created major organizations to help Mexican Americans.

Because of Corona's work and that of others like him, great strides have been made toward helping Mexican Americans improve their position in the United States. Although Corona, now in his seventies, has backed off from some of his leadership roles, he continues to be active in Hermandad. In his words: "Will I ever retire? No. I want to be able to do more things and see more things. I think we're entering into a very exciting epoch. . . . A lot of things will be happening that I'd like to be around to participate in and to see."

## Further Reading

García, Mario T., *Memories of Chicano History,* Berkeley: University of California Press, 1994.

García, Mario T., *Mexican Americans: Leadership, Ideology, and Identity, 1930–1960,* New Haven, Connecticut: Yale University Press, 1989.

Gutierrez, David G., *CASA in the Chicano Movement,* Working Paper Series, no. 5, Palo Alto: Stanford Center for Chicano Research, 1984.

Portes, Alejandro, and Rubén G. Rumbaut, *Immigrant America: A Portrait,* Berkeley: University of California Press, 1990. □

# Francisco Vásquez de Coronado

**Francisco Vásquez de Coronado (1510-1554) was a Spanish explorer and colonial official who is credited with one of the first European explorations of Arizona, New Mexico, and the Great Plains of North America.**

Francisco Vásquez de Coronado was born in Salamanca, the second son of Juan Vásquez de Coronado, a wealthy nobleman. As a younger son, Francisco could not inherit the family estates. He therefore went to the court of Charles I, where he secured a place in the service of Don Antonio de Mendoza, newly appointed viceroy of Mexico.

After his arrival in Mexico in 1535 Coronado rose rapidly in viceregal favor. In 1537 he married the wealthy Doña Beatriz de Estrada, daughter of the former treasurer of New Spain. In 1538 Mendoza appointed the young Coronado governor of the northern province of Nueva Galicia.

These were exciting times. The famous survivor of the Narváez expedition, Alvar Núñez Cabeza de Vaca, arrived at the viceregal court with stories he had heard of seven great cities in "Cíbola," far to the north. Mendoza, anxious to locate and conquer this reputedly golden land, dispatched Father Marcos de Niza and Cabeza de Vaca's companion Estevánico north. When Father de Niza returned in 1539 with a report that he had found the cities, the viceroy immediately outfitted a great expedition and named Coronado to lead it.

In February 1540 the army of more than 230 mounted Spanish gentlemen, 62 foot soldiers, several friars, and nearly 1,000 Indian allies headed north from Compostela. After a long march across northern Mexico and southern Arizona the army reached the Zuñi pueblo of Hawikuh in July. This spot Father de Niza identified as Cíbola, but to the disappointed Spaniards it was only "a little unattractive village" of mud and stone. Although discouraged by the lack of golden cities, Coronado dispatched several small exploring parties. One group marched west to the Colorado River, while another, under Pedro del Tovar, succeeded in reaching the Moqui (Hopi) pueblos north of Zuñi. A third group under García López de Cárdenas pushed northwest to the Grand Canyon. A fourth party under Hernando de Alvarado explored the upper Rio Grande. In the winter of 1540 Coronado moved his army to the Rio Grande and conquered the Tiguex pueblos near present-day Albuquerque.

At the Tiguex villages the Spaniards heard of a rich land called Quivira somewhere to the north. In the spring of 1541 Coronado set out to try to find this fabled kingdom. Marching eastward across the Pecos River, he turned north onto the Llano Estacado, the great grassland plains of North America; but when he arrived at Quivira on the Arkansas River, he discovered only a poor Indian village. Sickened by his failure to find gold and riches, Coronado left three missionaries to convert the Indians of Quivira and returned to Tiguex, where he gathered the remnants of his army and turned homeward. He arrived in Mexico in 1542, a bitter and disappointed man. For the next 2 decades the Spaniards forgot the northern lands and concentrated on developing their Mexican possessions.

In 1544 Coronado faced charges of neglect of duty and cruelty to the Indians and lost the governorship of Nueva Galicia. He returned to Mexico City, where he managed his estates and served as regidor, or member of the city council, until his death.

## Further Reading

The diaries and documents pertaining to Coronado's expedition can be found in such collections as George P. Winship, ed., *The Coronado Expedition, 1540-1542* (1896; repr. 1964), and George P. Hammond and Agapito Rey, eds., *Narratives of the Coronado Expedition, 1540-1542* (1940). The best biography of Coronado is Herbert E. Bolton, *Coronado: Knight of Pueblos and Plains* (1949). Also helpful are Arthur Grove Day, *Coronado's Quest: The Discovery of the Southwestern States* (1940; repr. 1964), and his brief *Coronado and the Discovery of the Southwest* (1967). □

# Jean Baptiste Camille Corot

**The fresh and often informal treatment of nature by the French painter Jean Baptiste Camille Corot (1796-1875) marked a significant departure from academic tradition and strongly influenced the development of landscape painting in the 19th century.**

On July 16, 1796, Camille Corot was born in Paris, the son of Louis Jacques Corot, a cloth merchant, and Marie Françoise Oberson Corot. At the age of 11 Camille was sent to the Collège de Rouen, and he completed his education at a boarding school in Passy in 1814. He went to work for a draper but announced his wish to become a painter. Although his parents did not approve, they did, upon the death of his youngest sister in 1821, transfer to Corot her annual allowance of 1500 livres, thereby enabling him to lead a carefree if modest existence and pursue his one real ambition.

Corot entered the studio of Achille Etna Michallon and received training in the painting of classical landscapes. When Michallon died, Corot studied with Jean Victor Bertin, who had been Michallon's teacher. During this period (1822-1825) Corot began sketching from nature in the forest of Fontainebleau near Paris and in Rouen.

## Italian Sojourns

In 1825 Corot made his first trip to Italy and remained there 3 years. He met the painters Léopold Robert, Edouard Bertin, and Théodore Caruelle d'Aligny and made the first attempts to record his fresh responses to landscape, free from the taste for classical arrangement. Although Corot always spoke of D'Aligny as his true teacher, it was the latter who, while watching Corot paint a view from the Farnese Gardens, exclaimed, "My friends, Corot is our master."

Corot was, indeed, rapidly master of his art, and if there is a weakness in these impressive early works, it lies only in some unconvincing attempts to conform to official expectations by introducing historical or biblical figures into his more ambitious scenes. From Corot's Italian journey dates the *Bridge at Narni* in Paris, a masterpiece that reveals his infallible sense for value and tone relationships. A second version, in Ottawa, more minutely executed and formally arranged, was shown at the Salon of 1827. Corot made two more trips to Italy during the summers of 1834 and 1843.

## Growth of His Reputation

In 1830 the tumult of the July Revolution drove the politically indifferent Corot to Chartres, where he painted *Chartres Cathedral,* one of his most originally composed early pictures. In 1831 the Salon accepted several of his Italian and French scenes; although they generally received little notice, the critic Delecluse remarked on their originality. In 1833 Corot's *Ford in the Forest of Fontainebleau* earned a second-class medal; although he also received this award in 1848 and 1867, the first-class medal was always denied him.

Corot's reputation grew steadily if undramatically. In 1840 the state acquired his *Little Shepherd* for the Metz museum, yet in 1843 the Salon jury rejected his *Destruction of Sodom*. In 1845 he was commissioned to paint a *Baptism of Christ* for the church of St. Nicolas du Chardonnet in Paris. He received the cross of the Legion of Honor the following year. At this time Corot found his first private client, Constant Dutilleux, whose future son-in-law, Alfred Robaut, later compiled the standard catalog of the painter's work.

During the liberalized Salon of 1848 Corot was a member of the jury and served again in this capacity the following year, and the state made further purchases of his work for the museums of Douai and Langres. It was only at the Salon of 1855, however, when the Emperor bought his *Souvenir of Marcoussis* that Corot achieved real fame and began to sell his work in quantity.

## Characteristics of His Art

Although Corot's art contributed to some aspects of impressionism (and Berthe Morisot received his guidance in 1861), he is appreciated even more for the realization of his poetical vision by means of a subtle and secure handling of his medium than for the historically forward-looking elements in his art. All who met him were impressed by his kindness and generosity as well as his genuine naiveté, which, the poet and critic Charles Baudelaire felt, was the source of the best qualities of his painting. Corot's *Self-Portrait* in Florence is perhaps the best indication of this innocent yet self-assured personality, who observed in one of his notebooks, "Never leave a trace of indecision in anything whatever."

Modern taste tends to prefer Corot's vigorous early and middle-period landscapes to those of his later years which, by contrast, appear somewhat sentimental in their dreamlike, silvery mellowness and suggest reliance on a successful formula. Curiously, it was while Corot was engaged in painting these landscapes (such as *Souvenir of Mortefontaine*) that the force of his early works was now expressed in a group of impressive figure compositions. In these paintings the note of nostalgia and suggestion of allegory (The Studio) are often integrated into convincing, technically bold pictorial conceptions (*Young Woman with Rose Scarf* and *Woman with Yellow Sleeve*). Corot exhibited only one of these pictures during his lifetime, the *Woman Reading in a Landscape,* in 1869.

In addition to his landscapes and figure pieces, Corot painted skillful portraits and a number of decorative ensembles. These include a bathroom for Maurice Robert's home at Mantes (1842) with six Italian views (now in the Louvre); the drawing room of the château of Gruyère (1857), and the home of Prince Demidov in Paris (1865).

Corot never married, convinced that family life would be incompatible with his activities as itinerant painter. He died in Paris on Feb. 22, 1875.

## Further Reading

Of the work done on Corot in English, an excellent recent study is Jean Leymarie, *Corot: Biographical and Critical Study,* translated by Stuart Gilbert (1966). An informative discussion of Corot's relationship to the Barbizon group is in Robert L. Herbert, *Barbizon Revisited* (1962).

## Additional Sources

Leymarie, Jean, *Corot,* Geneva: Skira; New York: Rizzoli, 1979.
☐

# Correggio

**The Italian painter Correggio (ca. 1494-1534) is famous for the grace and refinement of his art. He rendered nature with clarity and gentleness, as if it were all music, and he also was a pioneer in executing daringly foreshortened ceiling paintings.**

The real name of Correggio was Antonio Allegri, but he is known by the name of his birthplace, Correggio, near Reggio Emilia. He received his early training from fairly indifferent painters in his home town, but his earliest documented works, such as the *Madonna of St. Francis* (1515; Dresden), show him as a master who, much impressed with the monumentality of the works of Andrea Mantegna, knew how to join it to the traditions of the luminous and colorful art of Emilia. An early-17th-century source reports that Correggio worked for a time in Mantua, and several units of the decoration of Mantegna's funerary chapel in S. Andrea have been attributed to his hand.

As was true of most north Italian painters of the time, the art of the great Venetian and Florentine painters was reflected in Correggio's work. Many of his early pictures, such as the *Madonna and Child with the Infant St. John* (ca. 1515; Madrid) and the *Rest on the Flight into Egypt* (ca. 1516; Florence), show that he responded with particular happiness to the inventions and discoveries of Giorgione, Leonardo da Vinci, and Raphael. Another formative influence on his work was the engravings of Albrecht Dürer.

It is established with reasonable certainty that Correggio spent the better part of 1518 or 1519 in Rome. His later work shows that he received immense benefit from studying the works of Raphael and Michelangelo. Correggio was selective in what he adapted from their work, and he succeeded, in his most ambitious paintings, in reconciling and putting to splendid use the often conflicting lessons in the greatness of art that may be drawn from Raphael's Stanza della Segnatura and Michelangelo's Sistine Chapel ceiling.

## Mural Paintings

Correggio executed three elaborate fresco commissions in Parma. The first was the decoration of the abbess's drawing room in the Benedictine convent of S. Paolo (ca. 1518-1520). Over the fireplace is a painting of Diana in her chariot. The painted ceiling transforms the chamber into an artful green bower with garlands of fruit hanging down into the room. In the ceiling are simulated niches painted in grisaille with representations of divinities and allegories which look as if they are works of sculpture come to life. Above these niches is a cycle of lunettes in which cupids, painted in flesh color, display various attributes of the hunt.

Correggio's second commission was the decoration of the cupola, apse, and frieze of the church of S. Giovanni Evangelista (1520-1524). Especially in the cupola painting he put to the test the lessons in figure drawing and architectural perspective which only the Roman art of Michelangelo and Raphael can have taught him. Correggio filled the lower rim of the cupola with a majestic array of saints joined by angels. Some of them look down on the viewer; others look up raptly at the figure of Christ, who rises toward a myriad of angels all shining with golden light. Christ not only dominates the figures represented on the cupola but with a great, exhortative, and yet fleeting gesture calls toward himself the worshipers in every part of the church.

Even more ambitious are the frescoes Correggio painted in the Cathedral of Parma (ca. 1524-1530). He transformed the interior of the immense octagonal, fun-nelshaped Romanesque cupola into a vision of the heavens opened for the assumption of Mary. A host of music-making and dancing angels, portrayed in the most daring foreshort-ening, joyfully move about the clouds and, together with a number of saintly figures, surround a core of heavenly light, toward the source of which Mary, her arms opened in a gesture of bliss and grateful response, is being lifted. The archangel Gabriel, painted very large and almost in the center of the composition, has come to greet Mary and to fly on before her.

## Religious Panel Paintings

Correggio, in the period of his maturity, painted five great altarpieces: the *Madonna of St. Sebastian* (ca. 1525), the *Adoration of the Shepherds* (ca. 1530), the *Madonna of St. George* (ca. 1532; all in Dresden), the *Madonna of St. Jerome* (1528), and the *Rest on the Flight into Egypt* (1530; both in Parma). These works, though the presentation of their affecting subject matter is extraordinarily tender and moving, are painted, as befits their size, with a certain splendor of majesty.

In his smaller religious paintings, however, Correggio gave free rein to his lyrical imagination, as can be seen in his *Christ on the Mount of Olives* (ca. 1525; London). The great pathos of the kneeling Christ submitting himself with an open, giving gesture of the arms to the will of his Father is enhanced by the soft darkness of the night surrounding him and the singular gentleness and tearful beauty of his face lit up by a heavenly splendor.

When representing cheerful subjects, such as the *Mystic Marriage of St. Catherine* (ca. 1525; Paris), Correggio bestowed an infinite tenderness upon the scene. The picture shows us not only the happiness of a wonderful moment in the life of the saint but also brings us closer to an under-standing of the simplicity and exquisite fineness of the com-plete and loving surrender of a noble soul to its maker. Among Correggio's other great works in this genre the *Ma-donna of the Basket* (ca. 1523; London) and the *Madonna Adoring the Christ Child* (ca. 1525; Florence) are especially noted for their lyrical charm.

## Mythological and Allegorical Paintings

Correggio brought as much love and gentle under-standing to his mythological subjects as to his Christian topics. There are six mythological paintings by Correggio, all commissioned by the Duke of Mantua but not necessar-ily part of the same decorative project.

The *Education of Cupid* (ca. 1525; London) is a hu-manistic allegory ostensibly in praise of the love of learning, but the beauty of Venus's fully revealed body, her enigmatic smile, and the splendidly erotic glance of her wide-open and curiously musing eyes directed straight at the beholder triumphantly keep us from paying much attention to the allegorical significance of the story.

The other five paintings represent famous love affairs of Jupiter. In these works Correggio portrayed scenes of some-times quite absurd encounters, such as that of *Leda and the Swan* (ca. 1532; Berlin), with a literal accuracy and gentle delight which is, at once, tenderly amused and erotically compassionate. The most artful and affecting among these pictures is surely *Io Approached by Jupiter in the Form of a Cloud* (ca. 1532; Vienna), in which the cloud that softly envelops the enraptured nymph hides and yet reveals a very real physical likeness of the god in the fullness of the beauty of youth.

Correggio also painted two complex and not readily decipherable allegorical compositions for the *studiolo* of Isabella d'Este in Mantua (ca. 1533). One represents the exquisite tortures suffered by the man ruled by passions and vice; the other, the triumph of virtue and statecraft over vice. Characteristically the most impressive and engaging figure in this group is the cupid in the extreme foreground of the picture showing the triumph of the passions. He invitingly holds up a bunch of grapes and looks at us with an irresist-ibly knowing, sovereign, and vaguely malicious smile.

## Influence and Reputation

When Correggio died in 1534 in his native town, he was at the height of his creative life. He left behind no students worthy of his name, and in his immediate neigh-borhood only Parmigianino profited greatly from the exam-ple of his work. Correggio was famous in his lifetime, but since his works, especially the great frescoes in Parma, were in out-of-the-way places, he was at first more readily praised than seriously studied.

At the beginning of the 17th century the Carracci, touched by the facility and grace of Correggio's art, made him one of their greatest heroes. As their influence rose, so did his. Correggio's art of opening up ceilings illu-sionistically was adapted and, to a considerable extent, vul-garized during the 17th century.

Correggio's influence on 18th-century painting was all-pervasive. When the reputation of 18th-century art de-clined, the appreciation of Correggio's oeuvre declined with it. And it did not rise again significantly when 18th-century art was restored to critical favor, perhaps because the exquisite grace of Correggio's style demands a greater commitment of gentleness and refinement than does the charming playfulness generally associated with the rococo.

The painter Anton Raphael Mengs was one of the most perceptive and articulate students of the master's work. In his *Memorie sopra il Correggio* (*Opere*, 1783) he wrote that Correggio arrived at a perfection of painting because "he added to the representation of grandness and the imitation of nature a certain lightness which nowadays we are in the habit of calling 'good taste'; but in fact this good taste is simply the ability to delineate the true nature of things and to exclude all extraneous elements as insipid and useless."

## Further Reading

There is no modern appreciation in English of the complete work of Correggio. Arthur E. Popham's magisterial *Correggio's Drawings* (1957) transcends the limited scope indicated by its title and probably will remain one of the best introductions to Correggio's art. It also contains a concise critical review of the most important earlier publications on Correggio. Erwin Panofsky, *The Iconography of Correggio's 'Camera di San Paolo'* (1961), is concerned with the meaning of the allegories in the abbess's drawing room, and it also serves as an introduction to the social and political environment of the time. Works in Italian include A. C. Quintavalle, *L'opera completa del Correggio* (1970), which contains reproductions of all works generally attributed to Correggio, and Roberto Tassi, *Il duomo di Parma* (1966), a splendidly illustrated book on Correggio's ceiling paintings in the the Cathedral. □

# Corrigan and Williams

**Mairead Corrigan-Maguire (born 1944) and Betty Williams-Perkins (born 1943) were the founders of the women's peace movement in Northern Ireland in 1976. The movement sponsored marches by women from the rival communities in the province in protest against violence and drew international attention and acclaim. They were jointly awarded the Nobel Prize for Peace in 1976 when their efforts were credited with reducing the death toll in Northern Ireland by half.**

Corrigan (left), Williams (right)

Mairead Corrigan, born January 27, 1944, was the second child in a West Belfast Catholic working class family of five girls and two boys. She attended St. Vincent's Primary School and as a teenager went to Miss Gordon's Commercial College in Belfast, which qualified her for a clerical position. She advanced to become the confidential secretary to the managing director of the Guinness Brewery in Belfast. Her organizational involvement was primarily church-oriented, being an activist member of the Legion of Mary, a lay Catholic religious and welfare society, in which she supervised recreational activities for children and teenagers in the bleak West Belfast areas. This spurred her interest in assisting the community. As a Catholic, Corrigan was influenced by the traditions of her religion, but not those of the Republicans, those factions of Northern Ireland's Catholic minority who were fighting to unite the province with the Republic of Ireland.

Betty Williams was born on May 22, 1943, in a Catholic sector of Belfast known as Andersonstown, the eldest daughter of a mixed family (her father was Protestant and her mother Catholic, her grandfather Jewish). She attended St. Teresa's Primary School and St. Dominic's Grammar (high) School and afterwards took secretarial courses. When she was 13, her mother was incapacitated by a stroke and Williams was responsible for raising her younger sister. When she was 18 she married an English Protestant, Ralph Williams, an engineer in the merchant marine, and traveled with him considerably. They had a son and a daughter, although the marriage was ultimately dissolved. She worked as an office receptionist. Her involvement in social activism

was nonexistent until she witnessed the tragedy that occurred in front of her on a Belfast street in August 1976.

The hostility that lay between the minority Catholic and majority Protestant communities in Northern Ireland caused strife for years. The central issue were the contradictory aspirations of both factions: the Catholics wanted unification with the Republic of Ireland and the Protestants wanted to maintain their union with Britain. The era of troubles that began after 1969 was prompted specifically by Catholic complaints of discriminatory treatment by the Northern Irish state, especially in policing, welfare, social benefits, and public employment. The British, at the request of the Northern Irish Protestants, sent military forces to serve as peace keepers in 1969. What followed this intervention was guerrilla warfare and terrorism by revolutionary nationalists, especially the Provisional Irish Republican Army (IRA) within the Catholic community, and sectarian murders of Catholics by assorted Protestant militants such as the Ulster Volunteer Force. The loss of life because of the strife had reached an average of over 200 a year in a community were homicide had once been a rare phenomenon.

On August 10, 1976 Corrigan and Williams were brought together when three children of Mairead Corrigan's sister, Anne Maguire, were killed when hit by an IRA getaway car whose driver had been shot dead by British soldiers. Mairead Corrigan and her brother-in-law Jackie Maguire condemned the IRA on television for having brought on the tragedy. Betty Williams, who had witnessed the tragedy, went about in the Catholic areas securing 6,000 signatures to a peace petition which she read on television. The women met at the Maguire children's funeral and formed Women for Peace (renamed Community of the Peace People), which before the end of August held three peace marches, the last of which saw the Protestant women of the Shankill Road area receiving the Catholics from the Falls area at an assembly of over 35,000. With this broad-based non-sectarian character similar rallies continued elsewhere in Northern Ireland for the remainder of the year as well as supporting rallies in Dublin and London.

Sinn Fein, the political wing of the IRA, condemned the movement as "one-sided and deceptive" and for duping thousands of well-meaning people. There were physical attacks on the marchers for "selling-out" and Corrigan and Williams were suspected by both sides of "collaborating with the enemy." At times they were severely beaten and their lives threatened. However, they persisted spreading their word of peace throughout the world. It worked. International sympathy evoked hundreds of thousands of dollars in contributions to the peace movement.

In October 1977 a belated Nobel Peace Prize for 1976 was awarded to Corrigan and Williams, who also received honorary doctorates from Yale University and the Carl von Ossietzky Medal for Courage from the Berlin chapter of the International League for Human Rights. Corrigan was convinced that only reeducating the entire populace would stop the killing. "Unfortunately we never question our educational system. If we stop to evaluate a lot of our old ideas and concepts, we find that they're myths, that they're false; and that bigotry has created the fear and hatred that divides our peoples." Williams also found no sense in the violence, and in response to IRA calls for peace with justice she responded, "Where was the justice in the death of a child not yet three years old. . . . All I could see was that young men and boys of my area were becoming violent, aggressive, almost murderers; and that they were rapidly becoming the heroes of my community. Was that justice?"

By early 1978 the popular enthusiasm for the movement had waned. In addition, there appeared personal criticisms of the founders, who had been accepting an honorarium for their activities in view of their having given up their regular employment to devote full-time attention to the cause. Keeping a portion of the $140,000 Nobel Peace Prize enabled them to give up the honorarium but intensified such criticism even though a large part of the prize money went to the organization. The travels and renown of both ladies naturally invited jealousy and accusations of personal ambition. Accordingly, Corrigan and Williams resigned the leadership of the Peace People that year to give others a turn at directing the movement, although they remained active members.

Even before this the movement, which from the beginning had the journalistic and organizational advice of Ciaran McKeown, a Belfast correspondent for the *Irish Press,* had changed its tactics from mass rallies to lower level small group meetings, especially in troubled neighborhoods. It also sought to stimulate local community efforts for better youth recreational facilities and even to the encouragement of local industry. The group's criticism of established politicians was met by the politicians' disregard of a movement which was inherently outside of politics and regular political institutions. Furthermore, the Peace People had directed criticism at the authorities and the security forces as well as at the terrorists.

The tragedy that had inspired the formation of the peace group, the deaths of the Maguire children, was compounded on January 21, 1980, when their distraught mother Anne took her own life. The following year Mairead Corrigan married her widowed brother-in-law Jack Maguire, who had two surviving children, and they had a son. Corrigan-Maguire returned to the Community of Peace People (a.k.a. Peace People Organization) traveling throughout the world with her message of non-violent solutions to the world's great problems.

In 1982 Betty Williams married an educator, James T. Perkins with whom she has a daughter. She moved to Florida with her family in 1986 after 10 years of struggling for peace in Northern Ireland. She traveled the state lecturing for a nuclear freeze, and against the death penalty in keeping with her views of non-violence and justice. She also wrote children's fiction.

The rhetorical disregard by Corrigan and Williams for the political process obviously was insufficient for formulating a permanent solution to the Northern Irish problem. However, they were able to dramatically and memorably demonstrate to the province and the world the outrage in both communities at the bloodletting of the terrorists. Their own essentially non-political backgrounds made them appropriate figures for making such a statement for an end to violence. The peace movement must have had not a small part in explaining the striking reduction in casualties since 1976, as the number of deaths from violence dropped by about one-half to an annual average of under 100. In September 1994, the IRA called a cease fire in Northern Ireland and the following month most of the violent Protestant groups followed suit. These actions led to peace talks with the governments of Northern Ireland, the Republic of Ireland, and Great Britain. Sein Fein's leader Gerry Adams was also included in the discussions. Without the efforts of Corrigan-Maguire and Williams-Perkins, the peace process might never have been initiated. In an interview in 1993, Corrigan defined the philosophy that was the core of her involvement in the peace movement "I respect the life of each human person, and I will never take another human life. And that is my strongest identity, before any flag or religion. We need to recognize that life is sacred and that we are involved in a mystery. The human family is struggling toward a new kind of identity, allowing us to see people in the South of Ireland, people in England, people in Burma, people in Chicago as our brothers and sisters, who deserve absolute respect for their lives, opinions and welfare."

## Further Reading

A study of both women appeared the year immediately after the peace movement started: Richard Deutsch, *Mairead Corrigan/Betty Williams* (1977). Marcia Conta's *Women for*

*Human Rights* (1979) offers a general description of the women. More information about the peace movement and Mairead Corrigan's involvement can be found in the April 20, 1994 issues of the *Christian Century*'s article *Toward a higher identity: an interview with Mairead Corrigan Maguire.* For a general understanding of the issues see Paul Arthur, *The Government and Politics of Northern Ireland* (1980); Patrick Buckland, *A History of Northern Ireland* (1981); and Padraig O'Malley, *The Uncivil Wars* (1983). □

# Michael Augustine Corrigan

**American Roman Catholic clergyman Michael Augustine Corrigan (1839-1902) was archbishop of New York during years of rapid change and expansion.**

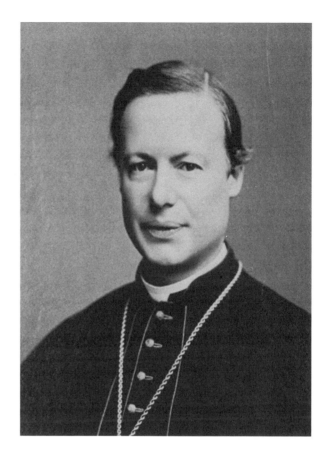

Michael Augustine Corrigan was born in Newark, N.J., the fifth of nine children of Thomas and Mary English Corrigan. His father had emigrated from Ireland in 1828 and was a successful grocer. Michael attended a private school conducted by a relative and spent 2 years at St. Mary's College, Wilmington, Del., graduating from Mount St. Mary's in Emmitsburg, Md., in 1859. Bishop James Roosevelt Bayley sent Corrigan to study for the priesthood as one of the first group of students to attend the new American College in Rome. In 1863 Corrigan was ordained a priest in Rome, and the next year he received his doctorate at the College of the Propaganda Fide.

Returning to New Jersey, Corrigan was named professor of theology and scripture at Seton Hall Seminary, and in 1868 he became the school's president, a post he held until 1876. He served during the same period as vicar general of the Newark diocese. In 1873 he became bishop of Newark, a diocese which covered the state of New Jersey. During his term he successfully systematized parish records and reports and promoted the building of parish schools. In 1880 he was elevated to the post of coadjutor to John McCloskey, Archbishop of New York, whom he succeeded in 1885.

Energetic, though somewhat colorless, and possessed by a passion for order and system, Corrigan developed clear lines of authority in his archdiocese, shored up church finances, adapted parishes to changing ethnic constituencies, sought out foreign-language priests for the hordes of new immigrants, and worked vigorously for the extension of the Catholic school system. Five diocesan synods clarified episcopal authority and clerical responsibility. Archbishop Corrigan completed the building of St. Patrick's Cathedral and constructed a diocesan seminary at Dunwoodie, which he endowed with a chapel from his personal inheritance.

Corrigan's centralization of diocesan affairs was opposed by some priests, whose protests to Rome exposed some of the canonical irregularities in the American system of diocesan management. Most notable was his highly publicized battle with Edward McGlynn, a brilliant priest who questioned the parochial school policy and supported reformer Henry George. Nationally, the archbishop joined other conservative prelates in opposing the more liberal programs advocated by Archbishop John Ireland of St. Paul. Corrigan defended the parochial school and advocated condemnation of secret societies and avoidance of ecumenical contact. He refused to assist the development of the Catholic University of America and staunchly defended the autonomy of his diocese. In later years, when controversy subsided, Corrigan devoted himself to local problems. He died suddenly in 1902.

## Further Reading

Frederick J. Zwierlein, *Letters of Archbishop Corrigan to Bishop McQuaid* (1946), is the major source for Corrigan's more controversial activities. Diocesan affairs are treated in John Talbot Smith, *The Catholic Church in New York,* vol. 2 (1908). For general background see Thomas T. McAvoy, *A History of the Catholic Church in the United States* (1969).

## Additional Sources

DiGiovanni, Stephen Michael, *Archbishop Corrigan and the Italian immigrants,* Huntington, Ind.: Our Sunday Visitor, Inc., 1994.

*The Diocesan journal of Michael Augustine Corrigan, Bishop of Newark, 1872-1880,* Newark: New Jersey Historical Society; South Orange: New Jersey Catholic Historical Records Commission, 1987. □

# Henry Cort

**The English ironmaster Henry Cort (1740-1800) made possible the large-scale and inexpensive conversion of cast iron into wrought iron, one of the most essential materials of the early industrial revolution.**

Henry Cort was born in Lancaster. His father was a mason and brickmaster. Young Cort became a supplier of naval provisions and by the 1770s had accumulated a small fortune.

In 1775, after years of experimenting with improved methods for wrought-iron production, Cort purchased a forge and slitting mill at Fontley. He tried to find an easy way to convert cast iron into wrought iron; traditionally a smith had hammered the iron in a forge. He patented grooved rollers in 1783 which replaced most of the hammering. By 1784 Cort worked out a process of pudding, whereby molten pig iron was stirred in a reverberatory furnace. As the iron was decarbonized by air, it became thicker, and balls of "puddled" iron could be removed as a pasty mass from the more liquid impurities still in the furnace. Puddled iron, like wrought iron, was tougher and more malleable than pig iron and could be hammered and finished with the grooved rollers. He also devised a process whereby red-hot iron was drawn out of the furnace through grooved rollers which shaped the puddled iron into bars, whose dimensions were determined by the shape of the grooves on the rollers. The rollers also helped squeeze out impurities, and preliminary shaping into bars made the iron more readily utilizable for the final product.

There were many advantages to these processes. Puddling used the plentiful coke, instead of the expensive charcoal. The combination of puddling and grooved rollers was a process that could be mechanized, for example, by the steam engine, which had just been introduced. The result was that production of wrought iron was increasingly carried out in a group of coordinated processes in a single economic unit, with reverberation processes in a single economic unit, with reverberation and blast furnaces operating side by side. This increased production at a greatly reduced cost, and for the first time iron became one of England's exports.

To obtain more capital, Cort took a partner, Samuel Jellicoe, who put up large sums of money. Jellicoe's father had embezzled these funds from the British government, and when this was discovered, Cort was completely ruined and lost his patent rights. As an acknowledgment of the value of Cort's patents, however, the government granted him a small pension in 1794. Cort died a poor man; he was buried in Hampstead, England.

## Further Reading

There is no biography of Cort. Material on him can be found in T. S. Ashton, *Iron and Steel in the Industrial Revolution* (1924; 2d ed 1951) and *The Industrial Revolution: 1760-1830* (1948;

rev. ed. 1964). John C. Hammond and Barbara Hammond, *The Rise of Modern Industry* (1925; 9th ed. 1966), is a classic study that includes information on Cort.

## Additional Sources

Mott, R. A. (Reginald Arthur), *Henry Cort, the great finer: creator of puddled iron,* London: Metals Society, 1983. □

# Gaspar and Miguel Corte Reál

**The Portuguese brothers Gaspar (died 1501) and Miguel (died 1502) Corte Reál were among the early explorers of the northeastern coast of America.**

The Corte Reál brothers were members of a noble Portuguese family. Gaspar was apparently the more aggressive of the two. In 1499 he learned of a grant from King Manoel I to a fellow Portuguese, John Fernandes, to undertake an expedition into the North Atlantic. Manoel sought to establish Portuguese control over a Northwest Passage to India and the Spice Islands. He also wanted someone who would establish Portugal's claims to any new lands that might be discovered in this area. Fernandes did not immediately make use of his grant from the King. Gaspar seized the opportunity to obtain royal permission to undertake his own exploratory expedition in May 1500.

Gaspar Corte Reál left Lisbon in the summer of 1500 in a fleet of three ships, financed by his family. He sailed first to Greenland and spent several months exploring its shoreline. During this time he contacted the natives, whom he compared to the wild natives of Brazil. His ships stayed in Greenland's waters until the winter icebergs forced them to leave. Gaspar and his ships returned to Portugal in late 1500.

The following year Gaspar organized another expedition, this time in conjunction with his brother Miguel. Their expedition departed in May 1501, again bound for unknown lands to the northwest. When they reached land after about 5 weeks, they found themselves on the shores of Labrador. They explored south along the coast, charting approximately 600 miles of shore.

At this point Miguel took two of the ships and returned to Portugal to report their findings. Gaspar, meanwhile, continued south and disappeared. Miguel, now back in Portugal, undertook an expedition to find him. This rescue mission was sanctioned by King Manoel, who also promised Miguel any new islands he might discover. Miguel set out in May 1502 with three ships. The three ships traveled together to Newfoundland, where they decided to divide and meet later. Two of them rendezvoused at the agreed-upon time, but Miguel Corte Reál, like Gaspar, was never seen again, presumably lost in a storm.

King Manoel, a friend of the Corte Reál family, financed a search expedition in 1503. He forbade a third brother, Vasqueanes, an important government official, from undertaking his own rescue attempt.

## Further Reading

Three useful works for the study of Gaspar and Miguel Corte Reál are Edgar Prestage, *The Portuguese Pioneers* (1933); Harold Lamb, *New Found World: How North America Was Discovered and Explored* (1955); and J. H. Parry, *The Age of Reconnaissance* (1963). □

# Hernán Cortés

**Hernán Cortés (c. 1485-1547) conquered the Aztec empire in Mexico and became the most famous of the Spanish conquistadores.**

Hernán Cortés was born in Medellin. His parents were of the small landed gentry of the region. As a youth, he studied Latin for 2 years at the University of Salamanca, but lured by tales of new discoveries in America, he abandoned student life and in 1504 sailed for the New World.

Cortés settled initially on the island of Santo Domingo (Hispaniola) but in 1511 joined an expedition to Cuba, where he became a municipal official and an intimate friend of Diego Velázquez, the governor of the island. When Velázquez determined to dispatch an expedition to Mexico, he named Cortés for the command, but Velázquez soon came to suspect Cortés of excessive ambition and determined to relieve him. Cortés, aware of this danger, managed to slip away with part of his followers before the governor could formally confront him. After meeting with other recruits, on Feb. 18, 1519, Cortés departed for Mexico with over 600 Spanish soldiers, sailors, and captains, some 200 Indian auxiliaries, and 16 horses.

Cortés's route took him first to Yucatán and thence up the Mexican coast to the vicinity of the modern city of Veracruz, where he founded a town, Villa Rica de Veracruz, which became the base for the conquest. There he arranged to have the municipal council—which he had appointed—name him captain general and principal judge, an act which gave him at least quasilegal status. He also negotiated alliances with adjacent Indian tribes and gathered intelligence about the Aztecs.

## War with the Aztecs

In August 1519 Cortés struck inland for Tenochtitlán, an island city in Lake Texcoco and the capital of the Aztec confederation ruled by Montezuma II. The most consequential episode in the march was an alliance which Cortés negotiated with the Tlascala, an Indian nation hostile to the Aztecs. In early November the expedition reached the shores of Lake Texcoco. Montezuma, unsure of the intentions of the Spaniards and, indeed, of whether they were gods or men, had offered no overt resistance to their approach and now invited them into Tenochtitlán.

The Spaniards were treated as not entirely welcome guests, and Cortés responded by seizing Montezuma as hostage. At this time Cortés was faced with the arrival of an expedition sent by Governor Velázquez to chastise him. Cortés hastened to the coast to meet the newcomers and, after a surprise attack on them, induced them to join his forces. Upon returning to Tenochtitlán, however, he found the inhabitants in arms and his forces beleaguered in their quarters. Judging the situation to be hopeless, on the night of June 30, 1520, he led his forces from the city to refuge with his Tlascala allies.

In Tlascala, Cortés rebuilt his forces with newly arrived Spaniards and Indian auxiliaries. In May 1521 he began an attack on Tenochtitlán supported by a small navy which had been built in Tlascala, transported to Lake Texcoco, and reassembled. After 75 days of bitter street fighting, on August 13 the city fell to the Spaniards.

## Founding of Mexico

Success won legal status for Cortés. On Oct. 15, 1522, Emperor Charles V appointed him governor and captain general of New Spain, the name applied by the Spaniards to the conquered region. It also provided Cortés with an opportunity to display new dimensions of his abilities. He rebuilt Tenochtitlán as the Spanish city of Mexico and dispatched his lieutenants in all directions to subdue other Indian groups. Within a short time most of what is now central and southern Mexico was brought under Spanish rule. Cortés encouraged the introduction of European plants and animals. He vigorously supported the conversion of the native population to Christianity, and his government was marked by consideration for the physical welfare of the Indians.

## Cortés's Retirement

The great conqueror's days of glory, however, were short. The Emperor was jealous of powerful and popular captains beyond his immediate control and soon began to withdraw or undermine the governmental powers conceded to Cortés. Royal officials were appointed to oversee the treasury of New Spain, royal judges arrived to dispense justice, and in 1526 he was deprived of the governorship. Cortés spent 2 years (1528-1530) in Spain defending himself against his enemies and attempting unsuccessfully to recover his administrative authority. He returned, retaining only the honorific military office of captain general but with the title of marquis of the valley of Oaxaca, which conferred on him a vast estate in southern Mexico.

Cortés remained in Mexico for the next 10 years, managing his estate and undertaking new expeditions which he hoped would recoup his power. His efforts were unsuccessful and in 1540 he returned to Spain, where he lived as a wealthy, honored, but disappointed man until his death in 1547. In compliance with his will, his remains were returned to Mexico, where they repose today in the church of the Hospital of Jesus in Mexico City, an institution which he himself had founded.

Cortés was unquestionably a man of immense abilities. As a conquistador, he displayed an exceptional combination of leadership, audacity, tenacity, diplomacy, and tactical skill. But he was more than a conqueror. He had a vision of a "New Spain" overseas and his statesmanship was instrumental in laying its foundations.

## Further Reading

The Letters of Cortés was edited by F. A. MacNutt in three volumes in 1908. The best studies of Cortés are F. A. MacNutt, Fernando Cortés and the Conquest of Mexico (1909); Salvador de Madariaga, Hernán Cortés, Conqueror of Mexico (1942), a fictionalized biography; and H. R. Wagner, The Rise of Fernando Cortés (1944). A useful contemporary account is Bernal Díaz del Castillo, The True History of the Conquest of New Spain, translated by A. P. Maudslay (5 vols., 1908-1916). The best single work on the conquest of Mexico is still W. H. Prescott, History of the Conquest of Mexico (1843; many later editions). See also R. C. Padden, The Hummingbird and the Hawk: Conquest and Sovereignty in the Valley of Mexico, 1503-1541 (1967). □

# Pietro da Cortona

**The Italian painter and architect Pietro da Cortona (1596-1669) was one of the main representatives of the first full flowering of the high baroque style in Italy.**

Pietro Berrettini, known as Pietro da Cortona from his birthplace of Cortona, a little town in Tuscany, was born on Nov. 1, 1596. In Rome, where he went in his teens, the paintings of Annibale Carracci and ancient Roman sculpture especially influenced him. With the encouragement of the learned archeologist Cassiano dal Pozzo he studied, as his contemporary G. B. Passeri tells us, "the statues and bas-reliefs of the ancient Romans, especially various columns, urns, and vases on which were represented sacrifices, bacchic revels, and other pagan ceremonies."

From such ancient sculpture Cortona usually selected those with the most dynamic compositions for his paintings. In his *Rape of the Sabines* (ca. 1629) the figures are arranged on planes parallel to the surface, almost as in a bas-relief, and the Roman architecture and Roman military dress are carefully rendered. But what is most evident is the violence of the individual gestures, the agitation and tumult that fill the whole composition. The highly active figures in Cortona's picture are painted in bright colors that are often laid on rapidly, so that the individual brushstrokes remain visible, much in the manner of the great Venetian artists of the 16th century such as Titian and Veronese.

Cortona's masterpiece of painting is the *Glorification of Pope Urban VIII* (1639), which covers the entire ceiling of the Great Hall of the Barberini Palace in Rome. It is painted to give the illusion that we are looking up into a wide stretch of open sky, partially interrupted by sections of an architectural framework. The sky is filled to overflowing with swarms of human figures who act out endless allegories as they drift back and forth over our heads and under the painted architecture like the last act in some theatrical spectacular in the sky.

Cortona's last major work, the ceiling paintings for the long gallery in the Pamphili Palace in Rome (1654), depicts the story of Aeneas. The gentler rhythms, the paler colors, and the uncrowded compositions with large stretches of open sky all seem to anticipate the 18th century.

Far less of Cortona's career was devoted to architecture, but here too he demonstrated the highest originality. His facade for the little church of S. Maria della Pace in Rome (1657) spreads across the front of a cloister on one side and an adjacent church on the other. A street runs through what looks like the right aisle. The whole surface of the building seems in motion. Sections of it rise and fall, bulge out or swing back, creating an orchestration as complex as his ceiling paintings and more sophisticated. Cortona died in Rome on May 16, 1669.

## Further Reading

The standard biography of Cortona is in Italian: Giuliano Briganti, Pietro da Cortona (1962). There are good chapters on Cortona in English in Rudolf Wittkower, Art and Architecture in Italy, 1600-1750 (1958; 2d ed. 1965), and Ellis K. Waterhouse, Italian Baroque Painting (1962). The section on Cortona in Robert Enggass and Jonathan Brown, Italy and Spain, 1600-1750 (1970), gives a detailed explanation of the meaning of Cortona's complicated ceiling painting in the Barberini Palace. □

# William Henry Cosby Jr.

**An entertainer for three decades, William Henry Cosby, Jr. (born 1937) starred in live performances, record albums, books, film, and television. His long-running, hugely popular "The Cosby Show" was in the top of the Nielson television ratings from its debut in 1984.**

William Henry Cosby, Junior, was born in Germantown, Pennsylvania, July 12, 1937, to Anna and William Cosby. There were four boys in the family, but one died from rheumatic fever at six years old. Soon after the young boy's death, William Cosby Sr., left his family and joined the Navy. Bill, the oldest son, became the man of the family and helped his mother pay the bills by doing odd jobs such as delivering groceries and shining shoes. He tried to keep up with his school work, but he dropped out of high school to join the Navy in the early 1950s. Cosby's mother had always stressed the importance of education to her children, and so eventually Bill earned his diploma through correspondence school and was accepted at Temple University in Philadelphia on an athletic scholarship.

The athlete at Temple still needed spending money, so he took a job as a bartender in a neighborhood café called The Underground. The bar had a resident comedian who often didn't show up for his act, so Cosby began to fill in, entertaining the crowd with jokes and humorous stories. His reputation as a funny bartender spread throughout the city, and Cosby soon got offers to do stand-up comedy in other clubs. His act was influenced by Mel Brooks, Jonathan Winters, Bob Newhart, and Lenny Bruce. Cosby's biggest chance came when he was asked to perform at the Gaslight Café, a Greenwich Village coffeehouse that regularly featured young performers such as Bob Dylan.

Cosby was soon making people laugh in large, well-known night spots all over the country, and he reached a point where his career showed him more promise than his education. He left Temple in 1962.

Cosby's first electronic medium for his comedy was the long-playing album. "Bill Cosby Is a Very Funny Fellow . . . Right!" (1963), produced by Roy Silver and Allan Sherman, was the comedian's first recording, as well as his first to win a Grammy Award. His second album, "I Started Out As a Child," released in 1964, received another Grammy honor as Best Comedy Album of the Year. All of Cosby's albums earned more than $1 million in sales. His popularity continued and he won consecutive Best Comedy Album awards every year from 1964 to 1969.

Allan Sherman was one of Cosby's biggest fans as well as his producer, and when Sherman filled in for Johnny Carson as guest host of "The Tonight Show" in 1963, he asked Cosby to be his guest. "The Tonight Show" producers were skeptical about having an African American comic on the show, but Sherman was adamant and Cosby was a big hit.

Sheldon Leonard, producer of mid-1960s hits including "The Danny Thomas Show," "The Dick Van Dyke Show," and "The Andy Griffith Show," was watching "The Tonight Show" the night Cosby was on. At the time, he was looking for a male actor to play opposite Robert Culp on a new dramatic series—and when he saw Cosby, he had his man. "I Spy" was an immediate success, and the fact that it was the first prime-time television program to star a black person added to its appeal. In 1967 Cosby won the Emmy Award for Best Actor in a Dramatic Series, and he did likewise in 1968 and 1969. His second prime-time series, "The Bill Cosby Show," began in 1969, just one year after "I Spy" went off the air. Starring Cosby as a high school sports instructor, it was number one in its first season. However, ratings steadily dropped over the next two years, and the show was canceled in the spring of 1971.

The following year marked the beginning of "Fat Albert and the Cosby Kids" as a regular series on CBS (it aired first in 1971 as a special). The Saturday afternoon cartoon featured a group of kids living and learning together in an urban area much like the impoverished section of Philadelphia where Cosby was reared. Cosby provided the voice for every character and bracketed the animated portion of the show in person to discuss the episode's message. So that his audience would learn good behavior and solid values, Cosby employed a panel of educators to act as advisers. The program won a variety of awards, and audience estimates numbered about six million.

Cosby made two more attempts at prime time with "The New Bill Cosby Show" and "Cos" in 1972 and 1976, respectively; both were unsuccessful variety shows which included dancing, skits, and monologue sessions.

Although Cosby dropped out of prime-time television for some time during the mid-1970s, he was still quite active in comedy, mostly through live performances and comedy albums such as "Why Is There Air?," "Wonderfulness," and "Revenge." The majority of the material for these albums came from Cosby's childhood experiences, such as plotting an escape from a bed he'd been told was surrounded by thousands of poisonous snakes, living through a tonsillectomy at age five, and having everything he ever made in shop class turn into an ashtray.

Cosby earned his undergraduate degree from Temple University in 1971 and in 1977 completed his Ph.D. in education at the University of Massachusetts. Cosby's commitment to education included regular appearances during the 1970s on "The Electric Company," produced by the Children's Television Workshop, which also produced "Sesame Street." He also appeared as the host of the Picturepages segment on "Captain Kangaroo" in the early 1980s.

Hollywood also employed the talent of Cosby, but with indifferent results. His first movie was "Man and Boy," a 1972 western film with Cosby in the lead; panned by critics, it quickly died at the box office. A much later movie (1978) with Richard Pryor, "California Suite," was written by Neil Simon. The film fared relatively well. In between, he made "Hickey and Boggs," "Uptown Saturday Night," "Let's Do It Again," "Mother, Jugs and Speed," "A Piece of the Action," "The Devil and Max Devlin," "Bill Cosby Himself," and "Leonard the Sixth."

By 1984 Cosby had become disillusioned with what he saw on television and came up with his own idea of a sitcom. The networks were skeptical, as his last two attempts at prime time were failures. Only NBC was interested; they ordered six provisional episodes only after seeing a pilot. Cosby gave them a segment featuring himself as Dr. Heathcliff Huxtable discussing sex with his two teenaged daughters. NBC liked it enough to agree to Cosby's major concessions, including complete creative control and a studio in New York. He would cast himself as an obstetrician-gynecologist married to an attorney. They would be parents to five children, and their names would be Huxtable (executives wanted him to change it to Brown). They would represent middle-class values and they would just happen to be black. They would not take on traditional television characteristics of blacks, neither Fred Sanford's dialect nor George Jefferson's anger. They would be a happy family dealing with everyday problems and incidents, and it would be called "The Cosby Show."

The first show aired in September 1984, and it was an immediate success. That season "The Cosby Show" finished as the third most watched prime-time television show, according to Nielsen ratings, and it was number one for the next four seasons. The show went into syndication in October 1988, and it sold to the Fox network for $550 million the rights to 182 programs to last for three and a half years.

On Jan. 16, 1997, Cosby's life took a dramatic turn, as headlines nationwide broke the shocking news that his only son had been murdered. Ennis, 27, had stopped to change a flat tire along a Los Angeles freeway when he was allegedly shot to death by an 18-year-old Ukrainian immigrant. Details of the fated night were sketchy at first, and it was not certain that the killer would be found. National tabloid the *National Enquirer* offered $100,000 for information leading to the arrest of the shooter, which prompted one witness, a friend of defendant Mihkhail Markhasev, to come forward to testify. The District Attorney's office announced in June, 1997, that it would not seek the death penalty for Markhasev.

Two days after the shooting, Cosby gained additional attention when a young woman alleged she was his illegitimate child. Prosecutors later claimed Autumn Jackson, 22, was one of three defendants who schemed to extort $40 million from the comedian. Cosby's lawyers alleged Jackson, along with failed children's television producer Jose Medina and Boris Sabas, tried to trash Cosby's reputation by threatening to sell the story to a supermarket tabloid. Cosby admitted to having had an affair with Jackson's mother, Shawn Upshaw, but has denied being Jackson's father. In July of 1997, Jackson was convicted of extortion.

Cosby and his wife, Camille, have been married since 1964 and have four daughters. Cosby has been his own manager and producer and wrote several books, including the best-selling "Fatherhood," published in 1986. He also became one of the most visible spokespeople in the nation, pitching products for Jell-O, Kodak, Del Monte, the Ford Motor Company and the Coca-Cola Company on television commercials.

"Cosby," which debuted in the fall of 1996 is the latest addition to the Cosby television archive. The CBS show, which also starred Madeline Kahn and Phylicia Rashad, was co-produced by Cosby for Carsey-Werner Productions.

## Further Reading

In addition to numerous articles in the popular media, Bill Cosby has been the subject of books by Bill Adler, *The Cosby Wit* (1986); Ronald L. Smith, *Bill Cosby in Words and Pictures* (1986) and *Cosby* (1986); James T. Olsen, *Look Back in Laughter* (1974); and Caroline Latham, *Bill Cosby—For Real* (1987). Cosby himself has written *Fatherhood* (1986), *Time Flies* (1988), and *Love and Marriage* (1989). All are anecdotal, humorous, and matter-of-factly make fun of everyday activities. □

# Liam Cosgrave

**The son of the head of the Irish Free State government, Liam Cosgrave (born 1920) became foreign minister and later prime minister (1973-1977).**

L iam Cosgrave was born in Dublin on April 30, 1920, the son of William T. and Louise (Flanagan) Cosgrave. He attended the Christian Brothers' School and St.

Vincent's College in Dublin. Studying law at the King's Inn, he was called to the bar in 1943 and became a senior counsel in 1958.

Cosgrave's father was the leader of the government of the newly independent Ireland (Irish Free State) from 1922 to 1932. They laid the foundation of Irish democracy in the aftermath of the bloody civil war with the British. William Cosgrave's government had to first wage a civil war against hardline nationalists unhappy with the terms of the independence and then restore constitutional normalcy after years of insurrection and civil war.

In 1932 Eamon De Valera, the leader of the defeated forces in the civil war, but who had in 1926 formed a constitutional opposition party, Fianna Fáil (Soldiers of Destiny), came to power. He would remain as head of the government with two brief exceptions (1948-1951 and 1954-1957) until 1959. Furthermore, his party would remain in power, after he had been elected to the more honorific presidency of Ireland, until 1973. With defeat, the elder Cosgrave's party, Cumann nan Gaedheal (League of Gaels), became absorbed in a new coalition of opposition groups that took the name of Fine Gael (Tribe of Gaels). That party was unable to dent the overwhelming electoral support given to the populist and economic nationalist program of De Valera.

Young Cosgrave entered politics and was elected a Fine Gael deputy to Dáil Eireann, the Irish parliament, in 1943. He served as a parliamentary secretary to the minister for industry and commerce in the 1948 to 1951 coalition

government, the first of the brief interruptions of the De Valera and Fianna Fáil ascendancy. More significantly, in the second coalition regime, 1954 to 1957, he was minister of external affairs and accordingly led the first Irish delegation to the General Assembly of the United Nations, to which Ireland had been admitted in 1955.

In 1965 he became the leader of the Fine Gael Party. This was a period when both major parties in Ireland were undergoing considerable change. Fianna Fáil, under Taoiseach, or prime minister, Seal Lemass and his successor, Jack Lynch, had turned its back on self-sufficiency and isolationist economic ideals and had opted for increased international trade and foreign investment as the means of Irish economic modernization, culminating in Ireland's entry into the European Economic Community (EEC). Younger members of the Fine Gael Party were trying to shed the party's economic conservative image and present themselves as a "social justice"-minded alternative to the freewheeling capitalistic flavor Fianna Fáil had seemed to assume. Cosgrave, personally more conservative, was able to hold together the more traditional elements in Fine Gael and the "Young Turks."

In February 1973, the month after Ireland's formal entry to the EEC, a national election was won by a coalition of Fine Gael and the smaller Labour Party. The coalition had campaigned on a "14 point program" emphasizing economic and social welfare issues, especially housing and unemployment. Cosgrave became Taoiseach and included in his government Fine Gael figures as conservative as himself and more liberal party members such as Garret FitzGerald, as well as pragmatic but brilliant Labour members such as Conor Cruise O'Brien.

At a conference at Sunningdale, England, December 6 to 9, 1973, the British and Irish governments and political leaders from Northern Ireland established a power-sharing or coalition executive for a devolved Northern Irish government, whereby the minority would have a proportionate number of cabinet positions, and a projected "Council of Ireland" to deal with mutual problems. Fears that the latter portended eventual unification of Ireland created widespread discontent among Northern Irish Unionists, the Protestant majority. British elections in February 1974 ousted the Conservative Prime Minister Edward Heath. His Labourite successor, Harold Wilson, was returned to power but had to govern without an absolute majority and capitulated to a Unionist general strike in Northern Ireland. This had brought the province to a standstill and toppled the power-sharing executive.

The violent spillover of the Northern Irish issue into the Irish Republic, such as the July 23, 1976, assassination of the British ambassador, prompted the Cosgrave government to push strict security measures. Before agreeing to sign the legislation which had been passed, the president of the Irish Republic, Cearbhall O'Dalaigh, exercised his constitutional option of referring the bills to the Supreme Court for advice on their constitutionality. His action provoked the minister for defense, Paddy Donegan, to label the president as "a thundering disgrace." O'Dalaigh interpreted the refusal of Cosgrave to dismiss a cabinet member who had made a partisan attack on the apolitical office of the presidency as grounds for himself to resign, which he did on October 22, 1976. The Cosgrave government sheltered itself from further embarrassment on the matter by not opposing the Fianna Fail nominee, Patrick Millery, as O'Dalaigh's successor. In July 1974 Cosgrave broke ranks with his own party and voted against an unsuccessful bid to liberalize the Irish law on contraceptives.

The coalition government with its promises of socially ameliorative programs came to power at the same time as the world-wide oil crisis, which had particularly severe effects on small nations such as Ireland with minimal natural resources, industry in a developing stage, and great dependence on imports. The efforts of the government to restrain a mainly foreign-induced inflation, to provide social services, to meet governmental expenditures, and to cope with serious unemployment were bound to weaken its political position. In June 1977 Fianna Fáil, running on a supply-side and populist manifesto promising economic recovery, job creation, and lessened taxes, swept the polls with a 20-seat majority and its greatest proportion of the vote in 39 years.

Questions have been raised that Liam Cosgrave was too conscious of his duty to follow in his father's footsteps that he failed to see the need to justify his actions and those of his government. He was a secretive man who never really revealed what motivated him. He used equivocation and ambiguity as a political tool, so much so that even his own party was uncertain as to his positions, such as on the controversial contraception issue. Because of this he called an early general election in 1977, completely misjudging the mood of the country. Had he waited a few more months to allow the country to experience the advantages of the upswing in the economy the election results would have been far different.

Probably the most significant feature of the Cosgrave government was its giving, by the Sunningdale Agreement, implied consent to the principle that Irish unity was dependent on the consent of the majority in Northern Ireland, a position from which succeeding Irish governments have not deviated.

Cosgrave resigned the leadership of the party and was succeeded by Garret FitzGerald. In 1981 he resigned from Dáil Eireann. He returned to public service, as Cathaoirleach of the Seanad (Leader of the Upper House) and served on the Industrial and Commercial Panel.

## Further Reading

An excellent study of Irish politics in the era of Cosgrave's prominence is Bruce Arnold, *What Kind of Country* (1984). Recent and authoritative studies of Irish history to the eve or early stages of the Cosgrave ministry are F. S. L. Lyons, *Ireland Since the Famine* (1973); John A. Murphy, *Ireland in the Twentieth Century* (1975); and Ronan Fanning, *Independent Ireland* (1983). In 1997, Stephen Collins examined *The Cosgrave Legacy* which focuses attention of Liam Cosgrave's role in government following his father's shining example. □

# Daniel Cosio Villegas

**A teacher and civil servant, Daniel Cosío Villegas (1898-1976) was best known for his broadranging studies of Mexican history. He came to be known for his lucidity and intellectual capacity in economics, history, and political science.**

Daniel Cosío Villegas was born into a lower middle class home in Mexico City in 1898. During his childhood his family lived in several Mexican cities. Later he received bachelor degrees in both arts and letters from the National Preparatory School. After studying a variety of subjects, including engineering and philosophy, he received a law degree from Mexico's National School of Jurisprudence in 1925. Cosío Villegas excelled as a student and was active in student affairs. He successively served as head of the Student Federation of the Mexican Federal District, of the Mexican National Student Federation, and of the International Student Federation.

Cosío Villegas' post-graduate studies reflected his broad-ranging interests. He studied economics at Harvard and agricultural economics at both the University of Wisconsin and Cornell University. Then he went to Europe, where he studied economics and political science. Upon his return to Mexico, Cosío Villegas began working at the Ministry of Education, starting a career in public service which would span over a third of a century.

At this time Cosío Villegas was heavily influenced by the recently concluded Mexican revolution. His post-revolutionary spirit led to a commitment to serve Mexican development. This desire in turn led him to concentrate on economics, a field which he felt was key to developing Mexico.

By the age of 30, Cosío Villegas was a secretary general of the University of Mexico. In that year he created a special economics section of the university, which developed into the National School of Economics. After economics classes began, Cosío Villegas observed a lack of economics texts available in Spanish. As a result, in 1934 he founded the Fondo de Cultura Económica, which became one of the most respected academic publishing houses in the Spanish-speaking world. Also in the 1930s he founded the magazine *Trimestre Económico,* which shifted the focus of Mexican economic discussion from abstract theory and considerations of European nations to the concrete reality of Mexico.

Cosío Villegas continued his public service and was appointed Mexican chargé d'affaires in Lisbon. He was serving there in 1937 as the Spanish Civil War intensified. He personally arranged for many Spanish intellectuals to come to Mexico. With the defeat of the Republican government in Spain, their stay in Mexico became permanent. The Spaniards taught and did research at the Casa de España, which Cosío Villegas helped organize for them. This institution later became the Colegio de México, which is one of the principal social science research centers in Latin America.

Cosío Villegas continued in government service as economic adviser to the Mexican secretary of treasury, to the Bank of Mexico, and to the Mexican embassy in Washington. In addition he was an adviser to Mexican delegations at various international conferences. From 1957 to 1968 he was Mexican ambassador to the Economic and Social Council of the United Nations.

Cosío Villegas combined government service with teaching at the National Preparatory School, the National University, and the Colegio de México in Mexico City. He also taught at the Central University of Madrid in Spain and at the University of Texas in Austin.

This middle period of his life was also one of prodigous scholarship in history, economics, international relations, and political science. In addition to *Trimestre Económico,* he founded and edited *Historia Mexicana* and a journal on international relations, *Foro Internacional.*

By the late 1940s Cosío Villegas began to feel what he described as a "general disillusion about the political climate" of Mexico, due to the emphasis on stability and economic growth rather than on social justice and political openness. Thus he shifted his attention to Mexican history, hoping that this would illuminate the priorities of Mexican society and make people aware of the original goals of the Mexican revolution.

His study of Mexican history occupied him for over a decade and led to the publication of the monumental ten-volume *Historia Moderna de México.* Harvard historian John Womack, Jr., called it the "greatest historical work on modern Mexico." Cosío Villegas wrote five of the ten volumes in the series and supervised the group of young Mexicans who wrote the other five. Thus he not only created a monumental scholarly work, but helped train a whole generation of Mexican historians.

Cosío Villegas' energy is indicated by his activity in his 60th year. He was still working to coordinate the *Historia Moderna de México,* was president of the Colegio de México and of the Economic and Social Council of Mexico, and was editing two of the magazines which he had founded, *Historia Mexicana* and *Foro Internacional.*

In 1968, after the bloody suppression of student demonstrations in Mexico, as Cosío Villegas stated in an interview, he began to feel a "general dissatisfaction about the situation of the country." Thus he left government service and became an essayist commenting on the Mexican scene. He wrote a regular column in *Excelsior,* Mexico's outstanding newspaper, and in addition published a series of popular books on the Mexican political system. The degree to which Cosío Villegas was in touch with the public is indicated by the press runs of his books. As many as 80,000 were printed, a phenomenal sales record for Mexico.

He continued in this role of critical essayist until the time of his death. After his death then-President of Mexico Luis Echeverría spoke of him as an "honest and courageous intellectual and teacher," and Mexican writer Octavio Paz noted his "incorruptible conscience." An obituary in the *American Historical Review* praised him as the "dean of historians of modern Mexico."

The honors Cosío Villegas received far exceed the space available to list them. Included were membership in the Colegio Nacional of Mexico, a life-time recognition limited to 20 members, and the presidency from 1957 to 1963 of the Colegio de México.

## Further Reading

No biography of Cosío Villegas has been published in English. However, several of his books, including *A Compact History of Mexico* (Mexico City, 1974), have been translated into English. Additional information about Mexico at this time can be found in *Change in Latin America: The Mexican & Cuban Revolutions* (1961); *The United States versus Porfirio Diaz* (1963); and *American Extremes* (1964).

## Additional Sources

Cosío Villegas, Daniel, *Memorias,* Mexico: J. Mortiz, 1976, 1977 printing.
Krauze, Enrique, *Daniel Coso Villegas, una biografia intelectual,* Mexico: J. Mortiz, 1980. □

# Elizabeth Cotten

**Versatile folk/blues singer, songwriter, and guitarist Elizabeth Cotten (1892-1987)—creator of the classic song "Freight Train"—performed in concert for the first time at age 67 and won a Grammy Award in 1985 at age 93.**

Amerian folk and blues musician Elizabeth Cotten, composer of the folk song classic "Freight Train" and recipient of a 1985 Grammy Award at age 93, began her career in music at an age when most people prepare for retirement. At 67 years of age Cotten, known as "Libba" by the folksinging Seeger family who discovered her talent, performed live in concert for the first time. A former maid, this versatile musician was also a songwriter and guitarist. Legendary for strumming left-handed on a guitar designed for right-handers, rather than reverse the strings she would play the guitar backwards, "pick[ing] with her left hand and chord[ing] with her right," wrote Martin F. Kohn of the *Detroit Free Press.* Playing the guitar and banjo, using "two-finger" and "three-finger" stylings, became her musical signature. This "Cotten style" of playing the guitar has made her one of the "finest fingerpickers on record," noted a contributor for *Guitar Player* magazine.

## Child's Play

Though "Libba" Cotten had not become a professional musician until she was 67 years old, she had composed folk songs and played the guitar and banjo as a child. By approximately eight years of age Cotten, then Elizabeth Nevills, taught herself how to play the banjo. Practicing on her brother's banjo, she created a style of guitar playing that, half a century later, was imitated by many guitarists across America. As Kristin Baggelaar and Donald Milton remarked in *Folk Music: More Than a Song,* "Libba Cotten's bass runs

are used frequently by other guitarists, and her basic picking styles have become standard patterns for folk guitar.'' At age 11 she composed the classic folk song ''Freight Train.'' Copyrights to the song, however, were not secured to her until 1957, some 50 years after its original composition. By age 14 she had collected a generous array of rag and dance tunes, some of which she had composed herself.

From approximately the ages of 12 to 15, Elizabeth worked as a housekeeper for neighbors in her hometown of Chapel Hill, North Carolina, a position she would hold on and off for most of her life. She earned 75 cents a month. When she had enough money saved, she bought her first guitar, a Sears & Roebuck Stella demonstrator guitar for $3.75, and kept her family up nights as she practiced religiously. Urged by the Baptist Church, however, to give up music and attend to more serious and appropriate activities for a young African American woman of her time, Elizabeth abandoned her guitar and took a walk down the aisle.

## The Domestic Life

Elizabeth Nevills married Frank Cotten in February of 1910 when she was 15 years old and had one child, a daughter, Lillie, by the time she was 16. She, Frank, and Lillie frequently moved between Chapel Hill, Washington, D.C., and New York City for Frank's business. They finally settled in New York City as a family where Frank eventually owned his own business. During this time Elizabeth held a string of odd jobs, mainly housekeeping and some work in a furniture store. The marriage was not a lasting one, however. As soon as their daughter married, Elizabeth and Frank

Cotten divorced, and Elizabeth moved to Washington, D.C., to live with her daughter, and eventually grandchildren and great-grandchildren.

In Washington, D.C., in late 1940s, Elizabeth Cotten worked in a popular downtown department store called Lansburgh's before the holidays. Elizabeth worked on the fifth floor where dolls were sold. One day a woman came to the store with her two daughters and bought some dolls from Elizabeth. The woman was Ruth Crawford Seeger, a noted music teacher and composer of folk songs and her husband, Charles Seeger, was a musicologist. As the dolls were being packaged, one of the little girls, Peggy Seeger, wandered away from her mother and sister. Elizabeth found the little lost girl and returned her to her mother. Ever grateful to her, Mrs. Seeger offered Elizabeth a job as her family's Saturday housekeeper. Shortly after her encounter with Ruth Seeger, Elizabeth quit her sales position at Lansburgh's and accepted Mrs. Seeger's offer. Elizabeth worked for the Seegers and remained friends with them for many years.

## A Musical Maid

The Seeger household provided fertile ground for Elizabeth's musical talent to take root and grow. It was in the Seeger home that Elizabeth Cotten, besides ironing and baking bread, developed her craft as a musician. Ruth Seeger was in the process of compiling a selection of folksongs for children and teaching her own children, Mike, Peggy, and Penny, about folk music when Elizabeth joined the family. ''Libba,'' Peggy's childhood nickname for Elizabeth, learned along with the kids. Elizabeth practiced on Peggy's guitar, fooled around with the chords every chance she got, and sang out a few tunes to accompany the music, often in the kitchen with the door closed. One Saturday, while the Seegers were practicing their music and singing together, ''Libba'' casually announced that she used to play the guitar. The Seegers, thus, first heard ''Freight Train'' in their own home.

The significance and subsequent popularity of ''Freight Train'' can be traced to its beginnings. The railroad train, explained Ed Badeaux in *Sing Out,* ''[from] its very first beginnings . . . , became a symbol of freedom and adventure to America's common folk.'' As a small child, Elizabeth and her brothers, not unlike the Seegers, would gather together, play the guitar and/or banjo, and compose their own songs. ''Freight Train'' was one song Elizabeth composed entirely by herself and, as Badeaux quoted Mike Seeger, '' 'was largely inspired by the train running near her [childhood] home.' '' The popular 1960s and 1970s folk-singing group, Peter, Paul, and Mary, performed and recorded their own version of ''Freight Train'' which became an American hit in 1963.

## A Second Career

After approximately ten years with the Seegers, in 1959, at age 67, Elizabeth Cotten performed professionally for the first time. She and Mike Seeger conducted a joint concert together, the first for both of them. ''Libba'' and Mike would perform together in coffee houses and at folk festivals throughout their careers as musicians. She would accompany him and his band the "New Lost City Ramblers." In turn, he would open shows for her, tune her instruments; they performed as a team.

Peggy Seeger also figured prominently in Elizabeth's development as a recognized musician. In 1957 Peggy took "Freight Train" to Europe as the popularity of folk music returned and made the song a hit abroad. Much to her regret, though, Peggy allowed some English gentlemen to tape her performance of the song, and they unfortunately later took full credit for composition of the song. As Ed Badeaux noted, "the rights to a song are oftentimes unfortunately a matter of public domain versus individual ownership. Vocalists perform and record other people's songs all of the time. Without proper documentation, it is almost impossible for a composer to protect his/her work from theft. Fortunately for Elizabeth Cotten, though, due to growing enforcement of copyright laws in the late 1950s, she was eventually rightfully credited with composition of the classic song."

From 1957, at 65 years of age, until her death in 1987 at age 95, Elizabeth Cotten recorded approximately six albums, performed live, and toured widely. She recorded her first solo album, *Negro Folk Songs and Tunes,* in 1957 for Folkways Records. Three other of her more well known albums are *Elizabeth Cotten, Volume II: Shake Sugaree,* 1967, *Elizabeth Cotten Volume III: When I'm Gone,* 1975, and *Elizabeth Cotten Live!,* 1983, for which she won a 1985 Grammy award. She was well into her seventies when she toured America with the popular blues singer, Taj Mahal. In the last 20 years of her life she performed at universities, music halls, and folk festivals across America, by which time she was a great-grandmother. She also performed on television and visited school children nationwide as involvement for projects sponsored by the National Endowment For The Arts. In 1978 she performed at Carnegie Hall in New York City, the most prestigious concert hall for musicians in the world. At 90 years of age she started a National Tour in 1983 called Folk City. The tour began in New York City where she opened with Mike Seeger.

## A Legendary Musician

Though born poor and black in the late 1800s, at a time when racial prejudice was very much alive in America and with only a fourth grade education, Elizabeth Cotten nonetheless became a highly respected musician. "There's no one like her . . . that was ever recorded," Mike Seeger had told Jon Pareles of the *New York Times* in 1983 at the opening of his and Elizabeth's National Folk City tour. Her distinctive "Cotten-Style" of playing the guitar, coupled with her simple, sincere love for guitar and song, made her a beloved personality in folk music.

A Burl Ives Awardee in 1972 for her vital role in folk music, a Grammy Award in 1985 for her album *Elizabeth Cotten Live!,* deemed best ethnic or traditional folk recording that year, and a National Heritage Fellowship from the National Endowment For The Arts, 1984, have secured her a place in American folk music history. "Libba had," said Ed Badeaux "what most of us can only strive for—a rich musi-

cal heritage and the ability to express that heritage beautifully through her playing." Her turn-of-the-century parlor music, a mixture of gospel, ragtime, and blues, was truly music composed, played, and sung from the heart.

## Further Reading

Baggelaar, Kristin, and Donald Milton, *Folk Music: More Than a Song,* Crowell, 1976.
"For These 'Youngsters' Life Begins at 80," in *Ebony,* February 1981, p. 62.
Harris, Sheldon, *Blues Who's Who,* Da Capo Press, 1979.
Lanker, Brian, *I Dream A World,* Stewart, Tabori, and Chang, 1989, pp. 156-57.
Hitchcock, H. Wiley, and Stanley Sudie, *The New Grove Dictionary of American Music,* Macmillan Press, 1986, p. 515.
"Ordinary Women of Grace: Subjects of the I Dream a World Photography Exhibit," in *U.S. News & World Report,* February 13, 1989, p. 55.
Southern, Eileen, *Biographical Dictionary of Afro-American and African Musicians,* Greenwood Press, 1982, pp. 85-86.
Lawless, Ray M., *Folksingers and Folksongs in America,* 2nd edition, 1965, pp. 504, 682-683.
Silber, Irwin, and Fred Silber, *Folksingers' Wordbook,* Oak Publications, p. 63.
"Blues With A Feeling," in *Guitar Player,* November 1994, p. 152.
"Elizabeth Cotten at 90, Bigger Than The Tradition," in *New York Times,* January 7, 1983, January 9, 1983, June 30, 1987.
"Elizabeth Cotten, 95, Noted Folk Singer, Dies," in *Jet,* August 17, 1987, p. 18.
Badeaux, Ed, "Please Don't Tell What Train I'm On," in *Sing Out,* September 1964, pp. 7-11.
"Life Begins at 71 For N.Y. Domestic," in *Detroit Courier,* December 25, 1967.
Kohn, Martin F., "The Freight Train lady brings her songs to town," in *Detroit Free Press,* March 21, 1977.
Gerrard, Alice, "Libba Cotten," in *Frets 2,* January 1980, pp. 26-29.
Reisner, Mel, "Maid Finally Wins Grammy," in *The Indianapolis Star,* September 1, 1985.
Lane, Bill, "Past 80 and Still Singing: Octogenarians Sippie Wallace, Elizabeth Cotten, & Alberta Hunter Don't Let Age Hold Them Back," in *SEPIA,* December 1980. □

# John Cotton

**John Cotton (1584-1652) was the leading clergyman of New England's first generation, a leader in civil and religious affairs, and a persuasive writer on the theory and practice of Congregationalism.**

John Cotton was born in Derby, Derbyshire, England. His father, Roland Cotton, was a lawyer and ardent Puritan; his mother was a deeply religious woman. He entered Trinity College, Cambridge, as a sizar in his thirteenth year, and earned a scholarship to Emmanuel, where he remained for 7 years, taking his bachelor of arts degree in 1603 and his master of arts in 1606. From childhood he had been inclined to the scholar's life, and he remained at Cambridge for 7 more years, taking a bachelor of divinity degree in 1613. Only one other first-generation New Englander held this advanced degree.

During his long experience in the cloistered Cambridge University life, Cotton had learned, in addition to his impressive fund of knowledge—biblical, theological, and ecclesiastical—certain political lessons as well, to be remembered to the last day of his life; among them how to disagree and yet conform, how to be true to his own convictions and yet at the same time to be safe. He saw both sides of every question in every controversy of his career, and when he took his own position with regard to any one of the issues involved, it would be, in his own words, "a middle way." To approach his mature life with this practical political secret in mind is to find the apparent enigmas about Cotton disappearing.

Aged 29, Cotton became the vicar of the church of St. Botolph in Boston, Lincolnshire. Conscientious Puritan that he was, from the beginning of his 20-year pastorate there, he substituted many simpler forms in the liturgy and succeeded in carrying most of his congregation with him in these changes. He escaped suspicion and remained presumably safe through the employment of a lecturer, a complete conformist, who conducted the more formal services, which would be more closely watched for strict conformity. Under the eye of Archbishop Laud, however, no service would go unwatched, concealment would not be so easy, and suspicion did come.

## Escape to America

In the spring of 1632 Cotton received a summons to the Court of High Commission. Knowing what was ahead, he did not appear but went into hiding. On May 7 he sent his resignation from the post of vicar at St. Botolph's to the bishop of London and remained in hiding. Later, with his newly married second wife, he embarked in disguise for New England. He was a close friend of John Winthrop, had preached the farewell sermon at Southampton to the vanguard of Winthrop's company in 1630, and had kept in touch with the New England Boston happenings since that date. His first thought for immediate escape had been Holland, but Thomas Hooker's report had changed his plan.

Cotton arrived in Boston on Sept. 4, 1633, and on Sept. 30 was made teacher of the Boston church, a post which he continued to hold for the 19 years he had yet to live. Through these years he was a leading figure in civil as well as religious affairs. Among pulpit men he was the most learned in America, not so eloquent as Thomas Hooker of Hartford and not so persuasive as John Davenport of New Haven, but these two men were his nearest rivals. He stood at the top.

One of Cotton's early civil services was the preparation of an abstract of the laws of New England which was, however, rejected by the colony in favor of one nearer to the Mosaic code. During his first 10 years he had a prominent part in the two controversies which rocked New England to its deepest foundations, the exile of Roger Williams and the heresies of Anne Hutchinson. The Williams controversy unearthed the basic question of the relation between church and state. Magistrates are God's deputies and their power goes as far as life and death, said Cotton. Roger Williams declared that a man's religious loyalties are untouchable by civil power. They were speaking for a future neither man would live to see. In the Anne Hutchinson controversy Cotton was in one of the most uncomfortable situations of his life. At the synod called to list her errors, he split hairs with the accusing brethren over scriptural interpretations to justify his own orthodox preaching; at her trial before the church he strenuously tried to guide her in an orthodox path, only to be obliged to turn against her at the end. This was no doubt a sad moment for him. He had tried to save her and orthodoxy at the same time, but it could not be.

## Cotton's Writings

Cotton's printed record is impressive. His exposition of early Congregationalism's purpose and practice is probably his most valuable contribution to American religious history. Among the several titles which illuminate this subject are *The Keyes of the Kingdom of Heaven* (1644), *The Way of the Churches of Christ in New England* (1645), and *The Way of Congregational Churches Cleared* (1645). A statement of his religious views called forth by the Anne Hutchinson controversy in 1636 appears in *Sixteen Questions of Serious and Necessary Consequences Propounded unto Mr. John Cotton with His Answers* (1644). The best volume for the two overlapping debates with Roger Williams is *The Bloudy Tennent Washed and Made White in the Bloud of the Lambe* (1644), together with *The Controversie concern-*

ing *Liberty of Conscience in Matters of Religion* (1646, 1649). Perhaps the most familiar title in his long list is *Milk for Babes, Drawn out of the Breasts of Both Testaments* (1646), which contains the substance of 100 sermons and recalls the discipline of uncounted children over three generations.

In his own day Cotton was of great importance. But in the long view of 3 centuries he was not a great man. He belonged to the 17th century and within tight limits. He did not see the changes that were already at work within his own Boston. He had no sympathy with the common man. But the world of willing obedience to authority would not be the world of the future in America. For these reasons his life and thought probably reveal more of what lay behind America's history in its first chapter than those of any other public man of his generation.

## Further Reading

Two early accounts of Cotton are by his grandson, Cotton Mather, *Magnalia Christi Americana: The Ecclesiastical History of New England* (2 vols., 1702), and by his friend Samuel Whiting, *Concerning the Life of the Famous Mr. Cotton,* which can be found in Alexander Young, *Chronicles of the First Planters of the Colony of Massachusetts Bay from 1623 to 1636* (1846). The best modern study is Larzer Ziff, *The Career of John Cotton* (1962). There is an extensive treatment of Cotton in Perry Miller, *Orthodoxy in Massachusetts, 1630-1650* (1933). Studies devoted to particular aspects of Cotton's life are Emery Battis, *Saints and Sectaries* (1962), which recounts Cotton's involvement in the Anne Hutchinson controversy, and Irwin H. Polishook, *Roger Williams, John Cotton and Religious Freedom* (1967), which attempts a balanced view of the Williams-Cotton controversy.

## Additional Sources

Norton, John, *Abel being dead, yet speaketh: a biography of John Cotton,* Delmar, N.Y.: Scholars' Facsimiles & Reprints, 1978.
☐

# Charles Edward Coughlin

**Charles Edward Coughlin (1891-1979) was a Canadian-born Roman Catholic priest who became a political organizer in the United States and, during the 1930s, a radical right-wing radio personality.**

Charles Edward Coughlin was born on October 25, 1891, in Hamilton, Ontario, Canada, and received his education in Catholic schools and at St. Michael's College of the University of Toronto. At the age of 20, he began studies for the priesthood, receiving his ordination in 1916. After assisting in several parishes in the Detroit area, Coughlin was formally incardinated into the Detroit diocese in 1923. Three years later, Coughlin's bishop assigned him to the new Shrine of the Little Flower Church in the suburban community of Royal Oak, Michigan.

In 1926, Coughlin started a weekly broadcast over the local radio station which proved so popular that, within four years, the Columbia Broadcasting System began carrying it nationally. A series of florid denunciations of communism in 1930 gave him a national reputation and occasioned his appearance before the Committee to Investigate Communist Activities, of the United States House of Representatives. By the end of the year, however, with the country in the throes of the Great Depression, Coughlin had shifted his broadcasts to emphasize the necessity for drastically altering American capitalism under a program keyed to monetary inflation called "social justice," which Coughlin based on the late-19th-century papal encyclical *Rerum novarum.*

In 1931, the network, worried by Coughlin's attacks on the Hoover administration and by other contentious material in his addresses, discontinued his weekly broadcasts. With contributions from his listeners, Coughlin organized his own radio network, which grew to 26 stations.

During the 1932 presidential campaign, Coughlin vigorously championed Franklin D. Roosevelt, proclaiming that America's choice was "Roosevelt or ruin." Roosevelt carefully cultivated Coughlin and benefited substantially from his support in the first year of the New Deal, but he always kept the priest at arm's length. Coughlin, however, saw himself as an unofficial member of the Roosevelt administration and assumed that the president would follow his advice for combating the Depression, particularly his advocacy of massive currency inflation through silver coinage. When Roosevelt refused to fully accept Coughlin's

schemes, the priest became a loud critic of the administration.

In 1934, Coughlin formed the National Union for Social Justice to combat communism and to fight for currency inflation and government control of big business. In 1936 Coughlin, determined to stop Roosevelt's re-election, made the National Union the nucleus for the Union party, which also amalgamated much of the followings of the late Huey Long and of Francis E. Townsend, a crusader for old-age pensions. Roosevelt was overwhelmingly re-elected, while the Union party's candidate polled less than 900,000 votes.

After 1936, Coughlin's influence declined rapidly. He organized the Christian Front to succeed the National Union and trained his oratorical guns on Roosevelt's foreign policy, which he believed would inevitably involve the country in another war. He also concentrated on the fancied internal menaces of Communists and Jews (who seemed interchangeable in Coughlin's thinking). Fascist Italy and Nazi Germany, he announced, were bulwarks against "Jewish-Communist" power in Europe. Coughlin enunciated a program for an anti-Semitic, fascist-style corporate state, under which established political institutions in the United States would virtually disappear.

Coughlin's anti-Roosevelt oratory became more shrill when World War II broke out in Europe in 1939 and the administration provided more and more assistance to the Allied governments. In 1940, the larger stations in Coughlin's radio network, acting on the basis of a recent National Association of Broadcasters ruling barring "controversial" speakers, refused to renew his broadcasting contract. When he continued his attacks on the government after Pearl Harbor, his bishop officially silenced him and the Post Office Department banned his weekly newspaper from the mail.

With his newsletter banned, his radio network gone, and his bishop silencing him, Coughlin confined his activities to those of an ordinary parish priest, in 1942. He retired from his pastorate at the Shrine of the Little Flower in 1966. He concerned himself with his newly-built home in Birmingham, Michigan, and still wrote pamphlets denouncing Communism.

Coughlin died on October 27, 1979 at his home in suburban Detroit. He was remembered as the fiery, vibrant, and opinionated priest who followed the directive of his church over his own feelings towards the government. Near his death, Coughlin said he "couldn't take back much of what [he] had said and did in the old days when people still listened to [him]."

## Further Reading

A biography officially authorized by Father Coughlin and written by a close friend and aide is Louis B. Ward *Father Charles E. Coughlin* (1933), it must be read with great caution. Charles J. Tull *Father Coughlin and the New Deal* (1965), is a detached, scholarly study of the radio priest's career during the 1930s. A fuller account of the Union party movement of 1936, in which Coughlin was the central figure, is given in David H. Bennett *Demagogues in the Depression: American Radicals and the Union Party, 1932-1936* (1969). For information on the up-

surge of Catholic social activism in the 1930s, which furnished much of the rationale for Coughlin's activities, see Aaron I. Abell *American Catholicism and Social Action: A Search for Social Justice, 1865-1950* (1960). There is also information about Coughlin in Arthur M. Schlesinger, Jr. *The Age of Roosevelt* (3 vols., 1957-1960), Rexford G. Tugwell *The Democratic Roosevelt* (1957), and George Wolfskill and John A. Hudson *All but the People: Franklin D. Roosevelt and His Critics, 1933-1939* (1969). Coughlin's obituary appears in the October 28, 1979 issue of the *New York Times*. □

# Charles Augustin de Coulomb

**The French physicist Charles Augustin de Coulomb (1736-1806) was famous for establishing the relation for computing the force between electrical charges. He also did pioneering work on sliding and fluid friction.**

Charles Augustin de Coulomb was born into a distinguished family of Angoulême on June 14, 1736. After being educated in Paris, he spent 9 years in Martinique as an army engineer. Ill health forced him to return to France in 1776, where during the next 13 years his scientific work brought him fame, military advancement, and membership in the Royal Academy of Sciences. He was appointed intendant of France's waters and fountains in 1784. The next 5 years were spent in writing his memoirs on electricity and magnetism. Coulomb had become a noted and influential figure in the academic world but resigned all his positions at the outbreak of the Revolution. He returned to Paris in 1802 for an appointment as one of the inspector generals of public instruction.

Coulomb's 1779 memoir, *The Theory of Simple Machines,* is a compilation of his early experiments on statics and mechanics in which he makes the first formal statement of the laws governing friction. In 1784 he studied torsional elasticity, finding the relationship between the various factors involved in the small oscillations of a body subjected to torsion.

His most notable papers are the seven which Coulomb presented before the academy in 1785 and 1786. In the first he announced the measurement of the electrical forces of repulsion between electrical charges. He extended this work to the forces of attraction in his second memoir. This led to further quantitative work and his famous law of force for electrostatic charges (Coulomb's law). The subsequent papers dealt with the loss of electricity of bodies and the distribution of electricity on conductors. He introduced the "proof plane" and by using it was able to demonstrate the relationship between charge density and the curvature of a conducting surface.

Magnetism was the subject of Coulomb's early studies and the one to which he returned in later years. He noted that magnetism obeyed a relation of attraction and repulsion similar to that for electrical forces. He also established the equation of motion of a magnet in a magnetic field, showing the derivation of the magnetic moment from the period of small oscillations.

In 1801 Coulomb published another important paper, in which he presented the results he obtained by allowing a cylinder to oscillate in a liquid, thus providing a way to find relative liquid viscosities.

Of Coulomb, Thomas Young wrote, "his moral character is said to have been as correct as his mathematical investigations." He remained in Paris until his death on Aug. 23, 1806.

## Further Reading

Most of the information on Coulomb is in French. In English, descriptions of his experiments are in William Francis Magie, *A Source Book in Physics* (1935); Duane Roller and Duane H. D. Roller, *The Development of the Concept of Electric Charge: Electricity from the Greeks to Coulomb* (1954); and Morris H. Shamos, ed., *Great Experiments in Physics* (1960). For general background on the scientific environment of the time see Abraham Wolf, *A History of Science, Technology and Philosophy in the Eighteenth Century* (1939). Brief references also appear in *A History of the Theories of Aether and Electricity: From the Age of Descartes to the Close of the Nineteenth Century* (1910), and Hugh Hildreth Skilling, *Exploring Electricity: Man's Unfinished Quest* (1948). □

# George Gordon Coulton

**The English historian and polemicist George Gordon Coulton (1858-1947) was the leading medievalist of his day. His primary interest was ecclesiastical history.**

George Coulton, the son of John James and Sarah Coulton, was born on Oct. 15, 1858, in King's Lynn. In 1877 Coulton entered St. Catharine's College, Cambridge, where he obtained his degree. He then studied for holy orders in the Anglican Church and was ordained deacon in 1883 and priest in 1884. The following year he resigned from the priesthood and began teaching at various private schools. In 1895 he sustained a nervous breakdown; after his recovery he left the academic life to work with a friend who ran a coaching company at Eastbourne. Spending 13 years there in relative financial security gave him the opportunity to pursue his own studies.

During this period Coulton decided to devote his life to the study of medieval life and thought, with special emphasis on the organization and operation of the ecclesiastical system of those centuries. He began to publish works in this field, such as *From St. Francis to Dante* (1906) and *Chaucer and His England* (1908). His developing reputation as a medievalist led to his appointment to the prestigious post of Birkbeck lecturer in ecclesiastical history at Trinity College, Cambridge, in 1910.

In 1919 Coulton was elected to what was then the sole university lectureship in English and later the same year was made a fellow of St. John's College, Cambridge. From that time onward, except during World War II when he was guest lecturer at Toronto, he remained at Cambridge.

Coulton's leading works are considered to be *Five Centuries of Religion* (4 vols., 1923-1950), *The Medieval Village* (1925), *Art and the Reformation* (1928), and *Medieval Panorama* (1938). His depictions in the area of ecclesiastical history, especially of monasticism, have been criticized as being unduly dark and pessimistic.

Throughout his life Coulton supported and vigorously argued in behalf of compulsory military service. He was also an unwavering advocate of what he termed the "moderate Protestant position." In both causes his rather uncompromising attitude was distasteful to many of his antagonists and colleagues. Nevertheless, he felt that his deep moral convictions left him no alternative on this subject. In the cause of compulsory military service he personally investigated conditions in France and Switzerland, spoke and wrote against pacifist views, and published many pamphlets and books, the best-known being *The Case for Compulsory Military Service* (1917). His polemics in religion also embroiled him in controversy throughout his life, particularly with Catholic historians. In fact, in the opinion of several critics his controversies generated more animosity and obfuscation than light.

## Further Reading

Coulton's autobiography is *Fourscore Years* (1943). Sarah Campion, *Father* (1948), is a biographical memoir by his daughter. □

# George S. Counts

**American educator and educational sociologist George S. Counts (1889-1974) was an authority on Soviet education and a leading spokesman for the social reconstructionist point of view in American education.**

George Sylvester Counts, son of James Wilson Counts and Mertie Florella (Gamble) Counts, was born on a farm near Baldwin City, Kansas, on December 9, 1889. His introduction to formal education consisted of two years spent in a one-room school house. Counts managed to complete the work of four grades in those two years, and the experience left him convinced of the merits of ungraded schools. He completed his education in the conventional public schools of Baldwin City, nevertheless, and graduated from high school in 1907.

Counts attended college at Baker University, a Methodist institution located in Baldwin City, and graduated at the head of his class with a B.A. degree in 1911. He then taught science and mathematics for a year at Sumner County high school in Wellington, Kansas. The following year he accepted a joint appointment as a teacher and school principal at the high school in Peabody, Kansas. This brief but rewarding exposure to teaching and school administration helped Counts decide to pursue advanced study in education, and he enrolled in the graduate school of the University of Chicago in 1913. Meanwhile, in September of 1913, he married Lois Hazel Bailey, the daughter of a Methodist minister. They had two daughters.

### Early Career in Education

At Chicago Counts majored in education and minored in sociology under such distinguished scholars as Charles H. Judd and Albion W. Small. Counts took his Ph.D. with honors in 1916 and was named head of the department of education and director of the summer school at Delaware College in Newark. During the next ten years he held successive teaching posts at Harris Teachers College, St. Louis (1918-1919); the University of Washington (1919-1920); Yale University (1920-1926); and the University of Chicago (1926-1927). In the fall of 1927 he became a member of the faculty at Teachers College, Columbia University, where he served as associate director of the International Institute from 1927 to 1932 and as professor of education until his retirement in 1956. During his career he also lectured at a number of leading universities, including Harvard, Illinois, Michigan, Stanford, and Virginia.

The author of 29 books and more than 100 articles, Counts was also an active participant in several professional and civic organizations, notably the American Academy of Political and Social Science, the American Association of

University Professors, the American Civil Liberties Union, the American Federation of Teachers, the American Historical Association, the American Sociology Society, the Liberal Party of New York State, the National Education Association, and the Progressive Education Association.

Prior to his appointment to the Teachers College faculty, Counts had served as a member of the Philippine Educational Survey Commission. This experience, together with his work in connection with the International Institute at Columbia, afforded him the opportunity to contribute to the relatively new field of comparative education. Counts focused his international studies on the social institutions and educational system of the Soviet Union and in due course became perhaps America's foremost authority on Russian education. *A Ford Crosses Russia* (1930), *The Soviet Challenge to America* (1931), *The Country of the Blind, Soviet System of Mind Control* (1949), and *The Challenge of Soviet Education* (1957) were some of his noteworthy writings on Soviet culture.

Apart from his concentration on Russian education, much of Counts's teaching and research was devoted to understanding the school as a social institution, its relations to other social institutions, and its potential for fostering social betterment. Some of his early efforts along these lines reflected the prevailing interest among educators, notably Counts's mentor Charles Judd, in the application of empirical and statistical methods to the study of education and signalled Counts' arrival as an authority in areas such as secondary education and educational sociology. With regard to the latter, his *School and Society in Chicago* (1928) was generally regarded as a landmark study of a school system within its social context.

*The Selective Character of American Secondary Education* (1922) and *The Social Composition of Boards of Education* (1927) were two other significant books published by Counts during the 1920s. The former argued that schools were partly responsible for the continuance of social inequality, and the latter pointed to the influence on American education of the existing power structure in society. In these and other works completed during the 1920s, Counts introduced themes that foreshadowed the social reconstructionism with which he was identified in the 1930s, and, indeed, anticipated many of the arguments advanced by social and educational theorists several decades later.

### A Different Approach to Education

In 1932, at the nadir of the Great Depression, Counts combined three speeches into a slim volume called *Dare the School Build a New Social Order?* The book led to his general acceptance as leader of the social reconstructionists, a group within the society-centered wing (as opposed to the child-centered wing) of the Progressive Education Association, that was intent on using the schools to initiate social change. With characteristic boldness, Counts argued for the replacement of traditional capitalism with some form of democratic collectivism in order to avert social and economic chaos. He called for educators to shape the attitudes of children so that they would be receptive to the idea that collective control of the economy was necessary. Thus schools, according to Counts, could become the incubators of a great society dedicated to cooperation rather than to exploitation. Anticipating the charge that his scheme smacked of indoctrination, Counts declared that all education entailed indoctrination to some extent.

Two years later Counts helped to launch *The Social Frontier,* a reformist journal that established itself as forum for social and educational debate and attracted some of the most distinguished liberal writers of the period to its pages. Counts was the first editor of the journal, serving in that capacity from 1934 to 1937.

All of this enhanced Counts's stature among the reconstructionists (or the "frontier group," as they were alternatively labeled) but also made him a prime target for the criticism of conservatives who viewed him as something of a communist sympathizer, bent on subverting the American way of life. Counts, however, described himself as "a cross between a Jeffersonian Democrat and a Lincolnian Republican, struggling with the old problem of human freedom and equality in the age of science and technology." It should be noted, in this connection, that Counts denounced Soviet communism in his later writings and vigorously opposed communist efforts to infiltrate the American Federation of Teachers during his term as president of that organization from 1939 to 1942.

Although Counts is probably best remembered for his ties to progressive education and social reconstructionism in the 1930s, he continued to explore the relationship between democracy and education throughout his career. His major post-war writings included *Education and the Promise of America* (1946), *Education and American Civilization* (1952), and *Education and the Foundations of Human Freedom* (1962).

Following his mandatory retirement from Columbia in 1956, Counts taught at the University of Pittsburgh, the University of Colorado, Michigan State University, and Northwestern University. He closed out his career as a distinguished visiting professor at Southern Illinois University from 1962 to 1971. Counts died on November 10, 1974.

## Further Reading

An autobiographical sketch of Counts may be found in *Twentieth Century Authors: First Supplement* (1955). Gerald L. Gutek, *The Educational Theory of George S. Counts* (1970) is the most comprehensive study of Counts's thought. John L. Childs, *American Pragmatism and Education* (1956) includes an informative chapter on Counts's career, and Lawrence A. Cremin, *The Transformation of the School* (1961), is an excellent background source. The August 1975 College of Education *Newsletter,* Southern Illinois University at Carbondale, was a memorial issue to Counts.

## Additional Sources

Counts, George S. (George Sylvester), 1889-1974., *George S. Counts, educator for a new age,* Carbondale: Southern Illinois University Press; London: Feffer & Simons, 1980.
Gutek, Gerald Lee, *George S. Counts and American civilization: the educator as social theorist,* Macon, GA: Mercer University Press, 1984. □

# Archibald Scott Couper

**The British chemist Archibald Scott Couper (1831-1892) shares with Kekulé the distinction of recognizing the tetravalency of carbon and the capacity of carbon atoms to combine to form chains, thereby providing the basis for structural organic chemistry.**

Archibald Scott Couper was born on March 31, 1831, at Kirkintilloch in Dumbartonshire, Scotland, the son of a prosperous cotton weaver. He commenced his university studies at Glasgow mainly in classics, spent the summer semester of 1852 in Berlin, and returned to Scotland to complete his university course in logic and metaphysics at Edinburgh. He spent the period 1854-1856 in Berlin and during this time decided to study chemistry.

Couper entered the laboratory of Charles Wurtz in Paris in the autumn of 1856 and remained there until his return to Scotland in 1858; during these 2 years he made all his contributions to chemistry: two papers containing experimental contributions and his now famous memoir "On a New Chemical Theory." A few months after his return to Edinburgh to be assistant to Lyon Playfair, in the autumn of 1858, he suffered a severe nervous breakdown, followed by a general breakdown in health. He retired to Kirkintilloch and lived there incapable of intellectual work and completely lost to chemistry until his death 34 years later.

## Work on the Element Carbon

The story of Couper's work, its subsequent disappearance from view, and its later recognition, largely through the efforts of Richard Anschütz, as a major piece of chemical history is one of the most remarkable in science. Early in 1858 Couper, then 27 and after only some 3 years' contact with chemistry, asked Wurtz to present Couper's manuscript "On a New Chemical Theory" to the French Academy. Wurtz, however, delayed taking any steps, and in the interim August Kekulé's paper "On the Constitution and Metamorphoses of Chemical Compounds and on the Chemical Nature of Carbon" appeared, containing essentially similar proposals. Couper protested to Wurtz about his procrastination but was, it is said, shown out of the laboratory.

Couper's paper was, however, finally presented by Jean Baptiste Dumas to the academy on June 14, 1858, and published in the *Comptes rendus;* fuller versions were subsequently published in English and French. After pointing out the inadequacy of current theories, Couper wrote in his paper: "I propose to consider the single element carbon. This body is found to have two highly distinguished characteristics: (1) It combines with equal numbers of equivalents of hydrogen, chlorine, oxygen, sulphur, etc. (2) It enters into chemical combination with itself. These two properties, in my opinion, explain all that is characteristic of organic chemistry. This will be rendered apparent as I advance. This second property is, so far as I am aware, here signalized for the first time."

### Valence and Aromatic Compounds

Couper also introduced the use of a line to indicate the valence linkage between two atoms and, had he used 16 rather than 8 for the atomic weight of oxygen, his chemical formulas would have been almost identical with those used today. It is also remarkable that in his paper he represents cyanuric acid by a formula containing a ring of three carbon and three nitrogen atoms joined by valence lines—the first ring formula ever published. The introduction of ring formulas is often ascribed to Kekulé, who in 1865 used this concept to develop his formula for benzene. It is interesting to speculate whether Couper might have anticipated Kekulé's formulation of aromatic compounds had he been able to continue his chemical work. But Couper's paper "On a New Chemical Theory" remains a landmark in the history of organic chemistry.

### Further Reading

Alexander Findlay, *A Hundred Years of Chemistry* (1937; 3d ed. 1965), discusses Couper's work and includes a short bibliography. See also Eduard Farber, *The Evolution of Chemistry: A History of Its Ideas, Methods and Materials* (1952; 2d ed. 1969). □

# James Hamilton Couper

**American agriculturist James Hamilton Couper (1794-1866), a leading Southern planter, was among the first to apply scientific research to agricultural operations.**

James H. Couper was born on March 4, 1794, in Sunbury, Ga. His father had emigrated from Scotland in 1775. The family moved several times, settling on Georgia's Atlantic coast, where Couper's father bought land on St. Simon Island and formed a plantation partnership with a friend, James Hamilton. Their business was raising long-fibered sea island cotton. In 1804 Couper's father bought another tract of land on the Altamaha River near Brunswick, Ga. Couper grew up the heir of a wealthy and influential family.

Among Couper's advantages was a college education; he graduated from Yale College in 1814 at the age of 20. He traveled to Holland to study methods of water control for possible use on the Georgia plantations. After his return he became manager of the estate on the Altamaha River. The family fortunes suffered reversals in the 1820s, and Couper's father failed in business in 1826. Hamilton paid off his partner's obligations in exchange for a half interest in the river estate. The younger Couper acquired Hamilton's half interest the following year and remained as manager. When he inherited his father's acres on St. Simon Island, he emerged as a leading Southern planter, supervising some 1,500 slaves.

Couper soon began scientific research and experimentation, setting the pace for his contemporaries and successors in the South. His scientific diking and drainage system at the Altamaha plantation was soon copied by others. Beginning as a cotton planter, he later raised several other commercial crops, including rice and sugarcane. At Altamaha in 1829 he built the most complete, modern sugar mill in the South. He was also the first American to build and operate a cottonseed oil mill; he erected two mills. Although he failed in the cottonseed oil business, his successors in the South found the industry a most prosperous one.

Couper was one of the South's planter aristocrats; he had impeccable manners, a graceful way in conversation, an extensive library, and high social prestige. The Civil War freed his slaves, claimed two of his sons, and destroyed his life. Couper died in 1866; few had better symbolized the meaning of the old, antebellum slavocracy.

### Further Reading

Couper's associate, Charles Spalding Wylly, wrote *The Seed That Was Sown in the Colony of Georgia: The Harvest and the Aftermath, 1740-1870* (1910), a good source of information on Couper's life. Other helpful works include Frances Butler Leigh, *Ten Years on a Georgian Plantation since the War* (1883); Ralph Betts Flanders, *Plantation Slavery in Georgia* (1933); and Lewis Cecil Gray, *History of Agriculture in the Southern United States to 1860* (2 vols., 1933-1941). □

# François Couperin

**François Couperin (1668-1733), called Couperin le Grand, was a French composer, organist, and harpsichordist. His harpsichord and organ works are the touchstones of the 18th-century elegant style.**

François Couperin was born on Nov. 10, 1668, in Paris. The Couperin dynasty was the most famous musical family in France during the 17th and 18th centuries. The first Couperin came to Paris from the region of Brie and became organist for the church of St-Gervais; his brothers soon followed. Couperin's father, Charles, succeeded his brother Louis on the latter's death in 1661. Charles died in 1679, and although François was only 11 years old he was named as Charles's successor at St-Gervais. The post was held open for François both on legal grounds and in the light of his extraordinary talent until he reached the age of 18.

In 1692 Couperin produced his first publications, pieces composed in the Italian manner. While retaining his post at St-Gervais, he entered the service of King Louis XIV in 1693 as one of the organists of the King's chapel at Versailles. Couperin prospered at court, being appointed master of music for the royal children in 1694 and ennobled in 1696.

Couperin composed much church music for use at Versailles. His keyboard and chamber music circulated in aristocratic circles. In 1713 the King granted Couperin the privilege of publishing his own music. He first issued a series of harpsichord suites (which he called *ordres*) written over the preceding 2 decades. In 1714 he published the three surviving sets from a projected group of nine *Leçons des Ténèbres. L'Art de toucher le clavecin,* his major theoretical work, appeared in 1716. The second *order* of harpsichord pieces came out in 1717, and the following year Couperin succeeded to the post of *ordinaire de la musique* to the King. Encouraged by the success of his publications, Couperin brought out sets and suites of earlier compositions in rapid order, and in 1730 his fourth *ordre* of harpsichord pieces was put together with the assistance of his family. He died on Sept. 12, 1733.

The bulk of Couperin's published work disappeared shortly after his death. Since his only son is presumed to have died in infancy, the post of organist at St-Gervais passed to a nephew. The position remained in the family until the French Revolution, and the dynasty itself died out in the 19th century.

## Harpsichord and Church Compositions

Couperin's harpsichord music is marked by a very elegant style and reflects the urbane, sophisticated quality of courtly and intellectual life as it was experienced in the last years of the reign of Louis XIV. Couperin arranged his harpsichord music into dance suites, with faintly suggestive or arcanely humorous titles; these character pieces represent the height of the cultured taste of the 18th-century connoisseur.

The music is not programmatic in the common sense of the term. Instead, Couperin only suggests or hints at the conditions of civilized life in the manner of a memoir. Such titles as *La Diane* and *La Charolaise* from Ordre I or *La Baccaneles* and *Le Réveil-matin* from Ordre II are but intimate suggestions or reminiscences; the titles are not descriptive any more than the music itself pretends to describe the actualities implied in the title.

Couperin's church music is marked by a solemn stateliness. Although not at all pompous it is entirely in keeping with the demands of the court, and in his old age Louis XIV preferred order, serenity, and restraint above all else.

## Manual of Performance Practice

*L'Art de toucher le clavecin* is the most important theoretical work with regard to performance practice surviving from 18th-century France. Here Couperin describes precise articulations for the very complicated style of ornamentation which dominated his harpsichord music. For Couperin ornamentation is not an additive process but one absolutely integral to the construction of the music itself; hence, accuracy is mandatory. This keyboard manual is also very illuminating with regard to such topics as fingering, phrasing, and *notes inégales* (the practice of performing evenly written notes unequally).

The accomplishments of Couperin le Grand are still among the least comprehended and appreciated of major 18th-century composers. Only with careful, scrupulously accurate re-creations in the proper style by the harpsichord

can one begin to understand Couperin's supreme compositional gifts.

## Further Reading

The standard work in English on Couperin's music is Wilfred H. Mellers, *François Couperin and the French Classical Tradition* (1950).

## Additional Sources

Beaussant, Philippe, *François Couperin,* Paris: Fayard, 1980. □

# Jean Desiré Gustave Courbet

**Jean Desiré Gustave Courbet (1819-1877) was a French painter whose powerful pictures of peasants and scenes of everyday life established him as the leading figure of the realist movement of the mid-19th century.**

Gustave Courbet was born at Ornans on June 10, 1819. He appears to have inherited his vigorous temperament from his father, a landowner and prominent personality in the Franche-Comté region. At the age of 18 Gustave went to the Collège Royal at Besançon. There he openly expressed his dissatisfaction with the traditional classical subjects he was obliged to study, going so far as to lead a revolt among the students. In 1838 he was enrolled as an *externe* and could simultaneously attend the classes of Charles Flajoulot, director of the École des Beaux-Arts. At the college in Besançon, Courbet became fast friends with Max Buchon, whose *Essais Poétiques* (1839) he illustrated with four lithographs.

In 1840 Courbet went to Paris to study law, but he decided to become a painter and spent much time copying in the Louvre. In 1844 his *Self-Portrait with Black Dog* was exhibited at the Salon. The following year he submitted five pictures; only one, *Le Guitarrero,* was accepted. After a complete rejection in 1847, the Liberal Jury of 1848 accepted all 10 of his entries, and the critic Champfleury, who was to become Courbet's first staunch apologist, highly praised the *Walpurgis Night.*

Courbet achieved artistic maturity with *After Dinner at Ornans,* which was shown at the Salon of 1849. By 1850 the last traces of sentimentality disappeared from his work as he strove to achieve an honest imagery of the lives of simple people, but the monumentality of the concept in conjunction with the rustic subject matter proved to be widely unacceptable. At this time the notion of Courbet's "vulgarity" became current as the press began to lampoon his pictures and criticize his penchant for the ugly. His nine entries in the Salon of 1850 included the *Portrait of Berlioz,* the *Man with the Pipe,* the *Return from the Fair,* the *Stone Breakers,* and, largest of all, the *Burial at Ornans,* which contains over 40 life-size figures whose rugged features and

static poses are reinforced by the somber landscape. A decade later Courbet wrote: "The basis of realism is the negation of the ideal. . . . *Burial at Ornans* was in reality the burial of romanticism. . . ."

In 1851 the Second Empire was officially proclaimed, and during the next 20 years Courbet remained an uncompromising opponent of Emperor Napoleon III. At the Salon of 1853, where the painter exhibited three works, the Emperor pronounced one of them, *The Bathers,* obscene; nevertheless, it was purchased by a Montpellier innkeeper, Alfred Bruyas, who became the artist's patron and host. While visiting Bruyas in 1854 Courbet painted his first seascapes. Among them is the *Seashore at Palavas,* in which the artist is seen waving his hat at the great expanse of water. In a letter to Jules Vallès written in this period Courbet remarked: "Oh sea! Your voice is tremendous, but it will never succeed in drowning out the voice of Fame shouting my name to the entire world."

Courbet was handsome and flamboyant, naively boastful, and aware of his own worth. His extraordinary selfconfidence is also evident in another painting of 1854, *The Meeting,* in which Courbet, stick in hand, approaches Bruyas and his servant, who welcome him with reverential attitudes. It has recently been shown that the picture bears a relationship to the theme of the Wandering Jew as it was commonly represented in the naive imagery of the popular Épinal prints.

Of the 14 paintings Courbet submitted to the Paris World Exhibition of 1855, 3 major ones were rejected. In retaliation, he showed 40 of his pictures at a private pavilion he erected opposite the official one. In the preface to his catalog Courbet expressed his intention "to be able to represent the customs, the ideas, the appearance of my own era according to my own valuation; to be not only a painter but a man as well; in short, to create living art."

One of the rejected works was the enormous painting *The Studio,* the full title of which was *Real Allegory, Representing a Phase of Seven Years of My Life as a Painter.* The work is charged with a symbolism which, in spite of obvious elements, remains obscure. At the center, between the two worlds expressed by the inhabitants of the left and right sides of the picture, is Courbet painting a landscape while a nude looks over his shoulder and a child admires his work. Champfleury found the notion of a "real allegory" ridiculous and concluded that Courbet had lost the conviction and simplicity of the earlier works. *Young Ladies by the Seine* (1856) only served to further convince the critic of Courbet's diminished powers.

But if Courbet had begun to disappoint the members of the old realist circle, his popular reputation, particularly outside France, was growing. He visited Frankfurt in 1858-1859, where he took part in elaborate hunting parties and painted a number of scenes based on direct observation. His *Stag Drinking* was exhibited in Besançon, where Courbet won a medal, and in 1861 his work, as well as a lecture on his artistic principles, met with great success in Antwerp. With the support of the critic Jules Castagnary, Courbet opened a school where students dissatisfied with the training at the École des Beaux-Arts could hear him extol the virtues of independence from authority and dedication to nature.

Courbet's art of the mid-1860s no longer conveyed the democratic principles so clearly embodied in the earlier works. He turned his attention increasingly to landscapes, portraits, and erotic nudes based, in part, on mythological themes. These include the *Venus and Psyche* (1864; and a variant entitled *The Awakening*), *Sleeping Women,* and *Woman with a Parrot* (1866).

In 1870 Courbet was offered the Légion d'Honneur, which, characteristically, he rejected. Now, at the height of his career, he was drawn directly into political activity. During the Franco-Prussian War he was named president of a commission charged with protecting works of art in Paris, and he also served as a member of another commission engaged in a study of the Louvre archives with the intent of discovering frauds traceable to the deposed government of Napoleon III. On March 19, 1871, the Commune was officially established, and a month later Courbet was elected a delegate. On May 8 the column in the Place Vendôme, long associated with Bonapartism, was pulled down, and on June 7, after the abolition of the Commune, Courbet was sentenced to a 6-month prison term for his part in the destruction of the column. He returned to Ornans in 1872, but the following year, when his case was reopened, he fled to Switzerland and settled near Vevey at La Tour de Peilz. In 1874 the government demanded the payment of 320,000 francs toward the reconstruction of the column and the public sale of his possessions. Already seriously ill with dropsy, Courbet was overwhelmed by the hopelessness of his situation. He died at La Tour de Peilz on Dec. 31, 1877.

## Further Reading

The only full biographical study of Courbet in English is Gerstle Mack, *Gustave Courbet* (1951), which is, however, poorly illustrated. Many good illustrations and a concise text are in Robert Fernier, *Gustave Courbet,* translated by Marcus Bullock (1969). *Gustave Courbet,* the catalog to the exhibition held at the Philadelphia Museum of Art and the Boston Museum of Fine Arts in 1959-1960, is noteworthy for its rich documentation of many works, good illustrations, and clear chronology. There is an important discussion of Courbet in John Rewald, *The History of Impressionism* (1946; rev. ed. 1961), and a study of the reception which his works received in "Courbet and His Critics" by George Boas, contained in the anthology edited by Boas, *Courbet and the Naturalistic Movement* (1938).

## Additional Sources

Courbet, Gustave, *G. Courbet, 1819-1877,* Milano: Fabbri, 1988.
Schumann, Henry, *Gustave Courbet,* Dresden: Verlag der Kunst, 1975. □

# Antoine Augustin Cournot

**The French mathematician, philosopher, and economist Antoine Augustin Cournot (1801-1877) was one of the founders of mathematical economics.**

Antoine Augustin Cournot was born at Gray, Haute-Saône, on Aug. 28, 1801. In 1821 he entered a teachers' training college and in 1829 earned a doctoral degree in mathematics, with mechanics as his main thesis supplemented by astronomy. While studying at the college, he also served (1823-1833) as private secretary to Marshal de Gouvion Saint-Cyr. From 1834 he held successive positions as professor of analysis and mechanics on the science faculty of Lyons, rector of Grenoble Academy, chief examiner for undergraduate students, and, finally, rector of Dijon Academy (1854-1862). He died, nearly blind, in 1877.

Although Cournot was above all a mathematician and a member of the teaching profession, his numerous works show him also to have been a philosopher and economist. In the field of mathematics, in addition to his thesis on the movements of rigid bodies and celestial bodies, he devoted his efforts to two great problems: the theory of functions and the calculus of infinity (1841), and the theory of chance and probability (1843). These theories, above and beyond their mathematical significance, seemed to Cournot to hold an important place in man's general understanding of the world, but more specifically an understanding of the place of economics in man's life.

Cournot was a profound thinker: his advanced ideas on order and chance, enlightening both for science and mankind in general, are still prophetic. His economic concepts were broad in scope; his theories on monopolies and duopolies are still famous. In the field of economics he wrote few books or treatises. One book, however, has had an immense bearing on modern economic thought: *Recherches sur les principes mathématiques de la théorie des richesses* (*Researches on the Mathematical Principles of the Theory of Wealth*) was published in 1838 and reedited in 1938 with an introduction by Georges Lutfalla.

Unfortunately, this book met with no success during Cournot's lifetime because the application of the formulas and symbols of mathematics to economic analysis was considered audacious. In an attempt to improve the comprehensiveness of this work, Cournot rewrote it twice: In 1863 under the title *Principes de la théorie des richesses,* and in 1877 in *Revue sommaire des doctrines économiques.* These last two works are oversimplified and less informative versions of the original, since they were stripped of the mathematical language. Researches can, however, be thought of as the point of departure for modern economic analysis.

Having introduced the ideas of function and probability into economic analysis, Cournot derived the first formula for the rule of supply and demand as a function of price $[D = f(p)]$. He made clear the fact that the practical uses of mathematics in economics do not necessarily involve strict numerical precision; economists must utilize the tools of mathematics only to establish probable limits and to express seemingly inaccessible facts in more absolute terms. Cournot's work is recognized today in the discipline called econometrics.

## Further Reading

S. W. Floss, *An Outline of the Philosophy of Antoine-Augustine Cournot* (1941), is a detailed, comprehensive study of Cournot's philosophic writings. Jacob Oser, *The Evolution of Economic Thought* (1963), includes a discussion of Cournot's theories. □

# Victor Cousin

**The French educator and philosopher Victor Cousin (1792-1867) helped to reorganize the French primary school system. He also established the study of philosophy as a major intellectual pursuit of the French secondary and higher schools.**

Victor Cousin was born in Paris in the midst of the Revolution on Nov. 28, 1792, the son of a poor watchmaker. Like most boys of humble birth at that time, Cousin languished in the streets awaiting the appropriate age to enter an apprenticeship. When he was 11, a fateful event altered the course of his life: in a street fight between schoolboys Cousin came to the rescue of the underdog, whose mother was looking on. A woman of means, she gratefully paid for Cousin's schooling at the Lycée Charlemagne, where he became one of the most brilliant students in the school's history. He continued his successful scholarly career first as a student at the prestigious École Normale, where he decided on a career in philosophy, and then as a teacher of philosophy and in several schools, and finally as a professor at the Sorbonne.

## Development of Eclecticism

In 1817 and again in 1818 Cousin traveled to Germany to meet the leading lights of German letters, J. W. von Goethe, Friedrich Schleiermacher, Friedrich von Schelling, and, most important of all, G. W. F. Hegel. According to Cousin's "eclecticism," as he called his approach, the human mind can accept all carefully thought-out and moderate interpretations of the world. No system of thought is seen to be false, merely incomplete. By studying the history of philosophy, and Cousin directed his students to choose from each system what is true in it and in so doing to arrive at a complete philosophy. The introduction of the history of philosophy and as a major discipline in higher schools in France is a lasting accomplishment of Cousin. He organized the history of philosophy in two major works: *Cours de l'histoire de la philosophie* (Course of the History of Philosophy), written and revised between 1815 and 1841, portions of which have been translated into English; and the widely read *Du vrai, du beau, et du bien* (1836), which has been translated into English under the title *Lectures on the True, the Beautiful, and the Good,* and which came out in 31 editions over 90 years.

## Political Pressures

During the repressive years of the Bourbon restoration (1820-1830), Cousin, considered too liberal, was fired from the Sorbonne. While traveling in Germany during that time, he was jailed for 6 months for being a liberal agitator, a charge that was wholly unfounded.

In the government of the July Monarchy (1830-1848) Cousin rose to the heights of power and success as an educator and statesman. As a member of the Council of State and later as a peer, he exercised the major influence over French schools and universities. Because of his knowledge of Germany, Cousin was sent to study the successful primary school systems of several German states, especially Prussia. His book *Report of the State of Public Instruction in Prussia* (1833), recommending reforms to the French, was read abroad and stirred many Americans, Horace Mann and Calvin Stowe among other, to visit Prussia to learn how the budding American common school could best be guided in its development. The Guizot Law of 1833, which was a constitution for the French primary school system, was written by Cousin and based on his *Report.*

The Revolution of 1848 left Cousin without a job. Yet his influence continued to be felt into the next two generations, since the leaders of the French nation were the graduates of the schools that for 18 years had felt the imprint of Cousin's dynamic style, thought, and personality. Cousin never married. His voluminous correspondence, which continued steadily until his death, attests to close friendships with many leaders in Europe and North America.

## Further Reading

The best book in English on Cousin, an affectionate and colorful biography, is Jules Simon, *Victor Cousin* (2d ed. 1882; trans. 1888). See also George Boas, *French Philosophies of the Romantic Period* (1925). □

# Norman Cousins

**Norman Cousins (1912-1990) was editor-in-chief of the *Saturday Review* for over 35 years. He was a tireless advocate for world peace and in his later years devoted much writing and study to the issues of illness and healing.**

N orman Cousins was born June 24, 1912 (although some sources give the date as 1915), in Union City, New Jersey. He was educated in New York City public schools and at Teachers' College, Columbia University. His journalistic career began in 1934, when he joined the staff of the *New York Evening Post.* The following year he moved to *Current History,* which first employed him as a book critic, subsequently as managing editor. *Current History* had its offices in the same building as the *Saturday Review of Literature,* and Cousins became friendly with members of its staff, notably Amy Loveman, Henry Seidel Canby, Christopher Morley, William Rose Benét, Harrison

Smith, and editor George Stevens. In 1940 Cousins became the *Saturday Review*'s executive editor, and two years later, after Stevens's resignation, he took over the editorship and presidency.

The *Saturday Review* had just been bought by the petroleum geologist Everette Lee De Golyer. In 1942 it had a circulation of roughly 20,000 and a reputation for an old-fashioned sort of literary aloofness. Cousins wasted no time in converting the magazine into a more broad-based publication which devoted a great deal of space to current events. His efforts at expansion were aided by the astute business manager Jack R. Cominsky, whom Cousins hired away from the *New York Times*. Cousins built up a stable of regular writers including Cleveland Amory, Bennett Cerf, John Mason Brown, Joseph Wood Krutch, and Irving Kolodin. Cousins's spirit of advocacy was reflected in his magazine. He exemplified the liberal democratic spirit of the Roosevelt era, and his ties with the government were close. During World War II he served on the board of the Office of War Information, co-chaired the Victory Book Campaign of 1943, and edited the magazine *U.S.A.*

## Campaigns for Peace and Health

His first book, *The Good Inheritance: The Democratic Chance* (with William Rose Benét, 1942), was a defense of the nation's liberal tradition. His second book, *Modern Man is Obsolete* (1945), began as an editorial published in the *Saturday Review* only 12 days after the second atomic bomb had been dropped on Japan. In it, he argued for a non-military use of atomic energy. "Man stumbles fitfully

into a new age of atomic energy for which he is as ill-equipped to accept its potential blessings as he is to counter-act or control its present dangers," he warned. He saw only one solution to this predicament—the unity of nations. "This is not vaporous idealism, but sheer, driving necessity. There is one way and only one way to achieve effective control of destructive atomic energy and that is through decentralized world government." Through its magazine and book publications, Cousins's text is estimated to have reached some 40 million readers. Meanwhile, he campaigned in favor of the United Nations and of Wendell Wilkie's One World Campaign and was named honorary president of the United World Federalists.

He supported the cause of the Ravensbrueck Lapins, 35 Polish women who had been victims of medical experimentation at the World War II Ravensbrueck concentration camp. His advocacy also helped the campaign to treat and rehabilitate the Hiroshima Maidens, Japanese women disfigured by exposure to the atomic bombings, and he and his wife, the former Ellen Kopf (married 1939), adopted one of them, Shikego Sasamori. In 1951 Cousins was sent by the U.S. government as a lecturer to India, Pakistan, and Ceylon and in 1953 to Japan. Out of his experiences in the subcontinent came his book *Talks with Nehru* (1951). Throughout the 1950s Cousins continued to fight for world peace. He chaired the Committee for Cultural and International Exchange, co-chaired the Citizens' Committee for a Nuclear Test Ban Treaty, and joined SANE. His books on the subject of peace include *Who Speaks for Man?* (1952), *The Last Defense in a Nuclear Age* (1960), and *In Place of Folly* (1961).

At the same time he maintained the *Saturday Review*'s campaigning stance, arguing against insufficiently tested "miracle drugs;" warning against the possible side effects of fluoridation, the consequences of cigarette advertising, and the increasing level of violence in entertainment; and editorializing in favor of pollution control and the nascent space program. All was not somber, though. Cousins enjoyed running hoaxes in his correspondence column, such as the series of letters from one K. Jason Sitwell complaining about a proposed congressional ban on golf. The *Saturday Review* had by this time become an institution, reaching a circulation of 260,000 by 1960. Owner De Golyer transferred ownership to Cousins in 1958, but the latter eschewed autocratic rule, distributing nearly half the stock to his staff while retaining a controlling 51 percent.

## Saturday Review Lost and Won

In 1961, however, the stockholders turned around and sold their share to the McCall's Publishing Company, owners of, among other things, *McCall's* and *Redbook*. McCall's signed Cousins to a ten-year contract as editor-in-chief. For 14 months in the late 1960s he served as editor of *McCall's* as well as of *Saturday Review*. This period saw no flagging of Cousins's public-spirited undertakings. In the early 1960s he quietly negotiated with Khrushchev on behalf of Pope John XXIII for the release of imprisoned Catholic clerics behind the Iron Curtain. He parlayed his acquaintance with the Pope, the Soviet head of state, and President Kennedy to establish communication among the three toward a nuclear test-ban treaty. These diplomatic adventures were described by him in *The Improbable Triumvirate* (1972). Cousins also found time to write a biography of Albert Schweitzer (*Dr. Schweitzer of Lambarene,* 1960), to serve as chairman of International Cooperation Year 1965, and to join the (New York City) Mayor's Task Force on Air Pollution.

In 1972 Norton Simon took over the McCall's Company and sold it for $5,500,000 to an investment group headed by Nicholas H. Charney and John J. Veronis, who had founded *Psychology Today.* The magazine that Cousins had redesigned and come to personify had reached an all-time high circulation of 650,000, but Cousins opted out, after 31 years, unable to agree with the new owners. This cannot have come as anything but a major blow to the man who once said: "Nothing in my life, next to my family, has meant more to me than the *Saturday Review.* To work with books and ideas, to see the interplay between a nation's culture and its needs, to have unfettered access to an editorial page which offered, quite literally, as much freedom as I was capable of absorbing—this is a generous portion for any man."

Undaunted, Cousins proceeded to launch *World* ("for the proper care of the human habitat"), which began in 1972 with 100,000 charter subscriptions. It scarcely had a chance to prove its mettle, however, because in 1973 Charney and Veronis declared bankruptcy and Cousins immediately returned to the *Saturday Review,* vowing to increase the "reportorial reach" of the new edition.

Cousins had a history of illnesses dating back to the tuberculosis that confined him to a sanatorium for a year when he was 11. In the mid-1960s he suffered a paralyzing collagen disease, which he claimed to have cured with massive injections of vitamin C. Reflections on mortality gave him the spur for his 1974 book *The Celebration of Life: A Dialogue on Immortality and Infinity,* in which he rejected existentialism, proposing in its stead the philosophy of "consequentialism," which, as the name would imply, fosters an awareness of the results of action. Around 1977 Cousins contracted cancer. He sold the *Saturday Review* to a former *Village Voice* staffer, Carll Tucker, remaining chairman of the editorial board and, after 1980, editor emeritus. His disease eventually went into remission, the whole struggle being described in *Anatomy of an Illness* (1979), which was later made into a CBS television movie starring Ed Asner and Cousins himself in 1984. Illness, both its prevention and cure, continued to interest Cousins, particularly after he suffered a near-fatal heart attack in 1980. It led him to write *The Human Option* (1981) and *The Healing Heart* (1983) and to compile the anthology *The Physician in Literature* (1981). Throughout Cousins's bouts with illness, he subscribed to the belief in a "laugh-cure", documenting his theories in his various books on health, and also in magazine articles. He also served as an adjunct professor at the University of California at Los Angeles School of Medicine.

In the late 1980s Cousins wrote *Head First* (1989), which further explored his theories about medicine and the doctor-patient relationship. His 1987 work, *The Pathology*

*of Power* was a treatise on world peace. Other of Cousins's later works include, *The Human Adventure: A Camera Chronicle* (1986), and *Albert Schweitzer's Mission: Healing and Peace* (1985).

On November 31, 1990, Cousins died in Westwood, California. The literary world mourned his loss, prompting even the politically opposed William F. Buckley to write in *National Review,* "He was a brilliant editor, a prolific writer, truly the man engaged. He was surpassingly generous, and I mourn his passing."

In his lifetime Norman Cousins received nearly 50 honorary degrees, and numerous awards. He received the Author of the Year Award from the American Society of Journalists and Authors in 1981, and was nominated for the American Book Award in 1982 for *Anatomy of an Illness.*

### Further Reading

Cousins is his own best source. Besides the titles cited in the article, many of which are autobiographical to one degree or another, there is a full-fledged autobiography, *Present Tense: An American Editor's Odyssey* (1968). □

# Jacques-Yves Cousteau

**Jacques-Yves Cousteau (1910-1997) was an undersea explorer, photographer, inventor of diving devices, writer, television producer, and filmmaker. He was also active in the movement to safeguard the oceans from pollution.**

"Calypso acquired a buoyant personality that has never left her. I decided from the beginning that those on board were companions in the adventure, whatever their jobs might be. There was no officers' mess; we all ate together. During the tumultuous and jocose mealtimes we discussed plans, made decisions, and learned from each other. No one shouted orders, and no one wore anything resembling a uniform. Pride of outfit began to develop, expressed in customs of our own."

On her first research voyage to the Red Sea the maritime and diving expertise of her crew was combined with the scientific expertise of academic scientists who came aboard. These expeditions advanced knowledge of the deep by the gathering of underwater flora and fauna and by extensive photographing of the underwater world, which is more vast than the surface above water. In this work Captain Cousteau and his companions achieved remarkable success, especially in very deep water photography. They discovered, by using nylon rope, a means of anchoring Calypso in water four and half miles deep in order to lower a camera to that depth.

When the French Ministry of Education finally provided grants to cover two-thirds of the expenses, Cousteau resigned from the navy in 1957 with the rank of lieutenant commander to become director of the Oceanographic Museum at Monaco. He continued deep-sea exploration, aided

by the bathyscaphe invented by Auguste and Jacques Piccard. He was also an adviser to the team that in 1959 made a "diving saucer" which resembled a flying saucer. For him the undersea world was the counterpart of the spatial world above and just as precious.

In 1960 Cousteau was an important initiator of the movement to prevent the dumping of French atomic wastes into the Mediterranean Sea. This movement ended in success and, mindful of the rich resources of large bodies of water, encouraged him to state, "Why do we think of the ocean as a mere storehouse of food, oil, and minerals? The sea is not a bargain basement. . . . The greatest resource of the ocean is not material but the boundless spring of inspiration and well-being we gain from her. Yet we risk poisoning the sea forever just when we are learning her science, art, and philosophy and how to live in her embrace." Modern civilization has become disastrous. "Never before has the marine environment been as raped and poisoned at it is today. All the urban and industrial effluents of 500 million Europeans and Africans flow freely—practically without treatment—into the Mediterranean, a near-closed sea that was once the cradle of civilization. Millions of tons of toxic chemicals are either dumped directly into the ocean or find their way there indirectly by way of river pollution or rain."

Throughout his life, Cousteau enjoyed much recognition for his tireless advocacy of ocean ecology. In 1959 he addressed the first World Oceanic Congress, an event that received widespread coverage and led to his appearance on the cover of *Time* magazine on March 28, 1960. In April of 1961 Cousteau was awarded the National Geographic's

Gold Medal at a White House ceremony hosted by President John F. Kennedy. It was Cousteau's television programs, however, that truly catapulted his work to world renown. In 1966 Cousteau's first hour-long television special, *The World of Jacques-Yves Cousteau,* was broadcast and received critical acclaim. The program's high ratings were instrumental in landing Cousteau a lucrative contract with the American Broadcasting Company (ABC) and in 1968 resulted in the series *The Undersea World of Jacques Cousteau.* The program ran for eight seasons and starred Cousteau, his sons, Philippe and Jean-Michel, and sea creatures from around the globe. In order to arouse public opinion against pollution he founded in 1975 the Cousteau Society, an international organization with branches in several countries (including the United States at Norfolk, Virginia). Two years later the *Cousteau Odyssey* series premiered on the Public Broadcasting Service (PBS) and reflected Cousteau's growing concern about environmental destruction. During the 1980s Cousteau produced programs on the St. Lawrence and Mississippi rivers, and called attention to threatened South American cultures with his *Cousteau Amazon* series. In all, Cousteau's television programs earned him more than forty Emmy nominations.

In honor of his achievements, Cousteau received the U.S. Presidential Medal of Freedom in 1985. In 1987 he was inducted into the Television Academy's Hall of Fame and later received the founder's award from the International Council of the National Academy of Television Arts and Sciences. In 1988 the National Geographic Society honored him with its Centennial Award and in 1989 France admitted him to membership in its prestigious Academy.

Cousteau died on June 25, 1997 at age 87. While some critics have challenged his scientific credentials, Cousteau never claimed "expert status" in any discipline. But perhaps to a greater degree than any of his more learned contemporaries, Cousteau enlightened the public by emphatically demonstrating the irreversible effects of environmental destruction.

Cousteau's major publications include: (with F. Dumas) *The Silent World* (1953); (with James Dugan) *The Living Sea* (1963); *World Without Sun* (1965); (with Philippe Cousteau) *The Shark: Splendid Savage of the Sea* (1970); *Life and Death in a Coral Sea* (1971); and *Dolphins* (1975). His other books dealt with sunken ships, corals, whales, octopi, and seals, as well as places explored by his divers. He also edited an encyclopedia, *The Ocean World,* in 20 volumes.

## Further Reading

Cousteau's books contain many facts about his activities and ideas. Also useful for information about his career are James Dugan, *Undersea Explorer: The Story of Captain Cousteau* (1957) and Muriel Guberlet, *Explorers of the Sea* (1964). J. Cousteau and Alexis Sivirine, *Jacques Cousteau's Calypso* (1983) provides a detailed description of the ship, well illustrated. □

# Miles Coverdale

**The English Puritan Miles Coverdale (1488-1569) was the first to translate the complete Bible into English.**

M iles Coverdale was a Yorkshireman of whose early education nothing is known. He joined the Augustinian friars at their great Barnwell Priory at Cambridge and became a priest, probably in 1514. He was very much influenced by his prior, Robert Barnes, an early and very active Lutheran, who was ultimately put to death under Henry VIII for his heretical opinions. Coverdale's increasingly heretical views caused him first to abandon his religious profession and then to leave England. By 1529 he had settled at Hamburg, Germany, and was engaged in assisting William Tyndale with his English translation of various parts of the Holy Scriptures.

By 1534 Coverdale was in Antwerp, where a merchant commissioned him to render the whole Bible in English. The printing of Coverdale's translation was completed by October 1535. This Bible, although allowed to circulate in England, lacked official approval because of its heretical tendentiousness and its inadequacy as a translation. Accordingly, Thomas Cromwell engaged Coverdale to work in England on a new version, using a revised edition of Tyndale's work known as Matthew's Bible. Coverdale's renewed efforts resulted in the publication in 1539 of the widely accepted Great Bible.

Meanwhile, Coverdale had taken a Scottish wife and with her went to Strassburg in 1540, when Henry VIII's approval of various executions made a longer stay in England dangerous. He returned to England, however, after Henry's death in 1547; he won favor, especially as a preacher, from the Privy Council and was rewarded with the bishopric of Exeter in 1551. As bishop, he earned a good reputation both from the fine example of his life and from his pastoral solicitude. But Coverdale was deposed soon after Mary I's accession to the throne in 1553. He would probably have been executed for heresy had not the king of Denmark successfully pleaded with Mary to allow him to depart for Copenhagen in 1555.

During his 4-year sojourn on the Continent, Coverdale visited various cities and worked on the Puritan version of the Bible, which appeared at Geneva in 1560. Then he returned to England. He was never restored to Exeter, probably because of his Puritanism, but he continued to preach and was warmly esteemed by his Puritan associates. He died in London on Jan. 20, 1569. His second wife, whom he married after his first wife's death in 1565, administered his estate. Of the two children by his first marriage, nothing seems to be known.

## Further Reading

The most recent study of Coverdale is James F. Mozley, *Coverdale and His Bibles* (1953), which outlines his life in the first chapter and has useful bibliographical appendices. An

earlier study is Henry Guppy, *Miles Coverdale and the English Bible, 1488-1568* (1935). ☐

# Pedro de Covilhão

**The Portuguese adventurer Pedro de Covilhão (ca. 1455-ca. 1530) was an explorer and diplomat, notably in eastern Africa.**

I n 1487 King John II commissioned Pedro de Covilhão to undertake an exploratory-diplomatic venture as part of Portugal's effort to break the Venetian hold on commerce with the East. Covilhão specific assignment was to gather information about trade routes and friendly ports throughout the Arabic world. He was also instructed to find out more about the mysterious kingdom of Prester John, the legendary priest-king, which was reputed to be somewhere in Africa, India, or China. Contact with a Christian king in the Moslem world would have been extremely valuable to Portugal.

Covilhão's background made him a likely candidate for the dual mission. Not only had he served John II as a spy, but he was one of the few Portuguese diplomats fluent in Arabic. He traveled to Alexandria and Cairo successfully disguised as a Moslem. Joining a caravan, he worked his way down the eastern coast of Africa, gathering information about the size and condition of facilities along the way. In

1490 Covilhão returned along the coast to Cairo. There he met messengers from King John and sent back with them a detailed report of his reconnaissance trip. His firsthand account of trade routes and ports, previously known only to Moorish traders, now made it possible for Portuguese expeditions to begin trading incursions along the eastern coast of Africa. His reports coincided with the discovery of a sea route around the Cape of Good Hope, thus further facilitating direct Portuguese contact with the Eastern world.

In order to pursue the legend of Prester John, Covilhão unilaterally decided to journey further east. He left Cairo in 1491 headed first for Mecca, this time disguising himself as a Moslem pilgrim. By so doing, he placed himself in grave danger, because discovery as an infidel meant certain death. He traced the legend of Prester John to Abyssinia (Ethiopia). While he did not find Prester John—who purportedly died years before his arrival in 1493—he did receive a warm welcome from the Abyssinian king. The king apparently recognized the value of this imaginative and bold foreigner, for he did not allow Covilhão to return to Portugal. Covilhão proved to be a valuable and useful servant; he was rewarded with titles and a substantial settlement of land, and he even married an Abyssinian.

Covilhão died sometime between 1527 and 1530. Before his death, however, he was able to be of further service to Portugal. When that government sent a diplomatic mission to Abyssinia in 1520, Covilhão served as interpreter and also informed the Portuguese envoys about the customs and traditions of his host's nation.

## Further Reading

Three useful works for the study of Covilhão are Arthur Percival Newton, *Travel and Travellers of the Middle Ages* (1926); Edgar Prestage, *The Portuguese Pioneers* (1933); and J. H. Parry, *The Age of Reconnaissance* (1963). □

# Noel Coward

**The English playwright, actor, and composer Noel Coward (1899-1973) was known for his genial urbanity and frequently acerbic wit.**

Noel Coward was born on December 16, 1899, in Teddingham, Middlesex, and studied intermittently at the Royal Chapel School in London. A restless and extroverted youth, he made his acting debut at the age of 12 and a year later won praise for his portrayal of Slightly in *Peter Pan.*

Coward's first play, *Rat Trap,* an exercise in psychological realism, was written in 1917 but not published until 1926. He played the leading role in his next play, *The Last Track* (1918). His first drama to be noted by the critics was *The Vortex* (1924), a serious play about narcotics addiction. During this period he was regarded as the spokesman for the younger generation, although his works were often condemned as immoral.

In 1929 Coward starred in the Broadway production of his *Bitter Sweet,* a romantic musical that was popular in both Great Britain and the United States. This play's popular song, "I'll See You Again," is one of his notable efforts as a composer; among his other songs are "Mad Dogs and Englishmen" and "I'll Follow My Secret Heart."

Coward's important plays of the next decade or so included *Private Lives* (1930), a sophisticated marital comedy; *Cavalcade* (1931), a patriotic depiction of British Victorian tradition; *Design for Living* (1937), a stylish comedy; and *Blithe Spirit* (1941), a fantasy concerning spiritualism. During World War II Coward entertained troops on the major battlefronts and later detailed his experiences in *Middle East Diary* (1945). In 1942 he wrote, codirected with David Lean, and acted in the motion picture *In Which We Serve,* which presented life aboard a British naval destroyer. He continued his collaboration with Lean on the filming of *Blithe Spirit* (1945) and on the scenario for *Brief Encounter* (1946), one of the screen's most tender love stories.

Although Coward's dramas of succeeding years— *Peace in Our Time* (1947), *Quadrille* (1952), *Nude with Violin* (1956), and *Sail Away* (1961)—lacked the freshness of his earlier works, he compensated for his eclipse as a writer by embarking on a career as an entertainer and raconteur. In 1960 he gave his finest performance as the secret agent in the Carol Reed-Graham Greene film, *Our Man in Havana.* Coward also wrote two volumes of autobiographical reminiscences, *Present Indicative* (1937) and *Future Indefinite* (1954); two collections of short stories, *To Step Aside* (1939) and *Star Quality* (1951); and a novel, *Pomp*

*and Circumstance* (1960), portraying British life on a South Seas island. He was knighted by Queen Elizabeth in 1970. Noel Coward died on March 26, 1973 in Kingston, Jamaica.

## Further Reading

In addition to Coward's autobiographical works, see Hoare, Philip, *Noel Coward: A Biography* (Simon & Schuster, 1996); Payn, Graham (with Barry Day), *My Life With Noel Coward* (Applause, 1994); and Fisher, Clive, *Noel Coward* (St. Martin's Press, 1992). For previous biographical material, see Robert Greacen, *The Art of Noël Coward* (1953), a brief biographical and critical study; James Agee, *Agee on Film* (1958); and Kenneth Tynan, *Curtains: Selections from Drama Criticism and Related Writings* (1961) and *Tynan Right and Left: Plays, Films, People, Places and Events* (1967). □

# Henry Dixon Cowell

**Henry Dixon Cowell (1897-1965) was an inventive and productive American composer, pianist, teacher, and author.**

H enry Cowell was born March 11, 1897, in Menlo Park, Calif. A precocious pianist and violinist, he began composing by the age of 8. He received his first systematic training under Charles Seeger at the University of California, prior to Army service in World War I.

During the 1930s Cowell, already established in America as a sort of maverick composer, pursued musicological studies in Europe, meanwhile touring as a pianist-composer. He often caused near-riots with audiences when playing works including "tone clusters"—a term and technique he originated that is used by many avant-garde composers. A tone cluster is produced by placing the fist, full hand, or full forearm over a section of the keyboard, while usually the other hand continues to play normally. Occasionally, Cowell rose and sat a moment on the keyboard. He sometimes delved into the innards of the piano, using fingers or plectra to stroke or pluck strings, playing while standing, his other hand on the keyboard, with pedal effects produced by a foot. Meanwhile, he was experimenting with new effects that could be produced on orchestral instruments. However, he was also composing comparatively simple pieces reflective of his Irish parentage and his love of American folklore.

Cowell became one of the most vocal champions of new and of older, neglected American composers. He founded the *New Musical Quarterly,* contributed to many musical magazines, and edited *American Composers on American Music* (1933). He and his wife wrote *Charles Ives and His Music.* He was confounder and often president or board member of the American Composers Alliance, an organization that made unpublished scores by both noted and younger composers available. Cowell even raised money during the 1930s and 1940s to sponsor recordings featuring the works of younger American composers. He later was a director-member of Composers' Recordings, Inc.

Meanwhile, teaching in a number of colleges and universities, he influenced many American and some foreign composers, who have since achieved success.

Cowell conjured a special American musical form of his own in which one will find some of his most significant music, aside from his many symphonies. He called it "hymn and fuguing tune." He was also an early experimenter with electronic instruments, such as the theremin, and pioneered in writing "serious" music for bands. His music, too prolific to list here, covers, often in depth, almost every thinkable musical combination. He was frequently disguisedly conservative in his compositions. For example, his invocation of "Americana" in certain works, except for certain subtle creative techniques employed, could sound "apple-pie American." Yet, especially in later years, traveling the world widely (especially Asia), he could dig deeply into the ancient musical lores of, for example, Iran or Japan, and produce an effective work sounding part Persian or part Japanese, part cosmopolitan-modern. He had set out to shock audiences, especially as a performing pianist-composer; later, he composed intricate, but somehow very accessible, music disturbing to practically no one. Cowell died on December 10, 1965, in Shady, New York.

Cowell once stated: "As a creator of music I contribute my religious, philosophical, and ethical beliefs in terms of creative sound: that sound which flows through the mind of the composer with a concentrated intensity that baffles description, the sound which is the very life of the composer, and which is the sum and substance of his faith and feeling." Virgil Thomson summed up: "Cowell's music covers a wider range in both expression and technic than any other living composer. . . . Add to this massive production his long and influential career as pedagog, and Cowell's achievement in music becomes impressive indeed. There is no other quite like it. To be fecund and right is given to few.''

## Further Reading

Information about Cowell is available in John T. Howard, *Our Contemporary Composers: American Music in the Twentieth Century* (1941); William W. Austin, *Music in the Twentieth Century* (1966); Peter Yates, *Twentieth Century Music* (1967); and David Ewen, *The World of Twentieth Century Music* (1968).

## Additional Sources

Lichtenwanger, William, *The music of Henry Cowell: a descriptive catalog,* Brooklyn, N.Y.: Institute for Studies in American Music, Conservatory of Music, Brooklyn College of the City University of New York, 1986.

Manion, Martha L., *Writings about Henry Cowell: an annotated bibliography,* Brooklyn, N.Y.: Institute for Studies in American Music, Conservatory of Music, Brooklyn College of the City University of New York, 1982.

Saylor, Bruce, *The writings of Henry Cowell: a descriptive bibliography,* Brooklyn: Institute for Studies in American Music, Dept. of Music, School of Performing Arts, Brooklyn College of the City University of New York, 1977. ☐

# Abraham Cowley

**The English writer Abraham Cowley (1618-1667) was among the first to use the Pindaric ode form in English poetry. He contributed importantly to the development of the familiar essay in English.**

The posthumous son of a merchant, Abraham Cowley was born in London and educated at Westminster and Trinity College, Cambridge, where he became a fellow in 1640. Like Richard Crashaw, he left Cambridge in 1643, when Oliver Cromwell's occupation of the city threatened the continuance of his fellowship, and joined the court at Oxford. He served the English court in Paris in 1646 and spent the next years on royal business. Returning to England in 1654, he was arrested the following year but after his release made his peace with Cromwell. He returned to Oxford to study medicine and earned a doctor of medicine degree in 1657.

With the Restoration in 1660 Cowley regained his fellowship together with some land whose rent provided a livelihood somewhat less than what he had hoped for from the court. For the rest of his life he lived in retirement studying botany and writing essays. He was one of the first to be nominated for membership in the Royal Society. His contemporary reputation as a poet was greater than it has been since, and his funeral at Westminster Abbey in 1667 was the most magnificent that had yet been afforded a poet.

Cowley's earliest volume, *Poetical Blossoms* (1633), published when he was only 15, comprises a schoolboy's imitations of Edmund Spenser and other Elizabethans. At Cambridge he wrote some plays, including *The Guardian* (1642), which was produced after the Restoration as *The Cutter of Coleman Street.* In 1647 he published *The Mistress,* a collection of poems, included with revisions in the *Poems* of 1656, which contained other poems as well, including his odes and the unfinished *Davideis,* a biblical epic. His odes made this form the vehicle for grandiose invention and influenced poetry for the next century. More verses appeared in 1663, and in 1668 his posthumous *Works* made additional poetry and his essays available.

The lyrics of *The Mistress* were influenced by metaphysical and cavalier traditions. They lack the virtues of the poetry they imitate, however, and thus served Dr. Johnson well in the next century when he chose them to illustrate the shortcomings of the metaphysical school. Cowley's religious epic, however, is the work of a man of common sense and rationality.

## Further Reading

The famous life of Cowley in Samuel Johnson's *Lives of the English Poets* appeared in 1779. A modern biography is Arthur H. Nethercot, *Abraham Cowley, the Muse's Hannibal* (1931). Studies of his poetry and its background are in George Williamson, *The Donne Tradition* (1930), and Douglas Bush, *English Literature in the Earlier Seventeenth Century* (1945; 2d ed. 1962).

**Additional Sources**

Cowley, Abraham, *Selected poems,* Manchester England: Carcanet Press, 1994.

Perkin, Michael Roger, *Abraham Cowley: a bibliography,* Folkestone: Dawson, 1977. □

# William Cowper

**The most characteristic work of the English poet William Cowper (1731-1800) is gentle and pious in mood and deals with retired rural life. He often anticipated the attitudes and subjects of romantic and Victorian authors.**

William Cowper was born on Nov. 26, 1731; his mother was a descendant of the poet John Donne. He studied law and was admitted to the bar in 1754. A love affair with his cousin ended unhappily in 1756, largely because the girl's father was concerned over Cowper's mental stability. In 1763 Cowper suffered a complete nervous breakdown as a consequence of worry about an examination he was to take for a clerkship in the House of Lords. After several attempts at suicide he was committed to a sanatorium.

After recuperating, Cowper spent his life under the care of several friends and patrons, notably Mrs. Mary Unwin (a clergyman's widow), the evangelical clergyman John Newton (whose religious zeal probably did not aid Cowper's troubled mind), and Cowper's cousin Lady Hesketh. In collaboration with Newton, Cowper wrote numerous hymns. His life after 1765 was one of rustic retirement, punctuated by severe breakdowns in 1773, 1787, and 1794. His intermittent mental breakdowns were generally characterized by severe religious gloom and often by a sense that he was irrevocably damned.

Cowper's most significant literary work was done in the last 2 decades of his life. In 1780-1781 he wrote a series of reflective essays in couplets; in 1782 he composed the immensely popular "John Gilpin's Ride," in which he burlesques the heroic ballad. In 1783 Cowper began his curious long poem *The Task* (published 1785), which begins with a mock-elevated disquisition on the historical evolution of the sofa from the humble three-legged stool (a lady had suggested the topic in response to Cowper's complaint that he lacked a subject for blank verse). It then treats a multitude of descriptive and reflective subjects and is probably Cowper's most typical poem. In it quiet meditation is mingled with atmospheric description of simple rural life and placid natural scenes.

Cowper's translation of Homer (1784-1791) demonstrated his opposition to what he considered the artificial elevatedness of Alexander Pope's version. In 1799 Cowper wrote the somber poem "The Castaway;" like the earlier "Lines Supposed to Be Written by Alexander Selkirk" (published 1782), it is a study of human isolation and has poignant religious overtones.

Cowper was one of the best and most prolific English letter writers. He also composed the texts of many well-known hymns, including "There Is a Fountain Filled with Blood," "God Moves in a Mysterious Way," and "Oh for a Closer Walk with God." He died on April 25, 1800.

## Further Reading

For Cowper's life see Maurice J. Quinlan, *William Cowper* (1953), and William N. Free, *William Cowper* (1970), which also contains a fine discussion of Cowper's poetry. Charles Ryskamp, *William Cowper of the Inner Temple* (1959), deals with the poet's early years. For critical comment see Morris Golden, *In Search of Stability: The Poetry of William Cowper* (1960), and Patricia A. Spacks, *The Insistence of Horror: Aspects of the Supernatural in Eighteenth-Century Poetry* (1962).

## Additional Sources

Cowper, William, *The letters and prose writings of William Cowper,* Oxford: Clarendon Press; New York: Oxford University Press, 1979-1986.

Cowper, William, *William Cowper, selected letters,* Oxford: Clarenden Press; New York: Oxford University Press, 1989.

Roy, James Alexander, *Cowper & his poetry,* Norwood, Pa.: Norwood Editions, 1977.

Roy, James Alexander, *Cowper & his poetry,* Philadelphia: R. West, 1978. □

# Archibald Cox

**Archibald Cox (born 1912), lawyer, educator, author, labor arbitrator, and public servant, was appointed special prosecutor to investigate the Watergate political scandal in 1973. Five months later he was fired in the "Saturday Night Massacre."**

Archibald Cox began an active life that took him in and out of public service on May 17, 1912, in Plainfield, New Jersey. He was one of six children born to Archibald and Frances Bruen (Perkins) Cox. He married Phyllis Ames on June 12, 1937. They had two daughters and one son.

In 1930 Cox began his long association with Harvard University, entering as an undergraduate student majoring in American history and economics and earning an A.B. degree in 1934. He attended the Harvard Law School, where he was elected to a position on the *Harvard Law Review* and received the LL.B. degree with honors in 1937. Thereafter, Cox was to be awarded about one dozen honorary degrees from universities in America, attesting to his distinguished career.

Admitted to the Massachusetts bar in 1937, he served as a law clerk for one year and became an associate with a law firm in Boston. He practiced law there for three years. In later years Cox would become a member of the American Bar Association.

As the nation prepared for its role in World War II, Cox served in the first of his many public posts beginning in 1941. He joined the staff of the National Defense Mediation Board. Shortly thereafter he took a position in the Office of the Solicitor General of the Department of Justice and later in the Department of Labor.

After the war he was appointed as a lecturer at the Harvard Law School. Within a year he was promoted to the rank of professor, becoming one of the youngest persons in the school's history to hold that rank. He stayed on to teach law, taking leaves of absence to reenter government service. From 1962 to 1965 he was a member of Harvard's board of overseers.

Cox's expertise and experience in labor relations was highlighted first with his appointment as co-chairperson of the Construction Industry Stabilization Commission in 1951 and then as chairperson of the Wage Stabilization Board in 1952. Several times throughout the decade that followed he was called upon to arbitrate nationwide labor disputes and college student rioting, to draft labor legislation, and to advise the U.S. Senate on labor matters. It was in the latter capacity that he worked with John F. Kennedy, then the junior senator from Massachusetts.

Having worked in Kennedy's successful 1960 Democratic presidential campaign, Cox was appointed as solicitor general of the United States. The solicitor general is the third ranking member of the Department of Justice and is responsible for supervising all the national government's legal suits before the U.S. Supreme Court. During his term of office (1961-1965), as well as in later years, Cox argued before the Supreme Court in several historic cases related to civil rights.

A major challenge faced Cox in 1973 when political scandal was confronting the White House. The "Watergate affair" developed following the break-in and electronic bugging in 1972 of the Democratic National Committee headquarters. Officials working with President Richard M. Nixon and with the committee to re-elect him president had been implicated in the break-in and related political and campaign finance activities and in attempts to hinder legal prosecution. The nation was shocked and confused.

Under pressure from the public and Congress in May 1973, Nixon approved the creation of the Watergate Special Prosecution Force to investigate those responsible for any illegal political activities or cover-up. Only a person of impeccable credentials and respect could be appointed to head that task. Cox was selected. He accepted, after receiving assurances that he would have independence to investigate, even if the evidence led to the White House staff or presidential appointees. The oath of office was taken on May 25, 1973.

Cox's first tasks were to create the structure, staff, and procedures for the special force and to comb through the background events and documents. His work took an unexpected turn on July 16, 1973, when Alexander Butterfield, a former White House staff member, made a shocking disclosure before the special Senate committee which was holding its own hearings on the Watergate affair. Butterfield testified that Nixon had been secretly taping conversations in the presidential offices. Two days later Cox wrote to the president's lawyer requesting eight tapes of specific conversations relevant to the investigation. On July 23 he received the answer: No.

Immediately thereafter, Cox sought a subpoena from U.S. District Court Judge John Sirica to compel release of the tapes. Within two days the White House invoked the doctrine of executive privilege, arguing that the president was immune from judicial orders enforcing subpoenas. Cox countered the arguments with a carefully drawn brief based on rare precedents. On August 29 Sirica ordered Nixon to release the tapes to him to determine if they were covered by executive privilege. Nixon appealed the order, and on October 12 the U.S. Court of Appeals upheld Sirica's action.

Nixon offered a compromise: Senator John Stennis (Democrat, Mississippi) would be asked to listen to the tapes and verify an edited written version that Nixon would submit to the grand jury and to the Senate committee. In addition, Cox was to make no further attempt to obtain tapes or other notes of presidential conversations. Cox rejected the proposal.

Attorney General Elliot Richardson was ordered by the White House to fire Cox. Having assured the Senate that Cox would be free to pursue the investigation, Richardson resigned rather than do so. Deputy Attorney General William Ruckelshaus was then given the task. He too refused to fire Cox and promptly quit his job in protest (and was simultaneously fired.) Finally, Solicitor General Robert Bork, next in line and appointed acting attorney general, was so ordered. He dismissed Cox. This quick series of events on October 20, 1973 ignited popular criticism and became known as the "Saturday Night Massacre."

Cox left Washington, D.C., and returned to Harvard to teach, write, practice law, and continue his public and political activities. At Harvard he served as Williston Professor of Law until 1976, as Carl M. Loeb University Professor from 1976 to 1984, and as a professor emeritus starting in 1984. He was also a visiting professor at Boston University starting in 1985.

In 1980 Cox became chairperson of Common Cause, a nationwide citizens' advocacy group, and held that position until 1992. He was also chairman of the Health Effects Institute starting in 1985. In the 1990s he was a member of the Free TV for Straight Talk Coalition, a nonpartisan group whose members included former CBS anchor Walter Cronkite, Christian Coalition leader Ralph Reed, actor Christopher Reeve, and a number of political figures from both parties, all united in urging that television networks voluntarily give free airtime to Presidential candidates. On the occasion of the 40th anniversary of the American Bar Foundation in 1993, Cox received that organization's Research Award.

Cox's name was often in the news in the 1980s and 1990s, not so much because of his current activities as because of his earlier role as special prosecutor. The decades following Watergate saw increased activity for special prosecutors, most notably Lawrence Walsh in the Iran-Contra hearings during the Reagan and Bush administrations, and Kenneth Starr in the Whitewater investigation of

President Clinton. Cox himself wrote an op-ed piece for the *New York Times* on December 12, 1996, in which he criticized what he described as overuse of the independent counsel and special prosecutor activities. He also made recommendations for "Curbing Special Counsels," the title of the article.

An important contributor to the fields of labor law and American justice, Cox authored or coauthored several books: *Cases on Labor Law* (1948, 11th edition 1981), *Law and the National Labor Policy* (1960), *Civil Rights, the Constitution and the Courts* (1967), *The Warren Court* (1968), *The Role of the Supreme Court in American Government* (1976), *Freedom of Expression* (1981), and *The Court and the Constitution* (1987.)

## Further Reading

Cox lacks a published biography in book form. Interesting reading on Cox's role in the Watergate affair, with insight into his personality and style, can be found in James Doyle, *Not Above the Law* (1977). Doyle was appointed special assistant for public affairs of the Watergate Special Prosecution Force and worked with Cox. Cox's successor as special prosecutor, Leon Jaworski, has written *The Right and The Power* (1976). Judge John Sirica's side of the Cox activities is found in his book *To Set the Record Straight* (1979). An overall report of the period is found in Bob Woodward and Carl Bernstein, *All the President's Men* (1974). □

# Harvey Cox

**Harvey Cox (born 1929) was professor of theology at Harvard Divinity School. In the mid-1960s he achieved international prominence because of his book *The Secular City*. After that he was a leading interpreter for the American church of the theological significance of cultural dynamics.**

Harvey Cox was born in 1929 and grew up in Malvern, a suburb of Philadelphia, Pennsylvania. His religious background was Baptist, and he described his faith journey not as a steady climb up the ladder of spiritual development, but rather as "desultory and meandering" with sometimes "sickening reversals and absurd contradictions." He titled an autobiography *Just As I Am* (1983) after the familiar gospel song, one verse of which he found especially meaningful:

Just as I am, though tossed about
With many a conflict, many a doubt,
Fightings and fears within, without,
O Lamb of God, I come, I come.
(Charlotte Elliott)

The metaphor of a faith journey is important to understanding Cox, for his creative theology was done less under the constraints of academia than in response to some exciting places he had been—Gdansk, Berlin, New Delhi, Cuernavaca, Mexico City, Rome, Tehran, Hiroshima—and experiences he had. Cox did theology by thinking through the implications of living where history was being made, and he spoke of the importance for him of "participating in history, not just watching it happen on TV." He was therefore concerned not so much with supposedly "eternal" truths as with truth for today, truth for action, and he suspected that a faith which responded primarily to ideas was more likely to be idolatrous and less likely to be redemptive than one that responded to events and experience.

The summer following his junior year in high school (1946) Cox responded to a call from the United Nations Relief and Rehabilitation Administration for volunteers to help ship cattle to Europe to replace the herds that had been devastated by war. His boat went to Gdansk, Poland. After completing his academic degrees—University of Pennsylvania (B.A.), Yale (B.D.), and Harvard (Ph.D.)—and following two brief terms as a college chaplain, first at Oberlin College and then at Temple University, Cox spent a year (1962-1963) in Berlin as an ecumenical fraternal worker. Having experienced this nexus of East-West tension, Cox returned to the United States and joined the civil rights struggle. He was in prison in Williamstown, North Carolina, when installed (in absentia) as assistant professor of theology and culture at Andover Newton Theology School in Boston.

Shortly thereafter Cox published *The Secular City* (1965), the cover adding "a celebration of its liberties and an invitation to its discipline" but formally subtitled "Secularization and Urbanization in Theological Perspective." Written in a popular style, it became an international best-seller (translated into 11 languages) and led to his appointment at Harvard. In that book Cox argued that secularization is itself a result of biblical faith and that secularization sets the agenda which gives meaning to the church's mission. The biblical commandment "no other gods" led historically to the "disenchantment" of nature and the relativization of politics and values. Therefore (following Bonhoeffer), the church must learn to "speak in a secular fashion of God," as the liberating power operative in nature and history that is discerned through the model of the Exodus.

In his second major book, *The Feast of Fools* (1969), described by Cox as "my favorite" and "intended as a companion piece," he explored the very different topics of festivity and fantasy, proposing that in addition to "world-changers" there is a need for "life-celebrators." Indeed, a world experiencing re-creation needs the festivity appropriate to the achievements of the past *and* the fantasy which, through myth and ritual, celebrates a world not yet arrived.

*The Seduction of the Spirit* (1973) begins as autobiography but develops as an analysis of the way individuals and institutions manipulate healthy religious instincts for purposes of selfish control and domination. *Turning East* (1977) is a critical but appreciative examination of Asian religion—especially Buddhism.

In *Religion in the Secular City* (1984) Cox suggested that mainline modern theology was written chiefly in response to intellectual critics of religion, to academics, to the supposedly "modern mind." He then evaluated the criticism of fundamentalist theology (the religious right) that modern theology is too accommodating to the intellectual establishment and the criticism of liberation theology (the religious left) that modern theology is too accommodating to the economic and political establishment. Seeking a constructive synthesis, Cox proposed that the theology of the future should be done not in dialogue with the cultural despisers of religion but instead with the despised— especially the poor. He found particularly inspirational the "base communities" that developed in association with liberation theology in Latin America. They understood the importance of "popular piety," so misunderstood and despised by modern theology. But in addition to myth, ritual, and popular devotion, it was necessary to come to grips with global religious pluralism. This set the agenda for a theology that could move beyond the secular city.

Cox continued to write about different religions and Christian denominations. In 1988 he wrote *Many Mansions: A Christian's Encounter with Other Faiths,* as well as *The Silencing of Leonardo Boff: The Vatican and the Future of World Christianity.* In 1996 he published *Fire From Heaven: The Rise of Pentecostal Spirituality.* The topic of Pentecostalism interested Cox, and in a 1997 book review in *World Policy Journal* he wrote, "If the market revolution is dramatically altering the world's economic landscape, the Pentecostal revolution is altering its spiritual topography just as radically."

Beginning in 1965, Cox taught at Harvard, first as an Associate Professor from 1965 to 1970, and then as a Victor Thomas Professor of Divinity from 1970 into the 1990s.

### Further Reading

*The Secular City Debate,* edited by Daniel Callahan (1966), provided a wide range of critical response to Cox's first important work. "Symposium on Religion in the Secular City," in *Christianity and Crisis* (February 20, 1984), has contributions from Douglas Sturm, Rosemary Reuther, Will Campbell, Cornel West, and Robert Imbelli evaluating Cox's reflections upon returning to the secular city 20 years later. □

# Tench Coxe

**American political economist and businessman Tench Coxe (1755-1824) vigorously defended the development of a balanced national economy in which agriculture, manufacturing, and commerce would all contribute to the general prosperity of the country.**

Tench Coxe was born in Philadelphia on May 22, 1755. His father, a respected merchant, was active in local politics. At the age of 16 Tench entered the College of Philadelphia (now the University of Pennsylvania) to study law. He was more interested in business than law, however, and when he came of age, he became a partner in his father's firm.

Coxe faced a dilemma during the American Revolution, as did many other established merchants. When the British invaded Philadelphia, he decided to remain neutral rather than declare his support for the Colonies. Some of his critics have claimed that Coxe was actually a royalist sympathizer and that he joined Gen. William Howe's army against the patriots. Considering his later career, however, this seems doubtful. More likely, the decision was based on economic rather than political motives. After the British withdrew from Philadelphia, his name was listed among those persons accused of treason. But the charges were dropped when no one appeared against him.

Following the Treaty of Paris (1783), Coxe turned his attentions to economic and social problems facing the new nation. In addition to serving on several local committees which attempted to restore order to both state and interstate commercial relations, he was a delegate to the Annapolis Convention (1786) and served briefly in the Continental Congress (1788). He also worked for banking reforms and served as secretary for an organization that promoted the abolition of slavery and relief for free Negroes held in bondage unlawfully.

Coxe began to consider national politics seriously after 1787. Although not a delegate to the Constitutional Convention, he worked enthusiastically for the adoption of the Constitution. He believed the new government would create a sound basis for establishing a national economy and would facilitate orderly economic growth. In 1790 he was appointed assistant to the treasurer, Alexander Hamilton. He supported assumption of state debts, full payment of the national debt, and creation of a national bank. His most influential contributions were made in Hamilton's *Report on Manufactures.* In 1792 he became commissioner of revenue. Although Coxe split with the Federalist party, he remained active in the government until 1797, when he was removed from office by John Adams. Having supported Thomas Jefferson in the election of 1800, he was appointed purveyor of public supplies and held this position until 1812.

Coxe played an important role in the development of American manufacturing. Called by some the father of the American cotton industry, he urged large-scale cultivation of cotton and in 1786 unsuccessfully attempted to import copies of Richard Arkwright's cotton-processing machinery. He died in Philadephia in 1824.

## Further Reading

Harold Hutcheson, *Tench Coxe: A Study in American Economic Development* (1938), is a thorough study of Coxe's economic philosophy. For Coxe's views on cotton production see George S. White, *Memoir of Samuel Slater: The Father of American Manufactures* (1836).

## Additional Sources

Cooke, Jacob Ernest, *Tench Coxe and the early Republic,* Chapel Hill: Published for the Institute of Early American History and Culture, Williamsburg, Va., by the University of North Carolina Press, 1978. □

# Jacob Sechler Coxey

**The American reformer and eccentric Jacob Sechler Coxey (1854-1951) was a well-to-do businessman who, distressed by the economic depression of the 1890s and impelled by the era's reform ideas, led a march of unemployed workers to Washington, D.C., in 1894.**

B orn in Selinsgrove, Pa., on April 16, 1854, Jacob Coxey quit school at 15 and went to work in the rolling mills of Danville. Ten years later he was an operator of a stationary engine. He briefly ran a scrap iron business, then moved to Massillon, Ohio, and in 1881 purchased a sandstone quarry supplying steel and glass factories. Business prospered and Coxey expanded his interests into agricultural holdings. By 1894 he was the wealthiest man in Massillon, his reputed fortune $200,000.

Like many men of his time, Coxey was interested in reform, especially in currency questions. He had been a Greenback Democrat and a member of the Greenback party. He was an unsuccessful candidate for the Ohio Senate in 1885. By the 1890s he was a Populist. In 1894, when he burst into national prominence, Coxey was 40 years old, of medium height, had a neatly trimmed mustache, and presented the general appearance of a prosperous, conservative citizen of the middle class. He was no outstanding orator but impressed people with his simple earnestness and sincerity.

This was the age of the "tramp problem"—tens of thousands of unemployed men on the road in search of work. Along with a colorful colleague, Carl Browne, Coxey conceived the idea of a march on Washington by a "Commonweal of Christ" to dramatize the plight of the country's unemployed. The object was to pressure Congress to adopt Coxey's two pet schemes, designed to relieve the distress of the unemployed while waging war on the interest-based wealth he despised. His Good Roads Bill called for the issuance of $500,000,000 to be expended on the construction of rural roads for wages of $1.50 for an 8-hour day. His Bond Bill authorized the Federal government to purchase bonds from local governments with fiat money, which the latter would use to employ men in constructing various public works, again paying Coxey's minimum wage.

The marchers left Massillon in late March 1894, traveled on foot about 15 miles a day through bad weather, and arrived in Washington on May 1. Coxey had predicted he would arrive with 100,000 men, but his band never numbered more than 300 on the road and his following in Washington was about 1000. (Other "armies" patterned after Coxey's sometimes numbered 2000.) The expedition ended in fiasco with Coxey and Browne arrested and sentenced to 20 days in jail for walking on the grass.

Coxey stuck to his ideas. He testified in Washington several times (including as late as 1946) and ran for innumerable offices for almost every political party. He was Republican mayor of Massillon (1931-1934). In 1932 he received 7,000 votes as the presidential nominee of his Farmer-Labor party. In 1944 he delivered the speech on the Capitol steps in Washington that he had begun exactly 50 years earlier. He died in Massillon on Jan. 14, 1951.

Coxey was an eccentric, but much of the substance of his 1894 proposals was subsequently adopted in government measures. The ideas which he propagandized were in the air during the 1890s. Coxey's contribution was to synthesize and promote them in a coherent program.

## Further Reading

The lack of a recent comprehensive study of Coxey must be attributed to the excellence of the standard work on the subject: Donald L. McMurry, *Coxey's Army: A Study of the Industrial Army Movement of 1894* (1929; rev. ed. 1968). The revised edition contains an excellent introduction by John D. Hicks that traces Coxey's career after the publication of McMurry's book. See also John D. Hicks, *The Populist Revolt* (1931). ☐

# Antoine Coysevox

**The work of the French sculptor Antoine Coysevox (1640-1720) reflected a shift in official French taste from the relatively severe classicism of the 1660s and 1670s to the more expressive and Italianate baroque style and foreshadowed the rococo.**

Antoine Coysevox was born in Lyons on Sept. 29, 1640. He studied at the Royal Academy in Paris (1657-1663). By the late 1670s he was employed at Versailles with many other sculptors engaged in the task of creating fountains and statues for the vast gardens. The artists working on this project were required to conform to the demand by the Royal Academy for a restrained, classical version of the baroque style. Although Coysevox never visited Italy, his personal taste tended to the more fluid, dramatic Italian baroque, and the garden sculpture he executed in the French classical manner is generally dull and uninspired.

During the 1680s the classicism which had dominated the Royal Academy became less constricting, and by the 1690s Louis XIV was himself inclined toward a more specifically Italian baroque style. These developments freed Coysevox's expressive talent, and he gradually began to overshadow François Girardon, his most important rival and the sculptor whose work most clearly reflected the earlier French taste for baroque classicism.

A brilliant example of Coysevox's fully developed personal style is the great stucco relief sculpture (1683-1685) of Louis XIV, which he executed for the Salon de la Guerre (Hall of War) at Versailles. In keeping with the name of this magnificently pompous reception room, Coysevox's relief presents the King on horseback as a conquering emperor riding victoriously over his fallen enemies. The bursting composition, the dramatic use of space, the boldly vigorous high relief, and the lively surface of this work are stylistic characteristics which constitute a break with French classicism.

Coysevox executed over 200 pieces of sculpture, including garden statues, religious works, portrait busts, reliefs, and tombs. His important tomb for Cardinal Mazarin (1689-1693; now in the Louvre, Paris) is surrounded by three richly draped bronze female figures personifying virtues and depicts Mazarin, in marble, kneeling on top of the tomb; the cardinal's gesture is lively and vibrant, and the long train of his vestment flows behind him in dramatic twists and folds and overlaps the edges of the tomb.

Coysevox's later works reveal marked tendencies toward the rococo, the light, delicate, intimate style which was to dominate the arts during the first half of the 18th century. These tendencies are especially to be seen in Coysevox's late portrait busts and in works such as the *Duchesse de Bourgogne as Diana* (1710) at Versailles. The duchess is shown as a lighthearted goddess of the hunt, her pose animated, her draperies gently agitated by her movement; the composition is pierced with space, and the surface presents a refined contrast of delicate textures. Coysevox died in Paris on Oct. 10, 1720.

## Further Reading

The most important works on Coysevox are in French and include Georges Keller-Dorian, *Antoine Coysevox* (2 vols.,

1920), and Luc Benoist, *Coysevox* (1930). For a brief but thorough and excellent analysis of Coysevox's place in 17th-century French art see Sir Anthony Blunt, *Art and Architecture in France, 1500-1700* (1953; rev. ed. 1957). □

# George Crabbe

**The English poet George Crabbe (1754-1832) is noted for his unsentimental realism in portraying people and events and his precision in describing visible nature.**

G eorge Crabbe was born on Dec. 24, 1754, in Aldeburgh, a poor fishing village in Suffolk. His father, part owner of a fishing boat and a customs master, had had some education. Therefore when George proved to have no promise as a seaman, his father sent him to schools at Bungay and Stow Market.

In 1768 Crabbe was apprenticed to a surgeon. But this master taught him little, and in 1771 he changed masters and moved to Woodbridge. There he met his future wife, Sarah Elmy, who accepted his proposal and had the faith and patience not only to wait for Crabbe but to encourage his verse writing.

In 1772 Crabbe had his first literary success; his poem on hope won a prize offered by *Wheble's Lady's Magazine*. Two years later his "Inebriety" was published. During the next years he completed his apprenticeship, studied midwifery in London, and attempted to practice in Aldeburgh. Then, in April 1780, Crabbe borrowed £5 and set off for London to try his literary fortunes. A poem, "The Candidate," was accepted, but the publisher's bankruptcy deprived Crabbe of any possible profit. In March 1781 he appealed in desperation to Edmund Burke, who recognized the merits of the man and his poems.

With Burke's aid Crabbe published three long poems: *The Library* (1781), *The Village* (1782), and *The Newspaper* (1785). *The Village* was much the best, the first example of Crabbe's special talent for telling with literal and compelling truth the often sordid stories of rural and village folk. In 1781 Crabbe took orders, and the following year he became the Duke of Rutland's chaplain.

In December 1783 Crabbe was at last able to marry. Although the duke died in 1787, Crabbe's life continued to be marked by happy domesticity and moderate advancement as a clergyman. A second period of publication, with much critical and some popular success, produced *The Parish Register* (1807), *The Borough* (1810), and *Tales in Verse* (1812), all in the vein of *The Village*. In 1813 his wife died, and in 1814 Crabbe moved to his last home and parish, in Trowbridge, Wiltshire. *Tales of the Hall,* his last volume of poems, was published in 1817. Crabbe died on Feb. 3, 1832, in Trowbridge.

## Further Reading

The first and fullest life of Crabbe is by his son, George Crabbe, Jr., *The Life of the Rev. George Crabbe, LLB* (1834). The best bibliography is in Frederick Clark's translation of René L. Huchon, *George Crabbe and His Times* (1907). Other critical studies are those of Robert L. Chamberlain, *George Crabbe* (1965), intended for general readers, and Oliver F. Sigworth, *Nature's Sternest Painter: Five Essays on the Poetry of George Crabbe* (1965), intended for specialists. A good brief critical biography is Thomas E. Kebbel, *Life of George Crabbe* (1888), in the "Great Writers" series.

## Additional Sources

Bareham, Tony, *A bibliography of George Crabbe,* Folkestone, Eng.: Dawson; Hamden, Conn.: Archon Books, 1978.
Crabbe, George, *Selected journals and letters of George Crabbe,* Oxford: Clarendon Press; New York: Oxford University Press, 1985. □

# Edward Gordon Craig

**Edward Gordon Craig (1872-1966) was an important actor, designer, director, and theoretician of the early 20th century European stage.**

Edward Gordon Craig was born in 1872. He was the son of Edward Godwin, an architect who also did stage designs, and Ellen Terry, one of the most revered actresses of the English stage. Craig's own stage career began at the age of 12 when he appeared as a gardener's boy with his mother at Henry Irving's Lyceum Theatre. At 17 he was accepted into the Irving company, and for the next ten years Craig's primary interest was in acting.

Despite Craig's successes as an actor, he ended that career at the age of 25. Part of the reason for this early retirement was Craig's belief that his idol, Henry Irving, personified the best in acting and that he, Craig, could contribute nothing more to the stage than a copy of Irving's style. From his mentor Craig had learned valuable theater lessons such as strict discipline in rehearsal; thorough rehearsal for a production including the actors, the lighting, and the technical elements; and attention to detail. Although these things seem standard today, they were innovations to early 20th-century theater.

Another reason that Craig left acting was his distaste for realism—the imitation of life—which was the predominant style of the period. As early as 1893 Craig had begun to experiment with music and woodcuts retaining only dominant forms and masses. He believed that art was not an imitation of life but rather an expression of the inexpressible.

Surprisingly, Craig's first work as a director, *No Trifling with Love* (1893), at the Uxbridge Town Hall, was executed in the style of historical realism. However, by 1899 he had developed his own form of theater which he displayed in his first major work, a production of *Dido and Aeneas*. This innovative production took eight months of rehearsal, included a cast of 80, introduced totally new lighting techniques, and completely broke from the realistic tradition. Designed, directed, and choreographed by Craig, the production evoked atmosphere and emotion rather than simply revealing time and place.

In Craig's next production, *The Masque of Love* (1901), he continued to develop his style, using three large cloths as the basis of the entire set and sacks stitched together for the costumes—again simplicity and mass created the entire illusion.

Edward Gordon Craig's practical work was not extensive, yet it helped to revolutionize the theater's growth in this century. In 1902 he directed and designed Handel's *Acis and Galatea;* in 1903 he presented *Bethlehem* and two productions which his mother acted in and produced, *The Vikings* and *Much Ado about Nothing.*

For several years Craig collaborated with other theater innovators, including Otto Brahm, Max Reinhardt, and Eleanora Duse. One of his most famous projects was a co-production with Stanislavsky (perhaps the most influential theater director/actor of the 20th century) of *Hamlet* (1912). This production, known primarily for its revolutionary setting of large moving panels, perhaps reveals the reasons that Craig left the practical theater world.

Aside from his difficulties with personality conflicts (Craig was known as an eccentric), his ideas were far ahead of his time. He believed in the director as the ultimate creator, one who must initiate all ideas and bring unity to a production. He created the idea of the actor as "ubermarionette," whose movement was not psychologically motivated or naturalistic, but rather symbolic. The actor should be like a mask for the audience to interpret. Finally, he introduced a new stagecraft—one based on the magic of imagination rather than on everyday details.

If Craig's actual work was limited, and sometimes impractical because of technical limitations, his writing was prolific. In 1898 he launched the theater journal *The Page;* in 1908 *The Mask* (until 1929); and from 1918 to 1919 he wrote *The Marionette*. He also published *The Art of the Theatre* (1905), *On the Art of the Stage, Towards a New Theatre, Scene, The Theatre Advancing,* and *Books and Theatres,* as well as biographies of Henry Irving and his mother.

Craig's work in the theater and his writings have influenced many of the 20th century's innovators, including Stanislavsky, Meyerhold, and Brecht. He continued to be a source of inspiration for many years—many of the ideas that he developed in the early part of the 20th century were not realized on the stage until the 1980s. Edward Gordon Craig died at the age of 94 in 1966.

## Further Reading

The most important and inclusive of Craig's own works are *On the Art of the Theatre* (1911) and *Index to the Story of My Days* (1957). For thorough examinations of Craig's life and his work, including illustrations, see Denis Bablet's *Edward Gordon Craig* (1981); Edward Craig, *Gordon Craig: The Story of His Life* (1968); J. Michael Walton, *Craig on Theatre* (1983), which includes selections from Craig's writings; and Laurence Senelick, *Gordon Craig's Moscow Hamlet: A Reconstruction* (1982).

## Additional Sources

Carrick, Edward, *Gordon Craig: the story of his life,* New York: Limelight Editions, 1968, 1985.

Craig, Edward Gordon, *Gordon Craig's Paris diary, 1932-1933,* North Hills, Pa.: Bird & Bull Press, 1982.

Craig, Ellen Gordon, *Edward Gordon Craig: the last eight years, 1958-1966: letters from Ellen Gordon Craig,* Andoversford, Gloucestershire: Whittington Press, 1983. □

# Lucas Cranach the Elder

**The German painter, engraver, and designer of woodcuts Lucas Cranach the Elder (1472-1553) is best known for the delightfully mannered style he practiced as court painter to the electors of Saxony.**

Lucas Cranach the Elder was born at Kronach, Franconia. He was apparently trained by his father, Hans, a painter, and from 1495 to 1498 undertook work at Kronach for Coburg and Gotha. There is evidence that Cranach resided in Vienna between about 1500 and 1504. In 1504 he married Barbara Brengbier of Gotha; they had three daughters and two sons, Hans (died 1537) and Lucas the Younger (1515-1586), both of whom were painters.

In 1505 Cranach established residence at Wittenberg, where he was court painter to three successive electors: Frederick the Wise, John the Constant, and John Frederick the Magnanimous. Cranach was a prosperous and respected citizen. He owned several houses and land, held the office of councilor, and was a burgomaster. He also worked for other princely patrons and was a follower and lifelong friend of Martin Luther.

In 1550 Cranach followed John Frederick the Magnanimous to Augsburg, where the elector was in exile, and in 1552 accompanied him to Weimar. Cranach died in Weimar on Oct. 16, 1553.

### Early Works

Cranach's earliest known works belong to the period of his Vienna residence and are strongly expressive in style, with figures and landscape dramatically united in movement; an interest in picturesque landscape manifests itself, anticipating tendencies peculiar to the so called Danube school. Characteristic examples are *St. Jerome in Penitence* (1502), the half-length portraits of Dr. Johannes Cuspinian and his wife Anna (ca. 1502-1503), and the *Crucifixion* in Munich (1503). In the composition of the *Crucifixion* Cranach broke sharply with iconographic tradition and em-

ployed bold foreshortening and other spatial devices that reflect a knowledge of the art of Michael Pacher and, through it, of Andrea Mantegna. In Cranach's first signed painting, *Rest on the Flight into Egypt* (1504), the spirit is idyllic and the actions of the figures are lively.

### Change in Style

Cranach's work became less emotional after he moved to Wittenberg in 1505, although the change was slower in the woodcuts than in the paintings. His woodcuts were technically inspired by Albrecht Dürer's but less finely cut and less clearly organized. In Cranach's woodcuts a dramatic emphasis prevailed, and a preference for tone led, by 1509, to the use of the chiaroscuro technique, as in the *St. Christopher* of 1506, reused or recut and printed with a color block in 1509. The change in style in the paintings may be seen in the *Martyrdom of St. Catherine* in Dresden (1506), in which the emphatic rendering of the garment patterns, the falling tongues of fire, and the crowding of the figures result in a loss of compositional unity and spatial clarity; and in the *Holy Kinship Altarpiece* (1509), painted soon after Cranach's trip to the Netherlands, in which Flemish influence accounts for the general disposition and costumes of the figures.

Thereafter Cranach's painting was increasingly distinguished by minimal modeling, stress on linear detail, clean contours, and, in the portraits and most pictures of one or two figures, unmodeled backgrounds. This may be observed in works of such diverse subject matter as the *Madonna and Child* in Breslau (ca. 1510), the model for many variants to issue from his workshop; *Cardinal Albrecht of Brandenburg as St. Jerome in His Study* (1525), based on Dürer's engraving *St. Jerome in His Study;* the *Judgment of Paris* (1530) and *Venus* (1532), in which the subjects are classical but the interpretation is pervaded by a naive charm due in large part to Cranach's curvaceous, gently erotic female nudes; the full-length portraits of Duke Henry the Pious and his wife Catherine (1514); the *Fountain of Youth* (1546); and Reformation pictures like the *Fall and Salvation* (1529) and *Christ Blessing the Little Children* (1538). Cranach also painted hunting scenes for the lodges of his princely patrons.

Cranach's drawings include eight pages of marginal illustrations for the Prayer Book of Maximilian (1515) and magnificent animal and portrait studies, like the head of Martin Luther's father (ca. 1527). His best-known engraving is the *Penance of St. John Chrysostom* (1509).

### Further Reading

A good summary of Cranach's life and art, with reproductions of his most characteristic work, is in Eberhard Ruhmer, *Cranach,* translated from the German by Joan Spencer (1963). For Cranach's drawings see Jakob Rosenberg, *Die Zeichnungen Lucas Cranach d. A.* (1960); and for the prints see F. W. H. Hollstein, *German Engravings, Etchings and Woodcuts, ca. 1400-1700,* vol. 6 (1954).

### Additional Sources

Cranach, Lucas, *Lucas Cranach,* Leningrad: Aurora Art, 1976. □

# Prudence Crandall

**American educator Prudence Crandall (1803-1890) made one of the early experiments in providing educational facilities for African American girls.**

Prudence Crandall was born on Sept. 3, 1803, in Hopkinton, R.I., to a Quaker family. Her father moved to a farm at Canterbury, Conn., in 1813. She attended the Friends' Boarding School at Providence, R.I., and later taught in a school for girls at Plainfield, Conn. In 1831 she returned to Canterbury to run the newly established Canterbury Female Boarding School. When Sarah Harris, daughter of a free African American farmer in the vicinity, asked to be admitted to the school in order to prepare for teaching other African Americans, she was accepted. Immediately, the townspeople objected and pressured to have Harris dismissed.

Crandall was familiar with the abolitionist movement and had read William Lloyd Garrison's *Liberator*. Faced with the town's resolutions of disapproval, she met with abolitionists in Boston, Providence, and New York to enlist support for the transformation of the Canterbury school into a school for African American girls. The *Liberator* advertised for new pupils. In February 1833 the white pupils were dismissed, and by April, 20 African American girls took up studies. A trade boycott and other harassments of the school ensued. Warnings, threats, and acts of violence against the school replaced disapproving town-meeting resolutions.

Abolitionists came to Crandall's defense, using the issue as a stand against opposition to furthering the education of freed African Americans. Despite attacks the school continued operation. On May 24, 1833, the Connecticut Legislature passed a law prohibiting such a school with African Americans from outside the state unless it had the town's permission, and under this law Crandall was arrested in July. She was placed in the county jail for one night and then released under bond.

A prominent abolitionist, Arthur Tappan of New York, provided money to hire the ablest lawyers to defend the Quaker school teacher at her trial, which opened at the Windham County Court on Aug. 23, 1833. The case centered on the constitutionality of the Connecticut law regarding the education of African Americans. The defense held that African Americans were citizens in other states, were so therefore in Connecticut, and could not be deprived of their rights under the Federal Constitution. The prosecution denied that freed African Americans were citizens. The county court jury failed to reach a decision. Although a new trial in Superior Court decided against the school, when the decision reached the Supreme Court of Errors on appeal, the case was dismissed for lack of evidence.

The judicial process had not stopped the operation of the Canterbury school, but the townspeople's violence against it increased and finally closed it on Sept. 10, 1834. Crandall had married a Baptist preacher, Calvin Philleo, on Sept. 4, 1834. He took her to Ithaca, N.Y., and from there

they went to Illinois and finally to Elk Falls, Kans., where she lived until her death on Jan. 28, 1890. In 1886 the Connecticut Legislature had voted her an annual pension of $400.

## Further Reading

Wendell P. and Francis J. Garrison, *William Lloyd Garrison, 1805-1879: The Story of His Life Told by His Children* (4 vols., 1885-1889), and John C. Kimball, *Connecticut's Canterbury Tale: Its Heroine Prudence Crandall and Its Moral for Today* (1886), are informative accounts of Prudence Crandall's work. See also Thomas E. Drake, *Quakers and Slavery in America* (1950), and Dwight L. Dumond, *Antislavery: The Crusade for Freedom in America* (1961).

## Additional Sources

Strane, Susan, *A whole-souled woman: Prudence Crandall and the education of Black women,* New York: W.W. Norton, 1990.

Welch, Marvis Olive, *Prudence Crandall: a biography,* Manchester, Conn.: Jason Publishers, 1983. ☐

# Hart Crane

**Hart Crane (1899-1932) was an American poet in the mystical tradition who attempted, through the visionary affirmations of his richly imagistic, metaphysically intense poetry, to counter the naturalistic despair of the 1920s.**

Hart Crane was born on July 21, 1899, in Garrettsville, Ohio, the son of the successful Cleveland manufacture of "Crane's Chocolates," and was raised in Cleveland. He violently repudiated the business values of his father and attached himself to his more cultivated mother. Crane's life was permeated with severe psychic disturbances perhaps originating in this nearly classic Oedipal situation; he eventually became an avowed homosexual and a severe alcoholic.

## Apprentice Poet

In 1916 Crane went to New York, where he held odd jobs to support himself while writing poetry. Later he worked in several midwestern cities before returning to New York in the early 1920s to align himself with the literary avant-grade. Immersing himself in the study of his American literary ancestors, particularly Herman Melville, Walt Whitman, and Emily Dickinson, Crane also managed to become familiar with the experimental verse being published in the "little magazines" of the period and to read the latest works of T. S. Eliot and Ezra Pound.

From 1925 until the end of his life Crane received financial assistance from the New York banker and art patron Otto Kahn. Thus he was able to prepare for publication his first volume of poetry, *White Buildings* (1926).

Earlier, in 1922, a reading of the *Tertium Organum,* written by the Russian mystic P. D. Ouspensky, had affected Crane profoundly, for it provided what seemed a cogent defense of Crane's own belief in the validity of mystical

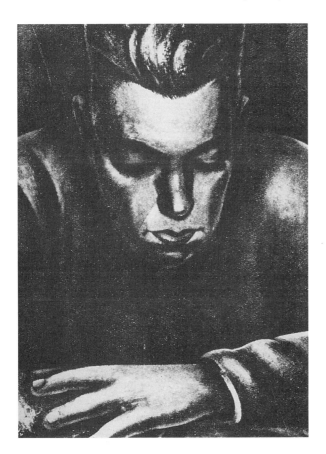

knowledge based on ecstasy and direct illumination. Ouspensky used Whitman as the chief example of a modern man possessed of mystic awareness, further enhancing Crane's interest in Whitman's poetry. This interest eventually resulted in Crane's most ambitious project, *The Bridge* (1930), a series of closely related long poems (inspired by Whitman's example) on the transcendent meaning of the United States, in which the Brooklyn Bridge symbolized the spiritual evolution of civilization. Crane attempted to build a metaphysical "bridge" between the individual and the race, the temporal and the eternal, and the physical and the transcendent.

The tortuous spiritual affirmations of Crane's poetry, with its illumination and exaltation, represented the positive side of an intense lifelong struggle against despair and self-disgust. On April 26, 1932, after a year in Mexico on a Guggenheim fellowship, Crane committed suicide by leaping into the Gulf of Mexico from the ship that was returning him to the United States. Thus the poet united himself with the sea that had so often served him as symbol of both the universal creative life-force and the threat of annihilation.

## Analysis of the Writings

Allen Tate's foreword to his friend's first volume, *White Buildings,* remains perhaps the best brief introduction to Crane's difficult and intense poetic vision. Tate wrote: "The poetry of Hart Crane is ambitious . . . . It is an American poetry. Crane's themes are abstractly, metaphysically conceived, but they are definitely confined to an experience of the American scene. . . . Crane's poems are a fresh vision of the world, so intensely personalized in a new creative language that only the strictest and most unprepossessed effort of attention can take it in. . . . Melville and Whitman are his avowed masters. In his sea poems . . . there is something of Melville's intense, transcendental brooding on the mystery of the 'high interiors of the sea.' . . . Crane's poetry is a concentration of certain phases of the Whitman substance, the fragments of the myth."

The best of *White Buildings,* "Repose of Rivers" and most of the "Voyages," are conceivably the greatest mystical poems in America since early Whitman.

Crane's "General Aims and Theories" (1926) is a rather tortured attempt to explain the terms of his mystical "way up" toward illumination and discovery through the creative adventure of art: "It is my hope to go through the combined materials of the poem, using our 'real' world somewhat as a spring-board . . . Its evocation will not be toward decoration or amusement, but rather toward a state of consciousness, an 'innocence' (Blake) or absolute beauty. In this condition there may be discoverable under new forms certain spiritual illuminations, shining with a morality essentialized from experience directly, and not from previous precepts or preconceptions. It is as though a poem gave the reader as he left it a single, *new word,* never before spoken and impossible to actually enunciate. . ." [Crane's italics].

But the best illustrations of Crane's poetic aims are found in the poetry itself. These poems are notoriously difficult to paraphrase, precisely because, when Crane is most successful, the mystical experience "described" in the poetry is actually simulated for the reader in the actual reading of the poem itself. In "At Melville's Tomb" Crane moves toward the achievement of religious illuminations by what he termed the "logic of metaphor." Often, as in "The Broken Tower," a late poem, the avenue to mystic vision is paved with erotic images similar to those employed by Whitman.

Although "The Proem" to *The Bridge* is surely one of Crane's greatest achievements, the work as a whole is disappointing in comparison with the best of *White Buildings.* Attempting no less than an esthetic distillation of the "Myth of America" while plunging ever deeper into personal despair and doubt, psychic disturbance, and alcoholism, Crane was unable to realize his enormous intentions.

The intent of the book, which grew out of Crane's devotion to Whitman and his desire to refute the spiritual desolation of Eliot's *Waste Land,* was to provide a defense of mystical experience in the age of modern science. Ouspensky's scientifically learned book had provided Crane with an invaluable weapon in the struggle, but the indispensable ally was Whitman. At the center of *The Bridge* is the poem "Cape Hatteras," which Crane himself described as "a kind of ode to Whitman." Within it, Crane echoes several of Whitman's works. For both poets, science and technology do not destroy faith based on mystical awareness but enlarge and promote it.

## The Achievement

But it was in "The Proem" that Crane had fully repaid his debt to Whitman. Affirmation and denial, dream and fact, in their paradoxical fusion and conflict, manage to incorporate both Whitman's vision and the materialistic temper of the 1920s that seemed to invalidate that vision. The parabolic curve of the actual bridge, which never closes in on itself, suggests the "inviolate curve" of the perfect circle of infinity and the upward movement of the spirit, while at the same time seeming to tend toward the finite closing of the arc in the intensely real steel girders of the span. The final line of the poem resolves its profound ambiguity in a plea for illumination which will "of the curveship lend a myth to God."

But Crane's attempt to demonstrate the possibility of spiritual experience in the modern wasteland through the creation of an "intrinsic," "secular" myth exacted a severe toll on the poet's already-strained psychological resources. Unable to trust completely in mystic intuitions derived largely secondhand from Whitman, and unsure of the validity of the supporting metaphysics supplied by Ouspensky but not fully corroborated in his own speculations, the poet sustained his fragile equilibrium mainly by strength of will. The excesses of Crane's personal life were probably as much the result of his tortured consciousness as of any purely clinical disorder. The failure of *The Bridge* to live up to its universal implications represented a collapse of will rather than a failure of the poet's art. The times were out of joint for the fulfillment of Crane's quest for transcendent certainty.

Although Crane published only two volumes of poetry in his brief career, he is regarded as one of the five or six greatest American poets of the 20th century. (Crane's *Complete Poems* and *Selected Letters and Prose* were published in New York in 1966.)

## Further Reading

*The Letters of Hart Crane, 1916-1932,* edited by Brom Weber (1952), is an invaluable source for the turbulent events of Crane's life. There are two excellent biographies of Crane: Philip Horton, *Hart Crane: The Life of an American Poet* (1937), and John Unterecker, *Voyager: A Life of Hart Crane* (1969), which introduces previously unpublished material. See also Brom Weber, *Hart Crane: A Biographical and Critical Study* (1948). A standard critical work is R. W. B. Lewis, *The Poetry of Hart Crane: A Critical Study* (1967).

## Additional Sources

Crane, Hart, *Letters of Hart Crane and his famil,* New York, Columbia University Press, 1974.

Crane, Hart, *O my land, my friends: the selected letters of Hart Crane,* New York: Four Walls Eight Windows, 1997.

Horton, Philip, *Hart Crane: the life of an American poet,* New York: Octagon Books, 1976, 1937.

Lindsay, Clarence B., *Hart Crane, an introduction,* Columbus: State Library of Ohio, 1979.

Unterecker, John Eugene, *Voyager: a life of Hart Crane,* New York: Liveright, 1987, 1969. □

# Stephen Crane

**Stephen Crane (1871-1900), an American fiction writer and poet, was also a newspaper reporter. His novel "The Red Badge of Courage" stands high among the world's books depicting warfare.**

After the Civil War, William Dean Howells, Henry James, and others established realism as the standard mode of American fiction. In the 1890s younger writers tried to enlarge the territory of realism with impressionist, symbolist, and even new romantic approaches. Of these pioneers, Stephen Crane was the most influential.

Crane was born on Nov. 1, 1871, the fourteenth and last child of Mary Helen Crane and the Reverend Doctor Jonathan Townley Crane, presiding elder of the Newark, N.J., district of the Methodist Church. A frail child, Stephen moved with his family from one parsonage to another during his first 8 years. In 1880, with the death of his father, his mother moved her family to Asbury Park, N.J. Stephen was exposed early to writing as a career: his mother wrote on religious topics and lectured for the Women's Christian Temperance Union, and his brother Townley worked as a newspaper reporter.

In 1888 Crane entered military school, where he made an impressive record on the drill field and the baseball diamond but not in the classroom. Without graduating he went to Lafayette College, then to Syracuse University. He flunked out, but whatever his academic record, his time had not been wasted: in his fraternity house Crane, aged 20, had

written the first draft of *Maggie: A Girl of the Streets.* Returning to Asbury Park as a reporter under his brother for the *New York Tribune,* Crane attended Hamlin Garland's lectures on the realistic writers. Garland was interested in the young writer, read his manuscripts, and guided his reading.

In 1891 Crane's mother died. Crane spent much of the next year in Sullivan County, N.Y., where another brother practiced law. Five "Sullivan County Sketches" were published in the *Tribune* and *Cosmopolitan* (his first magazine appearance). He went frequently to New York City, haunting the Bowery in search of experience and literary material. When he returned to Asbury Park, he lost his job on the *Tribune* (and his brother's too) by writing an accurate description of a labor parade that undermined his Republican publisher's standing in an election campaign. This year also brought unhappy endings to two romances.

### Career as Novelist

In autumn 1892 Crane moved to New York City. By spring he submitted a second version of *Maggie* to a family friend, Richard Gilder, editor of the *Century.* Gilder tried to explain his rejection of the manuscript, but Crane interrupted bluntly, "You mean that the story's too honest?" Honest the story is, and blunt and brutal. It shows Maggie as a simple, ignorant girl bullied by her drunken mother, delivered to a seducer by her brother, driven by the seducer into prostitution and, finally, to suicide. In approach the novel is akin to the "veritism" of Garland and the realism of Howells, but it differs stylistically in its ironic tone, striking imagery (especially color imagery), and its compression.

"Impressionism" is the term often applied to the very personal style Crane was developing. Convinced that no publisher would dare touch his "shocking" novel, Crane printed it at his own expense, using the pseudonym Johnston Smith. The book went unnoticed and unpurchased, except for two copies. Garland, however, admired it and called it to the attention of Howells, then America's most influential man of letters, who recognized Crane's achievement and tried unsuccessfully to get the novel reissued.

By summer 1893 Crane was well into what was to be a Civil War novel. As research he read *Century* magazine's series "Battles and Leaders of the Civil War" and, it is believed, traveled in Virginia to interview Confederate veterans. What he found missing from the history books was the actual sensation any single individual experiences in battle; this is what *The Red Badge of Courage* conveys. Just as Maggie represents every girl victimized by a slum environment, so Henry Fleming represents every recruit who reels through the noise and glare of war. Neither character had a name in Crane's first drafts: they are "every woman," "every man," buffeted by forces they neither control nor understand. Though there were delays—painful ones for the penniless author—this book was destined for early success. A shortened version was serialized in the *Philadelphia Press* and hundreds of other newspapers in 1894. The instant critical and popular enthusiasm spread to England when the complete book was published the following year. A revised version of *Maggie* was issued along with an earlier novel about slum life, *George's Mother,* in 1896. The syndicate that had arranged newspaper publication of *Red Badge of Courage* sent Crane to the West and Mexico to sketch whatever struck his fancy.

### Poet and Journalist

Crane's first book of poems, *The Black Riders,* was on the press before his departure. "A condensed Whitman," the *Nation* aptly called him. His "lines," as he called his poems, are terse, natural, and forceful; ironic and unsentimental. Their language is in the best sense journalistic, just as Crane's reportage had been from the beginning poetic.

The excursion west and to Mexico produced sensitive sketches and materials for a number of Crane's finest stories. Back in New York, he published newspaper articles critical of the city's corrupt police. The police made New York uncomfortable for Crane, so he departed for Cuba to report the anti-Spanish insurrection there. Enroute he stopped in Jacksonville, Fla., where he met Cora Stewart, a handsome New England woman in her late 20s, separated from her husband, the son of a British baronet. She was the owner of the Hotel de Dream, an elegant boardinghouse-cum nightclub-cum brothel and gave it all up to become (quite without clerical or legal formalities) "Mrs. Stephen Crane."

In spite of this "marriage," Crane left for Cuba aboard a small steamer. It sank on its first day out. Crane's heroic role in the disaster—he barely escaped with the captain and two other men—evoked his best short story, "The Open Boat."

## War Correspondent

For the Hearst newspapers Crane covered the war between Greece and Turkey. Crane, it appears, wanted to see if war was really as he had depicted it in *Red Badge of Courage:* it was. But the trip yielded mediocre war reportage and a bad novel, *Active Service* (1899). Cora had followed Crane to Greece; they next went to England, where Crane finished his powerful novella *The Monster* and three of his finest short stories, ''The Bride Comes to Yellow Sky,'' ''Death and the Child,'' and ''The Blue Hotel.''

The Spanish-American War in 1898 provided new employment. Crane sent distinguished reports to the *New York World.* He was with Cora in England when his second volume of poems, *War Is Kind,* appeared in 1899. Sick and aware of nearing death, he wrote furiously. That spring Cora took him to the Continent, where he died on June 5, 1900, in Badenweiler, Germany, of tuberculosis. His haunting tales of childhood, *Whilomville Stories,* and Cuban tales, *Wounds in the Rain* appeared later that year.

## Further Reading

Robert W. Stallman, *Stephen Crane: A Biography* (1968), is the authoritative source on Crane's life. The two most interesting studies—one biographical, the other critical—are by poets: John Berryman, *Stephen Crane* (1950), and Daniel G. Hoffman, *The Poetry of Stephen Crane* (1956). Also recommended are Maurice Bassan, ed., *Stephen Crane: A Collection of Critical Essays* (1967), and, for views of Crane in the context of his period, Warner Berthoff, *The Ferment of Realism* (1965), and Larzer Ziff, *The American 1890s* (1966). □

# Thomas Cranmer

**The English ecclesiastic Thomas Cranmer (1489-1556) was the first Protestant archbishop of Canterbury.**

Thomas Cranmer was born in Aslacton, Nottinghamshire, on July 2, 1489, the son of a village squire. He went to Cambridge University at the age of 14; though of indifferent scholarship, he received a bachelor's degree in 1511 and a master's degree in 1514. He also received a fellowship at Jesus College and seemed well on the way to an ecclesiastical career when, at 25, he abandoned his fellowship and married Black Joan of the Dolphin Inn at Cambridge. Very little is known of this girl, who died, as did his child by her, within a year of their marriage. Cranmer then returned to his former way of life. His fellowship was restored, and by 1520 he had been ordained a priest and become a university preacher. Five years later he received the degree of doctor of divinity.

A chance meeting in August 1529 with two members of King Henry VIII's administration led to Cranmer's employment in the royal service; he worked toward obtaining the annulment of Henry's marriage with Catherine of Aragon. In January 1532 he was sent as ambassador to the court of

Emperor Charles V at Ratisbon and at Nuremberg. At the latter town he made two acquisitions: Lutheran sympathies, if not convictions, and a young German wife, Margaret, a Lutheran and a niece of the prominent Lutheran scholar Andreas Osiander.

## Protestant Archbishop

Within a year of his appointment as ambassador, Cranmer was recalled and nominated for the office of archbishop of Canterbury. He knew that this appointment was given him in return for his future annulment of the King's marriage. The bulls of his appointment to the See of Canterbury were obtained, under compulsion and with great speed, from Pope Clement VII by March 1533, and Cranmer was consecrated archbishop on March 30. On May 23 he concluded the trial of Henry's marriage to Catherine of Aragon by declaring the marriage to have been invalid. On May 28 Cranmer publicly adjudged Henry's marriage to Anne Boleyn in the previous January to have been lawful; and on June 1, Whitsunday, he anointed and crowned her as queen of England in Westminster Abbey.

For the rest of his life Cranmer was a major instrument in establishing royal supremacy in spiritual matters as in temporal affairs and thus destroying the independence of the English Church. In 1536 he presided over a commission of bishops and divines which met at Lambeth Palace, his London home. This commission published the Ten Articles, a statement of the beliefs of the Henrician Church, which it was hoped could be accepted by Lutherans as well as Catholics.

On May 15, 1536, Anne Boleyn was condemned to death for treason by reason of her adultery. Her execution was postponed for 2 days, however, in order that Cranmer might declare her marriage to Henry invalid and thus bastardize their daughter, Elizabeth. On the day Anne died, Cranmer granted Henry a dispensation to marry Jane Seymour despite their consanguinity.

Disputes and negotiations over religious beliefs and practices filled these years. In 1539 Cranmer opposed the Act of the Six Articles; he believed the act was too Catholic despite the fact that Henry VIII himself had drawn up the final text. He helped, however, to put together the religious work known as the King's Book, although much of its content was contrary to his beliefs. His overwhelming Erastianism stifled his opposition to this book and allowed him to approve its use in his diocese.

## Liturgical Plans

In the last years of Henry's reign Cranmer's beliefs gradually became more Protestant, and his enemies at court sought to have him deposed, if not condemned, for heresy. Nevertheless, Henry, apparently well aware of all this, protected him and allowed him to develop the liturgical plans that were to bear such famous fruit. Cranmer published the English Litany in 1544 and the First Book of Common Prayer in 1549 during the reign of King Edward VI. A more Protestant version of the latter work, the Second Book of Common Prayer, was issued in 1552, and it proved to be the foundation of, and the most lasting formative influence in, the

Church of England. A. G. Dickens (1964) calls it "a devotional asset ranking second after the English Bible," and it exerted a most powerful influence on the development of the English language. Finally came the Forty-two Articles of Religion, which received royal approval a month before Edward's death in 1553. Cranmer and others had worked on these articles for many years, and they were the prototypes of the famous Thirty-nine Articles established in Queen Elizabeth's reign.

With the accession of Queen Mary, there remained for Cranmer, who had so injured her and her mother and had been so prominent in promoting the destruction of the Catholic Church, only imprisonment and death for heresy. Despite his recantations of his heretical views he vigorously affirmed his Protestantism as he was burned at the stake on March 21, 1556.

## Further Reading

A thorough biography is Jasper Ridley, *Thomas Cranmer* (1962). See also Francis E. Hutchinson, *Cranmer and the English Reformation* (1951), and Theodore Maynard, *The Life of Thomas Cranmer* (1956). For background material A. G. Dickens, *The English Reformation* (1964; rev. ed. 1967), and J. J. Scarisbrick, *Henry VIII* (1968), are useful.

## Additional Sources

Gilpin, William, *The life of Thomas Cranmer, Archbishop of Canterbury,* London: Printed for R. Blamire . . . , 1784.
MacCulloch, Diarmaid, *Thomas Cranmer: a life,* New Haven, CT: Yale University Press, 1996.
*Thomas Cranmer: churchman and scholar,* New York: Boydell Press, 1993. □

# Richard Crashaw

**The English poet Richard Crashaw (C. 1612-1649) was Roman Catholic in sensibility and ultimately in allegiance. His poetry is the single major body of work in English that can be called baroque.**

Richard Crashaw was born in London. His father, a stern Puritan who hated the Church of Rome as much as he did worldly pleasures—his son was to share the latter of his prejudices but not the former—was preacher at the Temple Church. Crashaw was educated at the Charterhouse, where he received a rigorous classical education under the tutelage of a royalist master. He had already indicated his poetic talent and religious sensibility in poems in Latin and Greek before he entered Pembroke College, Cambridge, in 1631.

At the university Crashaw found himself in the matrix of an extraordinary number of the period's best poets: John Donne, George Herbert, Andrew Marvell, Sir John Suckling, Abraham Cowley, and John Milton, to name some of the most important. His own college was High Church in ritual and spiritual allegiance. In 1634 Crashaw received a bachelor of arts degree, and in 1635 he was elected a fellow of

Peterhouse, which was strongly influenced by the conservative, High Church archbishop William Laud. In fact, the religious atmosphere of this college was scarcely distinguishable from Roman Catholicism. During the years that followed, Crashaw participated often in the life of the religious establishment at Little Gidding, a village near Cambridge. By 1639 he was an ordained preacher.

The civil war, however, changed his life. Cromwell seized Cambridge in 1643 and efficiently rooted out all traces of "popery." Crashaw did not wait to be ejected from his fellowship by the Puritans but left at the beginning of the occupation and spent the rest of his life in exile at Little Gidding and Oxford and on the Continent. The civil war deprived him of a successful career as preacher and probably of continued participation in the Anglican Church. His years of exile were dogged by poverty, ill health, and neglect by his patrons. Crashaw became a Roman Catholic in 1645. He died in 1649 in Loreto, Italy, where he was in the service of Cardinal Pallota.

Crashaw's major poetry appeared in *Steps to the Temple* in 1646 (enlarged in 1648). Though the title suggests the dominance of George Herbert, the major influences in fact are the spirit and esthetic techniques of the Continental Counter Reformation, which produced the arts known as baroque. The major poetic influence was the Italian Giambattista Marino, some of whose work Crashaw translated. Crashaw's baroque poetry, exemplified in "The Weeper," thrives on paradox, imagery flamboyant to the point of grotesquerie, stock religious symbols, and concern with martyrdom and mysticism.

## Further Reading

The standard work on Crashaw, equally useful for historical and literary backgrounds, biography, and critical interpretation, is Austin Warren, *Richard Crashaw: A Study in Baroque Sensibility* (1939).

## Additional Sources

*New perspectives on the life and art of Richard Crashaw,* Columbia: University of Missouri Press, 1990.
Willey, Basil, *Richard Crashaw (1612/13-1649): a memorial lecture delivered at Peterhouse, Cambridge, on 11 July 1949,* Norwood, Pa.: Norwood Editions, 1978. □

# Marcus Licinius Crassus Dives

**Marcus Licinius Crassus Dives (ca. 115-53 B.C.) was a Roman politician and member of the First Triumvirate, for which he provided financial backing. He spent much of his political career in frustrated rivalry with Pompey.**

Crassus was descended from a long line of distinguished senators. When, during the uprising of Cornelius Cinna in 87 B.C., his father committed suicide and his brother was murdered by the forces of Gaius Marius, Crassus fled to Spain. After the death of Cinna he came out of hiding, gathered a small military force, and eventually joined Sulla when he returned to Italy from the East. In command of the right wing at the battle of the Colline Gate in 82, Crassus was mainly responsible for the final victory of Sulla over the Marians. During the subsequent Sullan proscriptions he began to amass his enormous fortune by buying the property of the proscribed. Later he continued his speculations in real estate by buying fire-damaged properties. But in spite of his wealth, which he used for political purposes, he lived modestly, was temperate in his personal habits, and cultivated people in all walks of life. Through careful training he also became one of the most effective orators of his day.

## Early Public Career

Praetor in 73, Crassus was chosen by the Senate, after the defeat of both consuls in 72, to take over command in the war against Spartacus although he held no public office at the time. He drove Spartacus into Bruttium and there cut him off by building a wall across the toe of Italy. Although Spartacus broke through the wall during the winter, Crassus defeated him in two decisive engagements, but not until he had asked the Senate to summon for help M. Lucullus from Thrace and Pompey from Spain. Pompey caught a few stragglers from the final battle and characteristically claimed a share of Crassus' victory.

Pompey returned to Rome to run for the consulship of 70 B.C. with a program of reform in mind. Unwilling to be outdone, Crassus decided to run with him, but the rivalry of the two men was so great that they almost came to blows during their year in office, and Pompey captured the support of the people with his legislation to remove the restrictions on the tribunate and to open the jury courts again to the equestrians. As a result, Crassus had to stand by while Pompey was voted his great commands in the 60s.

While Pompey was absent in the East, Crassus sought to outmaneuver him politically in Rome. He used his money and his affability to support candidates for high political office, but apart from Julius Caesar, whom Crassus supported for aedileship in 65, all of his candidates failed because of Pompeian and senatorial opposition. In 65 Crassus was himself elected censor with Q. Lutatius Catulus. But his attempts to purge the Senate and win the support of Cisalpine Gaul with a grant of citizenship were vetoed by his colleague, and both men resigned from office prematurely. There is no concrete evidence that Crassus played an active part in the conspiracies of Autronius and Sulla in 66 or of Catiline in 63, although he may have hoped to profit from the unrest they caused.

## First Triumvirate

When Pompey returned and found himself checked politically by Cato and the senatorial leaders, Crassus' maneuvers finally paid off in the formation of the First Triumvi-

rate and the election of Julius Caesar to the consulship of 59 B.C. Pompey had been forced to turn to Crassus and Caesar for help. They tended to cooperate during Caesar's year in office to offset Pompey's enormous prestige and power.

In the years after 59 when Caesar was absent in Gaul, the rivalry between Pompey and Crassus broke out anew as Crassus used P. Clodius to harass Pompey and the two men competed for honors and commands. At one point Pompey complained to the Senate that Crassus was trying to assassinate him. Finally, in 56, the triumvirs met at Luca to compose their differences and make more realistic arrangements for sharing their power. Pompey and Crassus were to hold the consulship together for the second time in 55. Thereafter all three men would have coordinated commands for a period of 5 years, Caesar in Gaul, Pompey in Spain, and Crassus in Syria for a campaign against the Parthians.

As consuls in 55, Crassus and Pompey quelled opposition against the triumvirate. Toward the end of the year Crassus left for the East. In 54 he conducted a successful campaign across the Euphrates and was hailed by his troops. In the following year he again attacked, but he allowed himself to be drawn into the Mesopotamian desert, where his whole army of seven legions and 4,000 cavalry was surrounded and cut off by the Parthian mounted archers near the city of Carrhae. After losing his son, Crassus led the remnants of his legions to the city. To save themselves, his troops then forced Crassus to meet with the Parthian commander Surena. Crassus was treacherously slain at the conference on June 6, 53 B.C.

Plutarch says that in Crassus many virtues were obscured by one vice, avarice. In politics he was the spokesman for Roman financial interests. His failure was that he had no political goals beyond his own personal advancement or protection. The baton he briefly carried rightly passed to Caesar, a man of wider vision.

## Further Reading

The main ancient sources for Crassus are Plutarch's *Lives,* Cicero's speeches and letters, and Appian's *Roman History.* See also *The Cambridge Ancient History* (12 vols., 1922-1939) and H. H. Scullard, *From the Gracchi to Nero* (1959; 2d ed. 1963). □

# José Craveirinha

**José Craveirinha (born 1922) was a journalist in Mozambique, East Africa, who became the foremost lyric poet of his nation. His early poems inspired African pride and protest during the long (and successful) struggle for independence from Portugal.**

José Craveirinha was born on May 28, 1922, in Lourenço Marques, now Maputo, the capital of Mozambique. His father was an immigrant from the Algarve, Portugal's southernmost province, his mother a Ronga woman born in a village near Lourenço Marques. From her the boy gained his knowledge of African life and lore, while his father introduced him to great Portuguese prose and poetry of the 19th century.

"Zé," as he was called by his family and friends, received a good, European style education in his native city. Lourenço Marques was a cosmopolitan port, a beautiful modern city surrounded by teeming slums. People, ideas, and goods reached it from various parts of Africa, especially the nearby Republic of South Africa; from Asia, chiefly India; and from Europe, i.e., Portugal and Great Britain. For a bright young man it meant stimulation by the ideas of African consciousness, social justice, anti-colonialism and national independence that were agitating all of Africa by the time of World War II.

Mozambicans were called upon by a sociologist, Eduardo Mondlane, who studied and taught in the United States, to free themselves from European rule, just as two other African intellectuals were leading similar struggles for independence elsewhere: the physician Agostinho Neto in Angola and the agronomist Amílcar Cabral in Portuguese Guinea. In his book *The Struggle for Mozambique,* Mondlane showed how a small, educated, and therefore politically aware minority of urbanites had to perform the difficult task of organizing resistance among the mass of illiterate African country people, with whom they had little contact. They began "a purely cultural movement" by means of paintings and writings. Mondlane mentioned three pioneer poets of outrage and protest: Marcelino dos Santos, Noémia de Sousa, and José Craveirinha. They inspired a younger generation of intellectuals to join the armed struggle when it began in 1964. Craveirinha was to become the most effective poet of the three. He would be the only one to continue writing poetry long after the country had achieved independence in 1975.

Some of Craveirinha's poems appeared from 1955 on in the *Brado Africano* ("African Call"), for which he had been writing articles. Having played soccer, sports writing was a specialty of his. Eventually, after the outbreak of guerrilla warfare in the countryside, the Portuguese secret police and censors became suspicious. The poet-journalist was arrested, tried, absolved—and jailed with six other painters and writers. He spent four years in solitary confinement (1965-1969). In 1974, when the dictatorship was toppled in Portugal, Craveirinha was set free. He joined the government of the new state and was given various administrative posts, among them that of vice-director of the national press.

Many of Craveirinha's poems and all of his prose writings remain scattered in Mozambican and Portuguese periodicals; it has never been his ambition to be an author of books. However, part of his best poetry was collected and published. A first slender volume, *Chigubo,* named after a warriors' dance, was published without his knowledge by an overseas student association (Lisbon, 1964). The same group had awarded him a prize for a larger manuscript in 1962. It bore the title *Manifesto,* after the first poem. In it, he, the *Mestizo,* defiantly celebrated the African physique inherited from his mother—his hair, eyes, mouth, teeth,

lithe body. He identified himself with the peoples, lands, warriors, and hunters of Africa: "Oh! I am a Zulu chieftain once again, / I, a Bantu spear, / I, a drum . . ." His African readers understood whom he meant by "greedy locusts."

Hallucinating images and haunting drum beats characterize two other poems in that booklet, which was reedited and enlarged in 1980, *Sangue da minha mãe* ("My mother's blood") and *Grito negro* ("Black shout"). The latter remains one of his best known. It begins: "I am coal!/And you tear me brutally out of my hole./ Boss, I am the wealth you stole/ . . . but not for ever, boss, no!" His second best known poem, *Quero ser tambor* ("I want to be a drum") appeared in the collection *Karingana ua karingana* ("Once upon a time," Lourenço Marques, 1974), which he dedicated to his Black mother, white father, Maria de Lourdes his wife, his three children, friend Belinha, his native land, "and to some of my best enemies." The book, his largest, also contained an homage "to my beautiful father, the ex-emigrant," *Ao meu belo pai ex-emigrante:* "You, my former and pure Portuguese / who fathered me in a native girl's womb / me, one more Mozambican of a new breed / semi-light to be different from any other white / semi-black so as never to renege/ a drop of the Zambezis of my blood. . . ."

The bitter prison experience engendered *Cela I* ("Cell Number One", Lisbon: 1980), poems written for his wife Maria. During Maria's long illness and upon her death he wrote a large number of mournful poems in her memory, part of which were published as *Maria,* with a preface by fellow poet Rui Knopfli, an old friend of the couple (Linda-a-Velha, Portugal: 1988).

Craveirinha took the role of mentor in 1988, when he discovered a young woman of tremendous athletic ability competing on a male soccer team. Maria Mutola, then 15, was the youngest of six children of Joáo and Catarina Mutola, who lived in Macelala, near Maputo. Craveirinha's son, Stleo, a track and field coach, introduced Mutola to distance running. It wasn't until Craveirinha showed Mutola tapes of the 1984 Olympics that she became excited with the prospect of a career in track. Within months, she represented Mozambique at the 1988 Seoul Olympics, where she finished seventh in the 800 meter. Because of the lack of opportunity for Mutola in Mozambique, Craveirinha sent Mutola to the United States through an Olympic Solidarity Scholarship. Soon after her arrival in Eugene, Oregon, in 1991, Mutola finished fourth in the 800 meters at the Tokyo World Championships, then returned to Eugene to win the Oregon girls' cross-country. She finished fifth in the 1992 Olympics at Barcelona, and won the 800 meter at the 1993 World Championships. Mutola was ranked No. 1 in her event from 1993 to 1995. In an unexpected upset in the 800 meter, top-ranked Mutola gave up the gold and silver in the 1996 Olympics in Atlanta, winning the bronze. Less than a year later, she had established the world's best time in her event. Mutola enjoyed the rewards of her accomplishments and the lifestyle she led in the United States. She helped her family in Mozambique and supported athletics in her home country. The nurturing of Craveirinha led a young girl from a poor family in his native Mozambique through the doors to greatness.

What makes Craveirinha a great poet and person are human sympathy, unpretentiousness, a passionate sense of justice, attachment to his land and people, uninhibited lyrical eroticism, a powerful command of words, the directness and concentrated vigor of his verses, an extraordinary combination of reality and dream-like imagery, and a profound seriousness alternating with subtle irony. In 1979, during a private conversation, when the talk turned to the struggle for a better Mozambican society out of love for humanity, the poet wondered why there was so much hate and so little generosity even after the victory had been won. He concluded: "It is easier for man to be heroic than to be humble."

## Further Reading

Additional information on José Craveirinha can be found in R. A. Preto-Rodas, *Negritude as a Theme in the Poetry of the Portuguese-Speaking World* (1970), and Russell G. Hamilton, *Voices from an Empire: A History of Afro-Portuguese Literature* (1975). A few of Craveirinha's poems can be found in Eduardo Mondlane, *The Struggle for Mozambique* (1969), which includes a poem by J. Craveirinha in English translation in the section "The revolt of the intellectuals, and in Donald Burness, *A Horse of White Clouds* (1989), which includes Portuguese texts and English translations of four poems by José Craveirinha. □

# William Harris Crawford

**American politician William Harris Crawford (1772-1834) was a leader of the Old Republican wing of the Jeffersonian-Republican party.**

William H. Crawford was born in western Virginia on Feb. 24, 1772. At the end of the American Revolution, William's family moved to South Carolina but by 1786 settled near Augusta, Ga. For several years Crawford worked on the family farm and acquired the rudiments of an education. By 1804, having built a respectable law practice, he married and established a homestead (later expanded into a plantation) near Lexington, Ga.

Politics rather than law, however, was to be the focus of Crawford's considerable ambitions. Large in stature, handsome, magnanimous and affable though somewhat coarse, and with a limitless store of entertaining anecdotes, Crawford quickly became a popular figure. Building his career as the upland leader of a powerful coalition of well-to-do and conservative merchant and planter interests, Crawford secured election to the Georgia Legislature in 1803. Within 4 years he succeeded to the U.S. Senate. By 1808 he had emerged as the single most powerful political figure in the state. In the Senate, Crawford spoke for the Old Republican section of the Jeffersonian party, emphasizing states' rights, governmental economy, and simplicity.

The pragmatic search for office rather than ideological consistency was, however, Crawford's main characteristic.

In 1807 he opposed Thomas Jefferson's embargo and by 1811 had become not only an apologist for federally controlled internal improvements but one of the most enthusiastic advocates of rechartering the Bank of the United States. After a brief turn as U.S. minister to France, Crawford resigned and was appointed secretary of war and then secretary of the Treasury by President James Madison (a post Crawford held through both of James Monroe's administrations). In 1816, though publicly disavowing his candidacy, Crawford secured within the Jeffersonian-Republican caucus 54 votes to Monroe's 65 for the party's presidential nomination. During the next years Crawford worked vigorously to strengthen his national political base, using the patronage and influence provided by his control of the Treasury.

After Monroe's reelection in 1820, sparring for the election of 1824 began among the leading candidates—Crawford, John Quincy Adams, John Calhoun, Andrew Jackson, and Henry Clay. By 1823 Crawford had patched together an impressive, if motley, following of Southern Old Republicans and certain Northern commercial interests. For a while Crawford seemed the leading candidate. In 1823, however, he was stricken with paralysis. His followers vainly attempted to sustain his candidacy. In the final election Crawford ran a poor third.

With Crawford's physical condition permanently impaired and his political strength dissipated, his national career was at an end. He spent the rest of his life in Georgia, serving as judge of the state's Northern Judicial Circuit from 1827 until his death.

## Further Reading

Crawford's personal papers were lost shortly after his death; consequently, there can be no definitive biography. The best is Phillip Jackson Green's sympathetic *The Life of William Harris Crawford* (1965), although Green does not incorporate recent scholarship. Still useful is J. E. D. Shipp, *Giant Days: or, The Life and Times of William H. Crawford* (1909).

## Additional Sources

Mooney, Chase Curran, *William H. Crawford, 1772-18,* Lexington University Press of Kentucky 1974. □

# Bettino Craxi

**The Italian statesman Bettino Craxi (born 1934) was the youngest person and the first socialist to become prime minister of the Italian republic. He resigned after three and a half years in office due to problems with his coalition government. In the 1990s he was one of the targets of the largest corruption investigation in Italian post-war history and sentenced to 21 years in prison for his crimes. He went into self-imposed exile in Tunisia**

Bettino Craxi was born February 24, 1934, in Milan, Italy, where his lawyer father, a Socialist politician, had migrated from his native Sicily. Christened Benedetto, but known by the diminutive "Bettino" ever since he was a child, Craxi as a teenager once thought of becoming a priest. Instead, he turned to politics. At 14 he worked in his father's unsuccessful 1948 campaign for the Chamber of Deputies. At the University of Milan he enrolled to study law, but because of his political commitments he never completed his degree.

At 18 he joined the Socialist Party and was active in its youth movement and its publications. During the next few years he rose steadily through the party's ranks and was elected to local and then national offices. In 1957 he was made a member of the party's national central committee. In 1960, in his first electoral success, he won a seat on the Milan city council. In 1965 he was named secretary of the Socialist Party in Milan and a member of the national party's executive committee. In 1968 he won election to the Chamber of Deputies as a delegate from Milan. He retained that seat in each of the four succeeding general elections.

At the outset of his parliamentary career Craxi was an unknown. According to public opinion polls, 90 percent of the Italian people had never heard of him. Through patient organization and skillful use of contacts, Craxi worked his way to the leadership of the party. In 1970 Craxi became a deputy secretary of the Socialist Party and gradually began to build his power base within the organization. After the Socialists stumbled badly in the 1976 general election, Craxi made a bid for the party's leadership. On July 16,

1976, he became the compromise candidate for the position of party general secretary.

Craxi's great contribution to the Socialist Party was to revitalize it and to replace a traditional commitment to extremism with one of "pragmatism, gradualism and reform"—according to the platform adopted at the party's 42nd congress in Palermo, Sicily, in April 1981. Craxi tried to present the Socialists as a centrist organization capable of providing direction for a country whose governments had too often been immobilized by factionalism. Some observers have remarked that the Italian Socialist Party has often taken positions that resemble those of Germany's Social Democratic Party, for which Craxi had great admiration.

A vital aspect of Craxi's strategy was to give the Socialists an identity distinct from that of the Communists. Unlike their counterparts in France, Spain, Portugal, and Greece, Italy's Socialists have been constantly overshadowed by the Communists. The latter usually poll three times as many votes in elections and rank a close second in electoral strength to the dominant right-of-center Christian Democrats. In a symbolic gesture, Craxi changed the party's emblem from the hammer and sickle to a red carnation. Although he occasionally cooperated with the Communists to preserve left-of-center political control in some locales, he relentlessly attacked the Communists at the national level. Craxi, and other socialists, accused the Italian Communists of ideological dependence on the Soviet Union. He often expressed doubt publicly that a party with a Marxist-Leninist philosophy could play a legitimate role in a democratic and pluralist state. In addition to carrying on ideological warfare within his own party, Craxi purged extreme leftists, recruited more moderate replacements, and promoted younger leaders who were personally loyal to him.

Craxi's reforms were made with an eye to changing Italian electoral behavior. The voters, he noted, no longer responded to social class background and were far more sensitive to issue-oriented politics. Craxi also courted new groups emerging in the electorate, especially Italy's rising entrepreneurs, managers, and professionals.

Craxi's efforts to revitalize the Socialists bore fruit for him and for his party. In the party's first major trial of strength under his direction—the May 1978 local elections—the Socialists captured 13.1 percent of the vote, a 3.5 percent improvement over their performance in the general election of 1976. That showing prompted Craxi to nominate the Socialist Sandro Pertini for the presidency of the republic. Pertini was successful and returned the favor when in 1979 he first asked Craxi to form a government. Craxi's first attempt failed, but during the following four administrations between the autumn of 1980 and the spring of 1983, he played a critical role behind the scenes. In the general elections of June 1983 the Socialists made a modest showing with only 11.4 percent of the vote. Nevertheless, the party clearly held the balance of power, and President Pertini once again called on Craxi to form a government. This time he was successful and took office August 4, 1983.

In domestic affairs Craxi led a struggle against inflation and fought for an austerity budget. In foreign affairs he followed a strictly pro-American course. Despite his socialist ideology, Craxi was warmly received by President Reagan in Washington in mid-October 1983. Among the achievements of Craxi's administration were the signing of a concordat with the Vatican in which Roman Catholicism lost its status as the Italian state religion; the use of Italian peacekeeping troops in Lebanon; attacks on the crime "families" of Naples, Sicily, and Calabria; attempts at industrial renewal through new technology; and steps toward welfare and constitutional reform.

One of the major issues of the Craxi government was the growing problem of international terrorism. In 1985 the Italian cruise liner *Achille Lauro* was hijacked and an American was killed. Palestinian leader Mohammed Abdul Abbas Zaidan and three accomplices were captured in Sicily but released. Then during the Christmas holidays four terrorists attacked the Rome airport. Within five minutes 15 people, including three of the terrorists, were killed and 74 were wounded. By mid-1986 the Italian government had accumulated enough evidence against the ship hijackers to bring 15 to trial in Genoa—ten of them, including Abbas, were tried in absentia. Eleven were convicted. Meanwhile, Craxi's coalition government had stayed in power longer than any Italian government since World War II.

Craxi resigned as Prime Minister after three and a half years in office in March of 1987 citing rifts and irreconcilable differences in his five party coalition. He returned to leading the Italian Socialist Party and representing Milan in Italy's parliament.

In 1992, Mario Chiesa, a socialist politician who headed Milan's largest public charity, was caught pocketing a $6000 bribe. It set off an investigation "Operation Clean Hands" that went on to show that bribe collection was the most efficient and organized arm of the Italian government. Officials routinely skimmed 2 to 14 percent off government contracts for every public service, from airports and hospitals to theaters and orphanages. As the investigation unfolded, all major political parties were implicated: Socialist, Christian Democrat, Democratic Party of the Left (formerly the Communist Party). According to Giuseppe Turani and Cinzia Sasso in their book *The Looters*, "Operation Clean Hands has hit Italian Politics like a cyclone. After this nothing will be the same."

As head of the Socialist Party, Craxi was urged by party members to purge the party of the wrongdoers. Members of his family were directly involved—Craxi's brother-in-law Paolo Pillitteri was accused of personally accepting suitcases full of money while he was Mayor of Milan and his son Vittorio's election to local office was paid for by Mario Chiesa, whose arrest started the entire investigation. Craxi himself came under investigation, although he fought back, claiming that since all the political parties took the bribes, they must all answer for their crimes. This did not halt the investigation, and ruined Craxi's chances at a comeback as Prime Minister or President of Italy in 1992.

In 1994, Craxi went into self-imposed exile in Tunisia. He was sentenced, in absentia, to 13 years in prison for fraud and in 1996, an additional 8 years after having been found guilty of further corruption charges.

## Further Reading

Sources on Craxi in English are scarce. Joseph La Palombara's "Socialist Alternatives: the Italian Variant," in *Foreign Affairs* (Spring 1982) explains Craxi's role in the evolution of the Italian Socialist Party. Information concerning the scandal that toppled Craxi can be found in articles in the *Economist* January 23, 1993 and the *New Republic* August 10, 1992. A complete study of the scandal can also be found in *I Sacheggiatori (The Looters)* 1992 □

# Seymour Cray

**Seymour Cray (1925-1996) is one of the founding fathers of the computer industry. Seeking to process vast amounts of mathematical data needed to simulate physical phenomena, Cray built what many consider the first supercomputer, which represented a technological revolution to such fields as engineering, meteorology, and eventually biology and medicine.**

Seymour Cray is an electronics engineer and one of the founding fathers of the computer industry. His seminal work in computer design features the semiconductor as a component to store and process information. Cray's dense packing of hundreds of thousands of semiconductor chips, which reduced the distance between signals, enabled him to pioneer very large and powerful "supercomputers." Among his accomplishments was the first computer to employ a freon cooling system to prevent chips from overheating. However, Cray's most significant contribution was the supercomputer itself. Seeking to process vast amounts of mathematical data needed to simulate physical phenomena, Cray built what many consider the first supercomputer, the CDC 6600 (with 350,000 transistors). To such fields as engineering, meteorology, and eventually biology and medicine, the supercomputer represented a technological revolution, akin to replacing a wagon with a sports car in terms of accelerating research.

A maverick in both his scientific and business pursuits, Cray eventually started his own company devoted entirely to the development of supercomputers. For many years Cray computers dominated the supercomputer industry. A devoted fan of "Star Trek," a 1960s television show about space travel, Cray included aesthetically pleasing touches in his computers, such as transparent blue glass that revealed their inner workings.

Cray was born on September 28, 1925, in Chippewa Falls, Wisconsin, a small town situated in the heart of Wisconsin's dairy farm country. The eldest of two children, Cray revealed his talent for engineering while still a young boy, tinkering with radios in the basement and building an automatic telegraph machine by the time he was ten years old. Cray's father, a city engineer, and his mother fully

supported his scientific interests, providing him with a basement laboratory equipped with chemistry sets and radio gear. Cray's early aptitude for electronics was evident when he wired his laboratory to his bedroom, and included an electric alarm that sounded whenever anyone tried to enter his inner sanctum. While attending Chippewa Falls High School, Cray sometimes taught the physics class in his teacher's absence. During his senior year, he received the Bausch & Lomb Science Award for meritorious achievement in science.

While serving in the U.S. Army during the final years of World War II, Cray utilized his natural gifts in electronics as a radio operator and decipherer of enemy codes. After the war, he enrolled in the University of Wisconsin, but later transferred to the University of Minnesota in Minneapolis, where he received his bachelor's degree in electrical engineering in 1950 and a master's degree in applied mathematics the next year. Cray began his corporate electronics career when he was hired to work for Engineering Research Associates (ERA). When Cray joined the company, it was among a small group of firms on the cutting edge of the commercial computer industry. One of his first assignments with ERA was to build computer pulse transformers for Navy use. Cray credited his success on the project to a top-of-the-line circular slide rule that enabled him to make a multitude of calculations needed to build the transformers. In a speech before his colleagues at a 1988 supercomputer conference, Cray recalled feeling "quite smug" about his accomplishment until he encountered a more experienced engineer working at the firm who told Cray that he did not use complicated slide rules or many of the other standard engineering approaches in his work, preferring to rely on intuition. Intrigued, Cray put away his slide rule and decided that he would do likewise.

For his next computer project, Cray and his colleagues developed a binary programming system. With the addition of magnetic core memory, which allowed Cray and his coworkers to program 4,096 words, the age of the supercomputer dawned. Although devoted to his laboratory work, Cray was also interested in the business side of the industry; his efforts to market ERA's new technology resulted in the Remington Rand typewriter company buying out ERA. With a formidable knowledge of circuits, logic, and computer software design, Cray designed the UNIVAC 1103, the first electronically digital computer to become commercially available.

Despite his growing success, Cray became dissatisfied with the large corporate atmosphere of ERA, which had been renamed the Sperry Rand Corporation. A friend and colleague, William Norris, who also worked at Sperry Rand, decided to start his own company, Control Data Corporation (CDC), and recruited Cray to work for him. Lacking the financial resources of larger companies, Cray and Control Data set out to make affordable computers. Towards this end, Cray built computers out of transistors, which he purchased at an electronics outlet store for 37 cents each. Although the chips were of diverse circuitry, Cray successfully replaced the cumbersome and expensive tubes and radio "valves" which were then standard in the industry.

Control Data began developing a line of computers like the CDC 1604, which was immensely successful as a tool for scientific research. Cray went on to develop the CDC 6600, the most powerful computer of its day and the first to employ freon to cool its 350,000 transistors. In 1969, the corporation introduced the CDC 7600, which many considered to be the world's first supercomputer. Capable of 15 million computations per second, the 7600 placed CDC as the leader in the supercomputer industry to the chagrin of the IBM corporation, CDC's primary competitor. Even with a legion of researchers, IBM was unable to match CDC's productivity, and eventually resorted to questionable tactics to overtake CDC, which eventually filed and won an antitrust suit against IBM. But as Control Data grew, so did its bureaucracy. As Russell Mitchell recounted in *Business Week,* Norris once asked Cray to develop a five-year plan. What Norris received in return was a short note that said Cray's five-year plan was "to build the biggest computer in the world," and his one-year plan was "to achieve one-fifth of the above." After developing the CDC 8600, which the company refused to market, Cray, in 1972, decided to leave CDC and set up his own company, Cray Research Corporation. Norris and CDC graciously invested $500,000 to assist Cray in his fledgling business effort.

Cray Research immediately set out to build the fastest supercomputer. In 1976 the CRAY–1 was introduced. Incorporating a revolutionary vector processing approach, which allowed the computer to solve various parts of a problem at once, the CRAY–1 was capable of performing 32 calculations simultaneously, outpacing even the best CDC computer. When the National Center for Atmospheric Research met the computer's $8.8 million price tag, Cray Research finally had solid financial footing to continue building faster and more affordable computers. For Cray, this meant manufacturing one product at a time, a radical approach in the computer industry. The first CRAY–2 was marketed in 1985 and featured a phenomenal 2-billion byte memory that could perform 1.2 billion computer operations per second, a tenfold performance increase over the Cray–1. Capable of providing computerized models of physical phenomena described mathematically, the CRAY computers were essential catalysts in accelerating research. For example, in such areas as pharmaceutical development, supercomputer modeling of a drug's molecules and its biological components eliminated much trial and error, reducing the time necessary to solve complicated mathematical equations.

In 1983, Cray turned his attention to developing gallium arsenide (GaA) circuits. Although the CRAY–2 was based on silicon chips, Cray continued to develop GaA chips in the spinoff Cray Computers Corporation. Although extremely difficult to work with because of their fragility, gallium arsenide computer chips marked a major advance in computer circuitry with their ability to conduct electrical impulses with less resistance than silicon. Adding even more speed to the computer, the GaA chip also effectively reduced both heat and energy loss.

While Cray's advances in computer technology enabled him to corner the market on the supercomputer industry for many years, the advent of parallel processing allowed others in the industry to make inroads into the same market. Utilizing hundreds of mini-computers to work on individual aspects of a problem, parallel processing is a less expensive approach to solving huge mathematical problems. Although Cray for many years denounced parallel processing as impractical, he eventually accepted this approach and made plans with other companies to incorporate it into his computer research and business.

Cray's first wife, Verene, was a minister's daughter. Married shortly after World War II, they had two daughters and two sons, who have characterized their father as a man intensely dedicated to his work; in fact, Cray demanded their absolute silence while traveling in the car so that he could think about the next advance in supercomputers. In 1975, Cray and Verene divorced, and he wed Geri M. Harrand five years later. Although he engaged in outdoor pursuits with his new wife, such as windsurfing and skiing, Cray remained devoted to his research. In 1972, he was awarded the Harry Goode Memorial Award for "outstanding achievement in the field of information processing." As Cray looked forward to the future of supercomputers, especially to the use of GaA computer chips, many experts in the field characterized his vision as impractical. Nonetheless, Cray's numerous conceptual breakthroughs in computer and information science have firmly established him as an innovator in computer technology. Cray died on October 5, 1996, from injuries sustained in a car accident three weeks earlier.

## Further Reading

Slater, R, *Portraits in Silicon,* MIT Press, 1989, pp. 195–204.

Spenser, Donald, *Macmillan Encyclopedia of Computers,* Macmillan Publishing Company, 1992.

Anthes, Gary H, "Seymour Cray: Reclusive Genius," in *Computerworld,* June 22, 1992, p. 38.

Elmer-Dewitt, Philip, "Computer Chip Off the Old Block: Genius Seymour Cray and the Company He Founded Split Up," in *Time,* May 29, 1989, p. 70.

Krepchin, Ira, "Datamation 100 North American Profiles," in *Datamation,* June 15, 1993, p. 81.

Mitchell, Russell, "The Genius," in *Business Week,* April 30, 1990, pp. 80–88. □

# Crazy Horse

**The Native American Crazy Horse (ca. 1842-1877), Oglala Sioux war chief, is best known as the leader of the Sioux and Cheyenne renegades who won the Battle of the Little Bighorn, where Gen. Custer died.**

orn on Rapid Creek, S. Dak., near the present Rapid City, Crazy Horse (Tashunca-Uitco) was a strange, quiet Sioux youth, serious and thoughtful. His skin and hair were so light that he was mistaken for a captive white child and was called "Light-Haired Boy" and "Curly."

Crazy Horse grew to manhood wild and adventurous, implacably hating the reservations and the encroaching whites. He married a Cheyenne girl and thus had close ties with that tribe. After he came to prominence as a warrior, many Cheyenne followed him.

Crazy Horse probably participated in the Sioux wars of 1865-1868 but as a warrior, not a leader. By the last of these wars, in 1876, however, he had risen to prominence. He and his followers refused to return to the reservation by Jan. 1, 1876, as had been ordered by the U.S. Army following the outbreak occasioned by the Black Hills gold rush. Crazy Horse and his followers bore the first burden of this campaign. Their village of 105 lodges was destroyed by Col. J. J. Reynolds on March 17. The Native Americans' horses were captured, but Crazy Horse rallied his braves, trailed the soldiers 20 miles, and recaptured most of the horses. On June 17 he and 1,200 warriors defeated Gen. George Crook and 1,300 soldiers, turning them away from a rendezvous with the forces of Gen. Alfred Terry.

Crazy Horse next moved north, where he joined with Sitting Bull's followers on the Little Bighorn River. On June 25 he was in command of the warriors who massacred Gen. George Custer and 264 soldiers. Then, with 800 warriors he went into winter quarters in the Wolf Mountains near the headwaters of the Rosebud River. On Jan. 8, 1877, the village was destroyed in an attack led by Col. N. A. Miles.

Crazy Horse continued to fight for 4 months before surrendering on May 6 with 1,100 men, women, and children at Red Cloud Agency near Camp Robinson, Nebr. An army officer there described Crazy Horse as 5 feet 8 inches tall, lithe and sinewy, with a weathered visage; wrote Capt. John G. Bourke: "The expression of his countenance was one of great dignity, but morose, dogged, tenacious and melancholy. . . . He was one of the great soldiers of his day and generation."

On Sept. 5, 1877, the officers at the post, convinced that Crazy Horse was plotting an outbreak, ordered him locked up. Crazy Horse drew his knife and began fighting. In the struggle he was mortally wounded in the abdomen, either by a soldier's bayonet or his own knife. His death deprived the Oglala Sioux of one of their most able leaders.

## Further Reading

Details on Crazy Horse's life are in Mari Sandoz, *Crazy Horse: The Strange Man of the Oglalas* (1942), and Earl A. Brininstool, *Crazy Horse* (1949). A good, condensed version of his life is in Alvin M. Josephy, *The Patriot Chiefs* (1961). John G. Bourke, *On the Border with Crook* (1891), gives a contemporary assessment. □

# George Creel

**George Creel (1876-1953), American writer and journalist, was the first propaganda minister in American history.**

G eorge Creel was born on Dec. 1, 1876, on a farm in Lafayette County, Mo. His father, Henry Clay Creel, was a former Confederate officer. George spent his boyhood in Missouri, where he attended what public schools were available.

Creel's real education began at 20, when he secured a job as a reporter on the *Kansas City World*. In 1899 he became editor of the *Kansas City Independent*. After joining the Progressive wing of the Democratic party, he enjoyed considerable influence in Missouri politics. In 1909 he moved to Denver, Colo., where he edited the *Denver Post* (1909-1911) and the *Rocky Mountain News* (1911-1913). His pamphlets for the Democratic National Committee in 1916 brought him to the attention of President Woodrow Wilson, who named Creel chairman of the Committee on Public Information at the outbreak of World War I.

Creel directed the flow of government propaganda on the war and faced, for the first time in the 20th century, the issues of censorship, news manipulation, and the public's "right to know," so important to the freedom of the press in a democratic society. His task was to convince a divided country of the wisdom of Wilson's decision to join the war against Germany. Creel established a system of voluntary press censorship. He refused to distribute information on most of the cruder Allied atrocity stories; instead he blanketed the nation with official information which portrayed the United States as crusading for freedom and democracy

to save European civilization from Germany's brutish despoliation. Private American organizations such as the National Security League and the American Protective Association were far less careful in their publications than the Creel committee. Whoever was at fault, the result was an outbreak of war madness unparalleled in American history.

Creel always insisted that private groups rather than the Committee on Public Information were responsible for the wartime hysteria. In three books, *How We Advertised America* (1920), *The War, the World and Wilson* (1920), and his autobiography, *Rebel at Large* (1947), he defended his committee. But he never fully escaped the cloud that World War I cast over his name.

In 1920 Creel retired to private life. In the 1930s he helped moderate Democrats defeat Upton Sinclair's abortive EPIC (End Poverty in California) campaign in California. Creel remained active as a writer, newsman, and national commentator until his death on Oct. 3, 1953.

## Further Reading

Creel's autobiography, *Rebel at Large: Recollections of Fifty Crowded Years* (1947), is the best source for his life. For the Committee on Public Information see James P. Mock and Cedric Larson, *Words That Won the War: The Story of the Committee on Public Information, 1917-1919* (1939), and Horace C. Peterson, *Propaganda for War: The Campaign against American Neutrality, 1914-1917* (1939). For Creel and the New Deal see Arthur M. Schlesinger, Jr., *The Age of*

*Roosevelt,* especially volume 3, *The Politics of Upheaval* (1960). □

# Octave Crémazie

**Octave Crémazie (1827-1879) was a Canadian poet who was closely linked to the emergence of French-Canadian literature.**

Known as Octave, Claude-Joseph-Olivier Crémazie was born on Nov. 8, 1827, and educated in Quebec. He became the business associate of his brother Joseph in 1844. Octave used their bookshop as a base for his literary interests; buying, reading, and discussing recent works from France, particularly Victor Hugo's. A group around Crémazie formed what became known as the *École Patriotique* or the *École de Québec.* Nationally selfconscious and grandiloquently romantic, it created the first characteristic body of French-Canadian literature about 1860. Meanwhile, Crémazie's own affairs went badly, and in 1862 he fled to France to avoid pursuit for forging guarantors' signatures in order to gain credit for his failing business.

Crémazie's writings include occasional verse, more personal poems, various letters, and a diary. The poems which made his name commemorate events in Canadian history. Thus *Le Vieux soldat Canadian* celebrated the arrival in Quebec of the first French naval vessel (1855) since the British conquest in 1760, and *Le Drapeau de Carillon* celebrated the centenary of Montcalm's victory of 1758 at Carillon (now Ticonderoga, N.Y.). The latter poem also mentions the theme of *l'abandon,* the feeling that France failed its valiant Canadian colony, in spite of which, in Crémazie's opinion, the cult of France must be maintained.

Prolonged exile in France made Crémazie aware of his own outmoded, rhetorical style, and he expressed a preference for his lyrical poems, especially *La Promenade des trois morts,* which, however, he was too discouraged to complete.

Although direct contact with French literary circles crushed Crémazie as a poet, it stimulated him to write some valuable critical comments in his letters to Canada. He blamed the low standard of Canadian taste for his former success and felt that this had led him away from developing his finer talents. Canadian literature, he felt, could never excel either as a French or as an American creation.

These contradictions in Crémazie's attitude to his cultural context are indicative of French Canada's grave doubts about its cultural survival. In politics Crémazie supported right-wing positions generally and French imperialism in particular, but he was a liberal patriot at home. A similar deep contradiction is found in his poetic diction, for his attempts to imitate Hugo are overshadowed by his obvious affinity to the older style of the neoclassicists.

Crémazie was in Paris during the siege of 1870 and kept a diary containing details on living conditions and expressing anti-Communard sentiments. He died on Jan. 18, 1879, in Le Havre, where he had found modest employment.

### Further Reading

Crémazie's works were collected and published in 1883 as *Oeuvres complètes,* although there are many omissions. Maurice Dassonville, *Crémazie* (1956), contains useful biographical and bibliographical information. For background information see Ian Forbes Fraser, *The Spirit of French Canada: A Study of the Literature* (1939). □

# Thomas Alexander Crerar

**Thomas Alexander Crerar (1876-1975) was a Canadian political leader who, using farmers' organizations as a power base, represented the Western point of view in Canada's government.**

homas Alexander Crerar was born at Molesworth, Ontario, on June 17, 1876. The family moved west to Portage la Prairie, Manitoba, where Crerar was educated. After a stint of teaching in small rural schools, he turned to wheat farming and eventually to grain buying.

In 1907 Crerar became president of the Grain Growers Grain Company, a farmers' organization that had been established to fight the railway monopolies and the Eastern-controlled elevator companies. The Grain Growers quickly established a position of power, and Crerar, who was president until 1929, acquired a reputation as an articulate spokesman for the Western point of view.

Inevitably he was drawn into politics. During World War I Sir Robert Borden formed a Union government to ram conscription through Parliament. Crerar was one of several outsiders brought into the government by the Conservative leader, and he was minister of agriculture from 1917 to 1919. As such, he played a part in directing the war effort in its closing stages. But he also found himself part of a government that was dedicated to the maintenance of the high tariff and to the conscription of farmers' sons, both concepts that were anathema to Western farmers, who wanted cheap agricultural implements and a sure labor supply.

Crerar resigned in 1919 and turned to bolstering the farmers' organizations. In 1921 he led the newly formed Progressive party to the polls in the general election. The Progressives were a loose coalition of provincial farmers' groups, divided in aims and ideology, disparate in composition, and burdened with a startling naiveté about the workings of the political system. Despite their success in the election, Crerar did not find it easy trying to shepherd his party through the intricacies of parliamentary procedure, for most of his followers distrusted all political parties, including their own.

Crerar's desire was to link up with the governing Liberal party, using his farm support as a bludgeon to win real concessions for the West. But after his supporters balked and after a series of frustrating incidents, he resigned as leader in 1923. The party hung on for a few years, but its strength was broken.

Returning to Parliament as a Liberal in 1935, Crerar entered the Cabinet of Mackenzie King as minister of immigration and minister of the interior. In 1936 he became minister of mines and resources, a portfolio he held until 1945. In this department Crerar played an important part in mobilizing Canadian industry for war, and he was always the leading spokesman for Manitoba in the government. Just before the end of World War II, Crerar was appointed to the Senate, where he remained as vigorous and outspoken as ever until his retirement in 1966 at the age of 90. Thomas Crerar died on April 11, 1975.

### Further Reading

There is no biography of Crerar. The best book on the Progressive party is W. L. Morton, *The Progressive Party in Canada* (1950). Also important are Ramsay Cook, ed., *The Dafoe-Sifton Correspondence, 1919-1927* (1966) and his *The Politics of John W. Dafoe and the Free Press* (1963). □

# Edith Cresson

**The first woman prime minister of France and the fifth prime minister appointed by President François**

**Mitterrand, Edith Cresson (born 1934) was named to the office May 15, 1991.**

Edith Cresson was born January 27, 1934, in a fashionable Paris suburb of Boulogne-Billancourt. Her father was a senior civil servant. Raised by a British nanny, she became fluent in the English language. Cresson attended the School of Advanced Commercial Studies, earning a degree in business and later a doctorate in demography.

A successful businesswoman, she added a second career in politics when she met François Mitterrand in 1965. For the next 26 years the future president helped Cresson advance through the ranks of what is now the French Socialist Party, calling her "my little soldier."

After Mitterrand became president in 1981, Cresson served first as minister of agriculture (1981-1983), then as minister of external trade and tourism (1983-1984), as minister of industrial restructuring and external trade (1984-1986), and finally minister of foreign affairs (1988-1990). She resigned from the government on October 3, 1990, to work as a consultant on international development. Meanwhile she was three times elected a deputy to the National Assembly from the Vienne province (1981, 1986, 1988).

Then in May 1991, President Mitterrand asked Cresson to form a new government. Some experts believe Mitterand had grown dissatisfied with the failures of the government of Michel Rocard to gain majorities in the National Assembly.

Others believe the French president foresaw major international trade issues looming as the trans-European Union came into existence, and sought Cresson's expertise in trade affairs.

As prime minister, the combative Cresson planned to strengthen France's industrial power and to "protect" French and European trade from the inroads of Japanese and American products. In assembling her new cabinet of 29 members she chose a number of holdovers from the government of her predecessor. One, Pierre Brgovoy, was named to head a new superministry combining economic, trade, industrial, and technology affairs. His appointment served to restore trust in the French leadership in financial markets. She also appointed five women, three to posts in labor, development, and youth and sports.

When her appointment to prime minister drew misogynist remarks from some politicians of France's center and right parties, Cresson said, "Men are not in any sense irreplaceable except in one's private life." Nevertheless, more fair-minded criticism about her ability to command majorities in the National Assembly persisted.

The Cresson government moved aggressively to free what had become a stagnant economy, and on contentious domestic issues, frequently centered around immigrants. Quoted making strident and antagonistic comments about the Japanese "strategy of conquest," Cresson was greatly concerned over what she was convinced to be Japan's major threat to European trade and commonwealth. Diplomatically, her outspokenness was creating unease in international circles. Within four months of becoming president, the Cresson government had fallen precipitously in popularity. Subtle and not-so-subtle attacks on her gender continued, including a popular daytime television show featuring two puppet characters, one a sexy and servile female broadly seen as a Cresson parody. In April 1992, Cresson resigned. Since then she has served as Commissioner for Science, Research and Development to the European Commission.

Cresson's husband, Jacques, a retired executive of Peugeot, the French automobile and appliance company, remained supportive of his wife, and their relationship has been likened to that of Margaret Thatcher and her husband. Cresson has been compared to the British prime minister for her bluntness, energy, and stubbornness. They have two daughters.

### Further Reading

The appointment and career of Cresson was covered in the *Washington Post* (May 16 and May 18, 1991). See also "An Iron Lady Across the Channel?" *Business Week* (May 27, 1991) and "The Battle for Europe," *Business Week* (June 3, 1991). □

# St. John de Crèvecoeur

**Hector St. John de Crèvecoeur (1735-1813), a French-American farmer and writer, was one of the**

**most perceptive observers of American life in the late 18th century.**

Michel Guillaume Jean de Crèvecoeur was born in Caen, France, on Jan. 31, 1735. (Later he would sign his first book J. Hector St. John.) After a Jesuit education and a visit in England, where he learned English, he served as a map maker with Louis Montcalm's army in Canada from about 1755 to 1759. He left the army but stayed in the New World, where after a good deal of traveling, working as a surveyor, and note-taking, he became a farmer, first in Ulster County, then in Orange County, N.Y.

In 1769 Crèvecoeur married Mehitable Tippet, by whom he had three children, the eldest being named America-Francés. For a time his life was idyllic, but the American Revolution interrupted it. Unwilling to commit himself to either side at the time, he tried to visit France, which led to his imprisonment by the British for 3 months. Finally, in 1780 he returned to his old home in France via Dublin and London. While in London he arranged for publication of his most famous work, *Letters from an American Farmer* (1782). The book provides a comprehensive picture of American life, from Nantucket to Charleston: manners, customs, education, plant and animal life. Crèvecoeur posed as a provincial who sought to answer typical European questions about America. The most memorable portion is Letter Three, "What is an American?"

The book made Crèvecoeur famous. It was published in Philadelphia, as well as in Ireland, Holland, and Germany. He prepared a second edition, in French, much enlarged and more literary: *Letters d'un cultivateur américain* (1784). The original English versions of some of these letters were not published until 1925 (*Sketches of Eighteenth Century America*). In 1783, returning to America as French consul to New York, Connecticut, and New Jersey, he found that his wife had died and two children were missing. He located the children in Boston, then established a home in New York City. He developed packet-boat service between France and New York.

In time ill health largely incapacitated Crèvecoeur. In June 1785 he returned to France, seeking to improve commercial relations between France and America. He prepared a three-volume version of the French *Lettres,* published in 1789, the year of his return to America and to his position as consul. He was honored by election to the American Philosophical Society. Under the pen name of Agricola, his letters on potato culture, sheep feeding, sunflower oil, and other topics were published in various American journals.

In 1790 Crèvecoeur left America for the last time. For a while he lived quietly in his father's home in Normandy, for his health was poor and the French Revolution was in progress. He kept in touch with America through a son farming in New Jersey, and he wrote his longest work. It appeared in 1801 as *Le Voyage dans la Haute Pennsylvania et dans l'état de New-York* (available in English as *Eighteenth-Century Travels in Pennsylvania and New York,* 1961). It has never been as popular as the *Letters,*

Crèvecoeur spent 3 of his last years in Munich, where his son-in-law was minister plenipotentiary. He died in France in 1813.

## Further Reading

Two valuable studies of Crèvecoeur in English are Julia Post Mitchell, *St. Jean de Crèvecoeur* (1916), and Thomas Philbrick, *St. John de Crèvecoeur* (1970). □

# John Michael Crichton

**Michael Crichton (born 1942) is best known as a novelist of popular fiction whose stories explore the confrontation between traditional social and moral values and the demands of the new technological age. His most successful novel, *Jurassic Park* (1990), involves the re-creation of living dinosaurs from ancient DNA and examines what can go wrong when greedy people misconstrue the power of new and untested technologies.**

Crichton was born in Chicago and raised on Long Island. At fourteen years of age, he wrote and sold articles to the *New York Times* travel section, and, in 1964, earned a B. A. in anthropology from Harvard University. The following year, while on a European travel fellowship in anthropology and ethnology, he met and married Joan Radam; they eventually divorced in 1970. Returning to Harvard University in 1965, Crichton entered medical school, where he began to write novels under the pseudonym John Lange in order to support his medical studies. While doing postdoctoral work at the Salk Institute for Biological Studies in La Jolla, California, Crichton published *The Andromeda Strain* (1969), a technological thriller, which garnered literary acclaim and national prominence for the author. Upon leaving medical studies, Crichton began a full-time writing career. Eventually, he also directed his screenplay of his novel *Westworld* (1973), starring Yul Brynner, and wrote the screenplay for his book, *The Great Train Robbery* (1978).

Crichton's stories generally take place in contemporary settings and focus on technological themes, although his earliest works were traditional mystery novels. Writing under the pseudonym John Lange, Crichton published a mystery novel entitled *Odds On* (1966), followed by *A Case of Need* (1968), written under the pseudonym Jeffrey Hudson. *A Case of Need* received favorable reviews and the 1968 Edgar Allan Poe Award of Mystery Writers of America. In 1969, Crichton published *The Andromeda Strain,* a novel that, Crichton acknowledges, was influenced by Len Deighton's *The Ipcress File* (1962) and H. G. Wells *The War of The Worlds. The Andromeda Strain* is a technological thriller about a seemingly unstoppable plague brought to earth from outer space; it became a Book-of-the-Month Club selection and a 1971 motion picture, directed by Robert Wise and starring Arthur Hill. In *Westworld* (1973),

Crichton depicts the ability of technology to blur the line between reality and fantasy, and how that can affect people's lives. As the android creations of the Delos theme park begin to operate on their own recognizance, they attack and threaten the lives of the guests who have come there merely to play and live out their childhood fantasies in the make-believe Old West.

While *The Great Train Robbery* (1975) recalls the history of an actual train robbery in Victorian England, and *Eaters of the Dead* (1976) is set among tenth-century Vikings, and is supposedly the retelling of the *Beowulf* myth, *Congo* (1980) returns to the dangers of technology, greed, and power. *Congo* recalls the narrative tradition of Rider Haggard's novel *King Solomon's Mines,* as it relates the story of a behavioral specialist and Amy, a gorilla that is capable of communicating in human language. In the process of returning Amy to her African jungle home, the specialist and the gorilla encounter a series of dangers and catastrophes. These include the ruthless activities of a group of corporate-sponosored explorers who are searching for the Lost City of Zinj, where a race of hostile apes guards rare diamonds capable of nullifying humanity's need for nuclear weapons and energy. An encounter with alein life forms and alien technology is the central focus of Crichton's next novel, *Sphere* (1987). Scientists undertake an underwater excavation of an alien spacecraft, believed to have landed in the ocean three centuries earlier. While a raging storm maroons the scientists on board the spacecraft, which is one thousand feet below the surface of the sea, the aliens wreak havoc on the contact team.

In 1990, Crichton published his nationally acclaimed best-seller, *Jurassic Park,* which recounts the classic tale of greed and a technological experiment gone awry. A wealthy entrepreneur and his scientists lose control of their experiment to re-create living dinosaurs for a wild animal park on a deserted island off the coast of Costa Rica. Steven Spielberg's 1994 Academy award-winning film of *Jurassic Park* also helped to ensure the world-wide popularity and success of the novel. Turning to Japanese-American relations in today's competitive business world, *Rising Sun* (1992) begins with the bizarre murder of a young woman, which is pivotal to a plot that explores the exploitative and unprincipled actions of Japanese technocrats. *Rising Sun* is often criticized for its stereotypical presentation of Japanese villains and Japan-bashing—criticisms that Crichton rejects. *Disclosure* (1994) continues to focus on the technological business community and its handling of sexual harassment. In a role-reversal, the new female executive of DigiCom seduces a former lover and present employee, and then accuses him of sexual harassment when he spurns her advances. The story focuses on the fight to save his job and the truth of what actually happened. In 1995, Crichton returned to the theme of genetic engineering in *The Lost World.* Scientist Ian Malcolm and entrepreneur Lewis Dodgson of *Jurassic Park* join rival expeditions sent to investigate an island thought to be inhabited by dinosaurs. Once again, twentieth-century human technology is challenged by the raw force of prehistoric nature.

Crichton's works have received mixed reviews. While most critics applaud his ability to make technological information understandable and engaging, some fault his traditional and predictable plotlines, such as *Disclosure*'s battle-of-the-sexes plot and *Jurassic Park*'s the-dangers-of-new-science theme. And too, while many critics favorably comment on Crichton's well organized plots and use of clear and simple prose, they fault his ability to develop realistic characters. For instance, John Hammond and Nedry of *Jurassic Park* are the traditional unprincipled entrepreneur and scientific genius whose greed precipitates a technological disaster, while Meredith Johnson of *Disclosure* is the predictable evil enemy of Tom Sanders, the harassed and innocent victim-hero of the story. As Robert L. Sims points out, most of "Crichton's characters are one-dimensional figures whose psychological makeups are determined by the particular drama in which they are involved." A few commentators also remark at Crichton's ability to identify and successfully capitalize on current public issues and concerns. For example, *Disclosure* examines the issue of sexual harassment in the business world, while *Rising Sun* focuses on Japan's growing power in the world of American business. Nevertheless, in spite of traditional plotlines and simplistic characterizations, Crichton's concise prose style, tightly organized plots, contemporary themes, and engaging action continue to make his works popular and successful.

## Further Reading

*Authors and Artists for Young Adults,* Volume 10, Gale, 1993.
*Contemporary Literary Criticism,* Gale, Volume 2, 1974, Volume 6, 1976, Volume 54, 1989.
*Dictionary of Literary Biography Yearbook: 1981,* Gale, 1982.

*American Spectator,* May, 1992, p. 71.
*American Way,* September, 1975, pp. 66-69.
*Atlantic Monthly,* May, 1972, pp. 108-110.
*Best Sellers,* August 15, 1968, pp. 207-208; February, 1981, p. 388. □

# Francis Harry Crompton Crick

**The English molecular biologist Francis Harry Compton Crick (born 1916) contributed to the establishment of the double-helical model of the DNA molecule.**

Francis Crick was born June 8, 1916, in Northampton, England. At University College, London, he studied physics and mathematics and obtained his degree in 1937. Work on an advanced degree was halted by the coming of World War II, when Crick had to shift his interest from pure science to the design and production of magnetic mines. By the time the war ended, he had decided to pursue a career in biology, not physics. His decision was influenced by a reading of the book *What Is Life?* by physicist Erwin Schrödinger, with its message that an intensive investigation of the gene was likely to reveal the nature of life.

Crick began his study of biology at Strangeways Laboratory, Cambridge, in 1947, but within 2 years he left to join the Medical Research Council Unit for Molecular Biology at Cavendish Laboratory and to enroll as a doctoral student at Caius College, Cambridge. While at Cavendish he met (1951) the young American biologist James D. Watson, who shared his interest in the gene and the genetic material, deoxyribonucleic acid (DNA). In 1953 Crick and Watson jointly proposed their doublehelical model of the DNA molecule, which brought them the Nobel Prize in 1962, an honor they shared with English biophysicist Maurice Wilkins. In addition to the prize, Crick received distinguished lectureships, awards from scientific organizations, and membership in honorary societies, including the Royal Society of London (1959).

The discovery of the structure of DNA is considered to be one of the greatest events in 20th-century biology. Genes are responsible for transferring hereditary information from one generation to the next, and since they are DNA molecules, or segments of them, the structure of DNA provides the key to understanding the physical basis of heredity. The giant DNA molecule is a complex one, and Crick and Watson faced the difficult task of determining the exact arrangement of its molecular subunits. While Wilkins and others attempted to discover this arrangement by concentrating exclusively upon x-ray diffraction techniques, Crick and Watson approached the problem by conceiving and building large-scale models that would account for all the known physical and chemical properties of DNA. Watson first suggested the double helix as the basic feature of DNA, but it was Crick, with his background in physics, who supplied the theoretical and mathematical knowledge so important to the team's success.

Upon completion of the work on the structure of DNA, Crick began an investigation of the genetic code, that is, the precise manner in which the gene controls the synthesis of proteins.

## Further Reading

The personal and intellectual story of the discovery of the structure of DNA is told in James D. Watson's candid book *The Double Helix* (1968), in which Crick is depicted as a genius who exasperated many of his English colleagues but delighted his unconventional American friend. For Crick's statement of his philosophy of biology see his book *Of Molecules and Men* (1966). Crick is also the author of *What Mad Pursuit: A Personal View of Scientific Discovery* (1988) and *The Astonishing Hypothesis: The Scientific Search for the Soul* (1994). □

# Francesco Crispi

**The Italian statesman Francesco Crispi (1819-1901) fought for Italian unification and twice served as premier of Italy.**

Francesco Crispi was born on Oct. 4, 1819, in Ribera, Sicily. After studying law at the University of Palermo, in 1846 he became an attorney in Naples. He took an active part in the revolutionary struggle of 1848-1849, and after its failure he fled to Piedmont, where he engaged in radical journalism. Implicated in Giuseppe Mazzini's attempt to foment revolt in Milan in 1853, Crispi was expelled from Piedmont. In the following years he lived in Malta, London, and Paris and traveled throughout Europe.

In 1859 Crispi returned to Sicily and rejoined the independence movement. The following year he participated in Giuseppe Garibaldi's campaign in Sicily. When the kingdom of Italy was proclaimed in 1862, Crispi was elected deputy to the first Italian Parliament and became a leader of the left opposition to the premier, the Conte di Cavour. Although a zealous republican, in 1865 he became a supporter of King Victor Emmanuel II, after deciding that the monarchy could accelerate national unification.

In 1876 Crispi was elected president of the Chamber of Deputies. In December 1877 he became minister of the interior, but in March 1878 he resigned after being accused of bigamy. Although acquitted, he withdrew from political life for several years.

In 1887, after again serving briefly as minister of the interior, Crispi became premier. He broadened communal and provincial self-government, bettered public health conditions, and approved a more liberal penal code. However, he introduced severe regulations concerning public order and gave civil authorities the power to prohibit meetings and restrain freedom of association.

In the area of foreign policy Crispi supported Italian colonialism in Africa. He extended and unified Italian acquisitions in Africa and imposed an Italian protectorate on Ethiopia. He sought support of this policy from Germany and Austria-Hungary, Italy's allies in the Triple Alliance. Angered at French expansion in Africa, in 1887 Crispi influenced Parliament to refuse to renew the Italian commercial treaty with France. There then began a 10-year tariff war which greatly damaged the Italian economy.

In 1891, because of the unpopularity of his tariff and tax policy, Crispi was forced to resign. But in 1893, in an atmosphere of internal strife resulting from peasant riots and the growing worker movement, he again became premier. He outlawed all Socialist societies and associations of peasants and workers and disfranchised hundreds of thousands of Italians. He did not convoke Parliament in 1895 but ruled for 6 months as dictator.

Crispi continued his aggressive policy in Africa. But in 1896, following the crushing defeat of the Italian army at Adowa, Ethiopia, he was again forced to resign. He then lived in poverty and oblivion in Naples until his death on Aug. 11, 1901.

## Further Reading

Rich material on Crispi's life is in *The Memoirs of Francesco Crispi,* translated by Mary Prichard-Agnetti and edited by Thomas Palamenghi-Crispi (3 vols., 1912-1914). There is one biography of Crispi in English, *W. J. Stillman, Francesco Crispi: Insurgent, Exile, Revolutionist and Statesman* (1899).

## Additional Sources

Ganci, S. Massimo (Salvatore Massimo), *Il caso Crispi,* Palermo: Palumbo, 1976.

Tricoli, Giuseppe, *Francesco Crispi nella storiografia italiana,* Palermo, Italia: Editrice I.L.A. Palma, 1992. □

# Alfredo Cristiani

**Alfredo Cristiani (born 1947) sought to moderate the right-wing extremist image of the Alianza Republicana Nacionalista (ARENA) and led the party to victory when he was elected president of El Salvador in 1989.**

Alfredo Cristiani, nicknamed "Fredy," was a member of one of El Salvador's wealthiest families, whose interests included extensive holdings in coffee, cotton, sugar, and pharmaceuticals. Born in San Salvador on November 22, 1947, he enjoyed a privileged childhood. After attending the American School in the Salvadoran capital, Cristiani studied in the United States and graduated in business administration from Georgetown University. As a youth, he distinguished himself primarily as an athlete, excelling at squash and basketball, and eventually moving on to more expensive pursuits, such as motorcycling and aviation. Employed mostly in family enterprises before he became active in politics in the 1980's, Cristiani was known in his own country as a spokesperson for business interests. A free market enthusiast, he believed that economic development and social welfare were best left to the private sector.

The greatest political challenge facing Salvadoran elites of Cristiani's generation was the bloody civil war which began in the 1970's. Marxist insurgents, representing five different movements which united in 1980 under the banner of the Frente Farabundo Martí de Liberación Nacional (FMLN), waged a determined guerrilla struggle against a succession of military-dominated regimes. On October 15, 1979, progressive military officers, believing that El Salvador's centuries-old legacy of abuse and injustice lay at the root of the war, overthrew the despotic government of General Carlos Humberto Romero (1977-1979) and installed a reformist junta which included leftist civilians. The new government, which came to be dominated by Christian Democrats, initiated a land reform program and nationalized the banking and export industries, actions which threatened the interests of the wealthy class to which Cristiani belonged.

These reforms enjoyed the approval of the United States and resulted in a substantial increase in military and economic assistance, but they had little effect on the conflict. The FMLN and its allies on the left rejected the measures as superficial and condemned the regime for its failure to curb human rights abuses by the armed forces and the so-

called "death squads." Meanwhile, rightist elements denounced the reforms as Communist-inspired and called for a more ruthless prosecution of the war against the guerrillas.

In 1984 Alfredo Cristiani joined the right-wing ARENA as an organizer. He soon became leader of the party following the defeat in the presidential election that year of its founder, Roberto d'Aubuisson, a charismatic former intelligence officer widely believed to be involved in "death squad" activity. Cristiani owed his rapid elevation within the party to the fact that d'Aubuisson's violent reputation was a public relations liability—especially in the United States, upon whose continued financial support El Salvador depended. As leader of ARENA, Cristiani sought to moderate the party's extremist image and to expand its appeal to middle-class and poor voters. He represented a dramatic contrast with d'Aubuisson in background, style, and rhetoric, although d'Aubuisson's influence within the movement remained strong.

Cristiani's task of broadening ARENA's support base was made easier by the failures of the party in power, the Christian Democrats. José Napoleón Duarte, who had defeated d'Aubuisson in 1984 with covert assistance from the U.S. Central Intelligence Agency, was a popular politician, but as president he proved unable to achieve peace, to restore the economy, or to restrain the abuses of the armed forces. Corruption in his administration produced much resentment, and his own capacity to lead, always in doubt, was greatly reduced when he was found to be terminally ill with cancer. Under Cristiani's leadership, ARENA appealed effectively to voters' frustrations and won control of the Legislative Assembly and of many municipalities in 1988. The following year Alfredo Cristiani, running as ARENA's candidate, was easily elected president, winning 54 percent of the vote to 36 percent for Christian Democrat Fidel Chávez Mena in what was generally acknowledged to be, under the circumstances, a relatively free and fair election.

During the campaign, although almost always accompanied by d'Aubuisson, Cristiani had departed from previously held ARENA positions by promising not to dismantle the popular land reform enacted by the Christian Democrats and by expressing his willingness to negotiate with representatives of the FMLN. As president, he sought to keep these commitments and, also unusual for a Salvadoran conservative, emphasized the importance of addressing the problems of malnutrition and illiteracy, which he acknowledged to be among the causes of El Salvador's protracted civil conflict. Cristiani, however, rejected the statist solutions favored by the Christian Democrats in favor of free markets and privatization. An admirer of the economic policies of General Augusto Pinochet in Chile and of the development models followed by Taiwan and South Korea, Cristiani hoped to bring prosperity to El Salvador by lowering tariffs and creating incentives for foreign investment.

Cristiani's chances for success depended largely upon his ability to end the war, build a new political consensus, and maintain the confidence of the United States. However, these would not be easy tasks. Following unproductive early negotiations, the rebels, in November 1989, launched a major offensive against El Salvador. Although Cristiani showed personal courage in the crisis and the armed forces successfully repelled the attack, human rights remained absent in El Salvador. The government's response was brutal, especially in poor neighborhoods, and six prominent critics of the regime, all Jesuit priests, were murdered execution-style.

A border dispute between El Salvador and Honduras was peacefully resolved by Cristiani in 1992. Market reforms by the Cristiani government began to bear economic fruit with gross domestic product rising five percent in 1993. To a great degree, El Salvador's financial system was transferred from government to private control. Import tariffs were cut, price controls ended, while monetary policy was kept tight. His term in office expired in 1994. While no longer in the political spotlight, he continues to have signifigance in Salvadoran current events. He managed to survive an apparent attempt on his life, when a revolutionary group known as the "Popular Revolutionary Voice" planted a bomb outside Cristiani's new business, Compana Seguros e Inversiones S.A., a brokerage firm, in 1996.

## Further Reading

No major biography of Alfredo Cristiani has yet appeared in English. Sketches of his life and career have appeared in several magazines and newspapers. Particularly informative are Michael Massing, "Sad New El Salvador," *New York Review of Books* (May 18, 1989) and José Z. García, "Tragedy in El Salvador," *Current History* (January 1990). The best introduction to the Salvadoran crisis remains Tommie Sue Montgomery, *Revolution in El Salvador: Origins and Evolution* (2nd ed., 1984). □

# Benedetto Croce

**The Italian philosopher, critic, and educator Benedetto Croce (1866-1952) dominated Italian intellectual life in the first half of the 20th century. His many critical and philosophical writings brought Italian letters well into the mainstream of European thought.**

Born to a prosperous middle-class family, at the age of 9 Benedetto Croce began a rigorous Catholic education in Naples. When his parents and sister were killed in an earthquake in 1883, Croce went to Rome. While he never completed his law degree at the University of Rome, he reacted enthusiastically to the lectures on moral philosophy by Professor Antonio Labriola. Returning to Naples in 1886, Croce began a period of dedicated research, enriched by journeys to Spain, England, Germany, and France. Although his early works were largely historical, Croce transcended Positivistic scholarship and soon began inquiry into the nature of art and history and their relationship. He pursued this path relentlessly after his close study of G. W. F. Hegel and Giambattista Vico. With Labriola's

encouragement, Croce briefly (1895-1899) cultivated Marxism but refuted this doctrine in *Historical Materialism and Marxist Economics* (1900).

A long and fruitful collaboration with the philosopher Giovanni Gentile began in 1896. Working with Gentile, Croce edited *Classics of World Philosophy, Writers of Italy,* and *The Library of Modern Culture.* In 1903 Croce founded the bimonthly *La critica,* an international cultural review. For his contributions to Italian letters, in 1910 Croce was made a life member of the Italian Senate. Later, as minister of education (1920-1921), he conceived educational reforms implemented by Gentile, who subsequently occupied that office.

Croce's opposition to fascism, however, severed his association with Gentile. Through his "Manifesto of the Anti-Fascist Intellectuals" (1925), his denunciation of the Lateran Pact (1929), and his open criticism of Mussolini, Croce became the symbol of Italian intellectual freedom. After the fall of fascist Italy, he was a liaison between the Allies and the Italian monarchy but declined public office. In 1947 Croce established the Italian Institute for Historical Studies, to which he donated a large part of his house and extensive library.

## His Thought

The essence of Croce's thought may be found in his four-part *Filosofia dello spirito* (1902-1917; *Philosophy of the Spirit*), amplified and clarified in many subsequent writings. For Croce, philosophy is the science of the mind, or

spirit, wherein all reality resides. The mind's activity takes two distinct, interrelated but not opposite forms, the theoretical and the practical (or cognition and volition). The former perceives and understands reality, the latter creates and changes it. Within the sphere of theory, Croce distinguishes between intuition and logical thought. Similarly, in the realm of the practical, he separates the particular (utilitarian or economic) from the universal (ethical). These four interrelated divisions, none of which has primacy over the others, give rise to man's spiritual activities, which Croce treats in the four volumes of the *Filosofia: Aesthetics, Logic, Philosophy of Conduct* (*Economics and Ethics*), and *Theory and History of Historiography*.

In *Aesthetics* Croce declared that art is intuition. Realizing that intuition requires communication through language, he later spoke of "lyrical intuition" as creatively expressed impression. Still pursuing the theme in *La poesia* (1936), Croce distinguished between poetry ("achieved expression") and literature (which bears an external resemblance to poetry but fulfills another function).

As spokesman for an antimystical and antiutopian humanism which maintains that the goal of philosophy is an understanding of the course of human events, Croce has been criticized for not accepting an all-embracing belief, such as Catholicism or communism. He held, however, that there exists no final system or any eternally valid philosophy. Instead, Croce espoused "Historicism," a term by which he characterized the inherently evolutionary nature of his thought.

## Further Reading

In general, the most reliable translations of Croce's work are by Arthur Livingston and R. G. Collingwood. For a capsule portrait of Croce see Cecil J. S. Sprigge, *Benedetto Croce: Man and Thinker* (1952). A more complete study is Gian N. G. Orsini, *Benedetto Croce: Philosopher of Art and Literary Critic* (1961). There is a chapter on Croce in William Kurtz Wimsatt, Jr., and Cleanth Brooks, *Literary Criticism: A Short History* (1957). Henry Stuart Hughes, *Consciousness and Society: The Reorientation of European Social Thought, 1890-1930* (1958), includes a discussion of Croce.

## Additional Sources

Caserta, Ernesto G., *Studi crociani negli Stati Uniti: bibliografia critica (1964-1984),* Napoli: Loffredo, 1988.
Croce, Benedetto, *Carteggio,* s.l.: Bibliopolis, 1976.
Ocone, Corrado, *Bibliografia ragionata degli scritti su Benedetto Croce,* Napoli: Edizioni scientifiche italiane, 1993. □

# David Crockett

**David Crockett (1786-1836), American frontiersman and politician, became during his own lifetime a celebrity and folk hero, particularly to Americans living in the newly settled midwestern regions of the country.**

avy Crockett grew to manhood in a backwoods area. He experienced the crudeness and poverty of the frontier squatter and later used this knowledge in his political campaigns. A master storyteller, the semiliterate Crockett proved a formidable political campaigner, as well as the personification of the characters in the frontiersmen's "tall tales" of that day. Although he is known chiefly for his exploits as a hunter and soldier, Crockett's major contributions included political efforts to get free land for frontier settlers, relief for debtors, and an expanded state banking system for Tennessee.

Davy Crockett, the son of John and Rebecca Crockett, was born on Aug. 17, 1786, in Hawkings County, East Tennessee. John Crockett failed as a farmer, mill operator, and storekeeper. In fact, he remained in debt, as did Davy, all his life. Because of continuing poverty, Davy's father put him to work driving cattle to Virginia when he was 12 years old. Returning to Tennessee in the winter of 1798, Davy spent 5 days in school. After a fight there, he played hookey until his father found out and then, to escape punishment, ran away.

Crockett worked and traveled throughout Virginia and did not return home for nearly 3 years. Several years later he decided that his lack of education limited his marriage possibilities, and he arranged to work 6 months for a nearby Quaker teacher. In return Crockett received 4 days a week of instruction. He learned to read, to write a little, and to "cypher some in the first three rules of figures."

In 1806 Crockett married Mary Finely; the young couple began their life together on a rented farm with two cows, two calves, and a loan of $15. Frontier farming proved difficult and unrewarding to Crockett, who enjoyed hunting more than work. After five years he decided to move farther west. By 1813 he had located his family in Franklin Country, Tenn.

## Life on the Frontier

Shortly afterward the so-called Creek War began. During the summer of 1813 a party of frontiersmen ambushed a band of Creek Indian warriors in southern Alabama. Settlers in the area gathered at a stockade called Ft. Mims. The Native Americans attacked on Aug. 30, 1813, found the garrison undefended, and killed over 500 people. Within 2 weeks frontier militia units gathered for revenge, and Crockett volunteered for 3 months' duty that year. In September and October he served as a scout. During the famous mutiny against Andrew Jackson in December, Crockett was on leave, and reports that he deserted the militia during the Creek War are unfounded. He served again from September 1814 to February 1815. During this campaign Crockett was a mounted scout and hunter; apparently his unit encountered little fighting.

In 1815 Mary Crockett died. Within a year Crockett remarried. While traveling with neighbors in Alabama to examine the newly opened Creek lands during 1816, he contracted malaria and was left along the road to die. But he recovered and returned to Tennessee, pale and sickly, much to the surprise of his family and neighbors who thought he was dead. He has been quoted as remarking about his reported death, "I know'd this was a whopper of a lie, as soon as I heard it."

## Local and State Politics

In 1817 Crockett was a justice of the peace and the next year was serving also as a county court referee. In 1818 his neighbors elected him lieutenant colonel of the local militia regiment, and that same year he became one of the Lawrenceburg town commissioners. He held this position until 1821, when he resigned to campaign for a seat in the state legislature. During the campaign Crockett first displayed his shrewd ability to judge the needs of the frontiersmen. He realized that their isolation and need for recreation outweighed other desires. Therefore, he gave short speeches laced with stories, followed by a trip to the ever present liquor stand—a tactic well received by his audience, who elected him. Crockett appears to have been a quiet legislator, but his first-term actions demonstrate the areas of his future legislative interest. Having grown to manhood among the debt-ridden and often propertyless squatters, Crockett served as their spokesman. He proposed bills to reduce taxes, to settle land claim disputes, and in general to protect the economic interests of the western settlers.

When the legislative session ended in 1821, Davy went west again, this time to Gibson County, Tenn., where he built a cabin near the Obion River. Two years later he was elected to the Tennessee Legislature. This victory demon-

strates his improved campaign techniques and his realization that antiaristocratic rhetoric was popular. Again he worked for debtor relief and equitable land laws.

## Congressional Career

During 1825 Crockett ran for Congress; he campaigned as an antitariff man, however, and the incumbent easily defeated him. Two years later Crockett won the election. Throughout his congressional terms he worked for the Tennessee Vacant Land Bill, which he introduced during his first term. This proposal would have offered free land to frontier settlers in return for the increase in value which they would bring about because of their improvements.

In 1829, although he opposed several of President Andrew Jackson's measures, Crockett's campaign for reelection as a Jacksonian was successful. But during his second term in Congress, Crockett grew increasingly hostile to Jackson. He opposed the President on the issues of Native American removal, land policy, and the Second National Bank. In the election of 1831 Crockett was defeated. Two years later he regained his congressional seat by a narrow margin. By 1834 he had become such an outspoken critic of Jackson that Whig party leaders used Crockett as a popular symbol in their anti-Jackson campaigns. It was during these activities that several purported biographies and autobiographies of Crockett appeared. Their purpose was to popularize him and to show that not all frontiersmen supported the Jackson administration. These literary efforts failed to sway most of the voters, and Crockett was defeated in 1835, ending his congressional career.

During his three terms in Washington, Crockett tried to represent the interests of his frontier district. In doing so, he became enmeshed in a dispute with the Tennessee Jackson forces. The continuing fight with this group not only prevented him from making any lasting legislative contributions but also ended his political career.

## Death at the Alamo

In 1835 Crockett and four neighbors headed into Texas looking for new land. By January 1836 he had joined the Texas Volunteers, and within a month he reached San Antonio. In the first week of March he and the other defenders of the Alamo died during the siege and capture of that fort. Popular tradition places Crockett as one of the last defenders who died protecting the bedridden Col. William Travis during the final assault. The fact is, however, that Crockett was one of the first defenders to die, alone and unarmed.

Crockett's death at the Alamo engendered a notoriety and a lasting fame which his political activities would never have earned him. Through the newspaper accounts and other writings—fact and fiction—Crockett came to represent the typical westerner of that day. With the passage of time, tales and legends concerning his exploits grew. As a result, the popular image bears less relationship to the actual person than may be said about almost any other prominent figure.

Descriptions of Crockett are varied, but it is generally conceded that he was about 5 feet 8 inches tall, of medium weight, and with brown hair, blue eyes, and rosy cheeks. He was noted for a fine sense of humor, honesty, and ability as an entertaining public speaker. Those who knew him realized that he was a man of ability and character.

## Further Reading

A lack of source material has limited the scholarly studies of Crockett but has not prevented numerous popular accounts. Beginning with Matthew St. Clair Clarke's anonymously published *Life and Adventures of Col. David Crockett of West Tennessee* (1833), such accounts have continued to appear. Of the 19th-century books only *A Narrative of the Life of David Crockett, of the State of Tennessee* (1834), written by Crockett himself, is at all reliable.

The best work on Crockett is James A. Shackford, *David Crockett: The Man and the Legend* (1956), which separates the myths surrounding him from the historical person. Crockett's position in folklore is examined in Franklin J. Meine, ed., *Tall Tales of the Southwest: An Anthology of Southern and Southwestern Humor, 1830-1860* (1930), and Richard M. Dorson, ed., *Davy Crockett: American Comic Legend* (1939). For an understanding of politics in the Old Southwest see Thomas P. Abernethy, *From Frontier to Plantation in Tennessee: A Study in Frontier Democracy* (1932); Arthur M. Schlesinger, Jr., *The Age of Jackson* (1945); and Charles G. Sellers, *James K. Polk, Jacksonian: 1795-1843* (1957). □

# Herbert David Croly

**An American editor and author, Herbert David Croly (1869-1930) created the political philosophy known as "new nationalism" and was a founder of the magazine *New Republic*.**

Herbert Croly was born on Jan. 23, 1869, into an immigrant but middle-class family. Croly's father was editor of the *New York World* and the *New York Graphic,* and his mother wrote under the nom de plume Jennie June. Both parents were civic reformers.

Croly studied a year at the College of the City of New York and off and on for 11 years at Harvard before quitting academia in 1899 without taking a degree. So softspoken that he seemed to whisper, he was inordinately shy among strangers; according to his biographer his shyness approached the pathological. Croly's written words were as laborious as his spoken ones.

In 1892 Croly married Louise Emory of Baltimore, a wealthy socialite. He was editor of the *Architectural Record* from 1900 to 1913, when he quit to write books.

Croly wrote four books: *The Promise of American Life* (1909), *Marcus Alonzo Hanna: His Life and Work* (1913), *Progressive Democracy* (1914), and *Willard Straight* (1924), the biography of the banker who helped underwrite the *New Republic,* a magazine founded by Croly and two other journalists.

*The Promise of American Life* is the foundation of Croly's reputation. Despite the tortuous sentences, which often left readers confused, it attracted a following, and

*American Magazine,* at the height of the 1912 presidential campaign, hailed Croly as the "man from whom Colonel [Theodore] Roosevelt got his 'new nationalism.'" Croly first was attracted to his subject by the "dilemma of the artist or intellectual in an industrial society." He felt "empty individualism had run riot," that merit was measured by cash, and that industrial society was too mechanical. With the frontier gone, "automatic progress" was an end. He theorized that liberty and equality might actually conflict—despite America's heritage and the views of Jeffersonian Democrats. He pointed out that 19th-century "robber barons" cited slogans of individualism while forming monopolies.

Croly wanted "constructive discrimination" that would favor the weak. Equal rights for all, he argued, "merely left the great mass of people at the mercy of strong political and economic interests." He asserted that big government should control big business and big unions and that small businesses and nonunion people should be sacrificed as inefficient or failing parts of his system. Elite saint-heroes, or uncommon common men (like Abraham Lincoln), were to assure honesty of the system that Croly looked upon as "nationalized democracy."

Though he had suffered a paralytic stroke in 1928, Croly was still editor of the *New Republic* when he died on May 17, 1930.

## Further Reading

Charles Forcey, *The Crossroads of Liberalism: Croly Weyl, Lippmann, and the Progressive Era, 1900-1925* (1961), is the best study of Croly. See also Richard Hofstadter, *The Age of Reform: From Bryan to F.D.R.* (1955). ☐

# 1st Earl of Cromer

**The English statesman Evelyn Baring, 1st Earl of Cromer (1841-1917), ruled Egypt from 1883 to 1907.**

E velyn Baring was born on Feb. 26, 1841, at Cromer Hall in Norfolk. He entered Woolwich in 1855 to train for the Royal Artillery and in 1858 went with his battery to the Ionian Isles. After service in Malta and Jamaica he entered staff college in 1867, later moving into intelligence work for the War Office. In 1872 he was appointed private secretary to his cousin Lord Northbrook, the viceroy of India.

Baring returned to England in 1876, and the next year he was sent as commissioner to Egypt to represent British bondholders. But Khedive Ismail was attempting to rid himself of Anglo-French financial control, and in 1878 Baring resigned. When Ismael was deposed and Khedive Tewfik enthroned, Anglo-French control was reestablished, and in September 1879 Baring became British controller. Six months later, however, he returned to India as finance member on the viceroy's council.

In September 1883 Baring, now knighted, went to Egypt as British agent and consul general. Britain had occupied Egypt in the previous year and crushed the nationalists under Urabi. The country was bankrupt, and the Sudan in full rebellion under the Mahdists. To limit costs, Baring wished Egypt to evacuate the Sudan. His Egyptian ministers were opposed to his plan, but Baring forced them to obey, thus establishing British colonial control over theoretically independent Egypt.

By 1888 Baring had balanced Egypt's budget, which went into surplus in 1889. In the following years he abolished forced labor, reformed the systems of justice and administration, and extended direct British control over all aspects of interior government. Baring (who had already earned the nickname of "Overbaring" in India) became an almost viceregal figure.

In 1901 Baring was created Earl of Cromer. He opposed the growing Egyptian nationalist movement, which demanded that Britain's promises of withdrawal be fulfilled. The 1906 Denshwai incident, in which several Egyptian peasants were executed, incensed the Egyptian nationalists and gained them sympathy in Britain, where Henry Campbell-Bannerman's Liberal government insisted on progress toward self-government in Egypt. But Cromer could not adjust to these new policies and, his health failing, he resigned in March 1907.

Cromer took his seat in the House of Lords as a Liberal in 1908 but devoted most of his time to his writing. He died on Jan. 29, 1917.

## Further Reading

Cromer's *Modern Egypt* (2 vols., 1908) is a history of Egypt in the 19th century, culminating in an account of his own accomplishments there. His other works include *Abbas II* (1915), a study of his relations with the Khedive of Egypt, and *Political and Literary Essays* (3d series, 1916). Cromer's authorized biography is by the Marquess of Zetland, *Lord Cromer: Being the Authorized Life of Evelyn Baring, First Earl of Cromer* (1932). The most interesting and definitive modern scholarly study is by an Egyptian, Afaf L. al-Sayyid, *Egypt and Cromer: A Study in Anglo-Egyptian Relations* (1968). ☐

# Oliver Cromwell

**The English statesman and general Oliver Cromwell (1599-1658) won decisive battles in the English civil war. He then established himself and his army as the ruling force in England and later took the title Lord Protector of Great Britain and Ireland.**

O liver Cromwell was born on April 25, 1599, at Huntingdon. His father, Richard Cromwell, was a younger son of one of the richest men in the district, Sir Henry Cromwell of Hinchinbrook, known as the "Golden Knight." Cromwell's mother was the daughter of Sir William Steward, who managed the tithe revenues of Ely Cathedral. Little is known of Cromwell's childhood, except that his circumstances were modest and he was sent to the local school. His schoolmaster, Dr. Beard, was a devout Calvinist; most of Cromwell's intense religious convictions were derived from Beard, whom he venerated throughout his life.

In 1616 Cromwell entered Sidney Sussex College, Cambridge. He left the following year on the death of his father. For the next few years he lived in London, where in 1620 he married Elizabeth, the daughter of Sir James Bourchier, a wealthy leather merchant. Cromwell then returned to his small estate in Huntingdon, where he farmed his land and played a modest part in local affairs, acquiring a reputation as a champion of the poor and dispossessed. During these years Cromwell experienced periods of deep melancholy, suffused with religious doubt, but after much spiritual torment he became convinced that he was the instrument of God.

## Political Situation in 1640

When Cromwell entered Parliament for Cambridge in 1640, England had been ruled personally by Charles I for 11 years. The King had pursued an authoritarian policy in religion and finance which had distressed many country gentlemen, including Cromwell. Furthermore, Charles had plunged into war with Scotland, which had risen in revolt when Archbishop William Laud had persuaded him to impose the English Prayer Book on the Scottish Church. The Scots rapidly defeated the King; destitute of money and at the mercy of the Scots, Charles I was forced to call Parliament.

The mood of Parliament was highly critical, and there was a closely knit body of Puritan country gentlemen and lawyers who were determined that the power of the King and the Anglican Church should be limited by Parliament. Several of Cromwell's relatives, particularly the influential John Hampden and Oliver St. John, belonged to this group, which was led by John Pym. Cromwell threw in his lot with these men. A middle-aged man without parliamentary experience, he spoke rarely, but when he did it was usually in support of extreme measures. Cromwell soon established his reputation as a firm upholder of the parliamentary cause; he was dedicated to the reform of the Church and of the court and was highly critical of the King.

## Civil War

By 1642 the King and Parliament had become so antagonistic that armed conflict was inevitable. At the outbreak of war in August 1642, Cromwell headed a regiment whose prime duty was to defend East Anglia. He rapidly demonstrated not only his skill as a military leader by rapid raids into royalist territory combined with skillful retreat, but also his capacity to mold an effective army from his force of raw recruits.

Under the leadership of the Earl of Manchester, Cromwell's commander, regiments from other counties were brought together in a formidable body, known as the Eastern Association. In 1643 Cromwell's cavalry worsted the royalists in a number of sharp engagements—Grantham (May 13), Gainsborough (July 18), and Wincaby (October 13). These successes helped to create parliamentary supremacy in East Anglia and the Midlands. Cromwell's reputation as Parliament's most forceful general was made the next year, however, at the battle of Marston Moor (July 2, 1644), when his Ironsides routed the cavalry of Prince Rupert, the most successful royalist general. To Cromwell, whose religious convictions strengthened with every victory that he won, Marston Moor was God's work, and he wrote, "God made them stubble to our swords."

The victories in eastern England, however, were not matched by success elsewhere. After 2 years of war the King was still in the field, and there was a growing rift between Parliament and the army. Many disliked the price paid for alliance with the Scots (acceptance of the Presbyterian form of church government), and most longed for peace. Cromwell, however, yearned for victory. He bitterly attacked the Earl of Manchester, and after complex political maneuvering he emerged as the effective leader of the parliamentary armies. He proved his exceptional capacities as a general on June 14, 1645, when he smashed the royalists' army at Naseby in Northamptonshire. Within 12 months the royalist armies had capitulated.

In 5 years Cromwell had risen from obscurity to renown. A large man with a long, red face studded with warts, he nevertheless possessed considerable presence. His mood was usually somber, thoughtful, and deeply religious. His soldiers sang psalms as they went into battle, and every regiment had its preacher.

The next 3 years taxed Cromwell's skill and faith. His army became riddled with Levellers, whose radical doctrines called for a far more democratic social structure than Cromwell and his fellow generals would tolerate. Parliament and the Scots inclined not only to peace with the King but also to a rigid form of Presbyterianism, which Cromwell disliked. He claimed to believe in toleration, but excepted always Catholics and atheists.

In 1648 the royalists rose again, sided by the Scots, but in a lightning campaign Cromwell smashed both. The republicans were then determined to bring Charles I to trial, and Cromwell did nothing to stop them. At last agreeing that the King was "a man of blood" and should be executed, he signed Charles I's death warrant.

## Further Campaigns

The execution of the King settled nothing. Legally, the House of Commons, purged to such an extent that it was called the Rump, ruled. But the army, Scotland, and Ireland were soon in rebellion. The Scottish Presbyterians proclaimed Charles II (Charles I's son) their lawful monarch, and the Irish Catholics did likewise. In England the radicals were a rampant minority, the royalists a stunned majority, but neither had any respect for the Rump.

Cromwell suppressed the Levellers by force and then set about subduing first Ireland and then Scotland. In the former Cromwell fought a tough, bloody campaign in which the butchery of thousands of soldiers at Drogheda (Sept. 11, 1649) and hundreds of civilians at Wexford (Oct. 11) caused his name to be execrated in Ireland for centuries.

On June 26, 1650, Cromwell finally became commander in chief of the parliamentary armies. He moved against the Scots and got into grievous difficulties. At Dunbar in August 1650 he was pressed between the hills and the sea and was surrounded by an army of 20,000 men. But the folly of the Scottish commander, Leslie, enabled Cromwell to snatch a victory, he thought by divine help, on September 3. The next year Charles II and his Scottish army made a spirited dash into England, but Cromwell smashed them at Worcester on Sept. 3, 1651. At long last the war was over and Cromwell realized that God's humble instrument had been given, for better or worse, supreme power.

## Cromwell's Rule: 1653-1658

For 5 years after the execution of the King, Parliament tried to formulate a new constitution. Its failure to do this so exasperated Cromwell that on April 20, 1653, he went with a handful of soldiers to the House of Commons, where he shouted at the members, "The Lord be done with you," and ordered them out.

Until his death Cromwell tried to create a firm new constitutional base for his power. His first attempt to establish a constitution by means of a nominated Parliament in 1653 ended in disaster, so the Council of Army Officers promulgated the Instrument of Government, by which Cromwell became Protector in December 1653. He was assisted by a Council of State on whose advice he acted, for Cromwell believed sincerely in the delegation and sharing of power. For 8 months Cromwell and his Council ruled most effectively, sweeping away ancient feudal jurisdictions in Scotland and Ireland and uniting those countries with England under one Parliament, which was itself reformed. When the Parliament met in 1654, however, it soon quarreled with Cromwell over the constitution. He once more took power into his own hands and dissolved Parliament on June 22, 1655.

Cromwell's government became more authoritarian. Local government was brought under major generals, soldiers whom he could trust. This infuriated the radical left as well as the traditionalists. Again attempting to give his authority a formal parliamentary base and also needing additional revenue, Cromwell reconvened Parliament. His successes abroad and his suppression of revolts at home had greatly increased his popularity; thus when Parliament met, he was pressed to accept the crown, but after much soul-searching he refused. He took instead the title Lord Protector under a new constitution—the Humble Petition and Advice (May 25, 1657). This constitution also reestablished the House of Lords and made Cromwell king in all but name. But Cromwell was no Napoleon; there were definite limits to his personal ambition. He did not train his son Richard to be his successor, nor did he try to establish his family as a ruling dynasty. And at the height of his power he retained his deep religious conviction that he was merely an instrument of God's purpose.

Cromwell pursued an effective foreign policy. His navy enjoyed substantial success, and the foundation of British power in the West Indies was laid by its capture of Jamaica (1655). He allied himself with France against Spain, and his army carried the day at the battles of the Dunes in 1658. These victories, combined with his dexterous handling of Scotland and brutal suppression of Ireland, made his personal ascendancy unassailable, in spite of failures in his domestic policy. But shortly after his death on Sept. 3, 1658, Cromwell's regime collapsed, and the restoration of the monarchy followed in 1660.

## Critical Assessment

Cromwell's greatness will always be questioned. As a general, he was gifted yet lucky; as a statesman, he had some success but was unable to bring his plans to complete fruition. Although his religious conviction often appears to be a hypocritical cloak for personal ambition, his positive qualities are unmistakable. He believed in representative government (limited to men of property, however). He encouraged reform, and much of it was humane. He brought to the executive side of government a great degree of professionalism, particularly in the army and navy. Britain emerged from the Commonwealth stronger, more efficient, and more secure. Perhaps the most remarkable qualities of Cromwell were his sobriety and his self-control. Few men have enjoyed such supreme power and abused it less.

## Further Reading

Cromwell's letters and speeches are collected by Wilbur C. Abbott in *The Writings and Speeches of Oliver Cromwell* (4 vols., 1937-1947). The literature on Cromwell is enormous. The best and most complete biography of him is Sir Charles Firth, *Oliver Cromwell and the Rule of the Puritans in England* (1900; repr. 1961). An excellent brief biography is C. V. Wedgwood, *Oliver Cromwell* (1939). Maurice Ashley, *Oliver*

*Cromwell and the Puritan Revolution* (1958), is also valuable. The problems of Cromwell's character and policies are well explored in Richard E. Boyer, ed., *Oliver Cromwell and the Puritan Revolt* (1966). Equally valuable is Maurice P. Ashley, ed., *Cromwell* (1969). Cromwell's career as a general is best studied in C. V. Wedgwood, *The King's War* (1958); Alfred H. Burne and Peter Young, *The Great Civil War: A Military History of the First Civil War, 1642-1646* (1959); and Austin H. Woolrych, *The Battles of the English Civil War* (1961). The best bibliographical guide is Wilbur C. Abbott, *Bibliography of Oliver Cromwell* (1929). □

# Thomas Cromwell

**The English statesman Thomas Cromwell, Earl of Essex (ca. 1485-1540), was the chief minister of Henry VIII from 1532 to 1540 and was largely responsible for revolutionary reforms in the English Church and in administration of the state.**

Thomas Cromwell was born in Putney, near London. His father, Walter Cromwell, was a fuller and shearer of cloth who also worked as a blacksmith, innkeeper, and brewer. Perhaps an unruly youth, Thomas received little formal education. About 1504 he traveled to Flanders and Italy, where he served as a mercenary soldier. While abroad he had an opportunity to learn French and Italian and to observe something of the diplomatic maneuvers of the European powers. When he returned to England about 1513, he married Elizabeth Wykes, whose father was also a shearer. Their only son, Gregory, proved dull and despite an elaborate education never achieved prominence.

In 1514 Cromwell entered the service of Thomas Wolsey, the great cardinal who dominated both Church and state. Cromwell's administrative abilities were soon recognized, and he became involved in all of Wolsey's business, especially the suppression of certain small monasteries and the application of their revenues to new colleges founded in Ipswich and Oxford. During this period Cromwell evidently studied law; in 1524 he was admitted to Gray's Inn, one of the Inns of Court. He also entered Parliament and in 1523 may have delivered a famous speech denouncing Henry VIII's war in France and its accompanying taxation.

When Wolsey fell from power, Cromwell attached himself directly to the court. In 1529 he was elected to the Reformation Parliament, the later sessions of which he helped manage for the King. In 1532 he began to accumulate government offices, and he so gained the confidence of Henry VIII that he became the King's chief minister. He drafted the act in restraint of appeals, passed by Parliament in 1533 to allow Henry's divorce to be granted in England without interference from the Pope, and subsequent legislation which affirmed royal supremacy in religion and provided for a Church of England independent of Rome. His great ideal was the establishment of England as an "empire," completely self-contained and owing no allegiance to any external power.

Although he was not a priest, Cromwell was now named the King's vice-gerent, or deputy, in spiritual affairs. He was largely responsible for legislation which authorized the dissolution of the monasteries and the confiscation of their property by the King. Although more interested in politics than theology, he was probably a sincere Protestant and certainly a supporter of Archbishop Thomas Cranmer.

In secular affairs Cromwell sought efficiency above all. He instituted revolutionary reforms, especially in financial administration. His multiplicity of offices—the King's principal secretary, lord privy seal, master of the jewels, clerk of the hanaper, master of the rolls, chancellor of the Exchequer, and master of the court of wards—gave him control over virtually every aspect of government. Unlike Wolsey and his predecessors, Cromwell was never lord chancellor; he can be regarded as the first chief minister of a new type, a layman basing his influence on the office of principal secretary. In 1536 he was ennobled as Baron Cromwell of Oakham, in the county of Rutland, and in 1540 he was created Earl of Essex. Although his magnificence never approached Wolsey's, he enjoyed the considerable wealth which he acquired. He had four houses, all in or near London; friends and foreign ambassadors later recalled their pleasant walks in his gardens.

Cromwell always had his enemies, mainly religious conservatives like Stephen Gardiner, Bishop of Winchester, or members of the old aristocracy like Thomas Howard, Duke of Norfolk. After Cromwell arranged the King's disastrous marriage to Anne of Cleves, these foes combined to topple him, charging that he was an overmighty subject and a heretic. He was not given a trial but was condemned by a bill of attainder. On July 28, 1540, he was beheaded on Tower Hill. A clumsy executioner made the scene more than usually horrible, even by Tudor standards.

Although often criticized for his ambition, political ruthlessness, and plunder of the Church, Cromwell was a genuinely affable man, an administrative genius, and a loyal adviser to the King. It is doubtful that Henry VIII could have secured his divorce or devised his great scheme of ecclesiastical nationalization without Cromwell.

## Further Reading

Most of Cromwell's extant letters are printed in Roger B. Merriman, *Life and Letters of Thomas Cromwell* (2 vols., 1902). There is no satisfactory biography of Cromwell. His work in secular administration is best described in Geoffrey R. Elton, *The Tudor Revolution in Government* (1953), while his influence in the English Church is discussed in Arthur G. Dickens, *Thomas Cromwell and the English Reformation* (1959).

## Additional Sources

Beckingsale, B. W., *Thomas Cromwell, Tudor minister,* Totowa, N.J.: Rowman and Littlefield, 1978. □

# Walter Leland Cronkite Jr.

**Walter Leland Cronkite, Jr., (born 1916) was an American journalist and radio and television news broadcaster who became pre-eminent among the outstanding group of correspondents and commentators developed by CBS News after World War II.**

Walter Cronkite was born in St. Joseph, Missouri, the only son of his dentist father and the former Helena Lena Fritsch. While he was still a youngster the family moved to Texas. His reading about the exploits of foreign correspondents inspired his interest in journalism. Preparation for that vocation began with his work on his high school yearbook and newspaper.

In 1933 he entered the University of Texas at Austin and took a part-time job with the *Houston Post.* This set him on a professional career which led him to abandon college after two years to serve as a general reporter for the *Post,* a radio announcer in Kansas City, and a sportscaster in Oklahoma City. After that his principal employer for several years was United Press International (UPI), for whom he covered World War II in Europe (1941-1945) and served as chief correspondent at the Nuremburg War Crimes Trials (1945-1946) and in Moscow (1946-1948).

## Years at CBS

To this point Cronkite was largely unknown to the general public. In 1950 he joined CBS News where two years later he was narrator for "You Are There," a television program in which major historical events were re-created. In 1954 he became narrator of "The Twentieth Century," a

monumental television documentary which established Cronkite's recognition with the viewing public. That was reinforced by his quadrennial service as anchor of the CBS coverage of the national political party conventions, which he first covered in 1952. With the exception of the 1964 Democratic convention, he continued this role until his retirement in 1981.

When Cronkite assumed the duties of anchor and editor for the "CBS Evening News" in 1962, NBC's "Huntley-Brinkley Report" dominated viewer ratings. Gradually the CBS broadcasts gained ground on the renowned team at NBC, which broke up in 1970. From then until his retirement, Cronkite's program was consistently the most popular television news broadcast.

Although the evening news was his main platform, Cronkite maintained his prominence as narrator and correspondent on network specials, including space shots, major documentaries, and extensive interviews with world figures such as Presidents Truman, Eisenhower, and Johnson. After his retirement he continued this role in addition to the intermittent series, "Walter Cronkite's Universe."

For a society that emphasized youthfulness, it was a paradox that as Cronkite grew older his prestige increased. His white hair and moustache gave him a rather distinguished look, although Cronkite's reputation did not rest on appearance. He earned recognition and praise through hard work, a passion for accuracy, and an insistence on impartiality. Underlying that was a life-long competitive spirit that was sublimated before the microphone and camera but manifest in his leisure activities of sailing, tennis, and race car driving.

Among Cronkite's strengths were his believability, accuracy, and impartiality. He was also quite diligent about not becoming part of the story he was reporting. Yet there were memorable instances when he failed to remain completely detached from a story: his obvious emotional reaction when announcing the death of President John Kennedy in 1963; his characterization, on the eve of the 1968 Democratic convention, of the site as a concentration camp; his broadcast pronouncement in 1968, upon returning from Vietnam, that he doubted that U.S. policy for that region could prevail; and his undeniable enthusiasm when Neil Armstrong became the first person on the moon in 1969. Despite his philosophic disclaimer, Cronkite sometimes influenced the news, as in his televised interview with Anwar Sadat that led that Egyptian leader to visit Israel and the Israeli Prime Minister Menachem Begin to reciprocate. Inadvertently, Cronkite was a news topic in 1976 when John Anderson, running as an independent presidential candidate, mentioned Cronkite as his likely running mate.

The exceptions notwithstanding, Cronkite raised television news broadcasting to a level of professionalism that was lauded around the world. His credentials as a newspaperman and war correspondent, along with his unwillingness to deviate from a hard news format, demonstrated that acceptance and popularity in television news need not rest on superficiality.

The depth of respect for his work was reflected in the numerous awards he received: the Peabody for Radio and Television and the William Allen White Award for Journalistic Merit, as well as the Emmy. In 1981, during his final three months on the "CBS Evening News," Cronkite received 11 major awards, including the Presidential Medal of Freedom. In 1985 he became the second newsman, after Edward R. Murrow, to be selected for the Television Hall of Fame. At his retirement, Cronkite was the most commonly mentioned person on the "dream list" for lecturers at conventions, clubs, and college campuses.

### Post CBS Retirement

After retiring as anchor of the "CBS Evening News," Cronkite served as CBS News special correpondent and on the network's board of directors from 1981 to 1991. He also anchored the CBS News science magazine series "Walter Cronkite's Universe," (1980-82), and from the late 1980s until 1992, hosted "Walter Cronkite's 20th Century", a daily 90-second account of same-day historical events. In 1993 he formed his own production company and produced several award-winning documentaries for The Discovery Channel, PBS, and other networks. One of those, "Cronkite Remembers", was sheduled to air in early 1997 in conjunction with the late 1996 publication of his autobiography, *A Reporter's Life*. During the 1996 presidential campaign, Cronkite headed efforts to convince networks to offer free television time for presidential candidates. When not making documentaries, Cronkite enjoyed sailing his 48-foot yacht, the "Wynje".

### Further Reading

Cronkite tells the story of his years growing up in Kansas City and Houston; his early career working for newspapers, wire services, and radio stations; his time as a war correspondent for UPI; and his years at CBS in his autobiography *A Reporter's Life* (1997). An excellent overview of Cronkite's work habits, strengths and weaknesses, and rapport with his colleagues is "Uncle Walter," a chapter in *Air Time* (1978) by Gary Paul Gates. Briefer episodes of a similar vein about Cronkite are in *The Powers That Be* (1979) by David Halberstam. In *Challenge of Change* (1971), Cronkite set out his journalistic philosophy. The book is a collection of nine speeches he gave during 1967-1970. *Eye on the World* (1971) is useful mainly as an example of his editing skills. The volume is largely excerpts from interviews by other CBS newsmen on major topics of that period. Both philosophic and descriptive is his "What It's Like To Broadcast News," *Saturday Review* (December 12, 1970). *South by Southeast* (1983) with Ray Ellis and *South by Southwest* (1971) provide insight into Cronkite's leisure activities, especially sailing. One of Cronkite's daughters, Kathy, recorded her experiences as a child of a celebrity in *On the Edge of the Spotlight* (1981). □

# George Crook

**The American army officer George Crook (1828-1890) campaigned against Indians in the southwestern and northwestern United States, but he was also an outspoken champion of Indian rights.**

B orn on Sept. 8, 1828, on a farm near Taylorsville, Ohio, George Crook was appointed to the U.S. Military Academy in 1848. Four years later he graduated thirty-eighth in a class of 56 and was commissioned a lieutenant of infantry. Assigned to the Pacific Northwest, he spent the next 9 years exploring the area and fighting Indians.

During the Civil War, Crook was appointed colonel of the 38th Ohio Infantry, in command of the Department of West Virginia. By 1865, having distinguished himself in numerous battles, he was commissioned a major general of volunteers.

At the end of the Civil War, Crook reverted to the rank of lieutenant colonel and commanded the 23rd Infantry, which was headquartered at Boise, Idaho. He campaigned against Native Americans until 1871, when President Grant sent him to command the Department of Arizona. By this time he usually wore a weather-beaten canvas suit and a Japanese summer hat but no military trappings of any type, not even a symbol of his rank. Because of his manner of dress and his peculiar whiskers, the Apache dubbed him "Gray Fox."

Using unorthodox techniques, such as the enlistment of Apache scouts to guide his troops, Crook quickly brought peace to Arizona. For this feat he received a spectacular promotion in 1873, from lieutenant colonel to brigadier general.

In 1875 Crook was transferred to command the Department of the Platte, where he had to contend with the Sioux. His success on the northern plains was not so great as it had been in the Southwest, and in 1882 he returned to quell disorders in the Department of Arizona. He quickly restored order, forcing renegade Apache to return to their reservation. He also conducted the final Geronimo campaign of May 1885 through March 1886, which brought Geronimo to the conference table, where surrender terms were arranged. Geronimo returned to the Sierra Madre of Mexico, however, and Crook was pressured into asking for a transfer. Politics dictated a military solution to the Apache wars, while Crook believed in diplomacy.

In 1886 Crook resumed command of the Department of the Platte; then, in 1888, upon his promotion to major general, he was assigned the Division of the Missouri, with headquarters in Chicago. He died there on March 21, 1890.

Crook was a model soldier—fearless, modest, a good listener. He did not drink or use strong language. In his years in the West he fought corrupt Indian agents and spoke and wrote in favor of granting the Indians full citizenship and the right to vote. His wife, Mary, supported him throughout his long and colorful career.

## Further Reading

Martin F. Schmitt, ed., *General George Crook: His Autobiography* (1946), is the standard account of Crook's life; Schmitt pieced this work together from Crook's diary and letters and gave an excellent picture of the man. John G. Bourke, *On the Border with Crook* (1891; repr. 1962), is the account of

Crook's adjutant during many of his military years, while Crook's own work, *Résumé of Operations against Apache Indians, 1882-1886* (1887), indicates his attitude toward the Indians.

### Additional Sources

Crook, George, *General George Crook: his autobiography*, Norman: University of Oklahoma Press, 1986, 1960. □

# Sir William Crookes

**The English chemist and physicist Sir William Crookes (1832-1919) discovered the element thallium and invented the radiometer, the spinthariscope, and the Crookes tube.**

William Crookes was born in London on June 17, 1832. His education was limited, and despite his father's wish that he become an architect, he chose industrial chemistry as a career. He entered the Royal College of Chemistry in London, where he began his researches in chemistry. In 1859 he founded the *Chemical News*, which made him widely known, and remained its editor and owner all his life.

Most notable among Crookes's chemical studies is that one which led to his 1861 discovery of thallium. Using spectrographic methods, he had observed a green line in the spectrum of selenium, and he was thus led to announce the existence of a new element, thallium. While determining the atomic weight of thallium, using a delicate vacuum balance, he noticed several irregularities in weighing, which he attributed to the method. His investigation of this phenomenon led to the construction in 1875 of an instrument that he named the radiometer.

In 1869 J. W. Hittorf first studied the phenomena associated with electrical discharges in vacuum tubes. Not knowing of this, Crookes, 10 years later, made a parallel but more extensive investigation. In his 1878 report he pointed out the significant properties of electrons in a vacuum, including the fact that a magnetic field causes a deflection of the emission. He suggested that the tube was filled with matter in what he called the "fourth state;" that is, the mean free path of the molecules is so large that collisions between them can be ignored. Tubes such as this are still called "Crookes tubes," and his work was honored by naming the space near the cathode in low pressure "Crookes dark space."

Crookes also made useful contributions to the study of radioactivity in 1903 by developing the spinthariscope, a device for studying alpha particles. He foresaw the urgent need for nitrogenous fertilizers, which would be used to cultivate crops to meet the demands of a rapidly expanding population. Crookes did much to popularize phenol (carbolic acid) as an antiseptic; in fact, he became an expert on sanitation. Mention should also be made of the serious and

ing Crosby was born in Tacoma, Washington, on May 2, 1903 (although there is some dispute about the year, which is also variously stated as 1901 and 1904). He was one of seven children, all of whom were given music lessons by their musically inclined parents (one brother, Bob Crosby, later earned fame and fortune as a band-leader in the 1930s and 1940s). While he was still a boy the family moved to Spokane, Washington, where he grew up, graduating from a Jesuit high school in 1920 and for a while attending the Jesuit Gonzaga University.

He was christened Harry Lillis Crosby at birth, but was dubbed Bing while in grade school. According to his autobiography, he was an avid fan of a comic strip called "The Bingville Bugle" which appeared in one of the Spokane Sunday newspapers. Friends noticed that, like a number of characters in this strip, the young Crosby had large ears and took to calling him "Bingo" which in time was shortened to Bing. Publicity material issued during the 1930s, however, asserted that his name came from the fact that when he played cowboys and Indians as a child he shouted "bing" instead of "bang."

Crosby began singing professionally in the early 1920s. Throughout the decade he was active with a number of singing groups. The most notable of these groups was the Rhythm Boys, a trio which achieved a great deal of popularity through its association with the then immensely successful Paul Whiteman Orchestra. The trio became an important part of Whiteman's act, touring with the orchestra across America. But in time the trio decided to strike out on its own

active interest he took in psychic phenomena, to which he devoted most of 4 years.

Crookes was knighted in 1897. His marriage lasted from 1856 until the death of his wife in 1917; they had 10 children. He died in London on April 4, 1919.

### Further Reading

A biography of Crookes is Edmund E. Fournier d'Albe, *The Life of Sir Wm. Crookes* (1923). For background information see Alexander Findlay, *A Hundred Years of Chemistry* (1937; 3d ed. 1965), and Eduard Farber, *The Evolution of Chemistry: A History of Its Ideas, Methods and Materials* (1952; 2d ed. 1969).

### Additional Sources

Hall, Trevor H., *The medium and the scientist: the story of Florence Cook and William Crookes,* Buffalo, N.Y.: Prometheus Books, 1984. □

# Harry Lillis Crosby

**Harry Lillis Crosby (1903-1977) was one of the best-loved show business personalities of his time. He set a crooning style which was imitated for years, recorded over 1,600 songs, had his own radio show for over 20 years, starred in over 60 films, and made many guest appearances and specials for television.**

in Hollywood. Soon the group broke up, and in the early 1930s Crosby achieved recognition on his own.

## A Natural for Movies and Radio

Crosby's beautiful voice and engaging style were perfect for the movies, which had just converted to sound, and to radio broadcasting, which was just coming into its own as a national medium. As the knowledgeable Garson Kanin has pointed out with regard to Crosby at this time: "nothing is so powerful as a crooner who has met his time." Crosby's mellifluous voice, his laid-back persona, and his casual delivery set a crooning style for singers that was widely imitated for years. But he had no real competition until the 1940s and the advent of Frank Sinatra.

Crosby's radio career began in 1930 while he was performing in night clubs in Los Angeles as a band singer. By the following year he had his own 15-minute radio show, and he would have some kind of radio show for over two decades, until the mid-1950s. His theme song, "When the Blue of the Night Meets the Gold of the Day," became one of radio broadcasting's classic theme songs. Crosby is probably best remembered as a radio personality for his stint as the star of NBC's hour long Kraft Music Hall with which he was associated from 1935 to 1946.

When after World War II Crosby wanted to make use of newly developed technology to pre-record the show he met strong resistance from NBC and from the sponsor, Kraft. He moved to another network and easily found another sponsor. Crosby was a star in various mediums. His movies drew well at the box office; his records sold in the millions. But as journalist John Dunning convincingly argued, "radio first spread his name far and wide . . . , and kept Crosby synonymous with top show business for three decades."

Less good fortune marked Crosby's forays into television. He made many guest appearances before undertaking a weekly show in the mid-1960s. It lasted only a single season and was not a critical success. In 1966 Crosby did his first Christmas special; the last one was aired two months after his death. These specials attracted millions of Crosby's fans and were generally considered successful. Yet, overall, television was not a medium that was kind to Crosby.

## A Success in the Movies

The movies were another matter. Crosby was a top star for over 30 years, and for a period of time in the 1940s he was among the top ten box office draws in the United States. He made over 60 films, most of them for Paramount, which released 45 of the films. His association with the studio lasted for a quarter of a century. His movie career began in the Paul Whiteman film *King of Jazz* in 1930 as one of the Rhythm Boys.

His first important role in a Paramount film was in *The Big Broadcast* (1932), in which he played a happy-go-lucky crooner singing at a failing radio station. This film, which gave him his big break and which was successful at the box office, set the pattern for most of the other movies he made during the 1930s. These movies were light-weight comedies with Crosby as an easy-going singer with an affable style. It made no difference if the setting was on shipboard

(*Anything Goes,* 1936), at a girl's school (*Going Hollywood,* 1933), by a showboat (*Mississippi,* 1935), or in contemporary Los Angeles (*Sing You Sinners,* 1938).

While he continued to make some similar films during the 1940s, it was the "Road" films that moved his star even higher. In 1940 he embarked with Bob Hope and Dorothy Lamour on the *Road to Singapore.* Over the years there followed *Road to Zanzibar* (1941), *Road to Morocco* (1942), *Road to Utopia* (1945), *Road to Rio* (1947), *Road to Bali* (1952), and *Road to Hong Kong* (1962). All of these films were good-natured spoofs which played on the personalities of their leads and were filmed with amiable gags, outrageous quips, and a variety of send-ups.

Another important extension of his talents also took place during the 1940s when he played a relaxed amiable singing Irish priest in *Going My Way* (1944) and *The Bells of St. Mary's* (1945). Both these films were smash hits, and Crosby was critically acclaimed. For his first portrayal of Father O'Malley he was awarded an Oscar. These films were followed by more conventional musicals such as *Blue Skies* (1946), *Mr. Music* (1950), and *Just For You* (1952), which were no more or less than their titles indicate.

As the audience for such film fare began to diminish in the 1950s Crosby changed pace and undertook with considerable success a number of dramatic roles, including the part of the has-been alcoholic Broadway actor in the film version of Clifford Odets' bittersweet play *The Country Girl.* For his moving portrayal Crosby won an Oscar nomination and a New York Film Critics Award. His film career declined in the 1960s. His last major role, really a character part, was as a drunken doctor in the embarrassing remake (1966) of the classic 1939 Western *Stagecoach.* His last on-screen appearance was as one of the narrators in the nostalgic compilation film *That's Entertainment* (1974), which dealt with MGM's musical past.

## Millions of Records

One of Crosby's films—*Holiday Inn* (1942)—provided him with his greatest success as a recording artist. The Irving Berlin song "White Christmas," sung by Crosby in this film as the lament of a New Englander spending Christmas in snowless Southern California, struck a responsive chord during World War II when millions of soldiers were away from home during the holidays. Crosby's recording of that song has remained a best seller since then. It is estimated to be among the best selling singles ever recorded, having sold over 100 million copies. It has contributed to the fact that Crosby is among the greatest selling recording artists of all time. During his 51-year recording career Crosby recorded more than 1,600 songs and is estimated to have sold over 400 million records.

Bing Crosby was married twice. The first time, in 1930, was to the actress-singer Dixie Lee, who died of cancer in 1952. They had four sons—Gary (born 1934), Dennis and Phillip (born 1935), and Lindsay (born 1938). In 1957 Crosby married actress-starlet Kathryn Grant who was some 30 years younger than him. They had two boys (H. L. Crosby, Jr., born 1958, and Nathaniel, born 1961) and a girl (Mary, born 1959). Crosby died as the result of a massive heart attack on October 14th, 1977, while playing golf on a course in Spain. He is buried in Los Angeles.

During his years in show business Crosby earned a fortune, which he augmented by wise investments and careful management. At his death Crosby was estimated to be worth tens of millions of dollars, and his holdings were said to include everything from real estate and oil and gas wells to stock in the Coca-Cola company. He was one of the wealthiest show business personalities of his day and also one of the best loved. His popularity never really waned. He was, to use cinema historian John Kobal's words, "an American institution . . . relaxed to the point of disinterest, or so it seemed, but beneath that outward charm lay a tough showbusiness professional. . . ."

## Further Reading

Bing Crosby's autobiography is *Call Me Lucky* (1953). His second wife, Kathryn Crosby, has written an interesting memoir, *Bing and Other Things* (1967). The authorized biography is by Charles Thompson (1976). Other friendly biographies are by Bob Thomas (1978) and Barry Ulanov (1948). Crosby's son Gary also published a biography of his father, *Going My Own Way* (1983), and Kathryn Crosby released another memoir, *My Life with Bing* (1983). A quick once over of the films is by Robert Bookbinder (1977). Donald Shepherd and Robert L. Slatzer, *Bing Crosby: The Hollow Man* is an unfriendly biography (1981). ☐

# Samuel Adjai Crowther

**The Anglican bishop Samuel Adjai Crowther (ca. 1806-1891) was a pioneer African missionary and the first African Anglican bishop in Nigeria.**

Samuel Crowther, of the Yoruba tribe, was enslaved in 1821 and put aboard a ship which was captured by the British navy. The freed slaves were sent to Freetown, Sierra Leone, where Crowther was baptized and, in 1827, became the first teacher to graduate from the Church Missionary Society's Teacher Training College at Fourah Bay. He joined the 1841 Niger expedition, sent out by England to explore the Niger River, combat the slave trade, and open the country for legitimate trade. Climatic conditions prevented success, but Crowther distinguished himself. He was invited to England for further training and ordained in the Church of England in 1843.

Crowther worked as a priest in Sierra Leone but soon became a member of the Anglican Mission in Nigeria, first at Badgray and later at Abeokuta. There, by accident, he recognized his mother after 25 years of separation and baptized her in 1848.

Crowther preached in Yoruba, translated parts of the New Testament and the Book of Common Prayer and also published a *Vocabulary of the Yoruba Language* (1852). He believed that evangelization and trade should go together in order to bring peace and prosperity to the country.

In 1854 and 1857 Crowther was a member of two further Niger expeditions. The second suffered shipwreck, and Crowther did not return to Lagos until 1859. In 1855 he published *Journal of an Expedition up the Niger and Tshadda Rivers,* and in 1859, with J. C. Taylor, *The Gospel on the Banks of the Niger, 1857-1859.*

Crowther made frequent visits to England. In 1857 he was made head of the Niger Mission, and as the work prospered he was consecrated a bishop of the Church of England in West Africa in 1864 and also awarded an honorary doctor of divinity degree by Oxford University.

As a bishop, Crowther faced many difficulties. There was local opposition, both African and European; his duties and rights were not easily defined, and he was short of African helpers. Many of his African staff came from Sierra Leone and found it difficult to live in Nigeria. But the work prospered, and soon there were more than 600 Christians, with 10 priests and 14 teachers and catechists. His task was hard, but the fact that he was an African bishop inspired many African Christians in the years that followed. He died on Dec. 31, 1891, and was buried in Lagos.

## Further Reading

A full-length biography of Crowther is Jesse Page, *The Black Bishop: Samuel Adjai Crowther* (1908). Two more recent evaluations are in J. F. Ade Ajayi, *Christian Missions in Nigeria, 1841-1891* (1965), and E. A. Ayandele, *The Missionary Impact on Modern Nigeria, 1842-1914* (1966).

## Additional Sources

Page, Jesse, *The Black bishop, Samuel Adjai Crowther,* Westport, Conn.: Greenwood Press, 1979. ☐

# George Crumb

**The American composer and teacher George Crumb (born 1929) developed an immediately recognizable style based on the coloristic potential of instruments and voices, evoking mystery, sensuality, and great spatial dimension.**

George Crumb was born in Charleston, West Virginia, on October 24, 1929. He began writing music shortly after his tenth year, motivated by his father, who was a clarinetist and bandleader, and by the popular and religious music of his native Appalachia. The latter, especially, remained an influence in his mature compositions. His mother was also a cellist, so Crumb's childhood was saturated with musical inspiration, such that by nine years old he already played piano by ear. He earned degrees from Mason College, Charleston, (B.M., 1950); the University of Illinois (M.M., 1952); and the University of Michigan (D.M.A., 1959), where he studied with Ross Lee Finney. Crumb also studied with Boris Blacher at the Berkshire Music Center and at the Berlin Hochschule für Musik (1955-1956). An appointment at the University of

Colorado (1959-1965) and a position as creative associate at the Center of Creative and Performing Arts in Buffalo (1964-1965), preceded his longtime post at the University of Pennsylvania.

An extremely well-integrated eclecticism characterizes Crumb's mature works after the early 1960s. Although Crumb listed Debussy, Mahler, and Bartók as being his principal musical influences, the works themselves suggest far broader origins. The conciseness and attention to detail are reminiscent of Webern, and the delicacy of the line derives from Eastern music. Crumb utilized the vocabulary of extended vocal and instrumental techniques common to many 20th-century composers and expanded them considerably. Some of the more arresting effects are achieved in the following ways: striking a gong while lifting it in and out of a bucket of water (called the water gong); playing the violin and other stringed instruments "bottle-neck style" (that is, with a glass rod or tube on the fingerboard); playing directly on the piano strings, often with thimble-capped fingers; and dropping a light metal chain on the piano strings so that the strings, when sounded, will vibrate against it. The singer, too, was asked to produce non-traditional sounds and phonetical vocalizations, sometimes based on parts of a text, and often requiring great virtuosity.

For the most part, Crumb's sounds were produced acoustically, though with use of amplification to increase timbrel variation and to refine dynamic gradation. This coloristic basis also allowed the easy assimilation of folk, popular, and non-traditional instruments into his palette. These include banjo, mouth harp, harmonica, electric guitar, water glasses, and Tibetan prayer stones.

Almost all of Crumb's vocal music, comprising a large part of his total output, was based on the poetry of Federico García-Lorca, for whom the composer had a truly rare affinity. Regarding Ancient Voices of Children for soprano, boy soprano, and instruments (1970), Crumb wrote, "I have sought musical images that enhance and reinforce the powerful, yet strangely haunting, imagery of Lorca's poetry." The resonance of his timbrel effects and prolonged durations and slow harmonic rhythm combine to create a physical sense of vastness and helplessness that is very much akin to the spirit of Lorca's verse.

Quotation is another device occurring frequently in Crumb's compositions. He writes, also in regard to Ancient Voices of Children, "I was intrigued by the idea of juxtaposing the seemingly incongruous: a suggestion of flamenco with a baroque quotation, or a reminiscence of Mahler with a breath of the Orient." Again, the result was not simple collage; the quotations, though recognizable, were integrated into a total effect that was at once surreal and yet musically logical.

Crumb's music was largely freely ordered and non-tonal. Microtones, though used, did not have structural significance, as when the double strings of the mandolin are tuned one-fourth tone (the notes between adjacent keys of the piano) apart in Ancient Voices of Children to add pungency to the sound. Abstract forms did not play an important part in organizing even those works not built on the framework of a text. Frequently his forms were palindromic (they read the same forwards as backwards, such as ABCBA), and overall structure that is supported by sections written in "circular notation" (whereby the staff is in the shape of a circle). Where devices such as isorhythm (having a repeated scheme of time values) did appear, they usually reinforced a text—a throwback to Renaissance word-painting.

Visual aspects were also important to Crumb's music, evident both in the fine calligraphy of his scores and in the directions to performers, which often required the wearing of masks, as in Lux Aeterna for soprano, bass flute, recorder, sitar, and percussion (1970) and Vox Balanae for electric flute, electric piano, and electric cello (1971), or required processions and pose striking, as in Echoes of Time and the River for orchestra (1967). Off-stage placement of instrumentalists or singers enhanced both visual and acoustical-spatial dimensions previously described.

Because of the greater emphasis placed on pure musical imagination rather than on structural artifice, Crumb's music sounds more improvisatory than it actually is. Chance operations, when specified, permit choice of time and order of entry, but the notes themselves are fixed. The original version of Night Music I for soprano, celesta, piano, and percussion (1963) specified areas for improvisation, but for the 1979 recording Crumb wrote the passages out in full with the explanation that improvisation "rarely attains a consistent degree of stylistic congruity."

Other important compositions were: four books of Madrigals for soprano and various instrumental combinations (books I & II, 1965; books III & IV, 1969); Songs, Drones, and Refrains of Death for baritone, electric instruments, and percussion (1968); Night of the Four Moons for alto, banjo, alto flute, electric cello, and percussion (1969); Black Angels (Images I) for electric string quartet (1970); Makrokosmos I and II for amplified piano (1972, 1973), III: Music for a Summer Evening for two amplified pianos and percussion (1974), and IV: Celestial Mechanics for amplified piano, four hands (1978); Dream Sequence (Images II) for violin, cello, piano, and percussion (1976); the Gnomic Variations for piano (1982); and a Haunted Landscape for orchestra (1984).

Some of Crumb's later works included Star-Child for soprano, antiphonal children's voices, male speaking choir, bell ringers, and large orchestra (1977); Apparitions for soprano and amplified piano (1979); and The Sleeper for soprano and piano (1984). In this later period, Crumb composed some of his most elaborate pieces. Star-Child, for instance, has such an involved score that it requires four conductors to lead the eight percussionists, who perform on over 70 different instruments, ranging from pot lids, iron chains, and wind machines to other more traditional percussive instruments. But Crumb's later period wasn't limited to complex pieces; he also composed spare choruses, such as Apparitions, which was his first strictly vocal composition in over ten years.

Though he was one of the most celebrated American composers of the 1960s and 1970s, the popularity of Crumb's work faded in the 1980s and 1990s, when his style was overshadowed by emerging composers such as Phillip Glass. In the April 1995 issue of Commentary, Terry

Teachout wrote, "A quarter century after the fact, it is hard to remember how often Crumb's music used to be played, or why it once sounded so fresh and original; *Black Angels* now comes across as hopelessly thin in inspiration, a mere skeleton of spectacular instrumental effects without any connective music fabric."

Among the numerous grants, awards, and commissions he received were the following: Fulbright Fellowship (1955-1956); BMI prize in composition (1957), for the string quartet (1954), and the *Sonata* for cello solo (1955); Rockefeller Foundation grant (1965); Guggenheim Foundation fellowships (1965, 1971); Koussevitzky Foundation grant (1966) for *Madrigals, Books I* and *II;* election into the National Institute of Arts and Letters (1967); Pulitzer Prize in Music (1968) for *Echoes of Time and the River;* Elizabeth Sprague Coolidge Foundation Commission (1970) for *Ancient Voices of Children;* and From Music Foundation Commission (1974) for *Makrokosmos III.* Honorary doctorates were awarded him by Norris Harvey College, Marshall University, and Oberlin College. In 1967 Crumb was elected to the National Institute of Arts and Letters.

In his book, *American Composers,* David Ewen quotes Crumb on his life's work: "Music is tangible, almost palpable, and yet unreal, illusive. Music is analyzable only on the most mechanistic level; the important elements—the spiritual impulse, the psychological curve, the metaphysical implications—are understandable only in terms of the music itself."

## Further Reading

Short but informative descriptions placing Crumb in contemporary musical perspective are found in Eric Salzman's *Twentieth Century Music: An Introduction* and in Paul Griffiths' *Modern Music: The Avant Garde since 1945.* The most comprehensive book, compiled by Don Gillespie, is *George Crumb, A Profile of the Composer* (1985), which contains articles by Crumb himself as well as by others. Perhaps less accessible are articles written by Donal J. Henahan in *The Musical Quarterly* (1968); Carlton Gamer in *The Musical Quarterly* (1973); Robert Moevs also in *The Musical Quarterly* (1976); and Richard Steinitz in *The Musical Times* (1978). □

# Oswaldo Gonçalves Cruz

**Oswaldo Gonçalves Cruz (1872-1917) was a Brazilian microbiologist, epidemiologist, and public health officer who founded experimental medicine in Brazil and directed controversial programs to eradicate yellow fever and smallpox from Rio de Janeiro.**

Oswaldo Cruz was born in the province of São Paulo, the son of a doctor. He completed medical school at the age of 20, perhaps as much because of the elementary nature of medical instruction then provided in Brazil as because of his brilliance. In 1896 he went to Paris, where he worked at the Pasteur Institute for 3 years. Cruz returned to Brazil as the bearer of an entirely new outlook on medical problems. His understanding of modern principles regarding contagion was perhaps not unique even in Brazil, but he was exceptional in his ability to surmount the political obstacles to the application of this understanding to public health. He almost immediately demonstrated these abilities in the coastal city of Santos, where he stopped an epidemic of bubonic plague in midcourse in 1899.

In 1902 Cruz became the Brazilian director general of public health. Brazil's progress and effort to secure international respect had so far been severely hampered by the frequent epidemics that ravaged the population, discouraged immigration, upset the normal patterns of trade, and debilitated both workers and managers. With the President's backing, Cruz launched a vigorous campaign aimed at imposing sanitary standards first of all upon the capital city. He especially worked to eradicate the mosquito responsible for the transmission of yellow fever. Simultaneously he pushed through the Brazilian congress a law requiring compulsory smallpox vaccination of all citizens.

These programs encountered the resistance of a superstitious and conservative population. Alarmed by these newfangled ideas and the invasion of their privacy and individual freedom, the people were easily manipulated by opponents of the regime: urban riots and even an unsuccessful military revolt were the result. The President, however, continued to give Cruz his full support, and the campaign was successful. As of that time Rio de Janeiro ceased to be a synonym for epidemic disease.

Meanwhile, Cruz also became director of the newly formed Institute of Experimental Pathology. His energetic and progressive leadership soon made it world-famous in the field of tropical medicine. He personally conducted field experiments in the upper Amazon and began the long process by which malaria was effectively restricted in Brazil. His career was cut short by Bright's disease.

## Further Reading

Very little has been written in any language on Cruz. He is discussed briefly in Fielding H. Garrison, *An Introduction to the History of Medicine* (1913; 4th rev. ed. 1929), and in Arturo Castiglioni, *A History of Medicine* (trans. 1941; 2d rev. ed. 1947). □

# Cuauhtemoc

**Cuauhtemoc (ca. 1496-1525) was the last of the Aztec rulers and a heroic defender of his empire against the Spanish conquistadors. Cuauhtemoc is revered by many Mexicans as the symbol of the Indians and as the representative of Mexican nationality.**

Cuauhtemoc was born in Tenochtitlán (modern Mexico City), capital of the Aztec empire, the son of the Aztec emperor Ahuitzótl and the princess Tlilalcapatl. When he was 15, he entered the *calmecac,* or school for the nobility, devoted primarily to the study of religion, science, and art. Then he participated in a number of military expeditions to bring neighboring peoples under Aztec rule. Because of his military exploits he was appointed *techutli,* a term indicating an upper military and administrative position. In 1515 he was also appointed lordship of the region of Tlaltelolco.

In 1519 the Spanish conquistadors, led by Hernán Cortés, began the conquest of Mexico. Cortés captured the Aztec emperor Montezuma and ruled the empire from behind the throne. In 1520, however, the Indians under the leadership of Cuauhtemoc's uncle Cuitlahuac, who had succeeded Montezuma as Aztec emperor, rebelled and expelled the Spaniards. Cortés regrouped his men and prepared to recapture Tenochtitlán.

By this time Cuitlahuac had died, and Cuauhtemoc had inherited the throne. Cortés now faced a determined and courageous Indian leader. In May 1521 the Spaniards began the siege of the city. The Aztecs fought valiantly, but the water supply dwindled when the Spaniards cut the aqueduct, and by August, with most of the city in ruins, the Aztec defense finally collapsed. Cuauhtemoc attempted to escape but was captured by Cortés's men. Cuauhtemoc asked to be killed, but Cortés refused, taking him to his headquarters in Coyoacán and keeping him under house arrest.

Cuauhtemoc remained in captivity for a long time. On one occasion he was subjected to brutal torture because the Spaniards, believing that he knew where Aztec treasures were hidden, decided to force Cuauhtemoc to reveal the locations of the gold. Cuauhtemoc endured the suffering and revealed no secrets.

During his captivity Cuauhtemoc accompanied Cortés on several expeditions, including one to Honduras in October 1524. For months Spaniards and Indians traveled through Central America, and many of Cortés's Indian allies died of starvation. Cortés became convinced by his men that Cuauhtemoc was urging Indians to rebel. Although Cuauhtemoc protested that he was innocent, Cortés insisted that he and several other Indian leaders must die. Cuauhtemoc was hanged near the town of Itzancanal on Feb. 26, 1525.

## Further Reading

There is much written on Cuauhtemoc but mostly in Spanish. In English, Cora Walker, *Cuatemo: Last of the Aztec Emperors* (1934), is of dubious value. Some information on Cuauhtemoc as well as on the Aztecs in general is in J. Eric Thompson, *Mexico before Cortez: An Account of the Daily Life, Religion, and Ritual of the Aztecs and Kindred Peoples* (1933); George C. Vaillant, *Aztecs of Mexico: Origin, Rise, and Fall of the Aztec Nation* (1941; rev. ed. 1962); and Eric R. Wolf, *Sons of the Shaking Earth* (1959). □

# Ellwood Patterson Cubberley

**Ellwood Patterson Cubberley (1868-1941), an early 20th-century educator and university dean, wrote influential textbooks in the history of education and public school administration. He played a major role in the professionalization of teaching and administration and in elevating education to a university study.**

Ellwood Patterson Cubberley, the only child of Edwin Blanchard and Catherine Coryell Cubberley, was born in Antiock (later Andrews), Indiana, on June 6, 1868. His mother was of Delaware Quaker ancestry and his father, a druggist, was English. Ellwood attended the local schools of Antiock and the college preparatory school at Purdue University. In 1886, impressed by David Starr Jordan's lecture "The Value of a College Education," Cubberley persuaded his father to let him enter Indiana University where Jordan was then president. There he studied physical science and in his senior year became so skilled in managing the stereopticon lanterns that Jordan chose him as lantern assistant for his many illustrated lectures.

Cubberley also enrolled in Jordan's course on evolution, a course known later at Stanford as "bionomics." The study attempted to blend the "natural and social sciences with old fashion pietist religion." Later, Cubberley made the course a requirement for education students at Stanford. The relationship established between professor and student at this time was significant in Cubberley's career choices.

In 1888-1889 Cubberley interrupted his work at the university to teach in a one room school in Indiana. In the winter of 1891 he completed the A.B. degree from Indiana University and began teaching science at a Baptist college in Ridgeville. In the fall of that year he became professor of physical science at Vincennes University. At 25 he became president of the university, a post he held for the next three years. In June 1892 he was married to Helen Van Uxem, who had been a fellow student at Indiana.

## Move to California

In 1896, upon the recommendation of Jordan, then president of Stanford University, Cubberley was hired as superintendent of schools in San Diego, California, and immediately became the center of a political controversy. Several school board members who had wanted to hire a local person questioned the legality of Cubberley's credentials. The case was taken to court but was settled in Cubberley's favor. What disturbed the new superintendent was the functioning of the school board. It was the board rather than the superintendent that administered the schools. Cubberley worked hard to convince the board that it should act as a legislature and leave administration to him. From his experience in San Diego Cubberley's theories of school administration would later develop. He became convinced that school boards should be non-political and that executive autonomy was essential to efficiency in education.

In 1899 Cubberley accepted an appointment as assistant professor and acting head of the Department of Education at Stanford University. Once again he was to be associated with his mentor, Jordan. Within two months, Jordan made Cubberley's appointment permanent but gave him three years to "make education respectable" or have it abolished. The obstacles appeared insurmountable. In the first year Cubberley had to teach five courses in administration and the history of education, courses in a field for which he was not trained and in which there was little scholarly literature. Faced with the challenge of convincing his colleagues of education's worth, he had the additional burden of discovering what it was he should be teaching. Before the end of that year, however, Jordan had been persuaded to retain the Education Department. In 1906 Cubberley was made a full professor, and in 1917 the trustees created a professional school of education and made Cubberley its first dean. In 1901 Cubberley, taking a leave, attended Teachers College, Columbia, where he received the M.A. degree in school administration. He returned two years later as a student in the Ph.D. program and completed his dissertation on "School Funds and Their Apportionment."

The experience at Teachers College, where the new scientific method was being emphasized, intensified Cubberley's commitment to public education. His basic interest in social efficiency and his faith in science had been reaffirmed. Returning to Stanford, he wrote and published a brief essay, *Changing Conceptions of Education* (1909), in which ideas basic in his later writing were first explored. Recognizing the impact of the new industrial age, Cubberley saw education as social engineering and the schools as instruments of progress. In this new age children needed to acquire skills and knowledge taught in schools because no longer could the needs of an urban/industrial society be provided by informal processes. Moral direction, for so long the province of the home and church, must now be left largely to the school.

## The Challenge of Immigration

The school, too, must respond to immigrants from southern Europe who were crowding the cities of the Northern Atlantic and Central states. The school's task, Cubberley wrote, was "to break up these groups or settlements, to assimilate and amalgamate these people as part of our American race, and to implant in their children so far as can be done, the Anglo-Saxon conception of righteousness, law and order and popular government." Believing in Anglo-Teutonic superiority, Cubberley became convinced that the curriculum had to be adjusted to meet the needs of children of different abilities.

In order to achieve such an adjustment, Cubberley proposed a school system appropriate for such a task. He recognized in his *Public School Administration* (1916) that "Schools are in a sense factories in which the raw materials (children) are to be shaped and fashioned into products to meet the various demands of life." School boards must be non-partisan, teachers knowledgeable, and school superintendents should operate with the efficiency of industrialists.

In the many publications throughout his career Cubberley expanded and reinforced the social philosophy sketched in *Changing Conceptions of Education*. His biases, so obvious today, were not criticized during his lifetime, mostly because his students and readers shared these beliefs.

Although considered a pioneer in American educational history, Cubberley's abiding interest was administration. History to Cubberley became a useful tool for promoting his ideas of education. In this sense it celebrated the rise and development of universal public education, providing inspiration and direction for a developing profession. Because of his extensive use of the writings of school officials and reformers, his critics have suggested that the result was a narrowly construed "house history by and for schoolmen."

Cubberley's productive capacity was amazing. He was author or co-author of nearly 30 books and reports and numerous articles. Between 1911 and 1913 he served as departmental editor for the *Cyclopaedia of Education* in charge of educational administration. For this he wrote over 130 articles. The first edition of his *Public Education, in the United States* (1919) sold over 80,000 copies, and by 1939 nearly 70,000 copies of *History of Education* (1920) were in use.

As editor of Houghton Mifflin's Riverside Textbooks in Education, he edited almost 100 volumes in the fields of measurement, guidance, methodology, psychology, sociology, and administration in education. He was a popular speaker and lecturer and a pioneer of the school survey movement.

Cubberley retired in 1933 and spent his remaining years planning the disposition of a fortune amassed over the years through careful investment. He and his wife left to the Stanford School of Education over $770,000.

On September 14, 1941, Cubberley died of a heart attack. He was buried at Alta Mesa Cemetery near Palo Alto, California.

## Further Reading

Cubberley is listed in the *National Cyclopaedia of American Biography*. A comprehensive but devotional biography by Jesse B. Sears and Adin Henderson, *Cubberley of Stanford and His Contributions to American Education* (1957), is an excellent factual resource and includes a full listing of Cubberley's writings. Two significant criticisms of Cubberley's works (especially the histories) appeared in the 1960s: Lawrence Cremin, *The Wonderful World of Ellwood Patterson Cubberley* (1965); and Bernard Bailyn, *Education in the Forming of American Society* (1960). In this same vein two other sources of the 1960s merit attention: William W. Brickman, "Revisionism and the Study of the History of Education," *History of Education Quarterly* (December 1964); and Raymond E. Callahan, *Education and the Cult of Efficiency* (1962). A later, balanced treatment of Cubberley's historical works is found in Sol Cohen, "The History of the History of American Education, 1900-1960: The Uses of the Past," *Harvard Educational Review* (August 1976). An excellent appraisal of Cubberley's contributions to educational leadership is in David Tyack and Elisabeth Hansot, *Managers of Virtue: Public School Leadership in America, 1820-1980* (1982). □

# Ralph Cudworth

**The English philosopher and theologian Ralph Cudworth (1617-1688) was the most important of the Cambridge Platonists, a 17th-century circle which expounded rationalistic theology and ethics.**

R alph Cudworth was born in Aller, Somerset, where his father was rector. His father, who had also been a fellow of Emmanuel College, Cambridge, and chaplain to James I, died in 1624, and Cudworth therefore had his early education from his stepfather, Dr. Stoughton. He entered Emmanuel College in 1632 and received a bachelor of arts degree in 1635, a master of arts degree in 1639, and a bachelor of divinity degree in 1646. In 1645 he was appointed master of Clare College and regius professor of Hebrew. He served as rector of North Cadbury, Somerset, from 1650 to 1654, then returned to Cambridge as master of Christ's College. In 1654 he also married and subsequently had two sons, John and Charles, and a daughter, Damaris (later Lady Masham). His daughter's philosophical writing and her friendship with John Locke helped spread

Cudworth's ideas. The rest of his career was at Christ's College; he was involved in the political events of the time and served on and advised parliamentary committees.

Cudworth opposed excessive dogmatism in religion and advocated a predominantly moral conception of Christianity, with latitude in matters of ritual and organization. His earliest public statement of his position was a sermon preached before the House of Commons in 1647 and published later that year.

In *A Treatise on Eternal and Immutable Morality* Cudworth wrote, "It is universally true that things are what they are not by will but by nature." Thus truth, in morals, religion, and metaphysics, is discoverable by the use of reason. Those who set God's will or the will of a human sovereign above reason—Thomas Hobbes, the nominalists and Calvinists, even the rationalist René Descartes—were Cudworth's targets. Against Hobbes's alleged atheism, materialism, determinism, individualism, and ethical relativism, Cudworth defended theism, dualism, free will, organic political theory, and ethical absolutism.

Cudworth's metaphysical dualism asserts a distinction between active and passive powers, not the Cartesian distinction between thought and extension. Active powers, comprising unconscious "spiritual plastic powers" and deliberative operations, prudential and moral, are teleological. The passive powers are mechanical. In making reason active, Cudworth avoids the usual problems of moral psychology by reaffirming the Socratic identification: to know the good is to love it.

Cudworth's principal philosophical works are *The True Intellectual System of the Universe* (1678) and *A Treatise on Eternal and Immutable Morality* (1731). He died on June 26, 1688, and was buried in the chapel of Christ's College.

## Further Reading

For discussions of Cudworth the philosopher see John H. Muirhead, *The Platonic Tradition in Anglo-Saxon Philosophy* (1931), and Lydia Gysi, *Platonism and Cartesianism in the Philosophy of Cudworth* (1962). John Arthur Passmore, *Ralph Cudworth: An Interpretation* (1951), contains the most comprehensive bibliography.

## Additional Sources

Cudworth, Ralph, *A treatise of freewill and an introduction to Cudworth's treatise*, London: Routledge/Thoemmes Press, 1992. □

# Paul Cuffe

**The African American ship captain, merchant, and philanthropist Paul Cuffe (1759-1817) was active in the campaign for civil rights for blacks and Native Americans in Massachusetts. He is best known for his pioneering efforts to settle free African Americans in West Africa.**

Paul Cuffe was born on Jan. 17, 1759, near New Bedford, Mass., of a Native American mother and an African father, Cuffe Slocum, who had purchased his own freedom. Paul was the youngest of 10 children. His father died when Paul was a teenager, leaving the family to find its own means of support. Cuffe's education consisted of basic reading and writing, plus enough mathematics to permit him to navigate a ship. At the age of 16 he began his career as a common seaman on whaling and fishing boats. During the Revolutionary War he was held prisoner by the British for a time but managed afterward to start small-scale coastal trading. Despite attacks by pirates, he eventually prospered. He built larger vessels and successfully traded south as far as Virginia and north to Labrador. In later life he owned several ships which engaged in trading and whaling around the world.

Cuffe was a vigorous, pious, and independent man. He refused to use the name of his father's owner, Slocum, and adopted his father's given name, Cuffe (or Cuffee). In 1780 he and his brother John petitioned the Massachusetts government either to give African and Native Americans the right to vote or to stop taxing them. The petition was denied, but the case helped pave the way for the 1783 Massachusetts Constitution, which gave equal rights and privileges to all citizens of the state.

Cuffe was a devout and evangelical Quaker. He married at the age of 25. At his home in Westport, Mass., he donated a town school and helped support the teacher. Later he helped build a new meeting house. Through his connections with Quakers in other cities he became in-volved in efforts to improve the conditions of African Americans. Strongly opposed to slavery and the slave trade, he joined other free African Americans in the Northern states in their abolitionist campaigns.

When Cuffe learned of the Sierra Leone Colony in West Africa, which had been founded by English philanthropists in 1787, he began corresponding with English Quakers active in the movement to settle African Americans there. In 1811 he sailed with his all-African American crew to investigate the colony. Impressed and eager to start settling African Americans there who could evangelize the Africans, establish business enterprises, and work to stop the slave trade at its source, Cuffe returned to the United States after conferring with his allies in England. He planned to take a ship loaded with settlers and merchandise to Sierra Leone annually, but the War of 1812, between the United States and Britain, delayed him. Mean-while, he petitioned the American government for aid and actively recruited future settlers among the free African Americans of Baltimore, Philadelphia, New York, and Boston.

In 1815 Cuffe sailed with 38 settlers for Sierra Leone, where he helped them establish new homes with the cooperation of colonial authorities. Enthusiastic over his success, despite the heavy personal expense, he found increased interest in the project among African Americans. Soon, however, the newly formed American Colonization Society, which operated with support of Southern slave owners and advocated settlement of former slaves in Africa, began to frighten free African Americans, who feared forced deportation. Before Cuffe could pursue his own settlement project, his health failed.

On Sept. 9, 1817, Cuffe died, mourned by all who knew him.

## Further Reading

One biography of Cuffe is Henry N. Sherwood, *Paul Cuffe* (1923). Recent scholarship has added little to this fine study. Cuffe is also discussed in Benjamin G. Brawley, *Negro Builders and Heroes* (1937); Langston Hughes, *Famous Negro Heroes of America* (1954); William C. Nell, *The Colored Patriots of the American Revolution* (1968); and William J. Simmons, *Men of Mark: Eminent, Progressive and Rising* (1968).

## Additional Sources

Thomas, Lamont D. (Lamont Dominick), *Rise to be a people: a biography of Paul Cuffe,* Urbana: University of Illinois Press, 1986. □

# Ottobah Cugoano

**Ottobah Cugoano (ca. 1757-ca. 1803) was an African of Fanti origin from the Gold Coast in present-day Ghana. He became a prominent figure among the free Africans of late-18th-century London and in 1787 published an attack on slavery and the slave trade.**

Ottobah Cugoano was born near Ajumako and grew up in the household of the Fanti chief Ambro Accasa, ruler of Ajumako and Assinie. Cugoano was enslaved as a youth, taken to Grenada in the West Indies, and from there brought to England, where he was freed.

Educated while a slave and converted to Christianity, Cugoano soon emerged as a leader of opinion among the free Africans of London, where he corresponded under the adopted name of John Stewart, or Stuart, and became familiar with the abolitionist leaders Granville Sharp and Thomas Clarkson. Cugoano was a friend of Olaudah Equiano, with whom he collaborated in representing African interests.

Cugoano's book, *Thoughts and Sentiments on the Evil of Slavery,* was an impressively sustained intellectual assault which demolished the popular theological and biblical justifications for slavery and invoked the universality of the Christian God and His ethic, the equality of all men. It appealed to the humanitarian ideals of Enlightenment Europe and asserted the human right of Africans to freedom and dignity in the pursuit of their own destiny. Following the ideas of Adam Smith, Cugoano argued the economic insanity of slavery, previewing the later popular views of a "legitimate" commerce to replace the "illegitimate" slave trade. He proposed the outright manumission of all slaves 7 years or more in the colonies, the instruction of the rest in preparation for freedom, and a naval blockade in West Africa.

Several authorities believe that Cugoano's theological arguments were coached by Clarkson or Sharp, while his friend Equiano may have helped revise his book's first draft. Nevertheless, the work probably remains essentially a product of Cugoano's own thoughts and feelings, an articulate African's response to the impact of European expansion.

Very little is known of Cugoano's later career. In 1791 he was involved in Clarkson's scheme for recruiting Africans living in Nova Scotia and New Brunswick to Sierre Leone. The same year he published a shorter version of *Thoughts and Sentiments,* in which he gave notice of intent to establish an African school in London. The Italian-Polish patriot Scipione Piattoli knew Cugoano during his London years (ca. 1800-1803), and the French writer Henri Grégoire says Cugoano married an English woman. Beyond this, Ottobah Cugoano left no further record.

## Further Reading

Cugoano's work, *Thoughts and Sentiments on the Evil and Wicked Traffic of the Slavery and Commerce of the Human Species* (1787), was reissued in a second edition by Paul Edwards, entitled *Thoughts and Sentiments on the Evil of Slavery* (1969). Edwards added an informative introduction and appended five previously unpublished manuscript letters by Cugoano that are helpful in determining the authorship of *Thoughts and Sentiments.* The most useful and informative modern treatment of Cugoano is by Robert July, *The Origins of Modern African Thought: Its Development in West Africa during the Nineteenth and Twentieth Centuries* (1967), who considers Cugoano an important precursor of 19th- and 20th-century African thought. Prince Hoare, *Memoirs of Granville Sharp, Esq.* (1820), contains some letters from Cugoano and references to his relationship with Sharp. Christopher Fyfe, in *A History of Sierra Leone* (1962), agrees with Paul Edwards and doubts that Cugoano is the sole author of *Thoughts and Sentiments.* □

# Countee Cullen

**The American Countee Cullen (1903-1946) was one of the most widely heralded African American poets of the Harlem renaissance, though he was less concerned with social and political problems than were his African American contemporaries. He is noted for his lyricism and his artful use of imagery.**

Countee Cullen, whose real surname was Porter, was born May 30, 1903. Nothing is known about where he was born, and little is known of his parents. An orphan in New York City, he was adopted by the Reverend Frederick A. and Mrs. Carolyn Cullen, whose name he took. Following graduation from DeWitt Clinton High School, where he won a high school poetry contest, he attended New York University. In 1925 he took a baccalaureate degree, and his first book of poems, *Color,* was published. His metrical skill reminded many readers of the English poet Algernon Swinburne. He earned a master's degree at Harvard and then became assistant editor of *Opportunity: Journal of Negro Life,* which printed the fugitive pieces of African American writers and gave publicity to the African American artists who contributed so much to the cultural awakening of the 1920s.

Cullen knew what was going on in African American life, but he was not deeply involved. *Ballad of the Brown Girl* and *Copper Sun,* both published in 1927, contain mostly personal Keatsian lyrics, which, generally speaking, show no advance and no development from the poems in his first volume. The piece entitled "Heritage" is a noteworthy exception. In a critical preface to the collection of African American poetry, *Caroling Dusk* (1927), which he edited, Cullen argues that "Negro poetry . . . must emanate from some country other than this in some language other than our own." Though he later claimed that his poetry "treated of the heights and depths of emotion which I feel as a Negro," he did not want to be known as an African American poet.

Even after his marriage in 1928 to Yolande, the only daughter of the African American radical and activist W. E. B. Du Bois, Cullen stayed aloof from action and affirmative argument about race. His marriage lasted only through the first year of a 2-year visit to France, where he completed the long, narrative, parabolic poem "The Black Christ," which became the title poem of his fourth volume. *The Medea and Some Poems* (1935) was his last book of verse. From 1934 to 1945 he taught French in a New York public school.

Cullen's poetry is traditional in structure. His output in prose suffers from an absence of genuine commitment and is undistinguished. His novel, *One Way to Heaven,* satirizes

upper-class African American life. *The Lost Zoo* and *My Nine Lives and How I Lost Them* are children's books. Cullen collaborated on a musical play, *St. Louis Woman* (1946), but whatever emotional power and integrity it had was supplied by Arna Bontemps. The play opened on March 31, 1949. Cullen had died earlier, on Jan. 9, 1946. *On These I Stand,* his own selection of his best poems, was published in 1947.

## Further Reading

The only full-length work on Cullen is Blanche E. Ferguson, *Countee Cullen and the Negro Renaissance* (1966). Stephen H. Bronz, *Roots of Negro Racial Consciousness, the 1920's: Three Harlem Renaissance Authors* (1964), discusses Countee Cullen, James Weldon Johnson, and Claude McKay. Cullen is appraised in such anthologies and critical works as James Weldon Johnson, ed., *The Book of American Negro Poetry* (1922; rev. ed. 1931); Alain L. Locke, ed., *The New Negro: An Interpretation* (1925); J. Saunders Redding, *To Make a Poet Black* (1939); Margaret Just Butcher, *The Negro in American Culture: Based on Materials Left by Alain Locke* (1956); and Herbert Hill, ed., *Soon, One Morning: New Writings by American Negroes, 1940-62* (1963). □

nadian art and is particularly noted for his winter landscapes.

Maurice Cullen was born at St. John's, Newfoundland, and brought up in Montreal. He began his training as a sculptor under Philippe Hébert, and with a legacy from his mother he went to Paris in 1887 for further study at the École des Beaux-Arts. Once he saw the works of Claude Monet, however, he turned to painting and for the next few years sought out the favorite haunts of the French impressionists: Moret, Giverny, and Brittany. He exhibited at the Salon and was elected a member of the Société Nationale des Beaux-Arts.

With an established European reputation, Cullen returned to Montreal in 1895 and began to paint the winter landscapes along the St. Lawrence River in the vicinity of Quebec City and the night scenes of Montreal, for which he is best known. By 1897 he was a regular exhibitor with the Royal Canadian Academy, and he became a full member in 1907. In spite of this, his work was not immediately accepted by a public devoted to 19th-century European art, and he would have starved without the support of a few patrons, like Sir William Van Horne.

In 1900 Cullen managed to finance a second stay in Europe, this time for 2 years, and besides visiting familiar haunts in France with his old friend James Wilson Morrice, he ventured as far as North Africa. Between 1910 and 1912 he painted on the rugged coast of Newfoundland, and one of his larger canvases shows his native town of St. John's.

After World War I, in which Cullen served as a war artist, his reputation in Canada grew steadily. By the time he died in 1934 at his country retreat in Chambly, he was revered not only by the young rebels he had inspired in his lean years but by the wider Canadian public as well.

Unlike his friend Morrice, with whom he sometimes sketched on the Ile d'Orléans below Quebec, Cullen preferred to paint out of doors, even in the coldest weather, in order to capture the effect of sunlight on snow. He was one of the first Canadian artists to recognize the fact that snow shadows reflect the blue of the sky, and he did not hesitate to abandon the gentle haze of the French impressionists for the sharp clarity of the Canadian atmosphere. In his uncompromising honesty of subject and style, he was a true pioneer of the national school of landscape painting.

## Further Reading

The authoritative biography of Cullen is by his art dealer in Montreal, William R. Watson, *Maurice Cullen* (1931). For general background see J. Russell Harper, *Painting in Canada: A History* (1966). □

# Maurice Galbraith Cullen

**The Canadian painter Maurice Galbraith Cullen (1866-1934) was a pioneer of impressionism in Ca-**

# Edward Estlin Cummings

**The American poet Edward Estlin Cummings (1894-1962) presented romantic attitudes in technically experimental verse. His poems are not only ideas but**

**crafted physical objects which, in their nonlogical
structure, grant fresh perspectives into reality.**

In his publications E. E. Cummings always gave his name in lowercase letters without punctuation (e e cummings); this was part of his concern for the typography, syntax, and visual form of his poetry. He worked in the Emersonian tradition of romantic transcendentalism, which encouraged experimentation, and may have been influenced also by Walt Whitman, the poet that Ralph Waldo Emerson had personally encouraged.

Born in Cambridge, Mass., on Oct. 14, 1894, of a prominent academic and ministerial family, E. E. Cummings grew up in the company of such family friends as the philosophers William James and Josiah Royce. Had he lived in Emerson's time, he too might have been described as a "Boston Brahmin." His father, Edward Cummings, after teaching at Harvard, became the nationally known Congregational minister of the Old South Church in Boston, preaching a Christian-transcendentalist theology. Eventually Cummings came to espouse a positive position similar to that of his father, but not before an early period of rebellion against the stuffiness of Cambridge ladies, the repressiveness of conventional moralism, and the hypocrisy of the churches.

After receiving his bachelor of arts degree (1915) and master's degree (1916) from Harvard, Cummings became an ambulance driver in France just before America entered World War I. He was imprisoned for 3 months on suspicion of holding views critical of the French war effort, and this experience provided the material for his first book, *The Enormous Room* (1922), an experiment in blending autobiographical prose reporting with poetic techniques of symbolism.

## Early Career

Cummings's transcendentalism, which stressed individual feeling over "objective" truth in a period when critical canons of impersonal, rationalistic, and formalistic poetry were being articulated, resulted in early rejection of his work. For several decades he had to pay for the publication of his books, and reviewers revealed very little understanding of his intentions. His first volume of verse, *Tulips and Chimneys* (1923), was followed by a second book of poems 2 years later. Though Cummings received the Dial Award for poetry in 1925, he continued to have difficulty in finding a publisher.

In the 10 years following 1925 only two volumes of Cummings's poems were published, both at his own expense: *is 5* (1926) and *W* (*ViVa;* 1931). In that decade Cummings also arranged for the publication of one experimental play, *Him* (1927), and a diary like account of a trip to the U.S.S.R., *Eimi* (1933). With characteristic sarcasm Cummings named the 14 publishers who had rejected the manuscript of *No Thanks* (1935) in the volume itself and said "Thanks" to his mother, who had financed its publication.

## Poetic Techniques

Despite his dedication to growth and movement, and in contrast to his reputation as an experimenter in verse forms, Cummings actually tended to lack fresh invention. Especially in the 1930s, when he felt most alienated from his culture and his fellow poets, he repeated himself endlessly, writing many versions of essentially the same poem. He tended to rely too much on simple tricks to force the reader to participate in the poems, and his private typography, although originally expressive and amusing, became somewhat tiresome. Cummings's other stylistic devices—the use of low dialect to create satire and the visual "shaping" of poems—often seem selfindulgent substitutes for original inspiration.

However, Cummings's most characteristic device, the dislocation of syntax and the breaking up and reconstituting of words, was more than just another trick when it operated organically within the context of a poem's meaning. When he wrote, in one of his own favorite poems, "i thank You God for most this amazing," he emphasized the nonlogical quality of the statement by its syntactical ambiguity. "Most" intensifies the entire line in its displaced position and indicates why he thanks God; it moves "this amazing" toward "most amazing" in an authentic recreation of the miraculous process of the natural world. In general, Cummings's best dislocations expressed his belief in that miraculousness of the ordinary which logical syntax could not convey, bringing the reader to a freshness of perception that was Cummings's way toward illumination.

## Poetic Achievement

The love poems and religious poems represent Cummings's greatest achievements; usually the two subjects are interrelated in his work. For example, "somewhere i have never travelled, gladly beyond" is one of the finest love lyrics in the English language, and Cummings's elegy on the death of his beloved father, "my father moved through dooms of love," is a profoundly moving tribute. Often he used a dislocated sonnet form in these poems, but what makes them memorable is not their formal experimentalism but their unique combination of sensuality with a sense of transcendent spirit. Cummings wrote some of the finest celebrations of sexual love and the religious experience of awe and natural piety produced in the 20th century, precisely at a time when it was highly unfashionable to write such poems.

Early in his career Cummings had divided his time between New York and Paris (where he studied painting); later, between New York and the family home in North Conway, N.H. He was always interested in the visual arts, and his paintings and drawings, late impressionist in style, were exhibited in several one-man shows in the 1940s and 1950s.

## Ripening into Honor

After World War II a new generation of poets in rebellion against their immediate predecessors began to find in Cummings an echo of their own distinctly Emersonian ideas about poetry, and Cummings began to receive the recognition that had eluded him so long. In 1950 the Academy of American Poets awarded this self-described "failure" a fellowship for "great achievement," and his collected *Poems, 1923-1954* (1954) won praise in critical quarters which earlier had tended to downgrade Cummings for his unfashionable lyric romanticism.

Harvard University honored its distinguished alumnus by asking Cummings to deliver the Charles Eliot Norton Lectures in 1952-1953, his only attempt at formal artistic autobiography, later published as *i: six nonlectures* (1953). In the lectures Cummings said that perhaps 15 poems were faithful expressions of his stance as artist and man. The total number of truly memorable short poems is certainly higher than this modest figure but still only a fraction of the nearly 1,000 poems published in his lifetime.

Although Cummings did not "develop" as a poet either in terms of ideas or of characteristic style between the publication of *Tulips and Chimneys* and his final volume, *73 Poems* (1963), his work does show a deepening awareness and mastery of his special lyrical gift as poet of the mysteries of "death and forever with each breathing," with a corresponding abandonment of earlier defensive-offensive sallies into ideology and criticism. His finest single volume, *95 Poems* (1958), illustrates Cummings's increasing ability toward the end of his life to give content to his abstractions through the artifact of the poem-object itself, rather than depending entirely on pure rhetoric. If only a tenth of his poems should be thought worthwhile, Cummings will have been established as one of the lasting poets America has produced.

### Late Works and Influence

Cummings's *Collected Poems* was published in 1960. In addition to the works mentioned, Cummings published several other experimental plays, a ballet, and some 15 volumes of verse. Shortly before his death at North Conway on Sept. 3, 1962, Cummings wrote the texts to accompany photographs taken by his third wife, Marion Morehouse. Titled *Adventures in Value* (1962), this work exemplifies his lifelong effort to *see* intensely and deeply enough to confront the miraculousness of the natural. Poets of neoromantic inclinations consider him, along with William Carlos Williams, one of their artistic ancestors, although Cummings produced no significant stylistic followers.

### Further Reading

Good discussions of Cummings and his work include Charles Norman, *The Magic-Maker: E. E. Cummings* (1958); Norman Friedman, *E. E. Cummings: The Growth of a Writer* (1964); Barry A. Marks, *E. E. Cummings* (1964); and Robert E. Wegner, *The Poetry and Prose of E. E. Cummings* (1965). There is a section on Cummings in Hyatt H. Waggoner, *American Poets: From the Puritans to the Present* (1968). □

# Euclides Rodrigues Pimenta da Cunha

**Euclides Rodrigues Pimenta da Cunha (1866-1909) was a Brazilian writer whose account of the clash between the Brazilian army and fanatic followers of a backwoods mystic became a national classic.**

Euclides da Cunha was born in the province of Rio de Janeiro on Jan. 20, 1866. Orphaned at the age of 3, he was raised by aunts, interned in various boarding schools, and shuffled around a great deal. He was always moody, reserved, lonely, and unpredictable. At 18 he enrolled in the military academy, where he specialized in military engineering. Two years later he apparently suffered a nervous breakdown that led to a court-martial and dismissal for insubordination, but he was reinstated. The incident may already have reflected an abhorrence for war. In 1896 he resigned from the army as a first lieutenant and subsequently took up civil engineering while writing occasional newspaper articles.

When, in 1897, the army was forced to dispatch a fifth expedition into the backlands to crush a small messianic cult, Cunha accompanied the troops as a war correspondent for a leading Brazilian newspaper. Fighting in the searing heat of the drought-stricken region of northeast Brazil, the army proceeded to systematically exterminate the last of the sectarians, partially because they refused to surrender. Cunha not only wrote the commissioned articles but gathered the material for his broadly conceived, great book. In the next 5 years he directed engineering works by day and wrote at night. The result was *Os serões* (1902), translated as *Rebellion in the Backlands*.

Because of its vivid portrayal of the agony and bitterness of warfare, its anticipation of the technique of the documentary novel, its philosophical insights, and its perceptive interpretation of Brazil, the book was an immediate success. In it Cunha probed Brazil's developmental problems and drew attention to the misery and ignorance that still characterize Brazil's interior. Although he was grudgingly persuaded by the then current "scientific" ideas on racial superiority, his social Darwinism was tempered with admiration for the mestizos, who had been so brutally treated by the allegedly more civilized representatives of the coastal cities. In some ways it was an antimilitary tract, certainly a denunciation of man's inhumanity. At the same time, the book portrayed flesh-and-blood men caught up in a drama that moved inevitably to a tragic conclusion.

Cunha subsequently wrote several less important historical, biographical, geographical, and anthropological pieces, several of them dealing with the Amazon. A dispute over a woman led to his assassination at the age of 43 on Aug. 15, 1909.

**Further Reading**

The introduction by Samuel Putnam to Cunha's *Rebellion in the Backlands* (1902; trans. 1944), briefly surveys his life. See also Putnam's *Marvelous Journey: A Survey of Four Centuries of Brazilian Writing* (1948), and Erico Verissimo, *Brazilian Literature: An Outline* (1945). There are numerous works in Portuguese about Cunha. □

# Merce Cunningham

**The American Merce Cunningham (born 1919) was a solo dancer of commanding presence, a controversial choreographer, an influential teacher, and an organizer of an internationally acclaimed avant-garde dance company.**

Born in Centralia, Washington, on April 19, 1919, Merce Cunningham studied modern dance under Bonnie Bird in Seattle. Here he met the composer John Cage. From 1940 to 1945 Cunningham was a soloist with the Martha Graham Company, creating such roles as the Christ Figure in *El Penitente,* the Acrobat in *Every Soul Is a Circus,* March in *Letter to the World,* and the Revivalist in *Appalachian Spring.*

While still with the Graham Company, Cunningham began independent work, at first in solo concerts. His first important large creation was *The Seasons* (1947), with music by Cage. For the next quarter century, Cage acted as Cunningham's chief composer and musical adviser.

Cunningham's first substantial success came in 1952 (also the year he formed his own company-school) with his setting of Igor Stravinsky's "dance episodes with song," *Les Noces.* He continued working with music by experimentalist composers such as Erik Satie, Pierre Schaeffer, and Alan Hovhaness, as well as with Cage. Cunningham also danced to sounds produced solely by his own voice: grunts, shrieks, squeals, and howls.

Cunningham's personal dance style, reflected in his choreography, was usually athletic in forcefulness. But he could also effect a slow, nearly suspended motion which, when opposed sharply to the cross rhythms of accompaniments—either musical, or antimusical—produced unique effects. Cunningham never used such "tricks" as facial expressions to reach an audience, relying solely upon pure body movement to produce effects.

Cunningham experimented with Cage and others of futuristic thought from fields of dance, music, theater, visual arts, and even the technical sciences in combining abstract dance elements with *musique concrète,* electronic music, random sounds, lighting effects, action films or photo slides superimposed upon or backlighting stage action, pure noise, and even silence. But, though he worked frequently with "chance" methods, Cunningham remained a deadly serious creator who never really left anything to uncertainty. For example, in the late 1960s he worked on dances using body-attached cybersonic consoles which could increase, reduce, distort, unbalance, and then rebalance sounds by stage movements, according to the dimensions of different spatial areas; and on the control of stage lighting as affected by the dancers moving within range of electronic devices that changed hues and densities of illuminations.

In 1958 Cunningham's company began tours which took them to nearly every continent. Cunningham gave lecture-demonstrations or participated in symposiums at universities and museums around the world. By 1970 he had created nearly 100 ensemble dance works and dozens of solos for himself, had made significant documentary films on modern dance, and had authored a book.

Cunningham's awards include honorary member of the American Academy and Institute of Arts and Letters (1984), the Samuel H. Scripps American Dance Festival Award for lifetime contributions to dance (1982), the MacArthur Award (1985), the Laurence Olivier Award (1985), the National Medal of Arts (1990) and the Digital Dance Premier Award (1990).

*Ocean,* the final collaboration between Cunningham and John Cage, premiered at the University of California, Berkeley in April, 1996. In 1995, Cunningham developed a computer software program called LifeForms, to choreograph dances on computer.

**Further Reading**

Cunningham's partly autobiographical *Changes* (1968) mainly relates his ideas on dance. Pictures of his company's work are in Jack Mitchell, *Dance Scene U.S.A.* (1967), with commentary by Clive Barnes. Walter Sorell, ed., *The Dance Has Many Faces* (1951; 2d ed. 1966), includes good essays on modern dance and Cunningham's place in it. Cunningham was also featured in a public television broadcast of *Point in Space* (BBC, 1986). □

# Mario Matthew Cuomo

**Mario Matthew Cuomo (born 1932) was a progressive Democrat governor of New York state from 1982 to 1994. He emphasized lower taxes, balanced budgets, public education, and affirmative action, as well as a government-private sector partnership for economic progress. He was often mentioned as a possible Democratic candidate for president.**

Mario Matthew Cuomo was born on June 15, 1932, in New York City. His parents, Andrea and Immaculata (Giordano) Cuomo, had immigrated from Salerno, Italy, in the late 1920s. His father dug and cleaned sewers and by 1931 had saved enough to open an Italian-American grocery store in the South Jamaica section of Queens, a borough of New York City. Cuomo was born in the family's apartment above the store. He was the youngest of three children; he had a brother and a sister. He spent much of his early life watching his parents work incredibly hard and absorbing their values of respect for family, personal obligations, education, and the law.

Cuomo spoke only Italian until he started local public schools. Seeking a more rigorous academic education, he transferred to a Roman Catholic high school, St. John's Preparatory. A boy who always liked to play ball games, at 19 Cuomo was recruited by the Pittsburgh Pirates to become a professional baseball player. He was sent to play with its minor league team, the Brunswick (Georgia) Pirates, as a center fielder. His doubts about making sports a career won out after a head injury received from a fastball. He returned to school on a scholarship given by St. John's University. Cuomo earned his B.A. degree with high honors in 1953, then entered St. John's School of Law. In June 1954 he married Matilda Raffa, a student at St. John's, who became a school teacher. He earned his law degree in 1956, tied for first in his class.

After graduation, Cuomo became a law clerk with a New York state Court of Appeals judge. In 1958 he went into private practice, joining a Brooklyn law firm. In 1963 he started teaching law part-time at St. John's.

Cuomo soon was drawn into representing community groups in their legal problems. He earned a reputation as a skilled debater and arbitrator. Once, he represented a group of junkyard owners and scrap dealers who sought to save their businesses when their land was condemned by New York City as a proposed site for the 1964-1965 World's Fair. Another time he helped families save their homes from being bulldozed to build a school and athletic field in Corona, Queens. Mayor John Lindsey asked him to settle bit-terly hostile neighborhood disputes arising from a plan to build a large-scale low-income housing project in middle-income Forest Hills, Queens. His victories were heavily publicized and the recognition led to suggestions that he seek public office.

Cuomo, with a deep sense of civic obligation, decided to enter public service. In 1974 he ran for lieutenant governor of New York, but lost in a three-way Democratic primary that year. Governor Hugh Carey, an acquaintance from law school, appointed Cuomo secretary of state, beginning January 1975. Cuomo left his law partnership and teaching post to devote his full attention to the office, although he was not required to do so. He worked to expand the duties of secretary of state, intervening in a series of state-wide crises, including a Mohawk Indian lands claim dispute, nursing home practices problems, and rent strikes. The position offered him an extraordinary education in state government.

In 1977 he ran for mayor of New York City. He lost the Democratic primary, facing six rivals. However, he stayed in the race as the nominee of the Liberal Party. Cuomo was defeated by Edward Koch.

Carey, seeking re-election in 1978, asked Cuomo to run on his ticket as lieutenant governor. Cuomo received his party's support. The ticket won in the election. As lieutenant governor, Cuomo traveled the state in the role of ombudsman for citizen problems. He led President Jimmy Carter's 1980 re-election campaign in New York state and was a delegate that year to the Democratic National Convention.

When Carey announced that he would not seek a third term in office in 1982, Cuomo decided to enter the race. He faced his old opponent, Edward Koch, in the struggle for the nomination. Koch, more widely known and far better financed, lost this round. Relying on volunteers and upstate voters, Cuomo won the Democratic primary and, also, a place on the Liberal Party ticket. He narrowly defeated his millionaire Republican opponent in the general election to become New York's 52nd governor.

In 1984 Cuomo delivered the keynote address at the Democratic Party's national nominating convention in San Francisco. He electrified the crowd with his oratorical skills. In 1992 at the Democratic National Convention he gave the speech which nominated Bill Clinton as the Democratic candidate for President. Cuomo himself was sought after to run for the presidential nomination in 1984, 1988, and 1992, but each time he refused.

Cuomo won re-election in 1986 and again, for a third term, in 1990. His vote-gathering abilities broke state records for the percentage of votes received for governor. As governor, Cuomo pushed for lower taxes and balanced budgets. He made public education a top priority. He emphasized a partnership between business and government for economic development. His affirmative action efforts won praise.

In 1994, even after a campaign that was supported by New York City's Republican mayor, Rudolph Guiliani, Cuomo was defeated for re-election by his Republican challenger, George Pataki. Critics have said that Cuomo's brand of social liberalism had been discredited in the public mind, in favor of less government. In 1995, shortly after taking office, Pataki passed a death penalty law, after two decades of vetoes by his two Democratic predecessors.

Cuomo spoke of his political orientation as "progressive pragmatism." He was influenced by his ethnic, religious, and lower-class upbringing. He reminded people of America's immigrant heritage and the upward mobility of its people. His political philosophy was a "family kind of politics" that conceived of people sharing their burdens and blessings and understanding that their individual well-being depends on the well-being of the community. Thus, he believed that government has a responsibility to help those who through no fault of their own are either permanently or temporarily unable to help themselves.

Cuomo is an introspective person, keeping diaries to explore his own motivations and sort his thinking. He has been described as being a workaholic, competitive, having a quick temper, and refusing to delegate authority. Cuomo considers himself devoted to his family and friends. He doted on his three daughters and two sons. His elder son, Andrew, managed his father's campaigns and served as a chief adviser to the governor. Andrew Cuomo became Secretary of Housing & Urban Development in the second term of President Bill Clinton.

Mario Cuomo has authored books about public policy, social and cultural issues, New York, and his life, both personal and political. He also hosts a radio call-in show in New York City.

## Further Reading

Mario Cuomo has written two books recording major episodes in his life, based on his diaries. Both have biographical portions and personal meditations that give insight into the many forces that shape his character: *Forest Hills Diary: The Crisis of Low-Income Housing* (1974); and *Diaries of Mario M. Cuomo: The Campaign for Governor* (1984). He described New York State, its challenges and accomplishments in *The New York Idea: An Experiment in Democracy* (1994). He also released *More Than Words* and *Lincoln On Democracy* (which he co-edited). A fascinating biography is Robert S. McElvaine, *Mario Cuomo: A Biography* (1988). A study of Cuomo's political support and issues is Lee M. Miringoff and Barbara L. Carvalho, *The Cuomo Factor: Assessing the Political Appeal of New York's Governor* (1986). Information about Cuomo's political career can be followed in a biennial series, *The Almanac of American Politics,* by Michael Barone and Grant Ujifusa. □

# Marie Sklodowska Curie

**The Polish-born French physicist Marie Sklodowska Curie (1867-1934) pioneered radioactive research by her part in the discovery of radium and polonium and in the determination of their chemical properties.**

Marie Curie was born in Warsaw on Nov. 7, 1867, the youngest of the five children of Wladislaw and Bronislava Boguska Sklodowska. Marie was a brilliant student, gaining a gold medal upon completing her secondary education in 1883. As girls could not attend universities in Russian-dominated Poland, Marie at her father's suggestion spent a year in the country with friends. On returning to her father's house in Warsaw the next summer, she had to begin to earn her living through private tutoring, and she also became associated with the "Floating University," a group of young men and women who tried to quench their thirst for knowledge in semiclandestine sessions. In early 1886 she accepted a job as governess with a family living in Szczuki, but the intellectual loneliness she experienced there only stiffened her determination to achieve somehow her dream to become a university student. One of her sisters, Bronya, was already in Paris, successfully passing the examinations in medicine. In March 1890 she offered hospitality to Marie whose acceptance was a foregone conclusion, but it was not until September 1891 that she could leave for Paris.

When classes began at the Sorbonne in Paris in early November 1891, she enrolled as a student of physics. By 1894 she was desperately looking for a laboratory where she could work on her research project, the measurement of the magnetic properties of various steel alloys, and it was suggested that she see Pierre Curie at the School of Physics and Chemistry of the University of Paris. Their first meeting was movingly recorded in the future Madame Curie's recollections: "He seemed very young to me although he was

then age thirty-five. I was struck by the expression of his clear gaze and by a slight appearance of carelessness in his lofty stature. His rather slow, reflective words, his simplicity, and his smile, at once grave and young, inspired confidence. A conversation began between us and became friendly; its object was some questions of science upon which I was happy to ask his opinion."

Although she was insistent from the very start that she would go back to Poland in half a year to assist her subjugated country in whatever way she could, Pierre Curie was most intent to see her more and more often. The result was that she returned to Paris in October 1894 after spending the summer months in Poland. The next summer witnessed their wedding and the beginning of a most extraordinary partnership in scientific work. By mid-1897 Curie could list as her scientific achievements two university degrees, a fellowship, and a monograph on the magnetization of tempered steel. Their first daughter, Irène, had just been born, and it was in that euphoric atmosphere that the Curies' attention turned to the mysterious radiation from uranium recently discovered by Antoine Henri Becquerel. It was Curie's hunch that the radiation was an atomic property and therefore had to be present in some other elements as well. Her search soon established the fact of a similar radiation from thorium, and the historic word "radioactivity" was coined by her.

While searching for other sources of radioactivity, the Curies had before long to turn their attention to pitchblende, a mineral well known for its uranium content. To their immense surprise the radioactivity of pitchblende far exceeded the combined radioactivity of the uranium and thorium contained in it. From their laboratory two papers reached the Academy of Sciences within 6 months. The first, read at the meeting of July 18, 1898, announced the discovery of a new radioactive element, which the Curies named polonium after Curie's native country. The other paper, announcing the discovery of radium, was read at the December 26 meeting.

To substantiate the existence of the new elements and to establish their properties, the Curies had to have sufficiently large quantities. Fortunately, the Austrian government was willing to give the Curies a ton of pitchblende, but to process it a laboratory was needed. After long search, the Curies had to settle for a shed occupying part of a courtyard in the School of Physics and Chemistry. From 1898 to 1902 the Curies processed several tons of pitchblende, but it was not only the extremely precious centigrams of radium that rewarded their superhuman labors. The Curies also published, jointly or separately, during those years a total of 32 scientific papers. Among them was the one which announced that diseased, tumor-forming cells were destroyed faster than healthy cells when exposed to radium.

From abroad came the full measure of recognition which the French Academy of Sciences refused to give in 1902, when Pierre Curie presented himself as candidate for membership. In November 1903 the Royal Society in London gave the Curies one of its highest awards, the Davy Medal; and a month later followed the announcement from Stockholm that three French scientists, A. H. Becquerel and

the Curies, were the joint recipients of the Nobel Prize in physics for 1903. Finally even the academics in Paris began to stir and a chair in physics was created at the University of Paris, and a few months later Curie was appointed director of research associated with the new chair. In December 1904 their second daughter Ève, was born; while the next year brought the election of Pierre Curie to the Academy of Sciences and their travel to Stockholm, where he delivered on June 6 the Nobel lecture, which was in fact their joint address. Its concluding paragraph evoked in prophetic words the double-edged impact on mankind of every major scientific advance. Still Pierre Curie asserted his conviction that "mankind will derive more good than harm from the new discoveries."

The illustrious husband-and-wife team, now installed in more appropriate academic positions, had, however, their happy days numbered. The first academic year of Pierre Curie in his new professorship was not over when, on the rainy mid-afternoon of April 19, 1906, he was run down by a heavy carriage and killed instantly. Two weeks later the widow was asked to take over her late husband's post. Honors began to pour in from scientific societies all over the world on a woman left alone with two small children and with the gigantic task of leadership in radioactivity. In 1908 she began to give as titular professor at the Sorbonne the first, and then the only, course on radioactivity in the world. In the same year she edited the collected works of her late husband, and in 1910 she published her massive *Traité de radioactivité*. The next year the Academy of Sciences showed once more its true colors by denying with a one-vote majority the membership to the person who 11 months later became the first to receive twice the Nobel Prize, this time in chemistry.

In addition to the Nobel Prize the two finest honors that came to Curie in 1911 were her election as permanent member of the Solvay Conferences in physics and the erection in Warsaw of the Institute of Radioactivity, whose directorship was offered to her by a most distinguished group of Polish intellectuals. The first of these honors reflected on her stature as a scientist. The second honor was more of an emotional satisfaction and represented some temptation for her to turn her back on the unappreciative scientific establishment of her adopted country. But she decided to stay in France, though she did her best to assist the new institute in Warsaw in every possible way. A most important factor in Curie's decision to stay was the future of the laboratory which Dr. P. P.E. Roux, the director of the Pasteur Institute, proposed to build for her. The plan finally jolted the Sorbonne to join hands with the Pasteur Institute in establishing the famous Radium Institute. Its dedication took place in July 1914, a year after the institute in Warsaw had been dedicated in her presence.

Curie devoted much of her time during the 4 years of World War I to equipping automobiles in her own laboratory with x-ray (Roentgen) apparatus to assist the sick. It was these cars that became known in the war zone as "little Curies." By the end of the war Curie was past her fiftieth year with much of her physical energy already spent, together with her savings, which she had patriotically invested in war bonds. But her dedication seemed to be inexhaustible. The year 1919 witnessed her installation at the Radium Institute, and 2 years later her book *La Radiologie et la guerre* was published. In it she gave a most informative account of the scientific and human experiences gained for radiology during the war. With the end of the war also came the appointment of her daughter Irène, a physicist, as an assistant in her mother's laboratory.

Shortly afterward, a momentous visit took place in the Radium Institute. The visitor was Mrs. William B. Meloney, editor of a leading magazine in New York and representative of those countless women who for years had found in Curie their ideal and inspiration. A year later Meloney returned to tell her that a nationwide subscription in America had produced the sum of $100,000 needed to purchase a gram of radium for her institute. She was also asked to visit the United States with her daughters and collect in person the precious gift. Her trip was a triumph in the finest sense of the word. In the White House, President Warren G. Harding presented her with the golden key to the little metal box containing the radium.

On questions other than scientific, Curie rarely uttered public comment of any length. One of the exceptions was her statement at a conference in 1933 on "The Future of Culture." There she rallied to the defense of science, which several panelists held responsible for the dehumanization of modern life. "I am among those," she emphasized, "who think that science has great beauty. A scientist in his laboratory is not only a technician; he is also a child placed before natural phenomena which impress him like a fairy tale. We should not allow it to be believed that all scientific progress can be reduced to mechanism, machines, gearings, even though such machinery also has its own beauty."

The most heartwarming experience of the last phase of Curie's life was probably the marriage of Irène in 1926 to Frédéric Joliot (later Joliot-Curie), the most gifted assistant at the Radium Institute. Before long it was evident to her that their union would be a close replica of her own marvelously creative partnership with Pierre Curie.

She worked almost to the very end and succeeded in completing the manuscript of her last book, *Radioactivité*. In the last years her great support was her younger daughter, Ève. She was also her mother's faithful companion when, on July 4, 1934, death claimed the one of whom Albert Einstein aptly said, "Marie Curie is, of all celebrated beings, the only one whom fame has not corrupted."

## Further Reading

The classic biography of Marie Curie, written by her daughter, Ève Curie, is *Madame Curie* (trans. 1937), a work which emphasizes the human element. *Nobel Lectures: Physics, 1901-1921* (1967), published by the Nobel Foundation, includes a biographical sketch. General background works which discuss Curie include Gerald Holton and Duane H. D. Roller, *Foundations of Modern Physical Science* (1958), and Henry A. Boorse and Lloyd Motz, eds., *The World of the Atom* (2 vols., 1966). □

# Pierre Curie

**Pierre Curie (1859-1906) was a noted physicist who became famous for his collaboration with his wife, Marie Curie, in the study of radioactivity. Before joining his wife in her research, Curie was already widely known and respected in the world of physics.**

Pierre Curie was a noted physicist who became famous for his collaboration with his wife Marie Curie in the study of radioactivity. Before joining his wife in her research, Pierre Curie was already widely known and respected in the world of physics. He discovered (with his brother Jacques ) the phenomenon of piezoelectricity—in which a crystal can become electrically polarized—and invented the quartz balance. His papers on crystal symmetry, and his findings on the relation between magnetism and temperature also earned praise in the scientific community. Curie died in a street accident in 1906, a physicist acclaimed the world over but who had never had a decent laboratory in which to work.

Pierre Curie was born in Paris on May 15, 1859, the son of Sophie-Claire Depouilly, daughter of a formerly prominent manufacturer, and Eugène Curie, a free-thinking physician who was also a physician's son. Dr. Curie supported the family with his modest medical practice while pursuing his love for the natural sciences on the side. He was also an idealist and an ardent republican who set up a hospital for the wounded during the Commune of 1871. Pierre was a dreamer whose style of learning was not well adapted to formal schooling. He received his pre-university education entirely at home, taught first by his mother and then by his father as well as his older brother, Jacques. He especially enjoyed excursions into the countryside to observe and study plants and animals, developing a love of nature that endured throughout his life and that provided his only recreation and relief from work during his later scientific career. At the age of 14, Curie studied with a mathematics professor who helped him develop his gift in the subject, especially spatial concepts. Curie's knowledge of physics and mathematics earned him his bachelor of science degree in 1875 at the age of sixteen. He then enrolled in the Faculty of Sciences at the Sorbonne in Paris and earned his *licence* (the equivalent of a master's degree) in physical sciences in 1877.

Curie became a laboratory assistant to Paul Desains at the Sorbonne in 1878, in charge of the physics students' lab work. His brother Jacques was working in the mineralogy laboratory at the Sorbonne at that time, and the two began a productive five-year scientific collaboration. They investigated pyroelectricity, the acquisition of electric charges by different faces of certain types of crystals when heated. Led by their knowledge of symmetry in crystals, the brothers experimentally discovered the previously unknown phenomenon of piezoelectricity, an electric polarization caused by force applied to the crystal. In 1880 the Curies published the first in a series of papers about their discovery. They then studied the opposite effect—the compression of a

piezoelectric crystal by an electric field. In order to measure the very small amounts of electricity involved, the brothers invented a new laboratory instrument: a piezoelectric quartz electrometer, or balance. This device became very useful for electrical researchers and would prove highly valuable to Marie Curie in her studies of radioactivity. Much later, piezoelectricity had important practical applications. Paul Langevin, a student of Pierre Curie's, found that inverse piezoelectricity causes piezoelectric quartz in alternating fields to emit high-frequency sound waves, which were used to detect submarines and explore the ocean's floor. Piezoelectric crystals were also used in radio broadcasting and stereo equipment.

In 1882 Pierre Curie was appointed head of the laboratory at Paris' new Municipal School of Industrial Physics and Chemistry, a poorly paid position; he remained at the school for 22 years, until 1904. In 1883 Jacques Curie left Paris to become a lecturer in mineralogy at the University of Montpelier, and the brothers' collaboration ended. After Jacques's departure, Pierre delved into theoretical and experimental research on crystal symmetry, although the time available to him for such work was limited by the demands of organizing the school's laboratory from scratch and directing the laboratory work of up to 30 students, with only one assistant. He began publishing works on crystal symmetry in 1884, including in 1885 a theory on the formation of crystals and in 1894 an enunciation of the general principle of symmetry. Curie's writings on symmetry were of fundamental importance to later crystallographers, and, as Marie Curie later wrote in *Pierre Curie*, "he always retained a

passionate interest in the physics of crystals" even though he turned his attention to other areas.

From 1890 to 1895 Pierre Curie performed a series of investigations that formed the basis of his doctoral thesis: a study of the magnetic properties of substances at different temperatures. He was, as always, hampered in his work by his obligations to his students, by the lack of funds to support his experiments, and by the lack of a laboratory or even a room for his own personal use. His magnetism research was conducted mostly in a corridor. In spite of these limitations, Curie's work on magnetism, like his papers on symmetry, was of fundamental importance. His expression of the results of his findings about the relation between temperature and magnetization became known as Curie's law, and the temperature above which magnetic properties disappear is called the Curie point. Curie successfully defended his thesis before the Faculty of Sciences at the University of Paris (the Sorbonne) in March 1895, thus earning his doctorate. Also during this period, he constructed a periodic precision balance, with direct reading, that was a great advance over older balance systems and was especially valuable for chemical analysis. Curie was now becoming well-known among physicists; he attracted the attention and esteem of, among others, the noted Scottish mathematician and physicist William Thomson (Lord Kelvin). It was partly due to Kelvin's influence that Curie was named to a newly created chair of physics at the School of Physics and Chemistry, which improved his status somewhat but still did not bring him a laboratory.

In the spring of 1894, at the age of 35, Curie met Maria (later Marie) Sklodowska, a poor young Polish student who had received her *licence* in physics from the Sorbonne and was then studying for her *licence* in mathematics. They immediately formed a rapport, and Curie soon proposed marriage. Sklodowska returned to Poland that summer, not certain that she would be willing to separate herself permanently from her family and her country. Curie's persuasive correspondence convinced her to return to Paris that autumn, and the couple married in July, 1895, in a simple civil ceremony. Marie used a cash wedding gift to purchase two bicycles, which took the newlyweds on their honeymoon in the French countryside and provided their main source of recreation for years to come. Their daughter Irene was born in 1897, and a few days later Pierre's mother died; Dr. Curie then came to live with the young couple and helped care for his granddaughter.

The Curies' attention was caught by Henri Becquerel's discovery in 1896 that uranium compounds emit rays. Marie decided to make a study of this phenomenon the subject of her doctor's thesis, and Pierre secured the use of a ground-floor storeroom/machine shop at the School for her laboratory work. Using the Curie brothers' piezoelectric quartz electrometer, Marie tested all the elements then known to see if any of them, like uranium, emitted "Becquerel rays," which she christened "radioactivity." Only thorium and uranium and their compounds, she found, were radioactive. She was startled to discover that the ores pitchblende and chalcolite had much greater levels of radioactivity than the amounts of uranium and thorium they contained could account for. She guessed that a new, highly radioactive element must be responsible and, as she wrote in *Pierre Curie,* was seized with "a passionate desire to verify this hypothesis as rapidly as possible."

Pierre Curie too saw the significance of his wife's findings and set aside his much-loved work on crystals (only for the time being, he thought) to join Marie in the search for the new element. They devised a new method of chemical research, progressively separating pitchblende by chemical analysis and then measuring the radioactivity of the separate constituents. In July 1898, in a joint paper, they announced their discovery of a new element they named polonium, in honor of Marie Curie's native country. In December 1898, they announced, in a paper issued with their collaborator G. Bémont, the discovery of another new element, radium. Both elements were much more radioactive than uranium or thorium.

The Curies had discovered radium and polonium, but in order to prove the existence of these new substances chemically, they had to isolate the elements so the atomic weight of each could be determined. This was a daunting task, as they would have to process two tons of pitchblende ore to obtain a few centigrams of pure radium. Their laboratory facilities were woefully inadequate: an abandoned wooden shed in the School's yard, with no hoods to carry off the poisonous gases their work produced. They found the pitchblende at a reasonable price in the form of waste from a uranium mine run by the Austrian government. The Curies now divided their labor. Marie acted as the chemist, performing the physically arduous job of chemically separating the pitchblende; the bulkiest part of this work she did in the yard adjoining the shed/laboratory. Pierre was the physicist, analyzing the physical properties of the substances that Marie's separations produced. In 1902 the Curies announced that they had succeeded in preparing a decigram of pure radium chloride and had made an initial determination of radium's atomic weight. They had proven the chemical individuality of radium.

The Curies' research also yielded a wealth of information about radioactivity, which they shared with the world in a series of papers published between 1898 and 1904. They announced their discovery of induced radioactivity in 1899. They wrote about the luminous and chemical effects of radioactive rays and their electric charge. Pierre studied the action of a magnetic field on radium rays, he investigated the persistence of induced radioactivity, and he developed a standard for measuring time on the basis of radioactivity, an important basis for geologic and archaeological dating techniques. Pierre Curie also used himself as a human guinea pig, deliberately exposing his arm to radium for several hours and recording the progressive, slowly healing burn that resulted. He collaborated with physicians in animal experiments that led to the use of radium therapy—often called "Curie-therapie" then—to treat cancer and lupus. In 1904 he published a paper on the liberation of heat by radium salts.

Through all this intensive research, the Curies struggled to keep up with their teaching, household, and financial obligations. Pierre Curie was a kind, gentle, and reserved man, entirely devoted to his work—science conducted purely for the sake of science. He rejected honorary distinctions; in 1903 he declined the prestigious decoration of the Legion of Honor. He also, with his wife's agreement, refused to patent their radium-preparation process, which formed the basis of the lucrative radium industry; instead, they shared all their information about the process with whomever asked for it. Curie found it almost impossible to advance professionally within the French university system; seeking a position was an "ugly necessity" and "demoralizing" for him ( *Pierre Curie* ), so posts he might have been considered for went instead to others. He was turned down for the Chair of Physical Chemistry at the Sorbonne in 1898; instead, he was appointed assistant professor at the Polytechnic School in March 1900, a much inferior position.

Appreciated outside France, Curie received an excellent offer of a professorship at the University of Geneva in the spring of 1900, but he turned it down so as not to interrupt his research on radium. Shortly afterward, Curie was appointed to a physics chair at the Sorbonne, thanks to the efforts of Jules Henri Poincaré. Still, he did not have a laboratory, and his teaching load was now doubled, as he still held his post at the School of Physics and Chemistry. He began to suffer from extreme fatigue and sharp pains through his body, which he and his wife attributed to overwork, although the symptoms were almost certainly a sign of radiation poisoning, an unrecognized illness at that time. In 1902, Curie's candidacy for election to the French Academy of Sciences failed, and in 1903 his application for the chair of mineralogy at the Sorbonne was rejected, both of which added to his bitterness toward the French academic establishment.

Recognition at home finally came for Curie because of international awards. In 1903 London's Royal Society conferred the Davy medal on the Curies, and shortly thereafter they were awarded the 1903 Nobel Prize in physics—along with Becquerel—for their work on radioactivity. Curie presciently concluded his Nobel lecture (delivered in 1905 because the Curies had been too ill to attend the 1903 award ceremony) by wondering whether the knowledge of radium and radioactivity would be harmful for humanity; he added that he himself felt that more good than harm would result from the new discoveries. The Nobel award shattered the Curies' reclusive work-absorbed life. They were inundated by journalists, photographers, curiosity-seekers, eminent and little-known visitors, correspondence, and requests fr articles and lectures. Still, the cash from the award was a godsend, and the award's prestige finally prompted the French parliament to create a new professorship for Curie at the Sorbonne in 1904. Curie declared he would remain at the School of Physics unless the new chair included a fully funded laboratory, complete with assistants. His demand was met, and Marie was named his laboratory chief. Late in 1904 the Curies' second daughter, Eve, was born. By early 1906, Pierre Curie was poised to begin work—at last and for the first time—in an adequate laboratory, although he was increasingly ill and tired. On April 19, 1906, leaving a lunchtime meeting in Paris with colleagues from the Sorbonne, Curie slipped in front of a horse-drawn cart while crossing a rain-slicked rue Dauphine. He was killed instantly when the rear wheel of the cart crushed his skull. The world mourned the untimely loss of this great physicist. True to the way he had conducted his life, he was interred in a small suburban cemetery in a simple, private ceremony attended only by his family and a few close friends. In his memory, the Faculty of Sciences at the Sorbonne appointed Curie's widow Marie to his chair.

## Further Reading

Curie, Eve, *Madame Curie: A Biography by Eve Curie,* translated by Vincent Sheean, Doubleday, 1937.
Curie, Marie, *Pierre Curie,* Macmillan, 1923.
Giroud, Françoise, *Marie Curie: A Life,* Holmes & Meier, 1986.
Heathcote, Niels H. de V., *Nobel Prize Winners in Physics 1901–1950,* Henry Schuman, 1953.
Magill, Frank N., *The Nobel Prize Winners: Physics,* Volume 1: *(1901–1937),* Salem Press, 1989.
Reid, Robert, *Marie Curie,* Dutton, 1974.
Romer, Alfred, editor, *The Discovery of Radioactivity and Transmutation,* Dover, 1964.
Segre, Emilio, *From X-Rays to Quarks: Modern Physicists and Their Discoveries,* University of California Press, 1980.
Weaver, Jefferson Hane, *The World of Physics,* Simon & Schuster, 1987. □

# James Michael Curley

**The American politician James Michael Curley (1874-1958) was a magnetic political figure, particularly as mayor of Boston.**

James Curley was born on Nov. 20, 1874, in Boston, a city whose upper-class Yankee Protestant families despised Irish Catholics socially and discriminated against them politically. He became a symbol of the emergence of the Irish from their proletarian status to political dominance. Reared in politics, alienated from any sense of community, Curley formed a hard, unwavering, egocentric determination to succeed.

Curley overcame handicaps of birth and poor education, and his political ascendancy was meteoric. Elected to the Common Council in 1900, he then progressed to the Board of Aldermen and the Massachusetts Legislature. His Irish slum constituency elected him in 1911 to the first of four undistinguished terms in Congress. In 1928 he was a firm supporter of Governor Alfred E. Smith for president. Denied a place in the Massachusetts delegation to the 1932 Democratic convention, Curley managed to be chosen a delegate from Puerto Rico. His support was instrumental in winning the presidential nomination for Franklin D. Roosevelt, but he broke with Roosevelt after the President refused to appoint him ambassador to Ireland.

As governor of Massachusetts in 1935, Curley was criticized for his spending, job trading, and high-speed motorcades across the Commonwealth. In 1936 he was an unsuccessful candidate for the U.S. Senate.

Of his many political posts, Curley best enjoyed being mayor of Boston. He was elected in 1913, 1921, 1929, and 1945. In an age of such figures as Tom Pendergast of Kansas City and Frank Hague of Jersey City, Curley enjoyed his self-described role as political "boss." But whereas the others had powerful political machines, Curley's greatest strength lay in his personal magnetism. The core of his political support always came from the slums. Curley lacked a political philosophy beyond that of taking care of himself and his own.

Politics was a game he took as he found it; his only desire was to win, not to change or reform. He fabricated a Ku Klux Klan scare during his first gubernatorial campaign, and he regularly blackmailed Boston's propertied classes and social elite to subsidize his huge public works projects and padded city payrolls. He served two terms in prison: in 1904 for impersonating a friend in a civil service examination, and in 1947 for graft in connection with Federal contracts while serving as a member of Congress. His conduct frequently brought him into conflict with the Catholic hierarchy of Boston.

A political legend in Boston for more than half a century, Curley lived to see himself perpetuated as a literary legend. He was the prototype for Frank Skeffington, the principal figure in Edwin O'Connor's novel *The Last Hurrah.* Curley died on Nov. 12, 1958.

## Further Reading

Curley's autobiography, *I'd Do It Again: A Record of All My Uproarious Years* (1957), is a rambling and uneven document enlivened by the candidly brazen quality of the author's confessions. The beginning of the Curley legend and the first attempt to put his career in perspective is Joseph F. Dinneen, *The Purple Shamrock: The Honorable James Michael Curley of Boston* (1949). A frankly hostile account of Curley's governorship is Wendell D. Howie, *The Reign of James the First: A Historical Record of the Administration of James M. Curley as Governor of Massachusetts* (1936).

## Additional Sources

Beatty, Jack, *The rascal king: the life and times of James Michael Curley, 1874-1958,* Reading, Mass.: Addison-Wesley, 1992.
Curley, James Michael, *I'd do it again,* New York: Arno Press, 1976, 1957. □

# Sir Arthur William Currie

**Sir Arthur William Currie (1875-1933) was the leader of the Canadian Corps during World War I, the first native Canadian to head his country's forces in France and Flanders.**

Arthur Currie was born at Napperton, Ontario, on Dec. 5, 1875, and he was educated in the public schools of Strathroy. In 1894 he moved to British Columbia and taught in the public schools of Sidney and Victoria for 5 years. He then became involved with insurance and real estate, businesses which he practiced with little success and through which he became heavily indebted.

Currie's metier, however, was soldiering. He joined the 5th Regiment of Canadian Garrison Artillery in 1897 and received his commission in 1900. His rise through the ranks was swift, and in 1909 he was given command of the regiment. His command was one of the most efficient in Canada, and Currie's personal reputation was high with the minister of militia in Ottawa.

As a result, when war broke out in 1914, Currie was offered the command of a brigade in the 1st Canadian Division. After training in England, Currie led his troops to France in February 1915. Very shortly thereafter he and his untried men faced the first German gas attack at Ypres but stood their ground with incredible fortitude. In September 1915 Currie took charge of the 1st Canadian Division, and he led the troops through a series of terrific battles—Mont-Sorrel, the Somme, Fresnoy, and Vimy.

As a commander, Currie was not a brilliant strategist. But he was an excellent tactician, skillful in the use of artillery, meticulous in his planning. Most important, he was careful of the lives of his men, something for which World War I generals were not renowned. When the command of the Canadian Corps fell vacant in June 1917, Currie was the logical choice for the post. As with his previous commands, he did extraordinarily well, and he led the corps through the

horror of Passchendaele and through Arras and Amiens. The record of the corps was second to none, and Currie received and merited enormous praise.

After the war Currie was made general and named the inspector general of the military forces of Canada, a position he held until 1920, when he resigned to become principal of McGill University in Montreal. Often mentioned as a possible leader of the Conservative party, Currie decided to remain in academic life. He died on Nov. 30, 1933.

## Further Reading

There is a biography of Currie by Hugh M. Urquhart, *Arthur Currie* (1950), that is very discreet. The best study on the Canadian Corps and its commander, however, is John Swettenham, *To Seize the Victory: The Canadian Corps in World War I* (1965).

## Additional Sources

Hyatt, A. M. J., *General Sir Arthur Currie: a military biography,* Toronto: University of Toronto Press, 1987. □

# Currier and Ives

**Nathaniel Currier (1813-1888) and James Merritt Ives (1824-1895) were partners in the firm of Currier and Ives, the most important 19th-century litho-**

graphic company in America. Their prints were widely sold across the nation.

Nathaniel Currier, born in Roxbury, Mass., was apprenticed in his teens to a Boston lithographic firm. He established his own lithography business in New York City in 1835. The lithographer James Ives, born in New York City, entered into partnership with Currier in 1857. Currier retired in 1888, Ives a few years later; but the firm was carried on by their sons and flourished until 1907.

Lithography had begun in America in the 1820s. It was quicker and less expensive than engraving, hence the remarkable success of the firm of Currier and Ives. Soon after setting up business they produced extensive folios, usually based on paintings. Some of the work was crude, but the quality varied considerably. The star artists of the firm were Arthur F. Tait, who specialized in sporting scenes; Louis Maurer, who executed genre scenes; Fanny Palmer, who liked to do picturesque panoramas of the American landscape; and George H. Durrie, who supplied winter scenes.

So well known did Currier and Ives become that it was common to refer to any large mixed batch of prints as Currier and Ives prints. The firm was astoundingly prolific and produced prints on practically every aspect of the American scene. In the 1870s they issued four catalogs featuring 2800 subject titles.

Currier and Ives sometimes focused on current events. (In 1840 Currier produced what may have been the first illustrated "extra" in history when he depicted scenes of the fire that had broken out that year aboard the steamship *Lexington* in Long Island Sound.) Political cartoons and banners were commonly produced, like the *Presidential Fishing Party of 1848,* showing the candidates with fishing poles trying to hook fish on which names of various states are inscribed.

Historical prints were another field, and copies from the historical paintings of John Trumbull were especially popular. The Civil War print *Battle of Fair Oaks, Va., May 31, 1862* shows the first balloon ever used for warfare observation. Sentimental prints included one showing a married couple walking along a riverbank and another showing a girl taking care of her little sister. There were also prints for children, such as *Robinson Crusoe and His Pets* and *Noah's Ark;* country and pioneer home scenes, which included *Early Winter,* a beautiful scene of people skating on a frozen pond before a snow-covered country cottage; and lithographed sheet music. Still other categories were Mississippi River prints, including *On the Mississippi Loading Cotton* and *Midnight Race on the Mississippi;* railroad prints that sometimes featured minute descriptions of trains, as in *"Lightning Express" Trains Leaving the Junction;* and home prints, which were produced in especially large quantities.

Currier and Ives avoided controversial subjects, although there was at least one print showing the branding of slaves prior to embarkation from Africa. Prints of sporting events focused on prize fights (like the 1835 match between John C. Heeman and the English champion Tom Sayers),

boat races, and even, in the early stages of its development, baseball.

As America expanded, so did the demand for Currier and Ives prints. Today they provide a vivid picture of daily life in 19th-century America.

## Further Reading

Harry T. Peters, *Currier and Ives: Printmakers to the American People* (1942), is the authoritative work, containing 192 plates and an excellent introduction. Both Colin Simkin, *Currier and Ives' America* (1952), and Roy King and Burke Davis, *The World of Currier & Ives* (1968), contain useful introductions and reproductions. See also Currier's own *Currier & Ives Chronicles of America,* edited by John Lowell Pratt and with an introduction by A. K. Baragwanath (1968). □

# Jabez Lamar Monroe Curry

**The American politician Jabez Lamar Monroe Curry (1815-1903) was the main force behind improved education in the South in the latter half of the 19th century.**

Born on June 5, 1815, in Lincoln Country, Ga., J. L. M. Curry was the son of a slaveholding family that ultimately moved to Alabama. He graduated from the University of Georgia and the Harvard University Law School. While at Harvard, Curry heard a lecture by Horace Mann that awakened his zealous interest in universal education.

In 1845 Curry was admitted to the Alabama bar, and he quickly gained prominence as a lawyer. Three terms in the Alabama Legislature preceded 4 years as a member of the U.S. House of Representatives. During the Civil War he served first in the Confederate Congress and then as a colonel on the staffs of generals Joseph E. Johnston and Joseph Wheeler.

Shortly after his 1866 ordination as a Baptist minister, Curry accepted the presidency of Howard College in Alabama. He left that post in 1868 to become a professor of English, philosophy, and law at Richmond College, Va. Meanwhile, New England philanthropist George Peabody had donated $2,000,000 as a fund for the improvement of Southern schools. When the directorship of the Peabody Fund became vacant, Curry was immediately nominated. As one endorser stated: "He is so manysided, so clear in his views, so judicious and knows so well how to deal with all classes of men. His whole being is wrapped up in general education, and he is the best lecturer or speaker on the subject in all the South." In 1881 Curry received the appointment. He later became special agent for a similar educational endowment, the Slater Fund.

His supreme goal, Curry stated, was to "preach a crusade against ignorance." He practiced as well as preached, for he was the inspiration behind the establishment of nor-

mal schools in 12 Southern states; he was the chief organizer of elementary schools in a number of major cities; and he constantly prodded state legislatures to create more and better rural schools. His 40 reports and 10 addresses on education at this time dominated the subject. Two historians, Thomas D. Clark and Albert D. Kirwan, wrote: ''Scarcely a major educational advance was to be made in the South between 1881 and 1902 that was not influenced in some way by J. L. M. Curry; in fact his name became synonymous with public education.''

In his last years Curry served as special minister to Spain, president of the Board of Foreign Missions of the Southern Baptist Convention, and president of the Southern Historical Association. He died on Feb. 12, 1903, in Asheville, N.C., and is buried in Richmond, Va. His statue is one of two memorials placed by Alabama in the U.S. Capitol's ''Hall of Statuary.''

Curry's writings included *Constitutional Government in Spain* (1889), *William Ewart Gladstone* (1891), *The Southern States of the American Union* (1895), *The Civil History of the Government of the Confederate States* (1901), and a number of religious tracts.

## Further Reading

The best work on Curry is Jessie P. Rice, *J. L. M. Curry: Southerner, Statesman and Educator* (1949). An older study, still reliable and based in great part on Curry's writings, is Edwin A. Alderman and Armistead C. Gordon, *J. L. M. Curry: A Biography* (1911). Curry's *Civil History of the Government of*

*the Confederate States* (1901) contains many personal reminiscences. □

# Andrew Gregg Curtin

**The American politician Andrew Gregg Curtin (1815-1894) was the influential governor of Pennsylvania during the Civil War and one of Abraham Lincoln's most powerful supporters.**

Andrew Gregg Curtin's father was an Irish immigrant who settled in Pennsylvania in 1793 and became one of the first manufacturers of iron in that state. Curtin was born on April 23, 1815, at Bellefonte in Center County. Following an excellent tutorial education, he read law and was admitted to the bar in 1839. He promptly formed a partnership with John Blanchard, later a member of Congress. From the beginning, Curtin was a success. Magnetic, honest, and popular, he possessed a congenial manner, ready wit, and extraordinary power of speech.

Curtin entered Pennsylvania politics at the age of 25. As a Whig, he campaigned actively on behalf of the presidential candidacies of William Henry Harrison, Henry Clay, Zachary Taylor, and Winfield Scott. In 1854 he declined the nomination for governor and threw his support to the successful candidacy of James Pollock, who repaid Curtin with the high post of secretary of the commonwealth. Curtin's most notable achievement in that position was in fostering the cause of public education.

In 1860 Curtin was instrumental in securing the Republican presidential nomination for Abraham Lincoln. He himself agreed to run for governor against strong Democratic opposition. He won the election by a wide margin, and his victory was instrumental in swinging Pennsylvania to Lincoln in the national election a month later.

An ardent unionist, Curtin had an untarnished record as Pennsylvania's Civil War governor. He aroused such early and enthusiastic support for the North that five companies of Pennsylvania troops were the first soldiers to arrive in Washington for the capital's defense. When the state raised double its initial quota of 14,000 volunteers, Curtin organized the extra force into the Pennsylvania Reserve Corps. Throughout the war Curtin was ''ceaseless in his devotion to the wants and needs'' of Pennsylvania soldiers. He ensured that his regiments had the most up-to-date arms and equipment; he went to unparalleled lengths to care for the wounded; and he fathered a law providing for the education of war orphans in the state. These and similar endeavors earned him the sobriquet ''Soldier's Friend.''

Following a second term as governor, Curtin in 1869 accepted the ambassadorship to Russia. He returned to America in 1872 and supported the presidential candidacy of Horace Greeley, an action which alienated leading Republicans. Curtin then joined the Democratic party. Defeated in an 1878 bid for Congress, he ran again in 1880 and won the first of three consecutive terms in the national

legislature. Thereafter he retired to his mountain home, where he died Oct. 7, 1894.

## Further Reading

Curtin's messages and proclamations as governor of Pennsylvania were published by the state. No adequate biography of him exists. William H. Egle edited a series of laudatory sketches *Andrew Gregg Curtin: His Life and Services* (1895). For an analysis of Curtin's Civil War career see William B. Hesseltine, *Lincoln and the War Governors* (1948). □

# John Joseph Curtin

**John Joseph Curtin (1885-1945) was an Australian political leader who rose from trade union official and journalist to prime minister. His forthright approach to Australia's wartime difficulties and his rousing leadership gained him his countrymen's respect.**

John Curtin was born in Creswick, Victoria, on Jan. 8, 1885. He attended public schools and at the age of 13 took a job in a Melbourne printery while continuing his studies. The oratory of Tom Mann, Britain's "new unionism" figure, deeply influenced Curtin during Mann's Australian sojourn from 1902 to 1908.

Attending the Labour party's "college" for speakers and running unsuccessfully for a parliamentary seat, Curtin gained skill in public speaking and insight into campaign methods. From 1911 he was a union secretary, and in 1916 he also became secretary of the Anti-Conscription League, which opposed the plans of Prime Minister William Morris Hughes to make overseas service compulsory. Charged with failure to enlist for military service, Curtin was set free when the proclamation under which he had been detained was withdrawn. Separate proceedings against him on a sedition charge were dropped later.

In 1916 Curtin moved to Perth to become editor of the *Westralian Worker*. Between 1918 and 1934 he was elected several, but not consecutive, times to the House of Representatives, and he was Australian delegate to the International Labor Conference in Geneva in 1924.

By 1934 Curtin was stressing the dangers of impending war, and he urged greater defense preparedness while others in his party were speaking of disarmament. He also demonstrated a grasp of financial and economic issues. Elected as Labour's parliamentary leader in 1935, Curtin showed skill in healing a serious schism which had been weakening the party in New South Wales.

## Wartime Leader

In 1939 Curtin refused the invitation of the Liberal prime minister Robert Gordon Menzies to include Labour in an all-party wartime administration. Instead, in 1940, Curtin joined the interparty Advisory War Council and awaited a situation favorable for a Labour government. It came in September 1941, when two uncommitted members pledged their support, giving him a slim majority in the House.

After Pearl Harbor, with Australia directly threatened, Curtin called for an all-out war effort built around United States help. He quickly instituted a succession of measures designed to eliminate all activities absorbing manpower and resources that might be diverted to the war effort. Early in 1942 he successfully urged the U.S. government to send Gen. Douglas MacArthur to Australia as commander of a combined force capable of defending the country and ultimately converting it into a base for a northward drive against the Japanese. At the same time Curtin refused the British Cabinet's request to divert Australian ground forces—then returning from the Middle East—for the reinforcement of the Burma front, deciding that they should return to Australia to stave off any invasion. By his vigorous leadership Curtin gained national acceptance for his austerity measures designed to intensify all phases of the war effort.

Labour won the 1943 elections with majorities in both House and Senate. As the danger of invasion receded, Curtin decided to remove the long-standing ban on use of military conscripts beyond Australian territory. Labour had traditionally held firmly to the rule against overseas service for conscripts, but Curtin persuaded the party to update the law so that Australian land forces could accompany U.S. forces and Australian air and naval units in the northward drive.

## Preparations for the Postwar Era

Curtin constantly expressed his belief that the sacrifices being asked of fighting men should be honored by the creation of a postwar world with greater social Justice and enhanced opportunity for the individual, and a world in which causes of war were eliminated. As well as introducing progressive legislation to pave the way for general reconstruction and national advancement after the war, he began immediately to plan for the reintegration of armed services personnel into civilian life when peace was restored, and he mapped arrangements for a long-range immigration program. The government adopted full employment as a basic objective and, in international discussions on postwar economic planning, stressed this concept as the centerpiece of national policies.

In 1944 Curtin called for greater awareness of the regional significance of Australia and New Zealand—by now linked in the "Anzac" pact, which he and his external affairs minister, Dr. Herbert Vere Evatt, had been instrumental in developing. Curtin also gave the fullest support to the creation of the United Nations, sending a large and influential Australian delegation to the formulative meeting in San Francisco in June 1945, and encouraged the U.S. government to maintain an active role in the security of the Pacific. He died in Canberra on July 1, 1945.

## Further Reading

A useful biography of Curtin is Alan Chester, *John Curtin* (1943). Curtin's role in Labour party affairs is discussed in Louise Overacker, *The Australian Party System* (1952), and Leslie Finlay Crisp, *The Australian Federal Labour Party: 1901-1951* (1955). Comprehensive coverage of Australia's war role is contained in *Australia in the War of 1939-1945,* Series I to V (22 vols., 1952—). An economic analysis of Curtin's administration is E. Ronald Walker, *The Australian Economy in War and Reconstruction* (1947). The planning for a postwar immigration flow is outlined in Arthur A. Calwell, *How Many Australians Tomorrow?* (1945). The Curtin government's approach to international affairs is indicated in H. V. Evatt, *Foreign Policy of Australia: Speeches* (1945). □

# Benjamin Robbins Curtis

**Benjamin Robbins Curtis (1809-1874) was one of the most able lawyers on the U.S. Supreme Court in the 19th century.**

B enjamin Robbins Curtis was born into an old New England family in Watertown, Mass., on Nov. 4, 1809. He graduated second in his class at Harvard in 1829, then took a degree from Harvard Law School. In 1833 he married Eliza Maria Woodward, with whom he had five children. When she died in 1844, he married again and had three more children.

Through the influence of a prominent uncle, Curtis became a partner in a Boston law firm in 1834, remaining until 1851 and becoming one of the leading commercial lawyers in the United States. He was elected to the Massachusetts General Court in 1849 and 1851 and was largely responsible for the Massachusetts Practice Act of 1851, which eliminated many legal abuses. When what was then the New England seat on the U.S. Supreme Court became vacant in 1851, President Millard Fillmore appointed Curtis.

In his first term Curtis's ability to cut to the heart of a problem led to establishing a commonsense interpretation of the commerce clause in *Cooley v. Board of Wardens,* which allowed states to regulate local commercial matters while not diminishing Congress's power. Another precedent-setting case enabled administrative officers to determine and collect debts without a court order. He was also highly effective in conference, "educating" by persuasion his fellow justices.

Riding the New England circuit, Curtis continued to show concern for law and order and preservation of the Union. Though labeled a "slave-catcher judge" because of his strict enforcement of the Fugitive Slave Act, he dissented on the precedent-setting Dred Scott case (1852) and wrote a long minority opinion demonstrating that African Americans were U.S. citizens in 1787, that residence in free territory made a man free, and that Congress had complete authority to legislate for the territories, including prohibiting slavery. Misunderstandings with Chief Justice Roger B. Taney over dissemination of these opinions were partly responsible for Curtis's resignation from the Court.

Returning to a lucrative private practice, Curtis argued several important cases before the U.S. Supreme Court. When his second wife died in 1860, he married again. He supported the North in the Civil War but raised important questions about presidential power in a pamphlet critical of Abraham Lincoln's Emancipation Proclamation and of suspension of the writ of habeas corpus. He opposed Lincoln's reelection in 1864. When President Andrew Johnson was impeached, Curtis and William M. Evarts defended him before the Senate.

In 1874 Curtis suffered a brain hemorrhage and died at Newport, R.I., on September 15. His course of lectures at Harvard for 1872-1873, *Jurisdiction, Practice and Peculiar Jurisprudence of the Courts of the United States,* was published in 1880.

## Further Reading

There is no modern biography of Curtis. A eulogistic memoir by his brother and a volume of his writings edited by his son were published as *A Memoir of Benjamin Robbins Curtis, L.L.D., with Some of His Professional and Miscellaneous Writings* (2 vols., 1879; repr. 1969). Vincent C. Hopkins, *Dred Scott's Case* (1951), details Curtis's role in that case. His Court career appears in Leo Pfeffer, *This Honorable Court: A History of the United States Supreme Court* (1965). □

# George William Curtis

**American writer, orator, and, especially, civil service reformer, George William Curtis (1824-1892)**

was a patrician whose ideals and causes are blurred in historical retrospect by a personal elitism that bordered on priggishness and was out of step even in his own time.

George William Curtis was born into a very old New England family in Providence, R.I. After attending school in Massachusetts, he spent several years in New York City, where he worked as a clerk. Already a disciple of Ralph Waldo Emerson, Curtis lived for 2 years at the transcendentalist utopian colony, Brook Farm. He returned to New York City, then in 1846 left on the grand tour of Europe fashionable for well-to-do New Englanders. However, he added to this an unusual side trip to the Near East and wrote two books on his impressions of Egypt and Syria.

Curtis also published a satire of New York City life but in 1856 virtually abandoned "high" literature for journalism and politics. Curtis's New England sense of propriety showed clearly when, that same year, he assumed the debts run up by a magazine of which he was an editor, debts for which he was not legally liable. This sense of duty and rectitude characterized his whole career, as editor of *Harper's Weekly* during the Civil War and as a professional reformer.

Most of the well-known reforms of the century attracted Curtis. He was an abolitionist and a spokesman for woman's suffrage, and he spoke frequently on the need for reconciliation between industrial capitalists and laborers according to his concept of social justice. But he was best known and most active as an advocate of civil service reform in an age when politics seemed to mean little more than a scuffle for spoils.

Curtis was the classic "Mugwump," the name given to those Republicans who bolted the party in 1884 because its candidate, James G. Blaine, had some financial irregularities in his career. Curtis was genteel, hobnobbing with the prominent literati of his day, and more than a little condescending in his political dealings. In 1877, for example, the leading New York Republican spoilsman, Roscoe Conkling, denounced Curtis and other "snivel service" reformers in a vitriolic speech before the New York State Republican Convention. "It was the saddest sight I ever knew," Curtis noted in the patronizing tone that characterized much of his writing, "that man glaring at me in a fury of hate, and storming out his foolish blackguardism. I was all pity. I had not thought him great, but I had not suspected how small he was."

Curtis's personal life was exemplary and refined. To his admirers, of whom there were many, he was remembered— as one eulogist put it—as the "firm and sweet-souled leader of the public conscience." He died on Aug. 31, 1892.

## Further Reading

There is no recently published biography of Curtis. All standard accounts of the "gilded age" discuss his important role in the civil service reform movement, for example, Matthew Joseph-

son, *The Politicos, 1865-1896* (1938), and H. Wayne Morgan, *From Hayes to McKinley* (1969). □

# Glenn Hammond Curtiss

**The American aviation pioneer Glenn Hammond Curtiss (1878-1930) developed the first successful seaplane and manufactured the famous World War I Jenny training plane.**

Glenn Curtiss was born in Hammondsport, N.Y. After finishing grade school, he moved to Rochester, working for the telegraph company and later for the Kodak Company. But having acquired a taste for mechanics and a passion for speed, he returned to Hammondsport and opened a bicycle shop. He raced bicycles and won many prizes locally and statewide. When motorcycles became available, he began to race them as well, and in 1902 he started to make and sell first the motors, then the entire motorcycles, at his shop. He became famous as a racer and in 1906, riding an eight-cylinder cycle of his own construction, set a speed record of 137 miles per hour, which stood for 20 years.

After the dirigible balloonist Thomas Scott Baldwin ordered an engine for one of his balloons from Curtiss, Curtiss concentrated on the problems of flight. A balloon powered by a Curtiss engine won a major race at the St. Louis International Exposition in 1904. Baldwin moved to Hammondsport, and the two men manufactured the first dirigible adopted by the U.S. Army.

The successful flight of the Wright brothers in 1903 had demonstrated the potential of heavier-than-air craft, and Curtiss now turned in this direction. Alexander Graham Bell, the inventor of the telephone, for some years had been an enthusiastic supporter of airplane development, and in 1907 established the Aerial Experiment Association at Hammondsport, placing Curtiss in charge of experiments. A year later Curtiss won the *Scientific American* trophy flying his famous *June Bug*. During the next several years he won many air races in the United States and abroad. He barnstormed across the country, popularizing the idea of flying, and also established a number of flying schools, which benefited from the publicity his racing victories brought to him.

In 1908 Curtiss began to work on the problems of seaplanes and 3 years later successfully took off from, and landed again on, the water off San Diego, Calif. In 1912 he developed his famous flying boat; and in 1919 his NC4, developed for the U.S. Navy, became the first airplane to cross the Atlantic Ocean.

After the outbreak of World War I Curtiss moved his manufacturing facilities to Buffalo and built, by 1919, more than 5,000 Jennies. Although he had become wealthy, these years were marred by a court fight with the Wright brothers over the invention of the aileron, a wing device to maintain

igh offices in the British political and imperial structure at the end of the 19th century and the beginning of the 20th century were generally held by men chosen on the basis of highly restrictive family and educational connections. George Curzon was the epitome of this system, and it was useful to his political and social ambitions before World War I. Afterward, however, he was hurt by his connection with it and by his inconsistent actions that bordered on opportunism in his late drive for government leadership.

Curzon was born on Jan. 11, 1859, at Kedleston Hall, Derbyshire. His early life was dominated by the influence of a governess and a schoolmaster who were both strict disciplinarians; those years were not very happy ones for him, but he did exceptionally well at school. He was a leader and an outstanding student at Eton from 1872 to 1878 and at Balliol College, Oxford, from 1878 to 1882, although he was disappointed when he missed getting every honor. With an aristocratic appearance and a bearing that commanded attention, he put unrestrained energy into his work and was not satisfied unless he was in the center of every situation.

In the 3 years after leaving Oxford, Curzon traveled extensively in the Mediterranean world and used the knowledge he acquired to write articles on important issues. In 1885 Lord Salisbury, the prime minister, chose him as his assistant private secretary. Curzon lost his first election that year, but he won a seat the next year in the House of Commons. From 1887 to 1894 he continued to travel widely, choosing Asia as his particular interest and writing

vertical stability, which Curtiss had developed for Bell's association.

After the war Curtiss worked on automobiles and other devices as well as airplanes and was active in the Curtiss-Wright Corporation, but his real period of pioneering in aviation had ended by 1920.

## Further Reading

A standard biography of Curtiss is Alden Hatch, *Glenn Curtiss: Pioneer of Naval Aviation* (1942). His exploits are placed in a larger context in the contemporary account of Howard Mingos, *The Birth of an Industry* (1930), and in Welman A. Shrader, *Fifty Years of Flight: A Chronicle of the Aviation Industry in America, 1903-1953* (1953). The years after World War I are well covered by John B. Rae, *Climb to Greatness: The American Aircraft Industry, 1920-1960* (1968). □

# George Nathaniel Curzon

**The English statesman George Nathaniel Curzon, 1st Marquess Curzon of Kedleston (1859-1925), served as viceroy of India and as a member of several Cabinets.**

three outstanding books on Asian affairs: *Russia in Central Asia* (1889), *Persia and the Persian Question* (1892), and *Problems of the Far East* (1894).

Curzon began his government service in 1891 as undersecretary in the India office in Salisbury's government. The government fell from power in 1892, but when the Conservatives came in again in 1895, Curzon was named parliamentary undersecretary in the Foreign Office, directly under Salisbury, who was both prime minister and foreign secretary. Curzon was the principal government spokesman on foreign affairs in the House of Commons.

## Viceroy of India

Curzon was chosen viceroy of India in 1898. This position was perfectly suited to his desire for public attention, since he was in charge of the entire British administration of the Indian empire. He stayed in India for 7 years, ruling firmly in matters of domestic policy and making strong appeals in matters of foreign policy. In the latter, Curzon was particularly involved in the problem of defense along India's frontiers and in those areas of possible danger from Russian expansion and competition—Persia, Afghanistan, and Tibet.

Military matters were Curzon's undoing. He and Lord Kitchener, the commander in chief of the Indian army after 1902, became locked in a dispute over military organization; the government in England, then under Prime Minister Arthur Balfour, chose to sacrifice Curzon in favor of Kitchener, who was a more popular figure. Curzon returned to Britain in late 1905, out of favor with his own Conservative party leadership and, since the Liberals were coming into power, with no opportunity of remaking his reputation in another government assignment.

## War Cabinet and Foreign Office

Curzon was out of politics except as a member of the House of Lords, until he was included in the wartime coalition government formed in May 1915. When David Lloyd George became prime minister in December 1916, Curzon was brought into the five-man War Cabinet, and he participated in all the major decisions of the latter part of World War I. He was given the task of running the Foreign Office through most of 1919, while Lloyd George and the foreign secretary, Lord Balfour, were at the Paris peace conference, and in late 1919 he was named as Balfour's successor in the Foreign Office.

Curzon's service in the War Cabinet and as foreign secretary was the second peak in his career. But his role in the Foreign Office in the postwar era was not so satisfactory to Curzon as it would have been in an earlier era. British government was changing, and concentration of authority in the prime minister's hands had increased tremendously under Lloyd George's personal control and the emergency of wartime government. Curzon was a leading candidate for prime minister in May 1923; he was disappointed at the last moment, however, and Stanley Baldwin was chosen instead. Curzon was dismayed, but he stayed on to serve under Baldwin in the same post until the government fell in

January 1924. Curzon's public service ended then, and he died on March 20, 1925.

## Further Reading

The most complete work on Curzon is the Earl of Ronaldshay, *The Life of Lord Curzon* (3 vols., 1928). Two studies which are old but still worthwhile are Harold Nicolson, *Curzon, the Last Phase, 1919-1925: A Study in Post-war Diplomacy* (1934), and Arthur Anthony Baumann's sketch in Humbert Wolfe, ed., *Personalities: A Selection from the Writings of A. A. Baumann* (1936). Two other books essential to a full understanding of Curzon as a man are Leonard Mosley, *The Glorious Fault: The Life of Lord Curzon* (1960; published in England as *Curzon: The End of an Epoch*), and Kenneth Rose, *Superior Person* (1969). Michael Edwardes, *High Noon of Empire: India under Curzon* (1965), deals with India while Curzon was viceroy. Recommended for general historical background are R. C. K. Ensor, *England, 1870-1914* (1936); Gordon A. Craig and Felix Gilbert, eds., *The Diplomats, 1919-1939* (1953); *The Cambridge History of the British Empire,* vol. 3: E. A. Benians and others, eds., *The Empire-Commonwealth, 1870-1919* (1959); and A. J. P. Taylor, *English History, 1914-1945* (1965).

## Additional Sources

Curzon, George Nathaniel Curzon, Marquis of, 1859-1925, *A viceroy's India: leaves from Lord Curzon's note-book,* London: Sidgwick & Jackson, 1984.

Gilmour, David, *Curzon,* London: J. Murray, 1994 (1995 printing).

Goradia, Nayana, *Lord Curzon: the last of the British Moghuls,* Delhi; New York: Oxford University Press, 1993.

Parker, James G., *Lord Curzon, 1859-1925: a bibliography,* New York: Greenwood Press, 1991.

Rose, Kenneth, *Curzon, a most superior person: a biography,* London: Papermac, 1985. □

# Nicholas of Cusa

**The German prelate and humanist Nicholas of Cusa (1401-1464) was active in conciliating various schisms in the 15th-century Church and was a strong advocate of Church unity.**

T he son of a fairly prosperous boat owner and landholder, Nicholas was born in Cusa on the Moselle River. His early education was at Deventer under the Brothers of the Common Life, and he may have known Thomas à Kempis there. His university studies began at Heidelberg and continued at Padua, where he received a doctorate in canon law in 1423. After returning to his native Rhineland, he studied philosophy and theology at Cologne, where he also practiced law. In February 1432 he went to the Council of Basel.

The Council of Basel (1431-1449) had as its main subject the problem of Church unity and as its main task the avoidance of any repetitions of the Great Schism, which had recently split the Church. One suggested solution was the establishment of a supreme general council to oversee the papacy. At the beginning of his attendance at the council, Nicholas supported this plan (known as the conciliar movement). During the period from 1432 to 1434, Nicholas worked on, and submitted to the council, his famous political treatise, *De concordantia Catholica,* which deals with the problem of the respective roles of councils and popes in the government of the Church. This treatise supported the conciliar viewpoint of supremacy of the councils, but Nicholas eventually became disillusioned by the ineffectual committees working at the council and shifted his view to one of papal supremacy. In 1437 he began his services to Pope Eugene IV and his successors, as papal legate on various missions in Germany, as conciliator in the disputes between the Eastern and the Roman Churches, and as promoter of a crusade against the Turks.

In 1440 Nicholas completed his best-known work, *De docta ignorantia (Of Learned Ignorance).* In it he shows himself as an early skeptic, holding that true wisdom lies in a clear awareness of the limitations of human knowledge. After 10 years in the service of Pope Eugene IV, Nicholas was made a cardinal by the dying pope, an appointment confirmed in 1448 by Pope Nicholas V. In 1450 he was appointed bishop of Brixen (Bressanone) in the Tirol, where he had the difficult task of reforming the churches and monasteries of the diocese, then under the strong secular influence of Archduke Sigismund of Hapsburg. Nicholas left the Tirol in 1458 to serve his friend Aeneas Sylvius Piccolomini, the new Pope Pius II. Pius's proposals for papal reform reflect Cusa's own ideas concerning the role of the papacy.

Nicholas spent the remainder of his life in his reforming work in the churches of Bohemia. He died at Todi in Italy on Aug. 11, 1464.

## Further Reading

An introduction to Nicholas's life and thought and English translations of several of his works are in *Unity and Reform: Selected Writings of Nicholas of Cusa,* edited by John Patrick Dolan (1962). There is no definitive biography in English, but Henry Bett, *Nicholas of Cusa* (1932), is a standard source. Paul E. Sigmund, *Nicholas of Cusa and Medieval Political Thought* (1963), is the best modern study in English. □

# Harvey Williams Cushing

**The American neurosurgeon Harvey Williams Cushing (1869-1939) developed operative techniques that made brain surgery feasible.**

Harvey Cushing was born on April 8, 1869, in Cleveland, Ohio. He graduated from Yale University in 1891 and received a medical degree in 1895 from Harvard Medical School. After a year's internship at Massachusetts General Hospital he went to Johns Hopkins, where he was William Halsted's resident in surgery. From Halsted he learned meticulous surgical technique.

During a trip to Europe in 1900 Cushing worked with some of Europe's leading surgeons and physiologists, including Charles Scott Sherrington, Theodore Kocher, and Hugo Kronecker. They directed his attention to neurosurgery, to which he devoted the rest of his life. Shortly after his return to Johns Hopkins he was made associate professor of surgery. In 1902 he married Katharine Crowell.

In 1907 Cushing began studies of the pituitary gland. He unraveled many of the disorders affecting the gland and showed that a surgical approach to the pituitary was possible. In 1912 *The Pituitary Body and Its Disorders* was published. In that same year he accepted the Moseley professorship of surgery at Harvard and an appointment as surgeon in chief at Peter Bent Brigham Hospital in Boston. During World War I he served in France as director of Base Hospital No. 5. His wartime experiences formed the basis of a book, *From a Surgeon's Journal* (1936). Cushing's active affiliation with Harvard continued until 1932, when he was named professor emeritus. The following year he accepted the Sterling professorship of neurology at Yale.

Throughout his career Cushing studied brain tumors and published many important books on the subject, including: *Tumours of the Nervus Acusticus and the Syndrome of the Cerebellopontile* (1917); *A Classification of the Tumours of the Glioma* (1926), with P. Bailey; *Tumours Arising from the Blood Vessels of the Brain: Angiomatous Malformations and Hemangioblastomas* (1928), with Bailey; *Intracranial Tumours* (1932); and *Meningiomas: Their Classification, Regional Behavior, Life History, and Surgical End Results* (1938). He published numerous historical es-

says, and his biography of Sir William Osler (1925) received the Pulitzer Prize in 1926.

Cushing's use of local anesthesia in brain surgery was an outstanding achievement, as were his many special surgical techniques. In 1911 he introduced special sutures to control the severe bleeding that accompanies brain surgery and often made it impossible.

In 1937 Cushing accepted a position as director of studies in the history of medicine at Yale. He guided the development of a historical library to which he left his own excellent collection of historical books. He was especially interested in Andreas Vesalius, the 16th-century anatomist, and was at work on the *Bio-Bibliography of Vesalius* at the time of his death, on Oct. 7, 1939. The work was completed by his friends and published in 1943.

## Further Reading

The definitive biography of Cushing is John F. Fulton, *Harvey Cushing* (1946). A shorter biography for the general reader is Elizabeth Harriet Thomson, *Harvey Cushing: Surgeon, Author, Artist* (1950). On the occasion of Cushing's seventieth birthday, in 1939, *A Bibliography of the Writings of Harvey Cushing* was published by the Harvey Cushing Society.

## Additional Sources

Fulton, John F. (John Farquhar), *Harvey Cushing, a biography,* New York: Arno Press, 1980, 1946. □

# Charlotte Cushman

**The actress Charlotte Cushman (1816-1876) was the first great American-born tragedienne, in a career spanning 4 decades.**

Charlotte Cushman, who was descended from one of the original Pilgrim families, was born in Boston in 1816. Faced with poverty in her late teens, she determined to become an opera singer, a career for which her remarkable voice—a full contralto and almost full soprano—well suited her. But while performing in New Orleans, she strained her voice by reaching too high, and at the age of 19 her singing career ended.

Undaunted, Cushman decided to become an actress. Her debut as Lady Macbeth in New Orleans in 1835 began a career that lasted for 40 years and encompassed almost 200 roles. After her first success Cushman joined New York theater companies, where at least two plays were performed each evening and the bill was changed each day. Here she served a diligent apprenticeship; yet, after 8 years, she was still in "miserable, frightful uncertainty" about her career.

Then in 1843, William Macready, the great English actor, played Macbeth to her Lady Macbeth. He was so impressed by Cushman's undisciplined talent that he urged her to go to London for training. In appreciation for this fortuitous advice, she later said she had "groped in darkness until she met Mr. Macready and learned his method." By

1845 she was hailed in London as an actress with the "godlike gift" of genius. Three years later she played a command performance before Queen Victoria as Katherine in *Henry VIII.*

When Cushman returned to the United States in 1849, she found herself not only a celebrated actress but a symbol of the achievement of American culture. She sustained her reputation as the greatest American tragedienne until her retirement in 1875.

Her talent lay in portraying women of great passion and pathos; in such roles her muscular frame and powerful yet controlled voice could overwhelm and sometimes frighten the audience. The mysterious old gypsy Meg Merrilies in *Guy Mannering* was her most famous role, followed by Lady Macbeth, Queen Katherine, and Nancy in the dramatization of *Oliver Twist.* So strong was her presence that she won praise in men's roles, playing Romeo, Cardinal Wolsey, and Hamlet.

As early as 1852 Cushman made the first of many farewell appearances. She knew that she was suffering from cancer; the disease plagued her for the next 24 years and was finally the indirect cause of her death from pneumonia in Boston in 1876. Yet until the end she continued to act, and when her strength failed, she gave dramatic readings. Both on and off the stage she was a lady of dignity, passion, and majesty.

## Further Reading

The most intimate portrait of Charlotte Cushman was done by her friend Emma Stebbins, *Charlotte Cushman, Her Letters and Memories of Her Life* (1878). It is extremely sympathetic and somewhat sentimental but provides evidence of Cushman's strength and sensitivity in private and public life. William Winters includes private recollections and accounts of her performances in *Other Days* (1908) and *The Wallet of Time,* vol. 1 (1913). Two excellent if brief analyses of Cushman's talent and place appear in Lloyd Morris, *Curtain Time* (1953), and Garff Wilson, *A History of American Acting* (1966). □

# George Armstrong Custer

**No figure of the Indian wars in America so typifies that era as George Armstrong Custer (1839-1876). He is known universally for the massacre that bears his name and for the blundering that brought it about.**

George Custer was born in New Rumley, Harrison County, Ohio, on Dec. 5, 1839. His ambition from youth was to be a soldier, and he secured an appointment to West Point in 1857. A poor, mischievous student, he graduated at the bottom of his class in 1861, but was commissioned a second lieutenant in the 2d Cavalry.

The Civil War was in progress, and Custer fought on the Union side. For gallant conduct at the engagement at Aldie on June 16, 1863, he was breveted a brigadier general and given command of a brigade from Michigan. By the end of the war, at the age of only 25, he had been promoted to brevet major general. During the war he had married his childhood sweetheart, Elizabeth Bacon.

The conflict over, Custer reverted to his permanent rank of captain in the 5th Cavalry but soon was promoted to lieutenant colonel of the 7th Cavalry; he would actively hold this command until his death. In 1867 he was charged with absence from duty and suspended for a year but was reinstated by Gen. Philip H. Sheridan in 1868. On November 27 of that year he achieved a startling victory over Chief Black Kettle and the Cheyenne Indians at the battle of the Washita. His regiment was then fragmented, and he spent 2 years in Kentucky. In 1873 the regiment was reunited in the Dakota Territory. He was described at this time as tall, slender, energetic, and dashing, with blue eyes and long golden hair and mustache. At the post he wore velveteen uniforms decorated with gold braid, but in the field he affected buckskins. He rarely drank or used tobacco and spent his spare hours reading military history and studying tactics.

Rumors of gold in the Black Hills led to a government expedition in 1874, which Custer commanded. Scientists from the Smithsonian Institution confirmed the rumors, and the swarm of gold seekers to the area caused the Sioux Indians to go on the attack. Custer was to lead the campaign against the Sioux and Cheyenne in early 1876, but instead he was summoned to Washington to testify before a congressional committee investigating fraud in the Indian Bureau. Custer's testimony, unfavorable to Secretary of War W. W. Belknap, so angered President Grant that he removed Custer from command of the expedition to punish the Native Americans. Public outcry at the President's act, along with the request of Gen. Alfred Terry that Custer accompany the campaign, caused Grant to restore Custer to command of the 7th Cavalry, which then took the field.

On the Yellowstone River, Terry's scouts reported Indians in the vicinity, and Custer was sent to investigate, with orders to exercise caution. On the morning of June 25, 1876, he came upon a village later estimated to have contained from 2,500 to 4,000 Sioux and Cheyenne warriors under Chief Crazy Horse. Splitting his command into three parts, Custer personally led 264 men into battle. His force was surrounded on the hill that now bears his name, overlooking the valley of the Little Bighorn River. He and all the men under his personal command were massacred there, while Maj. Marcus Reno and Capt. Frederick Benteen took refuge on the bluffs overlooking the river and escaped.

The Custer massacre electrified the nation, although it had little effect on the outcome of the Sioux wars. Reno and Benteen were accused of cowardice by admirers of Custer, while Custer's detractors bemoaned the death of the troops under his command due to his rash order to charge so superior a Native American force. This controversy continues, for Custer was a man so paradoxical that he could fight corruption in the Indian Bureau to the disservice of his own carrier, yet also order a charge to kill Native Americans.

## Further Reading

So many books have been written about Custer that no one book can be singled out as best. Custer's autobiography, *My Life on the Plains: or, Personal Experiences with Indians* (1874), gives insights into his character, as do the books by his wife, Elizabeth Bacon Custer, *Boots and Saddle: or, Life in Dakota with General Custer* (1885) and *Tenting on the Plains: or, General Custer in Kansas and Texas* (1887). See also Marguerite Merington, ed., *The Custer Story: The Life and Intimate Letters of George A. Custer and His Wife Elizabeth* (1950). □

# Manasseh Cutler

**American clergyman, scientist, and politician Manasseh Cutler (1742-1823) was a member of the Ohio Company of Associates and coauthor of the Northwest Ordinance of 1787.**

M anasseh Cutler, the third child and eldest son of Hezekiah and Susanna Cutler, was born on May 13, 1742, in Killingly, Conn. He grew to manhood on his parents' farm. After graduating from Yale in 1765, he taught school in Dedham, Mass. The following year he married Mary Balch, and the couple moved to Martha's Vineyard, where Cutler ran a store. Cutler studied law, and by 1767 he was practicing in the Court of Common Pleas. The following year he returned to Yale to receive a master of arts degree and then began his study for the ministry. In September 1771 he was ordained and installed as pastor in the Congregational Church at Ipswich (later Hamilton), Mass.

Cutler's first church was to be his lifelong parish, although he frequently left Ipswich for business or for political activity. During the early years of the Revolutionary War he served as a chaplain.

Because of continuing financial difficulties, Cutler turned to studying medicine under the tutelage of a member of his congregation, and by 1779 he began practice. From medicine he turned to a study of the physical and biological sciences and began working with such varied instruments as sextants, telescopes, and microscopes, in addition to experimenting with an "electrical machine" and carrying out a widespread program of smallpox vaccination.

Among his widely varied scientific activities, botany became Cutler's particular interest. He examined and classified at least 350 species of plants found in New England, and during the 1780s he published an article, "An Account of Some of the Vegetable Productions Naturally Growing in This Part of America." In recognition of his untiring scientific activity, Cutler received membership in the American Academy of Arts and Sciences, the American Philosophical Society, the Philadelphia Linnaean Society, and the American Antiquarian Society. Yale gave him an honorary degree in 1789.

On March 1, 1786, Cutler joined a group of New England speculators who formed the Ohio Company of Associates. Hoping to take advantage of the Federal government's desperate need for funds, the company proposed buying Federal land with depreciated government securities issued during the Revolutionary War. The company sent Cutler to negotiate, and he suggested that Congress table its plan to sell land in small amounts to individual citizens and, instead, sell a vast tract at the confluence of the Muskingum and Ohio rivers to his company.

Finally, during July 1787, the secretary of the Board of Treasury, whose office handled land sales, intimated that Congress would accept Cutler's plan if members of the government could share in the profits. The result was a complex scheme under which the Ohio Company got its 1,000,000 acres of land, and a second group, the Scioto Company, got an option on several million acres more. On July 27, 1787, the Board of Treasury agreed to sell the land to the Ohio Company of Associates at a true cost of about 8 cents an acre.

Next, Cutler reminded Congress that few citizens would migrate to the new territory until Congress provided a system of orderly government there. This was no new idea. Congress had argued about the question for years. But Cutler's demand for a workable plan, coupled with the expectations of profits from increasing land sales, caused Congress to act. In early July 1787 Cutler helped to rewrite a proposal for establishing government in the West, and on July 13 the Ordinance of 1787, or the Northwest Ordinance, was adopted.

The ordinance established the territory northwest of the Ohio and provided for a series of steps through which the government of the region would move toward eventual statehood on an equal footing with the original 13 states. It created an American colonial system for the new territories and assured continuing political rights to citizens who wished to move to the frontier. For Cutler and the Ohio Company of Associates, the land sale and pattern for later government opened the area for settlement.

After visiting Ohio for a year, Cutler returned to Massachusetts, where he served a single term in the General Court and then represented his district for two terms in the U.S. House of Representatives. In 1804 he retired to private life. He continued his scientific activities and participated in the scholarly organizations to which he belonged. A tall, portly man with gracious manners, he was a striking figure in his black velvet suit, black knee stockings, and silver shoe buckles. Cutler died on July 28, 1823.

## Further Reading

There is no modern biography of Cutler, and historians have to depend on William P. and Julia P. Cutler, *The Life, Journals and Correspondence of Rev. Manasseh Cutler* (2 vols., 1888), for the basic factual information about his career. Cutler's activity in the Ohio Company may be traced in both the introduction and documents of Archer B. Hulbert, ed., *Ohio in the Time of the Confederation* (4 vols., 1918), and in Frazer E. Wilson, *Advancing the Ohio Frontier* (1953). Francis S. Philbrick, *The Rise of the West, 1754-1830* (1965), provides a balanced discussion of the era and its major developments. □

Soon after graduation, Cuvier became tutor to the D'Hericys family, Protestant nobles who lived in Normandy, with whom he remained until 1793. When his home district was absorbed into France that year, Cuvier became a French citizen. He served as secretary of Becaux-Cauchois until 1795 and then moved to Paris. He obtained a position as assistant to the professor of comparative anatomy at the Jardin des Plantes (later the National Museum of Natural History) and began his first course of lectures in comparative anatomy there in December. At the same time, he was elected a member of the anatomy and zoology section of the Institut de France. In 1800 Cuvier was appointed secretary for the physical sciences section of the Institute and professor of general natural history at the Collège de France.

From 1800 until his death Cuvier was very active both as a research scientist and as a scientific educationalist and administrator. Moreover, under successive French governments he held various offices of state and investigated and reported on state problems. These concerned not only science but also religion, as Cuvier remained a devout Lutheran throughout his life. In 1802 Napoleon appointed him inspector general of higher schools; later he was responsible for reorganizing education in Italy, the Netherlands, and other conquered territory beyond the borders of France. Also in 1802, he became professor of comparative anatomy at the Jardin des Plantes. The following year Cuvier was appointed one of the two permanent secretaries of the Académie des Sciences of the Institut de France. In 1807-1808

# Baron Georges Léopold Cuvier

**The French zoologist and biologist Baron Georges Léopold Cuvier (1769-1832) made significant contributions in the fields of paleontology, comparative anatomy, and taxonomy and was one of the chief spokesmen for science in postrevolutionary France.**

Georges Léopold Cuvier was born on Aug. 23, 1769, in Montbéliard, a small, French-speaking town in the duchy of Württemberg, where his father was commandant of the local artillery. Cuvier was christened Jean Léopold Nicolas Frédéric, but after the death of his elder brother, Georges, in 1769, he was known as Georges. His parents hoped that he would keep up the family tradition of one son from each generation training for the Lutheran ministry, but instead Cuvier attended the Académie Caroline in Stuttgart (1784-1788), studying commerce and economics, police and public administration, law, and chemistry, mineralogy, botany, and zoology. He was active in the school's natural-history society and studied privately under K. F. Kielmeyer, one of the early German *Naturphilosophes.*

he prepared a special report for Napoleon on the development of science since the French Revolution.

Cuvier married Anne Marie Coquet de Trazaille, a widow with four children, in 1804. Of their own four children, only one daughter survived infancy.

In the 15 years after his arrival in Paris, Cuvier was at his most active in scientific research. He published major works on animal classification, fossils, theoretical paleontology, natural history, and comparative anatomy. His later life was taken up more and more by administrative and state matters, so that although he continued to publish much scientific work it did not have the originality of his earlier publications.

Cuvier was appointed a councilor of the Napoleonic University of France in 1808. He was a member of the Council of State from 1813 until his death. In 1817 he became vice president of the Ministry of the Interior; the following year he was elected a member of the Académie Française. In 1820 he was made a baron. From 1821 to 1827 Cuvier was chancellor of the University of France. In 1822 he was appointed grand master of the Faculties of Protestant Theology in the University of Paris, and in 1826 he was made a grand officer of the Legion of Honor. In 1828 he became director of all non-Catholic churches in France. In 1831 Louis Philippe raised Cuvier to the peerage. He died on May 13, 1832.

In public life Cuvier was, above all, concerned for good order. His generally conservative attitudes were at least partly a response to the chaos and breakdown of social order which he had experienced in the years of the French Revolution. As a scientist who did not depend on his political activities for recognition or status, Cuvier was more concerned with the good working of the various institutions of French life than with party and personality politics. As an adviser to the state on education, he strongly opposed the influence of the Roman Catholic Church and particularly that of the Society of Jesus. He supported secular education and tried to see that it included a fair proportion of natural science.

## Contributions to Science

Cuvier's life spanned the period during which it became possible in France, for virtually the first time, to make a profession of science. He was not trained to be a scientist, as professional training in the sciences was virtually unknown when he went through college. He and his colleagues took part in setting up the first such courses in France.

Soon after Cuvier arrived in Paris in 1795, he took up the problem of the classification of animals and together with a colleague published a very important paper on the classification of mammals. Cuvier was concerned with the practical question of which features of an animal should be used to distinguish it from other species. Underlying the need for a practical system of classification was his search for a theoretical justification for the taxonomic system he advocated. Throughout his life he continued to be concerned with the problem of classification.

In 1798 Cuvier published an introductory textbook in natural history, *Tableau élémentaire de l'histoire naturelle des animaux,* which became the standard text for French colleges. He was also aware of the need for a comprehensive reference book and manual in zoology, and in 1817 he published the four-volume *Le Règne animal . . . ,* whose full title, "The Animal Kingdom, arranged according to structure, in order to form a basis for zoology, and as an introduction to comparative anatomy," well describes the functions he hoped it would serve. The work was revised and reissued in five volumes in 1829-1830; by then it had been translated into many languages and had become a standard zoological reference throughout the world.

Cuvier's lectures in comparative anatomy were collected and edited by two of his assistants and published in five volumes between 1800 and 1805 under the title *Leçons d'anatomie comparée.* His concern for classification led him to pay special attention to the anatomy of the various systems of organs as he developed his own theories about which systems should be used for purposes of classification.

Another area in which Cuvier carried out major research was the study of fossils. He believed that a study of fossil animals would clarify geological theories about the development and history of the earth. From 1796 until 1812 he published a series of papers on the fossil remains of animals and their significance for geology; they were collected in four volumes in 1812 as *Recherches sur les ossements fossiles de quadrupèdes.*

Appended to this collection was a summary of Cuvier's views about the formation of the different surface layers of the earth, which was later revised and entitled *Discours sur les révolutions de la surface du globe.* In this work he put forward the view that the earth had suffered successive catastrophes in the form of floods which had swamped all but the highest mountains. This view of geological history became known as catastrophism; it was opposed by the uniformitarians, who believed that the surface structure of the earth was due to ordinary everyday causes, which continued to be active up to the present, and not just catastrophic events.

## Cuvier and Classification

By the end of the 18th century biologists were faced with an enormous problem of classification because of the large number of new animal and plant specimens collected from different parts of the world. The ideas and practices which had been developed from the time of Carl Linnaeus were no longer satisfactory. One aspect of the problem of classification was its philosophical basis. For some naturalists a system of classification was merely an arbitrary but practical way to distinguish between and learn about different animals. Others, however, argued that there was a "natural" system of classification which indicated some sort of real relationship between the animals in the different parts of the system.

Cuvier believed that animals could be classified into different kinds and that each kind of animal could be represented for classification purposes by an ideal "type." The animal type would include all the characteristics distinguishing it from other types. According to Cuvier, types would not change from generation to generation. He arrived at the mature statement of his view on classification in 1812. He classified all animals into four main branches (*embranchements*) according to the construction of their nervous system; he used the nervous system because he considered it the most important system physiologically or functionally. Less important, or subordinate, systems of characteristics were used to create classificatory subdivisions within the four branches. He called this method of classification the principle of the subordination of characters.

Cuvier justified his system of classification philosophically by arguing along Aristotelian lines that animals were distinguished from other orders of creation by their ability to sense and perceive things. Hence, he argued, the most important, or the most "animalistic," physiological system was that responsible for sensation, namely, the nervous system. He then based his system of classification of animals on the differences of their nervous system. "In considering the animal kingdom from this point of view," he said, "... I have found that there exist four principal forms, four general plans, upon which all of the animals seem to have been modeled ..." (quoted in William Coleman, 1964). These four models, or branches, of the animal kingdom were the Vertebrata, the Mollusca, the Articulata, and the Radiata.

This new system of classification, together with the encyclopedic works which Cuvier based on it, greatly helped the naturalists of his day to assimilate and understand all the new information about animals. Despite its success, however, his system was immediately challenged by those whose philosophy of biology differed considerably from his own.

## Theory of Evolution

Cuvier did not live to see Charles Darwin propound his theory of evolution by natural selection, yet he is frequently portrayed as one of the most important anti-evolutionary figures in the history of biology. This reputation arose largely from the clash with his contemporaries Jean Baptiste de Lamarck and Étienne Geoffroy Saint-Hilaire, who supported evolutionary ideas.

Lamarck taught that there was no such thing as a constant species. He held that the more individual animals he examined, the less certain he became about saying that there were definite boundaries between the forms of different species. Moreover, he put forward the view that the form of species changed from generation to generation through the effects of use or disuse on the various parts of animals. The usage of different organs would change because of changes in the environment. Lamarck pointed to the fossil remains of animals as evidence supporting his theory. Among the fossils were animal forms no longer existing on earth. These, he claimed, were ancestor to the present array of animals.

Cuvier agreed with Lamarck that there was much variation among animals. But he held that most of the variation was among the secondary, or subordinate, characters of animals and that these were not important for the functional integrity of the animals. Organs such as the heart and lungs and the nervous and digestive systems—which were important for the functional integrity of an animal—varied slightly and within very definite limits in the one species, according to Cuvier. However, his strongest argument was that Lamarck could produce no evidence of the transformation of species, whereas Cuvier could show, from evidence recently brought back to France by Napoleon's army, that domestic animals had not changed since the time of the ancient Egyptians. Furthermore, he showed that the disappearance of various fossil animals was due to their becoming extinct rather than transforming into new species.

Both Lamarck and Geoffroy Saint-Hilaire supported the idea that all animals could be arranged into a "great chain of being" from the simplest to the most complex and that this was shown by certain similarities in the structures of all the species. Cuvier also strongly opposed this idea, which was used by some evolutionists. For him the four branches of the animal kingdom which he had postulated could in no way be likened to each other.

Cuvier's arguments against evolution fitted very well into his own conservative philosophy of biology and with his Christian faith, which supported the view that all present species must have descended from a common pair of ancestors created by God at the beginning of the world. Because his brilliant biological system fitted so well with the conservative point of view in both science and theology, his arguments against the evolution theory have been used countless times since his death.

## Further Reading

The best biography of Cuvier is William R. Coleman, *Georges Cuvier, Zoologist* (1964). Alexander B. Adams, *Eternal Quest: The Story of the Great Naturalists* (1969), has an excellent chapter devoted to Cuvier. □

# François Cuvilliés

**François Cuvilliés (1695-1768) was a Flemish-born, French-trained architect, interior decorator, and ornament designer who brought to Munich the new rococo style and produced there, particularly in the Amalienburg and the court theater, masterpieces of the Bavarian rococo.**

François Cuvilliés was born a dwarf in Soignies, Hainaut, on Oct. 23, 1695. Discovered about 1706 by Prince Elector Maximilian Emmanuel of Bavaria, who was in exile in Flanders, Cuvilliés was educated with the court pages, although he was officially the court dwarf. He returned with Maximilian Emmanuel from exile to Munich in 1715 and was allowed to work with the court architect, Joseph Effner.

Maximilian Emmanuel then sent Cuvilliés to Paris in 1720 to study under François Blondel the Younger, where he remained until 1724. On his return to Munich, Cuvilliés was appointed court architect in 1725, thus beginning his long career in the service of the house of Wittelsbach, the rulers of Bavaria. For them he produced such works as Schloss Brühl and the so-called Reiche Zimmer (the "rich rooms") and the Green Gallery of the Residenz in Munich between 1730 and 1737.

Cuvilliés's masterpiece, and one of the finest creations of the Bavarian rococo, is the famous Amalienburg, a hunting lodge built for the electress Maria Amalia on the grounds of the summer palace at Nymphenburg outside of Munich. This small palace, single-storied and with only six main rooms, is, in its exterior, very plain, but its interior, particularly the central round mirrored hall, decorated in pale blue and silver, and the flanking bedroom and sitting room, decorated in deep yellow and silver, are the masterpieces of Cuvilliés and Johann Baptist Zimmermann, who produced the stucco decoration after Cuvilliés's designs. The simplicity of the layout of the main rooms forms a suitable foil for the rich and fantastic ornament of the walls, the mirrors, and the doors, and even some of the furniture, especially the console tables of the central hall, all designed by Cuvilliés.

Cuvilliés repeated his triumph in the small court theater he built in the Residenz at Munich (1751-1753). Although the theater was destroyed during World War II, all the furnishings, the paneling, and carved decoration were saved; they were fully restored and are now installed inside the Residenz. The court theater is known as the Cuvilliés Theater, in honor of the architect. Cuvilliés other works in Munich are the Hohnstein Palace, now the Archbishop's Palace (1733-1737), the Preysing Palace (1740), and the facade of the Theatine church (1765-1768). Outside of Munich, the churches of Berg am Laim, Diessen, Schäftlarn, and Benediktbeuren all have altars or rooms decorated by Cuvilliés.

During the last 30 years of his life Cuvilliés also produced many designs for decorations and ornament, which, engraved and sold as pattern books, served to spread his personal mixture of French and German rococo throughout central Europe. His son, François Cuvilliés the Younger (1731-1777), assisted his father, engraved his designs, and, after the elder Cuvilliés's death on April 14, 1768, completed many of his works.

## Further Reading

In English, the following surveys deal with Cuvilliés: John Bourke, *Baroque Churches of Central Europe* (1958; 2d ed. 1962); Nicholas Powell, *From Baroque to Rococo* (1959); Eberhard Hempel, *Baroque Art and Architecture in Central Europe* (1965); and Henry-Russell Hitchcock, *Rococo Architecture in Southern Germany* (1968). □

# Aelbert Cuyp

**The landscapes of the Dutch painter Aelbert Cuyp (1620-1691) are famous for their golden light and alluring color. He painted Dutch rural life in its full variety.**

Born in Dordrecht, Aelbert Cuyp was probably first taught by his father, the painter Jacob Gerritsz Cuyp, known mainly for his portraits. Between 1640 and 1645 Aelbert painted skillful monochromatic dune and river landscapes with diagonal compositions, much in the manner of Jan van Goyen.

Because of the scarcity of dated works it is impossible to say precisely when Cuyp introduced the misty golden light that is the hallmark of his mature style, but it was certainly in the 1640s. This innovation was based in part on his observations of the optical effects of moist atmosphere; this was a time when optical experimentation attracted widespread interest among the Dutch. The many drawings and paintings Cuyp made of activities on the rivers that made Dordrecht a busy port in his day give evidence of his scrutiny of subtle variations in light effects. The major impetus for this interest, however, probably came from Jan Both, who returned from Italy to Utrecht in 1641 and painted there until his death in 1652. To Claude Lorrain's unprecedented demonstration of the unifying power of light in landscape painting, Both added a new specificity through attentive study of appearances at different times of day. This approach was central to Cuyp's mature achievement. The particular light of a given moment became part of his subject. In his ability to translate specific light effects into paint, he surpassed his models and created landscape paintings of unique poetic sensibility.

As is clear from his *Young Herdsmen with Cows* (ca. 1655) Cuyp ensconced his soft, golden luminosity in firmly structured compositions. The monumental cattle, silhou-

etted against the sky, emphasize the aerial perspective and create the illusion of a visual field of vast depth. Considered relationships and classical restraint likewise contribute to the calm perfection of his matchless scenes of moonlight on the water, for example, *Sailing Boats and Mill.* As Cuyp apparently never went to Italy, it seems that his Italianate scenes, such as *Travelers in a Hilly Landscape,* depend on works by Both and other Italianizing Dutch artists.

Having achieved sudden affluence through marriage in 1658, Cuyp painted little thereafter. There are no dated pictures after 1655.

## Further Reading

Wolfgang Stechow, *Dutch Landscape Painting of the Seventeenth Century* (1966), deals perceptively with Cuyp's development and his place within the Dutch landscape tradition. See also Jakob Rosenberg, Seymour Slive, and E. H. Ter Kuile, *Dutch Art and Architecture, 1600-1800* (1966). Two older works which include chapters on Cuyp are Eugène Fromentin, *The Masters of Past Time: Dutch and Flemish Painting from Van Eyck to Rembrandt* (1876; trans. 1913; new ed. 1948), and W. Bode, *Great Masters of Dutch and Flemish Painting* (1906; trans. 1909; rep. 1967).

## Additional Sources

Reiss, Stephen, *Aelbert Cuyp,* London: Zwemmer, 1975.
Reiss, Stephen, *Aelbert Cuyp,* Boston: New York Graphic Society, 1975. □

# Thascius Caecilianus Cyprianus

**Thascius Caecilianus Cyprianus (died 258) is known as St. Cyprian. As bishop of Carthage, he was the most prominent leader of Western, or Latin, Christianity in his time. He contributed to the development of thought on the nature and unity of the Church.**

Born to a high-ranking pagan family in Roman Africa probably during 200-210, Cyprian was converted to Christianity about 246. He was bishop of Carthage no more than 3 years later. Within months of his becoming bishop, the Roman imperial government inaugurated its first empirewide persecution of the Church. Cyprian retreated to an unknown spot in the country and directed Church affairs by letter and messenger.

During his exile and in the years following his return in 251, Cyprian faced a serious pastoral problem. Under torture and threat of death many Christians had either performed the required pagan sacrifices or so far complied with the government as to acquire papers certifying that they had performed them. These "lapsed" Christians penitently wished, however, to be readmitted to communion in the Church. Breaking with the traditional rigorism of the Church, Cyprian gradually moved to the position that all lapsed Christians could be fully readmitted after clear evidence of penitence. He differed crucially from dissident elements in Carthage and Rome, however, in his insistence that only the duly appointed bishop had authority to adjudicate the matter.

In arriving at his solution to this problem, Cyprian developed his constitutional theory of the Church. He believed that the "episcopate" was a single, divinely appointed, governing office shared by the many bishops, each of whom possessed the full authority of the office in his own locale. Christ's Apostles were the first bishops, and their plenary authority had continued in the duly elected and consecrated bishops who were their successors. To act apart from the bishop was to place oneself outside the Church and to lose the hope of salvation. Cyprian expressed these concepts in the treatise *De unitate ecclesiae.*

The last 3 years of Cyprian's life were marked by controversy with Stephen, the bishop of Rome. Disagreements among Christians over the problem of the lapsed had resulted in the emergence of dissident sects in Rome and Carthage. The question then arose whether persons baptized in a sect should be "rebaptized" if and when they decided to enter the Catholic Church. Cyprian, consistent with his principles, taught that baptism outside the Catholic Church was no Christian baptism at all; but Stephen, whose position ultimately prevailed in the Western Church, defended the traditional Roman policy of recognizing sectarian baptism and requiring that persons coming to Catholicism from the sects receive only the laying on of the bishop's hand.

When persecution of the Church was renewed, Cyprian went calmly and with dignity to his death as a martyr on Sept. 14, 258.

### Further Reading

The classic study of St. Cyprian is Edward White Benson, *Cyprian* (1897), which is still of great value as a comprehensive account of the man's life and times. See also G. S. Walker, *The Churchmanship of St. Cyprian* (1969).

### Additional Sources

Cyprian, Saint, Bishop of Carthage, *The letters of St. Cyprian of Carthage,* New York, N.Y.: Newman Press, 1984.
*Born to new life,* New Rochelle, N.Y.: New City Press, 1992. □

# St. Cyril

**St. Cyril (died 444) was bishop of Alexandria. A Doctor of the Church, he played a leading role in the controversies over the correct understanding of the person of Jesus Christ.**

Nothing certain is known concerning Cyril's early years except that he was born in Alexandria and was the nephew of Theophilus, his predecessor as bishop of that city. He was a member of his uncle's entourage at the infamous Synod of the Oak, where Theophilus was successful in bringing about the deposition of John Chrysostom from his post as bishop of Constantinople. Having become bishop in 412, Cyril soon brought about the seizure of property belonging to the Novatianists, an austere Christian sect. He also instigated the virtual dissolution of the Jewish community in his city.

About 430 Cyril began his campaign to bring about the downfall of Nestorius, the bishop of Constantinople. The bishops of Alexandria generally had tended to resent the new and rising prestige of the See of Constantinople. More particularly, Cyril had a deep and quite sincere conviction that the theology of Nestorius represented a serious threat to authentic Christian confession of faith in Christ. Nestorius represented the suspect theological traditions of another great and rival Christian metropolis, Antioch, whence he had been called to Constantinople.

According to Cyril, the Church's traditional belief in the Incarnation requires the acknowledgment that God the Word, the second "person" of the Trinity, is himself the one and only subject, or agent, in every deed and word acted and spoken by Jesus Christ; this implies for him that Mary, the mother of Jesus, is to be called *theotokos* (she who bears God). Nestorius dissented from such teachings, fearing that they destroyed the full humanity of Jesus and detracted from the dignity of God.

The Emperor summoned a general council of bishops to adjudicate the matter at Ephesus in 431. Once there, Cyril himself convened the council and swiftly accomplished the condemnation of Nestorius before Eastern bishops friendly

to the latter had arrived. After these irregular proceedings, Nestorius resigned voluntarily, and Cyril thereby accomplished one of his chief goals. Under government pressure in 433, however, Cyril made surprising concessions in reaching reconciliation with the more moderate of Nestorius's allies through a famous document, the *Formulary of Reunion.* Cyril's other writings include letters, theological and apologetic treatises, and commentaries on books of the *Bible.*

### Further Reading

There is no book-length general treatment of St. Cyril, though there are works in foreign languages on special aspects of his thought. In English, good general essays on him can be found in G. L. Prestige, *Fathers and Heretics: Six Studies in Dogmatic Faith* (1940), and Hans von Campenhausen, *The Fathers of the Greek Church,* translated by Stanley Godman (1959; rev. ed. 1962). □

# Saints Cyril and Methodius

**The Greek missionaries Saints Cyril (827-869) and Methodius (825-885) were the apostles of the Slavic peoples. Preaching Christianity in the native language, they brought the Slavic countries firmly into the sphere of the Christian Church.**

Methodius was 2 years old when his brother, Cyril, was born in Thessalonica in northeastern Greece in 827. Cyril was given the name Constantine at his baptism. Methodius entered the service of the Byzantine emperor and worked faithfully, if without distinction, for a number of years. Constantine studied at the imperial university in Constantinople but refused the offer of a governor's post and asked instead to be ordained a priest. He was more intellectually inclined than Methodius and spent some years as the official librarian of the most important church in eastern Europe, Hagia Sophia in Constantinople. He taught philosophy for a time at the imperial university and was sent by Patriarch Ignatius on one occasion to the Arabian caliph's court as a member of a delegation to discuss theology with the Moslems.

In the meantime Methodius had left government service and entered a monastery in Bithynia east of Constantinople. In 856 Constantine also decided to withdraw from the active life of a scholar-churchman and joined Methodius in the same monastery. The brothers' solitude lasted only 4 years. In 860 they were sent by Patriarch Ignatius to assure the Christian faith of the Khazars in Russia, who were wavering in the face of strong Jewish and Moslem influence. When they were on their return journey, Constantine discovered what he believed to be the bones of an early Christian pope, St. Clement of Rome, and carried them with him for the rest of his life.

From the time they were boys in Thessalonica, the brothers could speak Slavic. When the Moravian king Ratislav, unhappy with the Latin Christianity preached in his

**St. Cyril**

Slavic country by Charlemagne's German missionaries, turned to Constantinople for help, Constantine and Methodius were again summoned from their monastery and sent by Emperor Michael II to Moravia. This mission was to be their lifetime concern. In 863 the brothers reached the country (today the Czech Republic) and immediately began teaching and preaching in the Slavic language of the people. They started a school to train young men for the priesthood. They conducted the liturgical services in Slavic and eventually developed a special Slavic alphabet in order to put the *Bible* and the liturgy in writing.

For 5 years Constantine and Methodius worked steadily to establish Christian worship according to the forms and language of the Moravian people. They inevitably clashed with the German missionaries, who were committed to the Latin form of Christianity. The two brothers were invited to Rome in 868 by Pope Nicholas I to explain their work. The Pope was so impressed by their success that he made them both bishops and, contrary to expectation, authorized them to carry on their ministry in Slavic. Constantine, however, had no further desire for the active missionary life. He entered a monastery in Rome in 869 and took a new name, Cyril, as a sign of his new life. Fifty days later he died.

Methodius returned to Moravia and continued his efforts for 16 years more. An incident in 871 extended his influence still further. The visiting king of Bohemia was invited to dine with the Moravian king. The guest found that

he and his entourage were considered heathens and were expected to sit on the floor, while the host and Bishop Methodius, as Christians, were being served at a raised table. He asked what he could expect to gain by becoming a Christian. Bishop Methodius said, "A place higher than all kings and princes." That was enough. The king asked to be baptized, along with his wife and entire retinue, and returned to Bohemia to encourage many of his people to accept the Christian faith.

Methodius's difficulties with the Latin clergy continued to plague his later years. He was summoned to Rome again in 878 by Pope John VIII. This time the influence of the Latinists was stronger. The Pope decreed that Methodius must first read the Mass in Latin, then translate it into Slavic. The bishop returned, subdued. He died in 885. Cyril and Methodius were considered heroes by the people and were formally recognized as saints of the Roman Catholic Church in 1881.

## Further Reading

Most of the works on Cyril and Methodius are in Slavic or Russian. There are several helpful books in English, however. Francis Dvornik, *The Slavs: Their Early History and Civilization* (1956), describes the brothers' influence on the life and language of the people among whom they worked. Zdenek Radslav Dittrich, *Christianity in Great-Moravia* (1962), is a scholarly study of the history of the churches they helped found, and Matthew Spinka, *A History of Christianity in the Balkans* (1968), places their missionary results in the context of the history of eastern Europe. □

# Cyrus the Great

**Cyrus the Great (reigned 550-530 B.C.) was the founder of the Persian Empire. His reign witnessed the first serious contacts between Persians and Greeks and the permanent loss of political power by the peoples of the old centers of power in Mesopotamia.**

In the new Median Empire, which shared with Babylon the spoils of the fallen Assyrian power, the Persians were a subordinate group, though closely related to the Medes and speaking a similar Indo-European language. They were ruled by their own local kings, and one of these married a daughter of the Median king Astyages; their son was Cyrus. Astyages seems not to have been popular, and when, in 550 B.C., Cyrus revolted, Astyages's own troops went over to Cyrus. The Median Empire thus became the Persian Empire. It is worth noting that Cyrus treated his defeated grandfather with honor and that instead of sacking Ecbatana, the Median capital, he kept it as one of his own because Pasargadae, the Persian center, was too remote for use as a capital. Cyrus also continued to keep Medes in high office.

## War with the Greeks

The Medes and the Persians were so similar that foreigners tended to see only a change of dynasty (the Greeks still called the whole group Medes), but any such upset implied to the other powers a tempting weakness, and Cyrus soon found himself embroiled in new wars. The first was with Croesus, King of Lydia, a wealthy state in western Asia Minor whose subjects included the Greek cities along its coast. Croesus tried to find allies, including, with the aid of the Delphic oracle, the states of mainland Greece. But Cyrus moved too quickly. In a winter campaign he surprised and took Croesus's "impregnable" capital of Sardis. The Greek Herodotus says that Cyrus spared Croesus, though this has been questioned; Croesus may have committed suicide to avoid capture.

Cyrus then returned to the east, but he left Harpagus, a Mede, to complete the conquest. Over the next years Harpagus subdued the local peoples, including the Greek cities of the coast. The importance of this first serious contact between Greeks and Persians was doubtless unrecognized by either people, yet each was to become and remain for 2 centuries the main foreign preoccupation of the other.

## Conquest of Babylon

Nabonidus (Nabu-Naid) of Babylon had originally favored Cyrus, but border conflicts led to war, and in 539 Cyrus captured Babylon. Here again his victory was made easy by the aid of Nabonidus's own subjects, for Nabonidus had alienated many powerful interests, especially the priesthood of Marduk, Babylon's chief god. Cyrus posed as both a liberator and a supporter of the local gods and once in power pursued a careful policy of religious toleration. The most important example of this was his allowing the Jews to return to their homeland.

Not only the civilized states to the west but also the steppe peoples to the east engaged Cyrus's attention, and during his remaining years he pushed his frontiers to the Indus and the Jaxartes (modern Syr Darya). He died in 530 somewhere east of the Caspian Sea, fighting a tribe called the Massagetae.

Cyrus's right to be called "the Great" can hardly be questioned, and not only because his conquests were vastly larger than any before him anywhere on earth. The sudden emergence of Persia as the dominant power in the Near East is the most striking political fact of the 6th century B.C., while the conquest of Mesopotamia (Egypt was left for Cyrus's son Cambyses) marks the first time that a true Indo-European-speaking people had gained control of the old centers of civilization. Further, Cyrus's policy of generosity toward the conquered became standard Persian practice; among the imperial peoples of history, the Persians remain outstanding in their ready toleration of local customs and religions.

## Further Reading

Though business and government documents from the Persian Empire are extant, knowledge of the personal lives of the Persian kings comes almost entirely from Greek sources. Herodotus's *Histories* ranks first; Xenophon's *Cyropedia* is mainly a propaganda piece. Good recent treatments are in A. T. Olmstead, *History of the Persian Empire, Achaemenid Period* (1948); *Roman Ghirshman, Iran: From the Earliest Times to the Islamic Conquest* (1954); and Richard N. Frye, *The Heritage of Persia* (1962). □

# D

## Louis Jacques Mandé Daguerre

**Louis Jacques Mandé Daguerre (1787-1851), a French painter and stage designer, invented the daguerreotype, the first practical and commercially successful photographic process.**

Louis Daguerre was born on Nov. 18, 1787, at Cormeilles-en-Parisis. Abandoning his architectural training in 1804, he turned to scene painting and became a pupil of I. E. M. Degotti at the Paris Opéra. In 1822 Daguerre and Charles Bouton developed the diorama, a large-scale peep show in which a painting on a large translucent screen was seemingly animated by the skillful play of light on each side. Daguerre made dioramas for 17 years.

Daguerre used the camera obscura to make sketches for his stage designs and, like so many others, wished to avoid the tedious tracing and fix the image chemically. After several unsuccessful efforts he learned in 1826 that J. N. Niépce was working toward the same end and had made some progress. A cautious correspondence followed, in which Niépce revealed his heliograph process, and in 1829 Daguerre and Niépce formed a partnership to develop the method.

Heliography depended on the hardening action of sunlight on bitumen and the subsequent dissolution of the soft shadow parts of the image. Using this method on a glass plate, Niépce had obtained and fixed a photograph from the camera obscura in 1826. But his aspirations went beyond a visible image to a photoengraved plate from which he could pull prints. This goal led to his using bitumen on silver-coated copperplates and then iodizing the silver revealed after dissolving the unexposed bitumen. The removal of the hardened bitumen produced a silver-silver iodide image. But Niépce went no further.

365

Building on his partner's foundation, Daguerre discovered the light sensitivity of silver iodide in 1831 but was unable to obtain a visible image. His discovery in 1835 that the latent image present on a silver iodide plate exposed for so short a time as 20 minutes could be developed with mercury vapor marked a major advance. Fixing was achieved in 1837, when he removed the unreduced silver iodide with a solution of common salt. Having improved Niépce's process beyond recognition, Daguerre felt justified in calling it the daguerreotype. He ceded the process to the French government. He revealed his discovery on Aug. 19, 1839.

Daguerre retired to Bry-sur-Marne in 1840 and died there on July 10, 1851. He had little more to do with the daguerreotype, leaving its improvement to others. It was perhaps the invention which most caught popular fancy in the mid-19th century, but it proved to be a blind alley in the development of modern photography.

## Further Reading

Daguerre's life is fully documented in Helmut and Alison Gernsheim, *L. J. M. Daguerre: The History of the Diorama and the Daguerreotype* (1956). Their *The History of Photography* (1955) is an excellent overall discussion of photography.

□

# Roald Dahl

**A writer of both children's fiction and short stories for adults, Roald Dahl (1916–1990) is best known as the author of *Charlie and the Chocolate Factory,* the story of a poor boy who because of his honesty is selected by Willy Wonka to be the new owner of his world-famous chocolate factory. Dahl has been described as a master of story construction with a remarkable ability to weave a tale.**

Dahl was born in Llandaff, South Wales, to Norwegian parents, and spent his childhood summers visiting his grandparents in Oslo, Norway. After his father died when Dahl was four, his mother abided by her late husband's wish that Dahl be sent to English schools. Dahl subsequently attended Llandaff Cathedral School, where he began a series of academic misadventures. After he and several other students were severely beaten by the headmaster for placing a dead mouse in a cruel storekeeper's candy jar, Dahl's mother moved him to St. Peter's Boarding School and later to Repton, a renowned private school. Dahl would later describe his school years as "days of horrors" which inspired much of his macabre fiction. After graduating from Repton, Dahl took a position with the Shell Oil Company in Tanganyika (now Tanzania), Africa. In 1939 he joined a Royal Air Force training squadron in Nairobi, Kenya, serving as a fighter pilot in the Mediterranean. Dahl suffered severe head injuries in a plane crash near Alexandria, Egypt; upon recovering he was transferred to Washington, D.C., as an assistant air attache. There Dahl began his writing career, publishing a short story in the *Saturday Evening Post.* In 1961, he published his first work for children, *James and the Giant Peach,* and for the remainder of his life continued to write for both children and adults. He died in 1990.

Critical response to Dahl's children's books has varied from praising him as a genius to declaring his works racist and harmful. *Charlie and the Chocolate Factory* is his most popular and most controversial children's story. Many critics have censured this work for its alleged stereotyping and inhumanity, and have accused Dahl of racism for his portrayal of the Oompa-Loompas: in the original version of *Charlie and the Chocolate Factory,* they are described as black pygmies from deepest Africa who sing and dance and work for nearly nothing. In a revised edition, Dahl changed their appearance and gave them a mythical homeland. Dahl's supporters have argued that in *Charlie,* as in his other children's books, Dahl follows the traditional fairy tale style, which includes extreme exaggeration and the swift and horrible destruction of evildoers; they contend that children are not harmed by this approach.

Critics have compared Dahl's adult-oriented fiction to the works of Guy de Maupassant, O. Henry, and Saki. Praised by commentators as well crafted and suspenseful, Dahl's stories employ surprise endings and shrewd characters who are rarely what they seem to be. Of Dahl's work, Michael Wood has commented, "His stories are not only unfailingly clever, they are, many of them, *about* cleverness." Dahl also experimented with comic themes in his novel *My Uncle Oswald.* The title character, Oswald Hendryks Cornelius, is a charming man of the world who embarks upon a business venture to collect and preserve semen samples from geniuses and royalty, hoping to attract as clients wealthy women who desire superior offspring. Like Dahl's short stories, *My Uncle Oswald* features duplicitous characters, and some critics have observed that it shares a common theme with much of his short fiction: a depiction of the superficial nature of modern civilization.

## Further Reading

*Children's Literature Review,* Gale, Volume 1, 1976, Volume 7, 1984.
*Contemporary Literary Criticism,* Gale, Volume 1, 1973, Volume 6, 1976, Volume 18, 1981.
Dahl, Roald, *The Wonderful Story of Henry Sugar and Six More,* Knopf, 1977.
Dahl, Roald, *Boy: Tales of Childhood,* Farrar, Straus, 1984.
Dahl, Roald, *Going Solo,* Farrar, Straus, 1986.
Farrell, Barry, *Pat and Roald,* Random House, 1969.
McCann, Donnarae, and Gloria Woodard, editors, *The Black American in Books for Children: Readings in Racism,* Scarecrow, 1972. □

# Daigo II

**The Japanese emperor Daigo II (1288-1339) attempted to restore the power of the throne upon the destruction of the country's first military government, or shogunate, in 1333.**

Since the establishment of a centralized state in Japan under the influence of Chinese civilization in the 7th century, the Japanese sovereigns had gradually lost power. During most of the 10th and 11th centuries the Fujiwara family dominated the court at Kyoto as imperial regents. At the end of the 11th century and during the first half of the 12th, retired (or cloistered) emperors reasserted the authority of the imperial family in court politics. Yet, even as they did so, real power in Japan was shifting from the courtier class of Kyoto to an emergent warrior class in the provinces. This shift was climaxed by the founding of a shogunate by the warrior clan of Minamoto at Kamakura in the eastern provinces in 1185.

## Kamakura Shogunate

The founder of the Kamakura shogunate was Minamoto Yoritomo, who received the title of shogun, or "generalissimo," from the imperial court. But in the early 13th century actual control of the regime at Kamakura was seized by members of the Hojo clan, who established the office of shogunate regent. The Hojo regents allowed the imperial court little voice in the governing of the country. Emperors continued to reign but they did not rule.

The Hojo regents proved to be among the most effective administrators of medieval Japan, but by the end of the 13th century the Kamakura shogunate had nevertheless begun to decline. One of the chief reasons for this decline was the expense and effort required to repulse two attempts by forces of the Mongol dynasty of China to invade Japan in 1274 and 1281.

## Dispute over Succession to the Throne

After the Mongol invasions there arose a dispute over succession to the throne in Kyoto. At first the dispute was of little concern to the Hojo, since the throne exercised no political power. As Hojo rule continued to weaken in the early 14th century, however, discontented members of both the courtier and warrior classes began to turn to the court in opposition to the Kamakura shogunate.

Meanwhile, the contending branches of the imperial family had temporarily agreed to the practice of alternately providing successors to the throne. But when Daigo II of the so-called junior branch became emperor in 1318, he objected strongly to this procedure and determined to hold the throne permanently for himself and his line of descendants. In response to attempts by the Hojo to force continuance of alternate succession with the senior branch of the imperial family, Daigo II began to scheme to overthrow the Kamakura shogunate and to restore imperial rule.

Daigo II was apparently privy to an anti-Hojo plot that was uncovered in Kyoto in 1324, and in 1331 he actively encouraged an armed rising in the region of Kyoto that had to be put down by forces of the shogunate. The Hojo attempted to settle this second incident by exiling the Emperor to an island in the Japan Sea. Nevertheless, sporadic, guerrilla-type fighting continued in the central provinces around Kyoto, and in 1333 several great warrior chieftains, who had previously been the vassals of Kamakura, defected to the loyalist cause of Daigo II and helped bring about the sudden overthrow of the shogunate.

## Imperial Restoration

Upon his triumphal return to Kyoto in 1333, Daigo II sought to take the administrative powers of the country directly into his own hands and to launch an "imperial restoration." But this restoration, which was an anachronistic attempt to reverse the course of several centuries of history, lasted only a brief 3 years. The warrior class was in the ascendancy in Japan, and the imperial court, which was imbued with the governing techniques of an earlier age, was ill-equipped to meet its demands or to fulfill its needs.

As dissatisfaction with the restoration government grew, warriors throughout the land began to look for leadership elsewhere. The chieftain who came to the fore and who increasingly gave indications of his wish to open a new shogunate was Ashikaga Takauji. However, Daigo II, who opposed the sharing of national powers with anyone, steadfastly refused to appoint Takauji as the new shogun. And when, in 1335, Takauji showed signs of assuming shogunlike authority even without imperial approval, the Emperor commissioned Nitta Yoshisada, a keen rival of Takauji, to chastise the Ashikaga.

### War between the Courts

The effort to check the Ashikaga plunged Japan into a civil war that lasted for more than half a century. In 1336 Takauji occupied Kyoto and forced Daigo II to abdicate in favor of a member of the senior branch of the imperial family. But in the final month of the year Daigo II fled to Yoshino in the mountainous region to the south of Kyoto and proclaimed that he was still the legitimate sovereign.

The government that Daigo II opened at Yoshino is known in history as the Southern court to distinguish it from the Northern court in Kyoto, and the period of opposition between the two, which lasted until 1392, is called the age of war between the courts. Daigo II died in 1339, and the last spark of his movement to restore the throne to power was extinguished in 1392, when the Southern court abandoned its resistance.

### Further Reading

H. Paul Varley, *Imperial Restoration in Medieval Japan* (1971), provides a detailed analysis of Daigo II's attempt to restore imperial rule in the 14th century. For a good historical account of the country, and also Daigo's activities, see Sir George B. Sansom, *A History of Japan* (3 vols., 1958-1963). □

# Gottlieb Daimler

**The German mechanical engineer Gottlieb Daimler (1834-1900) was a pioneer in the development of the internal combustion engine and the automobile.**

Gottlieb Daimler was born on March 17, 1834, at Schorndorf near Stuttgart. He attended a technical school (1848-1852) in Stuttgart while serving as a gunsmith's apprentice. After 4 years (1853-1857) at a Strassburg steam engine factory, he completed his training as a mechanical engineer at the Stuttgart Polytechnic. He returned to Strassburg in 1859, but 2 years later, having recognized the need for a small, low-power engine capable of economic intermittent operation, he left to tour France and England. In Paris he saw E. Lenoir's new gas engine.

Daimler spent the next decade in heavy engineering. He joined Bruderhaus Maschinen-Fabrik in Reutlingen as manager in 1863 and there met Wilhelm Maybach, with whom he was to collaborate closely for the rest of his life. Daimler went to Maschinenbau Gesellschaft in Karlsruhe as director in 1869. When he joined Gasmotoren-Fabrik in Deutz as chief engineer in 1872, Daimler, N. A. Otto, and Eugen Langen perfected the Otto atmospheric (oil) engine. Daimler was asked by the Deutz board in 1875 to develop a gasoline-powered version, but this idea was dropped in favor of commercial exploitation of the four-cycle Otto engine.

### Daimler Motor Company

In 1882 Daimler and Maybach set up a factory in Stuttgart to develop light, high-speed, gasoline-powered internal combustion engines. Their aim from the start appears to have been to apply these engines to vehicles. During their early trials it seemed that ignition troubles were insurmountable, but in 1883 Daimler developed and patented a reliable self-firing ignition system using an incandescent tube in the cylinder head. Maybach worked to reduce the size while increasing the economy, and by 1885 their first gasoline-powered engine was fitted to a motorcycle. That year a more powerful, water-cooled unit was fitted into a carriage. They then developed a two-cylinder V engine, applied it to a motor car, and exhibited it at the 1889 Paris Exhibition. Though the public took little notice of the vehicle, it did attract R. Panhard and E. Lavassor, who developed the engine in France and began to manufacture automobiles in 1891.

In Germany the need for more capital led to the creation of Daimler-Motoren-Gesellschaft mbH (1890), but business disagreements led Daimler and Maybach to break away in 1893 and continue experimental development alone. They entered endurance trials and road races to establish the utility of the automobile and showed the way so clearly that Daimler returned to his company in full control in 1895. He died in Stuttgart on March 6, 1900.

### Further Reading

Perhaps the best recent study of Daimler is in Eugen Diesel and others, *From Engines to Autos: Five Pioneers in Engine Development* (1960). □

# Édouard Daladier

**The French statesman Édouard Daladier (1884-1970) represented his country at the Munich Conference in September 1938.**

The son of a baker, Édouard Daladier was born on June 18, 1884, at Carpentras. An ardent Dreyfusard schoolteacher and member of the Radical Socialist party, he was elected to Parliament in 1919. He attained ministerial rank under his former teacher Édouard Herriot in 1924 and served in most cabinets until 1940.

During his first premiership, from January to October 1933, Daladier signed the Four-Power Peace Pact with Great Britain, Germany, and Italy. Widely considered a "strong man," he was recalled to power in January 1934 to deal with disorders provoked by right-wing extremists. Undeterred, they rioted in Paris on Feb. 6, 1934, and forced Daladier to resign after only 11 days in office. A rival of Herriot and leader of the progressive Radicals, Daladier led his party into Léon Blum's left-wing Popular Front coalition, which won the parliamentary elections of May 1936. He then became minister of national defense.

As international tension mounted following Hitler's annexation of Austria, France once more turned to a "strong man," and Daladier resumed the premiership in April 1938. With France the prisoner of British foreign policy, Daladier was forced to support the appeasement policy of Neville Chamberlain. Consequently, he was compelled to acquiesce in the dismembering of Czechoslovakia at Munich in 1938. This act destroyed the security system of France in eastern Europe and encouraged Adolf Hitler in his policy of aggression and violence.

Daladier declared war on Germany after Hitler's invasion of Poland in September 1939. He continued in office until March 20, 1940, when he yielded to another "strong man," Paul Reynaud. He remained in the government, however, as minister of war and then as foreign minister until June 16, 1940. Arrested in September by Vichy authorities, he was sent to Riom for trial in 1942. Daladier defended himself with such courage and vigor that the proceedings were suspended. In 1943 he was deported to Germany, where he remained until his liberation in April 1945.

After the war Daladier sought to resume his political career but with little success. Although returned to Parliament, he was too much identified with the events which led to the fall of France to regain his prewar position of leadership. Even his tenure as president of the Radical party after the death of Herriot in 1957 was brief and inglorious. After his electoral defeat in the parliamentary elections of November 1958, he retired. Daladier died in Paris on Oct. 10, 1970.

## Further Reading

As with most French political leaders, Daladier has no biographer. His career before 1940, however, is intelligently

discussed in Alexander Werth, *The Twilight of France, 1933-1940* (1942); D. W. Brogan, *The Development of Modern France, 1870-1939* (1947; rev. ed. 1966); and Peter J. Larmour, *The French Radical Party in the 1930's* (1964).

## Additional Sources

Daladier, Edouard, *Prison journal, 1940-1945,* Boulder: Westview Press, 1995. □

# Dalai Lama

**The Dalai Lama (Lhamo Thondup; born 1935), the 14th in a line of Buddhist spiritual and temporal leaders of Tibet, fled to India during the revolt against Chinese control in 1959 and from exile promoted Tibetan religious and cultural traditions.**

The 14th Dalai Lama (loosely translated "Ocean of Wisdom") was born Lhamo Thondup on July 6, 1935, in Taktser, a small village in far northeastern Tibet. In 1937 a mission sent out by the Tibetan government to search for the successor to the 13th Dalai Lama, who had died in 1933, felt led to him by signs and oracles. It is reported that when they tested him, Lhamo Thondup correctly identified objects belonging to his predecessor, and a state oracle confirmed that he was the reincarnation of the previous Dalai Lamas. On February 22, 1940, he was officially installed as spiritual leader of Tibet, though political rule remained in the hands of the regents. He took the name Jamphel Ngawang Lobsang Yeshe Tenzin Gyatso.

As the 14th Dalai Lama, he followed in the line of Tibetan Buddhist spiritual and temporal leaders with roots in a reform movement led by Tsong-kha-pa (1357-1419), who sought to restore Buddhist monastic discipline and founded an order of Buddhist monks known as the Gelugpa or "Yellow Hat" sect. In 1438 the head of the order and the first Dalai Lama established a monastery at Tashilhundpo, but the second Dalai Lama established the monastery of Drepung, near Lhasa, as the permanent seat of the line. The third Dalai Lama (1543-1588) was first given the title "Dalai Lama" (*lama* is a Tibetan term that translates the Sanskrit *guru*, or "teacher"; *dalai*—"ocean, or all-embracing"—is apparently a partial translation of the third Dalai Lama's name) by a Mongol leader, Altan Khan, who led his followers to convert to Tibetan Buddhism. The grandson of Altan Khan was identified as the fourth Dalai Lama, thus solidifying Mongolian-Tibetan ties but threatening the Chinese rulers.

The Dalai Lama gradually gained his temporal power over Tibet through skillful use of Mongol and Manchu support. Finally, with the help of a western Mongol tribe, the fifth Dalai Lama (1617-1682) extended the rule of the Gelugpas over all of Tibet. He built the large winter palace, the Potala, in Lhasa, which has become a symbol of Tibetan nationalism. It was during his reign that the Dalai Lama was confirmed by "newly discovered texts" to be the reincarnation not only of the previous Dalai Lamas but also of the

Buddhist Bodhisattva Avalokiteshvara or Chenrezig, a celestial bodhisattva (enlightened being) who comes to the aid of people in need and often functions as do the gods of India and China, and, for some, as a patron deity of Tibet.

Repeated power struggles between western Mongols and Tibetans during the early 18th century, including a violent civil war in 1727-1728, resulted in intervention by the Ch'ing dynasty of China in 1720, 1728, and 1750. Their final solution was to firmly and finally establish the Dalai Lama in the position of full temporal power and Tibet as a protectorate of the Ch'ing Empire under the supervision of residents (*ambans*) from Peking.

The 13th Dalai Lama, Thupten Gyatso (1875-1933), took an interest in modern technology, sent Tibetan students abroad for education, and attempted to raise the standard of education of the Tibetan monastic community. The renewed assertion of control over Tibet by the Ch'ing government with broad reforms in 1908 proved so intense that when Chinese troops arrived in Lhasa in 1910 the Dalai Lama fled to India. He returned to Tibet in 1912 when the Chinese withdrew the troops in response to the 1911 revolution in China, and in January 1913 the Dalai Lama declared the independence of Tibet. The declaration was recognized by the British, who were colonizing South Asia, but not by China.

The 14th Dalai Lama, then, inherited his office on the basis of the belief that he was a reincarnation of each of the previous Dalai Lamas as well as the 74th manifestation of Avalokiteshvara, the first being an Indian Brahmin boy who lived at the time of the historical Buddha, Shakyamuni. Each Dalai Lama is "discovered" on the basis of omens and signs. Letters from the previous Dalai Lama are often cited in identification. Most important for determination is the Nechung oracle, who is believed to incarnate the god Pehar or Dorje Drakden, one of the protector deities of the Dalai Lama and with whom he consults at least annually. A medium enters a trance in which his face is said to be transformed. A 30-pound helmet is placed on his head; he wields a sword and dances slowly while speaking words of the deity which need interpretation. Consulting this and other oracles remains a regular element of the Dalai Lama's activity.

On October 26, 1951, Chinese troops again entered Lhasa. With the signing of the Sino-Tibetan Treaty, the Dalai Lama attempted to work within the strictures imposed by China, visiting Peking in 1954 and negotiating with Chinese leaders. He was attracted to Marxism but repulsed by Chinese activity in the "liberation" of Tibet. The Chinese attempted to use the Panchen Lama, the second spiritual leader, to counteract his influence, but this failed. With the Tibetan uprising in 1959, the Dalai Lama fled to India, where he set up his residence in Dharamsala, Himachal Pradesh.

The Dalai Lama received an extensive education in Buddhist thought and practice as part of his monastic training. His contacts with Westerners broadened his interest beyond Buddhism and he often spoke and wrote of the similarities of religions in the development of love and compassion and in the pursuit of goodness and happiness for all beings. Global peace and environmental concerns round out his popular message. In 1987 he was the recipient of the Albert Schweitzer Humanitarian Award and in 1989 he was awarded the Nobel Peace Prize.

The Dalai Lama remains an active and revered humanitarian throughout the world. His struggles for peace and freedom have made him one of the most recognized and regarded political/spiritual leaders in the world. He has spent much of his time traveling, speaking against communism and for peace. He has a devout following which includes individuals from all over the world and from all walks of life.

## Further Reading

*Freedom in Exile: The Autobiography of the Dalai Lama* (1990) introduces the life and personality of the 14th Dalai Lama. See also his *The Buddhism of Tibet* (1975) and *The Dalai Lama at Harvard: Lectures on the Buddhist Path to Peace* (1988). Several accounts of recent Tibetan history have been written by Tibetan leaders. See for example Chogyam Trungpa, *Born in Tibet* (1966), and Rinchaen Dola Taring, *Daughter of Tibet* (1970). The most accurate survey of Tibetan religion is Helmut Hoffman, *The Religions of Tibet* (1961). See also "The Dalai Lama" by Claudia Dreifus in the *New York Times Magazine* (November 28, 1993). □

# Sir Henry Hallett Dale

**The English pharmacologist and neurophysiologist Sir Henry Hallett Dale (1875-1968) shared the Nobel Prize in Physiology or Medicine for discoveries relating to the chemical transmission of nerve impulses.**

Henry Dale, son of C. J. Dale, a businessman, was born in London on June 9, 1875. He entered Trinity College, Cambridge, in 1894 with a scholarship, read physiology and zoology, and graduated bachelor of arts in 1898. During 2 years of postgraduate work at Cambridge he worked under W. H. Gaskell, J. N. Langley, and (Sir) F. Gowland Hopkins. In 1900 Dale started the clinical work at St. Bartholomew's Hospital, London, that was necessary for his Cambridge medical degree, which he took in 1903. After research at University College, London, and a period in Paul Ehrlich's research institute at Frankfurt am Main, Dale was invited by (Sir) Henry S. Wellcome in 1904 to accept the post of pharmacologist to the Wellcome Physiological Research Laboratories. Two years later he became director of the laboratories, a post which he held until 1914. He graduated as a doctor of medicine at Cambridge in 1909.

In 1914 Dale was appointed the first pharmacologist to the National Institute for Medical Research, newly established under the Medical Research Committee (later Council). He became its first director in 1928, a post from which he retired in 1942. Dale's work embraced important researches in four different subjects, all initiated while he was at the Wellcome Laboratories and continued at the National Institute.

## Problem of Ergot

A liquid extract of the fungus ergot had been used for centuries in obstetrics to stimulate the contractions of the pregnant uterus. Several alkaloids had already been isolated from this extract, and one of these was claimed to be the active principle. But this alkaloid, ergotine, was not nearly so powerful as the liquid extract, and, on Dale's appointment to the Wellcome Laboratories, Wellcome asked him to try to clear up the problem. Just before that the chemist George Barger, who was also working in the laboratories, had prepared other substances from ergot, and in 1906 Dale carried out a detailed pharmacological investigation of their activity. In succeeding years Barger and others isolated several more supposed "active principles," but Dale could not satisfy himself that any of these was the substance that made the watery extract so potent. It was not until 1935 that the real active principle, ergometrine, was isolated by Dale's former coworker Harold Ward Dudley. But the work that Dale carried out for some years on ergot was to give him pointers to nearly all his future work.

## Action of Pituitary Extracts

In 1909 Dale showed that an extract of the posterior lobe of the pituitary gland produced powerful contractions of the uterus of a pregnant cat. As a result, pituitary extract (pituitrin) was soon extensively used in obstetrics. He also showed that this effect was caused by an active principle of the extract different from that which produced a rise of blood pressure. In 1920-1921, with Dudley, he isolated and studied the active principle, oxytocin, that produced the powerful contractions.

## Histamine and Its Effects

In 1910 Barger and Dale, working on an ergot extract, discovered that a substance in it, later called histamine, had a direct stimulant effect on plain (smooth) muscle, especially that of the uterus and bronchioles. (Histamine had previously been synthesized, but it was not known to occur naturally, in the animal body or elsewhere.) They also showed that it caused a general fall in blood pressure and that its injection produced most of the features of anaphylactic shock. In 1911 they were the first to show that it could be present in animal tissues, as they had isolated it from the wall of the intestine.

No further work was done on histamine until the later years of World War I, when the problem of "secondary" surgical and traumatic shock had become of great practical importance. In 1918 Dale, working with Alfred Newton Richards, showed that small doses of histamine caused constriction of the arteries along with a general dilatation of the capillaries. In 1919 Dale, working with (Sir) Patrick Playfair Laidlaw, showed that massive doses of histamine produced a general dilatation of the blood vessels and capillaries, together with an exudation of plasma from the capillaries, a fall in body temperature, and respiratory depression. These features were almost identical with those found in surgical shock, and in a subsequent study Dale found that the dose of histamine necessary to produce the condition was much smaller if there had been previous hemorrhage. These discoveries were of great practical importance in surgery. Theoretically, they indicated that, in the case of injury to the tissues, histamine was produced by the body cells. But in 1919 there was no evidence that histamine was produced by the body cells, and it was not until 1927 that Dale and his coworkers showed that histamine is normally present in significant amounts in the lung and in the liver.

Meanwhile Dale had carried out various researches that were to lead to another aspect of the histamine problem. In 1913 he noticed the extreme sensitivity of the isolated uterus of a particular guinea pig when treated with a normally quite innocuous dose of horse serum. He later discovered that this particular guinea pig had already been used for the assay of diphtheria antitoxin and was therefore already sensitized to horse serum. By following up this chance observation Dale was able to produce in guinea pig plain muscle all the essential features of anaphylaxis, thus greatly advancing knowledge of the cause of this condition. In 1922 Dale and Charles Halliley Kellaway showed that anaphylactic phenomena are probably due to the location of the antibody in the cell substance. Ten years later other workers showed that in anaphylaxis histamine is actually released by the injured cells. The modern use of antihistaminic drugs stems essentially from Dale's work on histamine.

## Chemical Transmission of the Nerve Impulse

Even as late as the first 2 decades of the 19th century the manner in which an impulse, passing down a nerve to a muscle, causes the latter to contract was quite unknown. In 1904 Dale's friend Thomas Renton Elliott, then working in the same laboratory as Dale at Cambridge, suggested as a result of his research on adrenaline that sympathetic nerve fibers might act on plain muscle and glands by liberating this substance at their endings. But this suggestion was never actively followed up by anyone, though it profoundly influenced Dale's later research.

In 1914 Dale found unusual activities in a certain ergot extract, and the active principle responsible for these unusual effects was isolated by Dale's chemical coworker, Arthur James Ewins. It proved to be acetylcholine, the acetyl ester of choline. This work led to an important paper by Dale (1914), in which he showed that the action of acetylcholine on plain muscle and glands was very similar to the action of parasympathetic fibers, and that acetylcholine reproduces those effects of autonomic nerves that are absent from the action of adrenaline. These observations had no direct sequel at that time, because there was then no evidence that acetylcholine was normally present in the animal body. Nevertheless, this paper foreshadowed an understanding of the chemical transmission of the nerve impulse.

In 1921 one specialized form of chemical transmission was proved by Otto Loewi, who showed that the slowing of the frog's heart that occurred when the vagus nerve was stimulated was due to the liberation of a chemical substance. He suspected that this substance might be acetylcholine, but he cautiously called it the "vagus substance" because even then acetylcholine was not known to be present in the animal body. Indeed, it was not until 1933 that two of Dale's coworkers proved that Loewi's vagus substance was acetylcholine.

In 1929 Dale and Dudley found acetylcholine in the spleens of horses and oxen—the first occasion on which it had ever been found in the animal body—and the experiments of Dale and John Henry Gaddum (1930) strongly suggested that the effects produced by stimulation of parasympathetic nerves were due to the liberation of acetylcholine. But about this time Dale became convinced that, in laboratory animals, if acetylcholine was present at all, it must either be in very much smaller quantities than was found in the spleens of oxen, or alternatively it must be destroyed very rapidly.

In 1933 and 1934 the mode of action of impulses in sympathetic nerves was cleared up by Dale and his coworkers, (Sir) George Lindor Brown, Wilhelm Siegmund Feldberg, Gaddum, and others. It was known that, when fibers leading to a sympathetic ganglion were stimulated, a minute amount of a substance suspected to be acetylcholine was produced in the ganglion, but this substance was immediately destroyed by an esterase. But the action of this esterase was inhibited by eserine, so that, by adding eserine to the fluid used to wash out the ganglion, sufficient of the substance was collected for it to be tested. The substance was thus shown to be acetylcholine. They then showed that even a single nerve impulse in a single nerve fiber passing to a sympathetic ganglion, released an incredibly minute amount of acetylcholine, and this amount was approximately measured ($10^{-15}$ gram). It was shown that, having acted as a trigger at the synapse, the acetylcholine was immediately destroyed.

Dale and his coworkers then turned to the problem of a chemical transmitter in the case of voluntary muscle. This problem, which had eluded all others who had worked on it, was technically more difficult. But in 1936 they showed that the amount of acetylcholine liberated when a single impulse in one motor fiber reached the end plate of that fiber was also of the order of $10^{-15}$ gram. In 1936, also Dale, with Brown and Feldberg, showed that the direct injection—under certain conditions—of acetylcholine into the drained vessels in a muscle produced a contraction. The chemical transmission of the nerve impulse, in both parasympathetic and motor nerves, was now conclusively proved and its mode of action elucidated. For these researches Dale shared the Nobel Prize with Loewi in 1936.

## Later Life

From 1940 to 1947 Dale was a member of the Scientific Advisory Committee to the War Cabinet, and he was its chairman from 1942. When he retired from the directorship of the National Institute in 1942, he became Fullerian Professor and director of the Davy-Faraday Laboratory at the Royal Institution. From this post he retired in 1946. He had been chairman of the Wellcome Trust since its establishment in 1936, and he now devoted more and more of his time to the work of this scientific trust, of which he remained chairman until 1960.

Dale received very many honors. He was elected a Fellow of the Royal Society in 1914. He was its Croonian Lecturer in 1919; he received its Royal Medal in 1924 and the Copley Medal—its highest honor—in 1937. He was its Secretary from 1925 to 1935 and its President from 1940 to 1945. In 1947 he was President of the British Association and from 1948 to 1950 President of the Royal Society of Medicine. In 1922 he was elected a Fellow of the Royal College of Physicians, and he gave its Croonian Lecture in 1929.

Dale was knighted in 1932 and created Knight Grand Cross of the Order of the British Empire in 1943. In 1944 he was appointed to the Order of Merit. He received honorary degrees from 25 universities, and he was an honorary or corresponding member of over 30 foreign learned societies. He died at Cambridge on July 23, 1968.

## Further Reading

There is a short biography of Dale in *Nobel Lectures, Physiology or Medicine, 1922-1941* (1965); it also contains his Nobel Lecture, which deals solely with his work on the chemical transmission of the nerve impulse. Dale's work as a whole is discussed in some detail in C. Singer and E. A. Underwood, *A Short History of Medicine* (1962). More important, but more difficult, is Dale's own *Adventures in Physiology* (1953), in which he reprinted 30 of his most important scientific papers, with his later comments on each paper. □

# Richard J. Daley

**Richard J. Daley (1902-1976) was the Democratic mayor of Chicago from 1955 to 1976 and the last of the nation's big city bosses.**

The most powerful mayor in Chicago's history, Richard J. Daley, was born in a working class neighborhood on May 15, 1902, the only son of Michael Daley, a sheet metal worker, and Lillian (Dunne) Daley. His parents were Irish Catholics and sent young Richard to a Catholic elementary school, enlisted him as an altar boy, and then enrolled him at the Christian Brothers De LaSalle High School. Later, after several long years of night school, Daley earned a degree common to upwardly mobile Chicago politicians—a law diploma from De Paul Law School—in 1933. While a student Daley worked as a stockyards cowboy and clerked in the Cook County controller's office.

Richard J. Daley worked his way up through the precinct and ward organization and made his first successful run for public office as a state representative in 1936. Two years later he was elected to the Illinois senate, where he remained until 1946 when he suffered his only election loss—as a candidate for Cook County sheriff. Defeated but not without friends, Daley was selected by Governor Adlai Stevenson in 1949 to become director of the Illinois Department of Finance. While there Daley expanded his grasp of budgets and public finance, which later served him well as mayor. Daley then returned to Chicago and was elected Clerk of Cook County. Meanwhile, he had married Eleanor Guilfoyle on June 23, 1936, and was the father of four sons and three daughters. A devout Roman Catholic, Daley reportedly attended mass every morning.

## Begins Six Winning Elections

The key that opened his way to the mayor's office was Daley's election as chairman of the Cook County Democratic Central Committee in 1953. In 1955 Daley entered a Democratic primary election and defeated incumbent mayor Martin H. Kennelly. In the general election which followed, Daley beat Republican challenger Robert E. Merriam by a comfortable majority of the vote. During the next two decades Daley was reelected mayor over a series of nominally nonpartisan but generally Republican contenders in 1959, 1963, 1967, 1971, and 1975. The source of Daley's power derived from his dual role as mayor and party chairman. He ran a tightly organized party structure and made maximum use of about 35,000 city workers and patronage employees to bring out the vote. Daley also won public support because he paid attention to the delivery of municipal services and gave substance to the slogan "the city that works." His important role in helping John F. Kennedy win the Democratic nomination and the presidential election in 1960 brought Daley his first national recognition as a political strategist.

Dedicated to building and redeveloping Chicago's center, Daley encouraged the construction of downtown

skyscrapers, stimulated expressway expansion, improved mass transit facilities, and enlarged the world's busiest airport, O'Hare. His administrations also set a rapid pace for urban renewal, the demolition of blighted areas, and the building of additional public housing. As with all of his enterprises he mixed politics and business, and for the scoffers, Daley repeated over and again: "Good politics makes for good government." When taunted about the evils of the "machine," Daley generally snapped back to reporters: "Organization, not machine. Get that, organization not machine." Although evidence of venality occasionally tainted Daley's cronies, the mayor himself appeared to remain free of corruption. One notable exception was when a lucrative insurance contract was given over to a firm employing a Daley son. When chided, Daley exploded with rage over the issue, insisting that it was the duty of any good father to help out a son. Beyond that misdeed numerous clandestine investigations by public and private agencies and local newspapers failed to produce a single solid charge of peculation against the mayor personally.

### Some Setbacks in a Long Career

The year 1968 was a disaster for the Daley legend. In the wake of Martin Luther King's death in April 1968 a firestorm of arson, looting, and rioting swept through Chicago's Black West Side, and an enraged mayor issued an order which was broadcast across the newspaper headlines and television screens of the nation: "shoot to kill any arsonist . . . with a Molotov cocktail in his hand." Daley's command provoked the wrath of the liberal news media.

But that was only a foretaste of the bitter draught yet to come. Daley's attempt to host the 1968 Democratic presidential nominating convention in Chicago in August turned into a week of anti-war turmoil, street-violence by demonstrators, "a police riot," and a shambles that left Daley's reputation in low esteem. In newscaster hyperbole, Eric Savareid on national television compared that week in Chicago to the Russian invasion of Czechoslovakia with tanks. Daley's standing with the public plunged to its nadir.

For a few years thereafter some professional societies refused to schedule their annual meetings in Chicago. Media liberals predicted that Daley was finished, and the lockout of the Daley delegation from the 1972 Democratic National Convention by the George McGovern wing of the party seemed to support that view. Yet when New York and other cities teetered on the brink of bankruptcy in the mid-1970s, Daley's hard nosed business management kept his city solvent and its bond rating high, bringing about a recovery for his reputation. He went on to win his largest political victory ever in 1975, gaining an unprecedented sixth four-year term. Early in his new term, on December 20, 1976, Daley died and was buried at suburban Worth, Illinois. Daley's public esteem had ridden a roller coaster of highs and lows but had recovered in time for a glorious obituary by the city.

### An Evaluation of Mayor Daley

Daley's accomplishments during his 21-year tenure in office were numerous. The mayor had professionalized the police force and upgraded the fire department's services; he had continued the advantageous arrangement whereby suburban taxpayers paid for the support of Cook County Hospital, which served primarily city residents; he had solved a Chicago Transit cash shortage by the creation of a Regional Transit Authority which broadened the tax base; he had pushed through legislative action that transferred the cost and administrative responsibility for public assistance and welfare from Cook County and Chicago to the state; Daley had helped form a Public Building Commission to finance public construction by means of revenue bonds and at the same time protect the city's bond rating; he had prodded the Illinois legislature to create a Metropolitan Fair and Exposition Authority to operate Chicago's convention center, McCormick Place, without charge to the city; and, finally, he had persuaded the state to build a University of Illinois campus at the state taxpayers' expense in the heart of his city to serve primarily Chicago students. In short, Daley had expanded city services and shifted a large measure of the costs to the state, the county, and the Chicago area suburbs.

A year after the mayor's death a symposium was convened which included scholars, journalists, and practicing politicians who examined the Daley era and concluded: that Mayor Daley had won membership in a class of the best and most-effective big-city mayors of his time; that he had used the mayor's office in an instrumental way to rescue Chicago's downtown Loop from impending blight; that Daley's superior ability as a budget manager and an expert on public finances had helped steer Chicago away from the rocky shoals that nearly bankrupted New York

City; and that as a political broker and organizer Daley was with few peers in the nation.

The mayor earned lower grades from the experts for his reluctance to reach out to the growing suburbs; the Democratic Party's slowness in accommodating newcomer Blacks and Hispanics; and his often stormy and abrasive relationships with the media. On the other hand, the city's bankers and real estate interests were pleased with Chicago's solid financial footing and its high bond rating. On balance, the Daley mayoralty was judged a success. The key to Daley's success, as an expert put it, was that "he was more observant of detail, more canny in his analysis of the political possibilities, and when compromise failed, more powerful than his opponents."

## Further Reading

For the two best works on how the "machine" worked under Daley see Milton Rakove, *Don't Make No Waves: Don't Back No Losers; An Insider's Analysis of the Daley Machine* (1975) and *We Don't Want Nobody Nobody Sent* (1975). A knowledgeable and veteran city watcher and newsman who put together a most perspicacious life and death of the mayor is Len O'Connor in his *Clout: Mayor Daley and His City* (1975) and *Requiem: The Decline and Demise of Mayor Daley and His Era* (1977). For an appreciation of the mythic and Irish dimension of Daley see Eugene Kennedy's *Himself: The Life and Times of Mayor Richard J. Daley* (1978). A wickedly clever and entertaining hatchet job on Daley "da mare" can be read in Mike Royko's *Boss: Richard J. Daley of Chicago* (1971). For a larger perspective on the Daley era, the best single source remains a conference symposium, Melvin G. Holli and Peter d'A. Jones, "Richard J. Daley's Chicago: A Conference," October 11-14, 1977, Chicago.

## Additional Sources

Kennedy, Eugene C, *Himself!: The life and times of Mayor Richard J. Daley,* New York: Viking Press, 1978.

O'Connor, Len, *Requiem: the decline and demise of Mayor Daley and his era,* Chicago: Contemporary Books, 1977.

Royko, Mike, *Boss: Richard J. Daley of Chicago,* New York, N.Y.: New American Library, 1988, 1976.

Sullivan, Frank, *Legend, the only inside story about Mayor Richard J. Daley,* Chicago: Bonus Books, 1989. ☐

# 1st Marquess of Dalhousie

**The British statesman James Andrew Broun Ramsay, 1st Marquess of Dalhousie (1812-1860), served as governor general of India from 1848 to 1856. He is noted for his vigorous, often ruthless, expansion and westernization of British India.**

James Ramsay, the third and youngest son of the 9th Earl of Dalhousie, was born in the ancestral Dalhousie castle in Midlothian, Scotland, on April 22, 1812. He graduated from Christ Church, Oxford, in 1833 and married in 1836. He was elected to Parliament in 1837. As his brothers had both died, he succeeded to the title upon his father's

death in 1838 and entered the House of Lords. Dalhousie served as vice president of the Board of Trade in 1843 and as president in 1845 and early 1846. The following year he accepted the governor generalship of India.

Within 3 months of Dalhousie's assuming office in January 1848, the Punjab was aflame with renewed fighting between the British and the Sikhs. This hard-fought second Sikh war did not end until February 1849, when a British victory in Gujarat forced surrender upon the Sikhs. Dalhousie annexed the Punjab and helped make it the example of reformed imperial administration.

Although military conquest also served as a preliminary to the annexation of lower Burma in 1852, most of Dalhousie's extensions of British-controlled territory resulted from his strict application of the doctrine of lapse. Hindu princes under British influence needed British permission to adopt a male heir, and failure to obtain such permission meant forfeiture of the government, though not the private estate, of the ruler. Applying this policy, Dalhousie annexed Satara, Jaitpur, and Sambalpur in 1849, adding Jhansi and the major Maratha state of Nagpur in 1853.

While adding nearly 250,000 square miles to his government, Dalhousie also made important contributions to the integration and economic development of British India. In 1854 he freed himself and his successors from the minutiae of local government in Bengal by creating the post of lieutenant governor there. He gave real impetus to railway and canal construction, initiated telegraph services,

and overhauled the postal services to provide a uniform and inexpensive rate of postage within India.

Though in failing health, Dalhousie supervised the annexation of Oudh in February 1856. The following month he returned home to receive the thanks of Queen Victoria and a generous pension from the East India Company. The outbreak of the Indian Mutiny in 1857 brought bitter attacks upon him, but he was not well enough to reply to his critics. He died in Dalhousie castle on Dec. 19, 1860.

## Further Reading

J. G. A. Baird edited *Private Letters of the Marquess of Dalhousie* (1910). The standard biography is Sir William Lee-Warner, *The Life of the Marquis of Dalhousie* (2 vols., 1904). Manindra N. Das, *Studies in the Economic and Social Development of Modern India: 1848-56* (1959), is a thorough and favorable investigation of Dalhousie's policies. Aspects of Dalhousie's contribution are also assessed in R. J. Moore, *Sir Charles Wood's Indian Policy, 1853-1866* (1966). □

# Salvador Dali

**The Spanish painter Salvador Dali (1904-1989) was one of the best-known and most flamboyant surrealist artists. Possessed with an enormous facility for drawing, he painted his dreams and bizarre moods in a precise illusionistic fashion.**

S alvador Dali was born May 11, 1904 near Barcelona, Spain. According to his autobiography, his childhood was characterized by fits of anger against his parents and schoolmates and resultant acts of cruelty. He was a precocious child, producing highly sophisticated drawings at an early age. He studied painting in Madrid, responding to various influences, especially the metaphysical school of painting founded by Giorgio de Chirico, and at the same time dabbling in cubism.

Gradually, Dali began to evolve his own style, which was to execute in an extremely precise manner the strange subjects of his fantasy world. Each object was drawn with painstaking exactness, yet it existed in weird juxtaposition with other objects and was engulfed in an oppressive perspectival space which often appeared to recede too rapidly and tilt sharply upward. He used bright colors applied to small objects set off against large patches of dull color. His personal style was evolved from a combination of influences, but increasingly from his contact with surrealism. The contact was at first through paintings and then through personal acquaintance with the surrealists when he visited Paris in 1928. In 1929, Dali painted some of his finest canvases, when he was still young and excited over his surrealist ideas and had not yet developed so extensively his elaborate personal facade. He began to build up a whole repertoire of symbols, mainly drawn from handbooks of abnormal psychology, stressing sexual fantasies and fetishes.

## Paranoic-Critical Method

The surrealists saw in Dali the promise of a break-through of the surrealist dilemma in 1930. Many of the surrealists had broken away from the movement, feeling that direct political action had to come before any mental revolutions. Dali put forth his ''Paranoic-Critical method'' as an alternative to having to politically conquer the world. He felt that his own vision could be imposed on and color the world to his liking so that it became unnecessary to change it objectively. Specifically, the Paranoic-Critical method meant that Dali had trained himself to possess the hallucinatory power to look at one object and ''see'' another. On the nonvisual level, it meant that Dali could take a myth which had a generally accepted interpretation and impose upon it his own personal and bizarre interpretation. For example, the story of William Tell is generally considered to symbolize filial trust, but Dali's version had it as a story of castration. This way he had of viewing the world began early when he was told in art school to copy a Gothic virgin and instead drew a pair of scales. It meant that although Dali assumed many of the attitudes of madness this was, at least in part, consciously done.

A key event in Dali's life was his meeting with his wife, Gala, who was at that time married to another surrealist. She became his deliberately cultivated main influence, both in his personal life and in many of his paintings.

## Break with the Surrealists

Toward the end of the 1930s, Dali's romantic and flamboyant view of himself began to antagonize the surrealists. There was a final break on political grounds, and André Breton angrily excommunicated Dali from the surrealist movement. Dali continued to be extremely successful commercially, but his seriousness as an artist began to be questioned. He took a violent stand against abstract art, mixed with the fashionable world, and began to paint Catholic subjects in the same tight illusionistic style which had previously described his personal hallucinations.

In 1974, Dali broke with English business manager Peter Moore and had his copyrights sold out from under him by other business managers which gave him none of the profits. In 1980, A. Reynolds Morse of Cleveland, Ohio set up an organization called Friends to Save Dali. Dali was said to have been defrauded out of much of his wealth and the foundation was to put him back on solid financial ground.

In 1983, Dali exhibited a major retrospective at the Museum of Contemporary Art in Madrid, Spain. This show made him immensely famous in Spain and brought him further into favor with the Spanish royal family and major collectors around the world. After 1984, Dali was confined to a wheel chair after suffering injuries as the result of a house fire.

Dali died on January 23, 1989 at Pigueras Hospital in Figueras, Spain. Dali was remembered as the subject of controversy and substance, although in his last years, the controversy had more to do with his associates and their dealings then with Dali.

## Further Reading

Dali presents a fascinating though exaggerated vision of himself in his autobiographical writings, the best of which is *The Secret Life of Salvador Dali* (1942; rev. ed. 1961). A sober but admiring study is James Thrall Soby, *Salvador Dali* (1941; 2d rev. ed. 1946). Robert Descharnes, *The World of Salvador Dali* (trans. 1962), is lavishly illustrated. Biographical information on Dali is available in the 1940 and 1951 issues of *Current Biography*.

Dali's obituary appears in the January 24, 1989 issue of the *New York Times.* □

# Luigi Dallapiccola

**The Italian composer Luigi Dallapiccola (1904-1975) is best known for his twelve-tone compositions, often of highly lyrical and expressive nature.**

Luigi Dallapiccola was born on Feb. 3, 1904, at Pisino in Istria. The town (now Pazin; after World War I, part of Italy) belonged to the Austro-Hungarian Empire during his childhood. In 1917 the Dallapiccolas and other Italian families of that community were deported to Graz, Austria, for political reasons. There Dallapiccola had his

first opportunity to hear major operas, such as Wolfgang Amadeus Mozart's *Don Giovanni* and Richard Wagner's *Die Meistersinger* and *The Flying Dutchman*. At this time he decided definitely to become a musician, although his father, a professor of classical languages, insisted that he complete a classical education also.

In 1921 Dallapiccola graduated from high school. The next year he went to Florence, where he entered the harmony class of the conservatory in 1923. Two years later he composed three songs *Fiuri de Tapo* (texts by Biagio Marin); these remained unpublished and unperformed. In 1931 he became a professor at the Florence Conservatory. Dallapiccola's first major commission came in 1934: *Divertimento in quattro essercizi* for soprano and five instruments (on a 12th-century text), written for the group Le Carillon in Geneva.

In his early works Dallapiccola did not follow twelve-tone principles. However, he came to feel that the consistent use of the twelve tones would enable him to write richer and more expressive melodies. A fine example of such a melody occurs at the beginning of his opera *Volo di notte* (1937-1939; Night Flight; text after Saint-Exupéry). The *Canti di prigionia* (1939-1941; Prison Songs; texts by Mary, Queen of Scots, Boethius, and Savonarola) are united by a single twelve-tone row but still contain many free passages. His first work to use the strict twelve-tone method throughout is the *Cinque frammenti di Saffo* (1942). Dallapiccola was the first Italian composer to study and apply twelve-tone principles systematically. In applying them he also found his personal style. While he learned much from the

example of Arnold Schoenberg, Alban Berg, and Anton Webern, Dallapiccola's expressiveness is his own.

Most of Dallapiccola's important works are vocal. He often chose texts which glorified the idea of liberty. Three of his major compositions on this theme are the *Canti di prigionia; Il Prigioniero,* a one-act opera with prologue (1949; text after Villiers de l'Isle-Adam and Charles de Coster); and *Canti de liberazione* for choir and orchestra (1955; Songs of Liberation; texts from Castillio, St. Augustine, and the Book of Exodus). His opera *Ulysses* (1967) deals with Ulysses's quest for himself and his final delivery into the hands of God. He also composed *Sicut Umbra* (1970) and *Commiato* (1972). Dallapiccola died on February 19, 1975 and was buried in Florence.

## Further Reading

A biography available in English on Dallapiccola is Roman Vlad's brief study, *Luigi Dallapiccola* (trans. 1957). A lengthy biography appears in Thompson, Oscar, ed., *International Cyclopedia of Music and Musicians* (11th edition, Dodd, Mead & Co, Inc.,1985). □

# John Dalton

**The English chemist John Dalton (1766-1844) provided the beginnings of the development of a scientific atomic theory, thus facilitating the development of chemistry as a separate science. His contributions to physics, particularly to meteorology, were also significant.**

John Dalton was the youngest of three surviving children of a Quaker handloom weaver. He was born about Sept. 6, 1766 (no exact record exists), in Eaglesfield. Until he was 11, he attended school, then at the age of 12 became a teacher. For about a year he next worked as a farm helper, but at 15 he returned to teaching, privately for the most part, pursuing it as a career for the remainder of his life.

In his work Dalton used relatively simple equipment and has been accused of being "a very coarse experimenter." However, he had a gift for reasoning and for drawing correct conclusions from imperfect experiments. He himself attributed his success primarily to simple persistence.

## Studies in Meteorology

Dalton's lifelong interest in meteorology did much to make that study a science. He began keeping records of the local weather conditions—atmospheric pressure, temperature, wind, and humidity—in 1787 and maintained them for 57 years until his death. During this time he recorded more than 200,000 values, using equipment which for the most part was made by him.

Dalton's interest in the weather gave him a special interest in mixtures of gases, and his earliest studies were concerned with atmospheric physics. The formulation of his

law of partial pressures (Dalton's law) was announced in 1803. It defined the pressure of a mixture of gases as the sum of the pressures exerted by each component solely occupying the same space. In 1800 he studied the heating and cooling of gases resulting from compression and expansion, and in 1801 he formulated a law of the thermal expansion of gases. His work on water vapor concentration in the atmosphere, using a homemade dew-point hygrometer, and his 1804 study of the effect of temperature on the pressure of a vapor brought him international fame.

## Developing the Atomic Theory

The formulation of the atomic theory, Dalton's greatest achievement, was developed gradually, almost inadvertently, through a series of observations resulting from his preoccupation with gases. It began with an attempt to explain why the constituents of a gaseous mixture remain homogeneously mixed instead of forming layers according to their density. The theory was first alluded to in a paper presented before the Manchester Literary and Philosophical Society in 1803 on the absorption of gases by water and other liquids. In the last section of the paper was the first table of atomic weights. The acceptance of his theory prompted Dalton to expand it further, and finally he published it in his *New System of Chemical Philosophy* (1808). Although William Higgins claimed priority over Dalton, the consensus is that Dalton conceived the idea that the atoms of different elements are distinguished by differences in their weight. As contrasted to others who may have vaguely glimpsed the principle, Dalton presented it as a universal and consistent fact and applied it to the explanation of chemical phenomena.

Other, less significant contributions were his pioneering investigation of thermal conductivity in liquids and his 1794 paper in which he discussed color blindness.

## Later Life

Dalton lived a simple life, kept to the doctrines of his Quaker faith, and never married. During most of his life he had little money and was almost excessively economical; however, by tutoring and doing routine chemical work at low pay his few wants were met. He had no flair for lecturing: his voice was rather harsh, and he was inclined to be rather stiff and awkward in manner. He is said to have had no grace in conversation or in writing. Despite his lack of these social assets, he apparently lived a quite happy life and had many friends.

In 1810 Dalton refused an invitation to join the Royal Society but was finally elected in 1822 without his knowledge. As his fame grew, he received many honors, including a doctor's degree from Oxford in 1832, at which time he was presented to King William IV. For this occasion he had to wear the famous scarlet regalia of Oxford, which fortunately looked gray to his color-blind eyes and therefore was acceptable to him as an orthodox Quaker.

In 1837 he suffered a damaging stroke; the following year another left him with impaired speech. A final stroke came on the night of July 26, 1844.

## Further Reading

The most recent biography of Dalton is Frank Greenaway, *John Dalton and the Atom* (1966). See also L. J. Neville-Polley, *John Dalton* (1920), and Bernard Jaffe, *Crucibles* (1930). The background for Dalton's work, its influence, and biographical and historical material are contained in David Stephen L. Cardwell, ed., *John Dalton and the Progress of Science* (1968), which comprises essays presented by Dalton scholars at a conference marking the bicentenary of Dalton's birth. Dalton's scientific achievements are summarized in James R. Partington, *History of Chemistry*, vol. 3 (1962). A. L. Smyth, *John Dalton, 1766-1844: A Bibliography of Works by and about Him*, was published in 1966. □

# Marcus Daly

**American miner and business leader Marcus Daly (1841-1900) founded the Anaconda Copper Mining Company and was a power in Montana politics.**

Marcus Daly was born on Dec. 5, 1841, at Ballyjamesduff in County Cavan, Ireland. In 1856 he emigrated, settling first in New York City, where he found work as an errand boy and hostler. Five years later he moved to California and got a job as a mucker (clean-up man) in a gold mine. Despite his lack of education, Daly was intelligent and ambitious and soon had learned enough about good mining practice to become

foreman of a mine on the Comstock Lode in Nevada. He remained in the Virginia City area from 1862 to 1868 and then moved to Utah, where he operated several silver mines for a firm of Salt Lake City bankers and mine owners.

Daly's big opportunity came when this firm sent him to Butte, Mont., to examine their mining claims. Deciding to remain in Montana, Daly purchased the Alice silver prospect from his employers. He sold the mine at a large profit, which he then used in 1880 to purchase a small silver deposit known as the Anaconda from a prospector named Michael Hickey. Historians have speculated whether Daly actually knew that the mine contained a huge body of copper or was just lucky in his investment. Daly soon acquired adjoining claims, then entered into a partnership with three other men who provided the capital to develop the Anaconda.

Daly's partners were not enthusiastic about a copper mine in Montana. It was too far from the copper market, the market was limited, and what there was of a market was already monopolized by Michigan miners. But Daly, anticipating a great expansion in the use of copper, gambled that—with large-scale production—he could compete successfully with eastern mining interests. The rapid, phenomenal growth of Anaconda attests to Daly's business acumen.

From copper mining Daly branched out into related enterprises—banking, lumbering, and coal mining. He founded the town of Anaconda, constructed water and power facilities, went into ranching, bred racehorses, developed fruit orchards, built the largest smelter in the world, and constructed a railroad from Anaconda to Butte.

Daly also established a newspaper, the *Anaconda Standard,* which he used to further his political objectives. Although he personally sought no public office, he did finance the campaigns of Democrats for seats in the state and national legislatures. He also waged an expensive but unsuccessful fight to make Anaconda the state capital; Helena won the coveted prize by a margin of only a few thousand votes. But above all, Daly's political activities were directed toward frustrating the political ambitions of his archrival in copper mining, William Andrews Clark.

Until 1894 the Anaconda was operated as a partnership. Then the partners incorporated as the Anaconda Mining Company. When a Rothschild syndicate bought one partner's share of the property in 1895, the company reorganized as the Anaconda Copper Mining Company. In 1899 Standard Oil purchased Anaconda. Through all these changes Daly continued to serve as president of the company.

On Nov. 12, 1900, after a lengthy illness, Daly died in New York City. He was remembered as charitable, generous, and fair. His memory of his beginnings as an immigrant and a humble miner enabled him to maintain good relations with his workers. Anaconda had no labor disturbances so long as Daly remained at the helm.

## Further Reading

There is no biography of Daly, but material on his career may be found in Federal Writer's Program, *Copper Camp, Stories of* the World's Greatest Mining Town: Butte, Montana (1943); Isaac F. Marcosson, Anaconda (1957); and K. Ross Toole, Montana: An Uncommon Land (1959).

## Additional Sources

Powell, Ada, The Dalys of the Bitter Root, Montana: A. Powell, 1989. ☐

# Mary Daly

**Mary Daly (born 1928) was considered the foremost feminist theoretician and philosopher in the United States.**

Mary Daly was born in Schenectady, New York, on October 16, 1928. Educated in Catholic schools, she received her first Ph.D. from St. Mary's College/Notre Dame University in 1954. Between 1959 and 1966 she taught philosophy in Junior Year Abroad programs in Fribourg, Switzerland. She also received doctorates in theology and philosophy from the University of Fribourg in 1963 and 1965. After 1966 she was a member of the theology department of Boston College.

Daly was in the forefront of American feminist thinking, both in terms of her early appearance as a feminist writer and in terms of the depth, originality, and power of her work. Her first feminist book, The Church and the Second Sex (1968), was published at the very beginning of the women's liberation movement that emerged in the late 1960s. In that work Daly both documented the history of misogynism in the Catholic Church from the time of the early Fathers through the reign of Pope Pius XII and explored the limitations placed on women's development by the Church's perpetuation of the myth of the "Eternal Feminine." This was the belief that the true nature of women is to be self-sacrificing, passive, and docile, and that women are fulfilled only in physical or spiritual motherhood. Daly called for creative and independent women to exorcise the stifling image of the Eternal Feminine by "raising up their own image" and fulfilling their potential. She also urged the Church to contribute to the exorcism of antifeminism by ending discrimination against women in the ministry, eliminating the barriers that isolate nuns from the world, and examining the conceptual inadequacies that underlie and perpetuate androcentric theology. For example, the attribution of male gender to a transcendent God and the identification of women with sexuality, matter, and evil.

## Book Threatens Job

Considerable furor followed the publication of The Church and the Second Sex. Daly was threatened with the loss of her job at Boston College and was finally granted tenure only after some months of student protests and widespread media publicity. The experience radicalized her view of the oppressiveness of patriarchal structures and was the catalyst of her transformation from a reformist Catholic to a post-Christian radical feminist.

In her next book, Beyond God the Father (1973), Daly challenged the whole edifice of patriarchal religion. She argued that its myths and theological constructs, by legitimating male superiority and displacing evil onto the female as the prototypical Other, not only oppress half the human race but foster social structures and ways of thinking that produce racism, genocide, and war. She rejected not only the gender identification of God but the concept of God as a static noun (supreme being) rather than active verb (Be-ing). To "'hypostatize transcendence,' to objectify God as a 'being,'" she wrote, is to "envisage transcendent reality as finite. 'God' then functions to legitimate the existing ... status quo."

She saw in the women's movement an authentic challenge to patriarchal religion, a challenge that confronted the fathers' "demonic distortion of Be-ing" with an "ontological, spiritual revolution ... pointing beyond the idolatries of sexist society and sparking creative action in and toward transcendence." She attempted to salvage some traditional Christian images by radically transforming their content; she argued that redemption from the evils of the sexist order can be brought about only by women, that the New Being (theologian Paul Tillich's term for Christ) will be manifested in women, and that the prophecy of the Second Coming points to the re-emergence of a strong female presence capable of altering "the seemingly doomed course of human evolution."

## Departs Christian Symbolism

In the years following the publication of Beyond God the Father Daly left behind all Christian symbolism and rooted her theology completely in women's experience. Gyn/Ecology (1978) was concerned with the process of women's "becoming" (which Daly described in mythic terms as a journey to the Otherworld) and with the demonic obstacles to that process, the deceptive myths and sadistic practices of patriarchal culture. Subtitled The Metaethics of Radical Feminism, Gyn/Ecology was an attempt to see through the deceptive and confusing maze of patriarchal thinking about good and evil and to go beyond it into what Daly called the deep background of language and myth.

Daly explored the deadly "foreground" myths that shackle women's minds and recounted the psychological and physical destruction of women by such practices as Indian suttee, Chinese footbinding, African genital mutilation, European witchburning, and American gynecology.

Having named and described the male-created demons that block the passage to female Selfhood in the last section of the book, Daly then charted the deeper passages through which women spin and spiral into women-identified and woman-honoring consciousness. In the process of making this journey Daly reclaimed language—the "power of naming"—and forged it into an instrument for the liberation of women's minds from oppressive patriarchal myths and for the expression of deeper levels of women's psychological and spiritual experience. Though not always easy reading, this transformed language—incandescent, metaphoric, alliterative, playful, inventive, punning, charged with sheer energy, anger, and humor—is a brilliant manifestation of the emergence of a "metapatriarchal" women's consciousness.

## Language Key to Self

*Pure Lust* (1984), subtitled *Elemental Feminist Philosophy,* was concerned with First Philosophy, traditionally defined as ontology or the philosophy of being. Daly reiterated her earlier rejection of the objectified noun *being* as an inadequate expression of the constantly creating and unfolding Powers of Be-ing, and she defined the ultimate concern of feminist philosophy as "biophilic participation in Be-ing." Be-ing was not separated from nature in Daly's thinking; it was to be found in the elemental nature of the Self, the earth, and the cosmos; Daly saw matter and spirit as unified and the cosmos as enspirited and ensouled.

In *Pure Lust,* as in *Gyn/Ecology,* her method of discovering and connecting with the sources of Be-ing was through language: she explored the etymological roots of words and their multiple, double-edged, obscure, and obsolete meanings in order to discover and open up the deep meanings of words and make them suitable for women's journey toward fuller participation in Elemental Be-ing. Though that journey is both outward and inward—outward with the evolutionary unfolding of the cosmos—in *Pure Lust,* as in *Gyn/Ecology,* Daly focused primarily on the journey inward and back, through the mazes of patriarchal barriers, to women's Archaic origins and original Selves, to the rediscovery of their primordial life-affirming power, connectedness, and creativity.

Daly's *Websters' First New Intergalactic Wickedary of the English Language Conjured in Cahoots with Jane Caputi* was published in 1987. The book is an indictment of patriarchy and male dominated institutions in which Daly harnesses the power of naming to make her point. In the book, she defines "positively revolting hag," a term she uses to describe herself. For Daly it means, "a stunning, beauteous Crone; one who inspires positive revulsion from phallic institutions and morality. . . ." In Daly's lexicon, cockalorum means "a self-important little cock. Examples: Napoleon, Andy Warhol, Fiorello La Guardia, Mickey Mouse," and a crone is "a Great Hag of History, long-lasting one; Survivor of the perpetual witchcraze or patriarchy." Daly's dictionary was followed by *Outercourse: The Be-Dazzling Voyage,* based on her unpublished *Logbook of a Radical Feminist Philosopher.* This effort was followed by work for Daly's next book, to be called *Quintessence.* "This work is in some respects a successor to my philosophical autobiography, *Outercourse,* and in other ways it is a logical/ontological successor to my earlier works, *Beyond God the Father, Gyn/Ecology,* and *Pure Lust,*" wrote Daly.

During the 1980s and 1990s, Daly continued to lecture to audiences around the world. She was an outspoken critic of popular phenomena such as the Christian men's movement as personified by an organization called the Promise Keepers. Answering a reporter who asked, "who has hurt women?" Daly responded, "These creeps, the Promise Keepers, rightwing Christians. It's not just the ancient fathers of the church and it's not just the church. It's all the major religions."

Writing in *The New Yorker* in 1996, Daly articulated her thoughts on the empowerment of women. "Women who are Pirates in a phallocratic society are involved in a complex operation. First, it is necessary to Plunder—that is, righteously rip off—gems of knowledge that the patriarchs have stolen from us. Second, we must Smuggle back to other women our Plundered treasures. In order to invent strategies that will be big and bold enough for the next millennium, it is crucial that women share our experiences: the chances we have taken and the choices that have kept us alive. They are my Pirate's battle cry and wake-up call for women who I want to hear."

## Further Reading

There is no biography of Mary Daly. For biographical information, see *Contemporary Authors* (1st revision) and the autobiographical preface to the Harper Colophon edition of *The Church and the Second Sex* (1975).

## Additional Sources

Ratcliffe, Krista, *Anglo-American Feminist Challenges to the Rhetorical Traditions: Virginia Woolf, Mary Daly, Adrienne Rich,* Southern Illinois University Press, 1996. □

# Archibald Dalzel

**The Scottish slave trader Archibald Dalzel (1740-1811) was the author of the famous and authoritative *History of Dahomy,* which, though written in defense of the slave trade, dealt seriously with the traditions of that country.**

Archibald Dalzel (Dalziel until 1778) was born at Kirkilston on Oct. 23, 1740, the oldest of four brothers and one sister. Trained as a surgeon, he saw medical service in the Royal Navy during the Seven Years War but failed to enter private practice afterward. After several false starts he became a surgeon for the Committee of Merchants Trading to Africa (the African Committee). Sent to Anomabu in 1763, he was soon slave-trading on his own account, suppressing his initial qualms with the lucrative prospects of his new career.

From 1763 to 1778 Dalzel enjoyed steadily increasing success. In 1767 he was made director of the English fort at Whydah on the Slave Coast, main port of the kingdom of Dahomey, where he prospered, netting up to £1,000 a year, until he decided to retire to England. He arrived in London in 1771; his profits, however, had been inadequate, and he turned again to slaving, at first in partnership and then independently as the owner of three ships and a budding plantation in Florida. By 1778 Dalzel fancied himself ready to become a gentleman planter at Kingston, Jamaica, when he and practically his entire wealth were seized by a privateer while en route to England, where he arrived bankrupt.

Out of humiliation he changed his family name to Dalzel. He spent the next 13 years in irregular and often bizarre employments, by turns a candidate for the civil service, a pirate, a bookseller, and a Spanish wine merchant, failing in all and never, it seems, considering seriously the medical profession for which he was at least indifferently qualified. He then became a lobbyist for the slave-trading interests against the abolitionist movement in the 1780s. This brought him once more to the favorable notice of the African Committee, who in 1791 appointed him governor of their West African headquarters at Cape Coast Castle.

From 1792 until 1802 Dalzel labored energetically, yet in the end unsuccessfully, to restore the revenues of a declining company. Dalzel's governorship was a personal failure, as all his ventures had been, and he was still a poor man upon his retirement in 1802.

### History of Dahomy

Archibald Dalzel died bankrupt in 1811, but the events and circumstances of his disappointed life were lightened by a conspicuous achievement: his great book, *History of Dahomy*. Recognized since his time as a work of literary merit and intellectual power, it appeared in 1793 and was an unusual event for the 18th century, given the Enlightenment's scorn for the non-European past.

Dalzel conceived and wrote his book as an intellectual and moral defense of the slave trade. Notwithstanding this aspect of the work, his history continues to receive respect for its general accuracy, and recognition for its value as a colorful supplement to African traditions, because it deals seriously and with acute observation with the one state of the West African interior with which Europeans had direct contact over the entire course of its history.

### Further Reading

Elizabeth Donnan's classic *Documents Illustrative of the History of the Slave Trade to America* (4 vols., 1930-1935; repr. 1965) prints Dalzel's testimony on the slave trade to the Committee of the Privy Council in 1789. Dalzel's *History of Dahomy* (1793; new imp. 1967) contains an introduction by John D. Fage, who reviews Dalzel's career and gives him credit, despite Dalzel's antiabolitionist intent, as a historian of that African kingdom. The best account of the rise of Dahomey is I. A. Akinjogbin, *Dahomey and Its Neighbors, 1708-1818* (1967). Akinjogbin disagrees with Dalzel's and Robert Norris's theories of Dahomean motives for expansion. Dalzel gave, nonetheless, as Akinjogbin himself asserts, the best single account of Dahomey in the 18th century. Further mention of Dalzel's career is in John D. Hargreaves, *West Africa: The Former French States* (1967). □

# Carl Peter Henrik Dam

**The Danish biochemist Carl Peter Henrik Dam (1895-1976) shared the Nobel Prize in Physiology/Medicine for his discovery of vitamin K.**

Henrik Dam, the son of Emil Dam, an apothecary, was born in Copenhagen on Feb. 21, 1895. He graduated in chemistry at the Polytechnic Institute, Copenhagen, in 1920 and then held two instructor's posts in chemistry and biochemistry. In 1928 he was appointed assistant professor of biochemistry in the University of Copenhagen. In 1929 he was appointed associate professor, and in 1941 professor. In 1934 he graduated as a doctor of science of that university. While holding a Rockefeller Fellowship he worked at Freiburg (1932-1933) and at Zurich (1935).

In 1928 Dam started to work on the cholesterol metabolism of chicks. He fed them a practically sterol-free artificial diet to which vitamins A and D had been added. He proved that, contrary to the current view, chicks could synthesize cholesterol. But he also found that some chicks developed internal hemorrhages and delayed blood coagulation. In 1932 scientists in California claimed that this disease was due to the absence of vitamin C from the diet, but Dam showed that it was not cured by the addition of ascorbic acid (that is, pure vitamin C) to the diet. He also demonstrated that a diet rich in cereals and seeds prevented the disease, and in 1934 he announced that it was due to the absence from the diet of a hitherto unrecognized factor. He then found this factor to be fat-soluble, and in 1935 he announced that it was a new vitamin, which he designated vitamin K. The Californian workers rapidly confirmed his findings.

In 1939 pure vitamin K was first synthesized—from green leaves—by Dam, Paul Karrer, and their coworkers, and independently by E. A. Doisy and L. F. Fieser. In 1940 Doisy prepared from putrefied fish meal a similar vitamin, which he called $K_2$, and the original vitamin was thereafter called $K_1$. By 1939 Dam had shown that the blood of chicks fed on a vitamin K-free diet was very deficient in prothrombin, which is normally present and essential to clotting. He established a method of estimation, defined the vitamin K unit, and found the best sources to be green leaves and tomatoes.

In 1938 Dam and Glavind found that persons showing the cholemic bleeding tendency, which can cause complications in operations for obstructive jaundice, had vitamin K deficiency. In 1939-1940 Dam and his coworkers demonstrated that a prothrombin deficiency in newborn babies, causing them to bleed easily, could be effectively treated by administering vitamin K to the infant or to the mother before the birth.

In 1940, while Dam was lecturing in the United States, Germany invaded Denmark. As he was unable to return home until after the war, he worked during the war years at the Woods Hole Marine Biological Laboratories, at the University of Rochester, and at the Rockefeller Institute. During his absence he was appointed to the Copenhagen chair of biochemistry (1941),which he held until 1965, and continued as emeritus professor in biochemistry (Technical University of Denmark) until his death in 1976. He shared the Nobel Prize with Doisy in 1943.

In 1937 Dam showed that the absence of vitamin E from the diet of chicks caused excessive exudation of plasma from the capillaries. He subsequently showed that the diet had also to be deficient in certain fatty acids. Much of his later work dealt with fatty acids, and he was for a period (1956-1963) director of the division of biochemistry of the Danish Fat Research Institute. He was also the president of the Danish Nutrition Society from 1967-1970.

In addition to his Nobel Prize, Dam's many other honors included the Honorary Fellowship of the Royal Society of Edinburgh. He died on April 17, 1976.

## Further Reading

A biography of Dam is in *Nobel Lectures, Physiology or Medicine, 1942-1962* (1964), which also contains his Nobel Lecture. A discussion of his work is in Theodore Sourkes, *Nobel Prize Winners in Medicine and Physiology, 1901-1965* (1966). □

# Father Damien

**The Belgian missionary Father Damien (1840-1889) is known for his work among the lepers on Molokai in the Hawaiian Islands.**

Father Damien was born Joseph de Veuster in Tremeloo, Belgium, on Jan. 3, 1840, of pious and sturdy Flemish peasant stock. In 1860 he joined his brother in the Contemplative Congregation of the Sacred Heart of Jesus and Mary. After he experienced a vision of St. Francis Xavier, he was convinced that he had a missionary vocation. Without special preparation he substituted for his brother in a missionary party sailing for Hawaii in 1863. After arrival there he was ordained a priest and was then known as Father Damien.

After regular work in a parish, where he proved to be a true priest-workman, the great challenge of Father Damien's life came. He heard about the island of Molokai with its leprosarium, where incurable lepers were sent. He decided that these people "in darkness" needed a resident priest and volunteered for this service. "I am bent on devoting my life to the lepers," he said.

With his creative imagination the apostle brought new breath of hope to these people without hope. His down-to-earth Christian humanism led him to attempt the remaking of man's life even in the despair of Molokai, and he worked with the lepers to build houses, schools, and meeting places. At the same time he studied new ways of treating lepers. He also offered a context of celebration; he encouraged festivity to provide hope in the experience of decay and frustration. One of Father Damien's key words was participation. He had only intermittent coworkers from outside, and instead he recruited and trained coworkers from outside, and instead he recruited and trained coworkers from the lepers. The "prayer leaders" were the members of his team ministry, and his "model parish" eventually grew to become a sign of hope.

Father Damien received the highest Hawaiian decoration for his pioneering work with lepers, and his work received great publicity. He also earned a number of enemies because of his stubbornness and lack of organizational ability. In spite of many obstacles he persisted in his work even after 1878, when he was sure that he himself had leprosy. In one of his last letters he wrote, "My face and my hands are already decomposing, but the good Lord is calling me to keep Easter with Himself." He died on April 15, 1889. Above his grave on Molokai his friends set a black marble cross with the inscription, "Damien de Veuster, Died a Martyr of Charity." His body was reburied in Louvain, Belgium in 1936.

## Further Reading

Of the many biographies of Father Damien, a popular, although eulogistic, one is Omer Englebert, *The Hero of Molokai: Father Damien, Apostle of the Lepers* (1955). See also John Farrow, *Damien the Leper* (1937).

## Additional Sources

Bunson, Margaret, *Father Damien: the man and his era,* Huntington, Ind.: Our Sunday Visitor Pub. Division, Our Sunday Visitor Inc., 1989.

Lynch, Maud, *Father Damien of Molokai,* Dublin: Irish Messenger Publications, 1977. □

command an expedition to explore the Australian coastline. He reached Shark Bay, Western Australia, in August 1699, and using Tasman's charts, he sailed up the coast for a month seeking an estuary. After revictualing at Timor, he proceeded along the north coast of New Guinea and discovered New Britain but abandoned plans to explore the east coast of Australia because his ship, the H. M. S. *Roebuck,* was in poor condition. On the way home, the *Roebuck* was lost off Ascension Island, and the crew were rescued by returning East India men.

A court-martial in 1702 found Dampier unfit to command a naval vessel. During the next 4 years he led an unsuccessful privateering expedition in the South Seas. Between 1708 and 1711 he again sailed around the world as pilot for Capt. Woodes Rogers, a privateer sponsored by Bristol merchants. It was on this voyage that Alexander Selkirk, who had previously been marooned by the crew of a ship under Dampier's command, was picked up at one of the Juan Fernández Islands in the South Pacific. Dampier died in London in March 1715 before receiving his share of the expedition's spoils.

### Further Reading

An account of Dampier which notes both his achievements and defects is Christopher Lloyd, *William Dampier* (1966). See also Clennell Wilkinson, *Dampier: Explorer and Buccaneer* (1929). There is an exciting account of buccaneers in the Caribbean and Pacific in P. K. Kemp and Christopher Lloyd, *The Brethren of the Coast* (1960). □

# William Dampier

**The English privateer and author William Dampier (1652-1715) explored the Western Australian coastline and stimulated interest in the Pacific through popular travel books.**

William Dampier was born the son of a Somerset farmer in June 1652. He sailed to Newfoundland and the East Indies while still a boy and took part in the Third Dutch War (1672-1674). After a brief sojourn in Jamaica as undermanager of a plantation, he joined the buccaneers of the Caribbean in Capt. Morgan's heyday. In 1686 Capt. Swan of the *Cygnet,* in which Dampier was sailing, decided to seek prizes in the Pacific before returning to England. After spending 6 months in the Philippines, Swan's crew seized the ship and cruised in Far Eastern waters between China and Australia. Dampier accordingly spent the summer of 1688 at King Sound in Western Australia. After being marooned on one of the Nicobar Islands, he traveled by native canoe to Sumatra and served as a gunner at Bencoelen before returning to England.

Dampier recorded details of his amazing adventures along with navigational data in a diary on which he based *A New Voyage round the World* (1967) and *Voyages and Descriptions* (1699). Impressed with his work, the English Admiralty commissioned him with the rank of captain to

# Charles Anderson Dana

**The American journalist Charles Anderson Dana (1819-1897), as editor of the *New York Sun* in the late 19th century, created the first modern newspaper.**

Charles A. Dana was born on Aug. 8, 1819, in the small country town of Hinsdale, N.H., the son of an unsuccessful country storekeeper. When the family moved to upstate New York, Charles went to work in an uncle's general store in Buffalo. During the Panic of 1837, the store failed, and at the age of 18 Dana found himself with $200 saved but without a job. Luckily, he had spent much of his youth educating himself and had learned enough Greek and Latin to pass the entrance exams for Harvard College.

Dana attended Harvard for 2 years but was forced to leave because of failing eyesight and lack of money. An interest in the ideas of Charles Fourier, the French utopian socialist, led Dana to join the major Fourierist experimental community in the United States, Brook Farm in West Roxbury, Mass. Dana lived and worked there happily for 5 years until the community was disbanded after a fire. Because he had done some writing at Brook Farm, Dana gravitated toward journalism and in 1847 became city editor of Horace Greeley's *New York Tribune.*

In 1862, after a 15-year association, Dana and Greeley had a major falling-out and Dana was fired. The Civil War was raging, and Dana went to work for the Union government in various capacities, rising to assistant secretary of war under Edwin Stanton. He left the government in 1865 to become editor of a short-lived Chicago paper and then raised enough money among prominent Republicans in New York City to buy the failing *New York Sun*.

As editor, Dana rapidly transformed the Sun. Before the Civil War the prime "news" function of a newspaper had been to promulgate the editor's political opinions, but the dramatic firsthand accounts of battles during the Civil War had brought the news correspondent to prominence. In the *Sun* this trend was reinforced. Although Dana continued to expound his political beliefs on the editorial page, the emphasis in the paper became accurate, lively news stories. This approach contrasted with that of most American newspapers, which continued to imitate the turgid, third-person, literary style of the *London Times*. Dana also began running "human-interest" stories, which focused on the pathos or humor in the lives of ordinary people. Because of their popularity, human-interest stories became a hallmark of modern journalism throughout much of the world.

Dana's *Sun* was an immediate success, and it dominated New York journalism for about 15 years. However, his erratic political views worked against the newspaper. He was generally a Republican and continually attacked the New York City Democratic machine, but in national politics he frequently could not bring himself to support the Republican candidate. His failure to support either presidential

candidate in 1880 cost him considerable circulation and prestige. Shortly thereafter, the founding of Joseph Pulitzer's popular *New York World* cost even more in circulation. When Dana died in 1897, the *Sun* remained "a newspaperman's newspaper," but it had been displaced for the man in the street by the more sensational representatives of the new "yellow journalism," the Hearst and Pulitzer papers.

## Further Reading

James Harrison Wilson, *The Life of Charles A. Dana* (1907), is a sympathetic biography, but Charles J. Rosebault, *When Dana Was the Sun* (1931), is livelier and more colorful. The best serious study of Dana's ideas is Candace Stone, *Dana and the Sun* (1938). There are interesting sections on Dana in Frank M. O'Brien, *The Story of the Sun, New York, 1833-1928* (1918; new ed. 1928); Willard Grosvenor Bleyer, *Main Currents in the History of American Journalism* (1927); and Kenneth Stewart and John Tebbel, *Makers of Modern Journalism* (1952). □

# Richard Henry Dana Jr.

**American author and lawyer Richard Henry Dana, Jr. (1815-1882), wrote one of the most persistently popular nonfiction narratives in American letters, *Two Years before the Mast*. He was also an adviser in the formation and direction of the Free Soil party.**

S on of Richard Henry Dana, Sr. (1787-1879), the Massachusetts poet and editor, the younger Dana distinguished himself in 1834, when he abruptly left the security of Harvard undergraduate life and shipped round Cape Horn to California on a tiny hide-trading brig. He returned 2 years later, completed his studies, and in 1840 was admitted to the bar. In the same year *Two Years before the Mast* was published by Harper and Brothers, and though the publisher had deftly lifted the copyright (paying Dana just $250), the author hoped that the book would at least bring him some law practice.

Dana's hopes were realized—indeed his office filled with sailors and he became known as the "Seaman's Champion"—and he eventually shaped an impressive legal career. Still, the fact that his publisher realized $50,000 from the book did at times move Dana to complaint. He comforted himself with the knowledge that if he had lost money he had gained fame. The book was embraced by all factions—reformers, temperance crusaders, and romantic lovers of the sea, who saw the oceans as at least comparable to the prairies when it came to charting a frontier to explore. Since the day of its publication the book has never been out of print.

Years later, however, Dana wrote to his son: "My life has been a failure compared with what I might and ought to have done. My great success—my book—was a boy's work, done before I came to the Bar." There were other books: *The Seaman's Friend* (1841), a manual and hand-

book for sailors; and *To Cuba and Back* (1859), an interesting account of a vacation voyage.

But Dana's real commitments were to the law, where he finally prospered, and to politics, where he finally failed. Celebrated as the legal champion of fugitive black slaves, Dana consistently missed opportunities for high public office, even within the Free Soil party he had helped create. In 1878 he packed up and left for Europe, furious that his appointment as minister to England had failed of approval in the Senate.

In Europe Dana joined some of the brilliant expatriate circles then dominating Rome and seemed to find some peace. He called it "a dream of life," but even the dream ended, in January 1882, and he was buried in the same Italian graveyard that contained the remains of John Keats and Percy Bysshe Shelley.

## Further Reading

Charles Francis Adams, Jr., *Richard Henry Dana* (1890), and Samuel Shapiro, *Richard Henry Dana, Jr., 1815-1882* (1961), are recommended studies. Of interest also are two editions of *Two Years before the Mast,* one edited by Dana's son, R. H. Dana III (1911), and the other by John H. Kemble (1964). See also *The Journal of Richard Henry Dana* (3 vols., 1968). Background information is in D. H. Lawrence, *Studies in Classic American Literature* (1923; repr. 1964).

## Additional Sources

Dana, Richard Henry, *Two years before the mast: a personal narrative of life at sea,* Pleasantville, N.Y.: Reader's Digest Association, 1995. □

# Enrico Dandolo

**The Venetian doge Enrico Dandolo (ca. 1107-1205) made Venice the largest colonial power in all of Christendom.**

Although Enrico Dandolo held a number of public offices throughout his life, it was not until he became doge in 1192 at the age of 85 that his career acquired historical importance. In his first years as doge he defeated an armada from Pisa. He subsequently sent a powerful squadron to the canal of Otranto to break a blockade which the Pisans, aided by the king of Sicily, had set up to injure Venetian commerce.

Dandolo's most significant political achievement was his contriving to have Venetian ships hired for the Fourth Crusade (1202). Venice's direct participation with a powerful fleet was contingent upon its receiving half of the spoils of victory. But since the doge had not received full payment in advance for transporting the French cavalry, he refused to put them aboard, and the crusade did not take place. Instead, Dandolo induced the forces to attack the city of Zara, then in rebellion against Venice. And for thus turning Christian against Christian, he and all Venetians were excommunicated by the Pope.

After the bloody defeat of Zara the French crusaders wintered there, thus providing Dandolo with a ready body of men. These he employed in alliance with Alexis Angelus, son of Isaac II, the emperor of Constantinople, against Isaac's brother Alexis III, who had deposed and blinded the Emperor. In return, Alexis Angelus promised both the assistance of Byzantine forces in the crusade and the unification of the Greek and Latin churches. Dandolo moved with the crusaders against Constantinople. The siege of the city provoked an internal revolution which ousted Alexis III and effected the return of the Emperor and his son Alexis Angelus. But when the crusaders sought the union of the Greek and Latin churches, a second revolution took place which led to the imprisonment of the aged emperor and the death of his son.

In the face of this impasse Dandolo encouraged the crusaders to reconquer the city for themselves; and in April 1204 Constantinople fell to the Latins, who established a Latin empire on the ruins of the Greek one. Although Dandolo, who had personally directed all operations, was offered the crown of the new empire, he resolutely declined it, contenting himself with the enormous advantages which the conquest had brought to his city. From April 1204 until his death little is recorded of Dandolo's activities. He died on June 14, 1205.

Enrico Dandolo (top, left)

## Further Reading

Margaret Oliphant devotes a colorful and sympathetic chapter to Dandolo in *The Makers of Venice: Doges, Conquerors, Painters and Men of Letters* (1887). Also useful are Steven Runciman, *A History of the Crusades* (3 vols., 1951-1954), and Ernle Bradford, *The Sundered Cross: The Story of the Fourth Crusade* (1967). □

# Josephus Daniels

**The American journalist and statesman Josephus Daniels (1862-1948) was secretary of the Navy in Woodrow Wilson's Cabinet and served as Franklin D. Roosevelt's ambassador to Mexico.**

Josephus Daniels was born in Washington, N.C., on May 18, 1862. After his father was killed in the Civil War, his mother moved to Wilson, where he was raised and sent to school. In his early teens he developed an interest in journalism and upon graduating from high school became a partner in, and then the owner-editor of, the local weekly newspaper. He studied law at the University of North Carolina and eventually moved to Raleigh, where he edited two papers.

A dedicated and active Democrat, Daniels worked in Washington, D.C., in 1893 as chief clerk in the Department of the Interior. Upon returning to Raleigh, he bought the *News and Observer* and soon established himself as an influential man in the state. In national politics Daniels supported William Jennings Bryan, and during Bryan's three unsuccessful bids for the presidency Daniels stumped throughout the country on his behalf.

In 1911 Daniels supported Woodrow Wilson and was appointed the new president's secretary of the Navy. As his assistant secretary, Daniels chose an aristocratic young New York politician named Franklin D. Roosevelt.

Daniels had little previous experience with the Navy, but he did have some set beliefs about how American institutions should be run. He ran afoul of the officer corps by trying to abolish some of their traditional privileges and institute more humane and democratic treatment of enlisted men. A devout Methodist and a teetotaler, he is perhaps most famous in the Navy for having banned alcoholic beverages from ships. He served as secretary of the Navy until 1921, when the defeat of the Democrats sent him back to North Carolina to his lifelong love, journalism.

Roosevelt and Daniels had had some differences in the Navy Department (Roosevelt tended to sympathize much more with the Navy brass), but they had ended their association in Washington with deep mutual respect. Thus, when Roosevelt became president in 1933, he rewarded Daniels with the ambassadorship to Mexico. This aroused considerable consternation in Mexico, for Daniels had supervised the occupation of Veracruz during the Mexican Revolution in 1914.

Daniels however, turned out to be an ambassador with charm, good sense, and, above all, a deep concern for the Mexican people. In 1938, when the Mexican government nationalized the foreign-owned oil industry, Daniels argued for U.S. government restraint against Secretary of State Cordell Hull and the spokesmen for the oil interests, who demanded drastic retaliatory action. Daniels believed that the nationalization was an act of nationalism, not of communism, and that the long-run economic benefits to the United States, in terms of a higher Mexican standard of living and increased purchases from the United States, would far outweigh the short-run losses.

In 1941 Daniels retired to Raleigh and from there, even at an advanced age, continued to keep in touch with Mexican affairs and Mexican friends. He died in Raleigh on Jan. 15, 1948.

## Further Reading

In his later years Daniels wrote a long, rambling autobiography; the three volumes are *Tar Heel Editor* (1939), *The Wilson Era: Years of War and After, 1917-1923* (1946), and *Shirt-sleeve Diplomat* (1947). *The Cabinet Diaries of Josephus Daniels: 1913-1921*, edited by E. David Cronon (1963), is a useful source on both Daniels and the Wilson administration. The best single book on Daniels is Cronon's *Josephus Daniels in Mexico* (1960), which concentrates on his time as ambassador. Jonathan Daniels, *The End of Innocence* (1954), and Joseph L. Morrison, *Josephus Daniels: The Small-d democrat* (1966), are flattering portraits. □

# Gabriele D'Annunzio

**The Italian poet and patriot Gabriele D'Annunzio (1863-1938) was one of the last major representatives of fin-de-siècle decadence in European literature.**

G abriele D'Annunzio was born on March 12, 1863, at Pescara of well-to-do parents. He was educated at the Convitto Cicognini of Prato; he then attended the University of Rome but did not take a degree. Of small physique, bald at an early age, he nevertheless lived in Rome the life of a dandy and ladies' man. In 1883 he married the duchess Maria Hardouin di Gallese, with whom he had three sons. His daughter Renata (the Sirenetta of the novel *Notturno*) was born out of wedlock by a married woman, Maria Gravina Cruyllas, one of his many companions.

In 1910 D'Annunzio was forced to sell La Capponcina, a sumptuous villa near Florence, where he had lived since 1899. He moved to France, settling finally in Arcachon. In 1915 he returned to Italy to campaign for its entry into World War I. He made famous speeches at Quarto dei Mille and from the steps of Rome's Capitoline Hill. An active participant in the war, he flew over Trieste (1915) and Vienna (1918) and lost the sight of an eye after a bad landing. In 1919 he and his legionnaires occupied Fiume, thus anticipating its later union with Italy. D'Annunzio's rightist leanings made him sympathetic to the Fascist regime, which in 1924 conferred on him the title of Principe di Montenevoso. The government also gave him a villa, Il Vittoriale, on the Lake of Garda, where he resided until his death on March 1, 1938.

## Literary Works

One of the most prolific writers of modern Italian literature, D'Annunzio tried all genres with varying success. His accomplished virtuosity in technical matters is evident primarily in his poetry, where the search for new sensual experiences is one of his prime concerns. He also glorified heroic deeds in his patriotic poetry (*Odi navali,* 1892-1893). A synthesis and symphonic repetition of his earlier poetry is evident in the cycle *Laudi del cielo, del mare, della terra e degli eroi* (1903-1904; Hymns of the Sky, Sea, Earth and Heroes).

D'Annunzio collected the best of his short stories in the volume *Novelle della Pescara* (1902). As a story teller, he owes much to Gustave Flaubert and Guy de Maupassant. His novels are of an extreme autobiographical nature. He is Andrea Sperelli in *Il piacere* (1889; *The Child of Pleasure*), Tullio Hermil in *L'innocente* (1892; *The Intruder*), and Giorgio Aurispa in *Trionfo della morte* (1894; *Triumph of Death*). *Il fuoco* (1900; *The Flame of Life*) depicts his relationship to Eleonora Duse. Among D'Annunzio's numerous plays the best are *Francesca da Rimini* (1902) and *La figlia di Jorio* (1904; *The Daughter of Jorio*).

## Further Reading

Two major critical biographies of D'Annunzio in English are Tom Antongini, *D'Annunzio* (1938), and Anthony R. E. Rhodes, *The Poet as Superman: A Life of Gabriele D'Annunzio* (1959). On D'Annunzio's relationship with Eleonora Duse see Bertita L. Harding, *Age Cannot Wither: The Story of Duse and D'Annunzio* (1947), and Frances Winwar, *Wingless Victory: A Biography of Gabriele D'Annunzio and Eleonora Duse* (1956). □

# Joseph B. Danquah

**Joseph B. Danquah (1895-1965) was a Ghanaian political leader and a principal founder of the Gold Coast nationalist movement. As a scholar, he sought to accommodate the best of his country's tribal past to modernity.**

J oseph B. Danquah was born in December 1895 into the most prominent family in Ghana, the Ofori-Attas. In 1915 Danquah became secretary to his elder brother, Nana Sir Ofori-Atta, the paramount chief of Akim Abuakwa. In 1921 Danquah went to London for a higher education and by 1927 he had finished his doctorate with the thesis *The Moral End as Moral Excellence*. He also studied law, which became his principal mainstay and led him to politics in opposition to the British rulers.

## Independence and Opposition

After World War II, nationalist sentiment grew. Danquah was instrumental in founding the United Gold Coast Convention (UGCC), the elite party from which sprang all successive independence movements, until Kwame Nkrumah broke with Danquah in 1949 to found his own party. Danquah spent the rest of his life fighting Nkrumah and providing defense for Nkrumah's opponents. But Danquah won neither in the 1954 or 1956 parliamentary elections nor in the presidential election of 1960, in which he polled only 10 percent of the vote.

Danquah's last 5 years is a story of personal courage with few parallels in modern African history. He had neither the inclination nor the ability to rally his countrymen against the growing tyranny, but always he spoke out and encouraged the younger opposition members. After a railroad strike in 1961, which very nearly toppled Nkrumah's regime, Danquah was detained without charges. He was released in June 1962, but like few others the experience did not silence him. He hung onto his one semiofficial position as president of the Bar Association, and when Nkrumah tried to intimidate—and threatened to overthrow—the popular government of Sylvanus Olympio in Togo, Danquah characteristically protested both the legality and morality of the Ghanaian moves.

After an attempt on Nkrumah's life in January 1964, Danquah was again detained. The notion that Danquah was implicated in the assassination plot was nowhere taken seriously. But Danquah, and all he symbolized, did indeed threaten Nkrumah; and, no doubt, Nkrumah's insecurity explains the isolation and near-starvation diet of Danquah's last year. His only card left was his life, which he unwittingly played perfectly. In response to appeals from Bertrand Russell, Nkrumah planned to release Danquah dramatically to increase support, but before he could do so, Danquah died of heart failure on Feb. 8, 1965. No event did more to silence Nkrumah's remaining defenders or to isolate the regime internationally. A year after Danquah's death Nkrumah's regime was overthrown.

## Literary Output

Danquah's scholarly contributions spread throughout his life, and his political career must be seen in terms of his self-identification as a scholar proud of his past. Danquah's preoccupation with Christianity and the need to adapt it to local tradition led to his book *The Akan Doctrine of God* (1944). His historical research in the 1930s led him to propose that on independence the Gold Coast be renamed Ghana, after the early African empire. Earlier research led to *Gold Coast: Akan Laws and Customs and the Akim Abuakwa Constitution* (1928). His play, *The Third Woman*, appeared in 1943.

## Further Reading

Danquah's career may be traced in David Kimble, *A Political History of Ghana: The Rise of Gold Coast Nationalism, 1850-1928* (1963; rev. ed. 1965), and Dennis Austin, *Politics in Ghana, 1946-1960* (1964). □

# Dante Alighieri

**The Italian poet Dante Alighieri (1265-1321) wrote "The Divine Comedy," the greatest poetic composition of the Christian Middle Ages and the first masterpiece of world literature written in a modern European vernacular.**

Dante lived in a restless age of political conflict between popes and emperors and of strife within the Italian city-states, particularly Florence, which was torn between rival factions. Spiritually and culturally too, there were signs of change. With the diffusion of Aristotle's physical and metaphysical works, there came the need for harmonizing his philosophy with the truth of Christianity, and Dante's mind was attracted to philosophical speculation. In Italy, Giotto, who had freed himself from the Byzantine tradition, was reshaping the art of painting, while the Tuscan poets were beginning to experiment with new forms of expression. Dante may be considered the greatest and last medieval poet, at least in Italy, where barely a generation later the first humanists were to spring up.

Dante was born in Florence, the son of Bellincione d'Alighiero. His family descended, he tells us, from "the noble seed" of the Roman founders of Florence and was noble also by virtue of honors bestowed on it later. His great-grandfather Cacciaguida had been knighted by Emperor Conrad III and died about 1147 while fighting in the Second Crusade. As was usual for the minor nobility, Dante's family was Guelph, in opposition to the Ghibelline party of the feudal nobility which strove to dominate the communes under the protection of the emperor.

Although his family was reduced to modest circumstances, Dante was able to live as a gentleman and to pursue his studies. It is probable that he attended the Franciscan school of Sta Croce and the Dominican school of S. Maria Novella in Florence, where he gained the knowledge of Thomistic doctrine and of the mysticism that was to become the foundation of his philosophical culture. It is known from his own testimony that in order to perfect his literary style he also studied with Brunetto Latini, the Florentine poet and master of rhetoric. Perhaps encouraged by Brunetto in his pursuit of learning, Dante traveled to Bologna, where he probably attended the well-known schools of rhetoric.

A famous portrait of the young Dante done by Giotto hangs in the Palazzo del Podestà in Florence. We also have the following description of him left us by the author Giovanni Boccaccio: "Our poet was of medium height, and his face was long and his nose aquiline and his jaws were big, and his lower lip stood out in such a way that it somewhat protruded beyond the upper one; his shoulders were somewhat curved, and his eyes large rather than small and of brown color, and his hair and beard were curled and black, and he was always melancholy and pensive."

Dante does not write of his family or marriage, but before 1283 his father died, and soon afterward, in accordance with his father's previous arrangements, he married the gentlewoman Gemma di Manetto Donati. They had several children, of whom two sons, Jacopo and Pietro, and a daughter, Antonia, are known.

## Lyric Poetry

Dante began early in life to compose poetry, an art, he tells us, which he taught himself as a young man (*Vita nuova*, III, 9). Through his love lyrics he became known to other poets of Florence, and most important to him was his friendship with Guido Cavalcanti, which resulted from an exchange of sonnets.

Both Dante and Guido were concerned with the effects of love on the mind, particularly from a philosophical point of view; only Dante, however, began gradually to develop the idea that love could become the means of spiritual perfection. And while Guido was more interested in natural philosophy, Dante assiduously cultivated his knowledge of the Latin poets, particularly Virgil, whom he later called his guide and authority in the art of poetry.

During his youth Dante had known a young and noble Florentine woman whose grace and beauty so impressed him that in his poetry she became the idealized Beatrice, the "bringer of blessings," who seemed "a creature come from heaven to earth, A miracle manifest in reality" (*Vita nuova*, XXVI). She is believed to have been Bice, the daughter of Folco Portinari, and later the wife of Simone dei Bardi. Dante had seen her for the first time when both were in their ninth year; he had named her in a ballad among the 60 fairest women of Florence. But it was only later that Beatrice became the guide of his thoughts and emotions "toward that ideal perfection which is the goal of every noble mind," and the praise of her virtue and grace became the subject of his poetry.

When the young Beatrice died on June 8, 1290, Dante was overcome with grief but found consolation in thoughts of her glory in heaven. Although another woman succeeded briefly in winning Dante's love through her compassion, the memory of Beatrice soon aroused in him feelings of remorse and renewed his fidelity to her. He was prompted to gather from among all his poems those which had been written in her honor or had some bearing on his love for her. This plan resulted in the small volume of poetry and prose, the *Vita nuova* (New Life), in which he copied from his "book of memory" only those past experiences belonging to his "new life"—a life made new through Beatrice. It follows Dante's own youthful life through three movements or stages in love, in which Beatrice's religious and spiritual significance becomes increasingly clear. At the same time it traces his poetic development from an early phase reminiscent of the Cavalcantian manner to a foreshadowing of *The Divine Comedy*. In the last prose chapter, which tells of a "miraculous vision," the poet speaks of the major work that he intends to write and the important role Beatrice will have in it: "If it be the wish of Him in whom all things flourish that my life continue for a few years, I hope to write of her that which has never been written of any other lady."

The *Vita nuova*, written between 1292 and 1294, is one of the first important examples of Italian literary prose. Its 31 poems, most of them sonnets symmetrically grouped around three canzoni, are only a small selection of Dante's lyric production. He wrote many other lyrics inspired by Beatrice which are not included in the *Vita nuova;* in addition there are verses written to other women and poems composed at different times in his life, representing a variety of forms and stylistic experiences.

## Political Activities

Dante's literary interests did not isolate him from the events of his times. On the contrary, he was involved in the political life of Florence and deeply concerned about the state of Europe as a whole. In 1289 he had fought with the Florentine cavalry at the battle of Campaldino. In 1295 he inscribed himself in the guild of physicians and pharmacists (membership in a guild being a precondition for holding public office in Florence). He became a member of the people's council and served in various other capacities. For 2 months in 1300 he was one of the six priors of Florence, and in 1301 he was a member of the Council of the One Hundred.

In October 1301 Dante was sent in a delegation from the commune to Pope Boniface VIII, whose policies he openly opposed as constituting a threat to Florentine independence. During his absence the Blacks (one of the two opposing factions within the Guelph party) gained control of Florence. In the resulting banishment of the Whites, Dante was sentenced to exile in absentia (January 1302). Despite various attempts to regain admission to Florence—at first in an alliance of other exiles whose company he soon abandoned and later through his writing—he was never to enter his native city again.

Dante led the life of an exile, taking refuge first with Bartolommeo della Scala in Verona, and after a time of travel—to Bologna, through northern Italy, possibly also to Paris between 1307 and 1309—with Can Grande della Scala in Verona (1314). During this time his highest hopes were placed in Emperor Henry VII, who descended into Italy in 1310 to restore justice and order among the cities and to reunite church and state. When Henry VII, whose efforts proved fruitless, died in Siena in 1313, Dante lost every hope of restoring himself to an honorable position in Florence.

## Minor Works

During these years of wandering Dante's studies were not interrupted. Indeed, he had hoped that in acquiring fame as a poet and philosopher he might also regain the favor of his fellow citizens. His study of Boethius and Cicero in Florence had already widened his philosophical horizons. After 1290 he had turned to the study of philosophy with such fervor that "in a short time, perhaps 30 months" he had begun "to be so keenly aware of her sweetness that the love of her drove away and destroyed every other thought." He read so much, it seems, that his eyes were weakened.

Two uncompleted treatises, *De vulgari eloquentia* (1303-1304) and the *Convivio* (1304-1307), belong to the early period of exile. At the same time, about 1306, he probably began to compose *The Divine Comedy*.

In *De vulgari eloquentia,* a theoretical treatise in Latin on the Italian vernacular, Dante intended to treat of all aspects of the spoken language, from the highest poetic expression to the most humble familiar speech. The first book is devoted to a discussion of dialects and the principles of poetic composition in the vulgar tongue; the second book treats specifically of the "illustrious" vulgar tongue used by certain excellent poets and declares that this noble form of expression is suitable only for the most elevated subjects, such as love, virtue, and war, and must be used in the form of the canzone.

The *Convivio* was intended to consist of 15 chapters: an introduction and 14 canzoni, with prose commentaries in Italian; but only 4 chapters were completed. The canzoni, which are the "meat" of the philosophical banquet while the prose commentaries are the "bread," appear to be written to a beautiful woman. But the prose commentaries interpret these poems as an allegorical exaltation of philosophy, inspired by the love of wisdom. Dante wished to glorify philosophy as the "mistress of his mind" and to treat subjects of moral philosophy, such as love and virtue. The *Convivio* is in a sense a connecting link between the *Vita nuova* and *The Divine Comedy.* Thus in the latter work reason in the pursuit of knowledge and wisdom becomes man's sole guide on earth, except for the intervention of Divine Grace, in his striving for virtue and God. In the *Convivio* Dante also defends the use of the vernacular as a suitable medium for ethical and scientific subjects, as well as amorous ones.

The Latin treatise *De monarchia,* of uncertain date but possibly attributable to the time of Henry VII's descent into Italy (1310-1313), is a statement of Dante's political theories. At the same time it is intended as a practical guide toward the restoration of peace in Europe under a temporal monarch in Rome, whose authority proceeds directly from God.

During his exile Dante also wrote various Latin epistles and letters of political nature to Italian prices and cardinals. Belonging to a late period are two Latin eclogues and the scientific essay *Quaestio de aqua et terra* (1320). *Il fiore,* a long sonnet sequence, is of doubtful attribution.

In 1315 Dante twice refused pardons offered him by the citizens of Florence under humiliating conditions. He and his children were consequently condemned to death as rebels. He spent his last years in Tuscany, in Verona, and finally in Ravenna. There, under the patronage of Guido da Polenta and joined by his children (possibly also his wife), Dante was greatly esteemed and spent a happy and peaceful period until his death on Sept. 13 or 14, 1321.

## The Divine Comedy

The original title of Dante's masterpiece, which he completed shortly before his death, was *Commedia;* the epithet *Divina* was added by posterity. The purpose of this work, as Dante writes in his letter to Can Grande, is "to remove those living in this life from the state of misery and lead them to the state of felicity." The *Commedia* is divided into three parts: *Inferno* (Hell), *Purgatorio* (Purgatory), and *Paradiso* (Heaven). The second and third sections contain

33 cantos apiece; the *Inferno* has 34, since its opening canto is an introduction to the entire work. The measure throughout the poem is terza rima, consisting of lines in sets of 3, rhyming aba, bcb, cdc, and so on.

The main action of the literal narrative centers on Dante's journey to God through the agency of Beatrice; the moral or allegorical meaning that Dante wishes the reader to keep in mind is that God will do for everyman what he has done for one man, if everyman is willing to make this journey. Dante constructs an allegory of a double journey: his experience in the supernatural world points to the journey of everyman through this life. The poet finds himself in a dark wood (sin); he tries to escape by climbing a mountain illuminated by the sun (God). Impeded by the sudden appearance of three beasts, which symbolize the major divisions of sin in the *Inferno,* he is about to be driven back when Virgil (human reason) appears, sent to his aid by Beatrice. Virgil becomes Dante's guide through Hell, in a descent which is the first stage in his ascent to God in humility. The pilgrim learns all there is to know about sin and confronts the very foundation of sin, which is pride, personified in Lucifer frozen at the very center of the universe. Only now is he spiritually prepared to begin his ascent through the realm of purification.

The mountain of the *Purgatorio* is a place of repentance, regeneration, and conversion. The penitents endure severe punishments, but all are pilgrims directed to God, in an atmosphere of love, hope, and an eager willingness in suffering. On the mountain's summit Beatrice (divine revelation) comes to take Virgil's place as Dante's guide—for the final ascent to God, human reason is insufficient.

The *Paradiso* depicts souls contemplating God; they are in a state of perfect happiness in the knowledge of His divine truths. The dominant image in this realm is light. God is light, and the pilgrim's goal from the start was to reach the light. His spiritual growth toward the attainment of this end is the main theme of the entire poem.

### Further Reading

For an understanding of how little scholars know of Dante's life, see Michele Barbi, *Life of Dante,* edited and translated by Paul Ruggiers (1954). Recommended as important guides to the study of Dante are Charles A. Dinsmore, *Aids to the Study of Dante* (1903); Umberto Cosmo, *A Handbook to Dante Studies* (trans. 1947); and Thornes G. Bergin, *Dante* (1965). A variety of critical approaches to Dante are offered in Bernard Stambler, *Dante's Other World: The Purgatorio as Guide to the Divine Comedy* (1957); Charles S. Singleton, *Dante Studies I and II* (1958); Irma Brandeis, *The Ladder of Vision: A Study of Dante's Comedy* (1960); Mark Musa, *Essays on Dante* (1964); Jefferson B. Fletcher, *Dante* (1965); and Francis Fergusson, *Dante* (1966). □

# Georges Jacques Danton

**The French statesman Georges Jacques Danton (1759-1794) was a leader during the French Revolution. Called the "orator of the streets," he was the**

**most prominent early defender of popular liberties and the republican spirit.**

Born in Arcis-sur-Aube in Champagne on Oct. 26, 1759, Georges Jacques Danton was the son of a lawyer and minor court official. He was educated by the Oratorians at Troyes and in 1785 earned a degree in law at the University of Reims. He was employed in the office of public prosecutor in Paris and in 1787 purchased the office of advocate to the King's Council.

## His Character

Danton's massive stature, ready wit (which did much to overcome his physical ugliness), stentorious voice, and impromptu and fiery speeches made the public accept him as its champion of liberty. Danton was a pragmatist who believed that the Revolution could only succeed if it limited its program to the possible, which meant upholding the rights of property, ending the war as quickly as possible by negotiation, and restoring order through a strong central government.

Danton had tendencies toward laziness and the dissolute life, which often blunted the force of his actions and made him appear capricious and unreliable to many of his contemporaries. There seems to be little doubt that he was implicated in financial corruption, but this appears more the result of thoughtlessness than a deliberate attempt to profit from the Revolution. At heart Danton appears to have been

less a radical than an energetic and undisciplined individualist whose personality and the force of circumstances enabled him to become a great popular leader.

## Revolutionary Activities

Danton's part in founding the Cordeliers Club, which became the advance guard of popular revolutionary activity, suggests that from the beginning of the Revolution he inclined toward the "people's cause." He was involved in the fall of the Bastille on July 14, 1789, and was the most outspoken critic of the commune and the Marquis de Lafayette. Following King Louis XVI's unsuccessful flight in June 1791, Danton was among those who called for the creation of a republic, and his speeches were considered responsible for the popular agitation that culminated in the massacre of the Champ de Mars.

In December 1791 Danton was elected first deputy prosecutor of the Paris Commune. Following the invasion of the Tuileries on June 20, 1792, he was elected president of the Théâtre Française Electoral District. He spoke out against the distinction between active and passive citizens and thus became one of the first to espouse the modern conception of the legal equality of all citizens. At the same time he began to play the primary role in the conspiracy that led to the overthrow of the monarchy on Aug. 10, 1792. He had become convinced, as had others, that as long as the monarchy continued to exist the Revolution would be endangered.

Danton was subsequently named minister of justice and became the predominant member of the Executive Committee. In this capacity he rallied the nation against the invading Prussians. It appears that he could have done little to prevent the September Massacres (1792), but his silent complicity in them deepened the split between himself and the Rolandists, which did much to force the trial of the King. Although Danton opposed this trial since it would make a negotiated peace impossible, he eventually voted in favor of execution of the King.

During this period Danton delivered his famous speech to the National Convention, which stated that to protect the Revolution it was necessary for France to secure its natural boundaries, although this might mean a perpetuation of the war. On April 6, 1793, he was elected to the newly established Committee of Public Safety and to the Revolutionary Tribunal; he was thus enabled to act as an emergency dictator. Although Danton believed that it was necessary to destroy internal dissent, his diplomatic policies continued to be moderate. He thus alienated the Commune, which began to look to Robespierre and more radical Jacobins for leadership. Setbacks in the Vandée and his attempted protection of the Girondists, even after their exclusion from the National Convention, resulted in Danton's not being reelected to the Committee on July 10, 1793. The leadership of the Revolution passed to Robespierre.

In October Danton retired to his home in Arcis; he returned to Paris the following month at the insistence of his friends, who feared Robespierre's terrorist policies. The increasingly radical demands of the Hébertists, however, were more frightening to Danton, and he lent his support to

Robespierre. After the Hébertists had been suppressed, Robespierre moved against Danton, who had called for an end to the Terror. Danton and his followers were arrested and tried for antirevolutionary activity. On April 5, 1794, Danton went to the guillotine, which he had vowed to either pull down or die beneath.

## Further Reading

Danton has been the subject of a controversial literature. His great supporter was Alphonse Aulard, who unfortunately never wrote a biography of his hero. However, Aulard's *The French Revolution: A Political History, 1789-1804* (1901; trans., 4 vols., 1910) clearly indicates his admiration for Danton as the greatest example of revolutionary spirit. Louis Madelin, *Danton* (1914; trans. 1921), and his vignette of Danton in *Figures of the Revolution* (1928; trans. 1929) offer a more moderate but still favorable interpretation in which Danton's realism is praised. On the other side of the ledger are the works of Albert Mathiez, which condemn Danton as corrupt, vacillating in his diplomacy, insensitive to popular needs, and the tool of Orléans. Unfortunately, none of these works is in translation. Something of Mathiez's approach permeates Robert Christophe, *Danton: A Biography* (trans. 1967). Probably the best biography is Hermann Wendel, *Danton* (1930; trans. 1935), which provides an even and thoughtful approach.

## Additional Sources

Hampson, Norman, *Danton,* Oxford, UK; New York, NY, USA: B. Blackwell, 1988, 1978. □

In Darío's first volume of poetry, *Primeras notas* (1885), his liberal attitudes were clearly manifested. In 1886, hoping to find a more stimulating literary environment, he traveled to Valparaiso, Chile, where he wrote for the newspaper *La Epoca.* He began to read the French Parnassian and symbolist poets, whose influence on what he wrote in the next few years was fundamental.

Darío's *Azul* (1888) was a collection of the prose and poetry he had been writing in Chile. The elegance and refinement of his style were strikingly fresh in the Spanish language. *Azul* is generally considered to be the first book of the Spanish American literary tendency designated as modernism, which introduced new forms and standards of expression and effected a virtual renovation of Spanish American literary style.

## His Travels

Darío's subsequent travels were almost as influential as his writings in publicizing the new trend. He returned to Central America in 1889 and founded a newspaper in El Salvador, and another in Guatemala in 1890. He was married for the first time in 1890 and in 1891 settled in Costa Rica. In 1892 and 1893 he made his first visits to Europe, returning from the second trip directly to Buenos Aires, where he had been appointed the Colombian consul. Although he soon lost that appointment, he remained in Argentina until 1898, publishing his important works, *Los raros* (1896), a collection of essays dealing with writers Darío admired, and *Prosas profanas* (1896), the book with which the ground gained by the modernist tendency—now

# Rubén Darío

**Rubén Darío (1867-1916) was a Nicaraguan poet whose work is considered to have given the major impetus to the late-19th-century literary movement in Spanish America called modernism.**

R ubén Darío was born Félix Rubén García y Sarmiento on Jan. 18, 1867, in Metapa. Raised as an orphan in the home of an aunt, he showed at an early age an astonishing ability for versification. His early Jesuit training appears to have had little influence on his subsequent behavior, except perhaps to intensify his mystical inclinations. At 13, he published the first poem he was to sign as Rubén Darío, adopting the more euphonious last name of a paternal great-grandfather.

## Early Career

An intelligent, nervous, superstitious boy, Darío was taken by friends to the capital city of Managua in 1881. But in an effort to frustrate his announced plan to marry at age 14, he was sent to El Salvador. There he met the poet Francisco Gavidia, who introduced him to French literature and instructed him in new styles of versification. In 1884 Darío returned to Managua, took a job at the National Library, learned French, and set out on an intensive program of literary study.

being cultivated by poets throughout Spanish America—was consolidated.

In 1898 the Buenos Aires newspaper *La Nación,* with which Darío had been associated since 1889, sent him to Spain as a correspondent. He was soon transferred to Paris, which became the center of his activities for nearly 5 years. In his most mature collection of poetry, *Cantos de vida y esperanza* (1906), much of the surface brilliance of his earlier work is replaced by a more serious, human, meditative tone. Some of the elegance is missing, but it is replaced by the conscience of a man now aware of the world around him and the social and political circumstances of Spanish America at the turn of the century.

## Late Work

Between 1907 and 1915 Darío's life was complicated by continuous travel between Europe and Spanish America, the consequences of his chronic intemperance, and persistent marital troubles involving his second wife, from whom he had long been separated, and Francisca Sánchez, a Spanish woman who had borne him three children. He continued to write and publish his poetry, but these later volumes reveal a decline in his creative powers: *El canto errante* (1907), *El viaje a Nicaragua* (principally prose; 1909), and *Poema del otoño* (1910). He died in León, Nicaragua, on Feb. 6, 1916.

## Further Reading

The best source on Darío's life is Charles Dunton Watland, *Poet-Errant: A Biography of Rubén Darío* (1965). Much new Darío criticism appeared in commemoration of the centennial celebration of the poet's birth in 1967. Of the works in English, especially useful is George D. Schade and Miguel González-Gerth, eds., *Rubén Darío: Centennial Studies* (1970). Two excellent studies of distinct aspects of the poet's work are Donald F. Fogelquist, ed., *The Literary Collaboration and the Personal Correspondence of Rubén Darío and Juan Ramón Jiménez* (1956), and Dolores Ackel Fiore, *Rubén Darío in Search of Inspiration: Greco-Roman Mythology in His Stories and Plays* (1963). □

# Darius I

**Darius I (522-486 B.C.), called "the Great," was a Persian king. A great conqueror and the chief organizer of the Persian Empire, he is best known for the unsuccessful attack on Greece which ended at Marathon.**

Amember of a collateral branch of the Achaemenidian royal family, Darius apparently was not close to the throne when Cambyses died in 522 B.C. The story of Darius's accession is told most fully by the Greek Herodotus, whose version clearly reflects the official account set up by Darius's own order in the famous rock inscription at Behistun.

According to Herodotus, Cambyses had had his brother Smerdis (Bardiya) executed, but while Cambyses was absent in Egypt, a Magian priest named Gaumata, trusting in a chance resemblance, put himself forward as Smerdis and seized the throne. Cambyses started back but died en route, and the false Smerdis was generally accepted. Darius, with the aid of a few who knew that Smerdis was dead, murdered Gaumata and in his own person restored the royal line.

## Organization of the Empire

Though Darius was an excellent soldier and extended his empire east, north, and into Europe, he saw himself as an organizer and lawgiver rather than as a mere conqueror. Little of his work was startlingly original, but the blending of the old and new and the interlocked ordering of the whole gave his work importance. He divided the empire into 20 huge provinces called satrapies, each under a royally appointed governor called a satrap who had administrative, military, financial, and judicial control in his province. To check on such powerful subordinates, Darius also appointed the satrap's second-in-command, having him report to the King separately. Standing garrisons under commanders independent of the satrap were stationed strategically. However, since all these officials were more or less permanent, there remained the possibility that all three might conspire to plot revolt. Accordingly, a further set of

**Darius I (left)**

royal officials—inspectors called the King's "eyes" or "ears"—were frequently sent out.

Since in so huge an empire—it covered some 1 million square miles—there was always the problem of communication and transportation, Darius established a system of well-maintained all-weather roads and a royal courier system with posthouses and regular relays of horses and riders. The trip from Sardis in western Asia Minor to Susa in Persia normally took 3 months; a royal message could cover it in a week.

Darius also regulated the tribute, hitherto collected irregularly as needed, on a fixed annual basis according to the wealth of each satrapy. Though hardly low, this tribute does not appear to have been burdensome. He also instituted the first official Persian coinage.

## Military Organization

Militarily the empire was organized on the satrap system, but the results were less happy. Aside from the resident garrisons and the royal bodyguard there was no standing army. At need, satraps involved were ordered to raise a quota of men and bring them, armed and ready, to an appointed assembly point. Inescapably, a Persian army was thus long on numbers but short on uniformity; each contingent was armed and trained in its local fashion and spoke its native tongue. Persian infantry was usually of very poor quality; the cavalry, provided by the Persians themselves, the Medes, and the eastern steppe dwellers, was generally quite good. The Persian fleet was levied in the same manner as the army, but since the Mediterranean maritime peoples all copied from each other, there was little problem of diversity. The fleet's weakness was that, being raised entirely from among subject peoples, it had no real loyalty.

## Darius's Religion

Darius, himself a firm supporter of Ahura Mazda, the Zoroastrian god, said in the Behistun inscription that Ahura Mazda "gave" him his kingdoms, and with him Zoroastrianism became something like the national religion of the Persians. For the empire, however, he continued Cyrus's policy of toleration of local cults, and this mildness became and remained, except perhaps under Xerxes, a distinctive feature of Persian rule.

## War with the Greeks

Darius's first European campaign, about 513, was aimed not at Greece but north toward the Danube. Herodotus recorded that Darius intended to conquer the complete circuit of the Black Sea and that he was turned back north of the Danube by the native Scythians' scorched-earth policy. This may be, or it may be that Darius never intended any permanent conquest north of the Danube and that Herodotus turned a limited success into a grandiose failure in order to make all Persian operations in Europe at least partly unsuccessful. Darius did secure the approaches to Greece and the control of the grain route through the Bosporus.

The next act in the Greco-Persian drama was the so-called Ionian Revolt (499-494), an uprising against Persia of most of the Greeks of Asia Minor headed by the Ionians, and particularly by the city of Miletus. Though the revolt was put down by Darius's generals, its seriousness is indicated by its length and by the fact that the Ionians' appeal to the Greek homeland was answered, at least in part, by Athens and Eretria.

Darius had to take the Greek matter seriously. Not only did he have the duty of avenging the burning of his city of Sardis during the revolt, but he must have become convinced that to ensure the quiet of his Greek subjects in Asia Minor he would have to extend his rule also over their brothers across the Aegean. After the collapse of the revolt, the attempt of Darius's son-in-law, Mandonius, to carry the war into Greece itself ended when the Persian fleet was wrecked in a storm off Mt. Athos (492).

## Battle of Marathon

Perhaps Mardonius's ill-fated venture was really an attempt to conquer all Greece; the next effort certainly was not. Darius sent a naval expedition—he himself never set eyes on Greece—against only Athens and Eretria (490). The attack was perfectly well known to be coming, but the Greeks had their customary difficulties of cooperation, and Eretria, unsupported, fell and was burned in revenge for Sardis. Athens appealed to the Grecian states, but only 1,000 men from little Plataea reached Athens.

The Persians landed on the small plain of Marathon northeast of Athens, and the Greeks took up station in easily defendable nearby hills out of reach of the Persian cavalry. After some days' waiting, the Persians began to reembark, perhaps for a dash on Athens. The Greeks, led by Miltiades, were forced to attack, which they did with a lengthened front to avoid encirclement by the more numerous Persians. In this first major encounter between European and Asian infantry, the Greek closely knit, heavily armed phalanx won decisively. The Persian survivors sailed at once for Athens, but Miltiades rushed his forces back, and the Persians arrived to see the Greeks lined up before the city. Abandoning action, they sailed home, and the campaign of Marathon was over.

Though to the Western world Marathon was a victory of enormous significance, to the Persians it was only a moderately serious border setback. Yet this defeat and peace in Asia Minor called for the conquest of all Greece, and Darius began the mighty preparations. A revolt in Egypt, however, distracted him, and he died in 486, leaving the next attack for his son Xerxes.

## Further Reading

Herodotus's *History* is the principal source of information on Darius. Aeschylus's *Persae* is also important. The Behistun inscription is Darius's official account; it is contained in Roland G. Kent, *Old Persian: Grammar, Texts, Lexicon* (1950; 2d ed. rev. 1953). The fullest recent treatment of Darius is in A. T. Olmstead, *History of the Persian Empire* (1948; rev. ed. 1959), which asserts that Darius was a usurper. Roman Ghirshman, *Iran from the Earliest Times to the Islamic Conquest* (1954), is more traditional. Richard Frye, *The Heritage of Persia* (1963), is also of interest. □

# Clarence Seward Darrow

**As an American labor lawyer and as a criminal lawyer, Clarence Seward Darrow (1857-1938) helped sharpen debate about the path of American industrialism and about the treatment of individuals in conflict with the law.**

Clarence Darrow was born on April 18, 1857, in Farmdale, Ohio, to Amirus and Emily Darrow. He was introduced early to the life of the dissenter, for his father, after completing studies at a Unitarian seminary, had lost his faith and had become an agnostic living within a community of religious believers. Furthermore, the Darrows were Democrats in a Republican locale.

After completing his secondary schooling near Farmdale, Darrow spent a year at Allegheny College in Meadville, Pa., and another year at the University of Michigan Law School. Like almost all lawyers of the time, he delayed his admission to the bar until after he had read law with a local lawyer; he became a member of the Ohio bar in 1878. For the next 9 years he was a typical small-town lawyer, practicing in Kinsman, Andover, and Ashtabula, Ohio.

Seeking more interesting paths, however, Darrow moved to Chicago in 1887. In Ohio he had been impressed with the book *Our Penal Machinery and Its Victims* by Judge John Peter Altgeld. Darrow became a close friend of Altgeld, who was elected governor of Illinois in 1892. Altgeld not only raised questions about the process of criminal justice but, when he pardoned several men who had been convicted in the aftermath of the Haymarket riot of 1886, also questioned the treatment of those who were trying to organize workers into unions. Both of these themes played great roles in Darrow's life.

## Labor Lawyer

Darrow had begun as a conventional civil lawyer. Even in Chicago his first jobs included appointment as the city's corporation counsel in 1890 and then as general attorney to the Chicago and North Western Railway. In 1894, however, he began what would be his primary career for the next 20 years—labor law. During that year he defended the Socialist Eugene V. Debs against an injunction trying to break the workers' strike Debs was leading against the Pullman Sleeping Car Company. Darrow was unsuccessful, though; the injunction against Debs was finally upheld by the Supreme Court.

In 1906-1907 Darrow successfully defended William D. "Big Bill" Haywood, the leader of the newly formed Industrial Workers of the World, against a charge of conspiring to murder former governor Steunenberg of Idaho. But in 1911 disaster struck as Darrow, defending the McNamara brothers against a charge of blowing up the Los Angeles Times Building, was suddenly faced with his clients' reversing their previous plea of innocence to one of guilt. In turn, Darrow was indicted for misconduct but was not convicted. With this his career as a labor lawyer came to an end.

## Criminal Lawyer

Darrow had always been interested in criminal law, in part because of his acceptance of new, psychological theories stressing the role of determinism in human behavior. He viewed criminals as people led by circumstance into committing antisocial acts rather than as free-willing monsters. For this reason he was a bitter opponent of capital punishment, viewing it as a barbaric practice. Now he embarked on a new major career as a criminal lawyer.

Without a doubt Darrow's most famous criminal trial was the 1924 Leopold-Loeb case, in which two Chicago boys had wantonly murdered a youngster. For the only time in his career Darrow insisted that his clients plead guilty, then turned his attention to saving them from the death penalty. He was successful in this, partly because he was able to introduce a great deal of psychiatric testimony supporting his theories of the determining influences upon individual acts.

## Scopes Trial

During this period Darrow also participated in another great American case, the Scopes trial of 1925 in Dayton, Tenn. The issue was the right of a state legislature to prohibit the teaching of Darwinian theories of evolution in the public schools. Darrow, as an agnostic and as an evolutionist, was doubly contemptuous of the motives behind the fundamentalist law that had been passed, and he sought to defend the young schoolteacher who had raised the issue of evolution in his class. Technically, he was unsuccessful, for Scopes was convicted and fined $100 for his crime. But Darrow's defense, and particularly his cross-examination of William Jennings Bryan (the three-time Democratic candidate for president who spoke for the biblical, antiscientific, fundamentalist side) served to discredit religious fundamentalism and won national attention.

Two books among Darrow's many writings typify his concerns toward the end of his life. In 1922 he wrote *Crime: Its Cause and Treatment;* in 1929 appeared *Infidels and Heretics,* coedited with Wallace Rice, in which he presented the case for freethinking. To these two issue-oriented books he added in 1932 his autobiography, *The Story of My Life.*

Darrow's last important public service was as chairman of a commission appointed by President Franklin D. Roosevelt to analyze the operation of the National Recovery Administration. He died on March 13, 1938.

## Further Reading

The standard popular biography of Darrow is Irving Stone, *Clarence Darrow for the Defense* (1941). A more recent work is Miriam Gurko, *Clarence Darrow* (1965). A specialized, scholarly study is Abe C. Ravitz, *Clarence Darrow and the American Literary Tradition* (1962), which takes note of Darrow's participation in some of the literary controversies of his time. □

Hutton's uniformitarian view that present conditions and processes were clues to the past history of the earth, wrote his *Principles of Geology* (1830-1833), which Darwin on his *Beagle* circumnavigation found most apt for his own geological observations. Fossils in South America and apparent anomalies of animal distribution triggered the task for Darwin of assembling a vast range of material. A reading of Thomas Malthus's *Essay on the Principle of Population* in 1838 completed Darwin's conceptual scheme.

Critics, for whom the *Origin* is paramount among Darwin's considerable output, have accused him of vacillation and procrastination. But recent study of unpublished manuscripts and his entire works reveal a continuity of purpose and integrity of effort to establish the high probability of the genetic relationship through descent in all forms of life. Man is dethroned as the summit of creation and as the especial concern of the Creator. This revolution in thought has had an effect on every kind of human activity.

Darwin was born on Feb. 12, 1809, at Shrewsbury, the fifth child of Robert and Susannah Darwin. His mother, who was the daughter of the famous potter Josiah Wedgwood, died when Charles was 8, and he was reared by his sisters. At the age of 9 Charles entered Shrewsbury School. His record was not outstanding, but he did learn to use English with precision and to delight in Shakespeare and Milton.

In 1825 Darwin went to Edinburgh University to study medicine. He found anatomy and *materia medica* dull and surgery unendurable. In 1828 he entered Christ's College, Cambridge, with the idea of taking Anglican orders. He

# Charles Robert Darwin

**The English naturalist Charles Robert Darwin (1809-1882) discovered that natural selection was the agent for the transmutation of organisms during evolution, as did Alfred Russel Wallace independently. Darwin presented his theory in "Origin of Species."**

The concept of evolution by descent dates at least from classical Greek philosophers. In the 18th century Carl Linnaeus postulated limited mutability of species by descent and hybridization. Charles Darwin's grandfather, Erasmus Darwin, and the Chevalier de Lamarck were the chief proponents of evolution about 1800. Such advocacy had little impact on the majority of naturalists, concerned to identify species, the stability of which was considered essential for their work. Natural theology regarded the perfection of adaptation between structure and mode of life in organisms as evidence for a beneficent, all-seeing, all-planning Creator. Organic structure, planned in advance for a preordained niche, was unchanged from the moment of creation. Variations in structure in these earthly imperfect versions of the Creator's idea were minor and impermanent.

In 1815 William Smith had demonstrated a sequence of fossil populations in time. Charles Lyell, adopting James attended John Stevens Henslow's course in botany, started a collection of beetles that became famous, and read widely. William Paley's *Natural Theology* (1802) delighted Darwin by its clear logical presentation, and he later regarded this study as the most worthwhile benefit from Cambridge. He received his bachelor's degree in 1831.

## Voyage of the *Beagle*

On Henslow's recommendation Darwin was offered the position of naturalist for the second voyage of H. M. S. *Beagle* to survey the coast of Patagonia and Tierra del Fuego and complete observations of longitude by circumnavigation with a formidable array of chronometers. The *Beagle* left on Dec. 27, 1831, and returned on Oct. 2, 1836. During the voyage Darwin spent 535 days at sea and roughly 1200 on land. Enough identification of strata could be done on the spot, but sufficiently accurate identification of living organisms required systematists accessible only in London and Paris.

Darwin kept his field observations in notebooks with the specimens listed serially and their place and time of collection documented. On July 24, 1834, he wrote: "My notes are becoming bulky. I have about 600 small quarto pages full; about half of this is Geology the other imperfect descriptions of animals; with the latter I make it a rule to describe those parts which cannot be seen in specimens in spirits. I keep my private Journal distinct from the above." Toward the end of the voyage, when sea passages were long, he copied his notes and arranged them to accord with systematics, concentrating on range and habits. Geology was prepared with fewer inhibitions; he wrote from Mauritius in April 1836: "It is a rare piece of good fortune for me that of the many errant (in ships) Naturalists there have been few, or rather no, Geologists. I shall enter the field unopposed."

During the trip Darwin discovered the relevance of Lyell's uniformitarian views to the structure of St. Jago (Cape Verde Islands). He found that small locally living forms closely resembled large terrestrial fossil mammals embedded between marine shell layers and that the local sea was populated with living occupants of similar shells. He also observed the overlapping distribution on the continuous Patagonian plain of two closely related but distinct species of ostrich. An excursion along the Santa Cruz river revealed a section of strata across South America. He observed the differences between species of birds and animals on the Galápagos Islands.

## Publications Resulting from Voyage

Darwin's *Journal of Researches* was published in 1839. With the help of a government grant toward the cost of the illustrations, the *Zoology of the Voyage of the Beagle* was published, in five quarto volumes, from 1839 to 1843. Specialist systematists wrote on fossil and living mammals, birds, fish, and reptiles. Darwin edited the work and contributed habits and ranges of the animals and geological notes on the fossils. Two themes run through his valuable and mostly neglected notes: distribution in space and time and observations of behavior as an aid to species diagnosis.

He also published *The Structure and Distribution of Coral Reefs* (1842); he had studied the coral reefs in the Cocos Islands during the *Beagle* voyage.

Darwin abandoned the idea of fixity of species in 1837 while writing his *Journal*. A second edition, in 1845, had a stronger tinge of transmutation, but there was still no public avowal of the new faith. This delightful volume is his most popular and accessible work.

Darwin's Transmutation (Species) Notebooks (1837-1839) have recently been reconstructed. The notion of "selection owing to struggle" derived from his reading of Malthus in 1838. Earlier Darwin had read Pyrame de Candolle's works on plant geography, so his mind was receptive. The breadth of interest and profusion of hypotheses characteristic of Darwin, who could carry several topics in his mind at the same time, inform the whole. From this medley of facts allegedly assembled on Baconian principles all his later works derive.

It was not until Darwin's geological observations of South America were published in 1846 that he started a paper on his "first Cirripede," a shell-boring aberrant barnacle, no bigger than a pin's head, he had found at Chonos Island in 1835. This was watched while living, then dissected, and drawn while the *Beagle* sheltered from a week of severe storms. The working out of the relationship to other barnacles forced him to study all barnacles, a task that occupied him until 1854 and resulted in two volumes on living forms and two on fossil forms.

Darwin married Emma Wedgwood, his first cousin, in 1839. They lived in London until 1842, when ill health drove him to Down House, where he passed the rest of his life in seclusion. Four of their sons became prominent scientists: George was an astronomer and mathematician, Francis a botanist, Leonard a eugenist, and Horace a civil engineer.

## Development of Ideas on Evolution

In 1842 and 1844 Darwin wrote short accounts of his transmutation views. The 1844 sketch in corrected fair copy was a testament accompanied by a letter to his wife to secure publication should he die. Late in 1844 Robert Chambers's *Vestiges of Creation* appeared advocating universal development by descent. A great scandal ensued, and criticism of the amateur pretensions of the author was savage. Darwin decided to bide his time and become more proficient as a biologist.

In 1855 Darwin began to study the practices of poultry and pigeon fanciers and worldwide domesticated breeds, conducted experiments on plant and animal variation and its hereditary transmission, and worried about the problem of plant and animal transport across land and water barriers, for he was persuaded of the importance of isolation for speciation. The last step in his conceptual scheme had already occurred to him in 1852 while pondering Henri Milne-Edwards's concept of diversification into specialized organs for separation of physiological functions in higher organisms and the relevance of these considerations for classification when related to the facts of embryological development. Darwin's "principle of divergence" recognizes that the dominant species must make more effective use of the territory it invades than a competing species and accordingly it becomes adapted to more diversified environments.

In May 1856 Lyell heard of Darwin's transmutation hypothesis and urged him to write an account with full references. Darwin sent the chapter on distribution to Lyell and Sir Joseph Hooker, who were deeply impressed. Darwin continued his writing, and on June 14, 1858, when he was halfway through, he received an essay from Alfred Russel Wallace containing the theory of evolution by natural selection—the same theory Darwin was working on. Lyell and Hooker arranged for a reading of a joint paper by Wallace and Darwin, and it was presented at a meeting of the Linnaean Society on July 1. The paper had little effect.

### Origin of Species

On Nov. 24, 1859, Darwin published *On the Origin of Species by Means of Natural Selection, or the Preservation of Favoured Races in the Struggle for Life*. The analogy of natural selection was prone to misunderstanding by readers, since it carried for them an implied purpose on the part of a "deified" Nature. Herbert Spencer's phrase "survival of the fittest" was equally misleading because the essence of Darwin's theory is that, unlike natural theology, adaptation must not be too perfect and rigid. A mutable store of variation must be available to any viable population in nature.

The publication of Darwin's book secured worldwide attention for his hypothesis and aroused impassioned controversy. His main champion was T. H. Huxley. Darwin, remote in his retreat at Down House, took painstaking note of criticism and endeavored to answer points of detail in the five more editions of *Origin* produced during his lifetime. He avoided trouble and made several unfortunate concessions which weakened his presentation and made his views seem vague and hesitant. The first edition is easily the best.

### Later Works

In *On the Various Contrivances by Which British and Foreign Orchids Are Fertilised by Insects* (1862) Darwin showed how the welfare of an organism may be hidden in apparently unimportant peculiarities. It became hard to say what is "useless" in nature. His *The Variation of Animals and Plants under Domestication* (1868; rev. ed. 1875) expanded on a topic he had introduced in *Origin*. A chapter in *Origin* on man as the most domesticated of animals grew into the book *The Descent of Man and Selection in Relation to Sex* (1871). *The Expression of the Emotions in Man and Animals* (1872) developed from material squeezed out of the *Descent*.

Plants became an increasing preoccupation, the more so since Darwin had his son Francis as collaborator and amanuensis. Papers Darwin had published in 1864 were collected into *The Movements and Habits of Climbing Plants* (1875), and these ideas were further generalized on uniformitarian lines and published as *The Power of Movement in Plants* (1880). All plants, not merely climbing ones, were shown to execute to some degree exploratory "circumnutation" movements. Studies on fertilization of

plants by insects recorded as early as 1840 led to *The Effects of Cross and Self-Fertilisation in the Vegetable Kingdom* (1876) and *The Different Forms of Flowers on Plants of the Same Species* (1877). *Insectivorous Plants* (1873) pursued the reactions of plants to stimuli. Darwin's last work returned to observations he had made in 1837: *The Formation of Vegetable Mould through the Action of Worms, with Observations on Their Habits* (1881). He died on April 19, 1882, and was buried in Westminster Abbey.

### Further Reading

Primary sources on Darwin include *The Life and Letters of Charles Darwin*, edited by Francis Darwin (3 vols., 1887), which has an autobiographical chapter; *More Letters of Charles Darwin*, edited by Francis Darwin and A. C. Seward (1903); and his *Autobiography*, edited with appendix and notes by his granddaughter, Nora Barlow (1958; repr. 1969). An excellent, nontechnical account of Darwin's life and work is Sir Gavin de Beer, *Charles Darwin: Evolution by Natural Selection* (1964). Other biographical studies are Paul B. Sears, *Charles Darwin: The Naturalist as a Cultural Force* (1950), and Gerhard Wichler, *Charles Darwin: The Founder of the Theory of Evolution and Natural Selection* (1961). Gertrude Himmelfarb, *Darwin and the Darwinian Revolution* (1959), offers a provocative reinterpretation of the man and his impact.

A dramatic pictorial account of Darwin's trip around the world in the *Beagle* is Alan Moorehead, *Darwin and the Beagle* (1969), which incorporates excerpts from Darwin's autobiography, journal, and letters. Parts of Darwin's work are examined in P. R. Bell, ed., *Darwin's Biological Work: Some Aspects Reconsidered* (1959), and Darwin's vast influence is assessed in Michael T. Ghiselin, *The Triumph of the Darwinian Method* (1969). A good, succinct presentation of the essence of Darwin's ideas is Benjamin Farrington, *What Darwin Really Said* (1967), which can serve as a review of the major problems raised by Darwin's theories. □

# Mahmud Darwish

**Probably the foremost Palestinian poet of the late 20th century, Mahmud Darwish (born 1942) was one of the leading poets of the Arab world.**

Mahmud Darwish was born in al Birwah, a village that lies to the east of Acca (Acre), now in Israel, in 1942. In the 1948 war when he was a boy, Darwish fled with his family and walked across the mountains and forests to southern Lebanon. But when he returned with his family two years later, he found that his village had been completely razed by the Israeli forces and the land ploughed.

Darwish's impressions of this period of his life—the military government and the police harassment—remained with him and influenced much of his poetry, which he began to write at a young age. Darwish, who worked as a journalist in Haifa, became a victim of Israeli authorities as his poetry became more popular and widely read. His poetry, like other resistance poetry, was a strong indictment of

Israeli society and its attitude toward Palestinians. It reflected unyielding resistance to their conditions and a refusal to accept the *fait accompli*. The poetry was often recited in village meetings and in the fields because it served as an effective channel of political communication in a society with few political leaders. Darwish was sentenced to jail many times and his freedom of movement was restricted for several years. Several of his poems were written in prison.

During the early phase of his writing words such as refugees, Red Cross, security, occupation, UNRWA, Arabness, revolution, and love permeate his poetry. A growing shift from sorrow and grief to anger and challenge can also be discerned. Yet Darwish, despite his revolt against the challenge of what he viewed as an oppressive system, continued throughout much of his writings to emphasize the prospect of co-existence and pluralism as alternatives to exclusivism. Early on, Darwish complained bitterly about the barriers between Arab and Jewish literature, as was reflected in one of his articles, "The Siege." He often challenged liberal and humanist Israeli writers to interact with their Arab colleagues because of their common concerns in the areas of civil rights and liberties, social change, and opposition to militarism. Darwish's poetry has been characterized by various transformations both in content and in form, ranging from traditional verse in his early works to prose poetry, especially in his work in the late 1980s.

His poetic language was new in the sense that it created a metaphoric and symbolic atmosphere that transformed the ordinary meaning of words and contained hidden mean-

ings that could only be discovered in that atmosphere. The atmosphere is Palestine, in whose context words assume new meanings and new symbolic values and evoke different concepts and relationships. In the poetry of Darwish, love of the land, the woman, and the homeland (Palestine) merged together and became symbols of dignity, life, and the future. Merging of the three, as in "Lover from Palestine," comes to symbolize humanity and manhood as well as acts of declared opposition and resistance. Darwish's poetry of resistance became widely publicized and utilized by the Palestinian resistance as did the poetry of other resistance poets. Consequently, his poetry gained him much fame in the Arab world, particularly among Palestinians. In 1969 a book about him was published under the title "Mahmud Darwish: the Poet of Resistance."

In 1971 Darwish, in a move that stirred a great deal of controversy among Palestinian and Arab intellectuals, left his homeland to go to the U.S.S.R. He later settled in Beirut, which was then the cultural capital of the Arab world. Many believed that this was tantamount to a capitulation to Israel and an abandonment of his principles and of his compatriots. In Beirut, he edited *Shu'un Filastiniyya,* a journal focusing on Palestinian affairs and published by the Palestine Research Center. This self-imposed exile was widely credited with broadening his intellectual horizons.

This period ushered in a more complex and intricate form of poetry. Darwish, unlike a number of modern poets, showed that he could sustain an emotion for more than a few verses. He showed that he had the capacity to make his symbols undergo a number of transformations and to sustain them in long poems. It is easy to see in his earlier poems a poet experimenting in traditional form and a tendency to feel a voice instructing the poem from the outside. There is also a penchant toward oratory in evidence. In his later poetry, however, he seemed to achieve the dramatic voice that blurs the distinction between the poet and the poem, where the poet's individuality becomes an important function of the poet's power and impact. In his poems about Beirut, for example, he was able to eliminate the distinction by allowing the poem to stand on its own. This achievement, when it occurs, allows the poem to become more universal and to go beyond the question of Palestine, to delve into and deal with broader and universal moral issues the world over.

In 1982 Darwish was forced into a second exile when Israel invaded Lebanon. As an active member of the Palestine Liberation Organization (PLO), and as a member of its parliament, the Palestine National Council, he was compelled to leave Beirut. In 1990 he lived in Europe and edited the literary periodical *al-Karmel.*

Darwish published a number of volumes of poetry and was the subject of scholarly study in the Arab world. His poetry also received much attention outside the Arab world. Several of his poems have been translated into over 20 languages, including English, French, and Russian. He was the winner of the Lotus Prize, 1969, and the Lenin Prize, 1982. Some of his well-known works include "Ashiq min Filastin" (Lover from Palestine, 1966), "al-Asafir tamut fi al-Jalil" (Birds Die in Gallilee, 1970), "Muhawalah Raqm 7"

(Attempt Number 7, 1974), "A'ras" (Weddings, 1977), "Wda'an Aytuha al-harb wda'an Ayuha al'Salam" (Farewell to War, Farewell to Peace, 1974), Hisar li-mada'ih al Bahr (Siege of the Sea Songs, 1984), Tunis, Hiya Ughniyyat (She's a Song, 1986), Ma'sat alnarjis wa-malhat al-Fiddha (The Tragedy of Narcissus and The Comedy of Silver, 1989), Ara ma urid (I See What I Want, 1990), and Ihda ashar kawkaba (11 Planets, 1992). His most important prose work, focusing on his experiences in war-torn Beirut, is *Thakiratun lil-nusyan* (*A memory for forgetfulness,* 1987).

## Further Reading

Some of Darwish's works have been translated into English or published as part of anthologies of Palestinian or Arab poetry. In 1970 a number of his poems were included in N. Aruri and E. Ghareeb, editors/translators, *Enemy of the Sun: Poetry of Palestinian Resistance.* More of his poems were translated in other Arabic and Palestinian anthologies, including M. Khoury and H. Algar, editors, *An Anthology of Modern Arabic Poetry* (1974); A. al-Udhari, translator, *A Mirror for Autumn: Modern Arabic Poetry* (1974); A. al-Udhari, translator, *A Mirror for Autumn: Modern Arabic Poetry* (London: 1974); I. Boullata, editor/translator, *Modern Arab Poets 1950-1975* (1976); and A. Elmessiri, *The Palestinian Wedding* (1982). In 1980 a collection of Darwish's poetry, *The Music of Human Flesh,* was published in English. □

# Chitta Ranjan Das

**Chitta Ranjan Das (1870-1925) was an Indian lawyer and poet who became a nationalist leader. His main aim was swaraj, or self-rule, for India.**

Chitta Ranjan Das was born in Calcutta on Nov. 5, 1870, into a progressive Brahmo family. His father, Bhuvan Mohan, was a solicitor and a journalist who edited the English church weekly, *The Brahmo Public Opinion.* Das graduated from Presidency College in Calcutta in 1890 and went to England to compete in the Indian civil service examination. He failed the exams but joined the Inner Temple and was called to the bar in 1892.

Das returned to India in 1893 and started law practice in the Calcutta High Court. Following his successful defense of Aurobindo Ghose in the 1908 Alipur bomb conspiracy case, Das rose steadily and built a lucrative profession.

From his early youth Das was a nationalist. He was an active member of the Students' Association (1886), where Surendranath Banerjee had lectured on patriotism. At Presidency College, Das organized an undergraduate association and moved for permitting the use of Bengali in university examinations. He came in close contact with Bipin Chandra Pal and Aurobindo Ghose and helped them in publishing the *Bande Mataram,* an English weekly for propagating the ideals of *swaraj.*

Das was politically most active between 1917 and 1925. In 1917 he presided over the Bengal Provincial Conference and put forward a plan for village reconstruction through the establishment of local self-government, cooperative credit societies, and the regeneration of cottage industry. The same year he began to attend the Indian National Congress sessions regularly and was elected to all important committees. His powerful oratory, political foresight, and tact gave him a leading position in the Congress. He denounced the Montagu-Chelmsford Reform, which established a dyarchy for India, and joined Gandhi's noncooperation movement in 1920. He toured the whole country, carrying the new creed to every door. In 1921 he was arrested with his wife and son and sentenced to 6 months' imprisonment. The same year he was elected president of the Ahmedabad Congress.

On the failure of Gandhi's noncooperation movement, Das devised a new strategy. As president of the Gaya Congress (1922), he advocated an obstructionist policy inside the legislative councils with a view to mending or ending the dyarchy. But the majority in the Congress rejected his proposal. Thereupon, Das formed the Swarajya party with Motilal Nehru.

The Swarajya party gained tremendous success in Bengal and the central provinces and won majority seats in the legislative councils (1924). In Bengal the party inflicted repeated defeats upon the government, and the British bureaucracy in its earlier form met its doom in Bengal. In 1924 the Swarajists captured power in the Calcutta Corporation, and Das became the first popularly elected mayor of Calcutta.

Das realized that Hindu-Moslem unity was essential for the attainment of *swaraj.* In 1924 he formulated his famous Communal Pact to promote permanent peace between India's two major communities. He also wanted an assimilation of Eastern spirit and Western technique. He envisioned a pan-Asiatic federation of the oppressed nations and advocated India's participation in it. For his devotion to the cause of self-rule he gained the title Deshabandhu (friend of the country).

Das's genius was also revealed in the field of literature. He founded and published a literary magazine, *Narayan* (1914), and composed a number of poetical works. His first collection of poetry, *Malancha* (1895), raised a storm of protest among Brahmos. He was branded as an atheist, and in 1897 the Brahmo leaders boycotted his marriage. His successive works, *Mala* (1904), *Sagar Sangit* (1913), and *Kishore-Kishoree* and *Antaryami* (both 1915), reveal a Vaishnava devotionalism. Das died in Darjeeling on June 16, 1925.

## Further Reading

There are two major biographies of Das: Prithwis Chandra Roy, *Life and Times of C. R. Das* (1927), and Hemendra Nath Das Gupta, *Deshbandhu Chittaranjan Das* (1960). Critical treatments of Das's political, economic, and religious ideas are in Sukumar Ranjan Das, *Chitta Ranjan* (1922); Dilip Kumar Chatterjee, *C. R. Das and Indian National Movement* (1965); and Stephen N. Hay, *Asian Ideas of East and West* (1970).

**Additional Sources**

Roy Choudhury, Pranab Chandra, *C. R. Das and his times,* Mysore: Geetha Book House, 1979.

Sen, Rathindra Nath, *Life and times of Deshbandhu Chittaranjan Das,* New Delhi: Northern Book Centre, 1989. □

# Charles François Daubigny

**The French painter and etcher Charles François Daubigny (1817-1878), a member of the Barbizon school, was one of the first landscape painters to work out of doors in a systematic way.**

C harles Daubigny was born in Paris on Feb. 15, 1817. His father, Edmé François Daubigny, was a landscape painter, and his uncle and aunt were miniaturists. Daubigny made the customary trip to Italy (1835-1836) and did some ideal landscapes, but his eventual direction was more decisively shaped by Dutch landscape painting. In 1838 he enrolled as a student of the academic painter Paul Delaroche.

Although Daubigny enjoyed a reasonable success at the Salons, where he exhibited from 1838 on, graphic art in the form of etchings, woodcuts, lithographs, and illustrations contributed substantially to his income. *Pond with Storks* (ca. 1851), with its painstaking analytical detail, is a representative Barbizon school work; it also echoes Dutch art of the 17th century. Some of Daubigny's rarely seen drawings, such as *River Landscape* (ca. 1860), have an astonishingly light, airy, and evocative touch.

Daubigny painted in the forest of Fontainebleau near Barbizon, along the rivers of northern France, and on the coast. He assimilated many sources and worked in many different manners. The *Pond of Gylieu* (1853), balanced, meticulous in execution, and suffused with soft light, was a particularly popular picture. The *Lock at Optevoz* (1859), done in blocky masses and heavier impasto, is reminiscent of Gustave Courbet. Daubigny's *Banks of the Oise* (ca. 1860), which is more delicate and luminous, gives a foretaste of Alfred Sisley. In contrast, the heaviness and dark greens of *Landscape near Pontoise* (1866) call to mind the work of Camille Pissarro. Intimate forest pictures such as *Landscape* (ca. 1877), executed in softer greens with a fluttery touch, illustrate the persistence of Camille Corot's influence.

Daubigny, whose work was considered to be too much a matter of "impressions," gave help and encouragement to Claude Monet, who followed him even in the practice of using a houseboat as a floating studio. Daubigny visited England and the Netherlands in 1870-1872. He died at Auvers-sur-Oise on Feb. 21, 1878.

Lacking the boldness and imagination to be a major artist, Daubigny was a hardworking, conscientious craftsman who never stopped looking at art and nature and who never stopped producing fresh and appealing pictures—along with some that were dull, flat, and routine. Histori-

cally, his role was to bridge the gap between the popular but fading Barbizon school and the more audacious and original impressionist school.

**Further Reading**

Most of the literature on Daubigny dates from the 19th and early 20th centuries. David Croal Thomson, *The Barbizon School of Painters* (1902), is a representative work. Robert L. Herbert, *Barbizon Revisited* (1902), is a catalog of an important exhibition organized in part by the Boston Museum, and a thorough account of the whole movement. John Rewald includes some useful material in *History of Impressionism* (1946; rev. ed. 1961). □

# Alphonse Daudet

**The French novelist, dramatist, and short-story writer Alphonse Daudet (1840-1897) is remembered chiefly for his regionalist sketches of Provence and for his transitional role in the evolution of 19th-century theater.**

B orn in Nîmes, as a child Alphonse Daudet experienced the heady delights of a sun-drenched Provence and the darkening contrasts of his family's steadily worsening financial condition. His father, a silk manufacturer, had to abandon business there in 1849, moving the family north to Lyons; never fully recovering from the depression which followed the Revolution of 1848, the Daudets finally lost everything in 1857. The family became scattered, and Alphonse—never an enthusiastic student— found himself miserably placed as a *pion,* or monitor, in a provincial *Collège.* After a few months he was rescued by his elder brother Ernest, who brought him to Paris and generously encouraged the boy's already evident literary talents. A collection of undistinguished love verses, *Les Amoureuses,* represented a most traditional debut for Alphonse, but again through his brother's influence he was directed by the opportunities of journalism to contribute prose *chroniques,* stylish social sketches, which won him entry to the prestigious *Figaro* (1859); already in these early compositions, a mixture of what critics have called "rosewater fantasy" and often sharp satire reveals Daudet's most characteristic modes: sentimentality and imaginative flight.

**Early Career**

Until 1865 the young Daudet enjoyed financial security as a comfortable undersecretary to the Duc de Morny— a position accorded, in almost fairy tale manner, by a chance notice of the Empress Eugénie. In these years he collaborated in writing a number of one-act plays (*La Dernière idole,* 1862; *Les Absents,* 1864; *L'Oeillet blanc,* 1865), helped toward the stage by the Duc de Morny's influence. Daudet decided to live solely by his pen after the duke's death, and in 1866 the first of his regionalist sketches, or *Lettres de mon moulin* (*Letters from My Mill*),

**Alphonse Daudet (left)**

based on Provençal folklore began appearing in Paris papers.

Two years later Daudet's first long work, *Le Petit chose* (*The Little Good-for-nothing*), was completed; largely autobiographical, this early novel speaks of boyhood joys and travails but in the end leads its hero to the failure and obscurity which Daudet's recent successes were to forestall. The serial publication of his *Aventures Prodigieuses de Tartarin de Tarascon* (1869) assured Daudet a place in Parisian literary circles, and today—with *Lettres* and *Le Petit chose*—it represents his most lasting contribution to French letters. Full of boisterous good humor and the vitality of southern climes, Daudet's picaro Tartarin nevertheless stands in sharp contrast to the young hero of *L'Arlésienne,* originally one of the Provençal tales related in *Lettres,* and adapted for the stage as Daudet's most serious dramatic effort in 1872. Here somber passion and jealousy lead to suicide—a thematic shift typical of Daudet's search for personal and artistic maturity in these years. *L'Arlésienne* failed miserably before the theatergoers of 1872, and this reversal of fortune turned Daudet resolutely back to novel writing. The play remains important, however, for the transformation Daudet there attempted in established theatrical formulas. Augustin Scribe's "well-made play" and the "comedy of manners" fostered by Alexandre Dumas and Émile Augier had for 20 years held dominion over the French stage. The seemingly plotless, moody, sequential

arrangement of *L'Arlésienne* (with incidental music by Georges Bizet) produced shock and laughter, reactions of a prejudiced public erased only by a second, successful production in 1885, when Émile Zola's campaign for naturalistic reform in the theater as well as the novel had begun to condition audiences to a genre less dependent on formal contrivance, closer to the unconnected sequences of life.

## Later Works

Married in 1867, a father the following year, Daudet felt that the press of family responsibilities made success imperative; the shock of defeat and occupation after the Franco-Prussian War (1870) turned his imagination to a more serious vein, and it was at this time as well that he met regularly with Gustave Flaubert, Ivan Turgenev, Edmond de Goncourt, and Zola—all diversely arguing for an art expressive of nature in all its determinisms, of man in his natural milieu. Zola's formulation of "naturalism," weighted with scientific analogies, would not come until 1880, but Daudet followed the author of *Les Rougon-Macquart* as closely as his temperament permitted and over the next 20 years produced 10 long novels of his own (*Froment jeune et Risler aîné,* 1874; *Jack,* 1876; *Le Nabab,* 1877; *Les Rois en exil,* 1879; *Numa Roumestan,* 1881; *L'Évangéliste,* 1883; *Sapho,* 1884; *L'Immortel,* 1887; *La Lutte pour la vie,* 1889; *Le Soutien de famille,* 1896). Perhaps the most accomplished of the early, more determinedly objective works is *Jack,* the story of an illegitimate son reared below his station, forced to become a laborer, and eventually destroyed by the brutalizing world of industrial society. The novel contains one of the first protests heard in France against the dehumanizing effects of child labor.

As in all these realistic novels of manners, however, Daudet undermines both the force of *Jack'*s social protest and the novel's very artistic integrity with lacrimonious appeals to reader sentiment and verbose developments. Sentimentality is perhaps the hallmark of Daudet's fictional world. Daudet died after an apoplectic attack on Dec. 16, 1897.

## Further Reading

Daudet's works, particularly his novels, have found many translators; a version of *Letters from My Mill* is by John P. Macgregor (1966). Studies of Daudet in English include the early but still valuable book by R. H. Sherard, *Alphonse Daudet: A Biographical and Critical Study* (1894), and the general treatment by Murray Sachs, *The Career of Alphonse Daudet: A Critical Study* (1965). Daudet's theatrical works are studied by Guy Rufus Saylor in *Alphonse Daudet as a Dramatist* (1940).

## Additional Sources

Hare, Geoffrey E., *Alphonse Daudet, a critical bibliography,* London: Grant & Cutler, 1978. ☐

# Honoré Victorin Daumier

**Honoré Victorin Daumier (1808-1879) was a French lithographer, painter, and sculptor. A romantic real-**

**ist in style, he produced caricatures that are abiding commentaries on politics and social manners.**

I n some 40 years of political and social commentary Honoré Daumier created an enormously rich and varied record of Parisian middle-class life in the form of nearly 4,000 lithographs, about 1,000 wood engravings, and several hundred drawings and paintings. In them the comic spirit of Molière comes to life once again. After having been the scourge of Louis Philippe and the July Monarchy (1830-1848), Daumier continued as a satirist of Louis Napoleon and the Second Empire (1851-1870). Poor himself, the artist sympathized with the struggling bourgeois and proletarian citizens of Paris. As a man of the left, he battled for the establishment of a republic, which finally came in 1870. Liberals have always applauded Daumier; some conservatives, however, have been inclined to consider him woolly-minded.

Honoré Daumier, born on Feb. 26, 1808, in Marseilles, was the son of a glazier. When Honoré was 6, the family moved to Paris, where the elder Daumier hoped to win success as a poet. Honoré grew up in a home in which humanistic concerns had some importance. A born draftsman and designer who was largely self-taught, he received some formal instruction from Alexandre Lenoir, one of Jacques Louis David's students. An obscure artist named Ramelet taught Daumier the elements of the new, inexpensive, and popular technique of lithography. Daumier's style is so much his own that it is not easy to

disentangle influences from other artists. Rembrandt and Francisco Goya are usually mentioned, along with Peter Paul Rubens, the Venetian school, and photography.

**Early Works**

Under the sponsorship of Charles Philipon, publisher of *Caricature* and *Charivari,* Daumier drew political cartoons in the early 1830s until press censorship in 1835 forced him to do satiric pictures of bourgeois manners. Among his best-known early lithographs are *Lafayette Buried,* portraying the fat king as a hypocritical mourner, although the dark black shape of Louis Philippe is esthetically attractive; the *Legislative Belly,* depicting a group of potbellied legislators and organized in a broad light and shade pattern; and *Rue Transnonain,* concerned with police brutality and showing a family murdered in a bedroom, which is dramatically effective in its restraint.

In order to give a forceful character to his images of legislators, Daumier modeled busts of his targets in clay before executing his drawings. He was on friendly terms with several sculptors and periodically returned to the use of sculptured forms; some of them were later carried out in terra-cotta or cast in bronze.

Between 1836 and 1838 Daumier did a notable series of 100 lithographs about an imaginary swindler named Robert Macaire, who symbolized the get-rich-quick philosophy of the times. His character is tellingly suggested in a famous print entitled *The Public Is Stupid.*

In the early 1830s Daumier published a series of 50 devastatingly anticlassical lithographs entitled *Ancient History.* Delightfully comic in effect, they also effectively exploit the rich blacks possible in the lithographic technique. The *Abduction of Helen of Troy* and *Narcissus* are good examples: Paris, gleefully smoking a cigar, is riding in triumph on the shoulders of Helen; Narcissus, admiring his reflection, is hideously scrawny.

**Later Work**

The Revolution of 1848 gave Daumier another opportunity to do political cartoons, among them *The Last Meeting of the Council* and *Victor Hugo and Émile Girardin* (as supporters of Louis Napoleon). At this time he also began his serious work as a painter with a competition picture, heroic in conception, *The Republic;* an unfinished *We Want Barabbas;* and a revolutionary street scene, *The Uprising,* whose authenticity some scholars question.

In 1850, as Louis Napoleon seemed to be an increasing threat to the republic, Daumier fashioned a sculptured caricature, *Ratapoil* (''Ratskin''), which symbolized the whole class of Bonapartist followers and Napoleon himself. It is a strikingly novel pictorial conception of sculpture and seems almost to have been ''painted'' with some fluid material.

A decade later *The Laundress* (ca. 1863; two versions) reflects Daumier's deep interest in ordinary people and, in subject at least, belongs to the mid-century development of realism. *The Drama* (ca. 1860) is one of the few paintings directly related to a lithograph. A rather ambitious work for Daumier, it has a twofold psychological character: the amused detachment of the artist observing a melodrama and the excited absorption of the audience.

In the early 1860s, when Daumier had no regular employment, he did many small canvases, watercolors, and drawings. His persistent interest in the arts comes out delightfully in a little watercolor picture, *The Connoisseurs,* in which his skill in expressing human responses by silhouettes and physical attitudes is perfectly realized.

In the late 1860s Daumier gave a great deal of attention to the European scene, especially to the development of Prussia as a military threat. The menace of militarism is summed up in *European Equilibrium* (1867) and the devastation of the Franco-Prussian War in *Peace—an Idyl* (1871). The late lithographs are conceived in a new, open, and sketchily linear style.

Although Daumier, like Gustave Courbet, maintained that it was necessary to be of one's own time, he sometimes turned to literary sources, as in the long series of interpretations of Don Quixote, painted at the end of his career. *Don Quixote and Sancho Panza,* with its balancing of two eternal human types, reflects the balance in his own temperament of opposed romantic and realistic impulses.

During his own time Daumier was not widely recognized as a painter, and his only one-man show of paintings was held in 1878. He died the following year on February 11 in Valmondois.

## Daumier's Influence

Caricaturists and social critics have been keenly aware of Daumier's contribution for well over a century. In the field of painting his mark has been less considerable. Daumier was a draftsman and an almost monochromatic tonalist. Later artists put less emphasis on drawing and created their pictures primarily with touches of color. If Daumier's effective use of flat "stains" and abstract shapes in wash drawings and lithographs remind us of Édouard Manet, we cannot be sure that the parallelism is more than fortuitous. On the other hand, realistic café scenes such as *Absinthe* (1863) were followed by a whole line of similar works by Manet, Edgar Degas, and Henri de Toulouse-Lautrec.

## Further Reading

Bernard Lemann, *Honoré Daumier* (1946), is a carefully chosen selection of 240 lithographs, well reproduced, with a good introduction and notes. K. E. Maison, *Honoré Daumier* (1968), is a two-volume *catalogue raisonné* of the paintings, watercolors, and drawings; it is the most up-to-date study, with the main emphasis on authenticity and dating rather than on the interpretation of Daumier's work. Maison's *Daumier Drawings* (1960) is also a useful book in spite of its rather gray plates. Jacques Lassaigne's general survey, *Daumier* (1938; trans. 1939), remains a good introduction. Oliver W. Larkin, *Daumier: Man of His Time* (1966), is a solid and well-illustrated study. Howard P. Vincent, *Daumier and His World* (1968), is well written. Jeanne L. Wasserman's catalog of Daumier's sculptural works, *Daumier Sculpture* (1969), is very thorough. □

# John Davenport

**English Puritan clergyman and author John Davenport (1597-1670) founded the New Haven colony in America and was its theological ruler for its first 30 years.**

Of a distinguished English family, John Davenport was the fifth son of the mayor of Coventry. He attended the free grammar school at Coventry, then entered Oxford but had to withdraw for lack of money. Made vicar of St. Stephen's in London when he was 19, he became widely known as a pulpit orator. He returned to Oxford to take a bachelor of divinity degree. All this time he seems to have remained loyal to the Church of England, although he knew members of the Puritan party. Prior to his election to St. Stephen's he had written letters professing his conformity in order to allay suspicion and silence his opposition.

Davenport's Nonconformism evidently developed gradually. In 1629 he was one of the group actively working for a charter for the America-bound Massachusetts Bay Company, and he was a friend of John Cotton. Davenport's was a strictly orthodox Puritanism; in Holland (as later in New England) he opposed the baptism of the children of the unregenerate. His views brought him into conflict with the Dutch Classis, and he was denied the right to preach. Thus, on John Cotton's invitation, Davenport sailed for Boston in 1637, with his wife and his lifelong friend, the merchant Theophilus Eaton. In Boston, Davenport took part in the Antinomain crisis, which involved Anne Hutchinson's heretical idea of "grace." He founded the colony of New Haven in 1638 and became its pastor, while Theophilus Eaton became its governor.

Devoted to the life of the colony, Davenport also authored many tracts, including *The Knowledge of Christ* (1653) and *The Saints Anchor-hold in All Storms and Tempests* (1701). In *A Discourse about Civil Government in a New Plantation Whose Design Is Religion* (1633) he defended theocracy, which he defined as making "the Lord God our Governor." Davenport's political and theological positions were expressed with the intensity of one who acts in constant expectation of the Messiah. He preached sermons in support of the regicide judges Edward Whalley and William Goffe, who fled to America and were said to have found refuge in his house.

Davenport opposed assimilating New Haven into the larger Connecticut colony. When efforts against this union failed, Davenport in 1667, feeling Christ's interests "miserably lost," accepted the pastorate of the First Church in Boston. He died in Boston on May 30, 1670.

## Further Reading

*Letters of John Davenport, Puritan Divine,* edited by Isabel MacBeath Calder, was published in 1937. For information on Davenport see A. W. M'Clure, *The Lives of John Wilson, John Norton, and John Davenport* (1846), and Cotton Mather, *Magnalia Christi Americana: or, The Ecclesiastical History of*

*New-England* (1702; rev. ed., 2 vols., 1853-1855; repr. 1967). Robert G. Pope, *The Half-way Covenant: Church Membership in Puritan New England* (1969), includes an extensive chapter on Davenport. He is also discussed in Perry Miller, *The New England Mind: From Colony to Province* (1953). □

# David

**David, the second king of the Israelites (reigned ca. 1010-ca. 970 B.C.), was regarded as a model king and founded a permanent dynasty.**

D avid was born in Bethlehem, the youngest son of Jesse of the tribe of Judah. The prophet Samuel, after revoking Saul's designation as king, secretly anointed David as Saul's successor. David attained great popularity by killing the Philistine giant Goliath in combat (1 Samuel 17:49), although another biblical source attributes this feat to one named Elhanan (2 Samuel 21:19). A skilled harpist, David was brought to the royal court to divert Saul with music and alleviate the depression that Saul had succumbed to under the strain of his responsibilities. At court David won the undying friendship of the crown prince, Jonathan, whose sister Michal he married.

After Saul's jealousy had forced David to flee for his life, he had two opportunities to slay the King but magnani-

mously spared him. Saul eventually met his end at Gilboa, together with three of his sons, including Jonathan. After a period of mourning, David proceeded to Hebron, where he was chosen king by the elders of Judah. Saul's general Abner, however, proclaimed Ishbaal (Ishbosheth), a surviving son of the dead king, as the sovereign. In the civil war that ensued, Ishbaal and Abner were slain. Their deaths removed the last obstacles from David's path to the throne, and about 1010 B.C. he was crowned king of all the Israelites.

After numerous battles David liberated Israel from the yoke of the Philistines and ushered in a golden era for his people. He captured Jerusalem and made it his capital because of its strategic military position and its location outside the boundaries of any tribe. He placed the Ark of the Covenant in a tent near his residence, thereby making Jerusalem the religious, as well as the national, center of all of Israel and preparing the way for his son and successor, Solomon, to erect the Holy Temple there.

David expanded his kingdom to Phoenicia in the west, the Arabian Desert in the east, the Orontes River in the north, and Etzion Geber (Elath) in the south. But internal political troubles overtook David. His son Absalom led a rebellion which was finally suppressed when Joab, David's general, killed him, although the King had ordered that he be spared. David also had to quash an uprising of Saul's tribe, the Benjaminites.

The Bible idealizes David as a warrior, statesman, loyal friend, and gifted poet, yet it does not fail to mention his

faults and moral lapses. At one time David callously plotted the death in battle of one of his officers, Uriah the Hittite, so that he could marry Uriah's beautiful wife, Bathsheba. For this he was denounced by the prophet Nathan, and, recognizing that he had committed a great moral wrong, the King fasted and prayed in repentance.

Jewish tradition ascribes to David the authorship of the Book of Psalms and refers to him as the "sweet singer of Israel." The Messiah, too, was to come forth from "the stock of Jesse" (Isaiah 9:5, 11:10), and indeed the New Testament speaks of Jesus as a descendant of the House of David (Matthew 1:16). David's tomb, traditionally assumed to be on Mt. Zion, has become a venerated place of pilgrimage.

## Further Reading

The Bible portrays the life and achievements of David in 1 Samuel 16 through 2 Samuel 5, 2 Samuel 19-20, 1 Kings 1-2, and 1 Chronicles 10-29. The chapter on King David in Harry Meyer Orlinsky, *Ancient Israel* (1954), is recommended. See also Martin North, *The History of Israel* (1953; 2d ed. 1960); John Bright, *A History of Israel* (1959); and Mortimer J. Cohen, "David the King," in Simon Noveck, ed., *Great Jewish Personalities in Ancient and Medieval Times* (1959). □

# David I

**David I (1084-1153) reigned as king of Scotland from 1124 to 1153. He is noted for his introduction of Norman institutions into Scotland.**

David I came to the Scottish throne when his brother King Alexander I died in 1124 without an heir. David's two wars with England failed to bring northern English lands into his realm. He first marched south on the pretext of protecting the interests of his niece Matilda, daughter of Henry I, against Stephen, who had claimed the English throne. The Scottish army was routed at the Battle of the Standard, fought at Cutton Moor in 1138. David, however, was able to secure recognition of his son, Henry, as holder of Northumberland and Huntingdon, to which David's wife had been heiress. When a second invasion of England in 1140 proved as futile as the first, David gave up his program of expansion and devoted himself to internal Scottish affairs.

David brought a number of Norman nobles and churchmen with him when he traveled from England to take the Scottish crown. Norman nobles displaced Celtic leaders in the north, and their castles began to rise to symbolize the shift of political power. Landholdings based on Scottish customary rights were made subject to Norman charters, and Norman practices in law and administration were introduced. For the man in the field, however, it was a quiet revolution; no one was displaced, and the new system was grafted onto the old in a peaceful way.

Norman influences were especially apparent in the Church. David increased the number of dioceses from four to nine and named Normans as bishops of the new ones. He also founded 10 monasteries, welcoming to Scotland new orders that were popular south of the border, the Cistercians and the Augustinian canons regular. His active patronage of the Church won for David an enduring reputation for piety.

David was truly the father of the city, or burgh, in Scotland. He himself chartered only four or five burghs, but he allowed the development of private burghs under the aegis of his ecclesiastical and lay nobles. The rise of cities was related to a developing commerce, and to help the growing trade David broke new ground by issuing a silver penny, the first Scottish coinage. Within the cities a new class developed, the townsmen.

For Scotland, David was a constructive revolutionary: the language and customs of the Scots gave way to English speech and manners; the Church was organized on patterns akin to those of England and Rome; and the rise of burghs saw the emergence of the Scottish middle class.

## Further Reading

David's Normanizing work is covered in R. L. Graeme Ritchie, *The Normans in Scotland* (1954). A judicious appraisal of David's contributions is in *A New History of Scotland*, vol. 4: *Scotland from the Earliest Times to 1603*, written by William Croft Dickinson and George S. Pryde (1962; rev. ed. 1965). An interesting summary of the epoch is provided by Eric Linklater, *The Survival of Scotland: A New History of Scotland from Roman Times to the Present Day* (1968). □

# Jacques Louis David

**The French painter Jacques Louis David (1748-1825) was the leader of the neoclassic movement. His style set the artistic standards for many of his contemporaries and determined the direction of numerous 19th-century painters.**

Jacques Louis David early turned his back on the frivolous rococo manner, looking instead to antiquity for inspiration. Following the ideals of Nicolas Poussin, to whom the artist candidly admitted he owed everything, David sought to reduce classical principles to their barest, unencumbered essentials. In this endeavor he observed with avid interest the neoclassicism propounded by Johann Winckelmann and the illustrations of antiquity found in the paintings of Anton Raphael Mengs. An outspoken political firebrand, David espoused the cause of the French Revolution and under the Convention held sway as the virtual dictator of the arts; later when Napoleon came to power, he acted willingly as his artistic spokesman.

David was born in Paris on Aug. 30, 1748. His well-to-do bourgeois family placed him in the studio of that arch-practitioner of the rococo manner, the eminent painter François Boucher, to whom David was apparently distantly related. Perhaps because of his own advanced years, Boucher encouraged David to study under Joseph Marie Vien, a painter who had been attracted by the new wave of interest in antiquity while studying in Rome. In 1771 David won second prize in the Prix de Rome competition, but it was not until 3 years later and after severe mental frustration that he won the first prize with his painting *Antiochus Dying for the Love of Stratonice.*

## Early Works

David went to Rome in 1775 in the company of Vien, who had just been named the director of the French Academy there. David studied the ancient architectural monuments, marble reliefs, and freestanding statues. In addition, he strove for a clearer understanding of the classical principles underlying the styles of the Renaissance and baroque masters Raphael, the Carracci, Domenichino, and Guido Reni. The effects of David's Romanization were first witnessed in his *Belisarius Asking for Alms,* exhibited in Paris in 1781. When he returned to Paris in 1780, he was an artist already thoroughly imbued with the tenets of classicism. He was admitted to the French Academy in 1783 with his painting *Andromache by the Body of Hector.*

The following year David returned to Rome in order to paint the *Oath of the Horatii,* a work which was immediately acclaimed a masterpiece both in Italy and in France at its showing at the Parisian Salon of 1785. The painting reflected a strong interest in archeological exactitude in the depiction of figures and settings. Its carefully calculated severity of composition and its emphasis on a sculptural hardness of precise drawing, which David saw as more important than color, contributed to the forceful moralistic tone of the subject: the oath being administered to the

Horatii by their father, who demanded their sacrifice for the good of the state. In this single work, with its strong republican implications, those aspiring to do so could find a call to revolution, a revolution which was in fact only 5 years distant. The *Oath* was followed by other moralizing canvases such as the *Death of Socrates* (1787) and *Brutus and the Lictors Bringing Home to Brutus the Bodies of His Sons* (1789), both extolling the classical virtues.

## French Revolution

With the Revolution in full swing, David for a time abandoned his classical approach and began to paint scenes describing contemporary events, among them the unfinished *Oath of the Tennis Court* (1791), glorifying the first challenge to royal authority by the parliamentarians of the period. He also concentrated on portraits of the martyred heroes of the fight for freedom, including the *Death of Marat* (1793), the *Death of Lepeletier de Saint-Fargeau* (1793) and the *Death of Joseph Bara* (1794), all executed with an unvarnished realism. The artist was deeply involved with the political scene; elected to the National Convention in 1792, he served as a deputy to that all-powerful body and was one of those who voted for the execution of King Louis XVI.

David had apparently long harbored great animosity toward the French Academy, perhaps because it had failed to fully recognize his talents when he had first submitted works for the Grand Prix competition. Though an honored member by the time of the Revolution, in 1793 he hastened its dissolution, forming a group called the Commune of the Arts; this group was almost immediately supplanted by the Popular and Republican Society of the Arts, from whose ranks the Institute ultimately would be formed.

A friend of Robespierre, David nearly accompanied him to the guillotine when the Jacobin fell from power in 1794. Imprisoned for 7 months, first at Fresnes and then in the Luxembourg, the artist emerged a politically wiser man. It was while in prison that David executed one of his rare landscapes: the *Gardens of the Luxembourg* (1794), a view from his prison window. By 1798 he was busy on what he proclaimed his masterpiece, the *Rape of the Sabine Women.* The subject matter, derived from the classical legend described by Livy in which the Sabine women intervened in the battle between their fathers and brothers and their Roman husbands, represented a calculated appeal by David to end the internecine conflict that had ripped France asunder; further, the vast canvas was planned as a sort of manifesto proclaiming the validity of the antique.

## David and Napoleon

It was at this time that David met Napoleon Bonaparte, in whose person he recognized a worthy new hero whom he promptly proceeded to glorify. The Emperor in turn realized the rich potential of David as a propagandist born to champion his imperial regime, and it was probably with this in mind that he invited the artist to accompany him on his Egyptian campaign; that David declined to go was surely due only to the fact that he was then deeply absorbed in the creation of his avowed masterpiece, the *Sabine Women.*

Named "first painter," David executed a number of portraits of the Emperor, the most notable of which is probably that entitled *Bonaparte Crossing the St. Bernard Pass* (1800), in which the subject was idealized in physical stature and romanticized as the effortless man of action. Among the major commissions granted David by the Emperor were the colossal scenes treating specific episodes of his reign. The best-known of these are the *Coronation of Napoleon and Josephine* (1805-1807), containing over 100 portraits, and the *Distribution of the Eagles* (1810).

Though David would have preferred to be remembered for his history painting, he was at his best as a portraitist. Certain of his portraits, such as *Madame Sériziat and Her Daughter* and *Monsieur Sériziat* (1795), are done with an incredible directness and thus retain a freshness and vivacity not often encountered in David's more serious works. His unfinished portrait *Madame Récamier* (1800), with the subject shown in long, loosely flowing robes, vaguely reminiscent of the antique, summarizes the studied elegance of the neoclassic age.

With Bonaparte's defeat at Waterloo and the subsequent restoration of the Bourbons, David tried to retreat into quiet seclusion, but his earlier political affiliation and, more particularly, his actions during the heat of the Revolution were not calculated to warm his relations with the new rulers. He was declared persona non grata and fled to Switzerland. A short time later he settled in Brussels, where he continued to paint until his death on Dec. 29, 1825. His family's urgent request that his ashes be returned to France was denied. He was buried amidst great pomp and circumstance in the church of Ste-Gudule in Brussels.

## David's Influence

There was scarcely a young painter of the following generation who was not influenced by David's style, a style which had within it such diverse aspects as classicism, realism, and romanticism. Among his foremost pupils, each of whom developed various different facets of his style, were Antoine Jean, Baron Gros; Pierre Narcisse Guérin; François Gérard; Girodet de Roucy-Trioson; and perhaps most important, J. A. D. Ingres.

## Further Reading

Most of the vast literature on David is in French. In English, the best studies are W. R. Valentiner, *Jacques Louis David and the French Revolution* (1929), and David L. Dowd, *Pageant Master of the Republic: Jacques-Louis David and the French Revolution* (1948). David is also discussed in the following general studies of the period: Lionello Venturi, *Modern Painters* (2 vols., 1947-1950); Walter Friedlaender, *David to Delacroix* (1952); and Jack Lindsay, *Death of the Hero: French Painting from David to Delacroix* (1961).

## Additional Sources

Brookner, Anita, *Jacques-Louis David,* London: Chatto & Windus, 1980; New York, N.Y.: Thames and Hudson, 1980, 1987. ☐

# Arthur Bowen Davies

**American painter Arthur Bowen Davies (1862-1928) introduced a contemporary quality in a basically romantic style and was a pioneer in bringing American art into the mainstream of progressive Western painting.**

Arthur B. Davies was born in Utica, N.Y., on Sept. 26, 1862. He was sketching and painting scenes of the Mohawk Valley before he was 16, when his family moved to Chicago. He studied at the Art Institute there, worked for the board of trade, and went on an engineering expedition to Mexico. In 1887 he went to New York City and studied at the Art Students League, where Robert Henri and George Luks became his friends. Davies's earliest professional work (1888-1891) was magazine illustration. He married in 1890 and moved to a farm near Congers, N.Y.; soon afterward he competed unsuccessfully for the mural decorations of the Appellate Court in New York City. In 1894 the New York art dealer William Macbeth provided him with a studio over his gallery, gave him a one-man show, and introduced him to industrialist Benjamin Altman, who provided funds for his first trip abroad. In Europe he was impressed by the Venetians and by Delacroix, Puvis de Chavannes, and Whistler.

By 1900 Davies had found his characteristic theme: the female nude in a landscape setting, romantic, nostalgic, frequently with a mysterious ritualistic quality. The figures, small in scale, are often arranged in a friezelike procession against dark and forbidding backgrounds. The mood is poetic, with a peculiarly personal symbolism that is suggested by mythological themes or by obscure symbolic titles. A new grandeur was introduced in his work as the result of a trip to California in 1905 during which he made studies of mountains.

Davies was one of "The Eight" whose 1908 exhibition at the Macbeth Gallery challenged the authority and conservatism of the National Academy of Design. Five of the exhibiting artists stressed urban realism in subject matter; Davies and Maurice Prendergast established notes of fantasy and charm which were wholly personal. Davies was a master of many media—oil, watercolor, pastel, lithograph, etching, sculpture, murals, and tapestry designs.

From 1912 to 1914 Davies was president of the Society of Independent Artists, which had been formed to organize the Armory Show of 1913. This celebrated exhibition first introduced American artists and the American public to the European pioneers of 20th-century style. Davies's work for a period reflected a new cubist influence but returned eventually to the idyllic fantasies that were his natural language.

Though Davies was a habitual recluse and worked in considerable secrecy, he attracted devoted admirers and was generous in his admiration of progressive artists. During the 1920s he executed a series of murals and designed tapestries. He also became obsessed with the act of inhalation and believed that the character and quality of Greek art was due to the fact that it represented figures consciously controlling their breathing. It has even been said that his personal experiments in breathing led to his heart attack in 1923. After that he went again to Europe, where he painted a series of romantic landscapes in northern Italy. He died in Florence, alone in his studio, on Oct. 24, 1928.

## Further Reading

There is no comprehensive study of Davies. Royal Cortissoz, *Arthur B. Davies* (1931), is a brief but useful picture book. Davies's important role in formation of the Armory Show is documented in Milton W. Brown, *The Story of the Armory Show* (1963). There are interesting personal sidelights in Bennard B. Perlman, *The Immortal Eight: American Painting from Eakins to the Armory Show, 1870-1913* (1962).

## Additional Sources

Wright, Brooks, *The artist and the unicorn: the lives of Arthur B. Davies, 1862-1928,* New City, N.Y.: Historical Society of Rockland County, 1978. □

# Viscount Davignon

**Viscount Davignon (born 1932) was an important architect of European integration and unity as a member and later vice-president of the Commission of the European Communities.**

Viscount Etienne Davignon was born in Budapest (Hungary) on October 4, 1932, to a Belgian family of professional diplomats. His father had been a distinguished Belgian ambassador and his grandfather had been minister for foreign affairs (as a reward for his good services, he had been raised to the rank of nobility in 1916 by the King of Belgium).

Davignon studied law at the Catholic University of Louvain and thereafter joined the Ministry of Foreign Affairs in 1959 where he soon got involved in Belgium's most delicate post-war diplomatic action: negotiating a satisfactory way out of the turmoil in Africa surrounding the granting of independence to what had been the Belgian Congo. In 1961 he was nominated to serve in the office of the Foreign Minister Paul-Henri Spaak, who became the mentor and a close friend of the young diplomat. Davignon served as head of office from 1964 until 1969, remaining at this post under the next foreign minister.

A first major achievement in his career as an architect of European unity was realized when he became director general of the political department of the Ministry of Foreign Affairs from 1969 until 1976. He proposed the creation of a committee of all directors general of the European Communities (currently called the European Union), which then consisted of only six member countries. He successfully defended the idea of an institutionalized mechanism to coordinate the foreign policies of these countries. It was the first committee created through the European Communities (E.C.) that aimed directly at increasing the political coopera-

tion of the members, beside the already strongly institutionalized economic, commercial, and industrial cooperation. Davignon presided over this committee from 1974 until 1975, and his influence over it went so far that the committee carried his name. Davignon is rightly said to be one of the "founding fathers" of political cooperation in the European Communities.

## Appointment to Tackle Oil Crisis

In November 1974 he was appointed chairman of the governing board of the international Energy Agency created in response to the first world-wide oil crisis. He became one of the 13 commissioners of the European Economic Communities in December 1976. This meant that he had to act independently, in the interest of the E.C. as a whole and not as a Belgian representative anymore. During his first mandate (four years) at the commission he had responsibility for internal markets and industries. During his second mandate, from 1981 to 1985, Viscount Davignon also was chosen as one of the five vice-presidents of the commission, responsible for industry, energy, and research policies.

Decisions at the commission are collegial, and it is often hard to know whose product they are. Those related to Davignon's field of competence bear the distinctive mark of his influence and conceptions. His middle-of-the-road, pragmatic approach to solving the problems of Europe's traditional industrial sectors proved relatively successful, given the complex circumstances. He negotiated international agreements on textiles, steel, and shipyards to give European industry the indispensable breathing space it needed to reshape and adapt itself to prevailing world standards of competition. For example, his supervision of the steel industries within the European Communities resulted in the implementation of an anti-crisis plan also called "Plan Davignon." It was a response to protectionist moves by member countries who tried to protect their labor intensive steel industries in decline. The plan succeeded in preserving the openness of the European market for members as well as non-members of the European Communities. Other merits of Davignon's plan were that the difficult climate of solidarity among steel producers was maintained and that future government subsidies to the steel industry had to be submitted for approval by the commission. Similar plans were elaborated to save and restructure the also declining textile industry and the shipyards.

## Took on Trade Disputes

Trade disputes between the European Communities and the United States or Japan were frequent after the beginning of the world recession of the 1970s. Davignon took the lead in many of them, especially in settling the U.S.-E.C. steel dispute in 1982.

Davignon can also be credited for drawing up a wider strategy for encouraging the burgeoning high technology industries within the E.C. Common European standards had to be found in such new fields as computer technologies and telecommunications. Otherwise, a myriad of regulations would result in a sterile competition and too small internal markets would impede competition with products from the United States or Japan.

Davignon was also in charge of developing a common energy policy. The aim was to reduce energy consumption through more economic use of it. But declining oil prices and private initiatives made the policies obsolete. Though, still in the energy sector, Davignon insisted on the implementation of the Joint European Torus (JET) project, a research project to produce energy by nuclear fusion (instead of the classical fission). European governments have joined forces to build one of the most powerful experimental energy installations in the world.

After his second mandate at the commission of the European Communities, Davignon became a member of the governing board of the Société Générale de Belgique (SGB), Belgium's leading holding company and became chairman of the company in April 1989. SGB was known, half affectionately, half mockingly as La Vieille Dame (the old lady), a comment on SGB's "stuffy, old-fashioned traditions and its age." Davignon was also a partner at Kissinger Associates, Inc., a consulting office based in Washington, D.C.

In May 1991, Davignon became chairman of the Association for the Monetary Union of Europe. The Association was founded in 1987 by European industrialists who agreed on the objectives of monetary union and a single currency for the success of the single European market. Speaking on the need for a unified Europe, Davignon remarked, "More and more issues create problems when they don't get Europe-wide solutions. National frameworks don't work anymore."

## Further Reading

Little has been written on Davignon, and he himself published little. An excellent article by him is: "*Notre avenir dans l'Europe*" in *Réalités et perspectives* (1985, Banque Générale du Luxembourg). On political cooperation, see Philippe de Schoutheete, *La coopération politique européenne,* preface by Davignon, edited by Fernand Nathan (Paris, 1980). Davignon's papers are freely available at European Files and Documentations, Documentation Service, Bur. R/1 D, SDM8, Rue de la Loi, 200, B-1049 Brussels, Belgium. □

# Alexander Jackson Davis

**Alexander Jackson Davis (1803-1892) was a leading figure of the 19th-century Gothic revival in American architecture.**

Alexander Jackson Davis began as an apprentice architectural draftsman to Josiah Brady of New York in 1826, though his early painting ambitions remained evident in his lifelong picturesque approach to architectural design. In 1829 Davis joined Ithiel Town in what became the first architectural firm of a modern sort in the United States, lasting until Town's death in 1844.

Davis specialized in domestic architecture, leaving more public or monumental commissions to Town. Hun-

dreds of houses were built directly or indirectly from Davis's designs; he was also among the first architects to design furniture for his larger houses. He claimed to have been first to introduce to America "the English Gothic Villa with Barge Boards, Bracketts, Oriels, Tracery in Windows . . . in 1832" and also the Italianate villa, with a drawing exhibited about 1835. In the early 1840s Davis began moving into the orbit of A. J. Downing, illustrating Downing's book, *Country Houses,* in 1850. After Downing's death Davis designed and supervised all buildings in Llewellyn Park in West Orange, N.J., conceived by Downing and financed by Llewellyn P. Haskell as America's first "garden suburb" (1852-1869).

Picturesqueness was predominant in all Davis's works. Yet in his last major project, an unsuccessful submission in the 1867 competition for the New York City Post Office, he designed a metal and glass structure which clearly presaged 20th-century "functional" concepts. Far from being contradictory, however, both picturesqueness and functionalism were from the first inherent in the American—as distinct from English or French—Gothic revival.

In America, Gothic revival architecture never challenged the Roman or Greek revival in mass popularity; indeed, its associations were fundamentally "antiestablishment." Gothic was an "arty" style, associated with the idea of the "natural man." There was always something eccentric about it: a typical example was the exaggerated asymmetry and anticlassical proportions of Davis's H. K. Harral house in Bridgeport, Conn. (ca. 1846; demolished). Such stylistic self-consciousness inevitably encouraged self-conscious formalism—emphasis on the "naturalness" of Gothic forms and structure as an end in itself—and thence to the kind of "functionalism" exhibited in Davis's 1867 Post Office design. For historical reasons, however, the picturesque side of Gothic revival architecture predominated in America so that its chief legacy was the Arts and Crafts movement of about 1890 to about 1910, prefaced by the Romanesque of H. H. Richardson and climaxed by the early work of Louis Sullivan and Frank Lloyd Wright. Combining something of both trends, Davis has claim to be the most representative of all American Gothic revivalists.

## Further Reading

Though many articles have appeared in recent years on various aspects of Davis's life and career, the only book-length biography is Roger H. Newton, *Town & Davis, Architects: Pioneers in American Revivalist Architecture, 1812-1870* (1942), which has serious limitations. Davis's influence and career are discussed in Alan Gowans, *Images of American Living: Four Centuries of Architecture and Furniture as Cultural Expression* (1964).

## Additional Sources

Doumato, Lamia, *Alexander Jackson Davis, 1803-1892,* Monticello, Ill.: Vance Bibliographies, 1980.

Harmon, Robert B. (Robert Bartlett), *Greek revival architecture in America and the designs of Alexander Jackson Davis: a selected bibliography,* Monticello, Ill.: Vance Bibliographies, 1981. □

# Angela Davis

**A scholar, activist, and professed Communist, Angela Davis (born 1944) became a leading advocate of civil rights for blacks in the United States.**

I n August 1970 Angela Yvonne Davis was catapulted into the national spotlight when she was put on the list of the ten most wanted criminals in the United States. An armed black man, Jonathan Jackson, entered the Marin County, California, Civic Center on August 7, 1970, with a weapon owned by Davis and attempted, along with three San Quentin prisoners, to take hostages. Jackson's intention was to hold the hostages until several inmates of Soledad Prison, including Jackson's brother, George, were released. During the attempt three of the assailants and the presiding judge were killed and three others wounded. A warrant was issued for Davis's arrest. She fled, eluding the police until October 1970. After a total of 16 months in prison in New York—where she was apprehended—and in California, Davis's trial began.

The prosecutor alleged that Davis engineered the plan to kidnap the judge and jurors because of her love for George Jackson. The prosecution presented witnesses who testified that they had seen Davis with Jonathan Jackson in the days preceding the August 7 incident. Davis and her defense attorneys argued that Davis was a political activist concerned with prison reforms and the oppression of the poor in general and was not moved to a crime of passion because of her feeling for Jackson. The all-white jury, composed of eight women and four men, acquitted Davis on all counts in June 1972.

Davis, a self-avowed Communist, was born in Birmingham, Alabama, in 1944. Both her parents were college educated. Her mother was a teacher and her father, after teaching for a short time, went into business for himself. The Davises moved into an all-white neighborhood when Angela was very young. Racial antipathy was fomenting in the city and the Davises knew that they were not welcome in the neighborhood. The homes of several black families who moved in after the Davises were bombed, although the Davises' home was not.

Angela Davis encountered segregation in almost every area of her life. In housing, school, stores, church, and social life, the ubiquitous "white only" or "colored only" signs, both visible and invisible, were always there. Because Davis had the opportunity to travel to New York during many of her summer vacations her awareness of the difference in racial attitudes and social classes in the South and the North was heightened. Even as a teenager, Davis later wrote, she developed a desire to alleviate the plight of the black and the poor.

Because of superior achievement during her high school years Davis got the opportunity to study at Elizabeth Irwin High School in New York City. There she was regularly exposed to both socialist and communist philosophies and began to develop an interest in these subjects. She was especially interested in mass movements designed to overthrow political domination by elites. Davis's scholastic achievements earned her a scholarship to Brandeis University in Waltham, Massachusetts, where she was one of the few blacks on campus. At the university Davis studied French literature but continued to be interested in philosophy. She studied in France during her junior year. While there, she learned of the September 1963 bombing of a church in her hometown, Birmingham, that resulted in the death of four black girls. She knew three of them.

During her senior year at Brandeis, Davis studied philosophy with Herbert Marcuse, who later became her graduate adviser. After graduating magna cum laude and Phi Beta Kappa from Brandeis in 1965, Davis applied for a scholarship to study philosophy at the Goethe University in Frankfurt. After two years she returned to the United States to study for her doctorate with Marcuse, who was then teaching at the University of California at San Diego. While in graduate school she became politically active with groups such as the Black Panthers, the Student Non-Violent Coordinating Committee (SNCC), and Ron Karenga's US-Organization. In 1968 she became a member of the Communist Party and joined one of its local organs, the Che-Lumumba Club.

As a requirement for her doctorate Davis had to teach for one year and was appointed to the faculty at the University of California, Los Angeles. Her appointment was challenged because she had indicated on her application that she was a Communist. There was a regulation that Communists were not allowed to teach in California state universities. Consequently, the governing body of the university, the Board of Regents, and the governor, Ronald Reagan, attempted to fire Davis. She waged a court battle against her dismissal and won. Later, however, in June 1970, she was fired for her political activity.

After she was acquitted of the charges stemming from the August 7, 1970 incident, she taught black philosophy and women's studies at San Francisco State College. In 1980 and 1984 she ran on the Communist Party ticket for vice president of the United States. By 1983 she was working with the National Alliance against Racist and Political Repression and had been awarded an honorary doctorate from Lenin University.

Throughout the 1980s and 1990s Davis taught courses at several universities, and in 1997 continued to teach at the University of California at Santa Cruz. At the university she acted as presidential chair of a minority women's studies department. She has stated that she hopes young people will continue to seek new solutions. In *Essence* she said, "History is important, but it also can stifle young people's ability to think in new ways and to present ideas that may sound implausible now but that really may help us develop radical strategies for moving into the next century."

## Further Reading

Much has been written about Angela Davis. She is coauthor of a volume entitled *If They Come in the Morning* (1971) and the author of *Angela Davis, An Autobiography* (1974), *Women, Race and Class* (1983), and *Women, Culture & Politics* (1989). The transcript of the Marin County court case (#52613) is available on microfilm. Several other books discuss the same case. Some of these are Charles R. Ashman, *The People* vs. *Angela Davis* (1972); Regina Nadelson, *Who is Angela Davis?* (1972); J. A. Parker, *Angela Davis, the Making of a Revolutionary* (1973); and Bettina Aptheker, *The Morning Breaks* (1975). □

# Arthur Vining Davis

**Arthur Vining Davis (1867-1962) was the general manager of the Aluminum Company of America (ALCOA) for more than half a century. He also served as president of the company and as chairman of the board for shorter periods.**

Arthur Vining Davis was born on May 30, 1867, in Sharon, Massachusetts, the son of a Congregational minister. He was educated in Hyde Park, Massachusetts, and Roxbury Latin School in Boston. He then went on to Amherst College. Upon graduation in 1888 he moved to Pittsburgh to take a job at $14 a week with a new company planning to manufacture a new, light metal.

Although aluminum had been on the market for a number of years, it was an inordinately expensive product, selling for $8 a pound in the 1880s. In 1886, however, 22 year old Charles Martin Hall developed a process for making aluminum in an Ohio woodshed which would substan-

tially reduce the price. After trying for two years without success to interest anyone in the Ohio area in the process, Hall came to Pittsburgh in 1888. There he found a young metallurgist, Alfred E. Hunt, who recognized the value of the process. Hunt, in turn, was able to interest a group of young Pittsburghers to provide financial support for the project.

Hunt was a native of Massachusetts whose parents had attended Rev. Davis's Congregational Church in Hyde Park. When young Davis graduated from Amherst, his father asked Hunt to secure a position for his son in Pittsburgh. Hunt at that time was a partner in the Pittsburgh Testing Laboratory, but had just formed his association with Hall to manufacture aluminum. Davis, therefore, was present in Pittsburgh in time for Hunt to bring him into the company for the birth of the modern aluminum industry. Hunt and Hall had set up the Pittsburgh Reduction Company in July 1888 with a combined capital of just $20,000. With this money they built and equipped a small experimental plant which was able to demonstrate that Hall's process was commercially sound. Hall had put up no money, and Hunt had gotten a number of acquaintances in the steel industry, including George H. Clapp, Howard Lash, Robert Scott, Millard Hunsicker, and W. S. Sample, to contribute funds.

Davis at that time had no money and held no stock in the company. He was appointed assistant to Hall as they endeavored to work out technical problems with the process. Davis, however, early showed that his abilities lay outside the plant, becoming a superb salesman and executive. It was Davis who largely had the task of convincing

people that aluminum, still relatively expensive, could be used for a number of products. He particularly made important inroads in the kitchen utensil field, getting items fabricated in his company's plant and then sending a team of college students on the road to peddle them to housewives. In this way Davis convinced utensil manufacturers of aluminum's value. In 1891 Davis was made a stockholder in the firm, just shortly after Andrew W. and Richard B. Mellon provided important funds for the expansion of the enterprise. It was the Mellons, more than anyone else, who recognized the worth of Davis to the enterprise and persuaded the other partners to give Davis some of their stock.

Davis became general manager of the firm in the 1890s and was Hunt's right hand man. When Hunt died in 1899 he was succeeded by Richard B. Mellon, and Davis did not become president of the company, by then called the Aluminum Company of America (Alcoa), until 1910, although he had been acting manager of the concern during all those years. He became chairman of the board in 1928. It was Davis, working in tandem with the Mellons, who developed the aluminum industry in the United States. In turn, they made Alcoa the wholly dominant company in the field until the intervention of the government at the end of World War II.

Alcoa's domination of the aluminum industry had the company in continual conflict with the federal government. In 1913 Davis admitted to a House inquiry that an international agreement (cartel) covered the aluminum industry. From that time until 1937, when the federal government filed an anti-trust suit to force Alcoa executives to divest their holdings in the Aluminum Company of Canada, Ltd., Davis kept the government at bay. To forestall anti-trust activity, Davis had worked closely with the government during both world wars, insuring that there would be no shortages of the valuable metal. He played a particularly prominent role in the aluminum production drive during World War II, helping to attain an output vital to the Allied achievement of air superiority. For this work he got a Presidential Certificate of Merit. In spite of this, in a landmark decision in 1945 the Supreme Court found that Alcoa constituted a monopoly under Section 2 of the Sherman Act. This was the first major revision of the old "rule of reason," since it was admitted that Alcoa had not misused its monopoly position, but that the mere size of the company and its potential for misdeeds was illegal.

Although Davis remained chairman of Alcoa until 1957 he resigned from active management in 1948. At 80 he retired to Florida, seemingly ready for shuffleboard and canasta. Instead he began a second career in Florida real estate. Worth at that time some $350 million, he began buying vast tracts of raw acreage, soon becoming the most closely watched and controversial investor in the state. His belief in Florida real estate's "inevitable increase in value" was one of the factors bringing Davis to the area in 1948. His purchases of 125,000 acres included one-eighth of Dade County. He also bought 30,000 acres on Eleuthera Island in the Bahamas, where he developed a resort. He owned an ice cream plant, vegetable farms, a cement plant, a road building company, a steel fabricating plant, a furni-

ture plant, and an airline. He purchased the Boca Raton Hotel and Club for $22.5 million and property in Sarasota on the Gulf coast for $13.5 million. When asked by a reporter what he had in mind with all of these Florida purchases, Davis replied, "Making money. What else? Now go away, let me get on with it."

Davis had a reputation during his lifetime as a "terrible tempered tycoon," ruling Alcoa and his Florida enterprises with a desk-thumping autocracy. When he died in Florida on November 17, 1962, at age 95, he was, by his own admission, the fifth richest man in America. Although parsimonious in life, he was generous in his posthumous benefactions. One-fourth of his estate went for taxes and individual bequests, with $300 million left to trusts held by two banks in Miami and Pittsburgh. Earmarked for two A. V. Davis Foundations, the net income was to be used for "charitable, scientific, literary, and educational purposes." The income was expected to yield a minimum of $13.5 million annually. Davis had joined what *TIME* called "the most distinguished club in U.S. capitalism"—the founders of vast philanthropic foundations.

### Further Reading

There is no biography of Davis. The best information on him and the aluminum industry may be found in Charles Carr, *Alcoa: An American Enterprise* (1952). □

# Benjamin O. Davis Sr.

**Gen. Benjamin O. Davis, Sr. (1877-1970) was the first African American general in the regular United States Armed Services. He assisted in developing and implementing a plan for the limited desegregation of U.S. combat forces in Europe during World War II.**

Benjamin O. Davis was born on July 1, 1877, to Henrietta Stewart Davis and Louis P. H. Davis of Washington, D.C. He attended public schools and college in the nation's capital, ultimately graduating from Howard University.

Davis was commissioned a first lieutenant in the 8th U.S. Volunteer Infantry in 1898, thus beginning a distinguished military career which spanned half a century, four continents, and three major wars. Davis served in Cuba during the Spanish American War. Later he was stationed with the 9th Cavalry, one of two units of "Buffalo Soldiers" on the western frontier. The "Buffalo Soldiers," as the Indians called the African American regiments, were Indian fighters whose buffalo hide camouflage and reputation as fierce warriors won them their unusual nickname.

Subsequent tours of duty took Davis to the Philippines, Africa, Europe, and various places within the United States. He also taught military science at Tuskegee Institute and Wilberforce University. At retirement in 1948 General Davis was an assistant to the Army inspector general in Washington, D.C. He died November 26, 1970.

On October 25, 1940, Colonel Davis, then commander of the 369th Infantry of New York, was promoted to brigadier general. African Americans were elated over this long overdue appointment inasmuch as Davis, highly respected in the African American community, had been passed over for promotion many times while less senior white colonels had become generals. Although supportive of the Davis appointment, African American leaders contended that President Franklin Delano Roosevelt, whose office made the announcement only days before the general election, used it as a political ploy to regain the support of many disillusioned African American voters who were critical of the administration's racial policies. An October 16 news release reiterating the War Department's segregationist policies had angered many African Americans, as had the virtual elimination of African Americans from the officers' ranks. Indeed, War Department statistics indicate that in 1940 there were only five Black commissioned officers in the regular U.S. Armed Forces. Three were chaplains. The two combat officers were General Davis and his son, Capt. Benjamin O. Davis, Jr. In 1955 the younger Davis became the first African American general in the Air Force.

During World War II Davis, noted for his expertise in race relations, was summoned by the U.S. High Command to Europe where intense racial conflict among American troops had reached epidemic proportions. Davis's investigation indicated that racial strife was due primarily to discrimination against African American troops by their white countrymen. U.S. commanders not only strictly enforced segregation, but also urged Britons, more liberal in their racial attitudes and practices, to do likewise. Davis also found that African American troops deeply resented their exclusion from combat duty.

A shortage of combat troops, as well as political pressure and public demand, persuaded the American High Command in Europe to utilize African Americans in battle, thereby relieving some of the racial tension. Davis, long a proponent of integration of the Armed Forces, assisted in instituting a limited integration of forces in the European Theater. This experiment was successful, according to enlisted personnel, officers, and War Department officials; nevertheless, it did not lead to the full integration of the Armed Forces which Davis and others urged. (Full integration came only after a 1946 presidential directive by Harry S. Truman.)

## Further Reading

A biographical sketch of Davis, as well as considerable information on African American soldiers, is included in *Black Defenders of America, 1775-1973: A Reference and Pictorial History,* by Robert Ewell Greene (1974). William H. Leckie's monograph *The Buffalo Soldiers: A Narrative of the Negro Cavalry in the West* (1967) is an interesting and informative work about Black soldiers on the post Civil War frontier. Richard M. Dalfiume, *Desegregation of the United States Armed Forces: Fighting on Two Fronts, 1939-1953* (1969) and Gerald W. Patton, *War and Race: The Black Officer in the American Military, 1915-1941* (1981) are two useful books. □

# Henry Winter Davis

**The American congressman Henry Winter Davis (1817-1865) was a leading advocate of Radical Republican policies during the Civil War and a violent opponent of President Lincoln's more conservative course.**

Henry Winter Davis was born Aug. 16, 1817, in Annapolis, Md. He attended Kenyon College, studied law at the University of Virginia, and in 1840 established practice in Alexandria, Va. In 1850 he moved to Baltimore, where he became active in Whig politics, absorbing much of the strong nationalist perspective of that party.

Alarmed by the influx of Catholic immigrants in the early 1850s, Davis joined the Whigs and Democrats in the nativist Know-Nothing movement. He was elected to Congress three times as a Know-Nothing between 1855 and 1859. In 1860, as the Know-Nothing movement declined, Davis cooperated with the Republican party in Congress but maintained a measure of political independence by supporting the former Whig John Bell, the Constitutional Union candidate, for president. Davis was defeated for reelection in 1861.

Maryland's secession from the Union appeared to be a real possibility in 1861. Davis took the lead in rallying the unionist forces there in the fight to keep the state loyal. His militant unionism and dislike for the Democrats and conservative Republicans made him increasingly sympathetic to the Radical Republicans' crusade to crush secession and the slave power. Reelected to Congress as an unconditional unionist in 1863, Davis cooperated with the Radicals in attacking Lincoln's moderate policies on slavery and his conciliatory attitude toward the South and in seeking to wrench the initiative in policy making away from the President in favor of Congress.

In 1863 Lincoln issued a relatively mild Reconstruction plan permitting 10 percent of a seceded state's voters as of 1860 to form a new state government once they took a loyalty oath to the Union. Angered by the plan's moderation and restoral of a status quo in the seceded states, Davis and Senator Benjamin Franklin Wade of Ohio introduced a counterproposal (Wade-Davis Bill, 1864) which politically proscribed many Confederate sympathizers, required immediate emancipation, compelled repudiation of the Confederate war debt, and insisted that a majority of loyal electors, rather than 10 percent, set up any new government. When Lincoln pocketvetoed the measure, the two congressmen issued the Wade-Davis Manifesto, bitterly castigating the President for his "rash and fatal act" in defying Congress and Radical policies. But despite some initial support, they had overreached themselves. Most Republicans drew back from such violent assaults on the President in an election year. Davis, swallowing his disgust, even worked for Lincoln's reelection rather than chance a Democratic victory.

Davis's always precarious political position in conservative Maryland was weakened by his opposition to the President, and he was not renominated in 1864. He remained active in the lame-duck session of Congress in 1864-1865 as a critic of the administration and an advocate of further radical proposals, including African American suffrage. In December 1865 he contracted pneumonia and died on the 30th in Baltimore.

## Further Reading

The only biography of Davis is a poor one by Bernard C. Steiner, *Life of Henry Winter Davis* (1916). Charles Wagandt, *The Mighty Revolution: Negro Emancipation in Maryland, 1862-1864* (1964), is an excellent analysis of the fight for racial equality in Civil War Maryland and puts Davis's activities in useful perspective, as does Hans L. Trefousse, *The Radical Republicans: Lincoln's Vanguard for Racial Justice* (1969). □

# Jefferson Davis

**Jefferson Davis (1808-1889) was president of the Confederate States of America during the Civil War. His honesty, character, and devotion elevated his cause above a quest for the perpetuation of slavery to a crusade for independence.**

H istory has served Jefferson Davis badly by placing him opposite Abraham Lincoln. Davis is grudged even the loser's mite, for Fate chose Robert E. Lee to embody the "Lost Cause." Yet Davis led the Confederacy and suffered its defeat with great dignity, and he deserves a better recollection.

Davis was born on June 3, 1808, in what is now Todd County, Ky. The family soon moved to Mississippi. After attending Transylvania University for 3 years, he entered the U.S. Military Academy at West Point, from which he graduated in 1828. He served in the infantry for 7 years. At Ft. Crawford, Wis., he fell in love with Sarah Knox Taylor, daughter of post commandant Zachary Taylor. Col. Taylor disapproved of the proposed match. Davis resigned his commission in 1835, married Sarah, and took her to Mississippi; within 3 months she died of malaria. Davis contracted a light case of it, which, combined with grief, permanently weakened his health. From 1835 to 1845 he lived in seclusion at Brierfield, a plantation given him by his brother, Joseph. He and Joseph were close, shared reading habits, argued, and sharpened each other's wits and prejudices.

During these quiet years Davis developed a Southerner's fascination for politics and love for the land. In December 1845 Davis and Varina Howell, his new bride, went to Washington, where Davis took a Democratic seat in the House of Representatives. The Davises made a swift impression. Varina entertained well; Jefferson earned notice for his eloquence and the "charm of his voice."

War with Mexico interrupted Davis's congressional service. He resigned in 1846 to command a volunteer regi-

ment attached to Zachary Taylor's army. Col. Davis and his men won quick approval from the crotchety old general, and the earlier hostilities between the two men were forgotten. Distinguished service by Davis's outfit at Monterey, Mexico, was followed by real heroism at Buena Vista (Feb. 22, 1847). Wounded, Davis returned to Mississippi and received a hero's laurels. In 1847, elected to the U.S. Senate, Davis became chairman of the Military Affairs Committee. But in 1851 Mississippi Democrats called him back to replace their gubernatorial candidate, thinking that Davis's reputation might cover the party's shift from an extreme secessionist position to one of "cooperationist" moderation. This almost succeeded; Davis lost to Henry S. Foote by less than 1,000 votes.

## U.S. Secretary of War

When President Franklin Pierce appointed Davis secretary of war in 1853, Davis found his happiest niche. He enlarged the Army, modernized military procedures, boosted soldiers' pay (and morale), directed important Western land surveys for future railroad construction, and masterminded the Gadsden Purchase.

At the close of Pierce's term Davis reentered the Senate and became a major Southern spokesman. Ever mindful of the Union's purposes, he worked to preserve the Compromise of 1850. Yet throughout the 1850s Davis was moving toward a Southern nationalist point of view. He opposed Stephen A. Douglas's "squatter sovereignty" doctrine in the Kansas question. Congress, Davis argued, had no power to limit slavery's extension.

At the 1860 Democratic convention Davis cautioned against secession. However, he accepted Mississippi's decision, and on Jan. 21, 1861, in perhaps his most eloquent senatorial address, announced his state's secession from the Union and his own resignation from the Senate and called for understanding.

## Confederate President

Davis only reluctantly accepted the presidency of the Confederate States of America. He began his superhuman task with very human doubts. But once in office he became the foremost Confederate. His special virtues were revealed by challenge—honesty, devotion, dedication, the zeal of a passionate patriot.

As president, Davis quickly grasped his problems: 9 million citizens (including at least 3 million slaves) of sovereign Southern states pitted against 22 million Yankees; 9,000 miles of usable railroad track against 22,000; no large factories, warships, or shipyards; little money; no credit, save in the guise of cotton; scant arms and no manufacturing arsenals to replenish losses; miniscule powder works; undeveloped lead, saltpeter, copper, and iron resources; and almost no knowledge of steelmaking. Assets could be counted only as optimism, confidence, cotton, and courage. Davis would have to conjure a cause, anneal a new nation, and make a war.

With sure grasp Davis built an army out of state volunteers sworn into Confederate service—and thus won his first round against state rights. Officers came from the "Old Army" and from Southern military schools. Supplies, arms, munitions, clothes, and transportation came from often reluctant governors, from citizens, and, finally, by means of crafty legerdemain worked by staff officials.

When supplies dwindled drastically, Davis resorted to impressing private property. When military manpower shrank, Davis had to ask the Confederate Congress for the greatest military innovation a democracy could dare—conscription. In April 1862 Congress authorized the draft.

## Confederate Strategy

Nor was Davis timid in using his armies. Relying usually on leaders he knew, he put such men as Albert Sidney Johnston, Joseph E. Johnston, P. G. T. Beauregard, Braxton Bragg, James Longstreet, Thomas J. Jackson, Nathan Bedford Forrest, and Robert E. Lee in various commands. He developed a strategy to fit Confederate circumstances. Realizing that the weaker side must husband and hoard yet dare desperately when the chance came, Davis divided the Confederate military map into departments, each under a general with wide powers. He sought only to repel invaders. This strategy had political as well as military implications: the Confederacy was not aggressive, sought nothing save independence, and would fight in the North only when pressed. Davis's plan brought impressive results—First Manassas, the Seven Days, Second Manassas, and the clearing of Virginia by September 1862. Western results seemed equally promising. Shiloh, while not a victory, stabilized the middle border; Bragg's following campaign maneuvered a Union army out of Tennessee and almost out of Kentucky.

These successes led Davis to a general offensive in the summer and fall of 1862 designed to terrify Northerners, themselves yet untouched by war; to separate other, uncertain states from the Union; and to convince the outside world of Southern strength. Though it failed, the strategy had merit and remained in effect. Checks at Fredericksburg, Holly Springs, and Chancellorsville stung the North. When Union general U. S. Grant moved against Vicksburg in spring 1863, it looked as though he might be lost in Mississippi, with Gen. Joseph Hooker snared in Virginia's wilderness.

But Grant's relentless pressure on Vicksburg forced Davis to a desperate gamble that resulted in the Battle of Gettysburg, the loss of Vicksburg, and a cost to the South of over 50,000 men and 60,000 stands of arms. Men and arms were irreplaceable, and Davis huddled deeper in the defensive.

Davis had tried perhaps the most notable innovation in the history of American command when he adopted the "theater" idea as an expansion of departmental control. Joseph E. Johnston became commander of the Department of the West, taking absolute power over all forces from the Chattahoochee River to the Mississippi River, and from the Gulf of Mexico to Tennessee. It was a great scheme for running a remote war and might have worked, save for Johnston's hesitancy in exercising his authority. Davis lost faith in his general but not in his plan.

In 1864, after Atlanta's fall, Davis approved Gen. John Bell Hood's plan of striking along William T. Sherman's communications into Tennessee, with the hope of capturing Nashville. Logistical support for this bold venture was coordinated by P. G. T. Beauregard, the new commander of the Department of the West. But Beauregard also distrusted his own authority. Hood failed before Nashville; but by then things had so deteriorated that the blame could hardly be fixed on any one in particular.

## Wartime Innovations

Innovation was essential: the armies had to be supported—and in this quest Davis himself changed. Ever an advocate of state rights, he became an uncompromising Confederate nationalist, warring with state governors for federal rights and urging centralist policies on his reluctant Congress. Conscription and impressment were two pillars of his program; others included harsh tax laws, government regulation of railroads and blockade running, and diplomacy aimed at winning recognition of Confederate independence and establishing commercial relations with England and France. Davis came to advocate wide application of martial law. Finally he suggested drafting slaves, with freedom as the reward for valor. These measures were essential to avoid defeat; many were beyond the daring of the Confederate Congress.

Congress's inability to face necessity finally infuriated Davis. Though warm and winning in personal relations, he saw no need for politicking in relations with Congress. He believed that reasonable men did what crisis demanded and

anything less was treason. Intolerant of laxity in himself or in others, he sometimes alienated supporters.

## Southern Defeat

As Confederate chances dwindled, Davis became increasingly demanding. He eventually won congressional support for most of his measures but at high personal cost. By the summer of 1864 most Southern newspapers were sniping at his administration, state governors were quarreling with him, and he had become the focus of Southern discontent. The South was losing; Davis's plan must be wrong, the rebels reasoned. Peace sentiments arose in disaffected areas of several states, as did demands to negotiate with the enemy. Davis knew the enemy's price: union. But he tried negotiation. Yet when the Hampton Roads Conference in February 1865 proved fruitless and Davis called for renewed Confederate dedication, the Confederacy was falling apart, and there was almost nothing to rededicate. Confederate money had so declined in value that Southerners were avoiding it; soldiers deserted; invaders stalked the land with almost no opposition. Lee surrendered on April 9, 1865; Johnston surrendered on April 26. Davis and a small party were captured at Irwinville, Ga., on May 10.

## Years of Decline

Accused of complicity in Lincoln's assassination, and the object of intense hatred in both North and South, Davis spent 2 years as a state prisoner. He was harshly treated, and his already feeble health broke dangerously. When Federal authorities decided not to try him for treason, he traveled abroad to recuperate, then returned to Mississippi and vainly sought to rebuild his fortune.

Through a friend's generosity Davis and his family received a stately home on Mississippi's Gulf Coast. Here from 1878 to 1881 Davis wrote *Rise and Fall of the Confederate Government.* And here, at last, he basked in a kind of fame that eased his final years. He died in New Orleans on Dec. 6, 1889, survived by Varina and two of their six children.

## Further Reading

A primary source is Dunbar Rowland, ed., *Jefferson Davis, Constitutionalist: His Letters, Papers and Speeches* (10 vols., 1923), which includes an autobiography in volume 1. Biographies include Varina H. Davis, *Jefferson Davis: A Memoir* (1890); William E. Dodd, *Jefferson Davis* (1907); Allen Tate, *Jefferson Davis, His Rise and Fall* (1929); Robert W. Winston, *High Stakes and Hair Trigger: The Life of Jefferson Davis* (1930); Robert McElroy, *Jefferson Davis: The Unreal and the Real* (2 vols., 1937); and Hudson Strode, *Jefferson Davis* (3 vols., 1955-1964). See also Burton J. Hendrick, *Statesmen of the Lost Cause* (1939); Robert W. Patrick, *Jefferson Davis and His Cabinet* (1944); Frank E. Vandiver, *Jefferson Davis and the Confederate State* (1964) and *Their Tattered Flags* (1970). □

# John Davis

**English navigator John Davis (ca. 1550-1605), though remembered chiefly as a northern explorer, sailed many seas, took part in naval fighting, and invented a nautical instrument.**

ohn Davis, a Devonshire man, was friendly with the Gilbert and Raleigh families and at times sailed with members of both. One of the most proficient seamen of his day, he published both a practical and a theoretical work on navigation. The backstaff he invented for finding altitudes of heavenly bodies at sea (so named because the pilot using it turned his back to the sun) held the field for a century and a half.

Davis made his first exploration voyage in 1585 in search of the Northwest Passage to the Orient. He rounded Cape Farewell in Greenland, and went north to Godthaab (64°N) before crossing Davis Strait to Cumberland Gulf in Baffin Island, where the lateness of the season compelled his return to England. The next year he persuaded merchants, mostly in Devon, to send a larger expedition. He detached two vessels to explore Gilbert Sound and with a third continued investigation of Davis Strait without making a substantial discovery. Codfish caught and salted off Labrador helped defray costs of the expedition, but Davis found the Devon merchants unwilling to risk money for a new voyage.

Davis nevertheless acquired backing in London and in 1587 went again with three ships, though the pinnace *Ellen,* in which he sailed, made the only explorations. The result was no profit but considerable discovery, as Davis reached a point about 73°N on the west Greenland coast before turning across Davis Strait to explore Baffin Island further. Homeward bound, the *Ellen* visited the mouth of Hudson's Strait but did not penetrate it. When Davis reached England on Sept. 15, 1587, he had at least demonstrated the unlikelihood of anyone's pushing through to the Pacific in a single voyage.

This ended Davis's career as an explorer. He received unfair criticism for not having accomplished more; meanwhile, the great Spanish Armada was nearly ready to attack England. In the channel fighting against the Spaniards, Davis appears to have commanded the ship *Black Dog,* but his combat record is unknown.

Following the Armada's defeat, Davis took part in several voyages, but none involved discovery. He sailed with Thomas Cavendish in 1591 on an expedition intended to penetrate the Strait of Magellan, carry operations into the Pacific, and find the western outlet of the Northwest Passage. This came to nothing because of the bad condition of the ships; Davis did sight the Falkland Islands, though some historians believe these were earlier discovered by Amerigo Vespucci. His last expedition, to the East Indies under the orders of Sir Edward Michel-borne, resulted in his death at the hands of Japanese pirates in 1605.

Davis was married to Faith Fulford in 1582, but Faith proved faithless and with her paramour, a counterfeiter, brought false and unavailing charges against her accomplished husband, whom she had borne several sons.

## Further Reading

Source accounts of Davis's voyages and excerpts from his writings are contained in *The Voyages and Works of John Davis,* published by the Hakluyt Society (2 vols., 1880). Convenient summaries of the voyages are available in Edward Heawood, *A History of Geographical Discovery in the Seventeenth and Eighteenth Centuries* (1912). James A. Williamson, *Age of Drake* (1938; 5th ed. 1965), summarizes the explorer's career. Davis is also discussed in Samuel Eliot Morison, *The European Discovery of America: The Northern Voyages* (1971). □

# Miles Davis

**A jazz trumpeter, composer, and small-band leader, Miles Davis (1926-1991) was in the jazz vanguard for more than two decades. His legend continued to grow even after poor health and diminished creativity removed him from jazz prominence.**

iles Dewey Davis 3rd was born into a well-to-do Alton, Illinois, family on May 25, 1926. His father was a dentist, his mother a woman of leisure: there were two other children, an older sister and a younger brother. In 1928 the family moved to East St. Louis. At the age of 10 Miles began playing trumpet; while still in high school he met and was coached by his earliest idol, the great St. Louis trumpeter Clark Terry.

After fathering two children by a woman friend, Miles in 1944 moved to New York City. He worked for just two weeks in the talent-packed Billy Eckstine Band, then enrolled in the Juilliard School of Music, by day studying classical music and by night interning in jazz's newest idiom, bebop, with the leaders of the movement, notably Charlie Parker, Dizzy Gillespie, Fats Navarro, and Max Roach.

Miles' 1947-1948 stint in a quintet led by bebop genius Charlie Parker gained him a modicum of early fame; a fine trumpeter in the bebop idiom, he nevertheless began to move conceptually away from its orthodoxy. He felt a need to divest his music of bebop's excesses and eccentricities and to restore jazz's more melodic and orchestrated elements. The result was the seminal LP recording *Birth of the Cool* (1949), played by a medium-sized group, a nonet, featuring, in addition to Miles, baritone saxophonist Gerry Mulligan, alto saxophonist Lee Konitz, and pianist Al Haig. A highly celebrated record date, it gave "birth" to the so-called "cool," or West Coast, jazz school, which was more cerebral, more heavily orchestrated, and generally more disciplined (especially in its shorter solos) than traditional bebop, and it gave Miles a musical identity distinct from Parker and the other beboppers.

In the early 1950s Miles became a heroin addict, and his career came to a near halt for three years, but his ultimately successful fight against the drug habit in 1954 led to his greatest period, the mid-to-late 1950s. During that six-year span he made a series of small group recordings regarded as jazz classics. In 1954, with tenor saxophone titan Sonny Rollins, he made memorable recordings of three Rollins originals—"Airegin," "Doxy," and "Oleo"—as well as two brilliant versions of the Tin Pan Alley standard "But Not for Me." Additionally, in the 1954-1955 period Miles recorded with a number of other jazz giants—tenorist Lucky Thompson, vibist Milt Jackson, and pianist Thelonious Monk.

In 1955 Miles formed his most celebrated group, a remarkably talented quintet (later, a sextet, with the addition of alto saxophonist Julian "Cannonball" Adderley) that featured tenor saxophonist John Coltrane, pianist Red Garland, bassist Paul Chambers, and drummer Philly Joe Jones. Until Coltrane's defection in the 1960s, Miles' band was the single most visible and dominant group in all of jazz. The early 1960s saw a succession of personnel shifts until the band stabilized in 1964 around an excellent new rhythm section of pianist Herbie Hancock, bassist Ron Carter, and drummer Tony Williams, as well as a new tenor saxophonist, Wayne Shorter. Miles continued to be the greatest attraction (and biggest moneymaker) in all of jazz, but his new band couldn't match the impossibly high standards of its predecessor. Late in the decade his music took a radically new direction. In two 1968 albums, *Miles in the Sky* and *Filles de Kilimanjaro,* Miles experimented with rock rhythms and non-traditional instrumentation. For the last two decades of Miles' career his music was increasingly rhythm-and-drone and Miles himself became more of a jazz curiosity than a musician to be taken seriously.

A good part of Davis' fame owed less to his considerable musicianship than to his strange persona. He was notorious in performance for turning his back on audiences, for addressing them inaudibly or not at all, for expressing racial hostility toward whites, for dressing nattily early in his career and outlandishly later, and for projecting (especially in a series of motorcycle ads on television) a voice hoarse to a point of strangulation—all of which contributed to his charismatic mystique. Davis also had many health problems and more than his share of brushes with officialdom (widespread racism and his own racial militancy made the latter inevitable).

Miles was, in reality, a paradox. Himself the victim of a policeman's clubbing (reportedly, racially-inspired), he had the fairness and courage in the late 1950s to defy Black jazzmen's expectations by filling a piano vacancy with a white player, Bill Evans, but then, by all accounts, often racially taunted him. A physical fitness enthusiast (with his own private gym), he nevertheless ingested vast quantities of drugs (sometimes, but not always, for arthritic pain). Forbiddingly gruff and solitary, he was also capable of acts of generosity toward down-at-heels musicians, both African American *and* white.

Davis was married three times—to dancer Frances Taylor, singer Betty Mabry, and actress Cicely Tyson; all ended in divorce. He had, in all, three sons, a daughter, and seven grandchildren. He died on September 28, 1991, of pneumonia, respiratory failure, and a stroke.

Davis, in addition to the classic small group recordings of the 1954-1960 period, recorded memorable orchestral works with arranger and long-time friend Gil Evans, most notably *Miles Ahead* (1957), *Porgy and Bess* (1958), and *Sketches of Spain* (1960). Davis' extended works include scores for Louis Malle's film *Elevator to the Gallows* (1957) and for the full-length documentary *Jack Johnson* (1970). Among Davis' best-known shorter compositions are the early "Tune Up," "Milestones," "Miles Ahead," "Blue Haze," and "Four"; from 1958 on his best tunes, such as "So What" and "All Blues," are based on modal scales rather than chords. Early and late, both the compositions and the trumpet playing are trademarked by Davis' hauntingly "blue" sound.

## Further Reading

*Miles: An Autobiography* (1989), written with Quincy Troupe, is inadvertently self-revealing—opinionated, irreverent, egotistical, obscene, abusive, and wrong-headed (e.g., he is almost totally dismissive of his finest work and aggressively defensive of his worst). More balanced is Ian Carr's *Miles Davis* (1982). The two most rewarding articles are both negative assessments—Whitney Balliett's "Miles" in the *New Yorker* (December 4, 1989) and Stanley Crouch's "Play the Right Thing" in *The New Republic* (February 12, 1990), which labels Miles as "the most brilliant sellout in the history of jazz" (for having abandoned his early artistry in favor of jazz-rock fusion). A 1993 biography, *Miles Davis: The Man in the Green Shirt,* by Richard Williams is little more than a coffeetable book. □

# Ossie Davis

**Ossie Davis (born 1917) was a leading African American playwright, actor, director, and television and movie star.**

Ossie Davis was born in Cogdell, Ga., on Dec. 18, 1917. He grew up in Waycross. At Howard University in Washington, D.C., he was encouraged to pursue an acting career. He joined an acting group in Harlem in New York City and took part in the American Negro Theater, founded there in 1940.

Davis made his debut in the play *Joy Exceeding Glory* (1941). During Army service in World War II he wrote and produced shows. While playing his first Broadway role in *Jeb* (1946), he met actress Ruby Dee, and they were married two years later.

Davis's first movie role was in *No Way Out* (1950). This was followed by Broadway performances in *No Time for Sergeants, Raisin in the Sun,* and *Jamaica.* Other movie roles included *The Cardinal, Shock Treatment, Slaves,* and, in 1989, *Do the Right Thing.* An important achievement was his pioneer work as an African American actor in television,

appearing in dramas and on such regular series as *The Defenders* and *The Nurses.* He also wrote television scripts.

Equally talented, Davis and Ruby Dee played together many times on the stage, in television, cabaret, and movies. They starred in Davis's own play *Purlie Victorious* (1961) and in the movie based on it, *Gone Are the Days. Purlie Victorious* was published and also reprinted in anthologies. Davis coauthored the musical version of this hilarious satire, *Purlie* (1970), which enjoyed great success during its Broadway run.

In the late 1960s Davis pioneered in Hollywood as a African American film director with *Cotton Comes to Harlem,* among other films. With Ruby Dee he appeared on stage and television, reading the poetry of famous African Americans, and he made recordings of African American literature. Perhaps one of his most memorable endeavors was his eulogy on Malcolm X in 1965, when he called the slain leader "Our Shining Black Prince." Davis frequently lectured and read at universities and schools.

Davis's published essays include "The Wonderful World of Law and Order," "The Flight from Broadway," and "Plays of Insight Are Needed to Make the Stage Vital in Our Lives." He also wrote the play *Last Dance for Sybil* and the musical adaptation of Mark Twain's *Pudd'nhead Wilson.*

In his eighth decade, Davis remained very active, mostly in television, with a three-year run on the Public Broadcasting System (PBS) program *With Ossie and Ruby* as well as the popular series *Evening Shade.* He also helped to

usher in a new generation of African American film directors, spearheaded by Spike Lee. Davis even performed in three of Lee's films. As an author, fiction has proven to be fertile ground for Davis; his novel *Just Like Martin,* a paean to the civil rights movement, was published in 1992.

Davis had a deep love for his people and his heritage. He was an example of African American identity and pride, and he devoted much time and talent to the civil rights movement in America. He received a number of awards, including the Mississippi Democratic Party Citation, the Howard University Alumni Achievement Award in dramatics, and the Frederick A. Douglass Award (with Ruby Dee) from the New York Urban League. The Davises had three children and made their home in New Rochelle, New York.

### Further Reading

Lindsay Patterson, ed., *Anthology of the American Negro in the Theatre: A Critical Approach* (2nd edition, 1968), includes a short article by Davis. Other works which discuss him are Harry A. Ploski and Roscoe C. Brown, Jr., *The Negro Almanac* (1967); Mitchell Loften, *Black Drama: The Story of the American Negro in the Theatre* (1967); and Doris E. Abramson, *Negro Playwrights in the American Theatre, 1925-1959* (1969).
Bogle, Donald, *Blacks in American Film and Television,* Garland (New York), 1988.
*American Visions,* April/May, 1992. □

# Richard Harding Davis

**The American journalist Richard Harding Davis (1864-1916) was also a fiction writer and dramatist whose swashbuckling adventures were popular with the American public.**

Richard Harding Davis was born into a well-to-do and rather pious Episcopalian family in Philadelphia. His father, an editorial writer, and his mother, a well-known fiction writer, often entertained Philadelphia artists and visiting actors and actresses, and the boy from the start was completely at ease with celebrities. After graduating from Episcopal Academy and Lehigh University, he studied political economy during a postgraduate year at Johns Hopkins University. In 1886 Davis became a reporter for the *Philadelphia Press.* The editor and other reporters confidently expected the cocky young dandy to fall on his face, but he shortly proved to be a superb reporter and a talented writer. From 1888 to 1890 he was in New York writing special stories for the *Sun.* He also published two volumes of short stories, *Gallegher and Other Stories* (1891) and *Van Bibber and Others* (1892). At the age of 26 he became the managing editor of *Harper's Weekly* and soon was writing accounts of his worldwide travels, which were collected in books such as *Rulers of the Mediterranean* (1894), *About Paris* (1895), and *Three Gringos in Venezuela and Central America* (1896).

As a picturesque and alert correspondent for New York and London newspapers, always appropriately attired for each adventure, Davis covered the Spanish War and the Spanish-American War in Cuba, the Greco-Turkish War, the Boer War, and—toward the end of his life (he died in 1916)—World War I. He based a number of books upon his experiences. More short stories filled 10 volumes, including *The Lion and the Unicorn* (1899), *Ranson's Folly* (1902), and *The Scarlet Car* (1907). A number of Davis's novels covered the international scene; notable were *Soldiers of Fortune* (1897), *The King's Jackal* (1898), *Captain Macklin* (1902), and *The White Mice* (1909). In addition, Davis wrote about two dozen plays, of which dramatizations of *Ranson's Folly* (1904), *The Dictator* (1904), and *Miss Civilization* (1906) were the most successful.

The critic Larzer Ziff in *The American 1890's* admirably summarized Davis's significance: "He demonstrated to those . . . who would listen that their capacity for excitement was matched by the doings in the wide world. But he also demonstrated to an uneasy plutocracy . . . that their gospel of wealth coming to the virtuous and their public dedication to genteel manners and gentlemanly Christian behavior were indeed justified."

### Further Reading

For a complete list of Davis's writings consult Henry Cole Quinby, *Richard Harding Davis: A Bibliography* (1924). Two studies relate the author to his background admirably: Fairfax D. Downey, *Richard Harding Davis: His Day* (1933), and

Gerald Langford, *The Richard Harding Davis Years: A Biography of a Mother and Son* (1961).

### Additional Sources

Lubow, Arthur, *The reporter who would be king: a biography of Richard Harding Davis,* New York: Scribner; Toronto: Maxwell Macmillan Canada; New York: Maxwell Macmillan International, 1992. □

# Sammy Davis Jr.

**American entertainer Sammy Davis, Jr. (1925-1990) had a career that spanned more than five decades. He started in vaudeville and progressed to Broadway, film, and performing on the Las Vegas strip.**

S ammy Davis, Jr.'s death in 1990 robbed American audiences of a favorite entertainer, a star showman in the oldest vaudeville tradition. Davis was a well-rounded performer of the sort found only rarely these days: he could sing, he could act, he could dance, and he could make people laugh with clowning and impersonations. Davis's long career in show business was even more remarkable because he managed to break color barriers in an era of segregation and racism. His many honors and awards—including a prestigious Kennedy Center medal for career achievement—serve as reflections of the affection his fans felt for him.

Davis was a complete variety performer. With a microphone and a backup ensemble he could entertain solo for two hours at a time. He was one of the first blacks to be accepted as a headliner in the larger Las Vegas casinos and one of the very few stars, black or white, to receive Emmy, Tony, *and* Grammy Award nominations. *People* magazine contributor Marjorie Rosen notes that Davis "made beautiful music . . . and blacks and whites alike heard him and were touched by him. He was loved. And that, of course, is what he wanted most of all."

### Learned to Tap Dance Like a Master

Sammy Davis, Jr. began performing almost as soon as he could walk. Both of his parents were vaudevillians who danced with the Will Mastin Troupe. In 1928, when he was only three, Davis joined the Mastin Troupe as its youngest member. He became a regular in 1930 and travelled with his father on the dwindling vaudeville circuit. The demanding schedule of train rides, practice, and performances left little time for formal education, and Davis was always just one step ahead of the truant officer. His unconventional childhood did provide him with important lessons, however. Young Sammy learned how to please an audience, how to tap dance like a master, and how to move people with a smile and a song.

The motion picture industry all but forced most vaudeville entertainers out of business. Few acts survived the competition from the silver screen. The Mastin Troupe felt the strain, dwindling gradually until it became a trio—Sammy Davis, Sr., Will Mastin, and Sammy Davis, Jr. By 1940 Sammy, Jr. had become the star attraction of the trio, with his father and friend providing soft shoe in the background. The act was popular enough to receive billings in larger clubs, and in that environment Davis met other performers such as Bill "Bojangles" Robinson, Frank Sinatra, and various big band leaders.

Davis was drafted into the United States Army when he turned eighteen and was sent to basic training in Cheyenne, Wyoming. The boot camp experience was devastating for Davis. Although he was befriended by a black sergeant who gave him reading lessons, he was mistreated relentlessly by the white troops with whom he had to share a barracks. Transferred to an entertainment regiment, Davis eventually found himself performing in front of some of the same soldiers who had painted "coon" on his forehead. He discovered that his energetic dancing and singing could "neutralize" the bigots and make them acknowledge his humanity. This era may have marked the beginning of Davis's dogged pursuit of his audience's love, a pursuit that would sometimes earn him scorn in years to come.

### Headliner in Vegas and New York

After the war the Mastin Trio re-formed, playing on bills with Davis's friends like Sinatra, Mel Torme, and Mickey Rooney. Davis went solo after signing a recording contract with Decca Records. His first album, *Starring Sammy Davis, Jr.,* contained songs and comedy, but another work, *Just for Lovers,* was composed entirely of music. Both sold well, and soon Davis was a headliner in Las Vegas and New York, as well as a guest star on numerous television shows.

On November 19, 1954, Davis nearly lost his life in an automobile accident in the California desert. The accident shattered his face and cost him his left eye. While recuperating, he spent hours discussing philosophy with a rabbi on staff at the hospital, and shortly thereafter he converted to Judaism. Rather than end his career, the accident provided a burst of publicity for Davis. Upon his return to the stage he sold out every performance and received thunderous ovations. Even his well-publicized conversion failed to dampen his popularity. While some critics suggested that he might have had ulterior motives, others—especially blacks—applauded his thoughtful observations about Jews, blacks, and oppression.

Davis began the 1960s as a certified superstar of stage and screen. He had turned an average musical comedy, "Mr. Wonderful," into a successful Broadway show, and he earned critical raves for his performance in the film *Porgy and Bess.* As a member of the high-profile "Rat Pack," he hobnobbed with Frank Sinatra, Dean Martin, Tony Curtis, and Joey Bishop at fashionable bistros in Las Vegas and Los Angeles. In 1965 he starred in another Broadway play, "Golden Boy," in which he played a struggling boxer, and then he turned in creditable film performances in *A Man Called Adam* and *Sweet Charity.* Somehow he was also able to star in two television shows during the same years, "The Sammy Davis, Jr. Show" and "The Swinging World of Sammy Davis, Jr."

## Pitfalls of the "Swinging World"

Davis's "swinging world" had its pitfalls, however. His marriage to Swedish actress May Britt earned him the vitriol of the Ku Klux Klan. His "Rat Pack" habits of drinking and drug-taking threatened his health, and his ostentatious displays of wealth nearly bankrupted him even as he earned more than a million dollars a year. Throughout the 1960s Davis was a vocal supporter of the Black Power movement and other left-wing causes, but in the early 1970s he alienated blacks and liberals by embracing Richard Nixon and performing in Vietnam. By that time Davis was in the throes of drug and alcohol addiction. He developed liver and kidney trouble and spent some months in the hospital early in 1974.

The last fifteen years of Davis's life were conducted at the performer's usual hectic pace. In 1978 he appeared in another Broadway musical, "Stop the World—I Want To Get Off." He occasionally served as a stand-in host for the popular "Tonight Show," and he returned in earnest to the casino and show-hall stages. Even hip surgery failed to stop Davis from performing. His best-known act in the 1980s was a musical review with his friends Sinatra and Liza Minnelli, which played to capacity crowds in the United States and Europe just a year before Davis's death.

Doctors discovered a tumor in Davis's throat in August of 1989. The performer underwent painful radiation therapy that at first seemed successful. Then, early in 1990, an even larger cancerous growth was discovered. Davis died on May 16, 1990, as a result of this cancer—only some eight weeks after his friends of a lifetime feted him with a television special in his honor.

## A Mentor and Pioneer

During his lifetime, Sammy Davis, Jr. was not universally adored. Some observers—including some blacks—accused him of grovelling to his audiences, of shamelessly toadying for admiration. Those sentiments were forgotten, however, when Davis died at the relatively young age of sixty-four. In eulogies across the country, other black entertainers cited Davis as a mentor and as a pioneer who reached mainstream audiences even though he hailed from minority groups in both race and religion. Record producer Quincy Jones told *People:* "Sammy Davis, Jr. was a true pioneer who traveled a dirt road so others, later, could follow on the freeway. He helped remove the limitations on black entertainers. He made it possible for the Bill Cosbys, the Michael Jacksons and the Eddie Murphys to achieve their dreams."

Davis, the quintessential song-and-dance man, recorded albums throughout his career and performed a number of signature songs. Chief among these were his tribute to Bill Robinson, "Mr. Bojangles," the ballads "What Kind of Fool Am I" and "I've Gotta Be Me," and his biggest hit, the spritely "Candy Man." Davis's singing was like everything else in his performance—energetic, spirited, and played to maximum effect. Rosen sees Davis as "a personal link to a vibrant mainstream of American entertainment" who "poured his jittery energy into virtuoso performances with all the intimacy of a saloon singer."

In an interview for *Contemporary Authors,* Davis analyzed his position in show business. "Nobody likes me but the people," he said. "Though I have been treated extremely well overall by the critics, I have never been a critic's favorite. But the people always had faith in me, and they were supportive of me. . . . They laugh. They have good times, and they come backstage. It's a joy."

## Further Reading

*Contemporary Authors,* Volume 108, Gale, 1984.
Davis, Sammy, Burt Broyar and Jane Broyar, *Yes I Can: The Story of Sammy Davis, Jr.,* Farrar, Straus, 1965.
Davis, Sammy, Burt Broyar and Jane Broyar, *Why Me? The Sammy Davis, Jr. Story,* Farrar, Straus, 1989.
Dobrin, Arnold, *Voices of Joy, Voices of Freedom,* Coward, 1972.
Stambler, Irwin, *Encyclopedia of Pop, Rock & Soul,* St. Martin's, 1974.
*New York Times,* May 17, 1990.
*People,* May 28, 1990. □

# Stuart Davis

**Stuart Davis (1894-1964) was an American cubist painter whose colorful compositions, with their internal logic and structure, often camouflaged the American flavor of his themes.**

Stuart Davis was born in Philadelphia on Dec. 7, 1894. His father was the art editor of the *Philadelphia Press*. At the age of 16 Davis began studying art with Robert Henri, leader of "The Eight," a group of artists also known as the "Ashcan school." In the famous 1913 Armory Show, Davis exhibited five watercolors. His works of this period are close to the realistic style of "The Eight," but Davis soon began moving toward the more lively, Fauve manner, visible in *Gloucester Street* (1916).

Davis's new interest in cubism is partly explained by his statement that "a painting ... is a two-dimensional plane surface and the process of making a painting is the act of defining two-dimensional space on that surface." He experimented with the geometric visual language of Dutch painter Piet Mondrian in his own painting *The President* (1917) and tried synthetic cubist devices in the more pictorially ordered *Lucky Strike* (1921).

Davis's trip to New Mexico in 1923 manifested itself in more simply conceived, flatter paintings. *Still Life* and *Supper Table* (both 1925) reflect a move toward minimal pictorial elements, with a bold outline accentuating objects. The resolution of these earlier abstract tendencies can be found in the *Eggbeater Series* (1927-1930), still life paintings in which Davis sought to "focus on the logical elements" of the composition instead of establishing a "self-sufficient system" that worked apart from the objects. The late paintings in this series show a less abstract approach and an increased clarity of form and color.

In 1928 Davis traveled to Paris. In general, the work that followed reveals not only a greater interest in urban landscape but a move toward more lively, linear composition, often using sets of words within the picture to carry the rhythm. *Places des Vosges Number 2* (1928) juxtaposes line and color on a lightly textured surface, showing Davis's skill at rendering rhythmical equivalents of visual phenomena.

During the Great Depression, Davis became art editor of the Artists' Congress magazine, *Art Front*. Like many contemporary painters, he executed public murals: Men *without Women* (1932) at the Radio City Music Hall in New York City; *Swing Landscape* (1938), now at the University of Indiana; a mural for WNYC radio station in New York City; and the now-destroyed *History of Communication* (1939) for the New York World's Fair. But unlike many artists working under government auspices, Davis did not alter his esthetic outlook to accommodate public taste.

Davis's paintings during his last 2 decades (he died in 1964) show continued preoccupation with the lyrical order of visual experience. They draw on the tradition of Henri Matisse and Joan Miró, yet their content is indigenous to America. *Hot Stillscape for Six Colors* (1940), explosive with color and rhythm; *Visa* (1951); and *The Paris Bit* (1959) all integrate the visual feel of words with related color schemes and shapes.

Davis published a number of writings and taught in New York City at the Art Students League and the New School for Social Research.

## Further Reading

The most lively interpretation of Davis is E. C. Goossen, *Stuart Davis* (1959), which includes a useful bibliography and numerous illustrations. Autobiographical material can be found in James Johnson Sweeney, *Stuart Davis* (1945), and the exhibition catalog to the Museum of Modern Art show of the same year edited by Sweeney. A recent assessment of Davis's work is by H. H. Arnason in his *History of Modern Art* (1968). □

# William Morris Davis

**The American geographer and geologist William Morris Davis (1850-1934) formulated a concept of the cycle of erosion, but his theories of landscape evolution are now sharply contested.**

Of Quaker stock, William M. Davis was born in Philadelphia, Pa., on Feb. 12, 1850. He graduated from Harvard in 1869. From 1870 to 1873 he was a meteorological assistant at the Córdoba observatory in Argentina. In 1878 he returned to Harvard to teach geology and geography. Warned by senior colleagues that it would be difficult to gain promotion without publication, Davis soon became known for his contributions to journals. In all he wrote some 500 papers, chiefly on physical geography but also on the teaching of geography in schools and universities. These included 42 papers on meteorology and a textbook, *Elementary Meteorology* (1894).

In 1890 Davis became professor of physical geography at Harvard, and 9 years later he was appointed professor of geology. He retired from Harvard in 1912.

In 1889, in the first volume of the *National Geographic Magazine,* Davis published a notable paper on the rivers and valleys of Pennsylvania, followed in 1890 by a study of the rivers of northern New Jersey. For 10 years he published papers in this journal, which was then austerely academic; his work also appeared in numerous American and European journals. Steadily he developed his theory of the cycle of erosion under humid, arid, glacial, and other conditions. It provided a wonderful framework for teaching and research, profitably used by his disciples, notably the geologist Douglas W. Johnson. Block diagrams and sketches of unique clarity helped readers to visualize landscapes in three dimensions. For a time Davis's ideas on the evolution of landscapes were the basis of most geomorphological teaching. But there were always dissenting voices that called attention to the large assumptions on which some of the Davisian views were based, and at present some geomorphologists regard his views as interesting period pieces.

Davis was always anxious to bring geographers together, and through his enterprise the Association of American Geographers was founded in 1904. In 1911 he ran a 9-week "geographical pilgrimage" from Wales to Italy. He also organized the 8-week transcontinental expedition of the American Geographical Society in 1912 for European and American geographers. He was an enthusiastic fieldworker, and several of his papers were based on his careful fieldwork in Europe.

Davis was professor of physiographic geology at the California Institute of Technology from 1930 to 1934. He died in Pasadena on Feb. 5, 1934.

### Further Reading

Davis's *Geographical Essays,* edited by Douglas Wilson Johnson (1909), gives his most important papers. His work is discussed in Preston E. James and Clarence F. Jones, eds., *American Geography: Inventory and Prospect* (1954). □

# Sir Humphry Davy

**The English chemist and natural philosopher Sir Humphry Davy (1778-1829) isolated and named the elements of the alkaline-earth and alkali metals and showed that chlorine and iodine were elements.**

Humphry Davy was born on Dec. 17, 1778, in Penzance, Cornwall. He was apprenticed when he was 16 to an apothecary in Penzance, where he evinced a great interest in chemistry and experimentation, using as his guide Lavoisier's famous work, *Traité élémentaire de chimie.* His obvious talents attracted the attention of Gregory Watt and Davies Giddy (later Gilbert), both of whom recommended him to Dr. Thomas Beddoes for the position of superintendent of the newly founded Pneumatic Institution in Bristol. He worked there from October 1799 to March 1801.

The Pneumatic Institution was investigating the idea that certain diseases might be cured by the inhalation of gases. Davy, sometimes perilously, inhaled many gases and found that the respiration of nitrous oxide produced surprising results. Inhalation of "laughing gas," as it was soon called, became a novel form of entertainment, although nearly 50 years passed before it was actually used as an anesthetic. Davy also experimented with the newly invented voltaic pile, or battery.

Davy left Bristol to become the lecturer in chemistry at the Royal Institution in London. Sir Joseph Banks and Count Rumford had founded the Royal Institution in 1799 as a research institute and as a place for educating young men in science and mechanics. Here Davy's genius emerged full-blown. Not only did his brilliant lectures attract a fashionable and intellectual audience, but he also continued his electrical research. In 1806 he showed that there was a real connection between electrical and chemical behavior; for this achievement Napoleon I awarded him a prize. In 1807 he electrolyzed molten potash and soda and announced the isolation of two new elements, naming them potassium and sodium. In 1808 he isolated and named calcium, barium, strontium, and magnesium. Later he showed that boron, aluminum, beryllium, and fluorine existed, although he was not able to isolate them.

Lavoisier had claimed that a substance was an acid because it contained oxygen. Davy doubted the validity of this claim and in 1810 showed that "oxymuriatic acid gas" was not the oxide of an unknown element, murium, but a true element, which he named chlorine.

In 1812 Davy married a wealthy widow, Jane Apreece, and was knighted by the King for his great discoveries. Napoleon I invited him to visit France, even though the two countries were at war. Sir Humphry and his wife went to France in 1813, taking with them as valet and chemical assistant the 22-year-old Michael Faraday. The French presented them with a curious substance isolated from seaweed, and Davy, working in his hotel room, was able to show that this was another new element, iodine. When he returned to England, he was asked by a group of clergymen to study the problem of providing illumination in coal mines without exploding the methane there. Davy devised the miner's safety lamp and gave the invention to the world without attempting to patent or otherwise exploit it. Working in another area, he demonstrated how electrochemical corrosion could be prevented.

In 1820, after Sir Joseph Banks had died, Sir Humphry was made president of the Royal Society. He began the needed internal reform of the society, but bad health forced him to resign in 1827. The remaining years of his life he spent wandering about the Continent in search of a cure for the strokes from which he suffered. He died on May 29, 1829, in Geneva, Switzerland, where he was buried.

## Further Reading

Davy's own writings are the best source of information about his scientific work. They were edited in nine volumes by his brother, John Davy, *The Collected Works of Sir Humphry Davy* (1839-1840). A complete listing of all his writings is in June Z. Fullmer, *Sir Humphry Davy's Published Works* (1969). John Davy wrote a biography, *Memoirs of the Life of Sir Humphry Davy* (2 vols., 1839), to correct the excesses of John Ayrton Paris's biography, *The Life of Sir Humphry Davy* (2 vols., 1831). Recent biographies are Anne Treneer, *The Mercurial Chemist: A Life of Sir Humphry Davy* (1963), which discusses Davy's relationship to the romantic poets, and Sir Harold Hartley, *Humphry Davy* (1966), which concentrates on his life and importance as a scientist. □

# Henry Laurens Dawes

**As a U.S. senator, Henry Laurens Dawes (1816-1903) sponsored important legislation designed to assimilate Native Americans into the mainstream of national life.**

Henry Dawes was born near Cummington, Mass., on Oct. 30, 1816. After completing grade school and the academy at Cummington, he graduated from Yale College. He taught school for a few months, then began writing for local newspapers, read law, and was admitted to the Massachusetts bar in 1842. His first office was at North Adams, but he soon moved to Pittsfield. He served in the lower house of the Massachusetts Legislature in 1848-1849 and 1852, was elected to one term in the state senate in 1850, and became a member of the state constitutional convention of 1853.

In 1857, running as a Republican, Dawes was elected to the U.S. House of Representatives, a position he held until 1875. His seniority in the House brought him considerable power, which he used to write antislavery legislation. He was chairman for 10 years of the Committee on Elections, chairman of the House Committee on Appropriations in 1869, and chairman of the House Ways and Means Committee after 1871. He was a staunch believer in protective tariffs, especially for textiles, and he introduced the legislation to provide for daily weather reports that led eventually to the establishment of the U.S. Weather Bureau.

Dawes entered the U.S. Senate in 1875. A New England Yankee with high cheekbones and a gray beard, Dawes never achieved national prominence, but he was able to influence legislation to help the Native Americans. As chairman of the Senate Committee on Indian Affairs, he secured funds for educational facilities on the reservations and also brought the Native Americans under Federal criminal laws.

Dawes is best remembered as author of the Dawes Severalty Act (1887). Originating in his belief that Native Americans should be brought into the American political and economic system instead of clinging to their tribal ways, the act was aimed at breaking up the reservation system. It provided 160 acres to each head of family (and smaller amounts of land to others) who would leave the reservation. After a probationary period of 25 years, the Indians would be granted full title to the land and United States citizenship. At the time, this legislation was considered visionary.

After three terms in the Senate, Dawes retired to Pittsfield in 1892. He was consulted on national problems until his death on Feb. 5, 1903.

## Further Reading

George F. Hoar, *Autobiography of Seventy Years* (2 vols., 1903), contains excellent material on Dawes's service in Congress. His efforts on behalf of the Indians are recounted in Loring Benson Priest, *Uncle Sam's Step-children: The Reformation of United States Indian Policy, 1865-1887* (1942). He is briefly discussed in J. P. Kinney, *A Continent Lost—A Continent Won: Indian Land Tenure in America* (1937); Harold E. Fey and D'Arcy McNickle, *Indians and Other Americans: Two Ways of Life Meet* (1959); and George H. Mayer, *The Republican Party, 1854-1964* (1964). □

# William Levi Dawson

**African American composer, performer, and music educator William Levi Dawson (1899-1990) used the rich vitality of his musical heritage as a basis for all types of music, including arrangements of folk songs and original compositions.**

William Levi Dawson was born on September 26, 1899, in Anniston, Ala. At the age of 13 he entered Tuskegee Institute and graduated in 1921 with first honors. He received the bachelor of music degree from the Horner Institute of Fine Arts in Kansas City, Mo., in 1925. He studied composition under Felix Borowski at the Chicago Musical College and under Adolph Weidig at the American Conservatory of Music. In 1927 he received the master of music degree from the American Conservatory of Music in Chicago.

Dawson's membership in the band and orchestra at Tuskegee had been excellent professional preparation for serving as first trombonist with the Chicago Civic Orchestra from 1926 to 1930. In 1929 he won the *Chicago Daily News* contest for band directors, and in 1930 Wanamaker Contest prizes for the song "Jump Back, Honey, Jump Back" and the orchestral composition "Scherzo."

In 1931 Dawson became director of the School of Music at Tuskegee. From 1932 to 1933 Dawson conducted the institute's 100-voice a cappella choir in a month's engagement at the opening of the International Music Hall of Radio City, and in concerts at Carnegie Hall, New York City, the White House, and another at Constitution Hall, both Washington, D.C., and in a series of national and international broadcasts. In 1934, under the sponsorship of the President of the United States and the State Department, the Tuskegee Choir made a concert tour of international and interracial good will to the British Isles, Europe, and the former U.S.S.R. Leading critics in America and abroad praised the choir highly.

Dawson had wide experience as a director and consultant to festival groups. In 1956 Tuskegee Institute conferred upon him the honorary degree of doctor of music and he was sent by the U.S. State Department to conduct various choral groups in Spain.

Although Dawson's choral arrangements were popular, he was best known for his *Negro Folk Symphony,* which had its world premiere by the Philadelphia Symphony Orchestra under Leopold Stokowski (1934). In this work the composer used melodic and rhythmic language borrowed from Negro spirituals, along with original material in the same idiom. The symphony was imaginative, dramatic, and colorfully orchestrated.

In 1952 Dawson visited seven countries in West Africa to study indigenous African music. He later revised the *Negro Folk Symphony,* infusing it with a rhythmic foundation inspired by African influences.

Dawson was guest conductor with the Kansas City Philharmonic Orchestra (1966), the Nashville Symphony Orchestra (1966), the Wayne State University (Michigan) Glee Club (1970), and the Baltimore Symphony Orchestra (1975). He was named to the Alabama Arts Hall of Fame in 1975, and received the Alumni Merit Award from Tuskegee Institute in 1983. He died on May 4, 1990.

## Further Reading

For biographical information on William Levi Dawson, refer to Eileen Southern, *The Music of Black Americans: A History* (New York, 1971); J. Spady, *William L. Dawson: A Umum Tribute* (Philadelphia, 1981); and Hal Roach, *Black American Music: Past and Present* (1985). Dawson is also discussed briefly in Maud Cuney-Hare, *Negro Musicians and Their Music* (1936), and the *International Library of Negro Life,* vol. 5: *The Negro in Music and Art,* compiled by Lindsay Patterson (1967; 2nd edition, 1968). □

# Dorothy Day

**Dorothy Day (1897-1980) was a founder of the Catholic Worker Movement which joined radical social reform with the Roman Catholic faith in a movement for social justice and peace.**

Dorothy Day was born on November 8, 1897, in Brooklyn, New York, the daughter of John J. and Grace (Satterlee) Day. Her father was a newspaper sports writer whose search for a steady job caused the family to travel widely during her pre-adolescent years. She spent part of her youth (1904-1906) in California where her father worked until the San Francisco earthquake compelled him to find another job. In 1906 the family moved to Chicago where the elder Day was employed by a local newspaper. She felt extremely isolated from family and friends during

those pre-adolescent years, which she remembered in one of her many books as *The Long Loneliness* (1952).

Even as a youngster Day developed a taste for literature and writing and did much of both. She also had several religious experiences which would affect her later in life. In 1914 she finally escaped from her restrictive family milieu by matriculating as a student at the University of Illinois in Urbana. There she promptly fell in with a small crowd of radical students, many of whom were Jewish-Americans discriminated against by the general university community. Her closest friend at the university, a wealthy young Jewish woman from Chicago who shared Day's literary and political tastes, radicalized Dorothy politically (the friend later become a prominent Communist). Even before she left the university after only two years, during which academic studies grew sterile and failed to stimulate her, Day had become a part of the pre-World War I American youth rebellion against the conventions of their parents. She and her radical friends wanted to create a new and freer society—in the language of the day, "to transvalue all values."

Bored by academic life, excited by new social, cultural, and political ideas, it was natural for Day to seek to develop herself in what was then (1916) the center of an American bohemian culture. She moved to New York where she immediately joined in the lively life of the Greenwich Village and Lower East Side rebels and radicals. Day almost immediately found a job as a feature writer on the *New York Call,* the nation's largest and most influential socialist daily. Soon she was involved fulltime in the city's radical political and cultural scene, meeting and becoming close to many of

the era's most famous personalities. In the winter of 1917-1918 she became a close friend of the playwright Eugene O'Neill, whom she saw through many bouts with alcohol. Day also developed friendships with Floyd Dell and Max Eastman, who made her an assistant editor of their new magazine, *Masses*—one of the most famous radical cultural publications in American history.

But American participation in World War I led to government suppression of left-wing organizations and publications and left Day and her radical friends adrift. Troubled by her aimless life among Greenwich Village bohemians, in 1918 she took a position as a probationary nurse at Kings County Hospital in Brooklyn. Nursing, however, failed to satisfy Day's search for meaning in life, although it did involve her in her first serious and tumultuous love affair. In 1919 she left the hospital to work for a time as a writer on the successor journal to *Masses, The Liberator*. This, too, brought her little satisfaction, and in 1920, for reasons still unclear, she married Barkeley Tober, an oft-wed literary promoter. Only a year later Day dissolved this, her only formal marriage.

For the next several years she seemed to drift aimlessly, working as a reporter for the New Orleans *Item* in 1922-1923 and also as an occasional writer for the Catholic journal *Commonweal*. While in New Orleans she wrote and published a commercially successful, partly autobiographical novel, *The Eleventh Virgin* (1924). With the money from her novel, Day moved back to the New York area, buying a beach cottage on Staten Island. She resumed contact with the city's intellectuals and wrote occasional pieces for *The New Masses*. In 1925 she began living with a biologist and anarchist (one Foster Batterham), with whom she had a daughter, Tamar Teresa, born on March 3, 1927. After the daughter's birth Batterham left and Day began to immerse herself in religious literature and theology. Unknown to many of her old and close friends, Day on December 28, 1927, had herself and her daughter baptized in a small Staten Island Roman Catholic Church. For the remainder of her life she would remain a dedicated daughter of the Church. She had made a strange personal journey from a diluted childhood Protestantism through years as a rebellious bohemian, ultimately to find solace in the Catholic faith, a journey which she described poignantly in one of her autobiographical fragments, *From Union Square to Rome* (1938).

At first, however, even her new religious faith brought Day no clear purpose in life. In 1929 she toyed with scriptwriting in Hollywood but without satisfaction. A year later she moved with her small daughter to Mexico City, where they lived on the edge of poverty. That same summer she returned to the United States where the onset of the Great Depression swept her back into the movement for social reform. In December 1932 she went to Washington to report on a Communist-led hunger march. On her return to New York City she met Peter Maurin, a former French peasant and social agitator, who convinced her that radical social reform and the Roman Catholic faith could be united. Day now found a purpose in life that would remain with her for the remainder of her days. Together with Maurin she

founded a movement which would carry Jesus's original message to the most dispossessed of workers. They would prove that Catholicism served the poor as well as the rich, the weak better than the mighty. Through their newspaper, *Catholic Worker,* and hospitality houses which they established as havens for homeless workers, Day and Maurin promoted their singular version of Catholicism as a social reform movement.

For the next 50 years Day and the Catholic Worker Movement were at the forefront of all Catholic reform efforts. Young American Roman Catholics, eager to improve secular society while remaining faithful to their church, flocked to hear Day's message. The Berrigan brothers (Daniel and Philip), Michael Harrington, and many others fell under her spell, which turned them into radical social reformers. Other Catholics influenced by Day served as activists in the industrial union movement led by the Congress of Industrial Organizations, in the civil rights movement beginning in the 1950s, and increasingly in the peace movement which assumed growing importance in the nuclear age. Echoes of Day's approach to religion and reform could also be found in the "liberation theology" movement which emerged in Latin America in the 1960s.

By the time she died on November 29, 1980, Day had had an enormous impact on both American Catholicism and reform. It was an impact which lived on as revealed in the pastoral letters issued by the American Roman Catholic bishops in 1983 and 1984 on the issues of nuclear weapons and the economy.

## Further Reading

William D. Miller, *Dorothy Day, a Biography* (1982) is a full and excellent account of the subject's life and career. Two equally excellent books describe and analyze the history of the Catholic Worker Movement: William D. Miller, *A Harsh and Dreadful Love: Dorothy Day and the Catholic Worker Movement* (1972) and Mel Piehl, *Breaking Bread: The Catholic Worker and the Origin of Catholic Radicalism in America* (1982). Several of Day's own books, aside from the ones cited in the article, might also be profitably consulted, especially *House of Hospitality* (1939) and *On Pilgrimage: The Sixties* (1973). □

# Moshe Dayan

**The Israeli general and statesman Moshe Dayan (1915-1981) served as minister of defense of Israel, beginning in 1967.**

Moshe Dayan was born in the kibbutz of Degania, Palestine, in 1915. His father Samuel, a farmer, was a founder of Degania and Nahalal and a leader of the cooperative settlement (*moshavim*) movement. During the riots of 1936 to 1939 Dayan joined the Supplementary Police Force of Palestine under the British. Later he joined the first mobile commando platoons (*palmakh*) of the Haganah. In 1940 Dayan was arrested by the British because of his participation in the underground Haganah organization. After his release from prison in 1941, however, he joined the British army in order to fight against Nazi Germany. On a foray into Vichy-controlled Syria, he was wounded and lost his left eye. This scar, or rather the patch that covered it, would become his lifelong trademark.

During the struggle between the Palestine Jewish community and the British mandatory government in 1947, Dayan again served in the underground Haganah. During the War of Independence in 1948 he participated in the campaign against the Egyptian army. In 1949 he led the Israeli forces in the final battles around Jerusalem, and after the war he represented Israel at the Rhodes Armistice Conference. He was acclaimed a national hero for his part in the Sinai campaign against Egypt in 1956.

After retiring from the army in 1958, Dayan entered politics as a leading member of the "Young Mapai" and was appointed minister of agriculture in 1959, a post he occupied until 1964. Shortly after David Ben-Gurion's resignation as prime minister in 1963, Dayan also withdrew from government. But he soon returned to politics as a member of the Rafi opposition party, which Ben-Gurion formed in 1965.

In May of 1967 Dayan became minister of defense for Israel. Under his command and with the close collaboration of the chief of staff, General Itzhak Rabin, the Israeli armed forces won an unprecedented victory over the combined Arab military forces of Egypt (United Arab Republic), Jordan, Syria, Iraq, and Saudi Arabia in the Six Day War of June

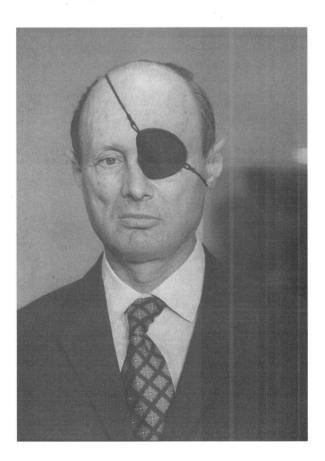

1967. As a result of its victory, Israel occupied vast Arab territories and blocked the Suez Canal to international navigation. After this conflict, Dayan continued to strengthen Israel's military forces in order to ensure the state's survival in the troubled Middle East. Dayan had a deep concern for the soldiers in the field and always paid meticulous attention to their safety and comfort. He became upset when, during retaliatory actions, lives were lost without territorial gains.

In the minority among Israel's leaders, Dayan foresaw a new war if the nation did not retreat from the Suez Canal. Mounting tensions exploded on October 6, 1973, the high holy day of Yom Kippur, the Jewish day of atonement. Forces from Egypt and Syria attacked Israel from north and south. Dayan predicted a grim, costly effort, yet he stood alone among Israel's military leaders. He flew to the Sinai after he received news of embattled Israeli troops, and reorganized command and strategy. Likewise, he worked with prime minister Golda Meir to organize an immediate airlift of supplies from the United States. The war turned in Israel's favor on October 10, and a cease-fire was declared by October 23.

Despite his efforts, Dayan was harshly criticized for what was seen as unpreparedness for the assault, and soon left the Ministry of Defense. In 1977 he was elected to the Ninth Knesset on the Labor party ticket, but continued to serve as foreign minister to the Begin administration until 1980. The next year he formed the Telem party and was its representative until he died on October 16, 1981, with his wife and his daughter by his side. He was buried in Nahalal, site of the Dayan family farm.

Dayan vigorously denied the allegation that he saw the problem of Arab-Israeli relations "through the sights of a gun." As minister of agriculture, he met frequently with Arab farmers and tried to give them every assistance. He always held that the Arabs of Israel should have equal rights and bear equal responsibilities with the other citizens of Israel.

Dayan's attitude toward prisoners of war and Arab civilians in the territories occupied after the Six Day War attested to his strong sense of justice. While energetically combating terrorist activities, he maintained a liberal policy toward the people of the occupied areas, giving them as much freedom as possible to run their own affairs and allowing commercial and social relations with Jordan.

Dayan had sides to his character that belied his image as a tough, unemotional fighter. He was passionately attached to the land and in particular to his farm in Nahalal. He had a great interest in archaeology, which he pursued through digging in his spare time and reading extensively on the subject. Dayan was also an author, and among his publications are *Israel's Border and Security Problems* (1955), *Diary of the Sinai Campaign* (1966), and *A New Map, New Relationships* (1969).

## Further Reading

One of the best books on Dayan's life is his own autobiography, *Moshe Dayan: Story of My Life*. A biography was written by his daughter, Yael Dayan, *My Father, His Daughter*. Naphtali

Lau-Lavie's *Moshe Dayan* (1968) is also a full-length biography. Moshe Ben Shaul, ed., *Generals of Israel* (trans. 1968), contains a succinct portrayal of Dayan by Doris Lankin. Two works that rely primarily on pictures are David Curtis and Stephen G. Crane, *Dayan: A Pictorial Biography* (1967), and Pinchas Jurman, ed., *Moshe Dayan: A Portrait* (1969). ☐

# Swami Dayananda Saraswati

**The Indian religious leader Swami *Dayananda Saraswati* (1824-1883) founded the Arya Samaj, or Society of Nobles, and epitomized the aggressive Hindu religious reformer.**

Dayananda Saraswati was born into a wealthy Brahmin family in Gujarat, a part of western India somewhat isolated from British colonial influence. He was raised in the orthodox Hindu tradition but soon found himself unsatisfied with the archaic teachings and practices, especially idol worship and other primitivisms imposed on him. At the age of 19 he left his family and undertook a long period of rigorous, ascetic study of the ancient Vedas—the oldest core of the Hindu religion.

Dayananda concluded that current religious beliefs and social institutions were hopelessly corrupt. With this conviction he began to preach an aggressive reforming doctrine which urged a return to the pristine Vedic tradition. While his commitments seemed basically "fundamentalist" and somewhat orthodox, in fact, he advocated radical reforms such as the abolition of idol worship, of child marriages, of the inequality of women, and of hereditary caste privileges. He praised the way of the Europeans and named as the causes of their advancement their representative assemblies, education, active lives, and the fact that they "help their countrymen in trade."

In his religious teaching he accepted the old doctrine of *karma* and transmigration, but he developed a highly sophisticated monistic philosophy which stressed ideals of self-perfection and ethical universalism: "I believe in a religion based on universal and all-embracing principles which have always been accepted as true by mankind—the *primeval eternal religion,* which means that it is above the hostility of all human creeds whatsoever." In 1875 Dayananda founded the Arya Samaj in Bombay as the institutional medium for the propagation of his teaching. He preached in vernacular Hindi in an effort to break through the elitist Sanskrit culture and to reach the masses. His society was open to all men and women on the basis of personal interest and commitment. His disciples perused the Vedas in minute detail, finding there the essential precursors of Western science and technology, including electricity, microbiology, and other modern inventions.

His outspoken criticism of Hindu tradition and his reforming interests provoked the hatred of many orthodox and conservative circles, and he argued abrasively with Moslem and Christian sectarians in favor of the universal philosophy of his own interpretation of the Vedas. Numerous attempts were made on his life, and he was finally poisoned in 1883.

The Arya Samaj was one of the most influential movements of the early modern period in India. It contributed to the rise of Indian nationalism by instilling a sense of pride in the integrity of the most unique and ancient traditions of Indian heritage while simultaneously undercutting the great bulk of conservative Hindu interpretation and law. Dayananda's personality and purifying reforms earned him the epithet "the Luther of India."

## Further Reading

Dayananda's *Light of Truth* was translated into English in 1906. A biography of Dayananda is Har Bilas Sarda, *Life of Dayananda Saraswati, World Teacher* (1946).

## Additional Sources

Arya, Krishan Singh, *Swami Dayananda Sarasvati: a study of his life and work,* Delhi: Manohar, 1987.

Bawa, Arjan Singh, *Dayananda Saraswati, founder of Arya Samaj,* New Delhi: Ess Ess Publications, 1979.

*Autobiography of Dayanand Saraswati,* New Delhi: Manohar, 1978.

Jordens, J. T. F., *Dayåananda Sarasvatåi, his life and ideas,* Delhi: Oxford University Press, 1978.

Lajpat Rai, Lala, *Swami Dayananda Saraswati: his biography and teachings,* New Delhi: Reliance Pub. House; New York, N.Y.: Distributed by Apt Books, 1991.

Pandey, Dhanpati, *Swami Dayanand Saraswati,* New Delhi: Publications Division, Ministry of Information and Broadcasting, Govt. of India, 1985.

Prem Lata, *Swami Dayåananda Sarasvatåi,* New Delhi: Sumit Publications, 1990. ☐

# Francis Deák

**The Hungarian statesman Francis Deák (1803-1876) was one of the creators of Austria-Hungary. Called the "Sage of the Nation," he was the architect of the Austro-Hungarian Compromise of 1867.**

The son of a nontitled nobleman and estate owner, Francis Deák was born at Söjtör on Oct. 17, 1803. After studying law, he joined the administration of his native Zala County. In 1833 he became one of his county's representatives at the national Diet at Pozsony (Pressburg, Bratislava), and from then on his activities became irrevocably linked with Hungarian national politics. At this time Hungary was under the control of the Austrian Hapsburgs, who, during the past 3 centuries, had made repeated efforts to integrate the country into their dynastic state. With the rise of 19th-century Magyar nationalism, however, the politically conscious Hungarian leading classes reacted and demanded the reestablishment of the original "personal union" relationship (partnership under a common ruler) with Austria, while also calling for liberal social and political reforms.

During the 1830s Deák championed such causes as the liberation of serfs, Polish liberties, religious freedom, and freedom of speech. During 1841-1842 he chaired the commission that recommended the elimination of corporal punishment, the death sentence, and the feudal courts and called for the introduction of a new court and jury system. However, the commission's proposals were defeated at the next Diet (1843-1844).

By this time Deák's unquestioned integrity, good judgment, and dedication to progressive goals had made him a most respected national leader, and in 1847 the factionalized liberals turned to him to draw up the program of the "united opposition." By combining Louis Kossuth's radical views and Baron Joseph Eötvös's centralist ones with his own, he formed the basis of the "March-April Compromise" of 1848, which transformed Hungary into a near-independent parliamentary state under its own responsible government.

Deák became the minister of justice in the new Batthyány government. In this post he devoted his attention both to the liquidation of the remnants of feudalism and to the prevention of a final break between Hungary and the dynasty. Following the Batthyány government's resignation (Sept. 28, 1848), Deák continued his parliamentary work. But in December he was unsuccessful in negotiating a compromise with Prince Alfred Windischgrätz, the commander in chief of the Austrian imperial forces sent to put down the Hungarian revolution. Deák then withdrew from politics and retired to his estate at Kehida.

Deák did not return to politics until 1854. In that year he moved to Pest, and thereafter his home became the center of Hungarian national politics. It was there that he worked out his successful policy of passive resistance and noncollaboration.

When Francis Joseph of Austria appeared willing to negotiate following the Italian defeat in 1859, Deák assumed the leadership in the negotiations and formulated specific conditions in parliamentary addresses to the throne. Aided by Eötvös and Count Julius Andrássy, Deák began serious negotiations in 1865, although they were interrupted by the Austro-Prussian War of 1866. Deák's partial retreat in accepting the idea of common foreign, military, and financial affairs, together with his refusal to raise his demands after Austria's defeat, helped result in the Compromise (*Ausgleich*) of 1867, which transformed the Hapsburg Empire into the dual state of Austria-Hungary.

Having attained his goal, Deák declined to head the new government or to serve in the Cabinet headed by his protégé Andrássy. Nor did he accept any titles or honors for his achievement, although he remained the acknowledged leader of the ruling political party, which bore his name. But age, infirmity, and increasing dissatisfaction with Hungarian liberalism as it developed during the 1870s gradually caused him to withdraw from active politics. A confirmed bachelor, Deák died in Budapest on Jan. 28, 1876.

## Further Reading

Anglo-American scholarship has been very remiss on Deák, and aside from Florence M. Arnold-Forster's slight and out-of-date account, *Francis Deák, Hungarian Statesman: A Memoir* (1880), there is virtually nothing available in English. Imre Lukinich, *A History of Hungary in Biographical Sketches* (1937), contains only a brief popular account. Those who read French can consult Louis Eisenmann, *Le Compromis Austro-Hongrois de 1867* (1904), which has much to say about Deák. Others must rely on general works on 19th-century Hungary and the Hapsburg Empire. The most detailed one-volume work on Hungary is Dominic G. Kosáry and Steven Bela Vardy, *History of the Hungarian Nation* (1969). On the empire, C. A. Macartney's monumental *The Hapsburg Empire, 1790-1918* (1968) supersedes all previous works. □

# Alfred Deakin

**Alfred Deakin (1856-1919) was an Australian political leader who established a remarkable record in colonial and federal politics in constructive and progressive causes.**

A lfred Deakin was born in the gold-boom city of Melbourne on Aug. 3, 1856. He studied law at the University of Melbourne, became a writer for the progressive newspaper *Age,* and in 1879 was elected to the legislative assembly of Victoria.

Deakin served in a succession of ministries. An ardent advocate of irrigation (then untried in Australia), he visited California in 1884-1885 and induced George and Benjamin Chaffey to develop an irrigation settlement on arid land along the Murray River in Australia. In 1886 he secured passage of the Irrigation Act to seal the arrangement.

When the proposals for federation of the Australian territories at the Federal Convention of 1891 lapsed in the colonial legislatures, he supported public calls for a popularly elected convention, and his powerful oratory warmed thousands to the federal cause; and in 1900 he was a member of the group which visited London to support the Constitution Bill.

A tall, slight man with a black beard and a plentiful crop of hair, Deakin was usually likened more to an academic than to an active politician. Some considered that he suffered from "mental remoteness," but others saw in him "an attractively refined and intellectual man."

Attorney general in the first federal ministry (1901-1903), Deakin succeeded Edmund Barton as prime minister. Refusing to accede to Labour party demands, he soon resigned, but in 1905, after Labour had made electoral gains, he formed a new Liberal ministry and stayed in office with Labour support until 1908. During this period, curbs on alien immigration were eased somewhat, pensions provided for the aged, and important commercial laws adopted. After a commission (set up in 1906) proposed that only factories paying "fair and reasonable" wages should be given the benefit of tariff protection, Deakin affirmed his New Protection doctrine of a benefit to the worker from tariffs; in 1907 a minimum, or "basic," wage was established.

Deakin lost support in 1908 but became prime minister for a third term (1909-1910) in a "fusion" with erst-while opponents on the non-Labour side. A significant defense measure was the creation of an Australian naval squadron. When Labour (under Andrew Fisher) replaced Deakin, many liberal measures advocated earlier by him were adopted. Deakin remained in the House of Representatives until 1913. He died in Melbourne, in retirement, on Oct. 7, 1919.

## Further Reading

Deakin's comments on the events leading to federation are contained in his *The Federal Story: The Inner History of the Federal Cause, 1880-1900* (1944; 2d ed. 1963). A biography by an admirer of Deakin's policies is Walter Murdoch, *Alfred Deakin: A Sketch* (1923). A fuller biography is J. A. La Nauze, *Alfred Deakin* (2 vols., 1965). Background on federation is provided in John Quick and Robert Garran, *The Annotated Constitution of the Australian Commonwealth* (1901); Bernhard Ringrose Wise, *The Making of the Australian Common-wealth: 1889-1900* (1913); and John Quick, *Sir John Quick's Notebook,* edited by L. E. Freedman (1965). The record of the Deakin administrations is covered in H. G. Turner, *The First Decade of the Australian Common-wealth . . . 1901-1910* (1911), and Arthur Norman Smith, *Thirty Years: The Commonwealth of Australia, 1901-1931* (1933).

## Additional Sources

Gabay, Al, *The mystic life of Alfred Deakin,* Cambridge England; New York: Cambridge University Press, 1992. □

# James Dean

**Actor James Dean (1931-1955) had a short-lived but intense acting career that began in 1952 and ended tragically in his death in September 1955. After his death he became a cult figure, and fans have marveled for decades at his ability to duplicate their adolescent agony on screen.**

Born on February 8, 1931, in Marion, Indiana, James Byron Dean was the only child of Winton and Mildred (Wilson) Dean. Winton, a farmer-turned-dental-technician, moved his family to Santa Monica, California. when Dean was six years old. Receiving a lot of attention from both parents, he was particularly close to his mother. James Byron, as she called him, entered first grade in 1937 at the Brentwood Public School. He took violin lessons, playing well for a young child although his school friends taunted him about this activity.

In July 1940 his mother died of cancer. His father sent him, then nine, back to Indiana to live with Marcus and Ortense Winslow, his sister and brother-in-law. In Fairmount Dean grew up in the rural Quaker home, helping with farm chores and enjoying a reasonably carefree existence. Underneath, however, he harbored great pain. "My mother died on me when I was nine years old. What does she expect me to do? Do it all alone?" Dean was later to say.

Still, he got along well, riding his motorcycle with friends and playing guard on the high school basketball team. He excelled at debate and drama, coached and trained by teacher Adeline Nall. He won several state titles for his abilities, and on April 14, 1949, the Fairmount *News* read, "James Dean First Place Winner in Dramatic Speaking."

After graduating in 1949 he left for Los Angeles, where he lived briefly with his father and stepmother and entered Santa Monica City College, majoring in pre-law. But it was drama in which he shone: he received Cs and Ds in law classes, As and Bs in acting. He transferred the following year to the University of California, Los Angeles, pledging Sigma Nu fraternity. Befriended by actor James Whitmore, Dean obtained a small part in a television drama, *Hill Number One.*

Soon Dean quit school, living precariously as a parking lot attendant and chasing auditions wherever they were available. In 1951, after landing only bit parts and a small role in *Fixed Bayonets,* a war picture, he left Hollywood for New York. There, in 1953, he landed a spot in the Actors Studio run by Lee Strasberg.

He obtained a small part in *See the Jaguar* which opened at the Cort Theatre on Broadway on December 3, 1952. After this his career took off. He did television plays and several more Broadway productions and developed a reputation as "difficult." Despite this he won the Daniel

Blum Theatre World Award for "best newcomer" of the year for his role in *The Immoralist*.

In March 1954 Elia Kazan, who knew Dean from Actors Studio days, offered him a Warner Brothers contract. The film was *East of Eden*. The film's New York preview was March 10, 1955, but Dean declined to attend. "I can't handle it," he said, and flew back to Los Angeles.

Dean finished filming *Rebel Without a Cause* (with Sal Mineo and Natalie Wood) in June 1955 and began work on *Giant*. He co-starred in this with Elizabeth Taylor and Rock Hudson. Completing *Giant* in September of that year, Dean was to start rehearsing for *The Corn Is Green*, a play for the National Broadcasting Company. But Dean had a few days free time in which he decided to do some car racing.

Intrigued with fast automobiles, Dean had bought a $6,900 Porsche Spyder which he planned to race at Salinas, California, in September. On September 30th, he and his mechanic, Rolf Wuetherich, were involved in a head-on collision at Paso Robles, California. The Porsche was crumpled, Rolf suffered a smashed jaw and leg fracture. James Dean, dead at the age of 24, was buried in Fairmount, Indiana, on October 8, 1955. Three thousand people attended his funeral.

Less than a month later, *Rebel Without a Cause* opened in New York City, and the Dean legend began. Warner Brothers received landslides of mail—fans were obsessed with the curt, swaggering Dean. In February 1956 he was nominated for a Best Performance Oscar for his role in *East of Eden*. He also received numerous foreign awards, including the French Crystal Star award and the Japanese Million Pearl award. By June 1956 there were dozens of fan clubs, and rumors flourished that Dean was not dead, only severely injured.

Dean, interviewed in March 1955, commented on his craft, offering this curiously fatalistic view of life: "To me, acting is the most logical way for people's neuroses to manifest themselves. To my way of thinking, an actor's course is set even before he's out of the cradle."

## Further Reading

Although countless articles appeared about James Dean during his short career and following his death, there are only a few substantial biographies. They include: William Bast's *James Dean* (1956), written by a former roommate and close personal friend; *James Dean: The Mutant King* (1974) by David Dalton; *James Dean, A Short Life* (1974) by Venable Herndon; and Dennis Stock's *James Dean Revisited* (1978). □

# Mario de Andrade

**Mario de Andrade (1928-1990), as a poet, critic, and political activist expressed the struggle of the people of Angola (and other Portuguese colonies) for independence from colonial rule.**

Mario Coelho Pinto de Andrade was born on August 21, 1928, in the town of Galungo Alto, Angola (then a Portuguese colony) on the southwest coast of Africa. Through his writings and actions, de Andrade sought to help liberate Angola from Portuguese colonial control and to assist it in its struggle for nationhood. Interestingly, in Brazil, another Mario de Andrade played a similar role—though somewhat earlier (1893-1945). The Brazilian sought to unite the Amazonian past with its Latin American present in a composite Brazilian literature, while the Angolan worked for an independent Angola to avoid any future need for reconciling with a Portuguese present. However, Angola today as an independent nation maintains vestiges of Portuguese influence in a number of spheres including the use of Portuguese as Angola's official language.

Mario de Andrade was educated in Luanda, the capital city of Angola, through his early high school years. He continued his education in Mozambique and then went on to Lisbon, Portugal, where he studied philosophy. Next he pursued the study of sociology at the university level in Paris at the Sorbonne.

Even before de Andrade was born, there was an incipient nationalist organization in Angola in the form of the Liga Africana, which was set up in 1923. However, the colonial government maintained control over African organizations in its territories to minimize threats to its power. In December 1956, the *Movimento Popular de Libertaçao de Angola* (MPLA), with Mario de Andrade as a leader, was secretly founded with the goal of overt opposition to Portuguese colonialism. The MPLA remained a secret organization until 1959 when a number of its leaders, suspected of anti-Portuguese activities, were arrested by the Portuguese secret police. This move forced the MPLA to set up headquarters outside the country—first in Guinea and later, in 1961, in Leopoldville (now Kinshasa, Congo). In January 1961, while de Andrade was head of the MPLA, another organization was set up in Tunis with member groups from Guinea Bissau and Goa. This group was known as FRAIN (*Frente Revolucionaria Africana para a Independencia das Colonies Portuguesas*) —that is, the African Revolutionary Front for Independence of the Portuguese Colonies. Such joining together of groups fighting for freedom in the other Portuguese colonies led next to the formation of CONCP (the Conference of the Nationalist Organizations of Portuguese Colônies), which was also chaired by de Andrade. This organization involved all Portuguese colonies except for Maçao and Timor.

## Led First Overt Rebellion

The liberation movement and ensuing armed struggle led by de Andrade in 1961 was the first overt rebellion in the Portuguese colonies. It was to be followed later by similar wars of liberation in Guinea-Bissau and Mozambique. Ironically, Angola was the last of these three colonies to achieve independence (1975) and its hard won independence came only in the wake of an army coup in Portugal in 1974. Still, the coup in Portugal was largely made possible by the fact that its dictatorship had been weakened by the colonial wars starting with the Angolan struggle in 1961.

Initially the MPLA sought a negotiated settlement of its quarrel with Portugal, but its overtures were met with an increase in the colonial military presence. In retaliation, the *Santa Maria*, a Portuguese luxury liner, was captured in January 1961. This incident triggered reprisals by Portuguese citizens against African political prisoners in Luanda, resulting in the death of 3,000 people. At that time de Andrade claimed that MPLA had a membership of 50,000.

A power shift in MPLA in 1962 saw de Andrade moved to the position of secretary of foreign affairs, while another poet (who was a physician as well), Agostinho Neto, became president. With Neto as MPLA's president, de Andrade removed himself from active participation in the organization, going eventually into exile in France. Neto went on to become independent Angola's first president under an MPLA government set up in 1976. Despite a vast amount of internal reshuffling and the death of Neto in 1979, the MPLA remained Angola's government.

De Andrade's exile resulted from rival nationalist groups fighting for Angolan independence, MPLA internal politics, and the fact that de Andrade's name appeared on a Portuguese list of "undesirables." In exile, he worked for the well-known French language journal of African literature, *Presence Africaine*.

In addition to his political activism, de Andrade was well-known as a poet and a scholar. He helped organize the Conference of Negro Writers in Rome in 1958 and wrote a number of sociology articles published in Angola, Brazil, and Portugal.

### Writings Don't Appear In English

A native speaker of Kimbundu, a Bantu language widely spoken in Angola, de Andrade wrote only in that language and in Portuguese. One of his best known poems was written in Kimbundu and published in Portuguese in a special issue of *Presence Africaine* entitled *New Sum of Poetry from the Negro World* (1966, vol. 57). None of his writings have appeared in English. The poem "Song of Sabalu" from the *New Sum* volume was translated from Portuguese to English for this article by anthropologist James B. Watson and is presented here to provide a sense of de Andrade as activist and poet. (*Aiue* is a vernacular Portuguese exclamation. São Tomé is an island off the Guinea coast with a prison colony on it. Prisoners were often shipped as slaves from there.)

Song of Sabalu

Our youngest child
They sent him to São Tomé
He had no documents
Aiue!

Our youngest child wept
Mama went crazy
Aiue!
They sent him to São Tomé

Our youngest child has gone
They sent him off in the hold of their ship
Aiue!
They sent him to São Tomé

Our youngest child is thinking
Of his land, of his home
They sent him to hard labor
They're watching him, watching him

Mama, he will come back
Ah, our luck must change
Aiue!
They sent him to São Tomé

Our youngest child did NOT return
Death took him

Aiue!
They sent him to São Tomé

Among de Andrade's other writings is an anthology of "Negro poetry expressed in Portuguese" published first in Lisbon but also clandestinely circulated in Angola and the other Portuguese colonies and a two-part volume on Portuguese African literature (poetry and prose) published in Algiers in 1967. Both the anthology and poetry/prose works were republished in 1970 by Kraus Reprint. The Laundan-based journal *Messagem* ("Message") has published de Andrade's story "Eme ngana, eme muene."

De Andrade died of a chronic disease in London in 1990 at the age of 62.

### Further Reading

None of de Andrade's writings have yet been officially translated into English. One may read about his work in both the political and literary spheres in the short biographical entry in Donald E. Herdeck's (ed.) *African Authors*, published by Black Orpheus press in 1973. The Portuguese version of "Song of Sabalu" translated into English here is published in *Presence Africaine* (1966). A book edited by John A. Davis and James K. Baker entitled *Southern Africa in Transition* (1966) has a chapter entitled "Nationalist Organizations in Angola: Status of the Revolt" by George M. Hauser which discusses de Andrade's role as a leader in the Angolan nationalist movement of the 1960s. His obituary appeared in the August 27, 1990 issues of the *New York Times* and the *Boston Globe*. □

# Silas Deane

**Silas Deane (1737-1789), a leading merchant and advocate of American independence, was a highly controversial commissioner to France from 1776 to 1778.**

Silas Deane was born Dec. 24, 1737, into a family long resident in Connecticut. He took his bachelor and master of arts degrees from Yale College and was admitted to the bar in 1761. He consolidated his standing among the commercial and political leaders of the colony by two marriages, first to Mehitabel Webb, and after her death to Elizabeth Saltonstall. After 10 years as a prosperous merchant and lawyer he was elected to his state's General Assembly in 1772, where he soon stood among the active foes of British measures.

In the first and second Continental Congresses, Deane worked to establish and equip colonial armed forces and personally supplied the expedition that captured Ft. Ticonderoga in 1775. Though for unknown reasons he was not reappointed delegate to Congress in 1776, he had earned national standing as one of the most energetic, resourceful leaders of the Revolution.

## Commissioner to France

In March 1776 Congress sent Deane to France, authorized to hasten war supplies to America and to gain French recognition of the soon-to-be-independent Colonies. Deane found France (and its ally Spain) eager to aid the Colonies against England, the ancient enemy of both countries. Yet, the French were unwilling to make open opposition, and he was confronted by numerous informal, clandestine arrangements. Authorized to extend credit for war material, Deane could never be sure what persons or groups in America stood behind his negotiations. Equally uncertain was the status of the French—were they giving, lending, or selling supplies? And were they private businessmen, agents of Louis XVI, or perhaps joint stock operators backed by both France and Spain? Opportunities for misunderstanding, fraud, and profiteering abounded.

The only certainties are that France, under the guidance of the foreign minister Comte de Vergennes, made funds and material available, and that Deane did get quantities of guns and uniforms that sustained American armies in the 1777 campaigns, including the vital victory at Saratoga. Deane also encouraged many European military officers to join the American army.

## Deane's Actions under Attack

In late 1776, when Benjamin Franklin came to France as a second commissioner, he endorsed Deane's arrangements without probing details, finding him generally "sincere and hearty in our cause." Less trustful was the third American commissioner, Arthur Lee, who suspected that Deane, and by acquiescence at least, Franklin, were in collusion with French profiteers who were billing Congress huge sums for worthless goods, materials never sent, or supplies meant to be gifts. Lee's charges led to Deane's recall soon after he signed (with Lee and Franklin) the French Alliance in February 1778.

## Unsolved Mystery

Called to account by Congress, Deane began appearances before that body in August 1778 to defend himself against charges brought by Lee's powerful friends. Lacking adequate records to prove either guilt or innocence, the hearings degenerated into personal bickerings and factional disputes, eventually leaving those disposed to trust and welcome French aid on Deane's side, and those deeply suspicious of it on Lee's. The acrimonious affair led to the resignation of Henry Laurens (who was against Deane) as president of Congress and his replacement by the more friendly John Jay. Deane published a vigorous self-defense, hurling countercharges at Lee; the ensuing "paper war" became fierce. Lacking reliable evidence, Congress postponed any decision.

After fretting, half-disgraced, for 2 years, Deane returned to Europe to seek evidence to clear himself. The necessary documents were lost, hidden, or nonexistent. Feeling ill-treated and worn down by poor health, Deane wrote despondently to American friends, advising them, in view of the disarray in the patriot cause, to reconcile with England. These letters, intercepted and printed in the loyalist press in New York, added to the cloud already hanging over Deane and seemed to prove him maliciously disloyal.

Sick and bankrupt, Deane spent his last years in England, where his only apparent friend was the notorious "double spy" Dr. Edward Bancroft, who during 1776-1777 had presented himself to Deane and Franklin to spy for them but was actually reporting every detail of the clandestine American negotiations to the British ministers.

Deane died mysteriously while on a ship about to leave for Canada. Recent material presented by historian Julian Boyd strongly implies that Bancroft poisoned Deane to silence incriminating testimony of further double-dealing.

Though in 1842 Congress awarded Deane's heirs $37,000 (a small fraction of their claim) in payment for losses Deane had incurred during the Revolution, no evidence has yet appeared to clarify the charges against him.

## Further Reading

No satisfactory, recent biography of Deane exists. Of the older accounts, George L. Clark, *Silas Deane: a Connecticut Leader in the American Revolution* (1913), is useful, as is a biographical notice by Charles Isham in volume 1 of *The Deane Papers, 1774-1790* in the *New York Historical Society Collections* (3 vols., 1887-1890). Further letters are in *The Deane Papers: Correspondence between Silas Deane, His Brothers and Their Business and Political Associates, 1771-1795* in the collections of the Connecticut Historical Society (1930). Samuel F. Bemis, *The Diplomacy of the American Revolution* (1935), discusses Deane's diplomatic activity in France. Edmund C. Burnett, *The Continental Congress* (1941), describes disputes over Deane in Congress. Carl C. Van Doren, *The Secret History of the American Revolution: An Account of the Conspiracies of Benedict Arnold* (1941), divulges as much as is known of the intrigues surrounding Deane's career.

## Additional Sources

James, Coy Hilton, *Silas Deane, patriot or traitor?*, East Lansing: Michigan State University Press, 1975. □

# Radhakant Deb

**Radhakant Deb (1783-1867) was a Bengali reformer and cultural nationalist who dedicated his life to the preservation of orthodox Hinduism.**

Historians have generally looked upon Radhakant Deb with disfavor, chiefly because he defended sati (suttee), the immolation of widows on funeral pyres of their dead husbands. Recent studies which focus on the psychology of Indian nationalism in opposition to British cultural imperialism have prompted a reevaluation of figures like Radhakant, Vivekananda, and Dayananda who, while ambivalent to forms of Westernization, were nevertheless modernizers of the Indian traditions.

Radhakant was a member of the Calcutta Hindu elite, which owed both its wealth and social status to profitable relations with Europeans. In the sophisticated atmosphere of the metropolis, Radhakant learned Arabic, Persian, Urdu, Sanskrit, Bengali, and English.

In 1816 Radhakant's father, Gopi Mohun Deb, contributed a large sum of money toward the establishment of Hindu College, the earliest institution of higher learning in Asia organized along European lines, and served on its first managing committee with members of the prominent Tagore and Mullick families. Some years later, Radhakant took his father's place on the committee.

Radhakant's intellectual development with respect to Western learning seems to have begun when he joined the newly formed Calcutta School Book Society and School Society in 1817-1818. He took an active role in the institutional operations of the School Society by becoming its "native" secretary and by personally supervising the reform of Calcutta primary schools.

His new cultural attitudes, intellectual development, and deepening social consciousness in the 1820s are best reflected in his publications for the School Book Society. His *Bangla siksa-grantha* (1821) was a small encyclopedia for student use and included an elementary analysis of language structure, spelling rules, geographical terms, and basic arithmetic. Also in 1821, Radhakant collaborated with J. D. Pearson in bringing out the first edition of the *Nitikatha* (Moral Tales), which drew on both Christian and Hindu traditions and was designed to inculcate a feeling of morality without sectarian bias. In 1822 Radhakant was coauthor of a book called *Strisikhar bidya,* which advocated female education. He also translated Western textbooks on the natural sciences, such as *Jyotibidya* (Astronomy), and on history, such as *Pracin itihaser sammacchay* (Essence of Ancient History).

Radhakant's dubious image as orthodox leader of Bengali Hindus began in 1830, when he and his followers founded the Dharma Sabha (Association in Defense of Hindu Culture) in opposition to Lord Bentinck's decree abolishing sati. Since the Sabha organized its defense of the indigenous culture against alien intrusion and used collective political means to articulate its position, it became modern India's first protonationalist movement. The founding of the Sabha proved to be the turning point in Radhakant's life, and for the next 30 years until his death, he increasingly sought ways and means of reconciling reformism with the demands of cultural nationalism.

## Further Reading

Radhakant is briefly referred to in most surveys of modern Indian history, and there is abundant material on his activities in articles on the Calcutta School Society, the British Indian Association, and the history of printing in Bengal. An evaluation of Radhakant's role in the 19th-century Bengal renaissance is in David Kopf, *British Orientalism and the Bengal Renaissance: The Dynamics of Indian Modernization, 1773-1835* (1969). See also Nemai Sadhan Bose, *The Indian Awakening and Bengal* (1960), and Ramesh C. Majumdar, *Glimpses of Bengal in the Nineteenth Century* (1960).

## Additional Sources

Sengupta, Syamalendu, *A conservative Hindu of colonial India: Raja Radhakant Deb and his milieu (1784-1867),* New Delhi: Navrang, 1990. □

# Michael Ellis DeBakey

**The American surgeon Michael Ellis DeBakey (born 1908) devised procedures for replacing diseased portions of the aorta, and was a leader in the development of the artificial heart.**

Michael DeBakey was born in Lake Charles, Louisiana, on September 7, 1908. From early on he had a keen interest in biology, and he received his bachelor of science degree in 1930, his medical degree in 1932, and a master of science degree for research on peptic ulcers in 1935, from Tulane University. He then served as a medical resident in Europe at the universities of Strasbourg and Heidelberg. He married Diana Cooper on Oct. 15, 1936.

In 1937, DeBakey became a member of the Tulane faculty. Except for service during World War II in the Surgeon General's Office, where he rose to become chief of the surgery consultants division, he remained at Tulane until 1948. DeBakey had already become an expert in blood transfusion and had developed a roller-type pump for use in transfusions. It became an important component of the heart-lung machine.

In 1948 DeBakey was appointed professor of surgery at Baylor University College of Medicine in Houston, Tex. A year later he assumed responsibilities as surgeon in chief at Houston's Ben Taub General Hospital. In the 1950s DeBakey originated complex surgical procedures for the correction of aneurysms and blockages of the aorta involving replacing the diseased part with Dacron tubing.

The work for which DeBakey is best known involves the artificial heart. He initially concentrated on developing a left ventricular bypass (half an artificial heart) and in 1967 successfully implanted his device. He worked toward the development of a completely artificial heart and believed that such a heart was the ultimate answer to human heart replacement in spite of others' interest in heart transplantation.

In 1969 a former colleague, Dr. Denton Cooley, implanted a completely artificial heart in a human. Since Cooley had worked closely with DeBakey and because he was assisted by Dr. Domingo Liotta, who had worked with DeBakey on the artificial heart, DeBakey claimed priority of development. Cooley's artificial heart was not successful, and DeBakey held that much more work was needed to perfect the device.

DeBakey earned numerous awards and honors. In 1963, he received the prestigious Albert Lasker Award for Clinical Research. The next year, he served on the President's Commission on Heart Disease, Cancer and Stroke. This Commission recommended, among other things, the establishment of intensive-care centers for these diseases and community centers for diagnosis. He received the Medal of Freedom with Distinction in 1969, and the Presidential Medal of Science in 1987. In 1976 his students from around the world established the Michael E. DeBakey International Surgical Society, and Baylor University founded the Michael E. Debakey Center for Biomedical Education and the DeBakey Lectureship. DeBakey has authored well over one thousand published medical-scientific articles and more extensive works. His books include *Battle Casualties, Incidence, Mortality, and Logistic Considerations* (1952) with G. W. Beebe and *Cold Injury, Ground Type* (1958) with T. F Whayne.

In addition to his other positions DeBakey was chairman of the Department of Medicine at Methodist Hospital in Houston, physician in chief at the Fondren-Brown Cardiovascular Research Center, and director of the DeBakey Heart Center of Baylor and Methodist Hospital. In 1996,

DeBakey again achieved international repute serving as consultant to the surgeons who performed heart bypass surgery on Russian President Boris Yeltsin.

## Further Reading

The greatest compilation of DeBakey's research can be found in his own *The Living Heart,* as well as in its sequels, *The Living Heart's Shopper's Guide* and *The Living Heart's Guide to Eating Out.* DeBakey's work is briefly discussed in Richard Hardaway Meade, *An Introduction to the History of General Surgery* (1968), and Robert G. Richardson, *Surgery: Old and New Frontiers* (1969), which is a revised and enlarged edition of *The Surgeon's Tale* (1958). □

# DeBartolo

**Edward John DeBartolo, (1919-1994), was a real estate developer whose firm, the Edward J. DeBartolo Corporation, specialized in large regional malls. His son, Edward John DeBartolo, Jr. (born 1946), was company president and also the owner of the San Francisco 49'ers football team.**

Edward John DeBartolo was born in Youngstown, Ohio, on May 17, 1919, the son of two Italian immigrants, Rose and Anthony Paonessa. His father died several months before his birth; his mother remarried, and Edward took the name of his stepfather, Michael DeBartolo, who raised him. Michael DeBartolo was a mason and general contractor in Youngstown, and during Edward's teens he worked on paving jobs and sometimes wrote the contracting bids for his Italian-speaking father. At his mother's urging he attended college at the University of Notre Dame, graduating in 1941 with a degree in civil engineering. In 1944 he married Maria Montani, and during World War II he served in the Army Corps of Engineers.

After the war DeBartolo returned to Youngstown and became president of his father's construction company. In 1948, however, he founded his own firm, the Edward J. DeBartolo Corporation. DeBartolo foresaw important developments in postwar America. As service people returned home, the suburbs expanded and the "baby boom" took off; retailing and commercial real estate development also changed. Traditional shopping centers were downtown, often along "Main Street," with one central area oriented toward public transportation. Now with cars and suburban growth, businesses moved to plaza or strip centers, usually a straight line of convenience stores (the "strip"). The first strip plazas served primarily as neighborhood centers, but in the 1950s the strip malls grew in size and complexity and became more regional in scope; the DeBartolo Corporation was at the forefront of these developments.

DeBartolo opened his first strip center, the Boardman Plaza, in 1951, in suburban Youngstown; Boardman remained a focus for DeBartolo in the 1990s, for both his home and corporate headquarters were located there. In the

**Edward DeBartolo, Jr.**

next 15 years DeBartolo opened some 45 strip centers across the country. Many were anchored by major department stores, which opened their first suburban branches in the 1950s. By 1960 retailing executives realized that two major stores in one center were complementary rather than competitive, and even larger regional centers proliferated.

The 1960s also saw the emergence of the enclosed mall as the typical regional shopping center. These large enclosed malls were not just places to shop, but centers for eating, browsing, socializing, exercise, and entertainment. DeBartolo was again a leader of the new pattern. According to one story, DeBartolo bought an airplane and flew over Midwest cornfields, choosing his mall sites close to major highway intersections. The story may be apocryphal, but it illustrates DeBartolo's conviction that the regional mall was retailing's future. In the 1960s and 1970s the developer opened four or five new malls a year; his Randall Park Mall outside Cleveland, with over 2.2 million square feet, was the largest mall in the world when it opened in 1976. By 1990 the corporation owned some 60 regional malls across the country, nearly a tenth of the nation's total mall retail space. The DeBartolo Corporation also developed office buildings, hotels, theaters, and condominiums. These holdings were nationwide, but DeBartolo had a particular cluster of malls in Florida. Again anticipating future developments, he bought huge plots of land in Florida in the 1960s at low prices; he gambled on population growth in

the Sunbelt and the success of Disney World, and both trends contributed to his long-term success there.

Despite its size, the DeBartolo Corporation remained a closely controlled family business, with all the stock held by DeBartolo and his two children. DeBartolo's personal fortune was estimated at over $1.4 billion. He was the chair of the board and chief executive officer in 1990. Son Edward J. DeBartolo, Jr., was the president and chief administrative officer of the company; daughter Marie Denise York was executive vice-president of personnel and public relations. "Mr. D.," as DeBartolo Senior was known to his employees, remained firmly in command. He arrived at his office every day at 5:30 a.m. and worked until 6:30 or 7:00 at night; he was tough and exacting, with a mind for the details of each project. The corporation was a vertical one, controlling each aspect of a real estate project from planning and land purchase through architecture and construction and finally leasing, marketing, and promotion.

Although the rapid building of the 1960s and 1970s had slowed by 1990, the DeBartolo Corporation continued to plan new malls and to expand and renovate existing malls to capitalize on its prime retail locations. New projects included updated strip centers built adjacent to the larger regional malls, and DeBartolo also experimented with a few urban malls.

In the late 1980s DeBartolo Senior became more involved in the world of Wall Street finance. In 1986 he bid on Allied Stores, a large retail chain which included Jordan Marsh and Brooks Brothers, to help forestall a takeover by Toronto real estate developer Robert Campeau. He lost that bidding war, but in 1988 he loaned Campeau $480 million toward his purchase of the Federated department store chain, including successful and trendy Bloomingdales. That loan also involved a proposal to build up to ten new DeBartolo malls a year, to be anchored by the Federated stores. Campeau and Federated later filed for bankruptcy, but the DeBartolo loans were secured. In late 1988 DeBartolo formed a partnership with Dillard Department Stores to purchase the Cleveland-based Higbee Company; despite Campeau's failure, DeBartolo believed that retailing and development could be successful complements.

Besides business, the DeBartolo family's other major interest is sports. DeBartolo Senior owned three race tracks, in Ohio, Louisiana, and Oklahoma, and he owned the Pittsburgh Penguins hockey team, of which his daughter, Marie, was the president. In 1980 he attempted to purchase the Chicago White Sox baseball team, but was voted down by the American League owners, under pressure from commissioner Bowie Kuhn. The ostensible reasons included his absentee ownership and his race track involvement, but many believed the unspoken objection was his reputed link to organized crime. A series of innuendoes followed DeBartolo beginning in the 1950s when there was a rash of bombings at his properties in Youngstown, where organized crime was strong, but FBI and Treasury Department investigations turned up no evidence. Nonetheless, his foray into baseball was rebuffed.

Not so his family's venture into football, which was the most successful of their sports ventures. In 1977 DeBartolo bought the San Francisco 49'ers for his son, Edward. Under his ownership the 49'ers won four Super Bowl championships, in 1982, 1985, 1989, and 1990, with star quarterback Joe Montana leading the team in each victory. In 1995, the 49'ers won their fifth Super Bowl championship. The De-Bartolo fortune was part of the team's success; the payroll was the highest in the National Football League and De-Bartolo, Jr., lavished first-class treatment on both players and their families. DeBartolo, Jr., enjoyed the glamour of his sports' affiliation, the locker-room camaraderie and celebrations, while his father was a more reclusive observer. DeBartolo Senior died in 1994.

## Further Reading

The DeBartolos and their real estate and sports interests are profiled in several articles in the *Chain Store Age Executive* (May 1981; May 1989; and November 1989). A more critical perspective is found in Jonathan R. Laing, "King of Malls," *Barrons* (June 12, 1989). DeBartolo is regularly listed in "The *Forbes* Four Hundred." Two accounts of the San Francisco 49'ers include material on the family: *TIME* (January 8, 1990) and *Sports Illustrated* (January 29, 1990).

Useful general accounts of shopping center development are William S. Kowinski, *The Malling of America* (1985); Horace Carpenter, Jr., *Shopping Center Management* (1978); and George Sternlieb and James W. Hughes, editors, *Shopping Centers: USA* (1981). □

# Simone de Beauvoir

**Simone de Beauvoir (1908-1986), a French writer, first articulated what has since become the basis of the modern feminist movement. She was the author of novels, autobiographies, and non-fiction analysis dealing with women's position in a male-dominated world.**

Simone de Beauvoir set out to live her life as an example to her contemporaries and chronicled that life for those who followed. Fiercely independent, an ardent feminist before there was such a movement, her life was her legacy and her work was to memorialize that life.

"I was born at four o'clock in the morning on the ninth of January 1908, in a room fitted with white-enameled furniture and overlooking the Boulevard Raspail." Thus begins the first of four memoirs written by de Beauvoir. It is through these autobiographies that de Beauvoir's readers best know her, and it is in her book *The Second Sex*, an early feminist manifesto, that de Beauvoir synthesized that life into the context of the historical condition of women.

The first child of a vaguely noble couple, de Beauvoir was a willful girl, prone to temper tantrums. Her sister, Poupette, was born when de Beauvoir was two and a half, and the two had a warm relationship. After World War I her father never fully recovered his financial security and the family moved to a more modest home; the daughters were told they had lost their dowries. Forced to choose a profes-

sion, de Beauvoir entered the Sorbonne and began to take courses in philosophy to become a teacher. She also began keeping a journal—which became a lifetime habit—and writing some stories.

## Link with Sartre

When de Beauvoir was 21 she joined a group of philosophy students including Jean-Paul Sartre. Her relationship with Sartre—intellectually, emotionally, and romantically—was to continue throughout most of their lives. Sartre, the father of existentialism—a school of thought that holds man is on his own, "condemned to be free," as Sartre says in *Being and Nothingness* —was the single most important influence on de Beauvoir's life.

In 1929 Sartre suggested that, rather than be married, the two sign a conjugal pact which could be renewed or cancelled after two years. When the pact came due, Sartre was offered a job teaching philosophy in Le Havre and de Beauvoir was offered a similar job in Marseilles. He suggested they get married, but they both rejected the idea for fear of forcing their free relationship into the confines of an outer-defined bond. It is indeed ironic that de Beauvoir, whose independence marked her life at every juncture, was perhaps best known as Sartre's lover.

The first installment of de Beauvoir's autobiography, *Memoirs of a Dutiful Daughter*, is the story of the author's rejection of the bourgeois values of her parents' lives. The second volume, *The Prime of Life*, covers the years 1929 through 1944. Written in the postwar years, she separated the events taking place in Europe that led to the war from her own, isolated life. By 1939, however, the two strands were inseparable. Both de Beauvoir and Sartre were teaching in Paris when the war broke out. Earlier she had written two novels that she never submitted for publication and one collection of short stories that was rejected for publication. She was, she said, too happy to write.

That happiness ended in the 1940s with the outbreak of World War II and the interruption of her relationship with Sartre. The introduction of another woman into Sartre's life, and then the anxiety and loneliness de Beauvoir felt while Sartre was a prisoner for more than a year led to her first significant novel, *She Came to Stay*, published in 1943. *She Came to Stay* is a study of the effects of love and jealousy. In the next four years she published *The Blood of Others*, *Pyrrhus et Cinéas*, *Les Bouches Inutiles*, and *All Men are Mortal*.

*America Day By Day* a chronicle of de Beauvoir's 1947 trip to the United States, and the third installment of her autobiography, *Force of Circumstances*, cover the period during which the author was formulating and writing *The Second Sex*, her feminist tract.

## The Second Sex

Written in 1949, *The Second Sex* is blunt and inelegant like her other writing. Its power comes from its content. Her themes and method of attack in *The Second Sex* are also the reoccurring issues of her work. The book rests on two theses: that man, who views himself as the essential being, has made woman into the inessential being, "the Other," and that femininity as a trait is an artificial posture. Both theses derive from Sartre's existentialism.

*The Second Sex* was perhaps the most important treatise on women's rights through the 1980s. When it first appeared, however, the reception was less than overwhelming. The lesson of her own life—that womanhood is not a condition one is born to but rather a posture one takes on—was fully realized here. De Beauvoir's personal frustrations were placed in terms of the general, dependent condition of women. Historical, psychological, sociological, and philosophical, *The Second Sex* does not offer any concrete solutions except "that men and women rise above their natural differentiation and unequivocally affirm their brotherhood."

If *The Second Sex* bemoans the female condition, de Beauvoir's portrayal of her own life revealed the possibilities available to the woman who can escape enslavement. Hers was a life of equality, yet de Beauvoir remained a voice and a model for those women whose lives were not liberated.

The fourth installment of her autobiography, *All Said And Done*, was written when de Beauvoir was 63. It portrays a person who has always been secure in an imperfect world. She writes: "Since I was 21, I have never been lonely. The opportunities granted to me at the beginning helped me not only to lead a happy life but to be happy in the life I led. I have been aware of my shortcomings and my limits, but I have made the best of them. When I was

tormented by what was happening in the world, it was the world I wanted to change, not my place in it."

De Beauvoir died of a circulatory ailment in a Parisian hospital April 14, 1986. Sartre had died six years earlier.

## Further Reading

The most complete biographies of Simone de Beauvoir are her four autobiographies, *Memoires of a Dutiful Daughter* (1958), *The Prime of Life* (1960), *Force of Circumstances* (1963), and *All Said And Done* (1972). Carol Ascher wrote an almost reverential analysis of the author's work, *Simone de Beauvoir—A Life of Freedom* (1981), which illustrates her effect on feminist thought. *Simone de Beauvoir* by Konrad Bieber (1979) and *Simone de Beauvoir* by Robert Cottrell (1975) both offer more critical analysis. □

# James Dunwoody Brownson De Bow

**An American business journalist, statistician, and protectionist, James Dunwoody Brownson De Bow (1820-1867) was a proslavery propagandist for Southern sectionalism.**

James D. B. De Bow, who was born in Charleston, S.C., on July 20, 1820, became an almost penniless orphan on the death of his father, a once prosperous merchant. After limited schooling and severe privations, he saved enough to enter the College of Charleston, graduating as valedictorian in 1843. Unsuccessful as a lawyer, he took up journalism in an effort to supplement his income. He contributed political and philosophical articles to the *Southern Quarterly Review* and became its editor in 1845.

De Bow was also actively involved in the campaign to promote Southern economic development, and at the 1845 commercial convention in Memphis he was a delegate and secretary for South Carolina. To further the cause of Southern commerce, he founded the *Commercial Review of the South and Southwest*, based in New Orleans. At first this monthly magazine was unsuccessful, and it was suspended in 1847. But it was revived with the aid of Maunsel White, a wealthy sugar planter, and eventually acquired a larger circulation than any other Southern magazine. In 1848 De Bow became professor of public economy, commerce, and statistics at the University of Louisiana, occupying a chair White founded for him, and he held a similar appointment at the Kentucky Collegiate and Military Institute.

## Advocating Sectional Bias

During the 1850s De Bow was an increasingly influential and partisan spokesman for the Southern viewpoint, and his writing undoubtedly helped to widen the breach in the country. He defended slavery, declaring that the South suffered neither competition between slave and free labor nor the conflict between immigrant and native workers which

occurred in the North. He advocated the reopening of the slave trade and favored tariff protection.

Predicting gloomy prospects for agriculture, De Bow called on Southerners to emulate the North by developing trade and manufactures and by providing state land grants for railroads. He believed railroads would enhance the region's strength and prosperity but, like John C. Calhoun, he regarded Federal internal improvements as corrupt and unconstitutional. De Bow strongly advocated the compilation of statistics to reveal and mobilize Southern economic resources, and in 1848-1849 he was head of the newly established Louisiana state government statistical bureau. Despite De Bow's strong sectional bias, President Franklin Pierce appointed him superintendent of the U.S. Census in 1850, a post he held until 1855. In addition to issuing the Seventh Census, he published *Industrial Resources of the South and Western States* (3 vols., 1853) and a compendium based on the census, entitled *Statistical View of the United States* (1854).

In the late 1850s De Bow was involved in plans to construct a Southern transcontinental railroad and to promote direct trade between the South and Europe. Although few of his schemes bore fruit, his importance was recognized by his presidency of the Knoxville Commercial Convention of 1857.

During the Civil War, De Bow was chief Confederate agent for the purchase and sale of cotton, and after the war he revived the *Review*. He died on Feb. 27, 1867.

## Further Reading

The two major sources are W. D. Weatherford, *James Dunwoody Brownson De Bow* (1935), and James A. McMillen, *The Works of James D. B. De Bow* (1940). The latter work contains a bibliography of De Bow's *Review*, a check list of his miscellaneous writings, and a list of references relating to him. See also the brief account in Joseph Dorfman, *The Economic Mind in American Civilization, 1606-1685*, vol. 2 (1947). □

# Louis de Broglie

**Louis Victor de Broglie, a theoretical physicist and member of the French nobility, is best known as the father of wave mechanics, a far-reaching achievement that significantly changed modern physics. For this groundbreaking work, de Broglie was awarded the 1929 Nobel Prize for physics.**

Louis Victor Pierre Raymond de Broglie was born on August 15, 1892, in Dieppe, France, to Duc Victor and Pauline d'Armaille Broglie. His father's family was of noble Piedmontese origin and had served French monarchs for centuries, for which it was awarded the hereditary title *Duc* from King Louis XIV in 1740, a title that could be held only by the head of the family. A later de Broglie assisted the Austrian side during the Seven Years War and was awarded the title *Prinz* for his contribution. This title was subsequently borne by all members of the family. Another of de Broglie's famous ancestors was his great-great-grandmother, the writer Madame de Stael.

The youngest of five children, de Broglie inherited a familial distinction for formidable scholarship. His early education was obtained at home, as befitted a great French family of the time. After the death of his father when de Broglie was fourteen, his eldest brother Maurice arranged for him to obtain his secondary education at the Lycée Janson de Sailly in Paris.

After graduating from the Sorbonne in 1909 with baccalaureates in philosophy and mathematics, de Broglie entered the University of Paris. He studied ancient history, paleography, and law before finding his niche in science, influenced by the writings of French theoretical physicist Jules Henri Poincaré. The work of his brother Maurice, who was then engaged in important, independent experimental research in X rays and radioactivity, also helped to spark de Broglie's interest in theoretical physics, particularly in basic atomic theory. In 1913, he obtained his Licencié ès Sciences from the University of Paris's Faculté des Sciences.

De Broglie's studies were interrupted by the outbreak of World War I, during which he served in the French army. Yet even the war did not take the young scientist away from the country where he would spend his entire life; for its duration, de Broglie served with the French Engineers at the wireless station under the Eiffel Tower. In 1919, after what he considered to be six wasted years in uniform, de Broglie returned to his scientific studies at his brother's laboratory.

Here he began his investigations into the nature of matter, inspired by a conundrum that had long been troubling the scientific community: the apparent physical irreconcilability of the experimentally proven dual nature of light. Radiant energy or light had been demonstrated to exhibit properties associated with particles as well as their well-documented wave-like characteristics. De Broglie was inspired to consider whether matter might not also exhibit dual properties. In his brother's laboratory, where the study of very high frequency radiation using spectroscopes was underway, de Broglie was able to bring the problem into sharper focus. In 1924, de Broglie, with over two dozen research papers on electrons, atomic structure, and X rays already to his credit, presented his conclusions in his doctoral thesis at the Sorbonne. Entitled "Investigations into the Quantum Theory," it consolidated three shorter papers he had published the previous year.

In his thesis, de Broglie postulated that all matter—including electrons, the negatively charged particles that orbit an atom's nucleus—behaves as both a particle and a wave. Wave characteristics, however, are detectable only at the atomic level, whereas the classical, ballistic properties of matter are apparent at larger scales. Therefore, rather than the wave and particle characteristics of light and matter being at odds with one another, de Broglie postulated that they were essentially the same behavior observed from different perspectives. Wave mechanics could then explain the behavior of all matter, even at the atomic scale, whereas classical Newtonian mechanics, which continued to accurately account for the behavior of observable matter, merely described a special, general case. Although, according to de Broglie, all objects have "matter waves," these waves are so small in relation to large objects that their effects are not observable and no departure from classical physics is detected. At the atomic level, however, matter waves are relatively larger and their effects become more obvious. De Broglie devised a mathematical formula, the matter wave relation, to summarize his findings.

American physicist Albert Einstein appreciated the significant of de Broglie's theory; de Broglie sent Einstein a copy of his thesis on the advice of his professors at the Sorbonne, who believed themselves not fully qualified to judge it. Einstein immediately pronounced that de Broglie had illuminated one of the secrets of the universe. Austrian physicist Erwin Schrödinger also grasped the implications of de Broglie's work and used it to develop his own theory of wave mechanics, which has since become the foundation of modern physics. Still, many physicists could not make the intellectual leap required to understand what de Broglie was describing.

De Broglie's wave matter theory remained unproven until two separate experiments conclusively demonstrated the wave properties of electrons—their ability to diffract or bend, for example. American physicists Clinton Davisson and Lester Germer and English physicist George Paget Thomson all proved that de Broglie had been correct. Later experiments would demonstrate that de Broglie's theory also explained the behavior of protons, atoms, and even molecules. These properties later found practical applica-

tions in the development of magnetic lenses, the basis for the electron microscope.

De Broglie devoted the rest of his career to teaching and to developing his theory of wave mechanics. In 1927, he attended the seventh Solvay Conference, a gathering of the most eminent minds in physics, where wave mechanics was further debated. Theorists such as German physicist Werner Karl Heisenberg, Danish physicist Niels Bohr, and English physicist Max Born favored the uncertainty or probabilistic interpretation, which proposed that the wave associated with a particle of matter provides merely statistical information on the position of that particle and does not describe its exact position. This interpretation was too radical for Schrödinger, Einstein, and de Broglie; the latter postulated the "double solution," claiming that particles of matter are transported and guided by continuous "pilot waves" and that their movement is essentially deterministic. De Broglie could not reconcile his pilot wave theory with some basic objections raised at the conference, however, and he abandoned it.

The disagreement about the manner in which matter behaves described two profoundly different ways of looking at the world. Part of the reason that de Broglie, Einstein, and others did not concur with the probabilistic view was that they could not philosophically accept that matter, and thus the world, behaves in a random way. De Broglie wished to believe in a deterministic atomic physics, where matter behaves according to certain identifiable patterns. Nonetheless, he reluctantly accepted that his pilot wave theory was flawed and throughout his teaching career instructed his students in probabilistic theory, though he never quite abandoned his belief that "God does not play dice," as Einstein had suggested.

In 1928, de Broglie was appointed professor of theoretical physics at the University of Paris's Faculty of Science. De Broglie was a thorough lecturer who addressed all aspects of wave mechanics. Perhaps because he was not inclined to encourage an interactive atmosphere in his lectures, he had no noted record of guiding young research students.

In 1929, at the age of thirty-seven, de Broglie was awarded the Nobel Prize for physics in recognition of his contribution to wave mechanics. In 1933, he accepted the specially created chair of theoretical physics at the Henri Poincaré Institute—a position he would hold for the next twenty-nine years—where he established a center for the study of modern physical theories. That same year, he was elected to the Académie des Sciences, becoming its Life Secretary in 1942; he used his influence to urge the Académie to consider the harmful effects of nuclear explosions as well as to explore the philosophical implications of his and other modern theories.

In 1943, anxious to forge stronger links between industry and science and to put modern physics, especially quantum mechanics, to practical use, de Broglie established a center within the Henri Poincaré Institute dedicated to applied mechanics. He was elected to the prestigious Academie Francaise in 1944 and, in the following year, was appointed a counsellor to the French High Commission of

Atomic Energy with his brother Maurice in recognition of their work promoting the peaceful development of nuclear energy and their efforts to bridge the gap between science and industry. Three years later, de Broglie was elected to the National Academy of the United States as a foreign member.

During his long career, de Broglie published over twenty books and numerous research papers. His preoccupation with the practical side of physics is demonstrated in his works dealing with cybernetics, atomic energy, particle accelerators, and wave-guides. His writings also include works on X rays, gamma rays, atomic particles, optics, and a history of the development of contemporary physics. He served as honorary president of the French Association of Science Writers and, in 1952, was awarded first prize for excellence in science writing by the Kalinga Foundation. In 1953, de Broglie was elected to London's Royal Society as a foreign member and, in 1958, to the French Academy of Arts and Sciences in recognition of his formidable output. With the death of his older brother Maurice two years later, de Broglie inherited the joint titles of French duke and German prince. De Broglie died of natural causes on March 19, 1987, at the age of ninety-five, having never fully resolved the controversy surrounding his theories of wave mechanics.

### Further Reading

Cline, Barbara Lovett, *Men Who Made a New Physics,* University of Chicago Press, 1987.
Guillemin, Victor, *The Story of Quantum Mechanics,* Scribner, 1968.
Heathcote, Niels H., *Nobel Prize Winners in Physics, 1901–1950,* Books for Libraries Press, 1953.
*Modern Men of Science,* Volume II, McGraw-Hill, 1968.
Weber, Robert L., *Pioneers of Science: Nobel Prize Winners in Physics,* Institute of Physics, 1980.
*Proceedings of the Royal Society,* Volume 34, 1988. □

# Eugene Victor Debs

**Eugene Victor Debs (1855-1926), a leading American union organizer and, after 1896, a prominent Socialist, ran five times as the Socialist party nominee for president.**

Eugene V. Debs was born on Nov. 5, 1855, in Terre Haute, Ind., where his French immigrant parents, after considerable hardship, had settled. Debs began work in the town's railroad shops at the age of 15, soon becoming a locomotive fireman. Thrown out of work by the depression of the 1870s, he left Terre Haute briefly to find a railroad job but soon returned to work as a clerk in a wholesale grocery company. Even though he was no longer a fireman, he joined the Brotherhood of Locomotive Firemen in 1874 and rose rapidly in the union. In 1878 he

became an associate editor of the *Firemen's Magazine.* Two years later he was appointed editor of the magazine and secretary-treasurer of the brotherhood.

Debs also pursued a political career in the early 1880s. A popular and earnest young man, he was elected city clerk of Terre Haute as a Democrat in 1879 and reelected in 1881. Soon after his second term ended in January 1884, he was elected to the Indiana Legislature, serving one term.

### Changing Concept of Unionism

During the 1880s Debs remained a craft unionist, devoted to "orthodox" ideals of work, thrift, and respectable unionism. With the Firemen's Brotherhood as his base, he sought to develop cooperation among the various railroad brotherhoods. A weak federation was achieved in 1889, but it soon collapsed due to internal rivalries. Tired and discouraged, Debs resigned his positions in the Firemen's Brotherhood in 1892, only to be reelected over his protest.

Debs's new project was an industrial union, one which would unite *all* railroad men, whatever their specific craft, in one union. By mid-1893, the American Railway Union (ARU) was established, with Debs as its first president. Labor discontent and the severe national depression beginning in 1893 swelled the union's ranks. The ARU won a major strike against the Great Northern Railroad early in the spring of 1894. Nevertheless, when the Pullman Company works near Chicago were struck in May, Debs was reluctant to endorse a sympathetic strike of all railroad men. His union took a militant stance, however, refusing to move Pullman

railroad cars nationally. By July, Debs felt the boycott was succeeding, but a sweeping legal injunction against the union leadership and the use of Federal troops broke the strike. Debs was sentenced to 6 months in jail for contempt of court, and his lawyer, Clarence Darrow, appealed unsuccessfully to the U.S. Supreme Court.

## Conversion to Socialism

Having moved from craft to industrial unionism, Debs now converted to socialism. Convinced that capitalism and competition inevitably led to class strife, Debs argued that the profit system should be replaced by a cooperative commonwealth. Although he advocated radical change, he rejected revolutionary violence and chose to bring his case to the public through political means. He participated in the establishment of the Social Democratic party in 1898 and its successor, the Socialist Party of America, in 1901.

Debs was the Socialist candidate for president five times. His role was that of a spokesman for radical reform rather than that of a party theorist. A unifying agent, he tried to remain aloof from the persistent factional struggle between the evolutionary Socialists and the party's more revolutionary western wing. As the party's presidential candidate in 1900 and 1904, he led the Socialists to a fourfold increase in national voting strength, from about 97,000 to more than 400,000 votes. While the party's vote did not increase significantly in 1908, Debs drew attention to the Socialist case by a dramatic national tour in the "Red Special," a campaign train. The year 1912 proved to be the high point for Debs and his party. He won 897,011 votes, 6 percent of the total.

## Imprisonment for Sedition

When World War I began in 1914, the party met with hard times. The Socialists were the only party to oppose economic assistance to the Allies and the preparedness movement. Debs, while refusing the Socialist nomination for president in 1916, endorsed the party view that President Woodrow Wilson's neutrality policies would lead to war. In 1917 America's entrance into war resulted in widespread antagonism toward the Socialists. When Debs spoke out in 1918 against the war and Federal harassment of Socialists, he was arrested and convicted of sedition under the wartime Espionage Act. He ran for the last time as the Socialist presidential candidate while in prison, receiving nearly a million votes, more actual votes (but a smaller percentage of the total) than in 1912.

On Christmas Day 1921, President Warren G. Harding pardoned Debs, but Debs could do little to restore life to the Socialist party, battered by the war years and split over the Russian Revolution. Debs had welcomed the Revolution; yet he became very critical of the dictatorial aspects of the Soviet regime, refusing to ally himself with the American Communist party. Debs died on Oct. 20, 1926, having won wide respect as a resourceful evangelist for a more humane, cooperative society.

## Further Reading

The most recent edition of Debs's writings is *Writings and Speeches of Eugene V. Debs,* with an introduction by Arthur M. Schlesinger, Jr. (1948). There are two excellent studies of Debs's career: Ray Ginger, *The Bending Cross: A Biography of Eugene Victor Debs* (1949), and H. Wayne Morgan, *Eugene V. Debs: Socialist for President* (1962). McAlister Coleman, *Eugene V. Debs: A Man Unafraid* (1930), is the best of the older biographies. Ira Kipnis, *The American Socialist Movement, 1897-1912* (1952), and David A. Shannon, *The Socialist Party of America* (1955), are invaluable sources on the Socialist party. □

# Achille Claude Debussy

**The French composer Achille Claude Debussy (1862-1918) developed a strongly individual style and also created a language that broke definitively with the procedures of classical tonality.**

The world having made peace with his innovations by the time of his death, Claude Debussy subsequently came to be regarded as the impressionist composer par excellence—a creator of poetic tone pictures, a master colorist, and the author of many charming miniatures (including *Clair de lune, Golliwog's Cake Walk,* and *Girl with the Flaxen Hair*). Only a handful of critics between World Wars I and II were concerned with the historical impact of his accomplishment, the scope of which is gradually coming to be recognized. It is generally accepted today that his coloristic harmonies do not simply "float" but "function" in terms of a structure analogous to the classical tonal structure and are governed by equally lucid concepts of tension and repose.

Claude Debussy was born on Aug. 22, 1862, at St-Germain-en-Laye into an impoverished family. Thanks to his godparents, he was able to enter the Paris Conservatory 10 years later. Although he worked hard to gain a solid grounding, the archaic and mechanical nature of much of what he studied there did not escape him. Still, certain aspects of his training were exciting, notably his introduction to the operas of Richard Wagner.

## Attitude to Wagner

In 1884 Debussy won the Prix de Rome for his cantata *L'Enfant prodigue.* In Rome the following year he was homesick for Paris, and he wrote that one of his few solaces was the study of Wagner's opera *Tristan und Isolde.* Not many years later Debussy harshly criticized Wagner, but his scorn seems directed more toward Wagner's dramaturgy than toward his music. Although Debussy could ridicule the *dramatis personae* of *Parsifal,* he did not neglect to add that the opera was "one of the finest monuments of sound that have been raised to the imperturbable glory of music." Throughout his life Debussy was fascinated by the chromatic richness of the Wagnerian style, but in keeping with Verlaine's epigram, "One must take eloquence and wring

its neck,'' he would categorically reject Wagnerian rhetoric. His inclinations were toward conciseness and understatement.

## Influence of the Gamelan Orchestra

At the height of his enthusiasm for Wagner, Debussy had an experience as important for his later development as Wagner had been for his beginnings: the revelation of the Javanese gamelan at the Paris World Exposition of 1889. This exotic orchestra, with its variety of bells, xylophones, and gongs, produced a succession of softly percussive effects and cross rhythms that Debussy was later to describe as a ''counterpoint by comparison with which that of Palestrina is child's play.'' What has come to be regarded as the typical impressionist texture—an atmosphere of melodic and harmonic shapes in which dissonant tones are placed so as to reduce their ''shock'' value to a minimum and heighten their ''overtone'' value to a maximum—was a logical conclusion to the explorations in sonority of 19th-century European composers. Yet without the specific influence of the gamelan Debussy might never have realized this texture in all its complexity.

The effect of the experience at the Exposition of 1889 was not immediately manifested in Debussy's work. It was the process of growth in the years 1890-1900 that brought the elements of the exotic music of the gamelan into play with others already discernible in his style and produced a new tonal language. The completion of this process toward the end of the decade can thus serve as a line of demarcation dividing the earlier years, not without their master-

pieces—*Ariettes oubliées* (1888), *Prélude à l'après-midi d'un faune* (1892; *Afternoon of a Faun*), and the String Quartet (1893)—from the period of maturity.

## Mature Works

Debussy's first large-scale piece of his mature period, the *Nocturnes* for orchestra (1893-1899), is contemporaneous with the work on his only completed opera, *Pelléas et Mélisande* (1894-1902), based on a play by Maurice Maeterlinck. The notoriety surrounding the premiere of *Pelléas* in 1902 made Debussy the most controversial figure in musical France and divided Paris into two strongly partisan camps.

Two years later Debussy abandoned his wife of 5 years, Rosalie Texier, to live with and eventually marry Emma Bardac, a woman of some means. The first taste of existence free from material worry seems to have had a beneficial effect on his productivity. During these years he wrote some of his most enduring works: *La Mer* (1905) and *Ibéria* (1908), both for orchestra; *Images* (1905), *Children's Corner Suite* (1908), and two books of *Préludes* (1910-1912), all for piano solo.

Debussy's pieces of the following years show certain marked changes in style. Not as well known as his works of the preceding years but in no way inferior, they have less surface appeal and are therefore more difficult to approach. It is ironic that just when he was exploring new avenues of thought he was in a sense relegated to the shadows by a ''radicalism'' more sensational than anything connected with *Pelléas* 10 years earlier. Debussy's ballet *Jeux*, his last and most sophisticated orchestral score, which had its premiere on May 15, 1913, was virtually eclipsed by the scandal of Igor Stravinsky's ballet *Sacre du printemps* (*Rite of Spring*) on May 29. Debussy's ambivalent attitude toward Stravinsky's music may reflect a certain resentment of the younger composer's noisy arrival on the scene. Debussy evinced a genuine, if limited, admiration for Stravinsky's work and even incorporated certain Stravinsky-like effects in *En blanc et noir* (1915) and the *Études* (1915). Whether or not Debussy's general tendency in his late pieces to achieve a drier, less ''impressionistic'' sound is the direct result of Stravinsky's influence is difficult to say.

When Debussy composed these last-mentioned works, he was already suffering from a fatal cancer. He completed only three of a projected group of six sonatas ''for various instruments'' (1915-1917). He died in Paris on March 25, 1918.

## Characteristics of Debussy's Music

A notable characteristic of Debussy's music is its finesse, but it is a characteristic applicable to almost every other aspect of his artistic behavior as well. His choice of texts to set to music (from Verlaine, Stéphane Mallarmé, and Maeterlinck), his own efforts in verse for the song set *Proses lyriques* (1894), and his fine prose essays (posthumously compiled under the title *Monsieur Croche, the Dilletante-Hater*) all attest to a culture that must have been mostly innate, since there is so little evidence of it in his early family life or formal education.

Finesse and understatement would seem to reinforce the mysterious and dreamlike elements in Debussy's music. In this respect his opera *Pelléas* is the key work of his creative life, because through it he not only achieved the synthesis of his mature style, but also in the art of allusion of Maeterlinck's play found the substance of what he could express in music more tellingly than anyone else. The words and actions of the opera pass as if in a dream, but the dream is suffused with an inescapable feeling of dread. Debussy brings to this feeling a disquieting intensity through music of pervasive quiet, broken rarely and only momentarily by outbursts revealing the underlying terror.

Similarly, in *Nuages* (*Clouds*), the first movement of the *Nocturnes,* the clouds are not cheerful billows in a sunlit sky but ominous signs—of what we cannot be sure. Characteristically, Debussy leaves us with a mystery: he presents us with the imminence of disaster but not disaster itself. Premonition is a force capable of disrupting the amiable surface of Debussy's music and is also one of the music's chief emotional strengths. What is more, it is a symbol of Debussy's position vis-à-vis European music at the turn of the century.

## Further Reading

The standard biography for many years was Léon Vallas, *Claude Debussy: His Life and Works* (trans. 1933). Its scholarliness and serious approach give it lasting value. It has been joined in recent years by Edward Lockspeiser's indispensable *Debussy: His Life and Mind* (2 vols., 1962-1965). This study places Debussy in the context of Paris at the turn of the century and gives a vivid picture of an extraordinary moment in France's cultural life. See also Oscar Thompson, *Debussy: Man and Artist* (1937); Rollo H. Myers, *Debussy* (1948); and Victor I. Seroff, *Debussy: Musician of France* (1956). "The Adventure and Achievement of Debussy" in William W. Austin, *Music in the 20th Century* (1966), is a valuable combination of biography and analysis. □

# Peter Joseph William Debye

**The main contribution of the Dutch-born American physical chemist Peter Joseph William Debye (1884-1966) was the development of methods based on induced dipole moments and x-ray diffraction for the investigation of molecular structures.**

Peter Debye was born on March 24, 1884, in Maastricht, Netherlands, the son of William and Maria Reumkens Debije. At the age of 17 Debye entered the Technical Institute of Aachen and earned his diploma in electrical engineering in 1905. He immediately obtained the position of assistant in technical mechanics at the institute. At the same time his interest in physics received strong promptings from Arthur Sommerfeld, then serving on the faculty. Debye followed Sommerfeld to the University of Munich and obtained his doctorate in physics by a mathematical analysis of the pressure of radiation on spheres of arbitrary electrical properties.

The dissertation and a 1907 paper on Foucault currents in rectangular conductors gave clear evidence of Debye's ability to produce the mathematical tools demanded by his topics. A fitting recognition of Debye's youthful excellence was his succession in 1911, at the age of 27, to Albert Einstein in the chair of theoretical physics at the University of Zurich. While in Zurich he worked out, on the basis of Max Planck's and Einstein's ideas, the first complete theory of the specific heat of solids and the equally important theory of polar molecules. Debye was professor of theoretical physics at the University of Utrecht from 1912 until 1914, when he received the prestigious post of director of the theoretical branch of the Institute of Physics at the University of Göttingen. In 1915 he became editor of the famed *Physikalische Zeitschrift* and served in that capacity for 25 years.

## X-ray Research

In Göttingen, Debye started a most fruitful collaboration with P. Scherrer. Their first paper, "X-ray Interference Patterns of Particles Oriented at Random" (1916), gave immediate evidence of the enormous potentialities of their powder method to explore the structure of crystals with very high symmetry. It also proved very useful in work with polycrystalline metals and colloidal systems. Two years later Debye and Scherrer extended the method from the study of the coordination of atoms to the arrangement of electrons inside the atom. It was in this connection that they formulated the important concept of "atomic form factor." Debye and Scherrer formed such a close team that when, in

1920, Debye became professor of experimental physics and director of the physics laboratory at the Swiss Federal Technical Institute in Zurich, Scherrer followed him there. The two inaugurated a most influential x-ray research center which attracted students from all over the world.

In the field of x-ray research Debye's signal success in Zurich was his demonstration in early 1923 that in the collision between x-rays and electrons, energy and momentum are conserved; he also suggested that the interaction between electromagnetic radiation and electrons must therefore be considered as a collision between photons and electrons. But Debye's principal achievement in Zurich consisted in the formulation of his theories of magnetic cooling and of interionic attraction in electrolyte solutions. The latter work, in which he collaborated with E. Hückel, was closely related to Debye's pioneering research on dipole moments. Debye had already been for 2 years the director of the Physical Institute at the University of Leipzig when his classic monograph, *Polar Molecules,* was published in 1928.

### War and Postwar Years

Debye's rather rapid moves from one university to another were motivated by his eagerness to work with the best available experimental apparatus. Thus in 1934 he readily accepted the invitation of the University of Berlin to serve both as professor at the university and as director of the Kaiser Wilhelm Institute. The latter establishment, now known as Max Planck Institute, was just completing, with the help of the Rockefeller Foundation, a new laboratory which was to represent the best of its kind on the Continent. During his stay in Berlin, Debye became the recipient of the Nobel Prize in chemistry for 1936. It was awarded to him "for his contributions to our knowledge of molecular structure through his investigations on dipole moments and on the diffraction of x-rays and electrons in gases."

Meanwhile, the Nazi government began to renege on its original promise that Debye would not be asked to renounce his Dutch citizenship while serving as director of the Kaiser Wilhelm Institute, a post with a lifetime tenure. Shortly after World War II broke out, he was informed that he could no longer enter the laboratory of the Institute unless he assumed German citizenship. As Debye refused, he was told to stay home and keep busy writing books. He succeeded in making his way to Italy and from there to Cornell University, which invited him to give the Baker Lectures in 1940.

Debye made Cornell his permanent home. He served there as head of the chemistry department for the next 10 years. His wartime service to his adopted country (he became a citizen in 1946) concerned the synthetic rubber program. In pure research he further investigated, in collaboration with his son, Peter P. Debye, the light-scattering properties of polymers, on which he based the now generally accepted absolute determination of their molecular weights. He was a member of all leading scientific societies and the recipient of all major awards in chemistry. His outgoing personality kept generating enthusiasm and goodwill throughout his long life, which came to an end on Nov.

2, 1966. Since 1913 he had been married to Mathilde Alberer, who shared his lively interest in gardening and fishing.

### Further Reading

The best sources available on Debye's life and on the various aspects of his scientific work are the introductory essays in *The Collected Papers of Peter J. W. Debye* (1954). A detailed biographical profile of Debye is in the Royal Society, *Biographical Memoirs of Fellows of the Royal Society,* vol. 16 (1970). Debye is discussed in Eduard Farber, *Nobel Prize Winners in Chemistry, 1901-1961* (1953; rev. ed. 1963); Aaron I. Ihde, *The Development of Modern Chemistry* (1964); and *Chemistry: Nobel Lectures, Including Presentation Speeches and Laureates' Biographies, 1922-41,* published by the Nobel Foundation (1966). □

# Stephen Decatur

**The American naval officer Stephen Decatur (1779-1820) is best known for his daring exploits in the Tripolitan War and as a successful commander in the War of 1812.**

Stephen Decatur was born on Jan. 5, 1779, at Sinepuxent, Md. He studied at the Episcopal Academy and then at the University of Pennsylvania. After working briefly in Philadelphia, Decatur accepted a midshipman's commission at the outset of the naval war with France (1798-1800). He won quick promotion to lieutenant in May 1799.

Decatur saw action in the war with Tripoli and, under Commodore Edward Preble, commanded the 12-gun schooner *Enterprise.* On Feb. 16, 1804, Decatur led the daring evening expedition that destroyed the captured frigate *Philadelphia* in the Tripoli harbor. He was quickly promoted to captain, and as such he commanded a division of gunboats in each of Preble's bombardments of Tripoli. In the first attack, on August 3, Decatur and his crew boarded and captured two Tripolitan gunboats; such feats made Decatur the most dashing figure of the war.

In 1806 Decatur married Susan Wheeler, daughter of a wealthy Virginia merchant. Two years later he was made commander of the southeastern naval forces. He also sat on the court-martial board in 1808 that suspended Capt. James Barron after the *Chesapeake-Leopard* affair. In 1811 he served as president of the court of inquiry following the *President-Little-Belt* affair.

In the War of 1812 Decatur was in command when the *United States* scored a victory over the British frigate *Macedonian* on Oct. 25, 1812, near Madeira off the Moroccan coast. When the *United States* was blockaded in New London, Conn., in 1814, Decatur and his crew were transferred to the *President.* In a violent storm on the night of Jan. 14, 1815, the *President* tried to run the British blockade but was grounded on a sandbar for 2 hours and somewhat damaged; the next morning it was sighted by the blockading fleet.

After a lengthy chase and moderate casualties suffered in a brisk fight with the *Endymion,* the American ship surrendered. A court of inquiry credited Decatur's capture to unforeseeable ship damage and praised him highly.

Following the War of 1812, Decatur led an expedition to the Mediterranean that successfully exacted payment from Algiers for damages inflicted on Americans during the war by the Barbary pirates. Fetes and dinners followed his return. Decatur gave the much-repeated patriotic response to one toast: "Our Country! In her intercourse with foreign nations may she always be in the right; but our country, right or wrong." From 1815 until his death Decatur served on the Board of Navy Commissioners. He died on March 22, 1820, in a duel near Bladensburg, Md., with Capt. James Barron, who held Decatur responsible for his own failure to be reinstated to command. First buried near Washington, D.C., Decatur's remains were transferred in 1846 to St. Peter's Churchyard, Philadelphia, beside his parents' grave.

## Further Reading

A competent biography is Charles Lee Lewis, *The Romantic Decatur* (1937). The source materials for Decatur's participation in the Barbary Wars are available in *Naval Documents Related to the United States Wars with the Barbary Powers* (7 vols., 1939-1944). A critical evaluation of Decatur's participation in the War of 1812 is Alfred Thayer Mahan, *Sea Power in Its Relation to the War of 1812* (2 vols., 1905). □

# Ruby Dee

**Ruby Dee's acting career has spanned more than 50 years and has included theater, radio, television, and movies. She has also been active in such organizations as the National Association for the Advancement of Colored People (NAACP), the Southern Christian Leadership Conference (SCLC), and the Congress of Racial Equality (CORE).**

## Early roles

Ruby Dee was born in Cleveland, Ohio, on October 27, 1924, but grew up in Harlem, attending Hunter College in New York. In 1942, she appeared in *South Pacific* with Canada Lee. Five years later, she met Ossie Davis while they were both playing in *Jeb.* They were married two years later.

Ruby Dee's movies roles from this period include parts in *No Way Out* (1950), *Edge of the City* (1957), *Raisin in the Sun* (1961), Genet's *The Balcony* (1963), and *Purlie Victorious* (1963), written by Davis. Since 1960, she has appeared often on network television.

In 1965, Ruby Dee became the first black actress to appear in major roles at the American Shakespeare Festival in Stratford, Connecticut. Appearances in movies including *The Incident* (1967), *Uptight* (1968), *Buck and the Preacher* (1972), *Black Girl* (directed by Davis) (1972), and *Countdown at Kusini* (1976) followed. Her musical satire *Take It from the Top,* in which she appeared with her husband in a showcase run at the Henry Street Settlement Theatre in New York premiered in 1979.

As a team, Ruby Dee and Ossie Davis have recorded several talking story albums for Caedmon. In 1974, they produced "The Ruby Dee/ Ossie Davis Story Hour," which was sponsored by Kraft Foods and carried by more than 60 stations of the National Black Network. Together they founded the Institute of New Cinema Artists to train young people for jobs in films and television, and then the Recording Industry Training Program to develop jobs in the music industry for disadvantaged youths. In 1981, Alcoa funded a television series on the Public Broadcasting System titled "With Ossie and Ruby," which used guests to provide an anthology of the arts. Recent film credits include *Cat People* (1982) and, with Ossie Davis, Spike Lee's *Do the Right Thing* (1989).

## "A neat piece of juggling"

Actress and social activist Ruby Dee expressed her philosophy in *I Dream a World: Portraits of Black Women Who Changed America:* "You just try to do everything that comes up. Get up an hour earlier, stay up an hour later, make the time. Then you look back and say, 'Well, that was a neat piece of juggling there—school, marriage, babies, career.' The enthusiasms took me through the action, not the measuring of it or the reasonableness."

Dee's acting career has spanned more than 50 years and has included theater, radio, television, and movies. She and her husband, actor Ossie Davis, have raised three children and been active in such organizations as the National Association for the Advancement of Colored People (NAACP), the Southern Christian Leadership Conference (SCLC), and the Congress of Racial Equality (CORE), as well as supporters of civil rights leaders such as Dr. Martin Luther King and Malcolm X.

Ruby Ann Wallace was born on October 27, 1924, in Cleveland, Ohio. Her parents, Marshall and Emma Wallace, in search of better job opportunities, moved the family to New York City, ultimately settling in Harlem. Emma Wallace was determined not to let her children become victims of the ghetto that the area was quickly becoming. Dee and her siblings studied music and literature. In the evening, under the guidance of their school-teacher mother, they read aloud to each other from the poetry of Longfellow, Wordsworth, and Paul Laurence Dunbar. The influence of this education became apparent early in Dee's life when as a teenager she began submitting poetry to the *New York Amsterdam News,* a black weekly newspaper.

## Pursued Education

Her love of English and poetry motivated Dee to study the arts, especially the spoken arts. Her mother had been an elocutionist who, as a young girl, wanted to be in the theater. Fully realizing the value of a good education, Dee decided that the public schools of Harlem, where so many of the black girls were being "educated" to become domes-

tics, were not for her. She underwent the rigorous academic testing required for admittance to Hunter High School, one of New York's first-rate schools that drew the brightest girls. The self-confidence and poise that Dee's mother had instilled in her helped Ruby adjust to her new environment populated with white girls from more privileged backgrounds. A black music teacher, Miss Peace, provided encouragement to the young Ruby, telling her to go as far and as quickly as she could.

While in high school, Dee decided to pursue acting. In an interview with the *New York Times,* she related that this decision was made "one beautiful afternoon in high school when I read aloud from a play and my classmates applauded." After graduation she entered Hunter College. There Dee joined the American Negro Theater (ANT) and adopted the on-stage name Ruby Dee. The struggling theater had little money, so in addition to rehearsing their parts the troupe sold tickets door-to-door in Harlem and performed all the maintenance duties in the theater, located in a basement auditorium of the 135th Street Library. Dee found the work she did with the ANT to be a memorable part of her training. Other young actors who started at the ANT and eventually became famous include Harry Belafonte, Earle Hyman, and Sidney Poitier.

While still at Hunter College, Dee took a class in radio training offered through the American Theater Wing. This training led to a part in the radio serial *Nora Drake.* When she graduated from Hunter College in 1945, Dee took a job at an export house as a French and Spanish translator. To earn extra income, she worked in a factory painting designs on buttons. Dee knew, however, that the theater was to be her destiny.

## Landed First Broadway Role

In 1946 Dee got her first Broadway role in *Jeb,* a drama about a returning black war hero. Ossie Davis, the actor in the title role, caught Dee's attention. After watching him do a scene in which he was tying a necktie, Dee experienced an awareness that she and Davis would share some type of connection. Critical reviews of the play were good, but the play ran for only nine performances. Dee's intuition, however, proved to be true. She and Davis became close friends and worked together in the road company production of *Anna Lucasta.* Later they played Evelyn and Stewart in Garson Kanin's *Smile of the World* and were married on December 9, 1948, during a break in rehearsals for that play.

Dee's first movie was *Love in Syncopation,* which was released in 1946. In 1950 she appeared in *The Jackie Robinson Story* as the legendary baseball player's wife. Also in that year she appeared in *No Way Out,* the story of a black doctor—played by Sidney Poitier—who is accused of causing the death of his white patient. The film was revolutionary for its time because it was the first American film in which blacks and whites confronted each other in a realistic way.

Over the next decade, Dee appeared in several plays and movies in which she was cast as the consummate wife or girlfriend—patient, always understanding, all-forgiving.

Such roles spurred at least one publication to refer to her as "the Negro June Allyson." A few parts helped Dee break free from this stereotyping. Of note is the role of the ebullient Lutiebelle Gussie Mae Jenkins in Davis's 1961 play *Purlie Victorious.* In this satire on black/white relationships, Davis plays the preacher Purlie who, with Lutiebelle's assistance, helps to outwit a white plantation owner. In 1963 this highly successful play was made into a movie titled *Gone Are the Days* and was later musicalized as *Purlie.*

Dee again was typecast as a long-suffering wife and daughter-in-law in the Broadway production of Lorraine Hansberry's *A Raisin in the Sun.* She recreated her role as Ruth Younger in 1963 film version of the play. Donald Bogle, in his book *Toms, Coons, Mulattoes, Mammies, and Bucks,* noted that prior to *A Raisin in the Sun,* Dee's roles made her appear to be "the typical woman born to be hurt" instead of a complete person. Bogle continued, "But in *A Raisin in the Sun,* Ruby Dee forged her inhibitions, her anemia, and her repressed and taut ache to convey beautifully the most searing kind of black torment."

## Broke Free From Typecasting

The one role Dee feels put an end to her stereotyped image was that of Lena in the 1970 production of Athol Fugard's *Boesman and Lena.* Fugard, a white South African dramatist, portrays the dilemma of South Africa's mixed race people who are rejected by both blacks and whites. Lena wanders the South African wilderness and ekes out a living with her brutish husband Boesman, played by James Earl Jones. Dee told interviewer Patricia Bosworth in the *New York Times* that "Lena is the greatest role I've ever had." It was also her first theater role since 1966, and she was not sure she could do it. Her husband encouraged her, saying that the part could have been written for her even though Fugard had originally written the role of Lena with a white actress in mind.

Dee immediately felt a bond with Lena. "I relate to her particular reality," she told Bosworth, "because it is mine and every black woman's. I can understand the extent of her poverty and her filth and absolute subjugation. . . . On one level [Boesman and Lena] represent the universal struggle of black against white, man against woman. But they are also victims of something that is permeating an entire culture."

Dee finally realized that she was being offered a great part at a time when few, if any, good parts were written for black actresses. In the *New York Times* interview she revealed, "I have always been reticent about expressing myself totally in a role. But with Lena I am suddenly, gloriously free. I can't explain how this frail, tattered little character took me over and burrowed so deep inside me that my voice changed and I began to move differently. . . . [I am as] alive with her as I've never been on stage." Critics took note of Dee's performance. Clive Barnes wrote in his *New York Times* review of the play: "Ruby Dee as Lena is giving the finest performance I have ever seen. . . . Never for a moment do you think she is acting. . . . You have no sense of someone portraying a role. . . . her manner, her entire being have a quality of wholeness that is rarely encountered in the theater."

Beginning in the early 1960s, Dee made numerous appearances on television including roles in the *Play of the Week* and in such television series as *The Fugitive, The Defenders, The Great Adventure,* and *The Nurses.* In 1968 she played Alma Miles, the wife of a neurosurgeon, on *Peyton Place,* the first black actresses to be featured in this widely-watched nighttime serial. Her performance in an episode of the series *East Side, West Side* earned her an Emmy nomination. In 1991 Dee's performance in *Decoration Day* won her an Emmy.

Dee and Davis collaborated on several projects designed to promote black heritage in general and other black artists in particular. In 1974 they produced *The Ruby Dee/ Ossie Davis Story Hour* which appeared on over 60 stations on the National Black Network. In conjunction with the Public Broadcasting System (PBS), they produced the series *With Ossie and Ruby* in 1981. It was work that Dee found particularly satisfying because she got to travel the country talking to authors and others who could put the black experience in perspective. She believes that the series made black people look at themselves outside of the problems of racism.

## Took Up Civil Rights Causes

Issues of equality and civil rights have long been a concern of Dee's. Her activism can be traced back to when she was 11 years old and her music teacher lost her job when funds for the Federal Music Program were cut. The teacher, terrified that she could not find another job in the Depression-ridden country, committed suicide. At a mass meeting following the teacher's death, Adam Clayton Powell was the principal speaker and Dee was chosen to speak in favor of restoring the music program. Several years would pass before Dee became actively involved in civil rights.

The year was 1953, and the cause was Julius and Ethel Rosenberg. The Rosenbergs had been convicted of wartime sabotage and were scheduled to be executed. Dee's vocal protest of the planned executions were expressed in several interviews with the press. Some accused her of being exploited by the Communists; others were convinced she was a card-carrying member of the party.

Dee's notoriety for denouncing the U.S. Government's decision to execute the Jewish Rosenbergs eventually parlayed itself into her first non-black part in a play. In *The World of Sholem Aleichem,* Dee played the Defending Angel. This experience helped Dee realize that racism and discrimination were not the exclusive provinces of black people—other races and cultures experienced it also. Dee began to understand how art and life blended together and how all human cultures are interrelated. She was inspired by these events to make a firm commitment to social activism.

Future events solidified this commitment. In September 1963, a hate bomb was thrown into a Birmingham, Alabama, church. The bomb killed four young black girls as they sat in their Sunday school class. People throughout the country were outraged by this senseless murder. Dee and Davis, along with other artists, formed the Association of

Artists for Freedom. The group launched a successful boycott against extravagant Christmas spending and urged people to donate the money to various civil rights groups. Dee and Davis were involved in and supported several other civil rights protests and causes including Martin Luther King's March on Washington. In 1970 the National Urban League honored them with the Frederick Douglass Award, a medallion presented each year for distinguished leadership toward equal opportunity.

### Established Dramatic Art Scholarship

By establishing the Ruby Dee Scholarship in Dramatic Art, Dee put into action her commitment to help others. The scholarship is awarded to talented young black women who want to become established in the acting profession. Both she and Davis have donated money and countless hours of time to causes in which they believe. They founded the Institute of New Cinema Artists as a way to train chosen young people for film and television jobs. Their Recording Industry Training Program helps develop jobs for disadvantaged youths interested in the music industry.

Dee has also used her talent to make recordings for the blind and to narrate videocassettes that address issues of race relations. She has reinterpreted West African folktales for children and published them as *Two Ways to Count to Ten* and *Tower to Heaven*. Dee returned to poetry, her early love, to edit *Glowchild and Other Poems* and to collect her poems and short stories in a volume titled *My One Good Nerve*.

Dee's remarkable acting talent has endured over the years. She continued to appear in theater, movies and television throughout the 1970s and '80s. In 1990 Dee appeared in the television movie *The Court Martial of Jackie Robinson*, playing Jackie Robinson's mother Mallie. John Leonard writing in *New York* laments that the movie gives Dee too little to do but commends Dee for "deliver[ing] one fine line" as she reprimands her son who is about to sabotage his courtship with Rachel. With fervor Dee, in the role of Mallie, states: "I didn't raise my boys to have sharecropper minds!" Leonard attributes the conviction with which Dee played her part to the fact that she played the role of Rachel herself over 40 years ago.

Director Spike Lee cast Dee in the role of Mother Sister—and Davis in the role of "Da Mayor"—for his controversial 1989 film *Do the Right Thing*. As Mother Sister, Dee plays a widow who lives in a brownstone and spends her time watching the neighborhood through a ground-floor window. In *New Republic* Stanley Kauffmann described Dee as "that fine actress with an unfulfilled career in white America" and described her role in Lee's movie "as a sort of neighborhood Delphic oracle." Davis plays a beer-drinking street philosopher who is in love with Mother Sister.

As racial tension rises in the neighborhood, Mother Sister and Da Mayor are unable to do anything to diffuse it. According to Terrence Rafferty in the *New Yorker,* these two characters "stand for the older generation, whose cynical, 'realistic' attitude toward living in a white society may have kept them from finding ways out of their poverty but may

also have helped keep them alive." Lee also cast the pair as the parents of the main character in *Jungle Fever.*

In 1988 *Ebony* featured Dee and Davis as one of "Three Great Love Stories." Explaining the success of their long marriage, Dee told *Ebony:* "The ratio of the good times to the bad times is better than 50-50 and that helps a lot. . . . We shared a great deal in common; we didn't have any distractions as to where we stood in society. We were Black activists. We had a common understanding." Davis added, "We believe in honesty. We believe in simplicity. . . . We believe in love. We believe in the family. We believe in Black history, and we believe heavily in *involvement.*"

### Further Reading

*Black Women in America,* Carlson, 1993.
Bogle, Donald, *Blacks in American Film and Television,* Garland, 1988.
Bogle, Donald, *Toms, Coons, Mulattoes, Mammies, and Bucks,* Viking, 1973.
*Directory of Blacks in the Performing Arts,* Scarecrow Press, 1990.
Fax, Elton C., *Contemporary Black Leaders,* Dodd, 1970.
Lanker, Brian, *I Dream a World: Portraits of Black Women Who Changed America,* Stewart, Tabori, Chang, 1989.
Salley, Columbus, editor, *The Black 100,* Citadel Press, 1993.
*Commonweal,* January 13, 1989, p. 21; July 14, 1989, p. 403.
*Cosmopolitan,* August 1991, p. 28.
*Ebony,* February 1988, p. 152.
*Essence,* May 1987, p. 28.
*Jet,* December 5, 1988, p. 55.
*Library Journal,* October 1, 1991, p. 153; January 1992, p. 198.
*Nation,* July 17, 1989, p. 98.
*National Review,* August 4, 1989, p. 45.
*New Republic,* July 3, 1989, p. 24.
*Newsweek,* July 3, 1989, p. 64.
*New York,* August 22, 1988, p. 142; October 22, 1990, p. 136; November 26, 1990, p. 165.
*New Yorker,* July 24, 1989, p. 78.
*New York Times,* June 23, 1970; July 12, 1970.
*People,* July 3, 1989, p. 13.
*Publishers Weekly,* June 10, 1988, p. 80; May 17, 1991, p. 63.
*School Library Journal,* October 1990, p. 76; July 1991, p. 67; March 1992, p. 196. □

# Ada E. Deer

**Ada E. Deer (born 1935) was the first woman to head the U.S. Bureau of Indian Affairs (BIA).**

L ife-long advocate for social justice, Ada E. Deer was the first woman to head the U.S. Bureau of Indian Affairs (BIA). As Assistant Secretary for Indian Affairs in the Interior Department, she was "turning the BIA upside down and shaking it," as she told hundreds of Navajos in Arizona a month after taking office in late July of 1993. For Deer, an activist for the rights of American Indians, youth, and women, turning things upside down was nothing new. Her career as a social worker, leader in numerous community and political organizations, and her successful fight to restore federal recognition to the Menominee Tribe all attest to her actions on behalf of human rights and her belief in coalition building. She told members of the Alaska Federation of Natives in August of 1993, as quoted in the *Tundra Times,* "I want to emphasize (that) my administration will be based on the Indian values of caring, sharing, and respect. . . . These values have been missing too long in the halls of government."

Deer was born in Keshena on the Menominee Indian Reservation in northeastern Wisconsin on August 7, 1935. She is the eldest of five children (her siblings are Joseph Deer, Jr., Robert Deer, Ferial Skye, and Connie Deer); four other children died in infancy. Her mother, Constance Stockton (Wood) Deer, is an Anglo-American from Philadelphia and a former BIA nurse. Her father was Joseph Deer, a nearly full-blood Menominee Indian who was a former employee of the Menominee Indian Mills; he died at the age of 85 on January 10, 1994. For the first 18 years of Deer's life, her family lived in a log cabin near the Wolf River with no running water or electricity. Deer told the Senate Committee on Indian Affairs at the hearing to confirm her as head of the BIA that "while all the statistics said we were poor, I never felt poor in spirit. My mother . . . was the single greatest influence on my life. She instilled in me rich values which have shaped my lifetime commitment to service."

This service began with a solid education in the Shawano and Milwaukee public schools. An outstanding student, Deer graduated in the top ten of her high school class before attending the University of Wisconsin-Madison on a tribal scholarship. She was one of two Native Ameri-

cans out of 19,000 students, and became the first Menominee to graduate from the university. She received her B.A. in social work in 1957; and in 1961, she went on to become the first Native American to receive a M.S.W. from Columbia University.

From the time she was a graduate student and over the next ten years, Deer held several professional positions. She was employed as a social worker in New York City and Minneapolis Public Schools. She also worked with the Peace Corps in Puerto Rico. It was between the years of 1964 and 1967 that Deer had her first job with the BIA in Minnesota as Community Service Coordinator. From 1967 to 1968, she served as Coordinator of Indian Affairs in the University of Minnesota's Training Center for Community Programs. During the same time, Deer served on the Joint Commission on Mental Health of Children, Inc., and in 1969 she became a member of the national board of Girl Scouts of the U.S.A., a post she held until 1975. During the summer of 1971, Deer studied at the American Indian Law Program at the University of New Mexico and then briefly attended the University of Wisconsin-Madison Law School. She left after one semester to work on an urgent tribal matter that was to become her major focus over the next several years.

## Fights to Regain Menominee Tribe Recognition

As part of the U.S. government's 1950s termination policy—an attempt to assimilate Indians forcibly—the U.S. Congress passed in 1954 the Menominee Termination Act. Fully implemented by 1961, it meant the loss of federal recognition of the Menominee Tribe and along with it, the closing of membership rolls, a loss of benefits such as health and educational services, and an imposition of state jurisdiction. The Menominees were taxed and had to sell off ancestral lands to pay the bills. As Deer testified in her confirmation hearing, the Menominees "literally went from being prosperous to being Wisconsin's newest, smallest and poorest county."

Deer left law school and returned to what was now Menominee County to help gather together tribal leaders to regain control of tribal interests from a group of Menominee elites, and to attempt to reverse termination. There, in 1970, Deer and many others created a new political organization known as Determination of Rights and Unity for Menominee Shareholders (DRUMS). With assistance from the Native American Rights Fund and local legal aid organizations, Deer and other leaders of DRUMS fought to regain federal recognition for the Menominees. Their tactics included a 220-mile "march for justice" from Menominee County to the capital in Madison. As a vital part of the restoration effort, in 1972 and 1973 Deer served as vice president and lobbyist in Washington, D.C., for the National Committee to Save the Menominee People and Forest, Inc.

Author Nicholas C. Peroff stated in *Menominee Drums* that Deer's positive attitude concerning restoration was evident in her comment to a *Washington Post* reporter in 1973: "Mainly I want to show people who say nothing can be done in this society that it just isn't so. You don't have to collapse just because there's federal law in your way. Change it!'' The efforts of Deer and the members of DRUMS resulted in national publicity for the issue of termination and finally the introduction of a bill in Congress to reverse this policy for the Menominees. On December 22, 1973, President Nixon signed the Menominee Restoration Act into law.

From 1974 to 1976, Deer chaired the Menominee Tribe and headed the Menominee Restoration Committee. After its work was completed, she resigned. In 1977, she became a Senior Lecturer in the School of Social Work and in the American Indian Studies Program at the University of Wisconsin-Madison, where she taught until 1993. Deer also moved into the democratic political arena more fully at this time, serving as legislative liaison to the Native American Rights Fund from 1979 to 1981. In 1982, Deer was a candidate for Wisconsin secretary of state. In 1984, she was delegate-at-large at the Democratic National Convention and vice-chair of the National Mondale-Ferraro Presidential Campaign. In 1992, Deer almost became the first Native American woman in Congress; after a strong showing in the Second Congressional District of Wisconsin, she lost in the general election to Republican Scot Klug. May of 1993, however, brought a nomination by President Clinton from a field of four candidates (including Navajo tribal chairman Peterson Zah) to head the BIA. Congress, with overwhelming support from its members and from tribal leaders, confirmed her nomination in July of 1993.

### Turning the BIA Around

With the BIA, Deer inherited an agency that is infamous for its bureaucracy and historically poor relations with tribes. Deer has had to contend with, among many issues, budget reductions for her agency; conflicts between tribes and localities over land management, water resources, and mineral rights; tribal recognition; education; and religious freedom. Deer is a strong proponent of Indian self-determination; this coincides with the BIA's planned reorganization which will shift more power to tribes. Her approach since being in office has been to visit individual Indian tribes, bringing them together with businesses, organizations, and government entities to find ways to work cooperatively, with the ultimate goal of helping tribes gain economic self-sufficiency. Deer, in her confirmation hearing, maintained: ''I want to help the BIA be a full partner in the effort to fulfill the Indian agenda developed in Indian country. The best way we can do this is for the tribes to decide what needs to be done and for the tribes to do it on their own terms, with our enthusiastic support.''

Deer's motto in life is ''one person can make a difference.'' For the difference she has made in her many spheres of activity, she has received numerous awards over her lifetime. Deer was one of the Outstanding Young Women of America in 1966. In 1974, she received the White Buffalo Council Achievement Award, along with honorary doctorates from the University of Wisconsin-Madison and Northland College. Other honors include the Woman of the Year Award from Girl Scouts of America (1982), the Wonder Woman Award (1982), the Indian Council Fire Achieve-

ment Award (1984), and the National Distinguished Achievement Award from the American Indian Resources Institute (1991).

There have been many achievements during Deer's tenure as Assistant Secretary. Some examples are: the recognition of over 220 Alaska Native villages, the increasing number of self-governance tribes and tribres who contract for programs previously administered by the federal government, and the reorganization of the Bureau. Deer is also active in many initiatives undertaken by the Clinton administration. She is a member of the President's Inter-Agency Council on Women which is charged with the implementation of the Platform for Action agreed upon at the UN's Fourth Conference on Women. In addition, she has testified before the UN Human Rights Committee and is the lead for the domestic activities in conjuction with the Decade of the World's Indigenous Peoples working closely with the State Department.

### Further Reading

*Biographical Dictionary of Indians of the Americas,* Volume 1, Newport Beach, California, American Indian Publishers, 1991; 181-182.

Deer, Ada, and R. E. Simon, Jr., *Speaking Out,* Chicago, Children's Press Open Door Books, 1970.

Deer, Ada, ''The Power Came from the People,'' in *I Am the Fire of Time: The Voices of Native American Women,* edited by Jane B. Katz, New York, Dutton, 1977.

*Department of the Interior:* ''http://www.doi.gov/bia/adabio.html,'' July 18, 1997.

Hardy, Gayle J., *American Women Civil Rights Activists: Bio-bibliographies of 68 Leaders, 1825-1992,* Jefferson, North Carolina, McFarland, 1993; 128-134.

*Native American Women,* edited by Gretchen M. Bataille, New York, Garland Publishing, 1993; 76-78.

*Native North American Almanac,* edited by Duane Champagne, Detroit, Gale Research, 1994; 1041.

Peroff, Nicholas C., *Menominee Drums: Tribal Termination and Restoration, 1954-1974,* Norman, University of Oklahoma Press, 1982.

*Reference Encyclopedia of the American Indian,* sixth edition, edited by Barry T. Klein, West Nyack, New York, Todd Publications, 1993; 504-505.

Cohen, Karen J., ''Ada Deer Tries to Start Fire Under Bureaucracy,'' *Wisconsin State Journal,* March 20, 1994; B1.

''Female BIA Chief 'Shaking Agency Up,''' *Denver Post,* September 2, 1993; B2.

Richardson, Jeff, ''Ada Deer: Native Values for BIA Management,'' *Tundra Times,* September 8, 1993; 1.

Worthington, Rogers, ''Woman Picked to Lead Indian Bureau,'' *Chicago Tribune,* May 20, 1993; A1.

*Nomination of Ada Deer: Hearing before the Committee on Indian Affairs, United States Senate, One Hundred Third Congress, First Session, on the Nomination of Ada Deer to be Assistant Secretary for Indian Affairs, July 15, 1993, Washington, D.C.,* Washington, D.C., U.S. Government Printing Office, 1993. □

# John Deere

**The American inventor and manufacturer John Deere (1804-1886) was one of the first to design agricultural tools and machines to meet the specific needs of midwestern farmers.**

John Deere was born in 1804 in modest circumstances in Rutland, Vt., the third son of William Rinold and Sarah Yates Deere. After receiving the limited education available to a country boy, Deere was apprenticed at 17 to a blacksmith in Middleburn, Vt. He completed his apprenticeship in 4 years and became a master craftsman.

In 1836 Deere left Vermont for Grand Detour, Ill., where he found ready employment in his trade. He prospered, for the farmers kept him fully occupied supplying their customary needs. They also presented him with an unusual problem posed by the local soil. The soil of Illinois and other prairie areas was not only difficult to plow because of its thick sod covering but also tended to clog the moldboards of plows. Deere tried covering the moldboard and cutting a plowshare from salvaged steel. Steel surfaces tended to shed the thick soil and were burnished by the abrasive action of the soil. Deere's new plows, introduced in 1839, sold readily, and within a decade the production of plows by Deere and his new associate, Leonard Andrus, exceeded 1,000 per year. Deere parted company with his partners to move to Moline, Ill., which was better situated for a market, transportation, and raw materials.

Repeated experiments produced an excellent moldboard and demonstrated that further improvements in the plow were dependent on using better-quality steel. Deere imported such steel from an English firm until a Pittsburgh firm cast the first plow steel in the United States for him. Deere's production of plows soared to 10,000 by 1857 as agriculture in the Midwest grew to meet the unprecedented demands of the growing home and export market.

The business was incorporated in 1868 with Deere and his son, Charles, in the executive positions. During the Civil War the company prospered as it diversified its output to include wagons, carriages, and a full line of agricultural equipment. It also adopted modern administrative practices and built an efficient sales, distribution, and service organization which reached into all parts of America. Deere remained active in the management of the company until his fatal illness in 1886. He was succeeded by his son.

John Deere married twice. His first wife, Demarius Lamb, died in 1865. Two years later he married her younger sister, Lucinda Lamb.

## Further Reading

Full-length studies of Deere are Neil M. Clark, *John Deere: He Gave to the World the Steel Plow* (1937), and Darragh Aldrich, *The Story of John Deere: A Saga of American Industry* (1942). See also Stewart H. Holbrook, *Machines of Plenty: Pioneering in American Agriculture* (1955), and Wayne D. Rasmussen, *Readings in the History of American Agriculture* (1960).

## Additional Sources

Broehl, Wayne G., *John Deere's company: a history of Deere & Company and its times,* New York, N.Y.: Doubleday, 1984.
Collins, David R., *Pioneer plowmaker: a story about John Deere,* Minneapolis: Carolrhoda Books, 1990. □

# William Deering

**American manufacturer William Deering (1826-1913) made improvements in the grain harvester that greatly increased production of grain throughout the world.**

Born in South Paris, Maine, William Deering intended to study medicine but, because of his father's need for help in his woolen mill, went to work there instead. During the next 20 years he made a considerable fortune selling woolen goods and speculating in western lands. In 1870 he lent $40,000 to E. H. Gammon, who was manufacturing the Marsh grain harvester in Illinois. When Gammon's health failed in 1873, Deering moved to Illinois to manage the company.

With the rapid expansion of wheat-growing in the Midwest during the 1870s and the efficient design of his machine, Deering's sales soared. His harvester had a mechanical grain lift that saved the labor of four men on ordinary reapers. To further improve his harvester, Deering experimented with an automatic wire binder. He finally purchased the rights to the still experimental Appleby twine binder.

In 1879 Deering became sole owner of the company and took a gamble by building 3,000 twine binders for the next harvest. Although the machines did not work perfectly, they represented a major technological break-through and established a standard design for harvesters throughout the world. Competition among the manufacturers of agricultural machinery grew fierce, and litigation over patents mounted to unprecedented levels. Between 1880 and 1885 the number of machines manufactured in a year rose from 60,000 to 250,000, while the number of manufacturers dropped from over 100 to about 20. The Deering Harvester Company, largely on the worth of its twine binder and Deering's business talent, swept ahead of most competitors. By 1890 the company's Chicago plant, with 9,000 employees, had a daily capacity of 1,200 machines of various kinds, which it sold all over the world.

During the 1890s the intense competition between Deering's company and his principal competitor, the McCormick Harvester Company, became damaging to both. As a result, when Deering retired, the two companies merged in 1902, thus forming the nucleus of the International Harvester Company.

A simple, unaffected man of complete integrity, Deering achieved success based on the huge demand for agricultural machinery at the time plus his own good business judgment and unremitting efforts to improve his products. He died in 1913.

## Further Reading

The best source of information about Deering is a privately printed volume, *William Deering* (no author, 1914), containing biographical sketches, testimonials, and reprints of newspaper obituaries. Accounts of his company and its bitter competition with the McCormick Harvester Company can be found in Herbert N. Casson, *Cyrus Hall McCormick: His Life and Work* (1909); William T. Hutchinson, *Cyrus Hall McCormick* (2 vols., 1930-1935); and Cyrus McCormick, *The Century of the Reaper: An Account of Cyrus Hall McCormick* (1931). □

# Morris S. Dees Jr.

**Civil rights attorney Morris S. Dees, Jr. (born 1936) used the rule of law to fight against hate groups in the United States.**

In the quarter of a century following the death of civil rights leader Dr. Martin Luther King, Jr. in 1968, there was an alarming rise in the number of hate groups and hate crimes in America. By 1994 it was estimated that there were over 250 hate groups across the United States, including the Ku Klux Klan, neo-Nazis, racist skinheads, and Christian Identity Movement, to name only a few of the most violent. Combatting these groups effectively was extremely difficult, since the very freedoms cherished in U.S. democracy, including and especially freedom of speech, allow bigots to spread their hateful ideas with little fear of prosecution by authorities.

One man made a stand against all of that. Morris S. Dees, Jr., a native of the deep South, led an innovative and effective campaign against America's most dangerous purveyors of hate by using the rule of law to put them out of business.

There is little in Dees' early biography that would hint of his later emergence as a crusader for the rights of minorities. He was born in 1936 in Shorter, Alabama, the son of a farmer and cotton gin operator. The South of his early youth provided equality for African Americans in theory only. Public schools and private institutions were segregated and most African Americans were eking out a living below the poverty line. In rural areas many lived on the land as sharecroppers, in effect little more than indentured servants to white landlords. There were few white citizens who ever questioned a system that rarely protected the rights of African Americans or provided them with opportunities to improve their economic status. Some, like Dees' uncle Lucien, were avowed racists. Others, while not fighting the status quo, still maintained a basic respect for their African American neighbors. Dees' father was such a man. He once took a belt to the young Dees when the teen called a worker a "Black nigger."

Originally, Morris Dees saw his future on the land; indeed, he was named the "star farmer" of Alabama in 1955. But his innovative business acumen would lead him on a different course. While an undergraduate at the University of Alabama, he founded a nationwide direct mail sales company that specialized in book publishing. He did not know it then, but Dees had not only discovered a way to secure his financial future, but a new way to communicate ideas directly to millions of Americans. In 1960 he graduated from the University of Alabama Law School, opened a law office in Montgomery, and continued to develop his direct mail business. Sales would reach $15 million, and eventually he sold his business to the Times-Mirror Corporation.

As Dees grew professionally, he and many other Southerners began to be deeply affected by the emerging civil rights movement of the 1960s. He decided to apply his legal knowledge to aid minorities in the courts. His most notable achievement was a 1968 lawsuit he filed that successfully led to the integration of the all-white Montgomery Young Men's Christian Association (YMCA).

In 1971 Dees co-founded the Southern Poverty Law Center, which engaged in civil lawsuits ranging from defending an African American female inmate in a North Carolina jail to the integration of the Alabama state troopers. Utilizing direct mail, Dees eventually won the financial support of some 300,000 Americans, which enabled the center to pursue critically important but highly unpopular civil rights cases. Throughout, Dees and his colleagues exhibited great courage in standing up for unpopular and powerless clients. But armed with the truth and a belief in the ultimate fairness of the American justice system, they prevailed against the odds.

In 1980 Dees founded Klanwatch as a direct response to resurgence of the virulently anti-African American, anti-Semitic, and anti-Catholic Ku Klux Klan (KKK) and related groups. In more than one instance, violent leaders of the Klan and the White Patriot Party planned to assassinate Dees. Combining great personal heroism and an aggressive use of the law, the Klanwatch struck telling blows against some of America's most dangerous hate groups.

In 1981 a Klan leader, Louis Beam, led a group of renegade American fishermen who sought to block immigrant Vietnamese fishermen from operating in the waters near Galveston, Texas. The new Americans were scared by the terror tactics of boat burnings and threats of physical violence and were on the verge of giving up their livelihoods when the law center entered the picture and successfully sued the Texas Knights of the KKK.

In his native Alabama, Dees successfully used the courts to sue the Klan. Not only were Klan leaders convicted of breaking the law, they were stripped of their assets and left virtually penniless. In one case, a unique aspect of the court-imposed settlement mandated that the leader of the racist assaults was required to attend a Brotherhood seminar convened by the husband of an African American woman who was the target of their attack. In Georgia, Klansmen had to pay $100,000 to their intended victims and their office equipment was transferred to the Raleigh branch of the

National Association for the Advancement of Colored People (NAACP). In 1984 Dees won a $7 million lawsuit against the United Klan following the lynching of an African American man by Klansmen. The suit forced the United Klan of America out of business.

The White Patriot Party, a paramilitary off-shoot of the KKK, had by the early 1980s some two thousand members who terrorized minorities in the Carolinas and Virginia. Some of the followers were actually active members in the United States Armed Forces. In 1985 legal action by Klanwatch against the group's leader, Glen Miller, led to the uncovering of thousands of dollars worth of explosives, including rockets stolen from the military, which were destined to be used in a "race war." Later, a Federal Bureau of Investigation (FBI) raid thwarted an assassination plot by Miller and his followers to kill Dees. As a result of the legal steps brought against them, the White Patriot Party no longer exists.

The legal and social basis of Dees' crusade can be shown in his summation before a Mobile, Alabama, court in 1987: "I do not want you to come back with a verdict against the Klan because they have unpopular beliefs. In this country you have the right to have unpopular beliefs just as long as you don't turn those beliefs into violent actions that interfere with someone else's rights. . . . But they put a rope around Michael MacDonald's neck and treated him to an actual death . . . so they could get out their message. . . . You have an opportunity to send a different message that will ring out all over Alabama and all over the United States: That an all white jury from the heart of the South will not tolerate racial violence in any way, shape or form. . . ." The jury found for the African American plaintiff and fixed damages at $7 million.

In the Southern Poverty Law Center's first quarter century the largest amount awarded by a court to the heirs and victims of a racist murder was the 1988 decision in Oregon to assess damages of $12 million against White Aryan Resistance leader Tom Metzger. His skinhead followers had murdered an Ethiopian immigrant. Obviously, money cannot compensate for murder and mayhem, but Dees had a remarkable track record in using the American justice system to financially bankrupt the groups and hate mongers who strove to promote racism in the United States.

Dees was honored by many groups and institutions. He received the Martin Luther King Jr. Memorial Award from the National Education Association. The American Civil Liberties Union presented him with the Roger Bladwin Award, and he was named the Trial Lawyer of the Year by the Trial Lawyers for Public Justice. He earned a reputation as a respected speaker and was asked to deliver the Ralph Fuchs lecture at Indiana University School of Law in 1996. He collaborated with James Corcoran to publish a chilling account of the militia groups in 1996. The book, *Gathering Storm: America's Militia Threat,* makes a strong case for the common thread which appeared to unravel from Ruby Ridge, Idaho in 1992, to Waco, Texas in 1993, to Oklahoma City in 1995.

## Further Reading

Two of the most important sources of information on Morris S. Dees, Jr., are books he co-authored with Steve Fiffer: *A Season for Justice: The Life and Times of Civil Rights Lawyer Morris Dees* (1991) and *Hate On Trial: The Case Against America's Most Dangerous Neo-Nazi* (1993). Dees also co-authored with James Corcoran a book about militia groups, *Gathering Storm: America's Militia Threat* (Harper Collins, 1996). Information on hate groups, chiefly the KKK, can be found in Robert P. Ingalls, *Hoods: The Story of the Ku Klux Klan* (1979); Andy Oakley, *"88": An Undercover News Reporter's Expose of American Nazis and the Ku Klux Klan* (1987); Craig Wyn Wade, *The Fiery Cross: The Ku Klux Klan in America* (1987); Susan S. Lang, *Extremist Groups in America* (1990); James Ridgeway, *Blood in the Face: The Ku Klux Klan, Aryan Nations, Nazi Skinheads, and the Rise of a New White Culture* (1990); and Bill Stanton, *Klanwatch: Bringing the Ku Klux Klan to Justice* (1991). See also *Klanwatch Intelligence Report: A Project of the Southern Poverty Law Center,* Southern Poverty Law Center, 1981 to present, a bimonthly. □

# Daniel Defoe

**The English novelist, journalist, poet, and government agent Daniel Defoe (1660-1731) wrote more than 500 books, pamphlets, articles, and poems. Among the most productive authors of the Augustan Age, he was the first of the great 18th-century English novelists.**

Daniel Defoe was the son of a dissenting London tallow chandler or butcher. He early thought of becoming a Presbyterian minister, and in the 1670s he attended the Reverend Charles Morton's famous academy near London. In 1684 he married Mary Tuffley, who brought him the handsome dowry of £3,700. They had seven children. Defoe participated briefly in the abortive Monmouth Rebellion of 1685 but escaped capture and punishment. From 1685 through 1692 he engaged in trade in London as a wholesale hosier, importer of wine and tobacco, and part owner and insurer of ships. In later life he also dealt in real estate and manufactured bricks.

Defoe evidently knew King William III; indeed, his bankruptcy in 1692 for the enormous sum of £17,000 was primarily because of losses suffered from underwriting marine insurance for the King. Although he settled with his creditors in 1693, he was plagued by the threat of bankruptcy throughout his life and faced imprisonment for debt and libel seven times.

Arrested in 1703 for having published *The Shortest Way with the Dissenters* in 1702, Defoe was tried and sentenced to stand in the pillory for 3 days in July. He languished in Newgate Prison, however, until Robert Walpole released him in November and offered him a post as a government agent. Defoe continued to serve the government as journalist, pamphleteer, and secret agent for the remainder of his life. The most long-lived of his 27 periodi-

cals, the *Review* (1704-1713), was especially influential in promoting the union between England and Scotland in 1706-1707 and in supporting the controversial Peace of Utrecht (1713).

Defoe published hundreds of political and social tracts between 1704 and 1719. During the 1720s he contributed to such weekly journals as *Mist's* and *Applebee's*, wrote criminal biographies, and studied economics and geography as well as producing his major works of fiction. He died in a comatose lethargy in Ropemaker's Alley on April 24, 1731, while hiding from a creditor who had commenced proceedings against him.

Defoe's interests and activities reflect the major social, political, economic, and literary trends of his age. He supported the policies of William III and Mary after the Glorious Revolution of 1688-1689, and analyzed England's emergence as the major sea and mercantile power in the Western world. He pleaded for leniency for debtors and bankrupts and defended the rights of Protestant dissenters. Effectively utilizing newspapers and journals to make his points, he also experimented with the novel form, which was still in its infancy.

### His Nonfiction

No brief account of Defoe's works can do more than hint at the range, variety, and scope of his hundreds of publications. His first major work, *An Essay upon Projects* (1697), which introduced many topics that would reappear in his later works, proposed ways of providing better roads,

insurance, and education, and even planned a house for fools to be supported by "a Tax upon Learning, to be paid by the Authors of Books."

In 1701 Defoe published *The True-Born Englishman,* the most widely sold poem in English up to that time. He estimated that more than 80,000 copies of this defense of William III against the attacks of John Tutchin were sold. Although Defoe's prose satire against the tyranny of the Church of England, *The Shortest Way with the Dissenters* (1702), led to his arrest, the popularity of his *Hymn to the Pillory* (1703) indicated the favor that he had found with the London public. From 1704 to 1713 in his monumental *Review,* Defoe discussed almost every aspect of the political, economic, and social life of Augustan England.

Defoe's allegorical moon voyage, *The Consolidator: Or Memoirs of Sundry Transactions from the World in the Moon* (1705), reviews the political history of the previous century, defends his political activities, and describes the ingenious machine which lifts the narrator to Terra Luna: a chariot powered by 513 feathers, one for each member of the British Parliament. His *Appeal to Honour and Justice* (1715) is perhaps his most moving and personal account of his services to the English crown.

### "Robinson Crusoe"

At the age of 59, after a full career as businessman, government servant, political pamphleteer, and journalist, Defoe embarked upon a career as novelist and within 6 years produced the half-dozen novels which have given him his greatest fame.

In April 1719 Defoe published his most enduring work, *The Life and Strange Surprizing Adventures of Robinson Crusoe.* The immediate success of the story of the shipwrecked Crusoe's solitary existence on a desert island for more than 20 years, of his encounter with the native Friday, and of his eventual rescue inspired Defoe to write *The Farther Adventures of Robinson Crusoe* later in 1719 and *Serious Reflections during the Life and Surprizing Adventures* in 1720. That year he published another travel novel, *The Life, Adventures, and Pyracies of the Famous Captain Singleton.*

The greatness of *Robinson Crusoe* lies not only in Defoe's marvelously realistic descriptive passages but in the fact that the novel recounts one of the great myths of Western civilization—man's ability to endure, survive, and conquer a hostile environment. As a fictional adaptation of the story of Alexander Selkirk, who had been stranded on an island near Chile early in the century, the novel shows Augustan England's interest in travel literature, religious allegory, and mercantilist economics.

### Other Major Fiction

Defoe published comparatively little in 1721 because he was hard at work on the three major books that were to appear the following year. In January 1722 he published *The Fortunes and Misfortunes of the Famous Moll Flanders,* probably the most successful of his novels. Its irony, vivid details, and psychologically valid individual scenes more than compensate for its structural weaknesses. The elderly

Moll writes of her early life, of her five husbands, of her life as a prostitute, and of her adventures as a thief.

A Journal of the Plague Year, issued in March 1722, presents a stunning picture of life in London during the Great Plague of 1665, and it was thought to be history rather than fiction for more than a hundred years. The third important novel to appear in 1722, The History and Remarkable Life of the Truly Honourable Col. Jacque, was published in December. In this study of a young man's rise to gentility, Defoe characteristically combined a brilliant command of detail and individual scene with an interesting but awkwardly plotted story.

Defoe published The Fortunate Mistress; or, . . . Roxana early in 1724. Though Roxana moves in a more fashionable world than did Moll Flanders, she shares with Moll native cunning and an instinct for self-preservation. Like Moll Flanders, Roxana juxtaposes moral homilies with titillating narrative passages. In 1724 Defoe also published A Tour Thro' the Whole Island of Great Britain, one of the most thorough and fascinating guide-books of the period.

The History of the Remarkable Life of John Sheppard (1724), one of Defoe's finest criminal biographies, was followed in 1725 by The True and Genuine Account of the Life and Actions of the Late Jonathan Wild. Defoe's intimate knowledge of London's underworld and of its prisons explains the vitality and accuracy of these hastily written criminal lives. These works also display his characteristically clear, strong, idiomatic English prose.

Although he continued to write until his death in 1731, only a few of Defoe's later works are worthy of note: The Complete English Tradesman (1725), The Political History of the Devil (1726), A New Family Instructor (1727), and Augusta Triumphans (1728), which was Defoe's plan to make "London the most flourishing City in the Universe."

## Further Reading

The standard bibliography of Defoe is John Robert Moore, A Checklist of the Writings of Daniel Defoe (1960). There are two major critical biographies: James R. Sutherland, Defoe (1937; 2d ed. 1950), and John Robert Moore, Daniel Defoe: Citizen of the Modern World (1958). Important critical studies of Defoe's works include Arthur W. Secord, Studies in the Narrative Method of Defoe (1924); Maximillian E. Novak, Economics and the Fiction of Daniel Defoe (1962) and Defoe and the Nature of Man (1963); and J. Paul Hunter, The Reluctant Pilgrim (1966). Recommended for general historical and social background are J. H. Plumb, England in the Eighteenth Century (1950); A. R. Humphreys, The Augustan World: Life and Letters in Eighteenth-Century England (1954); Ian P. Watt, The Rise of the Novel: Studies in Defoe, Richardson and Fielding (1957); and Ian P. Watt, ed., The Augustan Age (1968). □

# Lee De Forest

**The American inventor Lee De Forest (1873-1961) pioneered in radio, both in developing broadcasting and in inventing the audion. He is considered one of the fathers of radio.**

Lee De Forest was born in Council Bluffs, Iowa, in 1873, where his father was a minister. While Lee was still a boy, his father became the president of the College for the Colored in Talladega, Ala. Because of his father's association with African Americans, young Lee was shunned by playmates and sought relief from his loneliness in invention and mechanics. He took bachelor of science and doctor of philosophy degrees from Yale in 1896 and 1899. He then went to work for the Western Electric Company in Chicago.

During the 1890s Guglielmo Marconi transmitted radio waves over increasing distances; his work culminated in 1901 with a transatlantic message. The new field of radio attracted many inventors, among them De Forest. In 1910 he literally electrified the musical world by broadcasting the voice of Enrico Caruso by radio. In 1916 De Forest made what he believed to be the first news broadcast by radio.

The greatest single contribution De Forest made to the field, however, was his invention of the triode, or audion, as he called it, for which he received a patent in 1908. One of the major goals of inventors was to come up with a more powerful and sensitive detector, or receiver. In 1904 John Ambrose Fleming, a consultant to the Edison Electric Light Company, patented a two-electrode vacuum tube which he called a thermionic valve. Acting between the two elec-

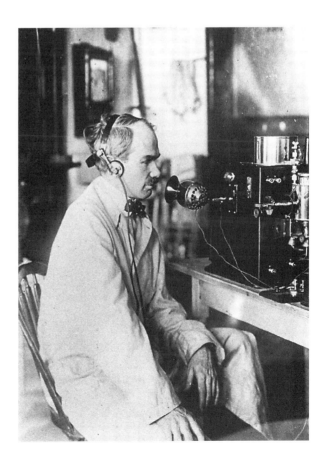

trodes, one of which was heated, the oscillating radio waves were made unidirectional. De Forest's contribution, which he claimed was made in ignorance of Fleming's earlier work, was to add a third element, thus converting the diode to a triode. This new element was a grid (or zigzag piece of wire) placed between the other two. Although no one, including the inventor himself, realized the importance or the exact action of the audion, it proved to be the basis of all subsequent radio development because it could be used to send, receive, or amplify radio signals better than any other device.

In 1902 De Forest became vice president of the De Forest Wireless Telegraph Company and in 1913 vice president of the Radio Telephone Company and the De Forest Radio Company. He worked on other electrical problems, including talking motion pictures and television, and eventually received over 300 domestic and foreign patents. He made and lost four fortunes during his lifetime and was extensively engaged in court litigation with such formidable foes as Irving Langmuir of the General Electric Company and Edwin Armstrong, with whom he disputed invention of the feedback circuit. This last dispute was decided in favor of De Forest in 1934. He retired to a private research laboratory in Hollywood, Calif.

## Further Reading

De Forest's autobiography is *Father of Radio* (1950). A more balanced account of his contributions is the standard history of radio, William R. Maclaurin, *Invention and Innovation in the Radio Industry* (1949). The business side of radio is covered in Erik Barnouw, *A History of Broadcasting in the United States* (1966). □

# Deganawida

**Deganawida was instrumental in founding the League of the Iroquois.**

Deganawida is best known as the great leader who, with Hiawatha, founded the League of the Iroquois. Although the story of Deganawida's life is based primarily on legend, all accounts of the league's formation credit Deganawida for his efforts. In addition to his persuasive vision of unified Iroquois tribes, Deganawida was instrumental in defining and establishing the structure and code of the Iroquois league.

It is believed that Deganawida was born around the 1550s in the Kingston, Ontario, area and was one of seven brothers born to Huron parents. According to legend, Deganawida's birth was marked by a vision his mother had that her newborn son would be indirectly responsible for the destruction of the Hurons. She, along with Deganawida's grandmother, tried to protect the Hurons by attempting three times to drown him in a river. Each morning after the attempts, Deganawida was found unharmed in his mother's arms. After the third unsuccessful attempt,

Deganawida's mother resigned herself to her son's existence.

## Creates the League of the Iroquois

When Deganawida was grown, he journeyed south to carry out his mission of peace among the Iroquois. He met Hiawatha (not the Hiawatha of Longfellow's poem), a Mohawk, who joined him in his efforts to create an alliance of the Oneidas, Cayugas, Onondagas, Senacas, and Mohawks. Deganawida acted as the visionary and, because Deganawida had a speech impediment, Hiawatha served as his spokesman. Deganawida's message to the Iroquois was that all men are brothers; therefore, they should cease their practices of killing, scalping, and cannibalism. Together, Deganawida and Hiawatha convinced the five tribes to make peace and join together in an alliance of friendship, rather than persist with their attempts to destroy each other. The powerful Onondaga chief, Thadodaho (also known as Atotarho, Adario), who initially had been strongly opposed to the union of the five tribes, marked the beginning of the alliance when he made the decision to join. Deganawida also tried, without success, to encourage the Erie and neutral tribes to join the alliance. Their refusal resulted in their eventual dispersal by the Iroquois in the 1650s. Deganawida's effort to persuade them to join may have been prompted by their friendly disposition toward the Hurons, unlike the other Iroquois. Sometime after Deganawida's death, his mother's earlier vision was realized when the Huron nation was destroyed by the Iroquois.

The alliance of the five tribes was referred to as the League of the Iroquois (also known as The Iroquois Five Nation Confederacy; after the Tuscaroras joined in the early eighteenth century, it was known as the Six Nations). The exact date of the founding of the league is unknown. The purposes of the league were to bring peace, to build strength, and to create goodwill among the five nations in order for them to become invulnerable to attack from external enemies and to division from within. The code of the league summarized the intent of Deganawida and the confederate chiefs to establish "The Great Peace." Out of this code was created the Pine Tree Chiefs. Deganawida served as one of those chiefs, who were chosen by merit rather than by heredity.

A grand council of all the chiefs of the five tribes gathered at Onondaga, the most centrally located of the five tribes, to establish the laws and customs of the league. Each tribe had an equal voice in the council despite the fact that the number of chiefs representing each tribe varied. As the council developed over the years, it became immersed in matters of diplomacy, including war and peace, associations with other tribes, and treaties with the European settlers on their borders. Deganawida is credited with the development of the advanced political system of the league, which was primarily democratic and also allowed women a major role. Many of the principles, laws, and regulations of the league are attributed to Deganawida.

By 1677, the league had developed into the most powerful of all the North American Indian confederations and consisted of approximately 16,000 people. The successful union begun by Deganawida flourished into the nineteenth century. After its peak of influence, the league began its collapse as a result of many contributing factors, including the influence of outsiders, the supply of trade goods, the control of military posts, the old covenants with the whites, the rivalry between warriors and chiefs, and structural weaknesses. However, the league owed the several centuries of influence it enjoyed to the prominent leadership of Deganawida, as evidenced by his astuteness in negotiations and by his wisdom in framing the laws and principles that served as the basis for the entire structure of the league.

## Further Reading

Dockstader, Frederick J., *Great North American Indians,* New York, Van Nostrand Reinhold, 1977; 71-72.

Graymont, Barbara, *The Iroquois in the American Revolution,* New York, Syracuse University Press, 1972; 14, 47, 128, 296.

*Handbook of American Indians,* edited by Frederick Webb Hodge, New York, Rowman and Littlefield, 1971; 383-384.

Leitch, Barbara A., *Chronology of the American Indian,* St. Clair Shores, Michigan, Scholarly Press, Inc., 1975; 82.

Tooker, Elisabeth, "The League of the Iroquois: Its History, Politics, and Rituals," in *Handbook of North American Indians,* edited by William C. Sturtevant, Smithsonian Institution, 1978; 422-424.

Waldman, Carl, *Who Was Who in Native American History,* New York, Facts on File, 1990; 96-97.

Wallace, Anthony F. C., *The Death and Rebirth of the Seneca,* New York, Knopf, 1969; 42, 44, 97-98. □

# Hilaire Germain Edgar Degas

**The French painter and sculptor Hilaire Germain Edgar Degas (1834-1917) is classed with the impressionists because of his concentration on scenes of contemporary life and his desire to capture the transitory moment, but he surpassed them in compositional sense.**

Edgar Degas was born on July 19, 1834, in Paris, the son of a well-to-do banker. From an early age Edgar loved books, especially the classics, and was a serious student in high school. His father hoped his son would study law, but Edgar enrolled at the École des Beaux-Arts in 1855, where he studied under Louis Lamothe, a pupil of J. A. D. Ingres. Degas always valued his early classical training and had a great and enduring admiration for Ingres, a painter with a decisively linear orientation.

In 1856 Degas went to Naples, where his sister lived, and eventually he settled in Rome for 3 years. He admired the Early Christian and medieval masterpieces of Italy, as well as the frescoes, panel paintings, and drawings of the Renaissance masters, many of which he copied. Back in Paris in 1861, he executed a few history paintings (then regarded as the highest branch of painting). Among these was the *Daughter of Jephthah* (1861), which is based on a

melodramatic episode from the Old Testament. He copied the works of the old masters in the Louvre, a practice he kept up for many years.

From 1862 until 1870 Degas painted portraits of his friends and family. In 1870, during the Franco-Prussian War, he served in the artillery of the national guard. Two years later he went to New Orleans to visit members of his family, who were in the cotton business. Between 1873 and 1883 Degas produced many of his paintings and pastels of the racecourse, music hall, café, and ballet. He had no financial problems, and even prior to the 1870s he had established his reputation as a painter. Degas stopped exhibiting at the respected Salon in 1874 and displayed his works with those of the less well-established impressionists until 1886. Although he was associated with the impressionists, his preoccupation with draftsmanship and composition was not characteristic of the group.

Beginning in the mid-1870s Degas suffered from failing eyesight. From the 1890s on he became increasingly miserly and more and more of a recluse. In the last years of his life he was almost totally blind and wandered aimlessly through the Parisian streets. He died on Sept. 27, 1917, in Paris.

## His Portraiture

Portraiture was more important for Degas than for any of the other impressionists. Some of his portraits are among the best produced in Western art since the Renaissance, and many reveal his profound understanding of human nature.

In the *Belleli Family* (1859), a group portrait executed in Naples of his aunt, her husband, and their two daughters, Degas caught the divisions within a family. Belleli's emotional separation from his wife is suggested by his pose and by his physical isolation within the room, as he sits cramped at a fireplace, with his back to the viewer. One of the daughters repeats the triangular form of her mother, who shields her, while the other, shown in a more unstable pose, seems to be divided in her loyalties. Among Degas's other portraits are the very soft *Head of a Young Woman* (1867), *Diego Martelli* (1879), and *Estelle Musson* (1872-1873), the blind wife of Degas's brother René, in which the silver and rose tones bring into relief the remote tenderness of the sitter.

## Depiction of the Modern Scene

By 1870 Degas had abandoned his desire to become a history painter, and he drew his characters instead from the contemporary Parisian scene. While the bourgeois fashionable world of the ballet, theater, and racetrack interested him considerably, he sometimes depicted squalid scenes of dissipation, as in *Absinthe* (1876). Degas was especially attracted by the spectacle of the ballet with its elegance of costume and scenery, its movement which was at once spontaneous and restrained, its artificial lighting, and its unusual viewpoints. Usually he depicted the ballerinas off guard, showing them backstage at an awkward moment as they fasten a slipper or droop exhausted after a difficult practice session. He seems to have tried deliberately to strip his dancers of their glamour, to show them without artifice.

On the surface Degas, operating in this candid-camera fashion, fits easily within the confines of impressionism as an art of immediacy and spontaneity. But these scenes of contemporary Parisian life are not at all haphazardly composed: the placement of each detail is calculated in terms of every other to establish balances which are remarkably clever and subtle and which are frequently grasped by the viewer only after considerable study. In *Dancers Practicing at the Bar* (1877) the perspective of the floorboards is so adjusted and the angle of vision so calculated that a resin shaker at the left of the canvas is able to balance in interest and compositional force the two dancers almost completely to the right of center.

Degas conceived of the human figure as operating within an environmental context, to be manipulated as a prop according to the dictates of greater compositional interest. Eccentricities of poses and cuttings of the figures, which were inspired to a degree by Japanese prints, do not occur accidently in his paintings. In *A Carriage at the Races* (1873) the figure in the carriage to the left is cut nearly down the middle. Had Degas shown more of this figure, an obvious and uninteresting symmetry would have been set up with the larger carriage in the right foreground.

## Degas's Techniques

In copying the Old Masters, Degas sometimes attempted to uncover their techniques. For example, when he copied Andrea Mantegna and some of the Venetians, Degas tried to simulate the Venetian method of building up the canvas with layers of cool and warm tones by a series of glazes. From the mid-1870s he worked increasingly in pastel; and in his last years, when his sight was failing, he abandoned oil completely in favor of pastel, which he handled more broadly and with greater freedom than before.

Pastel, for the most part an 18th-century medium, helped Degas produced qualities of airiness and lightness, as in the *Ballerina and Lady with Fan* (1885). However, Degas would endlessly experiment with unusual techniques. He would sometimes mix his pastel so heavily with liquid fixative that it became amalgamated into a sort of paste. He would do a drawing in charcoal and use layers of pastel to cover part of this. He would combine pastels and oil in a single work. He would even pass through a press a heavily pigmented charcoal drawing in order to transfer the excess of pigment onto a new sheet so as to make an inverse proof of the original. In his monotypes he used etching in a new way: he inked the unetched plate and drew with a brush in this layer of ink; then he removed all the ink in places to obtain strong contrasts of light and dark or painterly effects in this printing medium. Thus, in a variety of ways Degas succeeded in obtaining a richness of surface effects.

## Bronze Sculptures

After 1866 Degas executed bronze statues of horses and dancers, up to 3 or 4 feet high, which complemented his interest in these subjects in his paintings. His bronze and painted wax figures of dancers, like the *Little Dancer of Fourteen Years* (1880-1881), are often clothed in real costumes, an innovation that gives them a remarkable immediacy. In the statues of dancers, Degas catches the figures in a transitory moment, as they are about to change position. As in the paintings, Degas strips the dancers of glamour and sometimes reveals them as scrawny adolescents. The surfaces of Degas's bronzes are not smooth but retain the rich articulations of the wax and thereby complement the expressive surfaces of the impressionist painting.

## Further Reading

Jean Sutherland Boggs, *Portraits by Degas* (1962), is the definitive work on Degas and is thoroughly documented. John Rewald, *Degas: Works in Sculpture* (1944), shows a little-known aspect of Degas and contains 112 plates. Lillian Browse, *Degas Dancers* (1949), contains a fair text and over 150 good black-and-white illustrations of Degas's ballet dancers done in pastel, oil, and sculpture. Daniel Catton Rich, *Edgar Hilaire Germain Degas* (1951), glosses over Degas's debt to the art before him. □

# Alcide De Gasperi

**The Italian statesman Alcide De Gasperi (1881-1954) was one of the founders of Italian democracy after World War II.**

lcide De Gasperi was born on April 3, 1881, at Pieve Tesino in Trentino, then controlled by Austria. As a young man, he became active in the Irredentist movement to bring Italian-speaking people still under Austrian jurisdiction into the kingdom of Italy. In 1906 he began publication of the polemical journal *Il Trentino*. This brought him a good deal of attention, and in 1911 he was elected to the Austrian Parliament as deputy for Trentino, a post he held for 6 years.

De Gasperi then joined the new Catholic People's party (Partito Popolare Italiano), founded by the Catholic political leader Don Luigi Sturzo. Trentino became part of Italy following World War I, and De Gasperi served as a deputy in the Italian Parliament from 1921 to 1924. Hard work brought him a position of eminence, and when Don Sturzo was forced into exile in 1924, De Gasperi became general secretary of the party.

As Mussolini's hold on the Italian government grew stronger, the position of the party became ever more precarious, and in 1926 it was dissolved. De Gasperi was imprisoned but was released 3 years later when, amid the atmosphere of good feeling between Mussolini and the Vatican, the archbishop of Trent intervened on his behalf. De Gasperi found asylum and temporary peace in the Vatican, where he studied Catholic social doctrine.

During World War II De Gasperi became active in the underground and was one of the founders of the illegal Christian Democratic party (Democrazia Christiana). He also founded the newspaper *Popolo*. After the liberation of Italy in June 1944, he served as minister without portfolio and then as foreign minister; in December 1945 he became premier, a post he held until 1953. As chief of the Italian delegation at the World War II peace conference, he elicited concessions from the Allies that guaranteed Italian sovereignty.

After the formal end of the monarchy in June 1946, De Gasperi functioned as head of the Christian Democrats, the party that dominated Parliament for the next 8 years. As premier, he gave moderate guidance that kept a precarious balance, during this critical postwar period, between disparate elements within the party and the nation. By avoiding conflicts with the numerous Socialists and Communists, he managed with great delicacy to put Italian democracy on a firm foundation. Besides his successful negotiations with the Allied Powers, his most striking achievement in foreign policy was the agreement with Austria (September 1946) to establish the southern Tirol as an autonomous region.

When the Christian Democrats did not gain a majority in the elections of 1953, De Gasperi was unable to establish a workable Cabinet and was forced to resign as premier. The following year he also had to forgo the leadership of his party, and 2 months later, on Aug. 19, 1954, he died.

## Further Reading

Sources on De Gasperi in English are scarce. Elisa A. Carrillo, *Alcide de Gasperi: The Long Apprenticeship* (1965), covers his early life through his entry into the Quirinale as premier. Consult Denis Mack Smith, *Italy: A Modern History* (1959), for the political picture. English translations of the works by Luigi Sturzo that are helpful are *Church and State* (1939), *Italy and the Coming World* (1945), and *Italy and Fascism* (1967). □

# Charles André Joseph Marie De Gaulle

**The French general and statesman Charles André Joseph Marie De Gaulle (1890-1970) led the Free French forces during World War II. A talented writer and eloquent orator, he served as president of France from 1958 to 1969.**

harles De Gaulle was born on Nov. 23, 1890, in the northern industrial city of Lille. His father, Henri, was a teacher of philosophy and mathematics and a veteran of the Franco-Prussian War of 1870, in which the Prussians humiliatingly defeated what the French thought was the greatest army in the world. This loss colored the life of the elder De Gaulle, a patriot who vowed he would live to avenge the defeat and win back the provinces of Alsace and Lorraine. His attitude deeply influenced the lives of his sons, whom he raised to be the instruments of his revenge and of the restoration of France as the greatest European power.

From his earliest years Charles De Gaulle was immersed in French history by both his father and mother. For many centuries De Gaulle's forebears had played a role in French history, almost always as patriots defending France from invaders. In the 14th century a Chevalier de Gaulle defeated an invading English army in defense of the city of Vire, and Jean de Gaulle is cited in the Battle of Agincourt (1415).

Charles's great-great-grandfather, Jean Baptiste de Gaulle, was a king's counselor. His grandfather, Julien Philippe de Gaulle, wrote a popular history of Paris; Charles received this book on his tenth birthday and, as a young boy, read and reread it. He was also devoted to the literary works of his gifted grandmother, Julien Philippe's wife, Josephine Marie, whose name gave him two of his baptismal names. One of her greatest influences upon him was her impassioned, romantic history, *The Liberator of Ireland, or the Life of Daniel O'Connell*. It always remained for him an illustration of man's resistance to persecution, religious or political, and an inspiring example he emulated in his own life.

Perhaps the major influence on De Gaulle's formation came from his uncle, also named Charles de Gaulle, who wrote a book about the Celts which called for union of the Breton, Scots, Irish, and Welsh peoples. The young De Gaulle wrote in his copybook a sentence from his uncle's book, which proved to be a prophecy of his own life: "In a camp, surprised by enemy attack under cover of night, where each man is fighting alone, in dark confusion, no one

asks for the grade or rank of the man who lifts up the standard and makes the first call to rally for resistance."

## Military Career

De Gaulle's career as defender of France began in the summer of 1909, when he was admitted to the elite military academy of Saint-Cyr. Among his classmates was the future marshal of France Alphonse Juin, who later recalled De Gaulle's nicknames in school—"The Grand Constable," "The Fighting Cock," and "The Big Asparagus."

After graduation Second Lieutenant De Gaulle reported in October 1912 to Henri Philippe Pétain, who first became his idol and then his most hated enemy. (In World War I Pétain was the hero of Verdun, but during World War II he capitulated to Hitler and collaborated with the Germans while De Gaulle was leading the French forces of liberation.) De Gaulle led a frontline company as captain in World War I and was cited three times for valor. Severely wounded, he was left for dead on the battlefield of Verdun and then imprisoned by the Germans when he revived in a graveyard cart. After he had escaped and been recaptured several times, the Germans put him in a maximum security prison-fortress.

After the war De Gaulle went to general-staff school, where he hurt his career by constant criticism of his superiors. He denounced the static concept of trench warfare and wrote a series of essays calling for a strategy of movement with armored tanks and planes. The French hierarchy ignored his works, but the Germans read him and adapted his theories to develop their triumphant strategy of blitzkrieg, or lightning war, with which they defeated the French in 1940.

When France fell, De Gaulle, then an obscure brigadier general, refused to capitulate. He fled to London, convinced that the British would never surrender and that American power, once committed, would win the war. On June 18, 1940, on BBC radio, he insisted that France had only lost a battle, not the war, and called upon patriotic Frenchmen to resist the Germans. This inspiring broadcast won him worldwide acclaim.

## Early Political Activity

When the Germans were driven back, De Gaulle had no rivals for leadership in France. Therefore in the fall of 1944 the French Parliament unanimously elected him premier. De Gaulle had fiercely opposed the German enemy, and now he vigorously defended France against the influence of his powerful allies Joseph Stalin, Winston Churchill, and Franklin Roosevelt. De Gaulle once stated that he never feared Adolf Hitler, who, he knew, was doomed to defeat, but did fear that his allies would dominate France and Europe in the postwar period.

By the fall of 1945, only a year after assuming power, De Gaulle was quarreling with all the political leaders of France. He saw himself as the unique savior of France, the only disinterested champion of French honor, grandeur, and independence. He despised all politicians as petty, corrupt, and self-interested muddlers, and, chafing under his autocratic rule, they banded against him. In January

1946, disgusted by politics, he resigned and retreated into a sulking silence to brood upon the future of France.

In 1947 De Gaulle reemerged as leader of the opposition. He headed what he termed "The Rally of the French People," which he insisted was not a political party but a national movement. The Rally became the largest single political force in France but never achieved majority status. Although De Gaulle continued to despise the political system, he refused to lead a coup d'etat, as some of his followers urged, and again retired in 1955.

## Years as President

In May 1958 a combination of French colonials and militarists seized power in Algeria and threatened to invade France. The weakened Fourth Republic collapsed, and the victorious rebels called De Gaulle back to power as president of the Fifth Republic of France. From June 1958 to April 1969 he reigned as the dominant force in France. But he was not a dictator, as many have charged; he was elected first by Parliament and then in a direct election by the people.

As president, De Gaulle fought every plan to involve France deeply in alliances. He opposed the formation of a United States of Europe and British entry into the Common Market. He stopped paying part of France's dues to the United Nations, forced the NATO headquarters to leave France, and pulled French forces out of the Atlantic Alliance integrated armies. Denouncing Soviet oppression of Eastern Europe, he also warned of the Chinese threat to the world. He liberated France's colonies, supported the Vietnamese "liberation movement" against the United States, and called for a "free Quebec" in Canada.

De Gaulle had an early success in stimulating pride in Frenchmen and in increasing French gold reserves and strengthening the economy. By the end of his reign, however, France was almost friendless, and his economic gains had been all but wiped out by the student and workers protest movement in spring 1968.

De Gaulle ruled supreme for 11 years, but his firm hand began to choke and then to infuriate many citizens. In April 1969 the French voted against his program for reorganizing the Senate and the regions of France. He had threatened to resign if his plan was rejected and, true to his word, he promptly renounced all power. Thereafter De Gaulle remained silent on political issues. Georges Pompidou, one of his favorite lieutenants, was elected to succeed him as president. Charles De Gaulle died at Colombey-les-Deux-Églises on Nov. 9, 1970.

## Further Reading

De Gaulle's *War Memoirs* (3 vols., 1954-1959; trans. 1955-1960) is available in a single volume as *The Complete War Memoirs of Charles de Gaulle* (1964). The first volume of his postwar memoirs is *Memoirs of Hope* (trans. 1971). His *The Edge of the Sword* (1959; trans. 1960) is a personal credo on the qualities of leadership. Jean Lacouture, *De Gaulle* (1964; trans. 1966), is one of the best biographies, written by an astute French observer. Jean R. Tournoux, *Pétain and De Gaulle* (1964; trans. 1966), is a study of the relationship of the two men from World War I. A biography in three parts, examining De Gaulle's roles as soldier, savior of his nation, and statesman, is David Schoenbrun, *The Three Lives of Charles de Gaulle* (1966). Other more specialized studies include Jacques de Launay, *De Gaulle and His France: A Psychopolitical and Historical Portrait* (trans. 1968); Anton W. DePorte, *De Gaulle's Foreign Policy, 1944-46* (1968); and Raymond Aron, *De Gaulle, Israel, and the Jews* (1968; trans. 1969). □

# Thomas Dekker

**The English playwright and pamphleteer Thomas Dekker (ca. 1572-ca. 1632) is noted for his vivid portrayals of London life and his genial sympathy for the lower classes.**

Nothing is known of Thomas Dekker's parentage or education. Throughout his life he remained closely identified with London, where he was probably born about 1572. He acquired some knowledge of Latin, French, and Dutch, and he may have seen military service in his early years.

The first evidence of Dekker's association with the stage appears in the records of Philip Henslowe, the theatrical manager whose diary provides much valuable information about the more practical side of Elizabethan drama. Henslowe also reveals that Dekker was imprisoned for debt—a not uncommon fate for dramatists of the period.

Early in his career Dekker produced his most popular play, *The Shoemaker's Holiday* (1599). This engaging mixture of sentimental romance and homely urban realism shows Dekker's modest talents to best advantage. The principal focus of interest is the honest, convivial shoemaker Simon Eyre, who by virtue of industry and good luck rises to become lord mayor of London. Always mindful of his humble origins, the madcap lord mayor holds a grand feast for the apprentices of London and decrees that Shrove Tuesday be set aside as a holiday for shoemakers. Simon also plays a part in bringing together the wellborn lovers Rowland Lacy and Rose Otely and in restoring Rafe Damport to his wife, Joan. The play is seasoned with the diverting good humor of Dame Margery, Simon's talkative, down-to-earth wife, and the shoemakers Hodge and Firk.

About 1603 Dekker turned his hand to the writing of popular prose pamphlets. By 1610 he had produced at least 13 of these, *The Gull's Hornbook* (1609) being the best-known. While these works have little merit as literature, they do provide a fascinating picture of the seamier side of London life in the early 17th century.

During this period Dekker continued his dramatic work, usually as a collaborator. *The Honest Whore* (Part 1, 1604; Part 2, ca. 1605) and *The Roaring Girl* (ca. 1610, written with Thomas Middleton) are among the six or seven plays from this period of Dekker's career. From 1613 to 1619 he evidently wrote nothing; these years may have been spent in prison, but the evidence on this point is not conclusive. In 1620 he reappears as a pamphleteer and playwright. His later dramatic works (done in collaboration with such playwrights as Philip Massinger, William Rowley, and John Ford) reveal his abiding interest in London life, with his earlier sunny realism occasionally qualified by a note of bitterness.

Dekker composed the annual lord mayor's pageant in 1628 and 1629. He died shortly afterward, probably in 1632, heavily in debt.

### Further Reading

The basic biography is M. L. Hunt, *Thomas Dekker* (1911; repr. 1964). Critical studies include K. L. Gregg, *Thomas Dekker: A Study in Economic and Social Backgrounds* (1924); J. H. Conover, *Thomas Dekker: An Analysis of Dramatic Structure* (1969); and G. R. Price, *Thomas Dekker* (1969). □

# Fredrik Willem de Klerk

**Fredrik Willem de Klerk (born 1936) was state president of South Africa from 1989 to 1994. He abruptly pointed his country in a new direction in 1990 by opening negotiations with previously outlawed anti-apartheid organizations.**

In 1989 Fredrik Willem de Klerk was described by one observer of South African politics as "strongly loyal to National Party interests and a cautious, not bold, mover," an opinion shared by most analysts. Thus few were prepared for the dramatic news of February 11, 1990, when de Klerk announced the release of Nelson Mandela, the South African resistance leader, from prison after 27 years. At the same time, de Klerk restored to legality the African National Congress (ANC), the Pan-Africanist Congress, the South African Communist Party, and other opposition groups. These moves, far from cautious, thoroughly revolutionized the political landscape of South Africa.

### Brief Overview of South African History

De Klerk's actions as President went against a long tradition of suppression. In the early nineteenth century, England seized control from the Dutch of the Cape Colony at the southern tip of Africa. The Dutch-speaking inhabitants were displaced in power and influence by English-speaking settlers. In numerous ways, but especially in its more liberal treatment of African people, British rule angered many Dutch. Between 1836 and 1838, several thousand Dutch Boers (farmers) emigrated from the Cape Colony to establish new societies in the interior of South Africa, beyond the reach of British authority.

This mass emigration, known as the Great Trek, created two sorts of enemies for the Dutch, who began calling themselves Afrikaners. The first enemy was the British, from whose power they were attempting to escape. The second was a number of powerful Black African states, the Zulu being the best known, whose lands they were invading.

Over the next 150 years, the Afrikaners struggled against both.

By the 1960s, the Afrikaners seemed to have triumphed. The historic campaign to remove British power, the major confrontation being the Anglo-Boer War of 1899 to 1902, ended successfully with the election of a purely Afrikaner National Party government in 1948. As a result, South Africa withdrew from the British Commonwealth in 1960.

### National Party Established Apartheid

The National Party's policy of apartheid, which virtually eliminated Black African participation in government and reduced Black Africans to a powerless, cheap labor supply, appeared to have ended the Black African threat by the mid-1960s. Afrikaners, convinced that their success was the result of their unity of thought and action, brought schools, newspapers, television, and radio under government control to mold the minds of young Afrikaners. The Dutch Reformed Church, of which almost all Afrikaners were members, provided scriptural and moral support for apartheid. Opposing views were censored. Dissenters were branded traitors and treated accordingly.

### Black Protest Revived

Black protest revived in the 1970s. Strikes by Black workers, the uprising of school-children in Soweto and other Black townships in 1976, intensified sabotage by the ANC, and a growing campaign by people in other countries to isolate South Africa economically put intense pressure on the Nationalist government.

The response of National Party leaders was defiance. President John Vorster and his successor, P. W. Botha, suppressed dissent vigorously and assured the outside world that pressure would make Whites more resistant to change, not less. Botha instituted mild reforms. For example, in 1983 a new constitution was approved by White voters that gave a small bit of influence to people of Asian and mixed descent, though none to Black Africans. It also gave enormous power to the state president.

Largely because they had been denied any role in the new constitution, Blacks rose again in 1984. Demonstrations and riots were ruthlessly suppressed. Killings increased, rising into the thousands by 1986. Botha eased some "petty apartheid" laws, but left the system's basic structure intact. He declared a state of emergency, which suspended what civil liberties were left and led to the detention without trial of unknown numbers, perhaps thousands, of Black and White dissidents.

South Africa's economy suffered enormously, both from the effects of sanctions and from plunging investor confidence. The Rand, the basis of the currency, lost nearly two-thirds of its value. But Botha maintained his resistance to fundamental change. Into this situation stepped F. W. de Klerk.

## De Klerk's Early Years

De Klerk was born on March 18, 1936, in Johannesburg. J. G. Strijdom, a prime minister of South Africa in the 1950s who instituted many apartheid laws, was his uncle. De Klerk attended Potschefstroom University, a center of Afrikaner Nationalist thought. He was a member of one of the more conservative branches of the Dutch Reformed Church. While teaching law, he was elected to Parliament in 1972, representing the town of Vereeniging. All this activity was in the province of Transvaal, a focal point of Afrikaner political power and the location of most of the mineral wealth that is the basis of the South African economy.

He joined Vorster's cabinet in 1978, serving successively as minister of post and telecommunications, social welfare and pensions, sport and recreation, mineral and energy affairs, and internal affairs. De Klerk eventually became the chief of the Transvaal branch of the party.

## De Klerk Replaced Botha As Party Leader

In January of 1989, P. W. Botha suffered a stroke that forced him to resign as head of the National Party, though he remained state president. De Klerk replaced him as party leader. An extraordinary episode occurred in August when de Klerk, without Botha's knowledge, announced a meeting to talk about the South African situation with Zambia's President Kenneth Kaunda. Botha publicly chastised de Klerk and then suddenly resigned the presidency. De Klerk succeeded as acting president. In September of 1989, the National Party won parliamentary elections, though by a decreased margin. De Klerk thus became state president,

which set the stage for the extraordinary events of February 11, 1990.

While the sweeping nature of de Klerk's actions on that date surprised almost everyone, elements of his background aided his ability to discard the rigidity of Afrikaner nationalism. First, his brother, Willem de Klerk, was a founder of the anti-apartheid Democratic Party, which advocated a nonracial democracy for South Africa. Willem de Klerk described F. W. de Klerk as "open-minded," "pragmatic," and "very much inclined to find solutions for South Africa." Perhaps hinting that his views might have had some effect on F. W. de Klerk's, Willem de Klerk noted that their relationship was "basically sound."

Second, at the outset of his presidency de Klerk seemed to associate himself less with the security and military branches of the government, which have always favored greater repression, and more with the economic and foreign policy offices, which are more interested in South Africa's standing abroad.

Finally, there is de Klerk's undoubted loyalty to the National Party. As South Africa faced hard times in the 1980s, so did the party. Even P. W. Botha believed that South Africa must "adapt or die," and his halting steps toward reform split the party between those who wanted to strengthen and those who wanted to reform apartheid. Having inherited this fragmentation, de Klerk may have believed that the way to save the party was to attract reformers, many of them English-speaking, who had hitherto supported other groups.

On May 7, 1990, de Klerk and a government delegation had their first formal meeting with Mandela and representatives of the ANC, who had once been denounced by the government as terrorists. Both leaders reported the meeting to have been amicable, and each stated his regard for the integrity of the other. Mandela reported that "we are closer to one another." Both leaders were well aware that years of repression had produced many dangerous forces that could at any time sabotage the results of that meeting and its hope for South Africa's future. But de Klerk's role as the catalyst in changing the course of South Africa's history seemed secure. Additional evidence came September 24, 1990, when at a meeting with President George Bush he became the first South African head of state to visit the White House.

## De Klerk Became Second Vice President

De Klerk worked with Mandela to abolish apartheid and grant constitutional voting rights to all South Africans. In 1993 the two shared the Nobel Peace Prize. In April 1994, they saw their efforts come to fruition as they campaigned against each other in the first all-race election in South Africa. In this election, with Black South Africans casting the majority vote, Mandela became the first Black president of South Africa. De Klerk became the second vice president in Mandela's Government of National Unity. In 1996 the government adopted a new constitution that guaranteed equal rights. De Klerk was concerned, however, that the constitution would not protect minority group rights. The National Party, still led by him, broke away from Mandela, saying that South Africa needed a strong multi-party system. In August 1997, de Klerk resigned as head of the National Party and quit politics. At the news conference, he stated, "I am resigning because I am convinced it is in the best interest of the party and the county."

## Further Reading

Sketches of de Klerk's background can be found in such articles as Harald Pakendorf, "New Personality, Old Policies?" *Africa Report* (May-June 1989); Allister Sparks, "The Secret Revolution" *New Yorker* (April 11, 1994); *Los Angeles Times* (May 3, 1994). See also the interview with Willem de Klerk in *Africa Report* (July-August, 1989). Among the best accounts of Afrikaner ideology is Leonard Thompson, *The Political Mythology of Apartheid* (1985). A good account of the anti-apartheid struggle is Tom Lodge, *Black Politics in South Africa Since 1945* (1983). □

# Willem de Kooning

**The Dutch-born American painter Willem de Kooning (1904-1997) was a leader of the abstract expressionist movement of the 1940s and 1950s.**

B efore the 1940s the major advances in modern painting were forged on English and European soil. American artists, although aware of these advances, had not generally participated in their origin. After World War II, however, the United States, and in particular New York City, became a focal point for modernist developments. The most celebrated of these is known as abstract expressionism—abstract, because most of the new art eschewed all traces of visible reality; expressionism, because it appeared to have been created through uncontrolled and sometimes violent painterly gestures. Known also as action painting or painterly abstraction (historians have yet to agree on the most appropriate designation), abstract expressionism reached international scope and influence during the 1950s.

Willem de Kooning and Jackson Pollock are the best-known exponents of this new American style. Although their works inspired public ridicule at first, both artists are now recognized as major figures within the broader tradition of art history. For de Kooning this recognition is especially significant, because he always viewed himself as a link in the great tradition of painterly art that runs from the Renaissance to the present day.

Willem de Kooning was born in Rotterdam, Holland, on April 24, 1904. In 1916 he left school to work as a commercial artist, and he enrolled in evening classes at the Academy of Fine Arts in his native city, where he studied for eight years. During this period he became aware of the group called de Stijl, whose membership included Piet Mondrian and Theo van Doesburg, two of the most influential abstractionists of the early twentieth century.

## Early Career

In 1926 de Kooning immigrated to the United States. He took a studio in New York City and supported himself by doing commercial art and house painting. In his own painting he began to experiment with abstraction but, like many artists during the Depression, was unable to devote full time to his work. The opportunity to do so came in 1935, when he worked for a year on the Federal Art Project of the Works Project Administration.

In the 1940s de Kooning's career as a painter began to accelerate. He participated in several group shows and in 1946 had his first one-man exhibition in New York City. Among sophisticated patrons and dealers this show established de Kooning as a major figure in contemporary American painting. In the same year he married Elaine Fried, and two years later he taught at the experimental Black Mountain College, which was then under the direction of the influential color abstractionist Josef Albers.

De Kooning's paintings from the 1930s and 1940s reveal many of the same stylistic vacillations that characterize his better-known productions of the period after 1950. In the early work de Kooning approached the problems of abstraction cautiously. *Bill-Lee's Delight* (1946), for instance, is ostensibly devoid of subject matter from the visible world. Rough-hewn masses sweep toward the center of the composition, where they collide, overlap, and twist into painterly space. Many of the planes, however, particularly those on the periphery of the painting, appear to be remnants of the human body; their undulating contours loosely recall arms, legs, and torsos that have been distilled into pictorial entities. In other words, the painting retains figurative allusions in spite of its apparent abstractness.

## Retaining the Human Image

*Bill-Lee's Delight* indirectly reveals de Kooning's deep commitment to the image of the human body. Even earlier works show the character of this commitment more explicitly. *Queen of Hearts* (1943-1946) presents the three-quarter image of a seated woman whose head, breasts, and arms are drawn with loosely flowing contours. The figure is freely distorted and somewhat unsettling: the head is twisted, the facial anatomy is askew, and the limbs and breasts appear ready to twist off and float into space. In overall style the painting recalls European surrealism with its eerie interpretations of figurative content. It is also similar to the abstract, quasi-surrealist style of Arshile Gorky, with whom de Kooning had once shared a studio.

Some of de Kooning's finest paintings were executed in the period that ended in 1950; these include *Ashville* (1949) and *Excavation* (1950). Both works retain some figurative allusions, but they achieve a powerful, abstract flatness, thereby insisting upon their identity as paintings. Moreover, both canvases achieve this identity within a relatively restricted color range; this lends tautness to the compelling presence of each painting.

## De Kooning since 1950

In spite of the achievement marked by paintings like *Ashville* and *Excavation*, de Kooning was evidently uncomfortable with the problems of abstraction. In 1950 he returned to the human figure, embarking upon his famous "Woman" series. *Woman I* (1950-1952) is probably the most famous of the series. The figure is executed in a tortured, aggressive manner and emerges like some demonic presence. Paint itself is likewise assaulted—dragged, pushed, and scraped—with a technique that, for many viewers, is the ultimate of abstract expressionist style. When the "Woman" paintings were shown in 1953 in New York City, they catapulted de Kooning to fame and notoriety. Although he was honored with numerous awards and retrospective exhibitions after that, his work periodically revealed doubts and uncertainties about its direction.

During the late 1950s de Kooning again abandoned the human figure in favor of abstraction. The paintings from these years are sometimes called "landscapes" because their open, expansive space is suggestive of the space of the natural environment. In *Suburb in Havana* (1958), for instance, broad, earth-colored diagonals reach into space and extend toward a blue mass that resembles both sky and water. Because of the explosiveness with which they open pictorial space, these landscapes count among de Kooning's most spontaneous and exhilarating achievements.

From the early 1960s de Kooning's development seemed problematic and uncertain. Once again he returned to the human figure and a second "Woman" series. These works display the master's characteristic blend of technical gusto and emotional fervor, but they evoked mixed opinions

among his critics. Perhaps more historical perspective is needed before these paintings can be viewed objectively.

De Kooning's first retrospective took place in 1953 in Boston. In 1954 he enjoyed a second, at the Venice Biennale. The largest retrospective was held in New York City in 1969. He was elected to the National Institute of Arts and Letters in 1960, and he received the Freedom Award Medal in 1964.

Since the 1960s de Kooning continued to be one of the most powerful representatives of abstract art. The period from 1981 to 1989 was one of the most fertile of his life, giving rise to over 300 works. Sadly, this burst of creativity proved to be his last. Alzheimer's Disease, diagnosed in 1990, prevented further work for the remaining seven years of his life. De Kooning died on March 19, 1997, at his home in East Hampton, New York.

## Further Reading

Several monographs on de Kooning have been written, among them, Thomas B. Hess, *Willem de Kooning* (1959), and Harriet Janis and Rudi Blesh, *De Kooning* (1960). Also important is Hess's *Willem de Kooning* (1969), the catalog for the Museum of Modern Art's de Kooning retrospective of 1969. For a more general picture of de Kooning's relation to postwar American art see Barbara Rose, *American Art since 1900* (1967). For more information, please see Harry F. Gaugh, *De Kooning* (Abbeville Press, 1983); Paul Cummings, *Willem De Kooning: Drawings, Paintings, Sculpture* (Whitney Museum of American Art, 1983); and Diane Waldman, *De Kooning* (Abrams, 1987). □

# Ferdinand Victor Eugène Delacroix

**The French painter Ferdinand Victor Eugène Delacroix (1798-1863) repudiated the neoclassic manner and developed a freer and more romantic style with a particular emphasis on color.**

For 40 years Eugène Delacroix was one of the most prominent and controversial painters in France. Although the intense emotional expressiveness of his work placed the artist squarely in the midst of the general romantic outpouring of European art, he always remained an individual phenomenon and did not create a school. As a personality and as a painter, he was admired by the impressionists, postimpressionists, and symbolists who came after him.

Born on April 28, 1798, at Charenton-Saint-Maurice, the son of an important public official, Delacroix grew up in comfortable upper-middle-class circumstances in spite of the troubled times. He received a good classical education at the Lycée Impérial. He entered the studio of Pierre Narcisse Guérin in 1815, where he met Théodore Géricault.

### Early Style

Delacroix's public career was launched with a flourish at the Salon of 1822, in which he exhibited *Dante and Virgil in Hell.* Large, somewhat hastily painted, still traditional in its bas-relief type of design, it was nevertheless novel in subject matter and in the emotional intensity conveyed by powerful, contorted forms and smoldering, vibrant tones.

Delacroix shared the new Anglophilia of French culture, played the role of a dandy, read Shakespeare, Byron, and Scott, visited England, and was impressed by English artists such as Richard Bonington and John Constable. Indeed, Constable's landscapes are supposed to have influenced Delacroix's *Massacre at Chios,* shown in 1824. An immense canvas, almost 14 feet high, it was obviously designed to create an impression at the Salon. Although Baron Gros called it "the massacre of painting," the government purchased it. Based on an incident in the Greek war of independence, the painting is as exotic as Delacroix's later North African pictures and is filled with a romantic taste for violence.

Among the dozen paintings Delacroix submitted to the Salon of 1827-1828, the immense, baroque *Death of Sardanapalus,* based on a theme by Byron, is remarkable for its theatrical fervor and luxuriant color. *Liberty Leading the People,* inspired by the Revolution of 1830, closed the first phase of Delacroix's career. It is almost the only important work, except for the *Massacre at Chios,* that had any connection with contemporary history: the scene was Parisian but the interpretation was allegorical.

### Mature Style

The stimulus of a fortuitous 6-month trip to Morocco in 1832 had a lifelong effect on Delacroix's development and gave him an inexhaustible store of pictorial materials. The most immediate result was *Women of Algiers in Their Apartment* (1834), in which an Oriental subject allowed for the kind of "visual feast" and poetic effect that he always considered the proper aims of painting.

Also notable among the pictures of the 1830s and 1840s by Delacroix were historical scenes painted on commission, such as the *Battle of Taillebourg* (1837) and the *Entry of the Crusaders into Constantinople* (1840). They reflect his natural taste for the grand manner and for large-scale compositions, as well as his persistent enthusiasm for the dynamic style of Peter Paul Rubens and the mundane splendor of Paolo Veronese.

Those who believe that Delacroix turned back to classicism in the 1830s could point to his painting *Medea* (1838), a picture that could almost have been painted by Jacques Louis David. "I am a pure classic," Delacroix insisted at this time, only to confess in a paradoxical counterstatement, "If by romanticism they mean the free manifestation of my personal impressions . . . then I am a romantic and have been one since I was fifteen."

In 1833 Delacroix began his career as a mural painter, and in the next 28 years he executed paintings in Paris in the Chamber of Deputies (Palais-Bourbon), the Senate (Luxembourg Palace), the church of St-Denis-du-St-Sacrement, the Louvre, the City Hall, and St-Sulpice. Drawing heavily on classical and biblical themes and aided by assistants, he employed a technique in which the colors were mixed with wax. Although many of the subjects were traditional, the style in which they were carried out was full of romantic fire and excitement (*Attila Hemicycle,* finished 1847, Palais-Bourbon). In the ceiling panel of the Louvre, the *Triumph of Apollo* (1851), Delacroix achieved a highly successful baroque manner of his own. The murals are among the finest French decorative paintings.

### Late Style

In the 1850s Delacroix's natural tendency toward freedom in the treatment of form and looseness of touch became more marked: *Marphise* (1852) and the sketch for *Eurydice* (1856) are good examples. Such works are reminiscent of the boldness of the late Titian—and of the late Auguste Renoir. Brilliance and luminosity of color increase; all forms are fused together in a dense pictorial whole.

There is an appreciable increase in Christian themes in the final period of Delacroix's career. "I was much impressed by the Requiem Mass," he wrote in his *Journal* (Nov. 2, 1854). "I thought of all that religion has to offer the imagination, and at the same time of its appeal to man's deepest feelings." The *Christ on the Lake of Genesareth* (1854) in Baltimore illustrates the rough-textured, agitated, and tumultuous style that often appeared in his final years of painting. This theme, which seems to have had a broad symbolic significance for the artist, must have become truly obsessive, for there are seven different versions of it.

In the last 10 or 12 years of his life Delacroix showed a renewed interest in the "pagan" North African subjects of his Moroccan experience of 1832. Among the most striking are the tiger and lion hunts and scenes of animal violence, which were created as much from imagination and from Rubens as from direct observation of animal behavior in Africa or Paris. Perhaps the sketch *Lion Hunt* (1854), done in preparation for a large painting in Bordeaux, is the most astonishing of these works. The wild, explosive design, created by fluid patches of warm color, has very properly been considered an anticipation of Fauvism.

Charles Baudelaire's enthusiastic praise of Delacroix's contribution to the Salon of 1859 was not enough to outweigh the bitter criticism. In any case, the painter decided not to exhibit at the Salon again. In 1861, disappointed by the poor response to his new mural paintings in St-Sulpice (*Jacob Wrestling with the Angel*), Delacroix wrote that he did not see much point in continuing with work that interested only 30 people in Paris. And yet, if he had been offered other commissions and had had the strength to do them, he would have gone on. By that time artistic work had become his only passion, his only solace. Two years later failing health overcame his determined will, and Delacroix died in Paris on Aug. 13, 1863.

## Delacroix's Influence

In the early years of his career Delacroix found black a valuable "color." Later he said, "Gray is the enemy of all paintings"; and finally he wrote, "Banish all earth colors." Although he does not seem to have used a fully spectral palette, he moved in that direction, exploited complementary contrasts, and demonstrated the usefulness of separate touches and the possibility of constructing a picture by means of individual, interlacing brush-strokes and patches of color. These devices were developed further by the impressionists and postimpressionists. On the other hand, the symbolists followed Delacroix in the pictorial projection of inner, imaginative fantasies and in the abstractly expressive use of color.

## Further Reading

Delacroix's *Journal* was translated by Walter Pach in 1937. Lucy Norton did another translation of the greater part of the *Journal* in 1951. The most comprehensive study of Delacroix is René Huyghe, *Delacroix* (trans. 1963). The best short account is Lee Johnson, *Delacroix* (1963). Independent in outlook, and with many unfamiliar comparative illustrations, is Frank A. Trapp, *The Attainment of Delacroix* (1970). Two excellent but more specialized books are George P. Mras, *Eugène Delacroix's Theory of Art* (1966), and Jack J. Spector, *The Murals of Eugène Delacroix at Saint-Sulpice* (1967). □

# Miguel de la Madrid Hurtado

**Miguel de la Madrid Hurtado (born 1934) was elected president of Mexico in 1982 and served until 1988 at a time when the country was facing its most severe economic crisis in history. His substantial efforts to cope with the crisis won him more respect abroad than at home.**

Miguel de la Madrid Hurtado was born in the western Mexican state of Colima on December 12, 1934. The family roots in that state dated back to the 18th century. His father, Miguel de la Madrid Castro, placed a high premium on formal education for his children and sent young Miguel to Mexico City for his primary, secondary, and university schooling. Miguel de la Madrid completed his law studies at the National Autonomous University of Mexico in 1957 and was awarded his degree with distinction after defending a thesis entitled "The Economic Thought of the 1857 Constitution."

De la Madrid's professional interests lay in the field of economics, and shortly after graduation he secured employment in the Bank of Mexico. As he rose in the organization his responsibilities began to outstrip his formal training. He made the decision to move temporarily to the United States for additional graduate training. He studied at Harvard University from 1964 to 1965 and also earned a Masters degree in public administration while there.

De la Madrid Hurtado (center)

## Served in Treasury

Economic administration in the public sector would demand his energies for the next 15 years. From 1965 to 1970 he served as subdirector of the Credit Section of the Secretariat of the Treasury and then as subdirector of Finances for Petróleos Mexicanos, the state owned oil industry. In 1972 he moved back to the Treasury Ministry, this time as director general of credit. The record he established in public administration was an enviable one, and by 1979 President José López Portillo believed that Miguel de la Madrid, then only 45 years old, should be brought into the cabinet. He named him secretary of planning and programming, a position in which he served until he won the presidential nomination of the Partido Revolucionario Institucional in 1981. He won the Mexican presidency the following year.

## Inherited Economic Crisis

Miguel de la Madrid's rise to his country's highest political office was meteoric to be sure, but in spite of his relative youth he was perhaps better prepared for the tasks that lay ahead than any of his 20th-century predecessors. As he began his six-year term he inherited a country beset by economic problems so serious they threatened to disrupt the social order. The country was in its worst recession since the Great Depression of 1930. The inflation rate topped 100 percent in 1982 and approached that record again the following year. Increases in the costs of gasoline, corn, wheat, and electricity led the assault on the consumer price index. Negative publicity concerning the murder of a U.S. drug enforcement agent, the disappearance of several U.S. citizens in Guadalajara, and some political violence during the mid-term elections of 1985 discouraged U.S. tourism, further hampering the badly needed influx of U.S. dollars. The president's repeated assurances that tourists were safe in Mexico were true, but they proved unproductive.

Mexico's foreign debt under Miguel de la Madrid topped $90 billion, one of the highest debt loads in the world. During previous administrations, especially under López Portillo, Mexico had borrowed heavily to finance its modernization effort and had predicated its ability to repay the substantial loans on its petroleum wealth. But the world oil glut and the subsequent drop in the price for crude oil left the country without its leading source of foreign exchange earnings. Unemployment and underemployment demoralized the work force and pushed tens of thousands of Mexicans across the northern border into the United States in search of jobs. The peso began to slip against the dollar and then began its plunge in the free market. During the summer of 1985 it fell from 260 to 380 to the dollar along the U.S.-Mexico border.

President de la Madrid was forced to adopt stringent and unpopular austerity measures to restore some semblance of economic order and to rekindle some degree of confidence in the world's banking community and financial markets. Recognizing that government expenditures had to be drastically reduced, de la Madrid announced reductions in federal subsidies, the sale of inefficient and unprofitable state-owned enterprises, and a freeze on federal employ-

ment. Using the influence of the presidency he did his best to limit the size of wage increases in the labor force, and he also attempted to reduce the import of nonessential consumer goods. Finally, in a bold move, the president eliminated 51,000 federal jobs and cut back the salaries of many federal employees whose positions simply could not be eliminated.

## Refinanced Foreign Debt

President de la Madrid's austerity measures helped in some areas but not in others. Because the international banking community approved of his efforts, Mexico was able to refinance its huge foreign debt. Creditors agreed to give the country additional time to rebuild its economy. The 1984 inflation rate was held to 60 percent, a slight improvement, but in that same year Mexico's gross national product recorded its third consecutive decline as the country's population growth greatly outstripped a modest rate of economic growth.

De la Madrid was a strong and dynamic political figure, better thought of abroad than at home. The president sought improved relations with the United States, particularly with regard to trade, and was less critical than his predecessors of U.S. policies regarding Central America. However, particularly after a U.S. Drug Enforcement Agency employee was murdered in 1985, the issue of drug trafficking from Mexico to the United States remained a sore point.

De la Madrid was succeeded by Carlos Salinas de Gortari in 1988 after serving one six-year term. On his way out of office in 1988, de la Madrid sought a $3.5 billion loan to Mexico from the United States, ignoring a popular sentiment favoring a debt moratorium. He also announced plans to sell or liquidate up to 50 state-run companies. "De la Madrid is doing the dirty work now to make life easier for Salinas," said an official in Mexico's Energy, Mines & Federal Industry Secretariat.

In 1990, de la Madrid became director general of Fondo de CulturaECONÓOMICA. While in the mid-1990s, it had become popular with some of Mexico's living ex-presidents to break with the tradition called La Mordaza (the Muzzle) and criticize sitting President Ernesto Zedillo, de la Madrid refused to do the same.

## Further Reading

Miguel de la Madrid has not yet received full biographical treatment in English, and monographic analysis of his administration will have to await completion of his term of office. A brief biographical sketch can be found in Roderic A. Camp, *Mexican Political Biographies, 1935-1975* (1978). Preliminary studies of his economic policies are contained in *The Mexican Forum*, Vol. 5, No. 3 (1985), a newsletter published by the Office for Mexican Studies at the University of Texas. An early attempt to place de la Madrid in some historical perspective is found in Michael C. Meyer and William L. Sherman, *The Course of Mexican History* (1983). □

# Stephen DeLancey

**The American merchant Stephen DeLancey (1663-1741) founded an elite New York family and was an important colonial politician and entrepreneur.**

D uring the first half of the 18th century, when family connections meant everything in the commercial and political life of the American colonies and in New York particularly, Stephen DeLancey moved in the highest echelons of both spheres. He was born in Caen, France, offspring of a notable Huguenot family that was forced out of France in 1685 with other Huguenots by the Edict of Nantes. Shortly after his arrival in New York, DeLancey married into the well-to-do Van Cortlandt family, thus taking a place in the colony's aristocratic structure. By 1702 DeLancey was described as one of the "most distinguished" and active members of the New York legislative assembly. He remained so for more than a quarter century.

His given name in French, Étienne, long since dropped by DeLancey, was introduced anew in 1725 as a derisive reference to his French birth by New York's royal governor William Burnet. For political reasons Burnet was trying to remove DeLancey from the Assembly on the spurious grounds that, being foreign-born, he was ineligible to sit in that body. DeLancey not only survived this assault but also apparently improved his political position as a result. He epitomized the kind of "placeman" (elite representative of a key family) that dominated colonial American politics.

DeLancey also typified the enterprising and freewheeling trader who moved so successfully across the colonial landscape. He was, at various times, a commercial agent for several European merchant houses, a supplier of English troops quartered in different parts of the New World during successive colonial wars, merchant to English interests in Canada and to settlements in the New York wilderness, and moneylender to sundry enterprises sponsored by New York's colonial government. He was a shrewd, well-connected dealer at a time of wide-open economic opportunities. His efforts anchored the DeLancey fortune for future generations of the family.

Stephen's son, James DeLancey, born in New York in 1703, studied law in London and then returned to practice in his hometown. Becoming a judge of the New York State Supreme Court in 1731, he was its chief justice until his death in 1760. James and his son (also named James) took their place among New York's colonial elite. That they remained loyal to England during the American Revolution curtailed, but did not entirely end, the political and economic power the family wielded for nearly a century.

## Further Reading

While much has been written about later DeLanceys, there is almost nothing about the founder of the dynasty. The best secondary source for Stephen DeLancey's activities is Lawrence H. Leder, *Robert Livingston, 1654-1728, and the Politics of Colonial New York* (1961). See also Stanley Nider Katz, *Newcastle's New York: Anglo-American Politics, 1732-1753* (1968). □

# Martin Robinson Delany

**African American intellectual Martin Robinson Delany (1812-1885), a journalist, physician, army officer, politician, and judge, is best known for his promotion before the Civil War of a national home in Africa for African Americans.**

M artin Delany was born free in Charlestown, Va., on May 6, 1812. His parents traced their ancestry to West African royalty. In 1822 the family moved to Chambersburg, Pa., to find a better racial climate. At the age of 19 Martin attended an African American school in Pittsburgh. He married Kate Richards there in 1843; they had 11 children.

In 1843 Delany founded one of the earliest African American newspapers, the *Mystery*, devoted particularly to the abolition of slavery. Proud of his African ancestry, Delany advocated unrestricted equality for African Americans, and he participated in conventions to protest slavery. Frederick Douglass, the leading African American abolitionist, made him coeditor of his newspaper, the *North Star*, in 1847. But Delany left in 1849 to study medicine at Harvard.

At the age of 40 Delany began the practice of medicine, which he would continue on and off for the rest of his life. But with the publication of his book *The Condition, Elevation, Emigration, and Destiny of the Colored People of the United States, Politically Considered* (1852; repr. 1968), he began to agitate for a separate nation, trying to get African Americans to settle outside the United States, possibly in Africa, but more probably in Canada or Latin America. In 1854 he led a National Emigration Convention. For a time he lived in Ontario. Despite his bitter opposition to the American Colonization Society and its colony, Liberia, Delany kept open the possibility of settling elsewhere in Africa. His 1859-1860 visit to the country of the Yorubas (now part of Nigeria) to negotiate with local kings for settling African Americans there is summarized in *The Official Report of the Niger Valley Exploring Party* (1861; repr. 1969).

When Delany returned to the United States, however, the Civil War was in progress and prospects of freedom for African Americans were brighter. He got President Abraham Lincoln to appoint him as a major in the infantry in charge of recruiting all-African American Union units.

After the war Delany went to South Carolina to participate in the Reconstruction. In the Freedmen's Bureau and as a Republican politican, he was influential among the state's population, regardless of race. In 1874 he narrowly missed election as lieutenant governor. In 1876, as the Republicans began losing control of the state, Delany switched to the conservative Democrats. Newly elected governor Wade Hampton rewarded him with an important judgeship in

M azo de la Roche was born on Jan. 15, 1879, in the town of Newmarket near Toronto into a middle-class family. She was educated in suburban schools in and near Toronto and had firsthand experience with farm life when her family rented a homestead outside the town of Bronte, Ontario. Here the author, who had been writing stories for a number of years with little success, underwent formative experiences which helped to crystallize important ideas of a country squirearchy which would be central to her best-known work.

## Her Work

Beginning her career as a writer of short stories, Mazo de la Roche published her first novel, *Possession,* in 1923 and had several plays produced in the 1920s. International popularity came with the publication of *Jalna* (1927), which won the $10,000 Atlantic-Little Brown Award that year and which launched the Whiteoak family and the story of its dynastic ups and downs through a series of widely published and much-translated novels.

Mazo de la Roche spent all of her creative life in Canada except for the years 1929-1939, when she lived abroad, mainly in England. Her published work includes 22 novels written between 1923 and 1960; a novella, *A Boy in the House* (1952); four works with an autobiographical background, of which *Ringing the Changes* (1957) is an important if misleading autobiography; five produced plays, from *Low Life* (1925) to *The Mistress of Jalna* (1951), and an adaptation of *Whiteoaks of Jalna* which was created for the stage in London and New York; short stories, many of which have been anthologized; a history of Quebec; and two books for children. She died in Toronto on July 13, 1961.

## Whiteoak Family

The story of the Whiteoak family and of its ancestral seat of Jalna spans a period of a century; it is a masterful and imaginative portrayal of a large family of characters—often seen as a rich gallery of eccentrics—allowed to work out their lives against the backdrop of a genteel and idealized Ontario countryside. While the personages of the Whiteoak family are romantically conceived, they are, in the main, compelling characterizations of individuals, whose carefully constructed roles and situations are evoked by means of meticulous stage setting, psychological manipulation, and skillful and accurate description. Several of these in the Jalna gallery are real and memorable figures, and even the less significant characters benefit from the author's skill at allowing the nature of each individual to develop and grow while retaining a set of identifiable and basic qualities.

The major thrust of the Jalna series was to stave off the all-embracing sweep of a vulgar, democratized, and materialistic way of North American life and to celebrate and advance a set of low-key, aristocratic, but practical values. The sense of a spiritual connection with England is a strong and profoundly significant, if latent, motif.

There is some indication that while the novels of Mazo de la Roche enjoyed a favorable review press well into the 1930s, she was ultimately disappointed by what has been described as a lack of serious critical response to her writ-

Charleston. As a judge, Delany won the respect of people of all races. In 1878 he helped sponsor the Liberian Exodus Joint Stock Steamship Company, which sent one ill-fated emigration ship to Africa. The next year his *The Principia of Ethnology* argued for pride and purity of the races and for Africa's self-regeneration.

When his political base collapsed in 1879, Delany returned to practicing medicine and later became a businessman in Boston. He died on Jan. 24, 1885.

## Further Reading

A recent biography of Delany is Victor Ullman, *Martin R. Delany: The Beginnings of Black Nationalism* (1971). A contemporary account is Frank A. Rollin, *Life and Public Services of Martin R. Delany* (1868; repr. 1969). William J. Simmons, *Men of Mark* (1968), includes a biographical sketch. For the significance of Delany's black nationalist thought before the Civil War see Howard H. Bell, *A Survey of the Negro Convention Movement 1830-1861* (1970). □

# Mazo Louise de la Roche

**Mazo Louise de la Roche (1879-1961) was a Canadian author whose masterful and dramatic description of a family of Canadian country squires gained her international recognition.**

ing. Another source of annoyance was that whenever an extended appraisal of the *Jalna* novels was attempted, it was usually developed in terms of a comparison with John Galsworthy's saga of the Forsyte family, an approach not borne out by the profound but readily apparent differences in the intentions, backgrounds, personalities, and social attitudes of the two writers.

## Further Reading

The most satisfying study is Ronald Hambleton, *Mazo de la Roche of Jalna* (1966), a sympathetic and balanced assessment.

## Additional Sources

Givner, Joan, *Mazo de la Roche: the hidden life,* Toronto: Oxford University Press, 1989. □

# Robert Delaunay

**Robert Delaunay (1885-1941) was a French painter often credited with painting the first abstract canvases based on theories of pure color around the year 1913.**

Robert Delaunay was born in Paris on April 12, 1885, into a prominent family descended from French aristocracy; his mother used the title "Countess." His parents divorced when he was four years old, and he was subsequently raised by an aunt and uncle. An uninspired student, Delaunay did not pursue an education and instead apprenticed himself to a theater designer. Unlike most of the young painters of his generation, he had no formal art training. In 1910 he married Sonia Terk, a Russian painter who became a life-long collaborator and continued to work on shared ideas long after his death from cancer in 1941.

A prolific painter at an early age, Delaunay showed in the Salon exhibitions, the most important official shows in France, in his early 20s. He incorporated much of the restlessness of art during the first decade of the 20th century in his early work, passing through a Pointillist, a Nabi, then a Fauve phase. It was around 1912 that Delaunay came to believe that light could be expressed as pure color independent of any objective content. He declared that "color alone is form and content."

This idea ran counter to the Cubist ideas of Picasso and Braque, who were more interested in the analysis of physical form than in light. Cubist paintings between 1907 and 1913 are static and sculptural without emphatic color, whereas Delaunay's paintings of the same period are fluid and multi-chromatic. He began a series of paintings of the Eiffel Tower rendered in swinging arcs of color that suggest movement. The Cubists accused Delaunay of reverting to the optical effects of Cezanne, while Delaunay maintained that he was doing "pure" paintings that expressed the dynamism of the 20th century.

In 1913 he began a series of paintings of colored discs that have no reference to any object and are considered hallmark paintings in the evolution of abstract or nonobjective art. The poet Guillaume Apollinaire called Delaunay's new style of abstract work "Orphism" in reference to the musician Orpheus in Greek mythology whose music had magical powers. Early abstract artists found strong connections between their work and music because neither depended on the imitation of phenomena found in the natural world.

Delaunay's belief in the primacy of color over form placed him closer in temperment to the German Expressionist painters than to Cubists working in France. In 1911 he exhibited with the Blaue Reiter (Blue Rider) group organized around Russian painter Wassily Kandinsky and he also showed in the Der Sturm Gallery in Berlin. He was caught in Spain at the outbreak of World War I in 1914, and he stayed there and in Portugal with his wife and their son until 1921.

During this time he met Russian exiles Sergei Diaghilev, producer and choreographer of the famed Ballets/Russes, and the composer Igor Stravinsky. In 1918 the Delaunays designed costumes and decor for a Diaghilev production of *Cleopatra*. His wife worked along lines similar to her husband, applying their theories of color simultaneity—the interaction of colors in relationship to one another—to design as well as painting. She made clothing, fabric, wall-covering, upholstery, and furniture covered with patches of color. She had an automobile painted in this manner which was considered a shocking and innovative extension of an idea from the avant-garde into the world-at-large.

Back in Paris after the war Delaunay resumed painting in a semi-figurative manner somewhat in contradiction to his early theories of nonobjective art. He exhibited little during this time, and it is considered a period of regression in his work. He also painted frescos for which he invented new techniques for mixing additives to paint to create unusual textures and colors. He worked with painter Fernand Leger on murals for the International Exposition of Decorative Arts and he designed film and stage sets. He became friendly with artist Jean Arp and poet Tristan Tzara. In his 30s he continued to do commissioned wall paintings, completing a mural at the Palais des Chemin de Fer and at the Salon des Tuileries.

Delaunay's career as a painter was meteoric. He was a prominent spokesperson for a specific point of view at a time of much artistic fermentation in the years preceding World War I. Unlike such other highly regarded artists of that period as Picasso, Matisse, and Kandinsky, he did not sustain the innovations that propelled him into the limelight in his youth into his later work. As a result, his painting seems uneven after 1920 and his most significant work in the 1930s was murals and public commissions, an extension of his wife's early experiments. After his death in 1941 she continued to work prodigiously, designing books, tapestries, and fabrics, as well as interior decors and murals. Her work, as an extension of her husband's theories and early discoveries, helped to establish his reputation as a significant painter of the 20th century.

## Further Reading

There are a number of good books written on the work of both Robert and Sonia Delaunay. Gustav Vrieson's *Robert Delaunay: light and color* (1969) is a standard, as is *Robert Delaunay* (1975), translated from the French with a text by Bernard Dorival. A more recent monograph, *Robert Delaunay,* appeared in 1976. There are numerous catalogs of exhibitions in Europe but none in English. Several works on Sonia stand out. One is a catalog *Sonia Delaunay: rhythms and colors* (1972) with text by Jacques Remase, and a second is *Sonia Delaunay* (1975) by Arthur Cohen. □

# Max Delbrück

**Max Delbrück (1906-1981) has often been called the founder of molecular biology. In 1969 he shared the Nobel Prize for physiology or medicine for work in the area of molecular genetics.**

M ax Delbrück has often been called the founder of molecular biology. Although educated as a physicist, Delbrück quickly became interested in bacteriophages, a type of virus that infects bacterial cells. He perfected a method of culturing bacteriophages and found that they could infect a bacterial cell and, within twenty minutes, erupt out of the cell in a hundredfold their original number. Each of these offspring bacteriophages was then ready to infect another bacterial cell. Among his many contributions to the field, Delbrück and another researcher together discovered that bacterial cells could spontaneously mutate to become immune to the bacteriophages. He also found that two different types of bacteriophages could combine to create a new type of bacteriophage. Perhaps as much or more than his discoveries, he forged the field of molecular biology through his involvement in the work of so many other scientists. While he was highly critical and not easily convinced of a new discovery, Delbrück also inspired many scientists to new heights. His work paved the way for an explosion of new findings in the field of molecular biology, including the discoveries that viruses contain the genetic material deoxyribonucleic acid (DNA), along with the eventual unveiling of the structure of DNA itself. In 1969, Delbrück won the Nobel Prize for physiology or medicine, which he shared with Alfred Day Hershey and Salvador Edward Luria, for their work in molecular genetics.

Delbrück was born on September 4, 1906, in Berlin as the youngest of seven children to Hans and Lina Thiersch Delbrück. Many of his relatives were prominent academicians, including his father, who was a professor of history at the University of Berlin and editor of the journal *Prussian Yearbook;* his maternal great-grandfather, Justus von Liebig, is considered the originator of organic chemistry. Throughout his youth in the middle-class suburb of Grünewald,

Delbrück developed his interests in mathematics and astronomy, and carried those interests into college.

In 1924 he enrolled in the University of Tübingen, but switched colleges several times before enrolling at the University of Göttingen, where he obtained his Ph.D. in physics in 1930. Delbrück began writing a dissertation about the origin of a type of star, but abandoned it because of his lack of understanding of both the necessary math and English, the language in which most of the pertinent literature was written. He took up a new topic, and completed his dissertation by explaining the chemical bonding of two lithium atoms, and why this bonding is much weaker than the bond between two hydrogen atoms.

For the next year and a half, through a research grant, he did postgraduate studies in quantum mechanics at the University of Bristol in England. There, he became friends with other researchers, several of whom went on to make major contributions in the fields of physics and chemistry. In the early 1930s, he continued his research as a Rockefeller Foundation postdoctoral fellow under Neils Bohr at the University of Copenhagen, one of the major intellectual centers in the world. Bohr's beliefs had a strong impact on Delbrück. Bohr had developed a theory of complementarity, stating that electromagnetic radiation could be described by either waves or particles, but not both at the same time. He followed that by a now-famous lecture in 1932 called "Light and Life." In it, Bohr suggested that a similar paradox existed in living things: they could be either described as whole organisms or as groups of molecules. Delbrück was hooked. He began to study biology. In 1932,

Delbrück returned to Berlin and the Kaiser Wilhelm Institute. He remained at the institute for five years, and continued his shift from physics to biology. From 1932 to 1937, while an assistant to Professor Lise Meitner in Berlin, Delbrück was part of a small group of theoretical physicists which held informal private meetings; he was devoted at first to theoretical physics, but soon turned to biology. In his acceptance speech for the Nobel Prize, Delbrück recalled that "Discussions of (new findings) within our little group strengthened the notion that genes had a kind of stability similar to that of the molecules of chemistry. From the hindsight of our present knowledge," he said, "one might consider this a trivial statement: what else could genes be but molecules? However, in the mid-'30s, this was not a trivial statement."

In 1937, by virtue of his second Rockefeller Foundation fellowship, Delbrück immigrated to the United States, where he began to study biology and genetics and the reproduction of bacteriophages, in particular, at the California Institute of Technology in Pasadena. A year later, he met Emory Ellis, a biologist also working on these viruses, and together they designed experiments to study bacteriophages and the mathematical system to analyze the results.

By 1940, Delbrück had joined the faculty of Vanderbilt University in Tennessee and during the following summers continued his phage research intensively at the Cold Spring Harbor Laboratory on Long Island in New York. Also in 1940 he met Italian physician Salvador Luria, with whom he would eventually share the Nobel Prize. Luria was conducting bacteriophage research at the College of Physicians and Surgeons of Columbia University in New York City. Their collaborative work began, and in 1943 Delbrück and Luria became famous in the scientific community with the publication of their landmark paper, "Mutations of Bacteria from Virus Sensitivity to Virus Resistance." The paper confirmed that phage-resistant bacterial strains developed through natural selection: once infected with a bacteriophage, the bacterium spontaneously changes so that it becomes immune to the invading virus. Their work also outlined the experimental technique, which became a standard analytical tool for measuring mutation rates. The publication of this paper is now regarded as the beginning of bacterial genetics.

Also in 1943, the so-called Phage Group held its first informal meeting, with Delbrück, Luria and microbiologist Alfred Hershey in attendance. At group meetings, members discussed research and ideas involving bacteriophages. The number of members grew along with the excitement over the possibilities presented by this area of research. The meetings were much like those Delbrück had so enjoyed while he was working in Meitner's lab in Berlin. In the following year, the Phage Group drafted guidelines—called the Phage Treaty of 1944—to ensure that results gained from different laboratories could be compared easily and accurately. The treaty urged all bacteriophage investigators to conduct their studies on a specific set of seven bacteriophages that infect *Escherichia coli* strain B and its mutants. It also spelled out the standard experimental conditions to be used.

While on the faculty at Vanderbilt University, Delbrück organized the first of his summer phage courses at Cold Spring Harbor in 1945, the year he also became a U.S. citizen. The course became an annual event and drew biologists, geneticists and physicists who traveled from laboratories all over the world to learn not only about the experimental and analytical methods of phage research but also about its potential.

In 1946, Delbrück's and Hershey's labs separately discovered that different bacteriophage strains that both invade the same bacterial cell could randomly exchange genetic material to form new and unique viral strains. They called the phenomenon genetic recombination. According to *Biographical Memoirs of Fellows of the Royal Society*, this finding "led, about 10 years later, to the ultimate genetic analysis of gene structure by Seymour Benzer."

The following year, Delbrück returned to the California Institute of Technology as a professor in the biology department. In 1949, he delivered an address, "A Physicist Looks at Biology," that recalled his scientific journey. "A mature physicist, acquainting himself for the first time with the problems of biology, is puzzled by the circumstance that there are no 'absolute phenomena' in biology. Everything is time bound and space bound. The animal or plant or microorganism he is working with is but a link in an evolutionary chain of changing forms, none of which has any permanent validity. . . . If it be true that the essence of life is the accumulation of experience through the generations, then one may perhaps suspect that the key problem of biology, from the physicist's point of view, is how living matter manages to record and perpetuate its experiences." He described the cell as a "magic puzzle box full of elaborate and changing molecules (that) carries with it the experiences of a billion years of experimentation by its ancestors."

In the late 1940s and early 1950s, Delbrück expanded his interests to include sensory perception, eventually studying how the fungus *Phycomyces* uses light and how light affects its growth. As he did with the phage research, Delbrück formed a *Phycomyces* Group to gather and discuss ideas. Despite his shift, he and his work continued to have an influence in bacteriophage research. In 1952 Hershey, one of the original three members of the Phage Group, and Martha Chase confirmed that genes consist of DNA and demonstrated how phages infect bacteria. The following year molecular biologist Francis Crick and physicist James Watson, once a graduate student of Luria's, determined the three-dimensional, double-helix structure of DNA. While their work was in progress, Watson would frequently write Delbrück to discuss ideas and to tell him about their results, including the first details of the double-helix structure.

Delbrück remained busy throughout the 1950s and 1960s as investigators and students sought his knowledge and advice, despite his reputation for being a tough critic with a brusque manner. Following an investigator's explanation of his research and results, Delbrück would often respond, "I don't believe a word of it," or if it was a more formal presentation, "That was the worst seminar I have ever heard." Once, according to Seymour Benzer in *Phage and the Origins of Molecular Biology,* Delbrück wrote to Benzer's wife, "Dear Dotty, please tell Seymour to stop writing so many papers. If I gave them the attention his papers *used* to deserve, they would take all my time. If he *must* continue, tell him to do what Ernst Mayr asked his mother to do in her long daily letters, namely, *underline what is important.*" Yet, many scientists persisted in bringing their research to Delbrück. In his essay in *Phage and the Origins of Molecular Biology,* molecular biologist Thomas Anderson recalled Delbrück: "At each phase in our groping toward discovery, Max Delbrück seemed to be present not so much as a guide, perhaps, but as a critic. To the lecturer he was an enquiring, and sometimes merciless, logician. If one persevered, he would be fortunate to have Max as conscience, goad and sage."

Delbrück also had a lighter side. As reported in *Thinking About Science,* Delbrück remembered pitting his wits against those of his college professors. He would not take notes during the lectures, but would try to follow and understand the professor's mathematical argument. "When the professor made a little mistake, with a plus or minus sign or a factor of 2, I did not point that out directly but waited 10 minutes until he got entangled and then pointed out, to his great relief, how he could disentangle himself—a great game." When Delbrück joined the faculty ranks, he developed a rather unusual tradition with his students and peers. He often invited them along on camping trips with his family, including his wife and eventually their four children. Delbrück married Mary Adeline Bruce in 1941. They had two sons, Jonathan and Tobias, and two daughters, Nicola and Ludina.

In 1961, while still a professor at the California Institute of Technology, Delbrück took a two-year leave of absence to help the University of Cologne in Germany establish its Institute of Genetics. In 1966 back in California, the former Phage Group members celebrated Delbrück's sixtieth birthday with a book in his honor, *Phage and the Origins of Molecular Biology.* The book is a collection of essays by the group members, many of whom had gone on to make important discoveries in bacterial genetics. The larger scientific community also recognized Delbrück's contributions with a variety of awards. In December of 1969, Delbrück, Luria and Hershey accepted the Nobel Prize in physiology or medicine for their work in molecular biology, particularly the mechanism of replication in viruses and their genetic structure.

Delbrück continued his sensory perception research into the next decade. He retired from the California Institute of Technology in 1977, and died of cancer four years later in Pasadena on March 10, 1981. In *Phage and the Origin of Molecular Biology,* phage course alumnus N. Visconti recalled a conversation he had with Delbrück. "I remember he once said to me, 'You don't have the inspiration or the talent to be an artist; then what else do you want to do in life besides be a scientist?' For Max Delbrück it was as simple as that."

## Further Reading

*Biographical Memoirs of Fellows of the Royal Society,* Volume 28, Royal Society (London), 1982.
Fischer, Ernst P., and Carol Lipson, editors, *Thinking about Science: Max Delbrück and the Origins of Molecular Biology,* W. W. Norton, 1988.
Hayes, William, "Max Delbrück and the Birth of Molecular Biology," in *Social Research,* autumn, 1984, pp. 641–673.
Kay, Lily, "Conceptual Models and Analytical Tools: The Biology of Physicist Max Delbrück," in *Journal of the History of Biology,* summer, 1985, pp. 207–246.
*Physics Today,* June, 1981, pp. 71–74. □

# Théophile Delcassé

**The French statesman and journalist Théophile Delcassé (1852-1923) was the chief architect of the Triple Entente between France, Britain, and Russia.**

Théophile Delcassé was born on March 1, 1852, in Palmiers. After graduating from the University of Toulouse in 1874, he went to Paris and in 1879 began to write for Léon Gambetta's journal, *La République française.* He continued his association with that paper until 1888 and also contributed to the *Paris* from 1881 to 1889.

In 1889 Delcassé was elected to the Chamber of Deputies. He was undersecretary for the colonies from January to December 1893 and served as second minister of colonies from May 1894 to January 1895. His policies were governed by his belief that colonial strength would enhance France's position as a European power.

In June 1898 Delcassé was appointed minister of foreign affairs, and he retained this position until June 1905. His policies aimed to strengthen French interests and achieve the diplomatic isolation of Germany. He won both Spanish and American friendship by his successful mediation in the Spanish-American War of 1898. This opened the way for subsequent rapprochements with both the United States and Spain. Meanwhile, during the Fashoda crisis of 1898, Delcassé won a measure of respect from the British by withstanding their pressure for 6 weeks.

Between 1899 and 1903 Delcassé transformed the Franco-Russian alliance into an active instrument of policy by broadening its scope to include defense of the European balance of power. He achieved understanding with Italy, based on settlement of differences in Africa. This culminated in 1902 in mutual guarantees of neutrality. Three agreements of April 8, 1904, settled British and French colonial differences and became the foundation of the Entente Cordiale between Britain and France. Meanwhile, Delcassé also encouraged cooperation between Russia and Britain, which led in 1907 to the formation of the Triple Entente. Italian, British, and Spanish agreements guaranteed France a free hand in Morocco, but Delcassé was forced to resign in 1905 during the first Moroccan crisis, when the Cabinet refused to support his policy.

# Daniel De Leon

**The American Socialist theoretician and political leader Daniel De Leon (1852-1914) was, according to Lenin, "the greatest of modern Socialists—the only one who has added anything to Socialist thought since Marx." However, De Leon's Socialist Labor party remained a tiny sect.**

ccording to his own testimony, Daniel De Leon was born into a wealthy family on the island of Curaçao near Venezuela, but it is possible that he was American-born. He was also said to have studied languages, history, philosophy, and mathematics at Dutch and German universities between 1865 and 1871. In 1872 he came to New York City and briefly assisted Cuban revolutionaries editing a Spanish-language newspaper. De Leon taught at a preparatory school and in 1876 entered Columbia University Law School. He graduated in a year and in 1883 was appointed to an international law lectureship at Columbia. He left Columbia in 1889, when he was denied a promised promotion.

De Leon's career at Columbia apparently declined because of his support of Henry George's third-party mayoralty candidacy in 1886 and his interest in the Nationalist movement of Edward Bellamy. At any rate, De Leon joined a tiny, almost moribund German organization in New York, the Socialist Labor party (SLP), and within a few years became the acknowledged master of the organization. In 1891 he became editor of the party's paper and was never seriously shaken in his leadership of the SLP until his death, in 1914.

The stormy, radical career of De Leon caused him to be resented as a disrupter by most of the Socialists in the United States. Personally, he was arrogant, inflexible, and intolerant of dissent; he even expelled his favorite son, Solon, from the SLP for questioning one of his theses. His unsuccessful attempts to control labor unions earned him further enmity, and his dictatorship within the SLP caused the secession of many former followers.

De Leon's attempt to align the Knights of Labor as an auxiliary to the SLP in the early 1890s only hastened the decline of that union. After an unsuccessful attempt to "bore from within" the American Federation of Labor, he organized the Socialist Trades and Labor Alliance (STLA) in 1895. It grew no faster than the parent SLP, and in 1905 he merged it into the Industrial Workers of the World (IWW). Again, his collaborators suspected his intentions, and in 1908 he and the STLA were tacitly expelled from the IWW. De Leon claimed that his followers were the true IWW, and the fiction was maintained until his death.

A prolific and brilliant writer, De Leon turned out dozens of pungent pamphlets and essays on topics facing the revolutionary movement of his day. Like his writings, his speeches were models of clarity and logic, studded with vivid metaphors and aphorisms. But his insistence on a hard-and-fast ideology did not prosper, and the leadership

As minister of marine from March 1911 to January 1913, Delcassé reorganized and strengthened the French navy and engaged in joint naval planning with Britain. As ambassador to Russia between March 1913 and January 1914, he improved the joint military planning of France and Russia and accelerated development of Russia's strategic railroads. Early in World War I Delcassé was named minister of foreign affairs, but he resigned after 14 months, when Bulgaria joined the Central Powers, proving the failure of his Balkan policy. Delcassé refused to vote for the Treaty of Versailles, which he felt gave France "neither reparations nor security," and retired from public life after 1919. He died at Nice on Feb. 22, 1923.

## Further Reading

The best study of Delcassé in English is Charles W. Porter, *The Career of Théophile Delcassé* (1936), which concentrates on his writings, speeches, and political acts and implies that he must bear a considerable responsibility for developments leading to World War I. See also John Francis Parr, *Théophile Delcassé and the Practice of the Franco-Russian Alliance: 1898-1905* (1952), and Christopher Andrew, *Théophile Delcassé and the Making of the Entente Cordiale* (1968).

## Additional Sources

Porter, Charles Wesley, *The career of Théophile Delcassé*, Westport, Conn.: Greenwood Press, 1975. □

of American socialism passed to the more flexible Socialist Party of America even during his life-time.

## Further Reading

Most accounts of De Leon's career in histories of the American Socialist movement are essentially hostile to him. These include Ira Kipnis, *The American Socialist Movement, 1897-1912* (1952); Howard H. Quint, *The Forging of American Socialism* (1953); David A. Shannon, *The Socialist Party of America* (1955); and Melvyn Dubofsky, *We Shall Be All: A History of the Industrial Workers of the World* (1969). A helpful study is *Daniel De Leon, the Man and His Work: A Symposium* (1920), published by the Socialist Labor party. There is also an essay on De Leon in Charles A. Madison, *Critics and Crusaders: A Century of American Protest* (1947; 2d ed. 1959).

## Additional Sources

Coleman, Stephen, *Daniel De Leon,* Manchester, UK and New York: Manchester University Press, 1990. Distributed exclusively in the U.S.A. and Canada by St. Martin's Press.

Seretan, L. Glen, *Daniel DeLeon, the odyssey of an American Marxist,* Cambridge, Mass.: Harvard University Press, 1979.
□

# David Dellinger

**An unwavering nonviolent pacifist, David Dellinger (born 1915) devoted his life to the promotion of** peace through his writings, his organizational talents, and his personal acts of courage. He spoke up for what he believed and remained an active speaker well into the 1990s.

David Dellinger was born in Wakefield, Massachusetts, on August 22, 1915. His father was a lawyer, a Yale law school graduate, and a Republican. In high school David was an outstanding athlete, long distance runner, and tournament-level golfer. He was also a superb student and already a confirmed pacifist. He graduated from Yale University as a Phi Beta Kappa economics major in 1936 and was awarded a scholarship for an additional year of study at Oxford University in England.

On his way to Europe he went to Spain, then in the middle of its civil war. Dellinger was so moved by the spirit of brotherhood among the Loyalist communist troops that he nearly joined them. Instead, he spent his year at Oxford, then returned to America for graduate work at Yale and religious training at the Union Theological Seminary.

In 1940 the U.S. government instituted the military draft in preparation for entering World War II, and David Dellinger became one of its first conscientious objectors. He refused to serve in the army. War, he said, was evil and useless. His alternative to war was brotherhood and the abolishment of capitalism. He served a one-year prison term, again refused to enlist, and was jailed for another two years. Upon leaving prison he married Elizabeth Peterson

and embarked upon a career as a printer, a writer, a peace organizer, and, above all, a radical pacifist. Far from being the austere, serious prototype of a pacifist, Dellinger was a husky, happy man whom friends often described as a "cheery elf." He was a genial person of boundless energy and uncommon good sense.

Dellinger, A. J. Muste, and Sidney Lens became the editors of *Liberation* in 1956. It was a radical pacifist monthly magazine which stood for economic justice, democracy, and nonviolence, and it continued publication for 19 years. Its subscription lists grew as young Americans started to protest the nation's treatment of Black people and the U.S. military incursion into Southeast Asia. Now, as one of the spokespersons for the American radical left, Dellinger made two journeys to Cuba in the early 1960s, reporting enthusiastically on what the Castro revolution had done for the Cuban people.

In April 1963, Dellinger participated in a "peace walk" in New York City during which those who favored peace clashed with other marchers over the Vietnam War, and Dellinger was cast into the forefront of anti-Vietnam politics. He worked in 1964 with Muste and two radical Catholic priests, Daniel and Philip Berrigan, to produce a "declaration of conscience" to encourage resistance to the military draft. A year later (August 1965), with Yale professor Staughton Lynd and Student Nonviolent Organizing Committee organizer Bob Parris, Dellinger was arrested in front of the U.S. Capitol leading a march for peace and was jailed for 45 days. Two months later Dellinger became one of the organizers of the National Coordinating Committee to End the War in Vietnam—the group which staged the huge anti-war marches in Washington D.C. in 1970.

Dellinger made two trips to China and North Vietnam in the fall of 1966 and the spring of 1967. In America he helped in the production of the famed March on the Pentagon of October 1967, which would later be memorialized by author Norman Mailer in his prize-winning *Armies of the Night*. Dellinger spent much of 1968 travelling to Cuba and preparing for demonstrations at the Democratic party national convention in August. When the Chicago police attacked the demonstrators, the federal government indicted all demonstration leaders (Dellinger, Rennie Davis, John Froines, Tom Hayden, Abbie Hoffman, Jerry Rubin, and Lee Weiner) for conspiracy to cross state lines to incite a riot.

In July 1969 North Vietnam decided, as it had twice before, to release a few U.S. prisoners of war, and Vietnamese leaders requested that Dellinger come to Hanoi to receive them. He and three others, including Rennie Davis, his co-defendant in the aftermath of the Chicago riots, flew to Hanoi in August and escorted the Americans back to freedom.

The 1969 trial of the Chicago Seven (known officially as *U.S. vs. David Dellinger et al.* ) was one of the most celebrated court cases of the 1960s. In order to disrupt the proceedings in Judge Julius Hoffman's courtroom and to attempt to place the Vietnam War itself on trial, the defendants wore outrageous clothing, carried anti-war signs, and replied bluntly to the court's capricious rulings. They were all found guilty by Judge Hoffman and, in addition, given

innumerable contempt citations. But the entire trial was, on appeal, found to have been irrevocably tainted, and all "guilty" judgments were nullified.

By 1971 President Richard Nixon's planned withdrawal "with honor" of U.S. troops from Vietnam was lowering dissent on the home front. Dellinger was skeptical that there could be peace with honor because, as he saw it, the entire war had been without honor. He helped to plan the giant "Mayday" march on Washington, D.C. in spring 1971. But the next year American attention turned to the Watergate break-in, and Dellinger returned to his writing. *Liberation* ceased publication in 1975, and for the following five years he was the editor of *Seven Days* magazine. In the 1980s he moved to Peacham, Vermont, to teach at Vermont College and to write his memoirs, cheerfully referring to himself as a "failed poet, a flawed feminist, and a convinced pantheist."

Despite remaining an active protester and frequent public speaker, Dellinger found time to finish his memoirs and *From Yale to Jail: The Life Story of A Moral Dissenter* was published in 1993. In 1996, Dellinger and other activists who demonstrated at the 1968 Democratic National Convention had an opportunity of sorts to reprise the event. The 1996 Democratic National Convention was held in Chicago and attracted about 500 demonstrators protesting a host of causes. Dellinger was among them. He remarked to a reporter, "The numbers of people who came and the energy they had made it very successful. We made it clear there would be no violence."

## Further Reading

The best sources for material on the life of David Dellinger are the files of *Liberation* and two of his books: *Revolutionary Nonviolence* (1970) and *More Power Than We Know* (1975). Fred Halstead's *Out Now* contains many references. A brief article that might be of interest appears in the March-April 1997 issue of *The Humanist*. Dellinger is writing his own *Autobiography in the Form of a Novel*. □

# Vine Deloria Jr.

**Vine Deloria, Jr. (born 1933) is known as a revolutionary thinker who speaks out against the decadence of U.S. culture and insists that young Native Americans receive traditional teachings before exposing themselves to the philosophies of the dominant Euro-American culture. Through his widely published books, he has brought greater understanding of Native American history and philosophy to a vast global audience.**

Vine Deloria, Jr., of the Hunkpapa Lakota, became well-known as a political activist whose publications explained to the American people what the Native American rights movement was seeking. His family heritage combined with academic training gave him credibility in his writings. Deloria was born on March 26, 1933, in Martin, South Dakota, the son of Vine and Barbara (Eastburn) Deloria. He joined a distinguished family: his great-grandfather Francois Des Laurias ("Saswe") was a medicine man and leader of the White Swan Band of the Yankton Sioux tribe; his grandfather Philip Deloria was a missionary priest of the Episcopal Church; his aunt Ella C. Deloria was a noted anthropologist who published works on Indian ethnology and linguistics; and his father, Vine Deloria, Sr., was the first American Indian to be named to a national executive post in the Episcopal Church. Deloria's own comment about his family gave context to his first major book. In its afterword he wrote: "As long as any member of my family can remember, we have been involved in the affairs of the Sioux tribe. My great grandfather was a medicine man named Saswe, of the Yankton tribe of the Sioux Nation. My grandfather was a Yankton chief who was converted to Christianity in the 1860's. He spent the rest of his life as an Episcopal missionary on the Standing Rock Sioux reservation in South Dakota." From 1923 to 1982 the Indian Council Fire, an organization in Chicago, presented fifty-four achievement awards to recognize quality of Indian initiative and leadership. Of these awards, three were to members of the Deloria family: Vine, Sr., Ella, and Vine, Jr.

After attending grade school in Martin, South Dakota, the younger Deloria graduated from high school at St. James Academy in Faribault, Minnesota. He served in the Marine Corps from 1954 to 1956, then attended Iowa State University where he received his B.A. degree in 1958. In his youth,

he had considered following his father in the ministry, but exposure to his father's frustrations convinced him that church life did not have the bearing on Indian life that he wanted his career to have. Before he gave up the idea entirely, however, he earned a B.D. in theology at Augustana Lutheran Seminary, Rock Island, Illinois, in 1963. The following year he was hired by the United Scholarship Service in Denver to develop a program to get scholarships for American Indian students in eastern preparatory schools. He successfully placed a number of Indian students in eastern schools through the program.

He served as the executive director of the National Congress of American Indians (NCAI) in Washington, D.C., from 1964 to 1967, an experience he claimed was more educational than anything he had experienced in his previous thirty years. He was expected to solve problems presented by Indian tribes from all over the country, but found that unscrupulous individuals made the task impossible. He was frustrated by the feeling that the interests of tribes were often played against one other. In addition the NCAI had financial difficulties, and was often close to bankruptcy, so that a majority of time had to be spent resolving funding issues. Increased memberships and a research grant gave the organization enough strength to successfully win a few policy changes in the Department of Interior. Although Deloria felt the organization had been successful, especially because of the support and hard work of organization members, he realized that other tactics would have to be used to further the cause for Indian rights.

## Earns Law Degree

Two circumstances influenced his decision to return to college and earn a law degree from the University of Colorado in 1970. One was learning of the success of the National Association for the Advancement of Color People's Legal Defense Fund which had been established to help the black community. The second was the realization that local Indian tribes were without legal counsel and had no idea what their rights were. His goal when receiving his law degree was to start a program which would assist smaller tribes and Indian communities to outline their basic rights. Throughout his career his goal in life has been twofold: to support tribes through affiliation with various advocacy organizations and to educate Native Americans on aspects of the law through teachings and writings which stress the historical and political aspects of the relationships of Indians to other people. His role as an activist in the efforts of Native Americans to achieve self-government has focused on change through education rather than through violence.

From 1970 to 1972 Deloria was a lecturer at Western Washington State College in the division of ethnic studies. While there, he worked with Northwest Coast tribes in their effort to gain improved fishing rights. From 1972 to 1974 he taught at the University of California at Los Angeles. During the same period, from 1970 to 1978, he was the chairperson of the Institute for the Development of Indian Law, headquartered in Golden, Colorado. From 1978 to 1991 he was a professor of American Indian studies, political science, and history of law at the University of Arizona. In 1991 he moved to the University of Colorado in Boulder to join the faculty of the Center for Studies of Ethnicity and Race in America. In addition to his teaching positions, Deloria served in leadership positions in several organizations including the Citizens Crusade against Poverty, the Council on Indian Affairs, the National Office for the Rights of the Indigent, the Institute for the Development of Indian Law, and the Indian Rights Association.

## Publishes Indian Activist Views

Deloria has been an activist writer, dramatically presenting his case for Indian self-determination. *Custer Died for Your Sins: An Indian Manifesto,* written while he was attending law school, captured the attention of reviewers and critics and bolstered Native American efforts for recognition. Written at the time the American Indian Movement (AIM) was drawing public attention to Native American rights, Deloria's book was an articulation of the activist goal: to become self-ruled, culturally separate from white society and politically separate from the U.S. government. While blasting America's treatment of Indian people, Deloria explained the concepts of termination and tribalism. Although contemporaneous with the civil rights movement of other American groups, he distinguished between black nationalism and Indian nationalism, explaining that because Indian civil rights issues were based upon treaties they needed to be addressed in a different way. Deloria explained his reasons for writing the book in its afterword: "One reason I wanted to write it was to raise some issues for younger Indians which they have not been raising for themselves. Another reason was to give some idea to white people of the unspoken but often felt antagonisms I have detected in Indian people toward them, and the reasons for such antagonism."

Deloria's second book, *We Talk, You Listen: New Tribes, New Turf,* also addressed the issue of tribalism and advocated a return to tribal social organization in order to save society. His third book, *God Is Red: A Native View of Religion,* again captured a national audience. In this book Deloria offered an alternative to Christianity which he explained had failed both in its theology and its application to social issues. He proposed that religion in North America should follow along the lines of traditional Native American values and seek spiritual values in terms of "space" by feeling the richness of the land. Most critics applauded his presentation of Indian religious practice, but were offended by his attack on the Judeo-Christian tradition. His later book *The Metaphysics of Modern Existence* followed up on this theme by questioning non-Indian world views of modern life and recommending a reassessment of reality about moral and religious property.

In all of Deloria's writings, he has emphasized the failure of U.S. treaties to adequately provide for the needs of Indian people. Using his legal training, he has analyzed past relationships between the U.S. government and Native American groups and has continually pressed for renewed treaty negotiation in order to allow more Indian self-control over their culture and government. His book *Behind the Trail of Broken Treaties* provided an account of events

which led to the occupation of Wounded Knee, South Dakota, by supporters of the American Indian Movement. In this work he argued for reopening the treaty-making procedure between Indian tribes and the U.S. government. As an expert in U.S. Indian treaties, Deloria was called as first witness for the defense in the trial of Wounded Knee participants Russell Means and Dennis Banks in 1974. Later, in his writing about Indian activism of the early 1970s, Deloria blamed the failure of the Indian civil rights movement on the unwillingness of the American public to forget their perception of what an Indian should be. In the second edition of *God Is Red* he stated: "When a comparison is made between events of the Civil Rights movement and the activities of the Indian movement one thing stands out in clear relief: Americans simply refuse to give up their longstanding conceptions of what an Indian is. It was this fact more than any other that inhibited any solution of the Indian problems and projected the impossibility of their solution anytime in the future. People simply could not connect what they believed Indians to be with what they were seeing on their television sets." He castigated the American public for its avoidance of the real Indian world in a series of ironic contrasts between current events of the Indian movement of the 1970s and what the American public was reading. "While Dee Brown's *Bury My Heart at Wounded Knee* was selling nearly twenty thousand copies a week, the three hundred state game wardens and Tacoma city police were vandalizing the Indian fishing camp and threatening the lives of Indian women and children at Frank's Landing on the Nisqually River.... As Raymond Yellow Thunder was being beaten to death, Americans were busy ordering *Touch the Earth* from their book clubs as an indication of their sympathy for American Indians. As the grave robbers were breaking into Chief Joseph's grave, the literary public was reading his famous surrender speech in a dozen or more anthologies of Indian speeches and bemoaning the fact that oratory such as Joseph's is not used any more."

Deloria's writing style has been consistent. In his books he often attempts to peel away platitudes that his white readers have developed so that they begin to comprehend the issues and the Indian viewpoint. Not without humor, he cynically derides white culture, and then offers his replacement. He commented in an interview that Americans can be told the obvious fifty times a day and revel in hearing it, but not learn anything from it. Some critics have been disappointed that Deloria's books do not describe Indian culture. As Deloria stated in an interview in *The Progressive,* "I particularly disappoint Europeans. They come over and want me to share all the tribal secrets. Then I lecture and harangue about the white man." In the same interview he derided his own success as an Indian writer in the early 1970s. "I happened to come along when they [the media] needed an Indian. The writing is not very good at all. But Indians were new, so everybody gave *Custer* great reviews. I never fooled myself that it was a great book."

His second edition of *God Is Red,* published in 1992, built upon the arguments against Christianity he wrote in the first edition. Encouraged by trends in American society to be more concerned about religion and ecology, he raised additional issues in the revised edition. "I suggest in this revised edition that we have on this planet two kinds of people—natural peoples and the hybrid peoples. The natural peoples represent an ancient tradition that has always sought harmony with the environment." Hybrid peoples referred to the inheritors of Hebrew, Islamic, and Christian traditions who adopted a course of civilization which exploits the environment. When *The Progressive*'s interviewer asked Deloria his views on renewed interest in Native American spirituality, Deloria commented: "I think New Age shamanism is very interesting. Whites want to take our images, they want to have their Indian jewelry; at the same time, they need our valley to flood for a dam. People are desperately trying to get some relationship to Earth, but it's all in their heads. . . . New Age shamanism may be one of the few solutions." At the same time, he admitted his own dependence upon technology. "I wouldn't delude myself for a minute that I could go back to the reservation and live any kind of traditional life. I've been in the cities too long. . . . I would love to go back to the old shamanism. My great-grandfather was a very powerful man. But here I am in Tucson, Arizona, dependent upon Tucson Electric Power to stay comfortable."

Another of his major themes has been concern for the natural environment. He blames contemporary technological society for destroying the earth, and presents an apocalyptic view. He envisions the end of the earth if changes are not made soon to allow the natural environment to recover. He predicts in *The Progressive* interview that in 500 years "there will be fewer than 100,000 people on whatever this continent comes up as, there will probably be some Indians and all kinds of new strange animals—the Earth a completely different place, people talking about legends of the old times when iron birds flew in the air."

Other works by Vine Deloria include *Indians of the Pacific Northwest* (1977), *Of Utmost Good Faith* (1971), *A Better Day for Indians* (1976), *The nations within: the past and future of American Indian sovereignty* (1984), and *Behind the trail of broken treaties: an Indian declaration of independence* (1985).

## Further Reading

Bruguier, Leonard Rufus, "A Legacy in Sioux Leadership: The Deloria Family," in *South Dakota Leaders,* edited by Herbert T. Hoover and Larry J. Zimmerman, Vermillion, University of South Dakota Press, 1989; 367-378, 471.
*Contemporary Authors,* edited by Linda Metzger and Deborah A. Straub, Detroit, Gale, 20NR, 1987; 130-132.
*Contemporary Literary Criticism,* edited by Sharon R. Gunton, Gale, 21, 1982; 108-114.
Deloria, Vine, Jr., "An Afterword," in *Custer Died for Your Sins: An Indian Manifesto,* New York, Avon Books, 1970; 262-272.
Deloria, Vine, Jr., "Introduction" and "The Indians of the American Imagination," in *God Is Red: A Native View of Religion,* 2nd Edition, Golden, CO, North American Press, 1992; 1-3, 25-45.
Gridley, Marion E., *Indians of Today,* Chicago, I.C.F.P., 1971; 347.
*Native North American Almanac,* edited by Duane Champagne, Detroit, Gale, 1994; 1043-1044.
Paulson, T. Emogene, and Lloyd R. Moses, *Who's Who among the Sioux,* Institute of Indian Studies, University of South Dakota, 1988; 58-59.
*Reader's Encyclopedia of the American West,* edited by Howard R. Lamar, New York, Thomas Y. Crowell, 1977; 295.
*Something about the Author,* edited by Anne Commire, Gale Research, 21, 1980; 27.
Warrior, Robert Allen, "Vine Deloria Jr.: 'It's About Time to be Interested in Indians Again,'" *The Progressive,* 54:4, April 1990; 24-27. □

# Jacques Delors

**The French president of the European Commission, Jacques Delors (born 1925) was former minister for the economy and finance of France. He was the chief architect of Western Europe's drive toward market unity by 1992.**

The son of an employee of the French Central Bank, Jacques Delors was born in Paris on July 20, 1925. During his secondary school studies he went to two different schools: Lycée Voltaire (Paris) and Lycée Blaise-Pascal (Clermont-Ferrand). In 1943 Delors studied law at the University of Clermont-Ferrand. His studies were interrupted when the Germans closed the university in World War II. He was back in Paris in October, 1944, and soon found a job as an intern at the French Central Bank. In 1950 he was promoted to staff member for the director-general for securities and financial markets. During this period he became an active militant of a Christian trade union, the CFTC (Confédération Française des Travailleurs Chrétiens). He was put in charge of the trade union's studies center. In 1957 he became the expert for a CFTC publication called *Reconstruction.* In 1955 Delors had joined a political party called Jeune République (Young Republic). He left this party in 1960 shortly after he helped it merge with a small left-wing party to form the new Unified Socialist Party.

## Moving Through Government Ranks

In 1959 Delors became a member of the Planning and Investments Department of France's Economic and Social Council. He left the CFTC when he became a high government official to avoid conflicts of interests. In 1962 he became head of the Social Affairs Department of the Planning Commission. During this period he developed what would become one of the main principles of his political action in the future: the contractual policy. This means that some economic decisions (for example, the policy on salaries) should be reached through negotiations not only with the trade unions inside the company or industry concerned, but also with the authorities at the national level. Maybe because it was too revolutionary for that period, Delors' idea did not find its way into the council's Fifth Plan (1962-1965). Georges Pompidou, France's prime minister from 1962 to 1968 (and later president), would partly refer to this concept in his social policy.

In April of 1969, Delors became secretary-general of the Interministerial Committee for Professional Training. From 1969 to 1973 he also acted as adviser for social and cultural affairs to the new prime minister, Jacques Chaban-Delmas, and later as chargé de mission for economic, financial, and social affairs. In 1972, when Pierre Messmer became prime minister, Delors went back to the secretariat-general for professional training. He was dismissed from this post a few months later because he was accused of favoritism towards left-wing organizations. He started lecturing courses in company management at the University of Paris IX in 1973. That same year he returned to the French Central Bank as a member of its general council; a position he kept until 1979.

## Restarting a Political Career

In 1974 Delors decided to restart his political career by joining the Socialist Party (PS). At first, he had to face hostility from some of the party's leaders, due to his earlier participation in the right-wing Chaban-Delmas government. But thanks to the support of François Mitterrand, at that time secretary-general of the party, Delors became a member of the board of directors of the PS.

In 1979 Delors was elected as a member of the European Parliament (a body with little real legislative power within the European Community), where he soon became chairman of the Economic and Monetary Committee of the European Parliament. When François Mitterrand became French president in 1981, Delors was named minister for economy and finances. He was one of the most moderate members of the Pierre Mauroy government, which conducted rather far left economic and social policies. In 1984 Mitterrand chose Laurent Fabius to succeed Mauroy as prime minister, instead of Delors. Delors was disappointed but, given his interest and experience in European affairs, France strongly supported his nomination to the post of president of the European Commission, the permanent executive and administrative branch of the European Community.

When he became president of the European Commission in January 1985, Delors had to face the member states' unwillingness to make any further progress towards a closer integration inside the European Community (EC). The Council of the European Ministers, the ultimate governing body of the EC, was not able to undertake the indispensable changes toward this goal. This was due to disagreements among member states on a common European policy and their perception that the EC could not help them in coping with the economic crisis. This period of stagnation of the integration process is known as the period of "Eurosclerosis."

## European Frontier-Free Market

To solve the crisis, Delors launched in 1985 the idea of a European frontier-free market by the end of 1992. This ambitious long-term program (total free movement of persons, goods, services, and capital inside the European Community) was formalized into a commission White Paper. At first glance, it dealt only with the economic aspects of European integration. But it was obvious that it could not be achieved without important institutional changes. Therefore, the commission urged member states to modify some

provisions of the existing EC treaties in order to prepare for the necessary transfers of power from the member states to the EC. In 1986 a new treaty, called the "Single European Act," was approved by the member states. This act took over the commission's 1992 program and made it possible for the council (the real legislative power of the community) to make all the decisions concerning its achievement by majority (instead of the previously required unanimity). It also gave new powers to the community's institutions. This major progress in the European integration process represented a huge personal success for Delors.

During his first mandate Delors also strove for greater efficiency of the EC budget and for progress on such community issues such as agriculture, research and development, and external commercial relations. A second mandate as president of the European Commission was unanimously granted to him by the member states, who considered that he was the best qualified person to achieve the ambitious 1992 program he had promoted.

During his second four-year mandate, which started in January, 1989, Delors stressed the need for a wider social dimension to the EC's future single market. Unfortunately, the social charter approved by the council in December 1989 lacked real efficiency, despite the support of the European Parliament and of some influential member states, such as France. In 1989 Delors presented a report by the commission on the European Economic and Monetary Union for the creation of a new central bank of Europe and a single European currency.

Another important initiative on the road toward greater European integration was the European Political Union. In reaction to the dramatic events in Eastern Europe in late 1989, François Mitterrand launched the idea of a European confederation which would include the EC member states and the Eastern European countries. Fearing that any action undertaken to foster such a confederation could delay or even stop completely the whole European Community's integration process, Delors stressed the absolute priority that had to be given to reinforcing the European Political Union of the twelve members before considering the inclusion of Eastern Europe into a confederation. Delors favored the creation of a European federation of the twelve member states as a first step before moving to Mitterrand's European Confederation.

## The End of a Presidency

Delors' mandate as president of the European Commission expired at the end of 1993. Both supporters and detractors agreed on the importance of Delors' ten-year presidency of the commission. He was an architect of the program to create a single market and of the Single European Act; he was the driving force behind the social charter and the social chapter; his report on economic and monetary union led to the Maastricht treaty; and his advocacy of the European economic area not only helped to create a market of over $370 million but has led to the prospect of new members joining.

The key to Delors' success was his unique contribution of strategic sense, fierce dedication and negotiating skill.

Though born and brought up in a Paris working-class district and without a university education, he became a top-flight politician on the international level. As commission president, Delors could set the agenda but he relied on his relations with community leaders, above all with Helmut Kohl, for the implementation of his proposals.

The press often presented Delors as a potential candidate for the French presidency in 1995. He declined to run for the office, however, citing personal and political reasons. Delors was one of the most credible candidates on the political left, and polls had given him a clear lead. Delors knew his decision not to stand would sadden, even anger his supporters, but citing his age and his fears of sharing power with a right-wing parliament, he could not represent the Socialists. "I'm for a radical change in the way we regard politics. I want the French people to play an active role in our democracy and to help change society. I wouldn't have been able to guarantee that as president," Delors commented. In February 1997, Delors was selected as the recipient of the Erasmus Prize for exceptional services to Europe.

When away from his Brussels office Delors shares an apartment in Paris with his wife, Marie. They have a married daughter, Martine. Delors has served as television commentator for the annual Tour de France.

## Further Reading

Additional information on Jacques Delors can be found in his biography, Fabriel Milesi, *Jacques Delors* (Paris: 1985), written in French, with detailed background information on the evolution of the French political situation. Books written by Delors include *Les Indicateurs Sociaux* (Paris: 1971) and *Changer* (Paris: 1975). "The President of the European Commission presents the Commission's annual program to the European Parliament" provides insight on his work. The speeches of Delors can be found in the European Community Bulletins (edited by the European Commission) for the period 1985-1990. □

# Marcelo Hilario Del Pilar

**Marcelo H. Del Pilar (1850-1896) was a Philippine revolutionary propagandist and satirist. He tried to marshal the nationalist sentiment of the enlightened Filipino ilustrados, or bourgeoisie, against Spanish imperialism.**

Marcelo Del Pilar was born in Kupang, Bulacan, on Aug. 30, 1850, to cultured parents. He studied at the Colegio de San José and later at the University of Santo Tomas, where he finished his law course in 1880. Fired by a sense of justice against the abuses of the clergy, Del Pilar attacked bigotry and hypocrisy and defended in court the impoverished victims of racial discrimination. He preached the gospel of work, self-respect, and human dignity. His mastery of Tagalog, his native language, enabled him to arouse the consciousness of the masses to the need for unity and sustained resistance against the Spanish tyrants.

In 1882 Del Pilar founded the newspaper *Diariong Tagalog* to propagate democratic liberal ideas among the farmers and peasants. In 1888 he defended José Rizal's polemical writings by issuing a pamphlet against a priest's attack, exhibiting his deadly wit and savage ridicule of clerical follies.

In 1888, fleeing from clerical persecution, Del Pilar went to Spain, leaving his family behind. In December 1889 he succeeded Graciano Lopez Jaena as editor of the Filipino reformist periodical *La solidaridad* in Madrid. He promoted the objectives of the paper by contacting liberal Spaniards who would side with the Filipino cause. Under Del Pilar, the aims of the newspaper were expanded to include removal of the friars and the secularization of the parishes; active Filipino participation in the affairs of the government; freedom of speech, of the press, and of assembly; wider social and political freedoms; equality before the law; assimilation; and representation in the Spanish Cortes, or Parliament.

Del Pilar's difficulties increased when the money to support the paper was exhausted and there still appeared no sign of any immediate response from the Spanish ruling class. Before he died of tuberculosis caused by hunger and enormous privation, Del Pilar rejected the assimilationist stand and began planning an armed revolt. He vigorously affirmed this conviction: "Insurrection is the last remedy, especially when the people have acquired the belief that peaceful means to secure the remedies for evils prove futile." This idea inspired Andres Bonifacio's Katipunan, a secret revolutionary organization. Del Pilar died in Barcelona on July 4, 1896.

Del Pilar's militant and progressive outlook derived from the classic Enlightenment tradition of the French *philosophes* and the scientific empiricism of the European bourgeoisie. Part of this outlook was transmitted by Freemasonry, to which Del Pilar subscribed.

## Further Reading

An important source of information about Del Pilar is Magno S. Gatmaitan, *Marcelo H. Del Pilar, 1850-1896: A Documented Biography* (1966).

## Additional Sources

Gatmaitan, Magno, *The life and writings of Marcelo Hilario del Pilar,* Manila: Historical Conservation Society; Los Angeles, Calif.; Philippine Expressions Corp. distributor, 1987. □

# Agnes de Mille

**An American dancer and author, Agnes de Mille's (1905-1993) creative contribution to 20th-century ballet was as remarkable as her choreography for Broadway musical theater. She inspired awe for her**

**personal courage and determination in the face of declining health in later years.**

Agnes de Mille was born on September 18, 1905, in New York City into a theatrical family. Her father, William Churchill de Mille, wrote plays for David Belasco on Broadway and later became a Hollywood film producer. His brother, Cecil Blount de Mille, was a famous Hollywood film director. De Mille's maternal grandfather was Henry George, a social reformer and political economist who was famous for proposing the single tax.

When she was a child the family moved to Hollywood. The family's values were shaped by prevailing emphases on success and glamour as well as respect for intellectual life. During her teens her parents divorced and de Mille was torn between becoming a dancer and actress or pleasing her father, who was unsympathetic to a stage career. Having seen performances of Anna Pavlova and the Ballets Russes with Vaslav Nijinsky, as well as American dance pioneers Isadora Duncan and Ruth St. Denis, de Mille enrolled in ballet classes in Hollywood with Theodore Kosloff. While continuing ballet lessons, she agreed to attend college at the University of California, Los Angeles (UCLA), and graduated as an English major, *cum laude.* Later her mother gave support to her dance career, taking her to live in New York while her younger sister, Margaret, attended Barnard College and later helping to finance her trips abroad.

In New York she performed with the Grand Street Follies, choreographed a solo program (1928), and studied modern dance with Martha Graham, who opened her New York studio in 1927. In 1931 she appeared with Graham, Doris Humphrey, Charles Weidman, and Helen Tamiris in Dance Repertory Theater, a short-lived attempt at collaboration among the early pioneers of American modern dance.

De Mille left for Europe in 1932, performing recitals of her work in London, Paris, and Copenhagen. In London she staged dances for Cole Porter's *Nymph Errant* starring Gertrude Lawrence. Marie Rambert, with whom she studied ballet, invited her to join the Ballet Club where she worked with Frederic Ashton and Anthony Tudor, then young and emerging choreographers associated with Rambert. She created a role in the premiere of Tudor's *Dark Elegies* (1937).

On occasional return visits to the United States she appeared in Leslie Howard's Broadway production of *Hamlet* (1936) and the MGM film of *Romeo and Juliet* (1937). With the outbreak of World War II in Europe in 1939 she returned to New York permanently.

For the first season of Ballet Theatre (now American Ballet Theatre) in 1940 de Mille choreographed *Black Ritual* to Darius Milhaud's *Creation du Monde* with an African American cast. She earned the credit for convincing the company's managing director, Richard Pleasant, to invite Tudor to leave England and join Ballet Theatre, an important turn for American ballet history.

De Mille's big breakthrough as a choreographer came in 1942 with her ballet *Rodeo* for Ballets Russe de Monte Carlo. The original score was by Aaron Copland; the set design by Oliver Smith. She originally danced the Cowgirl, the female lead. This ballet remains in the repertories of many companies and is among her best known ballets, along with *Fall River Legend* (1948), a psychological study of Lizzie Borden based on her murder trial. *Rodeo*, a down-home story about cowboys and ranch life out West, provided de Mille with the invitation to choreograph Rodgers and Hammerstein's musical *Oklahoma* in 1943. This collaboration led to a life-long career with the Broadway musical, perhaps most significant of her choreographic achievements. *Oklahoma* was a landmark in that de Mille introduced the dream ballet to further the story through dance. This changed the course of the Broadway musical, making dance an integral part of the theatrical experience.

De Mille always saw dance as theatrical, expressive. She used body movement and motivated gesture as a kind of speech and drew from the technical vocabularies of classical ballet, modern dance, and folk and social dance. Although inspired by many subjects, her ballets were essentially American and favored themes dealing with its social history.

Known also as the author of many books, which she claimed she wrote in her "spare time," de Mille was a tireless and outspoken advocate for dance and for federal support for the arts. Drawing from her own experience as a choreographer, she was concerned that dances be copyrighted and that choreographers receive royalties. She served as first chairman of the dance panel of the National

Endowment for the Arts in 1965. She was also first president of the Society of Stage Directors and Choreographers in 1965.

De Mille founded two dance companies during her career: the Agnes de Mille Dance Theater (1953-1954) and the Heritage Dance Theater, a folk-oriented company formed in 1973, which used a lecture-demonstration format to present audiences with American dance history. The company toured widely until 1975, when de Mille suffered a cerebral hemorrhage just prior to a benefit performance at the Hunter College Playhouse in New York.

With extraordinary determination and courage, de Mille underwent extensive rehabilitation and learned to write with her left hand. She recovered sufficiently to re-sume her activities as a writer and choreographer, as well as spokesperson for dance.

De Mille was married to Walter Prude, a manager of concert artists, from 1943 until his death in 1988. (Her courtship and marriage are described in her autobiographi-cal work, *And Promenade Home*, and in *Martha.* ) She died of a stroke on October 7, 1993, in New York City at the age of 88. She was survived by a son, Jonathan Prude, and grandsons David Robert Prude and Michael James Prude.

De Mille received more than a dozen honorary de-grees. She was elected to the Theater Hall of Fame in 1973. She received the Handel Medallion, New York City's high-est achievement in the arts, in 1976; the Kennedy Center Award in 1980; and the National Medal of the Arts in 1986. Other awards include: Donaldson Award, Antoinette Perry (Tony) Award, Dance Magazine Award, Capezio Award, and De la Torre Bueno Award for writings on dance.

### Further Reading

The following are de Mille's ballets (listed chronologically): *Black Ritual* (1940); *Three Virgins and a Devil* (1941); *Rodeo* (1942); *Tally-Ho* (1944); *Fall River Legend* (1948), based on the Lizzie Borden murder trial; *The Harvest According* (1952), inspired by a Walt Whitman poem with material from the Civil War ballet in *Bloomer Girl; Rib of Eve* (1956); *The Bitter Weird* (1961); *The Four Marys* (1965), about Civil War slaves; *The Wind in the Mountains* (1965); *A Rose for Miss Emily* (1971), based on the William Faulkner story; *Texas Fourth* (1976); *The Informer* (1988), about the struggles between the English and Irish in 1917 and 1921; and *The Other* (1992), a symbolic depiction of the encounter between a young woman and death.

She choreographed the following Broadway musicals: *Okla-homa* (1943); *Bloomer Girl* (1944), a Civil War ballet; *Carou-sel* (1945); *Brigadoon* (1947); *Allegro* (1947), which she also directed; *Gentlemen Prefer Blondes* (1949); *Paint Your Wagon* (1951); *Goldilocks* (1958); *Kwamina* (1961); and *110 in the Shade* (1963).

De Mille's major article on Martha Graham, first published in *Atlantic Monthly* (1950), was later a chapter in *Dance to the Piper* (1952). Her last book, *Martha: The Life and Work of Martha Graham* (1991), a lively biography of the famous American dance pioneer, also contains much about the au-thor and her long friendship with Graham. Other personal memoirs include: *And Promenade Home* (1958); *Speak to Me, Dance with Me* (1973) about the years spent in London with Marie Rambert and the Ballet Club; *Where the Wings Grow* (1978), a recollection of her girlhood at the family's

summer colony in Sullivan County, New York; and *Reprieve* (1981), written in collaboration with her doctor, dealing with her first stroke in 1975 and her courageous recovery. Other works by de Mille include *To a Young Dancer* (1962), an advice book; *The Book of the Dance* (1963), an illustrated history of dance; *Lizzie Borden: A Dance of Death* (1968), about her choreography for *Fall River Legend; Portrait Gallery* (1990); ''Russian Journals'' in *Dance Perspectives* (1970); *The Dance in America* (1971); and *America Dances* (1980). □

# Cecil Blount DeMille

**Considered one of the founders of Hollywood, film producer and director Cecil B. DeMille (1881-1959) earned a place in moviemaking history with such religious epic films as *The Ten Commandments* and *King of Kings*.**

Although he is one of the most commercially suc-cessful film directors of all time, Cecil B. DeMille has for a long time been considered at best a direc-tor of mediocre quality. Still his place in the history of Hollywood movie making is central; in fact, more than any-one else, he deserves to be called the man who founded Hollywood. As Lewis Jacobs has said—as quoted in *World Film Directors:* ''If in the artistic perspective of American Film History, Cecil B. DeMille is valueless; in the social history of films, it is impossible to ignore him.''

### Religious and Theatrical Background

DeMille's father was split between wanting to be an actor and wanting to be an Episcopalian priest. It was an internal conflict strangely appropriate for the father of a man who would become identified with making sexually lurid motion pictures from Bible stories. The elder DeMille ended up teaching school until his friendship with David Belasco, the most successful American playwright of the late 19th century, led him to satisfy his theatrical urge by writing plays instead of acting in them. Both his sons followed him into the theater. Cecil's older brother broke in as a playwright, and Cecil tried to make it as an actor; but after ten years on the boards, he was still struggling to feed his family.

As he neared 30, DeMille gave up acting to join his mother in launching a theatrical agency. Working as the general manager, he met Jesse L. Lasky who along with a Samuel Goldfish—later to change his name to Goldwyn— was trying to break into motion picture production. At this time, feeling frustrated, DeMille was thinking of leaving show business altogether; but Lasky, after working on sev-eral musical plays with the younger man, convinced him to try his hand at directing a motion picture. After spending a day at Thomas Edison's studios in New York, DeMille took off for Arizona to shoot *The Squaw Man,* a melodrama based on a Broadway play and set in Wyoming. When the Arizona locations did not work out, DeMille got back on the train and headed off to the end of the line, Los Angeles.

## The Man Who Founded Hollywood

DeMille was not the first person to ever shoot a film in Hollywood, but when he arrived in late 1913, he decided to stay. The southern California climate was perfect for motion picture making, because even the indoor scenes could be shot outside on sets with three walls and no ceilings, since plenty of sun and not much rain let the crews shoot without having to set up lights, a huge savings in time and money. The barn on the corner of Vine Street in which DeMille set up shop would soon be the world headquarters for Paramount Studios; but at the moment they were sharing facilities with a stable of horses, and things did not always smell nice around the studio. DeMille was the consummate showman from the start and not only in the movies. Writing in *World Film Directors,* Philip Kemp speaks about DeMille's making of the image of the Hollywood Filmmaker: "To direct his first movie, DeMille adopted a distinctive costume which he retained largely unaltered throughout his working career and which came to represent the publicly accepted image of an old-style movie director: open-necked shirt, riding breeches, boots and puttees along with a riding-crop, a large megaphone, and a whistle on a neck-chord. Charges of theatricality were met with pained denial from DeMille who always insisted that his garb was strictly functional . . . . but his costume also undoubtedly reflected his favorite self-image—the movie director as bold and masterful adventurer, intrepid pioneer and empire-builder."

With the commercial success of *The Squaw Man,* DeMille's founding of Hollywood was complete. He had found the perfect location to make movies, he had developed the fashion style that would come to be associated with movie-making, and, now with the money he was making for Paramount, he proved the viability of his creation. The reviews of DeMille's early directorial efforts were very favorable. He worked with Alvin Wyckoff, one of the most important of the first generation of cameramen in Hollywood. Besides shooting motion pictures, Wyckoff invented new camera lenses that had the ability to work under difficult conditions. By the end of 1914, after only three DeMille films, Lasky moved his whole enterprise to California. He bought the barn next door and established a vast studio in the desert.

In 1915, DeMille made what many still consider his most impressive film. Writing in the *International Dictionary of Films and Filmmakers,* Eric Smoodin writes, "Although he made films until 1956, DeMille's masterpiece may well have come in 1915 with *The Cheat.* . . . . For the cinema's first 20 years, editing was based primarily on following action . . . . [but] in *The Cheat,* through his editing, DeMille created a sense of psychological space." DeMille was the first to use film editing in such an intrusive way to show off what a character is thinking.

## Produced First Epics

In the silent era, DeMille was fast becoming the middle-brow alternative to the high-brow films of D. W. Griffith, still the greatest innovator in film history, and the low-brow silent comedies pouring out of Mack Sennet's and Hal Roach's studios. In 1917, DeMille left his social comedies behind to make his first epic, *Joan the Woman,* the story of Joan of Arc. One of the longest and most extravagant pictures made to that time, it was a box office disaster. DeMille had made the first feature released in this country several years before, but audiences were not ready for the extra time he added to *Joan.*

The next years were difficult ones of DeMille. Two pictures he made with Mary Pickford flopped, and after several more mediocre films, he made *The Whispering Chorus.* The film meant a lot to him. In the film historian Kevin Brownlow's memorable phrase, he sunk not only his money, "but also his heart" into the film. The story of a man who tries to avoid a debt by faking his death, the film featured a chorus of whisperers who followed him through the movie, speaking his thoughts out loud. Whatever its artistic merit, it was a big failure. Some think it was the disappointment attendant on the reception of *The Whispering Chorus* which led DeMille to forsake artistic aspirations and concentrate on giving audiences what they wanted.

Still whatever his artistic disappointments, DeMille was able to regain his golden touch at the box office, primarily by making social comedies filled with both a bit of titillating sex and moralistic messages. Titles such as *We Can't Have Everything* and *Don't Change Your Husband* give a good sense of the message of these movies. By 1921, the critics held DeMille's work pretty much in contempt for the mix of sex and morality which he peddled so easily, satisfying his audience's erotic urges while at the same time satisfying their puritan tendencies. At the same time, DeMille was helping to set up the Hays Office, the self-policing branch of the Hollywood industry, which censored films for sexual or immoral content. DeMille's worry, shared by many in Hollywood at the time, was that if Hollywood did not censor itself, Congress would.

In 1923, he was powerful enough to return to the epic despite the failure of *Joan the Woman* at the box office. Costing $1,475,000, the first version of *The Ten Commandments* was probably the most expensive movie made to that time. Adolph Zukor, the studio head, threatened to pull the plug on the movie several times; but in the end, it was a blockbuster, making its huge budget back several times over. Some of the critics even liked it. He continued making expensive epics, but he did not return to the Bible until 1927 when he filmed a life of Christ entitled *King of Kings*. His first sound movie was *Dynamite*, which fared respectably, but his attempt to take advantage of the new medium to make a musical was another failure, *Madame Satan*.

*The Crusades,* another one of his epics, lost $700,000, perhaps the largest failure in Hollywood history up to that time. Five years later, after a couple of moderately successful westerns, DeMille made his first color film, *North West Mounted Police,* starring Gary Cooper. His next film, *Reap the Wild Wind,* distinguished itself by being the first motion picture edited by a woman, Anne Bauchens, to win the Oscar for Best Editing. Neither DeMille, nor any of his films had to that time an Oscar.

### End of His Career

After World War II, DeMille set a new tone for himself when he made *Samson and Delilah* with Victor Mature and Hedy Lamarr. It was widely viewed as one of the most tasteless American films ever made with its tacky special effects and heavy-breathing sexuality. In 1950, he returned to acting, playing himself in Billy Wilder's acid portrait of Hollywood, *Sunset Boulevard.* In 1952 he made *The Greatest Show on Earth,* a film often considered to be the closest movie to a self-portrait that DeMille ever made. It was the first film he made to win an Oscar. The best directing Oscar that year went to John Ford.

Unfortunately for DeMille, he was involved in another dispute with John Ford, one which would forever damage DeMille's reputation. DeMille, a politically conservative man, got wrapped up in the McCarthy anti-communist campaign in Hollywood and decided that he wanted to oust Joseph Mankiewicz as president of the Director's Guild. Mankiewicz was a successful director himself and politically liberal. DeMille thought he was soft on communism. A special meeting of the Director's Guild was called to air DeMille's charges. It was a very rancorous meeting attended by nearly every director in the guild. After four hours of debate, John Ford, who had not said a word as of yet, rose to speak. In an *Esquire* Magazine article, Peter Bogdonavich recounts the scene with Ford rising and introducing himself, "My name is Jack Ford—I make westerns." He then went on to praise DeMille's ability to produce pictures that appealed to the public—more so, Ford said, than anyone else in the room; he turned to look across the hall now directly at DeMille: "But I don't like you, C. B.," he said, "and I don't

like what you've been saying here tonight. I move that we give Joe a vote of confidence—and let's all go home and get some sleep."

It is worth noting that DeMille did not mention the episode in his memoirs. He also made his final film with one of the most conservative actors in Hollywood, Charlton Heston. Although the second version of *The Ten Commandments* is his most widely seen film, thanks to Easter-time television programming, it is not one of his most respected. Still it was a colossal success at the box office, capping a directing-producing career that was by far the most commercially successful of all time, at least until that of the much later director, Steven Spielberg. DeMille suffered a heart attack while shooting *The Ten Commandments,* but he refused to slow down; and soon after, in 1959, on a publicity tour for another picture, one which he produced but did not direct, he had another heart attack which led to his death.

### Further Reading

Eric Smoodin, *International Dictionary of Films and Filmmakers,* Nicholas Thomas, ed., St. James Press, 1991, pp. 204-207.
Bogdanovich, Peter, "The Cowboy Hero and The American West . . . as Directed by John Ford," in *Fifty Who Made a Difference,* ed. Lee Eisenberg, Esquire Press Book, 1984, pp. 347-348. □

# Süleyman Demirel

**Süleyman Demirel (born 1924) was a seven-time Turkish prime minister who later became president. He also led the now defunct Justice party. Throughout his career, Demirel was an outspoken proponent of secularism, holding fast to the political beliefs of Republic of Turkey founder Kemel Ataturk.**

S üleyman Demirel was one of the most important politicians of modern Turkey, representing the entry of the modernist, pragmatic technocrat into the political arena. Under his rule, the country made rapid economic progress. However, this led to grave socio-economic problems and to his own fall in 1971 and in 1980.

Demirel was born in 1924 in the village of Islamköy in the western province of Isparta—where the ancient city of Sparta was located—into a middle class family. After completing his schooling in the provinces, he went to Istanbul Technical University in 1942 and graduated in 1949 as a civil engineer. He entered state service and was sent to America for research at the Bureau of Reclamation in Washington, D.C., in 1949 and 1950. In 1954 Demirel was appointed director of the Bureau of Dams and came to be known as a supporter of the ruling Democrat party (DP) in the bureaucracy.

The 1950s were years of close relations between the United States and Turkey, especially after Turkey fought in Korea and joined the North Atlantic Treaty Organization

(NATO) in 1952. Demirel was a beneficiary of this relationship, for when the Eisenhower Exchange Fellowship was established in 1954 he was again sent to America as one of the first Turkish fellows in September. There he made contacts which served him well in private life and when he entered politics in the 1960s, acquiring the reputation of "friend of America." Upon his return to Turkey in 1955, Demirel was appointed director of the State Hydraulics Administration, a post he held until May 1960 when the Turkish army ousted the DP government of Prime Minister Adnan Menderes.

## Enters Politics

The military intervention of May 27, 1960, was a turning point in the politics of modern Turkey and in Demirel's life. Not only did the army remove the government, but it also closed down the Democrat party and thereby created a serious political vacuum in the country. Demirel, as a confirmed supporter of the defunct party, was forced out of state service and began working independently as an engineer. He worked as a consultant for Morrison-Knudsen, a major U.S. company, and also taught engineering at the Middle East Technical University in the capital, Ankara. But his most important decision was to join the Justice party (JP) when it was founded in 1961. He was elected to its administrative council the following year and became party chairman in 1964.

After the general election of 1961 the Justice party became the successor to the DP and began to play a crucial role in the coalition governments of the period. Demirel,

who was not as yet a member of parliament, directed the party from outside the Assembly in such a way as to make the governments of rival parties unstable. In February 1965 he forced the resignation of the Ismet Inönü coalition by having its budget defeated. The new coalition government, formed by an independent, non-party senator, Suat Ürgüplü, included Süleyman Demirel as deputy prime minister. When general elections were held in October 1965, the JP won an outright victory despite the provisions for proportional representation and ended the period of coalitions. Demirel was elected from his home town, Isparta, and was appointed prime minister, leading the government for the next six years.

Demirel's policies of rapid economic modernization, which undermined the small, traditional sectors while encouraging larger, innovative enterprises, had important political consequences. Many of his supporters were alienated and tried to remove him from the party's leadership. But they failed because his hold on the party was too firm. Consequently, his opponents were forced to leave the JP and join the small parties of the right, such as the conservative Democratic party, the religious National Salvation party (NSP), and the neo-fascist Nationalist Action party (NAP).

These were turbulent and difficult years for Turkey. The right criticized the government from one flank, the left from the other. The trade unions demanded higher wages to keep up with inflation, and radical students, inspired by their peers in European and American universities, also became involved in politics. By the late 1960s terrorism of the left and the right had also become a factor in Turkish politics. The constant instability affected the armed forces, and the commanders, convinced that Demirel could no longer control the situation, intervened and forced him to resign on March 12, 1971.

## Struggle to Survive

Despite this setback Demirel refused to give up his party's leadership, and the JP paid the price when it lost the elections in 1973. Demirel was forced into opposition, but not for long. The coalition government led by prime minister Bülent Ecevit resigned after Turkey's successful invasion of Cyprus in July and August 1974. Ecevit hoped that his newly-won popularity would enable him to win an early general election with a majority sufficient to form a party government. His hopes were dashed by the parties of the right, which refused to permit early elections.

Instead, Demirel formed a four-party coalition of the right, popularly known as the First Nationalist Front, including the NAP and the NSP, on March 31, 1975. He ruled until June 1977 when elections were held. Again Ecevit's Republican People's party won, though not with a sufficient majority to form a government on its own. Therefore, Demirel formed the Second Nationalist Front on July 21, 1977. But this coalition seemed so much under the influence of the NAP, a party directly involved in the rampant terrorism of the 1970s through the Gray Wolves organization, that there were resignations from the Justice party and Demirel's coalition fell on December 31, 1977. Ecevit now formed a coalition and ruled until November 1979. But since there was little he could do to solve the problems he had inherited—terrorism, economic stagnation, inflation, and unemployment—he lost his popularity and was forced to resign. Demirel formed Turkey's first minority government on November 12, but he too lacked the means to cope with the social, economic, and political crises that plagued the country in the 1970s. In the end the military commanders intervened again on October 12, 1980, and ousted Demirel. They were convinced that only an authoritarian regime could solve Turkey's problems.

### Barred From Politics

Under the military regime all political parties were abolished, and active politicians like Demirel were barred from all political activity for ten years. It was easy to pass such a law but virtually impossible to enforce it. Thus, when political activities were restored in April 1983 and new parties were formed, everyone knew that Süleyman Demirel was active behind the scene. One of the new parties prominent in Turkish politics, the True Path party, openly looked to Demirel for inspiration and guidance.

Demirel, who began his political career when he became a deputy in parliament from his home of Isparta in 1965, serving until 1980, returned to that post to serve from 1987 to 1991. He was chairman of the Justice party from 1965 until it was disbanded in 1980. Following the lifting of a ban on political activities by his and other parties in 1987, Demirel became chairman of the new True Path party and reentered parliament. In 1991 Demirel became prime minister for the seventh time since 1965 after his True Path party's victory in October elections and the formation of Turkey's first coalition government in more than 12 years.

### Becomes President

Only 18 months after Demirel became prime minister, the Turkish Grand National Assembly in May 1993 elected him to become the ninth president of the republic following the April death of President Turgut Ozal. While he was prime minister, Demirel had criticized President Ozal for overstepping the traditionally ceremonial powers of the presidency. At his swearing in—to which he wore a top hat, white tie and tails—Demirel said, "It is unthinkable that the president will ever take sides or take a stand that could cast a shadow over his impartiality. Yet it would be a mistake to interpret impartiality as avoiding national and international problems which have a political nature and as not becoming involved in issues at all." Observers noted clashes between Ozal and Demirel centered as much on personalities as on politics. Ozal championed linking Turkey to the central Asian republics and establishing close ties with Europe and the United States through broad, expansive schemes. Demirel was seen as a crafty political maneuverer and "a consummate deal maker."

### Unrest At Home

While during his presidency Demirel worked to strengthen ties with the United States and Europe, political turmoil at home also kept him busy. In October 1995, Demirel postponed a trip to the United States after Prime Minister Tansu Ciller lost a vote of confidence and resigned. The president quickly asked Ciller to form a new government and later in the month gave his approval for a coalition government of the center-right True Path party and a Social Democratic party to serve until the end of the year. In elections held in December 1995, Ciller's secularist and pro-Western True Path party was defeated by the pro-Islamic Welfare party. Demirel said at the time he would look to parties that could pass a parliamentary vote of confidence, which did not necessarily mean the victorious Welfare party. The following month, Welfare party leader Necmettin Erbakan was invited by Demirel to form a coalition government. Despite skepticism that he would succeed, Erbakan became prime minister.

However, Demirel remained an outspoken proponent of the secular system created by Kemel Ataturk, founder of the republic. In May 1996, Demirel escaped a would-be assassin's bullet unscathed. The pro-Islamic gunman was angered by an accord allowing Israeli jets to train in Turkish airspace. In newspaper interviews the following year, Demirel said Turkish laws made it clear what activities were crimes against the secular system and offered a veiled threat of a crackdown. "We do not want to be a country of bans but, if necessary, other laws can be passed on this subject." If anyone wants Islamic law, "it means he is not happy with the modern system and wants the old system, but Turkey does not want to retrogress. . ." Also, in seeming contradiction to his earlier criticism of former president Ozal, Demirel called for enhancement of presidential powers to allow the head of state to handle issues whenever Turkey was in what he called an uneasy state.

Although politics at home kept him busy, Demirel's activities abroad were numerous. A good deal of his effort went toward promoting Turkey for membership in the European Union. A December 1996 visit to Kazakhstan was aimed in part at strengthening bilateral relations and discussion of Turkish cooperation in the laying of an oil pipeline from Kazakhstan to a terminal near the Russian Black Sea port of Novorossiisk. Demirel also worked to strengthen ties with Iran. Following a meeting with Iranian President Akbar Hashemi Rafsanjani, Demirel said Turkey and Iran were two friendly neighboring countries sharing the same faith and deep cultural ties. Talks between Demirel and his Romanian counterpart, Emil Constantinescu, led to the signing of a free trade agreement between the countries and two other accords in April 1997. The following month on a visit to Poland, Demirel promoted a strategic partnership between Turkey and Poland and voiced support for the eastward expansion of the North Atlantic Treaty Organization (NATO).

Demirel's attention was soon called home again by political unrest. Following pressure from the Turkish military, which had been angered by attempts to chip away at secularism, Prime Minister Erbakan resigned in June 1997. Demirel was called upon to pick his successor and chose Motherland party leader Mesut Yimaz. Comments made by Demirel at about this time indicated his still strong support of secularism. "Secularism and modernism are required for civilization. This is the direction that Ataturk showed us."

## Further Reading

There is as yet no biography of Süleyman Demirel in English, but Feroz Ahmad, *The Turkish Experiment in Democracy 1950-1975* (1975) covers the years in which he was active. C. H. Dodd, *Democracy and Development in Turkey* (1979) and Walter Weiker, *The Modernization of Turkey: From Ataturk to the Present Day* (1981) throw light on the years after 1975. □

# Democritus

**The Greek natural philosopher Democritus (ca. 494-ca. 404 B.C.) promulgated the atomic theory, which asserted that the universe is composed of two elements: the atoms and the void in which they exist and move.**

Democritus was born in Abdera, the leading Greek city on the northern coast of the Aegean Sea. Although the ancient accounts of Democritus's career differ widely, they all agree that he lived to a ripe old age, 90 being the lowest figure. During that long career Democritus wrote many books. *Little Cosmology,* a veritable encyclopedia, has perished because its contents displeased those, such as the philosopher Plato, whose decisions determined which works should be preserved. Of all of Democritus's many-sided interests, his espousal of the atomic theory accounts for his renown and also for the disappearance of the treatises which won him that renown.

## Atomic Theory

Democritus did not originate the atomic theory; he learned it from its founder, Leucippus, the author of the *Big Cosmology.* While this work too has vanished, some conception of its contents may be obtained from Aristotle. He opposed the atomic theory, but in doing so he summarized its principal doctrines. Thus he attributed to Leucippus the ideas that the atoms are "infinite in number and imperceptible because of the minuteness of their size. They move about in empty space (for there is empty space) and by joining together they produce perceptible objects, which are destroyed when the atoms separate." The point at which Leucippus's elaboration of the atomic theory stopped and Democritus's contributions to it began can no longer be identified. In antiquity the theory's major features were sometimes ascribed to Leucippus and Democritus jointly and sometimes to Democritus alone.

Perhaps according to both of them and certainly according to Democritus, the atom was the irreducibly minimal quantity of matter. The concept of the infinite divisibility of matter was flatly contradicted by the atomic theory, since within the interior of the atom there could be no physical parts or unoccupied space. Every atom was exactly like every other atom as a piece of corporeal stuff. But the atoms differed in shape, and since their contours showed an infinite variety and could be oriented in any direction and arranged in any order, the atoms could enter into countless combinations. In their solid interior there was no motion, while they themselves could move about in empty space. Thus, for the atomic theory, the physical universe had two basic ingredients: impenetrable atoms and penetrable space. For Democritus, space was infinite in extent, and the atoms were infinite in number.

By their very nature the atoms were endowed with a motion that was eternal and not initiated by any outside force. Since the atoms were not created at any time in the past and would never disintegrate at any time in the future, the total quantity of matter in the universe remained constant: this fundamental principle of Democritus's atomic theory implies the conservation of matter, the sum total of which in the universe neither increases nor diminishes. Though Democritus's conception of the atom has been modified in several essential respects in modern times, his atomic theory remains the foundation of modern science.

For Democritus, "time was uncreated." His atomic universe was temporally everlasting and spatially boundless, without beginning and without end in either space or time. Just as no special act of creation brought Democritus's universe into being, so the operations of his cosmos did not serve any particular purpose. Consequently, Democritus's atomic theory was irreconcilable with the teleological view, which regarded the world as having been planned to fulfill some inscrutable destiny. As the founder of the atomic theory declared in his only surviving statement, "Nothing occurs at random, but everything happens for a reason and by necessity."

## Moral Teachings

Just as Democritus's cosmogony invoked no creator-god, so his moral teachings appealed to no supernatural judge of human conduct. He attributed the popular belief in Zeus and other deities to primitive man's incomprehension of meteorological and astronomical phenomena. To support his theory about the origin of worship of the various divinities, Democritus assailed the widespread notion that rewards for righteous actions and punishments for wrongdoing were administered in an afterlife. In the long history of Greek speculation Democritus was the first thinker to deny that every human being has an individual soul which survives the death of the body.

Democritus sought to diminish pain during life, of which "the goal is cheerfulness." Cheerfulness is identical not with pleasure, as he was misinterpreted by some people, but "with a calm and steady mind, undisturbed by any fear or superstition or other irrational feeling." Yet Democritus did not advocate a quiet life of repose. His was not the outlook of the retired citizen, drowsing in his rocking chair on the front porch and idly watching the world go by. Democritus taught a naturalistic morality, avoiding ascetic renunciation as well as excessive indulgence, and urging energetic participation in beneficial activities. In particular, "Democritus recommends mastering the art of politics as most important, and undertaking its tasks, from which significant and magnificent benefits are obtained for the people." Perhaps from his governmental experience in Abdera, Democritus learned that "good conduct seems to be procured better by the use of encouraging and convincing words than by statute and coercion. For he who is restrained by law from wrongdoing is likely to commit crime covertly. On the other hand, he who is attracted to uprightness by persuasion is unlikely to transgress either secretly or openly."

## Probing the Infinitesimal

Archimedes, the most brilliant mathematician of antiquity, gave Democritus credit for the discovery that the volume of a cone is one-third that of a cylinder having the same base and altitude. Archimedes added, however, that this theorem was enunciated by Democritus "without proof." In Democritus's time Greek geometry had not yet reached the stage at which it demanded rigorous proofs of its theorems. Democritus stated: "If a cone is cut by a plane parallel to its base, shall we regard the surfaces forming the sections as equal or unequal? If unequal, they make the cone uneven, having numerous indentations and protrusions, like a flight of stairs. But if the surfaces are equal, the sections will be equal and the cone comes to look like a cylinder, consisting of equal circles." Democritus's conception of the cylinder as being made up of an indefinite number of minutely thin circular layers shows him beginning to probe the momentous question of the infinitesimal, the starting point of a most valuable branch of modern mathematics.

## Further Reading

A comprehensive study of Democritus is Cyril Bailey, *The Greek Atomists and Epicurus* (1928). More recent discussions can be found in William Keith Chambers Guthrie, *A History of Greek Philosophy* (3 vols., 1962-1969); Andrew Thomas Cole, *Democritus and the Sources of Greek Anthropology* (1967); David J. Furley, *Two Studies in the Greek Atomists* (1967); and G. F. Parker, *A Short Account of Greek Philosophy from Thales to Epicurus* (1967). □

# Abraham Demoivre

**The Franco-English mathematician Abraham Demoivre (1667-1754) was a successful exponent of the calculus of Newton and Leibniz and an early writer on the mathematics of life insurance.**

Abraham Demoivre, the son of a surgeon living at Vitry, Champagne, was born May 26, 1667. He was given a Protestant schooling and at the age of 11 went to the Protestant University of Sedan. He studied logic at Saumur, and at the Collège d'Harcourt in Paris he learned the physics of the day, mainly according to the system of René Descartes. When Demoivre was 18, Louis XIV revoked the Edict of Nantes, which had granted toleration to Protestants, and the youth was forced to flee Paris, eventually settling in London.

Once in London, Demoivre earned a meager living as a private teacher and lecturer in mathematics and natural science. He obtained a copy of Isaac Newton's recently published *Principia* (1687) and studied it assiduously. It is said that he tore the book into sheets, carrying a few around at a time in his pocket to master it in his spare time. Demoivre made the acquaintance of Newton, Edmund Halley, and other members of the Royal Society. His mathematical talents were recognized, and in 1695 he presented his first paper to the society, "Method of Fluxions," on Newton's calculus. By 1697 he had been elected a fellow of the Royal Society.

Demoivre published a number of papers, but his most original work was a book on the subject of probability, *Doctrine of Chances* (1718). It contained several innovations, including methods for approximating to functions of large numbers. Isaac Todhunter, historian of theories of probability, contended that the subject owed more to Demoivre than any other mathematician, except possibly Pierre Simon de Laplace. It was as a natural extension of his writings on probability that Demoivre wrote *Annuities on Lives* (1725), the first mathematical work on this subject. It is based on a law of mortality that differs little from one devised by John Hudd in 1671. Though Demoivre's principles have since been modified, his work was still being defended by eminent actuarial mathematicians of the 19th century. Demoivre accused Thomas Simpson, a younger pioneer of the same subject, of plagiarism but later dropped the charge.

Demoivre was honored by many European societies. One important theorem applying complex or "imaginary" numbers to trigonometry bears his name. He died in London on Nov. 27, 1754.

## Further Reading

There is no biography of Demoivre. For background and a brief biographical sketch see David Eugene Smith, *History of Mathematics,* vol. 1 (1923). □

# Demosthenes

**Demosthenes (384-322 B.C.) is regarded as the greatest of Greek orators and perhaps the greatest orator of all times. He saw clearly the significance of the rise of an autocratic Macedonia and its implications for traditional Athenian and Greek political freedom.**

Demosthenes was the son of a wealthy manufacturer of weapons named Demosthenes of the deme of Paeania in Attica. The orator's father died when Demosthenes was 7 years old, and his estate was turned over to his two brothers, Aphobus and Demophon, and a friend, Therippides, who sorely mismanaged it.

## Early Career

Though a sickly child, Demosthenes was determined to obtain redress from his guardians. In order to prepare himself, he studied rhetoric and law under Isaeaus, and though by age 20 only about one-tenth of the capital remained for him, he successfully prosecuted his guardians. The four speeches dealing with this business are preserved in "Against Aphobus" and "Against Onetor."

Though the legend about his declaiming with pebbles in his mouth and practicing by the seashore midst the thunder of the waves may be apocryphal, there is no doubt that Demosthenes rigorously prepared himself to overcome any physical disabilities; and though apparently not a good improviser, he was closely familiar with the writings of Thucydides, Plato, and Isocrates. Demosthenes spent 15 years as a professional speech writer (*logographos*) and ranged over a wide variety of subjects with a mastery of oratorical form and of technical legal details. Thirty-two of these private orations are preserved, though only a third of these are generally considered genuine.

In 355 B.C. Demosthenes found himself employed as an assistant to the public prosecutors in the assembly, in the courts, and in other public places. The speeches against Androtion, Timocrates, and Aristocrates show evidence of a mind of considerable ability. His first public appearance in 354 in "Against Leptines" defends the policy of exempting from special taxation citizens who had performed outstanding services to the state. "Against Aristocrates" (352) shows him dealing with foreign policy, while "On the Navy Boards" (354), "For Megalopolis" (352), and "For the Rhodians" (351) show a Demosthenes keenly interested in foreign affairs and pushing hard for administrative reforms.

## Opponent of Macedon

The year 351 marks a turning point in Demosthenes's career since in a series of nine orations he began his famous "Philippics" (351-340), warning Athens of the threatening danger of an ever expanding Macedon and an ever imperialistically encroaching Philip. The "First Philippic" was succeeded by three "Olynthiac" speeches, centering on Olynthus, the strongest Greek city in the north, which was threatened by Philip. Demosthenes pleaded that the Athenians dispatch forces to help Olynthus out of its plight, but the Athenians were not convinced of the gravity of the situation and Olynthus fell in 348. Philip was not to be stopped as his attention was now directed southward. Once he became admitted to the Amphictyonic League in 346, Macedon became a Greek power with support in Athens itself.

Though Demosthenes supported the peace treaty with Philip in 346 in his oration "On the Peace," he soon saw that Philip had other plans. So in 344 in the "Second Philippic," in "On the Chersonese," and in the "Third Philippic" (341) he renewed his attack on Philip and his designs, while in "On the Embassy" (343) he attacked Aeschines, whom he accused of having betrayed the best interests of Athens. Gradually Demosthenes assumed the leadership of the opposition to the growing military and political aggrandizement of Philip, an opposition that developed into armed conflict and resulted in the crushing defeat of the Athenians and their allies at Chaeronea in 338. Demosthenes himself was among the defeated refugees.

Though defeated, Demosthenes was not broken in spirit. He continued to fight Philip, and for his services Ctesiphon proposed a golden crown be presented to him at the city Dionysia, a proposal that motivated Aeschines, Demosthenes's chief competitor, to bring charges against Ctesiphon on the grounds that an illegal proposal had been proferred. The trial took place in 330, and Demosthenes brilliantly defended Ctesiphon and himself in what is considered his masterpiece "On the Crown."

## Decline of Leadership

Thereafter Demosthenes's leadership waned. He was charged with having received money from Harpalus, the governor of Babylon and the treasurer of Alexander the Great, who had absconded with funds to Athens on the basis of a false rumor that Alexander was dead. Harpalus was refused admission to Athens because of an army of 6,000 that he had with him.

Upon demand Harpalus dismissed his troops and was admitted, but Alexander demanded his surrender. Demosthenes retorted by proposing that Harpalus be kept in custody and that the funds he had be deposited in the Parthenon. When Harpalus escaped there was a shortage of 370 talents, and Demosthenes was accused of having accepted a bribe of 20 talents to assist in the escape. Charged and brought to trial, Demosthenes was fined 50 talents, but because he was unable to pay he went into exile.

It is still not clear whether Demosthenes was actually guilty of misconduct in the Harpalus incident or not. At any rate, Demosthenes tried to organize support against Macedon in the Peloponnesus; was recalled to Athens, which was subsequently occupied by Macedon; and was condemned to death but escaped to the Temple of Poseidon in Calauria, where he committed suicide in 322.

## His Works

Sixty-one orations, six letters, and a book of 54 proems have been attributed to Demosthenes, though all are certainly not genuine. Private law court speeches include those against Aphobus and Onetor (363-362), "Against Dionysodorus" (323-322), "For Phormio" (350), and the first "Against Stephanus" (349). The subjects cover guardianship, inheritance, loans, mining rights, and forgery, among others.

The political law court speeches include "Against Androtion" (355), "Against Leptines" (354), "Against Timocrates" (353), "Against Aristocrates" (352), "Against Midias" (347), "On the Embassy" (343), "On the Crown" (330), and "Against Aristogeiton" (325-324). Topics covered include abolition of immunity from taxation for public-spirited citizens, embezzlement, assaulting a public official, bribery, and the private lives of Demosthenes and Aeschines.

Political speeches include "On the Navy Boards" (354), "For Megalopolis" (352), "For the Rhodians" (351), "First Philippic" (351), three "Olynthiacs" (349), "On the Peace" (346), "Second Philippic" (344), "On the Chersonese" (341), "Third Philippic" (341), "Fourth Philippic" (composite), "On the Halonnese" (342), and "On the Treaty with Alexander" (probably not by Demosthenes). The six "Letters" have been reinvestigated recently and the majority of them may be genuine. Both domestic Greek history and politics and foreign affairs are involved.

## His Significance

Demosthenes is generally acknowledged to be Greece's greatest orator, though he never lacked for rivals in his lifetime. It has been said that he united in himself the excellences of his contemporaries and predecessors. More than a master of rhetorical form, Demosthenes was a man of superior moral and intellectual qualities who knew how to use language for its best effects.

Perhaps most significant of all was Demosthenes's ability to see the implications of the rise of Macedonian political and military power and to become the staunchest and most persistent defender of individual Greek freedom against the new power; but he was not farsighted enough to see that the Greek city-state was no longer a viable political unit and that it would be replaced by the Hellenistic imperial state.

## Further Reading

Books on Demosthenes appear less frequently than they did in the past. A number of older works are still worth consulting: Samuel H. Butcher, *Demosthenes* (1881); Arthur W. Pickard-Cambridge, *Demosthenes* (1914); Charles D. Adams, *Demosthenes and His Influence* (1927); and Werner W. Jaeger, *Demosthenes: The Origin and Growth of His Policy* (1938). Jonathan Goldstein, *The Letters of Demosthenes*

(1968), provides a fascinating investigation into the question of the historical value and authenticity of the six letters attributed to Demosthenes.

## Additional Sources

Sealey, Raphael, *Demosthenes and his time: a study in defeat,* New York: Oxford University Press, 1993. □

# Jack Dempsey

**One of the world's greatest heavyweight boxers, William Harrison "Jack" Dempsey (1895-1983) was so popular that he drew more million-dollar gates than any prizefighter in history.**

William Harrison Dempsey, more commonly known as "Jack" after age 20, was born in Manassa, Colo., on June 24, 1895, the ninth child of Hyrum and Cecilia Dempsey, both sharecroppers. The family was so poor that Jack began farming at the age of 8. From age 16 to 19 he lived in hobo jungles.

Dempsey's early boxing often took place in back rooms of frontier saloons under the name "Kid Blackie." His first fight of record was in 1915 against "One-Punch" Hancock. Dempsey's one-punch win earned him $2.50; his highest purse. Eleven years later his purse was $711,000 for his first match with Gene Tunney. Eventually called the "Manassa Mauler," Dempsey earned more than $3,500,000 in all in the ring.

Dempsey's appeal lay in his punching ability: he was a ruthless tiger stalking his prey, fast as any big cat and deadly with either paw. He won the world's heavyweight title on July 4, 1919, against Jess Willard in Toledo. With his first real punch Dempsey shattered Willard's cheekbone and knocked him down seven times in the first round. Willard was unable to answer the bell for the start of the fourth.

Two years later Dempsey drew the world's first million-dollar gate against Georges Carpentier of France, in Jersey City, NJ, scoring a fourth-round knockout. Another million-dollar bout was in 1923 against Luis Angel Firpo of Argentina; few bouts have packed such unbridled fury and spectacular savagery. Dempsey was knocked down twice, once through the ropes and out of the ring; 10 times Firpo went down, the tenth time for keeps—all within the span of 3 minutes 57 seconds. The Mauler was dethroned in Philadelphia in 1926, when Gene Tunney outpointed him before the largest crowd ever, 120,757 spectators, to witness the championship game.

Dempsey knocked out Jack Sharkey before the second Dempsey-Tunney fight a year later in Chicago. This last bout became the focus of an enduring controversy. Dempsey floored Tunney in the seventh round but refused to go to a neutral corner according to the rules. The countdown was delayed, and Tunney, given this extra respite, recovered sufficiently to outbox Dempsey the rest of the way.

For several years after his defeat, Dempsey refereed, announced boxing matches, and mentored young fighters. He attempted a comeback in 1931-32 but failed.

During the years of the Great Depression, Dempsey concentrated on various business interests including retailing, real estate, and two restaurants in New York City. After the outbreak of World War II, Dempsey joined the Coast Guard, serving as director of the physical fitness program. As the war drew to a close in the Pacific, he was sent on a three month's tour of combat areas to assess needs for athletic and physical training.

During his time as a highly respected restauranteur on Broadway, Dempsey enjoyed a fantastic popularity, revered as one of the true titans of American sports. He died on May 31, 1983.

## Further Reading

The most authoritative book on Dempsey is his autobiography, *Dempsey,* written with Bob Considine and Bill Slocum (1960). The best statistical background is in *Nat Fleischer's Ring Record Book* (1970). Dempsey's manager, Jack ''Doc'' Kearns, appraises him in *The Million Dollar Gate,* written with Oscar Fraley (1966). The second Dempsey-Tunney fight is in Mel Heimer, *The Long Count* (1969). □

# Charles Demuth

**American painter Charles Demuth (1883-1935), distinguished for intimate watercolors and geometrized urban scenes, was one of the leading artists of precisionism, an American idiom of cubism in the 1920s.**

Charles Demuth was born in Lancaster, Pa., on Nov. 8, 1883. A childhood leg injury left him lame, and at an early age he began to draw and paint. After studying at the School of Industrial Art in Philadelphia, he entered the Pennsylvania Academy of Fine Arts in 1905 and took classes with William Merritt Chase and Thomas Anschutz.

In 1907 Demuth went to Paris, where Fauve painting with its expressive form and color affected his early work. *Studio·Interior* (ca. 1907), one of the few surviving works of this period, is a watercolor whose roughly outlined, loosely painted figures are reminiscent of those of Henri Matisse and Georges Rouault. It foreshadows the illustrational style Demuth employed, in refined form, later. He continued his studies at the Pennsylvania Academy (1908-1910), and his interest in figure drawing increased. As he refined his focus, the personages depicted became vehicles for acute psychological expression. In Paris again in 1912, he attended classes at the academies Julian, Colarossi, and Moderne. One of the few American artists of the period with firsthand understanding of the new European movements of cubism and Dada, Demuth evolved an art that transcended their literal and localized themes. In fact, he always remained receptive to a wide range of influences, and various styles found intelligent transmutation in his work.

Demuth's early watercolors, shown at the Pennsylvania Academy in 1912 and 1913, revealed a fragile, understated style; his landscapes, executed in delicate washes, evoked a gamut of European associations. Fauve references remained, but a new ***concern with formalism was evident, and there are parallels to Paul Cézanne's prismatic vistas in such paintings as *New Hope, Pennsylvania* (1911/1912). But even when Demuth employed the analytic approach of Cézanne or the cubist planes of Pablo Picasso, his art remained concerned with surface quality, not internal structure.

By 1915 Demuth was established as a major American artist through his landscapes, flower studies, and smallscale paintings of cabaret and circus performers. His figures have a weightless and phantomlike quality; in *Two Acrobats* (1918), entertainers dressed in tuxedoes float surrealistically through a vague landscape. Demuth's sensitive linear style was eminently suited to illustrating plays and novels such as Émile Zola's *Nana,* Henry James's *The Turn of the Screw,* Frank Wedekind's *Pandora's Box,* and Edgar Allan Poe's *The Mask of the Red Death.* These illustrations, not meant for publication, reflect Demuth's taste for the psychologically distorted and depict sexual conflict and social decadence.

In *White Architecture* (1917) Demuth used the cubist technique with delicacy and individuality and employed color sparingly to modify a complex of overlaid and intersecting structural planes derived from the building itself. He developed this style in his paintings of factories and industrial sites, beginning in 1918, and thus was a pioneer of the precisionist movement.

Demuth did a unique group of "poster portraits" (symbolic still-life paintings) that reflected the interests and attributes of friends, including painters Georgia O'Keeffe, Marsden Hartley, and Arthur Dove and poet William Carlos Williams. The best-known of these, *I Saw the Figure 5 in Gold* (1928), a "portrait" of Williams, whose title derives from a Williams poem, is a direct ancestor of pop art, using the numeral 5 in a repeated abstract arrangement. Demuth died in Lancaster on Oct. 25, 1935.

### Further Reading

The life and artistic development of Demuth are covered in A. C. Ritchie, *Charles Demuth* (1950), and Emily Farnham, *Charles Demuth: Behind a Laughing Mask* (1971). There is an essay on Demuth by Martin Friedman in the Walker Art Center Catalog *The Precisionist View in American Art* (1960). Older monographs include A. E. Gallatin, *Charles Demuth* (1927), and William Murrell, *Charles Demuth* (1931).

### Additional Sources

Eiseman, Alvord L., *Charles Demuth,* New York: Watson-Guptill Publications, 1982. □

# Deng Xiaoping

**Deng Xiaoping (Teng Hsiao-p'ing) (1904-1997) became the most powerful leader in the Peoples Republic of China (PRC) in the 1970s. He served as the chairman of the Communist party's Military Commission and was the chief architect of China's modernization and economic reforms during the 1980s.**

Born in Guangan, Sichuan Province, in 1904, Deng joined the Chinese Communist party (CCP) in 1924 while on a work-study program in France. Before returning to China in 1926 he went to Moscow, where he studied for several months.

During the fabled Long March of 1934-1935 Deng served first as director of the political department, and then as the political commissar, of the First Army Corps. After the war with Japan began in 1937 Deng was appointed political commissar of the 129th Division, one of the three divisions in the reorganized Communist Eighth Route Army, which was commanded by Liu Bocheng, also a native of Sichuan. The forces under the two Sichuanese grew into a large military machine and became one of the four largest Communist army units during the war. It was renamed the Second Field Army in 1946 when the civil war began. In the critical Huai-Hai battles in East China during November

1948-January 1949, Deng served as the secretary of a special five-man General Front Committee to coordinate the strategy of participating Communist troops and direct the military actions. In 1949-1950 the Second Field Army took Southwest China, and Deng became the ranking party leader there in the early 1950s.

Deng rose quickly in the leadership hierarchy after his transfer to Peking in 1952. He became CCP secretary-general in 1954 and a member of the Politburo the following year after he supervised the purge of two recalcitrant regional leaders. During the Eighth CCP Congress in 1956 Deng was elevated to the six-man Politburo Standing Committee and appointed general secretary, heading the party secretariat. By then, he had become one of the half dozen most powerful men in China.

### Exile and Return

By many accounts Deng was an able, talented, and knowledgeable man. He was nicknamed "a living encyclopedia" by his colleagues. Chairman Mao Tse-tung, the architect of the PRC, allegedly pointed Deng out to Khrushchev of the U.S.S.R. and said, "See that little man there? He is highly intelligent and has a great future ahead of him." Deng visited the Soviet Union several times in the 1950s and the 1960s, as he was closely involved in Sino-Soviet relations and their dispute over the international Communist movement.

Mao and Deng parted ways in the 1960s as they disagreed over the strategy of economic development and

other policies. Deng's pragmatism, embodied in his well-known remark, "It does not matter whether they are black cats or white cats; so long as they catch mice, they are good cats," was heresy to Mao's ears. Mao also resented Deng for making decisions without consulting him—he scolded Deng in a 1961 party meeting: "Which emperor did this?" In 1966 Mao launched the Great Proletarian Cultural Revolution (GPCR) and mobilized the youthful Red Guards to purge the "capitalist powerholders" in the party, such as Deng. From 1969 to 1973, Deng and his family were exiled to a "May 7 cadre school" in rural Jiangxi to undergo reeducation, in which he performed manual labor and studied the writings of Mao and Marx. Deng's elder son, Deng Pufang, was permanently crippled in an assault by Red Guards.

In the spring of 1973 Deng was brought back to Peking and reinstated a vice-premier in the wake of a major realignment of political forces, which resulted from the demise of Defense Minister Lin Piao and the purge of Lin's followers. Deng's ability and expertise were highly valued in the Chinese leadership and he quickly assumed important roles. In late 1973 he carried out a major reshuffle of regional military leaders and was elevated to the Politburo. In April 1974 he journeyed to New York to address a special United Nations session, in which he expounded Mao's theory of the "Three Worlds."

As Premier Chou Enlai was hospitalized after May 1974, the burden of leadership and administration increasingly fell on Deng's shoulders. In January 1975 Deng was elevated to a party vice-chairman, the senior vice-premier, and the army chief of staff. However, Deng's eagerness to carry out "four modernizations" and the political reforms alienated Mao and other radicals led by Mao's wife Chiang Ch'ing (Jiang Qing).

Thus, soon after Premier Chou died on January 8, 1976, Deng became the target of attack in the Chinese media, and on April 7 the party Politburo passed a resolution at Mao's urging to oust Deng from all leadership posts. After Mao's death in September 1976 Deng's allies prevailed and Deng was reinstated in July 1977, the opposition of new Party Chairman Hua Guofeng not withstanding.

After Deng's political comeback and in his struggle for ascendency thereafter, his foremost task was to destroy the cult of Mao and to downgrade Mao's ideological authority. Another powerful measure of de-Maoization was to put the "Gang of Four" on public trial, which began in Peking on November 20, 1980. These four radical leaders, including Mao's widow Chiang Ch'ing, were the late chairman's most ardent supporters and the prime movers behind the GPCR, on which they rode to power. The trial symbolized the triumph of veteran officials, led by Deng, who had fallen victim to the radical crusade between 1966 and 1976.

Moreover, Deng also used the trial as the *coup de grace* against Chairman Hua Guofeng. Although Hua was not a defendant, he did collaborate with the radicals before Mao's death. In a central committee plenum in June 1981 Hu Yaobang, Deng's protege, replaced Hua as the party chairman.

## Reform Leader

Deng's economic policies required opening China to the rest of the world in order to attract foreign investment and to educate students abroad in the latest technologies. Accordingly, the People's Republic of China in 1978 signed a Treaty of Peace and Friendship with Japan. In 1979, Deng obtained his nation's official recognition from the United States. Sino-Russian relations were gradually improved over the next decade, and he achieved the long-cherished goal of recovering the British colony of Hong Kong through an agreement scheduled for implementation in 1997.

These diplomatic successes supplemented and eased major changes in the domestic economy. Deng found China's industrial progress impeded by the imbalances of the Cultural Revolution, which stressed investment in heavy industry while virtually ignoring, consumer production, agriculture, transportation, and energy production. As a result, wages and farm prices were too low, and consumer goods were in short supply.

To combat this situation, Deng reduced capital investment in heavy industry, increased prices paid by the state to farmers, and arranged a series of bonuses to raise workers' incomes. Farmers were encouraged to sell more produce privately, and a rapid growth of free markets for farm produce occurred. The communal labor system was virtually eliminated from the rural communes, and fields were leased to farm families on terms that allowed them more autonomy in determining what crops to plant. Agricultural production increased dramatically while, at the same time, a significant proportion of the rural population transferred its activities from farming to various kinds of light industry and trade. More free markets sprang up for distribution of these products, and some state-owned factories were placed under the control of their managers, who were instructed to take into account the profitability and market conditions for their products.

## Fought to Maintain Political Stability

Throughout these reforms, Deng insisted upon maintaining China's socialist system. As ever greater reliance was placed on market forces to determine prices, it became increasingly difficult to balance socialist principles with capitalist effects. The reforms resulted in a generally improved standard of living but produced inequalities that were greatly resented. Inflation in the 1980s, a serious problem for the first time in a generation, accompanied increased unemployment and ever-growing disparities in living standards. Deng's inability to reform the blatant corruption and enrichment of many party and government officials and their families created new tensions.

Such tensions fed the long-smoldering discontent of academics who had opposed the party's dictatorship from the beginning and fueled repeated popular demands, especially among students, for a greater degree of democracy in China. In 1979, some of Deng's supporters had openly opposed his dictatorship and called for a democratic political system, and it was Deng himself who led the suppression of their democracy movement, imprisoned some of their leaders, and banned unofficial organizations and publications. Again in December of 1986, widespread unauthorized student demonstrations were repressed by the government. Hu Yaobang was blamed for this movement, forced to resign, and became a hero to the students. Zhao Ziyang replaced him as head of the party.

Deng's insistence through the 1980s on maintaining China's socialist system while putting his economic reforms into place had by 1989 forced him into an untenable corner of contradictions; he was presiding over increasing economic disparities in an ostensibly socialist society. The opposition's discontent ripened that year into plans for renewed student demonstrations on the 70th anniversary of the May Fourth Movement. When Hu Yaoband died in April, the demonstrators' leaders incorporated into their plans memorials that resembled their 1976 protests following Chou Enlai's death.

Focusing on demands for greater democracy, a series of student demonstrations at Tiananmen Square coincided with Mikhail Gorbachev's official state visit to Beijing and proved a serious embarrassment to China's leaders—one made worse by world-wide television coverage. The democracy movement quickly spread to other cities, threatening both social stability and Communist party leadership.

Deng, who began his political career 70 years earlier on one side of the May Fourth Movement of 1919, now found himself on quite another as party leaders began to weigh the possibility of compromise with the students. He chose, instead, confrontation. Restructuring his alliances, he forced Zhao Ziyang's resignation and relied on his old military friends to suppress the demonstrations. The violence that followed on June 4, 1989, is believed to have killed hundreds of demonstrators in Beijing alone.

### Final Years

Worldwide condemnation of the massacre in Tiananmen Square and the uneasy domestic peace that followed brought a tightening of controls over the Chinese people, but did not shake Deng from his dedication to the Communist party's dictatorship nor his pursuit of modernization and economic reform.

From time to time, Deng compromised with other leaders, slowed down the pace of reform, or shifted priorities to placate his critics, but this did not seriously effect Deng's control of the regime's direction. Recognizing his advanced age, Deng sought to assure continuation of his "open door" policy and other political and economic reforms by putting CCP General Secretary Hu Yaobang, Premier Zhao Ziyang, and many other like-minded younger officials in positions of responsibility. In November of 1989, Deng resigned his last official position as head of the Central Military Commission. However, he retained paramount authority and continued to guide Chinese policy from his retirement.

The failed Soviet coup in August 1991 and the subsequent collapse of the Soviet Communist party reinforced Deng's belief that the fate of China, as well as that of Chinese communism, depended heavily on the state of China's economy. Deng understood well that economic reform meant turning loose forces that might eventually topple the Communist party but believed strongly in the

party's ability to deliver economic growth and rising incomes. Deng's commitment to change and chastisement of those who dared oppose him forced many hard-line conservative elders to retire and cleared the way for Communist party to fully embrace his reforms. In 1992 the 14th Party Congress signalled the acceptance of Deng's ideas by making a socialist market economy a national goal for the year 2000.

In his last years Deng instigated debate within the Communist party on the need to balance economic reform with political stability, but was unable to impose a convincing plan for stability after his death. As Deng's health slipped into precipitous decline, the powerful patriarch became farther removed from his duties of daily decision-making. His last public appearance was during lunar new year festivities in early 1994, and on February 19, 1997 he died at age 92.

### Further Reading

For an excellent biographical article on Deng's life and the economic changes he brought to China see Patrick E. Tyler's essay in the *The New York Times,* February 16, 1997.
*Deng Xiaoping (Teng Hsiao-p'ing): Speeches and Writings* (1984) and Parris H. Chang, "Chinese Politics: Deng's Turbulent Quest," in *Problems of Communism* (January-February 1981) provide additional information on Deng's political activities. *TIME* magazine recognized his reforms by twice naming him "Man of the Year," in 1976 and 1985. □

# Rauf Denktash

**The Turkish Cypriot politician and statesman Rauf Denktash (born 1924) began his working life as a lawyer but became engaged in the struggle for his community's rights. In 1975 he became head of the "Turkish Federated State of Cyprus" and in 1985 president of the Turkish Republic of Northern Cyprus. He served in this office for three terms.**

Rauf Denktash was born January 27, 1924, in what became the British Crown Colony of Cyprus the following year. He came from a comfortable middle-class family, the son of a judge who worked in the British administration. After graduating from the English high school in Nicosia in 1941, he worked as an interpreter in the courts, taught for a year in the English school, and began to write articles on the problems of Cyprus' Turkish community for *Halkin Sesi (Voice of the People)*. In 1944 Denktash went to London to study law and was called to the Bar from Lincoln's Inn in 1947. He returned to Cyprus in 1948 and was appointed to the governor's "Constitutional Council." The following year he began to work in the prosecutor's office, where he remained until 1958.

These years coincided with the mounting Greek Cypriot agitation led by the National Organization of Cypriot Fighters, better known by its Greek acronym *EOKA*. This movement fought for self-determination and *enosis* or union with Greece, which the Turkish-Cypriot minority resisted strenuously. Denktash, now a respected figure in his community, realized that he must play an active role in the resistance movement. He therefore resigned from government service in February 1958 and was elected president of the Federation of Turkish Associations of Cyprus. He was also one of the founders of the Turkish Resistance Organization (TMT), the Turkish counterpart of *EOKA*. At the same time he continued his political journalism and published a weekly edition in the *Voice of the People* in order to present the Turkish thesis to the English-reading public.

## International Spokesman

By the late 1950s Denktash had become the spokesman for the Turkish case in the international arenas of London and New York. He led Turkish delegations in the constitutional talks and defended his community's interests in conferences in Athens and London. As a result of his activities his position within the community continued to grow and he became the second most important leader after Dr. Fazil Kuchuk.

Cyprus was declared an independent republic within the British Commonwealth on August 16, 1960. The constitution stipulated that political power would be shared proportionately between the two communities, each having its own legislature. Denktash was elected president of the Turkish Cypriot communal chamber as well as president of the executive committee. But the constitutional arrangements failed to work smoothly and President Makarios shelved the constitution in 1963. As a result, fighting broke

out between the two communities in December. Denktash went to London in January 1964 to defend the Turkish case in the five-power conference in which the two communities and the three guarantor powers (England, Greece, and Turkey) participated. In February Denktash went to the United Nations to present his case, the first of many visits.

Denktash was declared *persona non grata* by President Makarios and was therefore unable to return to Cyprus. As a result, he was forced to reside in Turkey until 1968, though he entered the island secretly from time to time to engage in the struggle against the Greek Cypriot government. He was caught by Greek forces in November 1967 and expelled again to Turkey. But Denktash was allowed to return to Cyprus in April 1968 and again became the president of the communal council and the deputy leader of the administrative council. From June 1968 onwards he led his community's team in the bilateral negotiations with the Greeks. These negotiations continued for the next six years but with no results. Time seemed to favor the Greeks; the Turkish community declined dramatically as a result of economic stagnation and emigration from the island.

The deadlock in negotiations was shattered in July 1974 by the Greek National Guard coup against President Makarios. Backed by the military junta in Athens (in power since 1967), their objective was to overthrow Makarios and bring about *enosis* by force. But the coup led to intervention by Turkey and the occupation of about two-fifths of the island in the north. In this area, the "Cyprus Turkish Federated State" was created on February 13, 1975, with Denktash as president of the Assembly. In the elections of June 20, 1976, held under the new constitution of June 8, 1975, Denktash was elected head of state for five years by a large majority. But he resigned from his office when he founded the National Union party, whose leader he became. Meanwhile, negotiations with the Greeks were again underway, Denktash proposing a two-state federal solution for the island. But this proposal proved unacceptable to the Greek Cypriot leadership.

## President of Breakaway Republic

Denktash was again elected his community's head of state in 1981. With negotiations between the Greek and Turkish communities at an impasse, the Turks proclaimed the Turkish Republic of Northern Cyprus on November 15, 1983, and Rauf Denktash was elected president on June 9, 1985. He was reelected president in April 1990. The new state was recognized only by Turkey but has acquired roots over the intervening years. Denktash won a third term in 1995 when he was 71. He defeated right-wing rival Dervish Eroglu. The same year, Denktash said Turkish-held parts of Cyprus would integrate with Turkey should the Cypriot government press its bid to join the European Union (EU). "We are not against accession to the EU ... we were never against accession to the EU. We will have full integration with Turkey as the south will have full integration with Europe, I think it is the only alternative we have," he told reporters.

The following year, Denktash rejected calls by Cypriot President Glafcos Clerides for demilitarization talks.

"Demilitarization on its own cannot be discussed. It should come up in the discussions of the Cyprus problem as a whole," he said at the time. Denktash accused the Cypriot president of trying "to deceive the world" by offering demilitarization. A Cypriot government decision to buy Russian ground-to-air missiles to defend air and naval bases under construction in Paphos further strained relations, said Denktash. However, in the first half of 1997 preparations were being made for direct talks between Denktash and Clerides. The two leaders had not met since 1994 when they talked informally under the auspices of the UN. In July 1997 the leaders met in New York City; however, a quick resolution was not in the offing. The Cypriot government rejected a Denktash proposal to set up a special bicommunal police force to assist UN peacekeepers in the island state's buffer zone. The Cypriot government also called on Denktash and Turkey to abandon attempts to seek recognition for the Northern Cyprus breakaway state.

Apart from being a politician and statesman, Denktash was also an accomplished photographer and author. Most of his publications are in Turkish but *The Cyprus Triangle* is in English and presents the Turkish-Cypriot perspective on the struggle for the island of Cyprus.

## Further Reading

There is as yet no English-language biography of Rauf Denktash. He is listed in such biographical dictionaries as *Who's Who in the World, International Yearbook and Statesmen's Who's Who,* and *International Who's Who of Intellectuals.* Therefore, to find more information on this Turkish Cypriot leader the reader will have to turn to the numerous books on the history of modern Cyprus. Recommended amongst these are the following: Pierre Oberling, *The Road to Bellapais* (1982); Tozun Bahcheli, *Greek-Turkish Relations since 1955* (1990); and Kyriacos Markides, *The Rise and Fall of the Cyprus Republic* (1977). If possible, the reader should try to find Rauf Denktash's own writings, especially *The Cyprus Triangle* (London, 1982). □

# Manoel Deodoro da Fonseca

**Manoel Deodoro da Fonseca (1827-1892) was the first president of Brazil. Perhaps his greatest contribution was the assumption of authority in the last days of the empire and his leading role in the establishment of the republic.**

Manoel Deodoro da Fonseca was born on Aug. 5, 1827, in Alagoas. In 1843 he entered the Military School in Rio de Janeiro and after graduation in 1847 began a series of assignments that took him to all parts of the empire. In 1864 he participated in military campaigns in Uruguay and later against Francisco Solano López in the Paraguayan War. He later rose to field marshal.

Militarism, nurtured during the Paraguayan War, became reality in the late 1870s. The army looked upon itself as the savior of the nation, and the Military School was the center of positivist propaganda. Deodoro's prestige had grown to such stature that when the Duque de Caxias died in 1880 the Conservative party hoped that Deodoro would assume the duke's role of pacifying the restive army. But Deodoro also had the admiration of the young officers, who were increasingly attracted to republicanism and positivism. Promoted to quartermaster general of the army, he was assigned to an office in Rio, where he became the military strongman around whom the officers and their sympathizers rallied.

As the military-civilian crisis intensified, Deodoro was first transferred to Mato Grosso and then returned to Rio in June 1889. Rumors of cutbacks in military personnel and troop transfers to the frontier to diminish the army's strength in Rio aggravated the growing conflict.

Pressed by militants to lead a coup and proclaim a republic, Deodoro believed that the military's honor could be maintained by merely overthrowing the ministry. After repeated entreaties he agreed to lead the revolt. Yet his real goal is still unclear. Even during the actual coup, led by Floriano Peixoto on Nov. 15, 1889, when Deodoro became ill, he seems to have thought it was simply a move against an antagonistic ministry. Emperor Pedro II was sent into exile the next day.

On November 17 the provisional government was formed with Deodoro as the chief executive. Unfortunately, he was ill-suited for the position. Accustomed to instant obedience, he had little patience or administrative ability. Receiving minimal cooperation from his ministers and daily attacks in the press, he became increasingly bewildered by his new responsibilities. On Jan. 20, 1891, his Cabinet resigned en masse. On February 24, however, the constitution was proclaimed, and the Constituent Congress elected Deodoro president and Peixoto his vice president.

Unpopular and frequently seriously ill, Deodoro faced chronic disorder within the country and fiscal chaos. He was in constant conflict with Congress, and Peixoto plotted against him. On Nov. 3, 1891, Deodoro dissolved Congress, proclaimed a state of siege in Rio and its environs, and ruled by decree. His dictatorial regime was short-lived, however, as he faced the rebellious disaffection of the army and continuing poor health. On November 22 he suffered a serious heart attack. Two days later he resigned and was succeeded by Peixoto.

Peixoto effectively crushed a revolt to restore Deodoro in January 1892, but by then Deodoro was suffering serious physical and mental decline. He died in Petrópolis on Aug. 22, 1892.

## Further Reading

The standard work in English on Deodoro is Charles Willis Simmons, *Marshal Deodoro and the Fall of Dom Pedro II* (1966). It provides a sympathetic treatment of a man thrust into a position of responsibility far beyond his own ambition and ability. For background see João Pandiá Calógeras, *A History of Brazil* (trans. 1939). □

# André Derain

**André Derain (1880-1954) was considered by leading critics in the 1920s to be the most outstanding French avant-garde painter and at the same time the upholder of the classical spirit of French tradition.**

Andŕe Derain was born on June 10, 1880, in Chatou. He began to paint when he was about 15. He studied at the Academy Carrière in Paris (1898-1899), where he met Henri Matisse. Derain was a close friend of Maurice Vlaminck, with whom he shared a studio in 1900 and also his radical views on painting, literature, and politics. Derain was drawn, through Vlaminck and Matisse, into the art movement known as Fauvism.

Derain's first artistic attempts were interrupted by military service (1901-1904), after which he devoted himself exclusively to art. He experienced impressionism, divisionism, the style of Paul Gauguin and Vincent Van Gogh, and Vlaminck's and Matisse's techniques by applying them to his own work. He copied in the Louvre and traveled a great deal in France to paint its various landscapes. He spent the summer of 1905 at Collioure with Matisse and that fall exhibited with the Fauves.

The art dealer Ambrose Vollard signed a contract with Derain in 1905, and the following year the artist went to London to paint some scenes of the city commissioned by Vollard. Derain's *Westminster Bridge* is one of his Fauve masterpieces.

About 1908 Derain became interested in African sculpture and at the same time explored the work of Paul Cézanne and early cubism. He became a friend of Pablo Picasso and worked with him in Catalonia in 1910.

In Derain's work, which comprises landscapes, figure compositions (sometimes religious), portraits, still lifes, sculptures, decors for ballets, and book illustrations, we can discern various periods, all of which are distinguished by masterpieces. About 1911 he was attracted by Italian and French primitive masters; he also admired the "primitive" art of Henri Rousseau. After World War I, during which Derain served at the front, he studied the masters of the early Renaissance and then Pompeian art. All these left traces in his work. Finally he emerged as a realist and intensified his contact with nature. In rejecting the cerebral art of cubism and abstraction, he defended the return of the human figure to painting. His development as an artist was dramatic, and although Picasso called him a *guide de musées,* in other words, not an innovator but a traditionalist, Derain's best work will survive many of the experimental attempts of his contemporaries because of its inherent painterly qualities.

Toward the end of his life Derain lived, practically forgotten, in his country home at Chambourcy. The retrospective exhibition in Paris in 1937 was the climax of his fame. He died in Garches on Sept. 2, 1954. The large retrospective exhibitions organized from 1955 to 1959 established a new appreciation of Derain as a major artist.

## Further Reading

Denys Sutton, *André Derain* (1959), gives an objective picture of Derain's development and the attitude of critics to his work. Other monographs are Malcolm Vaughan, *Derain* (1941), and Gaston Diehl, *Derain* (trans. 1964).

## Additional Sources

Lee, Jane, *Derain,* Oxford: Phaidon; New York: Universe, 1990.
    □

# Jacques Derrida

**The French philosopher Jacques Derrida (born 1930), by developing a strategy of reading called "deconstruction," challenged assumptions about metaphysics and the character of language and written texts.**

Jacques Derrida was born in El Biar, Algiers, in 1930. He went to France for his military service and stayed on to study at the Ecole Normale with the eminent Hegel scholar Jean Hyppolite. Derrida taught at the Sorbonne (1960-1964) and after 1965 he taught the history of philosophy at the Ecole Normale Superieure. He was also a visiting professor in the United States at Johns Hopkins University and at Yale. His scholarly contribution included work with

GREPH (Groupe de recherches sur l'enseignement philosophique), an association concerned about the teaching of philosophy in France.

Derrida gained recognition for his first book, a translation with lengthy introduction of Husserl's *Origin of Geometry* (1962), which won him the Prix Cavailles. His analysis of Husserl's phenomenology became the starting point for the criticism of Western philosophy developed in his numerous other works. Derrida was suspicious of all systematic metaphysical thought and sought to illuminate the assumptions and riddles found in language.

### 'Metaphysics of Presence'

Derrida depicted Western thought, from Plato onward, as a "metaphysics of presence." By this he meant the desire to guarantee the certainty of thought claims by finding an ultimate foundation or source of meaning and truth. This quest was seen in the Western preoccupation with such concepts as substance, essence, origin, identity, truth, and, of course, "Being." Moreover, he explored the way metaphysics is linked to a specific view of language. The assumption, Derrida contended, is that the spoken word is free of the paradoxes and possibilities of multiple meanings characteristic of written texts. He called this assumed primacy of the spoken word over text "logocentrism," seeing it closely linked to the desire for certainty. His task was to undo metaphysics and its logocentrism. Yet Derrida was also clear that we cannot easily escape metaphysical thought, since to think outside it is to be determined by it, and so he did not affirm or oppose metaphysics, but sought to resist it.

Derrida developed a strategy of reading texts called "deconstruction." The term does not mean "destruction" but "analysis" in the etymological sense of "to undo." Deconstructive reading attempts to uncover and undo tensions within a text showing how basic ideas and concepts fail to ever express only one meaning. Derrida's point was that language always defers any single reference to the world because it is a system of signs that are intelligible only because of their differences. He called this dual character of language "difference" linking deferral and difference. Traditional metaphysics, as the quest for a unequivocal mystery of meaning, is deconstructed by exposing the "difference" internal to metaphysical discourse.

### 'Nothing Outside the Text'

Derrida's famous phrase, stated in *Of Grammatology* (1976), that "there is nothing outside the text" sums up his approach. What texts refer to, what is "outside" them, is nothing but another text. "Textuality" means that reference is not to external reality, the assumption of much Western thought, but to other texts, to "intertextuality." Thus Derrida's criticism of logocentrism also entails an attack on the assumption that words refer to or represent the world. If texts do not refer to the world then it is impossible to secure through language a foundation for meaning and truth. This requires a revision of what we mean by philosophical thinking. It can no longer be seen as the search for foundations, but as the critical play with texts to resist any metaphysical drive of thought.

Derrida applied deconstructive reading to a variety of texts, literary and philosophical. In *Dissemination* (1972) he offered subtle and complex readings of Plato and Mallarme. In works such as *Margins of Philosophy* (1972) and *Writing and Difference* (1978) he wrote on topics ranging from metaphor to theater. He refused, in a way similar to Nietzsche, to accept simple distinctions between philosophical and literary uses of language. Interestingly, his challenge to philosophy and his affirmation of the ambiguity of texts meant that his own work called for deconstruction.

Derrida's deconstructive strategy has implications for the study of literature. His contention was that the search for meaning, ideas, the author's intention, or truth *in* a text are misguided. What must be explored is the meanings that words have because of linguistic relations in the text. This opens up an infinite play of meaning possible with any text. Put differently, there is no one meaning to a text, its meaning is always open and strictly undecideable. Deconstruction requires the close readings of texts that highlight linguistic relations, particularly etymological ones, and relations between a text and other texts found in our culture without seeking to determine "the" meaning of the work. In short, it requires taking seriously "difference" and intertextuality.

### Not Without Detractors

Derrida's work provoked the reconsideration of traditional problems and texts and suggested a strategy for reading. However, he did not offer a positive position but debunked metaphysic strains of thought found throughout Western philosophy and literature. His work had significant impact on philosophical and literary circles, particularly in France and the United States. Derrida and his ideas were not always accepted. Critics argued his philosophy undermines the rational dialogue essential to academic pursuits. Indeed, in 1992 a proposal to give Derrida an honorary degree from Cambridge University met with opposition.

Derrida's 1996 book *Archive Fever: A Freudian Impression*, explored the relationship between technologies of inscription and psychic processes. "Derrida offers for the first time a major statement on the pervasive impact of electronic media, particularly e-mail, which threaten to transform the entire public and private space of humanity," wrote one reviewer. Because of the complexity of his writing, the need to deconstruct his texts, and the limitless potential of deconstructive reading, the influence and importance of his work is still in question.

## Further Reading

Derrida is listed in *Contemporary Literary Criticism* (Vol. 24), which includes critical reviews by philosophers and literary critics. For a helpful study of Derrida's work see Geoffrey Hartman, *Saving the Text: Literature/Derrida/Philosophy* (1981). To see Derrida's relation to other contemporary philosophers and critics see David Couzen Hoy's *The Critical Circle: Literature and History in Contemporary Hermeneutics* (1978).

## Additional Sources

David Wood, *Of Derrida, Heidegger, and Spirit,* Northwestern University Press, 1993.
Newton Garver, *Derrida & Wittgenstein,* Temple University Press, 1995.
Richard Beardsworth, *Derrida & the Political,* Routledge, 1996.
Robert Smith, *Derrida and Autobiography,* Cambridge University Press, 1995
Ellen K. Feder; Mary C. Rawlinson; Emily Zaki; *Derrida and Feminism: Recasting the Question of Woman,* Routledge, 1997.
Mark Wigley, *The Architecture of Deconstruction: Derrida's Haunt,* Mit Pr, 1993.
James Powell, *Derrida for Beginners,* Writers & Readers, 1996.
Nancy J. Holland, *Feminist Interpretations of Jacques Derrida (Re-Reading the Canon),* Pennsylvania State University Press, 1997. □

# Francesco De Sanctis

**The Italian critic, educator, and legislator Francesco De Sanctis (1817-1883) was the foremost Italian literary historian of the 19th century.**

Francesco De Sanctis was born in Morra Irpina near Naples. His early inclination toward learning suggested a career in the priesthood. But his interest in pedagogy and his loss of religious faith after 1834 altered his course, and he turned toward education. Trained by the literary scholar and philologist Basilio Puoti, he founded an academy under Puoti's leadership.

De Sanctis supported the short-lived Neapolitan revolution of 1848 and proposed a series of scholastic reforms calling for free compulsory education, improved teacher training, and greater uniformity and continuity in schools. But the tide of reaction in 1849 annulled these proposals and forced De Sanctis to leave Naples. In December 1850 he was imprisoned on a fabricated charge of plotting to kill the king. When released two years later, De Sanctis traveled to Turin, the Piedmontese capital, where, consistent with his lifelong conviction, he advocated Italian unification under the house of Savoy. There he also delivered a series of distinguished lectures on Dante, for which he was invited to be professor of Italian literature at Zurich, a post he held from January 1856 to August 1860.

Returning to Italy and to political activity, De Sanctis worked to reform the University of Naples and was elected to Parliament. Appointed minister of education, he championed quality education as a matter of civic responsibility, though he realized the difficulty of carrying out such a program in a largely illiterate and tradition-bound nation. During the later stages of his legislative career, De Sanctis also served as professor of comparative literature at the University of Naples (1871-1878).

Although after 1865 De Sanctis continued to hold public office, his literary pursuits assumed greater importance. *Critical Essays* (1866), the revised *Essay on Petrarch* (1869), and the monumental *History of Italian Literature* (written in 1868-1871 as a teaching manual) represent his major contributions to literary criticism and historiography. Among the basic tenets of his critical approach are: art is the product of the fantasy of great men; the work of art is absolutely independent of science, morals, history, or philosophy; and art is the appropriate synthesis of content and form.

De Sanctis accepted the Positivists' demand for rigorous scholarship but maintained that minutiae are not a critic's central concern. Faulted by some for apparent inattention to detail and for focusing only on major figures, De Sanctis was defended eloquently by Benedetto Croce, who oversaw the posthumous publication of De Sanctis's other works. Later, elaborating on De Sanctis's esthetics, Croce recognized the lack of systematic theories and the consequent imprecision of terminology, but he praised De Sanctis's critical acumen and wide range of interests.

## Further Reading

In addition to numerous studies in Italian by Croce and others, one may profitably consult Louis A. Breglio, *Life and Criticism of Francesco De Sanctis* (1941). □

# René Descartes

**The French thinker René Descartes (1596-1650) is called the father of modern philosophy. He initiated the movement generally termed rationalism, and his *Discourse on Method* and *Meditations* defined the basic problems of philosophy for at least a century.**

To appreciate the novelty of the thought of René Descartes, one must understand what modern philosophy, or rationalism, means in contrast to medieval, or scholastic, philosophy. The great European thinkers of the 9th to 14th century were not incapable of logical reasoning, but they differed in philosophic interests and aims from the rationalists. Just as the moderns, from Descartes on, usually identified philosophy with the natural and pure sciences, so the medievals made little distinction between philosophical and theological concerns.

The medieval doctors, like St. Thomas Aquinas, wanted to demonstrate that the revelations of faith and the dictates of reason were not incompatible. Their universe was that outlined by Aristotle in his *Physics*—a universe in which everything was ordered and classified according to the end that it served. During the Renaissance, however, men began exploring scientific alternatives to Aristotle's hierarchical universe. Further, new instruments, especially Galileo's telescope, added precision to scientific generalizations.

By the beginning of the 17th century the medieval tradition had lost its creative impetus. But the schoolmen, so called because they dominated the European universities, continued to adhere dogmatically to the traditional philosophy because of its association with Catholic theology. The rationalists, however, persistently refused professorships in order to preserve their intellectual integrity or to avoid persecution. They rejected the medieval practice of composing commentaries on standard works in favor of writing original, usually anonymous, treatises on topics suggested by

their own scientific or speculative interests. Thus the contrast is between a moribund tradition of professorial disputes over trivialities and a new philosophy inspired by original, scientific research.

Descartes participated in this conflict between the scholastic and rationalist approaches. He spent a great part of his intellectual effort—even to the extent of suppressing some of his writings—attempting to convince ecclesiastical authorities of the compatibility of the new science with theology and of its superiority as a foundation for philosophy.

## Early Life

Descartes was born on March 31, 1596, in La Haye, in the Touraine region, between the cities of Tours and Poitiers. His father, Joachim, a member of the minor nobility, served in the Parliament of Brittany. Jeanne Brochard Descartes, his mother, died in May 1597. Although his father remarried, Descartes and his older brother and sister were raised by their maternal grandmother and by a nurse for whom he retained a deep affection.

In 1606 Descartes entered La Flèche, a Jesuit college established by the king for the instruction of the young nobility. In the *Discourse* Descartes tells of the 8-year course of studies at La Flèche, which he considered "one of the most celebrated schools in Europe." According to his account, which is one of the best contemporary descriptions of 17th-century education, his studies left him feeling embarrassed at the extent of his own ignorance.

The young Descartes came to feel that languages, literature, and history relate only fables which incline man to imaginative exaggerations. Poetry and eloquence persuade man, but they do not tell the truth. Mathematics does grasp the truth, but the certainty and evidence of its reasoning seemed to Descartes to have only practical applications. Upon examination, the revelations of religion and morals seem as mysterious to the learned as to the ignorant. Philosophy had been studied by the best minds throughout the centuries, and yet "no single thing is to be found in it which is not subject to dispute." Descartes says that he came to suspect that even science, which depends upon philosophy for its principles, "could have built nothing solid on foundations so far from firm."

## Travel and First Writings

The 18-year-old Descartes left college with a reputation for extreme brilliance. In the next years he rounded out the education befitting a young noble. He learned fencing, horsemanship, and dancing and took a law degree from Poitiers.

From 1618 to 1628 Descartes traveled extensively throughout Europe while attached to various military units. Although a devout Catholic, he served in the army of the Protestant prince Maurice of Nassau but later enlisted in the Catholic army of Maximilian I of Bavaria. Living on income from inherited properties, Descartes served without pay and seems to have seen little action; he was present, however, at the Battle of Prague, one of the major engagements of the Thirty Years War. Descartes was reticent about this period of his life, saying only that he left the study of letters in order to travel in "the great book of the world."

This period of travel was not without intellectual effort. Descartes sought out eminent mathematicians, scientists, and philosophers wherever he traveled. The most significant of these friendships was with Isaac Beeckman, the Dutch mathematician, at whose suggestion Descartes began writing scientific treatises on mathematics and music. He perfected a means of describing geometrical figures in algebraic formulas, a process that served as the foundation for his invention of analytic geometry. He became increasingly impressed with the extent to which material reality could be understood mathematically.

During this period Descartes was profoundly influenced by three dreams which he had on Nov. 10, 1619, in Ulm, Germany. He interpreted their symbols as a divine sign that all science is one and that its mastery is universal wisdom. This notion of the unity of all science was a revolutionary concept which contradicted the Aristotelian notion that the sciences were distinguished by their different objects of study. Descartes did not deny the multiplicity of objects, but rather he emphasized that only one mind could know all these diverse things. He felt that if one could generalize man's correct method of knowing, then one would be able to know everything. Descartes devoted the majority of his effort and work to proving that he had, in fact, discovered this correct method of reasoning.

From 1626 to 1629 Descartes resided mainly in Paris. He acquired a wide and notable set of friends but soon felt that the pressures of social life kept him from his work. He then moved to Holland, where he lived, primarily near Amsterdam, for the next 20 years. Descartes cherished the solitude of his life in Holland, and he described himself to a friend as awakening happily after 10 hours of sleep with the memory of charming dreams. He said his life in Holland was peaceful because he was "the only man not engaged in merchandise." There Descartes studied and wrote. He carried on an enormous correspondence throughout Europe, and in Holland he acquired a small, but dedicated, set of friends and disciples. Although he never married, Descartes fathered a natural daughter who was baptized Francine. She died in 1640, when she was 5.

## First Works

Descartes's research in mathematics and physics led him to see the need for a new methodology, or way of thinking. His first major work, *Rules for the Direction of the Mind,* was written by 1629. Although circulated widely in manuscript form, this incomplete treatise was not published until 1701. The work begins with the assumption that man's knowledge has been limited by the erroneous belief that science is determined by the various objects of experience. The first rule therefore states that all true judgment depends on reason alone for its validity. For example, the truths of mathematics are valid independently of observation and experiment. Thus the second rule argues that the standard for any true knowledge should be the certitude demanded of demonstrations in arithmetic and geometry. The third rule begins to specify what this standard of true knowledge en-

tails. The mind should be directed not by tradition, authority, or the history of the problem, but only by what can clearly be observed and deduced.

There are only two mental operations that are permissible in the pure use of reason. The first is intuition, which Descartes defines as "the undoubting conception of an unclouded and attentive mind"; the second is deduction, which consists of "all necessary inference from other facts that are known with certainty. "The basic assumption underlying these definitions is that all first principles are known by way of self-evident intuitions and that the conclusions of this "seeing into" are derived by deduction. The clarity and distinctness of ideas are for Descartes the conceptual counterpart of human vision. (For example, man can know the geometry of a square just as distinctly as he can see a square table in front of him.)

Many philosophers recognized the ideal character of mathematical reasoning, but no one before Descartes had abstracted the conditions of such thinking and applied it generally to all knowledge. If all science is unified by man's reason and if the proper functioning of the mind is identified with mathematical thinking, then the problem of knowledge is reduced to a question of methodology. The end of knowledge is true judgment, but true judgment is equivalent to mathematical demonstrations that are based on intuition and deduction. Thus the method for finding truth in all matters is merely to restrict oneself to these two operations.

According to the fourth rule, "By method I mean certain and simple rules, such that if a man observe them accurately, he shall never assume what is false as true . . . but will always gradually increase his knowledge and so arrive at a true understanding of all that does not surpass his powers." The remaining sixteen rules are devoted to the elaboration of these principles or to showing their application to mathematical problems. In Descartes's later works he refines these methodological principles, and in the *Meditations* he attempts a metaphysical justification of this type of reasoning.

By 1634 Descartes had written his speculative physics in a work entitled *The World.* Unfortunately, only fragments survive because he suppressed the book when he heard that Galileo's *Dialogue on the Two Great Systems of the Universe* had been condemned by the Catholic Church because of its advocacy of Copernican rather than Ptolemaic astronomy. Descartes also espoused the Copernican theory that the earth is not the center of the universe but revolves about the sun. His fear of censure, however, led him to withdraw his work. In 1634 he also wrote the brief *Treatise on Man,* which attempted to explain human physiology on mechanistic principles.

## *Discourse* and *Meditations*

In 1637 Descartes finished *Discourse on Method,* which was published together with three minor works on geometry, dioptrics, and meteors. This work is significant for several reasons. It is written in French and directed to men of good sense rather than professional philosophers. It is autobiographical and begins with a personal account of his education as an example of the need for a new method of conducting inquiry.

The work contains Descartes's vision of a unity of science based on a common methodology, and it shows that this method can be applied to general philosophic questions. In brief, the method is a sophistication of the earlier *Rules for the Direction of the Mind*. In the *Discourse* Descartes presents four general rules for reducing any problem to its fundamentals by analysis and then constructing solutions by general synthesis.

*Meditations on First Philosophy* appeared in 1641-1642 together with six (later seven) sets of objections by distinguished thinkers including Thomas Hobbes, Antoine Arnauld, and Pierre Gassendi and the author's replies. The *Meditations* is Descartes's major work and is one of the seminal books in the history of philosophy. While his former works were concerned with elaborating a methodology, this work represents the systematic application of those rules to the principal problems of philosophy: the refutation of skepticism, the existence of the human soul, the nature of God, the metaphysical basis of truth, the extent of man's knowledge of the external world, and the relation between body and soul.

The first meditation is an exercise in methodological skepticism. Descartes states that doubt is a positive means of ascertaining whether there is any certain foundation for knowledge. All knowledge originates either from the senses or from the mind. Examples of color blindness, objects seen in perspective, and so on testify to the distortions inherent in vague sense perception. The recognition of these phenomena as distorted suggests a class of clear perceptions which are more difficult to doubt. But Descartes then points out that such images appear as clear to man in dreams as in an awakened state. Therefore all sensory experience is doubtful because sense data in itself does not indicate whether an object is seen or imagined, true or false.

What about the realm of pure ideas? Descartes simplifies the argument by asking whether it is possible to doubt the fundamental propositions of arithmetic and geometry. Man cannot doubt that two plus two equals four, but he may suspect that this statement has no reality apart from his mind. The standard of truth is the self-evidence of clear and distinct ideas, but the question remains of the correspondence of such ideas to reality. Descartes imagines the existence of an all-powerful "evil genius" who deceives man as to the content of his ideas, so that in reality two plus two equals five.

The second meditation resolves these skeptical issues in a deceptively simple manner by arguing that even if it is doubtful whether sense images or ideas have objects, it is absolutely true that man's mind exists. The famous formula "I think, therefore, I am" is true even if everything else is false. Descartes's solution is known as subjectivism, and it is a radical reversal of previous theories of knowledge. Whereas nature had been assumed to be the cause of man's images and ideas, Descartes states that man is a "thinking thing" whose subjective images and ideas are the sole evidence for the existence of a world.

The third meditation demonstrates that God is "no deceiver," and hence clear and distinct ideas must have objects that exactly and actually correspond to them. Descartes argues that the idea of God is an effect. But an effect gets its reality from its cause, and a cause can only produce what it possesses. Hence either Descartes is a perfect being or God exists as the cause of the idea of God.

The fourth meditation deals with the problem of human error; insofar as man restricts himself to clear and distinct ideas, he will never err. With this connection between ideas and objects Descartes can emerge from his doubts about knowledge. The external world can be known with absolute certainty insofar as it is reducible to clear and distinct ideas. Thus the fifth meditation shows the application of methodology to material reality in its quantifiable dimensions, that is, to the extent to which material reality can be "the object of pure mathematics."

The sixth, and final, meditation attempts to explain the relation between the human soul and the body. Since Descartes believed in mechanism, there could be no absolute connection between a free soul and a bodily machine. After considerable hesitation he expresses the relation between mind and matter as a "felt union." The body is the active faculty that produces the passive images and imaginings man finds in his mind. Actually Descartes's explanation is logically impossible in terms of the "subjective" separation of mind; similarly, the unresolved dualism of the "felt union" violates the principle of assenting only to clear and distinct ideas.

The remainder of Descartes's career was spent in defending his controversial positions. In 1644 he published the *Principles of Philosophy,* which breaks down the arguments of the *Meditations* into propositional form and presents extra arguments dealing with their scientific application. In 1649 Descartes accepted an invitation from Queen Christina of Sweden to become her teacher. There he wrote *The Passions of the Soul,* which is a defense of the mind-body dualism and a mechanistic explanation of the passions. But Descartes's health was undermined by the severity of the northern climate, and after a brief illness he died in Stockholm in 1650.

## Further Reading

The most complete edition of Descartes's works in English is *The Philosophical Works of Descartes,* translated by Elizabeth S. Haldane and G.T.R. Ross (2 vols., 1955), although many editions of individual works in new translations are available in paperback. The standard biography is Haldane's *Descartes: His Life and Times* (1905; repr. 1966). The best general introductions to Descartes's philosophy are A. Boyce Gibson, *The Philosophy of Descartes* (1932); Stanley V. Keeling, *Descartes* (1934; 2d ed. 1968); and Albert G. A. Balz, *Descartes and the Modern Mind* (1952). Works on specialized topics of an analytic or critical nature include Norman Kemp Smith, *Studies in the Cartesian Philosophy* (1902) and *New Studies in the Philosophy of Descartes: Descartes as Pioneer* (1952); Jacques Maritain, *Three Reformers: Luther Descartes, Rousseau* (trans. 1928) and *The Dream of Descartes* (trans. 1944); and Leslie J. Beck, *The Method of Descartes: A Study of the Regulae* (1952). □

# Desiderio da Settignano

**The short working career of the Italian sculptor Desiderio da Settignano (1428-1464) was entirely centered in Florence. He was one of the most sensitive carvers of marble, especially in his images of children, in the history of this medium.**

Desiderio da Settignano was born in Settignano, the youngest of three sons of a mason, Bartolommeo di Francesco. All three sons joined the sculptors' guild in Florence; Desiderio matriculated in 1453. In 1456 Desiderio and his older brother, Gero, rented a studio in Florence. There are few certain details recorded of Desiderio's earlier training and later life. He must have been influenced by Donatello, but scholars now believe that Desiderio's actual training was under Bernardo Rossellino, with whom he may have worked on the tomb of Beata Villana in S. Maria Novella before 1451.

Desiderio must have had an established reputation by 1453, since he was then awarded the important commission for the tomb of the humanist scholar and state chancellor of Florence, Carlo Marsuppini, in Sta Croce. The date of completion of this monument is not known, nor is it certain when Desiderio began his second major project, the *Tabernacle of the Sacrament* in S. Lorenzo, but this was surely in place by 1461. The charming frieze of *putti* heads on the exterior of the Pazzi Chapel was probably completed in 1461. According to Giorgio Vasari, Desiderio's last work was the painted wooden statue of St. Mary Magdalene, left unfinished and completed by Benedetto da Maiano after Desiderio's death in 1464.

From the outset Desiderio's talent was distinct, assured, and very rare. His Marsuppini tomb, planned to balance Bernardo Rossellino's tomb of Leonardo Bruni on the opposite wall of Sta Croce, is at once a harmonious counterpart to its model and an independent achievement, animating and enriching the sober, dignified characterization of the deceased with the grace notes of an ornamental setting in which every detail is chiseled with an incomparable combination of featherlike delicacy and prismatic precision and strength.

The same seemingly effortless ease controls the astonishing inventions of Desiderio's *Tabernacle of the Sacrament* and invests his smaller separate reliefs and images, whether of the infant Christ Child or the aged St. Jerome, with a serene radiance that never degenerates into sentimentality and is never reduced to a formula. His subtle variations of expression, type, and design give such traditional themes as the Madonna and Child or youthful angels a new grace and humanity.

## Further Reading

The quality of Desiderio's sculpture can be appreciated in Clarence Kennedy's sensitive photographs in *Studies in the History and Criticism of Sculpture,* vol. 5: *The Tabernacle of the Sacrament, by Desiderio da Settignano* (1929). Both John

Pope-Hennessy, *Introduction to Italian Sculpture,* vol. 2: *Italian Renaissance Sculpture* (1958); and Charles Seymour, Jr., *Sculpture in Italy: 1400-1500* (1966), include important critical estimates of Desiderio's work. □

# Pierre Jean De Smet

**The Belgian Jesuit priest Pierre Jean De Smet (1801-1873) was a pioneer Roman Catholic missionary among the Native Americans west of the Mississippi River.**

Pierre Jean De Smet was born at Termonde on Jan. 30, 1801. At the age of 14 he entered the seminary at Malines. On Sept. 21, 1821, he arrived in the United States to enter the novitiate of the Jesuit order at White Marsh in Maryland. Two years later he was a member of a group that traveled overland to St. Louis whose purpose was to establish a new novitiate in the West. At his ordination as priest in 1827 he expected assignment as missionary among the Native Americans, but other pastoral assignments and serious illness delayed his dream for another decade.

Father De Smet's long missionary work among the Native Americans began in 1838, when he was sent among the Potawatomi Indians to found a mission. On this journey he began to keep the journals and write the long letters that were published later in book form and became the literary basis for his reputation. In 1840 he set out on the first of several long expeditions across the Northwest to evaluate the possibilities for missions among the Flathead and Nez Percé Indians in the Oregon country.

During 1841-1842 Father De Smet returned to Oregon, explored more of the territory, and established several missions. Finding that Canadian priests had already begun work in the Willamette Valley, he agreed to collaborate with them in extending the system of Catholic missions. He traveled to New Orleans and eastern cities and then went to six countries in Europe to solicit badly needed funds and personnel in 1843. Father De Smet returned directly to Oregon with several priests, nuns, and supplies the next year by sailing around Cape Horn. In future years he made many journeys through the West; he eventually crossed the Atlantic 19 times.

The entire region from St. Louis to the Pacific Northwest became his domain. Father De Smet was the leading "black robe" (Jesuit) to the Native Americans, and he was so respected that he was the only white man trusted by them. In turn, he loved the Native Americans and sought to keep white traders, settlers, or government agents from abusing them. Both the U.S. government and Native American tribes used him as mediator. He was especially important in this regard in 1851 at Ft. Laramie and in the Yakima War (1858-1859); he also undertook a number of peace missions to the Sioux. Eventually, he came to distrust government dealings with the Native Americans as much as he had earlier deplored Protestant missionary efforts among them.

**States, and was the first white man to cross the Mississippi River.**

Father De Smet's superiors increasingly recognized his appeal and thrust him into the work of propagandist and fund raiser for the Native American missionary work. Not as happy doing this as when working among the Native Americans, he nevertheless served faithfully until his health failed. He died at St. Louis on May 23, 1873.

## Further Reading

The best biography of De Smet is John Upton Terrell's well-written *Black Robe: The Life of Pierre-Jean De Smet: Missionary, Explorer, and Pioneer* (1964). *Life, Letters and Travels of Father Pierre-Jean De Smet,* edited by Hiram Martin Chittenden and Alfred Talbot Richardson (4 vols., 1905), is the basic source, containing nearly all the missionary's published materials.

## Additional Sources

Carriker, Robert C., *Father Peter John de Smet: Jesuit in the West,* Norman, OK: University of Oklahoma Press, 1995.

Laveille, E., *The Life of Father De Smet, S.J. (1801-1873),* Chicago: Loyola University Press, 1981. □

# Hernando de Soto

**The Spanish conqueror and explorer Hernando de Soto (1500-1542) participated in the conquest of Peru, explored the southeastern part of the United**

ernando de Soto was born at Jerez de los Caballeros in the province of Estremadura. Although of noble lineage, he was without wealth. "With only a sword and shield" he accompanied Pedrarias when the latter assumed his post as governor of Darien (Caribbean side of the Isthmus of Panama and Colombia). As Pedrarias's lieutenant, De Soto explored the area encompassing modern Costa Rica, Nicaragua, and Honduras in the 1520s.

Sailing from Nicaragua in 1531, De Soto joined Francisco Pizarro in the conquest of Peru, emerging from the conquest with a reputation as a skilled horseman and "one of the four bravest captains who had gone to the West Indies." With a fortune of 100,000 pesos in gold, De Soto returned to Spain in 1536, where Emperor Charles V rewarded his exploits by appointing him governor of Cuba and *adelantado* of Florida. As *adelantado,* he was commissioned to conquer and colonize, at his own expense, the entire region which is now the southern part of the United States.

De Soto returned to Cuba in 1538, where he assumed the governorship and prepared for his expedition to Florida. Hoping to find another Peru, De Soto and 620 men landed south of Tampa Bay on May 30, 1539. A reconnaissance party returned with Juan Ortiz, a survivor of the earlier ill-fated Narváez expedition, who had lived among the Indians

for 12 years. With Ortiz acting as interpreter, De Soto began a 3-year journey in search of treasure and an advanced Indian population. Marching up the west coast of Florida, he wintered near the present site of Tallahassee. In the spring of 1540 De Soto resumed the march through Georgia. At the Savannah River he met an Indian chieftainess who offered him a long string of pearls and told him more could be found in nearby burial grounds. After collecting 350 pounds of pearls, the expedition continued northward into what is present-day South and North Carolina, across the Smoky Mountains into Tennessee, and southward into Georgia and Alabama. Their severest battle with Indians, which resulted in heavy casualties and loss of the pearls, occurred in southeastern Alabama at a large town called Mavilla.

De Soto set out once again to the northwest into northern Mississippi. In May 1541 he sighted the Mississippi River south of Memphis. After crossing the Mississippi he explored Arkansas and established his winter quarters near the present site of Fort Smith. Now resolved to return to the sea, he reached the mouth of the Arkansas River, where he died of fever on May 21, 1542.

De Soto's men wrapped his body in mantles packed with sand and cast it into the river. The 311 survivors, under Luis de Moscoso, built seven brigantines, floated down the Mississippi, and coasted along the Gulf shore until they reached Tampico, Mexico, on Sept. 10, 1543.

## Further Reading

The most recent sources on De Soto are Garcilaso de la Vega, *The Florida of the Inca,* edited by John G. and Jeannette J. Varner (trans. 1951), and James A. Robertson, ed., *True Relation of the Hardships Suffered by Governor Fernando de Soto and Certain Portuguese Gentlemen during the Discovery of the Province of Florida* (trans., 2 vols., 1932-1933). Accounts of De Soto's career can be found in Woodbury Lowery, *The Spanish Settlements within the Present Limits of the United States, 1513-1561* (1901); Edward G. Bourne, *Spain in America, 1450-1580* (1904); and Herbert E. Bolton, *The Spanish Borderlands: A Chronicle of Old Florida and the Southwest* (1921). □

# Joan Jacques Dessalines

**Jean Jacques Dessalines (1758-1806) was a Haitian nationalist and the first ruler of a free Haiti. Although he was a courageous military leader during the war of independence, he failed as administrator and statesman.**

There is little detailed information on the exact origins of Jean Jacques Dessalines. Like the first great Haitian leader, Pierre Dominique Toussaint L'Ouverture, Dessalines was of African descent and born into slavery in northern Haiti. Unlike Toussaint, he remained illiterate all his life.

In the turbulent decade between the great slave revolt of 1791 and final independence on Jan. 1, 1804, Dessalines was one of Toussaint's principal lieutenants. During the period when Toussaint was operating against the mulattoes in southern Saint Domingue (later Haiti), Dessalines captured Jacmel, one of their main strongpoints, and followed up his campaign by exterminating the survivors. This ferociousness marked Dessalines throughout his career.

When Napoleon sent his brother-in-law, Captain General Charles Leclerc, to return the colony to slavery, Dessalines was the commander of the important port city of Saint-Marc. Many generals defected but not Dessalines. He and Toussaint retreated into the interior, where in March 1802 Dessalines was finally overwhelmed in the battle of Crête-à-Pierrot.

After Toussaint was captured and spirited away to France, Dessalines emerged as the principal figure of the Haitian war of independence. Gen. Leclerc's forces had taken heavy casualties in the campaigns against the armies of ex-slaves and were now trying to cope with guerrilla tactics and, at the same time, with yellow fever. Leclerc died of the disease in November 1802. A year later Dessalines defeated Leclerc's successor, Governor General Rochambeau, in the battle of Vertieres, near the present city of Cap-Haitien.

## Haitian Independence

On Jan. 1, 1804, Dessalines proclaimed Haitian independence at Gonaïves. Unfortunately for Haiti, Dessalines's

qualities of personal courage were not matched by desperately needed tolerance, statesmanship, and magnanimity. He had himself named governor general for life, with the right to choose a successor, following this by crowning himself Emperor Jean Jacques I, but without creating a nobility. In his own words: "Moi seul, je suis noble" (Only I am noble).

His hatred of whites continued after Haitian independence, and he methodically butchered any white Frenchman he could find. Obsessed with fear of French reconquest, he drained off great amounts of energy and money to maintain a large standing army and to build a series of forts.

Dessalines faced the task of rebuilding a shattered agricultural, labor-intensive economy the only way he knew—by order and discipline. A citizen was either a laborer or a soldier. Prosperity of a sort was restored but at the price of personal freedom and without the superb administration which Henri Christophe's regime would soon have in the north. Though the lower classes grudgingly accepted his decrees, the mulattoes, many of whom were longtime landholders and people of education and position, refused to bow to his increasingly harsh demands. Jean Jacques I was assassinated in an ambush near Port-au-Prince on Oct. 17, 1806.

## Further Reading

An excellent source on Haitian history and personalities is James G. Leyburn, *The Haitian People* (1941; rev. ed 1966). Other useful works include C. L. R. James, *The Black Jacobins* (1938; 2d ed. 1963); Ludwell Lee Montague, *Haiti and the United States, 1714-1938* (1940); Selden Rodman, *Haiti: The Black Republic* (1954); and Charles Moran, *Black Triumvirate* (1957). □

# Robert Nathaniel Dett

**African American composer, conductor, and music educator Robert Nathaniel Dett (1882-1943) elevated the African American folk spiritual into an art form.**

Robert Dett was born in Ontario, Canada, on Oct. 11, 1882, the youngest of four children of educated and musically talented parents. In 1893 the family moved to Niagara Falls, NY, where they operated a tourist home.

Dett studied piano in childhood and composed several pieces, but his serious music training began in 1901 on entering Halstead Conservatory, Brockport, NY. In 1903 he enrolled at the Oberlin Conservatory of Music, graduating in 1908 with a bachelor of music degree.

Dett began teaching in 1908 at Lane College, Jackson, Tenn. From 1911 he taught in Lincoln Institute, Jefferson City, Mo. But it was at Hampton Institute, Va., that he made his most significant creative contributions (1913-1932). He

organized the Hampton Choral Union to bring the people of the community and Hampton Institute closer together, and the Musical Art Society, which presented one of the country's outstanding college concert programs; and he directed the famous Hampton Institute Choir. He also organized and directed the school of music.

In 1920 Dett studied at Harvard University, winning one prize for his essay, "The Emancipation of Negro Music," and another for the best composition in concerted vocal music, *Don't Be Weary Traveler*. Other honors included an honorary doctor of music degree from Howard University, Washington, D.C., in 1924; an honorary doctor of music degree from Oberlin College in 1926; and the Harmon Award for creative achievement in 1928.

Dett was an idealist who loved humanity and was dedicated to uplifting his race through education. As a teacher, he sought to inspire rather than to dictate. As a choral conductor, he received national and international fame. Critics highly praised the concerts given by the Hampton Institute Choir in New York City, Boston, and Philadelphia. In a 1930 goodwill tour the choir gave concerts in the capitals of seven European countries.

As a composer, Dett was a skillful craftsman in the language and style of the romanticists. He achieved his goal—to give African Americans pride by creating something which would be musically his own yet would bear comparison with other peoples' artistic utterances. His published compositions include 5 piano suites and 12 piano solos, 23 vocal solos, 46 choral works, 2 collections of spirituals (one collection comprising four volumes), an oratorio with orchestral accompaniment and a violin selection.

## Further Reading

There is a brief biography of Dett in Wilhelmena S. Robinson, *Historical Negro Biographies* (1968). He is discussed in Maud Cuney-Hare, *Negro Musicians and Their Music* (1936); John P. Davis, ed., *The American Negro Reference Book* (1966); and the *International Library of Negro Life and History*, vol. 5: *The Negro in Music and Art,* compiled by Lindsay Patterson (1967; 2d ed. 1968).

## Additional Sources

Simpson, Anne Key, *Follow me: the life and music of R. Nathaniel Dett,* Metuchen, N.J.: Scarecrow Press, 1993. □

# Karl Wolfgang Deutsch

**The American political scientist Karl Wolfgang Deutsch (1912-1992) was ranked among the foremost social scientists of the post-World War II era. Few, if any, other thinkers in this field attained his level of intellectual originality, professional importance, and peer-group recognition.**

Karl Wolfgang Deutsch was born to German-speaking parents in 1912 in Prague, Czechoslovakia. His father Martin was an optician while his mother Maria (Scharf) was deeply involved in domestic and international political causes, eventually leading her to become one of Czechoslovakia's first woman parliamentarians. Young Deutsch graduated from the German Staatsrealgymnasium in Prague with high honors in 1931, whereupon he entered Prague's German university, completing his first degree there in 1934.

His continued studies at the same university were interrupted due to Deutsch's active opposition to the increasingly dominant Nazi presence which beset this university's faculty and student body by the mid-to-late 1930s. After a sojourn in England where Deutsch studied optics, he returned to Prague, gaining admissions to the Czech-national Charles University—a major distinction for a German-ethnic Czech—where he attained high honors in seven fields and received his doctorate in law in 1938. Shortly thereafter, Deutsch and his wife Ruth (Slonitz) left their increasingly troubled and intolerant homeland for a new life in the United States.

## Fleed Hitler

Deutsch thus became an integral part of that unique migration of European intellectuals who sought refuge from Hitler's barbarism in the New World. Like most in this group, Deutsch experienced a permanent effect from this profound transformation which was to manifest itself both in his scholarly work and in his relentless engagement on behalf of a general improvement of the human condition. It was at this time that the cornerstone of his life-long credo became firmly entrenched: "My life's aim has been to study politics in order to help people overcome the four chief dangers of our time: large wars, hunger, poverty, and vast population growth. For this end, I have sought more knowledge for greater competence and more compassion."

## Peron Expert

While enrolled at Harvard University in a doctoral program for political science as a recipient of a student-funded scholarship for refugees from Nazism, Deutsch never surrendered his immense talents to the sole pursuit of an academic career. Rather, he rendered his services to the United States government as an analyst of authoritarian political systems, in the course of which he became one of the main contributors to the famous "Blue Book" on Juan Peron's efforts to extinguish democracy in Argentina. Deutsch also participated in the International Secretariat of the San Francisco Conference of 1945 which was a direct precursor to the United Nations Organization.

In 1951 Deutsch completed his doctorate at Harvard, receiving the much-coveted Sumner Prize for his dissertation. Entitled "Nationalism and Social Communication," it represented a path-breaking study both of the cohesive integrating and also of the destructive-alienating dimensions of modern nationalism and its political manifestations. Spellbinding in its theoretical ambition and empirical scope, Deutsch's dissertation also broke new methodological grounds by using sophisticated quantitative analyses to illustrate the relationship between politics and society. Deutsch's book with the same title published two years later has remained a classic in the literature of political science to this day.

## Rose to the Top

Following his professorship at the Massachusetts Institute of Technology between 1952 and 1958, Deutsch accepted a teaching position at Yale University where, during the course of the 1960s, his influence and prestige reached the top of his profession. Here he published his seminal *The Nerves of Government,* which revolutionized the study of politics by introducing concepts derived from cybernetics for a more nuanced analysis of essential political mechanisms such as power, authority, governance, cohesion, conflict, guidance, and breakdown. It was mainly at Yale that Deutsch supervised the doctoral work of a large number of exceptional students, all of whom have since assumed prestigious posts at the world's leading universities where they continue to uphold his intellectual legacy.

Deutsch established the Yale Political Data Program, which is one of the most important organizations to develop quantitative indicators for testing significant theories and propositions in social science. In addition, his exceptional qualities as a teacher and educator were duly honored by the Yale Political Union, which awarded him the esteemed William Benton Prize for 1965 for having done most among the Yale faculty to stimulate and maintain political interest on campus. Deutsch left Yale University in 1967 for Harvard University where in 1971 he became the Stanfield Professor of International Peace, a post he held until 1983 when he was named an emeritus professor. He stayed at Harvard until 1985. After 1976 Deutsch was also invested with the directorship of the International Institute for Comparative Social Research of the Science Center in Berlin where he and his team of international scholars pioneered and refined the study of global modeling in political science.

## Numerous Awards

The most convincing testimony to Deutsch's eminence in political science emanates from the impressive accolades and prestigious awards his colleagues in the field bestowed upon him over the years. In addition to having lectured at well over 100 academic institutions all over the world, Deutsch was the holder of seven honorary doctorates from prestigious universities both in the United States and Europe. His colleagues' recognition of his merits also extends to having elected him president of the New England Political Science Association (1964-1965), of the American Political Science Association (1969-1970), and of the International Political Science Association (1976-1979), among a number of other leading scholarly organizations. Deutsch served on the editorial boards of six internationally prestigious academic journals. He was the frequent recipient of such coveted fellowships as the Guggenheim and was decorated with the Grand Cross of Merit, which is the Federal Republic of Germany's highest distinction bestowed upon a civilian. Deutsch was a member of the National Academy of Science and of the American Academy of Arts and Sciences.

Deutsch died of cancer in November 1992 at his home in Cambridge, Massachusetts.

## Further Reading

Deutsch's most important books are *Nationalism and Social Communication* (1953, revised 1966); *The Nerves of Government* (1963, revised 1966); *Arms Control and the Atlantic Alliance* (1967); *Nationalism and Its Alternatives* (1969); and *Tides Among Nations* (1979). He also has written two successful college textbooks entitled *The Analysis of International Relations* (1968, revised 1978) and *Politics and Government: How People Decide Their Fate* (1970, revised 1974, 1980). The most comprehensive analysis of Deutsch's work by leading scholars in the field can be found in Richard L. Merritt and Bruce M. Russett (editors) *From National Development to Global Community: Essays in Honor of Karl W. Deutsch* (1981). His obituary appeared in the November 3, 1992 edition of the *New York Times*. □

# Eamon De Valera

**The Irish revolutionary leader and statesman Eamon De Valera (1882-1975) served as prime minister and later president of Ireland (1959-1973).**

Eamon De Valera was born in New York City on October 14, 1882. In 1885, after the death of his Spanish father, he was sent to live with his Irish mother's family in Country Limerick. He graduated from the Royal University of Ireland in 1904 and became a mathematics teacher.

De Valera was an ardent supporter of the Irish language revival movement and also became a member of Sinn Fein and the Irish Volunteers. After the failure of the 1916 insurrection, he became the senior surviving rebel leader when his death sentence was commuted because of his American birth. Released by the British government in 1917, he was acclaimed in Ireland as the leader of the revolutionary independence movement. He became president of the Irish Republic established by the separatists after their victory in the election of December, 1918. In June, 1919, De Valera traveled to the United States, where he won much sympathy and financial support for the Irish cause. He returned to Ireland in December, 1920, as the guerrilla war with Britain was moving into its final phase.

De Valera accepted British proposals for a truce in July, 1921, and sent a delegation to London to negotiate a peace settlement. The British refused to accept his compromise plan for an Irish republic in external association with the British Empire and offered instead dominion status for Ireland, with the right of exclusion for loyalist Northern Ireland. In December, 1921, the Irish delegates accepted these terms, believing them to be the best obtainable without further war. De Valera, however, denounced the treaty as a betrayal of the republic which would mean continued subjection to Britain. Despite his protests the Republican Parliament, Dail Eireann, approved the treaty by a small majority in January, 1922. Continued dispute over the settlement led to civil war in June, 1922, and supporters of the new Irish Free State defeated the Republicans in May, 1923.

## Prime Minister

After the civil war De Valera led the Republican opposition to the pro-treaty government of William T. Cosgrave. In 1926 he broke with the extreme Republicans and founded a constitutional opposition party, Fianna Fail, which entered the Dail in 1927. Fianna Fail won the 1932 election, and De Valera formed a government which lasted for 16 years.

As prime minister, he removed the last remaining restrictions on Irish sovereignty imposed by the treaty. His refusal to continue payment of land-purchase annuities to Britain led to an economic war between the two countries, which enabled him to pursue plans to make Ireland more self-sufficient economically. His government also extended social services, suppressed extremist threats to the state, and introduced a constitution in 1937 which made the Free State a republic in all but name. In 1938 agreements made with Britain ended the economic war and British occupation of Irish naval bases retained under the treaty. De Valera was unable, however, to end the partition of Ireland.

De Valera had been a strong supporter of collective security through the League of Nations, but he maintained a policy of neutrality, with overwhelming popular support, throughout World War II. In the postwar period Fianna Fail alternated in power with two interparty governments, the first of which formally established the Irish Republic in 1949. Returned to office with a decisive majority in 1957, De Valera retired from active politics in 1959, when he was elected president of the republic. He was reelected in 1966, the fiftieth anniversary of his entry into Irish political life. Failing eyesight troubled him from the 1930s onward and left him almost blind before his retirement from active politics in 1973. Concurrently, he held the post of Chancellor of the National University of Ireland from 1921 until 1975. He died on August 30, 1975.

The wisdom of De Valera's policies has been widely disputed but not his unequaled impact on Irish life in the twentieth century. The charismatic appeal of "Dev" was firmly based on his understanding of the outlook and way of life of a large section of the Irish people and on his fellow citizens' great respect for his ability, austere dignity, and idealism.

## Further Reading

The most complete biography is *Eamon de Valera* (1970) by the Earl of Longford and Thomas P. O'Neill, written with the full cooperation of the subject. Background histories of Ireland include Timothy Patrick Coogan, *Ireland since the Rising* (1966); Desmond Williams, ed., *The Irish Struggle, 1916-1926* (1966); and T. W. Moody and F. K. Martin, eds., *The Course of Irish History* (1967). A feature film released by Warner Bros. in 1996, *Michael Collins,* covers early twentieth century Irish political history and includes a character representing De Valera. □

# Bernadette Devlin

**The youngest woman ever elected to the British Parliament, Bernadette Devlin (born 1947) personified the young radical Catholics of Northern Ireland at the onset of the modern troubles. She intermixed socialism, Irish republicanism, anti-clericalism, and feminism with general political impracticality and radical brashness.**

Bernadette Devlin was the third of the six children of John James and Elizabeth Bernadette Devlin of Cookstown, County Tyrone. Her mother's family, who were of strong farmer and publican background, opposed her parent's marriage because her father was from a laboring background. From both parents (her father who died when she was nine and her mother who died when she was 19) she developed a strong Irish Republican spirit and a sense of detestation for pharisaical piety and respectability. She attended St. Patrick's Academy, Dungannon, County Tyrone, and entered Queen's University, Belfast, in 1965 to study psychology.

## Took Part in Protests

This was a period when many in the younger Catholic community in Northern Ireland were turning away from both constitutional nationalism as represented by the socially respectable and bourgeois Nationalist party and the revolutionary Sinn Fein movement. In place of the immediately unlikely goal of Irish unity, they began to insist on civil rights for the minority (that is, the Catholic) community within Northern Ireland as appropriate for citizens of the United Kingdom.

Their specific grievances included the restricted franchise in local government elections (which de facto disenfranchised a higher percentage of Catholics), gerrymandered local government districts, and the consequent discriminatory treatment in public hiring and availability of benefits, especially public housing. They sought to emulate the tactics of African Americans by conducting a series of protest marches throughout Northern Ireland. Devlin took part in several of these marches, which met a combination of police obstruction and militant Protestant threats.

Devlin was one of the founders of People's Democracy, a student movement concerned with the civil rights cause and of decidedly socialist temperament. She was with that group in the celebrated march in January 1969 from Belfast to Derry which was assaulted by police auxiliaries and other Unionist militants at Burntollet Bridge along the route. People's Democracy entered the Northern Irish parliamentary election of March 1969, and Devlin unsuccessfully contested the South Derry constituency. A month later,

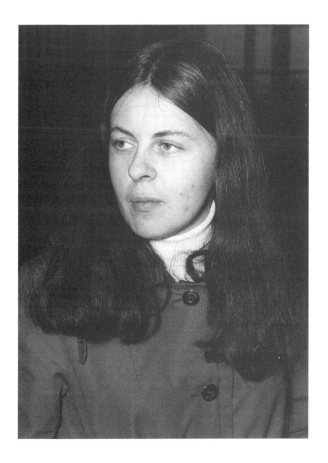

however, she emerged as the Unity candidate for the nationalist community in a by-election for the Mid-Ulster seat to the Westminster Parliament. She was elected, becoming the youngest woman ever to serve in Parliament and the youngest member of parliament in over 200 years.

## Battle of the Bogside

When the Protestant and Unionist Apprentice Boys' Parade in Derry on August 12, 1969, was followed by sectarian clashes and rioting, barricades were erected around the Catholic section, the Bogside, to exclude a police force of decided bias from the area. Devlin was a central figure in urging on the construction of the barricades and encouraging their defenders. That "Battle of the Bogside," which was followed shortly after by the intense community strife in Belfast that prompted the British government to send in its troops as peacekeepers, could be seen as the opening encounter in the troubles that continued in Northern Ireland for many years.

That same month Devlin came to the United States to raise funds for Northern Irish relief and also to meet the secretary-general of the United Nations. She soon alienated many of the older and more conservative Irish-Americans, including those who would become supporters of the violent Irish Republican Army (IRA), by her radicalism on issues other than Irish unity. A celebrated incident was her handing over to the Black Panthers, a racial radical group, the keys to the city of New York which had been presented to her by the mayor.

Her involvement in the Bogside disorder resulted in her conviction for incitement to riot and obstruction and disorderly behavior, for which she received a sentence of six months imprisonment. She entered prison after having been re-elected to Westminster in the June 1970 general election.

## Assault in House of Commons

In January 1972 she assaulted the home secretary, Reginald Maudling, in the House of Commons following the "Bloody Sunday" incident in Derry in which 13 people were killed by the army in the process of breaking up a meeting held against legal interdiction. In April 1973 she married a school teacher, Michael McAliskey. The following February she lost her seat when the Social Democratic Labour party, the amalgam of most moderate anti-Unionists, ran a candidate against her in the general election. She was linked with the Irish Republican Socialist party, which had broken away from the leftwing official Sinn Fein movement in 1974. In 1979 she ran unsuccessfully in Northern Ireland for the European Parliament, and she ran unsuccessfully for Dail Eireann (the Irish legislature) in two 1982 general elections. In early 1981 she and her husband were seriously wounded in an assassination attempt by members of the extremist Unionist Ulster Defense Association who were sentenced to long terms of imprisonment.

Her age and her bravery made her at the outset of the Northern Irish troubles a potential charismatic leader for the new wave of Northern Irish Catholics interested in civil rights more than in national unity. She also personified the soon-to-flourish cause of Irish feminism. However, her radical tactics and manner alienated many and her ideology, with its easy assumptions that the Protestant and Catholic working class could overcome cultural and religious hostility in a joint struggle for socialism and that Irish partition was ultimately founded on narrow capitalist self-interest, failed to draw substantial support. In addition, her message was too intermixed with other themes to satisfy those who supported the single-minded irredentism of the Provisional IRA.

## Daughter Arrested

In the 1990s, Devlin voiced her support for the Irish Lesbian and Gay Organization in its efforts to win gay men and lesbians the right to march in New York City's St. Patrick's Day Parade. In November 1996, Devlin's daughter Roisin McAliskey was arrested in Belfast on charges connected to an IRA bombing of a British Army barracks. Devlin protested her daughter's innocence and was at the center of a campaign to have her pregnant daughter released from jail to await trial. "I can think of more traumatic things than finding out that my daughter is a terrorist," Devlin told a reporter. The belief of Devlin and others of her daughter's supporters was that Roisin McAliskey's arrest was symbolic rather than directly related to the bombing investigation. "I have three children and not if the British government takes all of them will they stop me opposing the inhumanity and injustice of the state," Devlin said following her daughter's arrest.

## Further Reading

Devlin's own autobiography, written the year she became celebrated, *The Price of My Soul* (1969), is an excellent portrait of her personality and ideology, especially her socialism, feminism, and anti-clericalism. It indicates her contempt for regular politics, which no doubt explains her lack of success later. It should be accompanied by a reading of some general analyses of the Northern Irish question such as Padraig O'Malley, *The Uncivil Wars* (1983) and general accounts such as Simon Winchester, *In Holy Terror* (1974), a journalist's reporting of the events in Ulster in the opening phases of the troubles, the time Bernadette Devlin emerged to renown. An article about her daughter's arrest and Devlin's fight to free her appeared in *The Nation* March 17, 1997. Also see the biography G.W. Target, *Bernadette: The Story of Bernadette Devlin,* 1975, Hodder and Stoughton. □

# Hugo de Vries

**The botanist Hugo de Vries (1848-1935) worked in the fields of heredity and its relation to the origin of species, developing a mutation theory. He also brought the earlier work of Gregor Mendel to the attention of the scientific world.**

n the latter half of the 19th century, the field of botany was dominated by problems of heredity, variation, and evolution. Stemming both from Darwin's highly influential *On the Origin of Species by Natural Selection* (1859) and from intense interest in improving agricultural productivity, much investigation aimed at discovering the nature and extent of variation, its mode of inheritance, and the problem of how new varieties and species actually originate.

De Vries was a major figure in the study of heredity and its relation to the origin of species: in 1889 his book on *Intracellular Pangenesis* provided a theoretical outline for a particulate theory of inheritance; in 1900 he was one of the three rediscoverers of Gregor Mendel's laws of segregation and random assortment; and in 1901-1903 he published his massive, two-volume study, *The Mututation Theory* (*Die Mutationstheorie*), proposing a new mechanism which he called "mutations" or "sports" for the origin of species. By the early 1900s de Vries had become recognized as one of the leading botanists in the world and was elected to many scientific societies and was the recipient of a number of honorary degrees. While his theories of pangenesis and mutation gradually slipped into oblivion, in his own day de Vries was highly influential in focusing biologists' attention on heredity as a discrete process that could be studied experimentally and quantitatively.

De Vries was born in Haarlem, the Netherlands, on February 16, 1848, the son of Gerrit de Vries and Maria Everardina Reuvens. His father's family had been Baptist ministers and businessmen, and his mother's family scholars and statesmen. Educated first at a private Baptist school in Haarlem, young de Vries attended gymnasium (equivalent to high school) in the Hague, matriculating in the University of Leiden in 1866. Here, he read two works that greatly stimulated his interest in botany: Darwin's *Origin of Species* (1859) and Julius Sachs' *Textbook of Botany* (1868). Darwin's book raised de Vries' curiosity about variation and its relationship to the process of evolution, particularly the diversification of species. Sachs' textbook aroused de Vries' enthusiasm of quantitative, experimental work, as opposed to the old-style taxonomy that made up so much of the field of botany at the time. One of the weakest parts of Darwin's argument for evolution by natural selection had been his lack of coherent understanding of heredity and of how one ancestral population actually gave rise to two or more species. De Vries was eventually to make this issue central to his scientific investigations.

## Experimental Work with Sachs

Pursuing physiological studies at Leiden, de Vries earned his doctorate in plant physiology in 1870, but felt stifled by the university, where conditions for experimental work were crude and where there was open hostility to Darwinism. He therefore decided to continue his education in Germany, first at Heidelberg (1870) and then at Würzburg (1871) with Sachs. Sachs took a great interest in de Vries' career, helping him refine his experimental techniques and nominating him for several important posts over the next few years. Sachs was a strong proponent of experi-

mentation. Under his guidance de Vries began a series of detailed studies of osmosis, plasmolysis, and the effects of salt solutions on plant cells. He carried out these experiments at Würzburg, then at Amsterdam while teaching in a gymnasium (1871-1877), and finally at the University of Amsterdam where he was appointed lecturer in plant physiology in 1877 and professor in 1881; he remained at Amsterdam until compulsory retirement in 1918, when he moved to the small village of Lunteren.

In the late 1880s de Vries shifted from experimental work in plant physiology to the study of heredity. His first major publication on this subject was *Intracellular Pangenesis* in 1889, a critical review of the hereditary theories of Darwin, Herbert Spencer, August Weismann, and Carl von Nägeli. All of these writers had proposed some form of particulate theory of heredity. De Vries added to the list one of his own, the theory of "pangenes" (a term he borrowed from Darwin), unitary particles representing individual traits of an organism and manifesting themselves independently in the adult. De Vries considered the pangene a material unit that could combine and recombine in successive generations much like atoms in the formation of molecules. Although de Vries' hypothesis cannot be considered a forerunner of the Mendelian-chromosome theory that emerged in the 20th century, it was an elegant example of the sorts of theories of heredity and evolution that dominated much of later 19th-century biological thought.

As a result of his physiological training, de Vries was interested in studying heredity and evolution from a quantitative and experimental, rather than a purely theoretical, point of view. In the early to mid 1890s, he learned of the statistical work on variation being developed by Francis Galton in England. A strict Darwinian, Galton measured traits in animal populations and showed that they generally graphed as a smooth or "normal curve" of distribution. De Vries' studies showed that such curves also existed for many traits in plants. But he also found that many traits showed a bimodal or discontinuous distribution, suggesting that populations are often mixtures of varieties, or races, that can be separated from one another by selection. Crossing several closely related races of poppy, xenia, and other species that differed from one another by only one or a few traits, de Vries arrived independently (by 1896) at what is now known as Mendel's law of segregation. In 1900 he accidently came across and read Mendel's original paper of 1866 and incorporated a discussion of Mendel's results in his own work on the poppy, published in 1900. This publication appears to have triggered both Carl Correns and Erich von Tschermak-Seysengg to read Mendel's work and recognize its importance. The result was to bring to the attention of the scientific world the work of Gregor Mendel which was soon to lay the foundation for modern genetics.

## Working Out the Mutation Theory

It was for his work on the mutation theory, however, that de Vries ultimately became most well-known. In 1886 near Hilversum, outside of Amsterdam, de Vries noted what appeared to be several species of the evening primrose, *Oenothera lamarckiana*, growing side-by-side. Taking seeds from these plants and growing them in his experimental garden, de Vries found they produced many variant forms which he classified as new and distinct species. These suddenly-appearing variations de Vries called *mutations*, and in his *The Mutation Theory* (1901-1903) he suggested that evolution might occur more frequently by these large-scale jumps than Darwin's natural selection acting on slight individual variations. There were, de Vries noted, several types of mutations that occurred in plants: progressive (introducing a wholly new character, and usually making the plant a new species); retrogressive (loss of a trait); and degressive (activation of a trait long-latent in the species). While de Vries saw retrogressive and degressive mutations as following Mendel's laws (progressive mutations did not), he made little of the point. His major interest lay less in the problem of heredity and more in that of the origin of species.

De Vries' mutation theory was enthusiastically received by many investigators at the time as meeting many of the difficulties they saw in the Darwinian theory: lack of sufficient geological time for the slow and haphazard process of natural selection to produce new species; the problem of new traits being swamped or blended out by backcrossing with the parents; and the reliance of Darwinians on the heritability of slight, individual (as opposed to largescale) variations as the raw material on which selection could act. De Vries travelled widely lecturing on the mutation theory, going to the United States in 1904, 1906, and again in 1916, where he stimulated many investigators to seek in other organisms, including animals, large-scale mutations of the sort he had found in *Oenothera*. While no such mutations were forthcoming, de Vries' work did stimulate much interest in the experimental study of evolution, as investigators sought ways to produce mutations artificially and to detect their presence through experimental breeding. One result of de Vries' influence was that in 1908 Thomas Hunt Morgan at Columbia University began to search for mutations in the fruit fly *Drosophila melanogaster*, an organism whose favorable breeding characteristics were to become a major focus for experimental genetics in the 20th century.

Among his many honors, de Vries was the recipient of 11 honorary degrees and became a corresponding member of many foreign academies of science. His world-wide esteem was reflected in invitations to give the major lectures at the opening of the Station for Experimental Study of Evolution at Cold Spring Harbor, Long Island (1904), and at the dedication of Rice Institute in Houston, Texas (1916).

As influential as it was in his own day, de Vries' mutation theory did not pass the test of time. Between 1907 and 1915 various cytogeneticists showed that heredity in *Oenothera* involved a number of unusual chromosomal phenomena (polyploidy, or increased numbers of chromosomes; two groups of chromosomes attached end-to-end, each transmitted as a whole from parent to offspring) that gave only the illusion of new species. In reality the mutants of *Oenothera* were explicable not by de Vries' pet mutation theory but by the very Mendelian theory de Vries had helped to recover. Eventually, by the early 1920s, the mutation theory was abandoned as an explanation for origin of

species. (The modern term "mutation" refers only to small, discrete variations in particular traits, and thus has a much different meaning from de Vries' usage.)

## Further Reading

A biographical sketch of Hugo de Vries written by Peter van der Pas for the *Dictionary of Scientific Biography* includes a lengthy bibliography. For the reception of de Vries' work, see Garland E. Allen, "Hugo de Vries and the reception of the 'mutation theory'," *Journal of the History of Biology* (1969). For the relationship between de Vries and evolutionary problems, see: Lindley Darden, "Reasoning in scientific change: Charles Darwin, Hugo de Vries, and the discovery of segregation," in *Studies in History and Philosophy of Science* (1976) and Peter van der Pas, "Correspondence of Hugo de Vries and Charles Darwin," *Janus* (1970). De Vries' role in modern genetics is discussed in J. Heimans, "Hugo de Vries and the gene concept," in *Human Implications of Scientific Advance: Proceedings of the XV$^e$ International Congress of History of Science*, E. G. Forbes, editor (Edinburgh, 1978); in Malcolm Kottler, "Hugo de Vries and the rediscovery of Mendel's laws," *Annals of Science* (1979); and in Peter van der Pas, "Hugo de Vries and Gregor Mendel," *Folia Mendeliana* (1976). □

# William Castle DeVries

**William DeVries (born 1943) performed the first artificial heart transplant on a human patient.**

D r. William DeVries and his surgical team at the University of Utah Medical Center made medical history and national headlines on 2 December 1982, when they replaced the diseased heart of Barney Clark with the Jarvik-7, the first permanent artificial heart ever used for a human patient. DeVries was the only surgeon authorized by the federal Food and Drug Administration (FDA) to implant an artificial heart into a human.

## A Fateful Lecture

William DeVries was the son of a physician and a nurse. His widowed mother remarried and brought him up in Ogden, Utah. The young DeVries had an early mechanical bent and excelled in sports and his studies. During his first year in medical school at the University of Utah College of Medicine, he attended a lecture by Dutch-born Dr. Willem Kolff, a pioneer of biomedical engineering. Drawn to Kolff's work, DeVries asked him for a position on his research team. When DeVries introduced himself, Kolff replied, "That's a good Dutch name. You're hired!" In his work for Kolff, DeVries performed experimental surgery on the first animal recipients of the artificial heart. DeVries left Utah to do his internship and residency in cardiovascular surgery at Duke University, but returned to Kolff 's team in 1979.

## The Jarvik-7

When DeVries rejoined the team, he began to use Dr. Robert K. Jarvik's design for a mechanical heart. The Jarvik-7 replaced the ventricles of the human heart. Its pumping action came from compressed air from an electrical unit located outside the patient's body. After many experiments implanting the mechanism into animals, DeVries began the long and hard process of getting the permission required by the FDA to implant the heart into a human patient. After FDA approval in 1982, a panel of six members at the University of Utah Medical Center began reviewing heart patients. The decision made by DeVries, two cardiologists, a psychiatrist, a nurse, and a social worker had to be unanimous. The first patient they chose was sixty-one-year-old Barney Clark. After suffering a series of medical complications closely followed by the news media, Clark died 112 days after his artificial-heart surgery.

## Innovative Therapy or Hard-Core Experimentation?

Many people expressed philosophical, religious, and practical objections to the artificial-heart program. DeVries felt these slowed his work in Utah, so he left his post for a new position. The second implantation of the device occurred at DeVries's new appointment at the Humana Human Heart Institute International in Louisville, Kentucky. DeVries's patients at Humana also suffered setbacks widely covered by the media. DeVries and the Humana Institute were criticized for publicity seeking. *Life* magazine referred to "the Bill Schroeder Show" in an article about DeVries's second patient who suffered several strokes following implantation. After critics began to charge that the implant substituted mechanical heart disease for human heart disease, DeVries seemed to concede the dilemma when he said, "People always look at artificial hearts as innovative therapy. But the other part is hard-core experimentation. You may exchange one set of complications for another."

## An Unusual Eulogy

Doctors do not usually attend their patients' funerals because of an unwritten code about maintaining professional distance, but DeVries attended the funerals of several of his patients, including Barney Clark and Murray Haydon. At the widow's request, DeVries gave the eulogy at Bill Schroeder's funeral. By March 1987, forty-nine Jarvik-7 hearts were implanted by different surgeons in different parts of the world in dying patients as temporary bridges to transplantation. In January 1988 DeVries was close to performing his fifth artificial-heart transplant when a human donor heart was found for the patient. In January 1990 the FDA withdrew its approval of the Jarvik-7, ending the innovative program.

## Further Reading

The Schroeder Family with Martha Barnette, *The Bill Schroeder Story* (New York: Morrow, 1987).
Jeff Wheelright, Donna E. Haupt, and William Strode, "Bill's Heart; the Troubling Story Behind a Historic Experiment," *Life* (May 1985): 33 + . □

# Thomas Roderick Dew

**Thomas Roderick Dew (1802-1846), one of the earliest and ablest defenders in America of slavery, articulated the proslavery argument that dominated the Southern mind during the 30 years before the Civil War.**

Thomas Dew, the son of a wealthy planter, was born in King and Queen County, Va., on Dec. 5, 1802. He graduated from William and Mary College, and, after traveling in Europe and studying in Germany, he took the chair of political law at William and Mary in 1827. His major scholarly interest was political economy, and most of his published writings were in that field. In 1832 he became president of William and Mary, a post he held until his death in 1846.

In 1831 the bloody Nat Turner slave rebellion in Southampton County, Va., sparked the most intense critical discussion of slavery in the antebellum South. The Virginia Legislature vigorously debated the subject of slavery for a year, and motions for its abolition were only narrowly defeated. Prior to this, Southern intellectuals, following the lead of Thomas Jefferson, had generally treated slavery as a necessary evil, to be tolerated only until the problem of dealing with an unassimilable free black population could be resolved. Many Southerners were adherents of the American Colonization Society, which advocated gradual emancipation and colonization of freed slaves in Africa; this proposal figured prominently in the Virginia debate.

Dew had first contributed to the sectional controversy by publishing *Lectures on the Restrictive System* (1829), attacking the protective tariff. Now, in his *Review of the Debate in the Virginia Legislature of 1831-1832* he argued that colonization was economically impossible. He stated that the South's only alternatives were abolition, with the free slaves remaining and becoming "the most worthless and indolent of . . . citizens," or a continuation of slavery. He advocated the second course, strongly defending slavery on historical, economic, and theological grounds. He concluded, "It is the order of nature and of God that the being of superior faculties and knowledge should control and dispose of those who are inferior."

Dew's theories, developed and expanded, became staples of the proslavery argument that dominated the South politically for the following decades, finally generating the secession movement and the Civil War. Dew contracted pneumonia while on a trip and died in Paris on Aug. 6, 1846.

## Further Reading

There is no biography of Dew. Most general works on the history of the South and the Civil War note his work. The most useful treatments are in William E. Dodd, *The Cotton Kingdom* (1919), and William Sumner Jenkins, *Pro-slavery Thought in the Old South* (1935). His college career is treated in Herbert B. Adams, *The College of William and Mary* (1887). □

# George Dewey

**American naval officer George Dewey (1837-1917) was the celebrated victor of the Battle of Manila Bay in the Philippines during the Spanish-American War.**

George Dewey was born on Dec. 26, 1837, in Montpelier, Vt. After attending the local public schools and a private military academy, he entered the U.S. Naval Academy at Annapolis, graduating third in his class in 1858. He entered active service with the rank of lieutenant.

During the Civil War, Dewey saw hard combat at New Orleans, the opening of the Mississippi River, and the capture of Ft. Fisher. At war's end he had the rank of lieutenant commander and the respect of superiors who controlled his professional destiny.

During the 1870s and the early 1880s Dewey held routine assignments. As chief of the Bureau of Equipment and then as president of the Board of Inspection and Survey, between 1889 and 1897 Dewey played an important part in the construction of the new fleet of armored, steam-propelled steel warships.

In October 1897 with the backing of Assistant Secretary of the Navy Theodore Roosevelt, Dewey, now a commodore, was assigned to command the fleet's Asiatic squadron. Anticipating war with Spain, Roosevelt wanted an able officer who could aggressively carry out a plan for an attack on Manila, capital of the Spanish-held Philippines.

When Congress declared war in late April 1898, Dewey sailed for Manila with six light cruisers and an assortment of auxiliary vessels. On May 1, after a daring night run past the batteries guarding the harbor entrance, he attacked a Spanish squadron in Manila Bay that was similar in strength and composition to his own. When the firing ended, Dewey's force, without losing one man or ship, had sunk or set afire every Spanish vessel. This one-sided victory paved the way for the American conquest of the Philippines, and it transformed the obscure naval officer into a popular hero who was rewarded with parades, banquets, and triumphal arches upon his return to the United States.

Dewey's first wife had died in childbirth in 1872, and in 1899 he married Mildred McLean Hazen, a longtime friend. A brief Dewey presidential boom flared and fizzled. Promoted to admiral of the Navy, Dewey assumed the presidency of the newly created General Board of the Navy in 1900. During the next 15 years under Dewey's aggressive leadership, the Board became the nation's most influential military planning agency, working out basic war strategy and guiding the enlargement of the fleet. A few weeks before the outbreak of World War I in 1914, Dewey suffered a stroke that removed him from active duty. He died in Washington, D.C., on Jan. 16, 1917.

## Further Reading

*The Autobiography of George Dewey* covers his career to 1899. The most thorough biography is in Richard S. West, Jr., *Admi-*
*rals of American Empire* (1948). A full-length study is Laurin Hall Healy and Luis Kutner, *The Admiral* (1944). For the Manila campaign see French Ensor Chadwick, *The Relations of the United States and Spain: The Spanish-American War* (2 vols., 1911). John A. S. Grenville and George Berkeley Young, *Politics, Strategy, and American Diplomacy* (1966), contains new information on Manila and on Dewey's work with the General Board.

## Additional Sources

Dewey, George, *Autobiography of George Dewey, admiral of the Navy,* Annapolis, Md.: Naval Institute Press, 1987.
Spector, Ronald H., *Admiral of the new empire: the life and career of George Dewey,* Columbia, S.C.: University of South Carolina Press, 1988. □

# John Dewey

**During the first half of the 20th century, John Dewey (1859-1952) was America's most famous exponent of a pragmatic philosophy that celebrated the traditional values of democracy and the efficacy of reason and universal education.**

Born on Oct. 20, 1859, in Burlington, Vt., John Dewey came of old New England stock. His father was a local merchant who loved literature. His mother, swayed by revivals to convert to Congregationalism, possessed a stern moral sense. The community, situated at the economic crossroads of the state, was the home of the state university and possessed a cosmopolitan atmosphere unusual for northern New England. Nearby Irish and French-Canadian settlements acquainted John with other cultures. Boyhood jobs delivering newspapers and working at a lumberyard further extended his knowledge. In 1864, on a visit to see his father in the Union Army in Virginia, he viewed firsthand the devastating effects of the Civil War.

## Educational Career

Dewey's career in Vermont public schools was unremarkable. At the age of 15 he entered the University of Vermont. He found little of interest in academic work; his best grades were in science, and later he would regard science as the highest manifestation of human intellect. Dewey himself attributed his "intellectual awakening" to T. H. Huxley's college textbook on physiology, which shaped his vision of man as entirely the product of natural evolutionary processes.

Dewey later remembered coming in touch with the world of ideas during his senior year. Courses on psychology, religion, ethics, logic, and economics supplanted his earlier training in languages and science. His teacher, H. A. P. Torrey, introduced him to Immanuel Kant, but Dewey found it difficult to accept the Kantian idea that there was a realm of knowledge transcending empirical demonstration. Dewey also absorbed Auguste Comte's emphasis on the disintegrative effects of extreme individualism. The quality

of his academic work improved and, at the age of 19, he graduated Phi Beta Kappa and second in his class of 18.

Dewey hoped to teach high school. After a frustrating summer of job hunting, his cousin, principal of a seminary in Pennsylvania, came to his rescue. For 2 years Dewey taught the classics, algebra, and science, meanwhile reading philosophy. When his cousin resigned, however, Dewey's employment ended. He returned to Vermont to become the sole teacher in a private school in Charlotte, near his alma mater. He renewed acquaintance with Torrey, and the two discussed the fruits of Dewey's reading in ancient and modern philosophy.

## Intellectual Development

At this time most American teachers of philosophy were ordained clergymen who tended to subordinate philosophical speculation to theological orthodoxy. Philosophy was in the hands of laymen in only a few schools. One such school was in St. Louis, where William T. Harris established the *Journal of Speculative Philosophy*. Here Dewey published his first scholarly effort. Finally, Dewey decided to pursue a career in philosophy and applied for admission to the newly founded Johns Hopkins University, another haven for lay philosophers.

At Johns Hopkins in 1882 Dewey studied with George S. Morris, who was on leave as chairman of the philosophy department at the University of Michigan. Under Morris's direction Dewey studied Hegel, whose all-encompassing philosophical system temporarily satisfied Dewey's longing to escape from the dualisms of traditional philosophy. In 1884 Dewey completed his doctorate and, at Morris's invitation, went to teach at Michigan.

In Ann Arbor, Dewey met and married Alice Chipman. His interests turned toward problems of education as he traveled about the state to evaluate college preparatory courses. His concern for social problems deepened, and he adopted a vague brand of socialism, although he was unacquainted with Marxism. He still taught Sunday school, but he was drifting away from religious orthodoxy. In 1888 he accepted an appointment at the University of Minnesota, only to return to Michigan a year later to the post left vacant by Morris's death.

The next stage in Dewey's intellectual development came with his reading of William James's *Principles of Psychology*. Dewey rapidly shed Hegelianism in favor of "instrumentalism," a position that holds that thinking is an activity which, at its best, is directed toward resolving problems rather than creating abstract metaphysical systems.

In 1894 Dewey moved to the University of Chicago as head of a new department of philosophy, psychology, and pedagogy. Outside the academic world he became friends with the social reformers at Hull House. He also admired Henry George's analysis of the problems of poverty. To test his educational theories, he started an experimental school, with his wife as principal. The "Dewey school," however, caused a struggle between its founder and the university's president, William R. Harper. In 1904, when Harper tried to remove his wife, he resigned in protest. An old friend of Dewey's engineered an offer from Columbia University, where Dewey spent the rest of his teaching years. His colleagues, some of the most fertile minds in modern America, included Charles A. Beard and James Harvey Robinson.

## Peak of His Influence

Living in New York City placed the Deweys at the center of America's cultural and political life. Dewey pursued his scholarship, actively supported the Progressive party, and, in 1929, helped organize the League for Independent Political Action to further the cause of a new party. He also served as a contributing editor of the *New Republic* magazine and helped found both the American Civil Liberties Union and the American Association of University Professors. After World War I, reaching the peak of his influence, he became a worldwide traveler, lecturing in Japan at the Imperial Institute and spending 2 years teaching at the Chinese universities of Peking and Nanking. In 1924 he went to study the schools in Turkey and 2 years later visited the University of Mexico. His praise for the Russian educational system he inspected on a 1928 trip to the Soviet Union earned him much criticism.

As a teacher, Dewey exhibited the distracted air of a man who had learned to concentrate in a home inhabited by five young children. Careless about his appearance, shy and quiet in manner, he sometimes put his students to sleep, but those who managed to focus their attention could watch a man fascinated with ideas actually creating a philosophy in his classroom.

In 1930 Dewey retired from teaching. A year earlier, national luminaries had used the occasion of his seventieth birthday to hail his accomplishments; such celebrations would be repeated on his eightieth and ninetieth birthdays. He continued to publish works clarifying his philosophy. In public affairs he was one of the first to warn of the dangers from Hitler's Germany and of the Japanese threat in the Far East. In 1937 he traveled to Mexico as chairman of the commission to determine the validity of Soviet charges against Trotsky. His first wife having died in 1927, Dewey, at the ripe age of 87, married a widow, Roberta Grant. In the early years of the cold war Dewey's support of American intervention in Korea earned him criticism from the U.S.S.R. newspaper *Pravda*. He died on June 1, 1952.

## Dewey's Philosophy

In his philosophy Dewey sought to transcend what he considered the misleading distinctions made by other philosophers. By focusing on experience, he bridged the gulf between the organism and its environment to emphasize their interaction. He rejected the dualism of spirit versus matter, insisting that the mind was a product of evolution, not some infusion from a superior being. Yet he avoided the materialist conclusion which made thought seem accidental and irrelevant. While he saw most of man's behavior as shaped by habit, he believed that the unceasing processes of change often produced conditions which customary mental activity could not explain. The resulting tension led to creative thinking in which man tried to reestablish control of the unstable environment. Thought was never, for Dewey, merely introspection; rather, it was part of a process

whereby man related to his surroundings. Dewey believed that universal education could train men to break through habit into creative thought.

Dewey was convinced that democracy was the best form of government. He saw contemporary American democracy challenged by the effects of the industrial revolution, which had produced an overconcentration of wealth in the hands of a few men. This threat, he believed, could be met by the right kind of education.

The "progressive education" movement of the 1920s was an effort to implement Dewey's pedagogical ideas. Because his educational theory emphasized the classroom as a place for students to encounter the "present," his interpreters tended to play down traditional curricular concerns with the "irrelevant" past or occupational future. His influence on American schools was so pervasive that many critics (then and later) assailed his ideas as the cause of all that they found wrong with American education.

## Philosophical Works

To the year of his death Dewey remained a prolific writer. Couched in a difficult prose style, his published works number over 300. Some of the most important works include *Outlines of a Critical Theory of Ethics* (1891), *The Study of Ethics* (1894), *The School and Society* (1899), *Studies in Logical Theory* (1903), *How We Think* (1910), *The Influence of Darwin on Philosophy and Other Essays in Contemporary Thought* (1910), *German Philosophy and Politics* (1915), *Democracy and Education* (1916), *Reconstruction in Philosophy* (1920), *Human Nature and Conduct* (1922), *Experience and Nature* (1925), *The Public and Its Problems* (1927), *The Quest for Certainty* (1929), *Individualism Old and New* (1930), *Philosophy and Civilization* (1931), *Art as Experience* (1934), *Liberalism and Social Action* (1935), *Logic: The Theory of Inquiry* (1938), *Freedom and Culture* (1939), *Problems of Men* (1946), and *Knowing and the Known* (1949).

## Further Reading

For more information see Dewey's autobiographical fragment, "From Absolutism to Experimentalism," in George P. Adams and William Pepperell Montague, eds., *Contemporary American Philosophy: Personal Statements* (1930). His daughters compiled an authoritative sketch of his life in Paul Arthur Schilpp, ed., *The Philosophy of John Dewey* (1939), which also contains valuable summaries of aspects of his philosophy.

Indispensable for any examination of Dewey's thought is Sidney Hook, *John Dewey: An Intellectual Portrait* (1939). John E. Smith presents an excellent chapter on Dewey in *The Spirit of American Philosophy* (1963). Paul K. Conkin in *Puritans and Pragmatists: Eight Eminent American Thinkers* (1968) attempts an evaluation of Dewey's place in the context of American ideas. Morton G. White, *Social Thought in America* (1949), considers assumptions common to Dewey and his colleagues in other disciplines. Longer, more challenging treatments of Dewey's ideas are in George R. Geiger, *John Dewey in Perspective* (1958); Robert J. Roth, *John Dewey and Self Realization* (1962); and Richard J. Bernstein, *John Dewey* (1966). See also Jerome Nathanson, *John Dewey: The Reconstruction of the Democratic Life* (1951).

## Additional Sources

Campbell, James, *Understanding John Dewey: nature and cooperative intelligence*, Chicago, Ill.: Open Court, 1995.

Ryan, Alan, *John Dewey and the high tide of American liberalism*, New York: W.W. Norton, 1995. ☐

# Melvil Dewey

**The American librarian and reformer Melvil Dewey (1851-1931) established the Dewey decimal system of classifying books and played a prominent role in developing professional institutions for librarians.**

Melvil Dewey was born in Adams Center, N.Y., on Dec. 10, 1851, the youngest of five children of impoverished parents. His father, a boot maker and keeper of a general store, and his sternly religious mother inculcated principles of hard work and economy in the youth, along with a sense of self-righteousness that marked him throughout his life. He early demonstrated strong mathematical ability and a fascination with systems and classifications. His education was slowed by the need to earn money, and he did not enter Amherst College until he was 19, graduating in 1874.

Dewey worked in the college library during his last 2 years as a student and for the 2 years following his graduation. Although then still attracted to a missionary career, he carried out intensive investigations of other libraries and began to develop his own ideas. His work culminated in 1876, when he published *A Classification and Subject Index for Cataloguing and Arranging the Books and Pamphlets of a Library*. This system, still in use today in most public and some college libraries, was his major contribution to his profession.

Arranging the various fields of knowledge into a logical order and using a decimal system of notation to indicate the arrangement of books, Dewey's system proved easy both for librarians and users to understand, capable of expansion to suit the needs of large as well as small libraries, and applicable to a wide variety of books and ideas. Although he was not the first to come up with the basic idea, his version was both logical and workable. Pushed by Dewey and his students with missionary zeal, it triumphed over its competitors.

In 1876 Dewey left Amherst for Boston, where he founded the Library Bureau and worked for a number of reform movements, including the metric system, temperance, tobacco, and spelling. The spelling of his first name (he was baptized Melville) demonstrates his devotion to the last-mentioned cause. He played a major role in founding the American Library Association in 1876 and served as its secretary (1876-1890) and president (1890-1891, 1892-1893). He edited *Library Journal* (1876-1880) and all through his life contributed to it.

In 1883 Dewey accepted an offer to become librarian of Columbia College and vigorously proceeded to put his ideas into effect, reclassifying and recataloging the library and starting a library school. The zeal with which he applied his ideas was accompanied by a spirit of intolerance of disagreement and tactlessness toward others that aroused controversy and bitter opposition, climaxing in his suspension by the Columbia trustees in 1888. Although exonerated of the charges brought against him, he resigned later that year.

In 1888 Dewey was chosen director of the New York State Library and moved to Albany the following year, taking his library school with him. Again, he plunged into his work, expanding the scope and usefulness of his institution by enlarging its collections and establishing or improving the home education department, the extension division, and the traveling libraries. He helped found the Association of State Libraries in 1890 and was active in its deliberations. Again, his professional competence was counterbalanced by his inability to manage human relationships. Charges of profiting from financial transactions with his students were dismissed, but after he was rebuked by the board for his role in organizing a club at Lake Placid, N.Y., that discriminated against Jews, he resigned as of Jan. 1, 1906.

After leaving Albany, Dewey concentrated on the affairs of his club and a similar venture he began in Florida in 1927. He died of a cerebral hemorrhage on Dec. 26, 1931, in his Florida home.

## Further Reading

George Grosvenor Dawe, *Melvil Dewey: Seer, Inspirer, Doer* (1932), is an uncritical, family-sponsored biography that has many quotations from Dewey's letters and essays. Fremont Rider, *Melvil Dewey* (1944), is shorter and more critical though still favorable to its subject. No convenient collection of Dewey's writings, which are mostly periodical contributions, exists.

## Additional Sources

Wiegand, Wayne A., *Irrepressible reformer: a biography of Melvil Dewey*, Chicago: American Library Assoc., 1996. ☐

# Thomas Edmund Dewey

**Thomas Edmund Dewey (1902-1971) was governor of New York State from 1942 to 1954 and a Republican presidential candidate.**

T homas E. Dewey was born on March 24, 1902, at Owosso, Mich. In 1923 he received his bachelor of arts degree from the University of Michigan. After briefly studying music and law in Chicago, he entered Columbia University Law School. After his graduation in 1925, he toured England and France. Returning to New York, he entered the state bar, accepted a clerkship in a law office, and became active in the Young Republican Club. In 1928 Dewey married Frances E. Hutt; they had two children.

In 1931 the U.S. attorney for the Southern District of New York appointed Dewey his chief assistant. In addition to fundamental honesty and natural courage, Dewey possessed a capacity for careful and deliberate case preparation and an amazing self-control that enabled him to remain cool under pressure. With the resignation of the U.S. attorney in November 1933, Dewey took that position—at 31 the youngest U.S. attorney ever. When President Franklin D. Roosevelt appointed a Democrat to the position 5 weeks later, Dewey returned to private law practice. In 1935 he was appointed special prosecutor for the Investigation of Organized Crime in New York. His campaign against narcotics and vice racketeers obtained 72 convictions in 73 prosecutions. In 1937 he was elected district attorney for New York County.

In 1942 Dewey was elected governor of New York. He quickly established a reputation for political moderation and administrative efficiency, enjoying cordial relations with the legislature. Success as governor, added to his reputation in fighting New York racketeers, sent Dewey's political stature soaring. In 1944 he was the Republican party's presidential nominee. He ran well, despite Roosevelt's record as a war leader and Dewey's lack of experience in international affairs. Reelected governor of New York in 1946, he proceeded to ram a series of liberal laws through the legislature.

As the acknowledged front-runner in his second presidential campaign—against Democrat Harry Truman in 1948—Dewey refused to tax himself, made only a few speeches, avoided controversial issues, and scarcely recognized the opposition. He lost to Truman by a narrow margin. In 1950 he was elected to his third successive term as New York's governor.

At the suggestion of State Department adviser John Foster Dulles, Dewey visited 17 countries in the Pacific in 1951. In 1955 he reentered private practice with the New York firm of Dewey, Ballantine, Bushby, Palmer, and Wood. By 1957 Dewey had been awarded 16 honorary degrees. His books include *The Case against the New Deal* (1940), *Journey to the Far Pacific* (1952), and *Thomas E. Dewey on the Two Party System* (1966). He died on March 16, 1971, at Bal Harbour, Fla.

## Further Reading

Writings on Dewey remain limited. Stanley Walker, *Dewey: An American of This Century* (1944), was prepared for Dewey's first presidential campaign. Several good chapters on Dewey's race against Truman are in Irwin Ross, *The Loneliest Campaign: The Truman Victory of 1948* (1968).

## Additional Sources

Beyer, Barry K., *Thomas E. Dewey, 1937-1947: a study in political leadership*, New York: Garland Pub., 1979.
Smith, Richard Norton, *Thomas E. Dewey and his times*, New York: Simon and Schuster, 1982. ☐

# Mary Williams Dewson

**Mary Williams Dewson (1874-1962), widely known as Molly Dewson, was a reformer, government official, and organizer of women for the Democratic Party.**

Molly Dewson was born in Quincy, Massachusetts, on February 18, 1874. In her youth a number of influences awakened in her an interest in public affairs. Her father gave her an appetite for reading books on politics and government. Many of her neighbors and female relatives—such as her aunt Elizabeth Putnam, a pioneer in reforming delinquent girls—were active in public causes.

After attending private schools in the Boston area, she entered Wellesley College, where she was an excellent student. She was also president of her class in her junior and senior years, organized the Wellesley Athletic Association, introduced the Australian ballot for class elections, and began the Wellesley alumnae fund by raising money for the first class gift.

Upon graduating in 1897, she quickly established herself as one of the ablest of the generation of younger women who seconded the initiatives of such older women reformers of the progressive era as Jane Addams and Florence Kelley. Dewson got her first job when the Women's Educational and Industrial Union, the most important women's club in Boston, hired her to investigate and improve the living and working conditions of female domestics in the Boston area. Then, as the organizer and first superintendent of the Massachusetts Parole Department for delinquent girls between 1900 and 1912, she became a national authority on the rehabilitation of juvenile offenders.

As executive secretary of an investigating commission set up by the Massachusetts legislature she produced a report on the living conditions of women and children in industry. The report became the basis of the 1912 Massachusetts minimum wage act, the first such act passed in modern industrial America. Dewson went on to become a leader in the Massachusetts campaign of 1915 for the passage of a referendum favoring woman suffrage and then assumed the leadership of the state Suffrage Association.

After World War I Florence Kelley chose Dewson to take charge of the National Consumers League's national campaign for state minimum wage laws for women and children. Then switching to the New York Consumers League in 1924, she became the president. Dewson soon emerged as the leader of the Women's Joint Legislative Conference, most notably in lobbying for the passage through the New York legislature of a 1930 act limiting the hours of women and children in industry to 48 hours a week.

Starting in 1928 Eleanor Roosevelt, who was active in the Consumers League and in the Women's Division of the Democratic Party, persuaded Dewson to accept various positions of leadership within the Democratic Party in New York and on the national level in order to make women more effective in politics. As director of the Women's Division of the Democratic Party in Franklin D. Roosevelt's presidential campaigns of 1932 and 1936, Dewson led in trying to make women voters an important part of the voting coalition behind President Roosevelt. She believed that his New Deal program was the best hope for enacting national legislation to protect working men and women in industry.

Through the Women's Division Dewson developed many techniques to stimulate women who were timid about becoming politicians to be campaigners, party officials, and even candidates for office. She thus created the first effective nationwide vote-getting organization of women ever sponsored by a political party. This organization marked the decisive entrance of women into party politics on both the national and state levels.

Dewson found some time in the 1930s to promote industrial and welfare programs in such capacities as official adviser to Frances Perkins (secretary of labor) and as presidential appointee to the Social Security Board in 1937. But, due to chronic heart trouble, she resigned from the board in 1938 and, except for occasional participation in party affairs, retired to her home in Castine, Maine, where she died in 1962.

## Further Reading

A short biography of Dewson by Paul C. Taylor is in *Notable American Women: The Modern Period* (1980). She figures prominently in Susan Ware, *Beyond Suffrage: Women in the New Deal* (1981). Dewson's importance to Eleanor Roosevelt is illustrated in Joseph P. Lash, *Eleanor and Franklin* (1971) and to Frances Perkins in George Martin, *Madam Secretary: Frances Perkins* (1976).

## Additional Sources

Ware, Susan, *Partner and I: Molly Dewson, feminism, and New Deal politics,* New Haven: Yale University Press, 1987. □

# Sergei Diaghilev

**A Russian who inspired artists, musicians, and dancers, Sergei Diaghilev (1872-1929) took the ballet to new heights of public enjoyment.**

And what, dear sir, do you do in the company?" asked King Alfonso of Spain upon meeting Sergei Diaghilev, famed impresario of *Diaghilev's Ballets Russes.* "You don't conduct the orchestra or play an instrument. You don't design the *mise en scene,* and you don't dance. What do you do?" Ever charming and self-assured, Diaghilev replied, "Your Majesty, I am like you. I do no work. I do nothing, but I am indispensible."

Diaghilev's response was more than modest. He devoted his lifetime to promoting the arts—to a reverence for quality in the old and the new in music, painting, and the dance, and, eventually, to a merging of the three arts in the theatre form known as ballet.

Diaghilev was born in 1872 into an aristocratic, wealthy family on a country estate in Perm, a province of Russia. Serious conversations about poetry and literature, chamber music, and informal opera *soirees* were normal family activities. His studies from an early age included music and music theory. At home and at school his role as 'Young Master' was accepted as appropriate. There were those then, and later, who thought he was arrogant, but it was generally recognized that he possessed superior qualities.

His mother died at childbirth, but he was cared for and disciplined by a beloved step-mother. Throughout his life he remembered her admonition that he must never say "I cannot." Her message was, "When one wants to, one always can." He found the paths that let him do what he wanted to do and he was pleased when viewers were thrilled by his unconventional perceptions.

Diaghilev's life divides into three time units. The first and second, 18 years each, were secure preparations for the 21 years of high drama of the third.

## Career Change in Second Phase

In Perm he was effectively nurtured until he was sent off to be with distinguished relatives while studying law in St. Petersburg. In that city (Peter the Great's "window to the west") the country boy was citified. He learned much, including an awareness of the richness of Russian early painting and architecture.

Diaghilev soon discovered that he had little interest in the law, certainly far less than his love for music which remained throughout his life. Through his cousin he now became a member of a circle of writers, musicians, and painters that included Alexandre Benois and Leon Baskt. These two remained important colleagues for many years. It was already clear that Diaghilev's taste in art as well as music was exquisite, and that he had a flair for discovering talent, and a talent for discerning its possibilities. He began to write essays about artists and art trends, and soon found himself, along with Benois and Baskt, opposed to existing art criticism. Neither the conservative academics nor the realism of the political left was acceptable to the three friends, and they were vehement in their objections. Nonpolitical, they spoke for the new voice of art as the expression of the individual. From their fervor there came to life a new magazine titled *Mir Isskustva* (World of Art), which for five turbulent years shocked the art world.

One result was that outspoken Diaghilev was invited to join the Maryinsky Theatre, jewel of the Russian imperial theatres, to be in charge of "special missions." His first assignment was to edit the year book of the imperial theatres. He did it well and was then assigned the supervision of an opera, and after that a ballet. But his impatience and arrogance in dealing with the bureaucracy resulted in trouble, and in 1911 he left. It was at the Maryinsky that he became acquainted with Vaslav Nijinsky, Anna Pavlova, Michel Fokine, and other members of the Imperial Ballet and further developed an interest in the ballet.

Pursuing his interest in Russian art he travelled extensively through the country to collect and make possible exhibits of arts of the 18th and 19th centuries. In 1905 he was responsible for a major St. Petersburg exhibit titled *Russian Historical Portraits*. He took the exhibit to Paris in 1907, the first export of Russian art. From that beginning in Paris there developed the opera and ballet career that was to make the name of Diaghilev a shining light in the Western world.

## Fame in His Third Phase

In 1908 Paris was receptive to new ideas. There Diaghilev presented Mussorgsky's opera *Boris Godunoff,* with Maryinsky basso Feodor Chaliapin in the title role. The impact was ecstatic and resulted in an invitation to bring a troupe of Russian dancers to Paris. The result made history.

On October 19, 1909, the Ballets Russes presented five ballets, four of them choreographed by Fokine, who had already broken with the classical style and dared to invent dance movement appropriate to the ballet's subject. The ladies were not forever dainty, and the male dancers revealed an unprecedented energy and virtuosity. Nijinsky, Pavlova, Tamara Karsavina, Adolph Bolm, Mikhail Mordkin, and Ida Rubenstein were among the dancers. Fokine later wrote about opening night: " . . . the audience rushed and actually tore off the orchestra rail in the Chatelet Theatre. The success was absolutely unbelievable." Karsavina, in her book of recollections, *Theatre Street,* wrote "The atmosphere enveloping the Russian season had a subtle, light, gay intoxication. Something akin to a miracle happened every night—the stage and audience trembled in a unison of emotion."

In 1910 the ballet company returned to Paris, again on leave from the Maryinsky. But in 1911 Diaghilev decided he would set up a full-time, permanent company. With Baskt and Benois again as colleagues, he established the first privately supported company of people willing to give up pension, honors, and benefits to join *Diaghilev's Ballets Russes.* The company was already famous. It was soon to be augmented by other brilliant talents, men and women from countries other than Russia, attracted to collaborate in daring new ventures.

In the years between 1911 and Diaghilev's death in 1929 the company toured over and over again throughout Europe, South America, the United States. In England it inspired the beginnings of The Royal Ballet. In Boston a young Lincoln Kirstein, determined to be like Diaghilev, brought George Balanchine across the Atlantic to establish the School of American Ballet and the New York City Ballet. New Englander Lucia Chase, a ballet student of Mordkin (who had been Pavlova's concert partner as well a member of Ballets Russes), was encouraged by him to start Ballet Theatre. And many of today's ballet teachers in the United States trace their pedagogical heritage to the Russians who stayed behind to open up dance studios.

The long list of collaborators in *Diaghilev's Ballets Russes* included designers Bakst, Benois, and famous names from the world of art—Braque, Chagall, Cocteau, de Cherico, Derain, Laurencin, Matisse, Picasso (who designed posters, sets, and costumes and also married a company ballerina), Roerich and Utrillo. Among those who composed music for ballets were Debussy, de Falla, Milhaud, Poulenc, Prokofiev, Ravel, Satie, and Stravinsky.

In addition to Pavlova and Nijinsky, some of the company's famed dancers were Bolm, Dubrovska, Danilova, Dolin, Karsavina, Lifar, Lopokova, Markova, Mordkin, Sokolova, Spessivtzeva, Vilzak, Vladimirof, and Woizikovsky. While many of the dancers were not Russian-born, all of the choreographers were. Choreographers, and some of their ballets, were Fokine: *Les Sylphides, Spectre de la Rose, Petrouchka, Firebird,* and *Scheherazade;* Nijinsky: *Afternoon of a Faun, Jeux,* and *Sacre du Printemps;* Massine: *Parade, Boutique Fantasique,* and *Le Tricorne;* Nijinska: *Les Noces* and *Les Biches;* Balanchine: *Apollo* and *Prodigal Son.* While this is an incomplete list, it represents some of the Diaghilev ballets performed in company repertoires today, a remarkable reminder of Diaghilev "classics."

Diaghilev died of diabetes in his beloved Venice on August 19, 1929. He was the catalyst who helped open the door for the arts of the 20th century.

## Further Reading

Richard Buckle's *Diaghilev* is the most detailed of numerous biographies. In it are six pages, single spaced, of sources—books, articles, and documents relating to the life and work of the Russian impressario who created the Diaghilev Era. Of special interest is the first biography, *Diaghileff, His Artistic and Private Life,* by Arnold Haskell (1935; paperback, 1978); and Buckle's *In Search of Diaghilev* (London, 1958, New York, 1975).

## Additional Sources

Buckle, Richard, *Diaghilev,* New York: Atheneum, 1984, 1979.
Buckle, Richard, *In the wake of Diaghilev,* New York: Holt, Rinehart & Winston, 1983, 1982.
Garafola, Lynn, *Diaghilev's Ballets russes,* New York: Oxford University Press, 1989.
*Diaghileff, his artistic and private life,* New York: Da Capo Press, 1978, c1935. □

# Blaise Diagne

**Blaise Diagne (1872-1934) was a Senegalese political leader. He was the first African deputy elected to the French National Assembly and a pioneer of modern African and pan-African politics.**

B laise Diagne was born on the small island of Gorée off the coast of Dakar into a well-to-do Senegalese middle-class family. His family had the political rights of French citizens and were among the Africans who could elect a deputy to the French National Assembly.

In 1914 Diagne was elected to the National Assembly in Paris, defeating six European candidates. On Sept. 29, 1916, he achieved the enactment of a law that bears his name and which reaffirmed the rights of Franco-African

citizens at a time when there was a movement in France for their curtailment. In 1917 Diagne was appointed commissioner of the republic and placed in charge of conscription in West Africa. In this post he helped recruit over 180,000 men to fight for France in World War I.

Reelected deputy by large majorities in 1920 and 1924, Diagne also served as president of the 1919 international Pan-African Congress and cooperated with prominent Americans like W. E. B. Du Bois and Marcus Garvey.

In his first election manifesto Diagne told his followers that "your adversaries tremble at the idea of your political and social awakening." However, he sought his alliances with the various traditional elites and sought to reach the "masses" only indirectly. Diagne also bettered the status of Senegalese troops, giving them a sense of self-importance that persisted to independent Senegal's army.

Yet, as time passed, Diagne increasingly not only explicitly cast aside independence and even self-government as legitimate goals but defended every major aspect of the colonial system, including forced labor. By completely assimilating the cultural and political values of France and by acquiring positions of wealth and eminence, Diagne considered himself to be the personification and justification of French colonialism. He went on to become the first African to hold a high ministerial position in the French government. From June 26, 1931, until Feb. 19, 1932, he was undersecretary of state for the colonies.

While Diagne's first successes marked an important stage in the political evolution of Francophone Africa, new leaders, especially Léopold Senghor, soon rejected the legitimacy of French cultural hegemony.

## Further Reading

The best general background reading available in English on Diagne is Michael Crowder, *Senegal: A Study of French Assimilation Policy* (1962; rev. ed. 1967). See also Ruth S. Morgenthau, *Political Parties in French-Speaking West Africa* (1964), for a history of political development. See also S. O. Mezo and Ram Desai, eds., *Black Leaders of the Centuries* (1970). □

# David Diamond

**The American composer and teacher David Diamond (born 1915) wrote in a wide variety of styles and in virtually every medium. The strength of his music lies in its imposing formal design and its serious expression, which is, however, not without lyrical warmth and romanticism.**

D avid Diamond was born in Rochester, New York, on July 9, 1915. He was the son of Austrian-Polish Jewish immigrants who could not afford to cultivate the musical aptitude that he showed from about the age of six. Fortunately, the young boy's abilities also impressed others who were in a better position to help him. At a public school in Rochester he received a violin and free lessons, and in 1927, when the family moved to Cleveland, André de Ribaupierre taught him violin and theory without remuneration at the Cleveland Institute of Music.

Upon returning to Rochester in 1929 Diamond entered the preparatory department of the Eastman School of Music on a scholarship and studied violin with Effie Knauss and composition with Bernard Rogers. He continued at Eastman as an undergraduate after finishing high school in 1933, but left after one year to move to New York. Again on a scholarship he studied the Dalcroze method of Eurhythmics with Paul Boepple and composition with Roger Sessions at the New Music School from 1934 to 1936 and continued privately with Sessions until 1937.

Diamond made three trips to Paris in the mid-to-late 1930s (the last through funds from the first of three Guggenheim Fellowships), where he studied with the famous French teacher, Nadia Boulanger, and met many of the great artists then living in Paris, such as Albert Roussel, Igor Stravinsky, Maurice Ravel, André Gide, and Charles Munch. Important compositions from these Paris years include: the first of his three violin concertos (1936, 1947, and 1967); *Psalm* (1936) for orchestra (his first work to receive wide attention and also the Juilliard Publication Award in 1938); *Elegy* (1937) for strings and percussion in memory of Ravel; a cello concerto (1938); and *Heroic Piece* (1938) for small orchestra.

Germany's declaration of war on France in 1939 brought Diamond back to the United States for most of the next 12 years. During this time he composed prolifically both chamber and orchestral works. Among the former are the first three of his 11 string quartets (1940, 1943, 1946, 1951, 1960, 1962, 1963, 1964, 1966, 1966, and 1968); a piano quartet (1938) for which he won the Paderewsky Prize; a concerto (1942) for two solo pianos; a sonata (1947) for piano; and a *Chaconne* (1948) for violin and piano. Orchestral works of the period include the first four of his eight symphonies (1940, 1942, 1945, 1945, 1964, 1951, 1959, and 1960—note that the fifth symphony was completed after the eighth); *The Dream of Audubon* (1941), a ballet; music for Shakespeare's *The Tempest* (1944) for orchestra; *Rounds* (1944) for string orchestra; music for Shakespeare's *Romeo and Juliet* (1947) for orchestra; and a piano concerto (1950).

Diamond lectured on American music in Salzburg during the summer of 1949, and two years later went to Italy on a Fulbright Fellowship. He stayed, first in Rome and then in Florence, for 14 years, returning to the United States on two occasions (1961 and 1963) to teach at the State University of New York at Buffalo as Slee Professor of Music. The years in Italy proved productive as evidenced in the large amount of music written, including: *The Midnight Meditation* (1951), a cycle for voice and piano; a piano trio (1951); string quartets 4-8; symphonies 5-8; sonatas for solo violin (1954) and for cello (1956); Sinfonia Concertante (1954-1956); *The World of Paul Klee* (1957) for orchestra; a woodwind quintet (1958); *The Sacred Ground* (1962) for baritone, chorus, children's chorus, and orchestra; and *Elegies* (1963) for flute, English horn, and strings.

Returning to the United States in 1965, Diamond became chair of the composition department at the Manhattan School of Music; he resigned in 1967. A position as composer-in-residence at the American Academy of Rome drew him back to Italy during 1971 and 1972. After 1973 he was professor of composition at the Juilliard School of Music in New York. Some of his better-known compositions of the years 1964 to 1984 are: *We Two* (1964), *Hebrew Melodies* (1967), and *The Fall* (1970), cycles for voice and piano; *Music for Chamber Orchestra* (1969); *The Noblest Game* (1971-1975), an opera; a piano quintet (1972); and *Ode to the Morning of Christ's Nativity* (1980) for a cappella chorus.

Several writers have suggested that the early 1950s marked a rather abrupt change to a dissonant and nontonal style, some even stating that Diamond had taken up the 12-tone method. Diamond himself refuted this last statement in an article appearing in the *New York Times* (August 22, 1965), saying, "I am not now and never have been a twelve-tone composer." While his music became gradually lest tonal in later years, he always commanded a variety of styles, which he used according to the function of the music. The music for Broadway productions of Shakespeare plays, for instance, is quite lush and tonal, while the more absolute works, such as the fourth symphony, frequently involve a more complicated language (here polytonality).

The 1980s and 1990s saw works such as the ninth symphony in a series Diamond began nearly 45 years before. The symphonies were introduced steadily from 1940 until 1965, but it was not until 1985 that Diamond finally unveiled the ninth. In 1996 Juilliard Orchestra performed the world premiere of Diamond's *Concerto For String Quartet and Orchestra,* which the Juilliard School commissioned from Diamond in honor of the 50th anniversary of the Juilliard Quartet. The performance met high praise, notably from the *Village Voice*'s Leighton Kerner, who wrote, "American music boasts no composer more brilliant or more melodically imaginative, and this new concerto bears out the fact." Even at 81 years of age, Diamond seemed to have boundless reservoirs of creativity and energy, rising from his seat in the balcony to honor the Juilliard Quartet with a standing ovation.

New York publishers dismissed his 1936 *Sonata for Cello and Piano* as being avant-garde and "not suited for our purposes," but such luminaries as Igor Stravinsky and Arnold Schoenberg praised this same work. Fortunately, an editorial board for the publishing house of Theodore Presser, including Henry Cowell, Nicolas Slonimsky, and Charles Ives, also recognized its value and saw it through publication. Adhering to traditional formal structures, Diamond often cast his movements in sonata-allegro, rondo, or variation form. Contrapuntal textures and forms, such as fugues and passacaglia enhance the strength of his expression, which is, however, frequently softened by romantic, lyrical writing. Modern rhythmic complexities also energize later compositions such as *Warning* (1973) for chorus and tubular bells. While thus embracing some of the innovations of the 20th century, Diamond rejected others, most emphatically the aleatoricism of John Cage and his followers. Reflecting on his career, Diamond once commented, "one hopes the future will bring my music to a larger audience, one not interested in Trends and The Now, but music for All Time, for all humanity. . . ."

## Further Reading

Biographical information in David Ewen's *American Composers: A Biographical Dictionary* (1982) supersedes that which appears in Ewen's *Composers Since 1900* (1969). Other biographical information appears in *Contemporary Composers* (St. James Press, 1992). Young readers might enjoy Madeline Goss's somewhat fancified biographical account in *Modern Music Masters* (1952). "From the Notebook of David Diamond," *Music Journal* (April 1964) is a strong statement of his artistic credo, as is Richard Freed's article in the *New York Times*, "Music is Diamond's Best Friend" (August 22, 1965). Other sources include *Village Voice* (October 22, 1996). □

# Diana, Princess of Wales

**Lady Diana Frances Spencer (1961-1997) married Prince Charles in 1981 and became Princess of Wales. Retaining her title after the royal couple divorced in 1996, Diana continued her humanitarian work. She died in a tragic car accident in 1997.**

Lady Diana Spencer began enchanting the public and international press shortly before July 29, 1981, wedding to Prince Charles of Wales, heir to the British throne, in a ceremony that was broadcast worldwide. The media's obsessive fascination with the Princess of Wales hardly waned over the years and at times became frenetic, particularly in the mid-1990s as her marriage to Prince Charles became increasingly unstable.

On February 29, 1996, the Princess announced that she had agreed to a divorce. True to her high-profile image, in March of 1996 Diana suggested to Charles that they announce their divorce on television; according to *The Daily Telegraph*, Diana argued that such an appearance "would help the nation as much as themselves." After some stalling, Prince Charles agreed to the request and a hefty financial settlement of almost $23 million, plus $600,000 a year for the maintenance of Diana's private office. Diana, meanwhile, lost her title of Her Royal Highness and right to the throne, but kept the moniker Princess of Wales and continued to live in Kensington Palace. Just over a year after the divorce, Diana was killed in a car accident in Paris.

Rumors about the stability of Charles and Diana's marriage surfaced repeatedly over the years. Many royal watchers say the union was destined for trouble because the fairy tale wedding raised expectations that most couples would find impossible to meet. Others cited the difference in the couple's ages and interests, and Charles's long-time friendship with Camilla Parker Bowles, a woman he had once asked to marry him.

Diana Frances Spencer was born on July 1, 1961, in Norfolk, England, the third of the Lord and Lady Althorp's

four children. She grew up at Park House, a mansion in Norfolk located next door to the royal family's Sandringham estate. One of Diana's playmates was Prince Andrew, Charles's brother. Diana's mother, the Honorable Frances Shand-Kydd, is the daughter of a wealthy Anglo-Irish baron. Lady Fermoy, Diana's grandmother, was for years chief lady-in-waiting to the Queen Mother. Diana's father, the Viscount Althorp who became an earl in 1975, was a remote descendant of the Stuart kings and a direct descendant of King Charles II (1630-1685). The Spencers have served the Crown as courtiers for generations and are related to the Sir Winston Churchills and at least eight U.S. presidents, including George Washington, John Adams, and Franklin D. Roosevelt. Diana's younger brother Charles is Queen Elizabeth's godson, and her father was the late Queen Mary's godson and former personal aide to both King George VI and Queen Elizabeth.

Diana, a quiet and reserved child, had a relatively happy home life until she was eight years old, when her parents went through a bitter divorce, and her mother ran off with the heir to a wallpaper fortune. Her father eventually won the custody battle over their son and three daughters. Diana, who remained close to her mother, subsequently became depressed. In 1976 the Earl Spencer married Raine Legge, the daughter of British romance novelist Barbara Cartland. Apparently, the Spencer children and their stepmother had a stormy relationship.

Diana's academic career was unremarkable. She was tutored at home until the age of nine, when she was sent to Riddlesworth Hall in Norfolk. Her "major moment of academic distinction," according to *People,* was when she won an award for taking especially good care of her guinea pig, Peanuts. At the age of 12, Diana began attending the exclusive West Heath School in Sevenoaks, Kent, where she developed a passion for ballet and later Prince Charles. She hung his picture above her cot at the boarding school and told a classmate, as reported by *People,* "I would love to be a dancer—or Princess of Wales."

Diana became bored with academics and dropped out of West Heath at the age of 16. Her father sent her to a Swiss finishing school, Chateau d'Oex. She became homesick within a few months and returned to Norfolk. For a while she hired herself out as a cleaning woman, eventually finding work as a kindergarten teacher's aide. Her father bought her a three-bedroom flat not far from fashionable Sloane Street and Knightsbridge, where Diana helped her three roommates with housekeeping and cooking duties.

Although Prince Charles had known Diana, literally the girl next door, for virtually all of her life, he regarded her as a playmate for his younger brothers. He later dated Diana's older sister, Lady Sarah, who eventually became Mrs. Neil McCorquodale. Lady Sarah reintroduced Charles and Diana at a 1977 pheasant hunt at Althorp. "[Diana] taught him how to tap-dance on the terrace," a family friend once told *McCall's.* "He thought she was adorable . . . full of vitality and terribly sweet." Charles was struck by "what a very amusing and jolly and attractive 16-year-old she was," *Time* reported. Diana concluded that the prince was "pretty amazing."

Charles thought Diana was too young to consider as a marriage prospect, however, and the romance didn't bloom for another three years. In July of 1980 Diana visited the royal family's Balmoral Castle in Scotland to see her sister, Lady Jane, who was married to Robert Fellowes, the queen's assistant secretary. Once again Diana ran into Charles, and the two walked and fished together. Charles was quoted as saying in *Time,* "I began to realize what was going on in my mind and hers in particular." Diana was invited back in September.

Soon afterward, reporters began to suspect the nature of her relationship with Charles and began to hound Diana mercilessly, photographing her with the prince at her London flat and once while holding one of the children at the nursery school where she taught. To her horror, the sun behind her back clearly outlined her thighs through her skirt in a photo that has since been reprinted many times. At one point Diana's mother fired off a letter to the London *Times,* demanding, "Is it necessary or fair to harass my daughter daily?," as quoted in *Time.*

Charles proposed to Diana at dinner in his Buckingham Palace apartment on February 3, 1981. Diana was the first British citizen to marry the heir to the throne since 1659, when Prince James—later James II—married Lady Anne Hyde. In addition, Diana was an Anglican, presenting no legal obstacles to marriage with the man who, as king, would head the Church of England. Her past was pristine, a matter of great importance to the royal family. A well-known saying soon made the rounds in the press: Diana had a history, but no past.

According to a *Time* interview with the royal couple, Charles said the courtship was conducted "like a military operation" on national television. He proposed over dinner for two before Diana's February 6 departure for a vacation in Australia. "I wanted to give Diana a chance to think about it—to think if it was going to be too awful. If she didn't like the idea, she could say she didn't. . . . But in fact she said. . ." Diana interrupted, "Yes, quite promptly. I never had any doubts about it." When Diana returned from her trip, Charles asked the Earl Spencer for his daughter's hand. Diana resigned her teaching post and moved into the palace's Clarence House with the Queen Mother, where she was instructed in royal protocol.

The Archbishop of Canterbury and 25 other clerics officiated at the wedding of Prince Charles and Lady Diana on July 29, 1981. A congregation of 2,500 and a worldwide TV audience of about 750 million watched the ceremony under the dome of St. Paul's Cathedral. Five mounted military police officers led Diana in her glass coach from Clarence House to St. Paul's. Two million spectators—whose behavior was kept in check by 4,000 policemen and 2,228 soldiers—jammed the processional route.

Soon afterward, Diana's professional life became an endless round of ceremonial tree plantings, introductions, and public appearances. She was scheduled for 170 official engagements during the year following the royal wedding. In their first seven years of marriage, the Prince and Princess of Wales made official visits to 19 countries and held hundreds of handshaking sessions. But Diana was shielded from the press, never making any public statements—except for those approved by the palace—or giving a private interview to any reporter.

There seemed to be no doubts about Charles and Diana's love for each other in those early days. "Diana seems absolutely floating on air when she's around the Prince—squeezing his hand, nuzzling his cheek or leaning her head on his shoulder," Rita Lachman, a close friend of the Spencers, observed in *McCall's.* "And although the Prince's training has made his behavior more restrained, it is obvious how he feels about her." Later developments would make it appear that the relationship was rocky even before the marriage, but the public would only see the fairy tale facade.

On November 5, 1981, the palace announced that the Princess of Wales was expecting a child. Charles was present when his wife gave birth at London's St. Mary's Hospital 11 months after the royal wedding. Dr. George Pinker, Queen Elizabeth's gynecologist, attended the birth. Prince William, nicknamed Wills, was born in June of 1982. A second son, Harry, was born two years later in September of 1984. Diana was said to be a doting mother, trying to raise the children as normally as possible, away from the glare of publicity.

After giving birth, Diana dropped 30 pounds from her 5-foot 10-inch frame, according to a *People* correspondent, "leaving it lean and elegant—a splendid rack for the designer rags she assembled with impressive taste. Almost overnight a pretty girl was transformed into a statuesque belle." Around that time, reports alleging that Diana suffered from anorexia nervosa first began to surface.

Over the years, Diana immersed herself in numerous charitable causes. She became involved in such social issues such as homelessness and drug abuse, visited leprosariums in Nigeria and Indonesia, shook hands with patients at an AIDS ward in a Middlesex Hospital, and once visited victims of an IRA (Irish Republican Army) bombing in Northern Ireland. In 1990, *People* noted, Diana was the patron of 44 charities, making more than 180 visits on their behalf the previous year. "I don't just want to be a name on a letterhead," the princess was quoted as saying in the *Saturday Evening Post*.

In 1989 Diana became a patron of Relate, Britain's leading marriage counseling agency. She once addressed a crowd at Relate's Family of the Year ceremony, as quoted in *People*: "Marriage offers stability, and maybe that is why nearly 7,000 couples a week begin new family lives of their own. Sadly, for many, reality fails to live up to expectations. When that happens, most couples draw on new reserves of love and strength."

Ironically, Diana's own marriage apparently had been ailing for years. Rumors about marital problems surfaced just a few years after the wedding. The couple's first public spat, at a pheasant hunt at the queen's Norfolk estate, was followed two days later by another public row. The fairy tale turned into a soap opera, according to a British gossip columnist who characterized the situation as "*Dallas* in the palace." Many reports alleged that Charles quickly became disenchanted with his bride and that he was henpecked and obsessed with organic gardening and spiritualism. Diana was said to be bored, temperamental, self-absorbed, and clothes-mad.

Over the next few years Charles and Diana's widely varying intellectual and social interests became apparent: He was an intellectual who preferred to read philosophical and thought-provoking literature, while Diana was partial to romance novels. Charles enjoyed polo and horseback riding; Diana once fell off a horse and had lost any passion she had for riding. He enjoyed opera; she preferred ballet and rock music. The media began tracking the number of days the two spent apart, noting Charles's lengthy stays away from home. Diana once said in public, *People* reported, that being a princess "isn't all it's cracked up to be." Buckingham Palace maintained a stony silence.

The public's fascination with Diana fueled the media's insatiable hunger for sensational news about the princess. Coverage of the royal family was said to be more critical and crudely inquisitive than at any time since the early nineteenth century. As Suzanne Lowry, a writer for London's *Sunday Times* once wrote, according to *Time:* "What Diana clearly didn't understand when she took that fateful step [of marrying Charles] was that she could never get back into that nice, cozy private nursery again. . . . As James Whitaker [the London *Mirror's* royal watcher] might say to Diana with a nudge, 'You didn't know you were marrying us too, did you?'"

While some of Charles and Diana's problems were blamed on incompatibility, many royal watchers speculated that trouble stemmed from the attention lavished on Diana, while Charles was largely ignored. When the prince de-

livered a serious speech, for example, the newspapers would mention it briefly below a large photo of Diana in her latest fashion. One longtime insider revealed in *People*, "The problems of the marriage have come out in the open because Di's self-confidence has developed. She now appreciates her own incredible sexuality and the fact that the world is at her feet. This adoration used to terrify her. Now she quite enjoys the effect she has."

Media coverage of the royal family only increased after Prince Andrew married Sarah Ferguson in July of 1986. As *People* characterized it: "After five years in a corset of decorum, Di was ready to bust loose, and fun-loving Fergie was just the girl to help her unlace. . . . Soon the merry wives of Windsor were cutting up in public." Charles reportedly scolded Diana once for "trashing the dignity of the royal family," *People* reported, and Diana chided him for being "stuffy, boring and old before his time." The princess eventually tired of the antics and settled down.

In June of 1991, young Prince William sustained a skull fracture after being hit in the head with a golf club. Diana spent two nights with her son in the hospital, while Charles reportedly dropped in once, on his way to an opera. From that point on, *Time* pointed out, the "tabloids have smelled blood." A month later, Charles and Diana spent her 30th birthday apart. The press relished the news, ignoring the fact that Diana sported a new gold and mother-of-pearl bracelet the next day.

One of three biographies of Diana published in 1992, Andrew Morton's *Diana: Her True Story* alleged that Diana attempted suicide five times in the early 1980s—the first only six months after the wedding, while she was pregnant with William. The episodes were characterized as cries for help rather than serious attempts to end her life. Morton's book, along with the others, also claimed that Diana suffered from bulimia.

Morton's biography, sympathetic to Diana, is said to be the most damaging to the prince, portraying Diana as a martyr with a cold fish for a husband. The book was given more credence than others because, as *Newsweek* reported, the "revelations were unusually specific, extraordinarily well sourced and . . . they [made] sense in light of Charles and Diana's recent public behavior." Rumors surfaced that Diana collaborated with Morton—or at least approved the project, giving close friends and relatives permission to be interviewed. Diana's father, who died of a heart attack on March 29, 1992, had sold dozens of her childhood photographs to Morton's publisher.

Amid rumors in the fall of 1992 that a Wales separation announcement was forthcoming came intense media scrutiny of Diana's male friendships. A retired bank manager contacted the *Sun* in 1990, offering a tape recording of a chummy 1989 cellular telephone conversation between a man—supposedly Diana's close friend, James Gilbey—and a woman he believed to be Diana. The press subsequently resurrected old tales about an alleged dalliance between Diana and her riding instructor, Major James Hewitt. These claims were spelled out in Anna Pasternak's book *Princess in Love*. On December 9, 1992, it was formally announced that the royal couple was separating.

In 1993 Diana announced that due to exhaustion from the intense media scrutiny, she would be withdrawing from public life, though she would continue her charity work. For the next two years, with a few exceptions, she kept a fairly low media profile. During this time she sought government advice about how she might have some role as an ambassador for Britain, but no firm arrangements were made.

In 1994, Prince Charles granted a wide-ranging television interview to Jonathan Dimbleby, which was broadcast at the same time that Dimbleby's biography of Charles appeared in bookstores. In an uncharacteristically frank interview, Charles admitted his relationship with Camilla Parker Bowles, though he claimed this relationship began only in 1986, after his marriage with Diana had completely broken down. However, after the couple's divorce was announced in 1996, it seemed apparent that Charles had carried a torch for Camilla Parker Bowles since before his marriage to Diana, and it was speculated that he would marry her.

In November of the following year, Diana responded with a frank interview of her own, on BBC's *Panorama* program. The interview was particularly controversial because Diana had informed Queen Elizabeth of the interview only after it had already taken place, and just days before it was scheduled to be broadcast. The interview drew the largest viewing audience in *Panorama's* 43-year history—21.1 million viewers, from a total British population of 57 million. Typically, Diana's interview drew more attention than Charles' had; only 14 million people had watched his interview the year before.

According to a front page story in the *Daily Telegraph*, "her composure and fluency could have rivalled that of a statesman." While the BBC stated that Diana had not been given editorial control over the program, she was obviously well-prepared for the difficult questions. The *Daily Telegraph's* media correspondent pointed out that "no question took her by surprise, and no answers were fluffed. Some of the toughest ones produced distinctly unspontaneous lines, such as 'Well there were three of us in the marriage so it was a bit crowded,'" referring to Charles's long-standing affair with Bowles.

The *Panorama* interview seemed to put to rest any possibility of a reconciliation between the Prince and Princess of Wales. Shortly thereafter, the Queen took the unprecedented step of asking the couple to consider a divorce. On February 29, 1996, Diana gave her consent to a divorce—though again she violated protocol by not informing the Queen first. It was announced in July of 1996 that the royals had worked out the divorce terms. Diana would continue to be involved in all decisions about the children and the couple would share access to them, she would remain at Kensington Palace, and would be known as Diana, Princess of Wales—loosing the prefix H.R.H. (Her Royal Highness) and any right to ascend to the British throne. However, she kept all of her jewelry and received a lump-sum alimony settlement of almost $23 million, and Charles agreed to pay for the annual maintenance of her private office.

Diana continued her diplomatic role as Princess of Wales after the divorce. She visited terminally ill people in hospitals, traveled to Bosnia to meet the victims of land mines, and met Mother Teresa in New York City's South Bronx in June 1997. Romantically, the press linked her with Hasnat Khan, a Pakistani-born heart surgeon and Dodi al Fayed, whose father owned Harrods Department Store in London. However, her number one priority remained her two sons.

As Diana spent more time with Fayed, the paparazzi hounded the couple, who could not go anywhere without cameras following close behind. On August 31, 1997, the paparazzi followed the couple after they dined at the Ritz Hotel in Paris (owned by Fayed's father). The combination of the pursuing paparazzi, driving at a high rate of speed, and having a drunk driver behind the wheel, all played into the automobile accident which claimed Princess Diana's life. Some witnesses stated that photographers frantically snapped pictures and obstructed police officers and rescue workers from aiding the victims. The driver and Fayed died at the scene; Princess Diana died from her injuries a few hours later.

Photographers on the scene faced possible charges under France's "Good Samaritan" law, which requires people to come to the aid of accident victims on public roads. However, several blood tests showed that driver Henri Paul was legally drunk. Legal experts believed that the investigation into Diana's death was likely to take months, possibly years, to determine how much the paparazzi, alcohol, and speed were to blame.

The world mourned for "the people's princess" with an outpouring of emotion and flowers. People waited up to eight hours to sign condolence books at St. James Palace, and 100,000 people per day passed through Kensington Palace, where Diana lived. Her mother, Francis Shand Kydd, stated, "I thank God for the gift of Diana and for all her loving and giving. I give her back to Him, with my love, pride and admiration to rest in peace."

However, Britons and the British press soon lashed out at the royal family, who did not share in the public grieving. Headlines begged the family to "show us you care." Truly surprised by the backlash, Queen Elizabeth II went on live television the day before the funeral. It was only the second time in the queen's 45-year reign that she had appeared on live TV, not counting her annual Christmas greeting. She spoke as "your queen and as a grandmother," and stated "I want to pay tribute to Diana myself. She was an exceptional and gifted human being."

Diana's funeral was held in Westminster Abbey on September 6th. Her sons, Princes Willam and Harry, her brother, Earl Spencer, her ex-husband, Prince Charles, and her ex-father-in-law, Prince Philip, as well as five representatives from each of the 110 charities she represented, followed the coffin during part of the funeral procession. Elton John re-wrote the song "Candle in the Wind" and sang "Goodbye England's Rose" for his close friend. It was estimated that 2.5 billion people watched Princess Diana's funeral on television, nearly half the population of the world. One royal watcher stated, "Diana made the monarchy more in touch with people."

## Further Reading

Morton, Andrew, *Diana: Her True Story*, Simon & Schuster, 1992.

Morton, Andrew, *Diana: her new life*, Pocket Star, 1995.

Davies, Nicholas, *Diana: the lonely princess*, Carol Pub., 1996.

Clarke, Mary *Little girl lost: the troubled childhood of Princess Diana by the woman who raised her*, Carol Pub., 1996.

*Daily Telegraph*, November 29, 1994; November 15, 1995; November 22, 1995; February 12, 1996; February 29, 1996; March 4, 1996.

*Esquire*, June 1992.

*Maclean's*, July 24, 1989; August 5, 1991; June 15, 1992.

*McCall's*, June 1982.

*Newsweek*, October 28, 1985; February 6, 1989; June 22, 1992; September 15, 1997.

*New York Times*, March 30, 1992; June 9, 1992; June 20, 1992.

*People*, Spring 1988; July 16, 1990; September 14, 1992; September 15, 1997; September 22, 1997.

*Saturday Evening Post*, September 1989.

*Time*, March 9, 1981; August 3, 1981; February 28, 1983; November 11, 1985; July 29, 1991; September 15, 1997. □

# Bartolomeu Dias de Novais

**Bartolomeu Dias de Novais (died 1500) was a Portuguese explorer who discovered the Cape of Good Hope and opened the sea route to the Indian Ocean.**

It is not known when or where Bartolomeu Dias was born, and no information has survived about his early life. He emerged from obscurity only in 1487, when he sailed from Portugal with orders from King John II to continue exploration beyond a landmark raised by Diogo Cão in 1486 on the coast of South-West Africa. The King instructed Dias to discover a sea route to India which bypassed Moslem–dominated routes between the East and Europe and to seek information about the Christian empire of Abyssinia.

## Journey of Discovery

In command of two caravels, each of about 100 modern tons, and of a storeship of about double that size, Dias left the Tagus River in August 1487. Beyond the farthest point reached by Cão, Dias made a close coasting. On Jan. 6, 1488, off the Serra dos Reis, in modern South Africa, Dias left the coast and was out of sight of land for 13 days. He steered eastward and found no land so altered course to the north. He closed the coast again opposite a river, the Gouritz of today. The coast ran eastward, and on February 3 he entered and named the bay of São Bras (modern Mossel Bay). Here he took in fresh water and bartered livestock from the local inhabitants, the Khoi-Khoi (Hottentots).

Continuing east, Dias came to a bay which he called Golfo da Roca; it was soon to be known as the Baia da Lagoa, a name subsequently corrupted to Algoa Bay. In this bay the crews verged on mutiny: they protested their shortage of provisions, pointed out that they had reached the extremity of the continent, and urged Dias to turn for home.

A council agreed to this course, but Dias won consent to continue for a few more days.

At the end of the stipulated term the caravels reached a river which Dias called the Infante (probably modern Keiskama) after the captain of the second caravel. The coast was running decisively to the northeast, the sea became warmer, and it was clear that the expedition had indeed rounded Africa and reached the Indian Ocean. At the earliest conjunction of suitable site and favorable weather, at what came later to be called Kwaaihoek, 4 miles west of the Bushman's River, Dias landed and supervised the erection of a *padrão*, a square limestone pillar cut and inscribed in Portugal and surmounted by a block with the Portuguese coat of arms and a cross. It was a landmark, an assertion of Portuguese sovereignty, and a symbol of Christianity. Dedicated to St. Gregory, it was raised on March 12, 1488.

On May 16 Dias gave the name St. Brandon to a cape which soon became known as Agulhas. Dias discovered and named the Cape of Good Hope because, a contemporary recorded, "it gave indication and expectation of the discovery of India." There, on June 6, 1488, he probably raised another *Padrão*, dedicated to St. Philip. On Dias Point, west of Lüderitz, on July 25 he raised another *padrão*, dedicated to St. James. The caravels returned to the Tagus in December 1488. Dias had proved the sea route into the Indian Ocean.

## Later Career

Dias helped administer the Guinea gold trade until 1494, when King Manuel I appointed him to supervise the construction of two square-rigged ships for Vasco da Gama's expedition. Dias kept the squadron company as far as the Cape Verde Islands, when he turned off to Guinea.

On the return of Vasco da Gama, Manuel dispatched a fleet of 13 vessels under Pedro Álvares Cabral to the Indian Ocean to profit by the discoveries. In the fleet were 4 caravels under Bartolomeu Dias, who was instructed to found a trading station and fortress at the gold-exporting port of Sofala. The expedition left Brazil on May 2, 1500. On May 12 a comet came into view, "a prognostication of the sad event that was to take place," the Portuguese chronicler João de Barros remarked. The comet disappeared on May 23. The next day a sudden storm over whelmed 4 ships, which sank with all hands; among those lost was Dias.

## Further Reading

There are numerous books on the Portuguese voyages of exploration at the end of the 15th century. Recommended are Edgar Prestage, *The Portuguese Pioneers* (London: 1933) and "The Search for the Sea Route to India" in Arthur Percival Newton, ed. *Travel and Travellers of the Middle Ages* (New York: Alfred A. Knopf, 1930); Mary Seymour Lucas, *Vast Horizons* (New York: The Viking Press, 1943); Boies Penrose, *Travel and Discovery in the Renaissance, 1420-1620* (Cambridge: Harvard University Press, 1952); and Gerald R. Crone, *The Discovery of the East* (London: Hamish Hamilton, 1972).

Probably the best account of Dias's voyage is in Eric Axelson, *Congo to Cape: Early Portuguese Explorers* (New York: 1974). Boies Penrose, *Travel and Discovery in the Renaissance* (1955), and J. H. Parry, *The Age of Reconnaisance* (1963), are excellent surveys of European overseas expansion that include mention of Dias. Useful background is provided in Eric Axelson, *South-East Africa, 1488-1530* (1940). □

# José de la Cruz Porfirio Díaz

**José de la Cruz Porfirio Díaz (1830-1915) was a Mexican general and political leader. During his 34-year, virtually unchallenged rule of Mexico the economy grew and the country remained at peace despite its anachronistic social system.**

L atin American countries in the 19th century remained chained to a colonial past with few exceptions. Mexico, one of the Western Hemisphere's most poorly governed states, had suffered more than most. After half a century of independence its economy lay ruined, its people were exhausted by civil war, and over half its territory had been lost to the United States. The autocratic government of Porfirio Díaz sought to bring order out of this chaos and to make Mexico into a modern industrialized state. A charismatic and capable leader, he almost succeeded in this pro-

tean task, yet finally failed because he gave economic development far too high a priority over social justice.

Porfirio Díaz was born in the southern Mexican state of Oaxaca into a middle-class urban family of Spanish-Indian ancestry. His father, a moderately well-to-do veterinarian and innkeeper, died when Porfirio was only 3 years old. Though as a child he learned carpentry and shoemaking to help support his family, his mother sent him to study in a seminary in hope of his attaining the priesthood. But Díaz did not want to enter the clergy; he left the school and entered the Institute of Arts and Sciences in the city of Oaxaca, where he studied law under Benito Juárez. Díaz's legal training left him a convinced liberal determined to break the stranglehold that the professional army, the Church, and large landholders held over contemporary Mexico.

## Military Career

In 1846 Díaz had enlisted in the national guard to combat the North American invaders, but he did not participate in the fighting. He later attributed his anticlericalism to his witnessing priests distributing tracts favoring the foreign invasion. In the 1850s he served as a guerrilla officer against the conservative clerical forces seeking to prevent liberal reforms. In 1861 the victorious liberals appointed him a brigadier general.

The conservative defeat was rapidly followed by the French intervention, and Díaz again fought but this time to keep the Austrian Archduke Maximilian off the throne of

Mexico. In 1862 he participated in the successful Mexican defense of Puebla but was later captured when the city surrendered. He escaped, raised another liberal army, and laid siege to the city of Oaxaca. Again he was captured only to escape once more. By 1865 he had established a reputation as a brilliant guerrilla fighter and as a man able to overcome great odds despite adversity. Juárez, the liberal president, appointed Díaz commander of his eastern forces. Díaz governed eight states and commanded some 20,000 troops. In June 1867 Díaz took the city of Mexico from the conservatives, who had been abandoned by the French. He ruled the city as governor until July, when he presented it to Juárez, who welcomed him coldly. Díaz also handed over the eastern army's large treasury to the national government. At this time he was one of Mexico's most famous men and a threat to the determined Juárez, who believed himself the only one capable of governing Mexico.

## Politician and Rebel

In 1867 Díaz ran against Juárez for the presidency but was heavily defeated. In 1868 he retired from the army to his native state of Oaxaca, where the grateful citizens had given him a large farm, La Noria. Hoping to increase his prestige by a short retirement, Díaz devoted himself to the raising of sugarcane. In 1871 he again opposed Juárez for the presidency in an election marked by much bitterness over Juárez's decision to seek a fourth term. The election ended in a tie between Díaz, Juárez, and Sebastián Lerdo de Tejada, and the Mexican Congress made Juárez president and Lerdo vice president.

The disappointed Díaz retired to Oaxaca, where he staged a revolt whose program promised effective suffrage and no reelection. Juárez acted quickly by sending troops to Oaxaca to crush the rebellion, which cost Felix Díaz, Porfirio's brother, his life. Porfirio fled to the coastal state of Nayarit, but Juárez's victory was soon followed by his death in 1872, bringing Lerdo the presidency. Díaz accepted a general amnesty and opened a furniture factory in Veracruz, while he prepared for another try at the presidency. In 1876, after Lerdo announced plans to succeed himself, Díaz again revolted. Lerdo's regime, plagued by popular apathy and a querulous military, soon collapsed and Lerdo fled into exile. Díaz then ran unopposed and was elected to fill Lerdo's unexpired term.

## Ruler of Mexico

Díaz's 34-year rule is known as the *Porfiriato;* it was a period of relative peace and economic growth. During his first term Díaz began to reestablish the federal government's power over the diverse Mexican states. He enlarged and gave great power to a constabulary, the Rurales. They destroyed many of the bandit gangs which had proliferated during the civil wars and later crushed all political opposition to Díaz's rule. He also formed a compromise with the Catholic Church, by which the federal government would not harass the Church if the latter would not interfere in Mexican politics.

In 1880 Díaz left the presidency to Gen. Manuel González, a longtime supporter and friend. Díaz became governor of Oaxaca and watched while González ran the country into bankruptcy. Friends of the government made huge fortunes in public-land speculation, and foreign companies bought up huge tracts of Mexican land. The government reversed the old Spanish mining laws and allowed foreigners to purchase subsoil rights, or ownership of all oils and metals contained in the ground. The mining industry entered a boom period in which Mexico produced more gold and silver in 20 years than it had in the previous 4 centuries. Díaz, a widower, meanwhile had contracted his second marriage, to Carmen Romero Rubio, the daughter of a rich supporter of Lerdo. This marriage, sometimes called the "aristocratization of Porfirio Díaz," marked the rough mestizo general's entrance into the best Creole society. Carmen, a devout Catholic, not only made Díaz socially respectable but also helped form a tacit alliance between the government and the Mexican Catholic Church.

In 1884 Díaz abandoned his "no reelection" policy and again assumed the Mexican presidency. Continually reelected until his violent overthrow, Díaz was then free to pursue further the policies begun in 1876. Political peace was maintained through the Rurales and the policy known as "bread or club." Outstanding opponents were given government jobs or rich concessions; those who refused such bribes faced death, exile, or prison. Political power lay with Díaz, his old military cronies, and a small group of wealthy Creoles, known as the Científicos.

## Economic Progress

The Científicos, most prominent in the 1890s, cleverly adopted the positivism of the French philosopher Auguste Comte as a justification for their increasing monopoly over the nation's wealth. Defining their program as one of "freedom, order, and progress," they tried to establish a religion of science based on the cold indexes of Mexico's expanding economy. The Científicos saw Mexico's future best served by massive white European immigration, which would relegate other groups to a permanently inferior role. The army launched campaigns against the Yaquí tribes in the north and the Mayas in the south, while the government press defined the indigenous people as a "national burden."

In 1893 the prominent Científico José Ives Limantour became minister of finance, and Mexico became one of Latin America's most prosperous nations. By cutting the military budget, the astute banker gave Mexico its first budgetary surplus in years; railroad trackage increased to 16,000 miles as foreign trade quadrupled over the 1870 level. The new transportation system allowed domestic industries such as beer, pulque, and textile mills to develop along railroad lines. In 1903 Mexico built its first steel mill in Monterrey. By 1910 Mexico was producing some 800 million barrels of oil per year. Limantour also abolished the sales tax and put Mexico on the gold standard.

## Tides of Discontent

For most of rural Mexico the *Porfiriato* vaunted "order and progress" had meant economic and social disaster. In 1910 most rural workers earned about the same wage that they had earned in 1810. At the same time the cost of living had increased alarmingly. A rising population and a decreasing productivity of land resulted in many Mexican peasants' existing beneath subsistence level, while the fortunes of the Porfirian aristocracy grew yearly. Only a few peasants were able to find jobs on the railroads or in the growing industries, and many migrated to the United States seeking employment. Despite many promises illiteracy stood at about 87 percent.

The underdevelopment of rural Mexico was heightened by the government's actions. Laws requiring clear land title, surveying, and the dissolution of communal holdings led to the creation of huge estates at the expense of smallholders. The government sold off public lands to foreigners and cronies at bargain prices. Only the large estates could get improvement loans from the banking system. The government's policy of creating large efficient estates to produce export crops caused growing concern among those who held small ranches and farms. Later, those rural middle classes were to compose the backbone of the revolutionary forces. From 84 to 95 percent of the rural families had no land at all, while wealthy families often had estates running into millions of acres. The Terrazas family had 13.5 million acres in Chihuahua, while the Escandón estate in Hidalgo stretched for 90 miles.

## The Revolution

In 1910 the Porfirian elite prepared to celebrate a century of Mexican independence. Confident after 34 years of peaceful rule, they were unaware that their carefully contrived system stood on the verge of collapse. The young were impatient with foreign economic control, the destruction of the indigenous peoples, and the hoarding of political power by the Porfirian elite. The ranchers of the north and the communities of the south, still independent and armed, feared that they would become rapidly submerged into large haciendas, and labor in mining and textiles was becoming restive.

In 1907 Díaz made a critical political error. The aging president told James Creelman, a North American journalist, that Mexico was ready for democracy and that he was about to retire. The interview, published in English and intended for foreign consumption, soon reached Mexico. Opposition parties began to form throughout the nation as both the ambitious and the sincerely critical sought to find a form of government better able to reconcile development and social justice. After some confusion most opposition coalesced around Francisco Madero, the wealthy scion of a prominent Mexican family from the northern state of Coahuila.

Too late Díaz tried to correct his error. In 1910 he reelected himself and jailed Madero. The latter, now a national hero, escaped and called for revolution. As the country rose, the weak army collapsed. Díaz, deserted by many of his followers and without effective armed forces, resigned office on May 25, 1911. He fled to France, where he died in relative poverty on July 2, 1915.

## Further Reading

There is very little written in English on Díaz. The best biography is probably Carleton Beals, *Porfirio Díaz: Dictator of Mexico* (1932). Useful information may also be found in John Kenneth Turner, *Barbarous Mexico* (1911; 4th ed. 1914); Henry Bamford Parkes, *A History of Mexico* (1938; 3d ed. 1960); Daniel Cosío Villegas, *The United States versus Porfirio Díaz* (1956; trans. 1963); and James D. Cockcroft, *Intellectual Precursors of the Mexican Revolution* (1969). An excellent popular history of the revolution that began with the overthrow of Díaz is Ronald Atkin, *Revolution! Mexico, 1910-1920* (1970). □

# Bernal Díaz del Castillo

**The Spanish soldier Bernal Díaz del Castillo (ca. 1496-ca. 1584) was a member of the expedition that conquered the Aztec empire. His "A True History of the Conquest of New Spain" is the most complete contemporary chronicle of that event.**

Bernal Díaz del Castillo was born in Medina del Campo of a respectable although not distinguished family. He was enchanted by tales of the fortunes to be found in newly discovered America, and in 1514 he left for the New World in the entourage of Pedrarias, who had been appointed governor of Castilla del Oro (the Isthmus of Panama and adjacent mainland of South America). Díaz was soon disenchanted with the prospects in this area and moved on to Cuba. While based there, he participated in two expeditions which explored the coasts of the Gulf of Mexico in 1517 and 1518, respectively.

In 1519 Díaz joined the expedition organized by Hernán Cortés for the conquest of Mexico and participated in the campaigns which led in 1521 to the fall of Tenochtitlán, the Aztec capital. His exact status in the enterprise is not clear. He intimates that he exercised some authority and enjoyed the confidence of Cortés, but other evidence indicates that he was little more than a common foot soldier.

After the conquest of the Aztecs, Díaz settled in the province of Coatzacoalcos, southeast of Veracruz, where he had been awarded grants of land and native labor. These properties, however, provided him with only a modest livelihood, so in 1540 he went to Spain to plead for more substantial recognition of his merits and services. He was rewarded by a somewhat better allocation of lands and indigenous people in the province of Guatemala. Here he settled, probably in 1541, and became a respected citizen, a municipal official, and the father of a numerous progeny, legitimate and illegitimate. But until his death about 1584, he complained of poverty and bemoaned the inconspicuous rewards he had received for his services to the King.

## History of the Conquest

Possibly while still in Mexico, Díaz conceived the idea of recording his memories of the Conquest, but it was not until the early 1550s that he really began to write. The project progressed slowly. Then in the 1560s he read a book entitled *The History of the Conquest of Mexico* (1552), written by Francisco López de Gómara, a former chaplain of the Cortés family. Gómara's account appeared to glorify the role of Cortés at the expense of the common soldier, an interpretation that Díaz resented; it provided him with an incentive to complete his own account, which he entitled *A True History of the Conquest of New Spain*. In 1568, about age 72, he completed his task and in the mid-1570s sent a copy of the manuscript to Spain for publication. It did not appear in print, however, until 1632 and then only after the editor, Friar Alonzo Remón, had considerably altered the text. It was not until 1904-1905 that a true edition appeared, prepared by the Mexican historian Genaro García from the original manuscript, which had survived in Guatemala.

The *True History* begins in 1517 and terminates in 1568, but the bulk of it concentrates on the epic years 1519-1521. Díaz admitted and deplored his unpolished style, and it is in fact that of a common soldier. The narrative is prolix and digressive; events are sometimes transposed and observations and interpretations often naive. Yet he possessed a deep honesty and remarkable memory. For the most part his account is factually correct. He was also a superlative raconteur with a deep sense of personal involvement and a flair for the dramatic. The *True History* is not only a major historical document but also one of the greatest adventure stories of all time.

## Further Reading

Genaro Garcia's edition of Díaz's history was translated into English by Alfred Percival Maudslay and published by the Hakluyt Society as *The True History of the Conquest of New Spain* (5 vols., 1908-1916). Volume 1 contains useful notes on Díaz and his work. Several abridged English editions appeared subsequently. A good, recent biography of the chronicler is Herbert Cerwin, *Bernal Díaz: Historian of the Conquest* (1963). □

# Gustavo Díaz Ordaz

**Gustavo Díaz Ordaz (1911-1979) was president of Mexico from 1964 to 1970, a period of considerable world tension. His administration did not escape the turmoil as his government killed several hundred Mexican citizens in the attempt to quell student demonstrations in 1968.**

Gustavo Díaz Ordaz was born in San Andrés Chalchicomula (now called Ciudad Serdán), Puebla, on March 11, 1911, the son of a public accountant and a school teacher. His early schooling completed in Oaxaca, Guadalajara, and Mexico City, he returned to his home state, received his law degree from the University of Puebla in 1937, and worked briefly as a public prosecutor.

After teaching law at his alma mater for two years he made his political debut as a congressman from his home state. He served in Mexico's lower house from 1943 to 1946, when he was elected to the senate where he served until 1952. His national reputation began to flower when he was brought into the Secretariat of Gobernación as the director of the Department of Legal Affairs in 1953. Five years later President Adolfo López Mateos named him secretary of gobernación, a position long considered to be a training ground for future Mexican presidents. As a cabinet member he showed himself hyper-sensitive to anti-government demonstrations. In 1959 he crushed a strike of railroad workers and arrested a number of leftist politicians. This was only a preview of things to come. Other leftists, including David A. Siquieros, one of Mexico's most famous 20th century muralists, were jailed (1960-1964) on his orders.

By the time Díaz Ordaz received the nomination of the Partido Revolucionario Institucional for president in 1964 he had established a reputation for dedication, hard work, and efficiency. He was also reported to be the most conservative and most inflexible official party candidate of the post-World War II period. His election to the high office later the same year did nothing to challenge this reputation. The Mexican Revolution, however, had progressed too far to permit any significant change in orientation, especially in matters of foreign policy. When the United States administration of Lyndon B. Johnson intervened militarily in the Dominican Republic in 1965 the anticipated critical response of the Mexican government was forthcoming. Furthermore, in spite of his own personal doubts about the Cuban revolution, Díaz Ordaz refused to honor the diplomatic and economic sanctions voted by the Organization of American States against Fidel Castro's Cuba. Some of the social programs initiated by his predecessors continued. Educational initiatives, for example, received over one-fourth of the total Mexican budget under Díaz Ordaz. But wherever the president could moderate the liberal tendencies of previous heads of state, he did so.

## Business Prospered

Díaz Ordaz proved himself a good friend of the Mexican business community. As he placed the economic future of the country increasingly in the hands of the private sector, tariff protection on the importation of foreign goods and low interest loans catered to the nation's industrialists. The agrarian sector did not fare as well. Rural poverty prompted peasant invasions of private land in southern Mexico. Rather than address the root cause, the president simply dispatched troops to dislodge the squatters. Industrialization clearly took precedence over agrarian reform.

## Student Unrest Overshadowed Olympics

Discontent with the conservative policies of Díaz Ordaz began to grow noticeably in late 1965 and 1966. University students took the lead in organizing demonstrations against the government. Federal troops were called out to disperse students on campuses in Michoacán, Sinaloa, and Sonora, and a massive strike at the National Autonomous University of Mexico in the spring of 1966 culminated with the resignation of the rector. Each incident heightened political tension within the country, but the major confrontation was still two years away.

When the International Olympic Committee accepted Mexico's bid to host the summer games of 1968, President Díaz Ordaz placed his country's prestige squarely on the line. He planned an impressive "cultural olympics" to coincide with the athletic competition. Hundreds of millions of dollars were pledged to prepare Mexico City for the onslaught of tourists. The president wanted to use the extravaganza to portray Mexico to the world as a stable and prosperous republic. To his chagrin, the result was just the opposite.

The trouble began with a trivial street fight between students from two rival Mexican schools, but the rapid escalation defied imagination. President Díaz Ordaz and General Alfonso Corona del Rosal, mayor of the Federal District, ordered out the *granaderos,* a despised paramilitary riot force. The *granaderos* did put an end to the street fight, but in the process they further politicized Mexico City students. During the next several weeks the situation deteriorated as huge demonstrations provoked violence on the streets of Mexico City. The president named his secretary of gobernación, Luis Echeverría, to deal with the angry students, but the negotiations broke down and the students threatened to disrupt the opening ceremonies of the Olympic Games. The climax came on October 2, 1968, in the Mexico City district of Tlatelolco.

The student rally was not large by later standards, perhaps only 5,000. At 6:30 in the evening police units arrived in tanks and armored vehicles. When the demonstrators failed to disband, the *granaderos* moved in and began to disperse the crowd with billy clubs and tear gas. The shooting began moments later, and before it ended several hundred students were dead. As the violence was blared in the world press, tens of thousands of Olympic-bound tourists cancelled reservations made years in advance.

### His Legacy

The national shame that engulfed Mexico following Tlatelolco was much more severe than that of the United States after the 1970 Kent State shooting, a similar incident but one of lesser magnitude. The impact was so severe that when the Díaz Ordaz administration ended in 1970 it was not remembered for any of its accomplishments, but rather for the tragedy of October 2, 1968.

After leaving office, Díaz Ordaz remained politically active with his conservative constituency, and maintained ties with the new government. In 1977, he was appointed Ambassador to Spain, but resigned amid controversy after serving only four months.

He died of a heart attack at his home in Mexico City on July 15, 1979. Conservatives, particularly conservative businessmen, lamented the loss of a proponent of government intervention to quell the social and political protests that continued to plague Mexico.

### Further Reading

A critical view of the Mexican political system under Díaz Ordaz is found in Pablo González Casanova, *Democracy in Mexico* (1970) and in *Latin American Perspectives* (Summer 1993). The nature of the domestic conflict can be traced in Evelyn P. Stevens, *Protest and Response in Mexico* (1974) and in Judith Adler Hellman, *Mexico in Crisis* (1978). □

# Charles John Huffam Dickens

**The English author Charles John Huffam Dickens (1812-1870) was, and probably still is, the most widely read Victorian novelist. He is now appreciated more for his "dark" novels than for his humorous works.**

C harles Dickens was born on Feb. 7, 1812, at Portsea (later part of Portsmouth) on the southern coast of England. He was the son of a lower-middle-class but impecunious father whose improvidence he was later to satirize in the character of Micawber in *David Copperfield.* The family's financial difficulties caused them to move about until they settled in Camden Town, a poor neighborhood of London. At the age of 12 Charles was set to work in a warehouse that handled "blacking," or shoe polish; there he mingled with men and boys of the working class. For a period of months he was also forced to live apart from his family when they moved in with his father, who had been imprisoned in the Marshalsea debtors' prison. This experience of lonely hardship was the most significant formative event of his life; it colored his view of the world in profound and varied ways and is directly or indirectly described in a number of his novels, including *The Pickwick Papers, Oliver Twist,* and *Little Dorrit,* as well as *David Copperfield.*

These early events of Dicken's life left both psychological and sociological effects. In a fragmentary autobiography Dickens wrote, "It is wonderful to me how I could have been so easily cast away at such an age. . . . My father and mother were quite satisfied. . . . My whole nature was so penetrated with grief and humiliation of such considerations, that even now, famous and caressed and happy, I often forget in my dreams that I have a dear wife and children; even that I am a man; and wander desolately back to that time of my life."

The sociological effect of the blacking factory on Dickens was to give him a firsthand acquaintance with poverty and to make him the most vigorous and influential voice of the lower classes in his age. Despite the fact that many of England's legal and social abuses were in the process of being removed by the time Dickens published his exposés of them, it remains true that he was the most widely heard spokesman of the need to alleviate the miseries of the poor.

Dickens returned to school after an inheritance (as in the fairy-tale endings of some of his novels) relieved his

father from debt, but he was forced to become an office boy at the age of 15. In the following year he became a free-lance reporter or stenographer at the law courts of London. By 1832 he had become a reporter for two London newspapers and, in the following year, began to contribute a series of impressions and sketches to other newspapers and magazines, signing some of them "Boz." These scenes of London life went far to establish his reputation and were published in 1836 as *Sketches by Boz*, his first book. On the strength of this success he married; his wife, Catherine Hogarth, was eventually to bear him 10 children.

## Early Works

In 1836 Dickens also began to publish in monthly installments *The Posthumous Papers of the Pickwick Club*. This form of serial publication became a standard method of writing and producing fiction in the Victorian period and affected the literary methods of Dickens and other novelists. So great was Dickens's success with the procedure—summed up in the formula, "Make them laugh; make them cry; make them wait"—that *Pickwick* became one of the most popular works of the time, continuing to be so after it was published in book form in 1837. The comic heroes of the novel, the antiquarian members of the Pickwick Club, scour the English countryside for local points of interest and are involved in a variety of humorous adventures which reveal the characteristics of English social life. At a later stage of the novel, the chairman of the club, Samuel Pickwick, is involved in a lawsuit which lands him in the Fleet debtors' prison. Here the lighthearted atmosphere of

the novel changes, and the reader is given intimations of the gloom and sympathy with which Dickens was to imbue his later works.

During the years of *Pickwick*'s serialization, Dickens became editor of a new monthly, *Bentley's Miscellany*. When *Pickwick* was completed, he began publishing his new novel, *Oliver Twist,* in this magazine—a practice he continued in his later magazines, *Household Worlds* and *All the Year Round. Oliver* expresses Dickens's interest in the life of the slums to the fullest, as it traces the fortunes of an innocent orphan through the London streets. It seems remarkable today that this novel's fairly frank treatment of criminals like Bill Sikes, prostitutes like Nancy, and "fences" like Fagin could have been acceptable to the Victorian reading public. But so powerful was Dickens's portrayal of the "little boy lost" amid the lowlife of the East End that the limits of his audience's tolerance were gradually stretched.

Dickens was now embarked on the most consistently successful career of any 19th-century author after Sir Walter Scott. He could do no wrong as far as his faithful readership was concerned; yet his books for the next decade were not to achieve the standard of his early triumphs. These works include: *Nicholas Nickleby* (1838-1839), still cited for its exposé of brutality at an English boys' school, Dotheboys Hall; *The Old Curiosity Shop* (1840-1841), still remembered for reaching a high (or low) point of sentimentality in its portrayal of the sufferings of Little Nell; and *Barnaby Rudge* (1841), still read for its interest as a historical novel, set amid the anti-Catholic Gordon Riots of 1780.

In 1842 Dickens, who was as popular in America as he was in England, went on a 5-month lecture tour of the United States, speaking out strongly for the abolition of slavery and other reforms. On his return he wrote *American Notes,* sharply critical of the cultural backwardness and aggressive materialism of American life. He made further capital of these observations in his next novel, *Martin Chuzzlewit* (1843-1844), in which the hero retreats from the difficulties of making his way in England only to find that survival is even more trying on the American frontier. During the years in which *Chuzzlewit* appeared, Dickens also published two Christmas stories, *A Christmas Carol* and *The Chimes,* which became as much part of the season as plum pudding.

## First Major Novels

After a year abroad in Italy, in response to which he wrote *Pictures from Italy* (1846), Dickens began to publish *Dombey and Son,* which continued till 1848. This novel established a new standard in the Dickensian novel and may be said to mark the turning point in his career. If Dickens had remained the author of *Pickwick, Oliver Twist,* and *The Old Curiosity Shop,* he might have deserved a lasting reputation only as an author of cheerful comedy and bathetic sentiment. But *Dombey,* while it includes these elements, is a realistic novel of human life in a society which had assumed more or less its modern form. As its full title indicates, *Dealings with the Firm of Dombey and Son* is a study of the influence of the values of a business society on the personal fortunes of the members of the Dombey family and those with whom they come in contact. It takes a somber view of England at mid-century, and its elegiac tone becomes characteristic of Dickens's novels for the rest of his life.

Dickens's next novel, *David Copperfield* (1849-1850), combined broad social perspective with a very strenuous effort to take stock of himself at the midpoint of his literary career. This autobiographical novel fictionalized elements of Dickens's childhood degradation, pursuit of a journalistic and literary vocation, and love life. Its achievement is to offer the first comprehensive record of the typical course of a young man's life in Victorian England. *Copperfield* is not Dickens's greatest novel, but it was his own favorite among his works, probably because of his personal engagement with the subject matter.

In 1850 Dickens began to "conduct" (his word for edit) a new periodical, *Household Words*. His editorials and articles for this magazine, running to two volumes, cover the entire span of English politics, social institutions, and family life and are an invaluable complement to the fictional treatment of these subjects in Dickens's novels. The weekly magazine was a great success and ran to 1859, when Dickens began to conduct a new weekly, *All the Year Round*. In both these periodicals he published some of his major novels.

### "Dark" Novels

In 1851 Dickens was struck by the death of his father and one of his daughters within 2 weeks. Partly in response to these losses, he embarked on a series of works which have come to be called his "dark" novels and which rank among the greatest triumphs of the art of fiction. The first of these, *Bleak House* (1852-1853), has perhaps the most complicated plot of any English novel, but the narrative twists serve to create a sense of the interrelationship of all segments of English society. Indeed, it has been maintained that this network of interrelations is the true subject of the novel, designed to express Thomas Carlyle's view that "organic filaments" connect every member of society with every other member of whatever class. The novel provides, then, a chastening lesson to social snobbery and personal selfishness.

Dickens's next novel is even more didactic in its moral indictment of selfishness. *Hard Times* (1854) was written specifically to challenge the prevailing view of his society that practicality and facts were of greater importance and value than feelings and persons. In his indignation at callousness in business and public educational systems, Dickens laid part of the charge for the heartlessness of Englishmen at the door of the utilitarian philosophy then much in vogue. But the lasting applicability of the novel lies in its intensely focused picture of an English industrial town in the heyday of capitalist expansion and in its keen view of the limitations of both employers and reformers.

*Little Dorrit* (1855-1857) has some claim to be regarded as Dickens's greatest novel. In it he provides the same range of social observation that he had developed in previous major works. But the outstanding feature of this novel is the creation of two striking symbols of his views, which operate throughout the story as the focal points of all the characters' lives. The condition of England, as he saw it, Dickens sums up in the symbol of the prison: specifically the Marshalsea debtors' prison, in which the heroine's father is entombed, but generally the many forms of personal bondage and confinement that are exhibited in the course of the plot. For his counterweight, Dickens raises to symbolic stature his traditional figure of the child as innocent sufferer of the world's abuses. By making his heroine not a child but a childlike figure of Christian loving-kindness, Dickens poses the central burden of his work—the conflict between the world's harshness and human values—in its most impressive artistic form.

The year 1857 saw the beginnings of a personal crisis for Dickens when he fell in love with an actress named Ellen Ternan. He separated from his wife in the following year, after many years of marital incompatibility. In this period Dickens also began to give much of his time and energies to public readings from his novels, which became even more popular than his lectures on topical questions.

### Later Works

In 1859 Dickens published *A Tale of Two Cities*, a historical novel of the French Revolution, which is read today most often as a school text. It is, while below the standard of the long and comprehensive "dark" novels, a fine evocation of the historical period and a moving tale of a surprisingly modern hero's self-sacrifice. Besides publishing this novel in the newly founded *All the Year Round*, Dickens also published 17 articles, which appeared as a book in 1860 entitled *The Uncommercial Traveller*.

Dickens's next novel, *Great Expectations* (1860-1861), must rank as his most perfectly executed work of art. It tells the story of a young man's moral development in the course of his life—from childhood in the provinces to gentleman's status in London. Not an autobiographical novel like *David Copperfield*, *Great Expectations* belongs to the type of fiction called, in German, *Bildungsroman* (the novel of a man's education or formation by experience) and is one of the finest examples of the type.

The next work in the Dickens canon had to wait for the (for him) unusual time of 3 years, but in 1864-1865 he produced *Our Mutual Friend*, which challenges *Little Dorrit* and *Bleak House* for consideration as his masterpiece. Here the vision of English society in all its classes and institutions is presented most thoroughly and devastatingly, while two symbols are developed which resemble those of *Little Dorrit* in credibility and interest. These symbols are the mounds of rubbish which rose to become features of the landscape in rapidly expanding London, and the river which flows through the city and provides a point of contact for all its members besides suggesting the course of human life from birth to death.

In the closing years of his life Dickens worsened his declining health by giving numerous readings from his works. He never fully recovered from a railroad accident in which he had been involved in 1865 and yet insisted on traveling throughout the British Isles and America to read before tumultuous audiences. He broke down in 1869 and gave only a final series of readings in London in the following year. He also began *The Mystery of Edwin Drood* but died in 1870, leaving it unfinished. His burial in Westminster Abbey was an occasion of national mourning.

## Further Reading

The definitive biography of Dickens is Edgar Johnson, *Charles Dickens: His Tragedy and Triumph* (2 vols., 1952). This supersedes but does not render obsolete the long-standing "official" biography by John Forster, *The Life of Charles Dickens* (3 vols., 1872-1873; new ed., 2 vols., 1966). The most interesting psychological study is Edmund Wilson, "Dickens: The Two Scrooges," in *The Wound and the Bow: Seven Studies in Literature* (1941). The best critical interpretation is J. Hillis Miller, *Charles Dickens: The World of His Novels* (1958). F.R. and Q.D. Leavis, *Dickens the Novelist* (1970), contains essays on Dickens's major novels. For the earlier novels the most informative reading is Steven Marcus, *Dickens: From Pickwick to Dombey* (1965). The most useful book on the social and historical background of the novels is Humphry House, *The Dickens World* (1941; 2d ed. 1950). □

# Emily Dickinson

**One of the finest lyric poets in the English language, the American poet Emily Dickinson (1830-1886) was a keen observer of nature and a wise interpreter of human passion. Her family and friends published most of her work posthumously.**

American poetry in the 19th century was rich and varied, ranging from the symbolic fantasies of Edgar Allan Poe through the moralistic quatrains of Henry Wadsworth Longfellow to the revolutionary free verse of Walt Whitman. In the privacy of her study Emily Dickinson developed her own forms and pursued her own visions, oblivious of literary fashions and unconcerned with the changing national literature. If she was influenced at all by other writers, they were John Keats, Ralph Waldo Emerson, Robert and Elizabeth Barrett Browning, Isaac Watts (his hymns), and the biblical prophets.

Dickinson was born on Dec. 10, 1830, in Amherst, Mass., the eldest daughter of Edward Dickinson, a successful lawyer, member of Congress, and for many years treasurer of Amherst College, and of Emily Norcross Dickinson, a submissive, timid woman. The Dickinsons' only son, William Austin, also a lawyer, succeeded his father as treasurer of the college. Their youngest child, Lavinia, was the chief housekeeper and, like her sister Emily, remained at home, unmarried, all her life. The sixth member of this tightly knit group was Susan Gilbert, an ambitious and witty schoolmate of Emily's, who married Austin in 1856 and moved into the house next door to the Dickinsons. At first she was Emily's confidante and a valued critic of her poetry, but by 1879 Emily was speaking of her "pseudo-sister" and had long since ceased exchanging notes and poems.

## Early Education

Amherst in the 1840s was a sleepy village in the lush Connecticut Valley, dominated by the Church and the college. Dickinson was reared in Trinitarian Congregationalism, but she never joined the Church and probably chafed at the austerity of the town. Concerts were rare; card games, dancing, and theater were unheard of. For relaxation she walked the hills with her dog, visited friends, and read. But it is also obvious that Puritan New England bred in her a sharp eye for local color, a love of introspection and self-analysis, and a fortitude that sustained her through years of intense loneliness.

Dickinson graduated from Amherst Academy in 1847. The following year (the longest time she was ever to spend away from home) she attended Mount Holyoke Female Seminary at South Hadley, but because of her fragile health she did not return. At the age of 17 she settled into the Dickinson home and turned herself into a competent housekeeper and a more than ordinary observer of Amherst life.

## Early Work

It is not known when Dickinson began to write poetry or what happened to the poems of her early youth. Only five poems can be dated prior to 1858, the year in which she began gathering her work into hand-written fair copies bound loosely with looped thread to make small packets. She sent these five early poems to friends in letters or as valentines, and one of them was published anonymously without her permission in the *Springfield Republican* (Feb.

20, 1852). After 1858 she apparently convinced herself she had a genuine talent, for now the packets were carefully stored in an ebony box, awaiting inspection by future readers or even by a publisher.

Publication, however, was not easily arranged. After Dickinson besieged her friend Samuel Bowles, editor of the *Republican,* with poems and letters for 4 years, he published two poems, both anonymously: "I taste a liquor never brewed" (May 4, 1861) and "Safe in their Alabaster Chambers" (March 1, 1862). And the first of these was edited, probably by Bowles, to regularize (and thus, flatten) the rhymes and the punctuation. Dickinson began the poem: "I taste a liquor never brewed—/ From Tankards scooped in Pearl—/ Not all the Frankfort Berries/ Yield such an Alcohol." But Bowles printed: "I taste a liquor never brewed,/ From tankards scooped in pearl;/ Not Frankfort berries yield the sense/ Such a delicious whirl." She used no title; Bowles titled it "The May-Wine." (Only seven poems were published during her lifetime, and all had been altered by editors.)

## Friendship with T. W. Higginson

In 1862 Dickinson turned to the literary critic Thomas Wentworth Higginson for advice about her poems. She had known him only through his essays in the *Atlantic Monthly,* but in time he became, in her words, her "preceptor" and eventually her "safest friend." She began her first letter to him by asking, "Are you too deeply occupied to say if my verse is alive?" Six years later she was bold enough to say, "You were not aware that you saved my life." They did not meet until 1870, at her urging, surprisingly, and only once more after that. Higginson told his wife, after the first meeting, "I was never with anyone who drained my nerve power so much. Without touching her she drew from me. I am glad not to live near her."

What Dickinson was seeking was assurance as well as advice, and Higginson apparently gave it without knowing it, through a correspondence that lasted the rest of her life. He advised against publishing, but he also kept her abreast of the literary world (indeed, of the outside world, since as early as 1868, she was writing him, "I do not cross my father's ground to any house or town"). He helped her not at all with what mattered most to her—establishing her own private poetic method—but he was a friendly ear and a congenial mentor during the most troubled years of her life. Out of her inner turmoil came rare lyrics in a form that Higginson never really understood—if he had, he would not have tried to "edit" them, either in the 1860s or after her death. Dickinson could not take his "surgery," as she called it, but she took his friendship willingly.

## Years of Emotional Crisis

Between 1858 and 1866 Dickinson wrote more than 1100 poems, full of aphorisms, paradoxes, off rhymes, and eccentric grammar. Few are more than 16 lines long, composed in meters based on English hymnology. The major subjects are love and separation, death, nature, and God—but especially love. When she writes "My life closed twice before its close," one can only guess who her real or fancied

lovers might have been. Higginson was not one of them. It is more than likely that her first "dear friend" was Benjamin Newton, a young man too poor to marry, who had worked for a few years in her father's law office. He left Amherst for Worcester and died there in 1853.

During a visit to Philadelphia a year later Dickinson met the Reverend Charles Wadsworth. Sixteen years her senior, a brilliant preacher, already married, he was hardly more than a mental image of a lover. There is no doubt she made him this, but nothing more. He visited her once in 1860. When he moved to San Francisco in May 1862, she was in despair. Only a month before, Samuel Bowles had sailed for Europe to recover his health. Little wonder that in her first letter to Higginson she said, "I had a terror . . . — and so I sing as the Boy does by the Burying Ground—because I am afraid." She needed love, but she had to indulge this need through her poems, perhaps because she felt she could cope with it no other way.

When Bowles returned to Amherst in November, Dickinson was so overwhelmed she remained in her bedroom and sent a note down, " . . . That you return to us alive is better than a summer, and more to hear your voice below than news of any bird." By the time Wadsworth returned from California in 1870 and resettled in Philadelphia, the crisis was over. His second visit, in 1880, was anticlimax. Higginson had not saved her life; her life was never in danger. What had been in danger was her emotional equilibrium and her control over a talent that was so intense it longed for the eruptions that might have destroyed it.

## Last Years

In the last 2 decades of her life Dickinson wrote fewer than 50 poems a year, perhaps because of continuing eye trouble, more probably because she had to take increasing responsibility in running the household. Her father died in 1874, and a year later her mother suffered a paralyzing stroke that left her an invalid until her death. There was little time for poetry, not even for serious consideration of marriage (if it was actually proffered) with a widower and old family friend, Judge Otis Lord. Their love was genuine, but once again the timing was wrong. It was too late to recast her life completely. Her mother died in 1882, Judge Lord 2 years later. Dickinson's health failed noticeably after a nervous collapse in 1884, and on May 15, 1886, she died of nephritis.

## Posthumous Publication

How the complete poems of Dickinson were finally gathered is a publishing saga almost too complicated for brief summary. Lavinia Dickinson inherited the ebony box; she asked Mabel Loomis Todd, the wife of an Amherst astronomy professor, to join Higginson in editing the manuscripts. Unfortunately, they felt even then that they had to alter the syntax, smooth the rhymes, cut some lines, and create titles for each poem. Three volumes appeared in quick succession: 1890, 1891, and 1896. In 1914 Dickinson's niece, Martha Dickinson Bianchi, published some of the poems her mother, Susan, had saved. In the next 3 decades four more volumes appeared, the most important being *Bolts of Melody* (1945), edited by Mrs. Todd and her daughter, Millicent Todd Bingham, from the manuscripts the Todds had never returned to Lavinia Dickinson. In 1955 Thomas H. Johnson prepared for Harvard University Press a three-volume edition, chronologically arranged, of "variant readings critically compared with all known manuscripts." Here, for the first time, the reader saw the poems as Dickinson had left them. The Johnson text of the 1,775 extant poems is now the standard one.

It is clear that Dickinson could not have written to please publishers, who were not ready to risk her striking aphoristic style and original metaphors. She had the right to educate the public, as Poe and Whitman eventually did, but she never had the invitation. Had she published during her lifetime, adverse public criticism might have driven her into deeper solitude, even silence. "If fame belonged to me," she told Higginson, "I could not escape her; if she did not, the longest day would pass me on the chase . . . My barefoot rank is better." The 20th century has lifted her without doubt to the first rank among poets.

## Further Reading

Thomas H. Johnson edited *The Letters of Emily Dickinson* (3 vols., 1958). His three-volume variorum edition of her poems (1955) was followed by a one-volume *The Complete Poems of Emily Dickinson* (1960) and a selection of 575 poems, *Final Harvest* (1961).

The best of the early biographies of Emily Dickinson is George Whicher, *This Was a Poet: A Critical Biography of Emily Dickinson* (1938). It has been superseded by Richard Chase, *Emily Dickinson* (1951); Thomas H. Johnson, *Emily Dickinson: An Interpretive Biography* (1955); and David Higgins, *Portrait of Emily Dickinson: The Poet and Her Prose* (1967). Jay Leyda, *The Years and Hours of Emily Dickinson* (2 vols., 1960), is a valuable source book.

There are numerous critical studies. The best general appreciation is Charles R. Anderson, *Emily Dickinson's Poetry: Stairway of Surprise* (1960). More recent studies are Clark Griffith, *The Long Shadow: Emily Dickinson's Tragic Poetry* (1964); Albert J. Gelpi, *Emily Dickinson: The Mind of the Poet* (1965); Ruth Miller, *The Poetry of Emily Dickinson* (1968); and William R. Sherwood, *Circumference and Circumstance: Stages in the Mind and Art of Emily Dickinson* (1968). Richard B. Sewall edited *Emily Dickinson: A Collection of Critical Essays* (1963). Equally useful is Cesar R. Blake and Carlton F. Wells, eds., *The Recognition of Emily Dickinson: Selected Criticism since 1890* (1964).

Emily Dickinson's place in the history of American poetry is well established in Roy Harvey Pearce, *The Continuity of American Poetry* (1961), and Hyatt H. Waggoner, *American Poets from the Puritans to the Present* (1968). ☐

# John Dickinson

**John Dickinson (1732-1808), American lawyer, pamphleteer, and politician, helped guide public opinion during the clash between colonial and British interests prior to the American Revolution. Although he had opposed American independence, he worked to strengthen the new nation.**

After 1769 John Dickinson was without peer in the pamphlet war for colonial rights, which the moderates preferred to a shooting war. He was not a "man of the people," but he shared with most American Whigs the aspiration for self-government. He was cautious but not an obstructionist.

John Dickinson was born Nov. 13, 1732, in Talbot County, Md., the son of a judge. Dickinson began his legal studies in 1750 in Philadelphia, but 3 years later he went to London and became a reader at the Middle Temple.

In England, Dickinson studied the authorities, heard cases argued, and visited the theater and the family of Pennsylvania proprietor Thomas Penn. He took his law degree in 1757 and returned to America with the disillusioned view that Parliament was a school for corrupt bargainers of meager talents.

Dickinson was admitted to the Philadelphia bar, and after 1760, when his father died, he divided his time between Kent County, Del., and the thriving Pennsylvania capital. Elected to the colonial legislature in 1762, he showed little awe for the Penn family's proprietary interests but displayed a lifelong tendency to see both sides of an issue and then lean toward the middle ground. When the antiproprietary leaders insisted that the colony should be wrested from the Penns and converted into a royal province, Dickinson warned that the transition might exact a heavy price. The colony was torn between the Quaker party and the Scotch-Irish faction, and Dickinson insisted that a

change of masters was in itself no solution to their deep-rooted problems.

## Debating American Independence

No one could foresee the rapid deterioration of British-American relations set off by the Stamp Act in 1765, when local concerns finally gave way to larger problems. Whereas Benjamin Franklin at first saw no harm in the stamped paper, Dickinson sensed the dreaded implications it carried. As a delegate to the Stamp Act Congress, he met leaders of active antiparliamentary parties from other colonies. His "Declaration of Rights and Privileges" adopted by the Congress denounced taxes voted in England and collected in America. Regulation of trade was one thing, but levying taxes struck at the main artery of colonial government. Dickinson wrote several pamphlets which suggested that Britain would, if necessary, bleed the Colonies into obedience. In common with James Otis, the foremost pamphleteer of the day, Dickinson argued that "immutable maxims of reason and justice" supported the American discontent.

Repeal of the Stamp Act temporarily relaxed tensions, but the Townshend Acts of 1767 gave Dickinson renewed opportunity to serve as a moderate spokesman. In the maelstrom of American discontent, Dickinson's *Letters from a Pennsylvanian Farmer* capitalized on the shifting grounds of argument. The new duties were contrary to natural law, he argued, and clearly unconstitutional. Dickinson denied the sophistry that claimed there were internal and external duties and that Parliament might legally enact only the latter. Levying taxes, he argued, was the precious prerogative of the colonial assemblies alone but Parliament might enact regulatory duties on trade. Dickinson insisted that the point of tightened British controls was to keep Americans obedient rather than happy. Widely published in newspapers and as a pamphlet, his *Letters* (as Franklin said) echoed "the general sentiments" of the colonists. The tone was neither humble nor belligerent.

Dickinson tried to rouse the lethargic Philadelphia merchants into a more active stand and corresponded with James Otis and other resistance leaders. In 1770 he was elected to the Pennsylvania Assembly. He married Mary Norris the same year. In the backlash of the Boston Tea Party, Philadelphians debated both their role in aiding a sister city and their position in the imperial argument. Dickinson helped clarify matters in his pamphlet *An Essay on the Constitutional Power of Great Britain,* which granted Parliament power to regulate foreign trade but little else in American life. In the First Continental Congress he drafted both the cogent "Address to the Inhabitants of Quebec," a summary of the rights of Americans, and the petition to George III seeking reconciliation.

Dickinson's attitude characterized the Second Continental Congress, which John Adams saw as holding "the Sword in one Hand [and] the Olive Branch in the other." Dickinson's "Olive Branch" petition to the King boomeranged. By ignoring it, George III slammed the door on moderate Americans and placed Dickinson in a difficult position.

## Dickinson's Approach Too Moderate

By 1776 Dickinson was arguing against the inevitable; his opposition to the Declaration of Independence left him a conscientious but marked man. His proposed "Articles of Confederation" proved useful as Congress patched together a national government, but in state politics his ideas were rejected, and he was dropped from the congressional delegation. Exasperated, Dickinson challenged supporters of the ultrademocratic Pennsylvania Constitution by calling for an immediate revision of their work. Frustrated and convinced he was ill, he temporarily retired.

Gradually, Dickinson regained his old political form. In 1779 Delaware sent him back to Congress and in 1781 elected him its chief executive. A year later Pennsylvania also chose him as its president, and he briefly held both offices. Soon, however, he returned to Pennsylvania to serve 3 years as its president. Dickinson was sent to the Annapolis Convention and was a Delaware delegate to the Federal Convention in 1787. Age and health excused him from an active role in debate, but in the ratification campaign he wrote the "Fabius" letters in support of the United States Constitution.

Thereafter, Dickinson appeared rarely in public bodies. He helped draft the 1792 Delaware Constitution but took no part in a similar work for Pennsylvania. He veered away from the Federalists to attack Jay's Treaty. He supported the rising Republican party and Jefferson in 1800 but refused to become politically active himself. Dickinson died on Feb. 14, 1808, at Wilmington, Del.

## Further Reading

There is no satisfactory comprehensive biography of Dickinson. Charles J. Stillé, *The Life and Times of John Dickinson* (1891), is inadequate. David L. Jacobson, *John Dickinson and the Revolution in Pennsylvania, 1764-1776* (1965), is excellent for its analysis of a significant period. Dickinson's papers in the several leading Philadelphia archives have not yet been collected and edited by a competent scholar. *The Political Writings of John Dickinson,* edited by himself (1801), and Paul L. Ford, ed., *The Writings of John Dickinson* (1895), leave gaps.

## Additional Sources

Flower, Milton Embick, *John Dickinson, conservative revolutionary,* Charlottesville: Published for the Friends of the John Dickinson Mansion by the University Press of Virginia, 1983.
Fredman, Lionel E., *John Dickinson, American Revolutionary statesman,* Charlotteville, N.Y., SamHar Press, 1974. ☐